COVERS ALL
100% CERTIFIED
EXAM OBJECTIVES

Syngress knows what passing the exam means to you and your career. And we know that you are often financing your own training and certification; therefore, you need a system that is comprehensive, affordable and effective.

Boasting one-of-a-kind integration of text, and Web-based exam simulation, the Syngress Study Guide & Practice Exam guarantees 100% coverage of exam objectives.

The Syngress Study Guide & Practice Exam includes:

- **Study Guide with 100% coverage of exam objectives**
  By reading this study guide and following the corresponding objective list, you can be sure that you have studied 100% of the exam objectives.
- **Web-based practice exams** Just visit us at www.syngress.com/certification to access a complete exam simulation

Thank you for giving us the opportunity to serve your certification needs. And be sure to let us know if there's anything else we can do to help you get the maximum value from your investment. We're listening.

www.syngress.com/certification

SYNGRESS®

SYNGRESS®

NETWORK+

Study Guide & Practice Exams: Exam N10-003

Robert J. Shimonski

Michael Cross
Laura Hunter

Syngress Publishing, Inc., the author(s), and any person or firm involved in the writing, editing, or production (collectively "Makers") of this book ("the Work") do not guarantee or warrant the results to be obtained from the Work.

There is no guarantee of any kind, expressed or implied, regarding the Work or its contents. The Work is sold AS IS and WITHOUT WARRANTY. You may have other legal rights, which vary from state to state.

In no event will Makers be liable to you for damages, including any loss of profits, lost savings, or other incidental or consequential damages arising out from the Work or its contents. Because some states do not allow the exclusion or limitation of liability for consequential or incidental damages, the above limitation may not apply to you.

You should always use reasonable care, including backup and other appropriate precautions, when working with computers, networks, data, and files.

Syngress Media®, Syngress®, "Career Advancement Through Skill Enhancement®," "Ask the Author UPDATE®," and "Hack Proofing®," are registered trademarks of Syngress Publishing, Inc. "Syngress: The Definition of a Serious Security Library"™, "Mission Critical™," and "The Only Way to Stop a Hacker is to Think Like One™" are trademarks of Syngress Publishing, Inc. Brands and product names mentioned in this book are trademarks or service marks of their respective companies.

KEY	SERIAL NUMBER
001	HJIRTCV764
002	PO9873D5FG
003	829KM8NJH2
004	GHV99876HT
005	CVPLQ6WQ23
006	VBP965T5T5
007	HJJJ863WD3E
008	2987GVTWMK
009	629MP5SDJT
010	IMWQ295T6T

PUBLISHED BY
Syngress Publishing, Inc.
800 Hingham Street
Rockland, MA 02370

Network+ Study Guide & Practice Exams: Exam N10-003

Copyright © 2005 by Syngress Publishing, Inc. All rights reserved. Printed in Canada.
Except as permitted under the Copyright Act of 1976, no part of this publication may be reproduced or distributed in any form or by any means, or stored in a database or retrieval system, without the prior written permission of the publisher, with the exception that the program listings may be entered, stored, and executed in a computer system, but they may not be reproduced for publication.

Printed in Canada
1 2 3 4 5 6 7 8 9 0
ISBN: 1-931836-42-6

Publisher: Andrew Williams
Acquisitions Editor: Jaime Quigley
Cover Designer: Michael Kavish
Technical Editor: Robert J. Shimonski and
  Norris L. Johnson

Page Layout and Art: Patricia Lupien
Copy Editor: Amy Thomson
Indexer: Rich Carlson

Distributed by O'Reilly Media, Inc. in the United States and Canada.
For information on rights and translations, contact Matt Pedersen, Director of Sales and Rights, at Syngress Publishing; email matt@syngress.com or fax to 781-681-3585.

Acknowledgments

Syngress would like to acknowledge the following people for their kindness and support in making this book possible.

Syngress books are now distributed in the United States and Canada by O'Reilly Media, Inc. The enthusiasm and work ethic at O'Reilly are incredible, and we would like to thank everyone there for their time and efforts to bring Syngress books to market: Tim O'Reilly, Laura Baldwin, Mark Brokering, Mike Leonard, Donna Selenko, Bonnie Sheehan, Cindy Davis, Grant Kikkert, Opol Matsutaro, Steve Hazelwood, Mark Wilson, Rick Brown, Leslie Becker, Jill Lothrop, Tim Hinton, Kyle Hart, Sara Winge, C. J. Rayhill, Peter Pardo, Leslie Crandell, Regina Aggio, Pascal Honscher, Preston Paull, Susan Thompson, Bruce Stewart, Laura Schmier, Sue Willing, Mark Jacobsen, Betsy Waliszewski, Dawn Mann, Kathryn Barrett, John Chodacki, Rob Bullington, and Aileen Berg.

The incredibly hardworking team at Elsevier Science, including Jonathan Bunkell, Ian Seager, Duncan Enright, David Burton, Rosanna Ramacciotti, Robert Fairbrother, Miguel Sanchez, Klaus Beran, Emma Wyatt, Chris Hossack, Krista Leppiko, Marcel Koppes, Judy Chappell, Radek Janousek, and Chris Reinders for making certain that our vision remains worldwide in scope.

David Buckland, Marie Chieng, Lucy Chong, Leslie Lim, Audrey Gan, Pang Ai Hua, Joseph Chan, and Siti Zuraidah Ahmad of STP Distributors for the enthusiasm with which they receive our books.

David Scott, Tricia Wilden, Marilla Burgess, Annette Scott, Andrew Swaffer, Stephen O'Donoghue, Bec Lowe, Mark Langley, and Anyo Geddes of Woodslane for distributing our books throughout Australia, New Zealand, Papua New Guinea, Fiji, Tonga, Solomon Islands, and the Cook Islands.

And a special thank you to Rob Shimonski, Laura Hunter, Will Schmied, Norris Johnson, and Michael Cross for all their efforts in getting this book done. We appreciate all your help!

Lead Author and Technical Editor

Robert J. Shimonski (TruSecure TICSA, Cisco CCDP, CCNP, Symantec SPS, NAI Sniffer SCP, Nortel NNCSS, Microsoft MCSE, MCP+I, Novell Master CNE, Prosoft MCIW, SANS.org GSEC, GCIH, CompTIA Server+, Network+, Inet+, A+, e-Biz+, Security+, HTI+) is a networking and security expert and has designed, installed and managed hundreds of wide area and local area networks in corporate, military and educational facilities worldwide. Robert's specialties include network and security infrastructure design with the Cisco product line and systems engineering with Windows 2003 Server and Windows XP Professional.

Robert has also worked closely with CompTIA, the makers of the Network+ exam, for years. Robert has played a role helping CompTIA to build new exam as a Subject Matter Expert (SME), developing exam content for the eBiz+ and HTI+ certifications.

Robert is also a part-time author, having worked on over 30 book projects as both an author and editor. He has written and edited books on a plethora of topics such as security, networking, protocol analysis and Linux. Some of Robert's other Syngress Publishing titles are: *Sniffer Pro Network Optimization & Troubleshooting Handbook* (ISBN: 1-931836-57-4), *Building DMZs for Enterprise Networks* (ISBN: 1-931836-88-4), and the best selling *Security+ Study Guide & DVD Training System* (ISBN: 1-931836-72-8).

Robert can be found online at www.rsnetworks.net.

Contributing Authors

Laura E. Hunter (CISSP, MCSE: Security, MCDBA, Microsoft MVP) is a senior IT specialist with the University of Pennsylvania, where she provides network planning, implementation, and troubleshooting services for various business units and schools within the university. Her specialties include Microsoft Windows 2000 and 2003 design and implementation, troubleshooting, and security topics. Laura has over a decade of experience in the areas of Windows and Novell networking; her previous experience includes a position as the director of computer services for the Salvation Army and as the LAN administrator for a medical supply firm. She is a contributor to the TechTarget family of websites, and to Redmond magazine (formerly Microsoft Certified Professional Magazine).

Will Schmied, BSET, MCSE, CWNA, TICSA, MCSA, Security+, Network+, A+, is an Active Directory and Messaging Engineer for a Fortune 500 manufacturing company. As a freelance writer, Will has worked with many publishers, including Microsoft and Syngress. Will has also worked directly with Microsoft in the MCSE exam-development process. Will holds a bachelor's degree in mechanical engineering technology from Old Dominion University along with his various IT industry certifications. He also served in the US Navy for over 12 years in the nuclear power field. Will lives in Mississippi with his wife, Chris; their children, Christopher, Austin, Andrea, and Hannah; their dog Charlie; and their cats, Smokey, Evin and Socks. When he's not busy working, you can find Will enjoying time with his family, counting the days until hockey season starts or dishing out a serious frag-fest on his Xbox.

Michael Cross (MCSE, MCP+I, CNA, Network+) is an Internet Specialist / Computer Forensic Analyst with the Niagara Regional Police Service. He performs computer forensic examinations on computers involved in criminal investigations, and has consulted and assisted in cases dealing with computer-related/Internet crimes. In addition to designing and maintaining their Web site at www.nrps.com and Intranet, he has also provided support in the areas of programming, hardware, and network administration. As part of an Information Technology team that provides support to a user base of over 800 civilian and uniform users, his theory is that when the users carry guns, you tend to be more motivated in solving their problems.

Michael also owns KnightWare (www.knightware.ca), which provides computer-related services like Web page design, and Bookworms (www.bookworms.ca), where you can purchase collectibles and other interesting items online. He has been a freelance writer for several years, and has been published over three dozen times in numerous books and anthologies. He currently resides in St. Catharines, Ontario Canada with his lovely wife Jennifer and his darling daughter Sara.

Technical Editor and Reviewer

Norris L. Johnson, Jr. (MCSA, MCSE, MCT, CTT+, A+, Network +, CCNA) is a technology trainer and owner of a consulting company in the Seattle-Tacoma area. His consultancies have included deployments and security planning for local firms and public agencies, as well as providing services to other local computer firms in need of problem solving and solutions for their clients. He specializes in Windows NT 4.0, Windows 2000, and Windows XP issues, providing planning, implementation, and integration services. In addition to consulting work, Norris provides technical training for clients and teaches for area community and technical colleges in the classroom. He has co-authored *Configuring and Troubleshooting Windows XP Professional* (Syngress Publishing, ISBN: 1-928994-80-6) and *Hack Proofing Your Network, Second Edition* (Syngress, ISBN: 1-928994-70-9), and performed technical edits and reviews on *Hack Proofing Windows 2000 Server* (Syngress, ISBN: 1-931836-49-3) and *Windows 2000 Active Directory, Second Edition* (Syngress, ISBN: 1-928994-60-1). Norris holds a bachelor's degree from Washington State University. He is deeply appreciative of the support of his wife, Cindy, and three sons in helping to maintain his focus and efforts toward computer training and education.

CompTIA's Network+ Exam N10-003 Objectives Map and Table of Contents

All of CompTIA's published objectives for the Network+ Exam N10-003 are covered in this book. To help you easily find the sections that directly support particular objectives, we've listed all of the exam objectives below, and mapped them to the Chapter number in which they are covered. We've also assigned numbers to each objective, which we use throughout the book to identify objective coverage. In some chapters, we've made the judgment that it is probably easier for the student to cover objectives in a slightly different sequence than the order of the published Microsoft objectives. By reading this study guide and following the corresponding objective list, you can be sure that you have studied 100% of CompTIA's Network+ Exam N10-003 objectives.

Exam Objective Map

Domain I

Objective Number	Objective	Chapter Number
1.1	Recognize the following logical or physical network topologies given a diagram, schematic or description:	1
1.1.1	Star	1
1.1.2	Bus	1
1.1.3	Mesh	1
1.1.4	Ring	1
1.2	Specify the main features of 802.2 (Logical Link Control), 802.3 (Ethernet), 802.5 (token ring), 802.11 (wireless), and FDDI (Fiber Distributed Data Interface) networking technologies, including:	1
1.2.1	Speed	1

Domain I continued

Domain I continued

Domain II

Domain II continued

Domain II continued

Domain II continued

Domain III

Domain IV

Contents

Introduction

Welcome to Syngress Publishing's *Network+ Study Guide and Practice Exam.* Within these pages, you will learn much about the fundamentals of networking, as well as hone and polish or initially create the skills and knowledge you need to know to pass the CompTIA Network+ certification exam.

To deploy solutions, you need to know how to design, plan, and execute. To fix complex problems, you will need to have developed a well-rounded troubleshooting methodology. You may at times also need to consider "thinking outside of the box" or working by trial and error to fix complex issues. Sometimes you may have to recreate the problem altogether just to get a clue about what may have gone wrong. Frequently, problems come up, and the network is blamed immediately; it's your job to work your way toward proving that the network is indeed to blame, and to identify what the problem may be. As you can see, no matter what role you play in the networking arena, you will need to understand the basic principles behind network design, plans, and execution of plans.

Entry-level certifications such as the Network+ credential will help to make sure that the structural foundation of your basic knowledge is built before adding a single piece of advanced knowledge to it; the house builds up properly on the foundation, with the proper support laid out proactively in the beginning. This is much like networking—without understanding what class and range 10.1.1.1 fits into, you will be unable to design a network properly; it's just a fact. This guide closes that gap between very little knowledge (A+ is a recommended prerequisite, although it is not mandatory) and expert-level knowledge in granular disciplines such as Cisco internetworking and security design and deployment. However, that doesn't mean that the material in the book is overly fundamental. CompTIA is not asking you to know the "fundamentals" of "all" networking technologies; that material would fill a library. The current, up-to-date material in this book covers today's terminologies, trends, and the 2005 exam's objectives. Reading this book will provide you with a solid understanding of networking and prepare you for the Network+ exam. It also will prepare you for the networking industry if you are not already a part of it.

Passing the exam is no easy feat, but it is not impossible either. With the proper motivation, study habits, and effort, you can pass this exam on the first attempt. This book was assembled to provide you with all the tools you need to pass and obtain this credential by focusing material presented against every posted Network+ objective. All authors have taken the new Network+ exam; some even took the first beta ever presented. Some of the authors have even worked directly with and for CompTIA to help develop its exam content. Because of this experience, you simply won't find another study guide that prepares you quite like this one; the book's focus is from the perspective of authors who were themselves trained by CompTIA. All objectives are covered in detail, and you are tested on all concepts at the end of each chapter in the Self-Test sections.

So it's all up to you; we provide you with the tools, but you are the mechanic. Build yourself up to take and pass the exam with our help. Besides earning the Network+ credential, there are other benefits of reading this book; you will gain a wealth of knowledge from clearly written definitions, terms, explanations, exercises, and question items written by leading authors and proven specialists in the information technology (IT) industry. This book was written by experts following strict guidelines to bring you the best guide possible to learn from and pass the Network+ exam. Let's take a look at what makes up the Network+ exam.

What Is Network+?

More than half a decade ago, CompTIA released the first version of Network+ on April 30, 1999. Following the success of the A+ credential and since then, it has gone through multiple transformations and updates to the current version, the version this book covers. The 2005 objectives have been recently updated to remove old legacy information on the exam that no longer is important. Just like networks themselves, things get old, stagnant, and need updating. The older information has been replaced with new material that meets today's testing needs, such as moving testable questions from the limit of knowing Fast Ethernet to the new standards, Gigabit Ethernet and 10 Gigabit Ethernet. This is just one example of the path the exam takes and how you need to navigate it. If you were studying for any test before 2005, this exam guide is still pertinent, as 90% of the old material is still covered. Newer material is seeded in, and items have been updated. The new objectives update the Network+ exam on new technologies such as wireless networking and security technologies, keeping it current with the networking industry itself.

If this study guide is used correctly, you will also gain the Network+ credential, which is accredited in other popular certification programs today such as the Microsoft-based MCSE (Microsoft Certified Systems Engineer) and the Novell CNE (Certified Novell Engineer). Moreover, anyone embarking on a career in "networking" moving on to more advanced curricula and credentials such as the Cisco CCIE (Cisco Certified Internetworking Expert) will benefit greatly from starting with the Network+ credential from CompTIA. Any way you look at it, if you are interested in local and wide area networking, Network+ is a great place to start.

Successfully passing the CompTIA Network+ exam and understanding everything learned prepares you to successfully embark in the networking field and feel confident that you have learned the "basics of networking." In sum, the Network+ credential (and exam) makes sure that you, the candidate, are prepared to enter the world of networking with provable skills and knowledge. If the credential doesn't prove it, perhaps the book will give you the experience you need to get those skills so that you can enter the workforce. Either way, Network+ is a winning certification with a lot of great industry backing, especially from the program's creators and managers, CompTIA.org.

About CompTIA

CompTIA (Computing Technology Industry Association), an association located at www.comptia.org, is one of the leaders in the certification arena today, especially in the entry-level certification market. Starting with the well-known A+ credential, CompTIA has paved a path to certifying not only entry-level PC technician skills but also networking, home automation, security, and Web design. The CompTIA Network+ exam has become the leading entry-level network certification available and has enjoyed some of the same success as CompTIA's flagship certification, A+. It has also been around for almost half a decade as of the publishing of this book and continues to be updated and made better each time it is reexamined by CompTIA and its panel of subject matter experts, or SMEs. Network+ is also highly recognized in the industry. As part of many training centers' education program offerings, Network+ is one of the hottest certifications you can obtain today, especially if you are new to the networking world and need to master the fundamentals.

About the Book

The Network+ exam is thoroughly covered in this book. From every detail about how to get ready for test time all the way down to "full coverage" of the exam content and ways to prepare for the Network+ exam, it's all covered in this book and the Syngress Publishing Web site. Your book was also written by experts. In addition to being experts in writing and editing, the authors also are sought-after technology experts who work daily in the trenches of real-word networks—they design, manage, implement, and secure networks. The authors of this book have lived through all the technology listed in not only the Network+ objectives but also from a great many vendors of technology, such as Cisco, Microsoft, and Novell. The authors' biographies within this book show that this book was written by well-known published writers and full-time networking professionals, concentrating in the fields of network analysis, engineering, architecting, designing, implementing, and managing. The authors exemplify Network+ certified.

The book was written in a way to map directly to the CompTIA Network+ testable objectives. It gives you, the reader, a way to follow how CompTIA laid out the exam, learn the technology, and then focus on what is testable. The test questions at the end of each chapter also cover the essential information you need to pass the exam. Both elements combined give you a nice education on the technology, as well as a way to focus on how you will see the same material tested on the exam.

The exam is not hard, but it covers a lot of ground, and that is where the difficulty may come in for you. The exam also doesn't try to trick you; the questions are rather straightforward, but you may find yourself making mistakes you may have been able to avoid if you had read the questions more carefully. Remember, you are not in a rush; make sure you gauge your time so that you don't waste it or run out, but remember that if you prepared properly (with this study guide), then you should be able to move through the exam fairly rapidly (and carefully) and pass it on your first attempt.

Network+ Objectives

The new Network+ exam covers an updated set of objectives and has replaced the old Network+ exam as of the first quarter of 2005. Current holders of the CompTIA

Network+ certification will not need to take the new version of the test in order to retain their certification, as all of CompTIA's certifications are valid for life.

The objectives also broaden the scope somewhat, placing more emphasis on Linux as a viable networking operating system (NOS) and including AppleTalk as a network protocol. Although both Linux and AppleTalk have been covered on older versions of the exam, the topics have been refreshed to today's standards where Apple and Linux-based technologies are playing more and more of a role on many networks today. Because Novell and many other vendors are leaning very hard on using Linux (Novell's purchase of Germany-based SUSE, for example), it's important that it's covered in this book. You will see more and more of Linux as you progress in your work as a network technician. Moreover, once installed, Linux has a plethora of freeware tools that you can use (and will start to learn about in this book) to help you isolate and find problems on your network. So, in essence, just installing Linux will give you a new set of troubleshooting tools you may not have even known about—and this topic will be covered in depth in this study guide. You will learn about tools that run on Linux that will help you to manage your network; most of them are free or offered at very low cost.

The CompTIA Network+ objectives are laid out very similar to the older exams with minor updates. CompTIA sets the exam up into four separate categories:

- Media and Topologies 20%
- Protocols and Standards 25%
- Network Implementation 23%
- Network Support 32%

The list in the following section just gives you an idea on some of what is expected of you as you read the book and prepare for the exam.

Media and Topologies 20%

- You will need to know common media and topologies found on any typical or commonly seen network, local and wide (LAN and WAN).
- Understand the basic differences between Ethernet, Fast Ethernet, and Gigabit Ethernet.

- Understand and know the common types of Media such as 10BaseT, 10Base2, 10Base5, 100BaseTX, 100BaseFx, and Gigabit. as well as 10 Gigabit Ethernet.

- What is Token Ring and FDDI? Knowing about these older or uncommon Ring-based topologies is still needed for the exam. Other older technologies also need to be covered in little details (such as knowing 10Base2 or 10BaseFL; most times, you will not use these, but they are still out there en masse, unbelievably).

- What is the backbone segment of a network and what is commonly used at the location? Do you know the difference between a Bus backbone and a Star backbone?

- You need to know wireless, especially the 802 committee standards such as 802.11b, 802.11a, and 802.11g, and hardware such as Access Points and so on.

- Lastly, you must have a very solid understanding of switches, routers, hubs, bridges, firewalls and others such as IDS and the convergence of all of these devices into today's product offerings.

Protocols and Standards 25%

- TCP/IP was a Department of Defense (DoD) research project used to connect a number different networks designed by different vendors (or government agencies) into a single network of networks (called the "Internet"). To pass this exam, you will need to know TCP/IP fundamentals inside and out.

- You need to memorize the OSI and DoD models and what protocols in each protocol suite map to each layer of each stack.

- You need to also know port numbers such as HTTP (port 80), FTP (port 21), and SMTP (port 25). Others will be covered in the study guide.

Network Implementation 23%

- In this section of the exam you will receive questions on how to handle a particular situation or "scenario."

- Make sure you cover "how to" in this section. In the book you will get many exercises on how to configure protocols and so on; this material needs to be known for the exam. Windows, Novell, Linux, and so on are covered in the objectives.

Network Support 32%

- In this section of the exam you will be tested on how you support your network; this would include documentation, polices, and procedures.

- You will also need to know how to support your network via a plethora of troubleshooting tools on multiple platforms.

- Tools to focus on would be ping, ifconfig, winipcfg, ipconfig, nslookup, tracert, pathping, and so on. You must also know the "switches" used such as ping –a produces a different result than just using ping with a switch.

Network+ Study Tactics

There are quite a few things you should strategize about while preparing for the CompTIA Network+ exam. You should plan your studies around things such as your current experience and knowledge level, your available study tools, and your motivational focus, how well you prepare for exams in general.

Let's begin by discussing the needed study plan you will want to use or develop to pass this exam because just as you need a solid methodology to troubleshoot a network, you should also have a similar type of plan constructed for taking this exam.

It's very important that you fully prepare for the exam by studying correctly. Make sure that you do your due diligence when it comes to preparation; you are only going to cheat yourself if you don't. Try to set time aside each night to prepare properly by reading and working through the testable objectives in your mind, making sure you master the basics of each one so that you know what is expected of you come test time.

Now, lay out a study plan that fits into your time schedule, as well as a study location. Your study location is very important for preparation. A nice quiet place with few distractions is ideal for studying. Ask loved ones to give you some time alone, take the phone off the hook, or do whatever it takes to get some quality study time set aside so that you can prepare properly.

If you can, use a test system or build a test lab. A single PC or a dual-PC lab can really help you to practice and follow along with the exercises. Anything else you may have or be able to get (such as a hub, any cables, or connectors) will help as visual aids. Many questions on the Network+ exam expect you to know what things look like.

Experience helps, but is not mandatory. Some experience can be found in your lab; much of your true troubleshooting experience on full-sized networks will not. The more experience you have, the easier it will be for you to understand and digest the material. You will also learn how to use multiple types of tools on different systems. You will need to know multiple systems for this exam, so a lab can really help you gain the experience you need. It's strongly recommended. The exercises listed in the study guide are easy to follow and show you, step-by-step, what actions are being taken.

Don't underestimate the exam! Although in most cases the Network+ exam is considered fair, it can be tricky in some areas if you do not study.

How to Obtain Network+

To obtain the Network+ credential, you have to take and pass the CompTIA Network+ exam. There are no electives needed to take this exam. To take the exam, you can pay and register online or by phone. From each test provider's Web site, you can get up-to-date pricing information, as well as information about up-to-date, detailed information about the exam, such as the number of questions, time allotted, where in your area you can take the exam, and so on. The best way to prepare for the exam is to log on to the site, get all the way up to having to commit to taking the exam so you can read all the content about the exam without having to commit until you are ready. Between this and ensuring you visit the Network+ section of the CompTIA Web site, you are sure to have all the current information you need to be able to guide you in obtaining the Network+ credential.

Exam Day Experience

The CompTIA Network+ exam should be taken when you are ready; that is, after you have properly studied and reviewed all the material. Again, do not underestimate this exam, but don't overprepare for it either. The book covers all the testable material in a way that gives examples, tests you, and drives home points. By researching points online, you will also help to build up your knowledge. There is no escaping the posted objectives. Attack them as this book does, and you will be prepared.

The exam should be taken where you are comfortable. Dress comfortably and bring the right materials with you (proper identification, writing utensil, your test confirmation number in case there is a problem), and do not be late. Remember, you are helping no one if you rush or skim through the material.

The exam will have questions much like Microsoft's exams. You now have scenario questions. The Network+ questions are more straightforward. Straightforward does not mean "easy"; it just means that there are no 250-word scenarios. You won't need a scrap of paper to map out entire network topologies. It's much more to the point. Remember, this is a basic entry-level exam; the questions are made to be direct and expect a direct answer.

Links of Reference

Authors may use links of reference to the World Wide Web (www) throughout the book. As time goes on, these links may change and the reference rendered useless. Because of this inconvenience, we have provided a few solutions and some suggestions.

Lastly, your last benefit comes from the site **www.networkplusguide.com**, which was created to post any information related to the book that you may need. You can visit the site and find updates to the book, errata, and more information about the book, as well as updates on the exam. Between the book and the Web site, you should be able to find just about everything needed to pass the Network+ exam. Visit and send us (the authors) a note about the book or your success on the exam—we would love to hear your comments.

Pedagogical Elements and Practice Test

In this book, you'll find a number of different types of sidebars and other elements designed to supplement the main text. These include the following:

- **Head of the Class** These are discussions of concepts and facts as they may be presented in the classroom, regarding issues and questions that most commonly are raised by students during study of a particular topic.

- **Exam Warning** These focus on specific elements on which the reader needs to focus in order to pass the exam (for example, "Be sure you know the difference between symmetric and asymmetric encryption").

- **Test Day Tip** These are short tips that will help you in organizing and remembering information for the exam (for example, "When preparing for the exam on test day, it may be helpful to have a sheet with definitions of these abbreviations and acronyms handy for a quick last-minute review").

- **Configuring & Implementing** These are sidebars that contain background information that goes beyond what you need to know from the exam, but provide a "deep" foundation for understanding the concepts discussed in the text.

- **Security Alert** These are sidebars that point out potential security vulnerabilities and also attacks used by malicious hackers.

The book also includes, in each chapter, hands-on exercises in planning and configuring the features discussed. It is essential that you read through and, if possible, perform the steps of these exercises to familiarize yourself with the processes they cover.

You will find a number of helpful elements at the end of each chapter. For example, each chapter contains a *Summary of Exam Objectives* that ties the topics discussed in that chapter to the published objectives. Each chapter also contains an *Exam Objectives Fast Track,* which boils all exam objectives down to manageable summaries that are perfect for last-minute review. *The Exam Objectives Frequently Asked Questions* answers those questions that most often arise from readers and students regarding the topics covered in the chapter. Finally, in the *Self Test* section, you will find a set of practice questions written in a multiple-choice form that will assist you in your exam preparation These questions are designed to assess your mastery of the exam objectives and provide thorough remediation, as opposed to simulating the variety of question formats you may encounter in the actual exam. You can use the *Self-Test Quick Answer Key* that follows the *Self-Test* questions to quickly determine what information you need to review again. The *Self-Test Appendix* at the end of the book provides detailed explanations of both the correct and incorrect answers.

In addition to the questions included within this Study Guide, there is an additional Web-based practice exam. Just visit **www.syngress.com/certification** to take the exam. This will test your knowledge on all of the published certification objectives. The exam runs in both "live" and "practice" mode. Use "live" mode first to get an accurate gauge of your knowledge and skills, and then use practice mode to launch an extensive review of the questions that gave you trouble.

—Robert J. Shimonski, Network+ Certified
www.networkplusguide.com

NETWORK+
Domain I

Media and Topologies

Chapter 1

NETWORK+

Network Fundamentals

Domain I Objectives in this Chapter:

1.1 Recognize the following logical or physical network topologies given a diagram, schematic, or description:

    1.1.1 Star

    1.1.2 Bus

    1.1.3 Mesh

    1.1.4 Ring

1.2 Specify the main features of 802.2 (Logical Link Control), 802.3 (Ethernet), 802.5 (Token Ring), 802.11 (wireless), and FDDI (Fiber Distributed Data Interface) networking technologies, including:

    1.2.1 Speed

    1.2.2 Access method CSMA / CA (Carrier Sense Multiple Access/Collision Avoidance) and CSMA / CD (Carrier Sense Multiple Access / Collision Detection))

    1.2.3 Topology

    1.2.4 Media

3

Introduction

Networks have been around for many years, long before the first home computer was ever designed or created. Other forms of networking have been around since the dawn of time. Today, designing, planning, implementing, deploying, and managing computer networks is somewhat of a never-ending journey into technology as it develops and integrates, standardizes and grows. It's amazing to see where computer networks are today from just 15 years ago. Now, more than ever, computer networks are relied upon to produce not only data in the form of files or connectivity to a printer for printing… today, everything from surfing the Internet securely to making a call from New York to Tianjin, China over phone that solely works off the power of the network. Wired to wireless, satellites in the sky to home PC networks that allow 2 computers in your home to share the Internet at the same time. This is all done through networking. The wonderful world of networking is colorful, exciting, and is growing each and every day… routers, switches, and other infrastructure devices are deployed every day from companies such as Cisco, Juniper, Nortel, and 3Com to name a few. So who deploys them? Who plans, designs, and leads the way for all of this equipment to be planned, purchased, implemented, and managed? Each and every day technology grows more and more complicated, and it evolves as we do.

By the end of this chapter you will have learned what a network is, and you will start to build upon the initial concepts you need to develop to become a network technician, as well as to pass the Network+ exam. In this chapter we cover a brief history on the development of networks, as well where they originated from and where they are heading. We also cover the fundamental terminology you absolutely must know to perform your duties as a network technician and to pass the CompTIA Network+ exam. We cover network models such as centralized and decentralized, the differences between a local area network (LAN) and a wide area network (WAN). Network topologies such as bus, ring, mesh, and star are covered, as well as a discussion on wired and wireless networks. We then cover the IEEE (Institute of Electrical and Electronics Engineers), which is a standards committee aimed at making things in networking standardized, and easier to support and maintain. We cover in detail the most common standards, testable on the exam. Finally, we cover RFCs (Requests for Comments), a common source for networking professionals to get the definitive source on networking knowledge. So let us start from the very beginning… What exactly is a network anyway?

What is a Network?

Even someone who's new to computers has experienced the basic concept of networking; it is the difference between standing alone or being part of a group. Networks are systems that are interconnected in some way and provide a method of communication. If you think of your own experiences, you've probably networked with groups of colleagues, and perhaps discussed how you're planning on taking the Network+ exam.

Doing so provided a method of sharing information and possibly opened avenues to accessing important resources. Computers are the same; they can be standalone or part of a network.

A computer network exists when two or more machines are connected together, thereby allowing them to share data, equipment, and other resources. If there are no resources to share, then making a network is pretty useless. By using a combination of software and hardware the computers gain added functionality, including the ability to:

- Transfer data between machines.
- Save and access files on the same hard disks or other storage devices.
- Share printers, scanners, modems, and other peripheral devices.
- Allow messages to be exchanged via e-mail, instant messaging (IM), and other technologies.

TEST DAY TIP

It is wise to quickly review information dealing with the Network+ exam shortly before taking the exam itself. A fast approach to reviewing is to look over the Exam Watch information, Summary of Exam Objectives, and Exam Objectives Fast Track sections of this book. To make it easy to review items that you may have a problem remembering and that may appear on the exam, highlight or bookmark these items in the book so that you can review them at crunch time. They will provide a quick approach to re-examining important information.

Although networks may provide similar functions, they can be as different from one another as groups of people. Networks are characterized by a number of factors, which we'll discuss later in this chapter and throughout this book. Some of the elements that will define your network, and make it different from others include:

- **Hardware**, which includes the physical components of a computer or network, such as network interface cards (NICs) or network adapters that allow computers to transmit and receive data across the network. Other devices that fall into the category of hardware would include routers, switches, and hubs, which pass the data to other computers or networks (discussed in Chapter 3).
- **Media**, which consists of cables (discussed in Chapter 2) or wireless technologies (discussed in Chapter 4) that carry the data across the network.
- **Protocols**, which are sets of rules that control how the data is sent between computers. The most popular of these is the protocol used on the Internet, TCP/IP (Transmission Control Protocol / Internet Protocol), while other

protocols used on networks include IPX/SPX (Internetwork Packet Exchange/Sequenced Packet Exchange) and AppleTalk (discussed in Chapter 6).

- **Topology**, which is the shape of the network. It defines how the network is designed and describes how computers are physically connected together (discussed later in this chapter).

- **Network type**, which defines the size of the network and its scale within a geographical area (discussed later in this chapter).

- **Network model**, which determines the levels of security available to the network, and the components needed to connect the computers together (discussed later in this chapter).

- **Access**, which determines who can use the network and how, and if features of the network are available for private or public use (discussed in Chapter 7).

- **Network Operating Systems (NOS)**, such as Windows, NetWare, and Linux (discussed in Chapter 8). A NOS may be used for a server, which is a computer that provides services to numerous computers, and/or installed on computers that are used by individual users of the network. In some cases, such as with Novell NetWare, additional software may have to be installed on computers (*clients*) that use the server.

- **Other software and services**, such as access to internal websites, e-mail, databases, and so forth.

If some of these elements of a network seem foreign to you, don't worry. We'll expand on them as we move through the book, discussing areas of networking in great detail. Because there are so many components that make up a network, these factors influence the design of networks, so networks in different homes and offices aren't consistently the same. Networks may use different protocols, topologies, and other elements that make them unique. This means you can look at two networks in two different homes or businesses, and they can be completely different from one another.

Despite this, there are similarities that will exist among different networks. In all cases, a computer is configured to use the network (either by configuring its operating system or installing client software), and has a device capable of transmitting and receiving data, such as a network adapter or modem. Using a protocol like TCP/IP, the computer communicates with other computers and sends data over media (such as cables or wireless) to a device (such as a hub, router, or switch) that will send the data to its destination (such as another computer or device, such as a printer). Although the specifics may vary greatly, the basic aspects of a network remain the same.

Head of the Class...

Putting Things in Perspective

Many people who are new to networks may find the concepts overwhelming and difficult to process in their own mind. A good way of putting these concepts into perspective is to compare them to something that's already familiar. This not only makes the information easier to understand, but also provides mental cues that make it easier to remember.

You might compare networking to making a telephone call. A phone is a device that's used to transmit and receive information like a network adapter. When a call is made, you enter a number that uniquely identifies whomever you want to communicate with. On a TCP/IP network, this is called an IP address. This information is sent over a telephone network and routed to the person you're calling, just as a computer network sends data over various media and uses routers to ensure the correct computer gets the data being exchanged. Once you connect with the person you're calling, you use rules to communicate (such as not talking at the same time, or saying "Hello" and "Goodbye" to indicate the beginning and end of a conversation), just as networked computers use protocols to communicate and control how data is sent. Much of this is invisible to the person who is using the technology, which makes it easier to use.

What is an Internetwork?

Just as computers can be connected together, so can networks. An internetwork exists when two or more networks that are connected together. By connecting networks together, different businesses or locations can share data between their systems.

Internetworks are particularly important in organizations where sharing data is vital to the company's ability to function or operate effectively. For example, the police may have a network of computers in their cars, which connects to a network of computers located in police stations. If you're pulled over by the police, the officer may check your license plate number on the computer in his or her car. This computer would connect to a server used by the network of cars, and then pass along the request to a server on a different network that's used by other members of the organization, such as a Records department. If additional information was requested, the request might also be sent to networks belonging to state/provincial or federal police. By internetworking these different systems, the police can determine if the car is stolen, if it was used to commit a crime, or if the owner is wanted or believed dangerous.

As you've probably guessed from the name, the largest internetwork is the Internet. The Internet originated as a Department of Defense (DOD) project in 1969, when the Cold War was still going on between the West and the former Union of Soviet Socialist Republics (USSR). Under the direction of the DOD's Advanced Research Projects Agency (ARPA), the goal was to create a network that could withstand a nuclear attack.

If any part of ARPANET was destroyed, the other parts of it would continue to function. Initially connecting four universities (University of California Los Angeles (UCLA), Stanford Research Institute, University of California Santa Barbara, and

University of Utah), it allowed researchers and government to exchange information and quickly grew to include other organizations. Using the TCP/IP protocol suite that ARPA developed, additional computers and networks were added over the years, until finally in 1990, ARPANET was disbanded and removed from the Internet. Today, hundreds of millions of computers and networks connect to the Internet, making it a fundamental method of communication and data exchange.

Internetworks used by corporations and the Internet aren't to be confused with intranets. Intranets use the same technologies and features of the Internet, such as Internet browsers, websites, and so on. This allows users of a network to view documents, distribute data, share employee information, access shared databases, online programs, and other components that are needed or wanted by an organization. The major difference between an intranet and the Internet is that an intranet is used internally. While the Internet allows the public to view Web pages and other resources, intranets are private and available to employees of a company.

Configuring & Implementing

Knowledgeable Network Users

The Internet is a vast network of interconnected computers that your computer becomes a part of whenever it goes online. Since more people than ever before use the Internet, this means that many people are familiar with the basic concepts and features of networking without even being aware of it. This is a particular benefit in training the users of a network, as many will be familiar with using e-mail, having user accounts and passwords, and other technologies or procedures. Because the same or similar technologies are used, the skills gained in using the Internet are often transferable to the skills necessary to be a user of a corporate network.

Unfortunately, a little knowledge can also be a dangerous thing. When dealing with knowledgeable users, it is important to realize that they may have developed bad habits. After all, a user with years of experience will have found a few shortcuts and may have gotten lazy in terms of security. For example, the user may use easy-to-remember passwords that are easy to guess. In such a case, the solution would be to implement policies on using strong passwords (passwords with at least eight characters consisting of numbers, upper and lowercase letters, and non-alphanumeric characters), change passwords regularly, and not share passwords with others. If your company has an intranet, you can provide information on such policies to employees.

Another problem is that users may attempt to perform actions that aren't permitted in an organization, such as installing unapproved software or accessing restricted data. It is also important to set up security on a network so users can only access what they need to perform their jobs. This minimizes the chance that someone might modify or delete a file, view sensitive materials that are meant to be confidential, or install software that contains malicious programming or isn't work-related (such as games). Even in an environment with a trusting atmosphere, accidents happen and problems arise. Setting up proper security can prevent avoidable incidents from happening.

A Brief History on Networking and Communications

While the Network+ exam won't quiz you on the history of networking, learning about the foundations of networking and communications will give you a better understanding of more difficult topics discussed in later chapters. Understanding past achievements and how we've reached our present state of technology will also make you a better Network+–certified technician.

The history of networking and communications is rich and complex, stretching over a hundred years in the past, with massive changes in the later part of the 20th century. By looking at these changes, you will see the development of operating systems, hardware, and innovations that are still used today.

Early Telecommunications and Computers

Telecommunications got its start in 1870s in Brantford Ontario, when Alexander Graham Bell developed the idea of a telephone. After the first successful words were sent over the device on March 10, 1876, a revolution of communication began. Within decades of its conception, millions of telephones were sold, with operators connecting people using manual circuit switching. This method of calling the operator to have him or her connect you to another party was routine until the mid-20th century, when mechanical and electronic circuit switching became commonplace. These events would have a massive impact on the innovation of computers, even though they wouldn't be invented until sixty years after Bell's first successful phone call.

Although arguments could be made as to whether ancient devices (such as the abacus) could be considered a type of computer, the first programmable computer was developed by a German engineer named Konrad Zuse. In 1936, Zuse created the Z1, a mechanical calculator that was the first binary computer. Zuse continued making innovations to his design, and five years later had reached the point where the Z3 was able to accept programming. Although the next version of his computer would use punch cards to store programs, Zuse used movie film to store programming and data on the Z3 due to a supply shortage of paper during World War II. Just as his computers evolved, so did his programming skills. Zuse's achievements also extended to creating the first algorithmic programming language called Plankalkül, which later used to create the first computer chess game.

During this same time, John Atanasoff and Clifford Berry developed what is acknowledged to be the first electronic-binary computer. Created at the University of Iowa, the initial prototype acquired this team a grant that allowed them to build their 700-pound final product, containing over 300 vacuum tubes and approximately one mile of wire. Although an historic achievement, it wasn't initially recognized as such, as World War II prevented Atanasoff and Berry from completing a patent on their computer. Perhaps even worse, the computer itself met an unceremonious end when the Physics department needed storage space that was being used by the machine and dismantled it.

The distinction of being first initially went to John Mauchly and J. Presper Eckert for their ENIAC I computer, until a 1973 patent infringement case determined Atanasoff and Berry were the first. The ENIAC I (Electrical Numerical Integrator And Calculator) was developed with funding from the U.S. government, and was based on the work of John Atanasoff. Starting work in 1943, the project took two and a half years to design and build ENIAC I, at a cost of half a million dollars. The ENIAC I was faster than previous computers, and was used to perform calculations for designing a hydrogen bomb, wind-tunnel designs, and a variety of scientific studies. It was used until 1955 when the 30 ton, 1800 square foot computer was ultimately retired.

Another computer that was developed during this time was the MARK I computer, developed by Howard Aiken and Grace Murray Hopper in 1944 in a project co-sponsored by Harvard University and International Business Machines (IBM). Dwarfing the ENIAC at a length of 55 feet and 5 tons in weight, the MARK I was the first computer to perform long calculations. Although it was retired in 1959, it made a lasting mark on the English language. When the MARK I experienced a computer failure, Grace Murray Hopper checked inside the machine and found a moth. She taped it to her logbook and wrote "first actual bug found," giving us the terms "bug" for a computer problem, and "debug" for fixing it.

In 1949, Hopper went on from the MARK I project to join a company created by John Mauchly and J. Presper Eckert, which was developing a 1500 square foot, 40-ton computer named UNIVAC (UNIVersal Automatic Computer). UNIVAC was the first computer to use magnetic tape instead of paper cards to store programming code and data, and was much faster than the previous computers we've discussed. Whereas the MARK I took a few seconds to complete a multiplication operation, and ENIAC I could perform hundreds of operations per second, UNIVAC could perform multiplication in microseconds. What made UNIVAC popular in the public eye, however, was a 1952 publicity stunt where the computer accurately predicted the outcome of the presidential election. Although Dwight Eisenhower and Adlai Stevenson were believed evenly matched going into the November 4th election night, UNIVAC predicted that Eisenhower would get 438 electoral votes, while Stevenson would only get 93. In actuality, Eisenhower got 442 electoral votes, while Stevenson got 89. While political analysts had been unable to predict the outcome, UNIVAC did so with a 1% margin of error. Having earned its place in history, the original UNIVAC currently resides in the Smithsonian Institute.

Although UNIVAC was the more successful computer of its day, 1953 saw IBM release the EDPM 701. Using punchcards for programs, nineteen of these were sold (as opposed to 46 UNIVACs sold to business and government agencies). However, development of this computer lead to the IBM 704, considered to be the first super-computer. Because it used magnetic core memory, it was faster than its predecessor. This series of computers further evolved to the development of the 7090 computer in 1960, which was the first commercially available computer to use transistors, and the fastest computer of its time. Such innovations firmly placed IBM as a leader in computer technology.

The Space Age to the Information Age

While IBM and the owners of UNIVAC were contending for clients to buy their computers, or at least rent computer time, the former USSR launched Sputnik in 1957. Sputnik was the first manmade satellite to be put into orbit, and it initiated a competition in space between the USSR and the United States that pushed technology to new limits.

Sputnik launched a number of events that led to advances in computers and communication. While author Arthur C. Clark had published an article in 1945 describing manmade satellites in geosynchronous orbit being used to relay transmissions, communication satellites didn't appear until after Sputnik's historic orbit. In 1960, Bell Telephone Laboratories (AT&T) filed with the FCC to obtain permission to launch a communications satellite, and over the next five years, several communication satellites were orbiting overhead.

Obviously, the most notable result of Sputnik was the space race between the U.S. and USSR, with the ultimate goal of reaching the moon. The U.S. started the National Aeronautics and Space Administration (NASA), began launching space missions, and achieved the first manned landing on the moon in 1969. Using computers that employed only a few thousand lines of code (as opposed to the 45 million lines of code used in Windows XP), the onboard computer systems provided necessary functions and communicated with other computers on Earth. Communications between astronauts and Mission Control on Earth also marked the furthest distance of people communicating to date.

The Cold War and the space race also resulted in another important milestone in computer systems and communication systems. As we discussed earlier, the U.S. government started the Advanced Research Projects Agency, which developed such important technologies as:

- ARPANET, the predecessor of the modern Internet, which connected multiple institutions and areas of government together for research purposes.

- Packet-switched networks, where messages sent over a network are broken into packets. They are then sent over the network, and reassembled after reaching the destination computer.

- TCP/IP, which specifies rules about how data is to be sent and received over the network, and provides utilities for working over a network.

Although only a few educational institutions and the government were networked together through ARPANET, it lead to the first e-mail program being developed in 1972, and the first news server being developed in 1979. The Internet was years away, but its foundation was set here.

Hardware and Operating Systems

Major advances pushed the development of computers and networking in the 1970s. In 1971, Intel produced the first microprocessor, which had its own arithmetic logic unit and provided a way of creating smaller, faster computers. It was the first of many Intel processors produced over the years, including the:

- 8008 processor produced in 1972

- 8080 processor (an 8-bit processor) produced in 1974

- 8086 processor (a 16-bit processor) produced in 1978. Because other technology needed to catch up to the speed of the processor, an 8088 processor (an 8/16-bit processor) was released in 1979. It wasn't until 1983 that IBM released the XT with the 8086 processor (and option to add an 8087 match co-processor).

- 80286 (16-bit processor) produced in 1982

- 80386 (32-bit processor) produced in 1985

- 80486 (32-bit processor) produced in 1989

- Pentium (32-bit processor) produced in 1993, which ended the x86 naming scheme for processors. After this, Intel chips bore the Pentium name, inclusive up to the Pentium 75 (in 1994), Pentium 120, 133 and Pentium Pro 200 (in 1995), Pentium MMX and Pentium II (in 1997), and Pentium III (in 1999). As you would expect, each generation was faster than the last.

Just as processing changed in the 1970s, so did storage. In 1973, IBM developed the first hard disk, and an 8" floppy drive, replacing the need to store data and programs solely on magnetic tapes. This massive floppy was quickly replaced by the 5.25" floppy in 1976, which was later succeeded by the 3.5" floppy disk that was developed by Sony in 1980. These methods of storing data became commonplace until 1989 when the first CD-ROM was developed, and again changed in 1997 with the introduction of DVDs.

With the advances in technology, it was only a matter of time before someone developed a home computer. Prior to the mid-1970s, computers were still too large and expensive to be used by anyone other than large corporations and governments. With the invention of the microprocessor, a company called Micro Instrumentation and Telemetry Systems (MITS) developed the Altair 8800 using the Intel 8080 processor. Although it included an 8" floppy drive, it didn't have a keyboard, monitor or other peripherals that we're accustomed to today. Programs and data entry were entered using toggle switches at the front of the machine. Although it couldn't be compared to personal computers of today, it did attain the distinction of being the first.

The Altair also provided a point of origin for Microsoft, as Bill Gates and Paul Allen developed a version of the BASIC programming language for Altair that was based on a public domain version created in 1964. Microsoft went on to create an operating system called PC-DOS (which required users to type in commands) for the first IBM computer (named "The Acorn") in 1981, but maintained ownership of the software. This allowed them to market their operating system to other computer manufacturers and build their software empire. Microsoft went on to develop such operating systems as MS-DOS, Windows, Windows for Workgroups, Windows NT, Windows ME, Windows 2000, Windows 2003 Server, and Windows XP.

UNIX was another operating system that originated in the 1970s, and was the inspiration for developing another operating system that's widely used today. Ken Thomson and Dennis Ritchie of Bell Labs developed UNIX in 1970, which came to be used on high-end servers and (years later) Web servers for the Internet. Linus Torvalds used UNIX as the basis for developing Linux twenty years later. Linux is open source, meaning that the code is available to use for free, and is the only operating system that acts as competition for Microsoft and Apple today.

Apple Computer's start also originates in the 1970s, when Steve Jobs and Steve Wozniak incorporated their company on April Fools Day of 1976, and introduced the Apple II the next year. It wasn't until the 1980s, however, that Apple really made its mark. In 1981, Xerox developed a Graphical User Interface (GUI) that used the windows, icons, menus, and mouse support that we're familiar with in operating systems today. However, Xerox never released it to the public. Developing its Apple Lisa and Macintosh on the work done by Xerox, Apple introduced Lisa as the first GUI personal computer in 1983. The Macintosh was easy to use and made Apple the major competition of IBM after its release.

The WIMP (Windows, Icons, Menus, Pointer) interface that gave Apple and Windows their looks wasn't the only major contribution Xerox made to computers and networking. While working at Xerox's Palo Alto Research Center, Bob Metcalfe was asked to develop a method of networking their computers. What he created was called *Ethernet*. Ethernet was different from other networks like the Internet, which connected remote computers together using modems that dialed into one another, or dumb terminals that had no processing power and were only used to access mainframe computers. Ethernet connected computers together using cabling and network adapters, allowing them to communicate with one another over these physical connections. If you think that Ethernet sounds like many networks in use today, you'd be correct; Ethernet is an industry standard.

EXAM WARNING

Ethernet is the most popular type of networking used, and you can expect to see it covered or mentioned in questions on the exam. While its development is remarked on here, it is discussed in greater detail later in this chapter and in Chapter 2.

After Ethernet was developed, operating systems that were specifically designed for networking weren't far behind. In 1979, Novell Data Systems was founded with a focus on developing computer hardware and operating systems. In 1983 however, Novell changed focus and developed NetWare, thus becoming an industry leader in network operating systems. Unlike other operating systems that resided on a computer and could be used as either a standalone machine or a network workstation, NetWare was two components. The NetWare operating system is a full operating system and resides on a server, which processes requests from a network user's client machine. The computer that the network user is working on can run any number of different operating systems (such as Windows 9x, NT, etcetera), but has client software installed on it that connects to the NetWare server. When a request is made to access a file or print to a NetWare server, the client software redirects the request to the server. Due to its popularity as a network operating system, it is widely used on corporate and government networks.

The Information Age Appears

In the 1980s, computers became more commonplace in homes and businesses. Prices had dropped to the point where it was affordable to have a computer in the home, and powerful enough to be worth having a 286 or 386 computer. While many people found computers useful, they quickly outgrew the desire to have a standalone machine and wanted to be networked to others.

The 1980s and 1990s saw growing popularity in BBSs (Bulletin Board Systems), where one computer could use a modem and telephone line to directly dial another computer. Computers with BBS software provided the ability for users to enjoy many of the features associated with the Internet, including message boards, e-mail, chat programs (to send messages instantly to other users), the ability to download programs and other files, or play online games. Because communications were carried out over a modem, BBSs were largely comprised of computer users within a single community, although message networks were used to have discussions with people in other cities or countries.

While BBSs were eventually replaced by the Internet, the 1980s also saw changes that would affect the future of cyberspace. In 1983, the University of Wisconsin developed the Domain Name System (DNS). DNS provided a way of translating the IP addresses used to uniquely identify computers on TCP/IP networks. Using DNS, a number like 207.46.250.222 can be translated to a friendly domain name like microsoft.com. In 1984, DNS became part of ARPANET, and would eventually become a major part resolving domain names on the Internet.

Also during the mid-1980s, the backbone of the Internet was developed. The backbone was a central network that connected other networks on the Internet. Between 1985 and 1988, T1 lines were developed to accommodate a necessary increase of dataflow and speed on the Internet. The speed that data could be sent over the backbone was now increased to 1.544Mbps.

Perhaps the greatest defining moment in the shape of the Internet was Tim Berners-Lee's creation of HTML (HyperText Markup Language). In 1989, a textual version was created that supported hyperlinks, but this evolved into the language that was released by CERN in 1991, and used to create documents that can be viewed online (in the form of Web pages). In 1993, Mosaic became the first Internet browser, allowing users to view such Web pages, but others like Netscape and Internet Explorer soon appeared.

When ARPANET was retired in 1990, the first company to provide dial-up access to the Internet was formed. The World (www.theworld.com) provided the ability (for a fee) to dial into their system using a modem and connect to the Internet. In 1993, other Internet Service Providers (ISPs) appeared that provided this service, increasing the number of people using the Internet steadily. While initially used as a repository of programs, research, and other resources, this opened the Internet up to commercial use, which evolved into the entity we know today.

Networking Models

Since networks vary from one another depending upon a range of factors, it should come as no surprise that there are different network models. The network model you choose will affect a network infrastructure's design and how it is administered. Depending on the model or models used, it can have an impact on the location of computers, how users access resources, and the number of computers and types of operating systems required. The models available to choose from are:

- Centralized
- Decentralized (Distributed)
- Peer-to-Peer
- Client/Server

Centralized

When a centralized network model is used, a network's resources are centrally located and administered. This approach allows network administrators to have better access to equipment and better control over security issues. However, because responsibility for managing these resources now rests with the network administrator or IT staff, the workload of administering them increases.

A centralized model will affect the physical location of servers and certain other resources on your network. You'll remember that servers are computers that accept requests from client computers (which users of the network work on), and provide services and resources that the client has proper access to use. As we'll discuss later in this chapter, dedicated servers generally have larger hard disk space and memory, and have faster processors than the workstations accessing them. When a centralized model is used, these servers are generally located in a secure, central location, such as a dedicated server room. This secured room can also be used to house other resources, such as routers, switches, firewalls, Web servers, plotters, and other devices.

Because they are stored in a central location, additional work may be required to manage them. For example, let's say you had a plotter that was kept in a server room. Anytime anyone needed the plotter installed as a printer on his or her computer, you would need to set up permissions for him or her to use it. If the user sent a print job to this plotter, someone from the IT staff would need to enter the secure room to get the printout. In addition, there would also be the need to replace paper and toners used in the device. In a centralized model, administration of the resources is also centralized.

Despite the previous scenario, in some ways, managing resources can be easier with this model. By keeping these resources in one area, a network administrator can easily change backup tapes, replace hard disks, or fix other issues as required. Imagine the issues with having servers in offices throughout a city or region, and having to visit each of them whenever a tape had to be replaced after a tape backup. By keeping resources centralized, less work is required for their administration.

Depending on the requirements of an organization, the centralized network model can also mean that fewer servers or other devices are needed. Rather than each building having its own server on the premises, users can save their work to a dedicated server in a central location. This would keep everyone's files on one or more servers, allowing their work to be kept secure and regularly backed up.

Decentralized (Distributed)

When a decentralized network model is used, a network's resources are distributed through different areas of the network, and administration is shared by designating responsibility to system administrators or individual users. For example, printers may be scattered throughout an organization, with managers of each office being responsible for assigning permissions to user accounts to use specific printers. By sharing administrative burdens in this way, certain resources can now be managed by other members of the organization.

A decentralized network model has a variety of servers, equipment, and other resources distributed across the geographical area making up the network. While a network administrator may be able to access them over the computer network, such network components aren't readily accessible physically. As such, a network administrator must rely on people who are designated as system administrators in those locations. These people must be properly trained on the system, and responsible enough to take matters like security seriously. If not, something as simple as changing a backup tape could be problematic or even disastrous.

Even if an organization initially decides on having a centralized network, decentralizing the network may be the only viable option if cost factors or other issues come into play. For example, if a company had a slow network connection between buildings, users might find logging into the network, saving data to a server, or accessing network resources slow. A solution would be to put a server in each building so that computers could be authenticated and quickly access data on the server that's closest to them. By distributing servers in this instance, network performance would improve because users wouldn't have to authenticate or necessarily use the slow connection to the other server.

Head of the Class...

Centralized Access Control

Even when servers and resources are distributed throughout a network, it does not mean that access control can't be centralized. Centralized access control is when users achieve access to the network through a central point of authentication. Users log onto the network through some form of authentication, such as a username and password, which is passed to a server that processes the request for access. The server compares this information to a corresponding account that's stored in a database, and determines whether the user has correctly identified him or herself, and which resources this person is authorized to access.

Because users acquire access to resources through one source, it saves them from having to log onto each server. Early versions of network operating systems required users to determine which server they wanted to use, and then enter the username and password for their account on that server. By using centralized access control, the users only need to be authenticated once to be able to access resources on any server they are given permissions and rights to use.

Another benefit of centralizing access control is that administration of accounts can be done for an entire network through one control system. For example, on networks using Windows 2000 Server or 2003 Server, user accounts and information are stored in Active Directory, while Novell NetWare networks use Novell Directory Services (NDS) or eDirectory. Using ConsoleOne in NetWare or Microsoft Management Console (MMC) in Windows, a network administrator has the ability to connect to the directory containing user information, and control which folders a user can access, password requirements, when the user can log onto the network, and numerous other settings and controls. Rather than making changes to each server, the administrator only needs to make changes to one account to affect that user's access throughout the network. Because of this, centralized access control is often used in enterprises, where there are large numbers of computers and user accounts that have to be managed.

Peer-to-Peer

Years ago, most computers on a network weren't very powerful. Hard disks, memory, printers, and other components making up a computer system were expensive, creating a need for dedicated servers that other computers accessed to store data and access necessary resources. These dedicated servers could be mainframes or high-end computers with additional memory, storage space, and processing power. As technology progressed, computer workstations came to be as powerful as, or in many cases more powerful than the servers of years past, making peer-to-peer networks a viable solution for smaller networks.

In a peer-to-peer network, computers on the network act as equals, with each workstation providing access to resources and data. This is a simple type of network where computers are able to communicate with one another, and share what is on or attached to their computer with other users. It is also one of the easiest types of architectures to create.

Individual users have responsibility over who can access data and resources on their computers. Operating systems like Windows 2000 Professional and Windows XP allow accounts to be set up that will be used when others users connect to a specified computer. Accounts, passwords, and permissions are saved in a local database, and are used to determine what someone can do when connecting to your computer. For example, one account may allow a user to send print jobs to your printer, while another account may allow the user to access files in certain directories, but not to print.

Because peer-to-peer networks are generally small, creating one can be as simple as installing network adapters into each computer, attaching a network cable to the adapter and connecting the other end to a hub or router. If a wireless network is being created, then even the cables aren't necessary, as wireless adapters and a wireless router are all that's needed. Once this is done, each computer is configured to use the network adapter that's installed, and a protocol is configured to allow communication between the computers. In cases where operating systems like Windows XP are used, this configuration can be done through a wizard program, which takes you step-by-step through the configuration process.

One important issue with peer-to-peer networks is security. Each computer on this type of network may allow or deny access to other users, as access to data and resources are controlled on each machine. For example, a user could share a folder on his or her computer, allowing other users to access the files in that folder.

Because users can have the ability to control access to files and resources on their computers, network administration isn't controlled by one person. However, problems may exist when users grant access to data and resources based on friendship with another person instead of that person's need to perform his or her job. As such, peer-to-peer networks are generally used in situations where security isn't a major concern, as in the case of home networks or very small businesses.

Exam Warning

A peer-to-peer network uses share level access and allows users to control access to files and resources on their computers. Each computer is equal in this type of network. A client/server network has computers who act as clients to servers that share resources. Access on a client/server network is based on accounts, which can determine whether users and computers have access to files and other resources. If resources are located and administered in a central location, it is a centralized network, while resources that are distributed and administered across the network are decentralized. Remember the differences and relationships between different network types for the exam, as they may be covered either directly or incorporated in the scenarios used to cover other material.

Client/Server

In looking at the peer-to-peer network model, when one computer requests data or other services from another computer, it acts as a client, while the other computer delivering that data or service acts as a server. These roles seem obscured because both computers can act in either of these roles. In the client/server model, these roles are clearer because the model involves dedicated servers that provide services such as file and printer sharing and data to clients, without making similar requests of them.

The client/server model consists of high-end computers serving clients on a network, by providing them with specific services upon request. Years ago, each server generally performed a single role, such as:

- File server, which allows clients to save data to folders on its hard drive.

- Print server, which redirects print jobs from clients to specific printers.

- Application server, which allows clients to run certain programs on the server, and enables multiple users to common applications across the network.

- Database server, which allows authorized clients to view, modify and/or delete data in a common database.

Today, computers are more powerful and network operating systems are more effective, so each server may act in several different roles. For example, a server may be a Web server for the local intranet, but also allow users to access a database and store files in an area of its hard drive. The services provided by the server will vary greatly depending on how it has been configured and what's been installed.

The software that's installed largely dictates the roles a dedicated server can perform. First and foremost, the server needs to have a network operating system like Windows NT, Windows 2000 Server, Windows 2003 Server, UNIX/Linux, or Novell NetWare installed on it. These server operating systems provide features specifically for servicing clients, and can respond more efficiently to a greater number of client requests than standard operating systems like Windows 9x, NT Workstation, Windows 2000 Professional, or Windows XP.

Once a high-end computer has server software installed, the services provided by it have to be configured and other programs may have to be installed. Many of the server's functions are dependant on the server software installed on it. For example, a server that acts as an SQL server is a database server, but it has to have a program like Microsoft SQL Server installed on it. In the same way, a Web server on a Windows Server 2003 server would need Internet Information Services (IIS) configured. By installing server software on a dedicated server, you define the role that server will play on your network.

While a dedicated server may play a variety of roles, you should determine whether the load placed on the server is too great, thereby causing performance to decrease. Some services provided by a server may be accessed frequently, creating a larger workload for the server. Rather than creating a burden for the server, the server should be dedicated to performing a single role, or at least a decreased number of roles. For example, an e-mail server may be accessed frequently by users of the network who want to check for messages. Because it is used so often, many organizations will have one server performing this role alone to prevent it from being bogged down and providing slow access to e-mail. In the same way, if the service is essential to a business, such as Web server being necessary for a business that sells products on the Internet, that server will be dedicated to only that role. The more a server is dedicated to a specific or limited number of functions, the better its performance and the less chance there will be of everything becoming unavailable if one server fails.

Security Alert!

Only Use Servers as Servers

Although dedicated servers are designed to serve clients, many of the server operating systems have the ability to be used as if they were clients. For example, Windows servers have always had the same GUI as other versions of Windows for standalone computers or network workstations. This means you could install and use Microsoft Office, games, or any number of other software products. However, it is unwise to use a server as if it was any other client machine on your network.

Every time you run software on a computer, memory, processing, and other resources are used, which could otherwise be used for responding to client requests, and you run the risk of crashing the server. Think of the number of times a program has locked up your computer, and then think of the implications of what would happen if hundreds of users had been accessing it as a server and were now unable to do their work. The reason you have a server is for it to act as a server. Unless you are performing work on the server related to how it functions as a server, it is not advisable to use it for other purposes.

Network Types and Topologies

At the beginning of this chapter, we explained that a network exists when two or more computers are connected together so they can share various resources. While this defines the basic nature of a network, it doesn't provide an understanding of the different sizes and shapes a network can take as it's designed and developed. Having this understanding is important in determining the scope and physical layout of computers, cables, and other network components. It is also vital when considering the type of media that will be used, and whether additional components are necessary to expand your network.

Network Types

Just as we saw the Internet evolve from a relatively small network named ARPANET, networks can extend beyond their initial creation of a few computers connected together. A network can be in a single building, or comprised of computers connected together over a broader geographical area. To categorize the scope of a network, different terms have been created to classify these different network types. The types of networks that could be created include:

- Local area network
- Wide area network
- Metropolitan area network (MAN)
- Storage area network (SAN)
- Personal area network (PAN)
- Campus area network (CAN)

LAN and WAN

Local area networks and wide area networks were the first types of networks to be classified by the area they covered, and are still the ones most commonly referred to. While each of the names refer to an area, an exact range has never been firmly established and is left vague. Although IEEE (which we'll discuss later in this chapter) defines a local area as being up to 4 km, no one will accuse it of not being a LAN if it is slightly over that. LANs are networks spanning a limited distance, while a WAN is a network that is larger than a LAN. What distinguishes a LAN from a WAN in terms of area is ambiguous and speculative at best.

Local area networks are small- to medium-sized networks, and generally connect network devices that are no more than a few miles from one another. They include networks that have been set up in homes, offices, the floor of a building, an entire building, a campus or group of nearby buildings, or facilities that are relatively close to one another. Basically, if you can walk or drive the distance of the network in a short time, you're dealing with a LAN.

Another way to characterize a LAN is through ownership. Typically, the network is owned by a single person or organization, and is managed by a single person or group of people. For example, your home network would be a LAN that's owned and managed by you. In the same way, a large company with several buildings in a region that's run by a network administrator or IT department would also be a LAN. When you look at LANs in this way, you can see that most networks are actually local area networks.

Wide area networks can span great geographical distances and connect different LANs together using high-speed solutions or telephone lines. A WAN may connect LANs in different cities, regions, states/provinces, or even countries. This is something we saw when we discussed the first WAN, ARPANET, which connected the LANs of several institutions in different cities together. Over time, the number of computers and networks connecting to it grew until it spanned the world and became the Internet. By internetworking individual LANs together, the LANs become parts of a wide area network.

When looking at WANs, ownership isn't a defining factor. Wide area networks are often owned and managed by more than one organization. Each LAN that is part of the WAN may be managed by individuals or IT departments, who either maintain their connections to the rest of the LAN or hire outside parties to perform that function. For example, in the case of the Internet, you may maintain your home network, but you hire an ISP to maintain the connection to the World Wide Web. In the same way, a company with offices in different cities may hire the phone company to maintain a T1 line that connects the network together.

An effective way of understanding how a local area network is related to a wide area network is to look at how they are connected and how data is sent. This may differ from organization to organization, as there are several different ways of getting data from a LAN to a WAN, including:

- Modem, which is a device that allows you to connect to other computers and devices using telephone lines. Generally, when a modem is mentioned, it refers to a dial-up modem (as opposed to the digital modems for other methods mentioned below). This type of connection is slow, and allows connections at a maximum of 56Kbps (meaning that 56000 bits of data can be sent or received per second).

- ISDN (Integrated Services Digital Network), which also transmits data over telephone lines but at higher speeds, up to 128Kbps, but averaging 64Kbps using an ISDN modem or router.

- DSL (Digital Subscriber Line), which sends data across telephone lines at speeds ranging from 1.5Mbps (1.5 million bits per second) using a router or digital modem and configured phone lines.

- Cable, which transmits the data across cable lines using the same lines used for cable television at speeds of up to 1.5Mbps.

- Satellite, which transmits data to a satellite at speeds of up to 400Kbps.

- T1 and T3, which are dedicated connections that provide extremely high speeds. A T1 line provides speeds of 1.544Mbps, while a T3 line provides speeds ranging from 3Mbps to 44.736Mbps.

TEST DAY TIP

The speeds and types of media available for a network is an important area of study for the exam. While we'll discuss media in greater detail in Chapter 2 and WAN technologies in Chapter 7, you will need to memorize the characteristics and speeds of various media before taking the exam.

To illustrate the relationships between LANs and WANs, let's look at a situation that may be familiar to you: sending e-mail to another person. Using the e-mail program on your computer, you would click the **Send** button, and the data (your e-mail) would be sent to the device responsible for sending it to the Internet. As shown in Figure 1.1, this begins a process that will take the e-mail through a number of devices and possibly several LANs and WANs. If you have a dial-up account to the Internet, the device might be a standard modem. If you have a LAN in your home, the e-mail might be sent to a network adapter and sent over a network.

Figure 1.1 LANs and WANs

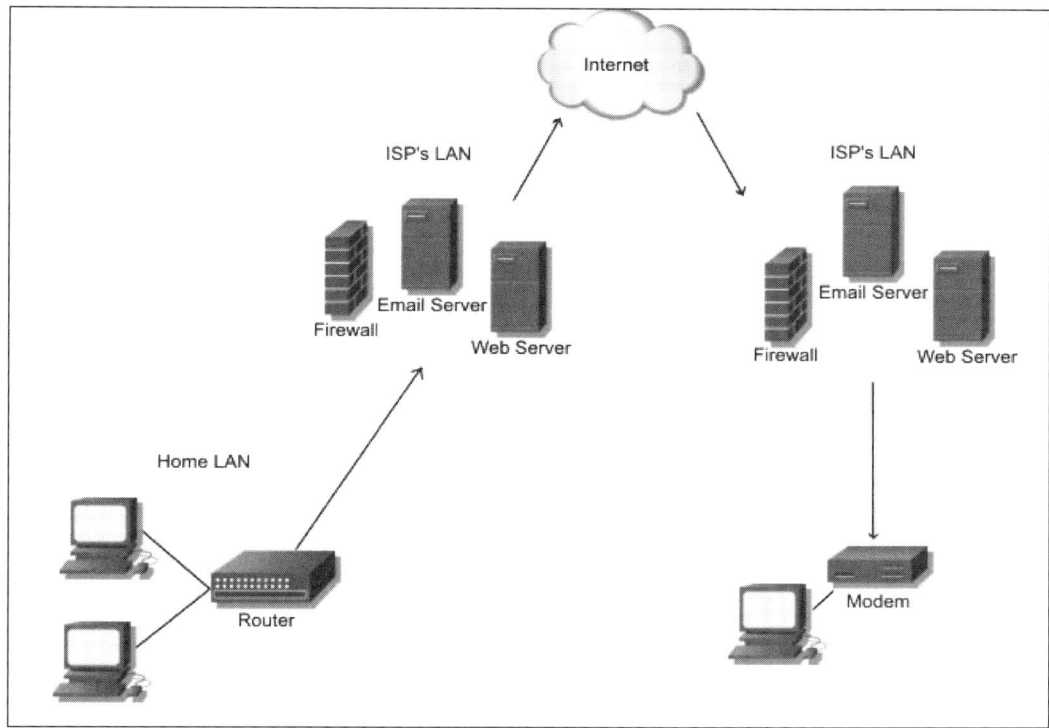

As we mentioned earlier, when a network is created, two or more computers are connected together. In a LAN, these computers are in the same locale, such as being in the same room. Each computer has a NIC installed in it, which transmits and receives data through a network cable or using wireless technology. When your data is sent to the network adapter, it is broken up into smaller chunks called *packets* that can be sent more efficiently over the network. As such, your e-mail would be broken into smaller packets, which would then be put back together by the computer receiving it.

If you used DSL, these packets would be transmitted over your home LAN to a router (or other termination device) that is used to connect to the ISP. Some of these devices come with the capability to act as hubs and switches, which allow them to be used to connect different computers on your LAN together. In cases where network cable is used, one end of a cable would be plugged into a network adapter and the other would plug into the router. Data is sent over the cable with information about its destination, and the router determines if it's for a computer on the LAN or has to be sent to the ISP who provides DSL to you. Since you're sending e-mail to someone who isn't on your home network, the router would use the DSL connection to send it from your LAN to the ISP's LAN. In doing so, the e-mail message has gone beyond the boundaries of your local network, and has been passed to a WAN.

When the ISP receives your e-mail, it also looks at where the data is destined. Because the ISP also has a LAN, it looks at whether the e-mail is destined for someone else who uses their service, a computer on their network, or another network connected to the Internet. Since you're sending the e-mail to someone who uses a different ISP, it sends the e-mail over the Internet, which is a giant WAN, to be received by the destination ISP's e-mail server.

When the destination ISP receives the data, it will store the e-mail you sent on its e-mail server, until your friend dials into the Internet using a modem. Your friend's computer connects to the ISP's server, and then requests any e-mail that the e-mail server might have. This data is again broken into packets, and sent over the telephone line so that your friend's modem can receive the data, and the computer can reassemble these packets and display them in your friend's e-mail program.

As you can see by this example, there are many different kinds of LANs and WANs that data may pass through. LANs may be as small as a couple of computers networked together, and a WAN may be as large as the Internet or as small as two LANs (yours and your ISP's) interconnected using routers. In each case, the LAN consists of computers that are part of the same network, and the WAN consists of geographically dispersed LANs that are internetworked.

EXAM WARNING

Being that the Network+ exam is an exam on networks, it should come as no surprise that questions dealing with LANs and WANs will appear. Make sure you know the difference between a LAN and a WAN, and that a WAN is a group of internetworked LANs. Other types of networks discussed below (MAN, SAN, CAN, PAN) aren't covered extensively on the exam. Specific elements of LANs and WANs are discussed throughout this book, and you will need to know them to pass the exam.

MAN

While most people refer to a network in terms of being either a LAN or a WAN, there are other terms to further categorize a network. One such category is a MAN, which is an acronym for a metropolitan area network. A MAN will generally cover a metropolitan area, like a city, but this isn't always the case. For example, if you lived in a small town and had your LAN connecting to another LAN in a neighboring town, you could also refer to this as a MAN. When LANs are connected together with high-speed solutions over a territory that is relatively close together (such as several buildings in a city, region or county), it can be considered a MAN. A MAN is a group of LANs that are internetworked within a local geographic area, which IEEE (an organization we'll discuss later in this chapter) defines as being 50 km or less in diameter. As shown in Figure 1.2, LANs can be joined together within this area to create a MAN, while still being part of a larger WAN.

Figure 1.2 LANs, MANs, and WANs

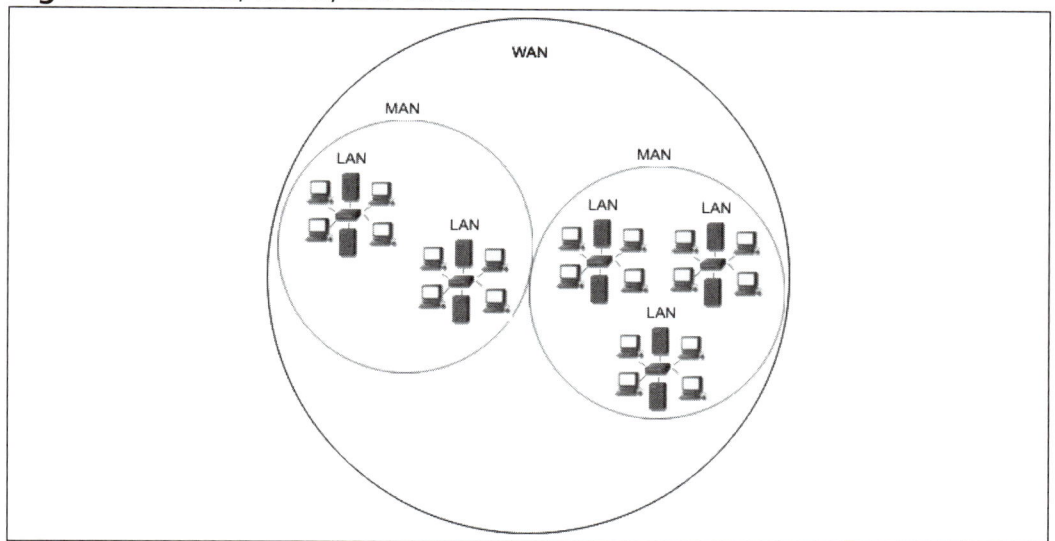

SAN

A SAN is a storage area network, and is used to connect storage devices together using high-speed connections. It is a segment of a network, and allows storage devices to be accessed by computers within the larger LAN or WAN. These storage devices consist of hard disks or other methods of storing data, and allow users of the network to view and/or save data to a centralized location.

PAN

A PAN is a personal area network, which is a wireless network that allows devices to exchange data with computers. Personal Digital Assistants (PDAs), cell phones, and other portable devices that support this technology have a wireless transmitter in them. When they are within a certain distance of a receiver that's installed on a computer, data can be exchanged between the computer and the device. Using a PAN allows you to do such things as update a calendar in a PDA or an address book in a cell phone, and other tasks that are supported by the device.

CAN

A CAN is a campus area network, and refers to a series of LANs that are internet-worked between several nearby buildings. This is a common type of network that's used in organizations with facilities that are close to one another, such as in a pool of office buildings or a campus. It is larger than a LAN, but smaller than a MAN.

NOTE

Wireless local area networks (WLANs) are covered in Chapter 4.

Network Topologies

Just as size defines a network, so does the way it's laid out. The topology of a network is the physical layout of computers, hubs, routers, cables, and other components. It provides a map of where things are and how the network is configured.

While networks are often unique, the topology of each network will share characteristics with others. Networks will use one or a combination of these topologies:

- Bus
- Star
- Ring
- Mesh
- Wireless

EXAM WARNING

One of the testable items on the Network+ exam is the ability to identify a topology based on either the description given, or a picture of the topology. Make sure you know each of the topologies covered in this section, and can identify them simply by looking at them before taking the exam.

Bus

The bus topology is an older topology that is rarely seen and not normally deployed in modern networks. As shown in Figure 1.3, all of the computers in a bus topology are connected together using a single cable, which is called a trunk, backbone, or segment. Coaxial cable is commonly used for the trunk, which is the same type of cable that's used to connect to your TV to receive cable television. The computers are attached to the 50ohm coaxial cable segment using T-connectors, which get their name because they're shaped like the letter T. Because all of these computers use the same cable, only one computer can send packets of data (which are electronic signals) onto the network at a time.

Figure 1.3 A Bus Topology

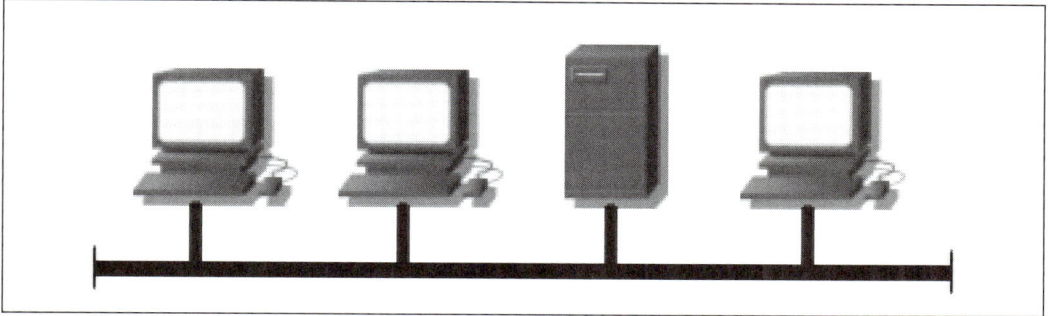

When a computer sends a packet of data onto the trunk, it is sent in both directions so that every computer on the network has the chance to receive it. Each of the computers on this type of topology listens to the network traffic, so that it can determine whether a packet being sent over the network is for it. When a computer listens to the network, any packets that aren't addressed to it are ignored, while any specifically sent to it are accepted. The exception to this is when a broadcast is made, in which packets are destined for every computer on the network.

Because the topology is linear, when data is sent over the trunk, it runs the length of the cable. To prevent data signals from staying on the cable indefinitely, the cable has to be terminated with 50ohm terminators at each end so electronic signals are absorbed when they reach the cable's end. The terminator absorbs the signal so that the cable is clear for other computers to send packets on the network. Without termination, a computer would send packets to another computer over the trunk, and the packets would bounce back and forth along the length of the cable making communication unreliable and prone to failure.

Bus topologies provide several benefits to organizations. While we mentioned that they are easy to set up, they are also a passive topology. In other words, when a computer is on a bus network, it only listens for or sends data. It doesn't take data and then resend or regenerate it, so each computer isn't essential to the network as a whole. If one computer fails, it doesn't crash the entire network.

Another benefit of this topology is that it is inexpensive, as less cable is used than in other topologies we'll discuss. As we'll see later, some topologies have redundant connections or require a significant amount of cable. In a bus topology, every computer is connected to a single cable.

Having a single cable, however, does cause other problems. If the trunk cable breaks, each segment has an end that isn't terminated, and the entire network goes down. If the trunk is long enough, it can be difficult to isolate where the break is.

Another disadvantage of this topology is that it isn't very scalable. The number of computers is limited to the length of the cable, and as your company grows, it can be difficult to change the size and layout of the network. Also, if changes or repairs are made to the cable, the network is down because there is no redundancy and termination of the cable is required.

EXAM WARNING

Although bus topologies are an outdated topology that should never be installed on a new network, it is a topology that is covered on the exam. You should be aware that it has historically been one on the easiest types of networks to set up, but star topologies have become the most popular topology in use on a LAN.

Star (Hierarchical)

In a star topology, computers aren't connected to one another, but are all connected to a central concentrator, commonly called a hub or switch. When a computer sends data to other computers on the network, it is sent along the cable to the hub or switch, which can then pass the packets to the other computers or devices connected to it. As shown in Figure 1.4, when the computers are cabled to the hub, each point in the network appears similar to points in a star (hence the name of this topology).

Figure 1.4 A Star Topology

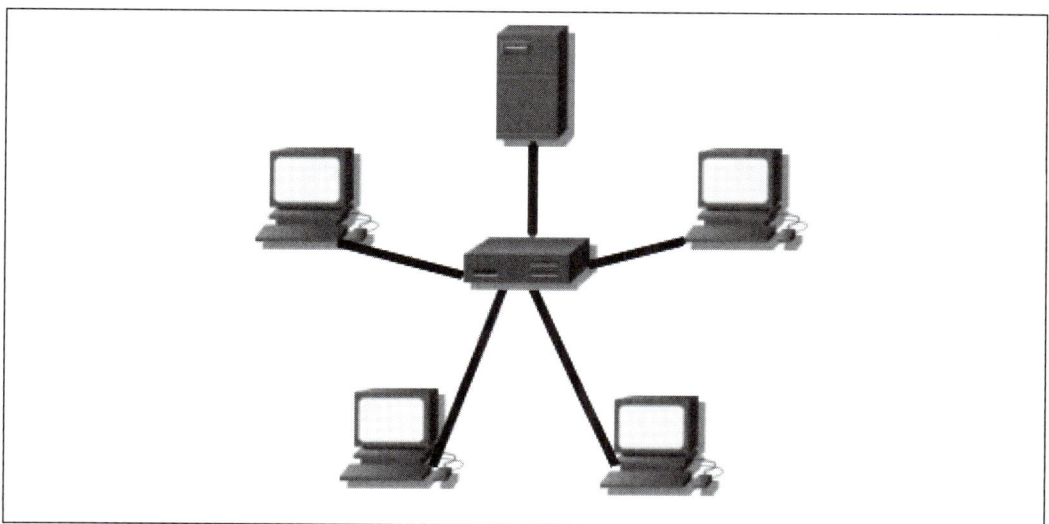

Although this is also considered an older topology that comes from the time when terminals were connected to mainframes as a centralized point, it is still a popular topology, having been reworked to today's needs and standards. In fact, the star topology is the most commonly used topology, thereby making it the one you will see most as a Network+ technician. Because cables run to a central point, if one cable breaks or fails in some way, only the computer that is connected to that cable is unable to use the network. Other computers are unaffected because they have their own cables running to the hub. This can also make it easier to repair because, unlike the bus topology, it is easy to see where the cable failure has occurred.

Another benefit of this topology is that it is scalable. As the network grows or changes, computers are added or removed from the hub. Unfortunately, because there is so much cabling that is being used to connect individual computers to a central hub, this also increases the cost of expanding and maintaining the network.

Mesh

A mesh topology has multiple connections, making it the most fault tolerant topology available. Every component of the network is connected directly to every other component. As shown in Figure 1.5, this creates a topology that provides redundant links across the network. If a break occurs in a segment of cable, traffic can still be rerouted using the other cables. In other words, if one connection fails, a computer can still access another computer or resource using another connection.

Figure 1.5 A Mesh Topology

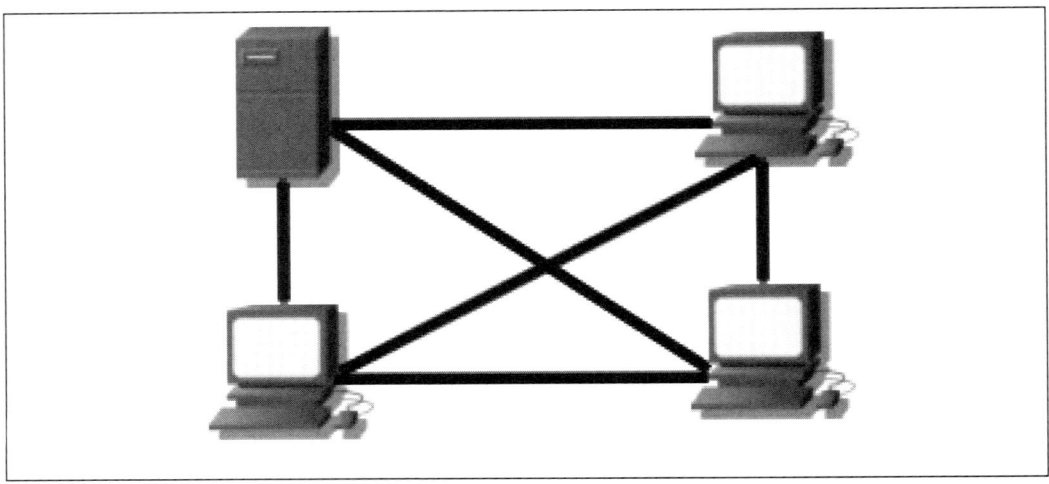

Although it is almost impossible for a cable fault to crash a mesh topology, this topology is rarely used. There is significant cost and work involved in having network components directly connected to every other component. This topology provides redundant cable connections, but exponentially increases the workload and cost of maintaining them, making them difficult to manage and creating a cost that's greater than other topologies.

Determining the number of cable connections required by a Mesh network can be done by using the following formula:

Ln=n(n-1)/2

In this connection *n* is the number of nodes (which is another term for the network's computers), while *Ln* is the number of connections required. If we were to use this formula on a mesh network with four computers (as depicted in Figure 1.5), then we would calculate it as follows:

4(4-1)/2

If we break this down, 4-1=3. When we multiply this by 4, we get 12. When we divide this by 2 we get 6. This would mean that in a mesh network of 4 computers, we need six connections between the computers. While this might seem reasonable on a small network, consider what happens when we use this same formula on a network of 100 computers:

100(100-1)/2.

Using the same formula, we find that on the network of 100 computers, 4950 connections would be needed to create a mesh network. When you consider the cost of purchasing this much cabling for the network, the reason why mesh networks aren't commonly used on LANs becomes clear.

Head of the Class...

Mesh Networks in Use Today

The only real benefit to having a mesh network is fault tolerance. Because there are so many connections being used, if one cable breaks, another can still be used to transmit messages between computers. This makes it nearly impossible to bring down the network when a failure occurs.

While mesh networks are rarely used in corporate environments, they can still be found in technologies that you've used. Telephone networks have multiple lines running between different locations and cities, so if one line breaks, another can still be used. Because telephone companies commonly provide ISDN, T1, and other connections used to interconnect different networks, it should come as no surprise that the Internet is another example of a mesh network. The Internet is made up of networks and individual nodes (computers) that are interconnected through multiple pathways. Much like the mesh of streets making up a city, if one path in the global village is unavailable, there is always another for traffic to use.

Network+
OBJECTIVE
1.1.4

Rings

A ring topology consists of computers connected to a cable that forms closed loop. As shown in Figure 1.6, there are no unconnected ends to the ring, so terminators aren't required. Data passes around the loop in one direction. As it reaches each computer, the computer examines each packet and determines if the destination address matches its network address.

If it isn't, the computer sends the packet on to the next computer in the ring. In doing so, each computer acts as a repeater, resending the packet and thereby boosting the signal. When the packet reaches the destination computer, it removes the packet from the network.

Figure 1.6 A Ring Topology

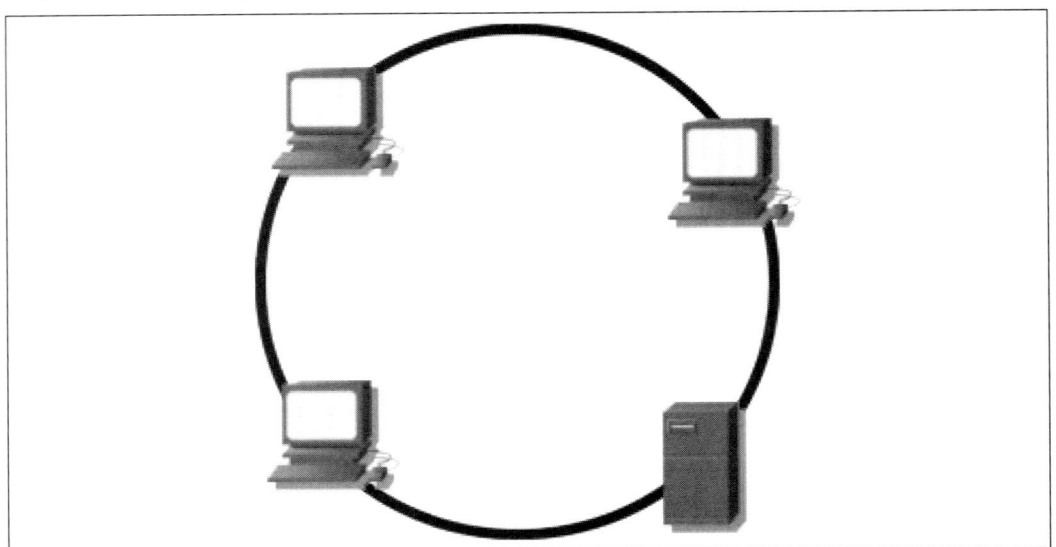

Ring topologies only allow one computer to have access to sending data on the ring at one time, which makes it *deterministic*. Deterministic access is the capability of computers to have regular turns at accessing the media (the cable making up the ring), and thereby always has an equal or predetermined chance to transmit data. This is different from the *contention* method of access that we saw earlier with a bus network, where computers must contend for access to the media.

A ring topology provides equal access to the network through a token-passing media access method. A signal called a *token* is passed from one computer to the next in the ring. When a computer has the token, it has access to the ring, and can send data. Because a computer can't use the ring without having the token first, this prevents two or more computers from transmitting on the network at the same time.

The Token Ring method of access provides equal access to each of the computers. This method of access is discussed further in this chapter, under the standard IEEE 802.5. When the token is passed, it is sent to its Nearest Active Downstream Neighbor (NADN). Once this computer takes the token from its Nearest Active Upstream Neighbor (NAUN), it now has the ability to transmit data.

On a Token Ring network, the first computer that is booted up and accesses the ring is called the *active monitor*. It has the responsibility of monitoring the ring for problems, such as a break in the ring, by sending out a packet of data to its NADN every seven seconds. This packet is passed around the ring until the active monitor receives it. This ensures that the ring is functioning without error. The role of the active monitor is important because a break in the cable means that the ring can't be completed and the network can't function properly.

Since the topology requires an unbroken ring, the active monitor takes further measures if it doesn't receive a packet from its NAUN, by beaconing and notifying the network if a break is detected. When a packet isn't received or is received later than every seven seconds, the active monitor sends out a packet with its address. This packet reaches the furthest point it can reach on the network, which indicates the location of a break or other problems. By detecting and reconfiguring the ring, it can now avoid the point where the break exists. By doing so, the network is able to function until the failed computer can be repaired.

Networks that use a ring topology operate at varying speeds. Token Ring networks operate at 4 and 16Mbps. While newer Token Ring cards run at 16Mbps, they provide backward compatibility to run at 4Mbps, allowing them to remain compatible with older Token ring equipment. When speed really comes into play in a ring topology, however, is when FDDI (Fiber Distributed Data Interface) is used, which operates at 100Mbps on rings of up to 100 kilometers in size.

Ring topologies that use FDDI also have other characteristics that differ from standard Token Ring networks. As shown in Figure 1.7, a FDDI ring topology uses two rings, which are fiber optic cabling. The primary ring is used at all times, while the secondary ring is only used if the primary ring fails. Each of these rings passes data in different directions. If a break occurs in the ring, the broken section can be bypassed by using the secondary ring. The token can be passed from one ring to another without causing a change in direction. By passing the token from one ring to another, much like a car making a U-turn and moving into the reverse lane, the ring essentially remains whole because the token can continue making a continuous loop.

Figure 1.7 FDDI

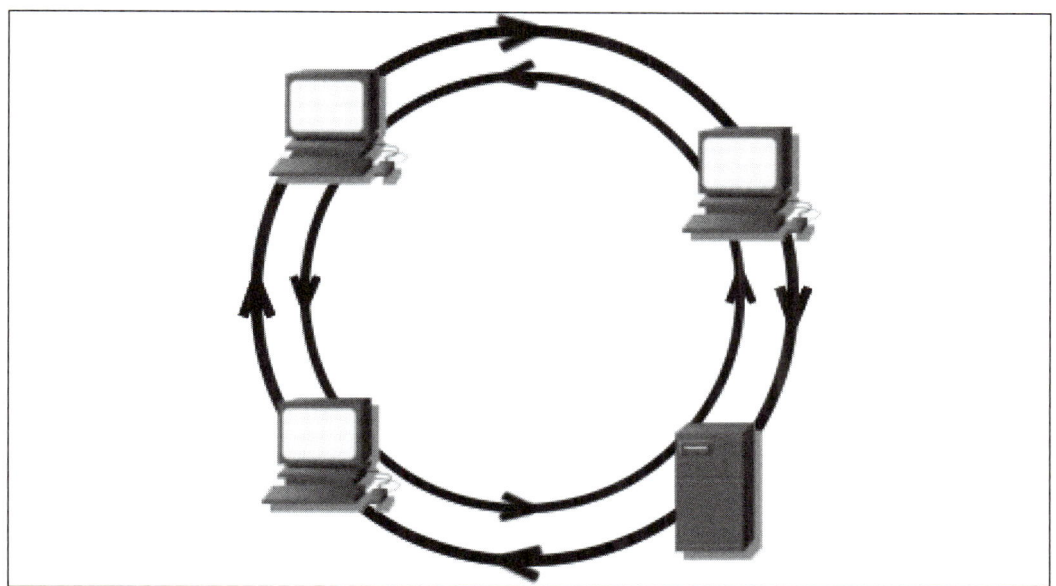

Another aspect of a FDDI ring is that priority levels can be set on specific machines, so that they have priority in getting the token. For example, if a higher priority was set on a server, the server would get the token more frequently, allowing it to transmit data over the cable. This allows the computer with priority to send more data than others on the network.

> **NOTE**
>
> FDDI is covered in Chapter 7 with other WAN technologies.

Wireless

A wireless topology broadcasts data over the air, so very few cables are used to connect systems together. As shown in Figure 1.8, this topology uses transmitters called *cells*, which broadcast the packets using radio frequencies (RF). The cells extend a radio sphere around the transmitter in the shape of a bubble that can extend to multiple rooms and possibly different floors in a building. Each cell is connected to the network using cabling so that it can receive and send data to servers, other cells, and networked peripherals. Computers and other devices have a device installed in them that transmits and receives data to and from the cell, allowing them to communicate with the network.

Figure 1.8 A Wireless Network

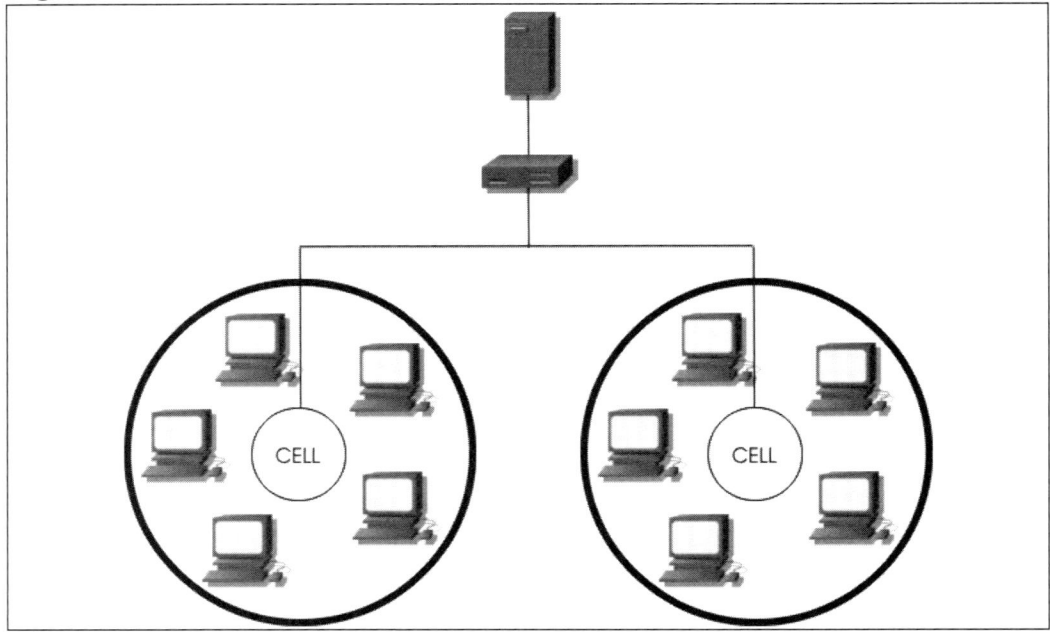

Wireless networks can also extend their transmission to wireless devices by implementing radio antennas that are situated on buildings or towers. The antenna serves as a cell that will cover a wider area, such as a building or campus. This type of wireless network is particularly beneficial for pools of buildings that are close together and have some difficulty in connecting LANs to each other using cables.

Another method of wireless networking uses infrared communications, which requires a direct line of site and close proximity for the communication to work. This type of wireless networking is similar to using a remote control for a TV, where each device has to be lined up and within range of one another. Because of these limitations, it isn't generally used for networking, but may be seen in a networked environment for connecting laptops and other computers to devices like printers.

Because very little may be directly cabled together on a wireless network, there is a greater chance of transmissions being blocked or experiencing interference. Machinery and other devices can emit radio frequencies or electrical interference that disrupts signals being exchanged between the cell and wireless devices. Also, some buildings using cinderblocks, large amounts of metal, or heavy insulation to prevent transmissions from interfering with equipment can interfere with a wireless signal enough so that a wireless network could be hampered from working between rooms. You may have experienced a blockage like this when you tried using a cell phone in certain buildings and found it didn't work. Signals are prevented from passing through these materials, and may require different frequencies to be used.

NOTE

Wireless technologies, WLAN, and RF are all covered in Chapter 4, "Wireless Technologies".

EXERCISE 1.1

BASIC NETWORK TOPOLOGY PLANNING

1. Determine what the needs of the network will be. Identify whether users will be routinely moving laptops or other networked devices between locations of the business. This will help to determine whether a particular type of LAN will be necessary, such as a wireless LAN.

2. Determine the types of data being moved over the network, and/or how much data is currently being moved over the existing LAN (that is, the amount of traffic). As we saw with ring networks, a standard Token Ring network provides lower bandwidth than a FDDI ring. As we'll discuss in

Chapter 2, different network media support different speeds and thereby will be able to move different amounts of data.

3. Determine whether the network is expanding over the next few years, and to what level that expansion will be. If mergers occur, the network may become a hybrid network with different topologies being used. If offices of computers are added (possibly in other buildings or cities), then additional nodes will be added to the topology, and the network will have to accommodate the extra computers and distances between sites. Distance is important to the network media being used, as we'll see in the next chapter.

4. Determine how software will be accessed by the machines. If computers have applications installed on them, they will be able to function if the network goes down (such as when a cable breaks, or another device fails). If applications are accessed from a server on the network, then additional bandwidth will be used by computers attempting to access these applications.

5. Choose the network topology that best meets the previous requirements, and draw out how it will be implemented. This includes the physical topology of how computers and devices are laid out (in a star, bus, mesh, or ring network), and the logical topology of IP addresses and subnetworks used on the network.

6. Review the requirements of the network to see if anything has changed before the new topology is implemented, or the existing one is modified. Sometimes, new conditions can affect the planning of your network, and will need to be modified to meet these conditions.

IEEE Committee

IEEE is an acronym for the Institute of Electrical and Electronics Engineers, which is an organization that develops and promotes standards dealing with various technologies. These standards serve as principles and guidelines of technology. While they aren't government regulations that need to be followed, they are industry standards that should be followed. The IEEE standards are agreed-upon standards that (when followed) ensure that networks and technologies can work together and are more secure. Although IEEE standards have been used when government regulations are created, manufacturers, developers, and technicians more commonly use the information in these standards.

Those who design and manufacture equipment and software look to these standards so their products can be compliant with IEEE standards. For example, if you bought a digital camera, you would want to be able to transfer the pictures to your computer. Without standards, cameras might use different cables or ports to transfer this data, meaning that you couldn't transfer the data easily to just any computer. Apple developed

FireWire as a method of connecting devices to computers and transferring large amounts of data quickly, and IEEE 1394 was developed as a nonproprietary standard of transferring audio and video. Without such standards, your devices would work with one type of computer (such as an Apple computer), but not with others (such as a PC). By adhering to these standards, products have the capability to be compatible with other technologies and can operate with other equipment.

History and Fundamentals of IEEE

The IEEE was formed in 1963 from a merger of two organizations: the American Institute of Electrical Engineers (AIEE) and the Institute of Radio Engineers (IRE). The AIEE was founded in 1884, as one of a number of engineering societies at that time. It succeeded in developing industry and professional standards for those involved in the electrical and engineering fields. As new technologies emerged, it formed committees to address specialized fields.

The Institute of Radio Engineers was founded in 1912 as an amalgamation of two earlier societies, and focused on obtaining international memberships. This organization focused on issues of standardization in radio, and not only affected manufacturing, but also assisted in developing broadcasting regulations and were part of conferences that led to the formation of the Federal Radio Commission in 1927, which later became the Federal Communications Commission (FCC). As technologies advanced, the IRE also assisted in standards dealing with FM radio and television.

While the IRE started as the smaller organization of the two, it eventually gained a greater membership than the AIEE. However, neither organization fully represented all fields associated with electrical or electronic engineering. This lead to a merger between the IRE and the AIEE in 1963, and inspired the name change to the Institute of Electrical and Electronic Engineers.

Over the years, the IEEE has developed and promoted numerous standards, provided education through publications and journals, and expanded its role in electricity, electronics and communications to also include computers. By creating committees to address emerging technologies and developments in computer engineering and computer science, they have been predominant in providing the standards used in computer hardware, software, and networking.

Exam Warning

The history behind the IEEE is very interesting and important to you as a working engineer. You do not need to know the history of the IEEE for the exam, but you need to understand the concepts behind the standardization and what those committees were created to do (such as the 802 standards), what those standards are, and which technologies they address.

802 Standards

IEEE standards use a numeric naming scheme to identify and group the technologies being addressed. Standards beginning with the number 802 relate to networking technologies and security, and are developed and evaluated by specialized committees within IEEE.

The 802 committee was first formed as a project in February 1980, and became known as Project 802 after the year (80) and month (2) it was created. After more than two decades, the members of the IEEE continue to review and provide industry standards for LANs, WANs, and issues related to the various types of networks.

The 802 committee is broken down into smaller sub-committees or working groups that focus on specific aspects of networking. The various groups that have worked on standards include:

- 802.1 Higher-Layer LAN protocols
- 802.2 Logical Link Control (Inactive)
- 802.3 CSMD/CD - Ethernet
- 802.4 Token Bus (disbanded)
- 802.5 Token Ring (inactive)
- 802.6 Metropolitan area network (disbanded)
- 802.7 Broadband (disbanded)
- 802.8 Fiber optic (disbanded)
- 802.9 Isochronous LAN (disbanded)
- 802.10 Security (disbanded)
- 802.11 Wireless LAN
- 802.12 Demand priority (inactive)
- 802.14 Cable modem
- 802.15 Wireless personal area network (WPAN)
- 802.16 Broadband wireless access
- 802.17 Resilient packet ring
- 802.18 Radio regulatory
- 802.19 Coexistence
- 802.20 Mobile broadband wireless access (MBWA)
- 802.21 Media independent handoff
- 802.22 Wireless regional area networks

TEST DAY TIP

In reading this book, you will find comments throughout that pinpoint areas where you need to focus your attention. Additional information may appear in the book that is useful to networking, or will enhance your understanding of various topics. In terms of IEEE standards, for example, not all of the IEEE standards will appear on the exam. Ensure that you know 802.2 (Logical Link Control), 802.3 (CSMD/CD), 802.5 (Token Ring), and 802.11 (wireless LAN).

Because technology changes, so do the working groups. New working groups are added to address emerging technologies, while others are disbanded or become inactive. Reasons for disbanding or making a group inactive vary, but when older technology isn't used as much or further standards aren't required, it makes sense to evaluate the need for a group. An up-to-date list of working groups and their status can be found on the IEEE website at http://grouper.ieee.org/groups/802/dots.html.

OSI and 802

The services and protocols specified in the 802 standards correspond to the lower layers of the OSI model. OSI is an acronym for Open Systems Interconnect, and the OSI model is a seven-layer structure that maps to a logical structure for network operations. It is often used to show how protocols work, and what happens when data is sent over a LAN. When communication is sent over a network, it starts at the topmost layer, and works its way down to the bottom layers. While we'll discuss OSI in great detail in Chapter 5, it's important that you understand the lower layers so you can fully comprehend what certain standards deal with.

The bottommost layers of the OSI model are the Data Link and Physical Layers. Earlier, we mentioned how data is broken into smaller pieces before it is sent over a network, which is a primary function of the Data Link Layer. When another computer receives these pieces of data, they are reassembled at the Data Link Layer, and passed up to higher layers so they can be further assembled into the data's original format and be used by an application.

The 802 standards break the Data Link Layer of the OSI model into two separate subcategories: Logical Link Control (LLC) and Media Access Control (MAC). The Logical Link Control is responsible for starting and maintaining connections with devices, while the Media Access Control allows multiple devices to share the media (such as coaxial cable, twist pair, etcetera) that data is being sent over. In other words, when you send data to another computer, it is the LLC that establishes the connection with the other computer, and it is the MAC that allows more than one computer to communicate on the network.

The Physical Layer of the OSI model deals with how data is moves on and off the network media. While it doesn't specify what media is used, it does identify how it is

Network+
OBJECTIVE
1.2.4

accessed. This includes the topology of the network, electrical and physical aspects of media, and the timing and encoding used for transmitting and receiving bits of data.

TEST DAY TIP

The Network+ exam will test you on the OSI layers covered in Chapter 3, and you will need to understand specific aspects of it like the Data Link Layer and Physical Layer. Remember that the Data Link Layer is separated into the Logical Link Control (LLC) and Media Access Control (MAC) by 802 standards.

Table of Standards (Complete)

IEEE working groups have generated a lengthy number of standards over the years. As you can see by these standards, each uses the numeric value of 802 to show it is part of the 802 committee's networking standards. A decimal value is used to designate the working group that developed it, and to show the standard it relates to, while a letter further categorizes specifications, supplements, and other addenda. While the 802 standards can be seen in the following table, a full listing of IEEE standards can be found on their website at http://info.computer.org/standards/standesc.htm.

TEST DAY TIP

Don't waste valuable study time memorizing each of the standards in Table 1.1. The Network+ exam doesn't expect you to memorize every IEEE standard available, but does expect you to know some of them. The ones you'll need to understand are 802.2, 802.3, 802.5, and 802.11, which are discussed in the next section of this chapter.

Table 1.1 Listing of 802 IEEE Standards

Standard	Subject / Description
802	Standard for LANs for Computer Interconnection. Provides compatibility between devices that have been made by different manufacturers.
802.1	Architecture & Overviews. Standard for allowing LAN or MAN to communicate with another LAN or MAN.
802.1b	LAN/MAN Management. Defines network management architecture and protocols at OSI layers 1 and 2.

Continued

Table 1.1 continued Listing of 802 IEEE Standards

Standard	Subject / Description
802.1d	MAC Sublayer Interconnection: MAC (Media Access Control) Bridges. Standard defining internetworking two or more LANs at the MAC sublayer.
802.1e	System Load Protocol. Standard on loading a LAN station's local address space.
802.1f	Recommended Practices for the Development of Layer Management Standards. Standard on common management activities across the OSI layers.
802.1g	MAC Sublayer Interconnection. Standard on internetworking two or more LANs at the MAC sublayer.
802.1h	LAN: Token Ring Access Method and Physical Layer Specifications.
802.1I	Standard MAC Bridges: FDDI Supplement.
802.1j	Managed Objects for MAC Bridges. Standard that manages objects for MAC bridges (corresponds to 802.1d).
802.1k	LAN/MAN Management Information for Monitoring and Event Reporting.
802.1m	System Load Protocol: Managed Object Definition and PICS Proforma. Specifies the System Load Protocol parameters for conformance.
802.2	Local Area Networks: Logical Link Control. Standard on the Link Layer protocol, which provides confirmation on the delivery of data over a LAN.
802.2a	Flow Control Techniques for Bridges – Local Area Networks.
802.2b	Acknowledged Connectionless-mode Service Type 3 Operation.
802.2c	Standard for Logical Link Control Conformance Requirements.
802.2d	Supplement to 802.2, Information Processing Systems: LAN Part2: Logical Link Control. Provides changes and corrections to the 802.2 standard.
802.2e	Supplement to 802.2, Information Processing Systems: LAN Part2: Bit Referencing.
802.2f	Standard for LLC Sublayer Management. Standard on sublayer management of the Logical Link Control.
802.2g	Supplement to 802.2, Logical Link Control Type 4 (High Speed, High Performance) Operation.
802.3	Local Network for Computer Interconnection (CSMA/CD). Standard for CSMA/CD or Ethernet. This provides a standard for communication devices to be compatible, so there is little to no need for customizing hardware and software.
802.3a	Medium Attachment Unit and Baseband Medium Spec. for Type 10Base2. Supplement for 10Mbps baseband media.

Continued

Table 1.1 **continued** Listing of 802 IEEE Standards

Standard	Subject / Description
802.3b	Section 11, Broadband Medium Attachment Unit and Broadband Medium Specifications. Supplement to add broadband capabilities to 10Mbps media.
802.3c	Local Area Networks: Repeater Unit. Defines a standard baseband repeater for 10BaseX networks, which allows the interconnection of multiple coaxial segments.
802.3d	Medium Attachment Unit and Baseband Medium Specification for Fiber Optic Inter-Repeater Unit. Specifications for fiber optic interconnections for 10Base5 and 10Base2 networks.
802.3e	Physical Signaling, Medium Attachment and Baseband Medium Specification, Type 1Base5. Implements a 1Mbps baseband Physical Layer for CSMA/CD, using twisted pair media on a star topology network.
802.3h	Layer Management. Supplement replaces a paragraph in the existing standard.
802.3I	Medium Attachment Unit and Baseband Medium Specs, Type 10BaseT. Specifications for a medium attachment unit and media on a LAN using CSMA/CD, so that it can operate at 10Mbps on twisted pair media.
802.3j	Fiber Optic Active and Passive Star Based 802.3 Segment. Supplement for 802.3
802.3k	Standard for Repeater Management (Revision).
802.3l	Supplement to Carrier Sense Multiple Access with Collision Detection CSMA/CD Access Method and Physical Layer Specifications: MAU, Type 10BaseT PICS Proforma.
802.3m	Supp. to CSMA with Collision Detection CSMA/CD Access Method and Physical Layer Specifications (Second Maintenance Ballot).
802.3n	Supplement CSMA/CD Access with Collision Detection CSMA/CD Access Method and Physical Layer Specifications (Third Maintenance Ballot).
802.3p	CSMA/CD Layer Management for 10 MB/S.
802.3q	CSMA/CD GDMO Format for Layer Managed Objects
802.3r	Supplement to Carrier Sense Multiple Access with CSMA/CD Access Method and Physical Layer Specifications: Type 10BASE5 Medium Attachment Unit (MAU) Protocol Implementation Conformance Statement.
802.3s	CSMA/CD Access Method and Physical Layer Specifications: Maintenance Revision #4. Revisions that provide corrections and updates.

Continued

Table 1.1 continued Listing of 802 IEEE Standards

Standard	Subject / Description
802.3t	Supplement to CSMA/CD Access Method and Physical Layer Specifications: Informative Annex for Support of 120 Ohm Cables in 10Base-T Simplex Link Segment.
802.3u	Supplement to CSMA/CD Access Method and Physical Layer Specifications: MAC Parameters, Physical Layer, Medium Attachment Units and Repeater for 100Mb/s Operation.
802.3v	Supplement to Carrier Sense Multiple Access with Collision Detection (CSMA/CD) Access Method and Physical Layer Specifications: Informative Annex for Support of 150 Ohm Cables in 10BASE-T Link Segment.
802.4	Revision LAN: Token-Bus Access Method.
802.4a	Fiber Optic Token Bus. Specifications for using fiber optic media and adding an additional Physical Layer to 802.4.
802.4b	Redundant Media Control Unit. Addendum that deals with connecting multiple media to a single MAC, and improving Physical Layer reliability.
802.5	LAN: Token Ring Access Method and Physical Layer Specifications.
802.5a	LAN: Station Management Revision.
802.5b	LAN: Telephone Twisted-Pair Media. Specification for using twisted-pair media in a token ring network.
802.5c	LAN: Token Ring Reconfiguration. Specification that adds automatic fault recovery.
802.5d	LAN: Interconnected Token Ring LANs. Specification on multi-ring operations.
802.5e	LAN: Token Ring Station Management Entity Specifications.
802.5f	LAN: 16 Mbit/s Token Ring Operations. Specifications for change 4Mbps Rings to 16Mbps.
802.5g	LAN: Conformance Testing.
802.5h	LAN: Operation of Logical Link Control III on Token Rings.
802.5I	LAN: Token Ring; Early Token Release.
802.5j	LAN: Fiber Optic Station Attachment.
802.5k	Token Ring Media Specification.
802.5l	Maintenance of Token Ring Standard. Revision of token ring access method and Physical Layer specifications.
802.5m	Recommended. Practice to Interconnection of Source Routed and Transparent Bridged Networks.
802.5n	Unshielded Twisted Pair at 4/16 Mbit/s. Standard for operating 4Mbps and 16Mbps Token Ring LANs on unshielded twisted–pair.

Continued

Table 1.1 continued Listing of 802 IEEE Standards

Standard	Subject / Description
802.5p	LAN: Part 2: Logical Link Control; End System Determination.
802.5q	LAN: Part 5: Media Access Control Revision.
802.5r	Revision of IEEE Standard 802.5 for Token Ring Station Attachment.
802.6	Standard for the Distributed Queue Dual Bus Metropolitan Area Networks. Standard used for MANs, which is used in specifying the MAC sublayer and Physical Layer.
802.6a	Multiple Port Bridging for Metropolitan Area Networks. Standard for services provided by multiple bridge ports, which are used to connect two or more Dual Bus sub-networks together.
802.6b	Standard for Premises Extension of DS3-Based 802.6 Metropolitan Area Networks.
802.6c	Standard for DS1 Physical Layer Convergence Procedures.
802.6d	Standard for SONET (SDH) Based Physical Layer Convergence Procedures for 802.6 MAN.
802.6e	Standard for Eraser Node for DQDB MAN.
802.6f	Conformance Statement (PICS Proforma).
802.6g	Standard for Layer Management for the 802.6 MAN.
802.6h	Standard for Isochronus Services Over the 802.6 MAN.
802.6I	Standard for Remote LAN Bridging Using the 802.6 MAN. Specifies protocols used between remote LAN bridges.
802.6j	Standard for Connection Oriented Services on a Distributed Queue Dual Bus Subnetwork of a Metropolitan Area Network.
802.6k	Distributed Queue Dual Subnetwork of a MAN. Supplement for MAC bridging.
802.6l	Point-to-Point Interface for Subnetwork of MAN. Specification for network between two locations in a MAN.
802.6m	Subnetwork of MAN.
802.7	Recommended Practices for Broadband LAN. Provides recommendations for the physical, electrical and mechanical practices of broadband coaxial media.
802.8	Fiber Optic Technical Advisory Group LAN. Standard for fiber optic technology.
802.9	Integrated Services (IS) LAN Interface at the MAC and Physical Layer. Standard for voice and data over twisted pair media.
802.9a	Supplement to Integrated Services LAN: IEEE 802.9 Isochronous Service with CSMA/CD MAC Service.
802.9b	Supplement for Functional Specification for AU to AU Interworking IEEE 802.9.

Continued

Table 1.1 continued Listing of 802 IEEE Standards

Standard	Subject / Description
802.9c	Supplement to 802.9, Management Object Conformance Statement.
802.9d	Supplement to 802.9, Protocol Implementation Conformance Statement.
802.10	Interoperable LAN Security (SILS). Standard for allowing secure LAN products to interoperate using encryption.
802.10a	Standard for Interoperable LAN Security (SILS) Part A: The Model.
802.10b	Standard for Interoperable LAN Security (SILS) Part B:Secure Data Exchange. Standard on protocol for secure data exchange at Data Link Layer.
802.10c	Standard for Interoperable LAN Security (SILS) Part C: Key Management. Standard on the management and distribution of cryptography keys.
802.10d	Standard for Interoperable LAN Security (SILS) Part D: Security Management.
802.10e	LAN: Recommended Practice of Secure Data Exchange on Ethernet 2.0. Specifies secure data exchange on LANs using Ethernet.
802.10f	Secure Data Exchange: Sublayer.
802.10g	Standard for Security Labeling Within Secure Data Exchange.
802.10h	Supplement to Interoperable LM Security: PICS Proforma/Security Data.
802.11	Standard for WLAN. Standard for MAC and physical layer for wireless networking.
802.12	Demand Priority Access Method, Physical & Repeater Specifications, 100Mb/s. Standard dealing with 100Mbs LANs.
802.14	Standard Protocol for Cable-TV Based Broadband Communication Network. Standard for cable modems.
802.15	Wireless Personal Area Network.
802.16	Broadband Wireless Access.
802.17	Resilient Packet Ring.
802.18	Radio Regulatory.
802.19	Coexistence.
802.20	Mobile Broadband Wireless Access (MBWA).
802.21	Media Independent Handoff.
802.22	Wireless Regional Area Networks.
1802.3-1991	IEEE Supplement to IEEE Std 802-1990: Methodology and Implementation for AUI Cable Conformance Testing.

Continued

www.syngress.com

Table 1.1 continued Listing of 802 IEEE Standards

Standard	Subject / Description
1802.3a	Supplement to CSMA/CD Access Method and Physical Layer Specifications: Methodology and Implementation for MAC Conformance Testing.
1802.3b	Supplement to CSMA/CD Access Method and Physical Layer Specifications: Methodology and Implementation for PLS, Type 10, Conformance Testing.
1802.3c	Supplement to CSMA/CD Access Method and Physical Layer Specifications: Methodology and Implementation for MAU, Type 10BASE-5, Conformance Testing.
1802.3d	Conformance Test Methodology for IEEE Standards for LAN and MAN Networks: CSMA/CD Access Method and Physical Layer Specifications Type 10BASE-T.

Table of Standards (Testable)

While numerous IEEE standards have been developed for networking, the Network+ exam only tests your knowledge on a limited number of them. The standards you'll be tested on, and that we'll discuss here, are:

- 802.2 Logical Link Control

- 802.3 CSMA/CD

- 802.5 Token Ring

- 802.11 Wireless

EXAM WARNING

IEEE standards are an important part of networking, and chances are that you'll see questions about them during the exam. You'll be tested on main features of Logical Link Control, CSMA/CD (Ethernet), Token Ring, and wireless technologies. Because Token Ring and wireless technologies are also part of the topologies we covered earlier in this chapter, you should review these topologies to have a firm understanding of the standards.

802.2 LLC

Earlier in this chapter, we explained how IEEE 802 standards break the Data Link Layer of the OSI model into two sublayers: the Media Access Control (MAC) and the Logical

Link Control (LLC). The Logical Link Control is used to establish connections between computers, and is used by other protocols defined by the 802 committee.

When the LLC receives data in the form of a *frame* from the layer above it (the Network Layer), it breaks the data apart into smaller pieces that can be sent over network media. It also adds header information that identifies upper layer protocols sending the frame, and can also specify destination processes for the data. The computer receiving the data will view this header information, and use it to reassemble the data into its proper format.

802.3 CSMA/CD

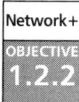

Based on the original Ethernet network from DIX (Digital-Intel-Xerox), 802.3 is the standard for Ethernet networks today. The only difference between 802.3 Ethernet and DIX Ethernet V.2 is frame type. The two Ethernet networks can use the same physical network, but devices on one standard cannot communicate with devices on the other standard.

The MAC sublayer uses Carrier Sense Multiple Access with Collision Detection (CSMA/CD) for access to the physical medium. CSMA/CD keeps devices on the network from interfering with one another when trying to transmit; if they do, a collision occurs. To reduce collisions, CSMA/CD devices listen to the network before transmitting. If the network is "quiet" (no other devices are transmitting), the device can send data. Since two devices can think the network is clear and start transmitting at the same time, resulting in a collision, all devices listen as they transmit. If a device detects another device is transmitting at the same time, a collision occurs. The device stops transmitting and sends a signal to alert other nodes about the collision. Then, all the nodes stop transmitting and wait a random amount of time before they begin the process again.

CSMA/CD doesn't stop collisions from happening, but it helps manage the situations when they do occur. In fact, collisions are a normal part of Ethernet operation. It's only when collisions begin to occur frequently that you need to become concerned.

Ethernet has evolved over the years to include a number of popular specifications. These specifications are due in part to the media variety they employ, such as coaxial, twisted-pair, and fiber-optic cabling.

- The 10Base5 specification, commonly referred to as Thicknet, was the original Ethernet specification and has a maximum distance of 500 meters (approximately 1640 feet) with a maximum speed of 2.94 to 10Mbps.

- The 10Base2 specification, commonly referred to as Thinnet, uses a thinner coaxial cable than 10Base5 does and has a maximum distance of 185 meters (approximately 607 feet) with a maximum speed of 10Mbps.

- The 10BaseT specification uses twisted-pair cabling with a maximum distance of 100 meters (approximately 328 feet) with a speed of 10 to 100Mbps.

802.5 Token Ring

Although Token Ring was first designed in the 1960s, IBM's token passing implementation did not become a standard until 1985. The 802.5 standard was modeled after the IBM Token Ring network, which had been in use for many years before the standard was developed.

The 802.5 network introduced a unique access method: token passing. The Token Ring IEEE 802.5 standard passes a special frame known as a *token* around the network. This token is generated by the first computer that comes online on the Token Ring network. When a workstation wants to transmit data, it grabs the token and then begins transmitting. This computer will send a data frame on the network with the address of the destination computer. The destination computer receives the data frame, modifies it, and sends it onto the network back to the original computer, indicating successful transmission of data. When the workstation is finished transmitting, the token is released back onto the network. This ensures that workstations will not simultaneously communicate on the network, as in the CSMA/CD method.

802.11 Wireless

The IEEE 802.11 standard addresses wireless networking, which we'll discuss in greater detail in Chapter 4. This standard includes the wireless access point (WAP) devices and the wireless network interface cards that are used to send and receive broadcasts from the cell or WAP device.

The WAPs and wireless NICs can be set to use different frequencies to allow for cell overlap. This technology does not include the same technology used by cell phones to manage the movement of PCs or mobile devices. The wireless NIC is set to a specific frequency and must be changed manually to be able to communicate with another cell. This means that a PC cannot be moved from one cell area to another without changing frequency, unless for some reason the cells operate on the same frequency and have no overlap of coverage area.

NOTE

802 standards will be revisited again in Chapter 5, "The OSI Model".

Request for Comments

Another set of standards is Request for Comments (RFC). RFCs are a series of documents that were originally started in 1969, before the Internet was even conceived of in its current form and was still in its infancy of being ARPANET.

While not all of the RFCs specifically deal with the Internet, all of the Internet standards are written as Requests for Comments. They focus on networking protocols, communication issues, procedures, concepts and other topics.

RFCs are created and maintained by the Internet Engineering Task Force (IETF). The IETF is an organization that consists of vendors, network administrators, designers, researchers, and other professionals who are interested in the operation and future of the Internet. These people can provide proposals to the IETF, who in turn provides a consensus on new standards that should be added. The proposals that are submitted are called "Internet Drafts," which are reviewed by working groups that specialize in specific areas. If a standard is developed as a result of the Internet Draft, it is written as an RFC and categorized as a standard.

Using RFCs

RFCs are categorized using a number that is preceded by the prefix "RFC". For example, the RFC dealing with the Domain Name System (DNS) is RFC 1034. In reading a RFC, you will find that there is a section that shows the category or status of the document. These categories include:

- Standards-track documents, which have the status of being a standard, draft standard, or proposed standard. This shows its current state in becoming a standard.

- Best Current Practice, which provides procedures and recommendations.

- Informational, which provides information on various subjects. This category also includes the IETF's parody RFCs, such as RFC1217 (Memo from the Consortium for Slow Commotion Research [CSCR]), and RFC1438 (Statements Of Boredom [SOBs]).

- Experimental, which designates a particular practice or topic as experimental in nature.

- Historic, which are standards that are no longer used.

Because the IETF doesn't remove RFCs, all of them are still available to view. The RFCs that aren't used are listed as being historic documents, but are still available for reference purposes. This provides those using RFCs with the ability to review practices, principles, and protocols that are no longer in use, but may be valuable when previous standards have to be reviewed.

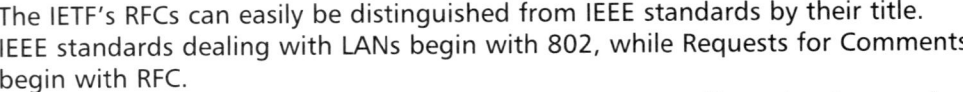

Test Day Tip

The IETF's RFCs can easily be distinguished from IEEE standards by their title. IEEE standards dealing with LANs begin with 802, while Requests for Comments begin with RFC.

RFCs may not explicitly appear in the exam, but you will need to know what RFCs are, as they may appear as an incorrect answer. Despite this, RFCs can still prove interesting and useful to review, and provide an additional source of information on networking-related topics. A full listing of RFCs can be found at www.ietf.org/iesg/1rfc_index.txt, or by using the RFC online database at www.rfc-editor.org/rfc.html.

As is the case with IEEE standards, the number of standards published by the IETF is massive. Rather than providing all of them here, Table 1.2 provides a list of the Internet standards, many of which also relate to intranets and networks using TCP/IP.

Table 1.2 IETF Internet Related Standards

RFC	Subject / Description
RFC768	User Datagram Protocol
RFC791	Internet Protocol
RFC792	Internet Control Message Protocol
RFC793	Transmission Control Protocol
RFC821	Simple Mail Transfer Protocol
RFC822	Standard for the format of ARPA Internet text messages
RFC826	Ethernet Address Resolution Protocol: Or converting network protocol addresses to 48.bit Ethernet address for transmission on Ethernet hardware
RFC854	Telnet Protocol Specification
RFC855	Telnet Option Specifications
RFC856	Telnet Binary Transmission
RFC857	Telnet Echo Option
RFC858	Telnet Suppress Go Ahead Option
RFC859	Telnet Status Option
RFC860	Telnet Timing Mark Option
RFC861	Telnet Extended Options: List Option
RFC862	Echo Protocol
RFC863	Discard Protocol
RFC864	Character Generator Protocol
RFC865	Quote of the Day Protocol

Continued

Table 1.2 continued IETF Internet Related Standards

RFC	Subject / Description
RFC866	Active Users
RFC867	Daytime Protocol
RFC868	Time Protocol
RFC891	DCN local-network protocols
RFC894	Standard for the transmission of IP datagrams over Ethernet networks
RFC895	Standard for the transmission of IP datagrams over experimental Ethernet networks
RFC903	Reverse Address Resolution Protocol
RFC907	Host Access Protocol specification
RFC919	Broadcasting Internet Datagrams
RFC922	Broadcasting Internet datagrams in the presence of subnets
RFC950	Internet Standard Subnetting Procedure
RFC959	File Transfer Protocol
RFC1001	Protocol standard for a NetBIOS service on a TCP/UDP transport: Concepts and methods
RFC1002	Protocol standard for a NetBIOS service on a TCP/UDP transport: Detailed specifications
RFC1006	ISO transport services on top of the TCP: Version 3
RFC1034	Domain names – concepts and facilities
RFC1035	Domain names – implementation and specification
RFC1042	Standard for the transmission of IP datagrams over IEEE 802 networks
RFC1044	Internet Protocol on Network System's HYPERchannel: Protocol specification
RFC1055	Nonstandard for transmission of IP datagrams over serial lines: SLIP
RFC1088	Standard for the transmission of IP datagrams over NetBIOS networks
RFC1112	Host extensions for IP multicasting
RFC1122	Requirements for Internet Hosts – Communication Layers
RFC1123	Requirements for Internet Hosts – Application and Support
RFC1132	Standard for the transmission of 802.2 packets over IPX networks
RFC1155	Structure and identification of management information for TCP/IP-based internets
RFC1201	Transmitting IP traffic over ARCNET networks
RFC1209	Transmission of IP datagrams over the SMDS Service
RFC1212	Concise MIB definitions

Continued

www.syngress.com

Table 1.2 continued IETF Internet Related Standards

RFC	Subject / Description
RFC1213	Management Information Base for Network Management of TCP/IP-based internets:MIB-II
RFC1350	The TFTP Protocol (Revision 2)
RFC1390	Transmission of IP and ARP over FDDI Networks
RFC1661	The Point-to-Point Protocol (PPP)
RFC1662	PPP in HDLC-like Framing
RFC1722	RIP Version 2 Protocol Applicability Statement
RFC1870	SMTP Service Extension for Message Size Declaration
RFC1939	Post Office Protocol – Version 3
RFC2289	A One-Time Password System
RFC2328	OSPF Version 2
RFC2427	Multiprotocol Interconnect over Frame Relay
RFC2453	RIP Version 2
RFC2578	Structure of Management Information Version 2 (SMIv2)
RFC2579	Textual Conventions for SMIv2
RFC2580	Conformance Statements for SMIv2
RFC2819	Remote Network Monitoring Management Information Base
RFC2920	SMTP Service Extension for Command Pipelining
RFC3411	An Architecture for Describing Simple Network Management Protocol (SNMP) Management Frameworks
RFC3412	Message Processing and Dispatching for the Simple Network Management Protocol (SNMP)
RFC3413	Simple Network Management Protocol (SNMP) Applications
RFC3414	User-based Security Model (USM) for version 3 of the Simple Network Management Protocol (SNMPv3)
RFC3415	View-based Access Control Model (VACM) for the Simple Network Management Protocol (SNMP)
RFC3416	Version 2 of the Protocol Operations for the Simple Network Management Protocol (SNMP)
RFC3417	Transport Mappings for the Simple Network Management Protocol (SNMP)
RFC3418	Management Information Base (MIB) for the Simple Network Management Protocol (SNMP)
RFC3550	RTP: A Transport Protocol for Real-Time Applications
RFC3551	RTP Profile for Audio and Video Conferences with Minimal Control

Continued

Table 1.2 continued IETF Internet Related Standards

RFC	Subject / Description
RFC3629	UTF-8, a transformation format of ISO 10646
RFC3700	Internet Official Protocol Standards
RFC3986	Uniform Resource Identifier (URI): Generic Syntax

Summary of Exam Objectives

In this chapter we discussed the fundamentals of networking, including what defines a network and how networks came to be. By providing an overview of these elements, we have provided a basic foundation for other topics covered throughout this book.

We also looked at the various network models available for a network. A network can use a centralized or distributed model, and be designed as a client/server model or peer-to-peer. Each of these models provides its own benefits and drawbacks in terms of administration and how resources are managed.

The differences in terms of the location and management of resources are clearly seen in centralized and decentralized models. When centralized models are used, the resources of the network are centrally located and managed by network administrators. This can increase the security of network resources, as they can be kept in a secure server room or in areas that limit access to the equipment and the data they contain. In a decentralized network, the resources are distributed across the network and are managed by system administrators or other network users who have been delegated responsibility over managing the resource.

The client/server and peer-to-peer models of networking also differ from with one another in terms of how resources and administration are handled. Client/server networks use dedicated servers that respond to clients' requests for services, data, and other resources. In this type of network, network administrators determine the levels of access specific users and computers will have to files, folders, and other resources on the network. Conversely, a peer-to-peer network allows each user to control access to resources on his or her machine. This is called share level access, where a user shares a particular file, folder, printer, or other resource on his or her computer.

In creating a network, we also discussed how it will use one or more topologies, which is the physical layout of network components. The topologies we covered in this chapter are bus, star, ring, mesh, and wireless.

Bus topologies aren't commonly used anymore, but they may appear on the exam as an alternative for smaller networks. With this type of LAN, the computers use T-connectors to attach the computers to a single cable segment. The single cable runs the length of the network and is terminated at each end using 50ohm terminators, which prevent signals from bouncing from one end of the segment to the other. Termination is necessary and only one computer at a time can transmit on this type of network.

Star topologies are the most commonly used topology, and have each computer on the network cabled to a central concentrator. The computers in this topology send data along the cable to the concentrator, which is a hub or switch, which then redirects the data to the proper machine or all machines on the LAN. Because everything is sent through the concentrator, it can be a single point of failure for the network.

Mesh topologies are the most fault tolerant because every device on the network is cabled to every other component. If one cable breaks, the computer or device is able to continue working on the network because it still has a redundant connection. Because of the number of connections that may exist on the network, it is also one of the most difficult topologies to manage, as the number of connections increase with each device added to the LAN.

Ring topologies have computers connected to a cable that is a closed loop and determines which computer can send data onto the loop through the use of a token. One type of ring uses Token Ring technology, which is covered under IEEE standard 802.5. Rings can also be a highly fault tolerant topology, when FDDI rings are used. FDDI networks use two rings that send data in different directions. If one of the rings fails, then the data can still be sent using the secondary ring.

Wireless topologies are different from other topologies, as very few cables are used to connect devices. Instead, data is broadcast over the air using devices that transmit data to points that are cabled to servers and other cabled devices. Wireless technologies are another type of topology that is covered under IEEE standards. IEEE 802.11 specifies how data is transmitted over airwaves using wireless technology.

Finally, the geographic scope of the network will determine which type of network you have. LANs are small networks within a limited area of a few miles, MANs are within a metropolitan area or a 50 km diameter, and WANs interconnect LANs over a wide area (such as cities or countries). These characteristics define your network, and will affect a wide variety of elements including security, media, and other features that make up your network as a whole. We also discussed various industry standards that ensure compatibility and consistency in network communication, hardware, and software. The Institute of Electrical and Electronic Engineers (IEEE) has an 802 committee that is responsible for standards in the networking industry. Their standards include 802.2 Logical Link Control, 802.3 CSMA/CD, 802.5 Token Ring, and 802.11 Wireless.

IEEE 802.2 breaks the Data Link Layer of the OSI model into two sublayers: Media Access Control (MAC) and Logical Link Control (LLC). In breaking apart the OSI model's layer in this way, it specifies how the Logical Link Control establishes connections between computers. The OSI model and LLC are discussed in detail in Chapter 5.

IEEE 802.3 is a standard that specifies how multiple computers can use the same media without interfering with the transmission of other computers, and how it will deal with collisions of data packets on LANs that require data to be sent by one computer at a time. This method is called Carrier Sense Multiple Access with Collision Detection (CSMA/CD). While it doesn't completely remove the possibility of collisions, it does determine how the network will deal with them.

IEEE 802.5 is the standard for Token Ring, which specifies how a frame is used to control how computers will have access to transmit data on a ring network. This frame is called a token, and the computer that has this frame has the ability to transmit data. By using the token method, computers are prevented from interfering with one another when data is transmitted onto a network.

Finally, we discussed how the Internet Engineering Task Force is another source of standards, providing Requests for Comments on various topics including Internet technologies. Each is a source of important information, common practices, and needed procedures that you will find references to as we continue through this book, when you take the exam, and as you work in the field of networking.

Exam Objectives Fast Track

What is a Network?

- ☑ A computer network exists when two or more machines are connected together, thereby allowing them to share data, equipment and other resources.

- ☑ An internetwork exists when two or more networks are connected together, as in the case of the Internet.

- ☑ A network protocol is a set of rules used to control transmission and reception of data on a networked computer. TCP/IP is a default protocol used by the Internet and many current operating systems, such as Microsoft Windows and Novell NetWare.

Networking Models

- ☑ A centralized network model has resources and administration that is centrally located. As resources are centrally located, this provides administrators with better access and control over security of equipment. However, management of these resources increases for network administrators, who must now administer and manage them.

- ☑ A decentralized network model has resources and administration that is distributed throughout the network. Management of these devices decreases for the network administrator, as designated users or system administrators are delegated responsibility over them.

- ☑ A peer-to-peer network model has computers on a network acting as equals, and acting as both clients and servers of the network. When one computer requests data or other services from another computer, it acts as a client, while the other computer delivering that data or service acts as a server.

- ☑ In a peer-to-peer network, the user of a computer can control access to resources on his or her machine. Using share level access, users can grant access to folders, files, and other resources on their computers to other network users.

- ☑ A client/server network model has dedicated servers that provide services and data to requesting computers (clients) who are authorized to access them.

☑ In a client/server network, a network administrator controls access to resources by setting appropriate levels of access to network accounts. The access given to the account of a user or computer determines which resources he or she can use.

Network Types and Topologies

☑ Local area networks (LANs) are small- to medium-sized networks, and generally connect network devices that are no more than a few miles from one another.

☑ Wide area networks (WANs) can span great geographical distances, and connect different LANs together using high-speed solutions or telephone lines.

☑ Metropolitan area networks (MANs) connect LANs together within a limited geographical radius. MANs generally exist within the same city or within a 50-km diameter.

☑ The topology of a network is the physical layout of computers, hubs, routers, cables, and other components. Common topologies include bus, star, ring, mesh, and wireless.

☑ Bus topologies are a linear topology in which computers are networked together through a single segment of cable called a trunk, backbone, or segment. The trunk must be terminated at each end or signals will bounce back and forth, preventing others from transmitting data.

☑ Star topologies have computers connected to a central concentrator, commonly called a hub or switch. It is the most commonly used topology today.

☑ Mesh topologies have every component of the network connected to every other component using multiple connections. It is the most fault tolerant topology available, but is also the most difficult to manage. The number of connections required by a mesh topology can be calculated using the formula $Ln=n(n-1)/2$.

☑ Ring topologies have all computers connected to a cable that creates a closed loop. The computer that can transmit data onto the cable is determined by which computer has a token. FDDI networks use two rings that send data in different directions and provide added fault tolerance. Token Ring networks operate at speeds of 4 and 16Mbps, while FDDI ring networks can operate at speeds of 100Mbps on rings that are up to 100 kilometers in size.

☑ Wireless topologies broadcast data over the air, and use few cables to connect systems together. This topology allows data to be sent between different locations without cabling, and is useful in areas where it's difficult or impossible to wire computers together.

IEEE

☑ IEEE is an acronym for the Institute of Electrical and Electronics Engineers, which is an organization that develops and promotes standards dealing with various technologies.

☑ The 802 committee is responsible for standards dealing with networks, and has subcommittees or working groups that develop industry standards.

☑ IEEE 802.2 is a standard for the Logical Link Control. It breaks the Data Link Layer of the OSI model into two sublayers: Media Access Control and Logical Link Control. The Logical Link Control is used to establish connections between computers, and is used by other protocols defined by the 802 committee.

☑ IEEE 802.3 is the standard for CSMA/CD (Carrier Sense Multiple Access with Collision Detection). It prevents devices from interfering with one another when data is transmitted onto a network, and specifies what will happen when a collision occurs.

☑ IEEE 802.5 is the standard for Token Ring, which specifies how a frame is used to control which computer will have access to transmit data on a ring network. It prevents devices from interfering with one another when data is transmitted onto a network.

☑ IEEE 802.11 is the standard for wireless networking, and specifies how data is transmitted over airwaves using technologies that support wireless networking.

☑ Another organization that provides standards is the Internet Engineering Task Force (IETF), which creates and maintains Requests for Comments (RFC).

Exam Objectives
Frequently Asked Questions

The following Frequently Asked Questions, answered by the authors of this book, are designed to both measure your understanding of the Exam Objectives presented in this chapter, and to assist you with real-life implementation of these concepts. You will also gain access to thousands of other FAQs at ITFAQnet.com.

Q: What is the purpose of a WAN, and how could it be applied to a network?

A: A WAN allows organizations in diverse geographical locations to be connected and function as if they were part of the same LAN. It can be applied to a network by implementing a high-speed connection between the two offices.

Q: Which networking component is the most likely to fail?

A: Cables. Cables are a common point of failure. Other network components have less chance of failing than a damaged or faulty cable.

Q: I am creating a home network that consists of one computer running an Apple iMac and another running Windows 2000 Professional. Each of them has a network adapter installed already. I want to network them together, but can't afford much in the way of additional equipment. What kind of network should I create?

A: Peer-to-peer. A peer-to-peer network is the simplest and least expensive type of network you can create. It doesn't require a machine running more expensive server software, and can be created by configuring these machines to be networked together, and connecting them to a hub (which is cheaper than a router) using network cabling. Being that security isn't an issue, peer-to-peer networks are ideal in these situations.

Q: My company wants to connect the LANs of an office in one city to an office in another city. They want the fastest possible connection. What type of cable should I get?

A: T3 lines are the fastest, but they are also the most expensive. T1 and T3 lines cost thousands of dollars a month, and may be more than your organization needs. Before deciding on a particular connection for your network, try to determine what users will be using it for, how often, and how much data will be transferred from one LAN to another.

Q: What is the most fault tolerant topology available?

A: The mesh topology is the most fault tolerant, because it uses multiple connections to the network. In this topology every computer is connected to every other computer, so if one cable breaks, the computer can continue using the network via another connection.

Q: My company is thinking of using wireless technology, but I've heard that hackers can access the data being transmitted using wireless. Should this be a concern?

A: Network security should always be a concern. Data being transmitted using wireless technology can be protected using data encryption methods, which can prevent unwanted individuals from being able to decipher the data they capture from wireless signals.

Q: What is the need for standards in networking?

A: Standards provide common methods and criteria for designing, developing, and manufacturing the hardware and software used in networks. It allows different devices to communicate with one another, regardless of who manufactured them, so that networks aren't limited to using proprietary equipment. It also provides best practices, recommendations, and information that is necessary to network communication (such as protocols that allow devices to transfer data).

Self Test

A Quick Answer Key follows the Self Test questions. For complete questions, answers, and explanations to the Self Test questions in this chapter as well as the other chapters in this book, see the Self Test Appendix.

1. You are creating a network for a small business with only four employees. Because employees often leave the office to visit clients, a maximum of one person is in the office and using a computer at any given time. Currently there are two computers in the office, but the company is willing to purchase more if needed to create a network. Due to budget constraints, they would like to avoid doing so if necessary. Based on this information, what is the minimum number of computers needed to create a network?

    A. One

    B. Two

    C. Three

    D. Four

2. The LAN used by your organization is on a single floor of a building. The network has servers and other resources that are kept in a secure server room. You are the only network administrator in the organization, and have sole responsibility for managing these resources and administration of network security for all of the users who are distributed throughout the network. What type of network model is being used?

    A. Centralized

    B. Decentralized

    C. Distributed

    D. Peer-to-peer

3. Your company's network is on several floors of a building. Due to the amount of data being stored, there are three file servers, a Web server for the intranet, an e-mail server for internal e-mail, and a SQL server that is used for several databases that have been developed in house. Due to security reasons, floppy disks and other devices to transfer or transmit data to and from the computer have been removed and aren't permitted. What type of network model is being used?

    A. Client/server

    B. Peer-to-peer

    C. MAN

    D. PAN

4. A company has hired you to create a network for their small business. Security isn't an issue, and there isn't enough money to hire or train a permanent network administrator. Users of the network routinely work on similar projects, and need to access one another's data on a regular basis. What type of network model will you use?

    A. Client/server

    B. Peer-to-peer

    C. Client

    D. Server

5. A company has multiple offices that are internetworked. Office A has a single computer that has the ability to dial into the Internet, but isn't connected to the other offices. Office B is in another part of the country from the other offices, but doesn't have its network interconnected to the other offices. Offices C and D are in separate states, but have a dedicated connection between them. Office C has twenty computers that access each other's machines, and provide services and data to one another. Office D has fifty computers that log onto the network using a single server. Based on this information, which of the offices are part of both a LAN and a WAN?

    A. Offices A and B

    B. Offices B and C

    C. Offices C and D

    D. The entire network (Offices A, B, C, and D)

6. An organization has offices in two countries. Office A is a small field office with two networked computers and is internetworked with Office B, which is across the road and has ten networked computers. Because they are a subsidiary of the main company, and perform different services from the rest of the organization, neither of these offices has been internetworked with the other offices, and is awaiting Internet connectivity to be provided next month. Office C is another field office that has a single computer, isn't networked with other offices, and only has an Internet connection. Office D is the headquarters of the company, has one hundred network users who are awaiting Internet connectivity to be added to the network, and has a network connection to Office E in London, which is their European office. Based on this information, which of the offices is connected to the largest WAN?

    A. Office A

    B. Office B

    C. Office C

    D. Office D

7. A company wants to create a WAN between two networks in different cities. To connect them, you want to have the fastest possible connection to meet their needs. Each network has massive amounts of data being sent between floors of their existing networked building, and you determine that at maximum, 1Mbps of data will have to be transmitted during normal business hours. Although they are a large business, and cost is not a major issue, they don't want to waste money on getting a solution with a bandwidth that's higher than they need. What type of connection will you choose in connecting these networks?

    A. Dial-up modem

    B. ISDN

    C. T1

    D. T3

8. A company has several offices that are networked together across the city. Each of the sales representatives uses PDAs to keep track of appointments with clients. The company has just implemented a new system where the appointments taken by receptionists are automatically uploaded to the PDAs whenever the sales staff enters

the main reception area. What types of networks are being used in this environment? Choose all that apply.

A. MAN

B. SAN

C. CAN

D. PAN

9. You have been hired by a company that uses the topology shown below. In looking at the physical layout of your network, which of the following types of topologies is being used?

Figure 1.9 Network Topology

A. Bus

B. Star

C. Mesh

D. Ring

10. Your network uses cells to send and receive data to and from computers. This allows computers in different buildings to be networked together so they can access data from servers in either building. A topology map has been created, using circles to identify the areas that computers can be placed to access the network. Based on this information, which of the following topologies is being used?

A. Star

B. Mesh

C. Wireless

D. Ring

11. You are training a new member of the IT staff, and decide to explain the topology of the existing network, shown below. What topology is currently being used?

Figure 1.10 Network Topology

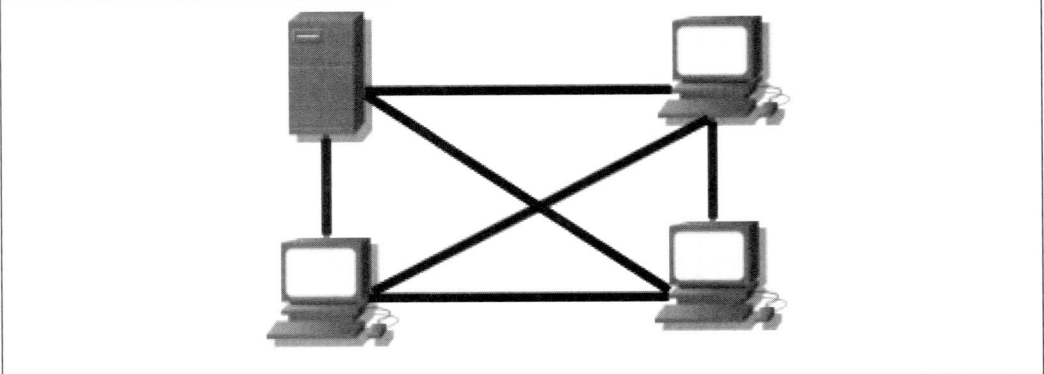

A. Bus

B. Star

C. Mesh

D. Ring

12. You are reviewing different topologies that will be used for a small network within your company. You want to ensure that all computers are enabled to the network using a minimal amount of cable. You also want to use a topology that is relatively easy to troubleshoot if a cable fails or breaks. Based on these criteria, which of the following topologies would you choose?

A. Bus

B. Mesh

C. Wireless

D. Ring

13. The IEEE 802 standards split a lower layer of the OSI model into two sublayers. One of these sublayers is used to establish connections between computers, and used by other protocols defined by the 802 committee. Which sublayer performs these actions, and which OSI layer is it part of?

A. Media Access Control, which is part of the Data Link Layer

B. Logical Link Control, which is part of the Data Link Layer

C. Physical Layer, which is part of the Data Link Layer

D. Data Link Layer, which is part of the Logical Link Control Layer

14. The network used in your organization uses the IEEE 802.3 standard. Before sending data onto the network, a computer will listen to ensure the network is clear so that two computers don't send data onto the cable at the same time. When two computers send out data at the same time, which of the following is true?

A. A critical network error will have occurred from a collision, and the network will crash.

B. The computer detecting the collision will send out a signal to all other computers. Because the collision has been detected, all devices will stop transmitting data for a random period of time, listen to see if the network is free of traffic, and then begin sending data again.

C. The computer detecting the collision will send out a signal to all the other computers. Because it detected the problem, it now has precedence over the other computers, and can send its data before any other computer.

D. None of the above. This cannot happen because the computers listen for network traffic before sending, which prevents data collisions from ever occurring.

15. Your network uses a ring topology in which computers are connected to a closed loop of cabling. A secondary ring of cabling is also used. If the primary ring of cabling has a break, what will happen?

A. The network will fail.

B. The secondary ring will be used, but the primary ring won't be used.

C. The primary ring will be used, but the secondary ring won't be used.

D. Both rings will be used.

16. You are designing a network for an organization that will have all components of the network connected to every other component. In designing this network, you need to determine the number of connections that will be necessary to achieve this topology. You find that there are 20 computers on this network. Based on this information, how many connections will be needed?

A. 20

B. 40

C. 150

D. 190

Self Test Quick Answer Key

For complete questions, answers, and explanations to the Self Test questions in this chapter as well as the other chapters in this book, see the Self Test Appendix.

1.	**B**		9.	**A**
2.	**A**		10.	**C**
3.	**A**		11.	**C**
4.	**B**		12.	**D**
5.	**C**		13.	**B**
6.	**C**		14.	**B**
7.	**C**		15.	**D**
8.	**A** and **D**		16.	**D**

Chapter 2

NETWORK+

Network Media

Domain I Objectives in this chapter:

1.3   Specify the characteristics (For example: speed, length, topology, and cable type) of the following cable standards:

       1.3.1   10BASE-T and 10BASE-FL

       1.3.2   100BASE-TX and 100BASE-FX

       1.3.3   1000BASE-TX, 1000BASE-CX, 1000BASE-SX and 1000BASE-LX

       1.3.4   10GBASE-SR, 10GBASE-LR and 10GBASE-ER

1.4   Recognize the following media connectors and describe their uses:

       1.4.1   RJ-11

       1.4.2   RJ-45

       1.4.3   F-Type

       1.4.5   ST

       1.4.6   SC

       1.4.7   IEEE1394 (FireWire)

       1.4.8   LC

       1.4.9   MTRJ

1.5   Recognize the following media types and describe their uses:

       1.5.1   Category 3, 5, 5e, and 6

       1.5.2   UTP

       1.5.3   STP

       1.5.4   Coaxial cable

       1.5.5   SMF optic cable

       1.5.6   MMF optic cable

Introduction

In this chapter, we'll take a look at what you will need to know about cable connections and termination for the Network+ exam. When working in the field of networking, it's nearly impossible to not come across physical cabling. Unless you have wireless media (covered in Chapter 4), you will need some form of cabling, and need some form of endpoint, or termination, to your transmission media and a way for it to physically connect to a device.

This endpoint is called a *connector*, and it terminates the end of the media, creating a way for it to connect to something else such as a patch panel, switch port, or other connection. This chapter shows you what you need to know about connecting and terminating the most common forms of cable in use today: copper in the form of twisted-pair cable, coaxial cabling, and fiber optics. The understanding of transmission media types, connectors, and termination is essential to being a networking professional. In this chapter we will learn the fundamentals of cabling, the connectors used with them, and the most common tools of the trade.

Cabling and Connectors Overview

The media that carries data makes up the basic infrastructure of a network. If you considered data as a vehicle that moves between two points, then cabling and connectors are the highways and interchanges that allow data to access and travel across that network. Connectors attached to the ends of the cables are plugged into or coupled in some way with a network card or other device on your network. In doing so, a physical link is created between this device and others on your network. Just as a car uses an on ramp to enter a highway, the connector provides an access point for data to move along the cable to its intended destination.

The purpose of a cable is to carry data across a network. In doing so, a network card passes an electronic signal onto a cable. A connector is used to connect the cable to the network card or other device to the cable. The data, in the form of an electronic signal, is passed through the connector to a wire or fiber in the cable. Just as the wires in your house carry electricity to the lights and wall sockets in each room, the cable carries these electronic signals to the computers, printers or other network devices meant to receive them.

While local area networks (LANs) of the past often used one type of cabling, many LANs today use a combination of different cable types. This is because different cables will carry the data at varying speeds and distances. While some cables can carry the data for a hundred meters or so, others can span greater distances, connecting widely spanned areas. In the same way, some cables will allow a network to transfer millions of bits data, while others can send a thousand times this amount. As we'll see later in this chapter, the features of a particular type of cable can vary greatly.

Because different types of cabling are available to use, it follows that there are also different types of connectors that may be used. The connectors fit on the ends of the cabling, and are designed to hold the wires or fibers within the cabling together, allowing them to make a connection when the connector is plugged into or coupled with a network device. If you think of a cable used on your telephone, each end of the phone cable has a connector that bundles the wires in the cable together in a specific way, so they can make a connection when the cable is plugged into the corresponding telephone or wall jack. The connectors on a network cable are the same, providing an interface for a device to connect to a cable.

Fundamentals of Cabling

Cabling is the wire or fiber medium that is used to connect computers and other network devices of your network together, and used to carry the data that is transmitted between them. While we'll discuss each of the types of cabling in greater detail later in this chapter, there are three types of physical media that can be used on a network:

- Coaxial cable
- Twisted-pair cable
- Fiber optic cable

Coaxial cable, also referred to as *coax*, is the same type of cabling you see in most cable television installations today. A single copper wire at the center of the cable core is used to carry the signals, and is surrounded by layers of insulation that protect the wire and its transmissions. On networks, there are higher grades and different types of coaxial that may be used: thin (10Base2) or thick (10Base5) are two examples.

The thin and thick kinds of coaxial cabling refer to the thickness of the cable. 10Base2 cabling, also known as *Thinnet*, is 0.25 inches while 10Base5 cabling, also known as *Thicknet*, is 0.5 inches. Because a thicker wire was used in 10Base5, it allows data to travel further than its thinner counterpart. This made 10Base5 ideal as a backbone for early networks, although the increased speeds and distances supported by fiber optic cabling has become a better solution for modern networks.

NOTE

A backbone segment is made up of high-speed lines and equipment normally located at the very center of your network.

Twisted-pair cable is a type of cabling that's used for telephone and network communications. When we mentioned the cable used to connect your phone to a wall jack, we were discussing a type of cable called twisted-pair. As shown in Figure 2.1, twisted-pair cables have one or more pairs of copper wires that are insulated and twisted around one another, which prevent the signals on the wires from interfering with one another. Common sources of interference are EMI (electromagnetic interference) and RFI (radio frequency interference). Problems may occur such as the untwisting of pairs. In this case, the twisted pairs may open up of loosen and will be more susceptible to EMI and RFI.

As we'll see later in this chapter, there are different categories of twisted-pair cabling, which are used for different purposes as well as to discuss common issues with interference.

Figure 2.1 Twisted-Pair Wiring

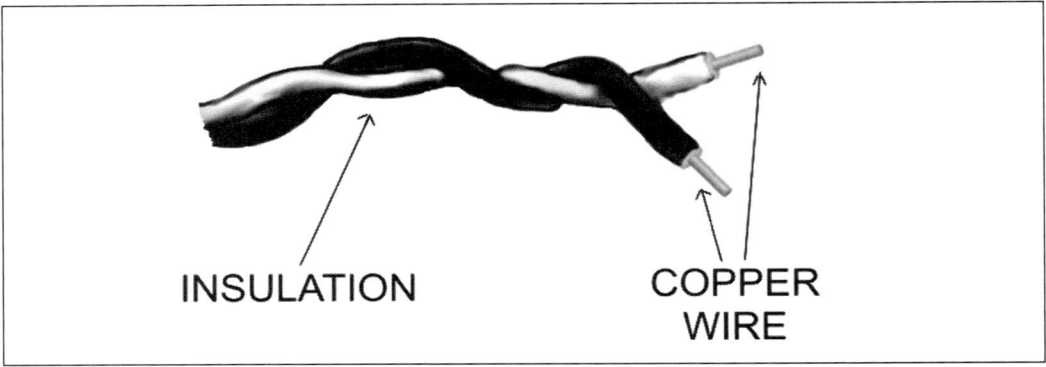

Twisted-pair cabling may be shielded or unshielded. The difference between unshielded twisted-pair (UTP) and shielded twisted pair (STP) is that STP has an extra layer of aluminum/polyester between the wire and the plastic covering. This acts as a shield against interference from outside sources that could corrupt data carried on the copper wire.

Fiber optic cabling is different from these other types of cabling, as it doesn't use copper wires to transmit data. Fiber optic cables use glass or plastic to transmit light pulses across the network. Because information is transmitted at the speed of light, it can carry more information faster than other types of cabling.

Fundamentals of Connectors

Connectors are used to hold the ends of the wires or fibers in a cable in place, so that it can then be plugged into a network card or other equipment on your network. As you can see when looking at the cable connectors used for your phone and cable television, these connectors may be plastic or metal, and differ greatly in appearance. This makes them easy to identify both in the real world and on the Network+ exam.

There are several different kinds of connectors that may be used with the different types of cabling, which we'll explain in detail later in this chapter. They are:

- BNC (Bayonet-Neill-Concelman) is a type of locking connector used to terminate coaxial cables. BNC is also referred to by many other names such as Bayonet Network Connector, British Naval Connector, or Bayonet Nut Connector.

- RJ (registered jack) is used with twisted-pair cables. RJ-11 is used for phone cables, while RJ-45 is a twisted-pair cable that is commonly used in networks.

- SC (standard connector) is used with fiber optic cabling.

- ST (straight tip) is used with fiber optic cabling.

- LC (local connector) is used with fiber optic cabling.

- MTRJ (mechanical transfer registered jack) is used with fiber optic cabling.

These different types of connectors attach a cable to network cards and other devices in different ways. Some, like RJ-11, RJ-45, and ST connectors are plugged into a port, while others like BNC and ST connectors have threading that is used to screw the connector into place. To put this into a perspective of something you're familiar with, the RJ connectors are plugged in just as you would plug your phone cord into the telephone. BNC connectors are screwed onto a corresponding port in the same way you attach you're the cable used for cable television to the back of your TV. Once the connector is attached to the network card or another device, it provides a connection between the device and the physical media that carries data across your network.

Media Issues

As with anything dealing with networks, there are issues that you'll need to consider when deciding on what's best for your organization. The different types of physical media available each have their own benefits and vulnerabilities that can affect network performance and the amount of work required to install, troubleshoot, and repair cabling. Some types of cabling can carry more data at faster speeds, and over longer distances. Other types are more susceptible to interference that can corrupt data or have security issues that make them more vulnerable to attack. By knowing the issues related to each media type, you can make a better decision on which cabling will best suit the needs of your network.

Interference

If you've ever listened to a radio during a storm, you've probably heard the crackles and pops of static when lightning interferes with the radio transmission. Just as the electricity of lightning can interfere with radio signals, similar interference can effect the transmission of data across a network cable. EMI is a low voltage, low current, high frequency signal that can interfere with the electronic signals transmitted over cabling. Because the EMI signals come from outside sources and interrupt the information sent over cabling, it is often referred to as *noise*.

EMI can result from numerous sources. Power lines, transformers, fluorescent lights and fixtures, industrial tools, engines, and other machinery and equipment that run on electricity can emit electromagnetic waves that affect other devices and data transmitted over cabling. The electromagnetic field generated by these devices is a natural byproduct of electricity being passed through the wiring, and its effects are not only seen in cabling, but also in other computer technology. For example, if you place a lamp or fan near your monitor, you may find that the screen flickers because the EMI of the lamp is causing interference with the monitor.

Similar to EMI is RFI, which is caused by electromagnetic radiation in the radio frequency range. RFI can be caused by radio and television broadcast towers, microwave satellite dishes, appliances, and furnaces. Just as with EMI radiation, RFI can result in data being corrupted during transmission.

The effects of EMI or RFI can be reduced or eliminated by properly grounding equipment, not placing cables close to sources of EMI or RFI, and using cables that use shielding or are more resistant to EMI/RFI. A shield is material in the cabling that's used to absorb EMI/RFI before it reaches the wires that carry data. Unshielded twisted-pair is the most vulnerable type of cabling because it doesn't use any shielding to protect the wires in the cable. Shielded twisted-pair is more resistant to EMI/RFI because of a layer of aluminum/polyester between the wire and the outer plastic covering of the cable. A similar shield is found in coaxial cable, which uses a wire mesh or foil shielding in the cable. The only cabling that is unaffected by EMI/RFI, however, is fiber optic cabling, which doesn't contain any copper wiring and uses plastic or glass that is non-conductive. While we'll discuss the internal components of these cables later in this chapter, using cables that provide shielding or aren't affected by EMI/RFI will prevent data from being corrupted during transmission.

Another type of interference that can occur in cabling is *crosstalk*. Crosstalk occurs when the electromagnetic field of one wire interferes with the transmission of another. That is, the signals from one wire essentially bleed onto another wire. You may have experienced this in a telephone system, when you hear someone else's conversation on your phone line. In networks, this type of interference can cause a loss or corruption of data.

Crosstalk can be reduced or eliminated by first ensuring that the twists in the wire pairs stay together and intact, by moving the cables further apart from one another or by using cables that use shielding. As with EMI/RFI interference, UTP is the most vulnerable to crosstalk, while STP and coaxial cable have shielding that protects the wire from outside interference. Fiber optic cabling is immune from crosstalk because it uses light rather than electronic signals to transmit data.

EXAM WARNING

Don't get crosstalk confused with EMI. Remember that when one cable has its data communications bleed onto another cable, it is crosstalk. EMI can come from any number of sources, including florescent lights or machinery.

Bandwidth

Bandwidth is a measurement of the amount of data that can be passed over a cable in a given amount of time. If you compare cabling to a highway, and data to vehicles traveling along the highway, then bandwidth would be the amount of traffic supported. Just as too many cars traveling on a highway would cause a traffic jam, there is a limit to the amount of data a cable can support before the network becomes bogged down.

Bandwidth is generally measured in increments of bits and bytes. A bit is short for *binary digit*, and is the smallest unit of data on a computer. When information is processed or sent across a wire or circuit board, it is passed as an electric current. The signal is either a high current or low current of electricity, and represented digitally by a 1 or 0. Each of these ones and zeros is referred to as a bit, and eight bits of data make a byte. A word is considered 4 bytes, which is essentially 32 bits… the same length as an IP (Internet Protocol) address, which we will learn about in Chapter 6.

The bandwidth capacity of a network cable is usually measured in the number of bits or bytes that can be transferred in a second. In modem connections, thousands of bits may be sent, with each thousand referred to as Kbps (kilobits per second). In network cabling, considerably more data can be sent more quickly. Bandwidth may be measured in megabits per second (Mbps), with each megabit representing a million bits of data transmitted each second, or in the gigabits per second (Gbps), meaning that 1000 million bits of data are transferred for every 1 gigabit supported. Table 2.1 shows the bandwidth capacity of different media standards, which we'll discuss in greater detail later in this chapter, and how this capacity varies depending on the media being used.

Table 2.1 Bandwidth Capacity of Physical Media

Media Standard	Cable Type	Bandwidth Capacity
10Base2	Coax	10 Mbps
10Base5	Coax	10 Mbps
10BaseT	UTP (Category 3 or higher)	10 Mbps
100BaseTX	UTP (Category 5 or higher)	100 Mbps
10BaseFL	Fiber optic	10 Mbps
100BaseFX	Fiber optic	100 Mbps
1000BaseT	UTP (Category 5 or higher)	1 Gbps (1000 Mbps)
1000BaseSX	Fiber optic	1 Gbps (1000 Mbps)
1000BaseLX	Fiber optic	1 Gbps (1000 Mbps)
1000BaseCX	Fiber optic	1 Gbps (1000 Mbps)
10GbaseSR	Fiber optic	10 Gbps
10GbaseLX4	Fiber optic	10 Gbps
10GbaseLR	Fiber optic	10 Gbps

TEST DAY TIP

An easy way of remembering the maximum bandwidth of the various media standards is to look at the number at the front of the standard, which refers to the number of megabits supported. In looking at 10Base5, the *10* symbolizes that the maximum transmission speed is 10 Mbps, while the word *Base* indicates that it is using a baseband technology (as opposed to broadband). The final portion of the media standard varies in meaning. Originally, the number at the end indicated the maximum distance of the cable. For example, the *5* in 10Base5 indicates that it has a maximum distance of 500 meters, while the *2* in 10Base2 was a rounded-up indication of its 185 meter maximum distance. This changed, however, with 10BaseT, which signifies that twisted-pair cabling is used.

If the amount of data exceeds the amount of bandwidth supported, the cabling can become a bottleneck because the transmission speed will be affected. Just like an example of plumbing with piping and water, as liquid being poured will slow when it reaches the narrow end of a tube, data transfers can slow if more data is being sent than the cabling can support. It should now make complete sense to you why bandwidth can be precious, especially for your wide area network (WAN) connections (discussed in more detail in Chapter 7). WAN links are costly and you will likely want to use every ounce of bandwidth you can squeeze out of it.

To follow a real world example, if 10BaseT UTP cable was used to transfer data between floors of a building, then upwards of 10 Mbps of data could be sent. If considerably more than this amount was being sent across the network on a routine basis, then cabling that supported a higher bandwidth (such as fiber optic) would be needed. When designing a network, it is important to consider the amount of data that will be transferred so the proper cabling can be initially installed. As the requirements of the network grow, replacing existing cabling with cables that support a higher bandwidth capacity may be necessary.

Length Problems

The length of cabling is an important consideration when deciding on the cable that will be used for a network. As signals travel the length of a cable, they will weaken over distance. The signals will eventually degrade until they reach the point where the data is lost. When this occurs, it is referred to as *attenuation*.

Because attenuation can occur, it is important that you don't exceed the maximum distance of a cable. Table 2.2 shows the maximum lengths of various media standards, which we'll discuss in greater detail later in this chapter. As you can see, physical media can have a maximum distance ranging from hundreds of meters to kilometers in length. If a cable has to be run longer than its maximum distance, then the signal will have to be regenerated. In the past, a device called a repeater performed this task. As we'll discuss in the next chapter, repeaters aren't generally found on modern networks, but this same functionality is found in other network devices, such as switches, routers and hubs.

TEST DAY TIP

Review the maximum cable lengths and the transmission speeds associated with the different media types before going into the exam. To ensure you know them, have someone quiz you on the various elements of each media standard. You can expect to see questions related to these elements of physical media on the exam.

Table 2.2 Maximum Distance of Physical Media

Media Standard	Cable Type	Maximum Length
10Base2	Coax	185 meters
10Base5	Coax	500 meters
10BaseT	UTP (Category 3 or higher)	100 meters
100BaseTX	UTP (Category 5 or higher)	100 meters
10BaseFL	Fiber optic	2 kilometers
100BaseFX	Fiber optic	400 meters (half-duplex) or 2 km (full-duplex)
1000BaseT	UTP (Category 5 or higher)	100 meters
1000BaseSX	Fiber optic	550 meters (multi-mode fiber)
1000BaseLX	Fiber optic	550 meters (multi-mode fiber) or up to 10 km (single mode fiber)
1000BaseCX	Fiber optic	100 meters
10GbaseSR	Fiber optic	Up to 300 meters over 2000Mhz.km multi-mode fiber
10GbaseLX4	Fiber optic	Up to 10 km over single-mode fiber
10GbaseLR	Fiber optic	Up to10 km over single-mode fiber

Fiber optic cabling doesn't suffer from attenuation as copper cabling does. While part of the electric signal passed along a copper wire will be absorbed by the cable and weaken over distance, fiber optic uses light and/or laser passed over glass or plastic fibers, so it doesn't suffer from the same problems. While twisted-pair and coaxial cables can span a distance of hundreds of meters, signals will run along fiber optic cable for kilometers without any noticeable signal degradation. It's for this reason that fiber optic cabling is used for connecting locations of a network that are separated by significant distance.

Security Issues

The security of cabling is another important issue that should be considered before installing a particular kind of cabling. Different organizations and locations may require different types of cabling to meet the security needs outlined in policies or regulations. In other situations, such as a small office home office (SOHO), security may be a minor issue. Because needs differ, you should try to establish what the security needs are before installation begins. In determining the kind of cable you'll install, you will also need to be aware of security issues that are inherent to certain types of cabling.

If you've watched any crime dramas on television, you've probably heard of wiretapping. Often, this refers to gaining access and listening to someone's telephone line without the person knowing about it. However, as we've said, the same or similar cabling used for voice communication is also used in networking. Wiretapping is as much a security risk for network cabling as it is for a business telephone line.

Wiretapping involves gaining physical access to a network cable. The cable must be cut or pierced so that the wires inside the cable can be accessed and then spliced or tapped. Because of the shield in STP cabling, this is more difficult to do than with UTP. Older networks that use coaxial cabling often recognize the risk of wiretapping because tapping is required on 10Base5 (Thicknet) cables to add new workstations. A tool called a *vampire tap* is used to clamp onto the coaxial cable and pierce it. A needle is then dropped into the hole in the cable, so that contact is made with the wire inside of the cable. This tap provides a connection so that 10Base2 cabling can be used to connect a computer to the cable, and access data traveling along the cable.

Fiber optic cabling is the least susceptible to wiretapping because of the glass or plastic fibers used to carry the data. It is difficult to tap into the cable without causing damage, although optical vampire taps do exist that allow a tap to be performed by clamping onto the cable. Generally though, a tap requires cutting the cable before tapping it, which may provide an obvious clue that a problem exists.

Another security issue related to cables is eavesdropping. Eavesdropping is the act of listening to data being sent over the wire without actually piercing the cable. As we learned earlier when we discussed crosstalk and EMI from other cables, the signals of a cable can bleed off and be picked up by other wires in neighboring cables. The same factors that make it possible for EMI to cause interference with cabling also make it possible for someone to obtain data from the cable without piercing it. To minimize the risk of eavesdropping, you should use cabling that is less susceptible to EMI (STP or coaxial) or immune to it altogether (fiber optic).

Security Alert!

Physical Security

Physical security is an important part of any network. In terms of cabling, you should try to keep as much cabling as possible out of public reach. Rather than running cable in the open, or having it accessible in waiting rooms or reception areas, most of your cabling should be run in secured conduits protected from damage behind walls, floors, or ceilings, with wall jacks placed to plug into the network in areas close to desks. Even if you do not use special cable management equipment, you can still keep the cabling neat and secure and out of reach so that you don't have issues with cut cables, broken cables, and so on. You don't want members of the public being able to access connections or cabling.

You should also perform routine inspections of cabling for physical damage, as this may indicate attempts to tap the wires and acquire data, or just alert you to a simple problem you may be able to proactively take care of before it gets worse. As mentioned in this section, fiber optic cabling and shielded cable will help to protect your cable from security issues, although fiber optic cabling is very sensitive to the touch and easy to break if handled incorrectly (this is one of its only flaws besides being pricier than copper cabling).

Remember that physical security is important and that in high security areas, more drastic and expensive methods are also available to add new levels of security, if needed, such as placing cables in steel conduits, or using conduits that are pressurized with gas and use monitors to determine pressure changes. This works like an alarm that someone may be attempting to access a cable.

Installation

The level of difficulty in installing physical media varies depending on the type used and where the cabling is being installed. In some situations, such as a home office, it can be incredibly simple, but in others, such as running cable down an elevator shaft to connect two floors of a building, the installation can be challenging. Depending on the cabling and the location, you may be able to easily install the cabling yourself, or may opt to outsource to a company that specializes in cable installation.

Installation of twisted-pair cable is relatively easy. UTP is similar to the cable used for phone lines, so it is thinner and more flexible than other types of cabling, making it easier to get around corners. STP is more difficult to bend than UTP because of the shielding. STP requires an electrical ground with the connectors, which is why it is easier to use pre-wired cables that already have the connectors installed. It is never recommended that you make cable if you either don't know how, or don't have equipment to test the cable that you made.

STP is thicker than UTP, making it more rigid, which can make it more difficult to install around corners. While the shielding providers greater benefits against EMI, the installation of the cabling can be more problematic. STP is also more difficult to make and more expensive than UTP.

Coaxial cable is also relatively easy to install. If you've ever extended the cable for your cable TV, you're probably familiar with some of the ease and difficulty you'll face. The connectors for coaxial cable are fairly simple to install, but the cable is relatively thick and rigid, and can require some finesse in navigating it around corners.

Installation of fiber optic cabling can be difficult, which is why many companies outsource the job of installing and maintaining it to other firms, such as a local phone company. Not only is it somewhat difficult to install, it is also difficult to test. Cable testers are your insurance that a line is good, tested ok, and is operational so you do not have to come back to fix it or spend more time troubleshooting it.

Because glass or plastic is used to carry the data, connecting two pieces of cabling together can prove difficult, as they must be fused together. Because of the cost of fiber optic cables, it generally isn't installed throughout an entire network. Rather, fiber is often used as a backbone for networks, connecting different buildings together so that data can be transmitted quickly between them. While other types of cabling are used within the buildings, a local phone company or another firm that specializes in fiber optic installation may be used to install and maintain the fiber optic cabling.

Troubleshooting

Experienced network administrators know that cabling is one of the most common causes of network failure. For this reason, you should check cabling early in the network troubleshooting process. Because you are often responding to a single workstation or group of computers that can't communicate within the network, start at that point and then work outward. There is no point in checking the backbone of the network if a single computer is having a problem. Also, because the workstation is probably using twisted-pair or 10Base2 coaxial cable, it is also the easiest to check first.

Most often, the cable running from the workstation to the wall jack is the one that will be the problem. This cable receives the most abuse, and may be damaged. Sometimes you may fix the problem by simply plugging the cable back in if it has fallen out or has otherwise been unplugged. Because of this, you should perform a visual inspection of cabling. Simply reviewing the cables and surrounding area will provide clues of possible wiretapping, tampering, electrical work that may have affected the cabling, or other things that are out of the ordinary.

If you believe a bad cable may be the culprit of a network-related problem, the most logical step is to test your hypothesis by replacing the cable with a known good cable. The results are simple: if you can communicate once again, then the old cable was the source of the problem. If you still cannot communicate with the known good cable, you need to continue troubleshooting or find another cable to test.

In troubleshooting cabling, you should also be aware that some apparent cabling problems may actually be hardware-related. You should determine whether the network interface card (NIC), which we'll discuss in Chapter 3, is faulty and not communicating with the network properly.

As you work outward from the problem, look for possible sources of interference, such as florescent lighting, machinery, or cables that are too close to each other. As we discussed earlier, interference from such sources can cause corrupt data and disrupt network communications.

Because there is a limit to how far cable can run before it suffers attenuation, you should also check cable distances. If the maximum distance for cabling has been reached, then you may need to install a device that will regenerate the data and pass it along to the next segment. We'll discuss such devices in Chapter 3.

Using tools that are designed for troubleshooting cable problems is another important factor in solving such problems quickly. As we'll see later in this chapter, there are a number of tools that can be used to check for breaks. These tools are a necessity to find where a problem exists in the cabling, and will save considerable time in solving cabling issues.

Repair

The ease with which different cabling types can be repaired depends on the cable type itself. The repair of copper cable is relatively easy. As we'll see later in this chapter when we discuss cabling and cable creation, twisted-pair and coaxial cabling may require replacement of a bad section with a new section of cable. Twisted-pair may require rewiring the individual wires of a new section to a connector, while coaxial could use male and female barrel connectors to attach a new section of cable to an existing one. Because copper wire is involved, this makes it a relatively simple procedure. Because of how inexpensive coaxial and twisted-pair cables are, it is often easier to simply replace the segment of cable with a new one, unless it is a particularly long segment.

Repair of fiber optic cabling is difficult, and requires professional training. If there is a bad section that has to be replaced, connecting a new section would require using either electric fusion or a chemical epoxy process to connect the segments together. Unless you have the necessary tools and training to perform such repairs, it is generally wiser to have a firm that specializes in such repairs do it for you. Repair of fiber optic cable is not just difficult; it is also costly. Most times, organizations need only a single fiber run, so it is cost-prohibitive to do this work yourself.

NOTE

For more information on how to make and test fiber optic cabling, visit www.thefoa.org/tech/FAQS/FAQ-TEST.HTM

Cable Testers and Troubleshooting

In many troubleshooting sessions, there is a time where a simple isolation of problems is just not feasible. In such situations, you will need to rely on electronic tools to determine what and where the problem is. Cable testers are tools that can analyze the capability of a cable to carry signals, and can find breaks or other problems in the wire. In addition to cable testers, there are also other tools that can be used in the troubleshooting process to identify problems on your network. In the sections that follow, we will look at the most common ones.

Tone Generator (Fox and Hound)

The *tone generator* is used to perform tests on phone and network lines by clipping to a wire, terminal panel, or standard modular jack, and will aid in the identification of wires during the wire tracing process. A tone generator can be connected to a data or voice line and it is used to find out where a cable end may be. A test signal is sent across a wire pair to transmit a tone (as in dial tone). You can quickly and easily trace pairs and locate broken pairs in the cabling, even those buried deep in the walls.

To use a tone generator, you begin by attaching the *fox* to the cable, jack, or panel that you would like to trace, and you continue with the *hound* on the other end of the cable to find the fox's tone. When you find the tone, you will know that you have correctly tracked the cable. This is very helpful in determining which cable in a group of many cables, such as a wiring closet, has gone bad and needs to be replaced, or if the cable installer did not correctly or properly mark the patch panel.

Time Domain Reflectometer

A *time domain reflectometer (TDR)* also uses signals it sends down the cable to identify problems. An electronic pulse travels down the cable until it is reflected back, much like how sonar technology works. The TDR then calculates the distance down the cable that the signal traveled before being reflected by measuring the amount of time it took for the signal to be returned. If this distance is less than your overall cable length, a cable problem exists. It will most likely be behind a wall or in a place where it will be very difficult to get to.

Wire Map Tester

A *wire map tester* is generally used on networks that use twisted-pair cabling. It will test for opens, shorts, and crossed pairs, and will provide information that may indicate improper wiring. Because they are a low-cost cable tester, they generally provide fewer features than other cable testers, such as TDRs.

Oscilloscope

An *oscilloscope* can determine if there are shorts or crimps in the cable. An oscilloscope formats its output in a graphical format. Oscilloscopes are commonly used to test cables that have been recently run through walls to ensure there are no problems with the cable prior to using it.

Network Monitors and Protocol Analyzers

Network monitors and protocol analyzers monitor traffic on the network and display the packets that have been transmitted across the network. If a particular type of packet is not being transmitted across the network, the problem may lie with that particular packet type. Since the network monitor enables you to view the contents of *all* packets on the network, in many cases, viewing the contents of these packets is considered unethical or even illegal. As such, you should determine the company's policy on using these tools before implementing them as part of the troubleshooting process.

Crossover Cable

A *crossover cable* appears to be just another twisted-pair cable, but two wires are crossed, which makes the cable unfit for plugging into a computer and a hub for normal use. The crossover cable is used to connect two computers to each other directly, without the use of a hub.

A crossover cable is also used to connect hubs in the event you need to cascade them. If you were to substitute a crossover cable for a regular twisted-pair cable to connect two hubs, it would not work correctly. Therefore, it is important that you mark your crossover cables or use a different color cable to designate a crossover cable. Many companies use yellow or black cables for regular cables and blue for crossover cables. You will not need many crossover cables, and you can make them yourself if you have the correct pinout. There are a few things to remember about making a crossover cable. First, make sure you label it or know how to distinguish it from other cables such as a straight through. This is because you may use the wrong type of cable and that may be the cause of your issues, when all along it could have been prevented with the proper labeling of the cable. Exercise 2.1 shows you how to make a crossover cable from a standard straight through cable.

EXERCISE 2.1

MAKING A CROSSOVER CABLE

This exercise will show you how to properly construct a crossover network cable from a preexisting straight through cable. In this exercise you will need tools to help you cut and create the wire. These tools (which will be discussed throughout the text and can be further researched online) are as follows.

You will need a preexisting cable. If you are already familiar with making cable, you can use a fresh length from a bulk cable spool if you have one available, but if not, then you can use a preexisting cable to perform this task. You will definitely want it to be Category 5 or above. You will also need connectors (RJ-45 modular plugs).You will also need a cutter to cut the wire. A cutter can be a standard pair of scissors or a high-end cutting tool made specifically for the job of cutting cable. Since cutting cable has to be exact, neat, and (most importantly) the 8 wires have to be cut evenly to fit in the RJ-45 connector, it's important to consider using the right tool for the job. A crimper is also needed to squeeze the RJ-45 connector onto the cable making it a permanent fit. This cannot be undone, nor do you want to. Mistakes here should be met with a new cut of the end of the Category 5 cable and a new end created. You will also need a stripper to pull the cable jacketing off the wire to expose it. Make sure that you do not damage any of the wires. Although making cable can be easy, a lot of care needs to go into its creation in order for it to work properly. Now that you have your tools ready and the cable you want to turn into a crossover cable, let's look at the actual steps involved in making the cuts and creating the cable.

1. Take a new (or tested) Category 5 UTP cable and ensure it is rated properly (check the outer jacket to ensure that this cable is Category 5 UTP). Now that that has been determined, take your cutter and snip off one of the ends of the cable you are about to make into a crossover cable.

2. Once you have made the cut, ensure that the cut is clean, meaning that there are eight wires cut evenly across with a hint of copper showing at the tip of each exposed wire. The copper ends will touch the contacts located within the RJ-45 connector. This is essentially why the cut has to be clean; it has to fit neatly into the connector and make connection with the contacts.

3. Now, strip off some of the excess jacket (about 1-3 inches) and reveal the inside wires so that you can work with them. You will have to untwist the pairs a bit to get them into the RJ-45 connector, but be careful not to untwist them too much, as the twists are what keep the phenomenon of crosstalk down. An example of exposed and twisted wire can be seen in Figure 2.2.

Figure 2.2 Viewing Exposed Cable

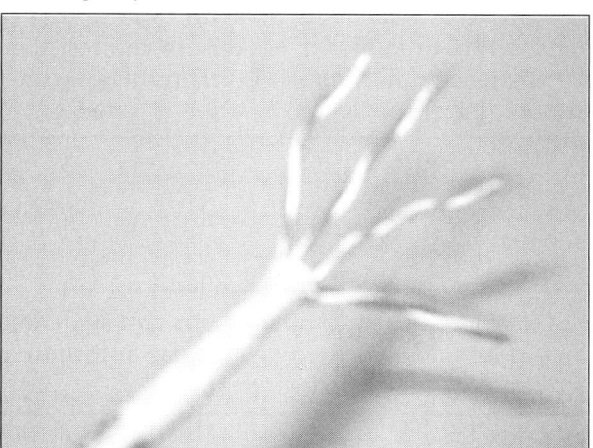

4. Once you have stripped off the jacket to expose the wires, you will need to spread the wires apart (carefully) in a fan so that you can clearly see the colors on each of the individual wires; 4 pairs of 2 wires each, each following a tip/ring combination of specific color codes.

5. Make absolutely sure that you hold on to the base of the jacket so that you can keep the twists tight at the base where you cut the wire's jacket. You do not want the wires to become untwisted down inside the jacket. Once you are ready, you have to re-order the cables so that the transmit (TX) and receive (RX) channels are reversed—hence the name *crossover*. Later in the chapter we will look at the wiring pairs in detail. To make a crossover cable, all you need to do is change one of the cable ends to a different standard.

6. 568A standard end on one side, 568B standard on the other end makes a crossover cable. Although cabling standards at this depth are not covered in the Network+ exam, it's still very important to know as a network technician. You will learn about the cabling pinouts later in the chapter.

7. Once you insert the cable pairs into the RJ-45 connector, you need to make absolutely sure that no cable is exposed outside of the RJ-45 connector. What this means is that if you cut the cable too long, it will have exposed wires, as the jacket is not able to protect them. Make sure that you cut the jacket so that the connector covers it so you don't have any open leakage for interference or wire pairs that can untwist themselves.

8. Take your crimper and insert the new end of the cable into it with the RJ-45 connector. Once you are ready, firmly place even pressure on the crimper so that the connector is seated and will not open up. Usually, once you crimp a connector, it cannot be uncrimped so if you make a mistake, you will be cutting the end off and starting again.

9. Now that you have finished the crimping job, you should have a perfectly good crossover cable that you can use that can be used for any connection that requires it. Make sure you test the cable, otherwise, you may experience other problems and not know where to look or troubleshoot.

NOTE

A crossover cable can be used to uplink hubs and switches to each other. However, some hubs and switching devices use autosense or have a manual way to switch the port to a crossover port.

Hardware Loopback Adapter

A *hardware loopback adapter* is a way to test the ports on a system without having to connect to an external device. For example, you can use a serial loopback adapter to verify that a transmitted signal is leaving your serial port and returning through the loopback adapter, ensuring that your serial port is working correctly.

Cable Tester

Cable testers provide a variety of tests that can be performed on network cabling. The features of a handheld cable tester will vary, so you should refer to the documentation that comes with the tester to familiarize yourself with what it can do and how the tests are performed. Some high-end testers will also combine the features of several testers, such as providing the features of a wire map tester and a TDR. A number of cable testers also have an auto-test feature, which provides the ability to automatically perform a series of tests on the cable, allowing you to review the results of each individual test.

In using a cable tester, you would check the segments of cable that are suspected to have a problem. For example, if you were performing a test on a network that uses 10Base2, you might separate the cable at a midway point. You could then check each half of the cable to determine which half has the problem. Once this is done, you could then perform the same test by checking the cable at the halfway point of that section, and repeat this until you have determined which where the defect in the cable was located.

Simplex, Half-Duplex, and Full Duplex

When data travels across the medium, it travels in a certain direction. To describe the movement of data across communication channels, certain terms are used, including:

- Simplex, which refers to data moving in a single direction.

- Half-duplex, which means data travels both ways on the medium, but in only one direction at a time.

- Full duplex, which means data travels in both directions simultaneously.

While these terms are often associated with network devices, as we proceed in this chapter, we will discuss how certain methods of network communication support simplex, half-duplex or full duplex.

Cabling

Cabling isn't just a term that refers to the cable being used. It is also a term that refers to the act of installing the cable and the work performed before installation begins. Because coaxial cable and twisted-pair cable are copper cables, and fiber optic cable uses glass or plastic fibers, different issues may arise for each type of cable. As we look at these types of cabling, we'll see that there are other significant differences in how they are created and installed.

Copper Cabling

Installation of cable requires a number of different tools. Because the major part of cable installation consists of running the cable where you want it and attaching the appropriate connectors at each end, having the right tools is crucial. Some of the tools will be common to any installation, such as electric drills to drill holes in walls, while others are specific to the cable itself. Tools are used to cut and strip the cable and to attach the proper connector to the end of the cable. These include:

- Cable cutter, which is used to cut the cable to the size you need.

- Cable stripper, which is used to strip the cable jacket and expose the copper wire inside.

- Crimp tool, which is used to attach the connectors to the cable.

- Connectors that will be attached at the ends of the cable

During the installation there are several points that need to be considered, including the pulling force used on the cable. The pulling force of cabling refers to the amount of force or tension that can be placed on the cable without damaging it. In other words, it is how hard you can pull on the cable when you're installing or working with it. For example, with Category 5 UTP cabling, if more than 25 pounds of force is applied to the cabling during installation, then it may be damaged and no longer meet the specifications associated with it. It is important that you refer to the pull tension specifications of the cabling being used before installation begins.

The minimum bend radius of a cable refers to how far the cable can be bent before it is damaged. If a cable is bent too far, the wire or other components in the cable can crack or break, or the electrical characteristics of the cable can be otherwise affected. Category 5 UTP cables allow a bend radius of 4 times the cable's diameter. For example, if the cable is 1/4 inch in diameter, you can bend it 1 inch. While the bend radius of cable can vary, depending on the materials making up the cable, it is generally four, six, or ten times the diameter of the cable.

Fiber Cabling

Fiber cabling also has bend radius and pull force ratings, and these will vary depending on the type of fiber cabling used and the number of fibers in the cable. The bend radius is usually specified with the cable, but will generally follow the rule of ten times the outside diameter of the cable. The pulling force of fiber optic cabling can also vary, with specifications ranging from 50 pounds to a few hundred pounds. If a string is used to pull the cable through areas during installation, at no time should you attach the pulling string to the fiber strands, as this will damage the fibers and make the cable unusable.

During installation, special tools will be needed to strip the cable so that the appropriate connector can be attached. These include:

- Cable stripper or ring tool, which is used to remove the plastic jacket of the cable without damaging the fibers.

- Kevlar shears, which is used to cut the kevlar inside the fiber optic cable.

- Connectors that will be attached at the ends of the cable.

Preparing Copper Cable

Preparing cable basically involves measuring out the amount of cable needed, exposing the wire inside of the cable, and attaching a connector. While this is obviously a compressed description of what has to be done, preparing copper cable is actually relatively easy.

The first step in preparing a cable is determining how much is needed for a particular run. Because you will probably be pulling the cable through false ceilings or areas that may be somewhat difficult to measure with a measuring tape, the easiest way of determining how much cable is needed is running the cable along the floor. By unrolling the cable along walkways where the cable will actually run through walls and ceilings, you will get a reasonable measurement of how much cable will go into a segment. It is important, however, to account for a little extra slack that may be necessary for cornering or to simply make it easier to work with the cable. Once you've determined how much cable is needed, use a cable cutter to cut the cable.

After you've got the proper length of cable, you will then need to strip the cable to expose the wires. Using a cable stripper, you remove the outer jacket of the cable. With UTP, you would remove about 3/4 of an inch from the cable, and then untwist the wires within the cable so you can work with them. Because four pairs of wires are used, this means that you will be working with eight wires that use a particular color code. The color code for UTP wiring is described in the next section.

Once the wires are untwisted, you trim the leads of all eight wires to a length of approximately 1/2 inch. Because the wires are thin, you should be able to cut all of them with a wire cutter simultaneously, ensuring they are all the same length. Having prepared the wires in this way, you are now ready to attach the cable to an RJ-45 connector.

UTP contains several sets of wires that are attached to an RJ-45 connector in a specific way. Once the leads are aligned, you insert them into the connector and push the wires forward until the copper wires can be seen through the transparent end of the connector. The connector and the cable are then inserted into a crimp tool, and with the wires pressed against the end of the connector, you squeeze the crimp tool's handle for a few seconds. Once this is done, the connector is now firmly attached to the cable, and is ready for installation.

Twisted-Pair Color Codes

If you look inside of a twisted-pair cable, you'll notice that the plastic sheaths covering the wires are colored differently. Twisted-pair cabling use color codes to specify the purpose of each wire and to make them easily identifiable. Because each wire belongs to a pair, the colors of each pair are the same, with one solid and the other striped. Table 2.3 shows the color scheme that corresponds to the Electronic Industry Association/Telecommunications Industry Association's Standard 568B used for a four pair UTP wire.

Table 2.3 Four Pair Cable Color Code

Pair	Solid Wire	Striped Wire
1	Blue	Blue and white
2	Orange	Orange and white
3	Green	Green and white
4	Brown	Brown and white

When connecting twisted-pair wire to an RJ-45 connector, the wires will have to be aligned so that they match up with the pins of the connector. Table 2.4 shows how the various wires of a four pair cable are installed.

Table 2.4 Twisted-Pair Wire/Pin Placement

Pin	Wire
1	Orange and white
2	Orange
3	Green and white
4	Blue
5	Blue and white
6	Green
7	Brown and white
8	Brown

Cable Installation

When installing cable, you first need to choose the location of the hub, switch or router. These devices will be where the cable will attach to, and as we'll see in the next chapter, are used to move data from one cable to another so it reaches its intended destination. In larger organizations a patch panel or cabinet may be used to accommodate numerous cables, or a separate hub, switch, or router will be used for each floor of a building. Using one of these devices on each floor will save time and require less cable.

Once the location of network devices has been decided, you should create documentation on where the cables will be installed. A map of wiring should include how many cables will be installed in ceilings, walls, and other locations. While creating the map, you will also be able to review issues that will arise during the actual cabling. such as holes that may have to be drilled or vertical runs of cabling down elevator shafts. When determining how the cable should run from an outlet to a hub, switch, or router, you should remember to keep the cabling at least three feet away from fluorescent lights and other sources of EMI.

Cables should be tested before they're actually installed. Even if new cable is being used for the installation, this doesn't guarantee that it isn't damaged in some way. It is easier to test the cable before installation than to determine where a section of bad cabling resides after installation is complete.

Once you're ready to actually start running the cabling along the paths you've planned out, you should ensure that you actually have more cable than is needed. In running 100 feet of cable, you don't want to find there is only 90 feet of cable left in the box. Having extra cabling will also ensure that you have enough slack to navigate the cable without problems.

Each end of a cable should be clearly marked, using masking tape or some other form of labeling. Because you may be installation several runs of cable at a time, you don't want to be confused as to which cable runs to a particular computer or location.

By labeling the cables, this confusion is removed, and you'll be able to focus on the installation.

If you need to bundle cable, you should only use cable ties. Cable ties are sturdy plastic strips that attach cables together into a ring. When using them however, you should allow enough space to fit a finger into the cable tie. Having a cable tie too tight can damage the cables and make it more difficult to cut when a cable has to be replaced. Using cable ties is the safest method of keeping cables together, as staples or other methods can damage cable.

LAN Technologies and Standards

In discussing the physical media that may be used on your network, it's important to understand the technologies that are used on them. While we'll discuss individual components of the network and technologies related to them throughout this book, we'll pause here to look at several technologies related to physical media. As networking technologies have developed over the years, it became apparent that standards were necessary so components of a network could work together effectively, and how data is transferred over the network cable. These standards include Ethernet, Fast Ethernet, and Gigabit Ethernet.

Ethernet

Ethernet is the standard for most of the networks today. As we discussed in the previous chapter, Bob Metcalfe originally developed Ethernet as a technology that networked together remote computers. Digital, Intel, and Xerox took the original specifications and extended it to accommodate speeds of 10 Mbps using coaxial cable or specific categories of twisted-pair cabling. In 1990, Ethernet was standardized by the 802.3 committee, and specifications under this correspond to 10Base2, 10Base5, and 10BaseT (each of which we'll discuss later in this chapter).

A major component of Ethernet is the use of *Carrier Sense Multiple Access with Collision Detection (CSMA/CD)* for access to the physical medium. CSMA/CD keeps devices on the network from interfering with one another when trying to transmit; when they do interfere with each other, a *collision* has occurred. To reduce collisions, CSMA/CD devices listen to the network before transmitting. If the network is *quiet* (no other devices are transmitting), the device can send its data. Since two devices can both think the network is clear and start transmitting at the same time, resulting in a collision, all devices listen as they transmit. If a device detects another device transmitting at the same time, both devices stop transmitting and send a signal to alert other nodes to the collision. Then all the nodes stop transmitting and wait a random amount of time before they begin the process again.

CSMA/CD doesn't stop collisions from happening, but it helps manage the situations when collisions occur. In fact, collisions are a very normal part of Ethernet operation. It's only when collisions begin to occur frequently that you need to become concerned.

Ethernet has evolved over the years to include a number of popular specifications. These specifications are due in part to the media variety they employ, such as coaxial, twisted-pair, and fiber-optic cabling.

Fast Ethernet

Fast Ethernet is a standard that provides transmission of data at speeds of 100 Mbps. It uses full duplex transmission, which enables data to pass in both directions at the same time. Because of the speeds available through this standard, Fast Ethernet is generally used as a backbone on local area networks to support workstations that have 10BaseT network cards. The Fast Ethernet standard corresponds to the 100BaseT specifications, which we'll discuss later in this chapter.

Gigabit Ethernet

An even faster standard in the evolution of Ethernet is Gigabit Ethernet, which provides speeds of 1 Gbps. To compare this to the 10 Mbps of Ethernet, which provides full duplex transmission speeds of 10 million bits per second, Gigabit Ethernet supports speeds of one billion bits per second. Because of the bandwidth available through this standard, it is often used as a backbone for many larger networks.

While Ethernet runs on either coaxial or twisted-pair, and Fast Ethernet runs on twisted-pair cable, Gigabit Ethernet uses both copper and fiber optic cabling to transmit data (www.pccables.com/02303.htm). The optical fiber in the cable allows data to transmit faster and over greater distances, making it useful for connecting different locations at high speeds.

Head of the Class…

Network+
OBJECTIVE
1.3.4

10 Gigabit Ethernet

In looking at how the speed of Ethernet has increased over the years, it should come as no surprise that even Gigabit Ethernet isn't fast enough to stop developing the standard. 10 Gigabit Ethernet isn't a standard yet, but at the time of this writing, it is currently in the process of becoming one. 10 Gigabit Ethernet provides transmission speeds of up to 10 Gbps (10 billion bits per second), while using technologies that already exist in most modern networks.

As with Gigabit Ethernet, 10 Gigabit Ethernet uses fiber optic cabling that allows it to transmit data over a longer distance, and uses full duplex transmission so that data can pass in both directions along the cable at the same time. Various types of 10 Gigabit Ethernet include:

- 10GBaseSR, which supports short distances over multi-mode (mm) fiber optic cable, and has a range of 26 meters and 82 meters depending on the cable type. It also supports distances of 300 meters over a new 2000 Mhz.km multi-mode fiber.

- 10GBaseLX4, which uses wavelength division multiplexing and supports ranges of 240 meters and 300 meters over multi-mode fiber, or 10 km over single-mode (sm) fiber.

Continued

- 10GbaseLR, which supports 10 km over single-mode fiber.
- 10GbaseER, which supports 40 km over single-mode fiber.

10 Gigabit Ethernet is gaining acceptance, and the 802.3a standard defines a version, but currently there is no commercial version available. As there are different methods of implementing this technology, it is not known whether it will become a LAN or WAN technology.

802.3 Media Standards

As we discussed in the previous chapter, the Institute of Electrical and Electronic Engineers (IEEE) is an organization that sets standards on a variety of technologies. Various committees are used to develop and promote these standards, including the 802 committee, which is broken down into smaller sub-committees or working groups that focus on specific aspects of networking. One of these sub-committees is the 802.3 working group, which has set standards for physical media used on networks.

10Base2, 10Base5, and Arcnet

10Base2 (also known as *Thinnet*) is a thin coaxial cable used on Ethernet networks. The cable used in 10Base2 is an RG-58 cable that is 6.3 mm or 1/4 inch in diameter, and supports transmission speeds of 10 Mbps. Used on bus topologies, the network cards are attached to the cable using a BNC T-connector, and the backbone cable is terminated at each end using a 50 Ohm terminator. The 10Base2 cable has a maximum length of 185 meters or 600 feet per segment, and workstations must be spaced a minimum distance of 1/2 meters from one another.

10Base5 (*Thicknet*) is a thicker type of coaxial cable that is 13 mm or 1/2 inch in diameter, and supports transmission speeds of 10 Mbps. The cable has a maximum length of 500 meters or 1640 feet per segment. Like 10Base2, 10Base5 is used on bus topologies, and must be terminated on each end using a 50 Ohm terminator. However, unlike 10Base2, 10Base5 generally isn't directly connected to workstations on the network. Instead, a vampire tap is used to pierce the cable so that a connection can be made to the cable. An N connector or a cabling tray and transceiver called a MAU (Media Attachment Unit) are connected to the cable. Another cable called an AUI (Attachment Unit Interface) that can be up to 50 meters in length is then run to the network card of the workstation. Each end of the AUI cable uses a 15 pin D-connector, which is also referred to as a DIX (Digital-Intel-Xerox) or DB-15 connector. While we'll discuss transceivers and connectors in greater detail later in this chapter, it's important to remember that a 10Base5 cable can have no more than 100 taps per cable segment, with each tap spaced 2 1/2 meters apart.

Determining how long a 10Base5 cable could be lengthened using different segments can be calculated using the 5-4-3 rule. A 10Base5 cable can have up to five segments, with four repeaters, with only three of the segments having devices attached to it. By using the maximum cable length with repeaters between each of the five segments, this would lengthen the cable to a maximum of 2,460 meters. However, because only three of the segments can have a maximum of 100 devices attached, this means that even by lengthening the cable in this manner you are limited to a maximum of 300 devices on the bus topology.

The problem with 10Base2 and 10Base5's cabling architechure cable is that a single fault in the cable can bring the entire network down. As we discussed in the previous chapter, each end of the cable must be terminated in a bus topology or the data will continue to bounce back and forth along the cable. This prevents any other workstations from being able to transmit data onto the network without causing collisions.

Arcnet is another technology addressed in the 802.3 standards that uses coaxial cable. Arcnet is a token bus technology, just as Ethernet, Token Ring, and FDDI are technologies used on a network. As with Token Ring, when a workstation on an Arcnet network receives a token, it has the opportunity to communicate on the network. If it doesn't have any data to send, then the next workstation on the bus then gets the token. If it does send data, then the receiving machine resets the token and others can then transmit data when they get the token.

With the various applications of coaxial (10Base2, 10Base5, and Arcnet), there are different coaxial cables that may be used. These include:

- RG-58 /U, which has a solid copper wire, and is used for 10Base2 networks.

- RG-58 A/U, which has a stranded copper wire, and can also be used for 10Base2 networks.

- RG-58 C/U, which is a military implementation of RG-58 A/U.

- RG-59, which is used for broadband transmissions (such as cable television), and is used for 10Base5 networks.

- RG-6, which is used for broadband, but supports higher transmission rates than RG-59.

- RG-62, which is used for Arcnet.

- RG-8, which is 10Base5 cable.

Security Alert!

Security Issues with Coaxial Cable

The coaxial cable used in both 10Base2 and 10Base5 share some of the same vulnerabilities. Unfortunately, it is relatively easy to perform a Denial of Service (DoS) attack on this type of network by cutting the cable or disconnecting a device. If communication is not able to flow completely up and down a coax network, the entire network is brought down. In addition, since connections to the network really cannot be controlled with a switch or hub, there is no way to prevent unauthorized connections. All an intruder has to do is tap into the network with either a T-connector or vampire tap for Thinnet or Thicknet, respectively.

These vulnerabilities exist due to the topology of coax networks. A coax network uses a bus topology, which basically means that all of the network devices are connected in a linear fashion. Each device on the network completes the circuit for the network as a whole. Due to this, if any device is removed from the network or if there is a break anywhere in the cable, the circuit is broken and the entire entire segments of the network is brought down unless it is the backbone which could then leave the entire network in a down state.

The main advantages to coax networks are the price and the ease of implementation. Since no expensive hubs or switches are required, cost is kept low. Since all that is required to set up the network is to run a coax cable as the backbone, connecting one computer to the next with T-connectors, this is one of the easiest networks to implement.

Most coax networks have been or are being replaced with unshielded twisted-pair/shielded twisted-pair (UTP/STP) or fiber optic cabling. Though you may never work with a coax network, it is important know how vulnerable it is to disruption of service or intrusion.

10BaseT and Beyond

In addition to the standards that use coaxial cable, there are also those that use twisted-pair and fiber optic cabling. These are more commonly used on today's networks, and knowledge of them is essential when designing or maintaining a network in the real world. The various types of media available are shown in Table 2.5.

Table 2.5 Media Standards Using Twisted-Pair and Fiber

Media Standard	Cable Type	Bandwidth	Cable Length
10BaseT	UTP (Category 3 or higher)	10 Mbps	100 meters
100BaseTX	UTP (Category 5 or higher)	100 Mbps	100 meters
10BaseFL	Fiber optic	10 Mbps	2 kilometers

Continued

Table 2.5 continued Media Standards Using Twisted-Pair and Fiber

Media Standard	Cable Type	Bandwidth	Cable Length
100BaseFX	Fiber optic	100 Mbps	400 meters (half-duplex) or 2 km (full duplex)
1000BaseT	UTP (Category 5 or higher)	1 Gbps (1000 Mbps)	100 meters
1000BaseSX	Fiber optic	1 Gbps (1000 Mbps)	550 meters (multi-mode fiber)
1000BaseLX	Fiber optic	1 Gbps (1000 Mbps)	550 meters (multi-mode fiber) or up to 10 km (single mode fiber)
1000BaseCX	Fiber optic	1 Gbps (1000 Mbps)	100 meters

EXAM WARNING

For the exam, you will have to memorize the characteristics of the various types of media. Questions may appear that specifically require this knowledge.

10BASET

10BaseT is one of the most common media standards found on networks. It is deployed on networks that use a star topology, which we discussed in the previous chapter. It uses UTP cabling to transmit data at speeds of 10 Mbps across cable segments that are up to 100 meters in length. Although it will work on Category 3 UTP, a higher grade of cable is recommended.

10BaseFL

10BaseFL is an older, but widely used fiber optic standard, and is sometimes referred to generically as 10BaseF. It uses fiber optic cabling to transmit data at speeds of 10 Mbps across cable segments that are up to 2 km in length.

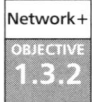

100BaseTX

100BaseTX uses UTP cabling to transmit data at speeds of 100 Mbps across cable segments that are up to 100 meters in length. The UTP must be Category 5 or higher. Another common term that relates to 100BaseT is Fast Ethernet. 100BaseTX cables use two sets of two pairs, or 4 wires.

100BaseFX

100BaseFX is another Ethernet standard that uses fiber optic cabling to transmit data at speeds of 100 Mbps. The distance that this standard can achieve depends upon whether half-duplex is used to achieve collision detection. If communication is half-duplex, it can transmit data across cable segments that are up to 400 meters in length. If full duplex is used, then it can transmit data up to 2 kilometers.

1000BaseT

1000BaseT is a Gigabit Ethernet standard that allows data to be transmitted over twisted-pair cabling at 1 Gbps. This means that 1000 megabits or 1 billion bits of data can be transmitted each second. 1000BaseT uses UTP cabling to transmit data at these speeds across cable segments that are up to 100 meters in length. For this to be used however, the UTP must be Category 5 or higher.

1000BaseCX

1000BaseCX uses fiber optic cabling to transmit data at speeds of 1 Gbps across cable segments that are up to 100 meters in length. Because it is an older standard, it isn't commonly used on newer networks.

1000BaseSX

100BaseSX uses multimode fiber optic cabling to transmit data at speeds of 1 Gbps across cable segments that are up to 550 meters in length.

1000BaseLX

1000BaseLX uses fiber optic cabling to transmit data at speeds of 1 Gbps. Using multi-mode fiber, data can be sent across cable segments that are up to 550 meters in length, while single mode fiber will allow longer distances of up to 10 km.

Connectors

While we've discussed a significant number of issues related to the physical media used on a network, it's important to remember that a cable is more than the wire or fiber that transmits the data. Cables have to be connected to the network interface card or other devices on a network. A connector is an interface that provides such a connection between a cable and a device. Because the media used on a network can differ, a number of different connectors have been developed over the years.

Twisted-Pair and Coaxial Cable Connectors

Several types of connectors are available for coaxial cable. Depending on the need, connectors that connect to different cable and devices are available for twisted-pair and coaxial. These include:

- D connectors
- RJ connectors
- DIX connectors
- BNC connectors
- F-Type connectors

D Connectors

The D connector gets its name from its shape. As shown in Figure 2.3, with some imagination, the D connector can be seen as looking like a letter D turned on its side. A male connector is one that has pins protruding from it, while a female connector has holes into which the pins fit. The number of pins used in a D connector varies, but always correspond to the number used in the D connector's name. These include:

- DB9, which has 9 pins.
- DB15, which has 15 pins, and which we'll discuss further in this chapter when we examine DIX connectors.
- DB25, which has 25 pins.

Figure 2.3 DB15 Connector

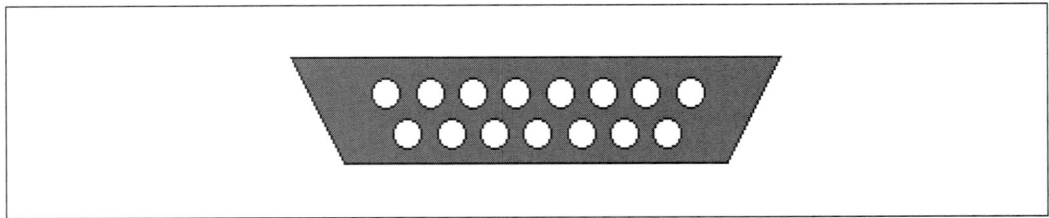

RJ Connectors

RJ connectors are used with twisted-pair cabling, and can be used to provide connectivity to a cable used by telephone and data devices. Because they are used for different purposes, there are several different variations of RJ connectors available.

RJ-11

RJ-11 connectors are used on twisted-pair cables that are used by telephones. You can easily find an RJ-11 connector in your home by looking at the ends of the cable running from your phone into the wall jack. They are also used to plug dial-up modems into the phone line so that computers can dial into the Internet or access networks remotely using the phone line. They are primarily used in North America, and are not widely used in other countries throughout the world.

RJ-11 connectors have four pins to support four of the wires in a twisted-pair cable. While the connector can be used with different categories of twisted-pair, only two pairs of wires are used, even if the cable contains more than four wires.

RJ-45

Network+
OBJECTIVE
1.4.2

The RJ-45 connector is used with twisted-pair cables that support data communication. As such, they can be used with Categories 3 and higher of UTP or STP cabling. They are commonly seen on today's networks, as they are used on both Ethernet and Token Ring networks.

As shown in Figure 2.4, an RJ-45 connector looks like a RJ-11 connector, but wider. RJ-45 connectors are similar to the phone connectors except that instead of four wires found in the home system, the network RJ-45 contains eight contacts. There are eight pins in the connector, hence eight wires in the cable are connected to it. Ethernet can use four of the wires or possibly all eight, depending on the media standard being used. As we saw earlier in this chapter, a special crimping tool is needed to make contact between the pins and the cable inside.

Figure 2.4 RJ-45 Connector

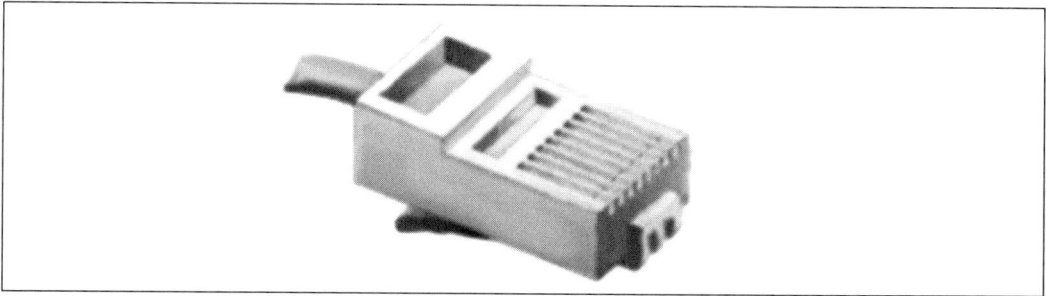

RJ-48 and RJ-25

In addition to the RJ-11 and RJ-45 connectors that are used for voice and data communication, there are also a number of other Registered Jack connectors that may be found in offices. The different types are used to provide different services, but are all used with twisted-pair cabling.

RJ-48 connectors are essentially the same as the RJ-45 connector, but used with STP cable. Like the RJ-45 connector, it uses eight pins to provide contact with the eight wires in a twisted-pair cable, although a different pin arrangement is used in connecting the wires.

Another example of a registered jack is the RJ-25 connector. RJ-25 connectors use six conductors to allow multiple phone lines to be used. They are often seen when telephones have three line connections.

DIX

Earlier in this chapter we discussed D connectors and how they consist of pins that are inserted into a female connector. One type of D connector is a DIX, which is used with an AUI that's used with 10Base5 cable. A DIX connector looks similar to the connector used for attaching a joystick to a joystick port. DIX connectors can be found on the back of some network cards, and allow the card to be used with different types of media.

BNC

The meaning of the acronym BNC is something that is a topic of argument. It is commonly referred to as a British Naval Connector, but is also referenced as meaning Bayonet Neill Concelman or Bayonet Nut Connector. Regardless of your preference, the BNC connector is used with coaxial cable.

If you've ever looked at the end of the cable used for your cable television, you've seen one that looks similar to what's illustrated in Figure 2.5. The copper wire running down the center of the cable protrudes from the center of a BNC barrel connector. The connector is threaded, allowing it to be screwed onto devices with a corresponding connector, so that the wire can fit into the female connection.

Figure 2.5 BNC Barrel Connector

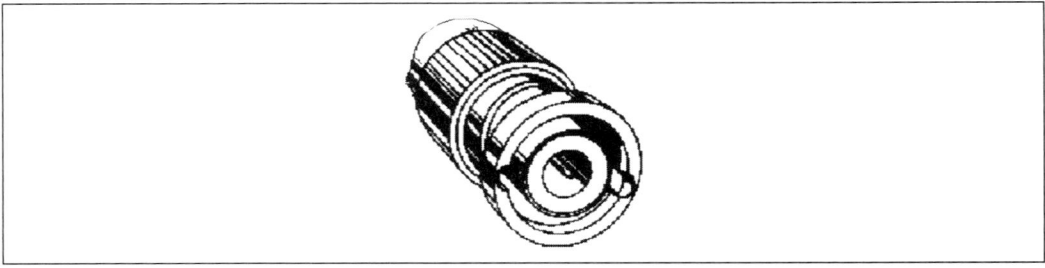

There are different variations of the BNC connector that can be used on a network. BNC connectors are used to connect 10Base2 coaxial cable to a hub, while a T-connector (shown in Figure 2.6) can connect a workstation's cable segment to the network backbone. A special crimping tool is used to put the connector on the end of the wire. The actual wire runs down the middle and must make contact with the end of the connector shown in the middle.

Figure 2.6 BNC T-connector

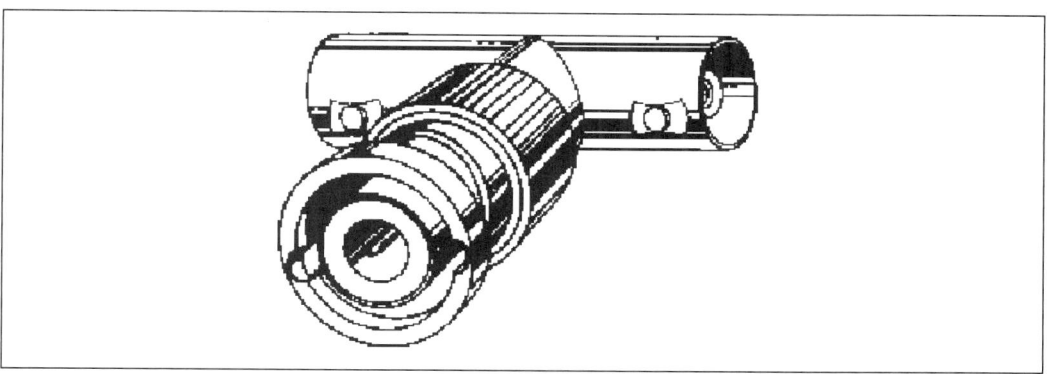

EXERCISE 2.2

TERMINATING A COAXIAL CABLE

Now that you have learned about coaxial cable and how identify it, we will learn how to terminate a coaxial connector on to a RG type cable.

1. As with twisted-pair cable termination, you will need to use crimping and stripping tools when terminating a coaxial cable, although the process itself is a little different. For one, you will need a stronger cutter that is sized properly for the job of cutting think coaxial cable.

2. To terminate the cable, you will need a ratchet crimper, a pair of coaxial cable strippers, the coaxial cable itself, and BNC connectors.

3. Use the cable cutter to cut a length of coaxial cable from a bulk spool if you have one available. The cable should be the proper length for the job, plus some extra slack for you to make some mistakes when cutting your cable. Remember, never cut cable (especially preexisting runs) without giving yourself a little extra cable to play with.

4. Next, use the cable stripper to remove the excess jacketing and outside coating of the cable.

5. Apply the RG-type connector on the cable and crimp it down.

6. Do both sides of the cable if not already done.

7. Make sure you test the cable and that it is within specifications.

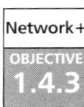

RG and F-Type Connectors

F-type connectors are used to terminate coaxial cable, and are commonly seen on RG-58 (Thinnet) and RG-59 (Thicknet) coaxial. Although it is an older type of connector, it is still frequently used. These connectors have the ability to screw onto televisions, VCRs, and devices for cable television, and are low in cost.

Fiber Connectors

There are a number of different connectors that are used with fiber optic cable. As is the case with some of the connectors available for twisted-pair and coaxial cable, some of these are used with older technology and are not routinely seen on modern networks. They include:

- Straight Tip
- Standard Connector
- Local Connector
- Mechanical Transfer Registered Jack

Standard Connectors

SC stands for *standard connector*, and is a suitable name, as it's the most common type of connector used with fiber optic cable. It is often used with Cisco equipment. As shown in Figure 2.7, the SC connector terminates the fiber optic cable by attaching to its end, using a locking mechanism that clicks into place.

Figure 2.7 SC Connector

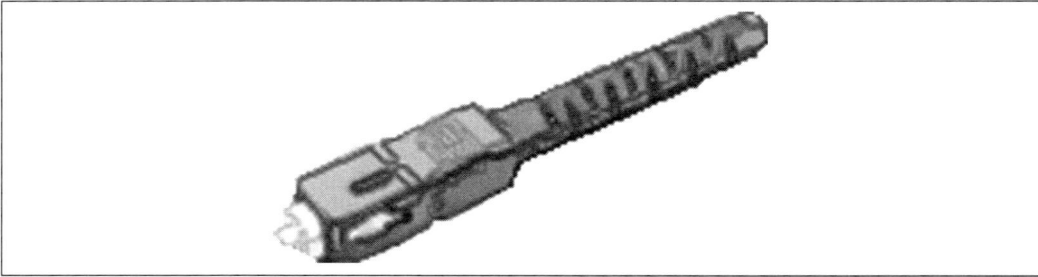

EXAM WARNING

An easy way to remember the SC connector is by thinking of its name (standard connector), which indicates that it's the most common one used today. An alternative method of remembering it is to think of SC as *stick and click*. This will help you to remember that it uses a click-into-place locking mechanism.

Straight Tip Connectors

Straight tip (ST) connectors are an older version of connector used on fiber optic cable. It is often seen on older 10BaseFL networks. The ST connector has a screw-on type of locking mechanism that attaches to the tip of a fiber optic cable and terminates it. In using this type of connector (shown in Figure 2.8), you will find that it has the look and feel of a BNC connector, making it easy to use.

Figure 2.8 ST Connector

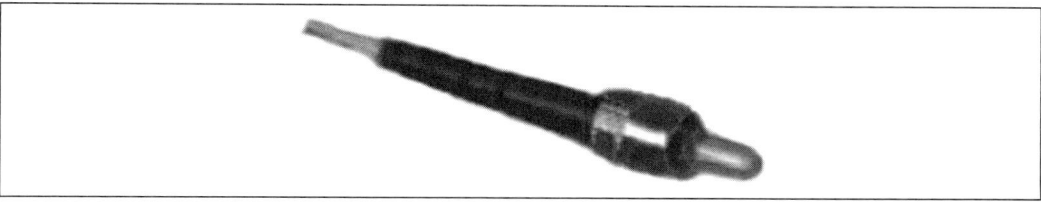

EXAM WARNING

An easy way to remember the characteristics of an ST connector is by using its nickname *stick and twist*. This will help you to remember that it is a screw-on type of connector, as you stick and twist it on.

Local Connectors

The Local connector (LC) is another common connector used on fiber optic networks. LC is a high-performance connector that is used on many networks. LC connectors use a locking mechanism that's similar to the SC connectors, which click into place. The connector is seated into place by pushing it in and snapping it into place.

EXAM WARNING

An easy way to remember the characteristics of an LC connector is by thinking of the term *lock and click*. This will help you to remember that its locking mechanism requires you to push and click it into place.

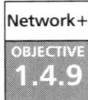 ## Mechanical Transfer Registered Jacks

The mechanical transfer registered jack is similar to the LC connector in that it is a duplex connector. As shown in Figure 2.9, it uses a form factor and latch that is similar to the RJ-45 connectors discussed earlier in this chapter. It is also easier to terminate and install than some of the other types of fiber optic connectors we've discussed, such as the ST and SC connectors.

Figure 2.9 MTRJ Connector

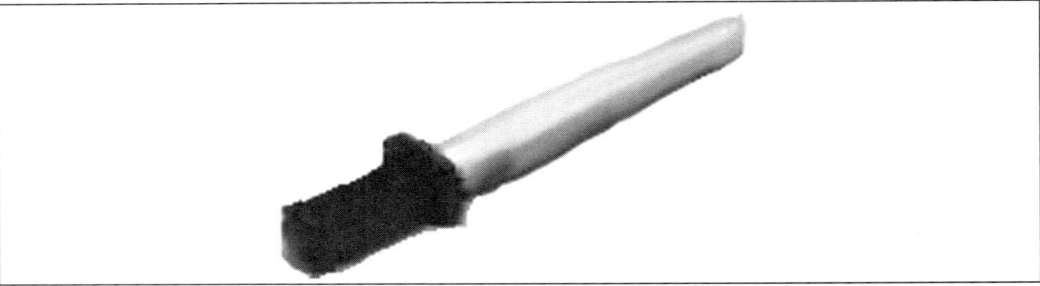

 # Recognizing Category 3, 5, 5e, and 6 UTP, STP, Coaxial cable SMF, Optic Cable MMF, and Optic Cable

While we've already provided you with a lot of information about cabling and their respective issues, it's time to go in depth into the types of cabling you'll find on networks and the Network+ exam. As we've discussed, there are three types of physical media that can be used on a network: coaxial cable, twisted-pair cable, and fiber-optic cable. These different media types can be further broken down into different categories and types of cabling, which are either used for specific purposes or provide greater bandwidth.

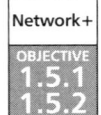 ## Category 3, 5, 5e, and 6 UTP

UTP cabling is the most common type of physical media on networks today. The typical twisted-pair cable for network use contains three or four pairs of wires. As shown in Figure 2.10, each pair of wires contained in the cable is twisted around each other, which helps shield against crosstalk and other forms of electromagnetic interference. Although the twisted wires do provide a certain amount of immunity from the infiltration of unwanted interference, this doesn't mean that UTP is the best solution against EMI. Twisted-pair cable is susceptible to interference and should not be used in environments containing large electrical or electronic devices.

Figure 2.10 Unshielded Twisted-Pair

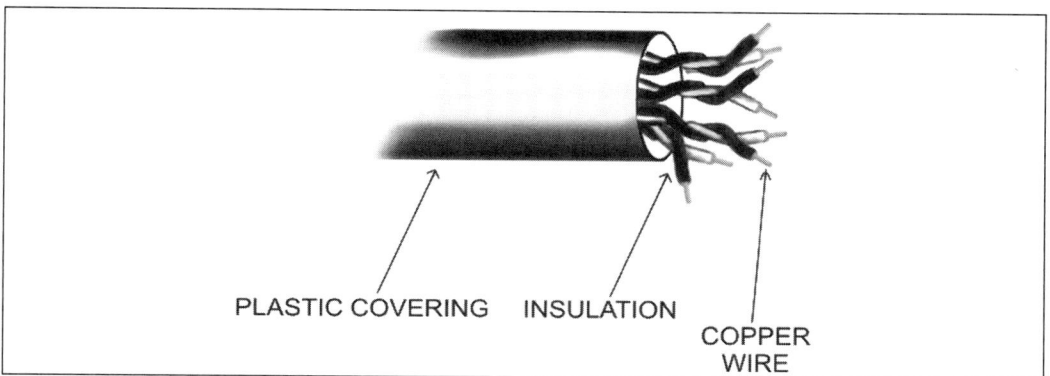

PLASTIC COVERING   INSULATION

COPPER
WIRE

Because UTP is used for everything from telephone cable to high-speed network cable, the Electrical Industry Association established different categories of UTP. These categories are rated by a number of factors, including the electrical characteristics, conductor size, and twists per foot. Because new categories are also an indication of enhancements in the wiring, the higher categories are also new evolutions of twisted-pair. The various categories, which are simply referred to as *CAT*, are shown in Table 2.6.

TEST DAY TIP

Although there are a number of different categories of UTP, the Network+ exam expects you to know the details of CAT 3, 5, 5e, and 6 cables. You should only review the other categories to know what is being offered as incorrect choices.

Table 2.6 Categories of Twisted-Pair Cabling

Category	Uses
CAT 1	Up to 1 Mbps. Voice communication in older analog telephone systems, and also used as doorbell wiring. This type of cabling is not suitable for data transmissions.
CAT 2	4 Mbps. Low performance cable; used for voice and low-speed data transmission.
CAT 3	16 Mbps. Voice communication in newer telephone systems. Rated at 10 MHz, this is the minimum category of UTP that can be used for data transmissions on networks; can be used for Ethernet, Fast Ethernet, and Token Ring.

Continued

Table 2.6 Categories of Twisted-Pair Cabling

Category	Uses
CAT 4	20 Mbps. Used for data and voice transmission; rated at 20 MHz; can be used for Ethernet, Fast Ethernet, and Token Ring.
CAT 5	100 Mbps (4 pairs). Typically used for Ethernet networks running at 10 or 100 Mbps. Used for data and voice transmission; rated at 100 MHz; suitable for Ethernet, Fast Ethernet, Gigabit Ethernet, Token Ring, and 155 Mbps ATM.
CAT 5e	1000 Mbps. Recommended for all new installations, and was designed for transmission speeds of up to 1 Gbps (Gigabit Ethernet). Similar to Category 5, but manufacturing process is refined; higher grade cable than Category 5; rated at 200 MHz; suitable for Ethernet, Fast Ethernet, Gigabit Ethernet, Token Ring, and 155 Mbps ATM.
CAT 6	Same as CAT5e, but higher standard. Rated at 250 MHz; suitable for Ethernet, Fast Ethernet, Gigabit Ethernet, Token Ring, and 155 Mbps ATM.
CAT 6e	Support for 10 Gigabit Ethernet. Similar to Category 6, but is a proposed international standard to be included in ISO/IEC 11801.
CAT 7	Not official standard at time of this writing. Still in development. Rated at 600 MHz; suitable for Ethernet, Fast Ethernet, Gigabit Ethernet, Token Ring, and 155 Mbps ATM.

Category 3 is the minimum grade of cable that supports networking, but it is not the best choice for networks. CAT3 is a voice-grade cable used in phone networks, and its only real benefit beyond being able to support data communication is that it already exists in most office buildings and homes. Regardless of this, CAT 5 or higher should be used in new networks.

Most of the UTP cable that's found in networks today is Category 5. CAT 5 is a multi-pair performance cable with eight wires (four pairs) that supports higher bandwidth, and is typically used for Ethernet networks that run at 10 or 100 Mbps. Until recent enhancements were made to UTP, this grade of cabling was the standard for new network installations.

Category 5e is essentially the same as CAT 5 cable, but adheres to more stringent standards that make it a better candidate for new installations that will use Gigabit Ethernet. It is designed for transmission speeds of up to 1 Gbps, and has been made an official standard.

Category 6 is another enhancement to the previous grades, and provides support for 10 Gigabit Ethernet. It is officially a part of the 568A standard, making it a standard grade of cable for UTP installations.

EXAM WARNING

Category 1 and 2 of UTP is for voice communications. Category 3 or higher can be used for data communications, but Category 5 or higher should be used. On the exam, you may see these categories abbreviated, so that they use the term *CAT* for category. Don't let this confuse you.

STP

As its name says, the difference between the unshielded and shielded varieties of twisted-pair is the shield. As shown in Figure 2.11, STP has a shield that's usually made of aluminum/polyester that resides between the outer jacket and the wires. The shield is designed to keep more interference out, protecting the wires inside from EMI caused by outside sources. STP also uses a much higher quality protective jacket for greater insulation.

Figure 2.11 Shielded Twisted-Pair

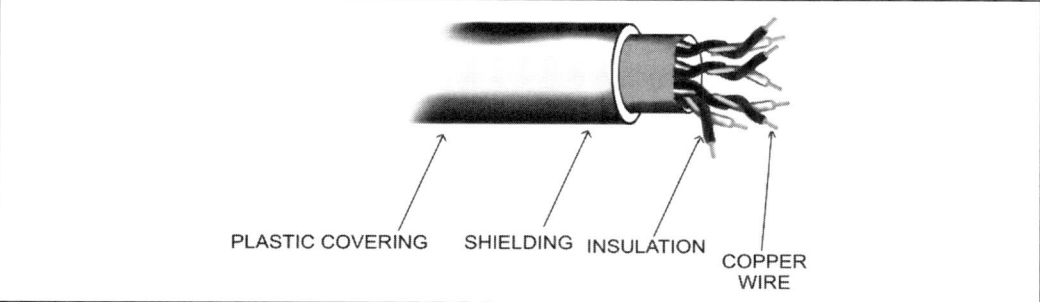

PLASTIC COVERING   SHIELDING INSULATION   COPPER WIRE

Coaxial cable

Coaxial (or coax) cable looks like the cable used to bring the cable TV signal to our television. As shown in Figure 2.12, one strand (a solid-core wire) runs down the middle of the cable. Around that strand is insulation. Covering that insulation is braided wire and metal foil, which shields against electromagnetic interference. A final layer of insulation covers the braided wire. Coaxial cable is resistant to the interference and signal weakening that other cabling, such as UTP cable, can experience. In general, coax is better than UTP cable at connecting longer distances and for reliably supporting higher data rates with less sophisticated equipment.

Figure 2.12 Coaxial Cable

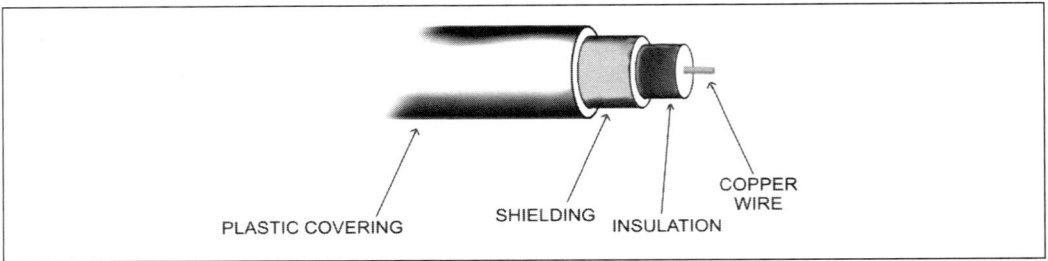

Just because the TV cable is coax does not mean it will work with computer networks. Network coaxial cable has very specific requirements, such as the gauge, the impedance, and the attenuation.

Thinnet refers to RG-58 cabling, which is a flexible coaxial cable about 1/4-inch thick. Thinnet is used for short-distance communication and is flexible enough to facilitate running and routing between workstations. Thinnet connects directly to a workstation's network adapter card using a BNC T-connector and uses the network adapter card's internal transceiver. 10Base2 refers to Ethernet LANs that use Thinnet cabling.

Thicknet coaxial cable can support data transfer over longer distances better than Thinnet can and is usually used as a backbone to connect several smaller Thinnet-based networks. The diameter of a Thicknet cable is about 1/2-inch and is harder to work with than a Thinnet cable. A transceiver is connected directly to Thicknet cable using a connector known as a piercing tap. Connection from the transceiver to the network adapter card is made using a drop cable to connect to the adapter unit interface port connector. 10Base5 refers to Ethernet LANs that use Thicknet cabling.

EXAM WARNING

While coax is not as commonly used as it used to be, the Network+ exam expects you to understand what it is and how it works. You will need to understand the lengths of cabling that can be used with Thinnet and Thicknet coax, as well as the transmission speeds.

Network+
OBJECTIVE
1.5.5

Single Mode Fiber Optic Cable

Optical fibers carry digital data signals in the form of modulated pulses of light. As shown in Figure 2.13, an optical fiber consists of an extremely thin cylinder of glass or optical fiber, called the *core*, surrounded by a concentric layer of glass, known as the *cladding*. A cable may contain two fibers per cable—one to transmit and one to receive—or a single fiber. However, often, multiple fibers are bundled into the center of the cable.

The fiber and cladding can be surrounded by a liquid gel that reflects signals back into the fiber to reduce signal lost, or a plastic spacer surrounded by kevlar fiber. Each of these components making up the fiber optic cable are further protected by a plastic covering that encases everything within the cable.

Figure 2.13 Fiber Optic Cabling

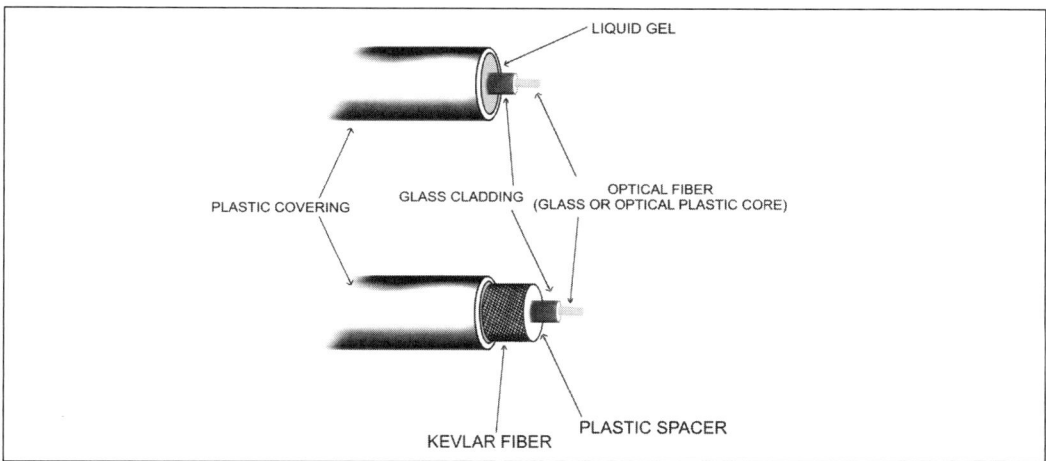

There are two different types of fiber optic cabling that may be used to carry data: Single Mode Fiber (SMF) and Multimode Fiber (MMF). SMF is optical fiber that's designed to transmit a single beam of light from a laser. The beam of modulated light provides greater bandwidth and allows cable to be run over longer distances. Because of these features, SMF is used for long distance transmissions such as in telephone and cable television networks.

Multimode Fiber Optic Cable

MMF is used to carry multiple beams of light at the same time, using a light emitting diode (LED) as a light source. Each of the beams is at a slightly different reflection angle within the core of the fiber. Because the light tends to disperse over distance, MMF is used for connecting locations within relatively short distances.

Other Media

While the cabling, connectors and other elements of a network we've discussed in this chapter are either traditional components of a network, or have grown to become standard, there are other technologies that are either new, not readily associated with networking, or often forgotten. Nevertheless, elements such as wireless technologies, FireWire, and transceivers are important to networking. Such media is not only covered on the Network+ exam, but is important to the design or development of your network.

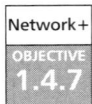

IEEE1394 (FireWire)

If you've ever hooked up a digital camera, digital video (DV) camera, or other devices that need to transfer large amounts of data to your computer, you may have used FireWire. FireWire is a proprietary name for an external bus that supports fast data transfer rates. Apple Computers originally developed the technology, but it has since been standardized as IEEE1394. Since then, other companies have developed their own trademark names, including Sony's iLink.

Devices that follow IEEE1394 allow data to be transferred at 400Mbps (in IEEE1394a) and 800Mbps (in IEEE1394b). In addition to this, it allows a single 1394 port to have up to 63 external devices connected to it. It is similar to USB in that can provide power to a device, and supports both plug and play and hot plugging.

Wireless Media

As we discussed briefly in the previous chapter, and will discuss in greater detail in Chapter 4, wireless networks require minimal cabling. Data is transmitted over the air using wireless adapters and wireless routers, so little to no cabling is required for network communication.

Transceivers (Media Converters)

The term *transceiver* is short for transmitter-receiver, which also describes its purpose on a network. Transceivers are the portion of a network interface that transmits and receives electrical signals across the transmission media. They are also the part of the interface that actually connects to the media. Transceiver types can be classified as being either on-board, which are built onto a network card, or external.

With an external transceiver, the actual media connection is made external to the network interface card using a small device that attaches via an extension cable to the network interface card. The types of transceivers and media that can be served by a network interface card determine the appropriate connector, and, as we saw earlier in this chapter, each media type has a typical connector type or connection method. One such connector is an AUI connector, which is also called a DIX connector. This type of connector can be found on the back of many network interface cards. The AUI connector enables a network card to be used with multiple types of media. A common implementation is to use this configuration for an Ethernet card that can be attached to twisted-pair, thickwire or thinwire coax by just changing the external transceiver type.

On networks that used 10Base2 and 10Base5 media, transceivers are used to connect to the cable and communicate with the network. 10Base5 networks use a device called a MAU, which taps into the thick cable and allows the workstation to connect to the network using an AUI cable. When a MAU and AUI cable are used on a 10Base5 network, the onboard transceiver of the network card isn't used. Instead, the transceiver in the MAU is used, which acquires power through the AUI cable from the network adapter card on the workstation. On 10Base2 networks, no more than 30 transceivers can be connected to any segment, while on 10Base5 networks no more than 100 taps can be performed per segment.

Because the network adapter's transceiver isn't used, the MAU detects collisions by sending out a signal called a heartbeat or SQE (Signal Quality Error) test signal. The MAU's heartbeat is sent to the workstation when a collision is detected, allowing it to deal with the collision accordingly, as we discussed in the previous chapter when discussing bus topologies. When a frame of data is successfully transmitted, the MAU will also send a heartbeat to determine whether the bus is active.

An exception to performing this test is when a repeater is used on the network, which resends data to other segments of the network. When a repeater receives the heartbeat signal, it will identify it as a collision, and send a jam signal. To prevent this, and thereby keep the network from becoming bogged down with these signals, the MAU's SQE test signal feature should be turned off if a repeater is used.

Summary of Exam Objectives

Cabling and connectors are essential to any network, providing a medium that allows computers to communicate and send data across the network. Cabling can be twisted-pair, coaxial, or fiber optic. Coaxial consists of a single copper wire to carry data, twisted-pair uses pairs of copper wires twisted together, and fiber optic cabling sends data across the network in the form of modulated pulses of light.

In using the various cables, there are a number of issues that may impact the performance of a network. Electromagnetic interference (EMI) can be caused by florescent lighting, machinery or other sources that put out a low voltage, low current, high frequency signal that can interfere electronic signals transmitted over cabling. Similar to this is radio frequency interference (RFI), which is caused by electromagnetic radiation in the radio frequency range. Putting cables too close to one another can cause another form of interference called crosstalk, where the electromagnetic field of one wire interferes with the transmission of another. Finally, data can weaken over distances, causing a problem called attenuation. These issues must be dealt with during the installation of network cable, or dealt with once cabling has been installed.

When problems present themselves, electronic devices called cable testers may be used to find the cause or location of a problem on the cable. Tools like tone generators, time domain reflectometers, wire map testers, and oscilloscopes can all provide information that is useful in fixing a problem.

We also saw that data can travel along a cable in several ways, using a simplex, half-duplex or full duplex data transfer. When simplex is used, data moves in a single direction. Half-duplex allows data to move in either direction, but in only one direction at a time. When full duplex is used however, data can move in either direction.

We discussed that Ethernet is a standard that's used on most networks today. Ethernet has specifications for 10Base2, 10Base5, and 10BaseT networks, and uses Carrier Sense Multiple Access with Collision Detection (CSMA/CD), which prevents devices from interfering with one another during transmission by detecting collisions of data. A newer variation of Ethernet is Fast Ethernet, which supports transfer speeds of up to 100 Mbps.

There is a wide variety of media standards, some of which have been around since the early days of networking. 10Base2 and 10Base5 are networks that use coaxial cable to transfer data, while 10BaseT, 100BaseTX, and 1000BaseT use UTP cabling. Finally, we also discussed various standards used for fiber optic networks, including 10BaseFL, 100BaseFX, 100BaseSX, 1000BaseLX, and 1000BaseCX.

Connectors are used to terminate cables and provide a method of connecting the cable to the device. There are a number of connectors available, including D, RJ, DIX, and BNC for coaxial and twisted-pair networks. SC, ST, LC, and MTRJ connectors are used for fiber optic cabling.

Just as there are various connectors, there are also a variety of media types. Twisted-pair cable comes in a variety of grades, ranging from CAT1 to CAT7. UTP Category 3 or higher can be used for data communications, but Category 5 or higher is recommended. The other form of twisted-pair is STP, which has a shield that helps to prevent interference. Coaxial cable also comes in more than one form. RG-58 cabling or Thinnet is thin coaxial cable (about 1/4 inch thick) used on 10Base2 networks, while RG-59 cabling or Thicknet is thick coaxial cable (about 1/2 inch thick) used on 10Base5 networks. Fiber optic cabling can be Single Mode Fiber (SMF), which is designed to transmit a single beam of light from a laser, while Multimode Fiber is used to carry multiple beams of light at the same time. Such variations show a wide variety of media types to choose from when designing a network.

Exam Objectives Fast Track

Cabling and Connectors Overview

☑ Cabling is the wire or fiber medium that is used to connect computers and other network devices of your network together, and used to carry the data that is transmitted between them.

☑ Coaxial cable, also referred to as *coax*, uses a single copper wire at the center of the cable to carry signals. The wire is surrounded by layers of insulation that protect the wire and its transmissions.

☑ Twisted-pair cables consist or pairs of wires that are twisted to reduce interference. This type of cabling may be unshielded or shielded.

☑ Fiber optic cable carries digital data signals in the form of modulated pulses of light.

Media Issues

☑ Electromagnetic interference (EMI) is a low voltage, low current, high frequency signal that can interfere with the electronic signals transmitted over cabling. EMI is also referred to as noise, as its signals come from outside sources and can corrupt data sent over cabling.

☑ Radio frequency interference (RFI) is caused by electromagnetic radiation in the radio frequency range.

☑ Crosstalk occurs when the signal of one wire bleeds onto another wire so that the electromagnetic field of one wire interferes with the transmission of another.

☑ Bandwidth is a measurement of the amount of data that can be passed over a cable in a given amount of time.

☑ Attenuation occurs when data transmitted over media weakens over distance.

Cable Testers and Troubleshooting

☑ Tone generators are used to perform tests on phone and network lines by clipping to a wire, terminal panel, or standard modular jack and will aid in the identification of wires during the wire-tracing process.

☑ Time Domain Reflectometers (TDRs) use signals that are sent down the cable to identify problems. An electronic pulse travels down the cable until it is reflected back, much like sonar.

☑ Wire map testers are often used on twisted-pair cabled networks to test for opens, shorts, or crossed pairs, and will provide information that may indicate improper wiring.

☑ Oscilloscopes can be used to determine when there are shorts, crimps, or attenuation in the cable.

Simplex, Half-Duplex, Full Duplex

☑ Simplex refers to data moving in a single direction.

☑ Half-duplex refers to data traveling both ways on the medium, but in only one direction at a time.

☑ Full duplex refers to data traveling in both directions simultaneously.

Cabling

☑ Ethernet is a standard for most networks used today, and includes specifications for 10Base2, 10Base5, and 10BaseT.

☑ Carrier Sense Multiple Access with Collision Detection (CSMA/CD) prevents devices from interfering with one another during transmission by detecting collisions of data.

☑ Fast Ethernet is a standard that provides speeds of 100 Mbps.

Media Standards

☑ 10Base2 uses coaxial cabling to transmit data at speeds of 10 Mbps across cable segments that are up to 185 meters in length.

☑ 10Base5 uses coaxial cabling to transmit data at speeds of 10 Mbps across cable segments that are up to 500 meters in length.

Cat5

☑ 10BaseT uses UTP cabling to transmit data at speeds of 10 Mbps across cable segments that are up to 100 meters in length. The UTP cabling must be Category 3 or higher.

Cat5

☑ 100BaseTX uses UTP cabling to transmit data at speeds of 100 Mbps across cable segments that are up to 100 meters in length. The UTP must be Category 5 or higher.

☑ 10BaseFL uses fiber optic cabling to transmit data at speeds of 10 Mbps across cable segments that are up to 2 kilometers in length.

☑ 100BaseFX uses fiber optic cabling to transmit data at speeds of 100 Mbps across cable segments that are up to 400 meters in length with half-duplex communication or 2 km for full duplex.

Cat5

☑ 1000BaseT uses UTP cabling to transmit data at speeds of 1000 Mbps across cable segments that are up to 100 meters in length. The UTP must be Category 5 or higher.

☑ 100BaseSX uses fiber optic cabling to transmit data at speeds of 1000 Mbps across cable segments that are up to 550 meters in length.

☑ 1000BaseLX uses fiber optic cabling to transmit data at speeds of 1000 Mbps across cable segments that are up to 550 meters (multi-mode fiber) or up to 10 km (single-mode fiber) in length.

☑ 1000BaseCX uses fiber optic cabling to transmit data at speeds of 1000 Mbps across cable segments that are up to 100 meters in length.

Connectors

☑ D connectors are shaped like the letter D, and have pins that connect to a female D connector.

☑ RJ connectors are used to connect devices used for voice and data communications.

☑ DIX stands for Digital Intel Xerox, who developed the connector for use with an AUI (Adapter Unit Interface) that's used with 10Base5 cable.

☑ BNC connectors are used to terminate coaxial cabling and provide connections to devices.

☑ There are a number of connectors available for fiber optic cabling, including SC (standard connector), ST (straight tip), LC (local connector) and MTRJ (mechanical transfer registered jack).

Media Types

☑ Twisted-pair cable comes in a variety of grades. UTP Category 3 or higher can be used for data communications, but Category 5 or higher is recommended.

☑ The difference between UTP and STP is that STP has a shield designed to keep interference out by protecting the wires inside from EMI caused by outside sources.

☑ RG-58 cabling or Thinnet is thin coaxial cable (about 1/4 inch thick) used on 10Base2 networks.

☑ RG-59 cabling or Thicknet is thick coaxial cable (about 1/2 inch thick) used on 10Base5 networks.

☑ Single Mode Fiber (SMF) is optical fiber that's designed to transmit a single beam of light from a laser. The beam of modulated light provides greater bandwidth and allows cable to be run over longer distances.

☑ Multimode Fiber is used to carry multiple beams of light at the same time, using a light emitting diode (LED) as a light source. Each of the beams is at a slightly different reflection angle within the core of the fiber.

Other Media

☑ FireWire is a proprietary name for IEEE1394, which is an external bus that supports fast data transfer rates of 400Mbps (in IEEE1394a) and 800Mbps (in IEEE1394b).

☑ Wireless media is used to transmit data without cable.

☑ Transceivers are the portion of a network interface that transmits and receives electrical signals across the transmission media. Transceivers may be onboard (on a network card) or external.

Exam Objectives
Frequently Asked Questions

The following Frequently Asked Questions, answered by the authors of this book, are designed to both measure your understanding of the Exam Objectives presented in this chapter, and to assist you with real-life implementation of these concepts.

Q: None of the workstations on the network are able to communicate with each other. They use a thinwire coax Ethernet to connect to each other.

A: The backbone has been severed or improperly terminated. Find the point at which the bus became severed and reconnect it. Make sure that the backbone is properly terminated.

Q: You have a brand new UTP cable, but the workstation is still not able to communicate on the network. The workstation worked with your test cable.

A: The brand new UTP cable may be a crossover cable. Obtain a regular UTP cable.

Q: A workstation was just moved to a new location and is no longer able to communicate on the network. There is nothing wrong with the workstation's configuration.

A: There are a number of reasons why the computer may no longer have network access – maybe it got moved to a different subnet, in which case its current configuration is wrong. Maybe the new location is further away than the supported cable length. Or perhaps cables were damaged in the move. Replace each cable one at a time to find the problematic cable.

Q: Is fiber the best networking media to implement in a standard office environment?

A: Normally, due to cost limitations, offices are wired with UTP or STP and the data center is wired with fiber. Fiber is also often used as a backbone to connect one building to another. This is typically the most cost-efficient manner of providing high-speed networking for your servers and providing acceptable access speeds to your users.

Self Test

A Quick Answer Key follows the Self Test questions. For complete questions, answers, and explanations to the Self Test questions in this chapter as well as the other chapters in this book, see the Self Test Appendix.

1. You are the network administrator of a 10BaseT network. On the weekend, when few people are working, you run 110 meters of cable to a new server that is being used as a file server. The cable is installed in a new section of the building, where no cabling currently exists. When you attempt to access files on the server, they are experiencing errors and corrupt data. Which of the following is most likely the cause of this problem?

   A. Bandwidth

   B. Attenuation

   C. Crosstalk from a neighboring cable

   D. CSMA/CD issues

2. Your company uses UTP cable for all of its network connections including work-stations and servers. The users have reported problems connecting to one of the most important servers on the network and you have been called in to look at it, due to a possible physical security breach by a former employee. While examining the server, you find that a small battery-powered motor has been placed and is running next to the server's network connection. What is causing the network problem?

   A. Electromagnetic interference

   B. Static electricity

   C. Transceivers

   D. Unknown, but the motor is probably unrelated

3. You are designing a new network and are concerned about interference from other wires. Which of the following is most susceptible to transmission errors due to crosstalk?

   A. Coaxial

   B. UTP

   C. STP

   D. Fiber optic

4. You are designing a new network for a grocery store. Cabling will have to run along the ceiling, where there are a significant number of florescent lights. You are concerned about interference from these lights. Which of the following cable types could be used, which would not be susceptible to this type of interference?

   A. Coaxial

   B. UTP

   C. STP

   D. Fiber optic

5. Your network uses vampire taps and AUI connectors to access data from the network cable. Which of the following cabling types is being used?

   A. Thinnet

   B. Thicknet

   C. STP

   D. Fiber optic

6. You are designing a 10Base2 network. In creating this network, what distance limitation will you be facing when installing the cabling?

   A. 100 meters

   B. 185 meters

   C. 500 meters

   D. 2 km

7. Examine the following illustration:

Figure 2.14 Determine Connectors for a 10Base2 Network

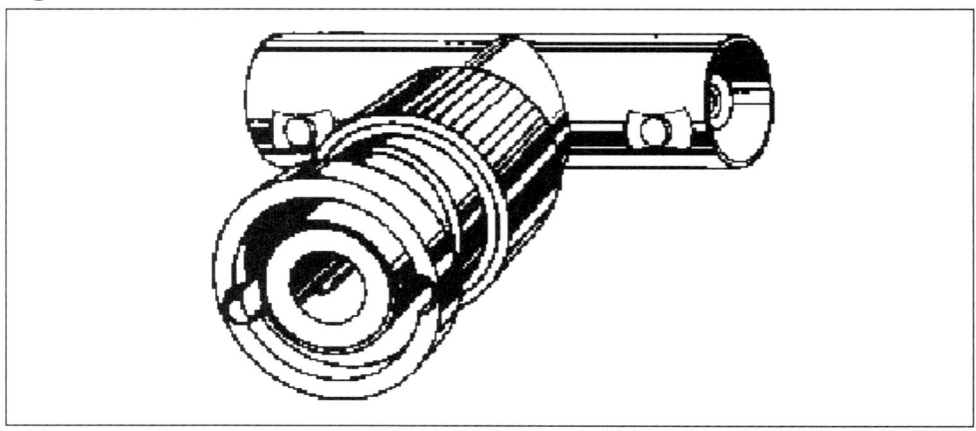

Your network is a 10Base2 network, and uses these connectors to attach to the network. Which of the following types of connectors is being used?

A. RJ-11

B. DIX

C. BNC Barrel Connector

D. BNC T-Connector

8. You have been hired by a small company to cable its network. The company has offices in two buildings that are 300 meters apart. Both of the offices have about 15 computers and the numbers are expected to grow in near future. All of the computers are within 90 meters of one another. You need to decide on the cabling that will be used both in the individual buildings, and which will be used to connect the buildings LANs together. Which of the following will you do?

A. Use UTP cabling in each of the buildings, and connect the two buildings together using 10BaseT cabling.

B. Use fiber optic cabling in each of the buildings, and connect the two buildings together using 10Base2 cabling.

C. Use 10BaseT cabling in each of the buildings, and connect the two buildings together using 10Base5 cabling.

D. Use 100BaseFX cabling in each of the buildings, and connect the two buildings together using 10BaseT cabling.

9. Your network uses 100BaseFX so that data can be transferred at higher speeds and up to distances of 400 meters. During transmission, data can travel in both directions, but only in one direction at a given time. Which of the following transmission methods is used?

   A. Simplex

   B. FireWire

   C. Half-Duplex

   D. Full Duplex

10. Examine the following illustration:

Figure 2.15 Determine Connectors in Star Topology

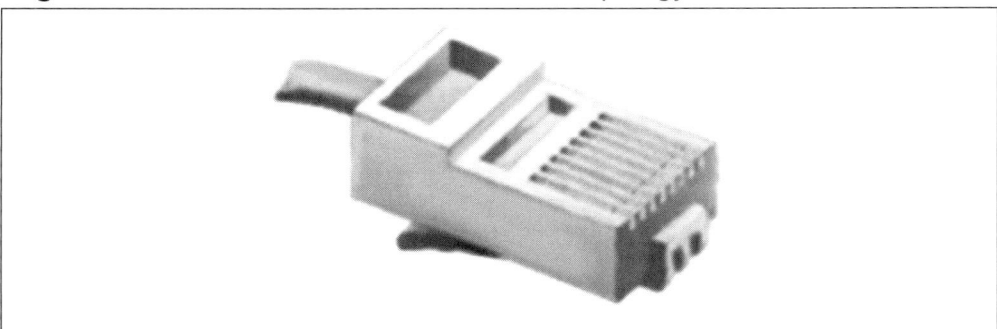

Your network uses UTP cabling in a star topology. Which of the following types of connectors is being used?

   A. RJ-45

   B. BNC

   C. ST

   D. SC

11.   As a Network technician for 123 LLC, you are asked by your CIO about the access method of Gigabit Ethernet. Which of the following access methods does Gigabit Ethernet use?

    A. FDDI

    B. CSMA/CD

    C. CSMA/CA

    D. Token passing

12.   You are the network engineer assigned to implement a new 100 Mbps network connection. You need to select the correct cabling, as well as the correct standard. From the selections below; choose which 100 Mbps networking standard makes use of only two pairs of a Category 5 UTP cable.

    A. 10BaseT

    B. 100BaseFL

    C. 100BaseTX

    D. 100BroadT4

Self Test Quick Answer Key

For complete questions, answers, and explanations to the Self Test questions in this chapter as well as the other chapters in this book, see the Self Test Appendix.

1.	**B**	7.	**D**
2.	**A**	8.	**C**
3.	**B**	9.	**C**
4.	**D**	10.	**A**
5.	**B**	11.	**B**
6.	**B**	12.	**C**

## Chapter 3

NETWORK+

Network Devices

Domain I Objectives in this Chapter:

1.6 Identify the purposes, features and functions of the following network components:

1.6.1 Hubs

1.6.2 Switches

1.6.3 Bridges

1.6.4 Routers

1.6.5 Gateways

1.6.6 CSU / DSU (Channel Service Unit / Data Service Unit)

1.6.7 NICs (Network Interface Card)

1.6.8 ISDN (Integrated Services Digital Network) Adapters

1.6.9 WAPs (Wireless Access Point)

1.6.10 Modems

1.6.11 Transceivers (media converters)

1.6.12 Firewalls

Introduction

A network is composed of many different devices, some of which perform a single function, and some of which perform a variety of functions, from routing data to applying security filters. As networking devices become more complex, they also become more versatile, in that they may be able to perform multiple roles that previously could only be carried out by individual devices. Some network devices are complex enough to warrant their own operating systems for intensive and detailed configuration. In some cases, these operating systems can be switched out, substituted, or used to configure the device to perform roles traditionally carried out by other devices. For example, a Layer 3 switch might be configured to combine both switching and routing functions. This coming together of technology within one device is called *convergence*.

In this chapter we will briefly discuss convergence, and we will look at the most common network devices in use today on small and large networks, including the Internet. These devices range from the very simple (such as an active hub, which simply repeats and sends out signals to all ports), to the more complex (such as a firewall that is responsible for controlling traffic and applying security features).

Network Devices

Network devices are components of a network that are required if the network is to grow, function, or provide certain functionality. There are a number of devices that fall into this category, including routers, switches, and other devices that we've mentioned briefly in previous chapters. These network devices provide functionality such as connectivity to physical media, security features, and the ability to connect to resources outside of the local area network (LAN). Before we discuss the current state of networking and the available devices, let's take a look at where the current devices evolved from.

Historical Network Devices

As we saw in Chapter 1, networks have been around for decades, so it follows that some devices have been around longer than others. As we'll see in the sections that follow, while some devices are as useful today as when they were initially introduced, others have become obsolete and are rarely if ever used on today's networks. In discussing these devices, we'll tell you about their purpose, features, and functions on a network.

Head of the Class…

OSI and Network Devices

A number of network devices can be mapped to the OSI (Open Systems Interconnect) networking model. OSI is a group of standards that provides a logical structure for network operations, and contains seven layers, which from highest to lowest are: Application, Presentation, Session, Transport, Network, Data Link, and Physical. The network devices we cover in this chapter map to that model, which is discussed in more detail in Chapter 5.

Network communication starts at the Application Layer of the OSI model and works its way down through the layers step by step to the Physical Layer. The information then passes along the cable to the receiving computer, which starts the information at the Physical layer. From there it steps back up the OSI layers to the Application Layer where the receiving computer finalizes the processing and sends back an acknowledgement if needed. Then the whole process starts over.

Table 3.1 shows the devices mapped to the OSI layers at which they operate.

Table 3.1 Mapping of Network Devices to the OSI Model

OSI Layer	Devices
Application	Gateway
Presentation	Gateway
Session	Gateway
Transport	Gateway
Network	Router, Layer 3 Switches, Gateway
Data Link	NIC, Bridge, Layer 2 Switches, Access Point, Gateway
Physical	Hub, MAU, Repeater, Gateway

Hubs

etwork+
OBJECTIVE
1.6.1

Even though hubs have been around since the early days of networking, they continue to be one of the most commonly used connection-based network components. Especially now that home networks are growing as more SOHOs (small offices home offices) are emerging, hubs are becoming a common household item. Some homes are even built today with a plan for a centralized wiring system, Internet access, routers, and hubs all included.

Hubs are predecessors of the switch, which we'll discuss later in this chapter, and are central locations for connecting network cabling. Multiple cables connect into the hub, providing a method for data to be passed from one cable to another. This is also why switches are sometimes referred to as *switching hubs*, although that terminology is not commonly used today.

As we discussed in Chapter 1, a star topology uses a hub to connect workstations, servers, and other devices. As shown in Figure 3.1, you can easily remember the layout of a hub if you think of a wheel and picture how the spokes go to the hub of the wheel. Each spoke is a connection and the hub of the wheel is the hub of the network where all the cables come together. Because all of the connections concentrate in the center, another term for a hub is a *concentrator*.

Figure 3.1 Hubs are Used in Star Topologies

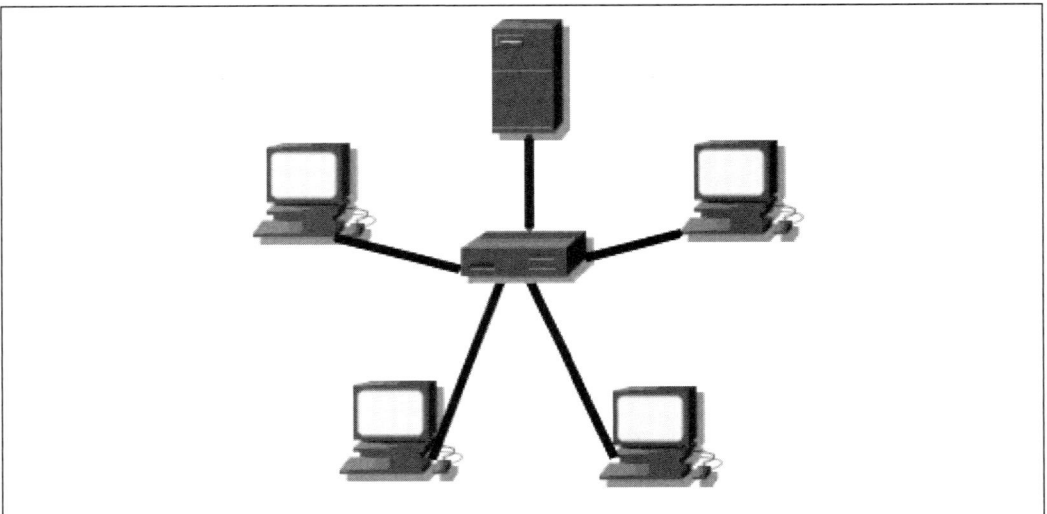

Each of the cables that extends to the hub from computers and other network devices is plugged into its own port on the hub. The port provides an interface between the cable and the hub. For example, because star topologies use unshielded twisted-pair (UTP) cable, UTP is a common cable type that is used with hubs. The RJ-45 connector (which we discussed in Chapter 2) of the cable plugged into a port on the hub. When data is sent from a computer, it is carried along the cable to the port that the RJ-45 connector is plugged into. The hub then takes this data and passes it to the other ports, allowing the data to travel along the other cables to workstations and devices that are attached to it. The number of ports on a hub will vary, but generally four or more are provided. Many hubs provide 24 or 28 ports, and can be attached together (or more commonly referred to as *uplinked* to each other) to provide connectivity to even more computers or network devices. There are rules, of course; when working with hubs you should always apply the 5-4-3 rule, which states that you can only connect a total of 5 segments linked together via 4 hubs and only 3 of those segments can be populated with network hosts such as PCs or printers. Breaking rules of this kind could lead to a degradation of performance and possible problems.

The two main types of hubs are *passive* and *active*. A *switching* hub is actually a type of switch that behaves like a hub.

EXAM WARNING

Hubs broadcast traffic on every single port. Because hubs only operate at the Physical Layer, they are deemed unintelligent. A hub is simple by design; a signal comes in from a connected PC and the hub just sends that signal out every port that it knows. For example, suppose an 8-port hub has 8 PCs attached. If PC 1 sends an e-mail to PC 2, that transmission will go to all 8 PCs. The data of course will get to its destination, but all six of the uninvolved PCs are interrupted because each has to examine the data to determine if it is the recipient. This process takes time, and if you multiply this over the traffic of a normal large-scale enterprise network, it's easy to see why hubs are typically limited to small networks.

Passive Hubs

In discussing hubs to this point, we have essentially been talking about passive hubs. A passive hub provides basic features of moving data from one port to another. Its function is simply to receive data from one port of the hub and send it out to the other ports. For example, an 8-port hub receives data from port 3 and then resends that data to ports 1, 2, 4, 5, 6, 7, and 8. It is as simple as that.

A passive hub contains no power source or electrical components. There is no signal processing. It simply attaches the ports internally and enables communication to flow through the network.

Active Hubs

An active hub provides the same functionality that a passive hub does, with an additional feature. Active hubs repeat (regenerate) the data while resending it to all of its ports. By using active hubs you can increase the length of your network beyond regular cable length limits. For example, UTP Category 5 cabling can be run a maximum of 100 meters. With an active hub, you can run Category 5 UTP 100 meters on each side of the hub, so that your cable now runs a length of 200 meters in total.

An active hub has a power source and built-in repeaters to boost the signal. There are extra electronics built into an active hub that allow for signal regeneration, which is how the incoming data on one port is repeated to the other ports. Because the signal is repeated in this way to the other ports, another term for an active hub is a *multiport repeater*.

Test Day Tip

The Network+ exam includes questions that deal with active hubs. Passive hubs aren't covered on the current version of the exam. This information is included for completeness.

Switching Hubs

While active and passive hubs will pass data to every other port on the hub, a switching hub will only send data to its intended port. Switching hubs are also referred to as *intelligent hubs*, as they can determine which port will get the data to its proper destination. The fact is, however, that even though it is referred to as a switching hub, these are the features of another device called a switch (which we'll discuss later in this chapter). While this term may be used in the real world to refer to a switch, for the Network+ exam it's best to keep the components separate in your mind. A switch is a switch, and a hub is a hub.

Exam Warning

Hubs operate at the Physical Layer of the OSI model (also known as Layer 1). Hubs are designed to simply forward data from one port of the hub to another, so they don't use upper-layer protocols like IP (Internet Protocol), IPX (Internetwork Packet Exchange), or MAC (media access control) addressing to ensure data reaches its intended destination.

Repeaters

A repeater is a device that is rarely seen on networks today, as its features are typically incorporated into other devices, such as active and switching hubs. The repeater will take a signal that may be weakening and regenerate it to its original strength. In doing so, it actually recreates the signal, making it the same strength that it was when it left the sending workstation.

To help you understand a repeater, imagine that you are with a friend and both of you are standing at opposite ends of a street. If you shouted something to your friend, the sound would fade over a distance. If someone stood between the two of you, however, and repeated your message, then it would be repeated strong and loud, allowing your friend to hear it. A repeater works in a similar fashion by repeating the data so it's in its original, strong form so the data doesn't corrupt as it weakens over distance.

Historically, repeaters were first created to fix a problem. Cables had length limitations, which were solved by connecting a repeater to two cable segments to extend the range beyond the regular distance limit. Repeaters were commonly used on Ethernet networks, such as those using UTP or coaxial cable, and provided networks with the ability to extend cable segments. 10BaseT limitations are 100 meters, or approximately 328 feet. Thickwire (or also known as 10Base5 or Thicknet) can normally transmit a distance of 500 meters, while thinwire (also known as 10Base2 or Thinnet) can normally transmit a distance of 185 meters. By putting a repeater between these segments, the distance that data can travel can be doubled. Remember, when using repeaters, greater lengths of cabling were allowed when planning a cabling scheme.

NOTE

Unlike previous versions of the Network+ exam, repeaters are no longer directly tested on the exam. The function of a repeater is to regenerate data so that it can be passed further than the maximum distance of a cable segment. The ability to regenerate data and perform this function is now found incorporated in other network devices, such as hubs and switches.

Bridges

A bridge is a network connectivity device that connects two different networks and makes them appear to be one network. It can connect two different LANs, or allow a larger LAN to be segmented into two smaller halves. The bridge filters local traffic between the two networks and copies all other traffic to the other side of the bridge.

Bridges are intelligent devices, and have the ability to forward packets of data based on MAC addresses. A bridge can look at a packet of data and determine the source and destination involved in the transfer of packets. It will read the specific physical address of a packet on one network segment and then decide to filter out the packet or forward it to another segment.

A bridge is another device that has largely become a thing of the past. Although bridges were a common component of older networks, its features are now typically incorporated into switches. One benefit of a switch over a bridge is that a bridge typically only has two ports, one for each segment that it is connecting. Switches may have many ports, and as we've already seen, incorporates features that were previously found in other devices, such as hubs.

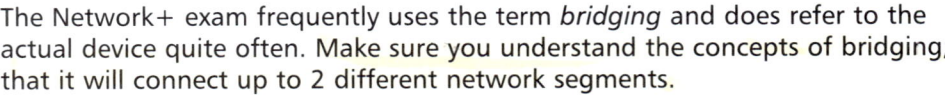

TEST DAY TIP

The Network+ exam frequently uses the term *bridging* and does refer to the actual device quite often. Make sure you understand the concepts of bridging; that it will connect up to 2 different network segments.

Network Segmentation

A bridge is a simple way to accomplish network segmentation. Placing a bridge between two different segments of the network decreases the amount of traffic on each of the local networks. Although this does accomplish network segmentation, most network administrators opt to use routers or switches, which are discussed later in the chapter.

Bridges segment the network by MAC addresses. When one of the workstations connected to one network has to transmit a packet, the packet is copied across the bridge as long as the packet's destination is not on its originating network segment. A bridge uses a bridging table to calculate which MAC addresses are on which network. The MAC address uniquely identifies computers and other devices on a network, just as the full address of your house uniquely identifies its location.

EXAM WARNING

Bridges operate at the Data Link Layer of the OSI model and use physical addressing to join several networks into a single network efficiently.

Multistation Access Units

Multistation access units (also known as MAUs or MSAUs) are used to connect workstations on a Token Ring network. Sometimes a MAU is referred to as a hub on the Network+ exam, but it shouldn't be confused with the active and passive hubs we discussed earlier, which are used on Ethernet networks. The features of a MAU are different than those of a standard hub.

A MAU typically has 8 or more ports that provide connections for workstations and other network devices on a Token Ring network. It is also generally non-powered, although some have been produced that are powered with lights to indicate connectivity and activity. A MAU is not something you will commonly find on newer networks simply because newer networks generally are installed as Ethernet, more typically Fast Ethernet or Gigabit Ethernet. MAUs are used with Token Ring networks, which are still present in today's environments, but are not as prevalent as Ethernet.

Head of the Class...

What Do I Need to Know About Token Ring for the Network+ Exam?

Although an aging technology, Token Ring is still supported on a great many networks. The reason is this: mainframes used to be the rulers of the world and many companies relied on them to store their data. They were accessed by dumb terminals that ran on UNIX .Many of those older networks ran Token Ring. As dumb terminals were replaced by PCs and the networks were migrated to Ethernet, the mainframes stood firmly in place. What some may not know is that because it was so expensive to replace a network card on a mainframe, it was often cheaper to just get a router with a Token Ring interface as well as an Ethernet one, so a great many Token Ring networks still exist as of this day!

So what exactly do you need to know about Token Ring? Well, it is important to know what it is not… Ethernet. Do not let questions trip you up. You could be asked about which type of hardware is used to connect your networking interface card (NIC) to your PC and MAU on an Ethernet network… Token Ring and Ethernet hardware are completely incompatible; they are completely two different standards. You would need some form of gateway to translate one technology to another, for instance, in the example above when the router was used to connect the two dissimilar networks together. Figure 3.2 shows an example of this in action:

Figure 3.2 Two Networking Technologies Connected via a Windows Server 2003 Router

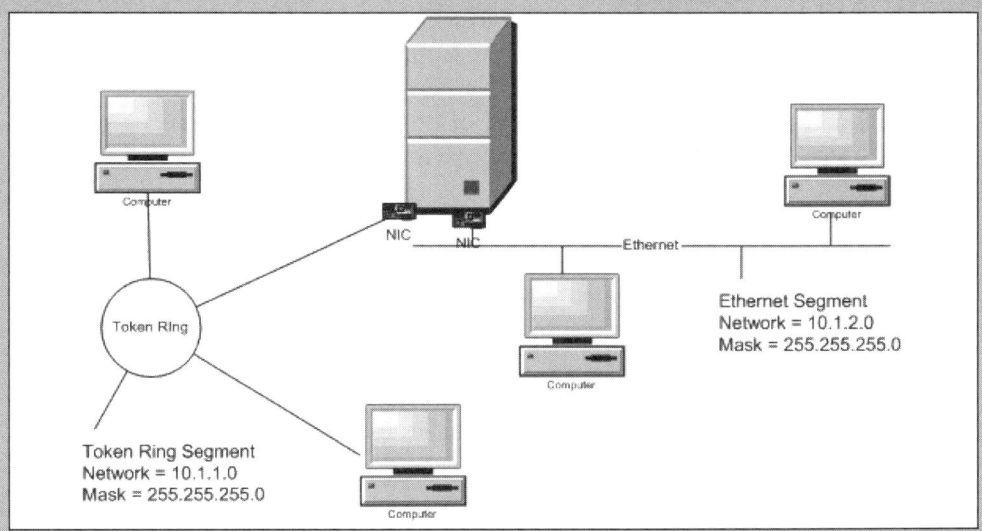

In our example, the Windows Server 2003 system has two NICs installed, one Ethernet, one Token Ring. The Routing and Remote Access Service (RRAS) is installed and functioning. This server is acting as a router and connecting two

Continued

different network segments together. The Token Ring NIC is connected to a MAU with two PCs attached to it. The Ethernet NIC is connected to a hub with 2 PCs also connected to it. Although both technologies coexist, do not think that they are interchangeable—they are not. Ethernet is Ethernet, and Token Ring is Token Ring. Be careful.

Concepts of Convergence

Over the years, a number of network devices have become obsolete or less necessary to a network because other devices have taken on their roles. Vendors will attempt to put as many features as possible into a device, and will even include functions that other devices provide. As we discussed earlier in this chapter, repeaters are no longer used on networks because switches provide the same functionality. The same will apply to other devices used on a home or office network. For example, a router used for Internet access may include a switch for networking devices together, a firewall, and perhaps even a wireless access point (WAP). As time goes on, you can expect to see other devices converging together, requiring networks to have fewer components.

When taking the Network+ exam, it is wise to consider such devices as separate, rather than as one device providing all features. For example, even though your router for the Internet has a firewall, you should consider a router and a firewall as two separate components of a network when taking the exam.

The Modem and Other Adapters

Over the past decade, having access to the Internet and remote access to networks has become as commonplace a method of communication as using a telephone. People have come to expect to be able to get the information they need quickly, and to be able to send messages and acquire data using a modem or other adapters. In the sections that follow, we'll look at a number of devices used for such access, and discuss related topics that may appear on the Network+ exam.

The modem gets its name from a combination of the terms *modu*lator and *de*modulator. In addition to analog modems, which typically provide connection speeds of up to 56 Kbps, there are other types of modems that provide higher speed connections. These include DSL (Digital Subscriber Line) modems, cable modems, and ISDN (Integrated Services Digital Network) adapters. In the sections that follow, we'll discuss each of these types of modems in greater detail.

Although there are many different types and makes of modems, they can be categorized into three areas: single external, single internal, and multi-line rack or shelf-mounted.

The external modem is commonly used to provide connectivity between computers, existing as a separate component that is attached to a computer using a cable. Many ISPs (Internet Service Providers) use pools of external modems to enable dial-in access. They are also common in server hardware, as many IT personnel include modems in production systems to allow for a backup communications link or for remote access.

The internal modem performs the same functions as the external modem. The only real difference is that it is located inside the computer chassis. While they are common in home computers, many companies don't use internal modems because external modems are easier to replace and troubleshoot. For example, internal modems do not have the LEDs that external modems do. This translates into a headache if you have to figure out why the modem won't connect to a remote host via the dial-up connection. Some modem manufacturers provide software interfaces; however, these generally are not as full-featured as for the external modem.

While internal modems are often adapter cards that are installed in desktop computers, another type of internal modem is used in laptop computers. Many laptop vendors integrate phone jacks into the chassis of the computer, allowing a connection to an internal modem inside the laptop. However, PC cards used with laptop computers can also be technically classified as an internal modem. The PC card bus, formerly known as PCMCIA, is an architecture designed primarily for laptops and other portable computers. Adapters for this bus are sometimes called credit card adapters after their size and shape, which is roughly equal to that of a credit card. Because of their small size, most have a receptacle to which an external adapter must be connected for attachment to the media. These modems are also sometimes combined with a NIC in a single card called a combo card.

Many vendors also offer a solution that is a single chassis containing a certain number of modem cards that can be connected directly to the network. Its modularity and its size are much more efficient than trying to maintain a shelf with a stack of external modems sitting on it. These have also been included in some new networking equipment. Manufacturers place analog modems in their equipment to facilitate redundancy features such as a backup network link.

Analog Modems

etwork+
BJECTIVE
.6.10

An analog modem is a communications device that enables a computer to talk to another computer through a standard telephone line. It does this by converting digital data from the computer to analog data for transmission over the telephone line and then back to digital data for the receiving computer. This is necessary because the Public Switched Telephone Network (PSTN) uses analog waves to transmit voice communications, while computers use digital data.

Because standard analog modems use a standard telephone line to acquire connectivity to the Internet or a remote network, they use the same type of telephone cable that's used by telephones. As we saw in the previous chapter, this type of cable uses an RJ-11 connector, allowing the device to dial out using the same system that you use to make telephone calls.

DSL and Cable Modems

While modems that dial up the phone number of an ISP or a computer network have been around for many years, new kinds of modems have gained popularity in recent years. Cable modems and DSL modems access technology that provides connection speeds in the megabit per second (Mbps) range.

Cable modems are used to access the Internet using the broadband technology of cable television lines. The cable modem is similar to an analog modem in that it translates data into a form that can be transmitted, and retranslates it into data the computer can understand. When data is sent using cable modems, the modem translates it into a coaxial-based technology, which is used to split Internet access from television signals. Regardless of the medium used however, the basic purpose of the modem remains the same—to allow you to access the Internet or remote networks.

The transmission speeds of a cable modem are typically as high as 1.544 Mbps. Although broadband Internet can provide greater speeds, allowing a download path of up to 27 Mbps, the cable service provider is generally connected to the Internet using a T1 line, which provides speeds of up to 1.544 Mbps.

Cable modems provide a constant connection to the cable service provider that also acts in the role of an ISP. The cable modem communicates with a Cable Modem Termination System (CMTS) provided by the cable service provider, but doesn't have the ability to directly access other cable modems. This is different from dial-up modems, which have the ability to dial directly into other computers.

Another type of modem uses a technology called DSL. With DSL, your local telephone company plays the role of ISP, providing access to the Internet through the twisted-pair cabling of your phone line. Unlike a standard modem that dials into an ISP over a telephone line, DSL allows simultaneous voice and data communication. In other words, you can surf the Web and talk on the phone at the same time.

While an analog modem converts digital data to an analog wave, DSL transmits and receives data digitally across the phone line's twisted-pair cable. Because data isn't converted, a higher bandwidth is available to transfer data. DSL typically provides transmission speeds of 1.544 Mbps, although it can provide data transfer rates of up to 6.1 Mbps. The speed of DSL does, however, decrease the further you are from a telephone company's offices or a repeater that regenerates the signal, because data rates decrease as they travel over cabling. The closer you are to the telephone company's offices, the faster your DSL connection will be.

There are several different variations of DSL available (shown in Table 3.2), which offer different data transfer rates and distance limitations.

Table 3.2 Types of DSL

Type of DSL	Bandwidth	Distance Limitations
Asymmetric Digital Subscriber Line (ADSL)	Downstream: 1.544 to 6.1 Mbps Upstream: 16 to 640 Kbps	Speeds decrease over distance. 1.544 Mbps at 18,000 feet, 2.048 Mbps at 16000 feet, 6.312 Mbps at 12,000 feet, and 8.448 Mbps at 9,000 feet
Consumer Digital Subscriber Line (CDSL)	Downstream: 1 Mbps Upstream: Under 1 Mbps	18000 feet
DSL Lite or G.Lite	1.544 to 6 Mbps	18000 feet
ISDN Digital Subscriber Line (IDSL)	128 Kbps	18000 feet
High Digital Subscriber Line (HDSL)	Varies depending on twisted pair lines. 1.544 Mbps duplex on two twisted-pair lines, or 2.048 Mbps duplex on three twisted-pair lines	12000 feet
Symmetric Digital Subscriber Line (SDSL)	1.544 Mbps	12000 feet
Very High Digital Subscriber Line (VDSL)	Downstream: 12.9 to 52.8 Mbps Upstream: 1.5 to 2.3 Mbps	Speeds decrease over distance. 4,500 feet at 12.96 Mbps, 3,000 feet at 25.82 Mbps, and 1,000 feet at 51.84 Mbps

ISDN Adapters

ISDN is a system of digital telephone connections that enables data to be transmitted simultaneously end to end. This technology has been available for more than a decade, and before DSL and cable modems, ISDN was an optimal choice for faster, clearer data communication. It came about as the standard telephone system began its migration from an analog format to digital.

History of ISDN

In the 1950s, the phone companies began looking at ways to improve communications. They began by sampling the analog signals that were passed during a phone conversation and attempted to convert them to digital signals. From this analog sampling, they determined that 64 Kbps would enable a digital signal to properly handle voice communications through the telephone network. This became the foundation of ISDN.

Because a standard did not exist among the different phone companies, the Consultative Committee for International Telephony and Telegraph (CCITT) began working on the Integrated Digital Network (IDN) in the late 1960s. IDN combined the functions of switching and transmission into one piece of hardware that could be set as the standard for all telephone companies to use. This initiative not only moved telephony services toward a standard, but also made the network much more efficient. It wasn't perfect, but was a step in the right direction.

The concept of ISDN was introduced in 1972. The concept was based upon moving the analog-to-digital conversion equipment onto the customer's premises to enable voice and data services to be sent through a single line. Telephone companies also began using a new kind of digital communications link between each central office. A T1 link could carry twenty-four of these 64 Kbps voice channels, and it used the same amount of copper wire as only two analog voice calls. Throughout the 1970s the telephone companies continued to upgrade their switching offices. They began rolling out T1 links directly to customers to provide high-speed access. The need for an efficient solution was greater than ever.

When ISDN was recognized by the ITU (International Telecommunications Union), an initiative was begun to define its standards. The initial recommendations were published in CCITT Recommendation I.120 (1984) and described some initial guidelines for implementing ISDN. In the early 1990s, an effort was begun to establish a standard implementation for ISDN in the United States. The NI-1 (National ISDN 1) standard was defined by the industry so that users would not have to know the type of switch they were connected to in order to buy equipment and software compatible with it.

Because some major office switches were incompatible with this standard, some major telephone companies had trouble switching to the NI-1 standard. This caused some problems when trying to communicate between these nonstandard systems and everyone else. Eventually, all of the systems were brought up to standard. A set of core services was defined in all BRIs (Basic Rate Interfaces) of the NI-1 standard. The services include data call services, voice call services, call forwarding, and call waiting. Most devices today conform to the NI-1 standard.

A more comprehensive standardization initiative, NI-2 (National ISDN 2) was adopted in recent years. Now, several major manufacturers of networking equipment have become involved to help set the standard and make ISDN a more economical solution. The NI-2 standard had two goals: standardize the Primary Rate Interface (PRI) as NI-1 did for the BRI, and simplify the identification process. Until this point, PRIs were mainly vendor-dependent, which made it difficult to interconnect them. Also, a standard was created for NI-2 for identifiers.

ISDN Channels

An ISDN transmission circuit consists of a logical grouping of data channels. With ISDN, voice and data are carried by these channels. Two types of channels are used for a single ISDN connection, a B channel and a D channel. Each channel has a specific function and bandwidth associated with it. The bearer channels (B channels) transfer data, and offer a bandwidth of 64 Kbps per each channel. A hardware limitation in some switches limits the B channels to 56 Kbps, or 56000 bytes.

The data channel (D channel) handles signaling at 16 Kbps or 64 Kbps. This includes the session setup and teardown using a communications language known as DSS1. The purpose of this channel is to enable the B channels to strictly pass data. You remove the administrative overhead from them by using the D channel. The bandwidth available for the D channel is dependent upon the type of service—BRIs usually require 16 Kbps and PRIs use 64 Kbps. Typically, ISDN service contains two B channels and a single D channel.

H channels are used to specify a number of B channels. The following list shows the implementations:

- **H0** 384 Kbps (6 B channels)
- **H10** 1472 Kbps (23 B channels)
- **H11** 1536 Kbps (24 B channels)
- **H12** 1920 Kbps (30 B channels)—Europe

ISDN Interfaces

Although B channels and D channels can be combined in any number of ways, the phone companies created two standard configurations. There are two basic types of ISDN service: Basic Rate Interface and Primary Rate Interface. BRI consists of two 64 Kbps B channels and one 16 Kbps D channel for a total of 144 Kbps. Only 128 Kbps is used for user data transfers. BRIs were designed to enable customers to use their existing wiring. This provided a low-cost solution for customers and is why it is the most basic type of service today intended for small business or home use.

PRI is intended for users with greater bandwidth requirements. It requires T1 carriers to facilitate communications. Normally, the channel structure contains 23 B channels plus one 64 Kbps D channel for a total of 1536 Kbps. This standard is used only in North America and Japan. European countries support a different kind of ISDN standard for PRI. It consists of 30 B channels and one 64 Kbps D channel for a total of 1984 Kbps. A technology known as Non-Facility Associated Signaling (NFAS) is available to enable you to support multiple PRI lines with one 64 Kbps D channel.

To use BRI services, you must subscribe to ISDN services through a local telephone company or provider. By default, you must be within 18,000 feet (about 3.4 miles) of the telephone company central office for BRI services. Repeater devices are available for ISDN service to extend this distance, but these devices can be very expensive. Special types of equipment are required to communicate with the ISDN provider switch and with other ISDN devices; you must have an ISDN terminal adapter and an ISDN router.

ISDN Devices

The ISDN standard refers to the devices that are required to connect the end node to the network. Although some vendors provide devices that have several functions included, a separate device defines each function within the standard. The protocols that each device uses are also defined and are associated with a specific letter. Also known as reference points, these letters are R, S, T, and U. ISDN standards also define the device types. They are NT1, NT2, TE1, TE2, and TA. The architecture for these devices and the reference points, which we'll discuss further in the next section, can be seen in Figure 3.3.

Figure 3.3 ISDN Device Architecture

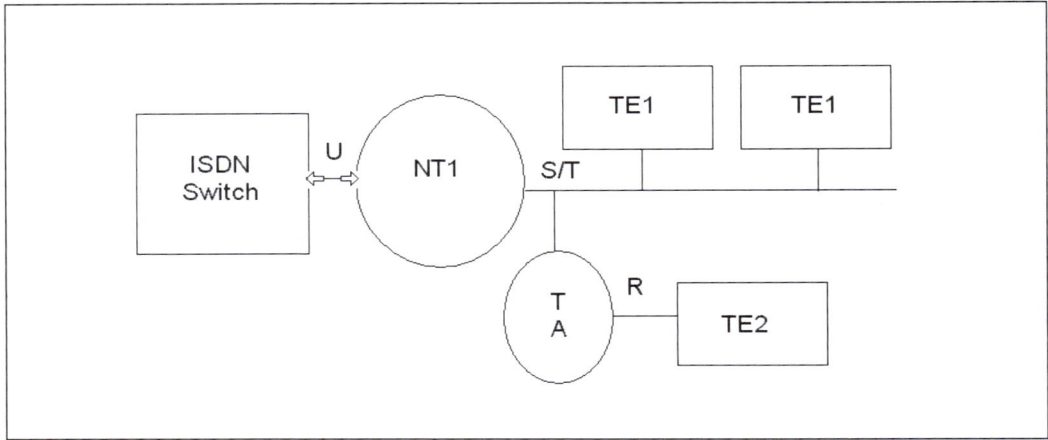

ISDN Reference Points

Reference points are used to define logical interfaces. They are, in effect, a type of protocol used in communications. The following list contains the reference points:

- **R** Defines reference point between a TE2 device and a TA device.
- **S** Defines reference point between TE1 devices and NT1 or NT2 devices.
- **T** Defines reference point between NT1 and NT2 devices.
- **U** Defines reference point between NT1 devices and line termination equipment. This is usually the central switch.

Network Termination 1 (NT1) is the device that communicates directly with the central office (CO) switch. The NT1 receives a U interface connection from the telephone company and puts out a T interface connection for the NT2. NT1 handles the physical layer portions of the connection, such as physical and electrical termination, line monitoring, and multiplexing.

Network Termination 2 (NT2) is placed between an NT1 device and any adapters or terminal equipment. Many devices provide the NT1 and NT2 device in the same physical hardware. Larger installations generally separate these devices. An example of an NT2 device is a digital PBX or ISDN network router. An NT2 device provides an S interface and accepts a T interface from an NT1. NT2 usually handles data link and network layer functions in network with multiple devices such as contention monitoring and routing.

Terminal Equipment 1 (TE1) is a local device that speaks via an S interface. It can be directly connected to the NT1 or NT2 devices. ISDN telephones and ISDN fax machines are good examples of TE1 devices.

Terminal Equipment 2 (TE2) devices are common everyday devices that can be used for ISDN connectivity. Any telecommunications device that is not in the TE1 category is classified as a TE2 device. A terminal adapter is used to connect these devices to an ISDN network and attaches through an R interface. Examples of TE2 devices include standard fax machines, PCs, and regular telephones.

A *terminal adapter (TA)* connects TE2 devices to an ISDN network. It connects through the R interface to the TE2 device and through the S interface to the ISDN network. The peripheral required for personal computers often includes an NT1 device. These are better known as ISDN modems.

Identifiers

Standard telephone lines use a ten-digit identifier that is permanently assigned. This is the telephone number. ISDN uses similar types of identifiers; however, they are not as easily used as a telephone number. ISDN uses five separate identifiers when making a connection. The provider assigns two of these when the connection is first set up: the Service Profile Identifier (SPID) and the directory number (DN). These are the most common numbers used because the other three are dynamically set up each time a connection is made. The three dynamic identifiers are TEI (Terminal Endpoint Identifier), BC (bearer code), and SAPI (Service Access Point Identifier).

The SPID is the most important number needed when using ISDN. The provider statically assigns this number when the ISDN service is set up. It usually includes the directory number plus a few extra digits. The SPID usually contains between 10 and 14 characters and varies from region to region. SPIDs can be assigned for every ISDN device, for the entire line, or for each B channel.

The SPID is unique throughout the entire switch and must be set up correctly. If it is incorrect, it is like dialing the wrong phone number—you will not be able to contact the person you are trying to reach. When an ISDN device is connected to the network, it sends the SPID to the switch. If the SPID is correct, the switch uses the stored information about your service profile to set up the data link. The ISDN device will not send the SPID again unless the device is disconnected from the network.

The directory number is the ten-digit phone number the telephone company assigns to any analog line. ISDN services enable a greater deal of flexibility in using this number than analog services do. Unlike with an analog line where a one-to-one relationship exists, the DN is only a logical mapping. A single DN can be used for multiple channels or devices. Also, up to eight DNs can be assigned to one device. Because a single BRI can have up to eight devices, it can support up to 64 directory numbers. This is why offices are able to have multiple phone numbers. Most standard BRI installations include only two directory numbers, one for each B channel.

A Terminal Endpoint Identifier identifies the particular ISDN device to the switch. This identifier changes each time a device is connected to the ISDN network. Unlike the SPID or directory number, the TEI is dynamically allocated by the central switch.

The Service Access Point Identifier identifies the particular interface on the switch that your devices are connected to. This identifier is used by the switch and is also dynamically updated each time a device connects to the network.

The bearer code is an identifier made up of the combination of TEI and SAPI. It is used as the call reference and is dynamic like the two identifiers included within it. The BC changes each time a connection is established.

Advantages of ISDN

ISDN offers several major advantages over conventional analog methods. First, it has a speed advantage over normal dial-up lines. The fastest analog modem connection currently available is 56 Kbps. Because this is an analog connection, many modems cannot reach this speed because they are limited by the quality of the connection. This accounts for your connecting at different speeds each time you dial in to a remote network. Because phone lines cannot actually transmit at 56 Kbps, a special kind of compression is used to enable these speeds. Two standards currently exist. For Internet Service Providers to appease everyone, they must support both standards, which could get expensive quickly.

ISDN enables you to use multiple digital channels at the same time to pass data through regular phone lines. The difference is that the connection being made from your computer is completely digital, with no conversion to or from analog. You can also use other protocols that enable you to bind channels together to get a higher bandwidth rate. In addition, ISDN takes half the time an analog line takes to make a connection.

In addition to speed, ISDN supports multiple devices set up in one link. In an analog system, a single line is required for each device attached. For example, a separate phone line is needed for a normal phone, a fax machine, or a computer modem. Since ISDN supports multiple devices, you can use each one of these items on a single line. It will also be clearer due to the fact that the data is being passed in a digital format.

Because ISDN uses a separate channel, the D channel for signaling, it removes the administrative overhead required. This means that the data is not hindered by the sessions setups and the communications required by the devices. The D channel keeps all of this information off the data streams. Because of the separation, the setup and takedown of each session is much faster. In addition, ISDN equipment is able to handle calls more intelligently.

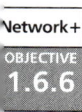

CSU/DSU

The somewhat lengthy acronym CSU/DSU is short for *Channel Service Unit / Data Service Unit* A CSU/DSU is a device that takes a signal from a digital medium and multiplexes it. Although a CSU and a DSU can be separate components, they are generally packaged as a single unit. The CSU is used to connect a terminal to a digital line, while a DSU performs diagnostic and protective functions.

A CSU/DSU terminates the end of a leased T-carrier line, which is a high speed line that can be used to connect a LAN to a WAN (wide area network). WANs are covered in greater depth in Chapter 7. The CSU/DSU is similar to a modem in that it connects to the media that will carry the data, but since the T-carrier transmits the data digitally, there is no need for device to modulate and demodulate between digital and analog formats. The CSU/DSU can be a separate component that attaches to a router and provides an interface between the router and the line, but many newer routers have more modular capabilities that allow you to purchase what are sometimes referred to as WAN interface cards, or WICs for short.

This is a card that incorporates the CSU/DSU into the actual port and cable connection so you do not have an external CSU; it's built directly into the router itself, thereby easing maintenance and management.

A T-carrier line is a leased telephone line that runs over fiber optic cabling and can provide different speeds depending on the level used. A T1 line consists of 24 separate channels called DS0s that are 64 Kbps each. In total, this equals 1.544 Mbps for a full T1 line. Because some companies may not need this amount of bandwidth, it is possible to lease only a portion of the channels. For example, if you rented two channels on a T1 line, you would have a 128 Kbps connection. When only a portion of the T1 line is used, it is referred to as *fractional T1*. If more than 1.544 Mbps of bandwidth were needed, a company could also lease another level of a T-carrier line called a T3 line, which provides speeds of 44.736 Mbps.

Configuring & Implementing

Multiplexing Defined...

Multiplexing is defined as the sending of multiple signals over one communications channel at the same time. The cable television system is a perfect example of multiplexing in action. Cable TV is a simple technology where your available channels are all sent along a single cable, and you are able to select a channel to view a specific program based on your numbered selection. In the world of data transmission, the technology very much the same. If you have a T1, for example, and you need to break that 1.544 Mbps of bandwidth down to smaller amount, you can do so with a *fractional T1*.

What about the rest of that bandwidth, is it wasted? Of course not; not with multiplexing. As a service provider, you can designate half of the bandwidth to company A and then the rest to company B. Data is sent along the whole T1 and no bandwidth is wasted. The technology of multiplexing is used in many ways to conserve bandwidth.

There are two different types of multiplexing, they are TDM and FDM. In Time Division Multiplexing (TDM), each signal is broken up into many segments, each having short durations or time slots on the whole of the available bandwidth. Frequency Division Multiplexing does the same thing as TDM except that TDM is based on digital signaling and FDM is based on analog. Instead of using time slots, all frequencies are given a percentage of the whole bandwidth.

Network Interface Cards

Network+
OBJECTIVE
1.6.7

Network interface cards, also referred to as network adapter cards or simply network cards, are the key components that allow computers or other devices to communicate with the rest of the network. Installed on workstations, servers, printers, and other network devices, it provides an interface to the network that allows data to be transmitted and received across the network media.

Simply put, the NIC performs the following functions:

- It translates data from the parallel data bus to a serial bit stream for transmission across the network.

- It formats packets of data in accordance with protocol.

- It transmits and receives data based on the hardware address of the card.

A NIC works as an interface between a computer's expansion bus and the medium that's used to transmit and receive data across the network. In many cases, this means that it attaches to the cable used on a network, but wireless NICs are also available that allow data to be transferred through the air. Although the NIC can be integrated into the system board, it is typically an add-on component for a computer, much like a video card or sound card is. The NIC is normally installed as an expansion board by plugging it into a bus slot, and has a connector that allows the network media to be attached to it.

Installing a NIC

Installing a NIC is like installing any other interface card in a computer. You have to determine the slot it will go in and have the right tools to remove the expansion slot cover and to remove and insert screws. Newer computers do not require any tools, not even screwdrivers. The ability to work on a computer with your hands free of tools is making any technician's job easier. The Network+ exam will challenge you to know what to do in certain situations. In this section you will learn several troubleshooting techniques and how to recognize the common issues that you will face with network interface cards.

NICs are built for computer bus types such as ISA (Industry Standard Architecture), EISA (Extended Industry Standard Architecture), MCA (Micro Channel Architecture), and PCI (Peripheral Component Interconnect). Most of the newer NICs support plug and play features and can be automatically configured by the operating system when the physical installation is done. This feature makes installation of the NIC considerably easier than with older cards.

Before you begin the physical installation of the NIC, or network adapter, be sure to address the following issues:

- Ensure that the adapter is compatible with the data bus, the protocol, the media, and the network operating system. In the case of Windows network operating systems, the hardware compatibility list (HCL) lists adapters that have been verified for use with a particular operating system (such as NT, 2000, 2003, and XP).

- Ensure that there is an open bus slot on the machine in which you want to install the adapter.

- Ensure that the adapter includes all items necessary for installation, including external transceivers or adapters, a T-connector for a thinwire Ethernet adapter, and product documentation.

- Ensure that the software, including the network driver and utilities for testing and configuring the adapter, is included. If a software driver is not provided, a driver may be included with operating system installation media. If not, drivers and driver updates may be available for download from the adapter manufacturer via the Internet or a bulletin board service.

- Remember that the NIC cannot do any useful work until high-level protocols and network services have also been installed and configured.

EXERCISE 3.01

ENABLING AND DISABLING A NIC CARD WITH WINDOWS XP PROFESSIONAL

In this exercise we will learn how to enable and/or disable a NIC card for security reasons. If you are not using an interface, disable it. Make sure you do not disable interfaces you need… check first.

To enable or disable an interface, you need to first open the Network Connections dialog box. To do this, double click **My Network Places** on your desktop. Click **View Network Connections** and you will see your current connections (as shown in Figure 3.4).

Figure 3.4 Viewing Your Network Connections

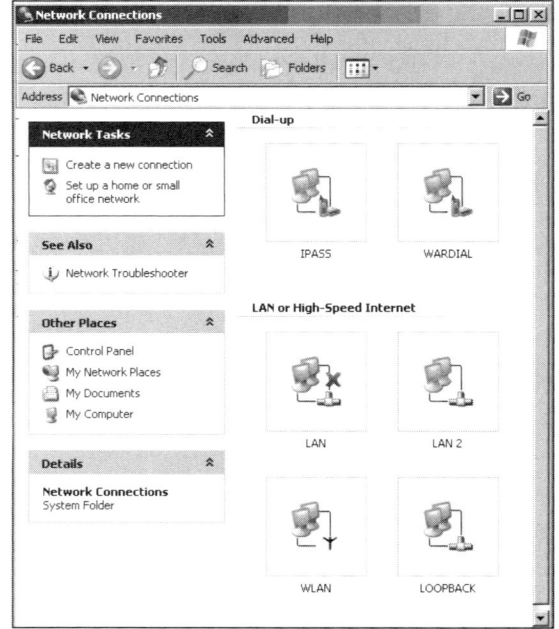

Note that in the Figure above, LAN has a red x. This indicates that the connection may have an issue, such as a disconnected RJ-45 connector on the NIC itself. LAN2 is grayed out. This indicates that the connection is disabled. To enable it, you only need to right click the connection select **Enable** from the shortcut menu (Figure 3.5). The NIC will enable itself barring any other issues, and the icon in the Network Connections window will be shown in full color.

Figure 3.5 Enabling a Connection with Windows XP Professional

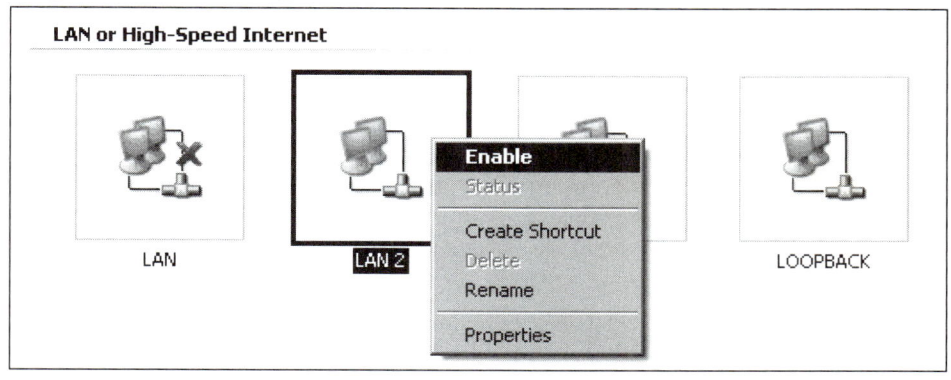

NIC Types and Operation

While NICs are all designed to allow computers and devices to access a network, not all NICs are the same. As we saw in Chapter 2, there are many different types of media and connectors that may be used on a network, which is why there are different NICs. Because of this, NICs are often defined by the following criteria:

- The type of Data Link protocol they support, such as an Ethernet or Token Ring
- The type of media they connect to
- The data bus for which they were designed

In using a NIC, the computer must have a software driver installed in order to interact with the NIC, just as it must for any other peripheral device. These drivers enable the operating system and higher-level protocols to control the functions of the adapter.

The NICs that exist in the various workstations on a network communicate with each other using their own unique addresses. The MAC address, or hardware address, is a 12-digit number consisting of digits 0-9 and letters A-F. It is basically a hexadecimal (base16) number assigned to the card by the manufacturer. The MAC address consists of two pieces: the first signifies which vendor it comes from, the second is the serial number unique to that manufacturer. This address must be unique on each network card on a network. You may wonder how a manufacturer can ensure uniqueness among all the network cards in the world. No doubt there are network cards that have the same address, but each manufacturer is assigned a range by the various network standards organizations, and they use only that range. Within the range, a manufacturer may have duplicates, but the duplicates are so spread out over time that it is almost impossible for a network, small or large, to have two devices with the same MAC address.

EXAM WARNING

NICs are the most common interface for a computer or device to connect to media on the network. They operate at the Data Link Layer of the OSI model

---

Transceivers

As we discussed in Chapter 2, the term *transceiver* is short for transmitter-receiver, and it is a component of a NIC that transmits and receives electrical signals across the transmission media. Transceivers are also the part of the interface that actually connects to the media. While transceivers can be external to the network card, they are typically built onto the NIC. A transceiver that's built onto a card is called an *onboard transceiver*.

While NICs are generally designed to connect to a particular type of media, they can also connect to multiple media types. A transceiver type setting is required for network adapters that are capable of attaching to more than one media type. Typical cards of this nature include Ethernet cards that have both twisted-pair and coaxial connectors. This is one of the more common oversights in configuring a network interface card and the card can be rendered nonfunctional if it is configured for the wrong media connection. To alleviate this problem, some cards of this type have an auto setting that causes the card to search for the transceiver that has media connected to it.

Modern Network Devices

While many of the devices we've discussed so far have been used since the early days of networking, a number of devices have either taken over the roles of these devices and/or are a predominant part of a modern network environment. These devices are crucial to a network's ability to handle data and ensure it reaches its intended destination as its being transmitted.

Switches

Switches provide services that are similar to those provided by Ethernet hubs. A switch takes data from a cable connected to its port, but unlike a hub that forwards the data through all of its other ports, a switch will forward the packet through a single port that leads to the computer that the data is intended for. The only time a switch will send out the data to all of its ports is when a broadcast message is sent.

Switches offer full duplex dedicated bandwidth to LAN segments or desktops. You can think of a switch as an intelligent hub that guarantees a specific amount (10, 100, or

1000 Mbps) of bandwidth to the computer that it is connected to. With a hub, you are guaranteed some of the bandwidth all of the time. This means that hubs are not intelligent enough to account for collisions on the network; you may be connected to a 10 Mbps port, but you may only be receiving 4 Mbps of throughput because of the amount of traffic on the network. With a switch, you are guaranteed the entire limit of your bandwidth because the switch is intelligent and can examine packets and send them in the right direction.

Configuring & Implementing…

Switches on Today's Network

In terms of devices that provide network connectivity, switches have become the future of networking. Today's computer networks have to support the combination of voice, video, and data, so many network administrators are beginning to favor intelligent switches over common shared hubs. Network switches enable you to have bandwidth on demand and ensure that you can use your network to the fullest capacity. If you have a switch that is capable of 100 Mbps, you are guaranteed that amount of bandwidth due to the way a switch can intelligently look at the packets. A shared hub, on the other hand, can sometimes supply only 40% of the potential bandwidth on the network.

Multiport Bridging

Switches are also sometimes referred to as *multiport bridges*, as they can perform the same functions as a bridge, which we discussed earlier. Unlike a bridge that can connect two LANs together or segment a large one into two smaller ones, a switch has multiple ports and thereby has the ability to connect more than two different segments of a network.

In multiport bridging, a switch automatically determines the MAC addresses of the devices connected to each port of the switch. The switch examines each packet it receives to determine its destination MAC address or IP address (depending on the OSI layer it works on, as we'll discuss later in this chapter), and sends it out on the appropriate port. It doesn't matter if the destination computer is on the same LAN as the computer that is sending the data. This allows two different networks to communicate with one another, yet still appear as part of the same network.

Network Performance Improvement with Switching

The primary benefit of implementing switching technology is that it improves network performance. It is important to note that if you are not having traffic problems on your network, adding a switch will probably not change your network's performance. If your network is having traffic problems, switching, when implemented properly, can greatly increase your performance.

Switching is a fairly involved process. For example, Computer A transmits a packet to Computer C. The packet enters the switch from Port 1 and then travels a direct route to Port 3. From Port 3 the packet is transmitted to Computer C. During this process, Computer B is unaware of the traffic between Computer A and C because there is a direct path within the switch and no shared bandwidth.

TEST DAY TIP

Switches are a topic that's tested on the Network+ exam and an important part of networking. It's wise to review the information about switches so that you're familiar with what they are and the roles they perform. Remember that it is a best practice to use switches whenever possible because of the increase in performance over a standard hub. When a standard hub is used, the network's bandwidth is shared by all users connected to the hub; with a switch, however, all users get the full network bandwidth. For example, a 10 Mbps network with an 8-port hub and 8 PCs will allow each user to have (10 / 8) Mbps bandwidth, but with a switching hub, each user would have a full 10 Mbps bandwidth.

Layer 2 Switches

A Layer2 switch is a common type of switch that looks at the MAC address of a packet to determine where it is destined. As we discussed earlier in this chapter when we talked about NICs, the MAC address is unique to the NIC and makes it identifiable on the network. When a packet of data is sent to the switch, it includes the MAC address of the destination computer, so the switch can tell which computer the data is meant for. Upon viewing this information, the switch can then send it through the appropriate port that will take it to this computer.

The reason this type of switch is called a Layer 2 switch is that it works at the Data Link Layer of the OSI model. The Data Link Layer handles many issues for communicating on a simple network. As we'll see in Chapter 5, where the OSI model is discussed in depth, the 802 standard defines the Data Link Layer as having multiple sublayers: Logical Link Control (LLC) and Media Access Control (MAC). The LLC sublayer starts, maintains, and manages connections between devices, while the MAC sublayer enables multiple devices to share the media. The MAC sublayer also maintains physical device addresses for communicating with other devices.

Layer 3 Switches

Layer 3 switches provide more features than Layer 2 switches, as they can handle routing. Routing functions at Layer 3 of the OSI model, hence the name. Layer 3 switches function as both a switch and a router simultaneously. As we'll see later in this chapter when we discuss routers, routing allows a device to determine the best way of sending the data to a destination computer through the use of internal routing tables. Because a Layer 3 switch provides similar features to those of a router, they can use network or IP addresses to identify the location of a computer on the network.

A Layer 3 switch works by utilizing switching tables and switching algorithms to determine how to send data via MAC addressing from host to host, device to device. Since switching is the process of sending data from segment to segment based on the MAC address, what happens when data has to be sent to a remote network? The data is sent to the default gateway (commonly a router), which sends the data to its destination. The time spent sending the data from the switch to the router and then the time spent by the router taking the packet off the wire to read it is now eliminated or shortened drastically by implementing a Layer 3 switch. This is because a Layer 3 switch is built into a Layer 2 switch so data does not have to be sent to a router; that is, the router is built into the circuitry of the switch so the data is routed as quickly as the switch can send it to itself – much quicker than one device trying to send data to another device. Now consider the speed at which a high-speed switch works. Consider the amount of packets that could be sent across that cable. Now you can start to see the benefits of a Layer 3 switch; having the two devices sandwiched together increases the efficiency of the transmission, thus speeding it up drastically as the volume of data increases.

EXAM WARNING

On the Network+ exam you may hear the term *brouter*. What is a brouter? It's a device that can route specific protocols and bridge others, thus combining the capabilities of a bridge and a router. So, simply put, a brouter is a network device that can perform the functions of both a bridge and a router, much like a Layer 3 switch can perform the same type of functionality – they are just two different devices with different names. A brouter is older terminology and technology, whereas a Layer 3 switch is today's terminology and technology.

Layer 4 and Beyond

Because of the success of Layer 3 switching and the performance gains it can provide, it was no surprise that switching would climb higher along the OSI's layered model. Layer 4 switches work at the Transport Layer of the OSI model, and have the ability to look at information in the packets it receives to not only identify the MAC address and IP address of the destination computer, but also the application protocols being used to send it. The switch can determine if HTTP (Hypertext Transfer Protocol), FTP (File Transfer Protocol), or other protocols in the TCP/IP (Transmission Control Protocol/Internet Protocol) suite are being used to send the packet, and can also identify the application that uses the data. Because the packet contains information about the application, priorities can be set on packets, as well as rules about how they are to be forwarded.

Layer 5 switches work at the Session Layer of the OSI model, and use information in the packet provided by this layer for routing. The Session Layer provides information such as Uniform Resource Locators (URLs) that allow the switch to route the packet more effectively to a destination computer. A URL is a method of addressing that is commonly used on the Internet. At the time of this writing, Layer 5 is the highest layer of the OSI model that switches work with.

EXAM WARNING

Switches operate at many layers of the OSI model. They work at the Data Link Layer (Layer 2), and sometimes at the Network Layer (Layer 3) of the OSI model. Layer 3 switches have an integrated router function that allows them to make decisions as to where the data should be sent.

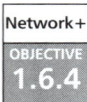

Routers

Routers route data packets across a network by opening the packet and making routing decisions based on the contents. On a network that uses TCP/IP as its communication protocol (which we'll discuss in great detail in Chapter 6), IP addresses are used as a method of identifying computers. This identification is used to ensure that data is sent to the correct computer on the network. In order for these computers to communicate, however, a device is needed to guide the TCP/IP network traffic to its destination. This is where routers come in.

Although we won't delve deeply into the OSI model until Chapter 5, we mentioned the Network Layer earlier in this chapter. The Network Layer, or Layer 3, is responsible for addressing messages and translating their logical addresses into an actual physical address. It is important to remember that a router is protocol-dependent. That means that a TCP/IP router can connect to a TCP/IP network. In other words, this is the layer of the OSI model that is responsible for determining where to send the TCP/IP packets to their destinations. Routers essentially separate different broadcast domains from one another and route traffic based on the destination, or Layer 3, address (the Layer 2 address is the MAC address).

When you want to communicate with another computer network, your computer essentially looks within the local network first before heading out to search for a remote address. For example, when your computer needs to access a file on another computer, your computer first checks its ARP (Address Resolution Protocol) cache to see if that computer has a recognizable MAC address. If it does not, your computer checks the local subnet by either broadcasting or asking a name server for help.

If the address is not found on the local subnet or network, your computer checks to see if you have a default gateway or router to send the information to. Your computer sends this information to your router and the router routes the message accordingly. The router receives the data with the address information and checks its routing tables to see where it should send your data. The type of router sometimes affects how quickly your data arrives at its destination.

Routers are either static or dynamic. In most cases, you'll only have to deal with a dynamic router—a router whose routing tables are populated automatically by receiving updates from other routers. Static routers have fixed routing tables that have to be updated manually. These static routers are at a disadvantage because they cannot communicate with any type of router in case a network route changes due to hardware failure or change to the network layout.

The main benefit of a dynamic router is that, depending on which type of routing protocol is used, it will attempt to route your network traffic to your destination as quickly as possible. For example, if you have a network that is standardized on Cisco routers (dynamic) that all communicate with one another using the OSPF (Open Shortest Path First) routing protocol (which is also a dynamic routing protocol). All of your routers are communicating with one another via broadcasts that they send whenever there is a change in their routing. This comes in very handy and adds a layer of redundancy so that if a segment of the network fails, your routers will be able to route the network traffic to other paths so that no matter what happens to the network, your data will always arrive at its destination.

If you were using a static router and you had a segment fail on your network, your network traffic would cease until the segment was repaired or another static route was mapped on the router. This puts static routing at a severe disadvantage in a large, complex network environment.

Understanding Static and Dynamic Routing

When it comes to routing, there is a huge difference between static and dynamic. Early routers had to be programmed with exactly which networks they could route between which interfaces, especially if there were many network interfaces. This is called static routing, and network administrators had to add, maintain, and delete routes of the network routing devices manually. In a small company this may not be much of a chore, but for medium to large networks, this can be nearly impossible. These larger networks almost always employ many logical subnets, which requires you to update the route tables on each routing device. If these remote subnets are connected by routers with static route tables, you have to add the exact static route in order to communicate between the two subnets. Table 3.3 shows an example of what is contained in the routing table.

Table 3.3 Information Contained in a Routing Table

Destination	Adjacent Router	Hops
Network 1	Router A	1
Network 1	Router B	2
Network 2	Router B	2
Network 2	Router C	3
Network 3	Router D	3

In this simplified table you can see how you only specify the router to be used to reach the destination, not the actual destination itself. The number of hops determines which route is the most efficient. If a route claims it can reach the destination in one fewer hop than the next router, then it is sent to that router. If there are two identical routes to the same destination, the route with the fewest hops will be used.

One change to a network address means visiting every routing device that employs static routing and updating the entry. What do we do if our network is fairly large and complex? We must then use routing devices capable of dynamically updating the route tables.

Dynamic routing does not require the network administrator to edit complex routing tables in order to communicate with other networks or segments. These routers communicate with each other using a powerful routing protocol such as Routing Information Protocol (RIP) or Open Shortest Path First (OSPF). They can also query other routers for updated route information, which can create more efficient paths for sending packets or locate an alternative route if the original route fails. The routers can broadcast the routes they have discovered to neighboring routers, and, in turn, accept routes from other neighboring routers. The Internet is comprised of many dynamic routers, which is an example of why dynamic routing is so important. Could you imaging having to update a static routing table on thousands of static routers? I don't think so.

These dynamic routers, however, cannot update the route tables of static routers or non-dynamic routers. There are a few situations in which integrating static and dynamic routers is acceptable:

- When you have a router at either end of a slow WAN link. This router will not increase traffic by broadcasting updated route information to the router on the other end of the link.

- When you require a packet to travel the same path each time to a remote network. Add the path you would like the packet to take in order to reach the destination network. You cannot enter the entire path over several routers, only the path to the first router.

- When you want to configure a static router to point towards a dynamic router to take advantage of the dynamic router *indirectly*. This is the next best thing to using a dynamic router. You can hand off the packet to the dynamic router and let this router determine the most efficient path to the destination based on the paths it has learned from neighboring dynamic routers.

EXAM WARNING

Routers operate at the Network Layer of the OSI model. The exam will deal with questions regarding both routers and the OSI model.

Switching Routers

As we discussed earlier in this chapter, switches have the ability to perform the tasks normally associated with other devices. A Layer 3 switch has the ability to open a packet and view the IP address and MAC address of the computer the packet is destined for. The switch can then review routing tables on the switch to determine the best route to send the data. By performing these functions, the switch is able to do the work of a router and get the packet to its intended destination by using the best route.

Security Integration

As reports of hacking, viruses, worms, and other attacks on networks become commonplace in the news, the need for security in network devices and networks in general continue to grow. Equipment and software can be added to a network, which can work with existing devices to protect your LAN and its data. Choosing which security measures to implement can be challenging, as there is an increasing number of products available. However, the more protected your network, the less chance there will be of it being damaged from outside sources.

Convergence of Security

Just as devices are including more and more features in them that make other devices obsolete or unnecessary to a network, devices are also including more security features that historically had to be purchased separately. Routers that are used for DSL or cable Internet include features such as a built in firewall with the router. The hardware-based firewall provides a barrier to incoming traffic from the WAN, and thereby prevents it from reaching your local computer or LAN. The hardware firewall, however, is limited in restricting and monitoring the incoming and outgoing traffic, and should be complemented by a software firewall and antivirus software.

Security Alert!

Monitoring Traffic Through Firewalls

As Internet access has become a more common fixture in organizations, so has monitoring the websites visited by personnel in those organizations. Firewalls are used to prevent unauthorized access to the internal network from the Internet, but also enable organizations to monitor what their employees are accessing on the Internet. Companies can check the firewall logs to determine what sites an employee visited, how long they spent there, what files they downloaded, and other information that the employee may consider private.

Companies may also stipulate the privacy of client information, or those with a presence on the Web may include or create a separate policy that deals with the privacy of a visitor to their website. In terms of actual clients (those people with whom a company does business), the policy should state the level of privacy a client can expect. This may include the protection of client information, including information on sales, credit card numbers, and so forth. In the case of police, this might include information on a person's arrest record that can't be concealed under the Public Information Act and Open Records laws, personal information, and other data. For both clients and visitors to websites, a company may stipulate whether information is sold to third parties that may send you advertisements, spam, or phone solicitations.

Firewalls

Network+
OBJECTIVE
1.6.12

A *firewall* protects a secure internal network from a public insecure network. Firewalls are devices or software that have the ability to control the traffic that's sent from an external network, such as the Internet, to an internal network or local computer. As we'll see later in this chapter, the features that are provided by a firewall will vary depending on the type you choose for your network.

The most common implementation today is the use of a firewall between an organization's internal network and the Internet. Firewalls can be very complex because they provide more features that just packet filtering. They can also provide multiple layers of protection, including actually scanning the information stored in the packets for malicious data as they pass through. They use advanced techniques to monitor connections, to log potential intrusions, and to act upon these incidents.

Firewall Architecture

A firewall is a combination of techniques and technologies used to control the flow of data between networks. A firewall enables all traffic to pass through to each network; however, it compares the traffic to a set of rules that determine how the traffic will be managed. If the traffic matches the rules for acceptable data, the traffic is passed on to the network. If the rule specifies that the data be denied, the traffic cannot continue and will be bounced back. Although some implementations may do this differently, the same basic functionality is used.

Dual-Homed Host Firewalls

A *dual-homed firewall* consists of a single computer with two physical network interfaces. This computer acts as a gateway between two networks. The server's routing capability is disabled so that the firewall can handle all traffic management. Either an application-level proxy or circuit-level firewall is run to provide data transfer capability. You must be careful not to enable routing within the network operating system or you will bypass your firewall software. Figure 3.6 shows a dual-homed host firewall configuration.

Figure 3.6 A Dual-Homed Host Firewall

Screened Host Firewalls

Screened host firewall configurations are considered by many to be more secure than the dual-homed firewall. In this configuration, you place a screening router between the gateway host and the public network. This enables you to provide packet filtering before the packets reach the host computer. The host computer could then run a proxy to provide additional security to this configuration. As packets travel into the internal network, they only know of the computer host that exists. Figure 3.7 shows an illustration of a screened-host configuration.

Figure 3.7 A Screened Host Firewall

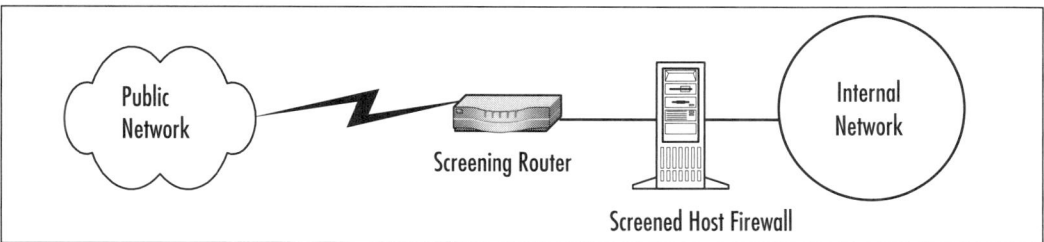

Screened Subnet Firewalls

A screened subnet firewall configuration takes security to the next level by further isolating the internal network from the public network. An additional screening router is placed between the internal network and the firewall proxy server. The internal router handles local traffic while the external router handles inbound and outbound traffic to

www.syngress.com

the public network. This provides two additional levels of security. First, by adding a link internally, you can protect the firewall host from an attack by an internal source. Second, it makes an external attack much more difficult because the number of links is increased. Figure 3.8 shows the screened subnet firewall configuration.

Figure 3.8 A Screened Subnet Firewall

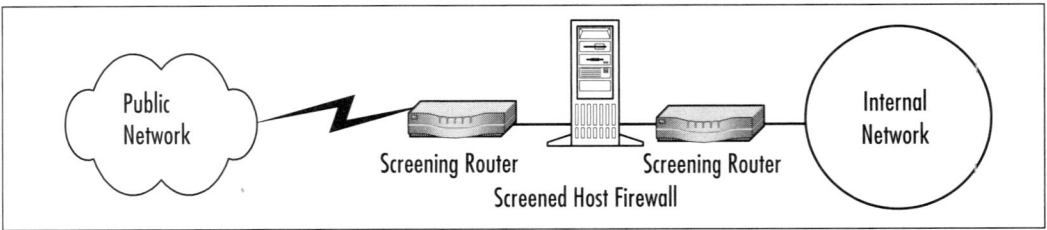

Firewall Types

There are three basic categories of firewalls: packet level, application level, and circuit level. Each uses a different security approach, thus providing different advantages and disadvantages. One additional feature that was discussed earlier is encryption services. Most firewalls provide some sort of cryptographic services for data transfers.

When you have a complete understanding of the features and type of security that is needed from a firewall, you can then determine the implementation that bests fits the environment.

Packet Level Firewall

A packet level firewall is usually a form of screening router that examines packets based upon filters that are set up at the Network and Transport Layers. You can block incoming or outgoing transfers based on a TCP/IP address or other rules. For example, you may choose to not allow any incoming IP connections, but enable all outgoing IP connections. You can set up rules that will enable certain types of requests to pass while other are denied. Rules can be based on source address, destination address, session protocol type, and the source and destination port. Because this works at only three layers, it is a very basic form of protection. To properly provide security to the network, all seven layers must be protected by a full-featured conventional firewall.

Application Level Firewall

The application level firewall understands the data at the application level. Application Layer firewalls operate at the application, presentation, and session layers. Data at the application level can actually be understood and monitored to verify that no harmful information is included. An example of an application level firewall is an Internet proxy or mail server. Many uses are available through some form of proxy, however these functions are usually very intensive to provide security at that level. In addition, often clients must be configured to pass through the proxy to use it. Proxy servers are also used to mask the original origin of a packet. For example, an Internet proxy will pass the request on; however, the source listed in the packet is the proxy server address. The overall server doesn't just filter the packets, it actually takes in the original and retransmits a new packet through a different network interface.

Circuit Level Firewall

A circuit level firewall is similar to an application proxy except that the security mechanisms are applied at the time the connection is established. From then on, the packets flow between the hosts without any further checking from the firewall. Circuit level firewalls operate at the transport layer.

Firewall Features

As firewalls have evolved, additional feature sets have grown out of or been added to these implementations. They are used to provide faster access and better security mechanisms. As encryption techniques have improved, they are being incorporated more in to firewall implementations. Also, caching is being provided for services such as the World Wide Web. This enables pages to be cached for a period of time, which can dramatically speed up the user experience. New management techniques and technologies such as virtual private networks (VPNs) are now being included as well.

Content filtering is another major feature of a firewall. Because of the possible damage a Java applet, JavaScript, or ActiveX component can do to a network in terms of threatening security or attacking machines, many companies filter out applets completely. Firewalls can be configured to filter out applets, scripts, and components so that they are removed from an HTML (Hypertext Markup Language) document that is returned to a computer on the internal network. Preventing such elements from ever being displayed will cause the Web page to appear differently from the way its author intended, but any content that is passed through the firewall will be more secure.

DMZ

DMZ is short for *demilitarized zone*, and is a military term used to signify a recognized safe area between two countries where, by mutual agreement, no troops or war-making activities are allowed. There are usually strict rules regarding what is allowed within the zone. In computer security, the DMZ is a neutral network segment where systems accessible to the public Internet are housed, and which offers some basic levels of protection against attacks.

The creation of these DMZ segments is usually done in one of two ways:

- Layered DMZ implementation
- Multiple interface firewall implementation

In the first method, the systems are placed between two firewall devices with different rule sets, which allows systems on the Internet to connect to the offered services on the DMZ systems, but prevents them from connecting to the computers on the internal segments of the organization's network (often called the *protected network*). Figure 3.9 shows a common installation using this layered approach.

Figure 3.9 A Layered DMZ Implementation

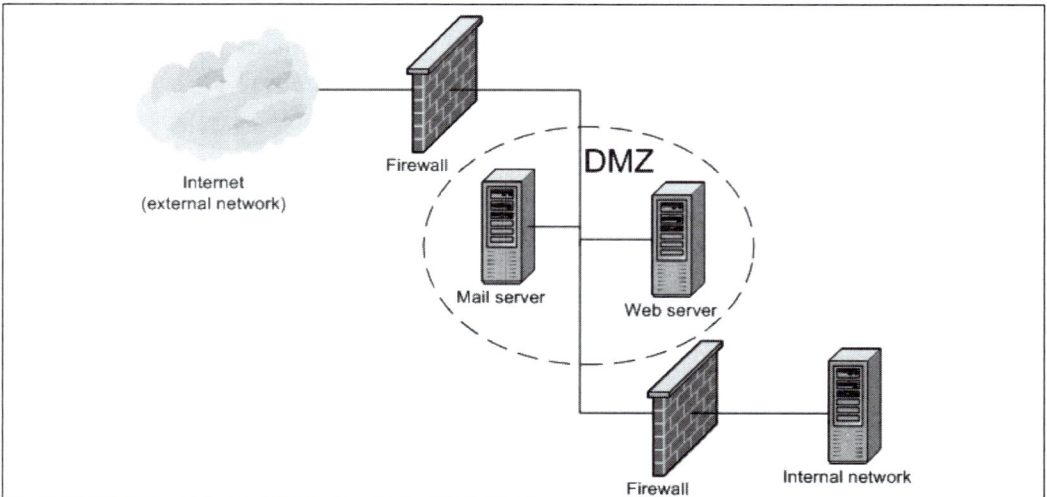

As shown in Figure 3.10, the second method is to add a third interface to the firewall and place the DMZ systems on that network segment. This allows the same firewall to manage the traffic between the Internet, the DMZ, and the protected network. Using one firewall instead of two lowers the costs of the hardware and centralizes the rule sets for the network, making it easier to manage and troubleshoot problems. Currently, this multiple interface design is the preferred method for creating a DMZ segment.

Figure 3.10 A Multiple Interface Firewall DMZ Implementation

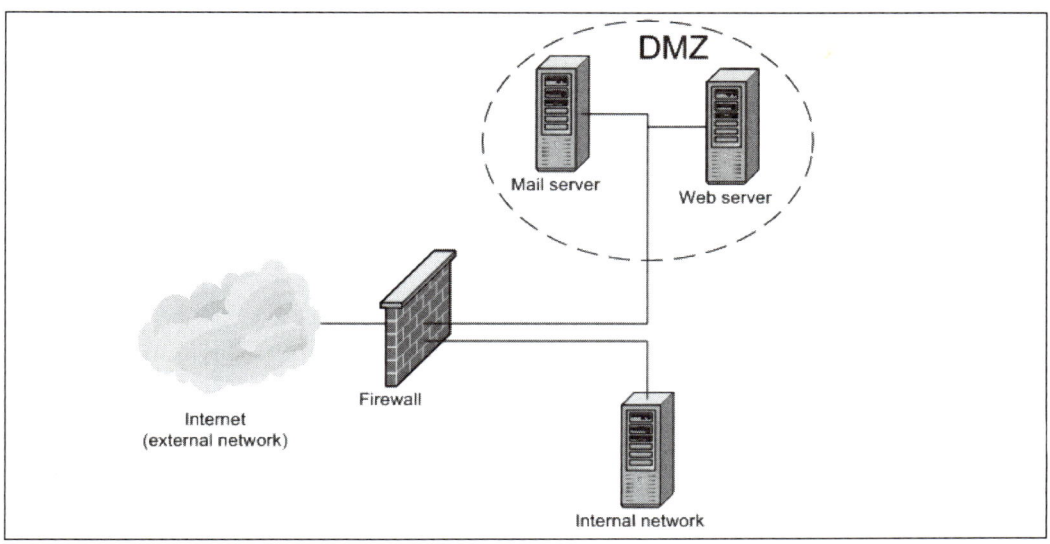

In either case, the DMZ systems offer some level of protection from the public Internet while they remain accessible for the specific services they provide to external users. In addition, the internal network is protected by a firewall from both the external network and the systems in the DMZ. Because the DMZ systems still offer public access, they are more prone to compromise and thus they are not trusted by the systems in the protected network. This scenario allows for public services while still maintaining a degree of protection against attack.

The role of the firewall in all of these scenarios is to manage the traffic between the network segments. The basic idea is that other systems on the Internet are allowed to access only the services of the DMZ systems that have been made public. If an Internet system attempts to connect to a service not made public, the firewall drops the traffic and logs the information about the attempt (if configured to do so). Systems on a protected network are allowed to access the Internet as they require, and they may also access the DMZ systems for managing the computers, gathering data, or updating content. In this way, systems are exposed only to attacks against the services that they offer and not to underlying processes that may be running on them.

TEST DAY TIP

DMZs can be a difficult topic to initially understand. In reviewing information about how they work, try to remember that the DMZ is a "no man's land" that provides a separation between your LAN and an external WAN like the Internet.

www.syngress.com

ACLs

ACLs are access control lists, which are used to control access to specific resources on a computer. An ACL resides on a computer, and is a table with information on which users have specific rights to files and folders on the machine. The operating system uses this attribute of the file or folder to determine whether a user is allowed or denied specific privileges to the object. By using the ACL you can provide users of the network with the rights they need to access these files or folders. However, in doing so, it is advisable that you only provide users with the minimum amount of access required by users to perform their jobs.

Proxy Server (Caching Appliances)

A proxy server is a server that performs a function on behalf of another system. In most cases this is a system that is acting as a type of gateway between the Internet and a company network. The employees who wish to access the Internet will perform actions as they normally would with their browser, but the browser will submit the request to the proxy server. The proxy server will then transmit the request on the Internet and receive the results. The results will then be sent to the original requester. A nice feature of the proxy server is that the Web pages that are not encrypted will be saved in a cache on the local hard disk. If another user requests the same page, the proxy server will not request the page from the Internet, but retrieve it from the hard disk. This saves quite a bit of time by not having to wait on Internet requests, which may be coming from an overburdened Web server.

The proxy server can cache information going both ways; since it can cache requests going out, it can also act as a proxy for Internet users making requests to the company Web server. This can help keep traffic minimized on the company network.

Another feature of the proxy server is that it can act as the physical gateway between the Internet and company network by filtering out specific information, especially if you use the proxy server to act as a proxy between the Internet and the company Web server. Filtering can be configured for allowing or not allowing packets if they meet one or more of the following: specific port, direction of transfer, or source or destination of packets.

Tunnels and Encryption

Tunneling is used to create a virtual tunnel (a virtual point-to-point link) between you and your destination using an untrusted public network as the medium. In most cases, this would be the Internet. When establishing a tunnel, commonly called a VPN (which we'll discuss in the next section), a safe connection is being created between two points that cannot be examined by outsiders. In other words, all traffic that is traveling through this tunnel can be seen, but cannot be understood by those on the outside. All packets are encrypted and carry information designed to provide authentication and integrity. This ensures that they are tamperproof and thus can withstand common IP attacks, such as the man-in-the-middle (MITM) and packet replay. When a VPN is created, traffic is private and safe from prying eyes.

NOTE

VPNs and the protocols used for encryption will be covered in great detail in Chapter 7.

VPNs

A VPN provides users with a secure method of connectivity through a public internetwork such as the Internet. Most companies use dedicated connections to connect to remote sites, but when users want to send private data over the Internet they should provide additional security by encrypting the data using a VPN.

When a VPN is implemented properly, it provides improved wide-area security, reduces costs associated with traditional WANs, improves productivity, and improves support for users who telecommute. Cost savings are twofold. First, companies save money by using public networks (such as the Internet) instead of paying for dedicated circuits (such as point-to-point T1 circuits) between remote offices. Second, telecommuters do not have to pay long-distance fees to connect to RAS (Remote Access Service) servers. They can simply dial into their local ISPs and create a virtual *tunnel* to the office. A tunnel is created by wrapping (or *encapsulating*) a data packet inside another data packet and transmitting it over a public medium. Tunneling requires three different protocols:

- **Carrier Protocol** The protocol used by the network (IP on the Internet) that the information is traveling over.

- **Encapsulating Protocol** The protocol (PPTP, L2TP, IPSec., Secure Shell [SSH]) that is wrapped around the original data.

- **Passenger Protocol** The original data being carried.
  Essentially, there are two different types of VPNs: site-to-site and remote access.

Site-to-Site VPN

Site-to-site VPNs are normally established between corporate offices that are separated by a physical distance extending further than a normal LAN. VPNs are available in software (such as Windows network operating systems) and hardware (firewalls such as Nokia/CheckPoint and SonicWALL) implementations. Generally speaking, software implementations are easier to maintain. However, hardware implementations are considered more secure, since they are not impacted by operating system vulnerabilities. For example, suppose Company XYZ has offices in Boston and Phoenix. As shown in Figure 3.11, both offices connect to the Internet via a T1 connection. They have implemented VPN-capable firewalls in both offices, and established an encryption tunnel between them.

www.syngress.com

Figure 3.11 A Site-To-Site VPN Established Between Two Remote Offices

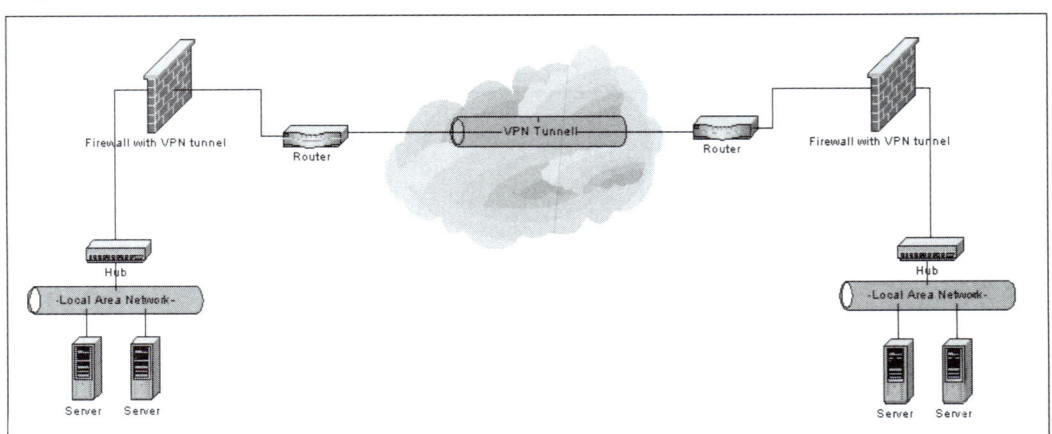

The first step in creating a site-to-site VPN is selecting the protocols to be used. Common protocols associated with VPN are PPTP (Point-to-Point Tunneling Protocol), L2TP (Layer 2 Tunneling Protocol), SSH (Secure Shell), and IPSec (IP Security). PPTP and L2TP are used to establish a secure tunnel connection between two sites.

Once a tunnel is established, encryption protocols are used to secure data passing through the tunnel. As data is passed from one VPN to another, it is *encapsulated* at the source and *unwrapped* at the target. The process of establishing the VPN and wrapping and unwrapping the data is transparent to the end user.

Most commercially available firewalls come with a VPN module that can be set up to easily communicate with another VPN-capable device. Microsoft has implemented site-to-site VPN tools on the Windows 2000 platform using either RRAS or the newest rendition of Microsoft's proxy server, Microsoft ISA Server 2000.

Whichever product or service is chosen, it is important to ensure that each end of the VPN is configured with identical protocols and settings.

Remote Access VPN

A remote access VPN, known as a private virtual dial-up network (PVDN), differs from a site-to-site VPN in that end users are responsible for establishing the VPN tunnel between the workstation and their remote office. An alternative to connecting directly to the corporate VPN is connecting to an enterprise service provider (ESP) that ultimately connects to the corporate VPN.

In either case, users connect to the Internet or an ESP through a point of presence (POP) using their particular VPN client software (see Figure 3.12). Once the tunnel is set up, users are forced to authenticate with the VPN server, usually by username and password.

Figure 3.12 A Remote-Access VPN Solution Using Regular Internet POPs

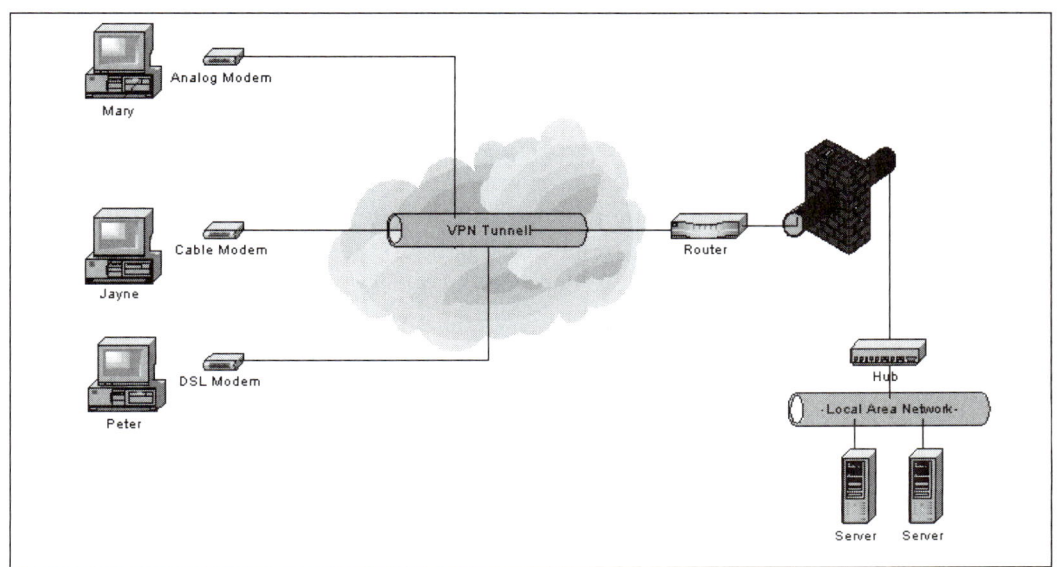

A remote access VPN is a great solution for a company with several employees working in the field. The remote access VPN allows these employees to transmit data to their home offices from any location. RRAS offers an easy solution for creating a remote access VPN.

IDS

IDS is short for an Intrusion Detection System, and it is designed to inspect and detect the kinds of traffic or network behavior patterns that match known attack signatures or that suggest potential unrecognized attacks may be incipient or in progress.

The simplest way to define an IDS is to describe it as a specialized tool that knows how to read and interpret the contents of log files from routers, firewalls, servers, and other network devices. Furthermore, an IDS often stores a database of known attack signatures and can compare patterns of activity, traffic, or behavior it sees in the logs it is monitoring against those signatures to recognize when a close match between a signature and current or recent behavior occurs. At that point, the IDS can issue alarms or alerts, take various kinds of automatic action ranging from shutting down Internet links or specific servers to launching backtraces, and make other active attempts to identify attackers and actively collect evidence of their nefarious activities.

By analogy, an IDS does for a network what an antivirus software package does for files that enter a system; it inspects the contents of network traffic to look for and deflect possible attacks.

To be more specific, intrusion detection means detecting unauthorized use of or attacks on a system or network. An IDS is designed and used to detect and then to deflect or deter (if possible) such attacks or unauthorized use of systems, networks, and related resources. Like firewalls, IDSs may be software-based or may combine hardware and software (in the form of preinstalled and preconfigured standalone IDS devices). Often, IDS software runs on the same devices or servers where firewalls, proxies, or other boundary services operate; an IDS *not* running on the same device or server where the firewall or other services are installed will monitor those devices closely and carefully. Although such devices tend to operate at network peripheries, IDS systems can detect and deal with insider attacks as well as external attacks.

Other Devices and Technologies

In addition to the security devices and other devices required for running a network, there are other devices that need to be considered when designing a network. Various devices are used to manage a network and provide additional features that make the network safer and more functional in day-to-day use.

Gateways

The term *gateway* has two meanings. First, a gateway is a bridge between two completely different technologies. For example, if you were to use an older IBM mainframe with the SNA (System Network Architecture) protocol running on it, and you want Windows clients to be able to print to it, you could facilitate the connection through a gateway.

The term *gateway* can also refer to the path out of a network. In this case, a gateway is a computer on a LAN that provides an entrance or exit into another network. It can also be an Ethernet port on a router, where all requests are sent when no other path is known. For example, if you have a computer that tries to access an IP address that isn't on the LAN, the default gateway configured on that machine will be used to forward the request to a specific server or router. When the gateway receives this, it will attempt to resolve the address by passing the request to another network, such as another server or router on the Internet. In this regard, although servers are commonly associated with being the gateway for a network, other devices can perform these tasks.

Gateways are used more and more in networking today because of the Internet. A gateway connects dissimilar systems. When UNIX wants to talk to NetWare, there must be a gateway for the two to communicate. A gateway is like a translator between two systems that are different from each other. The most common example of this is the Internet. Everyone who connects to the Internet, whether through a dial-up connection or through a LAN, must have a default gateway that his workstation points to.

Gateways can also be used to link networks that have different protocols, such as TCP/IP to IPX/SPX. The gateway can change an entire protocol stack into another or provide protocol conversion and routing services between computer networks. Gateways examine the entire packet and then translate the incompatible protocols so that each network can understand the two different protocols. For example, protocol gateways can also be used to convert ATM cells to Frame Relay frames and vice versa.

NOTE

An example of an application based gateway can be seen with Microsoft's HIS (Host Integration Server) product, which used to be called Microsoft SNA Server. For more information visit www.microsoft.com/hiserver.

Default Gateways and Subnetworks

The default gateway is needed only for systems that are part of the local network. Data packets with a destination IP address not on the local subnet, nor elsewhere in the route table, are automatically forwarded to the default gateway. The default gateway is normally a computer system or router connected to the local subnet and other networks that knows the network IDs for other networks in the internetwork (the whole network) and the best path to reach them. Because the default gateway knows the network IDs of the other networks in the internetwork, it can forward the data packet to other gateways until the packet is ultimately delivered to a gateway connected to the intended destination. However, if the default gateway becomes unavailable, the system cannot communicate outside its own subnet, except for with systems that it had established connections with prior to the failure. Since the default gateways are routers, they will either have to be adjusted manually, or—their routing protocols will learn of the downed segment and reconverge the network so that all routes for the downed segment are no longer available—dynamically.

Packets are routed to their destinations through routers and switches, and the routing tables used by them can be updated manually or dynamically. What gets the whole process rolling when we are routing packets to remote subnetworks, or subnets for short, is the use of the default gateway. The default gateway is what initially sends the packet on its way to the first router. When the packet reaches this first router, the router must determine if the destination computer is on the local network, or send the packet to the next router that will get the packet to its destination.

If the default gateway becomes unavailable, data packets cannot reach their destination. Multiple gateways can be used to prevent this from happening. However, if the default gateway becomes unavailable, the system cannot communicate outside of its own subnet.

Voice and IP Telephony

Voice and IP telephony refers to technologies that provide the ability to talk, fax or perform other tasks that are commonly associated with Public Switched Telephone

Networks. Telephony involves using the Internet Protocol's packet-switched connections to transfer voice and data communications. Using this technology, you can make local or long distance calls by having them sent as packets across the Internet, thereby avoiding the long distance phone charges that may be associated with the communication.

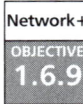

Wireless

Wireless networks require minimal cabling, as data is transmitted over the air using wireless adapters and wireless routers. Computers using wireless NICs use a transceiver that sends and receives signals over the air to a wireless router or hub. The wireless router is an access point, providing a method of communication that the computers with wireless NICs can connect to. The router serves in this way as a wireless access point (WAP) that can support data transfer rates of up to 11 Mbps and can support up to 32 wireless devices. Because the wireless devices use radio frequency (RF) transceivers, very little cabling is necessary on this type of network.

NAS

NAS is short for *Network Attached Storage*, and is refers to devices that are dedicated to providing storage of data on the network. NAS uses hard disks for storage, but instead of being installed on a server, the storage device is accessed through its own network address. This lowers the amount of overhead required to serve clients who want to access data, because memory and resources aren't being used for other purposes. Files are accessed by clients because they are mapped to a server by the NAS file server software, but programs and files are served faster because they are accessed directly from the storage device.

SANs

As we discussed in Chapter 1, a SAN is short for *Storage Area Network*, which is a network that is dedicated to transmission of data between servers and storage devices. Storage devices are networked together on a segment of the network, so that computers on a LAN can view and store data on them. Devices that may be used for storage purposes can include RAID (Redundant Array of Inexpensive Disks) arrays and NAS appliances, which we discussed in the previous section.

Summary of Exam Objectives

Media devices are a necessary part of a network, without which connectivity would be impossible. There are many devices that make up a network. Hubs are used to provide connectivity by passing from one port in the hub to the others, and thereby enabling data to move from one cable to another. An active hub takes this a step further by performing the role of a repeater, which is an older technology that takes data and regenerates it before resending it. In resending the data, the active hub will only send the data to the port that connects to the device the data is destined for. Another device called a MAU (Multistation Access Unit) is similar to this, in that it provides connectivity to a network, but is used on Token Ring networks. Bridges are another type of device that is used to connect two different LANs, or segment a large LAN into two smaller halves. In discussing these devices, we found that some (hubs, repeaters, and bridges) are either obsolete or serve functions that can be performed by more modern devices like switches.

In addition to devices on a LAN, we also discussed technologies that are used to connect to the Internet or acquire remote access to other computers. An analog modem is a communications device that enables a computer to talk to another computer through a standard telephone line. Other types of modems can also be used to connect to the Internet, such as cable modems that use broadband technology, or DSL, which provides high-speed connections via the twisted-pair cabling of telephone lines. DSL has gained increasing popularity over the last few years, and has largely grown from another technology called Integrated Services Digital Network (ISDN), which provides 128Kbps connections over telephone lines. Faster methods of communication can also be acquired using devices like CSU/DSU (Channel Service Unit / Data Service Unit), which provides an interface to T-carrier lines.

Today's local area networks rely on a significant amount of equipment for security and connectivity. The primary device used on a network is the network interface card (NIC), which is an interface between computers, printers, and other devices and the physical media on the network. The NIC transfers data to the cable, and retrieves it from the cable so the computer or other network device can then use it. Data on the network may be forwarded to its proper destination using either a switch or a router. A switch takes data from a cable connected to its port, but unlike a hub that forwards the data through all of its other ports, a switch will forward the packet through a single port that leads to the computer that the data is intended for. Switches can also provide the functions of a router, which is used to route data packets across a network by opening the packet and making routing decisions based on the contents.

Network security can be achieved through a variety of devices and concepts. Firewalls are used to secure an internal network from outside influence from a public insecure network. Firewalls control the traffic that's sent from an external network, such as the Internet, to an internal network or local computer using rules that are configured by a network administrator. A DMZ can also be used on the network as a neutral network segment where systems accessible to the public Internet are housed, which offers some basic levels of protection against attacks. In addition to this, proxy servers can shield the origins of where data was sent from, as they act on behalf of other systems.

By using these devices, your network is able to transfer data to other computers on the LAN and provide safe connectivity to external networks like the Internet. The functionality of many of these devices is a requirement for a functional network, while others are enhancements that provide greater levels of security to your network environment.

Exam Objectives Fast Track

Network Devices

☑ Hubs are used to provide connections between LAN devices. A passive hub will simply pass the data from one port in the hub to the others, enabling data to move from one cable to another. An active hub will regenerate the data, repeating it to the other ports so the signal is at its original strength.

☑ Repeaters are an older technology that takes data and regenerates it before resending it.

☑ Bridges are used to connect two different LANs, or segment a large LAN into two smaller halves. They also have the ability to forward packets of data based on MAC addresses and filter traffic on a LAN.

☑ A MAU is a device that multiple workstations are connected to in order to communicate on a Token Ring network.

☑ An analog modem is a communications device that enables a computer to talk to another computer through a standard telephone line. The modem converts digital data from the computer to analog data for transmission over the telephone line and then back to digital data at the receiving computer.

☑ Cable modems are used to access the Internet using the broadband technology of cable television lines.

☑ DSL provides high-speed connections to the Internet using a DSL modem.

☑ ISDN is a system of digital telephone connections that enables data to be transmitted simultaneously end to end.

☑ A CSU/DSU is a device that takes a signal from a digital medium and multiplexes it. The CSU is used to connect a terminal to a digital line, while a DSU performs diagnostic and protective functions.

☑ A T-carrier line is a leased telephone line that runs over fiber optic cabling. A T1 line consists of 24 separate channels called DSOs that are 64 Kbps each, providing up to 1.544 Mbps of bandwidth. A T3 line provides speeds of 44.736 Mbps.

☑ A NIC is the key component that allows a computer or device to communicate with the rest of the network.

☑ Switches provide services that are similar to those found in Ethernet hubs. A switch takes data from a cable connected to its port, but unlike a hub that forwards the data through all of its other ports, a switch will forward the packet through a single port that leads to the computer that the data is intended for.

☑ Layer 2 switches work at the Data Link Layer (Layer 2), and look at the MAC address of the packet to determine where it is to be sent.

☑ Layer 3 switches work at the Network Layer of the OSI model, and have an integrated router function that allows it to make decisions as to where the data should be sent.

☑ Layer 4 switches use information in the packet that identifies the application it belongs to, so that priorities can be set in routing the packets to the destination computer.

☑ Layer 5 switches use information from the Session Layer, allowing it to route packets using URLs.

☑ Routers are used to route data packets across a network by opening the packet and making routing decisions based on the contents.

☑ A dynamic router uses a routing table that is populated automatically by receiving updates from other routers.

☑ Static routers have fixed routing tables that have to be updated manually.

☑ A firewall protects a secure internal network from outside influence from a public insecure network. Firewalls are devices or software that have the ability to control the traffic that's sent from an external network, such as the Internet, to an internal network or local computer.

☑ A dual-homed firewall consists of a single computer with two physical network interfaces. This computer acts as a gateway between two networks.

☑ A packet level firewall is usually a form of screening router that examines packets based upon filters that are set up at the Network and Transport Layers.

☑ An application level firewall understands the data at the Application Layer. Application level firewalls operate at the Application, Presentation, and Session Layers. Data at the application level can actually be understood and monitored to verify that no harmful information is included.

☑ A circuit level firewall is similar to an application proxy except that the security mechanisms are applied at the time the connection is established.

☑ A DMZ is a neutral network segment where systems accessible to the public Internet are housed, and which offers some basic levels of protection against attacks.

☑ A proxy server is a server that performs a function on behalf of another system. In most cases this is a system that is acting as a type of gateway between the Internet and a company network.

☑ ACLs are used to control access to specific resources on a computer.

☑ Tunneling is used to create a virtual tunnel (a virtual point-to-point link) between you and your destination using an untrusted public network as the medium.

☑ A VPN provides users with a secure method of connectivity through a public internetwork such as the Internet.

☑ A gateway is a computer or device (such as a router) on a LAN that provides an entrance or exit into another network. The gateway is where all requests are sent when no other path is known.

☑ Voice and IP telephony refers to technologies that provide the ability to talk, fax or perform other tasks that are commonly associated with PSTNs.

☑ Wireless networks require minimal cabling. Data is transmitted over the air using wireless adapters and wireless routers, so little to no cabling is required for network communication.

☑ NAS refers to devices that are dedicated to providing storage of data on the network.

☑ A SAN is a network that is dedicated to transmission of data between servers and storage devices.

Exam Objectives
Frequently Asked Questions

The following Frequently Asked Questions, answered by the authors of this book, are designed to both measure your understanding of the Exam Objectives presented in this chapter, and to assist you with real-life implementation of these concepts.

Q: I need an inexpensive way to connect a small home network in a star topology using Ethernet standards. What type of device do I need?

A: A hub. A hub is a device that concentrates cabling to a central location, and will take data sent to it on one port and resends it to other cables. This allows the data to get from one cable to another on the network.

Q: I need an inexpensive way to connect a network in a star topology using Token Ring standards. What type of device do I need?

A: A MAU. A MAU or MSAU is a device that multiple workstations are connected to in order to communicate on a Token Ring network.

Q: I need a star network using Ethernet standards with enhanced performance. What type of network device do I require?

A: A switch. A switch is similar to a hub in that it will take data from one cable, regenerate the signal, and then resend it. What makes a switch different is that it will take the data sent to one port on the switch, and then determine which of the other ports will allow the data to get to its intended destination.

Q: I have an ISDN connection installed to my business. What is required for me to communicate on the ISDN medium?

A: ISDN modems are required to transmit local data packets onto the ISDN line and to receive the data packets from the ISDN connection and transmit them on the local network.

Q: My company has a firewall. Do I need to worry about worms or similar attacks?

A: Yes. Many users these days have laptop computers that are connected to a number of different networks. Each new network is a new vector for worm attack. Many companies stand to face outages caused by worms brought in on employee laptops.

Self Test

A Quick Answer Key follows the Self Test questions. For complete questions, answers, and explanations to the Self Test questions in this chapter as well as the other chapters in this book, see the Self Test Appendix.

1. Cables from workstations are connected to a central network connectivity device that takes data from one port and resends it to all of the other ports. In doing so, the data is regenerated so it is as strong as when it was originally sent. Which of the following devices is being used?

    A. Active hub

    B. Passive hub

    C. Switching hub

    D. Switch

2. Your network consists of a single large LAN that is in a star topology configuration. You have found that there are a significant number of collisions occurring on the network, and want to segment it into two smaller LANs. Which of the following devices will you use to segment this network, allowing each LAN to communicate with the other?

    A. NIC

    B. MAU

    C. Bridge

    D. Repeater

3. You want to get Internet access for a computer that is used by the IT staff to download drivers and updated software from the Internet. Because of the amount of data that is going to be downloaded, you want to use the fastest possible method of downloading data. Which of the following will you use?

    A. Analog modem with dial-up access to an ISP

    B. ISDN Digital Subscriber Line

    C. Consumer Digital Subscriber Line

    D. Very High Digital Subscriber Line

4. You are looking into purchasing a new switch for your network. You want the switch to be able to route packets of data based on the uniform resource locator included with the packet. Which switch type should you buy?

A. Layer 2 Switch

B. Layer 3 Switch

C. Layer 4 Switch

D. Layer 5 Switch

5. You have installed new cabling to accommodate a new section of the building that is being networked. Once computers are installed, you find that they are unable to connect to the network. You believe the problem is that the length of the cabling has exceeded the maximum distance allowed. You want to fix the problem with the least amount of cost and work. Which of the following will you do?

A. Remove the cabling and install cable that supports a longer distance.

B. Install a passive hub to increase the distance that data can travel along the cable.

C. Install a NIC to increase the distance that data can travel along the cable.

D. Install a switch to increase the distance that data can travel along the cable.

6. What will happen if the default gateway is not specified on your computer and you are trying to reach another network?

A. The packet will ask every router if they know the path to reach the destination.

B. The packet will broadcast for the IP address of the nearest router.

C. The packet will be forwarded to the DNS server.

D. The packet will not be sent.

7. You need to connect two networks that work on two different network protocols. Which of the following should be used?

   A. DMZ

   B. Firewall

   C. Gateway

   D. NAS

8. You have replaced all the hubs in your network with 10/100 Mbps switches. The switch ports are configured to work by automatically sensing the network speed. Most of the workstations already had 10/100 Mbps network adapters. Which of the following will you need to do in order to upgrade the speed of the entire network to 100 Mbps?

   A. Replace all 10 Mbps network adapters to 10/100 Mbps in the remaining workstations.

   B. Reconfigure all the ports on the switch to operate only at 100 Mbps.

   C. Reconfigure the 10 Mbps adapters in remaining workstations to operate only at 100 Mbps.

   D. None of the above.

9. You are implementing a firewall for a small company that wishes to establish an Internet presence. The company wants to use its dedicated Internet connection to allow employees to access the Internet as well as host a Web server. What is the best type of firewall to use in this situation?

   A. A packet filtering firewall

   B. A stateful inspection firewall

   C. An application layer gateway

   D. No firewall is necessary

10. What is the area of the network that typically contains public DNS servers and Web servers?

    A. Firewall

    B. DMZ

    C. VLAN

    D. VPN

11. Hannah wants to configure a VLAN on her network. What advantage can Hannah expect to get out of a VLAN?

    A. It will segment traffic on the internal network for increased security.

    B. It will create a DMZ to protect her Web servers from attacks.

    C. It will hide her internal network IP addresses from being seen on the Internet.

    D. It will provide a secure tunnel from her intranet to the intranet of a partner company.

12. To allow its employees remote access to the corporate network, a company has implemented a hardware VPN solution. Why is this considered a secure remote access solution?

    A. Because only the company's employees will know the address to connect to in order to use the VPN.

    B. Because VPNs use the Internet to transfer data.

    C. Because a VPN uses compression to make its data secure.

    D. Because a VPN uses encryption to make its data secure.

13. You have installed an Active IDS system onto your network. When an attack occurs and is detected by your new IDS, what might you expect it to do? (Choose all that apply)

    A. Inform the attacker that his or her actions may be monitored as part of the network AUP.

    B. Disable a service or services.

    C. Terminate the connection after a predefined amount of time.

    D. Shut down a server or servers.

14. You have an IDS system running only on one computer in your network. What type of IDS system is this?

    A. Active

    B. Host

    C. Network

    D. Anomaly

Self Test Quick Answer Key

For complete questions, answers, and explanations to the Self Test questions in this chapter as well as the other chapters in this book, see the Self Test Appendix.

1.	**A**	8.	**A**
2.	**C**	9.	**A**
3.	**D**	10.	**B**
4.	**D**	11.	**A**
5.	**D**	12.	**D**
6.	**D**	13.	**B, C,** and **D**
7.	**C**	14.	**B**

Chapter 4

NETWORK+

Wireless Technologies

Domain I Objectives in this Chapter:

1.7 Specify the general characteristics (For example: carrier speed, frequency, transmission type and topology) of the following wireless technologies:

    1.7.1   802.11 (Frequency Hopping Spread Spectrum)

    1.7.2   802.11x (Direct Sequence Spread Spectrum)

    1.7.3   Infrared

    1.7.4   Bluetooth

1.8 Identify factors that affect the range and speed of wireless service (for example, interference, antenna type, and environmental factors).

Introduction to the Wireless Network

Wireless networking has provided a new era of data connectivity unmatched by cabled networks. Increases in the speed of deployment, access to data, and scalability mean that the needs of specific user communities can be addressed in ways that were unavailable to network architects a few years ago.

New streams of end user applications and services are being developed to provide businesses and consumers with advanced data access and manipulation. The main benefits of wireless integration will fall primarily into two major categories:

- Convenience
- Productivity

Convenience

First and foremost in the minds of IT professionals, business leaders, and end consumers when discussing wireless networking is the aspect of convenience. This basic benefit more or less outweighs all other benefits combined in terms of user interest in wireless, and is predominantly the main reason for their deployments. Convenience can be broken down into three areas of interest:

- Flexibility
- Roaming
- Mobility

Flexibility

Wireless technologies provide the greatest flexibility of design, integration, and deployment of any networking solution available. With only transceivers (wireless network adapters) to install in the local station and a wireless hub or access point (AP) to be configured for local access, it is simple to retrofit wireless networking within existing structures, or to create access services where traditional networking infrastructures cannot go.

With traditional networking infrastructures that mostly rely on copper or fiber optic cabling, a physical path is required between the access concentrator (a *hub* or *switch*) and each of the end users of the network. This means that a cabling run has to be created from one end of the network to the other for users to communicate with each other, whether they are using workstations or servers.

Wired access drops are generally static in location in that the access is provided from a specified point that cannot easily be moved from one physical location to another. This also implies that if an existing access drop is in use, other users must wait their turn to gain access to the network if the next closest available drop is not conveniently located. The only other way to navigate this issue would be to install yet another concentrator (hub or switch) so that more users can share that preexisting cable drop. Existing environments may not always be "new installation friendly". Many older buildings, houses, and apartments do not provide facilities for installing new cabling. In these environments, building contractors and engineers may need to get involved to devise ways of running new cabling systems. When existing cable run facilities are available, they do not always offer the most optimum path between existing LAN (local area network) resources and new users. Security concerns also have to be addressed if a common wiring closet or riser is to be shared with other tenants. As such, the cost involved in installing new cabling can be prohibitive in terms of time, materials, or installation costs.

Another factor involved in the installation of new cabling is loss of revenue due to the unavailability of facilities during the installation itself. Hotel chains, convention centers, and airports stand to lose revenues during a cable installation retrofit project if a section of the building has to be closed off to customer access for safety reasons during the installation.

Intangible costs have to be explored as well when investigating the installation of new cable runs. These include customer dissatisfaction and loss of customer goodwill during and after the retrofit project.

With wireless networking, all that is required to create a new network is unrestricted radio wave access between end nodes and/or between an end node and a wireless AP within the vicinity of the end nodes. Radio waves can travel through walls, floors, and windows, which gives wireless network designers the flexibility to design wireless networks and install APs where needed. This means that a wireless AP, when properly placed, can be used to support multiple user environments at the same time.

An example of this in a wireless LAN configuration would consist of locating a wireless AP on the inside part of an eastern-facing exterior wall on the second floor of an office building. This one wireless AP could simultaneously serve the needs of a group of users on the eastern corner of the first floor, second floor, and third floor, along with those on the terrace located outside the first floor eastern corner. In this configuration, access is provided to users located on different floors inside and outside the building with a minimal commitment in terms of equipment and resources.

Another example of a wireless LAN configuration would consist of providing networking access within a large public area such as a library. In this scenario, properly placed APs could provide network coverage for the entire floor area without impacting the day-to-day use of the facilities. In addition, the APs could be located in an area of the library that has restricted access and is physically secure from daily activities.

Roaming

A wireless network access zone is an area of wireless network coverage. Compared to traditional wire-based networks, a wireless user is not required to be located at a specific spot to gain access to the network, although the user must be in range of the AP. A user can gain access to the wireless network provided he or she is within the area of wireless coverage where the radio signal transmissions to and from the AP are of enough strength to support communications. For a more flexible and robust solution, you can organize multiple APs to overlap coverage in a single area, thus allowing users to roam seamlessly between APs without a loss of connection. With the always-on connectivity provided by wireless LANs, a roaming user is one that has the ability to:

- Physically roam from one location to another within the wireless access zone.

- Logically roam a session from one wireless AP to another.

When discussing physical roaming, we would include both the movement of a user within a single AP's wireless network access zone or within the combined network access zones for all the APs that are part of this network.

When discussing logical roaming we refer to the transference of a networking session from one wireless AP to another without the need for any user interaction during the session reassociation process. When a user moves from one wireless AP's area of coverage to another AP's area of coverage, the user's transmission signal strength is assessed. As the signal reaches a threshold, the user credentials are carried over from the old "home base" AP to the new "home base" AP using a session token or other transparent authentication scheme.

This combination of physical and logical roaming allows users to keep data sessions active as they move freely around the area of coverage. This is of great benefit to users who require maintaining a data session with networked resources as they move about a building or facility.

An example of this would be an internal technical service agent. In their day-to-day activities, these agents may be called upon to service end stations where access to technical troubleshooting databases, call tickets, and other support resources may be required. By having access to these services over the wireless network, the technicians can move from one call ticket to another without being forced to reconnect to the wire line network as they move about. Another benefit to maintaining an always-on session is that they could provide live updates to the ticketing databases or order replacement supplies at the time of service.

Next, we take a look at a senior manager who is attending a status meeting in a conference room where a limited number of data ports will be available to access e-mail, databases, and other information stores. If this manager had access to wireless networking capabilities on their laptop, he or she could maintain a connection to the same services that are available at the local desktop. Real-time reports with up-to-the-minute metrics on business activities and critical information flows could be accessed more efficiently. The road to the top might actually be a little simpler.

As we mentioned earlier, the lack of wire lines provides the network architect with the ability to design networking solutions that are available anytime and anywhere through always-on connectivity. As noted in the previous examples, any networking solution using traditional wire line media would hit a hard limitation when exposed to the same requirements of access coverage. The costs in cabling materials alone would preclude any such contemplation.

Mobility

The last concept dealing with convenience is that of mobility. This benefit alone is often the biggest factor in an organization's decision to go for a wireless-based networking solution.

In traditional wire-line networking environments, once a cabling infrastructure is set in place, rarely does it move with tenants when they leave to a new facility or area of a building. Cabling installations are considered part of the cost of the move and are essentially tossed out.

With a wireless networking environment, the wireless APs can be unplugged from the electrical outlet and re-deployed in the new facility. Very few cables, if any, are left behind as a going away present to the building owner. This allows the network architects to reuse networking equipment as required to address the networking realities of each environment.

For example, it is possible to move part or all of a network from one functional area to another or from one building to another. This facilitates the job of IT managers who are constantly faced with network resource rationalizations and optimizations such as the decommissioning of access ports, or the moving of equipment and personnel from one area to another.

TEST DAY TIP

Mobility, roaming, and all the benefits of wireless network over that of wired networks covered in this chapter are all background information for you so that when items such as Wired Equivalent Privacy (WEP), frequency-hopping spread spectrum (FHSS), and Fresnel Zone are covered, you understand them well enough to sit the Network+ exam. It's very important to have a good background on wireless technologies. Even though this is not a wireless test, wireless technologies are spreading in use so quickly… it would be a career-limiting move not to understand the fundamentals.

Productivity

The net result of the increased level of flexibility, mobility, and convenience provided through wireless networking is increased productivity. Networked resources can become accessible from any location, thus providing the ability to design and integrate environments where users and services can be located where best suited. Wireless networking can provide opportunities for higher levels of service and productivity unmatched through cabled networking.

Radio Frequency and Antenna Behaviors and Characteristics

Before actually getting into the specifications and standards that define how wireless networks are constructed and operate, one must first have a good understanding of basic radio frequency (RF) behaviors and antenna characteristics. In the following sections, we will briefly examine these topics.

Radio Frequency Behaviors

The following radio frequency behaviors are important in your basic understanding of how wireless networks operate and interact with their environments.

Gain and Loss

Gain occurs when a signal has its strength increased, such as by passing through an amplifier. As you can see in the left-hand side of Figure 4.1, the lower wave represents the signal before passing through the amplifier and the higher wave represents the signal after passing through the amplifier. The difference in amplitudes between both signal strengths is the gain.

Loss is the exact opposite of gain, and occurs when a signal has its strength decreased, either intentionally through the use of a device such as an attenuator, or unintentionally such as through resistance losses in a transmission cable. As you can see in the right-hand side of Figure 4.1, the higher wave represents the pre-loss signal strength and the lower wave represents the wave signal strength after the loss has occurred.

Figure 4.1 Comparing Gain and Loss

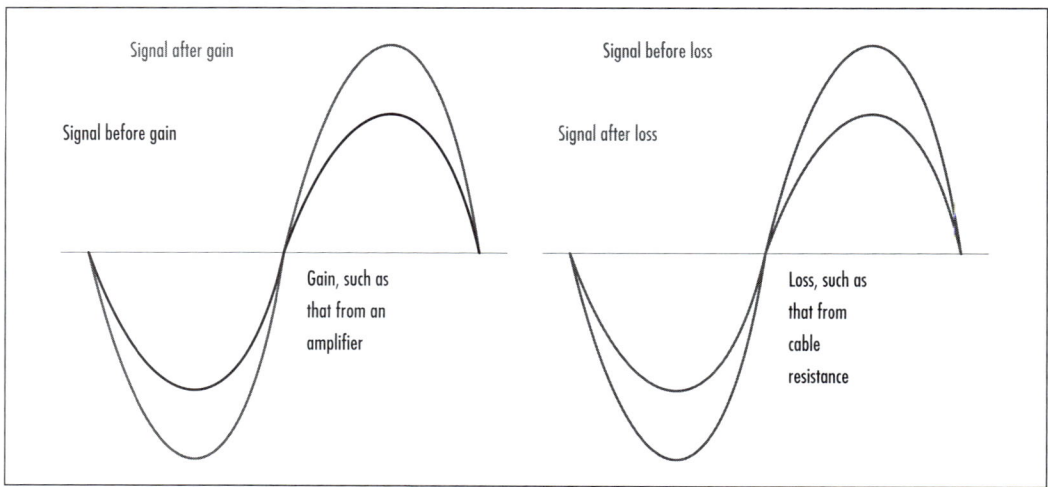

Reflection and Refraction

Some RF behaviors are similar to those of light waves, such as in the case of reflection and refraction. As you can see in the left-hand side of Figure 4.2, *reflection* has occurred because our electromagnetic radio frequency wave has impacted upon a surface that has a much larger cross-section than that of the wave itself. Many things cause reflection, such as doors, walls, floors, ceilings, buildings, and the curvature of the Earth to name a few. Assuming that the surface being impacted is relatively flat and smooth, a large majority of the original signal will be reflected off at a different angle than the entry signal. Some signal will be lost due to absorption and scattering (discussed later in this chapter). Surfaces that are less smooth or flat will cause a larger percentage of the original wave to be lost.

The right-hand side of Figure 4.2 depicts the behavior known as *refraction*. You've probably seen refraction for yourself if you've ever looked at a lake or pool of water. Refraction is a particular problem for long-range outdoor point-to-point links due to changing atmospheric conditions, notably differing air densities due to changes in air temperature. When a wave is refracted, it passes through a medium and changes course with some of the original wave being reflected away from the original wave's path. The longer an outdoor link is, the larger problem refraction could present.

Figure 4.2 Comparing Reflection and Refraction

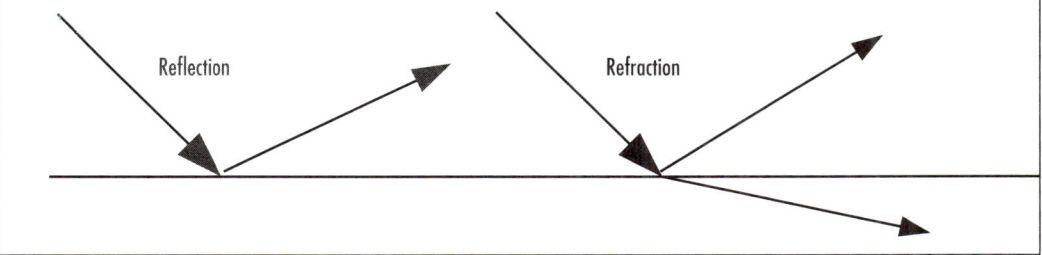

Absorption and Scattering

As disruptive as reflection and refraction are, absorption and scattering can absolutely destroy an electromagnetic signal wave and prevent it from reaching its intended destination. At least with reflection and refraction, the signal could still be received by the AP by chance.

As you can see in the left-hand side of Figure 4.3, the RF signal has been completely *absorbed* because it has impacted an object that does not pass it on through any means (reflection or refraction). In this case, no signal is left and the data contained in it is lost.

The right-hand side of Figure 4.3 depicts the behavior known as *scattering*. If you've ever played billiards, then you are undoubtedly familiar with this behavior. When an incoming electromagnetic wave hits a surface that is small compared to its wavelength, scattering will occur. This is the exact opposite of the effect of reflection. The resultant effect causes many lower magnitude waves to be sent off at various angles relative to the path of the original wave. Another practical example of scattering is the effect on satellite television during a heavy rain or snow storm; the incoming signal is degraded, and in some cases, completely destroyed, before arriving at the intended destination. Typical sources of scattering include trees, street signs and atmospheric conditions.

Figure 4.3 Comparing Absorption and Scattering

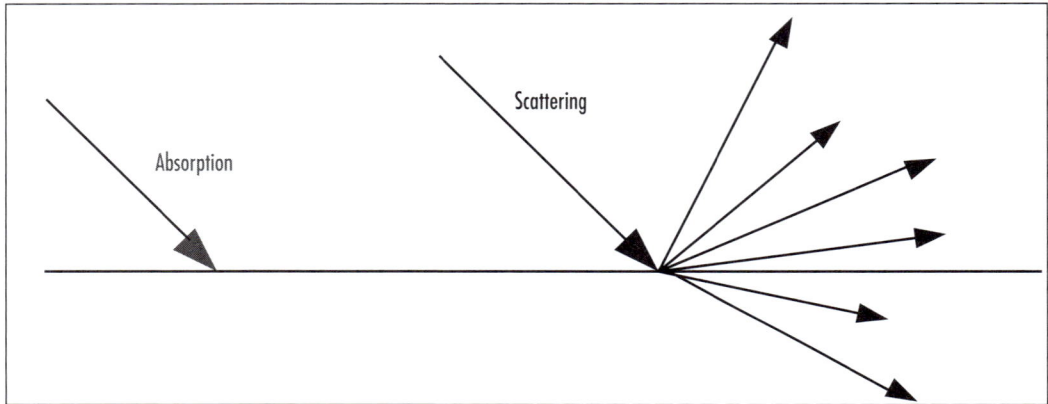

Antenna Characteristics

Since antennas are a key element of any electromagnetic wave-based system, including wireless networks, you should also have a good understanding of some basic antenna concepts. We'll examine the concepts of *line of sight* (LOS) and the Fresnel Zone in the next figure.

An antenna, by its very design, is an amplification device. There need be no specific manipulation of the incoming signal to cause amplification to occur—this is a result of the shape of the antenna itself. When RF energy is tightly focused into a smaller beam, it becomes amplified. Different antenna types cause different shapes of output signals, and thus different amounts of amplification.

Line of Sight and Fresnel Zone

Figure 4.4 illustrates another similarity that electromagnetic waves share with light waves – the visual line of sight. With light waves, if a straight line exists, it's implied that the line of sight exists. Once you have LOS, the light waves will be able to travel from point to point. The same basic concept holds true with RF waves, with one exception; RF waves are also subject to a phenomenon known as the Fresnel Zone (pronounced "frah-nell").

Figure 4.4 Line of Sight versus The Fresnel Zone

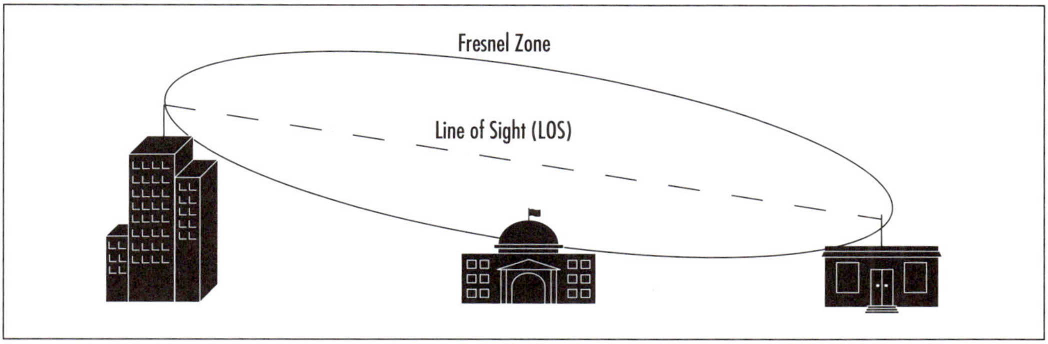

Fresnel Zone

Line of Sight (LOS)

When dealing with optics, visual line of sight is enough to ensure good signal transmission from point to point. With electromagnetic waves, this is not entirely true. Objects that extend into the Fresnel Zone, an elliptical region extending outward from the visual LOS, can cause signal loss through the methods we examined previously such as reflection, refraction and scattering.

The actual mathematic processes needed to calculate the width of the Fresnel Zone at its widest point is not important to know here. The key thing to take away from this discussion is that blockage of 20% or more of the Fresnel Zone can begin to cause RF signal loss from source to destination. Many common objects that can be encountered in a point-to-point link can cause Fresnel Zone blockage, including buildings and trees. To overcome any blockage you must either remove the object causing the blockage or raise one or both antennas in the link.

NOTE

A Fresnel Zone calculator is available at:
www.firstmilewireless.com/calc_fresnel.html.

Wireless Network Concepts

This section covers some of the most popular wireless technologies used today for wireless networking. In the past five years, two wireless network technologies have seen considerable deployment: Wireless Application Protocol (WAP) networks and Wireless Local Area Network (WLAN) networks based on the Institute of Electrical and Electronic Engineers (IEEE) 802.11 specification. While these are not the only wireless networking technologies available, they are the most popular and must be understood to pass the wireless objectives on the Network+ certification exam.

Overview of Wireless Communication in a Wireless Network

Wireless networks, like their wired counterparts, rely on the manipulation of an electrical charge to enable communication between devices. Changes or oscillations in signal strength from zero to some maximum value (amplitude) and the rate of those oscillations (frequency) are used singularly or in combination with each other to encode and decode information.

Two devices can communicate with each other when they understand the method(s) used to encode and decode information contained in the changes to the electrical properties of the communications medium being used. A network adapter can decode changes in the electric current it senses on a wire and convert them to meaningful information (bits) that can subsequently be sent to higher levels for processing. Likewise, a network adapter can encode information (bits) by manipulating the properties of the electric current for transmission on the communications medium (in the case of wired networks, this would be the cable).

Radio Frequency Communications

The primary difference between wired and wireless networks is that wireless networks use a special type of electric current known as radio frequency, which is created by applying alternating current (AC) to an antenna to produce an electromagnetic field (EM). Devices for broadcasting and reception use the resulting RF field. In the case of wireless networks, the medium for communications is the *EM field*, the region of space that is influenced by electromagnetic radiation. Unlike audio waves, radio waves do not require a medium such as air or water to propagate. As with wired networks, amplitude decreases with distance, resulting in the degradation of signal strength and the ability to communicate. However, the EM field is also dispersed according to the properties of the transmitting antenna, and not tightly bound, as is the case with communication over a wire.

Like the waves created by throwing a rock into a pool of water, radio waves are affected by the presence of obstructions and can be reflected, refracted, diffracted, or scattered, depending on the properties of the obstruction and its interaction with the radio waves. Reflected radio waves can be a source of interference on wireless networks. The interference created by bounced radio waves is called *multipath interference*.

When radio waves are reflected, additional wave fronts are created. These different wave fronts may arrive at the receiver at different times and be in phase or out of phase with the main signal. When the peak of a wave is added to another wave (in phase), the wave is amplified. When the peak of a wave meets a trough (out of phase), the wave is effectively cancelled. Multipath interference can be the source of hard-to-troubleshoot problems. In planning for a wireless network, administrators should consider the presence of common sources of multipath interference. These include metal doors, metal roofs, water, metal vertical blinds, and any other source that is highly reflective to radio waves. Antennas may help to compensate for the effects of multipath interference, but must be carefully chosen. Many wireless access points have two antennas for precisely this purpose. However, a single omnidirectional antenna may be of no use at all for this kind of interference.

Another source of signal loss is the presence of obstacles. While radio waves can travel through physical objects, they are degraded according to the properties of the object they travel through. For example, a window is fairly transparent to radio waves, but may reduce the effective range of a wireless network by between 50 percent and 70 percent, depending on the presence and nature of the coatings on the glass. A solid core wall can reduce the effective range of a wireless network by up to 90 percent or greater.

EM fields are also prone to interference and signal degradation by the presence of other EM fields. In particular, 802.11 wireless networks are prone to interference produced by cordless phones, microwave ovens, and a wide range of devices that use the same unlicensed Industrial, Scientific and Medical (ISM) or Unlicensed National Information Infrastructure (UNII) bands. To mitigate the effects of interference from these devices and other sources of electromagnetic interference, RF-based wireless networks employ *spread spectrum* technologies. Spread spectrum provides a way to "share" bandwidth with other devices that may be operating in the same frequency range. Rather than operating on a single, dedicated frequency such as is the case with radio and television broadcasts, wireless networks use a "spectrum" of frequencies for communication.

Spread Spectrum Technology

Conceived of by Hedy Lamarr and George Antheil in 1940 as a method of securing military communications from jamming and for eavesdropping during WWII, spread spectrum defines methods for wireless devices to use to send a number of narrowband frequencies over a range of frequencies simultaneously for communication. The narrowband frequencies used between devices change according to a random-appearing, but defined pattern, allowing individual frequencies to contain parts of the transmission. Someone listening to a transmission using spread spectrum would hear only noise, unless his or her own device understood in advance what frequencies were used for the transmission and could synchronize with them.

Two methods of synchronizing wireless devices are:

- Frequency hopping spread spectrum (FHSS)
- Direct sequence spread spectrum (DSSS)

EXAM WARNING

Make sure that you pay close attention to the next couple of sections in this chapter, as they directly relate to the exam. Most of what you learned to this point was background information to get you to the point where you can understand FHSS and DHSS. Make sure you study the next sections carefully.

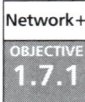

Frequency Hopping Spread Spectrum

As the name implies, FHSS works by quickly moving from one frequency to another according to a pseudorandom pattern. The frequency range used by the frequency hop is relatively large (83.5 MHz), providing excellent protection from interference. The amount of time spent on any given frequency is known as *dwell time* and the amount of time it takes to move from one frequency to another is known as *hop time*. FHSS devices begin their transmission on one frequency and move to other frequencies according to a pre-defined pseudorandom sequence and then repeat the sequence after reaching the final frequency in the pattern. Hop time is usually very short (200 to 300 ms) and not significant relative to the dwell time (100 to 200 ms). In general, the longer the dwell time, the greater the throughput and the more susceptible the transmission is to narrowband interference.

> **NOTE**
>
> One MHz represents one million cycles per second. The speed of microprocessors, called the clock speed, is measured in megahertz. For example, a microprocessor that runs at 200 MHz executes 200 million cycles per second. Each computer instruction requires a fixed number of cycles, so the clock speed determines how many instructions per second the microprocessor can execute. To a large degree, this controls how powerful the microprocessor is. Another chief factor in determining a microprocessor's power is its data width (that is, how many bits it can manipulate at one time).
>
> In addition to microprocessors, the speeds of buses and interfaces are also measured in MHz.

The frequency hopping sequence creates a channel, allowing multiple channels to coexist in the same frequency range without interfering with each other. As many as 79 FCC-compliant FHSS devices using the 2.4 GHz ISM band can be co-located together. However, the expense of implementing such a large number of systems limits the practical number of co-located devices to well below this number. Wireless networks that use FHSS include *HomeRF* and *Bluetooth*, which both operate in the unlicensed 2.4 GHz ISM band. FHSS usually operates at lower rates of data transmission (usually 1.6 Mbps, but as high as 10 Mbps) than networks that use DSSS.

Direct Sequence Spread Spectrum

DSSS works somewhat differently than FHSS. With DSSS, the data is divided and simultaneously transmitted on as many frequencies as possible within a particular frequency band (the channel). DSSS adds redundant bits of data known as *chips* to the data to represent binary 0s or 1s. The ratio of chips-to-data is known as the *spreading ratio*: the higher the ratio, the more immune to interference the signal is, because if part of the transmission is corrupted, the data can still be recovered from the remaining part of the chipping code. This method provides greater rates of transmission than FHSS, which uses a limited number of frequencies, but fewer channels in a given frequency range. Additionally, DSSS protects against data loss through the redundant, simultaneous transmission of data. However, because DSSS floods the channel it is using, it is also more vulnerable to interference from EM devices operating in the same range. In the 2.4 to 2.4835 GHz frequency range employed by 802.11b, DSSS transmissions can be broadcast in any one of fourteen 22 MHz-wide channels. The number of center-channel frequencies used by 802.11 DSSS devices depends on the physical location. For example, North America allows eleven channels operating in the 2.4 to 2.4835 GHz range, Europe allows thirteen, and Japan allows one. Because each channel is 22 MHz wide, the channels may overlap each other. Of the eleven available channels in North America, only a maximum of three (1, 6, and 11) may be used concurrently without the use of overlapping frequencies.

NOTE

When comparing FHSS and DSSS technologies, it should be noted that FHSS networks are **not** inherently more secure than DSSS networks, contrary to popular belief. Even if the relatively few manufacturers of FHSS devices were not to publish the hopping sequence used by their devices, a sophisticated hacker armed with a spectrum analyzer and a computer could easily determine this information and eavesdrop on the communications.

Wireless Network Architecture

The seven-layer open systems interconnect (OSI) networking model defines the framework for implementing network protocols. The OSI model will be covered in depth in chapter 5. Wireless networks operate at the *physical* and *data link* layers of the OSI model. The physical layer is concerned with the physical connections between devices, such as how the medium and low bits (0s and 1s) are encoded and decoded. Both FHSS and DSSS are implemented at the physical layer. The data link layer is divided into two sublayers; the media access control (MAC) and logical link control (LLC) layers.

The MAC layer is responsible for such things as:

- Framing data
- Error control
- Synchronization
- Collision detection and avoidance

The Ethernet 802.3 standard, which defines the Carrier Sense Multiple Access with Collision Detection (CSMA/CD) method for protecting against data loss as result of data collisions on the cable, is defined at this layer.

Exam Warning

802.11 networks operate at layer 1 (physical) and layer 2 (MAC and LLC) of the OSI model.

CSMA/CD and CSMA/CA

In contrast to Ethernet 802.3 networks, wireless networks defined by the 802.11 standard do not use CSMA/CD as a method to protect against data loss resulting from collisions. Instead, 802.11 networks use a method known as Carrier Sense Multiple Access with Collision Avoidance (CSMA/CA). CSMA/CD works by detecting whether a collision has occurred on the network and then retransmitting the data in the event of such an occurrence. However, this method is not practical for wireless networks because it relies on the fact that every workstation can hear all the other workstations on a cable segment to determine if there is a collision.

In wireless networks, usually only the AP can hear every workstation that is communicating with it (for example, workstations A and B may be able to communicate with the same AP, but may be too far apart from each other to hear their respective transmissions). Additionally, wireless networks do not use full-duplex communication, which is another way of protecting data against corruption and loss as a result of collisions.

Note

APs are also referred to as *wireless access points*. This is a more precise term that differentiates them from other network access points (such as dial-in remote access points), but in this chapter, we will use the acronym AP to avoid confusion with the Wireless Application Protocol (also known as WAP).

CSMA/CA solves the problem of potential collisions on the wireless network by taking a more active approach than CSMA/CD, which kicks in only after a collision has been detected. Using CSMA/CA, a wireless workstation first tries to detect if any other device is communicating on the network. If it senses it is clear to send, it initiates communication. The receiving device sends an acknowledgment (ACK) packet to the transmitting device indicating successful reception. If the transmitting device does not receive an ACK, it assumes a collision has occurred and retransmits the data. However, it should be noted that many collisions can occur and that these collisions can be used to compromise the confidentiality of Wired Equivalent Privacy (WEP) encrypted data.

CSMA/CA is only one way in which wireless networks differ from wired networks in their implementation at the MAC layer. For example, the IEEE standard for 802.11 at the MAC layer defines additional functionality, such as virtual collision detection (VCD), roaming, power saving, asynchronous data transfer, and encryption.

The fact that the WEP protocol is defined at the MAC layer is particularly noteworthy and has significant consequences for the security of wireless networks. This means that data at the higher levels of the OSI model, particularly Transmission Control Protocol/Internet Protocol (TCP/IP) data, is also encrypted. Because much of the TCP/IP communications that occur between hosts contain a large amount of frequently repeating and well-known patterns, WEP may be vulnerable to *known plaintext* attacks, although it does include safeguards against this kind of attack.

EXAM WARNING

Make sure you completely understand WEP and its vulnerabilities. WEP is discussed in more detail later in this chapter.

Wireless Network Protocols and Operation

Wireless local area networks (WLANs) are covered by the IEEE 802.11 standards. The purpose of these standards is to provide a wireless equivalent to IEEE 802.3 Ethernet-based networks. The IEEE 802.3 standard defines a method for dealing with collisions (CSMA/CD), speeds of operation (10 Mbps, 100 Mbps, and faster), and cabling types (Category 5 twisted pair and fiber). The standard ensures the interoperability of various devices despite different speeds and cabling types.

As with the 802.3 standard, the 802.11 standard defines methods for dealing with collision and speeds of operation. However, because of the differences in the media (air as opposed to wires), the devices being used, the potential mobility of users connected to the network, and the possible wireless network topologies, the 802.11 standard differs significantly from the 802.3 standard. As mentioned earlier, 802.11 networks use CSMA/CA as the method to deal with potential collisions, instead of the CSMA/CD used by Ethernet networks, because not all stations on a wireless network can hear collisions that occur on a network.

In addition to providing a solution to the problems created by collisions that occur on a wireless network, the 802.11 standard must deal with other issues specific to the nature of wireless devices and wireless communications in general. For example, wireless devices have to be able to locate other wireless devices, such as APs, and communicate with them. Wireless users are mobile and therefore should be able to move seamlessly from one wireless zone to another. Many wireless-enabled devices such as laptops and hand-held computers use battery power and should be able to conserve power when not actively communicating with the network. Wireless communication over the air has to be secure to mitigate both passive and active attacks.

WAP

The WAP is an open specification designed to enable mobile wireless users to easily access and interact with information and services. WAP is designed for hand-held digital wireless devices such as mobile phones, pagers, two-way radios, smartphones, and other communicators. It works over most wireless networks and can be built on many operating systems (OSs) including PalmOS, Windows CE, JavaOS, and others. The WAP operational model is built on the World Wide Web (WWW) programming model with a few enhancements and is shown in Figure 4.5.

Figure 4.5 WAP 2.0 Architecture Programming Model

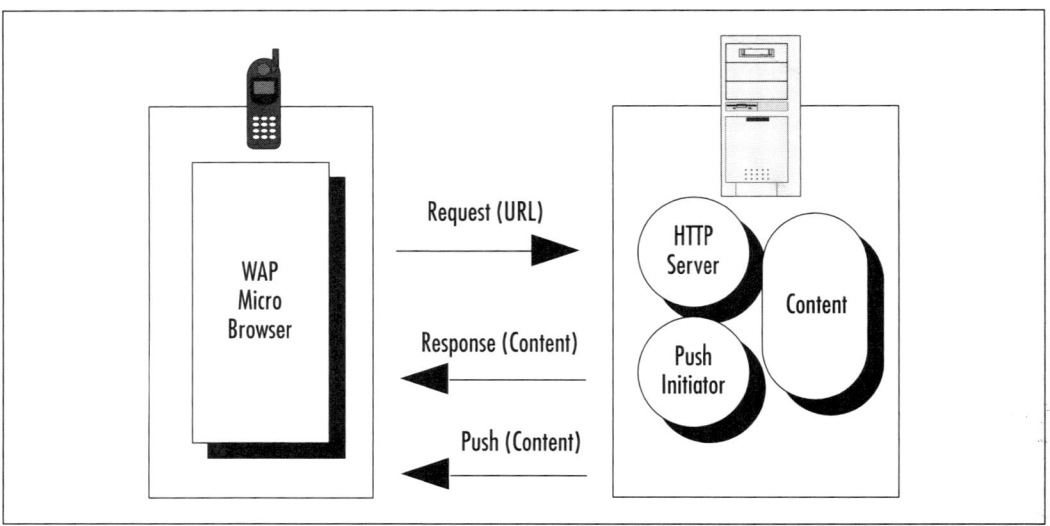

WAP browsers in a wireless client are analogous to the standard WWW browsers on computers. WAP URLs (uniform resource locators) are the same as those defined for traditional networks and are also used to identify local resources in the WAP-enabled client. The WAP specification added two significant enhancements to the above programming model: *push* and *telephony support* (Wireless Telephony Application [WTA]). WAP also provides for the use of proxy servers, as well as supporting servers that provide functions such as PKI support, user profile support, and provisioning support.

WTLS

Wireless Transport Layer Security (WTLS) is an attempt by the WAP Forum to introduce a measure of security into WAP. The WTLS protocol is based on the Transport Layer Security (TLS) protocol that is itself a derivative of the Secure Sockets Layer (SSL) protocol. However, several changes were made to these protocols to adapt them to work within WAP. These changes include:

- Support for both datagram and connection-oriented protocols
- Support for long round-trip times
- Low-bandwidth, limited memory, and processor capabilities

WTLS is designed to provide privacy as well as reliability for both the client and the server over an unsecured network and is specific to applications that utilize WAP. These applications tend to be limited by memory, processor capabilities, and low bandwidth environments.

Exam Warning

The following information must be mastered for the Network+ exam; you need to know the 802.11 standards, the speeds, operation, and so on for the Network+ exam. Make sure you follow the next sections very carefully as you study.

IEEE 802.11

The original IEEE 802.11 standard was developed in 1989 and defines the operation of wireless networks operating in the 2.4 GHz range using either DSSS or FHSS at the physical layer of the OSI model. This standard also defines the use of infrared for wireless communication. The intent of the standard is to provide a wireless equivalent for standards, such as 802.3, that are used for wired networks. DSSS devices that follow the 802.11 standard communicate at speeds of 1 Mbps and 2 Mbps and generally have a range of approximately 300 feet. Because of the need for higher rates of data transmission and to provide more functionality at the MAC layer, the 802.11 Task Group developed other standards (in some cases the 802.11 standards were developed from technologies that preceded them).

The IEEE 802.11 standard provides for all the necessary definitions and constructs for wireless networks. Everything from the physical transmission specifications to the authentication negotiation is defined by this standard. Wireless traffic, like its wired counterpart, consists of frames transmitted from one station to another. The primary feature that sets wireless networks apart from wired networks is that at least one end of the communication pair is either a wireless client or a wireless AP.

IEEE 802.11b

The most common standard used today for wireless networks, the IEEE 802.11b standard, defines DSSS networks that use the 2.4 GHz ISM band and communicate at speeds of 1, 2, 5.5, and 11 Mbps. The 802.11b standard defines the operation of *only* DSSS devices and is backward compatible with 802.11 DSSS devices. The standard is also concerned only with the physical and MAC layers: layer 3 and higher protocols are considered payload. There is only one frame type used by 802.11b networks, and it is significantly different from Ethernet frames. The 802.11b frame type has a maximum length of 2346 bytes, although it is often fragmented at 1518 bytes as it traverses an AP to communicate with Ethernet networks. The frame type provides for three general categories of frames: management, control, and data. In general, the frame type provides methods for wireless devices to discover, associate (or disassociate), and authenticate with one another; to shift data rates as signals become stronger or weaker; to conserve power by going into sleep mode; to handle collisions and fragmentation; and to enable encryption through WEP. Regarding WEP, it should be noted that the standard defines the use of only 64-bit (also sometimes referred to as 40-bit to add to the confusion) encryption, which may cause issues of interoperability between devices from different vendors that use 128-bit or higher encryption.

EXAM WARNING

Remember that IEEE 802.11b functions up to 11 Mbps in the ISM band.

IEEE 802.11a

In spite of its nomenclature, IEEE 802.11a is a more recent standard than 802.11b. This standard defines wireless networks that use the 5 GHz UNII bands. 802.11a supports much higher rates of data transmission than 802.11b. These rates are 6, 9, 12, 16, 18, 24, 36, 48, and 54 Mbps, although higher rates are possible using proprietary technology and a technique known as *rate doubling*. Unlike 802.11b, 802.11a does not use spread spectrum and Quadrature Phase Shift Keying (QPSK) as a modulation technique at the physical layer. Instead, it uses a modulation technique known as Orthogonal Frequency Division Multiplexing (OFDM). To be 802.11a compliant, devices are only required to support data rates of 6, 12, and 24 Mbps—the standard does not require the use of other data rates.

Although identical to 802.11b at the MAC layer, 802.11a is *not* backward compatible with 802.11b because of the use of a different frequency band and the use of OFDM at the physical layer, although some vendors are providing solutions to bridge the two standards at the AP. However, both 802.11a and 802.11b devices can be easily co-located because their frequencies will not interfere with each other, providing a technically easy, but relatively expensive migration to a pure 802.11a network. At the time of this writing, 802.11a-compliant devices are becoming more common, and the prices for them are falling quickly. However, even if the prices for 802.11b and 802.11a devices were identical, 802.11a would require more APs and would therefore be more expensive than an 802.11b network to achieve the highest possible rates of data transmission, because the higher frequency 5 GHz waves attenuate more quickly over distance.

EXAM WARNING

Remember that **IEEE** 802.11a functions up to 54 Mbps in the UNII band.

IEEE 802.11g

To provide both higher data rates (up to 54 Mbps) in the ISM 2.4 GHz bands and backward compatibility with 802.11b, the IEEE 802.11g Task Group members along with wireless vendors introduced the 802.11g standard specifications. To achieve the higher rates of transmission, 802.11g devices use OFDM in contrast to QPSK, which is used by 802.11b devices as a modulation technique. However, 802.11g devices are able to automatically switch to QPSK to communicate with 802.11b devices. 802.11g has advantages over 802.11a in terms of providing backward compatibility with 802.11b; however, migrating to and co-existence with 802.11b may still prove problematic because of crowding in the widely used 2.4 GHz band.

EXAM WARNING

Remember that **IEEE** 802.11g functions up to 54 Mbps in the ISM band.

Ad-Hoc and Infrastructure Network Configuration

The 802.11 standard provides for two modes for wireless clients to communicate: ad-hoc and infrastructure. The ad-hoc mode is geared for a network of stations within communication range of each other. Ad-hoc networks are created spontaneously between the network participants. In infrastructure mode, APs provide more permanent structure for the network. An infrastructure consists of one or more APs as well as a distribution system (that is, a wired network) behind the APs that tie the wireless network to the wired network. Figures 4.6 and 4.7 show an ad-hoc network and an infrastructure network, respectively.

Figure 4.6 Ad-Hoc Network Configuration

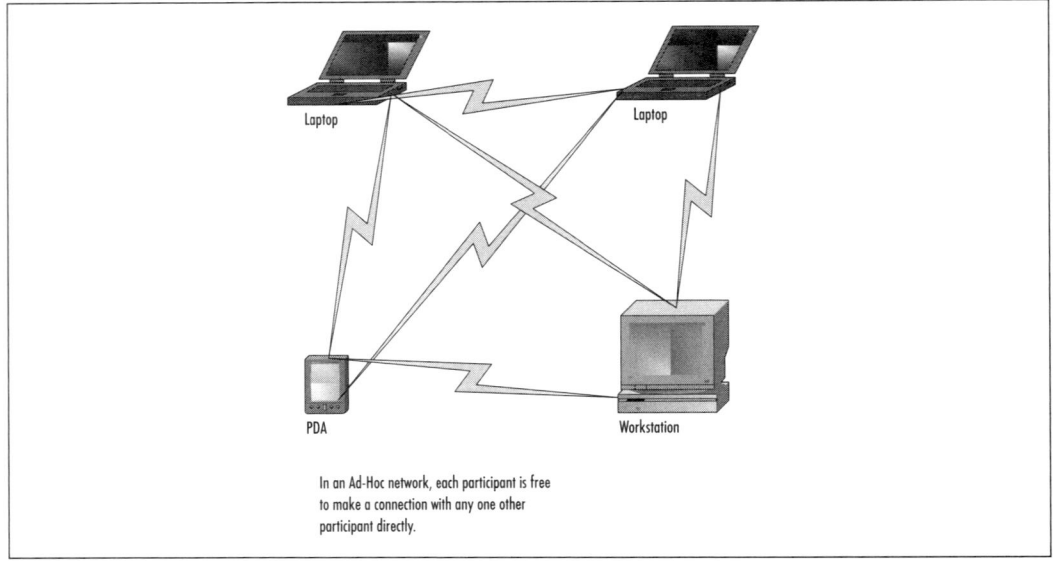

Figure 4.7 Infrastructure Network Configuration

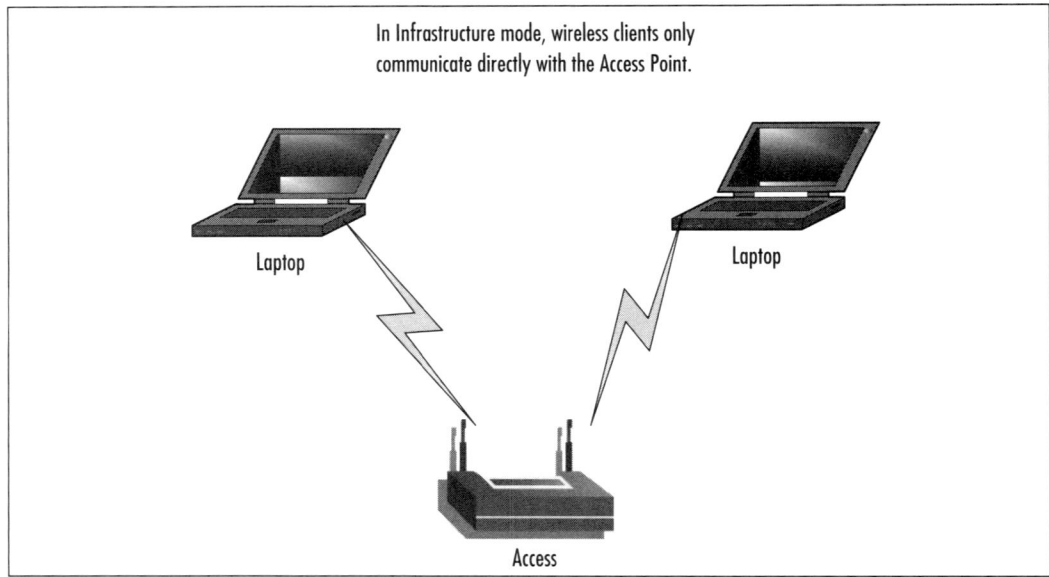

To distinguish different wireless networks from one another, the 802.11 standard defines the Service Set Identifier (SSID). The SSID is considered the identity element that "glues" various components of a wireless local area network (LAN) together. Traffic from wireless clients that use one SSID can be distinguished from other wireless traffic using a different SSID. Using the SSID, an AP can determine which traffic is meant for it and which is meant for other wireless networks.

802.11 traffic can be subdivided into three parts:

- Control frames
- Management frames
- Data frames

Control frames include such information as Request to Send (RTS), Clear to Send (CTS), and ACK messages. Management frames include beacon frames, probe request/response, authentication frames, and association frames. Data frames are 802.11 frames that carry data, which is typically considered network traffic, such as Internet Protocol (IP) encapsulated frames.

TEST DAY TIP

Remember for the Network+ exam that there are two main wireless networking models, ad-hoc and infrastructure.

IEEE 802.15 (Bluetooth)

Bluetooth uses the same 2.4 GHz frequency that the IEEE 802.11b and 802.11g wireless networks use, but unlike those networks, Bluetooth can select from up to 79 different frequencies within a radio band. Unlike 802.11 networks where the wireless client can only be associated with one network at a time, Bluetooth networks allow clients to be connected to seven networks at the same time. Bluetooth devices typically have a maximum useable range of about 10 meters (33 feet).

Bluetooth, by its very design, is not intended for the long ranges or high data throughput rates that 802.11 wireless networks have. This is largely due to the fact that the hop rate of Bluetooth devices is about 1600 hops per second with an average of a 625ms dwell time, thus producing exceptionally more management overhead than 802.11. While this exceptionally high hop rate does tend to make Bluetooth resistant to narrow band interference, it has the undesirable side effect of causing disruption of other 2.4 GHz-based network technologies, such as 802.11b and 802.11g. This high hop rate causes all-band interference on these 802.11 networks and can, in some cases, completely prevent an 802.11 wireless network from functioning.

Infrared

Infrared, unlike 802.11 and 802.15, is not a standard itself, but rather is the focus of the Infrared Data Association (IrDA). The IrDA was founded in 1993 as a member-funded organization whose primary function is to create and promote a standardized data transmission mechanism using infrared light. Infrared data transmission has been used for many applications in a non-nonstandard manner by Hewlett Packard calculators and printers. Now, most PDAs (personal digital assistants) and almost all portable computers do or can have infrared capabilities.

Infrared devices typically can achieve a maximum data throughput of 4 Mbps, but as it is a light-based technology, it is susceptible to light-based interference and the typical data throughput you can expect is around 100-125 Kbps. Also, since infrared is a light-based technology, it does not interfere in any way with RF-based wireless technologies. By that same token, infrared is a fairly secure technology in that an attacker would have to be in the direct path of the transmission, which is typically not very likely given the low power and low transmission range of infrared—the best theoretical outdoor distance you can get out of infrared is about 3280 feet (1000 meters), and this maximum drops off significantly with the presence of any other form of light.

WEP

The IEEE 802.11 standard covers the communication between WLAN components. RF poses challenges to privacy in that it travels through and around physical objects. Because of the nature of the 802.11 wireless LANs, the IEEE working group implemented a mechanism to protect the privacy of the individual transmissions, known as the WEP protocol. Because WEP utilizes a cryptographic security countermeasure for the fulfillment of its stated goal of privacy, it has the added benefit of becoming an authentication mechanism. This benefit is realized through a shared-key authentication that allows for encryption and decryption of wireless transmissions. Up to four keys can be defined on an AP or a client, and they can be rotated to add complexity for a higher security standard in the WLAN policy.

WEP was never intended to be the absolute authority in wireless security. The IEEE 802.11 standard states that WEP provides for protection from "casual eavesdropping." Instead, the driving force behind WEP was privacy. In cases that require high degrees of security, other mechanisms should be utilized such as authentication, access control, password protection, and virtual private networks (VPNs).

Despite its flaws, WEP still offers a level of security provided that all its features are used properly. This means taking great care in key management, avoiding default options, and ensuring adequate encryption is enabled at every opportunity.

Proposed improvements in the 802.11 standard should overcome many of the limitations of the original security options, and should make WEP more appealing as a security solution. Additionally, as WLAN technology gains popularity and users clamor for functionality, both the standards committees and the hardware vendors will offer improvements. It is critically important to keep abreast of vendor-related software fixes and changes that improve the overall security posture of a wireless LAN.

EXAM WARNING

Most APs advertise that they support WEP in 40-bit encryption, but often the 128-bit option is also supported. For corporate networks, 128-bit encryption–capable devices should be considered as a minimum.

With data security enabled in a closed network, the settings on the client for the SSID and the encryption keys must match the AP when attempting to associate with the network or it will fail. The next few paragraphs discuss WEP and its relation to the functionality of the 802.11 standard, including a standard definition of WEP, the privacy created, and the authentication.

WEP provides security and privacy in transmissions held between the AP and the clients. To gain access, an intruder must be more sophisticated and have specific intent to gain access. Some of the other benefits of implementing WEP include the following:

- All messages are encrypted using a CRC-32 checksum to provide some degree of integrity.

- Privacy is maintained via the RC4 encryption. Without possession of the secret key, the message cannot be easily decrypted.

- WEP is extremely easy to implement. All that is required is to set the encryption key on the APs and on each client.

- WEP provides a basic level of security for WLAN applications.

- WEP keys are user-definable and unlimited. WEP keys can, and should, be changed often.

None, 40 or 128 bit

EXAM WARNING

Do not confuse WAP and WEP. While it may seem that WEP is the privacy system for WAP, you should remember that WTLS is the privacy mechanism for WAP and WEP is the privacy mechanism for 802.11 WLANs.

Creating Privacy with WEP

WEP provides for three implementations: no encryption, 40-bit encryption, and 128-bit encryption. Clearly, no encryption means *no privacy*. When WEP is set to no encryption, transmissions are sent in the clear and can be viewed by any wireless sniffing application that has access to the RF signal propagated in the WLAN, unless some other encryption mechanism such as IPsec (IP Security) is being used. In the case of the 40- and 128-bit varieties (just as with password length), the greater the number of characters (bits), the stronger the encryption. The initial configuration of the AP includes the setup of the shared key. This shared key can be in the form of either alphanumeric or hexadecimal strings, and must be matched on the client.

WEP uses the RC4 encryption algorithm, a *stream cipher* developed by Ron Rivest (the "R" in RSA). The process by which WEP encrypts a message is shown in Figure 4.8. Both the sender and the receiver use the stream cipher to create identical pseudo-random strings from a known shared key. This process entails having the sender logically XOR (exclusive OR) the plaintext transmission with the stream cipher to produce ciphertext. The receiver takes the shared key and identical stream and reverses the process to gain the plaintext transmission.

The steps in the process are as follows:

1. The plaintext message is run through an integrity check algorithm (the 802.11 standard specifies the use of CRC-32) to produce an integrity check value (ICV).

2. This value is appended to the end of the original plaintext message.

3. A "random" 24-bit initialization vector (IV) is generated and prepended to (added to the beginning of) the secret key (which is distributed through an out-of-band method) that is then input to the RC4 Key Scheduling Algorithm (KSA) to generate a seed value for the WEP pseudorandom number generator (PRNG).

4. The WEP PRNG outputs the encrypting cipher-stream.

5. This cipher-stream is then XOR'd with the plaintext/ICV message to produce the WEP ciphertext.

6. The ciphertext is then prepended with the IV (in plaintext), encapsulated, and transmitted.

Figure 4.8 WEP Encryption Process in IEEE 802.11

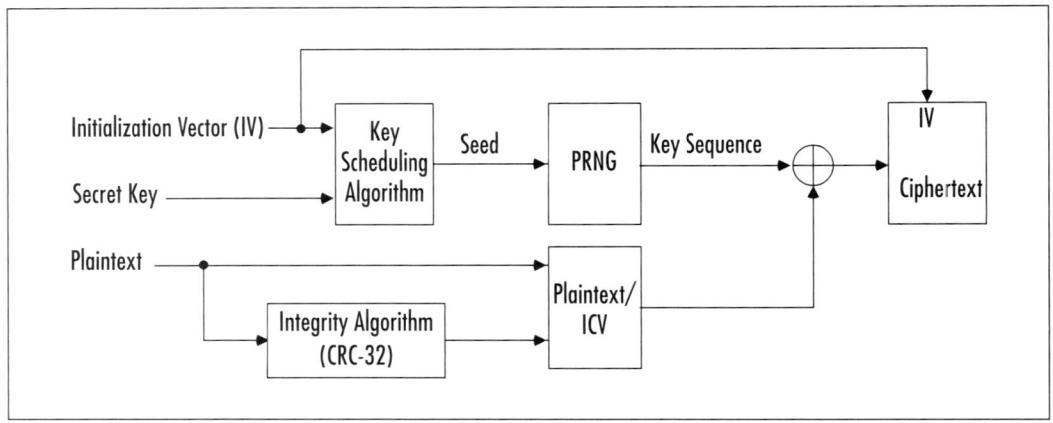

A new IV is used for each frame to prevent the reuse of the key from weakening the encryption. This means that for each string generated, a different value will be used for the RC4 key. Although this is a secure policy in itself, its implementation in WEP is flawed because of the nature of the 24-bit space. It is so small with respect to the potential set of IVs, that in a short period of time all keys are reused. When this happens, two different messages are encrypted with the same IV and key and the two messages can be XOR'd with each other to cancel out the key stream, allowing an attacker who knows the contents of one message to easily figure out the contents of the other. Unfortunately, this weakness is the same for both the 40- and 128-bit encryption levels, because both use the 24-bit IV.

To protect against some rudimentary attacks that insert known text into the stream to attempt to reveal the key stream, WEP incorporates a checksum into each frame. Any frame not found to be valid through the checksum is discarded.

Authentication

There are two authentication methods in the 802.11 standard: open and shared-key. Open authentication is more precisely described as device-oriented authentication and can be considered a null authentication—all requests are granted. Without WEP, open authentication leaves the WLAN wide open to any client who knows the SSID. With WEP enabled, the WEP secret key becomes the indirect authenticator. The open authentication exchange, with WEP enabled, is shown in Figure 4.9.

Figure 4.9 Open Authentication

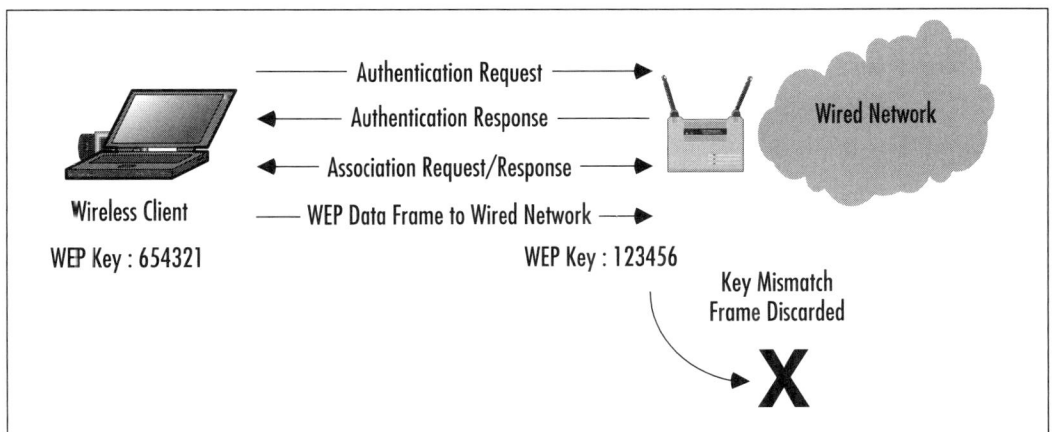

Exam Warning

Open authentication can also require the use of a WEP key. Do not assume that just because the Network+ exam discusses open authentication that a WEP key should not be set.

The shared-key authentication process shown in Figure 4.10 is a four-step process that begins when the AP receives the validated request for association. After the AP receives the request, a series of management frames are transmitted between the stations to produce the authentication. This includes the use of the cryptographic mechanisms employed by WEP as a validation. The four steps break down in the following manner:

1. The requestor (the client) sends a request for association.

2. The authenticator (the AP) receives the request, and responds by producing a random challenge text and transmitting it back to the requestor.

3. The requestor receives the transmission, encrypts the challenge with the secret key, and transmits the encrypted challenge back to the authenticator.

4. The authenticator decrypts the challenge text and compares the values against the original. If they match, the requestor is authenticated. On the other hand, if the requestor does not have the shared key, the cipher stream cannot be reproduced, therefore the plaintext cannot be discovered, and theoretically the transmission is secured.

Figure 4.10 Shared-Key Authentications

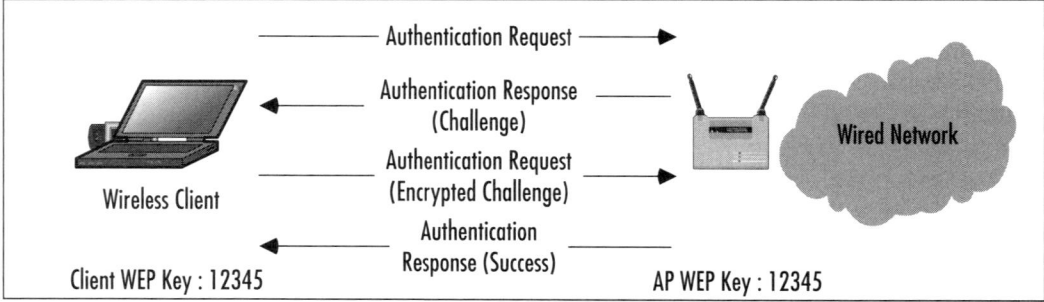

One of the greatest weaknesses in shared-key authentication is that it provides an attacker with enough information to try and crack the WEP secret key. The challenge, which is sent from authenticator to requestor, is sent in the clear. The requesting client then transmits the same challenge, encrypted using the WEP secret key, back to the authenticator. An attacker who captures both of these packets now has two pieces of a three-piece puzzle: the cleartext challenge and the encrypted ciphertext of that challenge. The algorithm RC4 is also known. All that is missing is the secret key. To determine the key, the attacker may simply try a brute force search of the potential key space using a dictionary attack. At each step, the attacker tries to decrypt the encrypted challenge with a dictionary word as the secret key. The result is then compared against the authenticator's challenge. If the two match, then the secret key has been determined. In cryptography, this attack is termed a *known-plaintext* attack and is the primary reason why shared-key authentication is actually considered slightly weaker than open authentication.

TEST DAY TIP

While the Network+ exam does not cover the authentication process in great detail, it is important to remember the two authentication mechanisms in the 802.11 standard: open and shared-key.

802.1x Authentication

The current IEEE 802.11 standard is severely limited because it is available only for the current open and shared-key authentication scheme, which is non-extensible. To address the weaknesses in the authentication mechanisms discussed above, several vendors (including Cisco and Microsoft) adopted the IEEE 802.1x authentication mechanism for wireless networks. The IEEE 802.1x standard was created for the purpose of providing a security framework for port-based access control that resides in the upper layers of the protocol stack. The most common method for port-based access control is to enable new authentication and key management methods without changing current network devices. The benefits that are the end result of this work include the following:

1. There is a significant decrease in hardware cost and complexity.

2. There are more options, allowing administrators to pick and choose their security solutions.

3. The latest and greatest security technology can be installed and should still work with the existing infrastructure.

4. You can respond quickly to security issues as they arise.

When a client device connects to a port on an 802.1x-capable AP, the AP port determines the authenticity of the devices. Before discussing the workings of the 802.1x standard, the following terminology must be defined:

- **Port** A single point of connection to a network.

- **Port Access Entity (PAE)** Controls the algorithms and protocols that are associated with the authentication mechanisms for a port.

- **Authenticator PAE** Enforces authentication before allowing access to resources located off of that port.

- **Supplicant PAE** Tries to access the services that are allowed by the authenticator.

- **Authentication Server** Used to verify the supplicant PAE. It decides whether or not the supplicant is authorized to access the authenticator.

- **Extensible Authentication Protocol Over LAN (EAPoL)** 802.1*x* defines a standard for encapsulating EAP messages so that they can be handled directly by a LAN MAC service. 802.1*x* tries to make authentication more encompassing, rather than enforcing specific mechanisms on the devices. Because of this, 802.11*x* uses Extensible Authentication Protocol (EAP) to receive authentication information.

- **Extensible Authentication Protocol Over Wireless (EAPoW)** When EAPOL messages are encapsulated over 802.11 wireless frames, they are known as EAPoW.

The 802.1*x* standard works in a similar fashion for both EAPoL and EAPoW. As shown in Figure 4.11, the EAP supplicant (in this case, the wireless client) communicates with the AP over an "uncontrolled port." The AP sends an EAP Request/Identity to the supplicant and a Remote Authentication Dial-In User Service (RADIUS)-Access-Request to the RADIUS access server. The supplicant then responds with an identity packet and the RADIUS server sends a challenge based on the identity packets sent from the supplicant. The supplicant provides its credentials in the EAP-Response that the AP forwards to the RADIUS server. If the response is valid and the credentials validated, the RADIUS server sends a RADIUS-Access-Accept to the AP, which then allows the supplicant to communicate over a "controlled" port. This is communicated by the AP to the supplicant in the EAP-Success packet.

Figure 4.11 EAP over LAN (EAPoL) Traffic Flow

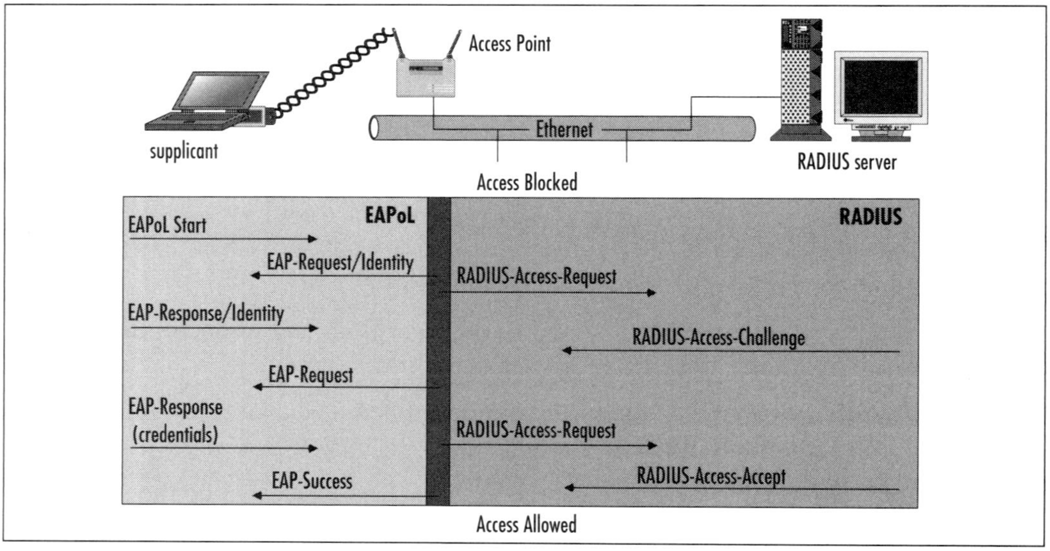

Head of the Class…

So What Exactly are 802.1x and 802.11x?

Wireless provides convenience and mobility, but also poses massive security challenges for network administrators, engineers, and security administrators. Security for 802.11 networks can be broken down into three distinct components:

- The authentication mechanism
- The authentication algorithm
- Data frame encryption

Current authentication in the IEEE 802.11 standard is focused more on wireless LAN connectivity than on verifying user or station identity. Since wireless can potentially scale very high in the sheer number of possible users, it is important to consider a centralized way to have user authentication. This is where the IEEE 802.1x standard comes into play.

User Identification and Strong Authentication

With the addition of the 802.1x standard, clients are identified by username, not by the MAC addresses of the devices. This design not only enhances security, but also streamlines the process of authentication, authorization, and accountability (AAA) for the network. 802.1x was designed to support extended forms of authentication using password methods (such as one-time passwords, or GSS_API mechanisms like Kerberos) and non-password methods (such as biometrics, Internet Key Exchange [IKE], and Smart Cards).

Dynamic Key Derivation

The IEEE 802.1x standard allows for the creation of per-user session keys. WEP keys do not have to be kept at the client device or at the AP when using 802.1x. These WEP keys are dynamically created at the client for every session, thus making it more secure. The Global key, like a broadcast WEP key, can be encrypted using a Unicast session key, and then sent from the AP to the client in a much more secure manner.

Mutual Authentication

802.1x and EAP provide for a mutual authentication capability. This makes the clients and the authentication servers mutually authenticating end points, and assists in the mitigation of attacks from man-in-the-middle (MITM) types of devices. Any of the following EAP methods provide for mutual authentication:

- **TLS** Requires that the server supply a certificate and establish that it has possession of the private key.

- **IKE** Requires that the server show possession of a preshared key or private key (this can be considered certificate authentication).

- **GSS_API (Kerberos)** Requires that the server can demonstrate knowledge of the session key.

Per-Packet Authentication

EAP can support per-packet authentication and integrity protection, but it is not extended to all types of EAP messages. For example, negative acknowledgment (NACK) and notification messages cannot use per-packet authentication and integrity. Per-packet authentication and integrity protection works for the following (packet is encrypted unless otherwise noted):

- TLS and IKE derive session key

- TLS cipher suite negotiations (not encrypted)

- IKE cipher suite negotiations

- Kerberos tickets

- Success and failure messages that use a derived session key (through WEP)

NOTE

EAP was designed to support extended authentication. When implementing EAP, dictionary attacks can be avoided by using non-password-based schemes such as biometrics, certificates, OTP, Smart Cards, and token cards. Using a password-based scheme should require the use of some form of mutual authentication so that the authentication process is protected against dictionary attacks.

Common Exploits of Wireless Networks

In general, attacks on wireless networks fall into four basic categories: passive, active, MITM, and jamming.

NOTE

While it may seem that we are deviating from the topic of networking here, the opposite in indeed the case. Security, especially in the case of wireless networking, is of paramount importance to you in your duties planning, implementing and maintaining any network. That said, we are likely diving a bit deeper in this section than you will likely be tested on during your Network+ exam.

Passive Attacks on Wireless Networks

A passive attack occurs when someone listens to or eavesdrops on network traffic. Armed with a wireless network adaptor that supports promiscuous mode, the eavesdropper can capture network traffic for analysis using readily available tools, such as Network Monitor in Microsoft products, or TCPDump in Linux-based products, or AirSnort (developed for Linux, but Windows drivers can be written). A passive attack on a wireless network may not be malicious in nature. In fact, many in the wardriving community claim their wardriving activities are benign or educational in nature. Wireless communication takes place on unlicensed public frequencies—anyone can use these frequencies. This makes protecting a wireless network from passive attacks more difficult.

Passive attacks are by their very nature difficult to detect. If an administrator is using DHCP (Dynamic Host Control Protocol) on the wireless network (this is not recommended), he or she might notice that an authorized MAC address has acquired an IP address in the DHCP server logs. Then again, he or she might not. Perhaps the administrator notices a suspicious-looking car sporting an antenna out of one of its windows. If the car is parked on private property, the driver could be asked to move or possibly charged with trespassing, but the legal response is severely limited. Only if it could be determined the wardriver was actively attempting to crack any encryption used on the network or otherwise interfering or analyzing wireless traffic with malicious intent would he or she be susceptible to being charged with a data-related crime, but this would depend on the country or state in which the activity took place.

Passive attacks on wireless networks are extremely common, almost to the point of being ubiquitous. Detecting and reporting on wireless networks has become a popular hobby for many wireless wardriving enthusiasts. In fact, this activity is so popular that a new term, "war plugging", has emerged to describe the behavior of people who actually wish to advertise both the availability of an AP and the services they offer by configuring their SSIDs with text such as "Get_food_here"!

Detecting Wireless Networks

Utilizing new tools created for wireless networks and the existing identification and attack techniques and utilities originally designed for wired networks, attackers have many avenues into a wireless network. The first step in attacking a wireless network involves finding a network to attack. The most popular software developed to identify wireless networks was NetStumbler (www.netstumbler.com). NetStumbler is a Windows application that listens for information, such as the SSID, being broadcast from APs that have not disabled the broadcast feature. When it finds a network, it notifies the person running the scan and adds it to the list of found networks.

As people began to drive around their towns and cities looking for wireless networks, NetStumbler added features such as pulling coordinates from Global Positioning System (GPS) satellites and plotting the information on mapping software. This method of finding networks is reminiscent of the method hackers used to find computers when they had only modems to communicate. They ran programs designed to search through all possible phone numbers and call each one, looking for a modem to answer. This type of scan was typically referred to as *war dialing*; driving around looking for wireless networks is known as *war driving*.

Similar tools are available for Linux and other UNIX-based operating systems. These tools contain additional utilities that hackers use to attack hosts and networks once access is found. A quick search on www.freshmeat.net or www.packetstormsecurity.com for "802.11" reveals several network identification tools, as well as tools used to configure and monitor wireless network connections.

Using NetStumbler

The NetStumbler program works primarily with wireless network adaptors that use the Hermes chipset, because of its ability to detect multiple APs that are within range and WEP, among other features (a list of supported adaptors is available at the NetStumber website). The most common card that uses the Hermes chipset for use with NetStumbler is the ORiNOCO gold card. Another advantage of the ORiNOCO card is that it supports the addition of an external antenna, which can greatly extend the range of a wireless network by many orders of magnitude, depending on the antenna.

> **NOTE**
>
> Wardrivers often make their own Yagi-type (tubular or cylindrical) antenna. Instructions for doing so are easy to find on the Internet, and effective antennas have been made out of such items as Pringles potato chip cans. Another type of antenna that can be easily homemade is the dipole, which is basically a piece of wire of a length that's a multiple of the wavelength, cut in the center and attached to a piece of cable that is connected to the wireless NIC (network interface card).

A disadvantage of the Hermes chipset is that it doesn't support promiscuous mode, so it cannot be used to sniff network traffic. For that purpose, you need a wireless network adaptor that supports the PRISM2 chipset. The majority of wireless network adaptors targeted for the consumer market use this chipset (for example, the Linksys WPC network adaptors). Sophisticated wardrivers will arm themselves with both types of cards, one for discovering wireless networks and another for capturing the traffic.

In spite of the fact that NetStumbler is free, it is a sophisticated and feature-rich product that is excellent for performing wireless site surveys, whether for legitimate purposes or not. Not only can it provide detailed information on the wireless networks it detects, it can be used in combination with a GPS to provide exact details on the latitude and longitude of the detected wireless networks. Figure 4.12 shows the interface of a typical NetStumbler session.

Figure 4.12 Discovering Wireless LANs Using NetStumbler

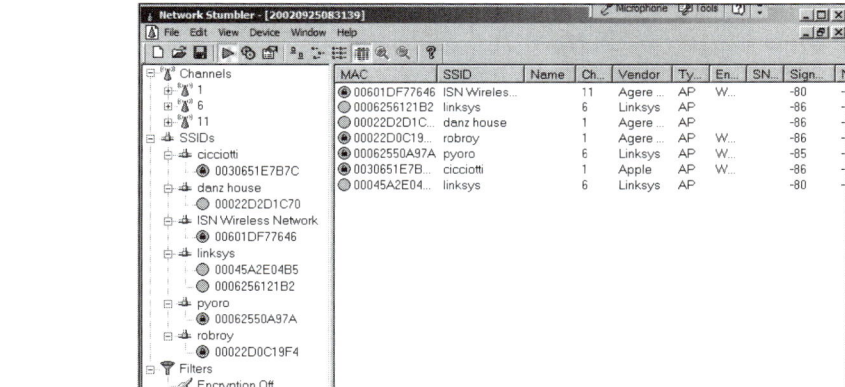

As you can see in Figure 4.12, NetStumbler displays information on the Service Set Identifier, the channel, and the manufacturer of the wireless AP. There are a few things that are particularly noteworthy about this session. The first is that a couple of APs are still configured with the default SSID supplied by the manufacturer, which should always be changed to a non-default value upon setup and configuration. Another is that at least one network uses an SSID that may provide a clue about the entity that has implemented it; again, this is not a good practice when configuring SSIDs. Finally, we can see which of these networks have implemented WEP.

If the network administrator has been kind enough to provide a clue about the company in the SSID or is not encrypting traffic with WEP, the potential eavesdropper's job is made a lot easier. Using a tool such as NetStumbler is only a preliminary step for the attacker. After discovering the SSID and other information, the attacker can connect to the wireless network to sniff and capture network traffic. This network traffic can reveal a lot of information about the network and the company that uses it. For example, looking at the network traffic, the attacker can determine which DNS servers are being used, the default home pages configured on browsers, network names, logon traffic, and so on. The attacker can use this information to determine if the network is of sufficient interest to proceed further with other attacks. Furthermore, if the network is using WEP, the attacker can, given enough time, capture a sufficient amount of traffic to crack the encryption.

NetStumbler works on networks that are configured as *open systems*. This means that the wireless network indicates that it exists and will respond with the value of its SSID to other wireless devices when they send out a radio beacon with an *empty set* SSID. This does not mean, however, that the wireless network can be easily compromised, *if* other security measures have been implemented.

Protecting Against Wireless Network Detection

To defend against the use of NetStumbler and other programs to detect a wireless network easily, administrators should configure the wireless network as a *closed system*. This means that the AP will not respond to empty set SSID beacons and will consequently be "invisible" to programs such as NetStumbler, which rely on this technique to discover wireless networks. However, it is still possible to capture the raw 802.11 frames and decode them through the use of programs such as ethereal and Wild Packet's AiroPeek to determine this information. As well, RF spectrum analyzers can be used to discover the presence of wireless networks. Notwithstanding this weakness of closed systems, you should choose wireless APs that support this feature.

Sniffing

Originally conceived as a legitimate network and traffic analysis tool, sniffing remains one of the most effective techniques in attacking a wireless network, whether it's to map the network as part of a target reconnaissance, to grab passwords, or to capture unencrypted data.

Sniffing is the electronic form of eavesdropping on the communications that computers transmit across networks. In early networks, the equipment that connected machines together allowed every machine on the network to see the traffic of all others. These devices, repeaters and hubs, were very successful for getting machines connected, but allowed an attacker easy access to all traffic on the network because the attacker only needed to connect to one point to see the entire network's traffic.

Wireless networks function very similarly to the original repeaters and hubs. Every communication across the wireless network is viewable to anyone who happens to be listening to the network. In fact, the person who is listening does not even need to be associated with the network in order to sniff!

The hacker has many tools available to attack and monitor a wireless network. A few of these tools are AiroPeek (www.wildpackets.com/products/airopeek) in Windows, Ethereal in Windows, UNIX, or Linux, and TCPDump or ngrep (http://ngrep.sourceforge.net) in a UNIX or Linux environment. These tools work well for sniffing both wired and wireless networks.

All of these software packages function by putting your network card in what is called *promiscuous mode*. When the NIC is in this mode, every packet that goes past the interface is captured and displayed within the application window. If the attacker is able to acquire a WEP key, he or she can then utilize features within AiroPeek and Ethereal to decrypt either live or post-capture data.

By running NetStumbler, or other software that can perform the same function, hackers are able to find possible targets. Once a hacker has found possible networks to attack, one of the first tasks is to identify the target. Many organizations are "nice" enough to include their names or addresses in the network name.

Even if the network administrator has configured his equipment in such a way as to hide this information, there are tools available that can determine this information. Utilizing any of the aforementioned network sniffing tools, an attacker can easily monitor the unencrypted network. Figure 4.13 shows a network sniff of the traffic on a wireless network. From this session, it is simple to determine the DNS server and the default search domain and default Web home page. With this information, an attacker can easily identify a target and determine if it is worth attacking.

Figure 4.13 Sniffing with Ethereal

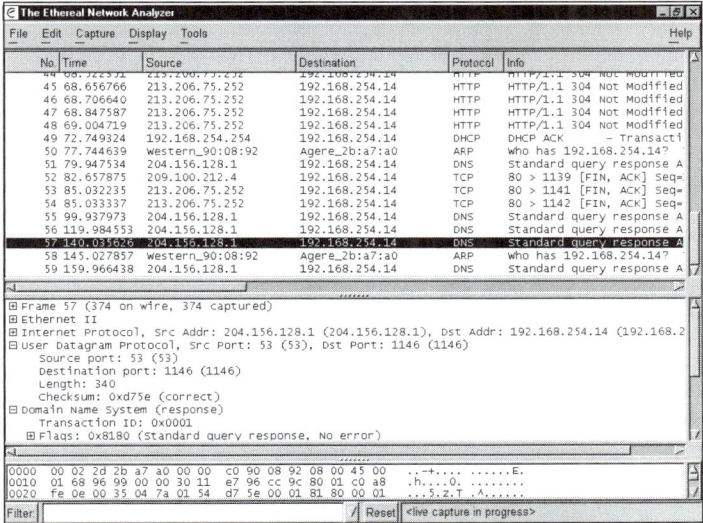

If the network is encrypted, the hacker will start by determining the physical location of the target. NetStumbler has the ability to display the signal strength of the discovered networks. Utilizing this information, the attacker only needs to drive around and look for a location where the signal strength increases and decreases to determine the home of the wireless network.

To enhance their ability to locate the positions of a wireless network, attackers can use directional antennas to focus the wireless interface in a specific direction. An excellent source for wireless information, including information on the design of directional antennas, is the Bay Area Wireless Users Group (www.bawug.org).

NOTE

Keep in mind that the most popular wireless network security scanning tools are Ethereal, NetStumbler, AiroPeek, and Kismet. This will help you analyze wireless networks in the field. Each tool has its benefits, so you may want to try them all if you have access to them.

Protecting Against Sniffing and Eavesdropping

As networking technology matured, wired networks were able to upgrade from repeaters and hubs to a switched environment. These switches would send only the traffic intended for a specific host over each individual port, making it difficult (although not impossible) to sniff the entire network's traffic. Unfortunately, this is not an option for wireless networks due to the nature of wireless communications.

The only way to protect wireless users from attackers who might be sniffing is to utilize encrypted sessions wherever possible: SSL for e-mail connections, SSH instead of Telnet, and Secure Copy (SCP) instead of File Transfer Protocol (FTP).

To protect a network from being discovered with NetStumbler, it is important to turn off any network identification broadcasts and, if possible, close down the network to any unauthorized users. This prevents tools such as NetStumbler from finding the network. However, the knowledgeable attacker will know that just because the network is not broadcasting information, that does not mean that the network cannot be found.

All an attacker needs to do is utilize one of the network sniffers to monitor for network activity. Although not as efficient as NetStumbler, it is still a functional way to discover and monitor networks. Even encrypted networks show traffic to the sniffer. Once they have identified traffic, attackers can then utilize the same identification techniques to begin an attack on the network.

Active Attacks on Wireless Networks

Once an attacker has gained sufficient information from the passive attack, the hacker can then launch an active attack against the network. There are a potentially large number of active attacks that a hacker can launch against a wireless network. For the most part, these attacks are identical to the kinds of active attacks that are encountered on wired networks. These include, but are not limited to, unauthorized access, spoofing, Denial of Service (DoS) and flooding attacks, as well as the introduction of *malware* (malicious software) and the theft of devices. With the rise in popularity of wireless networks, new variations of traditional attacks specific to wireless networks have emerged along with specific terms to describe them, such as "drive-by spamming" in which a spammer sends out tens or hundreds of thousands of spam messages using a compromised wireless network.

Because of the nature of wireless networks and the weaknesses of WEP, unauthorized access and spoofing are the most common threats to wireless networks. *Spoofing* occurs when an attacker is able to use an unauthorized station to impersonate an authorized station on a wireless network. A common way to protect a wireless network against unauthorized access is to use MAC filtering to allow only clients that possess valid MAC addresses access to the wireless network. The list of allowable MAC addresses can be configured on the AP, or it may be configured on a RADIUS server with which the AP communicates. However, regardless of the technique used to implement MAC filtering, it is a relatively easy matter to change the MAC address of a wireless device through software in order to impersonate a valid station. In Windows, this is accomplished with a simple edit of the registry, and in UNIX through a root shell command. MAC addresses are sent in the clear on wireless networks, so it is also a relatively easy matter to discover authorized addresses.

WEP can be implemented to provide more protection against authentication spoofing through the use of Shared Key authentication. However, as we discussed earlier, Shared Key authentication creates an additional vulnerability. Because Shared Key authentication makes visible both a plaintext challenge and the resulting ciphertext version of it, it is possible to use this information to spoof authentication to a closed network.

Once the attacker has authenticated and associated with the wireless network, he or she can then run port scans, use special tools to dump user lists and passwords, impersonate users, connect to shares, and, in general, create havoc on the network through DoS and flooding attacks. These DoS attacks can be traditional in nature, such as a *ping flood*, *SYN*, *fragment*, or *Distributed DoS (DDoS)* attacks, or they can be specific to wireless networks through the placement and use of *rogue access points* to prevent wireless traffic from being forwarded properly (similar to the practice of router spoofing on wired networks).

Spoofing (Interception) and Unauthorized Access

The combination of weaknesses in WEP, and the nature of wireless transmission, has highlighted the art of spoofing as a real threat to wireless network security. Some well-publicized weaknesses in user authentication using WEP have made authentication spoofing just one of an equally well-tested number of exploits by attackers.

One definition of spoofing is the ability of an attacker to trick the network equipment into thinking that the address from which a connection is coming is one of the valid and allowed machines from its network. Attackers can accomplish this in several ways, the easiest of which is to simply redefine the MAC address of the attacker's wireless or network card to be a valid MAC address. This can be accomplished in Windows through a simple registry edit. Several wireless providers also have an option to define the MAC address for each wireless connection from within the client manager application that is provided with the interface.

There are several reasons that an attacker would spoof. If the network allows only valid interfaces through MAC or IP address filtering, an attacker would need to determine a valid MAC or IP address to be able to communicate on the network. Once that is accomplished, the attacker could then reprogram his interface with that information, allowing him to connect to the network by impersonating a valid machine.

IEEE 802.11 networks introduce a new form of spoofing: authentication spoofing. As described in their paper "Intercepting Mobile Communications: The Insecurities of 802.11," Borisov, Goldberg, and Wagner (the authors) identified a way to utilize weaknesses within WEP and the authentication process to spoof authentication into a closed network. The process of authentication, as defined by IEEE 802.11, is very simple. In a shared-key configuration, the AP sends out a 128-byte random string in a cleartext message to the workstation that is attempting to authenticate. The workstation then encrypts the message with the shared key and returns the encrypted message to the AP. If the message matches what the AP is expecting, the workstation is authenticated onto the network and access is allowed.

As described in the paper, if an attacker has knowledge of both the original plaintext and ciphertext messages, it is possible to create a forged encrypted message. By sniffing the wireless network, an attacker is able to accumulate many authentication requests, each of which includes the original plaintext message and the returned ciphertext-encrypted reply. From this, the attacker can easily identify the key stream used to encrypt the response message. The attacker could then use it to forge an authentication message that the AP will accept as a proper authentication.

The wireless hacker does not need many complex tools to succeed in spoofing a MAC address. In many cases, these changes are either features of the wireless manufacturers or can be easily changed through a Windows Registry modification or through Linux system utilities. Once a valid MAC address is identified, the attacker needs only to reconfigure his device to trick the AP into thinking he is a valid user.

The ability to forge authentication onto a wireless network is a complex process. There are no known "off the shelf" packages available that will provide these services. Attackers will need to either create their own tools or take the time to decrypt the secret key by using AirSnort or WEPCrack.

If the attacker is using Windows 2000 and his network card supports reconfiguring the MAC address, there is another way to reconfigure this information. A card supporting this feature can be changed through the System Control Panel.

Once the attacker is utilizing a valid MAC address, he is able to access any resource available from the wireless network. If WEP is enabled, the attacker will have to either identify the WEP secret key or capture the key through malware or stealing the user's notebook.

Protecting Against Spoofing and Unauthorized Attacks

Protecting against these attacks involves adding several additional components to the wireless network. The following are examples of measures that can be taken:

- Using an external authentication source such as RADIUS or SecurID, will prevent an unauthorized user from accessing the wireless network and the resources with which it connects.

- Requiring wireless users to use a VPN to access the wired network also provides a significant stumbling block to an attacker.

- Another possibility is to allow only SSH access or SSL-encrypted traffic into the network.

- Many of WEP's weaknesses can be mitigated by isolating the wireless network through a firewall and requiring that wireless clients use a VPN to access the wired network.

Denial of Service and Flooding Attacks

The nature of wireless transmission, and especially the use of spread spectrum technology, makes a wireless network especially vulnerable to denial of service attacks. The equipment needed to launch such an attack is freely available and very affordable. In fact, many homes and offices contain the equipment that is necessary to deny service to their wireless networks.

A denial of service occurs when an attacker has engaged most of the resources a host or network has available, rendering it unavailable to legitimate users. One of the original DoS attacks is known as a *ping flood*. A ping flood utilizes misconfigured equipment along with bad "features" within TCP/IP to cause a large number of hosts or devices to send an ICMP (Internet Control Message Protocol) echo (ping) to a specified target. When the attack occurs, it tends to use a large portion of the resources of both the network connection and the host being attacked. This makes it very difficult for valid end users to access the host for normal business purposes.

In a wireless network, several items can cause a similar disruption of service. Probably the easiest way to do this is through a conflict within the wireless spectrum, caused by different devices attempting to use the same frequency. Many new wireless telephones use the same frequency as 802.11 networks. Through either intentional or unintentional uses of another device that uses the 2.4GHz frequency, a simple telephone call could prevent all wireless users from accessing the network.

Another possible attack would be through a massive number of invalid (or valid) authentication requests. If the AP is tied up with thousands of spoofed authentication attempts, authorized users attempting to authenticate themselves will have major difficulties in acquiring a valid session.

As demonstrated earlier, the attacker has many tools available to hijack network connections. If a hacker is able to spoof the machines of a wireless network into thinking that the attacker's machine is their default gateway, not only will the attacker be able to intercept all traffic destined for the wired network, but he or she would also be able to prevent any of the wireless network machines from accessing the wired network. To do this, the hacker needs only to spoof the AP and not forward connections on to the end destination, thus preventing all wireless users from doing valid wireless activities.

Not much effort is needed to create a wireless DoS. In fact, many users create these situations with the equipment found within their homes or offices. In a small apartment building, you could find several APs as well as many wireless telephones, all of which transmit on the same frequency. These users could easily inadvertently create DoS attacks on their own networks as well as on those of their neighbors.

A hacker who wants to launch a DoS attack against a network with a flood of authentication strings will also need to be a well-skilled programmer. There are not many tools available to create this type of attack, but (as we discussed earlier regarding the attempts to crack WEP) much of the programming required does not take much effort or time. In fact, a skilled hacker should be able to create such a tool within a few hours. This simple application, when used with standard wireless equipment, could then be used to render a wireless network unusable for the duration of the attack.

Creating a hijacked AP DoS requires additional tools that can be found on many security sites. These tools are not very complex and are available for almost every computing platform available.

Many apartments and older office buildings do not come pre-wired for the high-tech networks in use today. To add to the problem, if many individuals are setting up their own wireless networks without coordinating the installations, many problems can occur that will be difficult to detect.

Only a limited number of frequencies are available to 802.11 networks. In fact, once the frequency is chosen, it does not change until manually reconfigured. Considering these problems, it is not hard to imagine the following situation occurring:

A person goes out and purchases a wireless AP and several network cards for his home network. When he gets home to his apartment and configures his network, he is extremely happy with how well wireless networking actually works. Then, suddenly, none of the machines on the wireless network are able to communicate. After waiting on hold for 45 minutes to get through to the tech support line of the vendor who made the device, he finds that the network has magically started working again, so he hangs up.

Later that week, the same problem occurs, except that this time he decides to wait on hold. While waiting, he goes onto his porch and begins discussing his frustration with his neighbor. During the conversation, his neighbor's kids come out and say that their wireless network is not working.

So they begin to do a few tests (while still waiting on hold, of course). First, the man's neighbor turns off his AP (which is usually off unless the kids are online, to protect their network). When this is done, the original person's wireless network starts working again. Then they turn on the neighbor's AP again and his network stops working again.

At this point, a tech support rep finally answers and the caller describes what has happened. The tech-support representative has seen this situation several times and informs the user that he will need to change the frequency used in the device to another channel. He explains that the neighbor's network is utilizing the same channel, causing the two networks to conflict. Once the caller changes the frequency, everything starts working properly.

Protecting Against DoS and Flooding Attacks

There is little that can be done to protect against DoS attacks. In a wireless environment, an attacker does not have to even be in the same building or neighborhood. With a good enough antenna, an attacker is able to send these attacks from a great distance away.

This is one of those times when it is valid to use NetStumbler in a nonhacking context. Using NetStumbler, administrators can identify other networks that may be in conflict. However, NetStumbler will not identify other DoS attacks or other non-networking equipment that is causing conflicts (such as wireless telephones, wireless security cameras, amateur TV (ATV) systems, RF-based remote controls, wireless headsets, microphones and audio speakers, and other devices that use the 2.4 GHz frequency).

Man-in-the-Middle Attacks on Wireless Networks

Placing a rogue access point within range of wireless stations is a wireless-specific variation of a man-in-the-middle attack. If the attacker knows the SSID in use by the network (which, as we have seen, is easily discoverable) and the rogue AP has enough strength, wireless users will have no way of knowing that they are connecting to an unauthorized AP. Using a rogue AP, an attacker can gain valuable information about the wireless network, such as authentication requests, the secret key that is in use, and so on. Often, the attacker will set up a laptop with two wireless adaptors, where one card is used by the rogue AP and the other is used to forward requests through a wireless bridge to the legitimate AP. With a sufficiently strong antenna, the rogue AP does not have to be located in close proximity to the legitimate AP. So, for example, the attacker can run the rogue AP from a car or van parked some distance away from the building. However, it is also common to set up hidden rogue APs (under desks, in closets, etcetera) close to and within the same physical area as the legitimate AP. Because of their undetectable nature, the only defense against rogue APs is vigilance through frequent site surveys (using tools such as NetStumbler and AiroPeek,) and physical security.

Frequent site surveys also have the advantage of uncovering the unauthorized APs that company staff members may have set up in their own work areas, thereby compromising the entire network and completely undoing the hard work that went into securing the network in the first place. This is usually done with no malicious intent, but for the convenience of the user, who may want to be able to connect to the network via his or her laptop in meeting rooms or break rooms or other areas that don't have wired outlets. Even if your company does not use or plan to use a wireless network, you should consider doing regular wireless site surveys to see if someone has violated your company security policy by placing an unauthorized AP on the network, regardless of their intent.

Network Hijacking and Modification

Numerous techniques are available for an attacker to *hijack* a wireless network or session. And unlike some attacks, network and security administrators may be unable to tell the difference between the hijacker and a legitimate "passenger."

Many tools are available to the network hijacker. These tools are based upon basic implementation issues within almost every network device available today. As TCP/IP packets go through switches, routers, and APs, each device looks at the destination IP address and compares it with the IP addresses it knows to be local. If the address is not in the address table, the device hands the packet off to its default gateway.

The address table is used to coordinate the IP address with the MAC addresses that are known to be local to the device. In many situations, this is a dynamic list that is built up from traffic that is passing through the device and through Address Resolution Protocol (ARP) notifications from new devices joining the network. There is no authentication or verification that the request received by the device is valid. Thus, a malicious user is able to send messages to routing devices and APs stating that his MAC address is associated with a known IP address. From then on, all traffic that goes through that router destined for the hijacked IP address will be handed off to the hacker's machine.

If the attacker spoofs as the default gateway or a specific host on the network, all machines trying to get to the network or the spoofed machine will connect to the attacker's machine instead of to the gateway or host to which they intended to connect. If the attacker is clever, he will only use this to identify passwords and other necessary information and route the rest of the traffic to the intended recipients. If he does this, the end users will have no idea that this *man-in-the-middle* has intercepted their communications and compromised their passwords and information.

Another clever attack can be accomplished through the use of rogue APs. If the attacker is able to put together an AP with enough strength, the end users may not be able to tell which AP is the authorized one that they should be using. In fact, most will not even know that another is available. Using this technique, the attacker is able to receive authentication requests and information from the end workstation regarding the secret key and where they are attempting to connect.

These rogue APs can also be used to attempt to break in to more tightly configured wireless APs. Utilizing tools such as AirSnort and WEPCrack requires a large amount of data to be able to decrypt the secret key. A hacker sitting in a car in front of your house or office is noticeable and will generally not have enough time to finish acquiring enough information to break the key. However, if the attacker installs a tiny, easily hidden machine in an inconspicuous location, this machine could sit there long enough to break the key and possibly act as an external AP into the wireless network it has hacked.

Attackers who wish to spoof more than their MAC addresses have several tools available. Most of the tools available are for use in a UNIX environment and can be found through a simple search for "ARP Spoof" at http://packetstormsecurity.com. With these tools, the hacker can easily trick all machines on the wireless network into thinking that the hacker's machine is another machine. Through simple sniffing on the network, an attacker can determine which machines are in high use by the workstations on the network. If the attacker then spoofs the address of one of these machines, the attacker might be able to intercept much of the legitimate traffic on the network.

AirSnort and WEPCrack are freely available. While it would take additional resources to build a rogue AP, these tools will run from any Linux machine.

Once an attacker has identified a network for attack and spoofed his MAC address to become a valid member of the network, the attacker can gain further information that is not available through simple sniffing. If the network being attacked is using SSH to access the hosts, just stealing a password might be easier than attempting to break in to the host using an available exploit.

By just ARP spoofing the connection with the AP to be that of the host from which the attacker wants to steal the passwords, the attacker can cause all wireless users who are attempting to SSH into the host to connect to the rogue machine instead. When these users attempt to sign on with their passwords, the attacker is then able to first receive their passwords and then pass on the connection to the real end destination. If the attacker does not perform the second step, it will increase the likelihood that the attack will be noticed because users will begin to complain that they are unable to connect to the host.

Protection against Network Hijacking and Modification

There are several different tools that can be used to protect a network from IP spoofing with invalid ARP requests. These tools, such as ArpWatch, notify an administrator when ARP requests are detected, allowing the administrator to take the appropriate action to determine whether someone is attempting to hack into the network.

Another option is to statically define the MAC/IP address definitions. This prevents attackers from being able to redefine this information. However, due to the management overhead in statically defining all network adapters' MAC addresses on every router and AP, this solution is rarely implemented. There is no way to identify or prevent attackers from using passive attacks, such as from AirSnort or WEPCrack, to determine the secret keys used in an encrypted wireless network. The best protection available is to change the secret key on a regular basis and add additional authentication mechanisms such as RADIUS or dynamic firewalls to restrict access to the wired network. However, unless every wireless workstation is secure, an attacker only needs to go after one of the other wireless clients to be able to access the resources available to it.

Jamming Attacks

The last type of attack is the jamming attack. This is a fairly simple attack to pull off and can be done using readily available off-the-shelf RF testing tools (although they were not necessarily designed to perform this function). Whereas hackers who want to get information from your network would use other passive and active types of attacks to accomplish their goals, attackers who just want to disrupt your network communications or even shut down a wireless network can jam you without ever being seen. Jamming a wireless LAN is similar in many ways to how an attack would target a network with a Denial of Service attack—the difference is that in the case of the wireless network, the attack can be carried out by one person with an overpowering RF signal. This attack can be carried out by using any number of products, but the easiest is with a high-power RF signal generator readily available from various vendors.

This is sometimes the most difficult type of attack to prevent against, as the attacker does not need to gain access to your network. The attacker can sit in your parking lot or even further away depending on the power output of their jamming device. While you may be able to readily determine the fact that you are being jammed, you may find yourself hard pressed to solve the problem. Indications of a jamming attack include the sudden inability of clients to connect to APs where there was not a problem previously. The problem will be evidenced across all or most of your clients (the ones within the range of the RF jamming device) even though your APs are operating properly. Jamming attacks are sometimes used as the prelude to further attacks. One possible example includes jamming the wireless network, thereby forcing clients to lose their connections with authorized APs. During this time, rogue APs can be made available operating at a higher power than the authorized APs. When the jamming attack is stopped, the clients will tend to associate back to the AP that is presenting the strongest signal. Now the attacker owns all of the network clients attached to his rogue APs. The attack continues from there.

In some cases, you find that RF jamming is not always intentional and may be the result of other, non-hostile, sources such as a nearby communications tower or another wireless LAN that is also operating in the same frequency range. Baby monitors, cordless telephones, microwave ovens, and many other consumer products may also be sources of possible interference.

You can take some comfort in knowing that although a jamming attack is relatively easy and inexpensive to pull off, it is not the preferred means of attack. The only real victory with a jamming attack for most hackers is temporarily taking your wireless network offline.

Configuring Windows Client Computers for Wireless Network Security

Wireless LAN security is provided through a myriad of solutions. Some of these mechanisms are internal to Windows itself, while others are third-party solutions or part of the IEEE 802.11 standard. In this section, we will be focusing primarily on using WEP and 802.1x-based security on Windows 2000 Professional and Windows XP Professional computers. Whatever security mechanism you should decide to implement, you must ensure that you are diligent about getting it done right. There is rarely a second chance for security, especially when it comes to securing a wireless LAN.

Windows XP Professional

Windows XP has been hailed as the operating system of choice for wireless LAN users. Whatever your feelings are about this, it is a fact that Windows XP brings excellent support for 802.11 wireless networks and 802.1x security to the mainstream. The only flaw in Windows XP's solution is that it can in some cases take the majority of control away from a user—sometimes this can be a good thing, though. Configuring WEP and 802.1x security on a Windows XP Professional computer is outlined in Exercise 4.1.

EXERCISE 4.1

ENABLING WEP AND 802.1x SECURITY IN WINDOWS XP PROFESSIONAL

1. Click **Start | Settings | Control Panel | Network Connections**.

2. Double-click your wireless LAN connection.

3. Click the **Properties** button and switch to the **Wireless** tab, shown in Figure 4.14.

Figure 4.14 The Wireless Tab

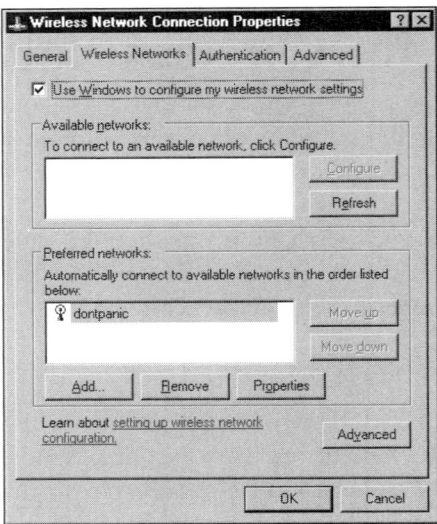

4. To configure a new connection, click **Add**. Configure all required
    information, including the WEP key, shown in Figure 4.15.

Figure 4.15 Configuring a New Connection

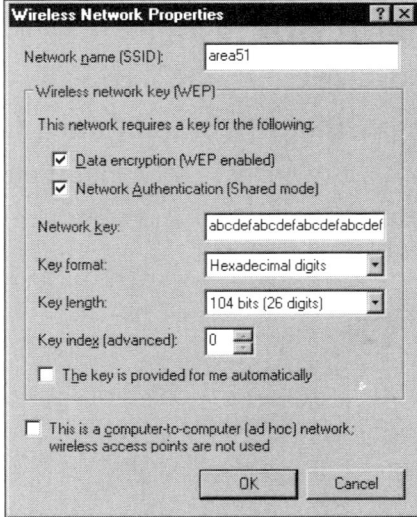

5. If your network uses a dynamic keying server, then you need only to
    select **The key is provided for me automatically** instead of speci-
    fying the WEP key specifics.

6. Click **OK** when you have entered all of the required information.

7. To configure 802.1x security on the network connection, change to the **Authentication** tab, shown in Figure 4.16.

Figure 4.16 Configuring 802.1x Security

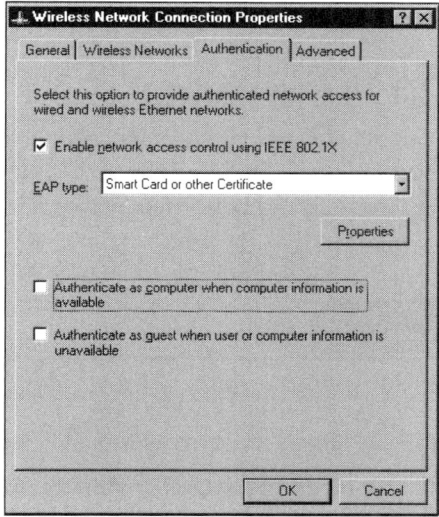

8. Select **Enable network access control using IEEE 802.1x**. Select your EAP type from the drop-down list. Most commonly, this is going to be **Smart Card or other Certificate**. By clicking **Properties** (see Figure 4.17) you can configure the certificate and certificate authority (CA) to be used for this authentication.

Figure 4.17 Configuring the Certificate Properties

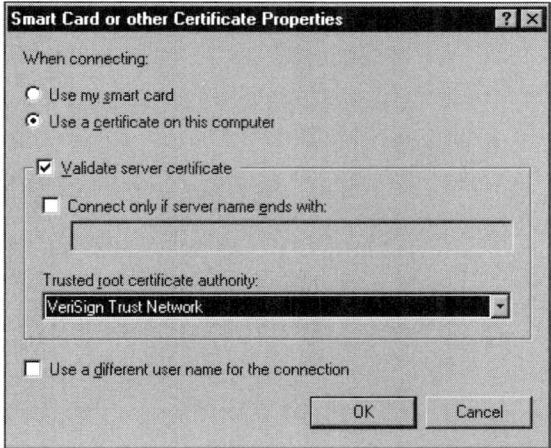

9. For increased security, ensure that the **Authenticate as computer when computer information is available** and **Authenticate as guest when user or computer information is unavailable** options are not selected. Click **OK** to accept the settings.

Windows 2000 Professional

Windows 2000 provides none of the built-in niceties for wireless networking that Windows XP does. All configuration and security is the job of the user. Exercise 4.2 outlines the process to enable WEP for a wireless network connection in Windows 2000 Professional.

EXERCISE 4.2

ENABLING WEP IN WINDOWS 2000 PROFESSIONAL

1. Click **Start** | **Settings** | **Control Panel** | **Network Connections**.

2. Double-click your wireless LAN connection.

3. Click the **Properties** button. Notice that the **Wireless** and **Authentication** tabs do not show up in Windows 2000 as they do in Windows XP (Figure 4.18).

Figure 4.18 Windows 2000 Network Adapter Properties

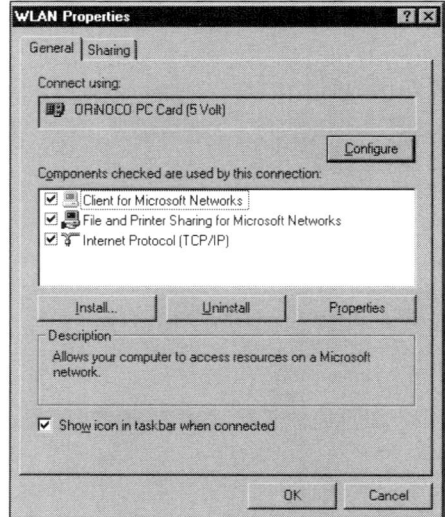

4. Close the network adapter Properties window.

5. Configure a wireless LAN connection profile using your WLAN network adapter client utility, such as the ORiNOCO Client Manager or the Cisco ACU. We will use an ORiNOCO network adapter for this example.

6. Open the Client Manager and click **Actions | Add/Edit Configuration Profile** (Figure 4.19).

Figure 4.19 Configuring a New Profile

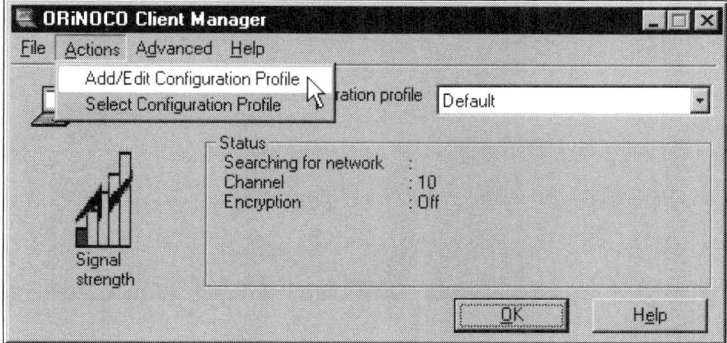

7. Click **Add** to create a new profile.

8. Enter the **Profile Name** and **Network Type** as shown in Figure 4.20 and click **Next**.

Figure 4.20 Specifying a New Profile

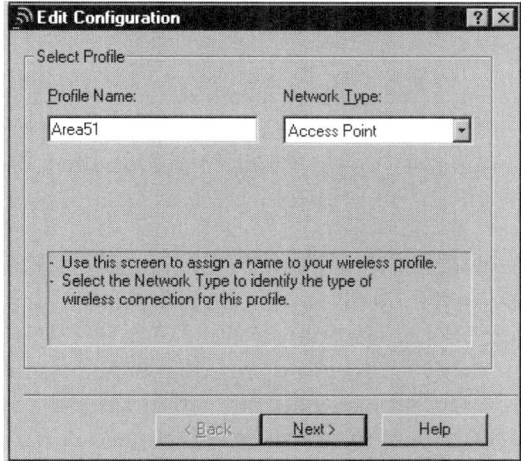

9. Enter the **Network Name** and click **Next**. This is the SSID of the network.

10. Select **Enable Data Security** and enter your WEP key or keys as shown in Figure 4.21. Click **Next** to continue.

Figure 4.21 Configuring the WEP Properties

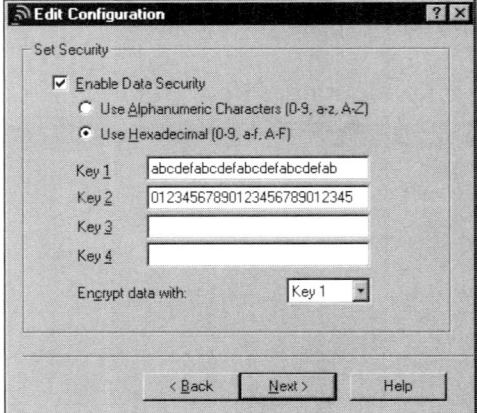

11. Configure the power management function you want and click **Next**.

12. Configure to renew the IP address of the network adapter upon connecting as desired and click **Next**.

Site Surveys

A site survey is part of an audit done on wireless networks. Site surveys allow system and network administrators to determine the extent to which their wireless networks extend beyond the physical boundaries of their buildings. Typically, a site survey uses the same tools an attacker uses, such as a sniffer and a WEP cracking tool (for 802.11 network site surveys). The sniffer can be either Windows-based (such as NetStumbler) or UNIX/Linux-based (such as Kismet). For WEP cracking, AirSnort is recommended.

Another tool that can be useful is a directional antenna such as a Yagi antenna or a parabolic dish antenna. Directional and parabolic dish antennas allow for the reception of weak signals from greater distances by providing better amplification and gain on the signal. These antennas allow wireless network auditors the ability to determine how far an attacker can realistically be from the source of the wireless network transmissions in order to receive from and transmit to the network.

Finally, another tool that is useful for site surveys is a GPS locator. This provides for the determination of the geographical latitude and longitude of areas where wireless signal measurements are taken. Using GPS, auditors can create a physical map of the boundaries of the wireless network.

EXAM WARNING

Site surveys are not likely to appear on the Network+ exam. However, you should be aware of them for your daily tasks, and the information is presented here in the event that you do see a question about some of the tools used to conduct these surveys. Remember that the tools used to conduct site surveys and audits are essentially the same tools an attacker uses to gain access to a wireless network.

Summary of Exam Objectives

Wireless LANs are attractive to many companies and home users because of the increased productivity that results from the convenience and flexibility of being able to connect to the network without the use of wires. WLANs are especially attractive when they can reduce the costs of having to install cabling to support users on the network. For these and other reasons, WLANs have become very popular in the past few years. However, wireless LAN technology has often been implemented poorly and without due consideration being given to the security of the network. For the most part, these poor implementations result from a lack of understanding of the nature of wireless networks and the measures that can be taken to secure them.

WLANs are inherently insecure because of their very nature; the fact that they radiate radio signals containing network traffic that can be viewed and potentially compromised by anyone within range of the signal. With the proper antennas, the range of WLANs is much greater than is commonly assumed. Many administrators wrongly believe that their networks are secure because the interference created by walls and other physical obstructions combined with the relative low power of wireless devices will contain the wireless signal sufficiently. Often, this is not the case.

There are a number of different types of wireless networks that can be potentially deployed. These include HomeRF, Bluetooth, 802.11b, and 802.11a networks. The most common type of WLAN in use today is based on the IEEE 802.11b standard.

The 802.11b standard defines the operation of WLANs in the 2.4 − 2.4835 GHz unlicensed Industrial, Scientific and Medical (ISM) band. 802.11b devices use direct sequence spread spectrum (DSSS) to achieve transmission rates of up to 11 Mbps. All 802.11b devices are half-duplex devices, which means that a device cannot send and receive at the same time. In this, they are like hubs and therefore require mechanisms for contending with collisions when multiple stations are transmitting at the same time. To contend with collisions, wireless networks use Carrier Sense Multiple Access with Collision Avoidance (CSMA/CA).

The 802.11a and 802.11g standards define the operation of wireless networks with higher transmission rates. 802.11a devices are not compatible with 802.11b because they use frequencies in the 5 GHz band. Furthermore, unlike 802.11b networks, they do not use DSSS. 802.11g uses the same ISM frequencies as 802.11b and is backward compatible with 802.11b devices.

The 802.11 standard defines the 40-bit Wired Equivalent Privacy (WEP) protocol as an optional component to protect wireless networks from eavesdropping. WEP is implemented in the MAC sub layer of the data link layer (layer 2) of the OSI model.

WEP is insecure for a number of reasons. The first is that, because it encrypts well-known and deterministic IP traffic in layer 3, it is vulnerable to plaintext attacks. That is, it is relatively easy for an attacker to figure out what the plaintext traffic is (for example a DHCP exchange) and compare that with the ciphertext, providing a powerful clue for cracking the encryption.

Another problem with WEP is that it uses a relatively short (24-bit) initialization vector (IV) to encrypt the traffic. Because each transmitted frame requires a new IV, it is possible to exhaust the entire IV keyspace in a few hours on a busy network, resulting in the reuse of IVs. This is known as IV collisions. IV collisions can also be used to crack the encryption. Furthermore, IVs are sent in the clear with each frame, introducing another vulnerability.

The final stake in the heart of WEP is the fact that it uses RC4 as the encryption algorithm. The RC4 algorithm is well known and recently it was discovered that it uses a number of weak keys. Airsnort and Wepcrack are two well-known open-source tools that exploit the weak key vulnerability of WEP.

Although WEP is not secure, it does nonetheless potentially provide a good barrier, and its use will slow down determined and knowledgeable attackers. WEP should always be implemented. The security of WEP is also dependent on how it is implemented. Because the IV keyspace can be exhausted in a relatively short amount of time, static WEP keys should be changed on a frequent basis.

The best defense for a wireless network involves the use of multiple security mechanisms to provide multiple barriers that will slow down attackers, making it easier to detect and respond to attacks. This strategy is known as defense-in-depth.

Securing a wireless network should begin with changing the default configurations of the wireless network devices. These configurations include the default administrative password and the default SSID on the access point.

The Service Set Identifier (SSID) is a kind of network name, analogous to an SNMP community name or a VLAN ID. In order for the wireless clients to authenticate and associate with an access point, they must use the same SSID as the one in use on the access point. It should be changed to a unique value that does not contain any information that could potentially be used to identify the company or the kind of traffic on the network.

By default, SSIDs are broadcast in response to beacon probes and can be easily discovered by site survey tools such as NetStumbler and Windows XP. It is possible to turn off SSID on some access points. Disabling SSID broadcasts creates a closed network. If possible, SSID broadcasts should be disabled, although this will interfere with the ability of Windows XP to automatically discover wireless networks and associate with them. However, even if SSID broadcasts are turned off, it is still possible to sniff the network traffic and see the SSID in the frames.

Wireless clients can connect to access points using either open system or shared key authentication. While shared key authentication provides protection against some denial of service (DoS) attacks, it creates a significant vulnerability for the WEP keys in use on the network and should not be used.

MAC filtering is another defensive tactic that can be employed to protect wireless networks from unwanted intrusion. Only the wireless station that possess adaptors that have valid MAC addresses are allowed to communicate with the access point. However, MAC addresses can be easily spoofed and maintaining a list of valid MAC addresses may be impractical in a large environment.

A much better way of securing WLANs is to use 802.1*x*. 802.1*x* was originally developed to provide a method for port-based authentication on wired networks. However, it was found to have significant application in wireless networks. With 802.1*x* authentication, a supplicant (a wireless workstation) has to be authenticated by an authenticator (usually a RADIUS server) before access is granted to the network itself. The authentication process takes place over a logical uncontrolled port that is used only for the authentication process. If the authentication process is successful, access is granted to the network on the logical controlled port.

802.1*x* relies on Extensible Authentication Protocol (EAP) to perform the authentication. The preferred EAP type for 802.1*x* is EAP-TLS. EAP-TLS provides the ability to use dynamic per user, session-based WEP keys, eliminating some of the more significant vulnerabilities associated with WEP. However, to use EAP-TLS, you must deploy a Public Key Infrastructure (PKI) to issue digital X.509 certificates to the wireless clients and the RADIUS server.

Other methods that can be used to secure wireless networks include placing wireless access points on their own subnets in wireless DMZs (WDMZ). The WDMZ can be protected from the corporate network by a firewall or router. Access to the corporate network can be limited to VPN connections that use either PPTP or L2TP.

New security measures continue to be developed for wireless networks. Future security measures include Temporal Key Integrity Protocol (TKIP) and Message Integrity Code (MIC).

Exam Objectives Fast Track

Radio Frequency and Antenna Behaviors and Characteristics

☑ Gain occurs when a signal has its strength increased, such as by passing it through an amplifier.

☑ Loss is the exact opposite of gain and occurs when a signal has its strength decreased, either intentionally through the use of a device such as an attenuator or unintentionally such as through resistance losses in a cable.

☑ Reflection occurs when an electromagnetic radio frequency wave has impacted upon a surface that has a much larger cross section than that of the wave itself.

☑ When a wave is refracted, it passes through a medium and changes course with some of the original wave being reflected away from the original wave's path.

☑ Absorption results when an electromagnetic wave has impacted an object that does not pass it on through any means (reflection, refraction or diffraction).

☑ When an incoming electromagnetic wave hits a surface that is small compared to its wavelength, scattering will occur.

☑ The Fresnel Zone is an elliptical region extending outward from the visual line of sight that can cause signal loss through reflection, refraction and scattering.

Wireless Network Concepts

☑ The most predominant wireless technologies consist of WAP (Wireless Access Protocol) and IEEE 802.11 Wireless LAN.

☑ Wireless Equivalent Privacy (WEP) is the security method used in IEEE 802.11 WLANs and Wireless Transport Layer Security (WTLS) provides security in WAP networks.

☑ WEP provides for two key sizes: 40-bit and 104-bit secret keys. These keys are concatenated to a 24-bit initialization vector (IV) to provide either a 64 or 128-bit key for encryption.

☑ WEP uses the RC4 stream algorithm to encrypt its data.

☑ 802.11 networks use two types of authentication: Open System authentication and Shared Key authentication.

☑ There are two types of 802.11 networks modes: ad-hoc and infrastructure. Ad-hoc 802.11 networks are peer-to-peer in design and can be implemented by two clients with wireless network cards. The infrastructure model of 802.11 uses access points (APs) to provide wireless connectivity to a wired network beyond the AP.

☑ To protect against some rudimentary attacks that insert known text into the stream to attempt to reveal the key stream, WEP incorporates a checksum in each frame. Any frame not found to be valid through the checksum is discarded.

☑ Used on its own, WEP does not provide adequate wireless local area network (WLAN) security.

☑ WEP must be implemented on every client as well as every AP to be effective.

☑ WEP keys are user definable and unlimited. They do not have to be predefined and can and should be changed often.

☑ Despite its drawbacks, you should implement the strongest version of WEP available and keep abreast of the latest upgrades to the standards.

☑ The IEEE 802.1x specification uses the Extensible Authentication Protocol (EAP) to provide for client authentication

Common Exploits of Wireless Networks

☑ Examining the common threats to both wired and wireless networks provides a solid understanding in the basics of security principles and allows the network administrator to fully assess the risks associated with using wireless and other technologies.

☑ Threats can come from simple design issues, where multiple devices utilize the same setup, or intentional denial of service attacks which can result in the corruption or loss of data.

☑ Malicious users aren't the source of all threats. Problems can also be caused by a conflict of similar resources, such as with 802.11b networks and cordless telephones.

☑ With wireless networks going beyond the border of the office or home, chances are greater that users' actions might be monitored by a third party.

☑ Electronic eavesdropping, or sniffing, is passive and undetectable to intrusion detection devices.

☑ Tools that can be used to sniff networks are available for Windows (such as Ethereal and AiroPeek) and UNIX (such as TCPDump and ngrep).

☑ Sniffing traffic allows attackers to identify additional resources that can be compromised.

☑ Even encrypted networks have been shown to disclose vital information in cleartext, such as the network name, that can be received by attackers sniffing the WLAN.

☑ Any authentication information that is broadcast can often be simply replayed to services requiring authentication (NT Domain, WEP authentication, and so on) to access resources.

☑ The use of virtual private networks, Secure Sockets Layer (SSL), and Secure Shell (SSH) helps protect against wireless interception.

☑ Due to the design of Transmission Control Protocol/Internet Protocol (TCP/IP), there is little that you can do to prevent MAC/IP address spoofing. Static definition of MAC address tables can prevent this type of attack. However, due to significant overhead in management, this is rarely implemented.

☑ Wireless network authentication can be easily spoofed by simply replaying another node's authentication back to the AP when attempting to connect to the network.

☑ Many wireless equipment providers allow for end users to redefine the MAC address for their cards through the configuration utilities that come with the equipment.

☑ External two-factor authentication such as Remote Access Dial-In User Service (RADIUS) or SecurID should be implemented to additionally restrict access requiring strong authentication to access the wireless resources.

☑ Due to the design of TCP/IP, some spoof attacks allow for attackers to hijack or take over network connections established for other resources on the wireless network.

☑ If an attacker hijacks the AP, all traffic from the wireless network gets routed through the attacker, so the attacker can then identify passwords and other information that other users are attempting to use on valid network hosts.

☑ Many users are susceptible to man-in-the-middle attacks, often entering their authentication information even after receiving many notifications that SSL or other keys are not what they should be.

☑ Rogue APs can assist the attacker by allowing remote access from wired or wireless networks. These attacks are often overlooked as just faults in the user's machine, allowing attackers to continue hijacking connections with little fear of being noticed.

☑ Many wireless networks that use the same frequency within a small space can easily cause network disruptions and even denial of service (DoS) for valid network users.

☑ If an attacker hijacks the AP and does not pass traffic on to the proper destination, all users of the network will be unable to use the network.

☑ Flooding the wireless network with transmissions can prevent other devices from utilizing the resources, making the wireless network inaccessible to valid network users.

☑ Wireless attackers can utilize strong and directional antennas to attack the wireless network from a great distance.

☑ An attacker who has access to the wired network can flood the wireless AP with more traffic than it can handle, preventing wireless users from accessing the wired network.

☑ Many new wireless products utilize the same wireless frequencies as 802.11 networks. A simple cordless telephone can create a DoS situation for the network.

Configuring Windows Client Computers for Wireless Network Security

☑ Windows XP provides support for 802.1x protection on wireless networking connections.

☑ Windows XP integrated wireless networking into the operating system to a high degree. Windows XP takes control of your network connection in most cases.

☑ Windows 2000 does not offer the high degree of integrated wireless networking that Windows XP does.

☑ Both Windows 2000 and Windows XP can support WEP 64 and WEP 128 as well as any third-party solutions on the market.

Site Surveys

☑ Tools used in site surveys include wireless sniffers, directional or parabolic dish antennas, and GPS receivers.

☑ Wireless sniffers that can be used in a site survey include the Windows-based NetStumbler and the UNIX/Linux-based Kismet or ethereal.

☑ Site surveys are used to map out the extent to which wireless networks are visible outside the physical boundaries of the buildings in which their components are installed.

Exam Objectives
Frequently Asked Questions

The following Frequently Asked Questions, answered by the authors of this book, are designed to both measure your understanding of the Exam Objectives presented in this chapter, and to assist you with real-life implementation of these concepts. You will also gain access to thousands of other FAQs at ITFAQnet.com.

Q: Do I really need to understand the fundamentals of security in order to prepare for the Network+ exam?

A: Yes. While you might be able to utilize the configuration options available to you from your equipment provider without a full understanding of security fundamentals to implement a wireless network, without a solid background in how security is accomplished, you will never be able to protect your assets from the unknown threats that will come against your network.

Q: Is 128-bit WEP more secure than 64-bit WEP?

A: Yes, but only to a small degree. This is because the WEP vulnerability has more to do with the 24-bit initialization vector than the actual size of the WEP key.

Q: Where can I find more information on WEP vulnerabilities?

A: Besides being one of the sources that brought WEP vulnerabilities to light, www.isaac.cs.berkeley.edu has links to other websites that cover WEP insecurities.

Q: If I have enabled WEP, am I now protected?

A: No. Certain tools can break all WEP keys by simply monitoring the network traffic (generally requiring less than 24 hours to do so).

Q: How can I protect my wireless network from eavesdropping by unauthorized individuals?

A: Because wireless devices are half-duplex devices, you cannot wholly prevent your wireless traffic from being listened to by unauthorized individuals. The only defense against eavesdropping is to encrypt layer 2 and higher traffic whenever possible.

Q: Are wireless networks secure?

A: By their very nature and by definition, wireless networks are not secure. They can, however, be made relatively safe from the point of view of security through administrative effort to encrypt traffic, to implement restrictive methods for authenticating and associating with wireless networks, and so on.

Q: My access point does not support the disabling of SSID broadcasts. Should I purchase a new one?

A: Disabling SSID broadcasts adds only one barrier for the potential hacker. Wireless networks can still be made relatively safe even if the AP does respond with its SSID to a beacon probe. Disabling SSID broadcasts is a desirable feature. However, before you go out and purchase new hardware, check to see if you can update the firmware of your AP. The AP vendor may have released a more recent firmware version that supports the disabling of SSID broadcasts. If your AP doesn't support firmware updates, consider replacing it with one that does.

Q: Why is WEP insecure?

A: WEP is insecure for a number of reasons. The first is that 24-bit initialization vector (IV) is too short. Because a new IV is generated for each frame and not for each session, the entire IV key space can be exhausted on a busy network in a matter of hours, resulting in the reuse of IVs. Second, the RC4 algorithm used by WEP has been shown to use a number of weak keys that can be exploited to crack the encryption. Third, because WEP is implemented at layer 2, it encrypts TCP/IP traffic, which contains a high percentage of well-known and predictable information, making it vulnerable to plaintext attacks.

Q: How can I prevent unauthorized users from authenticating and associating with my access point?

A: There are a number of ways to accomplish this. You can configure your access point as a closed system by disabling SSID broadcasts and choosing a hard-to-guess SSID. You can configure MAC filtering to allow only those clients that use valid MAC addresses access to the AP. You can enable WEP and Shared Key authentication. However, all of these methods do not provide acceptable levels of assurance for corporate networks that have more restrictive security requirements than are usually found in SOHO environments. For corporate environments that require a higher degree of assurance, you should configure 802.1X authentication.

Self Test

A Quick Answer Key follows the Self Test questions. For complete questions, answers, and explanations to the Self Test questions in this chapter as well as the other chapters in this book, see the Self Test Appendix.

1. What is the name of the behavior that occurs when the strength of an electromagnetic wave is changed, such as by an antenna?

    A. Refraction

    B. Absorption

    C. Gain

    D. Scattering

2. What is the name of the behavior that occurs when an electromagnetic wave is redirected in multiple directions, possibly resulting in a complete loss of usable signal at the destination?

    A. Reflection

    B. Scattering

    C. Refraction

    D. Loss

3. You suspect that your long range outdoor wireless link may be losing signal strength due to blockage of the Fresnel Zone by trees and buildings. At what percent Fresnel Zone blockage can you expect to start seeing signal loss?

    A. 50%

    B. 40%

    C. 30%

    D. 20%

4. What design feature causes an antenna to become an amplification device?

    A. It focuses the RF energy into a smaller beam.

    B. It focuses the RF energy into a broad beam.

    C. It is made of a ferrous metal.

    D. It is cylindrical in shape.

5. In long outdoor links, refraction of RF signals becomes a problem. Which of the following conditions is typically the reason for refraction in long outdoor links?

   A. Curvature of the Earth

   B. Rain or snow

   C. Differing air density

   D. Trees or buildings

6. In the United States, how many channels are available for usage by 802.11b and 802.11g wireless networks?

   A. 1

   B. 11

   C. 13

   D. 83

7. If you were implementing a new 802.11b or 802.11g wireless network in your large warehouse, what three channels could you safely use without having overlap? (Choose three correct answers)

   A. 1

   B. 2

   C. 4

   D. 5

   E. 6

   F. 10

   G. 11

8. Your supervisor has charged you with determining which 802.11 authentication method to use when deploying the new wireless network. Given your knowledge of the 802.11 specification, which of the following is the most secure 802.11 authentication method?

   A. Shared-Key Authentication

   B. EAP-TLS

   C. EAP-MD5

   D. Open Authentication

9. What are the two WEP key sizes available in 802.11 networks?

   A. 64–bit and 104–bit keys

   B. 24–bit and 64–bit keys

   C. 64–bit and 128–bit keys

   D. 24–bit and 104–bit keys

10. Which of the following is a weakness in WEP related to the initialization vector (IV)? (Choose all that apply)

    A. The IV is a static value, which makes it relatively easy for an attacker to brute force the WEP key from captured traffic.

    B. The IV is transmitted in plaintext and can be easily seen in captured traffic.

    C. The IV is only 24-bits in size which makes it possible that two or more data frames will be transmitted with the same IV, thereby resulting in an IV collision that an attacker can use to determine information about the network.

    D. There is no weakness in WEP related to the IV.

11. Bill, the network administrator, wishes to deploy a wireless network and use open authentication. His problem is that he also wants to make sure that the network is not accessible by anyone. How can he authenticate users without a shared–key authentication mechanism (choose the best answer)?

    A. Use MAC address filters to restrict which wireless network cards can associate to the network.

    B. Deploy a RADIUS server and require the use of EAP.

    C. Set a WEP key on the access points and use it as the indirect authenticator for users.

    D. Use IP filters to restrict access to the wireless network.

12. The 802.1x standard specifies a series of exchanges between the supplicant and the authentication server. Which of the following is not part of the 802.1x authentication exchange?

    A. Association Request

    B. EAPoL Start

    C. RADIUS-Access-Request

    D. EAP-Success

13. 802.1*x* provides for mutual authentication of the supplicant and the authenticator. Which of the following 802.1*x* methods support mutual authentication?

    A. EAP-MD5

    B. EAP-PWD

    C. EAP-RC4

    D. EAP-TLS

14. The 802.1*x* standard requires the use of an authentication server to allow access to the wireless LAN. You are deploying a wireless network and will use EAP-TLS as your authentication method. What is the most likely vulnerability in your network?

    A. Unauthorized users accessing the network by spoofing EAP-TLS messages.

    B. Denial of Service attacks occurring because 802.11 management frames are not authenticated.

    C. Attackers cracking the encrypted traffic.

    D. None of the above.

15. The tool NetStumbler detects wireless networks based on what feature?

    A. SSID

    B. WEP Key

    C. MAC Address

    D. CRC-32 Checksum

16. Some Denial of Service (DoS) attacks are unintentional. Your wireless network at home has been having sporadic problems. The wireless network is particularly susceptible in the afternoon and the evenings. This is most likely due to which of the following possible problems?

    A. The AP is flaky and needs to be replaced.

    B. Someone is flooding your AP with traffic in a DoS attack.

    C. The wireless network is misconfigured.

    D. Your cordless phone is using the same frequency as the wireless network and whenever someone calls or receives a call the phone jams the wireless network.

17. You suspect that someone is stealing data from your company, due to the fact that your closest competitor routinely seems to make it to market weeks before you on every product you introduce. You have conducted sweeps of your organization's

campus looking for surreptitious users and user actions, but have yet to locate any-thing out of the ordinary. What type of wireless network attack are you most likely being subjected to?

A. Spoofing

B. Jamming

C. Sniffing

D. Man-in-the-middle

18. Your wireless network does use WEP to authorize users. You do, however, make use of MAC filtering to ensure that only preauthorized client can associate with your access points. On Monday morning, you reviewed the AP association table logs for the previous weekend and noticed that the MAC address assigned to the network adapter in your portable computer had associated with your access points several times over the weekend. Your portable computer spent the weekend on your dining room table and was not connected to your corporate wireless network during this period of time. What type of wireless network attack are you most likely being subjected to?

A. Spoofing

B. Jamming

C. Sniffing

D. Man-in-the-middle.

19. The major weakness of WEP has to do with the fact that there are only a limited number of what available?

A. IVs

B. Packets

C. Frames

D. Beacons

20. In Windows 2000, how do you configure WEP protection for a wireless client?

A. Open the network adapter properties page and configure WEP from the Wireless Networks tab.

B. Install the high security encryption pack from Microsoft.

C. Issue the computer a digital certificate from a Windows 2000 Certificate Authority.

D. Use the utilities provided by the manufacturer of the network adapter.

21. In Windows XP, how do you configure WEP protection for a wireless client?

    A. Open the network adapter properties page and configure WEP from the Wireless Networks tab.

    B. Install the high security encryption pack from Microsoft.

    C. Issue the computer a digital certificate from a Windows 2000 Certificate Authority.

    D. Use the utilities provided by the manufacturer of the network adapter.

22. You are attempting to configure a client computer wireless network adapter in Windows XP. You have installed and launched the utility program that came with the adapter but you cannot configure the settings from it. What is the source of your problem?

    A. You are not a member of the Network Configuration Operators group.

    B. You do not have the correct Windows Service Pack installed.

    C. You do not configure wireless network adapters in Windows XP through manufacturer's utilities.

    D. Your network administrator has disabled SSID broadcasting for the wireless network.

Self Test Quick Answer Key

For complete questions, answers, and explanations to the Self Test questions in this chapter as well as the other chapters in this book, see the Self Test Appendix.

1.	**C**	12.	**A**
2.	**B**	13.	**D**
3.	**D**	14.	**B**
4.	**A**	15.	**A**
5.	**C**	16.	**D**
6.	**B**	17.	**C**
7.	**A, E** and **G**	18.	**A**
8.	**D**	19.	**A**
9.	**C**	20.	**D**
10.	**B** and **C**	21.	**A**
11.	**C**	22.	**C**

NETWORK+
Domain II

Protocols and Standards

## Chapter 5

NETWORK+

OSI Model

Domain II Objectives in this Chapter:

2.1   Identify a MAC address and its parts.

2.2   Identify the seven layers of the OSI model and their functions

2.3   Identify the OSI layers at which the following network components operate:

      2.3.1   Hubs

      2.3.2   Switches

      2.3.3   Bridges

      2.3.4   Routers

      2.3.5   NICs

      2.3.6   WAPs

Introduction

To prepare for the CompTIA Network+ exam, you should begin by reviewing the foundations of networking. Among these, you must understand the logical models on which networks are designed and created, the protocols they use to communicate, the addressing schemes by which they identify individual devices on the network, and the technologies they use to ensure that data reaches its destination. In this chapter, we will cover the OSI (Open Systems Interconnect) model in depth and then begin the discussion on TCP/IP (Transmission Control Protocol/Internet Protocol). Both are covered in great detail on the exam and need to be completely understood before sitting the exam if you want success.

The vast majority of networks today (including the Internet) use TCP/IP to transmit information among computers and networks in a wide area network (WAN). Together, TCP and IP are referred to as a protocol stack or as network/transport protocols because they work together at two different levels (called the Network and Transport layers) to enable computers to communicate with each other. This is important because TCP/IP, like other protocol suites (groupings) such as IPX/SPX (Internet Packet Exchange/Sequenced Packet Exchange), are arranged as suites of protocols that provide different functionality. If you want to send an e-mail to someone today, you will most likely need IP communications to establish communication and complete the transmission of the message. The models and the protocols (as you will see), tie very closely together, and that is why it's hard to discuss one without the other. As a matter of fact, no matter how long you are in networking you will find the OSI model is referenced on a daily basis all the way from the beginning student to a networking master.

In this chapter, we'll look at the networking models that provide guidelines for vendors of networking products, including the early Department of Defense (DoD) model as well as the International Organization of Standardization (ISO) OSI model.

Next, we'll move into some fundamentals of TCP/IP, although in this chapter we only start to touch on the protocol suite. The majority of TCP/IP fundamentals will be covered in Chapter 6. You'll also learn about the individual components of TCP/IP, a suite of protocols that are used throughout the network communication process to ensure that data sent from a computer reaches its intended destination. Now, let's start to pick apart the networking models and understand why they are so important.

Understanding the Purpose and Function of Networking Models

This chapter discusses several specific networking models, so it's important to begin our discussion with an overview of the purpose and function of networking models. Just about everywhere we look in the world today we can see examples of agreed-upon rules that help people work together more effectively and efficiently to achieve a specific aim. This is especially true in the world of technology where standards, specifications, and protocols are used to accomplish a particular task. Why is it you can pop a DVD in your player and watch it, regardless of who made the DVD, the DVD player, or the television? It's because everyone involved agreed to certain parameters such as the circumference of the DVD disk, the method of recording and reading the DVD, and the interface between the DVD player and the television.

The same is true in computer technology. A wide variety of methods can be used to transmit and receive data across a network. Models are used to broadly define the required elements. This helps break down complex tasks into more manageable segments. It also provides frameworks from which standards can be developed. Organizing networking tasks in this way provides standardization, which is critical for any technology to be widely adopted. It also reduces development time and cost because common tasks are defined and can be implemented without "reinventing the wheel." An excellent example of an organization dedicated to providing solid standards for networking is the IEEE (Institute of Electrical and Electronics Engineers), which will be covered shortly within this chapter.

The Department of Defense networking model was originally created to solve the problem of people needing to share information across large computer systems. That model was used as the basis for an expanded model known as the OSI model. In the next section of the text we will cover the DoD model. Although the exam primarily focuses on the OSI model, you should still be familiar with its existence and how it maps to the OSI model.

Understanding the Department of Defense Networking Model

In the mid-1960s, computer systems were huge mainframes that were all owned and maintained by large companies, universities, and governmental agencies. Users, especially in the academic, scientific, and governmental arenas, often needed to share data with other users. The problem was that mainframe computers all ran different proprietary software, and operating systems could not easily communicate with one another. In order to share data, programmers had to write code that would allow one mainframe to communicate with another specific mainframe.

This cumbersome one-to-one process was prohibitive, both in terms of the time and cost required to develop unique, proprietary solutions, and in terms of the limitations those solutions often imposed. After an interface was written, that mainframe still could communicate only with its specified counterpart. If either mainframe's operating system changed, the interface might be broken and programmers would have to be called back in to re-establish the communication system between the two mainframes.

The U.S. Department of Defense's *Advanced Research Projects Agency* (DARPA) tackled this problem with an experiment designed to demonstrate a way to share computer data across a wide area. This experiment was called ARPANET (Advanced

Research Projects Agency Network), and it became the foundation for what we know today as the Internet. It also resulted in the development of the TCP/IP protocols the late 1960s. TCP/IP is one of the few computer technologies from the 1960s that is still in prominent use today—a testament to the superb design of the TCP/IP suite. Although it has undergone some modifications over time, TCP/IP is still the protocol suite of choice for almost all large networks and for global connectivity to the Internet, which relies on TCP/IP.

The DARPA architecture, known as the *DARPA model* or the DoD model, defines four layers starting at the network cable (or interface) and working its way up. This model can be seen in Figure 5.1.

Figure 5.1 The Department of Defense Networking Model

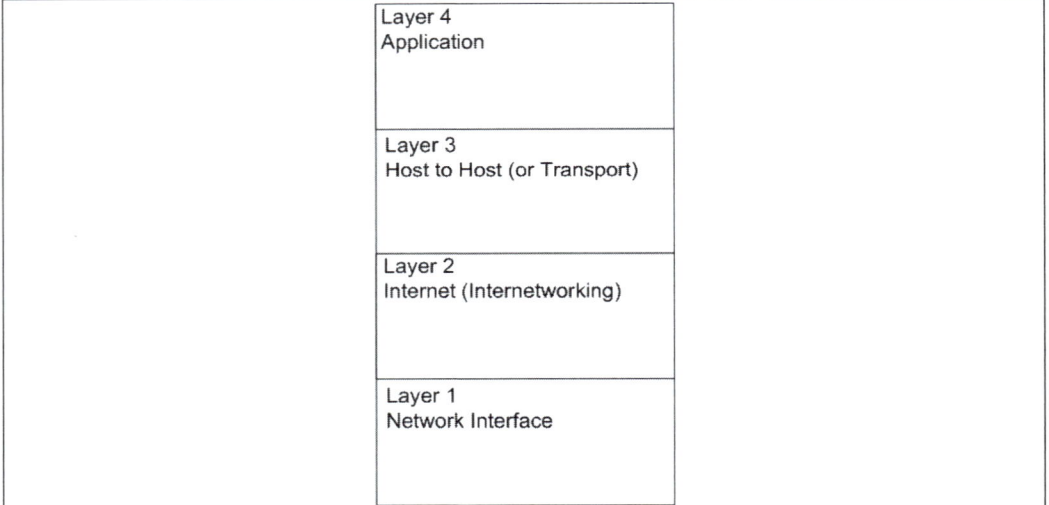

Each layer is designed with a specific function and together they provide the foundation for internetworking. Different protocols within the TCP/IP suite work at different layers, as you'll discover when we examine the individual components of the TCP/IP suite.

Layer One: Network Interface

The *Network Interface* layer of the DOD model corresponds to the lowest level of the TCP/IP protocol architecture and correlates to Layers 1 and 2 in the OSI model. The Network Interface layer provides most of the capabilities provided for in the Physical and Data Link layers of the OSI model.

Let's begin with a brief overview of the hardware involved in the network at this level. We have the network medium, which is typically coaxial, fiber optic or twisted-pair cabling (although wireless networking is increasing in popularity—see Chapter 4);

and we have the network interface card (NIC) that has both a physical MAC (Media Access Control) address and a logical IP address (we'll discuss the MAC and IP addresses a bit later). The NIC has logic (a circuit board and chips) built into it that gives it basic functionality. It uses a driver, which is a small software program that interfaces between the hardware and the operating system, to provide additional functionality.

The specifications related to how the network technology is implemented are defined by IEEE (called the "Eye-triple E" by industry members). The IEEE helps define common standards for use in a variety of technical fields, including computing. Although its may seem like humorous trivia, it's absolutely true that the standard known as the *802 standard*, was named so because the initial committee meeting was in 1980, in February (the second month). This standard defines specifications for the lower level networking technologies; that is, those at the Physical layer (NIC, connectors, and cables) and at the Data Link layer (access methods).

Exam Warning

For the Network+ exam, it's imperative that you understand the IEEE 802 model and its specific standards. Although there are many standards committees, you should definitely focus on the newer ones affecting today's current technologies (or areas of technology), such as Ethernet, wireless, and security. Most significantly, Ethernet is defined in 802.3, Token Ring in 802.5, and wireless networking in 802.11.

As you'll see, the standards vary, depending on the network technology (Ethernet, Token Ring, Asynchronous Transfer Mode [ATM], and Frame Relay). Because TCP/IP works independently of network technology, it can be used with each of these types of networks, and can be used to send information between two dissimilar networks as well. For more information on the IEEE, you can visit the IEEE at www.ieee.org.

The standards set by the 802 committee pertaining to networking are as follows:

- **802.1** Internetworking standards that deal with the management of local area networks (LANs) and metropolitan area networks (MANs), including bridges and the spanning tree algorithm used by bridges to prevent looping.

- **802.2** Logical link control (LLC), and the division of OSI Layer 2 into two sublayers, LLC and MAC.

- **802.3** CSMA/CD (Carrier Sense Multiple Access with Collision Detection), the media access control method used on Ethernet networks, and frame formats for Ethernet.

- **802.4** Token Bus networks that use 75 ohm coax or fiber optic cabling and the token passing access method.

- **802.5** Token Ring, the technology developed by IBM that uses a physical star and logical ring topology with twisted-pair cabling (shielded or unshielded) and the token passing access method.

- **802.6** MANs, networks of a size and scope that falls between that of the LAN and the WAN.

- **802.7** Broadband transmissions that use Frequency Division Multiplexing (FDM), including CATV.

- **802.8** Fiber optics networks, including Fiber Distributed Data Interface (FDDI) using the token passing access method.

- **802.9** Integrated services (voice and data) over ISDN (Integrated Services Digital Network).

- **802.10** Virtual private networking (VPN) to create a secure connection to a private network over the public Internet.

- **802.11** Wireless networking technologies, including the most common 802.11b, faster 802.11a, and newest 802.11g wireless communications methods.

- **802.12** The 100VG AnyLAN technology developed by Hewlett Packard, which uses the demand priority access method.

NOTE

Although some of this material may have been covered earlier, knowing it is imperative to passing the test, and repetition builds your ability to recall information when needed. The 802 standards need to be committed to memory, as you will definitely need to know them come exam time.

Media Access Control

Media access control refers to the method used to allocate use of the medium among the computers and devices on the network. The media access control method performs a function similar to the chairperson of a meeting, whose responsibility it is to recognize each speaker in turn and keep everyone from talking at once.

In networking, access control is important only when many devices share a common medium, such as a coaxial cable or twisted-pair cable—and then it is *very* important. Various schemes have been devised to control access to the media by the connected devices. If no methods were in place, all devices would send data whenever it suited them. On a small network, this might not be a problem, but if there are more than a few devices, it quickly causes congestion, collisions, and errors because everybody's talking at once. Therefore, as the size of the typical network grew, it was important to develop standard methods to control access to the shared media so that communication would proceed in an orderly and predictable manner. The access control method lays out rules defining how access is allocated, just as Robert's Rules of Order govern how meetings proceed (to see Robert's Rules of Order, visit www.constitution.org/rror/rror—00.htm).

Media Access Control is performed by MAC layer protocols. Although there are many different MAC protocols for a wide variety of media used by many different communications technologies (cellular, cable TV, satellite, etc.), we're going to concentrate on those that are most common in computing today. These include:

- CSMA/CD (Carrier Sense Multiple Access with Collision Detection)
- CSMA/CA (Carrier Sense Multiple Access with Collision Avoidance)
- Token passing

These will be discussed in detail later in this chapter.

Network Interface Hardware/Software

The network interface is established through the NIC. Each type of NIC uses a different type of connector to connect to the physical medium. The connector types are delineated in the IEEE 802 specifications. Each network technology is delineated in its own section of the 802 specification, as described previously. Again, most significantly, Ethernet is defined in 802.3, Token Ring in 802.5, and wireless networking in 802.11.

The NIC employs both hardware and software in connecting the device to the network media. The TCP/IP Network Interface layer defines protocols used by the NIC to receive, assemble, address, and transmit. For example, most Ethernet networks in use today employ an Ethernet NIC, which, among other things, uses CSMA/CD to control media access. The most common type of Ethernet NIC uses a Category 5 or greater unshielded twisted pair cable (typically referred to as UTP CAT5, CAT5e, or CAT6) with specified pin connections. In some cases (although not very common anymore by today's standards), Ethernet is still deployed occasionally over thin (1/4 inch diameter) or thick (1/2 inch diameter) coaxial cable.

Ethernet can also be deployed over fiber optic cable. Regardless of the cable type, Ethernet networks use the same contention-based access control method.

UTP cabling connects to the NIC via an RJ-45 modular plug and jack (similar to a large phone jack), and thin coax (thinnet) connects via a BNC connector (Bayonet Neill Concelman, after its twist-on style and the two men who invented it) shaped like a T. Thick coax (thicknet) is connected via a vampire tap (a metal pin that penetrates the cable) to an external transceiver, which in turn connects to the NIC. Other types of Ethernet NICs have the transceiver built onto the NIC itself. Some NICs (seen in older PC deployments), called combo cards, have connectors for more than one type of cable.

The Ethernet NIC is also responsible for receiving/sending and assembling/disassembling data to and from the network connection. The Network Interface layer in the

DoD model encompasses the functions of the OSI model's Physical and Data Link Control layers and controls media access and the assembly/disassembly of data at the lowest level of the hierarchy.

TEST DAY TIP

It's common to see new technologies being learned, standardized, and implemented at a very rapid speed, but it's also common to be replacing older technologies with said new ones. Therefore, it's common to see historical information on the Network+ exam, historical in that it covers technologies that are not commonly installed anymore, but are definitely commonly removed, migrated, upgraded, or replaced. Prevalent in older renditions of the exam was the need to know about things that were very common to older networking topologies such as coaxial cabling, 10Base5, 10Base2 technologies, Bus networking topologies, and so on. It still holds true today that you should know about these technologies for the exam, so do not overlook studying for them.

Layer Two: Internet (or Internetworking)

The next layer in the DARPA model is the *Internet* layer, which maps to the Network layer of the OSI model. The Internet layer, so called because of the addressing scheme that makes communications possible across a network of networks, or internetwork, is responsible for packaging, addressing, and routing the data. When this layer was originally conceived, the Internet as we know it today did not exist. The concept behind this layer was to define a framework for two computers to connect to one another to share data. This laid the foundation for widespread internetworking, which led to what we now know as the Internet.

Before data can be sent out over the network interface, it must have a standard format, size, and addressing scheme. The Network Interface layer is responsible only for taking the data it is given and translating it into signals on a physical medium. The Internet layer defines packet structure (what each bit of a data segment means), addressing, and routing.

Layer Three: Host-to-Host (or Transport)

Layer 3 in the DARPA model is the *Host-to-Host Transport* layer, sometimes called the *Transport* layer since this layer maps to the Transport layer (Layer 4) in the OSI model. As the name implies, this layer is responsible for transporting the data. It sets up communications between the Application layer and the lower layers. The Internet layer is responsible for formatting, addressing, and routing the data, and the Host-to-Host Transport layer is responsible for setting up the connection between hosts so that formatted data can be sent.

Because this layer establishes a connection, it can also take on some of the responsibilities of the Session layer of the OSI model. In TCP/IP, the two core protocols used at the Host-to-Host Transport layer are TCP and the *User Datagram Protocol* (UDP). TCP is a more complex protocol that provides reliable data transport—the application sending the data receives acknowledgement that the data was received. UDP is a much simpler protocol that does not provide acknowledgement messages. Although this makes UDP data transport less reliable, it is a very useful protocol in certain applications where fast, simple communication is required. Both of these protocols are discussed in detail later in this chapter.

Layer Four: Application

The *Application* layer of the DARPA model operates at the Session, Presentation, and Application layers of the OSI model. One of the main reasons why the DoD model is still used when referencing TCP/IP is because the TCP/IP protocol suite's protocols (such as FTP, Telnet and so on) do not map perfectly into the OSI model, They have overlap, and this is why you will see three OSI model layers under one layer in the DoD model. The DoD model's Application layer enables applications to communicate with one another and it provides access to the services of the other underlying layers (Network Interface [1], Internet [2], and Host-to-Host Transport [3]). There are wide varieties of Application layer protocols, and more are continually being developed because they can rely on all the services beneath them. If you think of how your computer's software is configured, you will realize that you use many different applications that rely upon the services of the underlying operating system. Each application does not have to provide duplicate services, such as a routine for accessing your disk drive. That is provided by the operating system and the application utilizes that functionality. This is how the Application layer of the networking model works as well. It relies upon the underlying services. In this way, developers do not have to write code continually to provide the underlying functionality, but can simply access that functionality by adhering to agreed-upon standards and specifications. We'll look at a number of Application layer protocols when we look at TCP/IP in detail.

We've discussed the four layers of the DARPA or DoD model of internetworking. Throughout this discussion, we've mentioned the OSI model. Now, let's take an in-depth look at the OSI model to understand how the OSI model expands upon the functionality defined in the DARPA model.

Understanding the OSI Model

The OSI model was originally developed at Honeywell in the mid-1970s, and expanded upon the DARPA model. In 1977, the International Organization for Standardization recognized the need to develop a communication standard for computing. They formed a subcommittee called the Open Systems Interconnection committee, and asked for proposals for a communication standard. Honeywell's solution, called *distributed systems architecture* (DSA), included seven layers for communications. This framework was adopted by the OSI, and is still used as the model for distributed communications. The OSI model is shown in Figure 5.2.

Figure 5.2 The Open Systems Interconnection (OSI) Networking Model

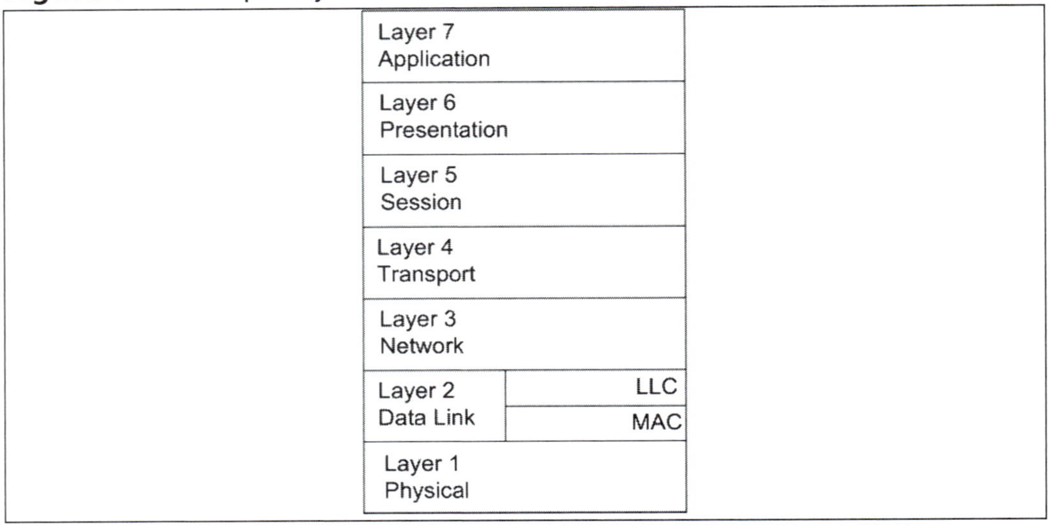

Layer 7 Application	
Layer 6 Presentation	
Layer 5 Session	
Layer 4 Transport	
Layer 3 Network	
Layer 2 Data Link	LLC
	MAC
Layer 1 Physical	

EXAM WARNING

Knowing the OSI model is imperative. You will need to know which devices and protocols function at each layer, so you need to know the layers to start with. Continue to draw the model shown in Figure 5.2 so that when you get to the exam, you can write it on scrap paper to help you with the exam.

We'll explore each of the seven layers of the OSI model in the following subsections. The first two layers of the OSI model involve both hardware and software. In the five upper layers (Layers 3 through 7), the OSI model typically is implemented via software only.

TEST DAY TIP

Some exams may ask you to identify the seven layers of the OSI model, as well as to identify the definitions of one or more of the layers. An acronym used to remember the seven layers of the OSI model is **A**ll **P**eople **S**eem **T**o **N**eed **D**ata **P**rocessing. This equates to **A**pplication, **P**resentation, **S**ession, **T**ransport, **N**etwork, **D**ata Link, and **P**hysical. By remembering this acronym, you'll easily remember the seven layers (in reverse order). Remember that numbering starts at the bottom of the model.

More commonly, the Network+ exam requires you to know and understand what happens at each layer, and which protocols operate there (rather than just rote memorization of the layers themselves) in order to be able to troubleshoot common networking problems.

The OSI model is represented as a *stack* because data that is sent across the network has to move through each layer at both the sending and receiving ends. The sending computer generally initiates the process at the Application layer. The data is then sent down the stack to the Physical layer and across the network to the receiving computer. On the receiving end, the data is received at the Physical layer and the data packet is sent up the stack to the Application layer. A good visualization of this can be seen in Figure 5.3, where Computer A wants to browse a website home page of Server B, such as www.syngress.com/index.htm.

Figure 5.3 Viewing a Web page using the OSI Model

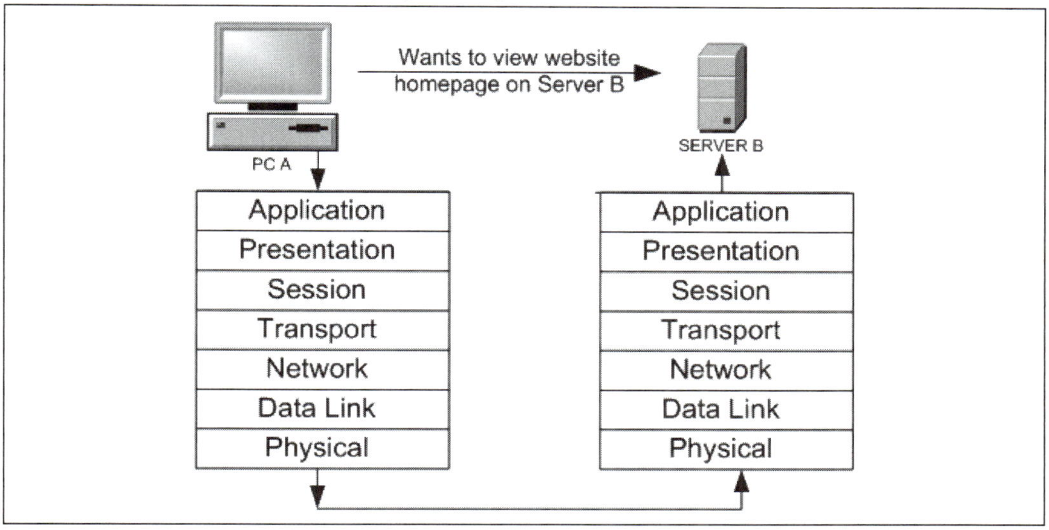

To view how this works, consider these facts. The home page **index.htm** is the file that is located in a folder (or directory) on the Web server, and this is what computer A wants to view. Computer A is connected to an ISP (Internet Service Provider) via a home PC, a NIC, a cable modem or whatever the ISP requires for connectivity. Computer A opens a Web browser (which is an application), the Web browser (not needing to know anything other than to make a request to the Web server), sends the request, and underlying protocols process it. The Application layer (not to be associated with the application itself), starts the process. Encapsulation (addition of small pieces of information relative to the transmission of information) happens at each layer, with each layer adding its information to the data to get it to the Web server, and then reversing the process to get information back again. As you can see, you only see the request; the Web server will answer back with **index.htm**. The beauty of this depiction is that it is very easy to see and clearly understand why you absolutely need to know the OSI model and what happens at each layer.

Head of the Class…

Advanced Networking

You don't need to know very advanced levels of networking for the exam. The testing will not dig down into packet headers, encapsulation types and so on, but if you want to make a career out of networking, you will eventually need to know this information. For that reason, let's dig into the OSI model a little more (Figure 5.4).

Figure 5.4 Viewing More Detail Within the OSI Model

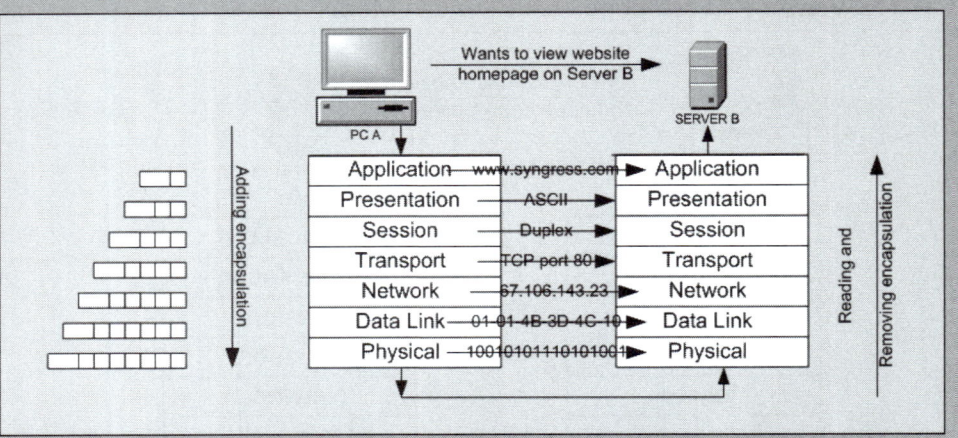

As computer A wants to visit the website of syngress.com, the Web browser on the local PC is where the URL (Uniform Resource Locator) is entered into the browser application's address area. In this example, www.syngress.com is entered, and then the real magic happens. As the request heads to the server, the

Continued

www.syngress.com

OSI model handles the request, and Figure 5.4 shows all the things that are happening, such as IP addressing information, MAC address information and so on. All of this will be explained in the following sections, but this is how you could mentally map the data transmission in your head. Remember that this chart and information is not needed for the exam, but for your general understanding of the topic.

Again, knowing the OSI model information provides a foundation for you to grow and build on. Let's now dig into the specifics of each layer starting from the lowest layer, the layer that makes use of the physical transmission medium, the Physical Layer.

Layer 1: Physical

The first, most basic layer of the OSI model is the *Physical* layer. This layer specifies the electrical and mechanical requirements for transmitting data bits across the transmission medium (cable or airwaves). It involves sending and receiving the data stream on the carrier—whether that carrier uses electrical (cable), light (fiber optic) or radio, infrared or laser (wireless) signals. The Physical layer specifications include:

- Voltage changes
- Timing of voltage changes
- Data rates
- Maximum transmission distances
- Physical connectors to the transmission medium
- Topology or physical layout of the network

Many complex issues are addressed at the Physical layer, including digital versus analog signaling, baseband versus broadband signaling, whether data is transmitted synchronously or asynchronously, and how signals are divided into channels (multiplexing).

Devices that operate at the Physical layer deal with signaling, such as the transceivers on the NIC, and the basic and simple connectors that join segments of cable.

Digital Versus Analog Signaling

These days, in the "digital age", there is hardly a day that goes by without the need surfacing for some form of electricity in your life. So what is this analog signaling and why so much concern? Well, because as a Network+ technician, you will need to understand how different types of technology work, and the perfect example to drive this home would be the *modem*, a device that a great many people utilize every day to access the Internet via their standard preexisting telephone lines.

A modem is a device that Mo... (Modulates) Dem... (Demodulates) a signal, or in easier to understand terms... the modem translates an analog system signal to a digital system signal and back again so that the signal can traverse along the plain old telephone service (POTS). It should then make sense to the PCs sending and receiving it, as the modem does the PC the favor of taking that analog signal and translating it into a digital one, which is what your PC natively understands.

EXAM WARNING

Modems translate analog to digital signals and back again. PCs are using digital technology to communicate, but the phone lines are using analog signaling. Therefore, the signal must be changed from one signaling method to the other as needed, such as when you want to connect your PC up to your ISP and surf the Internet.

So what is analog? Analog signals are electronic signals that are based on a wave that moves up and down continuously (as shown in Figure 5.5). A more technical definition of this technology is that analog signals are electronic signals that are transmitted by adding a signal of varying frequency or amplitude to a carrier wave of a given frequency of alternating electromagnetic current. For the Network+ exam, don't worry too much about the technical jargon here… understanding how this functions will help you to understand what the Physical layer of the OSI model is responsible for… and why.

Figure 5.5 Analog Signaling

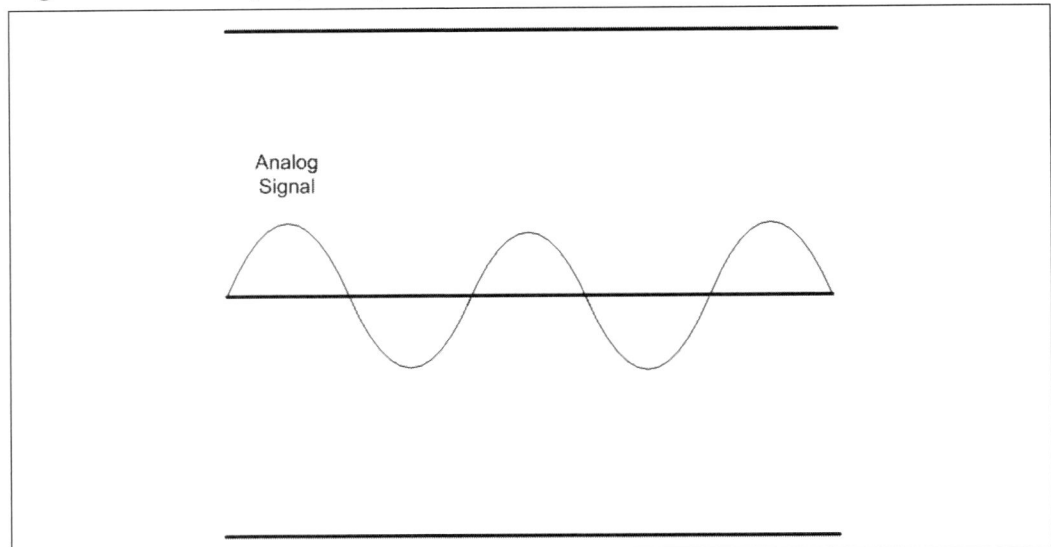

Analog signals, although commonly used today (consider the telephone in your home) are actually not commonly used for new installations. Nothing new implemented today in technology utilizes analog anymore: most if not all of it winds up in digital format. Digital communications are more compatible with PCs because that's how PCs operate, via digital technology. Digital signals are more reliable and easier to transmit. For this reason it should be clear as to why digital is so important to understand and learn. As shown in Figure 5.6, you should see that since computers operate on 1s and 0s, digital (either being on or off, like a light switch if you will) fits binary math perfectly. 1 or 0, on or off. Now that you have seen both signaling methods, let's move on to possible issues based on digital technology.

Figure 5.6 Digital Signaling

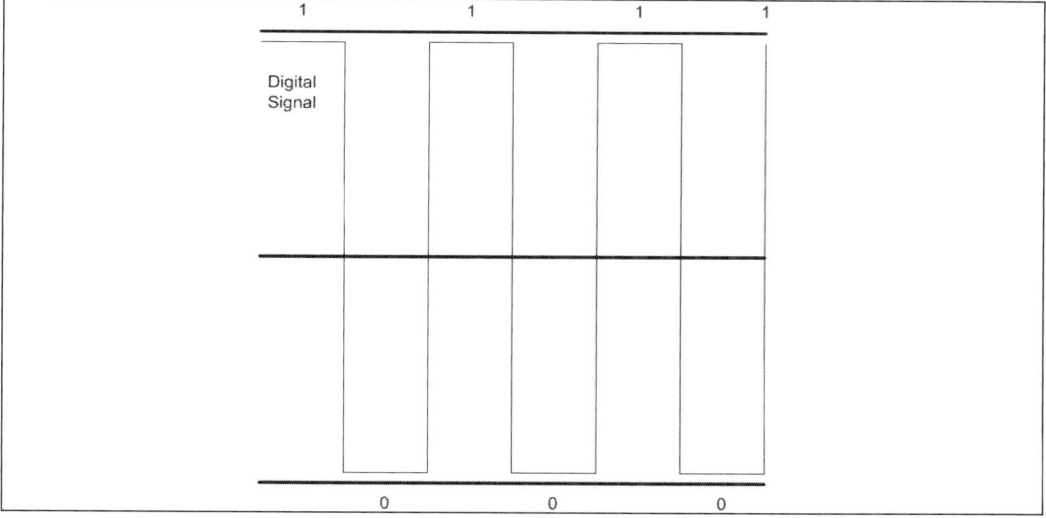

Issues like *attenuation* (degradation of the signal) can really ruin digital communications. For example, if you were installing a PC over 150 meters away from the concentrator it is connected to, (10BaseT technologies have a maximum allowed distance of about 100 meters or 328 feet), the signal is likely to degrade (Figure 5.7).

Figure 5.7 The Effects of Attenuation on a Digital Signal

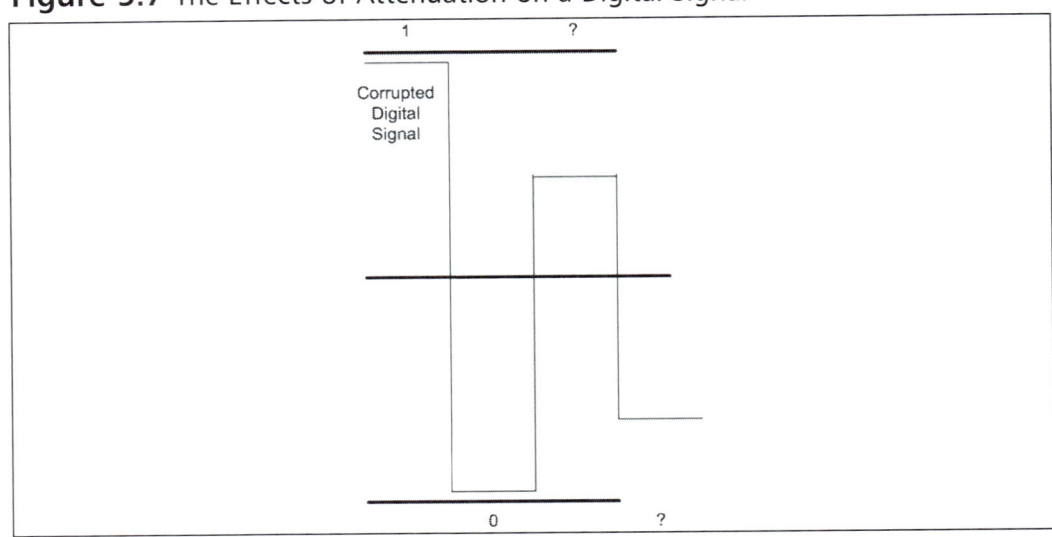

As Figure 5.7 shows, because the signal has degraded, the ones and zeros become "unknowns" because they fall short of being either a 1 or 0. This example demonstrates how exceeding maximum cable distances will in fact cause you issues later on.

TEST DAY TIP

Don't get confused about terminology such as Baseband and Broadband. Make sure you understand the following:

Baseband is a method of data transmission where all bandwidth on the transmission medium is used to transmit a single digital signal. As you saw in Figure 5.6, Baseband technology uses digital signaling.

Broadband is a method of data transmission where the bandwidth on the transmission medium is broken into channels that are capable of supporting a wide range of frequencies.

Make sure you are comfortable with the terminology and that you understand what each is and does. It will be important to understand, as you learn about 10BaseT, the *Base* stands for Baseband. 10BaseT runs at 10 Mbps, it has a 100 Meter limit on distance. The T is for *twisted-pair* cabling.

In sum, when dealing with the Physical layer, the data handled is in bits—literally 1s and 0s. These 1s and 0s are represented by pulses of light or electricity (on generally represents a 1 and off generally represents a 0). How these bits are arranged and managed is a function of the next layer in the OSI model.

Layer 2: Data Link

Layer 2 is the *Data Link* layer. This layer is responsible for maintaining the data link between two computers, typically called *hosts* or *nodes*. It also defines and manages the ordering of bits to and from data segments, called *packets*. *Frames* contain data arranged in an organized manner, which provides for an orderly and consistent method of sending data bits across the medium. Without such control, the data would be sent in random sizes or configurations and the data that was sent on one end could not be decoded on the other end. The Data Link layer manages the physical addressing and syn-chronization of the data packets (as opposed to the logical addressing that is handled at the Network layer). The Data Link layer is also responsible for flow control and error notification. Flow control is the process of managing the timing of sending and receiving data so that it doesn't exceed the capacity (speed, memory, etcetera) of the physical connection. Since the Physical layer is responsible only for physically moving the data onto and off of the network medium, the Data Link layer also receives and manages error messaging related to physical delivery of packets.

Network devices that operate at this layer include Layer 2 switches (switching hubs) and bridges. A Layer 2 switch decreases network congestion by sending data out only on the port to which the destination computer is attached, instead of sending it out on all ports, as a physical layer hub does. Bridges provide a way to segment a network into two parts and filter traffic by building tables that define which computers are located on which side of the bridge, based on their MAC addresses.

The Data Link layer is divided into two sublayers: the *Logical Link Control* (LLC) sublayer and the *Media Access Control* sublayer. These were originally seen in the OSI model diagram in Figure 5.2.

The LLC Sublayer

The LLC sublayer provides the logic for the data link, thus it controls the synchroniza-tion, flow control, and error checking functions of the Data Link layer. This layer can handle connection-oriented transmissions (unlike the MAC sublayer below it), although connectionless service can also be provided by this layer. Connectionless operations are known as Class I LLC, whereas Class II can handle either connectionless or connection-oriented operations. With connection-oriented communication, each LLC frame that is sent is acknowledged. The LLC sublayer at the receiving end keeps up with the LLC frames it receives (these are also called Protocol Data Units or PDUs), and if it detects that a frame has been lost during the transmission, it can send back a request to the sending computer to start the transmission over again, beginning with the PDU that never arrived.

The LLC sublayer sits above the MAC sublayer, and acts as a liaison between the upper layers and the protocols that operate at the MAC sublayer such as Ethernet, Token Ring, and so on (IEEE standards). The LLC sublayer itself is defined by IEEE 802.2.

Link addressing, sequencing, and definition of Service Access Points (SAPs) also take place at this layer.

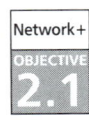

Network+
OBJECTIVE
2.1

The MAC Sublayer

The MAC sublayer provides control for accessing the transmission medium. It is responsible for moving data packets from one NIC to another, across a shared transmission medium such as an Ethernet or fiber optic transmission medium.

Physical addressing is addressed at the MAC sublayer. Every NIC has a unique MAC address, also called the physical address, which identifies that specific NIC on the network. The MAC address of a NIC is usually burned into a read-only memory (ROM) chip on the NIC. Each manufacturer of network cards is provided a unique set of MAC addresses so that (theoretically, at least) every NIC that is manufactured has a unique MAC address. Obviously, it would be confusing if there were two or more NICs with the same MAC address. A packet intended for NIC #35 (a simplification of the MAC address) would not know to *which* NIC #35 it was destined. To avoid this confusion, MAC addresses, in most cases, are permanently burned into the NIC's memory. This is sometimes referred to as the Burned-In Address or BIA.

EXAM WARNING

A MAC address consists of six hexadecimal numbers. The highest possible hexadecimal number is FF:FF:FF:FF:FF:FF, which is a broadcast address. The first three bytes contain a manufacturer code and the last three bytes contain a unique station ID. You must understand the functionality of a NIC card and what a MAC address is for the Network+ exam. On Ethernet NICs, the physical or MAC address (also called the hardware address) is expressed as 12 hexadecimal digits, arranged in pairs with colons between each pair, for example, 12:3A:4D:66:3A:1C. In binary notation, this translates to a 48-bit (or 6-byte) number, with the initial three bytes representing the manufacturer and the last three bits representing a unique network interface card made by that manufacturer. On Token Ring NICs, the MAC address is six bytes long, too, but the bits of each byte are reversed. That is, Ethernet transmits in canonical or LSB (least significant bit) mode, with the least significant bit first, whereas Token Ring transmits with the most significant bit first (MSB or non-canonical mode). Although duplicate MAC addresses are rare, they do show up because some manufacturers have started to use their numbers over again. This usually is not a problem because the duplicates almost never show up on the same network. Some cards allow you to change the MAC address by using special software to "flash" the card's chip. You can view the MAC address on most systems with the following commands.

Windows ME, 9x: **winipcfg** (navigate the GUI to find the MAC address)
Windows NT, XP, 2000, 2003: **ipconfig /all**
Linux: **ifconfig -a**
On Linux, an Ethernet network interface is commonly seen as **eth0**. Under this information you will find the relevant MAC for your system.

Another important issue that's handled at the MAC sublayer is media access control. This refers to the method used to allocate network access to computers and prevent them from transmitting at the same time, causing data collisions. Common media access control methods include Carrier Sense Multiple Access/Collision Detection, used by Ethernet networks, Carrier Sense Multiple Access/Collision Avoidance, used by AppleTalk networks, and token passing, used by Token Ring and FDDI networks. In Exercise 5.1, we'll go through the steps of identifying a MAC address on a Windows XP Professional system.

EXERCISE 5.1

LOCATING A MAC ADDRESS WITH WINDOWS XP PROFESSIONAL

1. Click **Start | Programs | Accessories | Command Prompt** to access the Windows Command Prompt.

2. Enter the command **ipconfig /all** to see the Physical Address for the adapter that corresponds with your current network connection. You will see the systems MAC address, similar to the one shown below.

   ```
   Physical Address. . . . . . . . . : 00-0C-F1-54-45-89
   ```

3. To close the Windows Command Prompt, type **exit**, then press **Enter**.

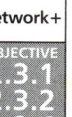

Layer 3: Network

As we travel up the OSI model, the next layer we encounter is the *Network* layer. At the Network layer, packets are sequenced and logical addressing is handled. Logical addresses are nonpermanent, software-assigned addresses that can be changed by administrators. The IP addresses used by the TCP/IP protocols on the Internet and the IPX addresses used by the IPX/SPX protocols on NetWare networks are examples of logical addresses. These protocol stacks are referred to as *routable* because they include addressing schemes that identify both the network or subnet and the particular client on that network or subnet. Other network/transport protocols, such as NetBEUI, do not have a sophisticated addressing scheme (nor the programming intelligence of high OSI model layers such as Network Layer and Transport Layer) thus crippling it and not allowing it to be routed across different networks. To make sure you understand what is meant by this, view Figure 5.8. Here, you see a network subdivided by different IP subnets (this will be covered in greater depth in Chapter 6).

Figure 5.8 TCP/IP Networks Subdivided and Connected Via Routers

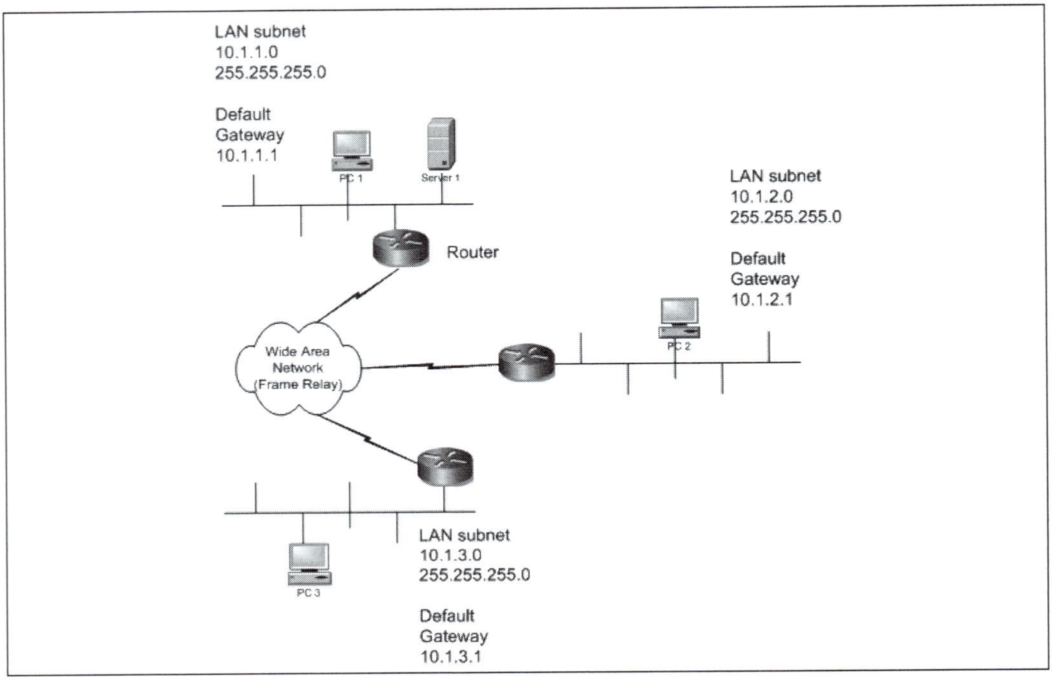

You can see that each LAN is connected to each other to via a WAN, using Frame Relay (both of which will be covered in depth in Chapter 7). The most critical fact here is that all of this logical addressing and routing are done at the Network layer of the OSI model. Each subnet must be unique, and each LAN will need to know how to get to the other LANs. That's where the WAN and the routers come in, acting as the default gateway for your network. Also, you need to understand that logical addressing (such as the 10.1.1.1 255.255.255.0 address being assigned to the router on the LAN as the default gateway), is important—it defines how and where the packets are sent, and so on. So, now that you have assigned the IP address, how does the MAC address tie in? Well, a TCP/IP protocol called ARP (Address Resolution Protocol) will help map an IP address to a physical machine address.

NOTE

To understand the difference between physical and logical addresses, consider this analogy: If you buy a house, it has a physical address that identifies exactly where it is located on the earth, at a specific latitude and longitude. This never changes (unless you have a mobile home that can be moved from one plot of land to another). This is like the MAC address on a NIC. Your house also has a logical address assigned to it by the post office, consisting of a street number and street name. The city can (and occasionally does) change the names of streets, or renumber the houses located on them. This is like the IP address assigned to a network interface.

The Network layer is also responsible for creating a virtual circuit (a logical connection, not a physical connection) between points or nodes. A node is a device that has a MAC address, which typically includes computers, printers, and routers. This layer is also responsible for routing, Layer 3 switching (which is nothing more than a Layer 2 switch with a Layer 3 router built into it), and the forwarding of packets.

Routing refers to forwarding packets from one network or subnet to another. Without routing, computers can communicate only with other computers that are on the same network via ARP broadcasts. Routing makes it possible for computers to send data through many networks to other computers that are on the other side of the world. Routing is the key to the global Internet, and is one of the most important duties of the Network layer. Easy to remember, routing is simple to understand. If you start with a LAN that has the 10.1.1.0 255.255.255.0 network, and you wanted to get to the 10.1.2.0 255.255.255.0 network (which has a different network number in the third octet) you would need a router with a routing table (so it knows where to send the packet) to get it there.

Finally, the Network layer provides additional levels of flow control and error control. As mentioned earlier, from this point on, the primary methods of implementing the OSI model architecture involve software rather than hardware.

Devices that operate at this layer include, most prominently, routers and Layer 3 switches.

Head of the Class...

Different Switches for Different Layers

Troubleshooting network problems requires that you understand which protocols and devices operate at which layers of the networking model. It's important to understand that all switches are not created equal. There are actually several different types of devices that are called switches, and they operate at different layers of the OSI model.

Layer 2 switches are sometimes called standard switches. They operate at the Data Link layer, and function like sophisticated hubs. When a computer sends data to a hub, the hub sends it back out on all ports, to all the connected computers. A switch sends the data only out the port to which the destination computer (based on the addressing information in the headers) is attached. This decreases the amount of unnecessary traffic on the network and also increases security.

Layer 3 switches operate at the Network layer, and are really a specialized type of router. They're sometimes called switched routers. Layer 3 switches use the information in the packet headers to apply policies, in addition to performing normal routing functions.

Layer 4 switches operate at the Transport layer (in addition to the lower layers) and can use the port number information from TCP or UDP headers. They can provide Access Control Lists (ACLs) to filter traffic for better security, and are able to control bandwidth allocation for load balancing purposes. Some routers also function as Layer 4 switches. These devices can help to identify application layer (layer 7) protocols, such as capable HTTP (Hypertext Transfer Protocol), FTP (File Transfer Protocol), and so on.

Layer 4: Transport

Layer 4 is the *Transport* layer. As the name implies, it is responsible for transporting the data from one node to another. It provides transparent data transfer between nodes and manages the end-to-end flow control, error detection, and error recovery.

The Transport layer protocols initiate contact between host computers and set up a virtual circuit. The transport protocols on each host computer verify that the application sending the data is authorized to access the network and that both ends are ready to initiate the data transfer. When this synchronization is complete, the data can be sent. As the data is being transmitted, the transport protocol on each host monitors the data flow and watches for transport errors. If transport errors are detected, the transport protocol can provide error recovery.

The functions performed by the Transport layer are very important to network communication. Just as the Data Link layer provides lower level reliability and connection-oriented or connectionless communications, the Transport layer does the same thing at a higher level. In fact, the two protocols most commonly associated with the Transport layer are defined by their connection state: The Transmission Control Protocol is connection-oriented, whereas the User Datagram Protocol is connectionless.

Head of the Class...

Connection-Oriented vs. Connectionless

What's the difference between a connection-oriented and a connectionless protocol? A connection-oriented protocol such as TCP creates a connection between the two computers before actually sending the data, and then verifies that the data has reached its destination by using acknowledgements (messages sent back to the sending computer from the receiving computer that acknowledge receipt). Connectionless protocols send the data and trust that it will reach the proper destination.

Consider an analogy: You need to send a very important letter to a business associate, containing valuable papers that must not get lost along the way. You call him before mailing the letter, to let him know he should expect it (establishing the connection). You might even insure it or send it via certified mail. After a few days have passed, your friend calls you back to let you know that he did receive the letter, or you get back the return receipt that you requested (acknowledgement). This is the way a connection-oriented communication works. It's different from mailing a relatively unimportant item, such as a postcard to a friend when you're on vacation. In that case, you just drop it in the mailbox and hope it gets to the addressee. You don't expect or require any acknowledgement. This is like a connectionless communication.

What else does the Transport layer do? It handles another aspect of logical addressing: ports. If you think of a computer's IP address as analogous to the street address of a building, you can think of a port as a suite number or apartment number within that building. It further defines exactly where the data should go.

A computer might have several network applications running at the same time: a Web browser sending a request to a Web server for a Web page, an e-mail client sending and receiving mail, and a file transfer program uploading or downloading information to and from an FTP server. There must be some mechanism to determine which incoming data packets belong to which application, and that's the function of port numbers. The FTP protocol used by that program is assigned a particular port, whereas the Web browser and e-mail clients use different protocols (HTTP and POP3 [Post Office Protocol] or IMAP [Internet Message Access Protocol]) that have their own assigned ports. Thus the information that is intended for the Web browser doesn't go to the e-mail program by mistake. Port numbers are used by the Transport layer protocols (TCP and UDP).

Finally, the Transport layer deals with name resolution. Because human beings prefer to identify computers by names instead of IP addresses (after all, it's easier to remember "www.microsoft.com" for Microsoft's Web server than "207.46.249.222", for example), but computers know only how to interpret numbers (and binary numbers, at that), there must be a way for names to be matched with numerical addresses so that people and computers don't drive one another crazy. Name resolution methods such as the Domain Name System (DNS) solve this problem, and they generally operate at the upper layers of the OSI model.

Layer 5: Session

After the Transport layer has established the virtual connection, a communication session can be established. A communication session occurs between two processes on two different computers. The *Session* layer is responsible for establishing, monitoring, and terminating sessions, using the virtual circuits established by the Transport layer.

The Session layer is also responsible for putting header information into data packets to indicate where the message begins and ends. Once header information is attached to the data packets, the Session layer performs synchronization between the sender's Session layer and the receiver's Session layer. The use of acknowledgement messages (ACKs) helps coordinate transfer of data at the Session layer.

A very important function of the Session layer is controlling whether the communications within a session are sent as full duplex or half duplex messages. Half duplex communication goes in both directions between the communicating computers, but information can travel in only one direction at a time (as with walkie-talkie radio communications, in which you have to hold down the microphone button to transmit and cannot hear the person on the other end when you do). With full duplex communication, information can be sent in both directions at the same time (as in a regular telephone conversation, in which both parties can talk and hear one another at the same time).

Whereas the Transport layer establishes a connection between two machines, the Session layer establishes a connection between two processes. A *process* is a defined task related to an application. An application may run many processes simultaneously to accomplish the work of the application. These processes are small executable files that together do the work required by the application. You can view the processes running on your Windows-based computer by pressing **CTL+ALT+DEL,** selecting **Task Manager**, and then clicking the **Processes** tab. You'll notice you have far more processes running than applications since each application typically runs more than one process at a time.

The Session layer, then, is responsible for setting up the connection between an application process on one computer and an application process on another computer, after the Transport layer has established the connection between the two machines.

> **N**OTE
>
> Earlier in this chapter we mentioned multiplexing. Computer communications can be in half duplex or full duplex mode. *Simplex,* or unidirectional (one-way) communication generally is not used in computer networking. It is the type of communication used for radio and over-the-air TV broadcasts (many CATV transmissions now use two-way signaling to allow for interactive TV).

There are a number of important protocols that operate at the Session layer, including Windows Sockets (the Winsock interface) and NetBIOS (the Network Basic Input/Output interface).

Layer 6: Presentation

Data translation is the primary activity of Layer 6, the *Presentation* layer. When data is sent from sender to receiver, the data is translated at the Presentation layer. The sender's application passes data down to the Presentation layer, where it is put into a common format. When the data is received on the other end, the Presentation layer changes the data from the common format back into a format that is usable by the application. Protocol translation, the conversion of data from one protocol to another so that it can be exchanged between computers that use different platforms or operating systems, takes place here.

This is the layer at which many gateway services operate. Gateways are connection points between networks that use different platforms or applications. Examples include e-mail gateways (which allow for communications between two different e-mail programs using a common protocol such as SMTP [Simple Mail Transfer Protocol]), Systems Network Architecture (SNA) gateways (which allow PCs to communicate with mainframe computers), and gateways that cross platforms or file systems (for example, allowing Microsoft clients that use the Server Message Block protocol for file sharing to access files on NetWare servers that use NetWare Core Protocol). Gateways are usually implemented via software, such as the Gateway Services for NetWare (GSNW). Software redirectors also operate at this layer.

This layer is also where data compression can take place, to minimize the actual number of bits that must be transmitted on the network media to the receiver. Data encryption and decryption take place in the Presentation layer as well.

Layer 7: Application

The *Application* layer is the point at which the user application program interacts with the network. This layer of the OSI model should not be confused with the application itself. This is very important to understand and remember, as they share the same name. Application processes, such as file transfers or e-mail, are initiated within a user application (for example, an e-mail program). Then the data created by that process are handed to the Application layer of the networking software. Everything that occurs at this level is application-specific. File sharing, remote printer access, network monitoring and management, remote procedure calls (RPCs), and all forms of electronic messaging occur at this level.

Both FTP (a common way of transferring files across a network) and *Telnet* function within the Application layer, as do SMTP, POP3, and IMAP4, all of which are used for sending or receiving e-mail. There are many other Application layer protocols, including HTTP, Network News Transfer Protocol (NNTP), and Simple Network Management Protocol (SNMP).

Be sure to distinguish between the protocols mentioned and applications that may bear the same names. There are many different FTP programs made by different software vendors, but all of them use the FTP protocol to transfer files.

TEST DAY TIP

Although it's important to *understand* the details of the OSI model for the exam, you're likely to run into a limited number of questions related to the specific layers of the model. Understanding the basic functions of each layer will help you easily identify correct answers to the questions you may see on the exam. It is especially important to remember that, when troubleshooting, you should start with Layer 1 (Physical) and work your way up. A common error among technicians and network administrators is starting to troubleshoot at Layer 7. Greater detail about troubleshooting with the OSI model can be found in Chapter 12, "Network Troubleshooting Methodology".

Encapsulation of Data

One last item to cover before we move on to new material is that you should make sure you understand what encapsulation is and how it works. Notice that each layer in Figure 5.9 adds a header to the data packet so that by the time it reaches the Physical layer (the last one on the bottom), it is much longer than when it started at the Application layer. When data are received by the receiving host, the headers are stripped off as the data moves back up the stack, one layer at a time, by the layer that corresponds to the one that added it. This means that each layer on the sending computer communicates only with the layer of the same name on the receiving machine.

Figure 5.9 Data Moving Through the OSI Layers

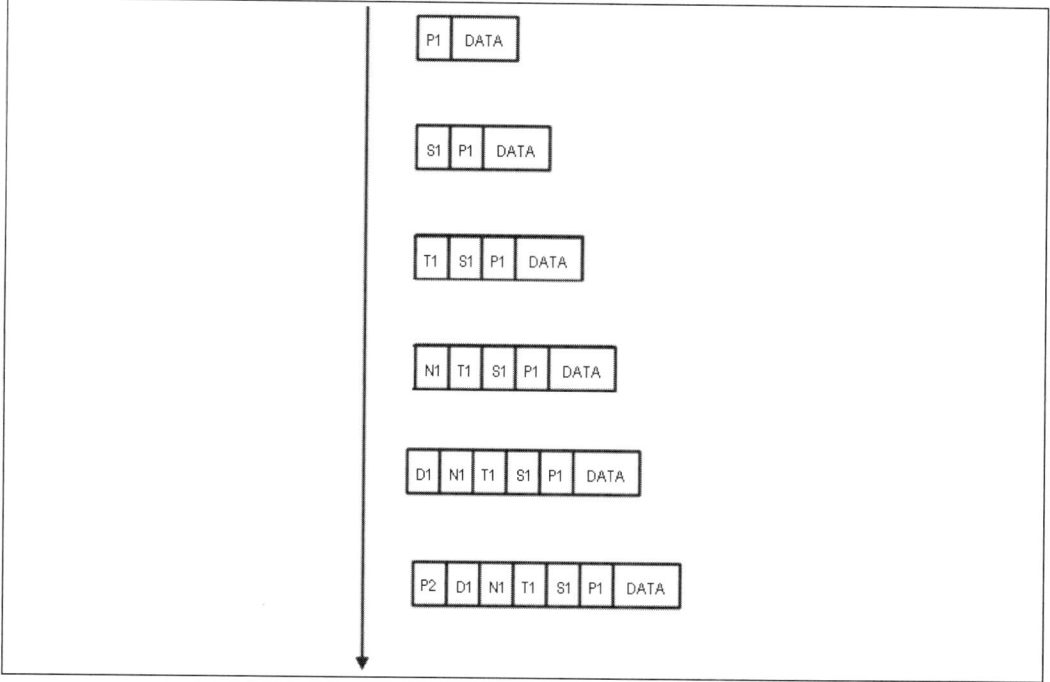

Now that the OSI model has been described for you, let's look at how Microsoft maps to this model. As you will see, many of the terms you may have heard in your training (such as API and NDIS) will be explained in the next few sections.

Test Day Tip

The information that follows is information only, and not directly related to the Network+, but reading it will definitely help you understand some key terms that you are definitely going to see on the Network+ exam, as well as in the real world of networking.

The Microsoft Model

Prior to the release of Windows NT 3.1, users who wanted to connect to a network had to obtain the TCP/IP protocol suite from a third party and install it. TCP/IP did not come bundled with the software. At times, the TCP/IP software that was purchased didn't work well with the operating system (OS) because it handled various tasks of network communication in a slightly different way than did the operating system. This sometimes led to intermittent network problems or time spent troubleshooting TCP/IP and operating system interoperability.

With the release of Windows NT 3.1, TCP/IP was built into the operating system, providing a seamless integration of networking functionality in the OS. Since that time, it has become standard to provide TCP/IP with the operating system since so many computers today connect to a network in one form or another.

The *Microsoft model* provides a standard platform for application developers. Its modular design enables the developer to rely on the underlying services of the OS through the use of standard interfaces. (Sound familiar to the discussion we had earlier on the DoD and OSI models?) These interfaces provide specific functionality developers can use as building blocks to develop an application. This makes development time shorter and provides common interfaces for users, making learning and using new applications easier.

Though the Microsoft model is used primarily by programmers, it's important to understand the framework of how TCP/IP works on a Microsoft Windows-based computer.

Understanding the Function of Boundary Layers

The Microsoft model describes software and hardware components and the connections between them that facilitate computer networking. This modular approach both allows and encourages hardware and software vendors to develop products that work together through the Microsoft operating system. Boundary layers are interfaces that reside at the boundaries of functionality. They interact with the layer below and the layer above, providing an interface from one layer to the next.

Within each layer, various components perform the tasks defined at that layer. A variety of components can provide similar functionality at any given layer. This modular approach provides flexibility for developers while providing common interfaces that reduce development time and cost. A vendor can provide new functionality at any of these layers, knowing their products will integrate with the other layers to provide seamless network communications. The interfaces defined by Microsoft are the *Network Device Interface Specification* (NDIS), *Transport Driver Interface* (TDI), and the *Application Program Interface* (API). Figure 5.10 shows the relationship of these boundary layers to both the OSI model and to the Microsoft Architecture.

The Windows OS is divided into three primary areas: the User, the Executive, and the Kernel. The Kernel is the core of the Microsoft operating system architecture and it manages the most basic operations including interacting with the hardware abstraction layer that interacts with the hardware (CPU, memory, etcetera). The Kernel also synchronizes activities with the Executive level, which includes the Input/Output (I/O) Manager and the Process Manager. The User level interacts with the Executive level; this is the level at which most applications and user interfaces reside.

Figure 5.10 The Microsoft Model

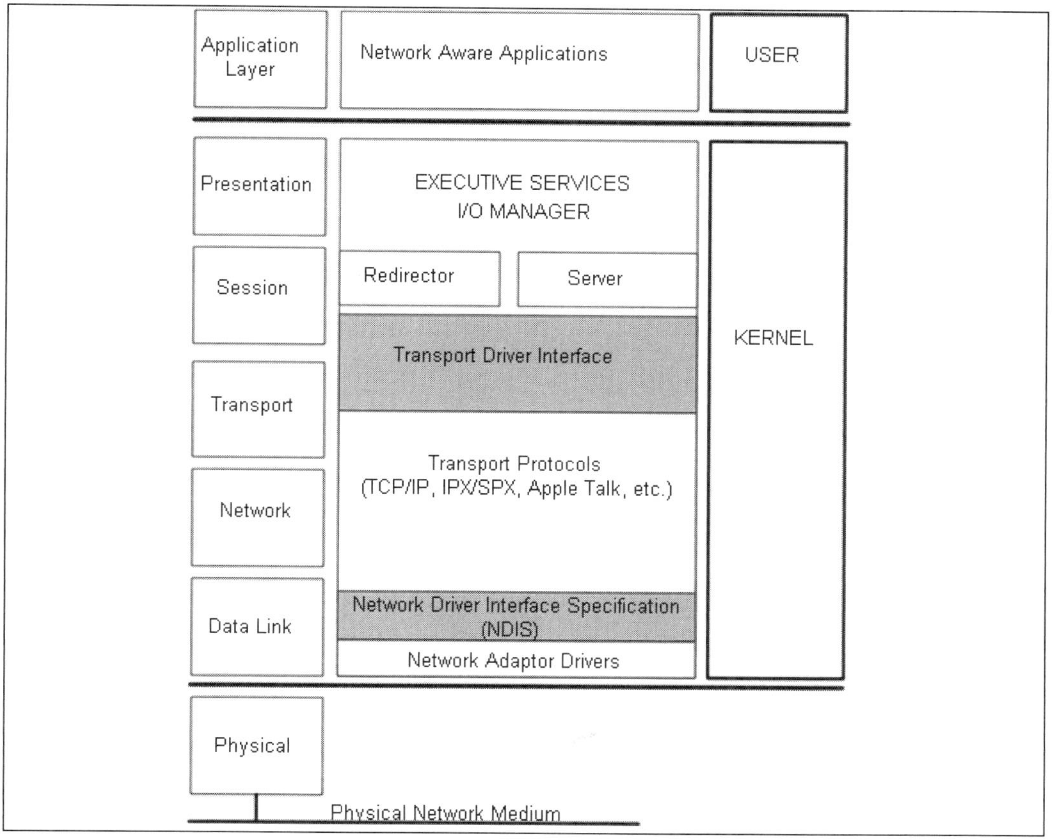

The Network Driver Interface Specification Boundary Layer

The Network Driver Interface Specification works at the bottom of the networking architecture and maps to the Data Link layer of the OSI model and the Network Interface layer of the DARPA model. The NDIS layer is the boundary between the physical network (Physical layer of the OSI model) and the higher-level transport protocols. This layer provides the standardized functions that allow various transport protocols to use any network device driver that is compatible with the specifications of this layer, providing both flexibility and reliability to developers. The earliest versions of NDIS were developed by a Microsoft and 3Com joint effort.

The Transport Driver Interface Boundary Layer

The Transport Driver Interface provides a portal into the transport protocols for kernel mode components such as servers and redirectors. In essence, it is the gateway between the Transport layer and the Session layer in the OSI model, providing a common interface that developers can use to access both Transport and Session layer functionality.

The Application Program Interface Boundary Layer

The Application Program Interface is the interface through which developers can access network infrastructure services such as various Application layer protocols. Dynamic Host Configuration Protocol (DHCP), DNS, and Windows Internet Name Service (WINS) all work at this level and connect to the lower layers through APIs. There are also Windows Sockets (WinSock), NetBIOS, telephony, and messaging APIs used to assist in carrying out lower level network functions.

Understanding Component Layers

Within each layer are component layers that provide very specific functionality.

The NDIS Wrapper

The NDIS wrapper is a library of common NDIS functions that can be used both by the MAC protocols beneath it and by TCP/IP above it. The NDIS wrapper is implemented by a file called *Ndis.sys*, which is software code that surrounds all NDIS device drivers. It provides a common interface for device drivers and protocol drivers. The NDIS wrapper is used to reduce platform dependencies during development of network interface devices.

Network Transport Protocols

Network transport protocols allow all applications or clients to send and receive data over the network. Although we're discussing TCP/IP specifically in this chapter, other network transport protocols include IPX/SPX, ATM, NetBEUI, Infrared Data Association (IrDA), AppleTalk, and SNA. These protocols are used on a variety of non-Microsoft operating systems including Novell, Apple, and IBM.

File System Drivers

The file system drivers are the *redirector* and the *server service*. When there is a request to open a shared file, the I/O Manager sends a request to the redirector, which selects the appropriate Transport layer protocol via the TDI layer. When there is a request to access a local file, the server service responds to requests from the remote redirector and provides access to the requested file. Named pipes, mailslots, server service, and redirector are file system drivers that work at both the Presentation and Session layers of the OSI model.

Applications and User Mode Services

Applications must interface with the lower layer protocols and must interact in some manner with the user. These services are implemented in a number of ways, but there are four commonly used APIs implemented at this point that provide access to lower transport protocols.

The WinSock API allows Windows-based applications to communicate with the lower layers. Winsock is a protocol-independent networking API that provides standard-ized access to datagram and session services over TCP/IP, IPX/SPX, AppleTalk, and others.

Telephony integrates computers with telephone technology and utilizes the Telephony API (TAPI) to provide a standardized interface to networking protocols for various telephony applications. The NetBIOS API has been used for developing client/server applications and is supported in Windows 2003 for backward compatibility. The Messaging API (MAPI) is an industry standard that assists applications in interfacing with messaging services via a single interface. Microsoft Exchange uses MAPI.

So in sum, although you won't be asked questions on the Network+ exam that directly relate to this information about the Microsoft model, not having it at all leaves massive gaps in your networking information. Understanding the Microsoft model helps to give you key terminology you will see so you understand what it means when you see it, to help differentiate wrong answers and so on. Now, let's jump into the OSI model again, but with a direct eye on TCP/IP so that we can prepare for Chapter 6.

Understanding the TCP/IP Protocol Suite

In the first section of this chapter, we discussed the DoD's DARPA model, which has four layers: Network Interface, Internet, Transport, and Application. Since TCP/IP is an outgrowth of the DoD's DARPA model, the TCP/IP protocol architecture uses those same four layers. However, there is a direct correlation between the OSI model's seven layers and TCP/IP's four layers, as shown in Figure 5.11.

Figure 5.11 The TCP/IP Protocol Suite and OSI Model

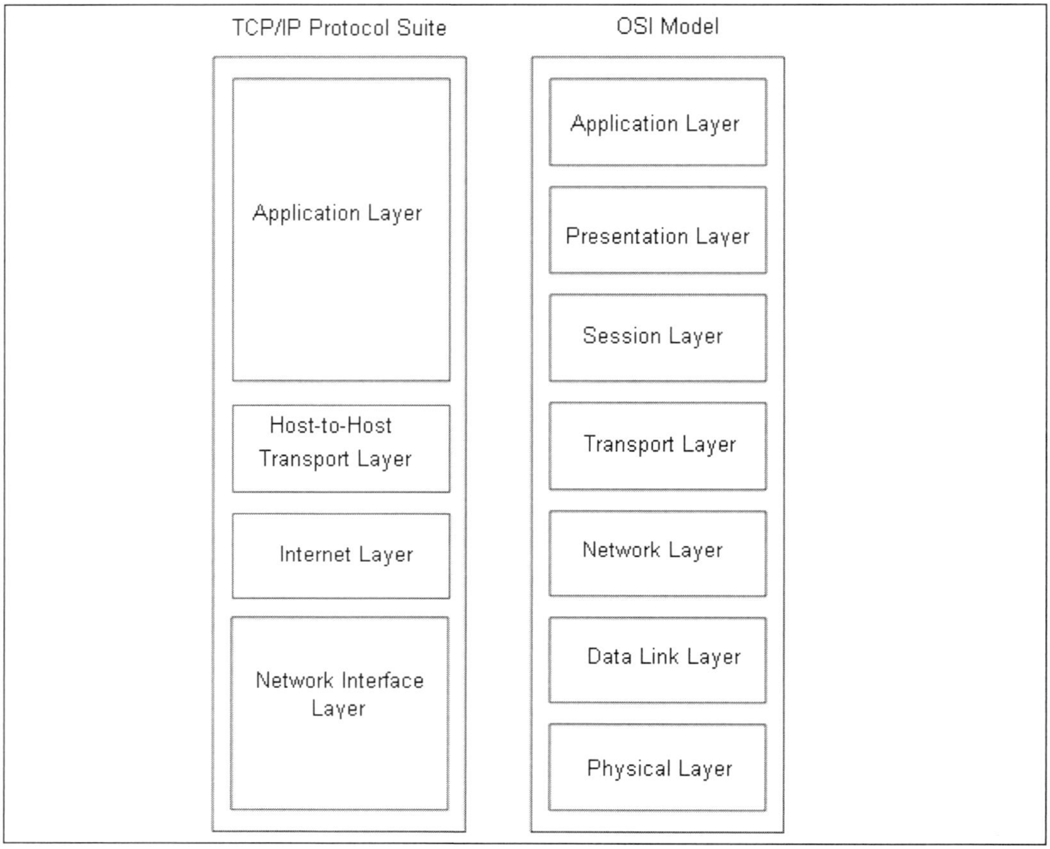

TCP/IP's Network Interface layer translates into Layers 1 and 2 of the OSI model, performing the same functions as the latter's Physical and Data Link layers. The TCP/IP Internet layer maps to the Network layer in the OSI model. In both models, the Transport layer is the next layer up, though in the DoD model, it originally was referred to as the Host-to-Host layer. The Application layer in the DoD model maps to the top three layers of the OSI model: Session, Presentation, and Application.

As you can see, the TCP/IP protocol suite, based on the DoD model, provides all the functionality delineated by the OSI model, but with a slightly different schema. As we discuss the protocols that comprise the TCP/IP suite, we'll continue to correlate the TCP/IP schema to the OSI model.

TCP/IP was designed to work independently of network design or architecture. It is independent of the access method, the frame format, and the medium (cable, airwaves, etcetera) itself. TCP/IP defines the details of networking activities at Layers 3 and above. Thus, it is used in many different types of networks, including Ethernet, Token Ring,

X.25, Frame Relay, and ATM. This independence provides the flexibility needed in today's networking environment.

TEST DAY TIP

It's common to find questions regarding the layers of the TCP/IP Protocol suite mapped to the OSI model, so make sure you pay close attention to this section while studying. Typically, on the Network+ exam you'll see questions regarding the OSI model and questions related to the various protocols within TCP/IP. By remembering how the TCP/IP protocols map to the OSI model, you'll be able to answer common questions about the individual protocols within TCP/IP and where they fall within the OSI model. This will also help you to remember what devices function at what layer.

Think about it, Layer 3... Network Layer, Routers, Routing... IP addressing, logical address... best effort transmission. Relying on upper layer protocols to provide more functionality... you will suddenly start to just memorize where everything goes... and why it's mapped there in the first place. For the exam, if you are having a lot of trouble remembering, start to draw the OSI model and fill it in once a day for a week until you have it down... then you can go into the test center, jot down your cheat sheet and begin. There is no crime in dumping your brains contents on paper – after you have sat down to prepare to take the live exam. Jotting down the OSI model and what maps to where would be one of the key things you should consider doing.

Layer 1: Network Interface (DoD) / Layers 1 and 2 Physical and Data Link (OSI)

The TCP/IP protocol suite provides networking protocols that work at all layers of the DoD model. TCP/IP generally follows the DoD model since they were developed at roughly the same time. There is not a clean mapping to the OSI model for TCP/IP, so we will utilize the DoD model, and make reference to what OSI model layers it maps to, which you should already know, as all of these layers were discussed earlier in the chapter. In this section, we're going to look at the TCP/IP protocols that work at each of the four layers defined in the DoD model (DARPA). Also known as the Physical and Data Link layers in the OSI model, the Network Interface layer combines both under one layer.

As you recall, the network interface layer maps to the Physical and Data Link layer in the OSI model. At the network interface layer, we're working with 0s and 1s being transmitted back and forth across the network medium (in many offices, the medium is twisted-pair Category 5 Ethernet cable). The Network Interface layer is responsible for controlling the movement of bits across the medium. As such, it must use some organized method of managing the sending and receiving of data. In Ethernet networks, the most common method is Carrier Sense Multiple Access/Collision Detection. However there are other, less common methods of managing data on the network, including Carrier Sense Multiple Access/Collision Avoidance and Token Passing. Each is discussed in turn in the next sections.

CSMA/CD

Ethernet, a common network architecture used in PC networking, uses Carrier Sense Multiple Access/ Collision Detection to manage media access. CSMA/CD is used on multiple access networks as defined in the IEEE 802.3 specification. Using this method, devices that have data to transmit listen for an opening on the line before transmitting (Carrier Sense). That is, they wait for a time when there are no signals traveling on the cable. When a device detects an opening, it transmits its data. The problem is that several devices may sense simultaneously that the line is clear and they may all transmit at the same time. When this happens, the data packets collide and the data is lost (this is called a collision), as shown in Figure 5.12.

Figure 5.12 A Collision on a Simple Network

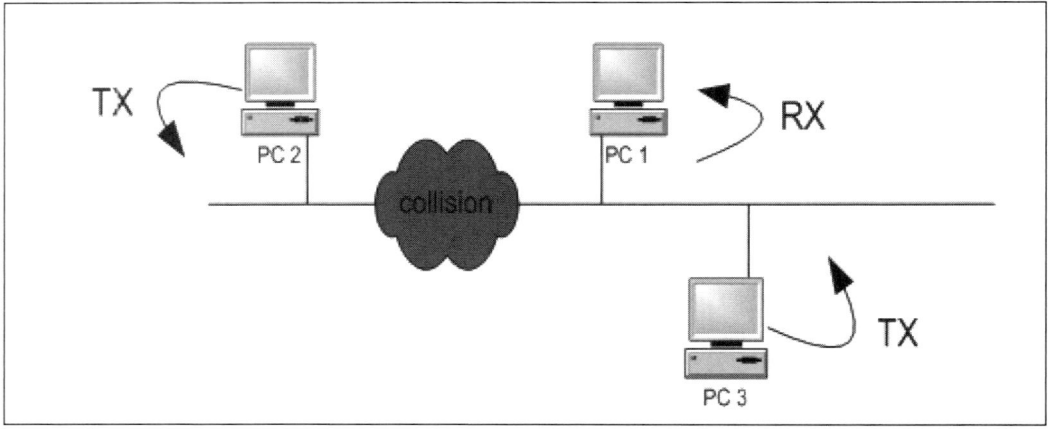

PC 1 has successfully received (RX) data from the network, but accidentally, PC 2 and PC 3 have transmitted (TX) at the same time, thus causing a collision on the network. Using the CSMA/CD protocol, the devices will detect that a collision has occurred (collision detection) and each of the devices that transmitted at the same time will wait a random amount of time and then retransmit. The likelihood of one or more devices *randomly* selecting the same delay is almost zero, so the retransmission is likely to be successful. Higher network traffic, larger numbers of computers on a network segment, and longer cables all contribute to an increased number of collisions, which in turn lowers the efficiency of the network because even more traffic is generated by larger number of retransmissions. A *collision domain* is a segment of cable on which two stations can't transmit at the same time without causing a collision. For example, all computers attached to the same hub in a star topology network, or all the computers on the same bus (linear segment) in a bus topology network, comprise a single collision domain. By using a switch, you can create separate collision domains and reduce network traffic.

With CSMA/CD, unlike with some access control protocols (such as demand priority) all stations or nodes are equal in their ability to send data when there is an opening; no station gets higher priority than any other.

A number of IEEE working groups continue to develop new standards for CSMA/CD, such as those pertaining to gigabit Ethernet and Ethernet over fiber (100BaseFX).

Head of the Class...

Collision and Broadcast Domains, what is the difference?

Now that you understand what a collision domain is, you should immediately know the difference between it and what's called a *broadcast domain*. A deeper explanation of a collision domain would be defined as all of the network interfaces (such as NICs) on one single network segment that can send data on the same physical wire. So, as seen in Figure 5.12 above, simultaneous transmission can result in a collision of the data being sent. When you use a hub (not a switch), all the nodes connected to the hub are in the same collision domain. A hub, as defined earlier in the book in Chapter 3, "Network Devices", is basically a repeater that regenerates and re-sends any signal it receives out each one of its ports. It doesn't discriminate, it sends all transmissions out every port, and this causes unneeded traffic on the network.

However, switches with enough internal memory can store MAC addresses, and send data from one port to another without having to send it out all ports, greatly reducing unneeded traffic on the network. A switch will in fact broadcast all ports when it is new on the network, because it has to "learn" who its neighbors are and properly record their unique MAC addresses and which ports they are located on within the switch. When a hub is used, every frame sent on the wire is seen by every node on the network. A Broadcast domain could be considered similar to a collision domain, but can consist of numerous collision domains. If one of those nodes on the network sends out a broadcast, all the nodes on that network can receive that broadcast on the physical wire are in the same broadcast domain. Remember that a broadcast copies and sends a transmission to every destination node on the network. Switches were designed to overcome the handicaps of a hub. As shown in Figure 5.13, although similar in appearance to a hub, the intelligence programmed within a switch keeps each port on a switch in its own collision domain. A switch can also be used to create smaller broadcast domains.

Figure 5.13 PCs Connected to Separate Broadcast Domains

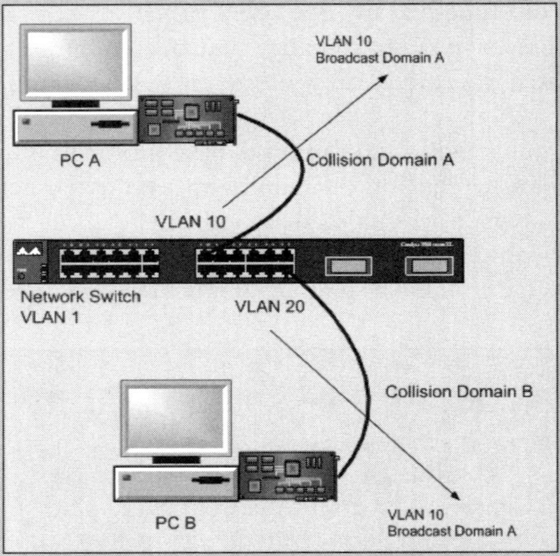

Only the devices on ports assigned to the same Virtual Local Area Network (VLAN) receive broadcasts from one another, and this design keeps things not only more efficient by removing some unneeded traffic off the network, but also more secure by keeping sensitive traffic to its own VLAN so that it is harder to eavesdrop on. A network engineer can assign certain devices to a VLAN as a way of creating smaller broadcast domains. A broadcast from a device connected to a port on VLAN 10 will only be seen by devices connected to ports assigned to VLAN 10. The same goes for VLAN 20, which the other PC is located on in Figure 5.13 above. VLANs are covered in depth in Chapter 9, "Network Infrastructure".

CSMA/CA

Network+
OBJECTIVE
2.3.6

A media access protocol that is related to CSMA/CD is Carrier Sense Multiple Access/Collision Avoidance, which is also used on multiple access networks such as Token passing or Wireless topologies. With CSMA/CA, a device listens for an opportunity to transmit its data just as devices do on CSMA/CD networks. However, when the device senses an opening, it does not immediately transmit the data; instead it transmits a signal notifying other devices that it is transmitting (a sort of warning message) before actually sending the data. This means data packets will never collide (although warning packets may).

Traditionally, CSMA/CA was most commonly used by AppleTalk networks. However, today most Apple computers can use Ethernet hardware, and this access method has fallen out of favor because it creates significant overhead—it adds unnecessary traffic to the network, slowing everything down. The preferred method of dealing with collisions is the collision detection method, which is the method now employed in Ethernet networking technologies.

As we learned in Chapter 4, "Wireless Technologies", in contrast to Ethernet 802.3 networks, wireless networks defined by the 802.11 standard do not use CSMA/CD as a method to protect against data loss resulting from collisions. Instead, 802.11 networks use CSMA/CA. CSMA/CD works by detecting whether a collision has occurred on the network and then retransmits the data in the event of such an occurrence. However, this method is not practical for wireless networks because it relies on the fact that every workstation can hear all the other workstations on a cable segment to determine if there is a collision.

In wireless networks (which are, of course, "multiple access"), usually only the AP (access point) can hear every workstation that is communicating with it (for example, PC A and PC B may be able to communicate with the same AP, but may be too far apart from each other to hear their respective transmissions). Additionally, wireless networks do not use full-duplex communication, which is another way of protecting data against corruption and loss as a result of collisions.

CSMA/CA solves the problem of potential collisions on the wireless network by taking a more active approach than CSMA/CD, which kicks in only after a collision has been detected. Using CSMA/CA, a wireless workstation first tries to detect if any other device is communicating on the network. If it senses it is clear to send, it initiates communication. The receiving device sends an acknowledgment (ACK) packet to the transmitting device indicating successful reception. If the transmitting device does not receive an ACK, it assumes a collision has occurred and retransmits the data. However, it should be noted that many collisions can occur and that these collisions can be used to compromise the confidentiality of Wired Equivalent Privacy (WEP) encrypted data.

CSMA/CA is only one way in which wireless networks differ from wired networks in their implementation at the MAC layer. For example, the IEEE standard for 802.11 at the MAC layer defines additional functionality, such as virtual collision detection (VCD), roaming, power saving, asynchronous data transfer, and encryption.

The fact that the WEP protocol is defined at the MAC layer is particularly noteworthy and has significant consequences for the security of wireless networks. This means that data at the higher levels of the OSI model, particularly Transmission Control Protocol/Internet Protocol (TCP/IP) data, is also encrypted. Because much of the TCP/IP communications that occur between hosts contain a large amount of frequently repeating and well-known patterns, WEP may be vulnerable to *known plaintext* attacks, although it does include safeguards against this kind of attack. Make sure you understand the fundamentals of CSMA/CA and Wireless for the Network+ exam.

EXAM WARNING

Be sure you understand the differences between CSMA/CD and CSMA/CA as well as which technologies utilize each.

Token Passing

In the 1980s and 1990s, IBM's Token Ring was a popular network technology. Its method of media access control involved the use of a token, a signal that was passed around the network (which was laid out in a logical ring configuration). A device that wanted to transmit data had to wait until it received the token. Once it had the token, it was free to transmit. This is referred to as a *noncontention* access method, because the devices don't contend or compete for access to the media. This certainly prevents packet collisions on the line, but it is also a slower process because of the time it takes for the token to pass from device to device. Token ring networks typically operate at 4Mbps or 16Mbps, so they have generally fallen out of favor as Ethernet has gained speed (going from 10Mbps to 100Mbps to 1000Mbps). Vendors such as IBM, Cisco, and 3Com have developed implementations of High Speed Token Ring (HSTR), including 100Mbps over copper and gigabit Token Ring over fiber, but high speed Ethernet had a big head start, and organizations such as the 10 Gigabit Ethernet Alliance (www.10gea.org) are devoted to taking it to even greater speeds.

However, FDDI networks are in use as high-speed backbones for mission-critical traffic. FDDI was designed to transfer data at 100Mbps, comparable to the most common implementation of Ethernet. FDDI uses a dual ring topology: traffic flows in opposite directions on the two rings. Stations on the network can be attached to both rings or to a single ring. Computers connected to both rings are called Class A stations, and those attached to only one are called Class B stations. The second ring usually is used for failover in case of problems with the primary ring. Unlike a Token Ring network, a FDDI network can have more than one frame traveling on the ring at the same time. Because it is faster than Token Ring, highly reliable, and fault tolerant, FDDI is great for networks that need both high bandwidth and high reliability. However, it is also relatively expensive.

Other network architectures have used the token passing method of access control. Attached Resource Computer Network (ARCnet), popular in the 1970s, used a special type of token passing in which the token moved from computer to computer in order of the node address on the NIC, rather than around a ring as with Token Ring and FDDI. ARCnet is slow (2.5Mbps in its original configuration, 20Mbps in a later version), so even though it is stable and reliable, it is slowly disappearing from the networking world.

Other Access Control Methods

There are other ways that computer networks can control access to the media, but they are limited in use. For example, Hewlett Packard designed an architecture it called 100VG-AnyLAN, based on the *demand-priority* access control method. These networks were designed in a tree configuration, with child hubs cascading off a root hub, and computers connected to each child hub. This creates multiple small collision domains, preventing problems associated with broadcasts that are sent to the entire network. The hubs (also called multiport repeaters because they boost the signals they receive before sending them back out) monitor the nodes that are attached to them, in a round-robin fashion, detecting requests to transmit on the network. An advantage of this access method is the fact that you can set priorities according to data type, to ensure that the most important data is processed first. The equipment, however, is proprietary, and despite its reliability, performance, and security advantages, demand-priority-based networks are not common.

TEST DAY TIP

When taking the exam, you should read each question carefully before reading the answers. Access control methods are needed only on networks where there are multiple connection points, not on point-to-point connections such as a one-to-one dial-up connection. This is an important distinction. You may see questions regarding how data is managed on the physical medium. Make sure you understand what the question is asking. The most frequently asked media access questions have to do with CSMA/CD, because it is the most widely used in networking today. However, you might find a tricky question that asks you to identify CSMA/CA instead.

Layer 2: Internet (DoD) / Layer 3 Network (OSI)

The TCP/IP suite has four core protocols that work at the Internet layer, which maps to the Network layer of the OSI model. The Internet layer is responsible for packaging, addressing, and routing the data. The four core protocols used in the TCP/IP suite are:

- The Internet Protocol
- The Internet Control Message Protocol
- The Internet Group Management Protocol (IGMP)
- The Address Resolution Protocol

IPv4

The Internet Protocol is probably the best known of the TCP/IP protocols. Many people, especially those who have even a passing familiarity with computer technology, have heard or used the term *IP address*. Later in this chapter, we'll take an in-depth look at how the IP protocol works and you'll learn the intricacies of IP addressing.

With regard to the TCP/IP architecture, IP is a routable protocol (meaning it can be sent across networks) that handles addressing, routing, and the process of putting data into or taking data out of packets. IP is considered to be *connectionless* because it does not establish a session with a remote computer before sending data. Data sent via connectionless methods are called *datagrams*. An IP packet can be lost, delayed, duplicated, or delivered out of sequence and there is no attempt to recover from these errors. Recovery is the responsibility of higher layer protocols including Transport layer protocols such as TCP.

IP packets (shown in Figure 5.14) contain data that include:

- **Source IP address** The IP address of the source of the datagram.

- **Destination IP address** The IP address of the destination for the datagram.

- **Identification** Identifies a specific IP datagram as well as all fragments of a specific IP datagram if the datagram becomes fragmented.

- **Protocol** Indicates to which protocols the receiving IP should pass the packets.

- **Checksum** A simple method of error control that performs a mathematical calculation to verify the integrity of the IP header.

- **Time-to-Live (TTL)** Designates the number of networks the datagram can travel before it is discarded. This prevents datagrams from circling endlessly on the network.

Figure 5.14 The IP Packet Header

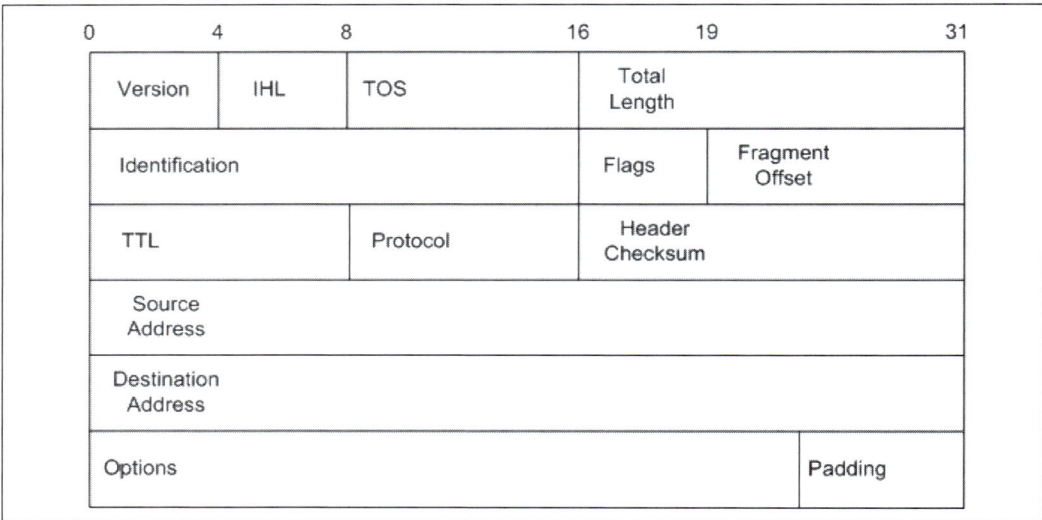

NOTE

We will cover IP and IPv6 in much more detail in the next chapter, "TCP/IP".

ICMP

The Internet Control Message Protocol is not as well-known as its famous cousin, IP, but is used so often that it would seem that you hear about this protocol more than IP. Many programs that you use as a network engineer rely on ICMP, such as Ping and Traceroute (Tracert). ICMP is responsible for handling errors related to IP packets that cannot be delivered. For instance, if a packet cannot be delivered, a message called *Destination Unreachable* is sent back to the sending device so it will know that there was an undelivered message. The Destination Unreachable message has several subtypes of messages that can be sent back to the host to help pinpoint the problem. For instance, *Network Unreachable* and *Port Unreachable* are two examples of *Destination Unreachable* messages that may be returned to help the host determine the nature of the problem.

If you have ever used the Ping utility (discussed at the end of this chapter) and received an error, it was ICMP that was responsible for returning the error. In addition to announcing errors, ICMP also announces network congestion (*source quench* messages) and timeouts (which occur when the TTL [time to live] field on a packet reaches zero). In Exercise 5.2 we will look at using ICMP on your network.

NOTE

For more information about ICMP, see RFC 792 at www.ietf.org/rfc/rfc792.txt, which defines the specifications for this protocol.

EXERCISE 5.2

USING TRACERT TO TEST YOUR NETWORK

1. Click **Start | Programs | Accessories | Command Prompt** to access the Windows Command Prompt.

2. Enter the command **tracert <destination>** to trace the route from your current location (source) to any <destination> you choose. In this example, we will utilize an ISP-based Internet connection to test the distance from a local PC to a website located out on the Internet somewhere.

```
C:\WINDOWS\SYSTEM32>tracert www.syngress.com


Tracing route to www.syngress.com [67.106.143.23]
over a maximum of 30 hops:


1     97 ms      71 ms     135 ms    10.9.0.1
2     18 ms      10 ms      25 ms    167.206.32.33
3     13 ms      12 ms      12 ms    r3-ge10-1.mhe.hcvlny.cv.net [167.206.32.9]
4     19 ms      21 ms      12 ms    r2-srp0-0.wan.hcvlny.cv.net [65.19.104.195]
5      *         23 ms      28 ms    r2-srp0-1.in.nycmny83.cv.net [65.19.96.70]
```

3. To close the Windows Command Prompt, type **exit**, then press **Enter**.

In this example, you can see the milliseconds in time it takes for packets to get from source to destination; very helpful when you want to find possible bottlenecks on your network. ICMP is responsible for reporting this information to the Traceroute program.

IGMP

The Internet Group Management Protocol manages host membership in multicast groups. IP multicast groups are groups of devices (typically called *hosts*) that listen for and receive traffic addressed to a specific, shared multicast IP address. Essentially, IP multicast traffic is sent to a specific MAC address, but processed by multiple IP hosts. As you'll recall from our earlier discussion, each NIC has a unique MAC address, but multicast MAC addresses use a special 24-bit prefix to identify them as such. IGMP runs on the router, which handles the distribution of multicast packets (often, multicast routing is not enabled on the router by default and must be configured).

Multicasting makes it easy for a server to send the same content to multiple computers simultaneously. IP addresses in a specific range (called Class D addresses) are reserved for multicast assignment. The IGMP protocol allows for different types of messages, used to join multicast groups and to send multicast messages.

A unicast message is sent directly to a single host, whereas a multicast is sent to all members of a particular group. Both utilize connectionless datagrams and are transported via UDP, which we'll discuss in the next section. A multicast is sent to a group of hosts known as an *IP multicast group* or *host group*. The hosts in this group listen for IP traffic sent to a specific IP multicast address. IP multicasts are more efficient than broadcasts because the data is received only by computers listening to a specific address. A range of IP addresses, known as Class D addresses, is reserved for multicast addresses. Windows Server 2003 supports multicast addresses and, by default, is configured to support both the sending and receiving of IP multicast traffic.

NOTE

For more information about IGMP, see RFC 1112 at www.ietf.org/rfc/rfc1112.txt, which defines the specifications for IP multicasting.

EXAM WARNING

Although their acronyms are very similar and they function at the same layer of the networking models, ICMP and IGMP perform very different functions, so be sure you don't get them confused on the test.

ARP

The Address Resolution Protocol is the last of the four core TCP/IP protocols that work at the Internet layer. As we've discussed, each NIC has a unique MAC address. Each NIC also is assigned an IP address that is unique to the network on which it resides. When a packet is sent on a TCP/IP network, the packet headers include a destination IP address (along with other information). The IP address must be translated into a specific MAC address in order for the data to reach its intended recipient. Without ARP, computers must send broadcast messages each time an IP address has to be matched to a MAC address.

ARP is responsible for maintaining the mappings of IP addresses to MAC addresses. These mappings are stored in the *ARP cache* so if the same IP address needs to be matched to a MAC address again, the mapping can be found in the cache; it's not necessary to repeat the discovery process.

The protocol includes four different types of messages: ARP request, ARP reply, RARP request, and RARP reply. RARP refers to Reverse Address Resolution protocol, which resolves addresses in the opposite direction (MAC address to IP address). These messages are used to discover the MAC addresses that correspond to specific IP addresses (and vice versa). When the MAC address is correlated to the specific IP address, the data can be sent to the proper host.

ARP was originally designed for DEC/Intel/Xerox (DIX) 10Mbps Ethernet networks, but is now used with other types of IP-based networks as well.

These are the four primary protocols involved in TCP/IP at the Internet layer, which is responsible for addressing, packaging, and routing packets of data. As we move up the protocol stack, we will examine the Transport layer.

EXAM WARNING

The Address Resolution Protocol is used to resolve the IP address to the Media Access Control address that is unique to each NIC manufactured. This concept is very important to understand. All network communication to a destination host requires knowledge of the MAC address to complete the transmission of data in the collision domain where that host is connected. ARP performs the function of resolving the IP (logical) address to the MAC (hardware) address so that the data can be delivered.

NOTE

For more information about ARP and RARP, see RFCs 826 and 903 at www.ietf.org/rfc/rfc826.txt and www.ietf.org/rfc/rfc903.txt.

Layer 3: Host-to-Host / Layer 4 Transport (OSI)

Layer 3 in TCP/IP is the *Host-to-Host Transport* layer, sometimes called the *Transport* layer. It maps to the Transport layer (Layer 4) in the OSI model. As the name implies, this layer is responsible for transporting the data. It sets up communications between the Application layer and the lower layers.

Because this layer establishes a connection, it can also take on some of the responsibilities of the Session layer of the OSI model. In TCP/IP, the two core protocols used at the Host-to-Host layer are TCP and UDP. As we discussed earlier, one of the key distinguishing features of these two protocols is that TCP is considered connection-oriented and UDP is connectionless.

TCP

The Transmission Control Protocol provides reliable one-to-one communications because it establishes a connection with the receiving host prior to transmitting and because it provides a number of control features to ensure reliable communications. TCP is connection-oriented because it establishes a TCP connection prior to sending data. This is similar to the way a modem works when the modem dials another computer and establishes a connection before data is transmitted. This ensures that someone is on the other end before data is sent. TCP sequences the packets, acknowledges sent packets, and helps recover lost packets. Data is transmitted in segments and each segment is numbered sequentially. When the receiving host receives data, it sends an Acknowledgement message to the sender. If the sender does not receive this ACK within a specified amount of time, the data segment is re-sent, based on the assumption that the data was not received.

Data from the Transport layer's TCP is organized into segments. These are sent down through the protocol stack and headers are added. Each network technology (Ethernet, Token Ring, etcetera) has a particular way it encapsulates data. This particular encapsulation is called the *frame format*. Each technology uses its own frame format. In Ethernet technologies, the frame of data is a fixed-length and is generally referred to as a *packet*. The Ethernet IP packet contains a preamble, destination and source address, data, and an error-checking sequence, among other things. The frame format describes the required data and the order in which is appears inside the data packet, which is the unit of data sent across the network medium.

Each TCP segment has a header that contains, among other things, the following important fields:

- TCP port to send the data

- TCP port to receive the data

- Sequence number for the segment

- Acknowledgment number

- Window size (not to be confused with the Microsoft Windows operating system), which indicates the current size of the TCP buffer on the sending host's end. The TCP buffer is used to hold incoming segments and must have room to accept additional segments when received.

Head of the Class…

TCP Window Size

The TCP window size is used to help control the sending and receiving of data between two hosts. The sender can send only as much data as the receiver's buffer can hold. New data is sent only when the receiver indicates its buffer is ready to receive more data. The sender can send only data that fits within the window and the window slides along the outbound and inbound data stream.

Using Windows XP Professional as an example, the TCP/IP maximum receive window is set to 16,384 bytes by default. The default maximum receive window is negotiated during the establishment of the TCP connection. The maximum receive window size can be set through the registry. There are two settings that are related to the TCP window size: GlobalMaxTcpWindowSize and TcpWindowSize.

The GlobalMaxTcpWindowSize is found in the following location:

HKEY_LOCAL_MACHINE\SYSTEM\CurrentControlSet\Services\Tcpip\Parameters

It sets the default maximum receive window for all interfaces unless that is overridden by the TcpWindowSize setting.

The TcpWindowSize setting is found in the following locations:

HKEY_LOCAL_MACHINE\SYSTEM\CurrentControlSet\Services\Tcpip\Parameters

and

HKEY_LOCAL_MACHINE\SYSTEM\CurrentControlSet\Services\Tcpip\Parameters\Interfaces\InterfaceGUID

Continued

In the case of both the GlobalMaxTcpWindowSize and the TcpWindowSize, values greater than 65,535 can be used only if window scaling is enabled and other computers support window scaling.

On older networks, the default window size is defined by RFC 793 and allows for a 16-bit field of data, which translates into 65,535 bytes of data. This means that the sender can send only 65K bytes of data before receiving an acknowledgement. Newer network technologies have much higher throughput and sending only 65K of data before awaiting a response is inefficient. RFC 1323 defines a larger window size called the *TCP window scale*. It provides a scaling factor that can be combined with the 16-bit TCP window to increase the maximum size of the window to 1,073,725,440 bytes (approximately 1 gigabyte). When supported, window scaling occurs when TCP establishes the connection and both hosts indicate their respective receive window sizes. This allows for a more flexible and efficient use of network bandwidth. Be aware that these settings do not exist by default and can be configured by an administrator if needed. All instructions on how to configure these settings can be found in the Microsoft online knowledgebase if more information is needed.

TCP also avoids sending and receiving small segments through a method called the *Nagle Algorithm*. The Nagle Algorithm named for its creator, John Nagle, and as described in RFC 896, works on the principle that only one small segment can be sent and not acknowledged. For interactive sessions such as Telnet, each individual keystroke entered is a single segment of data, which must make a round trip in order to be shown on the user's screen. Obviously, these small segments must be sent in order for the user to see on the screen what's been typed on the keyboard. Using the Nagle Algorithm, the many small segments (such as a user typing on a keyboard) are stored in a buffer. Once the first segment is acknowledged, the next segment is sent. That second segment may contain many smaller segments (for instance, several individual keystrokes).

Finally, there is a syndrome that occurs called *silly window syndrome* (SWS). Whenever data is sent to the receiver's Application layer protocol, the receive window opens and a new window size is advertised. Depending on a number of factors, this can cause one of several behaviors. Each time the Application layer protocol retrieves data, it may accept only one byte of data at a time. Thus, the sender's window advances by only one byte at a time. These are small segments that do not make optimal use of the network's total capabilities.

To avoid SWS, the receiver does not advertise a new window size unless it is half of the maximum receive window size or at least the maximum segment size (MSS).

In order to establish a connection, TCP uses a three-part handshake, which works as follows:

1. The client computer sends a SYN (synchronization request) message with a sequence number that is generated by the client.

2. The server computer responds with an ACK message. This consists of the original sequence number plus 1. The server also sends a SYN number that it generates.

3. The client adds a 1 to the SYN number that was sent by the server, and returns it as an ACK.

This process, with each computer acknowledging the other, results in the establishment of a connection. A similar process is used to terminate the connection. TCP establishes this one-to-one (host-to-host) connection and also adds header information to ensure reliable communications. The downside to this reliability is that it adds both time and data in the transmission, which slows down communication somewhat.

Figure 5.15 shows the process TCP uses to establish a connection. There are three distinct steps used to establish a reliable connection. These same steps are used to end a connection. This handshake process is what creates a reliable connection because both hosts must indicate that they are ready to send/receive and that they are finished sending/receiving. As you can see in Figure 5.15, the first step is to establish the connection. The sending host (we'll call it Host A for clarity) sends a TCP segment to the receiving host (Host B) with an initial Sequence Number for the connection and the TCP window size, which indicates the sender's receiving buffer size. The receiving computer, Host B, replies with a TCP segment that contains its chosen Sequence Number and its initial TCP window size. Host A sends a segment back to Host B acknowledging Host B's chosen Sequence Number.

Figure 5.15 The TCP Handshake

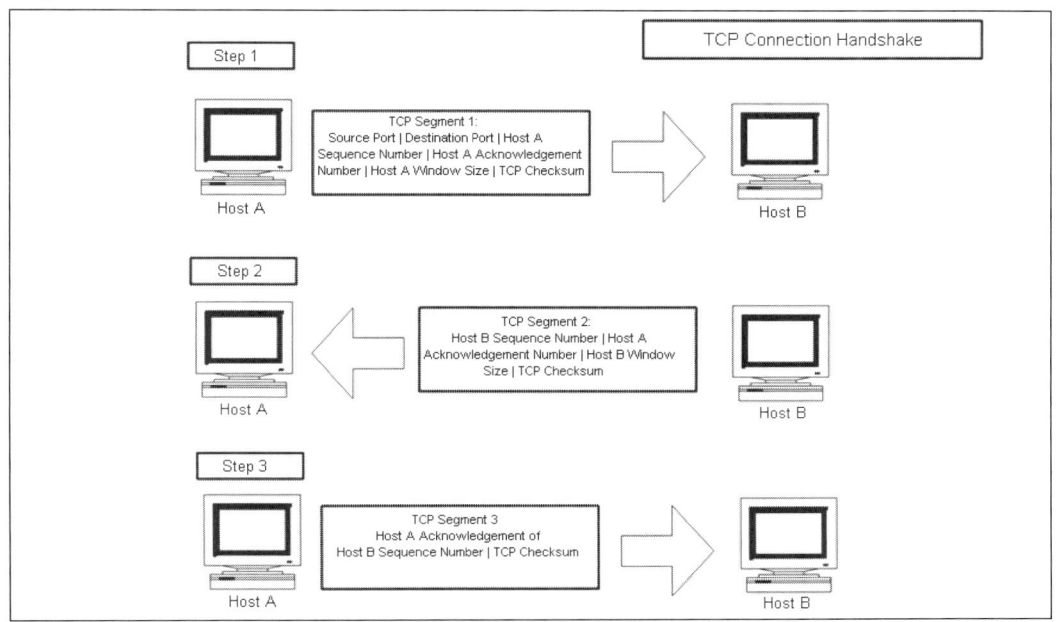

UDP

In some cases, it's appropriate to send a quick message without needing to sequence the data or to get an acknowledgement that it's been received. In these cases, an application developer might choose to use the User Datagram Protocol instead of TCP. Remember that protocols are agreed-upon rules that developers use to ensure their applications work within the TCP/IP framework. UDP is often described as connectionless or "best-effort delivery" because it does not establish a connection before sending, it does not sequence packets before sending, and it does not provide error control through retransmission. In short, it's a one-shot deal that is fast, but not always reliable.

The UDP header contains three important fields:

- The source port
- The destination port
- The UDP checksum

> **NOTE**
>
> The UDP checksum is the only error control mechanism within UDP. It is used to verify the integrity of the UDP header and data. UDP is used, for instance, in NetBIOS name service and SNMP because both of these use short data segments and do not require ACK messages.

Both TCP and UDP utilize port numbers, as we discussed previously. Port numbers are assigned by the Internet Assigned Numbers Authority (IANA). It is important to have a centralized body to assign these numbers so that everyone will use the same ports for the same functions. There are many well known TCP and UDP ports, as well as many obscure ports. When you secure a network server, it is usually advisable to disable all TCP and UDP ports that are not in use so they cannot be used by hackers looking for a back door.

TCP and UDP may use the same port numbers, but they are not the same ports. Each uses its own distinct set of ports. TCP port 20 is different from UDP port 20. A few of the common TCP and UDP ports are shown in Table 5.1.

Table 5.1 Common TCP and UDP Ports

Common TCP Ports	Common UDP Ports
Port 20 – FTP (Data Channel)	Port 53 – Domain Name System (DNS) Name Queries
Port 21 – FTP (Control Channel)	Port 137 – NetBIOS name service
Port 23 – Telnet	Port 138 – NetBIOS datagram service
Port 80 – HTTP	Port 161 – SNMP

For a list of commonly hacked (or probed) ports, see www.linux-firewall-tools.com/linux/ports.html. Although the site is a Linux site, the TCP and UDP ports used by TCP/IP services (and by hackers) are the same regardless of the operating system.

TEST DAY TIP

TCP versus UDP. You are very likely to run into some questions on the exam that are related to TCP and UDP. It's critical to understand the difference between these two transport protocols. UDP is an unreliable, connectionless, fast transport protocol used for sending short messages or messages that do not require acknowledgement of receipt. An easy way to remember the difference is: **TCP** is **T**rustworthy; **UDP** is **U**nreliable.

What's important to remember about TCP and UDP is that although one is considered reliable and the other unreliable, it does not mean that one is inherently better than the other. TCP establishes a connection before information is sent to the receiver; UDP does not. Many applications do not require acknowledgement that sent data was received because it sends the data in small amounts. In these scenarios, using a connectionless UDP datagram is far more efficient. Therefore, UDP datagrams are used in a variety of applications including NetBIOS name service, NetBIOS datagram service, SNMP, and DNS.

Layer 4: Application (DoD) / Layers 1, 2, 3 Session, Presentation and Application (OSI)

The Application layer protocols of the TCP/IP protocol suite operate at the Session, Presentation, and Application layers of the OSI model. In the DoD model, this layer enables applications to communicate with one another and it provides access to the services of the other underlying layers (DoD Layers 1 through 3). There is a wide variety of Application layer protocols, and more are being developed because they can rely on all the TCP/IP services beneath them in the protocol stack.

We briefly mentioned some of the Application layer protocols in our discussion of the OSI Application layer. In the following sections, we will describe some of these in more detail. We won't cover every single Application layer protocol in use today (we couldn't, without turning this book into an encyclopedia set), but we will cover some of the protocols and services that you're not only likely to work with on the job as a network technician, but that you're also likely to encounter on the Network+ certification exam.

NetBIOS over TCP

NetBIOS over TCP as a naming service has been largely supplanted by the use of DNS. However, in organizations running operating systems or applications that cannot use DNS for name services, NetBIOS over TCP must still be enabled.

NetBIOS over TCP (NetBT) is an Application layer set of protocols that provides name, session, and datagram services for NetBIOS applications. NetBIOS was originally developed for IBM by Systek Corporation to extend the capabilities of the BIOS (Basic Input Output System) to include the ability to work across a network. It is a software interface and a naming convention, not a protocol (although you will see it referred to in some documentation as the *NetBIOS protocol*). NetBIOS over TCP supplies the programming interface provided for by NetBIOS, along with communication protocols provided for by TCP.

- NetBT's *name* service allows host computers to attain and retain (or defend) a NetBIOS name. It also assists other hosts in locating a computer with a specific NetBIOS name. Additionally, the name service resolves a specific NetBIOS name to an IP address. This process utilizes *broadcast* messages that are sent to all hosts on the network. The name service uses UDP port 137.

- The *session* service of NetBT provides for the reliable exchange of messages between two NetBIOS applications, typically on two different computers. The session service uses TCP port 139.

- The *datagram* service within NetBT provides connectionless, unreliable message delivery between NetBIOS applications via UDP port 138. As mentioned earlier, when data length is short or reliability is not critical, the datagram service is a faster method than session-based communication.

Together, the session and datagram services provide the NetBIOS applications with the ability to exchange information with one another.

EXAM WARNING

Remember the following for the Network+ exam:
- The name service uses UDP Port 137.
- The datagram service uses UDP Port 138.
- The session service uses TCP Port 139.

WINS

Windows Internet Name Service, or WINS, is a NetBIOS name server that NetBIOS clients can use to attain, register, and resolve NetBIOS names. WINS is specific to Microsoft networks and is not used (or available for use) on non–Microsoft operating system-based computers. Computers running UNIX, Linux, and other non–Microsoft operating systems typically use DNS for name resolution, although there are other, non–WINS NetBIOS name services available. Generally other operating systems will be concerned with NetBIOS names only when they're on a network with Microsoft machines; for example, when using SAMBA (a Linux-based file and printer sharing application).

WINS provides NetBIOS functionality, but expands it by replicating this information for faster name resolution services across a large network. WINS generates a database that contains each NetBIOS name and its associated IP address. A WINS server resolves NetBIOS names and provides the associated IP addresses when it receives requests.

EXAM WARNING

NetBIOS name resolution can be done via a centralized WINS server or via a local lmhosts file, both of which will be able to keep traffic down on your network by mapping NetBIOS names to IP addresses.

WINS is implemented in two parts: the server service and the client service. The server service maintains the database containing both NetBIOS names and associated IP addresses. It also replicates the database to other WINS servers for faster name resolution across a large network. This reduces network broadcast traffic because names can be acquired and defended using direct requests to the WINS server, rather than by using network broadcasts. The client service runs on the individual computers and it uses WINS to register the computer name, as well as to provide name resolution services to the local applications and services.

For backward compatibility, Windows-based clients and servers also provide support for using the lmhosts file. This plain text file is unique to Windows-based computers and provides a map of the computer's NetBIOS name with an IP address. This static file was used prior to the implementation of dynamic Windows name resolution found in WINS. WINS will be covered in greater detail in Chapter 6.

EXAM WARNING

NetBIOS name resolution uses four different node types to resolve names to IP addresses: Broadcast (B-node), Peer-to-Peer (P-node), Mixed (M-node), and Hybrid (H-node).

SMB/CIFS

The Server Message Block (SMB) protocol was originally developed by IBM in the 1980s and later expanded upon by IBM, Microsoft, Intel, and 3Com. SMB was primarily used for file and print sharing, but is also used for sharing serial ports and abstract communications technologies such as named pipes and mail slots. SMB is also now known as *Common Internet File System* (CIFS); both names are used interchangeably.

CIFS is a protocol that, like many Application layer protocols, is operating system-independent. It evolved from SMB and NetBIOS file and print sharing methods in earlier versions of the Windows operating system. It can be used by different platforms and operating systems and across different network/transport protocols; it is not TCP/IP-dependent. The connection from client to server can be made via NetBEUI or IPX/SPX. After the network connection from client to server is established, then SMB commands can be sent to the server so that the client can open, read and write files, and so on.

CIFS is being jointly developed by Microsoft and other vendors, but no published specification currently exists. UNIX and Linux clients can connect to SMB shares using *smbclient* from SAMBA or *smbfs* for Linux. Server implementations of SMB for non-Microsoft operating systems include SAMBA and LAN Manager for OS/2 and SCO.

NOTE

For more detailed information about SMB, go to:
http://samba.anu.edu.au/cifs/docs/what-is-smb.html

IPP

The Internet Printing Protocol (IPP) is related to SMB and CIFS. It provides the ability to perform various printing operations across the network (including an internetwork) using HTTP version 1.1.

NOTE

There are a large number of RFCs that define different specifications for IPP. For more information, see the IEEE's PWG (Printer Working Group) Web site at www.pwg.org/ipp/

Windows Sockets

Windows Sockets is a Microsoft Windows API that provides a standard programming interface for accessing TCP/IP in Windows. Sockets were originally developed at the

University of California in Berkeley, and Microsoft developed Windows Sockets (also referred to as *Winsock*) to work specifically in the Windows operating system environment.

Vendors who develop software that runs on Windows can use this API to access standard TCP/IP functionality. A number of built-in Windows tools rely on Windows Sockets, including *Packet InterNet Groper* (ping) and *Trace Route* (tracert). In addition, the FTP and DHCP servers and clients use Windows Sockets, as does the Telnet client.

Telnet

Telnet is a terminal emulation protocol that allows you to log onto a remote computer. The remote computer must be using TCP/IP and have the Telnet server service running. To connect to a remote host, you must start the Telnet client and must possess a username and password for the remote host computer. In Windows Server 2003, the Telnet server service is present, but must be started in order to service Telnet clients.

If you have never used the command prompt in Windows, here's how: click **Start | Run** and type **cmd** in the dialog box (in Windows operating systems prior to Windows 98, the 16-bit command was **command**. In Windows 98 and beyond, the 32-bit command, **cmd**, is supported). This will open a command window. Type **telnet** at the prompt. Type **help** for a list of commands and **quit** to close Telnet. Use **exit** to close the command prompt window.

Exam Warning

Remember that Telnet uses port 23 (both TCP and UDP) for communication, SSH (which stands for Secure Shell and is essentially encrypted Telnet) runs on port 22 (also TCP and UDP). Telnet information is sent in plaintext so it's very easy to capture packets and read the contents such as usernames and passwords.

DHCP

The Dynamic Host Configuration Protocol is used to automatically (or dynamically) assign IP addresses to host computers on a network running TCP/IP. Prior to DHCP, network administrators had to assign IP addresses to host computers manually. This was not only a time-consuming endeavor, but also made it easy for errors (either in IP assignment or in entering in the IP address) to creep in and cause network problems.

Why is DHCP so important? Because each host must have a unique IP address, and a problem occurs when two hosts have the same IP address. DHCP was devised as an efficient method to alleviate both the problems caused by errors and the time it took to assign and resolve errors. It does this by maintaining a database of the assigned addresses, ensuring that there will never be duplicate addresses among the DHCP clients.

DHCP is implemented as both a server service and a client service. The DHCP server service is responsible for assigning the IP address to individual hosts and for maintaining the database of IP address information, including IP addresses that are assigned, IP addresses that are available and other configuration information that can be conveyed to the client along with the IP address assignment. The DHCP client service interacts with the Server service in requesting an IP address and in configuring other related information including the *subnet mask* and *default gateway* (both are discussed in detail later in this chapter and in the next chapter, "TCP/IP").

SMTP

The Simple Mail Transfer Protocol is a protocol used to transfer e-mail messages and attachments. SMTP is used to transmit e-mail between e-mail servers and from e-mail clients (such as Microsoft Outlook or Linux's sendmail) to e-mail servers (such as Microsoft Exchange). However, most e-mail clients use other protocols, such as POP3 or IMAP4, to *retrieve* e-mail from the server. These two server applications (SMTP and POP or IMAP) may exist on the same physical server machine.

As with the other protocols and services discussed in this section, SMTP operates at the Application layer and relies on the services of the underlying layers of the TCP/IP suite to provide the actual data transfer services.

Exam Warning

Remember that SMTP uses port 25 for communication.

POP

Post Office Protocol is a widely used e-mail application protocol that can be used to retrieve e-mail from an e-mail server for the client application, such as Microsoft Outlook. The current version of POP is POP3.

POP servers set up mailboxes (actually directories or folders) for each e-mail account name. The server receives the mail for a domain, and sorts it into these individual folders. Then a user uses a POP client program (such as Outlook or Eudora) to connect to the POP server and download all the mail in that user's folder to the user's computer. Usually, when the mail messages are transferred to the client machine, they are deleted from the server.

EXAM WARNING

Remember that POP3 uses port 110 for communication.

IMAP

IMAP, like POP, is used to retrieve e-mail from a server, and creates a mailbox for each user account. It differs from POP in that the client program can access the mail and allow the user to read, reply to, and delete it while it is still on the server. Microsoft Exchange functions as an IMAP server. This is convenient for users because they never have to download the mail to their client computers (saving space on their hard disks), but especially because they can connect to the server and have all of their mail available to them from any computer, anywhere. When you use POP to retrieve your mail, old mail that you've already downloaded is on the computer you were using when you retrieved it, so if you're using a different computer, you won't be able to see it. IMAP is preferred for users who use different computers (for example, a home computer, an office computer, and a laptop) to access their e-mail at different times.

EXAM WARNING

Remember that IMAP4 uses Port 143, (both TCP and UDP) for communication.

HTTP

Hypertext Transport Protocol is the protocol used to transfer files used on the Internet to display Web pages. When you type an Internet address (a URL) into your browser's **Address** field, it uses the HTTP protocol to retrieve and display the files located at that address.

A URL typically contains a server name, a second level domain name, and a top-level domain name, with the parts of the address separated by dots. Individual folder and file names may follow, separated by slashes. For example, www.rsnetworks.net/index.htm indicates an HTML document (Web page) on a Web server named www in the rsnetworks.net domain. The first part of the URL may also be entered as an IP address if it is known.

HTTP was defined and used as early as 1990. However, there were no published specifications for HTTP in the beginning, and different vendors modified HTTP as they saw fit. As the World Wide Web continued to evolve and grow to be the enormous resource that it is today, additional functionality was needed in HTTP. The first formal definition was labeled HTTP/1 and it was later replaced by HTTP/1.1.

Exam Warning

Remember that HTTP uses port 80 for communication. Do not confuse this with https:// which is SSL (Secure Sockets Layer) encrypted Web traffic running on port 443.

NNTP

The Network News Transfer Protocol is similar to SMTP in that it allows servers and clients to exchange information. In this case, however, the information is exchanged in the form of news articles. This feature originally was implemented in the Internet's predecessor network, ARPANET. Network bulletins were exchanged using this protocol. Today there are thousands of newsgroups devoted to discussion of every topic imaginable. Usenet has grown into a huge network of news servers hosting news groups. Newsgroups differ from other forums such as Internet mailing lists (in which all messages posted come into your inbox if you're a member) and Web discussion boards (which are accessed through the browser).

NNTP is now implemented as an Application layer client/server protocol. The news server (for example, msnews.microsoft.com) manages news articles and news clients. A news client is an application that runs on a client computer and is used to both read and compose news articles. Outlook Express contains a news reader component. For more information about Usenet newsgroups, see the Usenet FAQ and references at www.faqs.org/usenet/

Exam Warning

Remember that NNTP uses port 119 for communication.

FTP

The File Transfer Protocol is used to transfer files from one host to another, regardless of the hosts' physical locations. It is one of the oldest Application layer protocols and was used on ARPANET to transfer files from one mainframe to another. Still in use today, FTP is widely used on the Internet to transfer files. One of the problems with FTP is that it transmits users' passwords in clear text, so it is not a secure protocol.

In contrast to the single connections used by NNTP, HTTP, and SMTP, two separate connections are established for an FTP session. One transmits commands and replies and the other transmits the actual data. The command and control information is sent, by default, via TCP port 21. The data, by default, is sent via TCP port 20.

Configuring & Implementing…

FTP Ports

Understanding the configuration and implementation of FTP is important for a number of reasons. FTP ports 20 and 21 are used for FTP data and FTP control, respectively. It is possible to modify the ports used for data and control transmissions when developing or implementing an application. However, by default, a program interface that uses FTP listens at TCP port 21 for FTP traffic. Thus, if your application is sending TCP control information on a different port, the other application interface may not hear the FTP traffic.

TCP ports 20 and 21 are well-known port numbers and hackers often try to exploit these ports. As a security measure, all servers that are not running the FTP server service should have TCP ports 20 and 21 disabled. This prevents attackers from exploiting these ports to gain unauthorized access to the server, and perhaps to the entire network. RFC 1579, "Firewall-Friendly FTP" is definitely worth a read if you want even more in depth information on how FTP uses ports. This information is not related to the exam, but may interest you for futures in the security field. www.ietf.org/rfc/rfc1579.txt.

DNS

The Domain Naming System is used to resolve a hostname to an IP address in order to facilitate the delivery of network data packets. As mentioned previously, DNS is now the primary method used in Microsoft Windows Server 2003 to resolve hostnames to IP addresses. DNS is also the protocol used on the Internet to resolve hostnames (such as those in URLs) to IP addresses.

Prior to DNS, hostname-to-IP resolution was accomplished via a text file called *hosts*. In the days of ARPANET, this file was compiled and managed by the Network Information Center at the Stanford Research Institute. This plain text file contained the name and address of every single computer, but there were only a handful of computers on the network at the time. When a new computer was added, or a computer changed its IP address, the file had to be edited manually and distributed to all the other computers. As computers and networks proliferated, another, more automated solution had to be devised and the specifications for a distributed naming system, called the Domain Naming System, were developed.

DNS servers on the Internet store copies of the DNS database. Due to the explosive growth of the Internet in the past decade, DNS databases are specialized. For instance, a set of databases is responsible for top-level domain information only. Examples of top-level domains are .com, .gov, .edu, .net, .org, and so on. All requests for an address ending with .com will be forwarded to a particular set of DNS servers. These servers will query their databases to find the specific .com domain requested (for example, microsoft.com). DNS databases are replicated periodically to refresh the data.

EXAM WARNING

Remember that DNS uses port 53 for communication..

RIP

As the name implies, the Routing Information Protocol (RIP) is used to exchange routing information among IP routers. RIP is a basic routing protocol designed for small- to medium-sized networks. It does not scale well to large IP-based networks (including the Internet). Windows Server 2003 computers can function as routers, and as such, they support RIP. Routing is covered in more depth in Chapter 6, where WAN standards and remote access are covered.

NTP

Network Time Protocol (NTP) is a protocol that provides a very reliable way of transmitting and receiving an accurate time source over TCP/IP-based networks. NTP, defined in RFC 1305 (www.ietf.org/rfc/rfc1305.txt), is useful for synchronizing the internal clock of the computers to a common time source. Some systems like Novell NetWare's Novell Directory Services (NDS, or now known simply as e-Directory) as well as Microsoft Windows Server 2003 and 2000, rely on a time source to keep things running right. For system maintenance, troubleshooting of issues, and documentation, it is important that all systems be time synchronized. In addition, for prosecution of security breaches or attacks, security logs need to be accurate, and so on. NTP, when used properly, can have a hierarchical disaster recovery system designed into it, with primary sources of time as well as secondaries. Having the correct time on your system(s) is very important. Many problems can surface if networked machines are not synchronized.

EXAM WARNING

Remember that NTP uses port 123 for communication. Do not confuse this with NNTP, which uses port 119.

SNMP

The Simple Network Management Protocol is used for communications between a network management console and the network's devices, such as bridges, routers, and hubs. This protocol facilitates the sharing of network control information with the management console. SNMP employs a management system/agent framework to share relevant network management information. This information is stored in a *Management Information Base* (MIB) and contains a set of objects, each of which represents a particular type of network information such as an event, an error, or an active session. SNMP employs UDP datagrams to send messages between the management console and the agents.

Now that we have covered the OSI model (as well as the DoD model) in depth… you should now have a good idea of the importance of it, and why it's so important to know for the Network+ exam. This modular approach to network communications makes development less time-consuming and more consistent across vendors, networks, and systems. As a result, new Application layer protocols are constantly being developed. This section is not meant to serve as an exhaustive look at the wide array of application protocols available today, but to give you a better idea of the more common protocols and services that operate at this layer and provide an understanding of how the layered approach works.

We've reviewed the seven layers of the OSI model (starting from the lowest level, Physical, Data Link, Network, Transport, Session, Presentation, and Application) and the four layers of the DARPA (TCP/IP) model (Network Interface, Internet, Host-to-Host, and Application) and we've learned how these layers map to one another.

We've also taken a look at the very different Microsoft networking model. We've examined many of the common protocols of the TCP/IP protocol suite that work at each layer and looked the services and functions that each provides. In the next chapter, you'll learn in depth about the IP protocol and how it is used to send data to the correct location, no matter where the destination host resides.

Summary of Exam Objectives

In this chapter we covered the OSI model in depth. For those of you unfamiliar with working with network models, it should be clear now that working with them can bring many benefits, such as ease of development and troubleshooting. Networking models can be very helpful to you. In this chapter we covered three of them in particular: the OSI model, the DoD model, and the Microsoft model, all of which are similar and share common core elements, but have differences as well.

From the DARPA experiment came the understanding that networking would become increasingly common—and increasingly complex. The OSI model was developed, based on the original DoD DARPA model, and approved by the Open Systems Interconnection (OSI) subcommittee of the International Organization for Standardization (ISO). The OSI model defined seven layers for standard, reliable network communications: Physical, Data Link, Network, Transport, Session, Presentation, and Application. The acronym commonly used to remember this is (in reverse order): **A**ll **P**eople **S**eem **T**o **N**eed **D**ata **P**rocessing.

If you were to follow each layer and map to it a protocol and a device, then by reading this chapter you would remember that the Physical layer is responsible for signaling, transmission medium, and ones and zeros traversing the wire. As we move up the model, things get increasingly more complex. The next layer, the Data Link layer, is where your MAC address is located. We discussed the functionality of a NIC card and what a MAC address is. On Ethernet NICs, the physical or MAC address (also called the hardware address) is expressed as 12 hexadecimal digits, arranged in pairs with colons between each pair, for example, 12:3A:4D:66:3A:1C. In binary notation, this translates to a 48-bit (or 6-byte) number, with the initial three bytes representing the manufacturer and the last three bits representing a unique network interface card made by that manufacturer. The Data Link layer is subdivided into two sublayers, known as the LLC and MAC layer. The LLC or Logical Link Control sublayer is responsible for providing the logic for the data link, and thus it controls the synchronization, flow control, and error checking functions of the Data Link layer.

The TCP/IP protocol suite provides the functionality specified in the OSI model using the four related layers of the DoD model: Network Interface, Internet, Host-to-Host, and Application. The Network Interface maps to the Physical and Data Link layers and the Internet layer maps to the OSI Network layer. The Host-to-Host layer maps to the Transport layer and DoD's Application layer maps to the Session, Presentation, and Application layers of the OSI model. Some of the more commonly known Application layer protocols are FTP, HTTP, POP3, WINS, DNS, and DHCP. Understanding the details of the TCP/IP protocol suite is fundamental to managing computers in today's networked environment. Being able to subnet, assign IP addresses, create subnet masks, and set up routing are essential skills you'll need on the job and to successfully master the material on the Network+ exam. In our next chapter, we will get more intimate with the TCP/IP suite, delving into Internet Protocol Version 4.

Exam Objectives Fast Track

Identify a MAC (Media Access Control) Address and its Parts

☑ The Data Link layer is where the MAC address is located.

☑ On Ethernet NICs, the physical or MAC address (also called the hardware address) is expressed as 12 hexadecimal digits, arranged in pairs with colons between each pair: 12:3A:4D:66:3A:1C.

☑ In binary notation, the MAC address translates to a 48-bit (or 6-byte) number, with the initial three bytes representing the manufacturer and the last three bits representing a unique network interface card made by that manufacturer.

☑ The Data Link layer is subdivided into two sublayers (defined in the IEEE 802 specifications), known as the LLC and MAC layers.

☑ The MAC sublayer is responsible for providing control for accessing the transmission medium. It is responsible for moving data packets from one NIC to another, across a shared transmission medium such as an Ethernet or fiber optic transmission medium.

☑ Physical addressing is addressed at the MAC sublayer. Every NIC has a unique MAC address, also called the physical address, which identifies that specific NIC on the network. The MAC address of a NIC usually is burned into a read-only memory (ROM) chip on the NIC card.

☑ The LLC or Logical Link Control sublayer is responsible for providing the logic for the data link, thus it controls the synchronization, flow control, and error checking functions of the Data Link layer.

Identify the Seven layers of the OSI (Open Systems Interconnect) Model and Their Functions

☑ The Department of Defense (DoD) model was originally designed to share computer data across a wide area between several large, mainframe computers.

☑ The DoD's Advanced Research Projects Agency (DARPA) formed an internetworking experiment called ARPANET.

☑ The DoD model used four layers: Network Interface, Internet, Host-to-Host, and Application.

☑ The OSI model is based on the DARPA model and has seven defined layers.

☑ The seven layers of the OSI model are Physical, Data Link, Network, Transport, Session, Presentation, and Application.

☑ An acronym commonly used to remember the seven layers is All People Seem To Need Data Processing.

☑ Each layer of the OSI model is responsible for a specific set of network communication functions.

☑ FTP and Telnet are both implemented at the Application layer.

☑ The IEEE 802.3 standard was originally developed by Xerox. It was eventually standardized as the IEEE 802.3 based on the Ethernet DIX standard. The DIX standard comprised of companies who originally created the specification which are Digital, Intel, and Xerox, hence DIX.

☑ The IEEE 802.3 standard covers all Ethernet based networks such as 10 megabits per second (Mbps), 100 Mbps, and 1000 Mbps networks. One thing to consider is that Ethernet is not Fast Ethernet; they are different standards, so they rate different subcommittees. For example, Ethernet Encapsulation Standards / Ethernet (802.3), Fast Ethernet (802.3u), Gigabit Ethernet (802.3z) and Gigabit Ethernet over copper (802.3ab), but they are all primarily 802.3.

☑ In 1995, the IEEE defined the 802.3u Fast Ethernet standard (100BaseTX, 100BaseT4, 100BaseFX)

☑ 802.3 is based on CSMA/CD.

☑ Port 20 maps to FTP.

☑ Port 21 maps to FTP.

☑ Port 22 maps to SSH.

☑ Port 23 maps to Telnet.

☑ Port 25 maps to SMTP.

☑ Port 53 maps to DNS.

☑ Port 80 maps to HTTP.

☑ Port 110 maps to POP3.

☑ Port 119 maps to NNTP.

☑ Port 123 maps to NTP.

☑ Port 143 maps to IMAP4.

☑ Port 443 maps to HTTPS.

☑ Port 137 (UDP) maps to the name service.

☑ Port 138 (UDP) maps to the datagram service.

☑ Port 139 (TCP) maps to the session service.

Identify the OSI (Open Systems Interconnect) Layers at Which the Following Network Components Operate such as Hubs, Switches, Bridges, Routers, NICs and APs

☑ Hubs operate at the Physical layer of the OSI model.

☑ Switches operate at the Data Link layer of the OSI model.

☑ Bridges operate at the Data Link layer of the OSI model.

☑ Routers operate at the Network layer of the OSI model.

☑ NICs operate at the Data Link layer of the OSI model.

☑ APs operate at the Data Link layer of the OSI model.

Exam Objectives Frequently Asked Questions

The following Frequently Asked Questions, answered by the authors of this book, are designed to both measure your understanding of the Exam Objectives presented in this chapter, and to assist you with real-life implementation of these concepts. You will also gain access to thousands of other FAQs at ITFAQnet.com.

Q: How likely am I to see a question related to the DoD DARPA model or ARPANET on the exam?

A: It's unusual to see a question directly related to these topics, but you will see questions that rely upon your understanding of both the OSI model and the TCP/IP suite. Understanding the origins of these models will help you answer questions related to the networking models.

Q: Isn't ARPANET the same thing as the Internet? Why do I need to know this anyway?

A: ARPANET was the first working implementation of internetworking. The structures devised in the experiment as well as the knowledge gained during that project form the foundation of the Internet. The ARPANET was a network of a few mainframe computers and was not universally available, as the Internet is today, nor was it a commercial network (all nodes were located at universities or government ager.cies). It is possible that you'll see an exam question that uses ARPANET as an answer. Understanding the origins of the Internet can help you answer other questions on the exam, sometimes by simply helping you eliminate wrong answers.

Q: How exactly does the Network Interface layer of the DoD model map to the Physical and Data Link layers of the OSI model?

A: The DoD's Network Interface layer maps directly to the Physical and Data Link layers of the OSI model, with one notable exception. There are two parts to the Data Link layer—the Logical Link Control and the Media Access Control sublayers. TCP/IP does not implement the Logical Link Control element at the Network Interface layer. This function is handled further up the protocol stack at the Host-to-Host (Transport) layer.

Q: There are a lot of Application layer protocols in the TCP/IP suite. Am I expected to memorize them all?

A: There is an ever-expanding set of Application layer protocols in use today. It's important to get a firm understanding of the most common protocols and to have at least a familiarity with the less common protocols. At the very least, you should be very familiar with NetBIOS over TCP, Windows Sockets, DNS, DHCP, WINS, Telnet, SMTP, HTTP, FTP, RIP, and SNMP.

Self Test

A Quick Answer Key follows the Self Test questions. For complete questions, answers, and explanations to the Self Test questions in this chapter as well as the other chapters in this book, see the Self Test Appendix.

1. What is the unique physical address (Burned in Address—BIA) that is found on all NICs called?

   A. DNS Address

   B. NAT Address

   C. IP Address

   D. MAC Address

2. Which of the following is a valid MAC address?

    A. 00:05:J6:0D:91:K1

    B. 10.0.0.1 – 255.255.255.0

    C. 00:05:J6:0D:91:B1

    D. 00:D0:A0:5C:C1:B5

3. When working with MAC addresses, which layer of the OSI model do MAC addresses, frames and switches associate to?

    A. Data Link

    B. Host to Host

    C. Presentation

    D. Application

4. You are the system administrator for a small company that runs two Windows servers (Windows Server 2003) and two Linux servers (SUSE Linux). You need to lock down the connections to the switch via port security; this essentially means you will need to retrieve the MAC addresses on the systems. MAC addresses are found on Linux server by issuing which command?

    A. ipconfig /a

    B. ifconfig /a

    C. winipcfg /a

    D. ifconfig –a

5. You are the system administrator for a small company that runs two Windows servers (Windows Server 2003) and two Linux servers (SUSE Linux). You need to lock down the connections to the switch via port security; this essentially means you will need to retrieve the MAC addresses on the systems. MAC addresses are found on Windows Server 2003 systems by issuing which command?

    A. ipconfig /a

    B. ifconfig /all

    C. winipcfg /all

    D. ipconfig /all

6. You are the system administrator for a small company that runs two Windows servers (Windows Server 2003) and two Linux servers (SUSE Linux). You have 20 desktop systems, half of which are running Windows 98 SE. You need to lock down the connections to the switch via port security for the Windows 9x systems; this essentially means you will need to retrieve the MAC addresses on the systems. MAC addresses are found on Windows 9x systems by issuing which command?

    A. ipconfig /a

    B. ifconfig /a

    C. winipcfg

    D. ifconfig –a

7. From the list of choices, which of the following media access methods is used for an IEEE 802.5 network?

    A. Direct sequence

    B. Token passing

    C. CSMA /CD

    D. CSMA /CA

8. Which of the following provides NetBIOS name to IP address resolution?

    A. hosts

    B. lmhosts

    C. services

    D. protocols

9. Which OSI model layer is responsible for frame sequencing?

    A. The Physical Layer

    B. The Transport Layer

    C. The Data Link Layer

    D. The Application Layer

10. POP3 is identified by which TCP/IP port number?

    A. UDP Port 21

    B. TCP Port 23

    C. UDP Port 25

    D. TCP Port 110

11. Standards for CSMA/CD are specified by which IEEE 802 sublayer?

    A. 802.1

    B. 802.2

    C. 802.3

    D. 802.5

12. From the choices listed, which of the following protocols represents e-mail protocols? Please choose two from the list below.

    A. POP3

    B. SMNP

    C. IMAP4

    D. Telnet

13. From the following protocols listed, select the protocol that network management applications use to monitor network devices remotely.

    A. SNMP

    B. DNS

    C. SMTP

    D. DHCP

14. Which of the following can you use to connect with a UNIX server using terminal emulation software?

    A. Web Browser

    B. FTP

    C. Telnet

    D. NNTP

15. When discussing the OSI model and the DoD model, which layers of the OSI model handle what you would find in the Application layer of the DoD model? Choose all that apply.

    A. Application

    B. Presentation

    C. Transport

    D. Session

16. You are a network administrator looking to implement technology into a company. You are told you need to build a network utilizing the IEEE 802.11 standard. From the list below, the IEEE 802.11 standard maps to which of the following? (Select only one answer).

    A. Token Ring

    B. Wired Ethernet

    C. Metropolitan Area Network (MAN)

    D. Wireless in Infrastructure mode

17. You are a network technician assigned to install a new network hub. Which layer of the OSI model does a standard hub operate at? Select only one answer.

    A. Physical Layer

    B. Data Link Layer

    C. Network Layer

    D. Transport Layer

18. You are a network technician assigned to install a new network switch. Which layer of the OSI model does a standard switch (or bridge) operate at? Select only one answer.

    A. Physical Layer

    B. Data Link Layer

    C. Network Layer

    D. Transport Layer

19. You are a network technician assigned to install a new network Router. Which layer of the OSI model does a standard router operate at? Choose all that apply.

    A. Physical Layer

    B. Data Link Layer

    C. Network Layer

    D. Transport Layer

20. You are a network technician assigned to install a new NIC in a PC. Which layer of the OSI model does a NIC operate at? Select only one answer.

    A. Physical Layer

    B. Data Link Layer

    C. Network Layer

    D. Transport Layer

Self Test Quick Answer Key

For complete questions, answers, and explanations to the Self Test questions in this chapter as well as the other chapters in this book, see the Self Test Appendix.

1.	**D**	11.	**C**
2.	**D**	12.	**A** and **C**
3.	**A**	13.	**A**
4.	**D**	14.	**C**
5.	**D**	15.	**A, B** and **D**
6.	**C**	16.	**D**
7.	**B**	17.	**A**
8.	**B**	18.	**B**
9.	**C**	19.	**C**
10.	**D**	20.	**B**

Chapter 6

NETWORK+

Network Protocols

Domain II Objectives in this Chapter:

2.4   Differentiate between the network protocols in terms of routing, addressing schemes, interoperability, and naming conventions.

2.5   Identify the components and structure of IP addresses and the required setting for connections across the Internet.

2.6   Identify classful IP ranges and their subnet masks.

2.7   Identify the purpose of subnetting.

2.8   Identify the differences between private and public network addressing schemes.

2.9   Identify and differentiate between the IP addressing methods.

2.10   Define the purpose, function, and use of the protocols used in the TCP/IP suite.

2.11   Define the function of TCP/UDP ports.

2.12   Identify the well-known ports associated with the commonly used services and protocols.

2.13   Identify the purpose of network services and protocols.

Introduction

TCP/IP, (short for Transmission Control Protocol/Internet Protocol) is a term we recognize easily due to its ever-increasing function in connecting our computers to the Internet. TCP/IP is a network protocol used to provide the logical communication structure needed to send and receive data on a computer network. This logical communication structure is the complicated part, and what we will be primarily learning about in this chapter. The Network+ exam calls for an understanding of routable and routing protocols in terms of routing, addressing schemes, interoperability, and naming conventions. This chapter, as well as sections of the next chapter, will cover many aspects of TCP/IP , especially those areas made testable by the Network+ posted objectives.

In this chapter we will also be covering other not-so-well-known network protocols still in use in some networks, such as AppleTalk, IPX/SPX (Internetwork Packet Exchange/Sequenced Packet Exchange) and the rarely used NetBEUI (NetBIOS Enhanced User Interface). However, this chapter's main focus will be on TCP/IP. The reasoning for this is simple; not only is TCP/IP one of the most thoroughly tested knowledge areas on the exam, it is the most widely used and integrated protocol in use today around the world. Not knowing TCP/IP can be somewhat career-limiting when considering becoming a network engineer. The TCP/IP protocol suite is primarily what keeps the Internet running as well it does. TCP/IP is also used to provide network communication in most of the world's companies, universities, and countries. Anywhere there is a network connection, it is most likely that TCP/IP is in use. Keep in mind that this chapter does in no way explore all there is to know about TCP/IP, as that could literally take volumes to cover.

By the end of this chapter you should be comfortable with navigating numbering schemes, have a better understanding of the protocol suite, and have the ability to work your way through any problem presented to you (on the Network+ exam and in real life).

TCP/IP has rattled many test takers in the past who have taken exams where TCP/IP fundamentals are tested extensively. Since Network+ is somewhat of an entry-level exam, you will not have to have TCP/IP addressing and design perfected or mastered, but you will have to have the fundamentals of it. Learning about network protocols is not too tough an issue once you understand the underlying mechanics. The intent of this chapter is to ensure that you have the foundation and fundamental knowledge needed to pass the exam and build the rest of your studies on. Now, let's delve into these network protocols and see exactly what we need to know for the Network+ exam as well as in your day-to-day activities as a network administrator.

NOTE

This chapter covers the TCP/IP protocol in depth and also looks briefly at other protocol suites such as AppleTalk and IPX/SPX. These protocols will show up on the exam, but not as much as TCP/IP. Although the information in this chapter is good for test preparation purposes, as a working network engineer, you should know more about somewhat obscure and less-commonly used protocols.

Network Protocols

Network protocols keep the network communications world running. They provide for continuing data exchange, they keep e-mails going back and forth from source to destination, and take care of all of the network–based operations that we take for granted Just about anything done on a network today is handled by the accurate design and implementation of routable network protocols. Commonly seen and used today is TCP/IP. Since most of this chapter focuses on TCP/IP, we will cover it last. Before we do, let's look at some other network protocols that you will encounter, not only within your travels and working as a network technician, administrator, or engineer, but also on the CompTIA Network+ exam.

Understanding network protocols is not as difficult as most would make it out to be. Understanding some basic math, addition and subtraction, and basic multiplication skills, are nearly all you need to become a good network engineer working with network protocols—that, and an understanding of how the protocols work. Armed with both, you will be able to work on any network protocols you encounter.

IPX/SPX

IPX is a connectionless Layer 3 network protocol. Its counterpart, SPX, operates at Layer 4. Although multiple Novell protocols also operate at Layer 4, SPX is the most commonly implemented. SPX, a reliable, connection-oriented protocol, was derived from the XNS (Xerox Network System) protocols of the 1970s. Network Core Protocol (NCP) provides interaction between clients and servers by defining connection control and service request/reply. Service Advertisement Protocol (SAP) allows servers to advertise their addresses and the services they provide.

IPX/SPX is an old Novell-based protocol that has been around for many years, and is still used in some legacy Novell network environments. Over time it is being gradually phased out in favor of TCP/IP. IPX/SPX will see very few new installs. You will, however, undoubtedly come across IPX/SPX currently installed in older networks, and as such, knowledge of the IPX/SPX protocol suite is still tested on the Network+ exam.

At its beginning, Novell adapted IPX from the Xerox Network System Internet Datagram Protocol (IDP). IPX is a *connectionless* datagram protocol. This means that when a process running on a particular node uses IPX to communicate with a process on another node, no connection between the two nodes is established. IPX packets are addressed and sent to their destinations, but there is no guarantee or verification of successful delivery. As a Network Layer protocol, IPX addresses and routes packets from one location to another on an IPX network. IPX bases its routing decisions on the address fields in its header and on the information it receives from RIP (Routing Information Protocol), or NLSP (NetWare Link State Protocol). IPX uses this information to forward packets to their destination nodes or to the next router providing a path to the destination node. RIP and NLSP are routing protocols that make routing decisions based on a RIT (Routing Information Table). Figure 6.1 shows how the IPX/SPX protocol suite maps to the OSI (Open Systems Interconnect) model.

Figure 6.1 Comparison of the IPX/SPX Protocol Suite and the OSI Model

OSI Model	IPX/SPX Suite
Application	SAP, NCP, NetBIOS
Presentation	
Session	
Transport	SPX
Network	IPX, RIP, NLSP
Data Link	
Physical	Ethernet, Token Ring

NOTE

In Figure 6.1, we see the use of RIP at the Network Layer of the OSI model. This is not the same version of RIP used for TCP/IP; it's actually IPX/SPX-based RIP. Small intricacies will not stump you on the actual exam, but can surely ruin your day on the job. Make sure you continue your studies of protocols and protocol suites after moving past the material in this publication.

EXAM WARNING

Figure 6.1 shows only a handful of protocols available in the IPX/SPX suite. You should understand basic placement of the most commonly used IPX/SPX protocols on the OSI model by layer. For more information on the OSI model, reference Chapter 5.

IPX Addressing

An IPX address consists of two parts: the network number and the node number. IPX addresses are 80 bits long, with 32 bits for the network number and 48 bits for the node number. IPX simplifies mapping between Layer 3 and Layer 2 addresses, using the Layer 2 address as the host portion of the Layer 3 address. This eliminates the need for address resolution, such as that provided by the Address Resolution Protocol (ARP) for the IP suite. IPX addresses are generally written as hexadecimal digits in the *network.node* format.

Unlike IP, IPX has no concept of subnetworking. The IPX network number is manually assigned and must be unique for each network segment. Each node number on a given IPX network segment must be unique.

NOTE

IPX supports multiple Ethernet frame types: Ethernet II, IEEE 802.3, IEEE 802.3 SNAP, and Novell 802.3 RAW. It is possible to use multiple encapsulation types on a single network segment as long as a unique network number is assigned to each encapsulation type. It is important to note that hosts that use different encapsulation types will not be able to directly communicate with each other. You won't be tested on this intricate detail of the protocol, but it's important to know as a network engineer, as frame types are very important when configuring specific protocols.

Node numbers do not have to be unique across networks because the network number and node number are used together to identify a particular host.

Internal Network Numbering and Server Addresses

IPX contains two types of network numbers: internal network numbers and network numbers assigned to local area network (LAN) and some wide area network (WAN) interfaces (sometimes called *external* network numbers). The *internal* network number identifies a virtual network segment inside your server. This means that the internal network is another (virtual) segment on the network. Therefore, if you configure an internal network number on a computer running IPX, a router will add an extra hop in its route to that computer.

The use of an internal network number allows for improved fault tolerance on the network. IPX resources are referenced by SAP names that point to an IPX address. Using an internal network number as a part of the SAP address means that in the event of a failure of a particular network segment, only the IPX route, not the SAP tables, will have to be adjusted to an alternate path.

The internal network number is an eight-digit hexadecimal number between 0x1 to 0xFFFFFFFE and must be unique across the entire IPX network. Although 0xFFFFFFFE was originally allowed for use as an address, this changed after the introduction of Network Link Services Protocol. Both NLSP and IPX RIP have been modified since then to recognize 0xFFFFFFFE as the default route. When you use the internal network number, the host portion of the IPX address is set to 1.

How to Translate an IPX Address

Figure 6.2 shows an IPX address in more detail. The first 32 bits of the address are the network number, which is configured by the network administrator. This number must be a hexadecimal value between 0x00000001 and 0xFFFFFFFD. In this case, the network number is configured as the hexadecimal value 0xBEEF. The last 48 bits of the address are the same as the Media Access Control (MAC) address of the device's NIC (network interface card). In this case, the MAC address of the NIC is 00-20-E0-88-80-74, which is also used as the IPX node number.

Figure 6.2 Example of an IPX Address

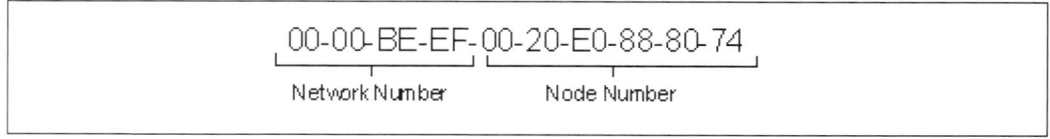

00-00-BE-EF-00-20-E0-88-80-74

Network Number   Node Number

Exam Warning

IPX does not have a broadcast network number (such as 0xFFFFFFFF). In addition to network number 0, the numbers 0xFFFFFFFF and 0xFFFFFFFE are reserved for specific purposes. For this reason, they should not be assigned to any IPX network.

TEST DAY TIP

Prepare for your exam with these very important pieces of information. For the Network+ exam, please remember that UNIX and Linux do not support IPX/SPX. Windows 2000 and 2003 natively support TCP/IP, IPX/SPX, and NetBEUI. Any system running a protocol such as IPX/SPX or NetBEUI is most likely doing so for backward compatibility with older applications or systems. Do not get confused when you are asked, "what is the best protocol to use for this situation" and the answer is IPX/SPX… and you think it's incorrect because its being phased out. This could lead you into putting incorrect answers down if you read the question and answer set too quickly.

NetBEUI (Network Basic Input / Output System Extended User Interface)

NetBEUI is an enhanced version of the NetBIOS (Network Basic Input Output System) protocol used by network operating systems such as LAN Manager, LAN Server, Windows for Workgroups, Windows 95, and Windows NT. NetBEUI was originally designed by IBM for their LAN Manager server and was later extended by Microsoft and Novell.

NetBEUI is rarely ever used or seen today. NetBEUI was originally designed for very small, non-routable networks, and is broadcast-based. NetBIOS is an API (application program interface) that augments the MS-DOS (Microsoft Disk Operating System) BIOS by adding special functions for LANs. Almost all Windows-based LANs for PCs are based on and use NetBIOS. Some LAN manufacturers have even extended NetBIOS, adding additional network capabilities. NetBIOS is still very much in use today. NetBIOS will be covered in more detail later in the chapter.

EXAM WARNING

IPX/SPX and TCP/IP are routable; NetBEUI is not.

AppleTalk / AppleTalk over IP

Apple Computer developed AppleTalk as a plug-and-play protocol for use on Macintosh computers. AppleTalk was designed to allow sharing of resources such as files and printers among multiple users. Any device attached to an AppleTalk network is known as a *node*. Figure 6.3 shows how the AppleTalk protocol stack maps against the OSI reference model.

Figure 6.3 Layers of the AppleTalk Protocol Stack

OSI Model	AppleTalk Suite
Application	AFP
Presentation	
Session	ASP, ADSP, ZIP, PAP
Transport	AEP, ATP, NBP, RTMP, AURF
Network	AARP, DDP
Data Link	EtherTalk, TokenTalk
Physical	Ethernet, Token Ring

AppleTalk supports four media-access protocols:

- **EtherTalk** AppleTalk over Ethernet

- **LocalTalk** AppleTalk over phone wire

- **TokenTalk** AppleTalk over Token Ring

- **FDDITalk** AppleTalk over Fiber Distributed Data Interface (FDDI)

At the Data Link Layer, each of these physical media technologies has its own corresponding Link Access Protocol (LAP): EtherTalk LAP (ELAP), LocalTalk LAP (LLAP), TokenTalk LAP (TLAP), and FDDITalk LAP (FLAP).

At the Network Layer of AppleTalk are two protocols: AppleTalk Address Resolution Protocol (AARP), and Datagram Delivery Protocol (DDP). AARP can be compared to ARP in TCP/IP, and DDP can be compared to IP in TCP/IP. DDP is responsible for transmitting and receiving packets and provides socket-to-socket connectivity between nodes.

Five key protocols exist at AppleTalk's Transport Layer:

- **AppleTalk Echo Protocol** (**AEP**) This protocol is responsible for testing the reachability of network nodes.

- **AppleTalk Transaction Protocol** (**ATP**) This protocol is responsible for ensuring that communications between a source and destination socket occur without any loss.

- **Name Binding Protocol (NBP)** This protocol is responsible for mapping user-friendly entity names to numeric network addresses.

- **Routing Table Maintenance Protocol (RTMP)** This distance-vector routing protocol for AppleTalk is based on IP RIP.

- **AppleTalk Update-Based Routing Protocol (AURP)** This protocol is an extension to RTMP that allows two noncontiguous AppleTalk networks to talk to each other by tunneling their traffic through IP using UDP (User Datagram protocol) encapsulation.

The Session Layer of AppleTalk consists of four protocols:

- **AppleTalk Session Protocol (ASP)** This protocol is responsible for establishing and maintaining logical connections between clients and servers. ASP runs on top of ATP.

- **AppleTalk Data Stream Protocol (ADSP)** This protocol is responsible for reliable transmission of data after a session has been established between two nodes. ADSP runs directly on top of DDP.

- **Zone Information Protocol (ZIP)** This protocol maintains network-to-zone-number mappings.

- **Printer Access Protocol (PAP)** This protocol is used to establish connections between clients and servers (usually print servers). PAP runs on top of ATP.

The most important of the AppleTalk protocols is AFP (AppleTalk Filing Protocol) AFP sits at the Presentation and Application Layers and allows files and directories to be shared over a network. AFP relies on ASP, ATP, and AEP. AFP is covered in more detail later in the chapter.

AppleTalk Addressing

Like TCP/IP and IPX/SPX, AppleTalk uses addresses to identify and locate devices on a network. AppleTalk addresses consist of three elements:

- **Network number (2 bytes)** The network number specifies the value of a unique AppleTalk network. Valid network numbers in AppleTalk are 1 through 65,279. The network number 0 is reserved for the local network. Network numbers 65,280 through 65,534 are reserved for the startup process.

- **Node number (1 byte)** The node number specifies a unique AppleTalk node attached to a particular network. Valid node numbers are 1 through 253 (255 is reserved for broadcasts, and 0 and 254 are not allowed).

- **Socket number (1 byte)** The socket number specifies a particular socket running on a node. Sockets in AppleTalk are similar to ports in TCP/IP; they represent a process or a service on a host. Sockets addresses are 8 bits long; there can be a maximum of 254 sockets on a node (socket numbers 0 and 255 are reserved). Sockets 1 through 127 are statically assigned, and sockets 128 through 254 are available for dynamic assignment.

AppleTalk addresses are generally written as three decimal values (network number, node number, socket number) separated by periods. For example, the address 5.3.20 means *network 5*, *node 3*, and *socket 20*.

Addresses are assigned dynamically using AARP. When an AppleTalk node boots up, it selects an arbitrary node number on the network. It then sends an AARP request to see if any other node on the network is using that address. If no response is received, the node keeps the address. If another node is already using the address, this node selects a new node number and sends another request to ensure that no other nodes are using that node number. The process repeats itself until no AARP response is received. An AppleTalk device stores the last used network address in NVRAM (non-volatile random access memory) and attempts to reuse that network address the next time it boots up. AARP is also used for AppleTalk node to Layer 2 address mapping, similar to how ARP works in IP. Layer 3 to Layer 2 address mappings are stored on an AppleTalk host in the address mapping table (AMT).

There are two types of AppleTalk networks, Phase 1 and Phase 2. Phase 1 networks (also known as *non-extended networks*) have a limit of 253 nodes on a network. Phase 2 networks (also known as *extended networks*) overcome the 253-host limitation by using the concept of a *cable range*. Instead of a single network number, as in Phase 1, a Phase 2 segment can be assigned a sequential range of network numbers. This range of network numbers behaves as a single network and is known as a *cable range*. Each network number in a cable range can have 253 nodes. A cable range is expressed as a pair of hyphen-separated network numbers. For example, the cable range 4001-4004 encompasses the network numbers 4001, 4002, 4003, and 4004. Note that a cable range could consist of just a single network number. For example, the cable range 4005-4005 consists of the single network number 4005.

Zones and AppleTalk Communication

A *zone* in AppleTalk consists of a logical grouping of network devices. The idea behind zones is to enable users to locate network services easily. The *Chooser* program on an Apple Macintosh computer identifies all services within a zone and presents them in a single list. Zone names are assigned arbitrarily by network administrators and are generally based on geographic or organizational boundaries. A host can belong only to one zone, and all services published by the host appear within that zone.

A single zone can span one ore more networks, and multiple zones can exist on a single network. The Zone Information Protocol operates at the Session Layer and is responsible for mapping networks to zone names throughout the network. When a host boots up on the network, ZIP provides it a list of zone names.

Head of the Class…

Too Many Protocols to Know? Get Ahead With Simple Tips For Study.

There will be many protocols you will come across in your travels and working as a network technician. It will be impossible to remember or memorize them all without starting somewhere. In this chapter you will be bombarded with a great deal of information about network protocols and what their uses are, which port numbers are assigned to them, and so on. The Network+ exam's questioning does not go to the detailed level that this text does. The text is based on getting you to understand the concepts surrounding the technology. For instance, you will not need to know everything about AppleTalk to pass the Network+ exam, but be prepared to know about AFP (as it's a testable objective), as well as its mapping to the OSI model. This is only one example. Other examples of AppleTalk (or any other protocol showing up on the exam) can be used as distracters for other questions.

If you want to prepare properly for the Network+ exam, make sure you are comfortable with placement of protocols within their respective suites, their basic functionality, and the differences between them come test time. Questions can range in difficulty. You may see AppleTalk (and IPX/SPX) show up many times as incorrect answers to TCP/IP-based questions. Because of this, it's recommended that you do your best to commit these protocols to memory if you can.

For more information on the OSI model, refer to Chapter 5. Use scrap paper and practice recreating the models so come test time, you can duplicate this information right before the exam and reference it from your scrap paper.

TCP/IP

In the 1970s, IP was developed as part of the Transmission Control Protocol effort to provide logically addressed and structured networking. Since then, IP has matured greatly and can convey a wide array of information and services. The primary role of IP is to provide logical addresses and support the routing of traffic to its destination. Recent efforts to expand the capacity of IP addresses (which are nearly exhausted) have resulted in the next generation of the protocol, IP version 6 (IPv6). IP supports the ability to send to a group via multicasting. These topics are covered in the next sections, starting with IP version 4 (IPv4).

IP provides the Network Layer addressing and functions for the TCP/IP protocol stack, as shown in Figure 6.4. The TCP/IP protocol stack does not map neatly to the OSI model, as the OSI model was developed after TCP/IP.

Figure 6.4 TCP/IP Protocol Stack

OSI Model	DoD Mode	TCP/IP Suite
Application		FTP, HTTP, Telnet, SMTP
Presentation	Application	
Session		
Transport	Host to Host	TCP, UDP
Network	Internet	IP, ICMP, IGMP, RIP, OSPF
Data Link		Ethernet, Token Ring
Physical	Link	

IPv4 has structure and processes developed around its address space. Information is transported in IP packets, in which the header remains consistent in terms of size and fields.

NOTE

We will cover the TCP/IP protocol stack later in more detail when we discuss TCP/IP-based protocols such as SMTP (Simple Mail Transfer Protocol), Telnet and FTP (File Transfer Protocol). This is only the beginning … there are over one hundred protocols covered in the TCP/IP suite. The Network+ exam only covers the most basic and fundamental ones—the ones more commonly seen on the job and in production environments.

IPv4

IP is responsible for addressing and delivery by providing a logical address scheme. The original version of IP (referred to as IPv4) consists of 32 bits spread over four 8-bit octets, expressed in *dotted decimal* format. For example, a 32-bit address may look like this in binary:

```
00001010000010110000110000001101
```

To improve readability, the 32-bit IP address splits into four blocks of 8 bits like this:

`00001010      00001011      00001100      00001101`

Finally, each 8-bit block is converted to decimal and the decimal values are separated with periods or dots. The converted IPv4 address, expressed as a dotted decimal address, is:

`10.11.12.13`

It is much easier to remember an IP address of 10.11.12.13 than to remember a string of bits such as 00001010000010110000110000001101. IP addresses and their values and uses are discussed in detail later in this chapter.

All information transported over IP is carried in IP packets with the format shown in Figure 6.5. The header length can vary somewhat depending on whether the options field is present and the number of bits that are used to specify these options. This variation in length adds to the processing burden, as predictability and consistency are not achieved.

Figure 6.5 The IPv4 Header

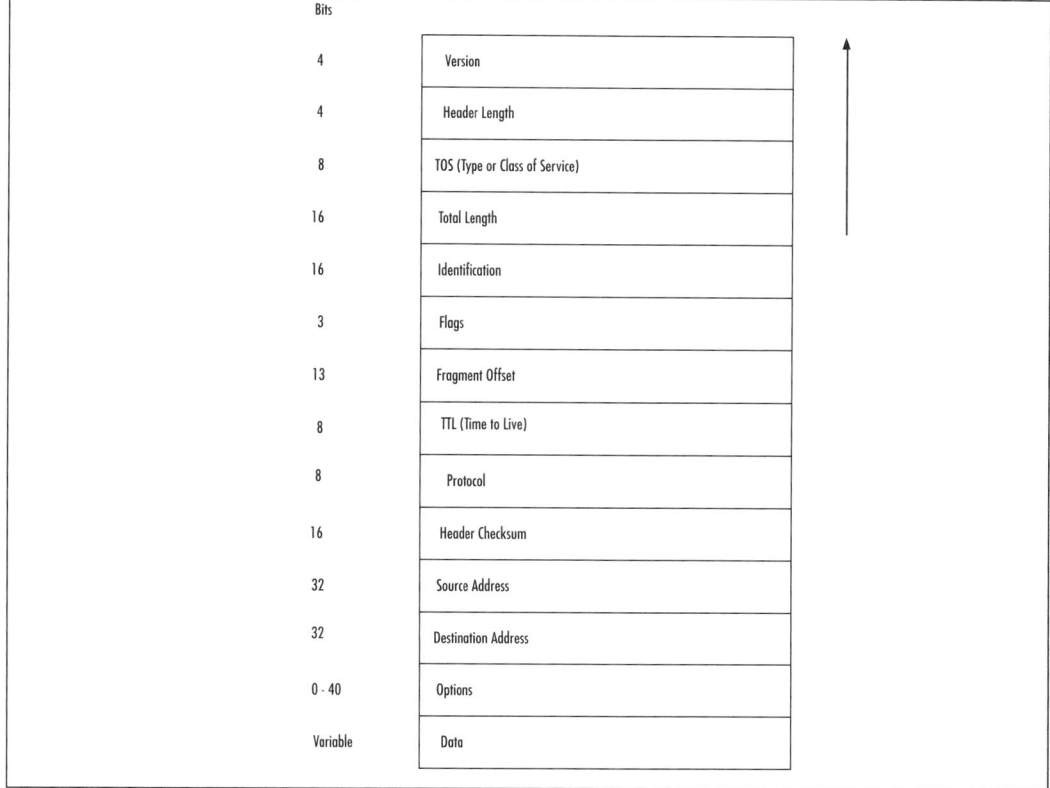

■ **Version** 4-bit field. Identifies the version of IP (4 or 6). Makes IPv6 backward-compatible with IPv4.

■ **Header Length** 4-bit field. Indicates the length of the header, as the IPv4 header is a variable between 20 and 64 bytes.

■ **Type of Service (ToS)** Identifies the priority of packet.

■ **Total Length** The entire length of the IP portion of the packet. Called *payload length* in IPv6.

■ **Identification, Flags, Fragment Offset** Handles the fragmentation and reassembly of packets. Not necessary in the IPv6 header, as they are handled by the source.

■ **Time To Live (TTL)** Limits the number of hops the packet is allowed to transit. At each hop, a router decrements (reduces) this field, and when it reaches zero, the packet is removed from the network.

■ **Protocol** Indicates the next protocol (header) following the IPv4 header, such as TCP or UDP.

■ **Header Checksum** Maintains the integrity of the IPv4 header.

■ **Source and Destination Address** 32-bit addresses that identify the source and destination for this packet.

■ **Options** If enabled, each intermediate node in the path needs to examine it, which can cause inefficient router performance.

Familiarity with the IP address classes, masks, and structure are essential to mastering and using IP. The most fundamental aspect of IP is its addresses.

TEST DAY TIP

Understanding the inside of the IP packet is not crucial to passing the Network+ exam, but if you want to intimately understand TCP/IP and how it works (which is basically what the entirety of this chapter is based on), you should understand how an IP packet works, what it is made of, and some of the fields within it. In Chapters 11 and 12, when we look at network troubleshooting, having an intimate understanding of the internals of the packet will greatly help. Also, using tools such as a network sniffer, which essentially captures traffic for you to analyze and dissect, relies on your knowledge of the internals of the packet.

IPv6

Issues such as address exhaustion that made IPv4 inadequate require robust solutions. While 32 bits of address space were originally thought to be more than enough, time and growth have proven this to not be the case. Address space depletion will be covered later in this chapter. IPv6, if implemented fully in the future, will solve the depletion problem, as the newer version of the IP protocol allows for far greater amounts of addressing to be deployed than its predecessor, IPv4. Additionally, IPv4 suffers from a lack of hierarchical structure; while addresses may be sequentially allocated and summarized, they are not optimized by routing or allocation.

Designers of IPv6 worked diligently to ensure that the same issues would not be encountered. Members of the Internet community who were responsible for developing the protocol carefully scrutinized each new RFC (Request for Comment) penned for IP. This section covers IPv6, which was developed to overcome the exhaustion of IPv4 addresses, and to improve on it in general. As defined in RFC 1884 and later revised in RFC 2373, IPv6 addresses are 128-bit identifiers for interfaces and sets of interfaces, not nodes. Three general types of addresses exist within IPv6 (IP version 6); unicast, anycast, and multicast. IP addresses are structured as follows:

- Expanded addressing moves us from 32-bit address to a 128-bit addressing method.

- Provides newer unicast and broadcasting methods.

- Hexadecimal fused into the IP address format.

- Uses ":" instead of "." as delimiters.

- To write 128-bit addresses so that they are more readable to human eyes and not a complete chore to apply, IPv6 allows for using a hexadecimal format. IPv6 is written as 32-hex digits, with colons (:) separating the values of the eight 16-bit pieces of the address.

- IPv6 addresses are written in hexadecimal format: 7060:0000:0000:0000:0006:0600:100D:315B

- Leading 0s in each 16-bit value can be omitted, so this address can be expressed as follows: 7060:0:0:0:6:600:100D:315B

- IPv6 addresses may contain consecutive 16-bit values of 0, one such string of 0s per address can be omitted and replaced by a double colon (::). As a result, this address can be shortened even more: 7060::6:600:100D:315B

Benefits of IPv6

The following sections look at the two main problems solved by IPv6—address depletion and routing scalability—in more detail. Some added benefits that IPv6 gives to network designers and administrators include:

- Increased IP address size

- Increased addressing hierarchy support

- Simplified host addressing (unified addressing: global, site, local)

- Simplified auto-configuration of addresses (easier readdressing, DHCPv6 (Dynamic Host Configuration Protocol version 6), and neighbor discovery instead of ARP broadcasts)

- Improved scalability of multicast routing

- The *anycast* address

- A streamlined header

- Improved security (security extension headers, integrated data integrity)

- Better performance (aggregation, neighbor discovery instead of ARP broadcasts, no fragmentation, no header checksum, flow, priority, integrated quality of service [QoS])

IPv4 versus IPv6

How does IPv6 compare with its predecessor, IPv4? IPv6 eases the network administrator's burden, in that *aggregatable global unicast* addresses do not require address translation when used to access external networks such as the Internet. In IPv4, private address spaces are used when global addresses are unavailable. These private addresses must be translated to a limited set of global addresses when accessing external networks. IPv4 address translation schemes include NAT (network address translation) and PAT (port address translation). IPv6 virtually eliminates the need for address translation as a means of accessing external networks.

Table 6.1 illustrates the reduced address administration burden placed upon IPv6 network administrators.

Table 6.1 Address Administration Comparison

Address Administration Issues	IPv4 Private Class A Block	IPv6 Aggregatable Global Unicast
Address Length	32 bits	128 bits
Length of Pre-assigned Upstream Fields	8 bits	48 bits

Continued

Table 6.1 Address Administration Comparison

Address Administration Issues	IPv4 Private Class A Block	IPv6 Aggregatable Global Unicast
Length of Delegated Addressing Fields	24 bits	80 bits
Host Identifier Length	24 subnet bits	64 bits
Subnet Identifier Length	24 host bits	16 bits (SLA ID)
Allocate host addresses for subnet identifiers	Yes	No
Determine subnet identifiers	Yes	Yes
Determine host identifiers	Yes	No
Address Translation Required (NAT/PAT)	Yes	No

Header Comparison

In IPv6, five fields are eliminated, including the variable-length IPv4 *options* field. Removal of the variable-length field and other fields permits the IPv6 header to have a fixed header of 40 bytes in length. A comparison of the two types of headers is summarized in Table 6.2.

Table 6.2 Header Comparison

Header	IPv4	IPv6
Header Format	Variable	Fixed
Header Fields	13	8
Header Length	20 to 60 bytes	40 bytes
Address Length	32 bits	128 bits
Header Checksum	Yes	No
Fragmentation Fields	Yes	No
Extension Headers	No	Yes

To provide for additional options, IPv6 defines the following extension headers, which are used to provide specific information needed for particular operations.

- Hop-by-Hop Options header
- Destination Options header
- Routing header
- Fragment header

- Authentication header (AH)
- Encapsulating Security Payload header

There is not much you need to master about IPv6 for the Network+ exam. A firm understanding of its development and its differences (such as being able to identify an IPv6 address over an IPv4 address) will be sufficient.

Head of the Class…

Making the Transition, IPv4 and IPv6 Backward Compatibility

IPv6 will hopefully one day become the de facto standard, but until then both will have to coexist, and because of this fact, you need to understand how IPv6 is backward compatible with IPv4.

IPv4 addresses are embedded within IPv6 addresses. This method takes regular IPv4 addresses and puts them in a special IPv6 format so they are recognized as being IPv4 addresses by certain IPv6 devices. IPv6 devices will know when they receive packets that have IPv4 addresses embedded within them.

TEST DAY TIP

You may or may not see a question that directly relates to IPv6 and information about it, but you may see questions where IPv4 is the focus and IPv6 is used to test your understanding of the basic differences. The more you know about IP, the easier the exam becomes, even though the exam focus is on version 4. Make sure you know the basic differences between versions 4 and 6 so you can pick the correct answer.

Feature Comparison

The IPv6 architecture contains integrated features that are not contained in IPv4. Table 6.3 contrasts the features of IPv4 and IPv6.

Table 6.3 IPv4 and IPv6 Features

Feature	IPv4	IPv6
Anycast Address	No	Yes
Multicast Scoping	No	Yes
Security Support	No	Yes
Mobility Support	No	Yes
Autoconfiguration	No	Yes
Router Discovery	No	Neighbor Discovery
Multicast Membership	IGMP	Multicast Listener Discovery
Router Fragmentation	Yes	Source only

NOTE

For more information on IPv6, visit www.ipv6.org.

Understanding IP Addressing

IPv4 is widely used today as the foundation of network addressing in both private networks and across the Internet. It is widely known simply as TCP/IP. In order to effectively manage a network in today's complex environment, it's critical to understand IP addressing in depth. IP addressing is used to assign a unique logical address to a host for identification purposes. Assigning the IP address to a host is a relatively simple process, especially if the host uses DHCP to automatically acquire that address. However, most networks are divided into more efficient segments called *subnets*.

Understanding addressing related to subnets is a bit more complex, so we'll begin by exploring some of the mathematics underlying this process. Let's start by dissecting the IP address and learning how to manipulate it.

IP addresses are expressed in four sets of three numbers, such as 136.14.117.5. Each of the numbers between the dots is called an *octet* because, when converted to binary notation, it represents eight binary digits (bits). Binary notation is covered in the next section. Every IP address has 32 bits and can be notated as *www.xxx.yyy.zzz or w.x.y.z*. This is called *dotted decimal notation*. When the value of any one of the octets is less than three digits, it is written without leading zeroes. Therefore, you'll see IP addresses with one, two, or three digits in each section, such as 254.4.27.112. However, when the value of the octet is zero, it is still written as zero because each octet must be represented (for example, 129.48.0.95). The notation is often shortened to *w.x.y.z* to represent the four octets. The longer notation, *www.xxx.yyy.zzz* is used to indicate that each position can be a maximum of three digits. In this chapter, we'll use both notations.

Each IP address contains two elements, the network address space and the host address space. Throughout this text, we'll use *address* and *ID* interchangeably, and we may also refer to the *network ID* or the *host ID*. Understanding how to work with IP addressing is a fundamental skill that will be used throughout your career in Information Technology and throughout many other certification exams, not just the Network+ exam. Take the time to understand this information thoroughly if you want to ensure your success on the exam and on the job.

EXAM WARNING

You must understand the IP address to successfully navigate the Network+ exam. Make absolutely certain that you read the following sections until you are comfortable with the material within.

Converting from Decimal to Binary

In everyday life, we use the decimal numbering system for counting. The decimal system relies on the digits 0 through 9. This is the system we use for the standard math that we do in our heads. However, this is not the only way to denote numbers. The binary system relies on only two digits: 0 and 1. It's the language of the computer because electrical components are either on or off, and thus electrical signals (or RF signals or light impulses) can easily represent 0 with an off status and 1 with an on status. Although there are some exceptions, for the purpose of this discussion, we will use this convention. Each binary digit is called a *bit* and in IP addressing, eight bits form an *octet*. An IP address has four octets, or a total of 32 bits.

Any whole number from our decimal system can be represented in binary. Each location, or bit position, in a binary number has a certain weight, just as in our commonly used decimal system. For example, we know that in the decimal system, a digit in the first position from the right represents ones, a digit in the second position represents tens, a digit in the third position represents hundreds, and so forth. When we see the number 384, we don't even have to stop and think to know that it means 3 hundreds, 8 tens (eighty) and 4 ones.

As with decimal, the weighting in a binary number moves from low-order on the right to high-order on the left. Although our eyes are accustomed to understanding decimal numbers when we read them left to right, many people find it easier to work with binary numbers from right to left.

EXAM WARNING

It is unlikely that the exam will contain any straightforward conversion questions such as "what does the binary number 1001 0001 1111 1011 represent in decimal?" If only it was that easy! Instead, you'll need to know how to do the conversion as part of a more complex process, usually in calculating subnet masks. It's easy to calculate subnet masks if you understand the basic fundamentals of binary and decimal conversion.

Binary numbers typically are counted beginning with bit 0, the right-most bit. This has a value of 2^0, or 1. Each bit to the left is raised (exponentially) to the next power, which effectively doubles the number. Thus, bit 1 is 2^1 or 2, and so forth, as shown in Table 6.4. This formula is typically expressed as 2^n where n is the bit number.

Table 6.4 Binary and Decimal Values

Bit Number	Bit 7	Bit 6	Bit 5	Bit 4	Bit 3	Bit 2	Bit 1	Bit 0
Notation	2^7	2^6	2^5	2^4	2^3	2^2	2^1	2^0
Decimal Value	128	64	32	16	8	4	2	1

If you're not familiar with binary numbers, you may be wondering why this numbering system is set up this way. If you take the right-most position, the bit 0 position, and set it to 0, the number is 0. If you set bit 0 to 1, the number is 1. How do we get to 2? We set the next bit, bit 1, to 1 and reset bit 0 to 0. This is just like in the decimal numbering system in which you count, in the right-most position, from 0 to 9. After nine, you move to the next position, set it to 1 and reset the first position to 0, resulting in the decimal number 10. Binary works the same way, except that each bit position can be only 0 or 1, thus you need more positions in order to represent decimal numbers.

To create a binary number, we set the desired bit to 1. For instance, to represent the number 128, we would set the 8th position, or bit 7 (remember, we're counting from 0 to 7, not 1 to 8), to 1. What if we wanted to create the number 132? We'd set bit 7 and bit 2 to 1. The rest of the bits would remain 0, as shown in Table 6.5. Any number can be expressed this way, limited only by the number of bits in a defined field (in TCP/IP, we use only eight bits for each number).

Table 6.5 Setting Bits to Create Dotted Decimal Values

Bit Number	Bit 7	Bit 6	Bit 5	Bit 4	Bit 3	Bit 2	Bit 1	Bit 0
Notation	2^7	2^6	2^5	2^4	2^3	2^2	2^1	2^0
Decimal Value	128	64	32	16	8	4	2	1
Bit Values for 132	1	0	0	0	0	1	0	0

To convert a binary number to decimal, add the value of each bit position set to 1. Thus, the binary number 10000100 converts to decimal 132.

To convert a decimal number to a binary number, look at the decimal number and find the largest binary bit represented. If we want to convert 184 to binary, we do the math shown in Table 6.6. For each number we subtract, we set the corresponding bit to 1.

Table 6.6 Calculating Binary Bits from Dotted Decimal

Converting Decimal to Binary	Subtraction
Decimal number	184
Largest binary number (in octet) that can be subtracted from this number	−128
Remainder	56
Largest binary number that can be subtracted	−32
Remainder	24
Largest binary number that can be subtracted	−16
Remainder	8
Largest binary number that can be subtracted	−8
Remainder	0

Using this example, 184 can be notated as 10111000 with the 128, 32, 16, and 8 bits set to 1, and the rest set to 0. As you become accustomed to working with both binary and decimal conversions, you may not need to do this lengthy math; eventually you might simply be able to do this in your head. Let's look at Exercise 6.1, which will help you master the concept of converting decimal and binary numbers.

EXERCISE 6.1

CONVERTING DECIMAL AND BINARY NUMBERS

This exercise is designed to reinforce what we've learned about binary and decimal conversions. Remember, you will not get a question that explicitly asks you to do these steps, but you may be required to do them to figure out if a subnet mask is incorrectly shown on the exam. Understanding this conversion process is the cornerstone of understanding the IP addressing system.

1. Convert the following number to binary: 24. Using the technique described in this section, we first write out the bit values of an octet: 128 64 32 16 8 4 2 1. Next, we look for the highest value that is less than the number given. In this case, the highest number is 16. We set bit 4, which is equivalent to decimal 16, to 1. Next we subtract 16 from our number: 24 − 16 = 8. We set bit 3, equivalent to decimal 8, to 1. We subtract 8 − 8 = 0 and we have no remainder. Thus, we have the 16 and 8 bits set to 1, and all other bits are zero: 00011000.

2. Convert the following number to decimal: 00001011. In this case, we have to do just the opposite of what we did in the first conversion. Now, we write the bit values of the octet and add up any bit values set to 1. The octet numbers are 128 64 32 16 8 4 2 1. The following bits are set to 1: 8, 2, 1. We add 8 + 2 + 1 to yield 11, the decimal equivalent of this binary notation.

3. Convert the following number to binary: 255.0.132.2. Let's work on each octet, one at a time. Let's begin with the left-most octet, 255. By now, you might recognize that the 255 is all 1s. If not, this is a handy fact to remember. To calculate its value, we begin by subtracting the highest bit value less than 255. (The bit value being subtracted is in **bold** to make it easier to read). In this case, that's 128. 255 − **128** = 127. Again, we subtract the largest bit value: 127 − 64 = 63. Repeating this process we get: 63 − **32** = 31. 31 − **16** = 15. 15 − **8** = 7. 7 − **4** = 3. 3 − **2** = 1. 1 − **1** = 0. For each bit value we subtract (128, 64, etcetera) we set the corresponding bit position to 1. Thus, the binary equivalent is 11111111. The next octet (x) is easy; it's all 0s. The octet is written as 00000000. The third octet (y) is equal to 132. Using our subtraction technique, we know that the 128 bit will be set to 1. 132 − 128 = 4. Thus, we set the 4 bit to 1, yielding this octet: 10000100. The final octet (z) is 2. This is easy to figure out—the second bit is set to 1, the rest of the bits are 0. The octet is 00000010. Putting this all together, we have 11111111.00000000.10000100.00000010

4. Convert the following number to dotted decimal notation: 00001000.00001111.00101101.10101010. In this case, we need to convert this number to dotted decimal by adding the values of each bit position set to 1. Again, we'll start on the left. In the first octet, the only position set to 1 is the 8 position. In the second octet, the right-most four bits are set to 1. If you're becoming familiar with the different bit patterns, you'll immediately recognize 15. Otherwise, add the bit values of 1, 2, 4, and 8 together to yield 15. The next octet (y) has the following bit positions set to 1: 32, 8, 4, 1. If you have difficulty with this, write out the bit values 128 64 32 16 8 4 2 1, and then write out the octet underneath. You'll see which bit positions are set to 1 and you can add those values. In this case, it equals 45. The final octet, z, has the following bit positions set to 1: 128, 32, 8, 2. Adding these results yields 170. The resulting dotted decimal notation for this is 8.15.45.170.

5. Convert the following number to binary: 112.64.117.3 Again, we'll use our subtraction method to find the largest bit value that is lower than the number and subtract it from the number. We'll repeat the process until the remainder is 0. For each number we subtract (shown in bold), we set the corresponding bit to 1. Our answer looks like this:

First octet (*w*): 112 – **64** = 48. 48 – **32** = 16. 16 – **16** = 0 = 01110000

Second octet (*x*): 64 – **64** = 0 = 01000000

Third octet (*y*): 117 – **64** = 53. 53 – **32** = 21. 21 – **16** = 5. 5 – **4** = 1. 1 – **1** = 0 = 01110101.

Fourth octet (*z*): 3 – **2** = 1. 1 – **1** = 0 = 00000011

Putting the four octets together yields this dotted decimal notation: 01110000.01000000.01110101.00000011

Although the adding and subtracting may seem simplistic, it's important to practice this over and over, so you can actually look at an octet and add up the values in your head or at least recognize the values and add them with a calculator. It's simple math that simply requires close attention to detail. It's easy to inadvertently miss a bit position. Writing down the sequence can help you avoid these kinds of errors.

It's a good idea to practice converting binary to decimal, as you'll need to know how to do this when working on your network and as well as the Network+ exam. The key is to break each octet down individually and check your work by adding up the value of the bits you've set. This will help ensure that your math and your logic are both correct and will reduce common errors when you set up subnets, subnet masks, and other IP addresses.

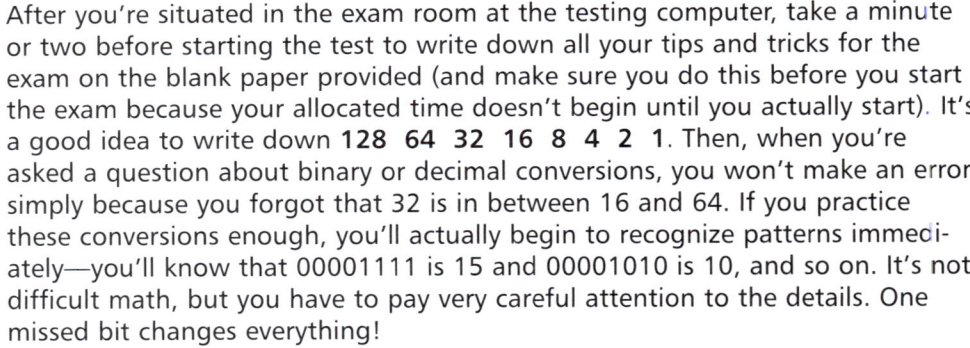

Test Day Tip

After you're situated in the exam room at the testing computer, take a minute or two before starting the test to write down all your tips and tricks for the exam on the blank paper provided (and make sure you do this before you start the exam because your allocated time doesn't begin until you actually start). It's a good idea to write down **128 64 32 16 8 4 2 1**. Then, when you're asked a question about binary or decimal conversions, you won't make an error simply because you forgot that 32 is in between 16 and 64. If you practice these conversions enough, you'll actually begin to recognize patterns immediately—you'll know that 00001111 is 15 and 00001010 is 10, and so on. It's not difficult math, but you have to pay very careful attention to the details. One missed bit changes everything!

Network ID and Host ID

Now that you've learned how to convert binary to decimal and back again, let's look at the principals underlying networking with IP addresses. An IP address has two elements, the *network address* and the *host address*. As we've discussed, the IP address is a unique address assigned to a computer or device (printer, router, etcetera) connected to the network. The network address is a fixed address used to identify a common network. Within each IP address is a network address (shared by all computers on that network) and a unique host address. When combined, the result is a single unique IP address on the network.

All hosts (also called *nodes* when talking about connected network devices) on the same network segment must have the same network ID. A good analogy is the U.S. zip code system. There are many houses on a street, each with a unique street address (host ID) but all of them have the same zip code within a certain area (network ID). The street address combined with the zip code is a unique combination that identifies a particular house or building just as an IP address identifies a particular host. Figure 6.6 illustrates this concept.

Figure 6.6 Network and Host IDs

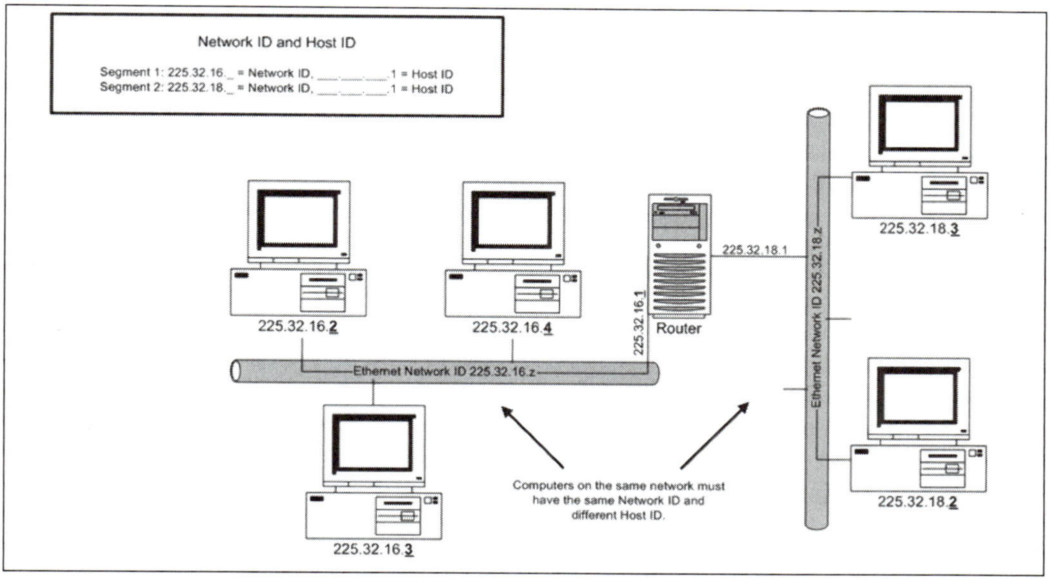

Large networks are usually divided by routers. Routers (first covered in Chapter 3, "Network Devices") separate one segment from another and only pass along data destined for external networks (those on the other side of the router). If the data is intended for a host within the segment, the router does not forward it to the external segment(s). This reduces network traffic and increases response times. In order for this to work, however, each segment of the network must have a unique identifier, which is the network address or network ID. Primary network IDs are managed by the *Internet Network Information Center* (InterNIC), an organization that manages top-level network addresses to prevent two organizations from using the same network ID. Two networks connected to the Internet cannot use the same network ID (networks that are completely standalone and have no connection to the Internet can use any network ID you wish).

Originally, network IDs were divided into classes: Class A, B, C, and D. Each class had a specific purpose and a defined range of allowable addresses. The goal was to provide for three common scenarios in networking:

- Small number of very large networks (large number of nodes per network)

- Moderate number of medium-sized networks

- Large number of very small networks (small number of nodes per network)

This class-based system worked well for quite some time. However, in the 1990s, when the Internet boom period (the massive growth of the Internet) began, it became clear that the addressing scheme would not support the many hundreds of thousands of networks that were popping up (and getting connected to the global network) around the world. A new *classless* system was devised. It still uses IP addressing fundamentals, but it extends the original concept. The class-based system now often is referred to as *classful*, to differentiate it from the *classless* addressing system. We'll discuss the classless system (also called *variable length subnet masking or VLSM for short)* later in this chapter. For now, let's look at the class-based system to understand network addressing fundamentals.

The 32-bit IP address is subdivided into two portions: the network address space and the host address space. The use of 32-bits does not change, but the use of the bits *within* the 32-bit address changes in order to define four classes of addresses. There are currently five defined address classes: Class A, B, C, D, and E. Microsoft Windows Server 2003 supports four address classes: A, B, C, and D. It does not support Class E addresses, which are considered experimental at this time. In addition, there are several guidelines regarding allowable or legal addresses for network IDs and for host IDs. As we learned earlier, the notation used is called *dotted decimal* and is also represented as *w.x.y.z* to denote the four octets used.

Exam Warning

The 32-bit IP address is subdivided into two portions: the network address space and the host address space. You must know how to identify IP addresses correctly on the Network+ exam. You must also know how to identify an IP address by its class, as well as its default subnet masks. Please pay very close attention to these areas as you proceed through the text. A lot of the material here is to get you to learn how to do this, not just memorize it for the exam. You can't fake the understanding of IP addressing on the exam, and rote memorization is no cure either. You must be able to clearly identify IP addressing issues on the Network+ exam and how to solve them. You will not be asked to create an elaborate design for a complex network, but you may see diagrams of segments that you need to work with. Understanding IP addressing will help you to successfully navigate these questions and pass these section objectives on the exam.

Rules for Network IDs

The following rules apply to creating or using network IDs in a class-based system.

- Network IDs cannot begin with 127 as the first octet, such as 127.14.102.6. 127.x.y.z is reserved for loopback addresses. A loopback address is used to test IP software on the host computer and is not associated with the computer's hardware.

- A Network ID cannot have all bits set to 1. This configuration is reserved for broadcast addresses.

- A Network ID cannot have all bits set to 0. This configuration is reserved for indicating a host on the local network.

- A Network ID must be unique to the IP network. If you have three network segments in your corporate network, each segment must have a unique network ID.

Rules for Host IDs

The following rules apply to creating and assigning host IDs.

- A Host ID cannot have all bits set to 1. This configuration is reserved for broadcast addresses.

- A Host ID cannot have all bits set to 0. This configuration is reserved for the expression of IP network IDs.

- A Host ID must be unique to the network on which it resides.

Just like modern day humanity, there is obviously a class system with IP addressing and this one is needed to keep the IP address space organized and readily available for use. In the next section we will cover the IP addressing class system.

Class A Addresses

Class A addresses are designed for very large networks with few logical network segments and many hosts. Class A addresses always have the high-order bit (or left-most bit) set to zero. The first octet (the left-most eight bits) is used to define the network ID. The host addresses use the second, third, and fourth octets. This can also be represented as w = network ID, $x.y.z$ = host ID (using the convention that all IP addresses are composed of four octets and represented as $w.x.y.z$). Let's look at an example: **0111**0000 00000000 00001100 00001111 is a Class A address. The network ID (in **bold**) is 112. The host ID is 0.12.15. Thus, this IP address is 112.0.12.15. Other hosts on the same network would all have IP addresses that begin with 112.

With the high-order bit set to 0, by definition, a Class A address cannot be greater than 127 since a value of 128 would require the left-most bit be set to 1. To calculate the number of possible networks, use the formula 2^n or 2^n, where n is the number of bits in the octet that can be used. In this case, we cannot use the left-most bit, so n in this case is 7. 2^7 or 2^7 equals 128. However, we know that we cannot have a network set to 127 (loopback) and we cannot have a network of all 0s or all 1s. Therefore, we have 126 useable network addresses. We can also calculate how many possible host addresses we have in a Class A network by using the same formula. In this case, we're using three octets for host IDs. Therefore, we have 2^{24} or 16,777,216. Again, we cannot use addresses of all 0s or all 1s, so we have 16,777,214 useable host addresses available.

Class B

Class B addresses are used for medium-sized networks that have a moderate number of hosts connected to them. Class B addresses always have the first two high-order bits (left-most) set to **10**. The Class B network ID uses the first *two* octets for the network ID. This allows for more network IDs and fewer hosts than a Class A network. Since it uses an additional octet for the network, there is one fewer octet available for host IDs, reducing the number of hosts that can be addressed on this network by approximately a factor of two.

Here's a Class B IP address: **10010001 00001100** 00001010 00001001. This translates into 160.12.10.9. The first two octets (160.12) represent the network ID and the last two octets (10.9) represent the host ID portion of this IP address. Thus, the schema is *w.x* = network ID, *y.z* = host ID. Notice that the two high-order bits are set to 10.

Class B networks use the first two octets for the network ID. However, we cannot set the second bit to 1 (Class B left-most two bits must be 10). Therefore, we can calculate that there are a total of 2^{14} or 16,384 Class B network addresses (16 bits for network ID, but we cannot use the first two bits because they must be set to 10). Since we are required to set the first two bits to 10, we will not end up with a network address that is all 0s or all 1s; therefore we do not need to subtract from our total network IDs to find available network IDs. To calculate the number of hosts on a Class B network, we know that we use 16 bits (two octets) for the host ID. Thus, we have 65,536 total host IDs and we cannot use all 0s or all 1s, resulting in 65,534 available host IDs on a Class B network.

Class C

Class C addresses are for small networks with few hosts. These addresses have the first three high-order bits set to **110**. Class C addresses use the first *three* octets for the network ID and the last octet for the host ID. Using your understanding of IP addressing at this point, how many host addresses will be available in each Class C network? If you answered 256 (0 through 255), you'd be close. If you add each bit (128 + 64 + 32 + 16 + 8 + 4 + 2 + 1), it totals 256, but remember we cannot use an address of all 0s or all

1s. We're left with 254 possible addresses. The schema for the Class C IP address is *w.x.y* = network ID, *z* = host ID.

Class C networks use the left-most three bits set to 110. To calculate the number of networks available, we calculate the total bits available, in this case 24 (three octets) − 3 (first three bits must be 110) = 21. Using the formula 2^{21} we see that the number of Class C networks is 2,097,152. Again, because the left-most three bits must be set to 110, we do not need to subtract for network IDs of all 0s or all 1s. As we saw, the number of host IDs is 254 based on $2^8 − 2 = 256 − 2$ or 254.

Class D and Class E

Class D is reserved for IP multicast addresses. The first four high-order bits are set to 1110. The remaining 28 bits are used for individual IP multicast addresses. *Multicast Backbone on the Internet* (MBONE) is an extension to the Internet that supports IP multicasts and uses Class D addresses. MBONE allows a single packet to have multiple destinations and is most often used in real-time audio and video applications. Multicasting will be covered later in this chapter.

Class E addresses are reserved for future use. This class is considered experimental and the addresses are defined as "reserved for future use." The first five high-order bits are set to 11110.

Address Class Summary

This is by far one of the most important sections for the Network+ exam. IP addresses are 32-bit addresses divided into four octets. Each octet has eight bits and a maximum value of 255, which is when all eight bits are set to 1. Each address class defines the maximum number of networks (or subnets, actually) and hosts. These are summarized in Tables 6.7 and 6.8.

Table 6.7 Network Address Classes

Address Class	Octets Used	First Network ID	Last Network ID	Number of Networks
Class A	1	1.x.y.z	126.x.y.z	126
Class B	2	128.0.y.z *	191.255.y.z	16,384
Class C	3	192.0.0.z	223.255.255.z	2,097,152

* Remember that a valid network address cannot begin with 127.0.0.0, which is reserved for loopback addresses.

Table 6.8 Host Address Classes

Address Class	Octets Used	First Host ID	Last Host ID	Number of Hosts
Class A	3	w.0.0.1	w.255.255.254	16,777,214
Class B	2	w.x.0.1	w.x.255.254	65,534
Class C	1	w.x.y.1	w.x.y.254	254

TEST DAY TIP

It would be helpful for you to be able to recall this information (especially the default address classes and ranges) for the Network+ exam. It's always helpful to practice writing this information down, therefore, when you get to the test center you can jot this down before the exam and have it handy while you are taking the exam.

Network+
OBJECTIVE
2.7

Understanding Subnetting

A Class A network could theoretically have 16,777,214 hosts. However, in a real world application, this would be impractical. Most networks are broken down into smaller segments that are easier to manage. It is possible to assign such a network, although it would be very flat, and very large by default. As you recall, there are some instances when information is broadcast on a network. Imagine broadcasts to and from 16 million hosts. The network would come to a grinding halt from all that traffic. Therefore, although a company may have a Class A network ID, it will segment (divide) that network to avoid having 16 million hosts per network. This process of segmenting is called *subnetting*. Each segment or subnet must have a unique identifier so that traffic can be sent to the correct location. Since the network ID is a fixed number assigned by the InterNIC, a method was devised to subdivide the assigned network ID by borrowing bits from the *host* address space, not the *network* address space. An assigned Class A network assigns the network ID using only the first octet. A subnetted Class A network might use bits from the second and third octets to create new subnetworks.

Although it's theoretically possible to use any host octet bits, in practice they are always used starting from the left-most host address space bit moving to the right. In other words, we take the high-order host address bits first. Table 6.9 shows the resulting number of subnets and number of host bits used when subnetting a Class A network.

Table 6.9 Subnets Using Host ID Bits

Number of Subnets	Number of Host Bits Used in Network ID	Binary (network ID in bold)
0	0	**01000010** . 00000000 . 00000000 . 00000000
1–2	1	**01000010** . 0**0**000000 . 00000000 . 00000000
3–4	2	**01000010** . **00**000000 . 00000000 . 00000000
5–8	3	**01000010** . **000**00000 . 00000000 . 00000000
9–16	4	**01000010** . **0000**0000 . 00000000 . 00000000
17–32	5	**01000010** . **00000**000 . 00000000 . 00000000
33–64	6	**01000010** . **000000**00 . 00000000 . 00000000
65–128	7	**01000010** . **0000000**0 . 00000000 . 00000000
129–256	8	**01000010** . **00000000** . 00000000 . 00000000

The process is identical to extend the number of subnets on a Class A network beyond 256 by taking additional host address bits from the next octet (where *w.x* and *y* are used for network and only *z* is left for host addresses). This process is similar for Class B and Class C networks as well, although the number of subnets and hosts will vary.

We can identify the number of bits used for the network by notating how many total bits (counting left to right) are used in the network address. From there, we can calculate how many bits remain for host addresses. A Class A network subdivided to allow up to 16 subnets uses 12 bits for the network ID, leaving 20 bits for host addresses. This is commonly denoted with a */12* to show that 12 bits are used for the network ID. An example of this notation is 66.192.15.4/12. This is sometimes referred to verbally as "slash 12". As a reminder, your understanding of subnet masks is important. For the exam, you will not need to do very hard calculations, and you will not need to understand IP addressing at the level explained within this chapter. You will be asked questions that are far less complex than those within this chapter's exercises. The point of the chapter is to get you so good at IP addressing and give you such a solid explanation of it that when you do get IP addressing questions on your Network+ exam, you can annihilate them with ease and waste little time on what will be common knowledge to you come test time.

Head of the Class...

Calculating the Number of Hosts

When you begin subnetting, each bit you take from the host address space reduces the number of hosts by a factor of 2. If you can have a maximum of 65,534 hosts and you take 1 bit from the host address space, you reduce the number of hosts you can have by approximately half, or 32,767 (65,534 / 2). If you keep this in mind, you'll have an easier time assessing correct scenarios on the exam and in configuring subnets on the job.

There are two ways to calculate the total number of possible hosts on any given network. First, you can determine the number of host address bits and total the bit values for each bit position that is a host bit. Although we've discussed only the weighted binary values up to 128, they extend far beyond that. To extend these values further to the left, (writing this in reverse order to make it easier to read) we would have 1 2 4 8 16 32 64 128 256 512 1024 2048 4096 8192 16384, and so on. To place this sequence in the proper order, we simply write it from right to left: 16384, 8192, 4096, 2048, and so on. If we want to calculate the number of hosts, we just keep adding, from right to left, the number of host bits. Since a traditional Class A network uses the first octet (w) as the network address, that generally leaves 24 bits for host addresses. You would have to extend the previous example out to 24 bits (the previous example goes out to only 15 bits), doubling the previous number. Remember, though, that you must subtract 2 from any result since legal addresses cannot be all 0s or all 1s in the classful addressing scheme.

Another way to calculate this, which is much faster and easier if you have a scientific calculator function available to you, is to use the formula $[(2^n)-2]$. Most people can't do this kind of math in their heads but you can use the **x^y** function on the Windows Calculator. Start the Calculator by selecting **Start | Run** and typing **calc** in the **Run** dialog box, and then pressing **Enter**. Choose **View | Scientific** from the menu. Enter the number **2**, click the button labeled **x^y**, then enter the number of bits used for the problem and press **Enter** or click **=**. For instance, 2^{21} equals 2,097,152. If you're using 21 bits for the host address space, you will have (2,097,152 – 2) bits available to you, or 2,097,150. The same holds true for network addresses. So, rather than memorizing the many different configurations, use this formula to check your logic, your math, and your answers.

To become familiar with the conversions, we recommend creating conversion tables for yourself by writing a conversion on an index card and running through these flash cards until you're doing conversion in your sleep.

Understanding Subnet Masking

Large networks are subdivided to create smaller subnetworks to reduce overall network traffic by keeping local traffic on the local subnet and sending all non-local traffic to the router. In order to create a subnetwork, we need to have a system for addressing that allows us to use the network ID and host ID within the class-based system. This is accomplished through the use of a *subnet mask*. In essence, a subnet mask is a 32-bit number that is combined with the IP address (network address and host address) to shield or mask certain bits, thus creating a new, unique number.

The 32-bit IP address is composed of the network ID and the host ID. The number of host IDs on a network is variable, but the network ID must be the same for all hosts on a segment. For example, in a Class C network, you can have from 1 to 254 hosts. Suppose you wanted to divide your Class C network into two networks with 100 hosts each? You could use your Class C network ID with a subnet mask and virtually divide your network into two parts. This is done by borrowing bits from the host ID portion of the IP address. When you take bits from the host address space, you reduce the number of potential host addresses roughly by a factor of two. If this sounds a bit confusing, don't worry. We're going to walk through this step-by-step. The underlying concept of subnets and subnet masking involves a binary process called *bitwise ANDing*. ANDing is actually a fairly simple concept to understand and perform.

How Bitwise ANDing Works

The term *ANDing* comes from a form of mathematics called Boolean algebra. Computers use *Boolean operators* in their circuitry. Integrated circuits contain components known as gates and inverters. A gate (or inverter) has one or more inputs. Their output is based on the *state* of those inputs. The state can only be off (0) or on (1). In Boolean terms, it can only be true (1) or false (0). AND gates will return (or output) 1 if *all* inputs are 1 and will return 0 if *any* input is not 1. An OR gate will return 1 if *any* input is 1 and will return 0 only if no input signals are 1.

You may be familiar with Boolean operators in using search engines. You can refine your search by using Boolean operators, including AND and OR. There are other, less commonly used operators such as *NAND* (not AND) and *XOR* (exclusive OR), but these are outside the scope of this discussion.

Bitwise ANDing simply means that we are performing the logical AND function on each bit. The simple AND statements can be expressed as shown here. Rather than a mathematical *plus* function, this is a comparison between two (or more) values.

- $0 + 0 = 0$
- $0 + 1 = 0$
- $1 + 0 = 0$
- $1 + 1 = 1$

Notice that the logical AND function results in a 1 only when *both* inputs are 1; otherwise, the result is 0. Next, let's take a slightly more complicated example, still using bitwise ANDing. Look at Table 6.10 to see the results.

Table 6.10 Calculating the results of ANDing

First input	1010	1010	1010
Second input	0001	1000	1100
Result of ANDing	0000	1000	1000

Again, the result is 1 only when both inputs are 1; otherwise the result is 0. Now let's explore how bitwise ANDing is used in subnetting.

EXERCISE 6.2

BITWISE ANDING

Exercise 6.2 is designed to give you practice with bitwise ANDing. Each question is followed by a step-by-step answer.

1. What is the result of the following bitwise ANDing? Convert your answer from binary to dotted decimal. Compare 146.64.160.9 and 255.255.224.0.
    Answer: The result is 146.64.160.0

Inputs	Dotted Decimal Notation	Binary Notation
IP address	146.64.160.9	10010001.01000000.10100000.00001001
Subnet mask	255.255.224.0	11111111.11111111.11100000.00000000
Result	146.64.160.0	10010001.01000000.10100000.00000000

As you can see, the result from our bitwise ANDing of an IP address and our subnet mask is the underlying network ID, in this case 146.64.160.0. Once you have delineated your subnet IDs and determined your subnet mask, you can check your work by performing the ANDing process to verify the result is the underlying subnet network ID.

2. What is the result of the following bitwise ANDing? Convert your answer from binary to dotted decimal. Compare 146.64.195.36 and 255.255.224.0.
    Answer: The result is 146.64.192.0

Inputs	Dotted Decimal Notation	Binary Notation
IP address	146.64.195.36	10010001.01000000.11000011.00100100
Subnet mask	255.255.224.0	11111111.11111111.11100000.00000000
Result	146.64.192.0	10010001.01000000.11000000.00000000

In this example, the underlying network ID was not readily apparent. By using bitwise ANDing, we were able to extract the network ID.

3. What is the network ID of this IP address: 146.64.187.112/20? As you recall, the notation /20 indicates we're using 20 bits from the network address space. Thus, we know that our subnet mask must use 1 in the left-most 20 locations. Our bitwise ANDing results in a network ID of:

Inputs	Dotted Decimal Notation	Binary Notation
IP address	146.64.187.112	10010001.01000000.10111011.01110000
Subnet mask	255.255.240.0	11111111.11111111.11110000.00000000
Result	146.64.176.0	10010001.01000000.10110000.00000000

NOTE

You will not need to know ANDing for the Network+ exam; it's only needed to help with the conversion of IP addresses, testing, and so on. You will need to know how to perform ANDing for your own purposes, but will not be asked direct questions on its function.

Default Subnet Mask

A subnet mask is a four-octet number used to identify the network ID portion of a 32-bit IP address. A subnet mask is required on all class-based networks, even on networks that are not subnetted. A *default subnet mask* is based on the IP address classes we discussed earlier and is used on networks that are not subdivided. If your network is not subnetted, you must use the subnet mask associated with your IP address class. The default subnet masks are shown in dotted decimal format in Table 6.11.

Table 6.11 Default Subnet Masks

IP Address Class	Default Subnet Mask
Class A	255.0.0.0
Class B	255.255.0.0
Class C	255.255.255.0

We've already discussed the fact that a Class A network uses the first octet as the network address. You can see from the default subnet mask shown in the preceding table that the first octet is set to all 1s (dotted decimal 255). Recall that a network ID cannot be set to all 1s. Thus, when you use logical ANDing with any Class A network and the default subnet mask, it will always yield the Class A network ID. For example, if the Class A network ID is 66.x.y.z, it would be represented as 01000010.x.y.z. The default subnet mask is represented as 11111111.x.y.z. The logical AND function, shown in Table 6.12, yields 01000010.x.y.z.

Table 6.12 ANDing Network ID and Default Subnet Mask

Class A Network ID = 66	01000010
Default Subnet Mask = 255	11111111
Bitwise AND result = 66	01000010

Custom Subnet Mask

Most networks are subnetted because the number of hosts allowed in both Class A and Class B networks is well beyond what could be used in practical application. Subnetting is accomplished by using bits from the host address space for the network address space.

The custom subnet mask (also called a variable length subnet mask) is used *to identify the bits used for a network address versus the bits used for a host address*. Custom subnet masks are used when *subnetting* or *supernetting*. As we've discussed, subnetting is the process of dividing one network into many. Supernetting uses a single IP address to represent many unique IP addresses. *Supernetting* is the process of allocating a range or block of network IDs (typically Class C) instead of a single Class A or B network ID to preserve Class A and B networks for uses that require a large number of host addresses.

To determine the appropriate custom subnet mask (typically referred to simply as *subnet mask*) for a network, you must first:

1. Determine the *number of host bits to be used* for subnetting.
2. Determine the *new subnetted network IDs*.
3. Determine the *IP addresses for each new subnet*.
4. Determine the appropriate *subnet mask*.

Determine the Number of Host Bits to Be Used

We can create a subnet mask by using bits that would normally be used for host addresses. *The number of required subnets will determine the number of host bits to be used*. An important element of this process is determining the maximum number of subnets you may need in the future, to avoid having to reassign addresses when your network grows. Allow for more subnets than you plan to use, within reason. Also keep in mind that the more host bits you use for subnets, the fewer host IDs you'll have left for assigning to your connected devices. There is a trade-off between allowing for adequate subnet growth and retaining adequate host IDs for all connected devices.

Let's look at an example using a Class B network, which uses the two left-most octets for the network ID and the two right-most octets for the host ID. If you had no subnets, you would have 65,534 host addresses available to use. Suppose you wanted to have two subnets? How would you determine your subnet mask and how many host IDs would you have available to you?

If you take one bit from the host address space, you would be able to create two networks, each with 32,768 host addresses. If you take two bits from the host address space, you can create three to four subnets of 16,384 host addresses per subnet. Remember, we can't use host addresses with all 0s or all 1s, so the number of *available* host addresses is reduced by two each time.

NOTE

The rule that network IDs could not consist of all 0s or all 1s came about because at one point in time, router software wasn't capable of handling such network IDs. The routers being made today are perfectly capable of handling network IDs of all 0s or all 1s, so this rule—while still imposed by Microsoft on their networks—no longer is a technical limitation, but merely one of convention. However, although network IDs of all 0s and all 1s are permissible now, you still cannot use host IDs that consist of all 0s or all 1s.

For this section, we're going to use the following data. We're going to use a Class B network with the IP address of 145.64.0.0. We'll assume we need up to eight subnets to handle our future expansion. We'll also assume that having up to 8,190 host addresses per subnet will be acceptable for our configuration. We've determined our maximum number of subnets and the resulting number of host addresses per subnet.

Now that we've decided we need a maximum of eight subnets, we must next determine how many host bits we'll need to use to accomplish this. Thus, we use bits from the third octet (y) and determine how many we'll need to create eight (remember, counting starts with 0). We can see that we need three bits from the third octet to give us up to eight subnets. We know that 00000111 = 7. Since we're including 0, using three bits would allow a total of eight subnets. It's important not to get confused between bit values and number of bits. At this point, we simply need to figure out how *many* bits are needed, so we start on the right. If we needed 64 networks, we'd need six bits (00111111 = 63) and so on. Table 6.13 shows the bit configuration for up to eight subnets using our sample network 145.64.0.0.

Table 6.13 Dotted Decimal and Binary Configuration for Subnetted Networks

Network Dotted Decimal	Binary (network address in bold)	Subnet Range
145.64.0.0	**10010001.01000000.0**0000000.00000000	Undivided Class B network
145.64.0.0	**10010001.01000000.**00000000.00000000	First subnet address
145.64.224.0	**10010001.01000000.**11100000.00000000	Last subnet address

Notice that we used three bits—the three bits contiguous to our original network ID. Essentially these bits extend the network address space by three bits. An important thing to remember is that these bits retain their original bit value and that they stay in their original octet—we don't move the decimal place. For example, the left-most bit of the third octet, while incorporated into the network ID, still retains its value of 128. When we add together the values of the four left-most bits from the third octet, it results in 224 (128 + 64 + 32), yielding our highest network ID.

Determine the New Subnetted Network IDs

Once we've taken the number of host address bits we need to create our requisite number of subnets, we must determine the resulting addresses of our new subnets. There are two steps in this process.

1. List all the possible binary combinations of the bits taken from the host address space.

2. Calculate the incremental value to each subnet and add to the network address.

The possible combinations of the four bits taken from the host address space are shown in Table 6.14. The number of combinations can be denoted as 2^n, where n is the number of bits. In this case, we could represent all possible combinations as 2^3 or 8.

Table 6.14 Binary Combinations

Combination Number	Binary Representation
1	000
2	001
3	010
4	011
5	100
6	101

Continued

Table 6.14 continued Binary Combinations

Combination Number	Binary Representation
7	110
8	111

Next, we need to calculate the incremental values. Again, we begin with the bit that is contiguous with the original network ID. Table 6.15 shows the results.

Table 6.15 Incremental Binary Values

Network Dotted Decimal	Binary (network address in bold)
145.64.0.0	**10010001.01000000.00**000000.00000000
	10010001.01000000.00000000.00000000
	10010001.01000000.00100000.00000000
	10010001.01000000.01000000.00000000
	10010001.01000000.01100000.00000000
	10010001.01000000.10000000.00000000
	10010001.01000000.10100000.00000000
	10010001.01000000.11000000.00000000
	10010001.01000000.11100000.00000000

Determine the IP Addresses for Each New Subnet

Earlier we learned that we could denote the number of network ID bits by using the convention w.x.y.z/## where ## is the total number of network ID bits. In this case, we have a Class B network, so we know we're starting with 16 bits for the network. We've taken three bits from the host address space, so our total network bits are now 19. Thus, we can denote our new subnetted network in this way: 146.64.0.0/19. Each of the subsequent subnet IDs can be denoted in a similar fashion as shown in Table 6.16.

Table 6.16 Incremental Dotted Decimal and Binary Values

Network Dotted Decimal	Binary (network address in bold)
145.64.0.0 /16	**10010001.01000000.**00000000.00000000
145.64.0.0 /19	**10010001.01000000.00**000000.00000000
145.64.32.0 /19	**10010001.01000000.001**00000.00000000
146.64.64.0 /19	**10010001.01000000.01**000000.00000000
146.64.96.0 /19	**10010001.01000000.011**00000.00000000
146.64.128.0 /19	**10010001.01000000.10**000000.00000000

Continued

Table 6.16 continued Incremental Dotted Decimal and Binary Values

Network Dotted Decimal	Binary (network address in bold)
146.64.160.0 /19	**10010001.01000000.101**00000.00000000
146.64.192.0 /19	**10010001.01000000.110**00000.00000000
146.64.224.0 /19	**10010001.01000000.111**00000.00000000

TEST DAY TIP

As a reminder, you do not have to be able to subnet networks on the Network+ exam, but understanding how they are created is essential to your job and your future in the networking job market. Understanding subnetting will help you prepare for your exam and eliminate any wrong answers that you may see.

Creating the Subnet Mask

We've determined our subnets, and now we need to create a subnet mask that will work with each subnet ID we created. Recall that we use bitwise ANDing to compare the bits of the IP address and the subnet mask. The result of the comparison is the network ID. Using Table 6.16, we know that we need to set to 1 any bits used for the network ID portion of the IP address. In this case, the subnet mask would be set to:

11111111.11111111.11100000.00000000

Notice that we have set the left-most 19 bits to 1. Thus, our subnet masks can be written in dotted decimal notation as 255.255.224.0. Let's compare this subnet mask to a sample IP address from within our subnetted addresses to see how this works.

146.64.193.14 IP address	= 10010001.01000000.11000001.00001110
255.255.224.0 subnet mask	= 11111111.11111111.11100000.00000000
Result of bitwise ANDing	= 10010001.01000000.11000000.00000000
Underlying network ID	= 146.64.192.0

EXERCISE 6.3

DEFINING SUBNET MASKS

In this exercise, we'll practice defining subnets and subnet masks. Use the following scenario: Your brand new start-up company has been assigned a Class C address.

You have only six computers, one router, and three printers attached to your network. You'd like to subnet your network before your company's planned expansion and you'll need a maximum of six to seven networks in the future.

1. How many host address bits will you need to take from the host address space to create seven subnets? To solve this problem, we need to think in terms of the bit value of the binary bits in an octet. Which bit values, when added together, equal 7? The answer is the right-most three bits, or 00000111. This tells us we need three bits from the host address space to add to the network address space. However, it's important to remember that we don't *use* the right-most bits. This may be confusing, but we used the bit values simply to determine how many bits we'll need. We use the bits closest to the octet used for the network ID.

2. What is the binary representation of the subnet mask used for this configuration? Class C uses the *w.x.y* octets for network ID. Therefore, we know that the default subnet mask is 255.255.255.0. We've determined that we need to take three bits from the host ID space. We take the three left-most bits from the fourth octet so they remain contiguous with the network address space. The result is a subnet mask with the 1s in 27 of the 32 bits, moving left to right, as shown. 11111111.11111111.11111111.11100000

3. What is the dotted decimal value of the binary configuration shown in Problem 2? 255.255.255.224

4. What is one way of representing this network configuration, given that we are using three bits from the host address space for network IDs? As you may recall, a common notation for showing how many bits represent the network ID (and therefore the subnet mask) is *w.x.y.z* /27 where *w.x.y.z* are the dotted decimal values of the four octets that comprise an IP address and the /27 denotes the number of bits used for the network address.

5. If we use three bits from the host space for network IDs, what is the maximum number of hosts we can have per subnet? We know that an IP address has 32 bits and that we're using 27 of those bits for network addresses. 32 – 27 leaves 5 bits for host addresses. If we use the formula 2^n, we have 2^5, or 32 addresses. However, this includes an address of all 0s and all 1s, both of which cannot be used, resulting in 30 possible host addresses per subnet.

This exercise should help you find out if you have any areas of confusion. If so, go back and work on the specific area that is giving you trouble. The Network+ exam is not likely to have questions that rely upon this knowledge to make you figure out a subnet, create one, or otherwise. You need to understand the concept behind subnetting, and the subnet mask, and understand the differences between the host ID and the network ID as well as their relationship. Understanding the process of subnetting can help to drive that home for you.

Head of the Class...

Creating Subnet Masks

This topic always causes some confusion in the classroom because it requires us to work left to right *and* right to left. As we work through examples, some people get it immediately and some people don't. Usually the area of most confusion deals with taking bits from the host address space. This is because we use the bits with the lowest bit values first. However, when we're using those bits, they shift over to the left because we always want to use the bits contiguous with the network address space.

We emphasize that the bits retain their weighted binary values within the octets, regardless of their use. In the preceding exercise, we saw that there were both *network* and *host* bits in the fourth octet (the *z* octet). Although the bits are used for two different purposes, they must be calculated into a single dotted decimal number. The first thing we always calculate is how many subnets we're going to need. We convert that number to weighted binary, to determine how many bits we need. This essentially tells us how many possible bit combinations there are and therefore how many subnets we can delineate.

One example we use to make this point clear is a simple one. If we need one network ID, we don't need any bits from the host address space. There is only one combination. If we need two networks, we need one bit. Why? Because that one bit can be either 0 or 1, and that's two different combinations.

If we need one bit, we take that bit and use it on the left side of the octet. That's where some people get confused. After we figure out how many bits we need, we extend the network address space by that number of bits, which is the reason they shift to the left while retaining their weighted value based on their placement within the octet.

You should work through lots of examples so that you can fully understand both the concepts and the practical applications of subnetting. Work through the examples in this chapter and make up some of your own. If you have a study buddy, you can help each other by testing your knowledge of this crucial topic. Tables 6.17, 6.18, and 6.19 show the possible subnet masks that can be used in Class A, Class B, and Class C networks, respectively. These tables are useful for quickly determining the amount of hosts per subnet that would be achieved with a particular mask.

Table 6.17 Class A Subnet Table

Subnets	Hosts	Mask	Subnet Bits	Host Bits
2	8,388,606	255.128.0.0	1	23
4	4,194,302	255.192.0.0	2	22
8	2,097,150	255.224.0.0	3	21
16	1,048,574	255.240.0.0	4	20
32	524,286	255.248.0.0	5	19
64	262,142	255.252.0.0	6	18

Continued

Table 6.17 continued Class A Subnet Table

Subnets	Hosts	Mask	Subnet Bits	Host Bits
128	131,070	255.254.0.0	7	17
256	65,534	255.255.0.0	8	16
512	32,766	255.255.128.0	9	15
1,024	16,382	255.255.192.0	10	14
2,048	8,190	255.255.224.0	11	13
4,096	4,094	255.255.240.0	12	12
8,192	2,046	255.255.248.0	13	11
16,384	1,022	255.255.252.0	14	10
32,768	510	255.255.254.0	15	9
65,536	254	255.255.255.0	16	8
131,072	126	255.255.255.128	17	7
262,144	62	255.255.255.192	18	6
524,288	30	255.255.255.224	19	5
1,048,576	14	255.255.255.240	20	4
2,097,152	6	255.255.255.248	21	3
4,194,304	2	255.255.255.252	22	2

Table 6.18 Class B Subnet Table

Subnets	Hosts	Mask	Subnet Bits	Host Bits
2	32,766	255.255.128.0	1	15
4	16,382	255.255.192.0	2	14
8	8,190	255.255.224.0	3	13
16	4,094	255.255.240.0	4	12
32	2,046	255.255.248.0	5	11
64	1,022	255.255.252.0	6	10
128	510	255.255.254.0	7	9
256	254	255.255.255.0	8	8
512	126	255.255.255.128	9	7
1,024	62	255.255.255.192	10	6
2,048	30	255.255.255.224	11	5
4,096	14	255.255.255.240	12	4
8,192	6	255.255.255.248	13	3
16,384	2	255.255.255.252	14	2

Table 6.19 Class C Subnet Table

Subnets	Hosts	Mask	Subnet Bits	Host Bits
2	126	255.255.255.128	1	7
4	62	255.255.255.192	2	6
8	30	255.255.255.224	3	5
16	14	255.255.255.240	4	4
32	6	255.255.255.248	5	3
64	2	255.255.255.252	6	2

(handwritten note: Take 2 off each time)

These subnet mask tables make it easier to determine which subnet mask to use for any given situation. As the table shows, the number of subnets increases and the number of hosts in each subnet decreases. As the number of subnet bits increases, the number of host bits decreases. Since there are a fixed number of bits to work with in each class of network address, each bit can be used in only one way as specified by the mask. Each bit must be either a subnet bit or a host bit. An increase in the number of subnet bits causes a reduction in the number of host bits, and vice versa.

Use these tables to help you memorize placement.

Strategies to Conserve Addresses

Several strategies have been developed and implemented to help the Internet community cope with the exhaustion of IP addresses. These strategies help reduce the load on Internet routers and also help administrators use globally unique IP addresses more efficiently. The following three strategies were mentioned in previous sections, and are discussed in more detail in the following paragraphs:

- Classless InterDomain Routing (CIDR)
- Variable-Length Subnet Mask
- Private Addressing

Classless InterDomain Routing

CIDR (RFCs 1517, 1518, and 1519) reduces route table sizes as well as IP address waste. Instead of full Class A, B, or C addresses, organizations can be allocated subnet blocks. For example, if a network needed 3,000 addresses, a single Class C network (256 addresses) would be insufficient. However, if a Class B network was assigned (65,536 addresses), 62,000 addresses would be wasted. With CIDR, a block of 4,096 addresses can be allocated—the equivalence of 16 Class C networks. This block of addresses covers the immediate addressing needs, allows room for growth, and uses global addresses efficiently.

Variable-Length Subnet Masks

VLSMs conserve IP addresses by tailoring the mask to each subnet. Subnet masks are appropriated to meet the amount of addresses required. The idea is to assign just the right amount of addresses to each subnet. Many organizations have point-to-point WAN links. Normally, these links comprise a subnet with only the 2 addresses required. By using a routing protocol that supports VLSM, administrator's can use a block of addresses much more efficiently. An example of a VLSM used on a WAN link can be seen in Figure 6.7.

Figure 6.7 A VLSM in Use

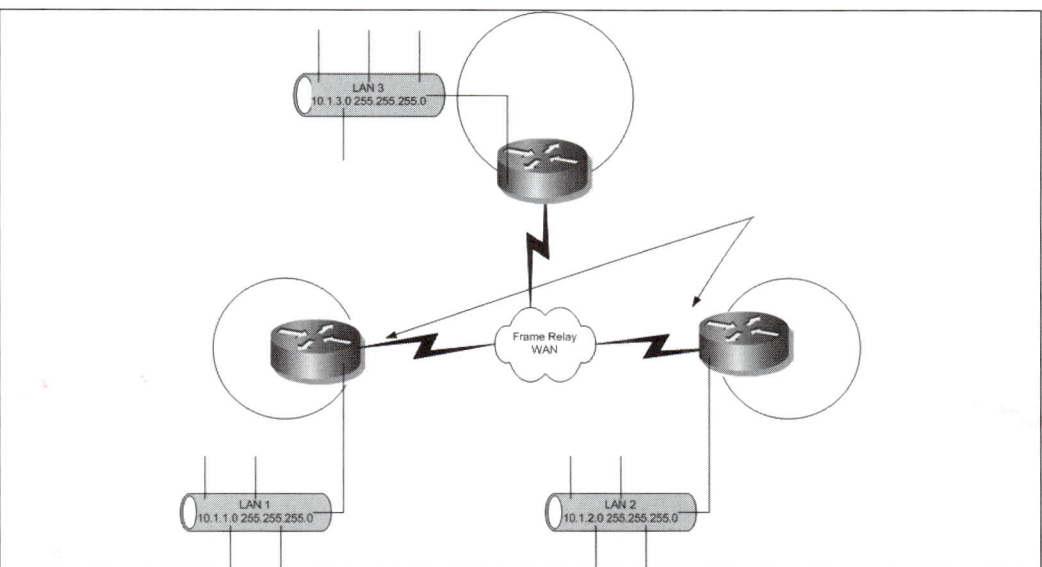

EXAM WARNING

Using VLSMs on WAN links on your network is very common. You don't need to know how to do this for the Network+ exam, but you should understand it so when you see it in use, you understand that this is a common use of VLSMs. You will learn more about WAN technologies in the next chapter.

Private Addresses

The most effective strategy for conserving globally unique (public) IP addresses is not using any. If an enterprise network is using TCP/IP protocols, but is not communicating with hosts in the global Internet, public IP addresses are not needed. If the internetwork is limited to one organization, the IP addresses need only be unique within that organization. Only networks that interface with public networks such as the Internet need public addresses. Using public addresses on the outside and private addresses for inside networks is very effective. Network address translation is used to convert those private (inside) addresses to public (outside) addresses.

Public versus Private Address Spaces

The IP requires that each interface on a network have a unique address. If the scope of a network is global, the addresses must be globally unique. Since global uniqueness must be assured, a centralized authority must be responsible for making sure IP address assignments are made correctly and fairly.

To meet the demands of a growing Internet community, the Internet Assigned Numbers Authority (IANA) was replaced by the Internet Corporation for Assigned Names and Numbers (ICANN). If an organization wants to use IP protocols and applications in its network, but is not connecting its network to the global Internet, the IP addresses it uses do not have to be globally unique. A network of this type is called a *private network*, and the addresses used are called *private addresses*.

RFC 1918—Private Network Addresses

RFC 1918 conserves globally unique IP addresses by providing three blocks of addresses that are never officially allocated to any organization. These blocks can then be used in private networks without fear of duplicating any officially assigned IP addresses in other organizations. With the explosive growth of the Internet, the InterNIC realized that some devices may never connect directly to the Internet. A good example of this is that many computers in a company connect to the Internet via an intermediate device such as a firewall, proxy server, or router. Consequently, those devices behind the firewall or other intermediate device don't need globally unique IP addresses. Three address blocks are defined as private address blocks, for situations in which the host does not connect directly to the Internet.

- **10.0.0.0/8** This is a private Class A network address with the host ID range of 10.0.0.1 through 10.255.255.254. This private network has 24 bits that can be used for any subnetting configuration desired by the company.

- **172.16.0.0/12** This scheme uses Class B addresses and allows for up to 16 Class B networks, or 20 bits can be used for host IDs. The range of valid addresses on this private network is from 172.16.0.1 through 172.31.255.254.

- **192.168.0.0/16** This configuration can provide up to 256 Class C networks, or 16 bits can be used for host addresses. The value range of IP addresses in this private network is 192.168.0.1 through 192.168.255.254.

These private addresses are not assigned publicly and therefore will never exist in Internet routing tables. This makes these private addresses unreachable via the Internet. If a host using a private network IP address requires access to the Internet, it must use the services of an Application Layer gateway such as a proxy server, or it must have its address translated into a legal, public address. A process called *network address translation* performs this translation before sending data out to the Internet from a private address host ID. NAT will be covered in more depth later in this chapter.

Another use of private addressing is called automatic private IP addressing (APIPA). If a computer (Windows 98 or later) is configured to obtain its address automatically from a DHCP server and it cannot locate a DHCP server, it will configure itself using APIPA. The computer randomly selects an address from the 169.254.0.0/16 address range and then checks the network for uniqueness. If the address is unique, it will use that address until it can reach a DHCP server. If the address is not unique, it will randomly select another address from that range.

EXAM WARNING

You must know the private address ranges as well as the APIPA IP address range for the Network+ exam. Also, do not forget the reserved loopback Class A address of 127.0.0.0.

TEST DAY TIP

Consider the following type of question on your Network+ exam. You may see a situation where you cannot get on the network because every node on the subnet is in the 10.0.0.0 to 255.255.255.0 range, and one node is having a problem because it has an APIPA address, so it won't be on the same subnet. Either that or the DHCP server is down and because of this the nodes on the network revert their addressing to the APIPA range. Think about this chapter and what you have learned so far and how it all ties together. All nodes on a subnet have to be in the same IP address range to communicate. There will be problems that arise where APIPA comes into play and you will need to know how to handle that situation. Make sure you consider this for the Network+ exam.

Table 6.20 summarizes the private address blocks defined by RFC 1918. Notice the CIDR shorthand for the mask. As a reminder, /8 would be equal to 255.0.0.0.

Table 6.20 Private IP Address Blocks

Address Block	Classful Equivalent	Prefix Length	Number of Addresses
10.0.0.0–10.255.255.255	1 Class A 256 Class B 65,536 Class C	/8	16,777,216
172.16.0.0–172.31.255.255	16 Class B 4,096 Class C	/12	1,048,576
192.168.0.0–192.168.255.255	1 Class B 256 Class C	/16	65,536

Considerations

The address blocks in Table 6.20 can be used in any network at any time. However, devices using these addresses will not be able to communicate with other hosts on the Internet without some kind of address translation. Some benefits of using private addresses are:

- **Number of Addresses** There are plenty of addresses for most internal networking needs.

- **Security** Private addresses are not routable on the Internet. The translation from private to public addresses further obscures internal network information.

- **Renumbering** If using NAT, no readdressing of privately addressed networks is necessary in order to access public networks.

- **Networks** Treating private addresses as public addresses when allocating ensures that efficiency and design are maximized.

Configuring & Implementing

Is Private IP Addressing Really a Free-For-All?

One would think that with that much IP address space available to them, network engineers, managers, administrator, and technicians would have a lackadaisical attitude when assigning IP space. Quite the contrary (as was learned earlier when we covered VLSMs); this is not the case. One of the greatest challenges that you will face when working within any network is that it's always designed to grow. As more technology develops, and as newer technologies emerge and more and more of a need is placed on the network, the more logical addressing you will need to provide it. You should always work to conserve your address space, never wasting it. You never know what you will need in the future. The tighter you lock down the procedures early on, the less of a chance you will have to go back and fix it later. In networking, this is always a problem because you never have the time to go back. In the networking world, if you do manage to have the time, depending on the size and use of your network, you may have to schedule an outage to change things over. An IP addressing change on a LAN-sized or larger scale is always a lot of work and is somewhat time consuming. Design it right the first time and do not go back if you do not have to, as it will be more difficult later to redo it. Make sure you get into a good habit of conserving (and documenting) your address space. Use DHCP whenever possible and when it is not a security risk. Always ensure that you consider future growth in the way of acquisitions and mergers, which will bring up the issues of duplicate IP addressing, as most of the space used is in the same private range. This is why NAT is so prevalent, and why you need to know it for the Network+ exam. NAT will be covered later in this chapter.

Static and Dynamic Assignments

On the Network+ exam, you will be responsible for not only knowing APIPA, but knowing the whole concept behind dynamic and static assignments. As mentioned earlier, DHCP is responsible for handing out a subset of IP addresses that an administrator configures into what is called a *scope*. The scope contains the leaseable address space that has been preconfigured. If your network uses TCP/IP as its network protocol, the nodes will, of course, need an IP address to communicate once they are up and running on the network. To configure each node statically (to go to the node itself, its physical location, or connect via remote administration) and configure an actual usable IP address on that node can become very unwieldy and it is highly discouraged if your network is large enough to warrant the use of DHCP.

In a more technical definition, DHCP is a communications protocol that allows you to manage IP addressing usage centrally and to automate the assignment of logical addresses in an organization's network. Remember, each host on the network needs a unique IP address to be able to communicate. When an organization sets up its computer users with a connection to the Internet, an IP address must be assigned to each machine. Without DHCP, the IP address must be entered manually at each computer and, if computers move to another location in another part of the network, a new IP address must be entered. DHCP lets a network administrator supervise and distribute IP addresses from a central point and automatically sends a new IP address when a computer is plugged into a different place in the network.

DHCP uses the concept of a *lease*, or amount of time, that a given IP address will be valid for a computer. The lease time can vary depending on how long a user is likely to require the Internet connection at a particular location. It's especially useful in education and other environments where users change frequently. Using very short leases, DHCP can dynamically reconfigure networks in which there are more computers than there are available IP addresses.

DHCP supports static addresses for computers containing Web servers that need a permanent IP address; you can make reservations for such addresses.

DHCP is an extension of an earlier network IP management protocol, Bootstrap Protocol (BOOTP). DHCP is a more advanced protocol, but both configuration management protocols are commonly used and DHCP can handle BOOTP client requests. Some organizations use both protocols, but understanding how and when to use them in the same organization is important. Some operating systems, including Windows NT/2000, come with DHCP servers. A DHCP or BOOTP client is a program that is located in (and perhaps downloaded to) each computer so that it can be configured.

NOTE

DHCP and its operation are thoroughly covered within the DHCP RFC. www.rfc-editor.org/rfc/rfc2131.txt

DHCP Operations

DHCP was covered briefly earlier in the chapter. DHCP is responsible for automatic and dynamic addressing of your network. It has a lot of complexity to it as well. For example, to get DHCP broadcasts to get to remote sites that are connected only by routers and T1 links, you would need to configure those routers to pass the DHCP broadcast from the client to the server; if the router is not configured to do so, then it will not pass. This is a common problem seen on the Network+ exam. Consider the following: You need to allow your clients to communicate with the DHCP server to get an address so they can participate on the network, accessing services and so on. You have three clients on one remote subnet that cannot get a valid IP address, but all other clients can. This is a common issue. Since all other sites work just fine (eliminating the possibility that it could be a server issues affecting all sites) the problem may be that the remote site's router is not configured to pass the broadcast from the client to the server, which will then give that client a lease on an IP address so it can participate on the network. In this section we cover the basics of DHCP operations.

As just mentioned, when a DHCP-based client is booted up, unless already configured with an IP, the client attempts to communicate with a DHCP server to get its TCP/IP configuration information. The following is a list of DHCP message types exchanged between client and server. You will not need to memorize these for the Network+ exam, although understanding these messages simplifies the understanding of DHCP itself and better prepares you for the exam.

- **Dhcpdiscover** The first time a DHCP client computer attempts to start on the network, it requests IP address information from a DHCP server by broadcasting a Dhcpdiscover packet. The source IP address in the packet is 0.0.0.0 because the client does not yet have an IP address. The attempt is sent out from the client on the network and as long as the packet can get to the server, the request process can be officially completed by the server.

- **Dhcpoffer** When the DHCP server receives the request, it selects an unleased IP address from the range of available IP addresses and offers it to the DHCP client. The lease is generally configured as part of a scope, mentioned earlier. The lease is good generally for a week by default, although this can be changed. In most cases, the DHCP server also returns additional TCP/IP configuration information, such as the subnet mask and default gateway in a Dhcpoffer packet. More than one DHCP server can respond with a Dhcpoffer packet, and the client accepts the first Dhcpoffer it receives.

- **Dhcprequest** When the client receives the Dhcpoffer packet, it responds by broadcasting a Dhcprequest packet that contains the offered IP address.

- **Dhcpdecline** A message from the DHCP client to the server indicating that the offered configuration parameters are invalid.

- **Dhcpack** The DHCP server acknowledges the client's Dhcprequest for the IP address by sending a Dhcpack packet.

- **Dhcpnack** If the IP address cannot be used by the client because it is no longer valid or is now used by another computer, the DHCP server will respond with a Dhcpnack packet.

- **Dhcprelease** A message from the DHCP client to the server that releases the IP address and cancels any remaining lease.

DHCP Relay Agents

When the DHCP server receives the request from the DHCP client computer, it dynamically assigns an IP address to the requesting computer from the range of valid IP addresses contained within the DHCP scope. The DHCP server allocates the IP address with a lease that defines how long the IP address can be used by the client computer. The DHCP server can also establish other configuration parameters, such as subnet mask and DNS (Domain Name System) and WINS (Windows Internet Name Service) server identification for the client computer. DNS and WINS are both covered within this chapter. It's important to remember that when configuring DHCP for clients, it's not just an IP address that is delivered to the client, but many other parameters such as DNS server address, WINS server address, subnet mask, default gateway and routing metrics, all of which are covered within this chapter.

In order to get this information to the client so that it can be used, the client must be able to contact the DHCP server. As mentioned before, if it cannot, then you may have a router issue that prevents the broadcast request from getting through. Understanding and configuring DHCP relay agents on a router is a very important part of DHCP to consider as a network engineer. TCP/IP networks are interconnected by routers that connect network segments (subnets) and pass IP packets between the subnets. Because routers do not pass broadcasts by default, a configuration change must be added to the router. As mentioned earlier, one of the major components of the DHCP specification is the DHCP protocol for communications between DHCP servers and clients. If this communication is disrupted or not allowed, DHCP will not function on your network.

On the Network+ exam, you may come across a question of two that tests your knowledge of RFC 1542 and broadcast-based communications when working with an RFC 1542-compliant router. A DHCP server can only provide IP addresses to clients in multiple subnets if the router that connects the subnets is an RFC 1542-compliant router. The configuration is commonly called an *IP helper address* in Cisco Systems-based routers. If the router cannot function as a relay agent, each subnet that has DHCP clients requires a DHCP server.

A relay agent is a program used to pass specific types of IP packets between subnets. A DHCP/BOOTP relay agent is simply a hardware or software program that can pass DHCP/BOOTP messages (packets) from one subnet to another subnet according to the RFC 1542 specification.

NOTE

BOOTP is described in RFC 951 and RFC 1084, and is used for booting diskless nodes. Updated in RFC 1395 and RFC 1497 and superseded by DHCP, BOOTP is still supported for legacy applications on most, if not all DHCP server implementations. The way it works is that when the client is ready to boot up on the network, it sends out a broadcast message requesting information and waits for a reply. The client only has to know its own hardware (MAC) address. With this information, the BOOTP server will respond with an IP address.

Now that you understand the basics of network protocols such as IPX/SPX, AppleTalk, and TCP/IP, let's continue learning about the TCP/IP suite's other functionalities, services, applications, and protocols. In the next section we will briefly cover the use of multicasting and the TCP/IP protocols used to provide it.

Multicast, Broadcast, and Unicast

With the continuously expanding use of networks, more and more people are deciding that one-to-one networking is not enough anymore. The need to have one-to-many networks has become more important. This is true for large corporations who benefit from e-mail, file sharing, and mirrored servers in two different cities (or countries). New technologies are developed every day.

Multicasting can reduce travel expenses while maximizing benefits. Imagine the cost of sending several employees halfway around the world for a conference that lasts less than a day. Not only would you incur the cost of travel, but also the cost of the employees' time as they travel.

A better solution in this case would be to videoconference (which is a very popular and always-developing technology), which allows viewing a presentation in one window while watching the speaker in another. Questions can be typed while the presentation is in progress, and prioritized for answering at the end of the conference. These are just a few of the features that can be provided by multicasting. Other benefits can include interactive distance learning and corporate announcement transmissions.

Multicasting benefits are not limited to video/audio needs. Multicast can be used to push updates to multiple hosts simultaneously, thus reducing the effort and time involved in doing one update at a time. Multicasting can also push computer operating system images to their hosts.

The possibilities seem endless and are rapidly growing. The following sections cover the basics of multicasting and how the multicasting addressing scheme is laid out.

Understanding the Basics of Multicasting

For the Network+ exam, you will not need to understand the dozens of commands that you can program into a router to enable and control multicasting, nor will you need to know the exact detailed operation of how multicasting protocols such as IGMP (Internet Group Management Protocol) work. However, you do need to know about multicasting fundamentals for the exam. You have already learned about Class D addressing space, which is where multicasting was originally mentioned. Why is there so much concern about it? Well, for one, since the use of it is growing, it must mean that the pressure placed on networks today is warranting its use. Bandwidth utilization is the first thing most network technicians and administrators think about when discussing streaming video and other live information feeds to an individual's PC or across a WAN link that may not have the bandwidth to accommodate it. To simply increase your bandwidth because of a single application's requirements could be expensive when dealing with telecommunications providers.

To understand multicast traffic completely, we have to discuss the other types of traffic. It is important to understand the differences between unicast, broadcast, and multicast traffic. Multicasting is UDP-based. While UDP is not a great example of reliability, it makes more sense for multicasting than TCP. For starters, having a multitude of hosts acknowledge receipt of a multicast packet stream would be counterproductive. Additionally, UDP has lower overhead, which provides the speed necessary to support the traffic needs of multicasting.

Multicast addresses cannot be used as source addresses for any traffic. While multicast addresses can be associated with particular interfaces on particular devices (such as 224.0.0.5 for OSPF [Open Shortest Path First]enabled interfaces on a router), traffic cannot be sourced from a multicast address because it does not identify a specific host; rather, a multicast address identifies a group of hosts sharing the same address.

Multicast addresses are not *assigned* to a device, rather, a device proceeds to listen for and receive traffic destined to a multicast group that it has joined by some process. For example, routers can join the OSPF multicast group on their network by having OSPF configured, and having interfaces configured to participate in OSPF routing. In this case, it means that the router will receive traffic destined to multicast IP addresses reserved for OSPF routing. Hosts can opt to join a multicast group by having certain applications (such as videoconferencing software) installed and configured.

NOTE

Remember, the Network+ exam does not dig as deeply into these concepts as this chapter does (such as our last discussion on OSPF). You need to remember facts, such as which protocols are used, which IP address class is used, which IP range is within that class, as well as being able to single out any wrong answers that may be placed in the question as a distracter. Knowing this other information is only going to help you understand what you are memorizing.

Understanding multicasting is very important as a network engineer, especially if you are working with videoconferencing or any of the many other applications that use multicasting as an underlying technology.

As mentioned earlier, IGMP allows host computers on the Internet to participate in IP multicasting. A multicast address identifies a transmission session instead of a particular physical destination. This allows for sending a message to a large number of recipients without the necessity for the source computer to know the addresses of all the recipients. The network routers translate the multicast address into host addresses. The protocol used to facilitate this is IGMP. IGMP was originally defined in RFC 1112. Extensions have been developed and are included in IGMP version 2, addressed in RFC 2236.

A computer uses IGMP to report its multicast group memberships to multicast routers. IGMPv2 allows group membership terminations to be reported promptly to the routing protocol. IGMP is required to be used in host computers that wish to participate in multicasting. IGMPv3 is also available for use. Knowing all the version types is not necessary for the Network+ exam, but it's important to know if you need to use IGMP, as some versions have (obviously) more functionality, enhancements, and security than others.

Unicast Traffic

What is most commonly seen (and wanted on your network) is what is called unicast traffic. Unicast is the transmission of data from one host to another, one host at a time. This is a one-to-one session between one host and another, such as a client and server arrangement. Unicast can be used to support multiple sessions (that is, multicasting) by establishing multiple one-to-one communications to transport the same data stream to multiple hosts. An example of this is shown in Figure 6.8.

Figure 6.8 Unicast Network Video Feed Example

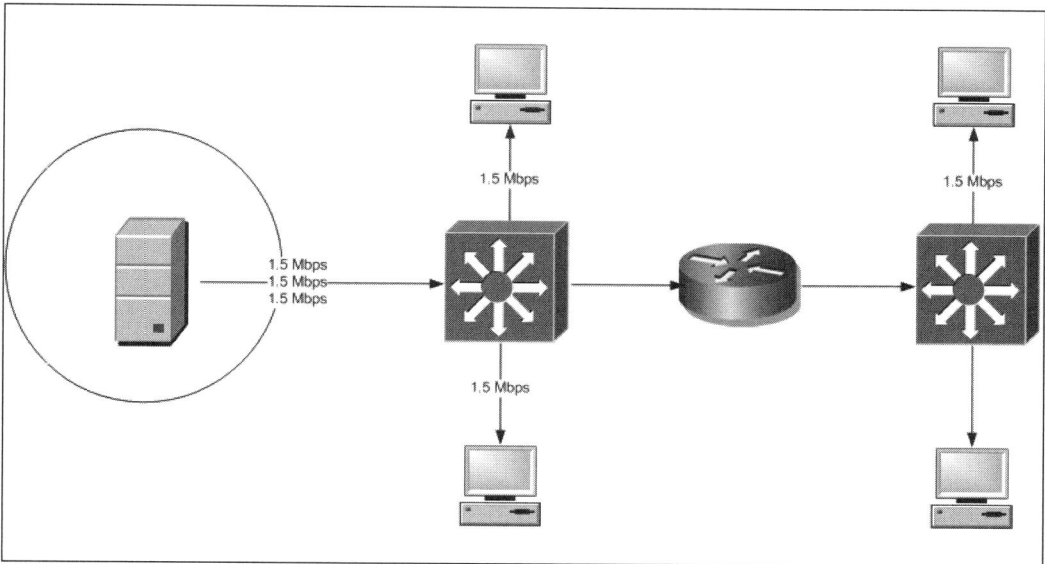

If the session is required by multiple hosts, a one-to-one connection is established, with the same data transmitted repeatedly to each host. This form of transmission will not transmit to every computer on a network; however, multiple requests for the same conference or data would cause that data to be pushed across the network media at the same time. Thus, as shown in Figure 6.8, a video feed of 1.5 Mbps unicasted to 10 computers on a network requires 15 Mbps of bandwidth. While this might not seem significant, it can degrade network performance as the feed size and quantity increase.

The toll of network usage is realized on the network equipment traversed from source to destination for the video feed. All of the routers and switches will have a considerable amount of data traffic to process.

Broadcast Traffic

Broadcast is another option that can be used for transmitting data to a large number of host systems simultaneously. Broadcasts can consume a significant amount of bandwidth; connections are based on a one-to-all method transmission. This can be seen when using the NetBIOS and ARP protocols, as well as many others. Any hosts on a network where a broadcast is generated will process that broadcast (at least far enough to know it is not intended for that system). An example of a broadcast can be seen in Figure 6.9.

Figure 6.9 Broadcast Network Video Feed Example

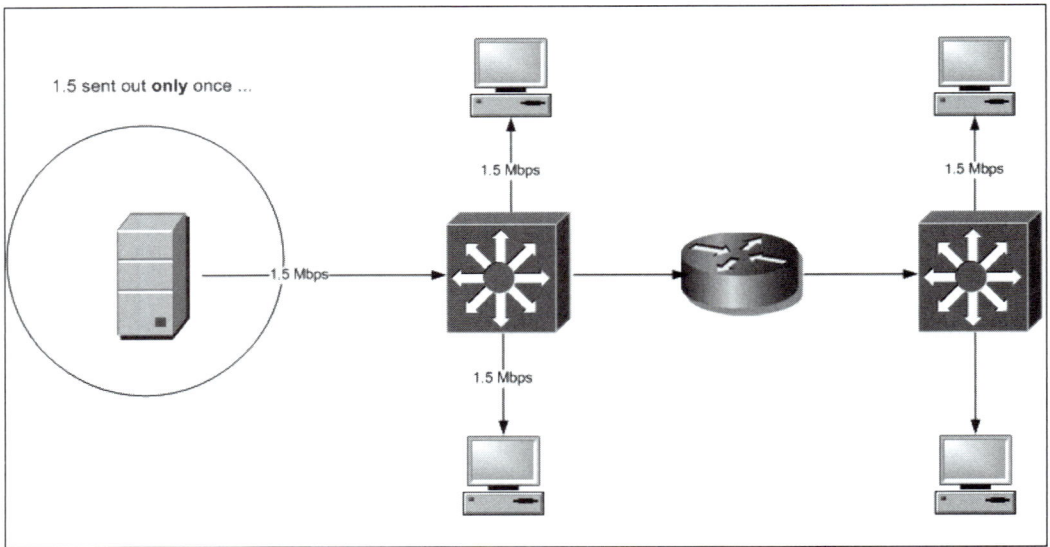

As shown in Figure 6.9, the broadcast traffic is sent to all computer systems that can be reached on the network. This process launches the 1.5 Mbps video stream to all the interfaces possible, thus not creating the intense bandwidth consumption of a unicast.

The problem is that each host receiving the broadcast has to process the 1.5 Mbps data stream continuously until it is finished. If the receiving host does not want the broadcast traffic, valuable resources of the host will still accept the datagram and then determine what to do with it—accept it or reject it. Because this is also a video feed, this large piece of data has to be processed, which can take a considerable toll on the host system.

Another disadvantage of using the broadcast transmission for video feeds is the network architecture. On a small network with no routers, this may be a desirable option.

On larger networks, or if there are any routers in the path to a host, the default action is to filter (block) the broadcast, meaning that broadcasts must be explicitly allowed to traverse the path to the host.

Multicast Traffic

Obviously, neither unicast nor broadcast is optimized to handle traffic destined for multiple hosts, especially if those hosts are logically assigned to a specific group. Multicasting and the protocols discussed address this need. Multicast traffic establishes a one-to-many type of transmission. This allows the data traffic to only be sent to those who specifically requested the information, and only sends one stream of traffic to each requesting broadcast domain. A multicast example is shown in Figure 6.10.

Figure 6.10 Multicasting in Action

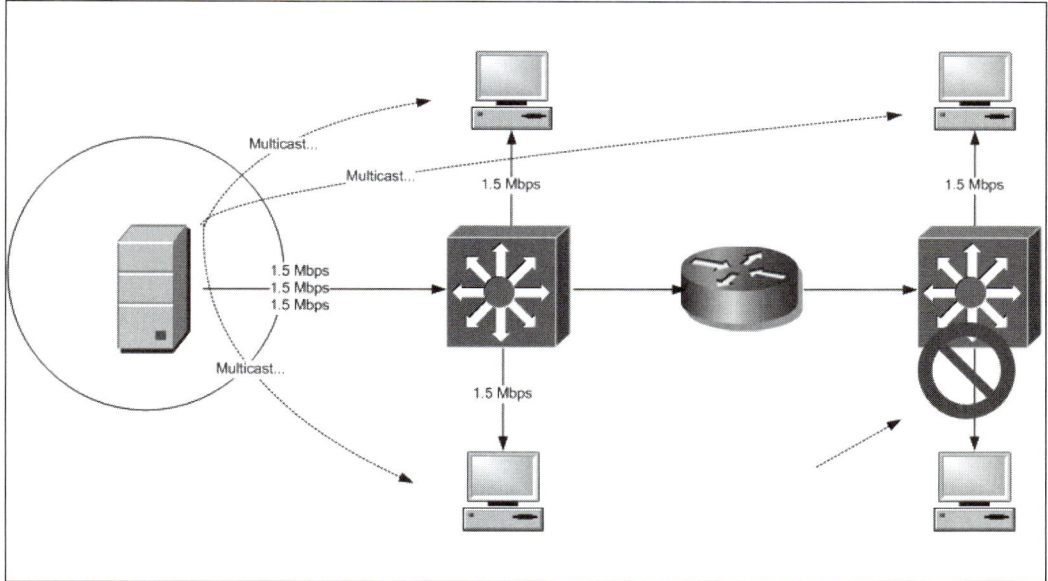

Multicast (RFC 1112) is a technology used to address multiple hosts as a group. A source host multicasts to a group of hosts by sending an IP packet to a special IP address associated with that group. The IP address that defines a multicast group is a Class D address (224.0.0.0 to 239.255.255.255), with unique groups allocated their own IP address in that range. This allows multiple multicast groups to be defined at the same time with different IP addresses. Multicasting sends the data stream only to the group of hosts that specifically want it. All other hosts ignore and do not process the multicast traffic.

Multicasting differs from broadcasting because multicasting sends traffic to a group of hosts, not to all hosts on a network. Hosts that are not part of the group will not process the multicast packet because it is not addressed to them.

As mentioned earlier in the section, a typical multicast application is videoconferencing. Not all network users want or need to participate in a videoconference; only those users that need to will join the multicast group to receive the video feed.

The advantage of multicasting becomes apparent when you consider that using unicast addresses would result in an individual video feedback to each receiver. More users and demand mean more bandwidth used. By using multicasting, only one channel is used, regardless of the number of users: 1,000 users only require one channel. Multicast traffic is bi-directional: a host can receive or send multicast packets.

As mentioned briefly before, it's important to understand the need for the group. If only one data stream is being transmitted, how can all of the requesting systems receive the data? Multicasting uses IP addresses to establish multicast groups, which host systems can join to receive multicast data. The multicast data is sent to the group IP address and all listed group members receive the traffic.

Multicast IP Address Designations

Class D IP addresses comprise the whole range of multicast addresses, with a range of 224.0.0.0 through 239.255.255.255. Multicast IP addresses are easily recognized by their binary numeration, as their high-end bits are always 1110. For instance 11100000 is equal to 224 and 11101111 is equal to 239. These first 4 bits account for a portion of the IP address; the remaining 28 bits are used for multicast group identification. Two types of multicast IP addresses are used: *dynamic* and *static*.

Transient (dynamic) addresses are used for the duration of the session, and are relinquished when no longer needed. Dynamic multicast IP addressing allows applications to acquire an IP address for the length of the multicast transmission. This IP address allocation has a certain expiration time and must be considered by the application requesting the address in order to retain functionality. For example, a transient address is used to multicast a videoconference of an event. After the event is finished, the transient address can be reused. Transient addresses must be coordinated to ensure that two people or organizations do not use the same transient address for different needs.

Static multicast IP addresses are a group of IP addresses, ranging from 224.0.0.0 to 224.255.255.255, that have been specifically assigned by the IANA. The permanent addresses are defined in the protocol itself, such as the all-hosts (224.0.0.1), all-routers (224.0.0.2), or RIPv2 group (224.0.0.9) addresses. Permanent addresses can also be assigned by the IANA for other protocols or uses. These addresses are reserved for particular purposes and are referred to as *well-known* addresses. Table 6.21 shows some of these assigned static IP addresses. For a complete listing of statically assigned Class D IP address, see www.iana.org/assignments/multicast-addresses.

Table 6.21 Permanent (Static) Multicast Addresses

Static IP Address	Assigned Use
224.0.0.0	Base IP address for multicasting
224.0.0.1	All host systems on a subnet
224.0.0.2	All routers on a subnet
224.0.0.3	Unassigned
224.0.0.4	All Distance Vector Multicast Routing Protocol (DVMRP) routers, (covered later)
224.0.0.5	All OSPF routers
224.0.0.6	All OSPF designated routers
224.0.0.7	ST routers
224.0.0.8	ST hosts
224.0.0.9	All RIPv2 routers
224.0.0.10	All Interior Gateway Routing Protocol (IGRP) routers
224.0.0.11	Mobile agents
224.0.0.12	DHCP server or relay agent
224.0.0.13	All Protocol Independent Multicast (PIM) routers, (covered later)

All reserved static Class D addresses that are used for multicast management and multicast data are never forwarded to these addresses. Static addresses such as 224.0.0.2 include all multicast-enabled router interfaces. Multicast-enabled routers automatically join this "all routers" group upon initialization. In turn, all multicast-enabled hosts must join the all-host systems group 224.0.0.1. Others become active upon activation or configuration of some features such as OPSF on a router.

TEST DAY TIP

Memorize the Class D range, not the specific assignments for the exam. The specific assignments are for your own knowledge.

Understanding Basic IP Routing

In this section, we're going to explore how data is routed on a network using the IP protocol. We'll begin by discussing how names and addresses are resolved. Then, we'll look at how packets of data are sent from one network to another to understand the process of basic IP routing. Understanding how routing works will help you to understand the concepts behind routing protocols such as those found within the network protocol suites we already mentioned in this chapter (TCP/IP, IPX/SPX, and AppleTalk). In this section we will thoroughly cover how data is transmitted on a TCP/IP network. This knowledge is easily converted to other suites (such as IPX/SPX). Less commonly used protocols are not covered as thoroughly on the exam, hence we are focused on TCP/IP in this section (and chapter). However, you will need to know how to use protocols and services within the other suites to be able to function in a production environment that may not solely rely on TCP/IP for communication. Consider this as you wrap up your studies for this exam. Think about moving on to other protocols later and dig into them at a much more involved level.

Head of the Class…

Network+ Exam is Focused on TCP/IP… Period.

For those of you taking the Network+ exam, you will need to know TCP/IP in detail. It's the most commonly used protocol today and the most tested on the exam. On the Network+ exam, the term IPX/SPX (as well as the others) will come up a lot so it may appear as if many questions are on IPX/SPX, AppleTalk, or NetBEUI. It's important to understand that many times, in this scenario, you are being asked fundamental knowledge that was already acquired earlier in this chapter, such as the fact that IPX/SPX uses NLSP as a dynamic routing protocol, whereas TCP/IP will use something such as OSPF. NLSP is an IPX/SPX-based dynamic routing protocol, while OSPF is a TCP/IP-based one. Most of the exam is focused on details about TCP/IP, so don't get too upset that you see IP-based protocols covered here in depth, whereas, others are not.

Name and Address Resolution

Names are often used for computers and devices because it's much easier for humans to remember names than numbers. You're more likely to remember that your computer name is XP-1 than to remember that your IP address is 196.55.141.6. There are two types of names—*NetBIOS names*, which are used by NetBIOS applications and *hostnames*, used by Windows sockets applications and TCP/IP applications. Since names are often used, there must be a method for translating or resolving names—both NetBIOS and hostnames—to unique IP addresses.

Hostname Resolution

A hostname is a name, or alias, assigned to a device (also called *host* or *node*) to identify it as a TCP/IP host device. This hostname can be up to 255 characters long, can contain both alphabetic and numeric characters, and can contain the hyphen (-) and .dot, or period (.) characters. A computer or device can actually have multiple hostnames assigned to it. In Windows version 2000 and later, the hostname and computer name do not have to be the same.

Window sockets-based applications can use either the hostname or the IP address. Both Internet Explorer and FTP are examples of Windows sockets-based applications that use either the hostname or IP address. If a hostname is used for the destination, it must be resolved to the IP address associated with the hostname.

Hostnames take a variety of forms, but the two most common are nicknames (aliases) and domain names. A nickname might be "Galileo" or "JohnS". Domain names are hostnames that follow the commonly-known Internet naming conventions.

The InterNIC created a hierarchical namespace called *Domain Name System* (DNS), which allows organizations to create custom names based on an agreed-upon hierarchy. This system is similar to a directory structure on a disk drive. A unique name for the host within this type of hierarchy is referred to as a *fully qualified domain name* (FQDN). An example of an FQDN is *server01.example.somecompany.com*. The root is indicated with a null "". The top-level domain is *com*, familiar to most people in today's environment. *Somecompany* represents the second-level domain, *example* represents the third-level domain, and *server01* is the host (computer name). The unique hostname is the entire string. It is possible, for example, to have a host named server01 on another domain, such as *example2*, in which case the FQDN would be *server01.example2.somecompany.com*. Each name is still unique because the entire string serves as the name. Domain names are not case-sensitive. FQDNs have to be resolved to IP addresses in order for data to be sent and received properly. Hostnames (whether alias or FQDN) can be resolved through the use of a static hosts file, through the use of a DNS server for lookup, or through a combination of the two.

NOTE

DNS will be covered again later in the chapter.

Hosts File

UNIX has long used the *hosts* file to store hostname-to-IP address mappings. This file can also be used on Windows-based computers. On UNIX systems, the hosts file typically is located in /etc/hosts. On a Windows Server 2003 machine (or Windows 2000), it is located in the \%SystemRoot%\system32\drivers\etc directory. The file is a simple text file (but saved *without* the .txt extension) that lists the IP address and the hostname of each defined device. The top of the next page illustrates an example of a hosts file.

```
#
# Table of IP addresses and host names
#
127.0.0.1    localhost
132.14.29.1  router
191.87.221.2 server2.example.somecompany.com
191.87.221.3 server3.example.somecompany.com  galileo
```

Notice that the IP address is given first, then the hostname. On the last line of this sample hosts file, notice that there are two names: *server3.example.somecompany.com* and *galileo*. In a hosts file, you can map both a FQDN and an alias (nickname) to the same associated IP address. Thus, there are three ways someone could reach that device: using *galileo*, *server3.example.somecompany.com*, or *191.87.221.3*. Hosts files in Windows NT, 2000, and 2003 are not case-sensitive and are named *hosts*. In other operating systems, such as in UNIX, the hosts file is case-sensitive.

There are two big problems with using a hosts file. First, it is a static file. If any names or addresses change, they must be changed manually in the hosts file. If you have a hosts file on 1,500 computers that defines the location and name of a router and information changes, you may have a big job ahead of you when you need to change that hosts file on all 1,500 computers and other devices that use that router. Also, if the number of defined hosts in a hosts file gets long, it can take a long time to parse the file. This results is a delay as your computer reads through a long file in an attempt to locate a hostname and associated IP address.

DNS Name Resolution

An alternative to the hosts file is to use a DNS server. DNS servers store FQDN-to-IP address translations. A computer runs the DNS client called the *DNS resolver*, which is configured with the IP address of the DNS server. When an IP address is needed, the DNS resolver requests the information from the DNS server by first translating the FQDN provided into a *DNS name query*. When the IP address is returned from the DNS server, the DNS resolver provides that information to the requesting application. DNS is a distributed system, so not all mappings reside on all DNS servers. Each DNS server is responsible for a particular segment of the names and it either returns the requested information or forwards it to the appropriate DNS server. We'll learn more about DNS later in this book. In the Windows implementation of TCP/IP, both a hosts file and DNS are used to resolve hostnames. The hosts file is checked first and if the desired mapping is not present, DNS will be queried.

NetBIOS Name Resolution

NetBIOS, as we learned earlier, stands for Network Basic Input Output System, and is an API that augments the DOS BIOS by adding special functions for LANs. Almost all Windows-based LANs for PCs are based on the NetBIOS name resolution method. Some LAN manufacturers have even extended it, adding additional network capabilities. Windows-based computers, although striving to use DNS only, still rely heavily on NetBIOS. Much of this reliance on NetBIOS is from all the older implementation of it already in existence today. There are essentially four ways a NetBIOS name can be resolved:

- The client's NetBIOS name cache is checked to see if the NetBIOS name-to-IP address has already been resolved and is sitting in memory.

- A WINS server can be queried to see if the information is in a WINS database.

- The client can use a file called lmhosts (which works like the hosts file for hostnames).

- The NetBIOS name is converted to a hostname, and hostname resolution methods are employed

The method by which NetBIOS names are resolved depends on the node's configuration. There are four types of configurations, described in Table 6.22, that are referred to as NetBIOS node types.

Table 6.22 NetBIOS Node Types

Node Type	Description of Node
B-node (Broadcast) **Benefit**: Broadcast sends message to network for response. **Potential Problem**: Increased network traffic.	B-node clients broadcast a message to the local network. If the queried name exists on the local network, a positive *name query response* is generated, which contains the IP address of the associated NetBIOS name. Once resolved, this information resides in the NetBIOS cache until it times out.
P-node (Peer-to-peer) **Benefit**: Message is sent only to WINS server, reducing network traffic. **Potential Problem**: Names may be resolved over WAN, which is both slower and less efficient.	P-node clients send a unicast (a directed message) to the defined WINS server. If the WINS server database contains the needed information, it responds with a positive name query response along with the requested IP address. If the WINS server does not respond, the client will try additional WINS servers.

Continued

Table 6.22 continued NetBIOS Node Types

Node Type	Description of Node
M-node (Mixed) **Benefit**: Useful when the client is on the other side of a WAN link from the desired resource. **Potential Problem**: Broadcasts may cause increased traffic on the local network.	M-node clients use B-node to resolve the name-to-address first. If this is unsuccessful, it will then use P-node for resolution.
H-node (Hybrid) **Benefit**: Works well if names are located on a WINS server and are resolved via WINS. **Potential Problem**: Can still generate excess local network traffic through the use of broadcasts.	H-node clients use a process just the opposite of M-node clients. Resolution is first attempted using P-node and if unsuccessful, B-node is used.

You may be thinking that a single broadcast to resolve a name on a network may not be significant in increasing network traffic. However, depending on the number of hosts on a subnet, the attempts at name resolution could cause substantial network traffic. It's also important to remember that these broadcasts use UDP datagrams. If you recall our earlier discussions, UDP datagrams are connectionless and are therefore not reliable. If a client does not receive a positive response from a name query, the client doesn't really know whether the request ever reached its destination. In order to make sure the request is received, these UDP datagram broadcasts are sent out three times with a 750-millisecond delay in between. Thus, each attempt at name resolution generates three packets, not just one. The number of attempts and the delay can be changed in the registry, though these default settings are typically adequate.

In Windows Server 2003 (and going as far back as Windows 98), a client can be configured with up to twelve WINS servers, significantly increasing the chances of receiving a positive name query response from a configured WINS server. However, if the name is still not resolved using these methods, the client will continue to try to resolve the name.

How Packets Travel from Network to Network

Now that we understand how names are translated into IP addresses, let's look at how a data packet from one host travels to another across the span of networks. After a sending host receives the needed IP address, the packet is sent from the host through the TCP/IP suite to the physical medium for delivery at the target IP address. Routing is the process of sending the packet to its destination. A *router* is a device that forwards packets from one network to another and is also referred to as a *gateway* (the term gateway is used in several different contexts; in all cases, a gateway connects one thing with another). Gateways are covered in more detail in Chapter 3, "Network Devices".

When the sending host has a packet ready, it already has determined the destination's IP address by using one of the many name-to-IP resolution methods discussed. However, it may not know where that IP address is located if it is not located on the same subnet as the sending host.

When TCP/IP on a host is initialized, it automatically creates a routing table, which consists of default entries, manual entries, and entries made automatically through communication with network routers. In order to route the packet properly, the IP layer of a host will consult with the routing table that is stored in memory. Depending on whether the destination is on the same network or across the network boundaries (which is determined by examining the network ID of the destination address), the packet will be sent by *direct delivery* or *indirect delivery*.

Direct delivery is when the router is not used to forward the packet because the destination is on the same network (subnet or network segment) as the sending host. In this case, the packet is sent directly to its destination. When the packet leaves the sending host, the data is encapsulated in a frame format for the Network Interface Layer with the destination's physical address included (as you'll recall, the physical or MAC address that matches the IP address in the destination header is determined by ARP).

If the packet is destined for another network, it is sent to an intermediate point for forwarding. This is called indirect delivery. The IP data is encapsulated in a frame format that is actually addressed to the physical address of the network interface of the IP *router* that is on the sending computer's subnet. Thus, the packet is sent from the sending host directly to the router. The router takes a look at the packet and determines where it should be sent in order to reach its final destination. The router passes the packet from its *internal interface* (the one with an address on the same subnet as the sender) to its *external interface* (the interface that's on a different subnet). From there, the packet may make its way across many routers before reaching the subnet or network on which the destination computer resides.

IP Routing Tables

Any IP node that initializes the TCP/IP stack will generate a default routing table based on the configuration of that node. For instance, when your network-connected desktop boots up and initializes the TCP/IP stack, it will create a default routing table based on your computer's unique IP address, which includes the network ID as well as the default gateway (default router) and subnet mask. The table also contains the logical or physical interface, typically the network interface card, to be used to forward the packet.

IP Routing Table Entries

Routing table entries can be default, manual, or dynamic.

- The default values are created when the TCP/IP stack is initialized, as shown in Figure 6.11.

- Manual entries can be placed in the table for specific routes that may be desired. Some organizations, for instance, want specific traffic to go through specific routers. In that case, those routes can be entered into the routing table manually.

- Routes can be added dynamically if the router supports dynamic routing tables.

Figure 6.11 Default Routing Table Entries

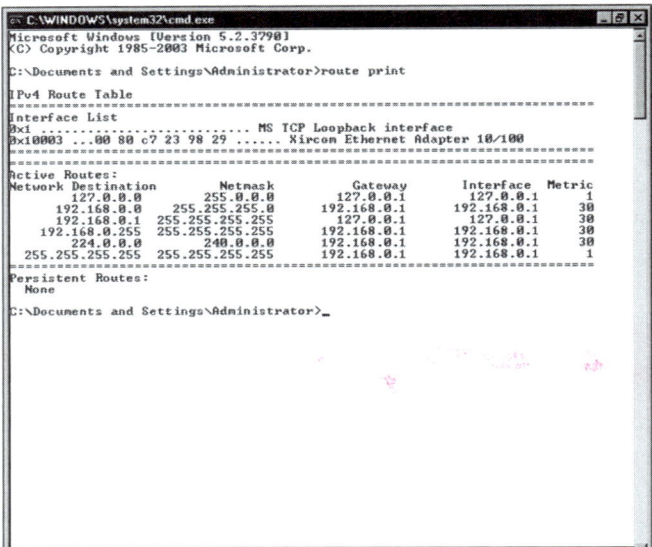

We'll discuss the differences between manual and dynamic routing in a moment. For now, let's look at the specific entries in a routing table. Routing table entries contain a number of elements in a specified order. Each of those elements is required and each is described briefly here. Figure 6.11 shows a typical routing table.

- **Network Destination** The network ID can be class-based, subnetted, or supernetted.

- **Netmask** The mask used to match the destination network with the IP address in the data.

- **Next Hop or Gateway** The IP address of the next router (a hop is one segment between routers. If a packet has to go through two routers, that would be two hops).

- **Interface** Identifies which network interface is used to forward the packet. Remember that every router has at least two interfaces.

- **Metric** The metric is a number used to help determine the best route for the packet. This typically is used to identify the route with the fewest hops. The metric is often expressed as the *cost of the route*.

Routing tables can also store four specific types of routes:

- **Directly Attached Network IDs** For packets destined for the local or attached network. If the sending and receiving hosts are both on the same subnet, for instance, the packet will be sent via this method.

- **Remote Network IDs** Any packets destined for networks reachable via routers will be sent via this routing method.

- **Host Routes** A host route is a route to a specific IP address. This type of route allows a packet to be sent to a specific IP address. The network ID is the IP address of the destination host and the network mask is 255.255.255.255.

- **Default Route** The default route is used when a more specific network ID or route cannot be found. When all else fails, the default route is used. This is defined as a network ID of 0.0.0.0 and the network mask is 0.0.0.0.

NOTE
_____

In this section we used a server (multi-homed with two NICs) as a router. When using RRAS (Routing and Remote Access Service), you can use Windows Server 2003 (or 2000) as a router. Since most people have more access to a copy of the server than to a Cisco router, this made the most sense. However, it will be most commonly seen on a vendor router such as Cisco or Juniper. For the exam you will not be asked to analyze different vendor-based RITs, so this example is all that you need in order to learn the concepts about routing to be able to pass the exam. Make sure that when you get an opportunity, try to work with commonly used equipment whenever possible, especially Cisco's offerings.

_____

Route Determination Process

Each IP packet has a destination IP address, which is used to determine how the packet will be routed. Using the logical ANDing process, the destination IP address and the subnet mask (or netmask) are compared. If they match, the packet stays on the local network and is sent directly to the destination IP address.

If the destination IP address and the subnet mask do not match, the entries in the routing table are compared to the destination IP address. If a match is found (that is, if the destination IP address and the subnet mask AND to a value found in the routing table), the packet is sent to the gateway listed in the routing table. If no matching entries can be found, the packet is sent to the defined default gateway. If more than one match is found in the routing table entries, the *metric* is used and the route with the fewest hops is typically selected. Table 6.23 on the following page shows a sample routing table list. To view the route table on a Windows Server 2003 computer, access the command prompt and type **route print**.

If there is no matching entry in the routing table, the packet will be sent to the default gateway for forwarding. When this process is complete, the resulting IP address (either destination IP address or gateway IP address) is then resolved to a physical address. This process uses ARP.

Physical Address Resolution (Using ARP)

ARP resolves IP addresses to physical addresses. ARP is used to resolve the next-hop IP address to a physical MAC address. This is done using network broadcasts. The resolved MAC address is placed in the header of the packet as the destination MAC address.

ARP Cache

Just as a routing table is stored on the local host, so too is a list of the resolved IP-to-MAC addresses. This information is held in the ARP cache. Each time a request and resolution occur, both the sender and receiver store the other's IP-to-MAC address mapping. When a packet is received, the ARP cache is checked to see if the resolution has already been added to the cache. If so, the packet is immediately forwarded to the resolved address. If the ARP cache does not contain the listing, a process must be initiated to resolve the IP address to the MAC address. Resolved entries are stored for a specified period of time and then discarded. If the same IP address is used within the specified time frame, the MAC address is already known and the packet is simply forwarded. If the ARP cache entry has expired, it no longer exists and the discovery process must be used, even if the MAC address was previously discovered.

ARP Process

There are two steps involved in resolving the IP address to a MAC address: the *ARP request* and *ARP reply*. The node responsible for forwarding the packet (either the sender or a gateway) will use the ARP request message to request the MAC address for the next-hop IP address. The format of the ARP request is a MAC-level broadcast that is sent to all nodes on the same physical segment as the sender. Whichever node sends the ARP request message is called the *ARP requester*.

The ARP reply is the return process. The node whose address matches the MAC address in the ARP request will respond by sending an ARP reply. This is a unicast (directly back to the sender only) MAC frame sent by the node called the *ARP responder*. The ARP responder's unicast message contains both its IP address and its MAC address.

Table 6.23 Sample Static Routing Table

Destination IP	Subnet Mask	Gateway	Interface	Metric	Purpose
0.0.0.0	0.0.0.0	166.42.8.1	166.42.14.62	20	Default route
127.0.0.0	255.0.0.0	127.0.0.1	127.0.0.1	1	Loopback network
166.42.8.0	255.255.224.0	166.42.14.62	166.42.14.62	20	Directly attached network
166.42.14.62	255.255.255.255	127.0.0.1	127.0.0.1	20	Local host
166.42.255.255	255.255.255.255	166.42.14.62	166.42.14.62	1	Network broadcast
224.0.0.0	224.0.0.0	166.42.14.62	166.42.14.62	1	Multicast address
255.255.255.255	255.255.255.255	166.42.14.62	166.42.14.62	1	Limited broadcast

Once this process is complete, both nodes now have new information about an IP address and the associated MAC address. This information is stored in the ARP cache for a specified amount of time. When it expires, if this address is needed again, the same request and reply process is used.

> **NOTE**
>
> The process of resolving an address to its physical (MAC) address is a very important one and is likely to be the subject of at least one exam question. Typically, questions have to do with how ARP actually resolves the address. Remember that the *ARP request* is a broadcast datagram and the *ARP reply* is a unicast datagram. Datagrams, unlike other messages, do not require the ACK message to acknowledge receipt. The broadcast datagram is sent out to all hosts, which process the ARP request. If a host's IP address matches the ARP request, it sends an ARP reply. The ARP reply is a unicast because it is sent from the matching host directly back to the requesting host. No other hosts receive this datagram. If it does not match the request, the ARP request is simply discarded.

RARP (which is Reverse ARP), is the complete opposite of ARP. Where ARP is the process of resolving a known IP address to its MAC address, RARP will resolve an IP address to a known MAC. Remember, it's simply the opposite of ARP and very easy to remember simply by its name alone.

Although not necessarily testable on the Network+ exam, there are other forms of ARP that you should be aware of as a Network+ technician that you will see in use in your day-to-day activities.

Inverse ARP

On non-broadcast-based multiple access (NBMA) networks, such as wide area technologies including ATM (Asynchronous Transfer Mode), Frame Relay, and X.25, the network interface address is not the MAC address. Instead, it is a virtual circuit. In these cases, the IP address is mapped to the virtual circuit over which the packet is traveling. In resolving addresses in NBMA networks, the virtual circuit identifier is known, but the receiving node's IP address is not. Inverse ARP (InARP) is used to resolve the IP address on the other end of the virtual circuit. InARP was specifically designed for Frame Relay circuits. InARP uses a query on each virtual circuit to determine the IP address of the interface on the other end. A table is built using the results of these queries for use in resolving addresses in NBMA networks.

Proxy ARP

Proxy ARP occurs when one node answers ARP requests on behalf of another node. This is typically the case in subnets where no router is present. An ARP proxy device is placed between nodes on the network. This device is aware of all nodes on its physical segment and can respond to ARP requests and facilitate the forwarding of packets on the network. An ARP proxy device is often a routing device, but it does not act as an IP router.

Static and Dynamic IP Routers

Routing tables can be updated manually or dynamically. If the table must be updated manually, it is considered to be *static*. If the table can be updated automatically, it is considered to be *dynamic*. Static routing works well in small environments, but does not scale well to larger networks. Another useful application of static routing is in subnets that are separated from the rest of the network. Rather than using routing protocols across WAN connections, static routes can be entered manually at both the main office and remote office routers to make each network segment reachable. A third common use of static routes is to connect a network to the Internet. A Windows Server 2003 computer can be used as a static router when it is configured as a multi-homed computer. This entails installing two or more network interface cards, each with a separate IP address and subnet mask. Static routes can then be configured for the two (or more) networks directly attached to the multi-homed computer.

Dynamic routing occurs when routing tables are automatically and periodically updated. Dynamic routers rely upon routing protocols. The two most commonly used IP-based routing protocols, are:

- Routing Information Protocol
- Open Shortest Path First

The Routing Information Protocol was originally designed for use on classful networks. RIP is a *distance vector* routing protocol and determines routes based on the number of hops (how many routers it must pass through). Any route more than 15 hops away is considered unreachable. For this reason, RIP does not scale well to large networks. RIP routing tables are dynamically updated using a route-advertising mechanism.

In contrast to RIP, OSPF is a *link state* routing protocol. The method of dynamically updating routing information is through link state advertisements (LSAs) that have information containing both the connected networks and their costs. The *cost* of each router interface is determined by the administrator in order to use best connections first. The combined cost of a connection using this classless routing protocol must be less than 65,535.

A Windows Server 2003 computer can be configured as a dynamic router, using either of these protocols. As with static configurations, multiple NICs must be installed and RRAS must be enabled. In dynamic routing, default routes are seldom used. Thus, it is not necessary to configure a default gateway on any NIC. When the Routing and Remote Access Service is enabled, static routing is enabled. To enable dynamic routing, add the RIP and OSPF protocols and enable them on your NICs by adding your NICs to the appropriate routing protocol. RIP is more appropriate for small-to medium-sized networks and OSPF is appropriate for large networks. Therefore, you are most likely to enable one or the other protocol, depending on your network configuration.

TEST DAY TIP

One or more questions about routing protocols may come up on the exam. Remember that RIP and OSPF both support dynamic routing, but RIP is not a good choice for a larger network. Look for questions that may include more than 16 hops—you'll immediately know that RIP can't be used in this case. Since OSPF was specifically designed for Frame Relay circuits, questions about OSPF will likely revolve around Frame Relay as opposed to other NBMA types of networks. Also keep in mind that a multi-homed computer must have RRAS enabled to function as a router, and that it sets up static routing by default. The only way dynamic routing occurs is if you install the RIP or OSPF protocols and bind your NIC to them.

Routing Utilities

There are four commonly used routing utilities. Each typically is run from the command line (**Start | Run | cmd**). The specific command line options available are displayed when the command is typed in at the prompt. See Figure 6.12 for an example of the command line options available for the **tracert** and **ping** commands.

- **route** Used to view and modify the entries in the routing table.

- **ping** Used to verify reachability of intended destinations using ICMP (Internet Control Message Protocol) Echo messages.

- **tracert** Used to send ICMP Echo messages to discover the path between a node and a destination.

- **pathping** Used to discover the path between a host and destination or to identify high-loss links.

Figure 6.12 *tracert* and *ping* Command Line Options

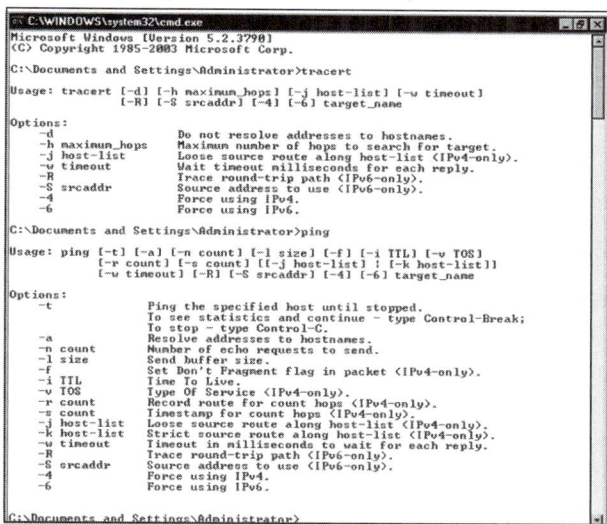

A very common use of the ping utility is to check connectivity from one computer to another. From your computer, you can run the ping utility from the command window. You can ping using an IP address or hostname. If your computer cannot connect to the network, you can try to ping a known server or another computer (by IP address or name) on your network. If that does not work, the next step is to ping the local computer, which tests the internal network communication functions of your computer (NIC and TCP/IP stack) by using the following command: **ping localhost** or **ping 127.0.0.1** (the loopback address). If this fails, the problem is with the configuration of the TCP/IP stack on your computer. If pinging the loopback address is successful, the problem is probably external to the NIC.

EXAM WARNING

Before exam day, try each of these utilities on a networked computer. Once you see how the utility works and what the return values are, you'll have a much clearer idea of how each is used. Scenarios based on using these utilities may trip you up if you're not certain which utility has which function. Memorize the functions of these four utilities. You'll probably see one or more of them used in a network scenario. You will learn more about these commands and utilities as well as troubleshooting in general in Chapters 11 and 12 respectively.

IP routing involves using both direct and indirect routes to deliver packets to their intended destinations. Static and dynamic routing tables are used to determine how to best send the packet. With the use of the IP protocol and other associated protocols (Application Layer protocols, UDP datagrams, ICMP messages, or routing protocols), messages are reliably and quickly encoded, sent, and decoded.

Example of a Simple Classful Network

Class A, B, and C networks are often subnetted to increase efficiency of the network. Broadcasts are kept on local subnets, preventing wider distribution of broadcast traffic, and IP data that is intended for a host on the local subnet is kept local and not passed across a router. Routing tables are used to determine how an IP packet will be sent. If its destination IP address matches the local network, the data is sent to the destination host. If the address does not match the local network ID, the packet is sent to the router, or gateway for forwarding. Figure 6.13 shows two segments of a Class B network and a sample routing table for a host on Subnet A.

Figure 6.13 Example of Classful Network and Routing Table

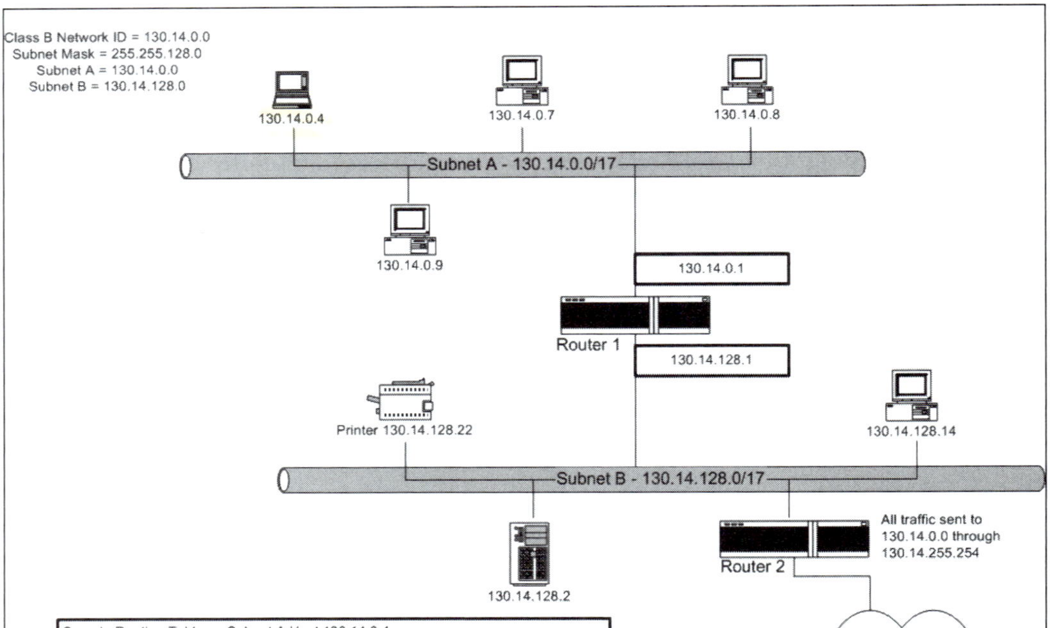

Sample Routing Table on Subnet A Host 130.14.0.4

Network Destination	Netmask	Gateway	Interface	Metric
0.0.0.0	0.0.0.0	130.14.0.1	130.14.0.4	1
127.0.0.0	255.0.0.0	127.0.0.1	127.0.0.1	1
130.14.0.0	255.255.128.0	130.14.0.4	130.14.0.4	1
130.14.0.4	255.255.255.255	127.0.0.1	127.0.0.1	1
130.14.128.22	255.255.128.0	130.14.0.1	130.14.0.1	1

The routing table contains several entries that should look familiar. The first entry is the default route, which is used if no other entries in the routing table match the destination IP's network ID. Notice that the gateway is Router 1 and the interface is the IP address for the host. The second entry in the routing table is the loopback address, which is the same for each host. The third entry is for the directly attached network. The Class B network ID is 130.14.0.0 with a subnet mask of 255.255.128.0. Data intended for the directly attached network is not forwarded to a router, but is delivered directly to the destination IP address from the source address. The gateway and interface IP addresses are set to the host IP address to indicate the data originated at the host. The next entry, 130.14.0.4, is the host address. Data sent from the host to the host is looped back, as reflected by the gateway and interface addresses of 127.0.0.1. Finally, a route exists to the printer on Subnet B. The destination IP address is on the other subnet and the gateway and interface addresses are those belonging to Router 1. As you can see, classful subnetting and routing is relatively easy to understand conceptually, but can be quite complex in its implementation.

NOTE

Classless routing and CIDR were covered earlier in this chapter.

Services and Applications

In this section we will look at some of the various protocols and services that operate within the TCP/IP protocol suite. We have covered the TCP/IP suite as it stacks up against the OSI model and examined not only its operation, but also the other protocols and functions that work within it. As we mentioned in an earlier section, there could be volumes of books dedicated to this subject, and sometimes to each specific protocol. For instance, RIP is a protocol within the TCP/IP protocol suite and there are many books dedicated to how to configure it to function on Cisco or 3COM routers. Make sure that you do expand your reading on these protocols, as they are very important to know as a working network engineer. You will be working with many different products, so starting to familiarize yourself with them is essential to your success beyond this exam.

Using protocols like Telnet, SSH (Secure Shell), and FTP are daily, if not hourly occurrences. As a joke, I tallied up how many times I remotely connected to devices in one hour of one day at about 10:00 A.M. Within that hour, I remotely connected to over 54 devices using a plethora of tools, such as Telnet and SSH for terminal emulation to UNIX servers and Cisco routers located at that company. Now that you understand how many times you possibly may be using this protocol (or already do), you should spend some time digging into the operation of each one so that you understand the underlying way the protocols and services work.

Knowing a little about how each protocol operates as well as some of the distinctive nuances (such as knowing the differences between TCP and UDP) that set them apart can really give you an edge when it comes to doing your job, administration, troubleshooting, and so on. Questions like, "what are the benefits of using a UDP port when using TFTP (Trivial File Transfer Protocol)?" should be easy enough for you to answer silently in your mind. The answer here would be, "because when using TFTP, you do not need all the overhead of FTP, which makes it quicker and much easier to use." That makes sense, but on the other hand, using TFTP is a security risk on tightly controlled networks because it doesn't have the overhead that FTP does to allow for a more secure login and so on. This may mean you need to steer clear of using it, if not allowed by your company's security policy. All of these decisions and suggestions can only be decided upon and made if you have knowledge of the technology. In this section we will cover the services and applications you need to know for the Network+ exam. Let's start to learn more about these protocols and services and see what they offer.

In this section we will define the purpose, function and use of the following protocols used in the TCP/IP protocol suite: TCP, UDP, FTP, SFTP (Secure File Transfer Protocol), TFTP, SMTP, HTTPS (HyperText Transfer Protocol Secure), POP3/IMAP4 (Post Office Protocol version 3/Internet Message Access Protocol version 4), Telnet, SSH, ICMP, ARP, RARP, NTP (Network Time Protocol), SCP (Secure Copy Protocol), LDAP (Lightweight Directory Access Protocol), IGMP, LPR (line printer remote). The protocol suite is not limited to these protocols; there are obviously many more, as shown in Figure 6.14.

Figure 6.14 The TCP/IP Protocol Suite Mapped to the OSI Model

Application	FTP, SFTP, Telnet, SSH, X-Windows, HTTP, IMAP4, POP3, NTP, TFTP , HTTP, HTTPS, Tacacs+, SLP, RADIUS, etc.
Presentation	
Session	NetBIOS, DNS, LDAP
Transport	TCP, UDP
Network	IP, ICMP, IGMP, RSVP, DHCP, BOOTP, BGP, RIP, OSPF
Data Link	ARP, RARP (also works in the Network layer)
Physical	Ethernet, Token Ring, FDDI

The protocols listed and covered here in the text are directly from the Network+ testable objectives. Make sure that if you expand your studies of TCP/IP you definitely learn about the other protocols and services available, such as BGP (Border Gateway Protocol).

Protocols and Ports

Before we cover the protocols and services themselves, a discussion on the use of ports is essential. Thanks to the multitasking capabilities of most modern operating systems, you can use more than one network application simultaneously. For example, you can use your Web browser to access your company's homepage at the same time your e-mail software is downloading your e-mail. By now, you should know that TCP/IP uses an IP address to identify your computer on the network and get the messages to the correct system, but how does it separate the response to your browser's request from your incoming mail when both arrive at the same IP address?

That's where ports come in. The two parts of an IP address that represent the network identification and the host (individual computer) identification are somewhat like a street name and an individual street number. In this analogy, the port number would identify the specific apartment or suite within the building.

TCP and UDP, the Transport Layer protocols, assign port numbers to each application so the data intended for the Web browser in Apartment A doesn't get sent to the e-mail program living in Apartment B.

Commonly Used Port Numbers

Although we have covered ports quite a few times throughout the text, this is where it should finally sink in and make total sense, because now you know how TCP and UDP work and now have a clear definition of ports when used with TCP/IP. For the Network+ exam, you will be expected to know how TCP and UDP ports function.

TCP ports, UDP ports, and protocol numbers are important to TCP/IP networking and to how networking takes place, especially when it comes to Internet access and firewall usage. Ports and protocol numbers provide access to host computers. However, they also create a security hazard by allowing uninvited access. Therefore, knowing which port(s) to allow or disable increases a network's security. You can allow or disallow certain traffic to pass a firewall (or ACL—access control list) based on a port number so if you didn't want Telnet through a firewall, you can block that port, which would be TCP 23. If the wrong ports or protocol numbers are disabled on a firewall, router, or proxy server as a security measure, essential services might become unavailable. You should also understand that port numbers are duplicated from TCP to UDP. You will have TCP and UDP ports 23, but because Telnet is a program that requires more overhead than TFTP, it will require the usage of TCP, so it's TCP 23, whereas, TFTP would be UDP 69. You will only need to memorize the port numbers for the exam, not really the concepts behind it as just mentioned. In Table 6.24, the ports you need to know for the Network+ exam are listed per the objectives.

Table 6.24 Commonly Used Ports

Protocol	Port (in numerical order)
FTP	20 and 21
SSH	22
Telnet	23
SMTP	25
DNS	53
TFTP	69
HTTP	80
POP3	110
NNTP	119
NTP	123
IMAP4	143
HTTPS	443

NOTE

These are the ports that are covered by the objectives. There are thousands of ports in use, and many of them will be services you configure on proprietary products, and so on. It's important to know where you can find more port information if you need it. You can visit www.iana.org/assignments/port-numbers.

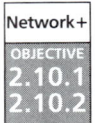

TCP and UDP

If you were going to study any two protocols in depth for the Network+ exam, it would obviously be TCP and IP. We just spent time covering IP in depth. Now, since you understand how IP and ports work, let's delve into TCP and its lesser variant, UDP.

Two types of connection services are used at the Transport Layer or the OSI model:

- Connection-oriented
- Connectionless

Which is most appropriate for sending a given message depends on whether reliability or speed is of highest priority. This is what we need to uncover. In TCP/IP communications, data is sent over the network as a sequence of datagrams. A datagram is a collection of data sent as a single message. Each datagram is sent across the network individually. To recap, 0s and 1s are sent across the network medium at Layer 1, the Physical Layer. Data Link Layer is responsible for framing and the Network Layer is responsible for packets. Datagrams (or segments) are covered at Layer 4, the Transport Layer. Now, with TCP (and UDP) at the Transport Layer of the OSI model, we dig deeper into their specific operations as data is sent over the network as a sequence of datagrams. Let's look at the major differences between connection-oriented versus connectionless communications.

TCP and UDP Communications (Transport)

A connection-oriented protocol such as TCP offers better error control than UDP, but its higher overhead means a loss of performance. A connectionless protocol such as UDP, on the other hand, suffers in the reliability department, but, unhampered by error-checking duties, is faster.

As a provider of connection-oriented services, TCP first establishes a virtual connection between the sending and receiving computers. This is done through the use of acknowledgments and response messages. An acknowledgment message is sometimes referred to as an *ACK*. There are other forms of messages such as *SYN* and *FIN*, which when sent back and forth from source to destination confirm that information is synchronized, or finished. There are other tags, but this is enough to give you an idea of how TCP provides connection-oriented services.

The most commonly used analogy for differentiating between connection-oriented and connectionless communications compares different services available from the post office. If you need to send an important report to the manager of your company's branch office in El Paso, you could put it in an envelope, affix the required amount of postage, and drop it in the corner mailbox. This would be the easiest, quickest way to take care of the task, but you would have no idea whether or when the report reached its destination.

On the other hand, you could go to the post office and fill out a card to send the report via registered, certified mail, with a return receipt requested. It would cost more and it would take more time and effort on your part, but it would be a more reliable form of communication. You would get back an acknowledgment when the package was delivered, showing that it was indeed received by the person to whom it was addressed.

Connection-oriented services are more like the second example, although they actually go one step further: They establish the connection before sending the data. This would be as if, before you sent your certified mail, you first got on the telephone with the El Paso manager and let him know the report was coming so he could be on the lookout for its arrival. If you're really detail-minded (or paranoid), you could even ask that he call you back when it gets there, and let you know that all the pages are there in sequence and it wasn't damaged along the way. You've taken pains to make sure your communication is as reliable as possible, but at a cost in time (and long distance charges) to both you and the intended recipient.

UDP performs the same basic function as TCP—transport of datagrams—but does so in a "bare bones" manner. It does not acknowledge receipt of the messages, nor does it sequence the datagrams. UDP should be used when speed is of high priority and assured delivery of the messages is less critical.

A connectionless transport protocol like UDP doesn't provide the same acknowl-edgment of receipt process as the connection-oriented TCP does. Since UDP doesn't sequence the packets that the data arrives in, an application program that uses UDP has to be able to make sure that the entire message has arrived and is in the right order. To save processing time, network applications that have very small data units to exchange, and thus very little message reassembling to do, may use UDP instead of TCP. For example, DNS hostname lookup messages that will always fit in a single datagram can effectively use UDP. For these very short queries, you don't need all the complexity of TCP; if you don't receive an answer after a few seconds, you can just ask again.

Examples of applications that use UDP for communication include TFTP, RIP, RADIUS (Remote Authentication Dial-In User Service) accounting, and some imple-mentations of Kerberos authentication.

UDP doesn't split data into multiple datagrams, as TCP does. It doesn't keep track of what it has sent, data can be resent if needed, and it doesn't guarantee delivery or protect against duplication. However, it is not completely irresponsible: it does provide for a checksum capability, to ensure that data arrives intact, and it provides port numbers to distinguish between the requests sent by different user applications.

The UDP header is shorter and simpler than the TCP header. It has the source and destination port numbers and a checksum, but it doesn't include a sequence number, since UDP doesn't do any sequencing.

In sum, The TCP/IP suite includes two Transport Layer protocols, TCP and UDP. As already discussed, TCP is the connection-oriented protocol that should be used when error control is of high priority. TCP provides highly reliable, full-duplex transport ser-vices, and supports sequence numbering so that large messages can be broken down and then reassembled at the receiving end. We learned about full duplex communications in Chapter 2, "Network Media", and the same theory applies to TCP. If you want to have communications simultaneously in both directions—you are operating in full duplex.

TEST DAY TIP

Be prepared to answer questions about the major differences between TCP and UDP for the Network+ exam.

FTP, SFTP, and TFTP (Application Layer)

FTP was covered earlier in the chapter. To recap, the File Transfer Protocol is used for copying files from one computer to another and is optimized to do so with some overhead added to it to provide such functionality. With commands like get, mget, put, and mput, as well as options to change files into binary format and others, FTP was born to transfer files.

Do not forget about the other forms of FTP. One such version that is very important to remember for the Network+ exam is SFTP, the security-conscious, encrypted form of FTP. FTP is an unsecure protocol because it doesn't contain the overhead to protect itself with encryption. If you send your credentials to an FTP server to log in, the authentication attempt can be grabbed off the wire with a packet sniffer and used against you because the credentials are sent in cleartext and easily read. An inherent weakness in the IPv4 version of TCP/IP is that it was not designed with security in mind and most of what is sent across the network is sent in cleartext, which means in plain view. If the data is intercepted, the data can be read in any standard Sniffer, or other capture tool. SFTP protects against data theft, manipulation, or any other attack that exploits the inherent weaknesses of FTP.

EXAM WARNING

FTP has a lot of overhead to transfer files, but what if you wanted a protocol that quickly transferred files without the need for the overhead? TFTP is one such protocol. As mentioned earlier, TFTP was made to quickly transfer files. It is commonly used with Cisco router hardware and software offerings.

Exercise 6.4 covers the use of FTP on a Windows XP Professional workstation. You should be familiar with basic operations of FTP to pass the Network+ exam. Of course, you will be using FTP in your place of work very frequently as a network technician. Let's take a look at how to use FTP.

EXERCISE 6.4

USING FTP WITH WINDOW XP PROFESSIONAL

This exercise is designed to reinforce what we've learned about FTP, so now we will delve into its usage.

1. To open the FTP program supplied with Windows XP, access the command prompt by clicking **Start | Programs | Run**. Type **cmd** and press **Enter** to continue.

2. Type **ftp** and press **Enter**.

3. Type **?** and press **Enter**. You will see all the available commands you can utilize. The list of available commands is shown in the output that follows.

```
C:\>ftp
ftp> ?
Commands may be abbreviated.  Commands are:


!           delete       literal     prompt        send
?           debug        ls          put           status
append      dir          mdelete     pwd           trace
ascii       disconnect   mdir        quit          type
bell        get          mget        quote         user
binary      glob         mkdir       recv          verbose
bye         hash         mls         remotehelp    cd
help        mput         rename      close         lcd
open        rmdir
ftp>
```

4. After familiarizing yourself with available commands, let's use a few to learn how to manipulate the FTP client while working with a server, such as an FTP server waiting to supply you with the files you may need. To transfer files from the FTP server to a local directory on your workstation, you need to be familiar with the put, get, mput, and mget commands. To get a file from a FTP server, you must first connect and authenticate to the FTP server. To do so, you would need to know the IP address, or the DNS name of the FTP server to connect to. You can connect using the following commands.

```
C:\>open ftp.novell.com
ftp> dir
```

5. Once you can see what is located at the FTP site, you can request files and send or receive them based on which commands you select and use. For instance, put is used to **put** files on a server from the client, and **get** is used to get them; obvious and easy. When using **mput** or **mget**, the m stands for *multiple* and it simply means that you are getting or putting multiple files on the server at one time, so you don't have to specify them separately.

6. Another handy command to learn is how to change data formats. You may have data stored on a server in binary format, but need it converted to ASCII text. You can do that with the ASCII and binary commands.

Remember to practice using FTP, as you will be expected to know it not only for the Network+ exam, but just about anywhere you work.

HTTPS ↑ρ·

The HyperText Transfer Protocol (HTTP) is perhaps the most familiar of the Application Layer protocols because it is used on the World Wide Web (WWW). HTTP allows computers to exchange files in various formats (text, graphic images, sound, video, and other multimedia files) via client software called a Web browser. Web browsers such as Netscape Navigator or Internet Explorer are only two of many various vendor offerings.

A computer running a Web server program, such as Microsoft's Internet Information Server (IIS), stores files in HyperText Markup Language (HTML) format that can be accessed by the client browser. These HTML pages often contain hyperlinks for quickly and automatically connecting to other files on the Internet, on an intranet, or on the local machine. Other types of pages can also be kept on the server and accessed, such as XML (eXtensible Markup Language), but HTML is the most common one that you will be accessing.

The current version is HTTP 1.1, which was developed by a committee of the IETF (Internet Engineering Task Force). It contains enhancements that allow for faster transfer of information. The specifications for HTTP 1.1 are defined in proposed RFC 2068, which can be accessed on the Web at www.ics.uci.edu/pub/ietf/http/rfc2068.txt.

HTTPS is the encrypted version of HTTP. Just like FTP and SFTP, HTTPS cures some of the inherent weaknesses in HTTP such as clear transmission of data. If you caught a Web request from a source address, you could easily see the URL (Uniform Resource Locator) used to get that Web page. HTTPS is also known for its use with Secure Sockets Layer (SSL), used mostly in e-transactions to protect the buyer purchasing goods online using HTML pages. With HTTPS, the pages and transmissions can be secured from prying eyes.

EXAM WARNING

HTTPS uses port 443. HTTPS is also known as SSL. S-HTTP is NOT HTTPS; it's a different version of the protocol, not a typo. Whereas SSL is designed to establish a secure connection between two computers, S-HTTP is designed to send individual messages securely. You will only need to know HTTPS for the Network+ exam.

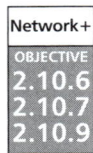

SMTP, HTTP, POP3, and IMAP4

Every time you send and receive e-mail, you are not only using TCP/IP, but are also using higher-level Application Layer protocols such as SMTP, POP3, and IMAP4. The SMTP is used for sending e-mail on the Internet. SMTP is a simple ASCII protocol and is non-vendor-specific. Because SMTP has limited capability in queuing messages at the receiving end, most e-mail client programs use SMTP for *sending* e-mail, and either POP3 or IMAP4 for *receiving* the messages that come in and are stored on a server. For more information about SMTP, see RFC 821 at www.cis.ohio-state.edu/htbin/rfc/rfc821.html. SMTP is the lifeblood of e-mail across the world, as it ensures that e-mail data is transferred from server to server and from clients to servers.

POP3 is a scaled-down protocol that allows you to use a thin e-mail client and access your e-mail quickly; it has less overhead than SMTP and is commonly used with ISP accounts and remote user accounts in production networks.

IMAP4 is a scaled-up version of POP3 with more functionality than POP3. Knowing very explicit differences between IMAP4 and POP3 is not needed for the exam, other than knowing that IMAP4 has more overhead and functionality than POP3. POP3 and SMTP are still the most widely used e-mail protocols.

EXAM WARNING

SMTP (Simple Mail Transfer Protocol) uses port 25.
POP3 (Post Office Protocol version 3) uses port 110.
IMAP4 (Internet Message Access Protocol version 4) uses port 143.

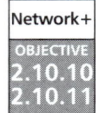

Telnet and SSH

Out-of-band (OOB) management of systems requires to use of a program to facilitate it, such as terminal emulation. If you are trying to connect to a remote system that is running a service or daemon that allows for the use of Telnet to the system, then by simply using TCP/IP on your own system (UNIX, Windows, or otherwise), you can use a program like Telnet (with the Telnet protocol) to achieve this functionality.

Telnet is a TCP/IP-based service that allows users to log on to, run character-mode applications, and view files on a remote computer. Windows Server 2000 and 2003) include both Telnet server and client software. UNIX has always used Telnet as its terminal emulation solution. UNIX was the first network operating system (NOS) to work with Telnet. Telnet differs from FTP in that you cannot transfer files from one computer to another (upload or download) using Telnet. Telnet is often used to access a UNIX shell account on an ISP's server and delete e-mail messages directly from the server without downloading them to the local machine. The Telnet protocol itself is used to establish the initial connection to FTP and SMTP servers from the host's user agent.

SSH, sometimes known as *Secure Socket Shell* or simply as *Secure Shell*, is a protocol for securely getting access to a remote computer. It's nothing more than encrypted Telnet. It is widely used by network administrators to control Web and other kinds of servers remotely. SSH is actually a suite of three utilities: slogin, ssh, and scp, which are secure versions of the earlier UNIX utilities, rlogin, rsh, and rcp. SCP will be covered later in the chapter. SSH commands are encrypted and secure in several ways. Note that UNIX commands must be in lowercase.

Both ends of the client/server connection are authenticated using a digital certificate, and passwords are protected with encryption. SSH uses RSA public key cryptography for both connection and authentication. Encryption algorithms include Blowfish, DES, and IDEA. IDEA is the default.

EXAM WARNING

Telnet uses port 21 and SSH uses port 22. This is very easy to remember as they are in numerical order. Make sure that you memorize these port assignments for the Network+ exam.

ICMP

ICMP, which stands for the Internet Control Message Protocol, is known as a *maintenance* protocol. It lets two computers on an IP network share IP status and error information. When working on a network, it's important to be able to test the functionality of that network. How would you know if data could be transmitted without knowing you have a complete path from the source to the destination? That being said, how could you test that path? ICMP provides you with two tools that can be used to test a path; ping and tracert. ICMP packets will be able to help send information about errors, control, and other informational messages.

EXAM WARNING

Computers and routers using IP can report errors, and exchange control and status information via ICMP. Ping and traceroute (tracert) exclusively use the ICMP protocol.

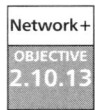

ARP/RARP DataLink Layer

ARP and RARP were covered earlier in this chapter. Remember that ARP works to resolve physical addressing to logical addressing, which we know as MAC addresses and IP addresses.

ARP translates the logical IP addresses to physical MAC addresses. ARP discovers this information by way of broadcasts, and keeps a table of IP-to-MAC entries. This table is referred to as the ARP cache.

RARP is a similar protocol that does just the opposite: instead of starting with an IP address and finding the matching MAC address, it uses the MAC address to find the IP address. Exercise 6.5 covers the operation of ARP, especially viewing the ARP cache and changing it if needed. .

EXERCISE 6.5

ADDING AN ARP ENTRY ON A WINDOWS XP PROFESSIONAL WORKSTATION

This exercise is designed to reinforce what we've learned about ARP. In this exercise we will look at the ARP cache utilized on a Windows XP Professional workstation. In this exercise we will alter the ARP cache to add a static entry.

1. To use the ARP program supplied with Windows XP, access the command prompt by clicking **Start | Programs | Run**. Type **cmd** and press **Enter**.

2. Type **arp –a** and press **Enter**. The ARP cache on your local system will be displayed.

```
C:\>arp -a


Interface: 10.8.53.218 —- 0x4
  Internet Address      Physical Address      Type
  10.8.53.217           00-06-25-a3-69-a8     dynamic


  C:\>
```

4. To add an entry, you can use the **arp –s** command. You can add a static ARP assignment by typing the following at the command prompt:

```
C:\>arp -s 157.55.85.212    00-aa-00-62-c6-09
```

5. If you now look at your ARP cache again, you will see the assignment in the ARP cache, and its Type will be listed as *static*.

TEST DAY TIP

This chapter covers a lot of information on the ARP process. You must understand how ARP operates. Go through the exercise of viewing an ARP cache and
make sure you know how to verify whether something is dynamically or statically located in your table.

NTP   *Application Layer*

For the Network+ exam, you need to be aware of NTP, its use and what protocol it uses
to communicate with. Network Time Protocol provides a reliable way of transmitting and
receiving the time over TCP/IP networks. NTP, defined in IETF RFC 1305, is useful for
synchronizing the internal clock of the computers to a common time source. This can be
very important in directory-based systems such as Novell NetWare's Novell Directory
Services (also knows as NDS or eDirectory) and Microsoft Windows Active Directory.
Also, having a reliable time source ensures that your security logs (or logs in general) have
the correct time stamps on them to help aid in the troubleshooting effort. Nothing works
better than knowing when something happened. If you don't have accuracy, and happen to
have the wrong time on a device and then check its logs, it would be impossible to find
out when something happened that you may want to trace or analyze.

EXAM WARNING

NTP uses port 123 for communications.

NNTP

NNTP is used for managing messages posted to private and public newsgroups. NNTP
servers provide for storage of newsgroup posts, which can be downloaded by client software called a newsreader.

Windows 2000 Server and Windows Server 2003 both include an NNTP server
with IIS. Outlook Express version 5 and later, which is part of the Internet Explorer
software included with just about any current version of Windows, provides both an e-
mail client and a newsreader.

EXAM WARNING

NNTP uses port 119 for communications.

SCP

Secure Copy Protocol is used to securely copy files between hosts on a network. It uses SSH for authentication and data transfer, thus gaining the features of strong authentication and secure encrypted communications. SCP is the main replacement on UNIX systems for the ftp and rcp commands. You could say SCP as an encrypted version of rcp.

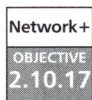

LDAP *SessionLayer*

LDAP is series of IETF Internet-standard specifications for a lightweight version of the X.500 global directory service. DAP, the original form of the protocol, and had too much overhead, so LDAP was developed and since then has been used in a great many applications, including NDS (eDirectory) and Active Directory, as well as the Netscape Directory and many others. A typical LDAP server is a simple network-accessible database where an organization stores information about its authorized users and what privileges each user has.

LDAP is a very important protocol to learn about since you will definitely need to use it in the future if you are not using it already. The current series of specifications is known as LDAP version 2 and is covered in RFC 1777, RFC 1778, and RFC 1779. Both X.500 and LDAP define the interactions between directory components to provide a global directory service. LDAP is used by several PKI (public key infrastructure) implementations, often with X.501 directories and X.509 certificates. For the Network+ exam, you need to know the fundamentals of LDAP, as well the port it uses (port 389).

> ### EXAM WARNING
>
> LDAP uses port 389 for communications.

IGMP *NetworkLayer*

IGMP is defined in RFC 1112 as the standard for IP multicasting. IGMP will establish host memberships in particular multicast groups on a single network.

IGMP was primarily designed for hosts on multi-access networks to inform locally attached routers of their group membership information; groups are created to ease the burden of broadcast transmission on a TCP/IP network. Hosts inform routers by multicasting IGMP host membership reports. Once multicast routers receive these reports, they can exchange group membership information with other multicast routers. This reporting system allows distribution trees to be formed to deliver multicast datagrams.

IGMP and multicasting were covered in greater detail earlier in the chapter, so if you missed the section, you may want to go back and ensure that you read it for the exam.

LPR

LPR was used primarily in UNIX environments and is a printer protocol, but has grown in use over the years to multiplatform environments. LPR uses TCP/IP to establish a connection between a printer and a workstation requesting its use.

LPR is nothing more than a UNIX print command. The way the protocol works is by copying (or linking) the files you want to print to a separate spool area. From this area a daemon copies the spooled file to an assigned printer.

More Services, Protocols, and Applications

In this section we will cover more network protocol services, protocols and applications that you will need to know for the Network+ exam.

DNS

When the Internet was in its infancy, hostnames were resolved to IP addresses via a plain text file named hosts.txt. This file was located at the Stanford Research Institute's Network Information Center (SRI-NIC). Whenever a machine was added to the network, or an existing machine's IP address was changed, the hosts.txt file had to be edited. This hosts.txt file then had to be downloaded from SRI-NIC so that all machines on the network would have an accurate list of hostnames and IP addresses for host name resolution.

As mentioned earlier in the chapter, an alternative to the hosts file is to use a DNS server. DNS servers store FQDN-to-IP address translations. A computer runs the DNS client called the *DNS resolver*, which is configured with the IP address of the DNS server. When an IP address is needed, the DNS resolver requests the information from the DNS server by first translating the FQDN provided into a *DNS name query*. When the IP address is returned from the DNS server, the DNS resolver provides that information to the requesting application. DNS is a distributed system, so not all mappings reside on all DNS servers. Each DNS server is responsible for a particular segment of the names and it either returns the requested information or forwards it to the appropriate DNS server. We'll learn more about DNS later in this book. In the Windows implementation of TCP/IP, both a hosts file and DNS are used to resolve hostnames. The hosts file is checked first, and if the desired mapping is not present, DNS will be queried.

> **NOTE**
>
> Microsoft operating systems can still use a hosts file for resolution of FQDNs; however, this hosts file does not use the .txt (or any) extension. A common mistake in creating a hosts file in Notepad or other text editors is that the application saves it with the .txt extension, which means it will not work. Make sure that you understand the hosts file.

A Hierarchical Naming System

As discussed earlier in the chapter, we could use a hosts file for name resolution, but in the past, this has presented several problems. First, the hosts file uses a flat namespace like that seen in NetBIOS. The flat namespace requires each computer to have a different name. Second, as more and more machines joined the network, traffic at SRI-NIC became a significant bottleneck to network communications. Third, the size of the hosts.txt file got increasingly large, which led to long download times, which reduced performance for lookups. To solve these problems, Paul Makapetris in 1987 developed and proposed the Domain Naming System. DNS was designed to be a hierarchical naming system, and responsibility for the DNS database was distributed. In a distributed database, hostname lookup times are significantly reduced, and there is fault tolerance for the DNS, as no single location is responsible for maintaining the contents or the integrity of the DNS database.

Domain Levels

At the top of the DNS hierarchy is the root domain. The root domain is sometimes represented as a period surrounded by quotation marks ("."), or as a space surrounded by quotation marks. If you have read many books on TCP/IP, you've probably seen it represented both ways. Which one is correct? We will come back to that question when we finishing discussing FQDNs.

Top-Level Domains

Just underneath the root domain are the top-level domains. The top-level domains consist of a two- or three-letter designation, such as .com, .net, .org (called generic domains), or .au, .us, .de (country codes). The top-level domains are intended to subdivide the DNS namespace into logical groups based on the nature of the organization participating in a specific top-level domain space hierarchy. For example, organizations participating in the .com hierarchy were originally meant to be commercial, profit-making entities. Groups in the .org hierarchy were expected to be nonprofit entities. The .net domain was intended for network providers such as ISPs (Internet Service Providers). The two-letter designations are country codes, although some countries use a two-letter designation to denote the type of organization within a specific country code hierarchy; for example, www.bbs.co.uk.

Second-Level Domains

The second-level domains lie below the top-level domains. These second-level domains typically represent the organizations that own the domain names. A second-level domain name can be obtained from a *domain registrar*, such as Network Solutions, Inc. (NSI). NSI was the only registrar for second-level domains in the United States until 1999. There are other domain registrars participating in second-level domain registrations now, but

NSI continues to be the primary purveyor. New domain name registrars are being approved on a continuous basis.

For an up-to-date listing of authorized registrars, see ICANN's website at **www.icann.org/registrars/accredited–list.html**. The second-level domain name places your organization in a unique position in the DNS hierarchy. Examples of second-level domains are microsoft.com, syngress.com, and rsnetworks.net.

Subdomains

The root domain, top-level domains, and second-level domains are the only centralized aspects of the Domain Naming System. After you have registered your second-level domain name with a domain registrar, you are free to create as many subdomains as you like. For example, Microsoft might want to create subdomains for their marketing and development divisions, so they could create subdomains named marketing.microsoft.com and dev.microsoft.com.

The Domain Tree

Each domain in the DNS hierarchy represents a branch in the "tree." Each branch terminates with a leaf object (an endpoint object that cannot contain other objects), which is a hostname for a machine that belongs to a specific domain. The Microsoft subdomain dev.microsoft.com might have machines with the hostnames like www and vbs. Those hostnames, then, are leaf objects, or termination points in the DNS tree.

Each leaf object (or host) can be identified by its location in the tree. Remember that only the root, top-level, and second-level domains are centrally managed. It is the responsibility of the DNS administrator to maintain the DNS database of hostnames and IP addresses for all objects within the subdomain, and any subdomains contained within his/her subdomain. In this example, the DNS administrator responsible for the dev.microsoft.com subdomain and must manage the resources represented by hosts www and vbs, which includes their IP address entries in the DNS database.

Fully Qualified Domain Names

In order to identify a host participating in the DNS, you must include more than just the hostname. Each computer, or host, belongs to a specific domain, and it is identified by its domain membership. The combination of a hostname and its domain name is referred to as its fully qualified domain name. All hosts participating in the DNS are identifiable via their FQDNs.

The FQDN is comparable to a full path location for a file on a machine's hard drive. For example, if you have a file called cache.dns located in the dns subdirectory, which is in the system32 subdirectory, which is in the WINNT subdirectory, which is contained on the C: drive, the full path to the cache.dns file would be:

```
C:\WINNT\system32\dns\cache.dns
```

The location moves from general to specific as you move from left to right in this file path example. When specifying an FQDN, however, the path moves from specific to general. For example, in the FQDN www.dev.microsoft.com, the leftmost entry (www) is the hostname of the machine. The *dev* domain is a subdomain of the larger Microsoft domain, which in turn is a subdomain of the larger *com* domain.

Each level in the FQDN is separated by a dot, or period. The information between the dots is referred to as a *label*, and each individual label can contain up to 63 octets or characters. The entire FQDN is limited to 255 octets. You should be aware that although labels and FQDNs are allowed a defined number of octets, many applications will not accept labels of this length. Domain registrars have traditionally limited domain names to 22 characters.

In order to be fully qualified, the name must be terminated with a dot. This is an error that many network administrators fail to appreciate when they run into problems. This is typically not a problem when users enter FQDNs into a WinSock application such as a Web browser or e-mail client, but can be a major issue when using DNS diagnostic tools such as nslookup. Nslookup is a tool that you can use to query a DNS server using the Windows command prompt. Chapter 11, "Network Troubleshooting Tools," covers the usage of Nslookup.

EXAM WARNING

DNS uses port 53 to communicate.

NAT

NAT is designed for IP address simplification and conservation. NAT is a feature of most systems, including Microsoft servers used as routers and configured with RRAS, and Cisco devices that use IOS (Internetwork Operating System—the OS that Cisco devices use). NAT permits an organization's IP address structure to appear differently to outside networks than the actual address space it is using. This allows organizations to connect to the Internet without having to use globally unique addressing schemes internally. It enables private IP networks that use non-registered RFC1918 IP addresses to connect to the Internet.

Generally, NAT is used when a company's internal addresses are not globally unique and thus cannot be routed on the Internet (for instance, using RFC 1918 private addresses), or because two separate networks that need to communicate are using an overlapping IP address space.

In most cases, NAT allows hosts on a private network (inside network) to transparently communicate with destination hosts (outside network) in a global or public network.

This is achieved by modifying the source address portion of an IP packet as it traverses the NAT device. The NAT device tracks each translation (conversation) between the source host (inside network) and the destination host (outside network), and vice versa.

NAT converts IP addresses from the private address space to the public address space. When a device performing NAT receives a packet from the internal network, it changes the source IP address, recalculates the appropriate checksums, and sends it to the Internet. This obscures the true source address.

NAT is a method by which IP addresses are mapped from one address realm to another. This type of translation provides transparent routing from host to host. There are many variations of address translation that assist in translating different applications. Figure 6.15 shows a common use of NAT in an enterprise environment. In this example, someone at home wants to surf rsnetworks.net. When they do, the request goes to the server that holds that information by DNS over the Internet. Once the request packets are sent to the Web server's network, the router that sits on the perimeter performs network address translation on the packets. In this example, the packets are sent to a server inside the network with an IP address of 192.168.1.10. When the data that was requested is sent back, the router maintains the information needed to return the packets in its internal tables. Some router vendors call these *translation tables*. Cisco calls them *xlate* on their PIX firewalls.

Figure 6.15 Basic NAT Transaction

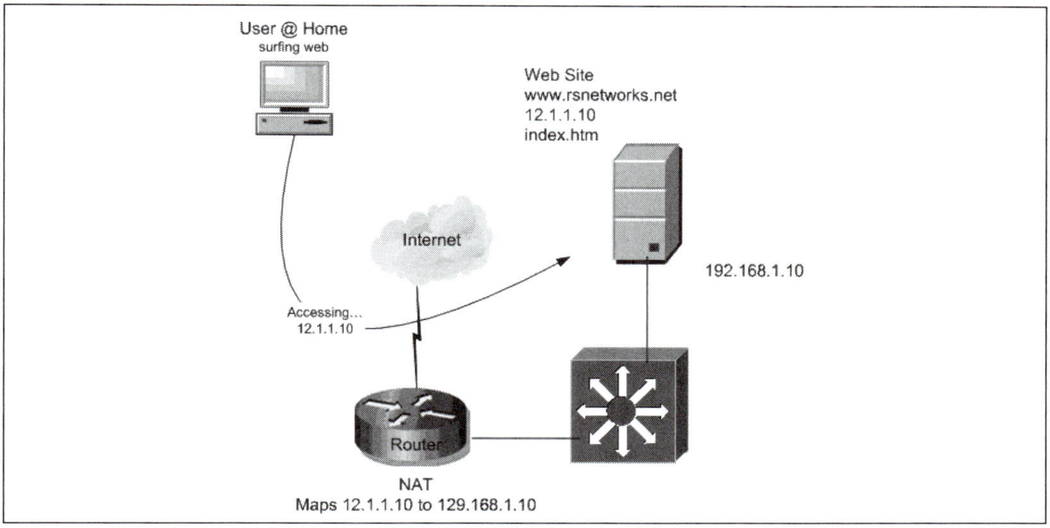

Another commonly used technology, although not on the listed objectives, but equally important, is PAT. PAT extends the concept of translation one step further by also translating transport identifiers like TCP and UDP port numbers and ICMP query identifiers. This allows the transport identifiers of a number of private hosts to be multiplexed into the transport identifiers of a single global IP address. PAT allows numerous hosts from the internal network to share a single external network IP address. The advantage of this type of translation is that only one global IP address is needed, whereas with NAT, each internal host must translate to a unique external IP address. PAT can be particularly useful for locations or users connected via cable modem, Digital Subscriber Line (DSL), or other similar arrangement wherein they are provided a single global, public IP address. In such scenarios, all inside addresses are translated to this single address.

> ## EXAM WARNING
>
> NAT hides the local internal IP addresses from external Internet users, which provides a layer of security to your network.

Internet Connection Sharing

Much like the example just used with the rsnetworks.net Web server, Internet Connection Sharing (ICS) also performs translation from one NIC to another NIC. ICS is Microsoft's answer to NAT. Apply the same concepts of NAT to ICS and you are already starting to understand what ICS does. When you run a home PC, you can share a small network inside of your home out to the Internet through a computer currently connected to the Internet ifICS is configured correctly.

With ICS there is a small amount of configuration necessary. In order to permit traffic to flow from within your network out to the Internet, you must add the ICS service and its operational settings. You may do so by entering the **Services Definition** on the **Services** tab of the ICS or Internet Connection Firewall (ICF) host computer.

The operational settings provide the parameters that are required in order for ICF to allow traffic to travel from the Internet to the network and ICS to forward traffic. If all is configured correctly, you will be able to access the Internet from within your small network. The information needed to add a service definition includes:

- The description of the service
- The name or IP address of the computer hosting the service
- The TCP or UDP port number of the service

Services like FTP, e-mail, Telnet, and Web Services are examples of built-in services that come predefined in ICF and ICS. ICS is intended for use in a network where the ICS host computer directs network communication between computers and the Internet and vice versa.

WINS

The Windows 2000 Windows Internet Name Service is a service designed solely to service NetBIOS requests for Windows-based systems. The Windows Server 2003 WINS server is fully RFC-compliant and includes many extra features that optimize its use on Windows networks. In this section, we'll examine the types of exchanges that take place between the WINS client and WINS server.

When a WINS client starts up, it will register its NetBIOS name with a configured WINS server via a *NetBIOS name registration request*. If the WINS client's name does not already exist in the WINS server's database, the WINS server will send a *positive NetBIOS name registration response* to the WINS client.

If the WINS client's name is already in the WINS database, the WINS server returns a WACK (wait for acknowledgement) message to the WINS client. The WINS server then issues a challenge (*NetBIOS node adapter status* message) to the IP address associated with that NetBIOS name in its database. If there is no response from the registered owner of the NetBIOS name, the WINS server will return a positive NetBIOS name registration response to the WINS client, and its name and IP address will be recorded in the WINS database. If the owner does respond to the challenge, the WINS client that is attempting to register the name will receive a *negative NetBIOS name registration response* and will not be able to initialize its TCP/IP stack. If the computer that is registering its name and the IP address is the same as the one in the WINS database, it will be treated as a refresh of the WINS database entry, and the renewal date will be updated for the entry.

A WINS database entry must be renewed periodically. The amount of time that can pass before the WINS client must renew its name is the *renewal Interval*, which is configured at the WINS server. The default for the Windows 2000 WINS server is 6 days, or 144 hours (this is correct. Six days is 144 hours. If you have read some of the Windows NT 4.0 books on the market, you might have noticed that many of them state the Windows NT 4.0 WINS server's default renewal interval was "4 days, or 144 hours." While you might have figured this was just "WINS new math," it was in fact an error in the Windows NT WINS server help file that was then perpetuated by the authors of several popular books).

Head of the Class...

The lmhosts File

The lmhosts file is a static, manually updated text file that contains NetBIOS name and IP address mappings for NetBIOS hosts. In this respect, the lmhosts file is similar to the hosts file used for host name resolution for WinSock programs (which we discussed in a previous section). However, the lmhosts file has added functionality because Microsoft has added *tags* that can be placed in an lmhosts file to provide extra information other than just NetBIOS names and IP addresses. The lmhosts file is a very simple file to create, and resolves NetBIOS names by reading the file from top to bottom. This means the most frequently accessed computers should be listed on top, while less frequently accessed files should be placed toward the bottom.

There are a number of useful tags you can place in the lmhosts file that provide added functions. For example, let's look at two of the tags, #PRE and #DOM. The #PRE tag causes its associated entry to be placed in the NetBIOS remote name cache during system startup, and it will remain there for the entirety of that machine's session. The #DOM tag indicates that the machine is a domain controller.

The lmhosts file is placed in the %systemroot%\system32\drivers\etc folder.

EXAM WARNING

You may get exam questions that ask you about WINS and a proxy server. Be very careful when you see this type of question. A WINS proxy agent is a machine configured to listen for NetBIOS name query requests and forward these to a WINS server. WINS proxy agents are useful when you have non-WINS-enabled machines on a segment that need NetBIOS name resolution services. A proxy server like ISA (Internet Security and Acceleration) from Microsoft, is used to act as a *proxy* between internal Web clients and the websites that they surf. The proxy server acts as the go-between and protects the internal clients, as well as caching the pages for them for quicker access and retrieval. Although you may not get a question on a WINS proxy agent, it may be used as a distracter, so stay alert when taking the test.

You do not need to be a master of WINS to pass the Network+ exam, but you do need to understand what it is and how to define it as well as understand its basic functionality. As you progress into networking with NetBIOS, WINS, and Samba (which is the Linux-and UNIX-based NetBIOS name service) you will need to master this technology.

SNMP

The Simple Network Management Protocol provides a way to gather statistical information. An SNMP management system makes requests of an SNMP agent, and the information is stored in a Management Information Base (MIB). The MIB is a database that holds information about a networked computer (for example, how much hard disk space is available or a temperature reading from a sensor). SNMP is a very handy management protocol.

SNMP is not a utility in and of itself. Rather, it is a protocol used to communicate status messages from devices distributed throughout the network to machines configured to receive these status messages. Machines that report their statuses run SNMP agent software, and machines that receive the status messages run SNMP management software. One way to remember how this works is to think of the agent software as the "secret agent" that gets information about a network device, and then reports the information to his "manager" at headquarters.

While the name of the protocol itself would lead you to believe that the primary function is to allow you to manage objects on the network, management in this context is more related to monitoring, rather than actually effecting any changes to the devices themselves. Administrators typically think of managing something as taking an active role in configuring or changing the behavior of a device, so don't let the name of the protocol fool you.

SNMP allows you to audit the activities of servers, workstations, routers, bridges, intelligent hubs, and just about any network-connected device that supports the installation of agent software. In order for agent software to collect information regarding a particular service, a MIB must be created. The MIB is a database and a collection of instructions about how and what information should be gathered from a system. The MIBs included with Windows 2000 allow the agent software to communicate a wide range of information.

The agent is responsible for reporting the information gathered by the MIB. However, agents rarely volunteer information spontaneously. Rather, the agent must be queried by an SNMP management system before it gives up its knowledge.

There is an exception to this: a *trap* message. A trap message is sent spontaneously by an agent to an SNMP management system. For example, we could set a trap message for indicating that the World Wide Web service is hung. We would then configure the agent to send a trap message to the IP address of our computer running the SNMP management software so that we can quickly handle this catastrophic event. Remember, in sum, SNMP is a set of protocols for managing networks. SNMP works by sending messages, called protocol data units (PDUs). SNMP-compliant devices, called agents, store data about themselves in MIBs and return this data to the SNMP requesters. Management systems can be deployed to help you manage your network or system use SNMP.

NOTE

SNMP uses ports 161 and 162 for communication. SNMP messages themselves are sent to UDP port 161 for typical GET and SET messages, and UDP port 162 for trap messages.

Network File System

Network File System (NFS) is a distributed file system protocol suite developed and licensed by Sun Microsystems that allows different makes of computers running different operating systems to share files and disk storage.

In actuality, NFS is simply one protocol in the suite. NFS protocols include NFS, RPC (remote procedure call), XDR, and others. These protocols are part of a larger architecture that Sun refers to as ONC (Open Network Computing). The original version of RPC was defined in RFC 1050. Version 2 of RPC is defined in RFC 1057. The ONC RPC version 2 is defined in RFC 1831.

Server Message Block

SMB, short for Server Message Block, is a Microsoft-based protocol developed for file and print sharing. SMB is a message format used by DOS and Windows to share files, directories, and devices. NetBIOS is based on the SMB format, and many network products use SMB. These SMB-based networks include LAN Manager, Windows for Workgroups, and so on. There are also a number of products that use SMB to enable file sharing among different operating system platforms.

A product called Samba enables UNIX and Windows machines to share directories and files. Samba is an open source implementation of the SMB file sharing protocol that provides file and print services to SMB/CIFS clients. CIFS stands for the Common Internet File System, the advanced version of SMB.

Samba allows a non-Windows server to communicate with the same networking protocol as the Windows products. Samba was originally developed for UNIX, but can now run on Linux, FreeBSD, and other UNIX variants. It is freely available under the GNU General Public License (GPL).

TEST DAY TIP

You may not be asked questions about protocols like NFS or SMB such as which RFC is associated with NFS, or what the packet decode of a captured SMB transmission is. You could see questions such as, "You want to apply NAS (Network Attached Storage) to your network and you want to ensure that you can allow this information to be accessible on a Windows and UNIX network. What protocols could you use to ensure that the NAS is accessible?"

Zero Configuration

Zero configuration (Zeroconf) IP networking is a method of networking devices via an Ethernet cable without requiring configuration and administration. Zeroconf is able to allocate addresses without a DHCP server, translate between domain names and IP addresses without a DNS server, and find services, such as a printer, without a directory service. This is meant to be used in small networks.

Zeroconf has one goal in mind, and that is to enable networking in the absence of configuration and administration. As crazy as this may sound, Zeroconf is destined to make this a reality.

Zero configuration networking is required for environments where administration is impractical or impossible, such as in the home or small office, embedded systems plugged together, as in an automobile, or to allow impromptu networks built on-the-fly as needed. Because networking can be somewhat complicated, having systems that configure themselves can seem ideal.

EXAM WARNING

Do not confuse APIPA with Zeroconf, which is a different type of service with a similar concept.

AFP

AppleTalk File Protocol sits at the OSI Presentation and Application Layers and allows files and directories to be shared over a network. AFP relies on ASP, ATP, and AEP. AppleTalk was covered in detail earlier in this chapter.

AFP is the client/server file sharing protocol used in an AppleTalk network. A non-Apple network can only access data from an AppleShare file server by first translating into the AFP language.

Line Printer Daemon

The Line Printer Daemon (LPD) is the UNIX standard print service daemon. Used in conjunction with LPR, the LPD software typically is stored in the printer or print server and the LPR software must be installed in the client device. The LPR client sends the print request to the IP address of the LPD printer/server, which in turn queues the file and prints it when the printer becomes available.

LPD listens on TCP port 515. The service will listen for print service requests. Once received, the request will be serviced.

Summary of Exam Objectives

Understanding TCP/IP from the ground up is required to effectively manage a network whether local (LAN) or wide (WAN). TCP/IP is a suite of protocols originally developed by the Department of Defense in a project called the Advanced Research Projects Agency (DARPA). The first wide area network implemented using these protocols was called the Advanced Research Projects Agency Network (ARPANET). It was during this time that TCP/IP was designed and developed as a standardized way for computers to communicate across a network.

From the DARPA experiment came the understanding that networking would become increasingly common—and increasingly complex. The OSI model was developed, based on the DARPA model, and approved by Open Systems Interconnection (OSI) subcommittee of the International Organization for Standardization (ISO). The OSI model defined seven layers for standard, reliable network communications: Physical, Data Link, Network, Transport, Session, Presentation, and Application. The acronym commonly used to remember this is (in reverse order): **A**ll **P**eople **S**eem **T**o **N**eed **D**ata **P**rocessing. The OSI model was covered in depth in Chapter 5. It will, however, continue to be used through the rest of the text. As you can see, the use of it becomes very important when discussing network protocols, the heart of this chapter's content. For the Network+ exam, make certain that you memorize the OSI model and the placement of TCP/IP protocols within it.

The TCP/IP protocol suite provides the functionality specified in the OSI model using the four related layers of the DoD model: Network Interface, Internet, Host-to-Host, and Application. This is because it's hard to map TCP/IP protocols to the OSI model, also discussed in the previous chapter. The Network Interface maps to the Physical and Data Link layers; the Internet Layer maps to the OSI's Network Layer. The Host-to-Host Layer maps to the Transport Layer and DoD's Application Layer maps to the Session, Presentation, and Application Layers of the OSI model. Some of the more commonly known Application layer protocols are FTP, HTTP, POP3, WINS, DNS, and DHCP. Within these layers are protocols that are covered in this chapter, all of which you must remember for the exam.

At the Internet Layer is the Internet protocol used for addressing data for delivery across a network. Understanding IP addressing is a fundamental skill needed both on the job and for this exam. IP addresses are 32-bit addresses represented in dotted decimal format ($w.x.y.z$). The 32 bits contain both a network and host ID. To understand IP addressing, you must first understand how to convert the dotted decimal numbers into binary and back to decimal. In order to send data to the correct location, the IP address in the packet is compared, using bitwise ANDing, to the subnet mask. If the result is the local network address, the packet stays on the local network. If ANDing indicates that the network address is external to the local network, the packet is sent to the defined default gateway for forwarding.

Network addresses were originally designed in a class-based system. Class A networks use the first octet (w) and have an address range of $1.x.y.z$ to $126.x.y.z$. Class B networks use the first two octets for the network ID and have an address range of $128.0.y.z$ to $191.255.y.z$. Class C networks use the first three octets for the network ID and have an address range of $192.0.0.z$ to $223.255.255.z$. Each class of network, when undivided, uses a default subnet mask, which identifies which bits of the IP address represent the network ID. The default subnet masks are: Class A: 255.0.0.0; Class B: 255.255.0.0; Class C: 255.255.255.0.

Classful networks can be subdivided for greater efficiency by reducing the number of hosts per segment, thus reducing network traffic. Subnetting requires the subdividing of the class-based network IDs using custom subnet masks. These are developed by using bits from the host address space. The number of subnets that can be created from the network ID depends on the number of bits taken from the host address space. There is an inverse relationship between the number of subnets and the number of hosts per subnet. Typically, organizations choose to have a maximum of 256 devices per subnet for the most efficient use of network bandwidth.

Packets destined for networks that are not local are forwarded using gateways or routers. IP routing involves resolving the hostname or NetBIOS name to an IP address and resolving the IP address to a MAC address. NetBIOS name resolution uses four different node types to resolve names to IP addresses: broadcast (B-node), peer-to-peer (P-node), mixed (M-node), and hybrid (H-node). Names can also be resolved by using a hosts file or through the Domain Name Service (DNS). Names must be resolved to IP addresses. The Address Resolution Protocol (ARP) is used to resolve the IP address to the Media Access Control (MAC) address that is unique to each Network Interface Card (NIC) manufactured.

Routing on a network can be static or dynamic, depending on whether or not dynamic routing protocols are installed. Many computers designed as routers include this function, but a Windows Server 2003 computer can be set up as a router by installing two NICs, enabling the Routing and Remote Access Service (RRAS) via the registry and installing and configuring both the Routing Information Protocol (RIP) and Open Shortest Path First (OSPF) dynamic routing protocols. Four commonly used routing utilities are route, ping, tracert, and pathping. Each can be run from the command line in Windows. Protocols such as APIPA and DHCP help to get systems logically addressed dynamically. Protocols such as DNS and WINS help to provide name resolution as well.

In this chapter we also covered the use of protocol ports and the importance of them. You must memorize these port assignments for the Network+ exam. You will definitely not only see them there, but also need to use them daily on the job as a Network+ certified technician.

Understanding the details of the TCP/IP protocol suite is fundamental to managing computers in today's networked environment as well as to passing the Nework+ exam.

Exam Objectives Fast Track

Differentiate Between the Network Protocols in Terms of Routing, Addressing Schemes, Interoperability and Naming Conventions

☑ IPX / SPX (Internetwork Packet Exchange / Sequence Packet Exchange) is used primarily on Novell NetWare systems. IPX is a network layer protocol used in the file server operating system and SPX is a transport layer protocol built on top of IPX and used in client/server applications.

☑ NetBEUI stands for Network Basic Input / Output System Extended User Interface. It is rarely used and is non-routable.

☑ AppleTalk / AppleTalk over IP (Internet Protocol) is a network protocol developed by Apple Computer. The most important protocol to remember when using AppleTalk is AFP, AppleTalk Filing Protocol. This is the protocol that non-Apple networks use to access data on an AppleTalk server.

☑ TCP / IP (Transmission Control Protocol / Internet Protocol) is the most commonly used protocol today, and the lifeblood and backbone of the Internet.

Identify the Components and Structure of IP Addresses and the Required Setting for Connections Across the Internet

☑ IP addresses are 32-bit addresses expressed in dotted decimal notation of four octets, *w.x.y.z.*

☑ IP addresses contain the network address space followed by the host address space.

☑ Originally, IP addresses were assigned four classes: A, B, C, and D. Class E is considered experimental and is not supported in Windows Server 2003.

☑ The growth of networking required a new solution. CIDR was implemented as a classless addressing schema.

☑ Dotted decimal notation can be converted to its binary equivalent by using weighted binary bits notated with 2^n where *n* is the number of bits.

☑ Packets are sent with a destination name or IP address included in the packet headers.

☑ Name resolution occurs using WINS or an lmhosts file (for NetBIOS names) or DNS or a hosts file (for hostnames).

☑ NetBIOS name resolution occurs using one of four types of broadcasts: broadcast node (B-node), peer-to-peer node (P-node), mixed node (M-node), and hybrid node (H-node).

☑ IP address resolution of host names occurs using hosts files or DNS.

☑ IP address to MAC address resolution occurs through ARP request and reply messages. The reverse, MAC to IP resolution, uses Reverse ARP (RARP) requests and replies.

☑ Routers can use static or dynamic routing. Static routing requires new entries to be entered manually. Dynamic routing updates route information automatically.

☑ Dynamic routing means that a protocol like Route Information Protocol (RIP) or Open Shortest Path First (OSPF) is used to handle the routing instead of you statically having to configure each routers routing information table (RIT).

Identify Classful IP Ranges and Their Subnet Masks

☑ In the following table, Class A, B, and C addresses are listed for quick recall. It's imperative for the Network+ exam to have the following information memorized.

Address Class Networks	Octets Used	First Network ID	Last Network ID	Number of
Class A	1	1.x.y.z	126.x.y.z	126
Class B	2	128.0.y.z	191.255.y.z	16,384
Class C	3	192.0.0.z	223.255.255.z	2,097,152

Remember that 127.0.0.0, is reserved for loopback addresses.

Identify the Purpose of Subnetting

☑ Default subnet masks are defined for undivided Class A, B, C, and D networks.

☑ The default subnet masks for Class A, B, C, and D are, respectively, 255.0.0.0, 255.255.0.0, 255.255.255.0, and 255.255.255.255.

☑ Custom subnet masks (also called variable length subnet masks) are used when a network is divided, by using bits from the host address space that are added to the network address space.

☑ A logical bitwise AND comparison is used to compare the bits of the IP address to the subnet mask. The result of the comparison is the network ID.

Identify the Differences Between Private and Public Network Addressing Schemes

☑ Public IP addresses are IP addresses that fall in a range other than those designated as private. Public IP addressing is addressing assigned to you for use on the public Internet. Two such organizations were created to manage the use of such addressing: Internet Assigned Numbers Authority (IANA) and the Internet Corporation for Assigned Names and Numbers (ICANN).

☑ RFC1918 conserves globally unique IP addresses by providing three blocks of addresses that are never officially allocated to any organization. Those address ranges are as follows:

Address Block	Classful Equivalent	Prefix Length	Number of Addresses
10.0.0.0– 10.255.255.255	1 Class A 256 Class B 65,536 Class C	/8	16,777,216
172.16.0.0– 172.31.255.255	16 Class B 4,096 Class C	/12	1,048,576
192.168.0.0– 192.168.255.255	1 Class B 256 Class C	/16	65,536

Identify and Differentiate Between the IP Addressing Methods: Static, Dynamic, and APIPA

☑ Static IP addressing is done manually. It is hard to manage and adjust, as you have to visit every system that has an address if you want to change the addressing scheme from one range of IP addresses to another, such as from 192.168.1.0 to 10.1.1.0.

☑ Dynamic IP addressing is done automatically. This can be done with DHCP or with APIPA.

☑ Self-assigned (APIPA [Automatic Private Internet Protocol Addressing]) is a Microsoft Windows-based service (but available to any OS) that will allow for a Windows 98, ME, 2000, 2003, or XP system to assign itself an address from a designated private block ranging from 169.254.0.1 to 169.254.255.254, with a subnet mask of 255.255.0.0.

Define the Purpose, Function and Use of the Protocols Used in the TCP / IP Suite

☑ TCP (Transmission Control Protocol), together with Internet Protocol (IP), is one of the core protocols underlying the Internet. TCP enables two computers to establish a connection and exchange information and is a connection-oriented protocol. TCP guarantees delivery of data and also guarantees that information packets will be delivered in the same order in which they were sent

☑ UDP (User Datagram Protocol) is a connectionless, unreliable, Transport Layer protocol that provides multiplexing and error detection for applications that require a low-overhead protocol for one-shot transactions that do not promise guaranteed delivery. Protocols such as TFTP rely on UDP.

☑ FTP (File Transfer Protocol) is a very common protocol used to move files from one location to another. FTP was created to transfer files and is optimized to do so. You use FTP by logging in using an account name (commonly seen as "anonymous").

☑ SFTP (Secure File Transfer Protocol) is very similar to FTP, but performs all operations over an encrypted SSH transport, which adds a layer to security to the unsecure FTP. IPv4-based protocols in the TCP/IP protocol suite in that version were commonly unsecure, hence the development of IPv6, which clears up many inherent weaknesses in its predecessor. When you use SFTP, you gain the benefits of public key encryption and compression.

☑ TFTP (Trivial File Transfer Protocol) is used to quickly send files across the network with fewer security features than FTP. It is meant to be quick and easy to use.

☑ SMTP (Simple Mail Transfer Protocol) is the de facto protocol used to send e-mail on the Internet and in many of the world's networks today.

☑ HTTP (HyperText Transfer Protocol) is used to transfer files and other data across the Internet. HTTP is the most important protocol used in the World Wide Web (WWW) today. It is also very unsecure.

☑ HTTPS (HyperText Transfer Protocol Secure) is a Web protocol developed by Netscape that encrypts and decrypts user page requests as well as the pages that are returned by the Web server. It runs over SSL (Secure Sockets Layer).

☑ POP3 (Post Office Protocol version 3) is the most common protocol used to retrieve e-mail from a mail server. If you have your e-mail on a server, with the right credentials you can set up a POP3 client on your local PC and download your e-mail for reading.

☑ IMAP4 (Internet Message Access Protocol version 4) allows a client to access and manipulate e-mail messages on a server just like POP3, but with several enhancements. IMAP includes operations for creating, deleting, and renaming mailboxes; checking for new messages; permanently removing e-mail, and so on.

☑ Telnet will allow you to open a remote session over TCP/IP networks to a remote host. Telnet performs terminal emulation. Commands you enter from your own system are executed exactly as if you were sitting in front of a remote system.

☑ SSH (Secure Shell) is a protocol that allows you to encrypt all data traveling from one system to another using different types of encryption algorithms. The server you are connecting to must be running SSH, and you must be running a SSH client on your own machine.

☑ ICMP (Internet Control Message Protocol) operates at the level of the IP protocol in the Network Layer of the OSI model. ICMP is used on IP-based networks so you can receive notification of errors. If you use a tool such as ping, you can test connectivity between two hosts. ICMP is the protocol used to provide the messaging for errors.

☑ ARP (Address Resolution Protocol) is used to map an IP address to a physical machine address or MAC address. RARP (Reverse Address Resolution Protocol) does the exact opposite; it maps a MAC address to an IP address. This could be used in diskless workstation setups.

☑ NTP (Network Time Protocol) is used to keep time standardized from one (as well as backup) sources.

☑ NNTP (Network News Transport Protocol) is a protocol defined for posting and management of news messages. NNTP is commonly used when you work within a newsgroup.

☑ SCP (Secure Copy Protocol) is a program to copy files between hosts on a network. It uses SSH for authentication and data transfer.

☑ LDAP (Lightweight Directory Access) is a set of protocols used for accessing information directories, namely X.500.

☑ IGMP (Internet Group Multicast Protocol) was primarily designed for hosts on multi-access networks to inform locally attached routers of their group membership information. Multicasting is a message sent to a group, which differs from unicast (message to one) or broadcast (message to all).

☑ LPR (Line Printer Remote) is the UNIX print command.

Define the Function of TCP / UDP Ports

☑ When you use more than one service at a time on an IP-based system, you need to differentiate between all the different things going on, such as sending a file using FTP, sending an e-mail using SMTP, and connecting to a router to change something using Telnet. You have one NIC, one IP address. How do you run all three at once? With ports, because 10.0.0.1:23 and 10.0.0.1:25 are unique due to the port difference. Make sure you memorize the most common ports for the Network+ exam.

Identify the Well-known Ports Associated with the Commonly Used Services and Protocols

☑ Port 20 maps to FTP (File Transfer Protocol).

☑ Port 21 also maps to FTP (File Transfer Protocol).

☑ Port 22 maps to SSH (Secure Shell).

☑ Port 23 maps to Telnet.

☑ Port 25 maps to SMTP (Simple Mail Transfer Protocol).

☑ Port 53 maps to DNS (Domain Name System).

☑ Port 69 maps to TFTP (Trivial File Transfer Protocol).

☑ Port 80 maps to HTTP (HyperText Transfer Protocol).

☑ Port 110 maps to POP3 (Post Office Protocol version 3).

☑ Port 119 maps to NNTP (Network News Transport Protocol).

☑ Port 123 maps to NTP (Network Time Protocol).

☑ Port 143 maps to IMAP4 (Internet Message Access Protocol version 4).

☑ Port 443 maps to HTTPS (HyperText Transfer Protocol Secure).

Identify the Purpose of Network Services and Protocols

☑ DNS (Domain Name System) is used to map names to IP addresses and vice versa. Domain Name Servers maintain central lists of domain name to IP addresses mappings.

☑ NAT (Network Address Translation) is the translation of an IP address used within one network to a different IP address known within another network.

☑ ICS (Internet Connection Sharing) is a Microsoft solution that is used to allow for more than one computer to share an Internet connection through the system configured with more than one NIC, a valid Internet connection, and ICS.

☑ WINS (Windows Internet Name Service) is the same as the NetBIOS Name Service, a term created by Microsoft. Similar to DNS (which maps hostnames to IP addresses), WINS is used for the mapping of NetBIOS names to IP addresses. WINS servers cut down on the amount of broadcast traffic on your network.

☑ SNMP (Simple Network Management Protocol) is used for gathering statistical data about just about anything from network traffic all the way to reading the temperature on a firewall's chassis. SNMP uses MIBs, which define what information is available from any manageable network device.

☑ NFS (Network File System) is a protocol suite developed and licensed by Sun Microsystems. NFS will allow for data sharing between different vendors versions of computers as well as running different operating systems.

☑ Zeroconf (Zero configuration) is a service developed to ease the network configuration of devices by setting up the most commonly setup things (such as IP address, gateway address, etcetera) for you.

☑ SMB (Server Message Block) is Microsoft's file and print sharing protocol.

☑ AFP (AppleTalk File Protocol) allows access to Apple shared servers from dissimilar systems such as Windows.

☑ LPD (Line Printer Daemon) is the standard print service daemon and is the standard when it comes to printing on UNIX systems.

Exam Objectives
Frequently Asked Questions

The following Frequently Asked Questions, answered by the authors of this book, are designed to both measure your understanding of the Exam Objectives presented in this chapter, and to assist you with real-life implementation of these concepts. You will also gain access to thousands of other FAQs at ITFAQnet.com.

Q: There are a lot of Application Layer protocols in the TCP/IP suite. Am I expected to memorize them all?

A: There is an ever-expanding set of Application Layer protocols in use today. It's important to get a firm understanding of the most common protocols and to have at least a familiarity with the less common protocols. At the very least, you should be very familiar with NetBIOS over TCP, Windows Sockets, DNS, DHCP, WINS, Telnet, SMTP, HTTP, FTP, RIP, and SNMP. For the Network+ exam, make sure you review the testable objectives and absolutely know the protocols and services as well as you can.

Q: I'm still a bit rusty with binary, dotted decimal, conversions, and so forth. Can't I use a program to do all this for me when I'm working on my corporate network?

A: Yes, there are programs available that will do all the conversions and subnet calculations you need. However, those won't be available on the exam and they may not always be available to you on the job. Keep working through the conversions and examples in this chapter until you feel confident of your understanding and application of the material.

Q: Will I be given a table of Class A, B, and C networks, subnets and subnet masks for the exam?

A: No, you will not. You'll need to memorize the definitions of Class A, B, and C networks, along with their associated default subnet masks. You will not need to calculate complex subnet masks for the Network+ exam, but you will need to understand the concepts behind it, as well as logical addressing of network protocols in general.

Q: When preparing for the Network+ exam, do I need to worry about memorizing all the assigned ports in the commonly used range? Ports are important; do I need to remember these?

A: No, you do not. For the exam you need to remember the following protocol ports: Port 20 maps to FTP (File Transfer Protocol), Port 21 also maps to FTP (File Transfer Protocol), Port 22 maps to SSH (Secure Shell), Port 23 maps to Telnet, Port 25 maps to SMTP (Simple Mail Transfer Protocol), Port 53 maps to DNS (Domain Name System), Port 69 maps to TFTP (Trivial File Transfer Protocol), Port 80 maps to HTTP (HyperText Transfer Protocol), Port 110 maps to POP3 (Post Office Protocol version 3), Port 119 maps to NNTP (Network News Transport Protocol), Port 123 maps to NTP (Network Time Protocol), Port 143 maps to IMAP4 (Internet Message Access Protocol version 4) and Port 443 maps to HTTPS (HyperText Transfer Protocol Secure). Knowing the rest is important on the job, but not for the Network+ exam. As for memorizing all of them, you should only be concerned about the ones listed here. You can always visit the IANA website to look up a forgotten port number within seconds if you have an Internet connection.

Q: Will I be expected to know about private addressing for the Network+ exam?

A: Yes, you will. You need to master the ranges listed. They are: 10.0.0.0–10.255.255.255, 172.16.0.0–172.31.255.255 and 192.168.0.0–192.168.255.255. You will be expected to know these, not only for the exam, but also on the job.

Q: Will I need to know how to configure an e-mail server for this exam? With all this talk about e-mail protocols such as SMTP, what do I need to focus my studies on?

A: No, you will not need to know how to configure anything for the exam. The exam is more straightforward asking you very simple paths to get to places in Windows that are very common. Other than that, all other questioning is pretty straightforward.

Self Test

A Quick Answer Key follows the Self Test questions. For complete questions, answers, and explanations to the Self Test questions in this chapter as well as the other chapters in this book, see the Self Test Appendix.

1. You are the network administrator assigned to building a new network within a new facility. You want to implement a protocol that identifies nodes through the use of the MAC address as part of its address scheme. You need to choose the best protocol to suit the job. Which protocol should you use?

   A. TCP/IP

   B. IPX/SPX

   C. AppleTalk

   D. NetBEUI

2. Which protocol from the options shown is non-routable by design?

   A. TCP/IP

   B. IPX/SPX

   C. AppleTalk

   D. NetBEUI

3. Your computer seems to have a problem with name resolution and you decide the problem may be in your hosts file. Your computer's IP address is 66.212.14.8. You open the hosts file and spot the likely problem. Which line from the hosts file is the most likely the cause of your name resolution problem?

   A. 66.214.41.1 router1

   B. 127.0.0.1 localhost

   C. 191.87.221.2 server.company.com pisces

   D. 66.212.14.8 localhost

4. You've just accepted a job at a small company as the IT Manager. The company network is not yet connected to the Internet and you've been asked to make this your top priority. You examine the IP addresses on several computers and find these addresses in use: 192.168.0.4, 192.168.0.19, and 192.168.0.11. What is the next step you would have to take to connect your network to the Internet?

   A. Purchase, configure, and install a server to act as a firewall for Internet connectivity.

   B. Apply to the InterNIC for the appropriate IP address assignment.

   C. Install and configure the common Internet protocols including SMTP, FTP, and HTTP.

   D. Subnet the current network configuration using a custom Class C subnet mask.

5. A user contacts you to let you know his computer won't connect to the corporate network. You ask the user to go into his Network Connections properties and tell you both his IP address and subnet mask. He tells you his IP address is 180.10.254.36 and his subnet mask is 255.255.240.0. Based on this information, what is the correct binary representation of the network ID to which this user is connected?

   A. 10110100.00001001.11110000.00000000

   B. 10110100.00001010.11100000.00000000

   C. 10110110.00001010.11110000.00000000

   D. 10110100.00001010.11110000.00000000

6. Another IT staff person, Mike, tells you about a problem he's troubleshooting. He says that Jake's computer doesn't connect to the corporate network. The network uses DHCP to automatically assign IP addresses to computers, so he believes the IP address is correct and unique. He's tried pinging the localhost and that works fine, but when he pings a server that is on the same subnet as Jake's computer, he gets an error message. What is the most likely cause of this problem?

   A. Mike's NIC card has a duplicate IP address.

   B. Mike's NIC card has a duplicate MAC address.

   C. Mike's NIC card has no IP address.

   D. Mike's Ethernet cable is loose.

7. You're designing a network scheme from a Class A network address. You want to be able to have about 16,000 hosts on each subnet. Based on this, what is the maximum number of host address bits you can take to still allow up to 16,000 hosts per subnet?

   A. 8

   B. 16

   C. 24

   D. 17

8. The company for which you work has three locations in three different states. The WAN links are dedicated T1 lines, which are heavily utilized. Your current network ID is 166.12.0.0. The subnet mask is 255.255.192.0. Each location has grown significantly over the past three years and the network at each site is slow. Given this information, what is the most effective change you could make that would increase network speed for all users?

    A. Replace static routers with dynamic routers.

    B. Subdivide each of the three sites into smaller subnets.

    C. Add additional bandwidth between the sites.

    D. Reduce the number of hosts on each subnet.

9. You receive an e-mail from your supervisor, Lisa. She says that the IT director decided to go ahead with one of the subnetting plans you and Lisa developed. Lisa's e-mail simply says, "Let's use the 132.12.0.0/21 configuration we discussed. Please work up the network address ranges as soon as possible. I'll get to work on a list of the devices using static addresses we'll need to change. Thanks, Lisa." Based on Lisa's e-mail, what is the last (highest) network ID that will be created?

    A. 132.12.0.0

    B. 132.12.224.0

    C. 132.12.248.0

    D. 132.12.240.0

10. The company for which you work has three locations in three different states. You were assigned a Class B network ID from the InterNIC and your predecessor subdivided the network for better efficiency. Your current network ID is 166.12.0.0. The subnet mask is 255.255.192.0. Given this information, how many subnets did your predecessor create at the time he subdivided the network?

    A. 192

    B. 3 to 4

    C. 16,382

    D. 2

11. From the list of IP addresses shown, which IP address is a public IP address?

    A. 11.1.1.1

    B. 10.0.1.1

    C. 192.168.1.1

    D. 172.17.1.1

12. You are the technician assigned to deploy a Windows Server 2003 server and 20 Windows XP Professional clients all with default installations. Your DHCP server is currently down and all your XP clients are complaining that they cannot surf the Internet, whereas 60 minutes ago they could. You see that all your clients currently have addresses in the 169.254.xx.xx range. What is most likely the problem?

   A. There is a duplicate DHCP server on the network with a scope in the 169.254.xx.xx range.

   B. The DHCP server is currently not available so APIPA is used.

   C. You suspect that static addressing was configured without your knowledge.

   D. The 169.254.xx.xx range is automatically configured by a service called Zeroconf.

13. You are a network administrator at your company. Your company has a firewall that blocks all communication. You need to allow users in your organization to send e-mail messages as part of their daily business activities. Which protocol should you allow through the firewall so that users can send e-mail messages?

   A. FTP

   B. TFTP

   C. POP3

   D. SMTP

14. You are the network administrator at your company. Your company's network includes a Web server and an SMTP server. The network has a permanent connection to the Internet protected by a network firewall. Because you are concerned about the threat of hackers gaining access from the Internet, you decide to enforce HTTPS on your Web server, which is SSL over HTTP. After configuring HTTPS, your Web server is no longer accessible from the Internet, but can still be accessed by your internal network users. What is the likely cause of this problem?

   A. Your DNS server is down.

   B. Your Web server address has changed.

   C. Your firewall is blocking port 389.

   D. Your firewall is blocking port 443.

15. You are developing a new application for your company. This application needs to send and receive data across the corporate network. In order to make this application work correctly, you need to be sure that the data sent is accurately received on the other end and that data sent from the other side is accurately received. Which TCP/IP protocol would you implement to accomplish this?

    A. ICMP

    B. TCP/IP

    C. IP

    D. TCP

16. You work as a network administrator at your company. The company's local network includes multiple services and has a permanent connection to the Internet. You are concerned about hackers gaining access to the local network from the Internet. You decide to implement a firewall and configure it to filter ports 100 through 150. Which service might be affected by the firewall?

    A. FTP

    B. NTP

    C. HTTP

    D. SMTP

17. POP3 is identified by which TCP/IP port number?

    A. 80

    B. 110

    C. 25

    D. 21

18. Telnet is identified by which TCP/IP port number?

    A. 80

    B. 23

    C. 119

    D. 161

19. You've just upgraded from Windows 2000 Server to Windows Server 2003 Enterprise Edition. Your client computers are configured to use WINS for resolving NetBIOS names on the network. However, users are complaining that they can't reach certain resources on the network now. What is the most likely cause of the problem?

A. The Enterprise Edition of Windows Server 2003 no longer supports WINS.

B. The WINS service is not enabled.

C. The WINS service can be enabled only on the client side to allow for NetBIOS name resolution.

D. The WINS client must be enabled on client computers first.

Self Test Quick Answer Key

For complete questions, answers, and explanations to the Self Test questions in this chapter as well as the other chapters in this book, see the Self Test Appendix.

1.	**B**		11.	**A**
2.	**D**		12.	**B**
3.	**D**		13.	**D**
4.	**B**		14.	**D**
5.	**D**		15.	**D**
6.	**D**		16.	**B**
7.	**B**		17.	**B**
8.	**B**		18.	**B**
9.	**C**		19.	**B**
10.	**B**			

Chapter 7

NETWORK+

WAN and Security
Standards and Services

Domain II Objectives in this Chapter:

Introduction

In this chapter we will cover WAN (wide area network) standards and security protocols that you will see not only on the CompTIA Network+ exam, but also in a large production environment. Most of these protocols and standards are used often and you will need to know about them for the Network+ exam. For the Network+ exam, be familiar with the speeds, capacities, and the types of media used for each WAN technology covered.

By the end of this chapter, you will know the specifics of the following WAN protocols: ISDN (Integrated Services Digital Network), T1, E1, and X.25. You will also understand the basic characteristics of specific WAN technologies, such as how packet switching and circuit switching differ.

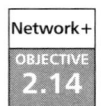

What is a WAN?

A wide area network is a computer network covering a wide geographical area, including more than one remote location and typically a *core* network where all resources are kept. A WAN is common to any company doing business with remote sites that are connected via a network topology. The remote sites build on the core site and a WAN is born. Chapter 1 discussed the basics of WANs, and in this chapter, we'll dig in a little deeper into how WANs operate and which types are the most commonly used.

WANs may be created in different configurations, with the most common being some combination of public networks and private networks. When working within the realm of a public network, you are working with networks that are publicly accessed and most likely connected to the Internet. IPSec (Internet Protocol Security) and VPN (virtual Private Network) technologies allow you to build a WAN over the Internet. When working in the realm of private networks, you are working with networks that are accessed only by designated individuals. This means that you are most likely running a private access network using Frame Relay or MPLS (Multi-Protocol Label Switching), or a similar technology, and not allowing access to anybody except the company paying for it. This means that the network users aren't at the mercy of the public Internet where you do not get a guarantee of delivery.

Test Day Tip

A WAN is a data communications network that covers a relatively broad geographic area and that often uses transmission facilities provided by common carriers, such as telephone companies. WAN technologies generally function at the lower three layers of the OSI (Open Systems Interconnect) reference model: the Physical Layer, the Data Link Layer, and the Network Layer. X.25 is a good example of a WAN technology that operates at all 3 layers, whereas Frame Relay only operates up to Layer 2.

Switching Methods

When working with WANs, the operations you do are transparent to you, so you may be unaware of the underlying technology that gets data from one location to another. There are a number of methods by which data is processed through the network to get from point A to point B. WANs operate within two types of switching methods: circuit switching and packet switching.

Although almost all WAN protocols in use today are packet switched, there are still some old networks out there using circuit-switching technologies. Technologies such as X.25 and Frame Relay are always available—their connections are constant, so they do not have to be set up every time they are used. Packet switching technologies are always available, but circuit switching is not. Circuit switching requires a separate setup for each connection session. That is the biggest difference between these two types of switching methods.

Circuit Switching

Circuit switched networks are not always available, as connections have to be initiated before transmission can take place. This means that when you use technologies such as ISDN (Integrated Services Digital Network), you will find that the call must first be initiated (to set up the circuit) and then data can traverse it. Once competed, the circuit can be taken down. If a router at a site has to send data to another router at a remote site, the circuit is initiated (brought up and online for use). The switched circuit is initiated with the circuit number of the remote network. In the case of ISDN, the setup will use a SPID (service provider ID) number, which is essentially a phone number that the router dials to initiate the circuit with the WAN switch. An example of a sample carrier network is shown in Figure 7.1. The cloud represents the carrier's telecommunications network.

Figure 7.1 Viewing a Carrier Network

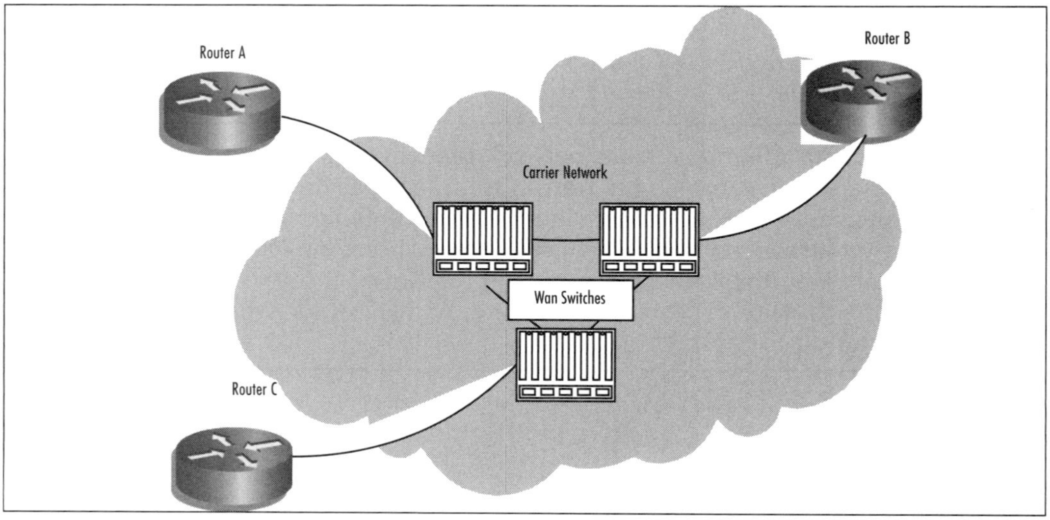

Packet Switching

Packet switching is the method of sending data from location to location on a WAN that is always available. There is no need to initiate a call to a WAN switch, as the connection is already up and running from the start. When you set the carrier's link up (let's use Frame Relay for this example), it stays up. The only time this link should drop is during scheduled outages, problems, and emergencies. Other than that, consider packet-switched networks to always be available. Some examples of packet-switching networks include Asynchronous Transfer Mode (ATM), Switched Multi-megabit Data Services (SMDS), and X.25, to name a few.

Packet-switched networks will also divide the transmitting data into packets, and each packet is sent individually from the source to the destination. All packets are given sequence numbers so that they can all be put back together again in the right order at the destination. The benefit of this is that each packet can take a different route to get to its destination. Once there, the message will be recompiled and take its original form. Packet switched networks are often *shared*. This doesn't open you up to security issues, but it does open you up to bandwidth challenges. Just be aware that packet-switched networks are not the same as point-to-point private lines that provide dedicated bandwidth to the purchaser.

EXAM WARNING

The telephone service provided by your carrier is most likely based on a circuit switching technology. Circuit switching is ideal when data must be transmitted quickly and must arrive in the same order in which it's sent. Packet switching is the opposite of circuit switching. Packet switching is more efficient and robust, and it is commonly used for data that can withstand some delays in transmission.

WAN Standards and Protocols

Now that you have reviewed the underlying concepts of the WAN and covered some of the methods in which they transmit data, let's take a good look at some of the technologies that make up the WAN. In this section we will discuss the Network+ objectives based on WAN protocols and standards such as T carriers, ISDN, and FDDI (Fiber Distributed Data Interface is discussed in Chapter 1). You must be able to understand and respond to questions about the speeds, capacity, and media for the Network+ exam.

T/E Carrier

T1 lines have been around for a long time and are still very much in use as of today. The name *T* (Terrestrial) and the number following it denotes the type of line. If it is a *T1*, then it is a dedicated media connection supporting data rates of 1.544Mbps. This speed is derived from 24 individual channels of 64Kbps (only 23 are available for data transfer and network use). If it is a *T3*, the line can support data rates of about 43 Mbps, which is created with 672 channels of 64Kbps. E1 and E3 lines are similar, but they are European-based, and J lines are used within Japanese carrier systems.

For any Network+ technician in the field, it's common to work with T1 and E1 lines very often. Users can also access just a fraction of the whole bandwidth, which would mean that you have leased lines with specific data rates. A T1 line, with its 24 individual channels, can be configured to carry voice or data traffic. Most telephone companies allow you to buy just some of these individual channels, known as fractional T1 access. T3 lines are used mainly by Internet Service Providers (ISPs) connecting to the Internet backbone, although many private companies have implemented T3 lines in some of their core networks and data centers.

As stated earlier, an E1 line is similar to the North American T1 line. E1 is the European format for digital transmission, and is similar to a T1 line, but has higher data transmission rates. E1 carries signals at 2 Mbps (32 channels at 64Kbps, with 2 channels reserved for signaling and controlling). An E3 is the European equivalent to the T3, but the T3 has a higher data rate (E3 lines carry data at a rate of about 34.368 Mbps, usually rounded up to 35 Mbps).

T1 channels are sometimes known as DS0s (digital signal Zero). In T-carrier systems, DS0 is a basic digital signaling rate of 64 Kbps, corresponding to the capacity of one voice or data channel. Twenty-four DS0s (24 x 64 Kbps) equal one DS1. A full T1 is equal to a DS1; a full T3 is equal to a DS3.

> ### EXAM WARNING
>
> Make sure you are familiar with the speeds of the T- and E-carrier links, as well as the number of channels that make up a T1. T3 lines are faster than T1 lines because they have more bandwidth. Use common sense on the exam when determining which has a higher capacity. A T3 has a higher capacity than an E3 and a T3 has a higher capacity than an E1, and so on. You may be asked to determine which line would you recommend based on the needs of the client, so be able to respond by knowing which technologies offer which benefits.

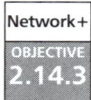

ISDN

ISDN is a WAN protocol based on an international communications standard for sending voice, video, and data over digital telephone lines or normal telephone wires. ISDN is commonly seen in the corporate offices of companies worldwide. Mostly used for WAN links from one company to another, ISDN is unique, in that it is *call initiated* and *call terminated*, so you only pay for what you use. ISDN, which uses telephone number-like entities called SPIDS to dial from peer to peer to bring up the line when traffic has to be sent across it. Once the call is deemed over due to inactivity, the call is ended and so is the billing for that usage. ISDN supports data transfer rates of 64 Kbps (64,000 bits per second) per channel, and most ISDN circuits used today are configured as two channels to provide 128Kbps of throughput.

There are two types of ISDN: basic rate interface (BRI) and primary rate interface (PRI). BRI consists of two 64-Kbps B channels and one D-channel for transmitting control information. BRI ISDN has a maximum speed of 128Kbps. PRI consists of 23 B-channels and one D-channel (in North America) or 30 B-channels and one D-channel (in Europe). The B channel is used for control.

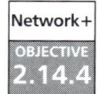

Fiber Distributed Data Interface (FDDI)

Although considered more of a LAN technology, and debated to be a LAN technology, FDDI (whether based on the LAN or WAN), is a technology that is used to provide very high speed, redundant backbone service to your network. Listed in the Network+ objectives, it's imperative that you understand the underlying technology used with FDDI. FDDI, which is based on *fiber*, is the standard for a 100 Mbps dual ring token passing technology. Also based on copper cable, Copper Distributed Data Interface (CDDI) provides high speed, redundant transmission of data. The Fiber Distributed Data Interface (FDDI) is generally used as a backbone technology due to its redundant design, and high speed. Figure 7.2 shows FDDI's overall design.

Figure 7.2 Fiber Distributed Data Interface (FDDI)

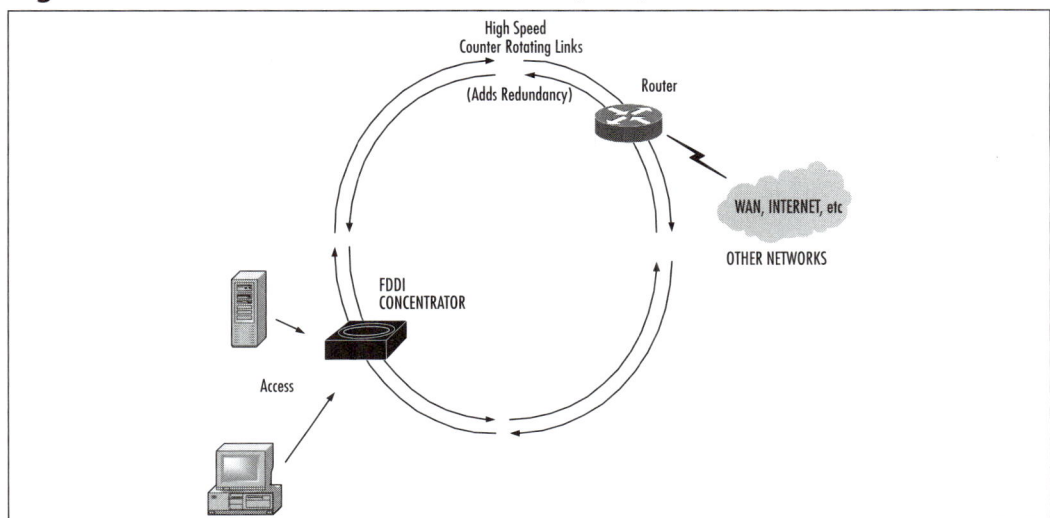

FDDI works by using a dial ring token passing architecture that allows for bidirectional traffic—traffic traveling opposite directions—which is also called counter rotation. FDDI and its primary and secondary rings are based on providing high speed service reliably. The dual rings offer redundancy in case of failure, the traffic can traverse the other link.

NOTE

XTACACS is rarely deployed in modern installations, and is not a topic of the Security+ exam.

Basic Rate Interface

The BRI ISDN service uses two B channels and one D channel (2B+D). Now that you understand what a T1 is, it should be pretty simple to understand that a channel represents a DS0. You would use two channels at 64 Kbps to total 128 Kbps, which is the rate of an BRI ISDN service. If you want to get more then that basic rate, you can move to a PRI.

The B channels are used to send and received data; the D channel is used for signaling. BRI B-channel service operates at 64 kbps and is meant to carry user data; BRI D-channel service operates at 16 kbps and is meant to carry control and signaling information, although it can support user data transmissions under certain circumstances. The D channel signaling protocol comprises Layers 1 through 3 of the OSI reference model.

BRI also provides for framing control and other overhead, bringing its total bit rate to 192 kbps.

TEST DAY TIP

Remember the following: the ISDN basic rate interface service offers two B channels and one D channel (2B+D). BRI B-channel service operates at 64 kbps and is meant to carry user data; BRI D-channel service operates at 16 kbps and can also carry user data but is normally used for management purposes such as signaling.

Primary Rate Interface

PRI offers 23 B channels and 1 D channel in North America and Japan, yielding a total bit rate of 1.544 Mbps (the PRI D channel runs at 64 kbps). In Europe, Australia, and other parts of the world, PRI provides 30 B channels plus one 64-kbps D channel and a total interface rate of 2.048 Mbps. The PRI Physical Layer specification is ITU-T I.431. This is essentially the same as getting a full T1, except you are getting the ISDN service benefits.

TEST DAY TIP

Remember that PRI service offers 23 B channels and 1 D channel in North America and Japan, yielding a total bit rate of 1.544 Mbps (the PRI D channel runs at 64 kbps).

In Europe (and other parts of the world), PRI provides 30 B channels plus one 64-kbps D channel and a total interface rate of 2.048 Mbps.

It is important to remember that ISDN is comprised of digital telephony and data-transport services offered by regional telephone carriers using preexisting telephone wiring. ISDN is also used very often as backup links since they are circuit switched. They can be brought up when needed, as in the case of an emergency where the main link to a site is down. In these cases, ISDN can be used to fix the problem. Figure 7.3 shows an example of both circuit-switched and packet-switched networks in use simultaneously.

Figure 7.3 Circuit and Packet Switching Technologies Used Together

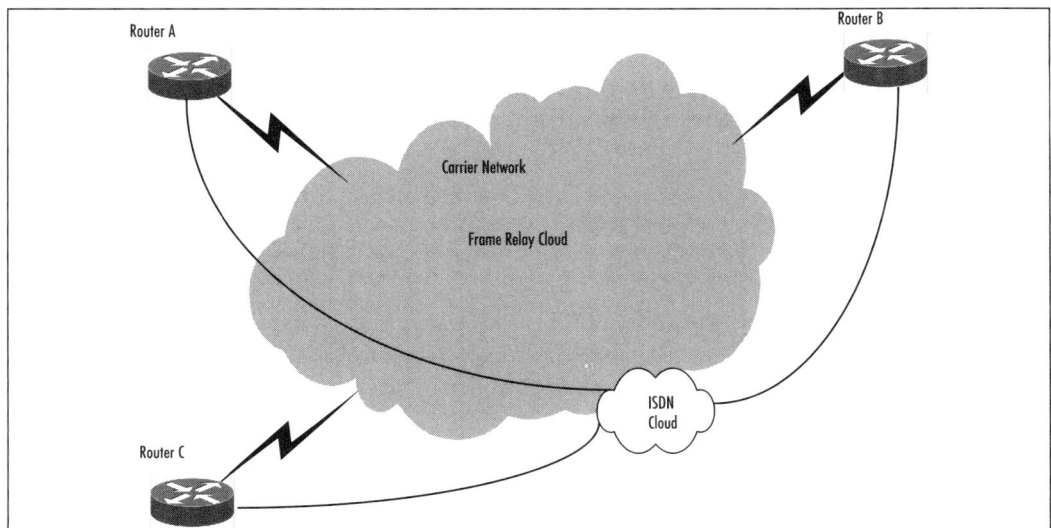

You can save money using a hybrid network as well. Since you pay for Frame Relay service to be up at all times, it becomes your primary network, and is where your data mainly travels. At the same time, each router is conveniently configured with another technology (in this example, ISDN), which provides a failsafe or backup network in case of failure of the frame circuit, providing high availability to the network users.

NOTE

If you would like to research this technology and design more thoroughly, visit the Cisco ISDN DDR page at:
www.cisco.com/warp/public/793/access_dial/britobribackup.html.

Frame Relay

Frame Relay is a packet-switching protocol for connecting devices on a WAN. Frame Relay networks in the United States support data transfer rates at T1 (1.544 Mbps) and T3 (45 Mbps) speeds and can be purchased as DS0s. This allows you flexibility, so you could have a Frame Relay link from one site to another and need 128 Kbps of available circuit bandwidth. You could then purchase 2 channels at 64 Kbps each and that would be your circuit speed for your Frame Relay link.

Frame Relay, when used in the WAN, is often used between a company's core and remote sites and sized very perfectly to whatever bandwidth is needed between the sites.

The sizing is done so that the you can take advantage of *bursting* which is when the carrier allows you to use some of the space on the rest of the whole line (up to 1.544Mbps on a T1, for example) if available.

Frame Relay has a high transmission speed, very low network delay if configured properly and sized correctly, and is fairly reliable. Because of how the system is maintained in the carrier's internal network, it's easy to make mistakes, as there is a lot to configure when you use Frame Relay. This is especially true if you are an engineer working on routers or WAN switches inside a carrier's network. Since the service is not highly reliable at all times, it's common to back up a Frame Relay network with another network such as ISDN.

Frame Relay is based on the older X.25 packet-switching technology, which was designed for transmitting analog data such as voice conversations, and is the skeleton for the MPLS solutions now being used in most enterprises today. See the following "Notes from the Underground" section for more information on MPLS.

Although it is losing ground to other technologies that operate using purely Layer 3 communications (Frame Relay primarily operates at Layer 2 of the OSI model), Frame Relay is one of the most prevalent technologies used in wide area networking today. Because carriers quickly move to update (and upgrade) their infrastructures to stay competitive, Frame Relay and ATM technologies are quickly losing ground in favor of pure IP-based Layer 3 WAN infrastructure, as this is more compatible with today's voice and video applications. Frame Relay networks are still used in many enterprises today and must still be supported. Many companies and other institutions using Frame Relay have no need at this time to upgrade their networks and will continue to use Frame Relay until they do need to migrate to another technology. In any case, much like X.25, Frame Relay is a becoming a less frequently used technology. Frame relay is no longer covered directly as an objective in the Network+ exam, but the concepts involved in the technology related to packet switching are still covered on the exam.

Security Alert!

Multi-Protocol Label Switching

MPLS is a new WAN technology that is becoming very popular because of its many benefits, including its pure Layer 3 design and the fact that it is IP–based. Furthermore, MPLS allows you to label data to have a specific priority based on the application type. The QoS (Quality of Service) mechanisms in MPLS are quite sophisticated. MPLS is able to use labels to mark packets as they come in and out of the MPLS network. When the packets enter the MPLS network fabric, it is quickly routed to its destination based on its label and what that label specifies. MPLS operates at Layer 3 of the OSI model and is an excellent choice for voice and video applications. RFC 3031 (www.faqs.org/rfcs/rfc3031.html) shows many fine details on the inner workings of the technology and how MPLS operates.

X.25

At one time, X.25 was a popular standard for packet-switching networks, but new installations are few and far between these days. Heavily used at one time, it is now slowly fading away. X.25 is a WAN protocol that operates at Layers 1, 2, and 3 of the OSI model. X.25 is very versatile, designed to operate in almost any environment. It was not as fast as other technologies, but added a very robust error-checking mechanism that virtually guaranteed error-free delivery of data. When network communications were carried on much poorer network media than we enjoy today, this was a very important protocol for WAN transmission. You can see an example of an X.25 WAN in Figure 7.4.

Figure 7.4 An X.25 Wide Area Network

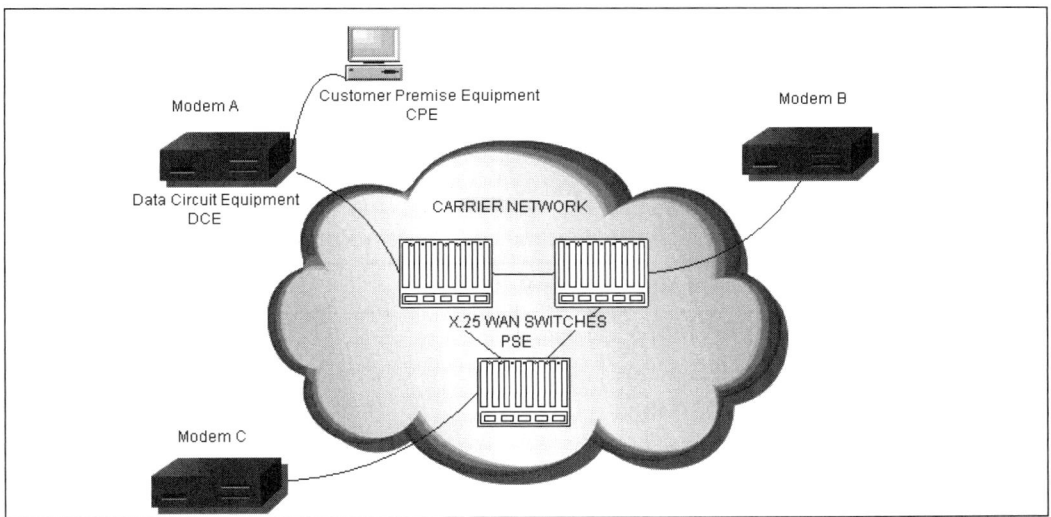

Although X.25 is a fading technology and not used too often anymore, the terminology that stems from it is, in fact, still widely in use. For instance, when viewing Figure 7.3, you will see terminology in use such as PSE (packet switching exchange), CPE, and DCE (data circuit-terminating equipment).

When looking at an X.25 network, you will see that it is primarily made up of these three groupings: data terminal equipment (DTE), DCEs, and PSEs. The PSE is no different than the networks we talked about earlier—X.25 is a packet-switched type of network. The X.25 WAN switches facilitate the transfer within the carrier's network; this is essentially the PSE.

Data terminal equipment devices are systems on your network that are not related to the WAN; DTEs are usually PCs, terminals, or other hosts found on your local network. DTE is not the responsibility of the carrier, however; DCEs usually are.

DCE devices are communications devices, such as modems and Channel Service Unit/Data Service Unit's (CSUs/DSU), that provide the interface between DTE devices and a PSE, and are normally located within the carriers' network, or can be onsite at the customer's premises, although the carrier still maintains responsibility for the device.

As you can see, the terminology used for X.25 is used interchangeably with other network technologies. CSUs/DSUs, modems, PCs, terminals, and WAN-based packet switches are all common devices found when describing most WAN technologies found in use today.

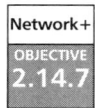

SONET

Short for Synchronous Optical Network, SONET is an older, extremely high-speed network that provides a standard interface for communication carriers to connect networks based on fiber optic cable. The SONET system uses fiber in dual counter-rotating rings. SONET is designed to handle multiple data types such as voice and video. The SONET standard defines a hierarchy of interface rates that allow data streams at different rates to be multiplexed (as shown in Table 7.1). SONET establishes OCx levels from 51.8 Mbps to 40 Gbps. OCx is short for Optical Carrier <number>. The number denotes the level of speed that comes with that level of Optical Carrier. The base rate of OC-1 is 51.84 Mbps.

Table 7.1 Optical Carrier Levels and Data Transmission Rates

Optical Carrier Level	Data Transmission Rate
OC-1	51.84 Mbps
OC-3	155.52 Mbps
OC-12	622.08 Mbps
OC-24	1.244 Gbps
OC-48	2.488 Gbps
OC-192	10 Gbps
OC-256	13.271 Gbps
OC-768	40 Gbps

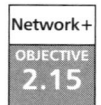

Internet Access Methods

In this section we will look at Internet access technologies such as Digital Subscriber Line (DSL), cable, POTS (plain old telephone service)/PSTN (public switched telephone network), satellites, and wireless.

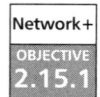

DSL

DSL is commonly seen as xDSL, where the *x* specifies what type of DSL is in use. DSL is commonly used to access the Internet from both residential and business locations to provide high-speed access to the Internet. DSL became very popular as dial-up technologies become increasingly unable to meet the demand for fast access to the Internet. Downloading MP3s, video files, and pictures has pretty much stretched the limitations (and life span) of dial-up to its very limits. DSL (and other high speed technologies) are slowly displacing dial-up service to the Internet. DSL is one of the most highly used because it can use preexisting phone lines in your home, so installation is a bit cheaper and less intrusive.

One benefit of DSL is that it is not a shared medium, unlike cable networks, which use shared access. Shared access means that when there is heavy usage of the system, less bandwidth is available to individual users. DSL is dedicated bandwidth so the only one using that bandwidth is you.

One drawback of DSL, however, is that the quality of service is dependent on the user's distance from the central office (CO). The CO is where the network endpoint is located, and is generally run by your ISP. The farther you are from the CO, the worse (slower) the service is.

There are many forms of DSL, although only a couple are commonly used. The most common forms of DSL are *ADSL* (Asymmetric DSL) and *SDSL* (Symmetric DSL)

ADSL

ADSL is the most widely deployed form of DSL technology. Most homes and small businesses currently using DSL technology use ADSL. ADSL is used to transmit digital information on preexisting phone lines. Although using the phone lines, it is still much quicker than dial-up, so don't be fooled. Also, unlike dial-up, ADSL provides an *always on* connection to the Internet. ADSL is also able to place voice and data information on the same line.

The main design feature of ADSL is that is it asymmetric. This means that ADSL is designed to provide more bandwidth in one direction than in the other. The reason for this is quite practical; think of how much data you download from the Internet (every time you access a Web page, you are downloading). For most users, the amount of information that is uploaded is minimal, so in ADSL, bandwidth is allocated where it's needed (on the downstream channel). ADSL generates downstream speeds of about 8 Mbps and upstream speeds of up to 640 Kbps.

SDSL

SDSL is typically used in larger companies, and the upstream and downstream channels are the same size; that is, the download speed and upload speed are equal. SDSL operates at about 2-2.5 Mbps.

EXAM WARNING

Other forms of DSL not covered by the exam, but worth researching are Very High Speed Digital Subscriber Line (VDSL), High speed Digital Subscriber Line (HDSL), Symmetrical High Speed Digital Line Subscriber (SHDSL), ISDN Digital Subscriber Line (IDSL) and HDSL-2 (HDSL 2nd Generation). You will have to be familiar with ADSL and SDSL not only for the exam, but also for your own use if you plan on working on DSL. These are the most commonly used types and will surely be something you will want to know about in more depth if the situation arises where you may be working with this technology. For the exam, you will need to know how to troubleshoot problems with DSL, although DSL itself may not be the problem. Look for misleading types of questions that ask you about DSL technology, although the questions are not essentially focused on that particular technology. The Network+ exam is notorious for these types of scenario questions. Be able to isolate what the cause of a problem may be, whether it be an ISDN, DSL, or WISP (Wireless ISP) connection based on the technology *and* the underlying network—as well as problems may also be occurring there that are misleading you into the wrong answer. Finally, make sure that you remember that DSL and ISDN are both digital technologies, not analog.

Broadband Cable

OBJECTIVE
2.15.2

Broadband cable access requires the use of a modem designed to operate over cable TV lines. Because the coaxial cable used by cable TV provides much greater bandwidth than telephone lines, a cable modem can be used to achieve extremely fast access to the World Wide Web (WWW). Cable modems are commonly used in small and home offices. Figure 7.5 shows a typical cable network setup.

Figure 7.5 A Typical Cable Network

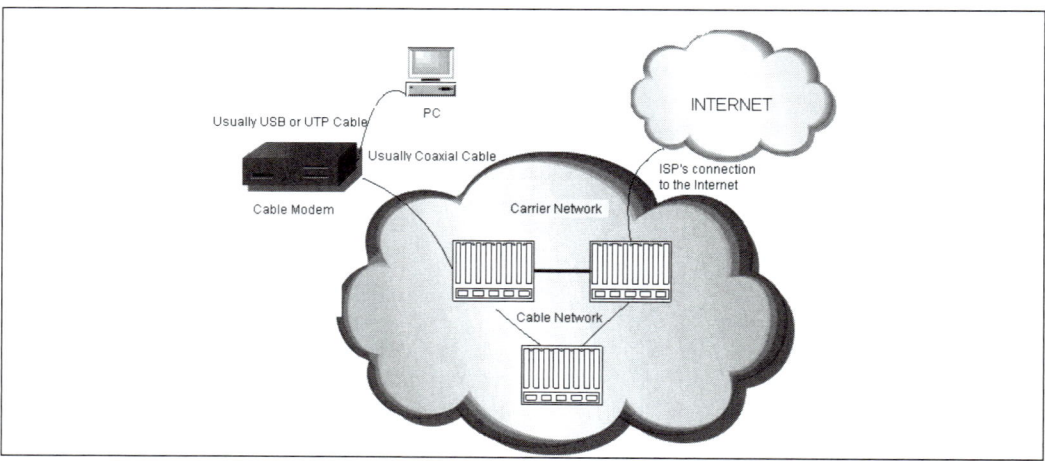

Many cable providers are working diligently to provide the best access at the lowest cost, and to be less intrusive into your home or office. Cable networks provide a shared access to the users on the network, so heavy usage can slow it down, unlike DSL, which has dedicated user access. However, DSL has generally slower upload speeds than download speeds, unlike cable networks. Since cable networks do not use preexisting phone lines in the home, cable companies will have to install a line into your home (at an additional cost) if one doesn't already exist.

Cable networks provide speeds up to about 10 Mbps, which is much faster than ADSL, which usually ranges from 64 to 256 Kbps. Even with shared access, cable is often faster at most times. As the ISP's networks get cluttered, normally scheduled upgrades to the network will usually be conducted to solve those issues as they occur, or most times, proactively before they occur.

Unfortunately, cable networks are not available everywhere yet. DSL has more availability at this time than cable networks.

Exam Warning

Some of the most common questions that you are likely to have to solve will be in the form of how to troubleshoot network devices or which one is better and faster than the other. Which one should you use and for what reasons? Refer to Chapters 11 and 12, which discuss how to troubleshoot networking devices.

POTS / PSTN

The term Public Switched Telephone Network refers to the international telephone system based on copper wires carrying analog voice data. Telephone service carried by the PSTN is often called plain old telephone service (POTS) which refers to the standard telephone service that most homes use. When referring to either, we are generally referring to dial-up technologies where you would use a dial-up modem to connect to your ISP to get to the Internet. In Figure 7.6, you can see a standard dial-up session taking place so that a user can access the Internet through the telephone carrier's network from within his home. Refer to Table 7.2 for typical dial-modem speeds.

Figure 7.6 Dialing up to the Internet

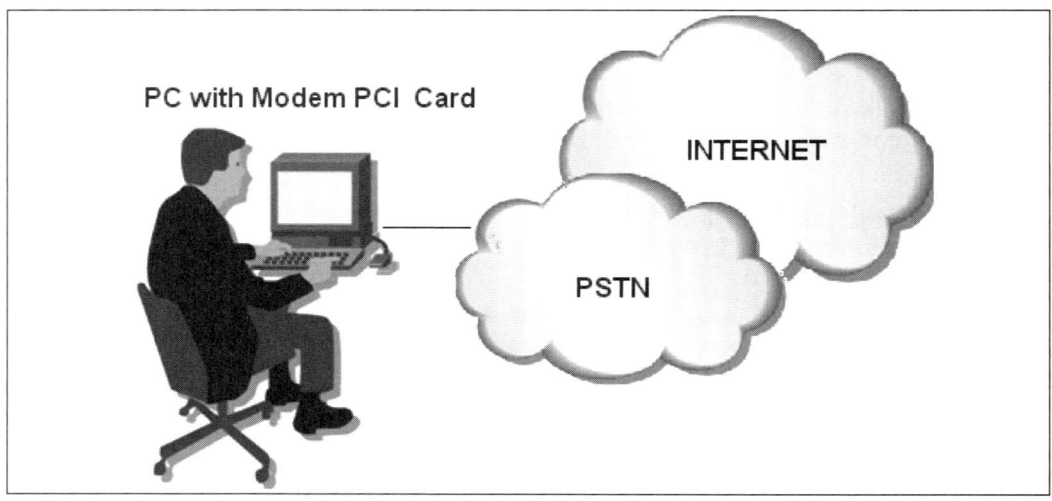

Table 7.2 Typical Dial-Up Modem Speeds

Modem	Speed
V.90	56 Kbps (receive only)
V.34	33.6 Kbps
V.32 bis	14.4 Kbps

NOTE

A few notes about Table 7.2: First, *bis* means *second edition*. Also, theoretically, an analog telephone line has a maximum speed of about 35 Kbps, so you can consider the V.90 modem to be the fastest, and since it can only receive, it's a pretty good assumption that dial-up Internet access is going to be slow (in the Kbps range) and any faster speeds can only be reached by using other methods of Internet access such as DSL or cable.

As mentioned before, the speeds for dial-up are not very fast (dialup does not provide speeds above 56 Kbps). Try not to get confused between ISDN and dial-up. Both use dialing, but dial-up is based on the telephone system and use analog lines, whereas ISDN (and DSL) are both digital. For the Network+ exam, you will need to have a clear picture of each technology and its basics, and you must be able to differentiate between them.

Wireless

Wireless ISPs (WISPs) provide Internet access anywhere that it has coverage. Many locations that have very little access to a good last mile source utilize this technology to connect to the Internet. Homes also use this very often to get Internet access. You can access the Internet from an antenna in your local PC, no matter where you are, as long as you can access an antenna and have a clear shot to the antenna you want to connect with. We will look at the most commonly used ways to access the Internet with a wireless connection later in the chapter. Wireless is also covered extensively in Chapter 4, "Wireless Technologies."

Satellite

Satellite dishes are starting to gain popularity as a way to access the Internet. Many times (as is the case with cable), your carrier or ISP will provide you with television service, or some other form of service, so you can use the satellite dish for multiple purposes. Also, the dish is less intrusive into your home because it's mounted with very little need for wires or a run to a CO. Satellite is becoming a very convenient way to connect to the Internet without having any wires run into your home.

Mobile and remote users (users who travel often and usually use a laptop) are starting to use satellite to access the Internet more frequently. These mobile users want to link their laptops to the Internet no matter where they are located. If you sign up with an ISP that uses satellite to provide Internet access, then you will be able to work through them to get the coverage plan you need.

A typical satellite-based network is shown in Figure 7.7. A satellite is used to allow a user with a laptop, PDA (personal digital assistant), or PC with wireless satellite capabilities to connect to the Internet from anywhere within the coverage area. Figure 7.7 shows the use of LEOs (low Earth orbit satellites) and MEOs (medium Earth orbit satellites). LEOs are primarily used with Internet-based satellite communications and are typically located about 1800 to 2000 miles above Earth. MEOs orbit at about 9,000 to 10,000 miles above Earth. There are also GEOs (geosynchronous Earth orbits), which are typically used for the carrier's or ISP's trunk lines. GEOs orbit at about 22,000 to 23,000 miles above Earth. All play an essential role in allowing you to access the Internet from just about anywhere in the world.

While satellite communications are often costly and slow, the ease of use and flexibility of wireless communications are always the same—slower, more costly, but flexible in use. Wireless systems and satellites are commonly used in geographical areas that are far from a CO or when extreme flexibility is needed.

Figure 7.7 A Satellite-Based Network

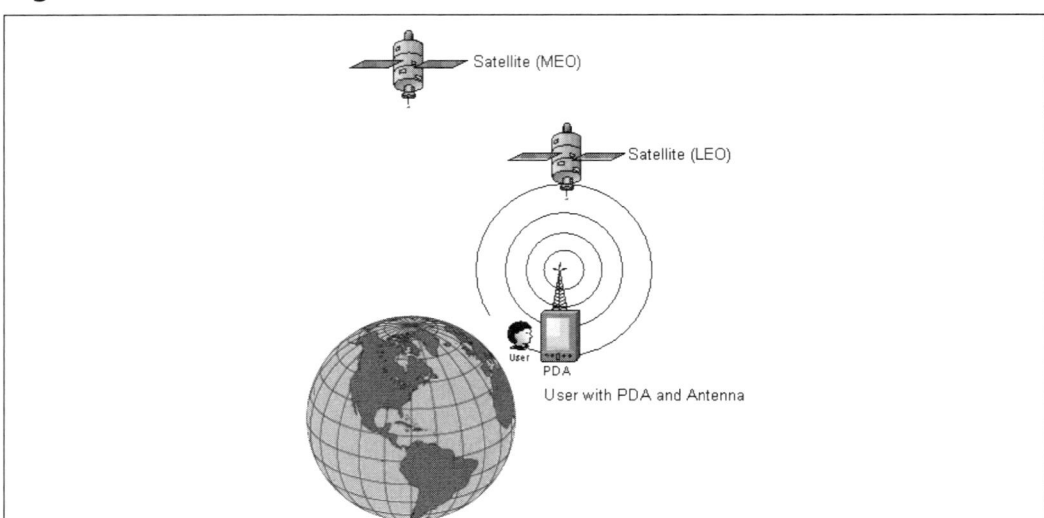

Remote Access Protocols and Services

In this section, we will discuss remote access protocols. Remote access protocols are used to help make connections from clients to servers when you want to work remotely and securely from your office. You can create a dial-in connection or connect directly over the Internet to your corporate office, authenticate to a server, and use your company's internal resources within minutes, all from the comfort of your home. For the Network+ exam you will need to know about the Remote Access Service (RAS), protocols such as PPP (Point-to-Point Protocol), SLIP (Serial Line Internet Protocol) and PPPoE (Point-to-Point Protocol over Ethernet), and what a VPN is as well as the Remote Desktop Protocol.

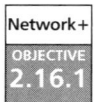

RAS

Remote Access Service is a common method of allowing users of a corporate network to access network resources either from home or on the road. RAS servers typically have an array of modems and dial-in lines available for users to connect through to the corporate network. They provide some form of authentication and then connect the user to the corporate network as if his or her system was physically located on the local area network (LAN). The authentication for RAS servers is typically done with Challenge Handshake Authentication Protocol (CHAP), Microsoft Challenge Handshake Authentication Protocol (MS-CHAP), Password Authentication Protocol (PAP), or Extensible Authentication Protocol (EAP). CHAP and MS-CHAP are more secure than PAP, as they do not send an actual password to the RAS server. EAP offers additional features in that it can be configured to accept a plethora of third-party authentication methods. This could include smart cards, Kerberos, or biometric authentication. Most RAS servers also offer additional security features such as *mandatory callback*. This feature requires users to connect from a number the administrator has entered into the system. After initial connection and authentication, the server disconnects and dials the user's callback number. The user's system is then required to answer this call to complete the connection process. Some RAS servers use caller ID to identify the number the user is connecting from and then to either authorize the connection based on the number or log it.

NOTE

RAS sometimes stands for *Remote Access Server* as well as *Remote Access Service*. Also, Microsoft has implemented a new Management Console (beginning with Windows 2000) called RRAS, which stands for Routing and Remote Access Server. The console has a lot of routing and remote access management tools used for both technologies.

RAS is a feature built into Windows (and other operating systems) that enables users to log into a LAN using a modem or WAN link. RAS works with several major network protocols, including TCP/IP (Transmission Control Protocol/Internet Protocol).

SLIP

Serial Line Internet Protocol is used to encapsulate data for transmission. Developed long ago and primarily used on UNIX systems, SLIP is rarely used now (PPP is typically used instead). SLIP only works with IP, whereas PPP can use other protocols within its own suite to handle IPX/SPX (Internetwork Packet Exchange/Sequenced Packet Exchange), for example. PPP also works in Layer 3 of the OSI model. SLIP also requires static IP addressing, which makes it extremely cumbersome for wide use.

PPP

Point-to-Point Protocol is used to encapsulate data for transmission. PPP is more stable than the older SLIP protocol and provides error-checking features. Working in the Data Link Layer of the OSI model, PPP sends the computer's TCP/IP packets to a server that in turn sends the packets to the Internet. Additionally, PPP allows ISPs to use DHCP (Dynamic Host Configuration Protocol) to assign addresses to clients accessing their networks, greatly expanding the ability of ISPs to provide service to more users.

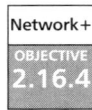

PPPoE

Point-to-Point Protocol over Ethernet relies on two widely accepted standards: PPP and Ethernet. PPPoE is a specification for connecting the users on an Ethernet to the Internet through a common broadband medium, such as DSL or cable modem.

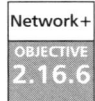

What is a VPN?

A VPN provides users with a secure method of connectivity through a public internetwork such as the Internet. Most companies use dedicated connections to connect to remote sites, but when users want to send private data over the Internet they should provide additional security by encrypting the data using a VPN.

When a VPN is implemented properly, it provides improved wide area security, reduces costs associated with traditional WANs, improves productivity, and improves support for users who telecommute. Cost savings are twofold. First, companies save money by using public networks (such as the Internet) instead of paying for dedicated circuits (such as point-to-point T1 circuits) between remote offices. Second, telecommuters do not have to pay long-distance fees to connect to RAS servers. They can simply dial into their local ISPs and create a virtual *tunnel* to the office. A tunnel is created by wrapping (or *encapsulating*) a data packet inside another data packet and transmitting it over a public medium. Tunneling requires three different protocols:

- **Carrier Protocol** The protocol used by the network (IP on the Internet) that the information is traveling over.

- **Encapsulating Protocol** The protocol, such as PPTP (Point-to-Point Tunneling Protocol), L2TP (Layer 2 Tunneling Protocol), IPSec, or Secure Shell (SSH), that is wrapped around the original data.

- **Passenger Protocol** The original data being carried.

Essentially, there are two different types of VPNs: site-to-site and remote access.

Site-to-Site VPN

Site-to-site VPNs are normally established between corporate offices that are separated by a physical distance extending further than normal LAN media covers. VPNs are available as software (such as Windows VPN, available on Windows NT and Windows 2000) and hardware (firewalls such as Nokia/Check Point and SonicWALL) implementations. Generally speaking, software implementations are easier to maintain. However, hardware implementations are considered more secure, since they are not impacted by operating system vulnerabilities. For example, suppose that Company XYZ has offices in Boston and Phoenix. As shown in Figure 7.8, both offices connect to the Internet via a T1 connection. They have implemented VPN-capable firewalls in both offices, and established an encryption tunnel between them.

Figure 7.8 A Site-To-Site VPN Established Between Two Remote Offices

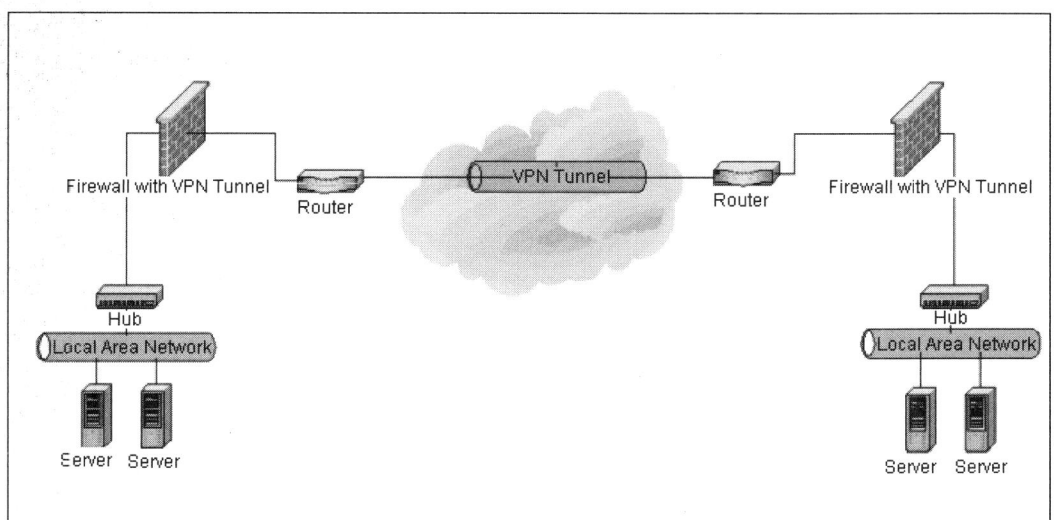

The first step in creating a site-to-site VPN is selecting the security protocols to be used. Common protocols associated with VPN transmission security are PPTP, L2TP, SSH, and IPSec.

PPTP and L2TP are used to establish a secure tunnel connection between two sites. Once a tunnel is established, encryption protocols are used to secure data passing through the tunnel. As data is passed from one VPN to another, it is *encapsulated* at the source and *unwrapped* at the destination. The process of establishing the VPN and wrapping and unwrapping the data is transparent to the end user.

Most commercially available firewalls come with a VPN module that can be set up to easily communicate with another VPN-capable device. Microsoft has implemented site-to-site VPN tools on the Windows 2000 platform using either RRAS or the newest rendition of Microsoft's Proxy server, Microsoft ISA Server 2004. Whichever product or service is used, it is important to ensure that each end of the VPN is configured with identical protocols and settings.

NOTE

A common mistake that network security professionals make is setting up a site-to-site VPN, then disregarding other types of security. Access control (such as Windows NTFS permissions) should also be implemented so that users on remote networks cannot access the local network freely.

Remote Access VPN

A remote access VPN, known as a private virtual dial-up network (PVDN), differs from a site-to-site VPN in that end users are responsible for establishing the VPN tunnel between their workstation and their remote office. An alternative to connecting directly to the corporate VPN is connecting to an enterprise service provider (ESP) that ultimately connects users to the corporate VPN.

In either case, users connect to the Internet or an ESP through a point of presence (POP) using their particular VPN client software (see Figure 7.9). Once the tunnel is set up, users are forced to authenticate with the VPN server, usually by username and password.

Figure 7.9 A Remote-Access VPN Solution Using Regular Internet POPs

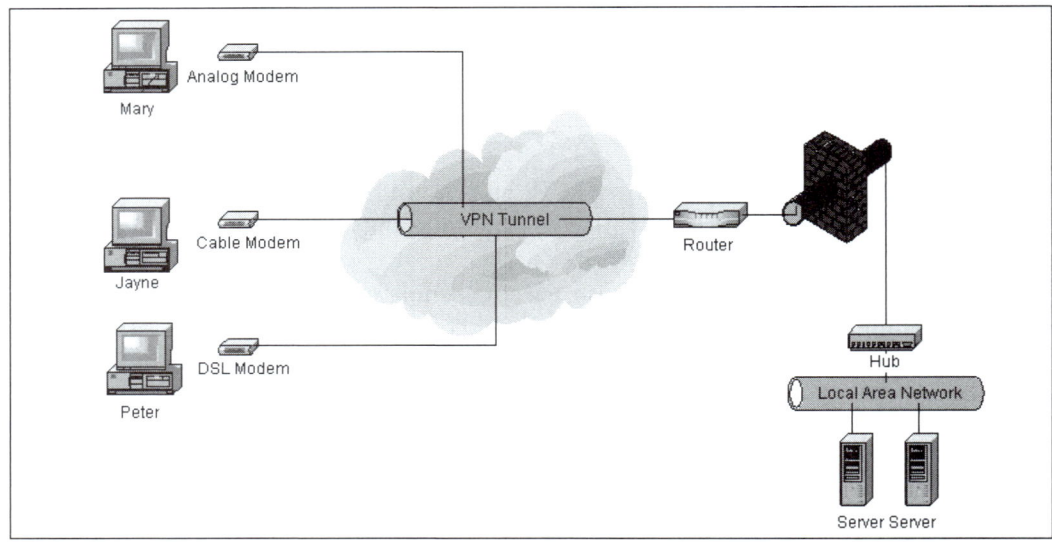

A remote access VPN is a great solution for a company with several employees working in the field. The remote access VPN allows these employees to transmit data to their home offices from any location. RRAS offers an easy solution for creating a remote access VPN.

RDP

Network+
OBJECTIVE
2.16.7

The Remote Desktop Protocol (RDP) is a Presentation Layer protocol that allows a Windows-based system to communicate with another Windows-based system remotely. RDP allows you to connect to a client computer and display and input data to that device. The technology is often used in Microsoft-based networks to remotely connect clients to terminal servers, and as an administrative tool to manage Windows servers. This feature was added to Windows 2000 servers and is still available in Windows Server

2003. It was also added to Windows XP to provide the ability to remotely assist users having problems with their systems, as the protocol allows interactive desktop connections to be established and may be used by technicians to remotely assist end users who are having difficulty with their machines. In the following exercise, you can set up an RDP connection using Windows XP Professional. This connection will allow you to access other Windows systems remotely.

Network+
OBJECTIVE
2.16.7

EXERCISE 7.1

USING RDP WITH WINDOWS XP PROFESSIONAL

In this exercise we will build an RDP-based connection using Windows XP Professional.

1. To create an RDP connection, access **Start | Programs | Accessories | Communications | Remote Desktop Connection.** The Remote Desktop Connection screen (Figure 7.10) will be displayed

Figure 7.10 Remote Desktop Dialog Box

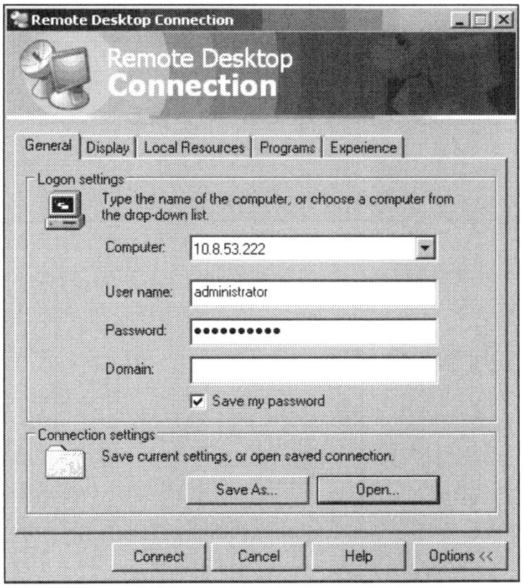

2. In the **Computer** field, enter the IP address of the system you want to connect to, or use the drop-down list to select the IP address. Enter the **User name** and **Password** required to access the remote system. In this exercise, the administrator account is being used with a hard-to-guess password.

3. Click **Connect** to start the connection to the remote system. If the remote system has remote desktop sharing enabled, you will be able to access the system.

It is a good idea to save your profile for a later date. Don't save over the default RDP connection (Figure 7.11); create new connections based on your needs. Name the profiles in a way that helps you remember what they are used for.

Figure 7.11 Default RDP

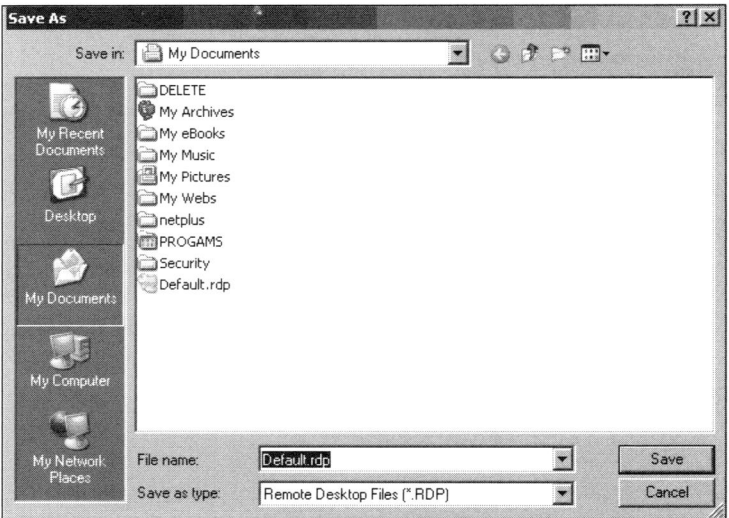

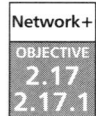

Security Protocols

For the Network+ exam, you will need to define, describe and identify how the following security protocols function. In this section we will cover the most common of tunneling protocols: IPSec, and ISAKMP. We will also cover other tunneling protocols such as PPTP and L2TP. We will also look at SSH, an encrypted alternative to Telnet for remote access to hosts. Other security protocols covered are SSL for Web transactions, as well as initiatives to keep Wireless networking secure, such as WPA, WEP and 802.1x.

IPSec

The IPSec protocol, as defined by the IETF (Internet Engineering Task Force), is "a framework of open standards for ensuring private, secure communications over Internet Protocol networks, through the use of cryptographic security services." This means that IPSec is a set of standards used for encrypting data so that it can pass securely through a public medium, such as the Internet. Unlike other methods of secure communications, IPSec is not bound to any particular authentication method or algorithm, which is why it is considered an open standard. Also, unlike older security standards that were imple-mented at the Application Layer of the OSI model, IPSec is implemented at the Network Layer.

EXAM WARNING

Remember that IPSec is implemented at the Network Layer, not the Application Layer.

The advantage of IPSec being implemented at the Network Layer (versus the Application Layer) is that it is not application-dependent, meaning users do not have to configure each application to IPSec standards. IPSec can also be implemented in two different modes of operation:

- **Transport Mode** IPSec implemented in transport mode (Figure 7.12) speci-fies that only the data (or *payload*) is encrypted during transfer. The advantage of this is speed—since the IP headers are not encrypted, the packets are smaller. The downside to transport mode is that a hacker can sniff the network and gather information about end parties. Transport mode is used in host-to-host VPNs (this provides connection and protection from end to end).

- **Tunnel Mode** Unlike transport mode where only the data is encrypted, in tunnel mode (Figure 7.13) both the data and the IP headers are encrypted. The advantage is that neither the payload nor any information about end par-ties can be sniffed. The disadvantage is speed, since the size of the encrypted packet is larger. Tunnel mode is used in host-to-gateway or gateway-to-gateway VPNs (this protects the session, for example, between two ISPs or two routers, but does not provide protection from those points to the hosts involved in the network communication).

Figure 7.12 Using IPSec in Transport Mode Only Encrypts the Data Payload

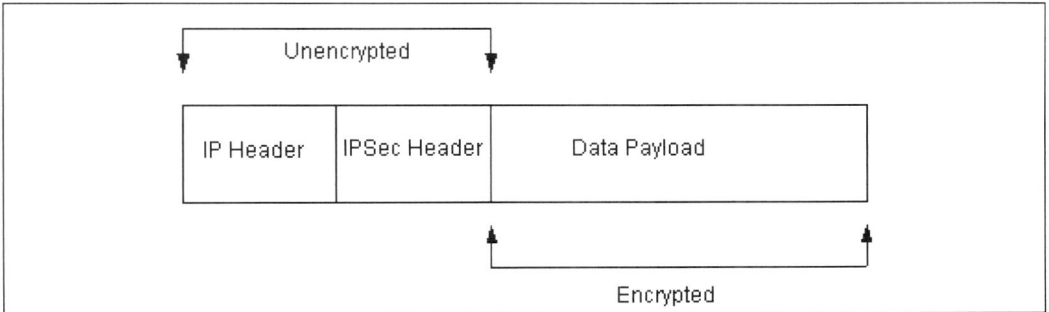

Figure 7.13 Using IPSec in Tunnel Mode Encrypts Both the Data and IP Headers

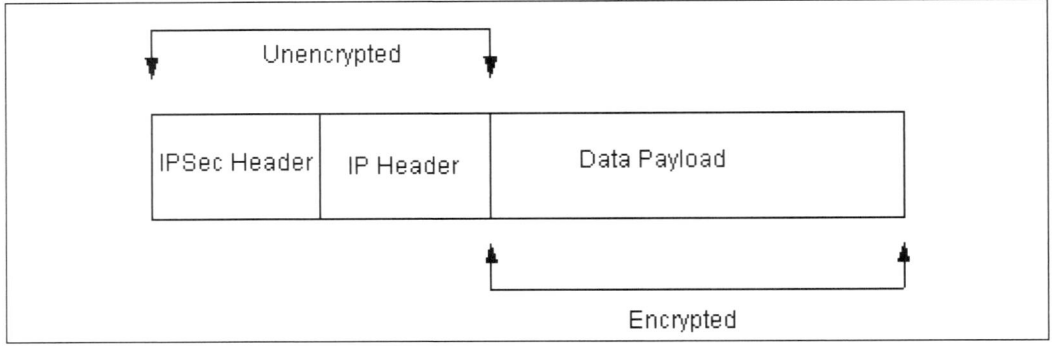

IPSec is made up of two separate security protocols. Authentication header (AH) protocol is responsible for maintaining the authenticity and integrity of the payload. AH authenticates packets by signing them, which ensures the integrity of the data. Since the signature is specific to the packet being transmitted, the receiver is assured of the data source. Signing packets also provides integrity, since the unique signature prevents the data from being modified. Encapsulating security payload (ESP) protocol also handles the authenticity and integrity of payloads, but also adds the advantage of data confidentiality through encryption. AH and ESP can be used together or separately. If used together, the entire packet is authenticated. It is also important to note that since AH signs the packet with its original IP address, most implementations of Network Address Translation (NAT) will change the packet's address and cause failure of the AH authentication mechanism. ESP encrypts the entire packet and adds a new IP header, which is not subject to the same rejection due to change in a NAT process.

TEST DAY TIP

An easy way to remember the difference between AH and ESP is to use the E in ESP to remember *encryption*.

IPSec Authentication

To ensure the integrity of data being transmitted using IPSec, there has to be a mechanism in place to authenticate end users and manage secret keys. This mechanism is called Internet Key Exchange (IKE). IKE is used to authenticate the two ends of a secure tunnel by providing a secure exchange of a shared key before IPSec transmissions begin.

For IKE to work, both parties must use a password known as a *pre-shared* key. During IKE negotiations, both parties swap a *hashed* version of a pre-shared key. When they receive the hashed data, they attempt to recreate it. If they successfully recreate the hash, both parties can begin secure communications.

IPSec also has the ability to use digital signatures. A digital signature is a certificate signed by a trusted third party called a certificate authority (CA) that offers authentication and *non-repudiation*, meaning the sender cannot deny that the message came from him or her. Without a digital signature, one party can easily deny he or she was responsible for messages sent.

Although *public key cryptology* (user A generates a random number and encrypts it with user B's *public key*, and user B decrypts it with his *private key* [described in Chapter 10]) can be used in IPSec, it does not offer non-repudiation. The most important factor to consider when choosing an authentication method is that *both parties must agree on the method chosen*. IPSec uses an SA (security association) to describe how parties will use AH and encapsulating security payload to communicate. The security association can be established through manual intervention or by using the Internet Security Association and Key Management Protocol (ISAKMP). The Diffie-Hellman key exchange protocol, described in detail in Chapter 9, is used for secure exchange of pre-shared keys.

ISAKMP

The advantage of using IKE over the manual method is that the SA can be established when needed, and can be set to expire after a certain amount of time. RFC 2408 describes ISAKMP as a framework for establishing, negotiating, modifying, and deleting security associations between two parties. By centralizing the management of security associations, ISAKMP reduces the amount of duplicated functionality within each security protocol. ISAKMP also reduces the amount of time required for communications setup by negotiating all of the services at once.

Network+
OBJECTIVE
2.16.5
2.17.2

PPTP/L2TP

As mentioned earlier, there are several standard tunneling protocol technologies in use today. Two of the most popular are PPTP and L2TP, which are Layer 2 (Data Link Layer) encapsulation (tunneling) protocols using ports 1723 and 1701, respectively. However, PPTP and L2TP do use different transport protocols: PPTP uses TCP and L2TP uses UDP (User Datagram Protocol).

TEST DAY TIP

Create a mental grid for remembering the difference between PPTP and L2TP. PPTP/1723/TCP and L2TP/1701/UDP.

PPTP

PPTP's popularity is mainly due to the fact that it was the first encapsulation protocol on the market, designed by engineers at Microsoft. Thus it is supported in all Windows operating systems (L2TP is not supported in Windows 9x/ME or NT 4.0, although these OSs (except Windows 95) can create L2TP connections using the Microsoft L2TP/IPSec VPN client add-on. PPTP establishes point-to-point connections between two computers by encapsulating the PPP packets being sent. Although PPTP has helped improve communications security, there are several issues with it.

- PPTP encrypts the data being transmitted, but does not encrypt the information being exchanged during negotiation. In Microsoft implementations, Microsoft Point-to-Point Encryption (MPPE) protocol is used to encrypt the data.

- PPTP is protocol-restrictive, meaning it will only work over IP networks.

- PPTP cannot use the added benefit of IPSec.

EXERCISE 7.2

CREATING A CLIENT CONNECTION IN WINDOWS 2000

Microsoft has made it easy to create VPN client connections in their newer OSs. In Windows 2000, users can create VPN connections as easily as they can create dial-up connections to the Internet. Let's walk through the steps of creating a VPN client connection.

1. Click **Start| Settings| Network and Dial-up Connections**.
2. Click the **Make New Connection** icon.
3. On the Network Connection Wizard screen (Figure 7.14), click **Next**.

Figure 7.14 Network Connection Wizard Welcome Screen

4. Select **Connect to a private network through the Internet** (Figure 7.15) and click **Next**.

Figure 7.15 Selecting the Network Connection Type

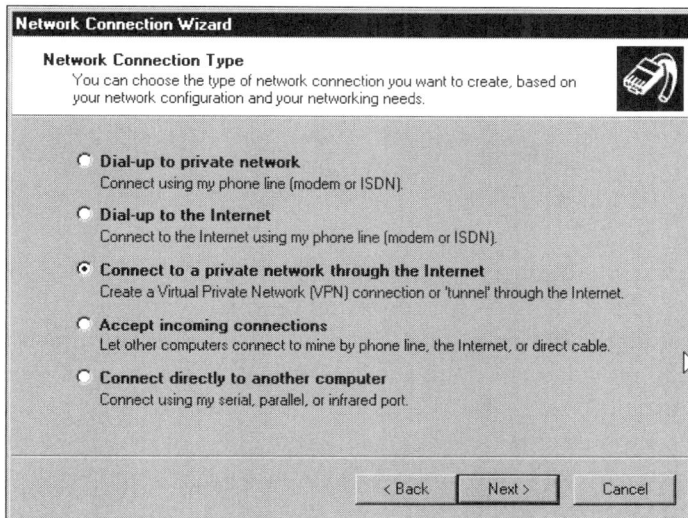

5. When prompted to select a public network, select **Do not dial the initial connection** and click **Next**.

6. Next, you will be prompted to select the destination address (Figure 7.16). Type **vpn.xyzcompany.com** and click **Next**.

Figure 7.16 Selecting the Destination Address

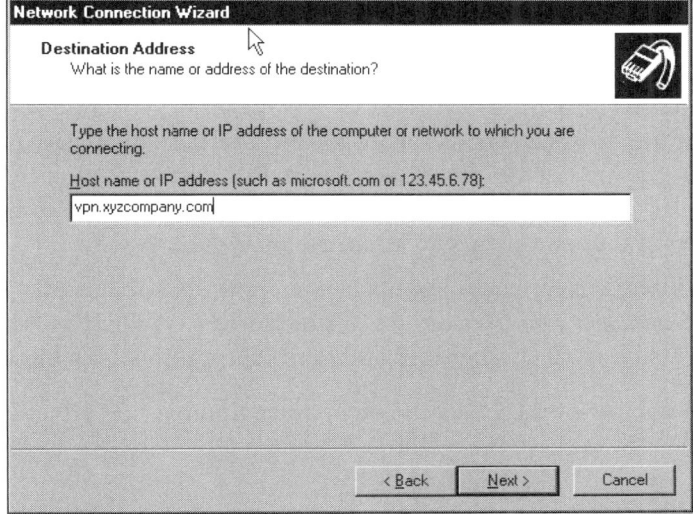

7. On the Connection Availability screen, select **For all users** and click **Next**.

8. Click **Next** again.

9. Name the VPN connection and click **Finish** to complete the wizard setup.

10. To begin the VPN connection, double-click on the new icon.

L2TP

As with TACACS+ (Terminal Access Controller Access Control System +), Cisco believed they could design a better tunneling protocol, which was the creation of the Layer 2 Forwarding (L2F) protocol. Unfortunately, L2F was not much better than PPTP. Specifically, L2F provided encapsulation (tunneling), but it did not encrypt the data being encapsulated.

To use the features of both PPTP and L2F, L2TP was developed through a joint venture between Microsoft and Cisco. L2TP was a major improvement, but still did not offer encryption. To remedy this, L2TP was designed to use IPSec for encryption purposes. The differences between PPTP and L2TP that you need to know for the Network+ exam are:

- L2TP requires IPSec in order to offer encryption.

- L2TP offers RADIUS (Remote Authentication Dial-In User Service) and TACACS+, where PPTP does not.

- L2TP is often implemented as a hardware solution, while PPTP is not.

- L2TP can run on top of protocols such as IP, IPX, and SNA (Systems Network Architecture), while PPTP can work only on IP networks.

- Using L2TP with IPSec provides per-packet data origin authentication (proof that the data was sent by an authorized user), data integrity (proof that the data was not modified in transit), replay protection (prevention from resending a stream of captured packets), and data confidentiality (prevention from interpreting captured packets without an encryption key).

- L2TP/IPSec connections require two levels of authentication: *computer-level authentication* using certificates or pre-shared keys for IPSec sessions, and *user-level authentication* using PPP authentication protocol for the L2TP tunnel.

Some advantages of the L2TP/IPSec combination over PPTP are:

- IPSec provides per-packet data origin, data integrity, replay protection, and data confidentiality. In contrast, PPTP only provides per-packet data confidentiality.

- L2TP/IPSec connections require two levels of authentication: computer-level authentication and user-level authentication.

- PPP frames exchanged during user-level authentication are never sent unencrypted because the PPP connection process for L2TP/IPSec occurs after the IPSec security association is established.

SSH

Developed by SSH Communications Security Ltd., secure shell is a program used to log into another computer over a network, to execute commands in a remote machine, and to move files from one machine to another. It provides strong authentication and secure communications over insecure channels. It is a replacement for rlogin, rsh, rcp, and rdist, which are all UNIX-based protocols used for remote management of the system. SSH protects a network from attacks such as IP spoofing, IP source routing, and DNS spoofing. An attacker who has managed to take over a network can only force SSH to disconnect.

SSH is a cryptographically secure replacement for standard Telnet, rlogin, rsh, and rcp commands. SSH consists of both a client and a server that use public key cryptography to provide session encryption. It also provides the ability to forward arbitrary ports over an encrypted connection.

SSH has received wide acceptance as *the* secure mechanism for access to remote systems interactively. SSH was conceived and developed by Finnish developer, Tatu Ylonen. When the original version of SSH became a commercial venture, the license became more restrictive. A public specification was created, resulting in development of a number of versions of SSH-compliant client and server software that do not contain the restrictions (most significantly, those that restrict commercial use).

SSH deals with the confidentiality and integrity of information being passed between a client and host. Since programs such as Telnet and rlogin transmit usernames and passwords in cleartext, sniffing a network is easy, and it's incredibly important that such data is encrypted. By beginning an encrypted session *before* the username and password are transmitted, confidentiality is guaranteed. SSH protects the integrity of the data being transmitted by the use of *session keys*. The client keeps a list of user keys for servers with which it previously established secure sessions. If the key matches, the secure session is established and the integrity of the data being transmitted is confirmed. Using SSH helps protect against different types of attacks including packet sniffing, IP spoofing, and manipulation of data by unauthorized users.

How SSH Works

When a client wants to establish a secure session with a host, the client initiates communication by requesting an SSH session. Once the server receives the request from the client, the two perform a *handshake*, which includes the verification of the protocol version. Next, session keys are exchanged between the client and server. Once session keys have been exchanged and verified against a *cache* of host keys, the client can begin the secure session. Figure 7.17 depicts the SSH authentication process.

Figure 7.17 SSH Communications are Established in Four Steps

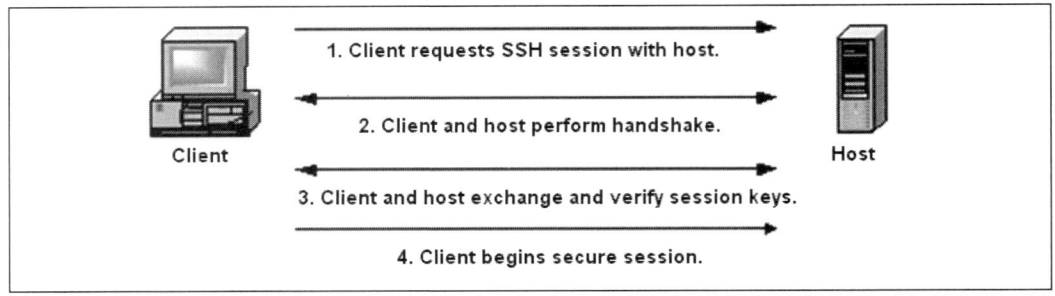

EXERCISE 7.3

USING SSH WITH WINDOWS XP PROFESSIONAL

1. To access a system using SSH, you will need to install a third-party tool or freeware. You can get one similar to Figure 7.18 online, such as putty. Here is one you can use. www.ssh.com/support/downloads/secureshellwks/non-commercial.html

2. Once installed, you can open SSH and create an encrypted and secure connection to another remote host without worrying about your data being intercepted in transit.

Figure 7.18 SSH Secure Shell

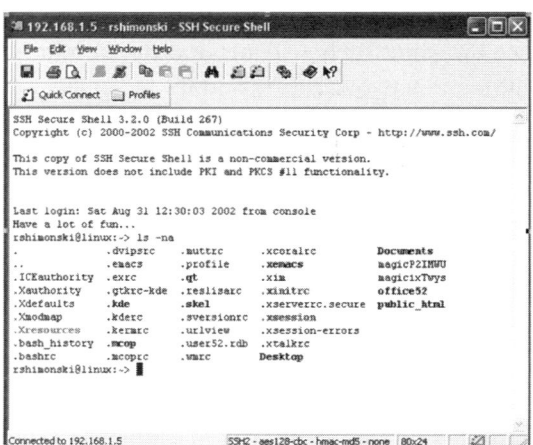

SSL and HTTPS

etwork+
BJECTIVE
.17.3

SSL (Secure Sockets Layer) is a public key-based protocol that was developed by Netscape and is supported by all popular Web browsers. It is widely used on the Internet for Web transactions such as sending credit card data. It can be utilized for other protocols as well, such as Telnet, FTP (File Transfer Protocol), LDAP (Lightweight Directory Access Protocol), Internet Message Access Protocol (IMAP), and Simple Mail Transfer Protocol (SMTP), but these are not commonly used. Transport Layer Security (TLS), on the other hand, is an open IETF-proposed standard based on SSL 3.0. RFCs (Requests for Comments) 2246, 2712, 2817, and 2818 define TLS. The name is misleading, since TLS happens well above the Transport Layer. The two protocols are not interoperable, but TLS has the capability to drop down into SSL 3.0 mode for backward compatibility, and both can provide security for a single TCP session.

SSL and TLS provide a connection between a client and a server, over which any amount of data can be sent securely. Both the server and browser generally must be SSL- or TLS-enabled to facilitate secure Web connections, while applications generally must be SSL- or TLS-enabled to allow their use of the secure connection. However, a recent trend is to use dedicated SSL accelerators as VPN terminators, passing the content on to an end server. The Cisco CSS Secure Content Accelerator 1100 is an example of this technique.

For the browser and server to communicate securely, each must have the shared session key. SSL and TLS use public key encryption to exchange session keys during communication initialization. When a browser is installed on a workstation, it generates a unique private/public key pair.

443 → HTTPS is simply HTTP (Hypertext Transfer Protocol) over SSL. HTTPS is the protocol responsible for encryption of traffic from a client browser to a Web server. HTTPS uses port 443 instead of HTTP port 80.

When a URL begins with "https://," you know you are using HTTPS. Both HTTPS and SSL use a X.509 digital certificate for authentication purposes from the client to the server. For highly detailed information about SSL and HTTPS, visit Netscape's website at http://wp.netscape.com/eng/ssl3/ssl-toc.html.

EXAM WARNING

SSL must be understood for the Network+ exam. Remember key items like the port it uses (443) and its basic functionality.

SSL suffers from security vulnerabilities caused by small key sizes, expired certificates, and other weaknesses that can plague any public key implementation. Many servers running SSL on the Internet are still using an older, flawed version (SSLv2), or they use 40-bit encryption, or their certificates are expired or self-signed.

S-HTTP

It is important not to confuse HTTPS with Secure HTTP (S-HTTP). Although they sound alike, they are two separate protocols, used for different purposes. S-HTTP is not widely used, but it was developed by Enterprise Integration Technologies (EIT) to provide security for Web-based applications. Secure HTTP is an extension to the HTTP protocol. It is a secure message-oriented communications protocol that can transmit individual messages securely (whereas SSL establishes a secure connection over which any amount of data can be sent). S-HTTP provides transaction confidentiality, authentication, and message integrity, and extends HTTP to include tags for encrypted and secure transactions. S-HTTP is implemented in some commercial Web servers and most browsers. An S-HTTP server negotiates with the client for the type of encryption that will be used, several types of which exist.

Unlike SSL, S-HTTP does not require clients to have public key certificates because it can use symmetric keys to provide private transactions. The symmetric keys are provided in advance using out-of-band communication.

WEP   *up to 4 WEP keys on an AP (access point) RC4 encryption*

Network+
OBJECTIVE
2.17.4

The IEEE (Institute of Electrical and Electronic Engineers) 802.11 standard covers the communication between WLAN (wireless local area network) components. RF poses challenges to privacy in that it travels through and around physical objects. Because of the nature of the 802.11 wireless LANs, the IEEE working group implemented a mechanism to protect the privacy of the individual transmissions, known as the WEP (Wired Equivalent Privacy) protocol. Because WEP utilizes a cryptographic security countermeasure for the fulfillment of its stated goal of privacy, it has the added benefit of becoming an authentication mechanism. This benefit is realized through a shared-key authentication that allows for encryption and decryption of wireless transmissions. Up to four keys can be defined on an access point (AP) or a client, and they can be rotated to add complexity for a higher security standard in the WLAN policy.

WEP was never intended to be the absolute authority in wireless security. The IEEE 802.11 standard states that WEP provides for protection from casual eavesdropping. Instead, the driving force behind WEP was privacy. In cases that require high degrees of security, other mechanisms should be utilized such as authentication, access control, password protection, and VPNs.

Despite its flaws, WEP still offers a level of security provided that all of its features are used properly. This means taking great care in key management, avoiding default options, and ensuring adequate encryption is enabled at every opportunity.

Proposed improvements in the 802.11 standard should overcome many of the limitations of the original security options, and should make WEP more appealing as a security solution. Additionally, as WLAN technology gains popularity and users clamor for functionality, both the standards committees and the hardware vendors will offer improvements. It is critically important to keep abreast of vendor-related software fixes and changes that improve the overall security posture of a wireless LAN.

EXAM WARNING

40 or 128

Most APs advertise that they support WEP in 40-bit encryption, but often the 128-bit option is also supported. For corporate networks, 128-bit encryption-capable devices should be considered as a minimum.

With data security enabled in a closed network, the settings on the client for the service set identifier (SSID) and the encryption keys must match the AP when attempting to associate with the network or it will fail.

WEP provides security and privacy in transmissions held between the AP and the clients. To gain access, an intruder must be more sophisticated and have specific intent to gain access. Some of the other benefits of implementing WEP include the following:

- All messages are encrypted using a CRC-32 (cyclic redundancy check-32) checksum to provide some degree of integrity.

- Privacy is maintained via RC4 encryption. Without possession of the secret key, the message cannot be easily decrypted.

- WEP is extremely easy to implement. All that is required is to set the encryption key on the APs and on each client.

- WEP provides a basic level of security for WLAN applications.

- WEP keys are user-definable and unlimited. WEP keys can, and should, be changed often.

NOTE

Chapter 4 covers Wireless technologies and WEP in depth.

WPA (Wi-Fi Protected Access)

Network+
OBJECTIVE
.17.5

For the Network+ exam you will need to know about another form of wireless security called WPA (Wi-Fi Protected Access), created by the Wi-Fi Alliance. WPA is a technology that was created to help overcome the limitations of WEP. The way it does this is by using a technology called Temporal Key Integrity Protocol (TKIP). TKIP is a protocol used to add more encryption benefits to wireless transmissions to include a message integrity check. Since using TKIP eliminates all known vulnerabilities to WEP, there really should be no reason to even use WEP at this point if you can use WPA.

Another great benefit of WPA is that it uses authentication protocols such as EAP and 802.1x (both explained shortly) to allow for a central authentication method based on a RADIUS server as an example.

802.1x

In Chapter 4, users will become familiar with wireless local area networks and the IEEE 802.11 standard for wireless networking. It is so simple to implement wireless networking technology that most novice users can install it themselves. What most users do not realize is that as soon as they transmit their first piece of data across the new network they have opened up a can of worms!

Head of the Class

The Dangers of a Wide-Open WLAN

My first experience with wireless security issues occurred while I was working as a networking consultant at a boarding school. A staff member set up an access point on the school's network. Consequently, a student working on a laptop (with a wireless NIC installed) was able to access the school's network! The caller's concern was that if one student accessed the WLAN, how many others have? The message is: know your network, know what is attached to it, and make sure you have security measures in place to protect it.

This is where the 802.1x standard enters. 802.1x is a WEP protocol designed to enhance the level of security offered on a WLAN.

TEST DAY TIP

The argument can be made that wireless technologies are part of a LAN, not a remote access technology. For the Network+ exam, think of wireless as being a *remote access* because there is no direct physical (cabled) connection from a laptop or PDA.

When a wireless user (or *supplicant*) wants to access a wireless network, 802.1x forces him or her to authenticate to a centralized authority called an *authenticator*. 802.1x uses the Extensible Authentication Protocol for passing messages between the supplicant and the authenticator. When communication begins, the authenticator places the user into an *unauthorized state*. While in this unauthorized state, the only messages that can be transmitted are EAP start messages. At this point, the authenticator sends a request to the user asking for his or her identity. The client then returns his or her identity to the authenticator, which in turn forwards it to the *authentication server,* which is running an authentication service such as RADIUS.

The authentication server authenticates the user and either accepts or rejects the user based on the credentials provided. If the user provides the correct credentials, the authenticator changes the user's state to *authorized*, thus allowing the user to move freely within the WLAN. Figure 7.19 depicts how the authentication process works.

Figure 7.19 The 802.1*x* Authentication Process

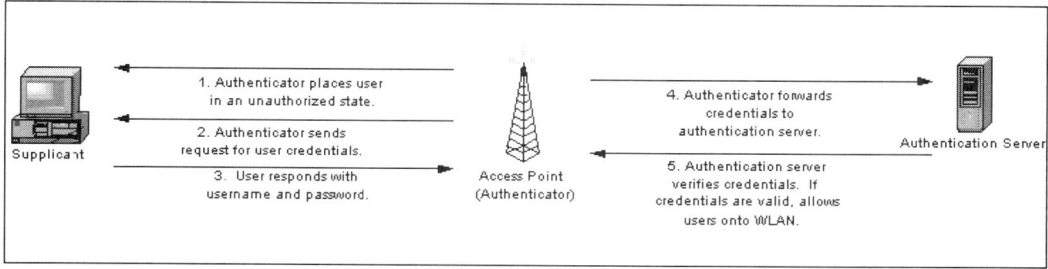

Identifying Authentication Protocols

Applying authentication protocols such as CHAP, Kerberos, RADIUS and/or EAP are common in today's network environment. For the Network+ exam, you will be expected to be able to identify different authentication protocols. The process of authentication is a security measure used to verify the identity of a person, process, or host trying to access a system. For example; authentication protocols handle the identification process.

CHAP

One of the methods that can be used protect information when using remote access to a resource is the Challenge Handshake Authentication Protocol. CHAP is a remote access authentication protocol used in conjunction with PPP to provide security and authentication to users of remote resources. You will recall that PPP replaced the older Serial Line Internet Protocol. PPP not only allows for more security than SLIP, but also does not require static addressing to be defined for communication. PPP allows users to use dynamic addressing and multiple protocols during communication with a remote host. CHAP is described in RFC 1994, available at www.faqs.org/rfcs/rfc1994.html. The RFC describes a process of authentication that works in the following manner:

CHAP is used to periodically verify the identity of the peer using a three-way handshake. This is done upon initial link establishment, and may be repeated anytime after the link has been established.

1. After the link establishment phase is complete, the authenticator sends a challenge message to the peer.

2. The peer responds with a value calculated using a one-way hash function.

3. The authenticator checks the response against its own calculation of the expected hash value. If the values match, the authentication is acknowledged; otherwise the connection should be terminated.

4. At random intervals, the authenticator sends a new challenge to the peer, and repeats steps 1 to 3.

CHAP operates in conjunction with PPP to provide protection of the credentials presented for authentication and to verify connection to a valid resource. It does not operate with encrypted password databases, and therefore is not as strong a protection as other levels of authentication. The shared secrets may be stored on both ends as a clear-text item, making the secret vulnerable to compromise or detection. CHAP may also be configured to store a password using one-way reversible encryption, which uses the one-way hash noted earlier. This provides protection to the password, because the hash must match the client wishing to authenticate with the server that has stored the password with the hash value. CHAP is better than Password Authentication Protocol, however, since PAP sends passwords across the network in cleartext.

MS-CHAP

Microsoft created its own extensions for CHAP and called it MS-CHAP. This protocol is not standardized, but is widely used in Microsoft Windows deployments. Its current version, (MS-CHAPv2) is an enhancement that allows a client to change his or her account password if it has expired on the RADIUS server. MS-CHAP is only as secure as the passwords that users choose, and this is basically why it's still not entirely a secure protocol to use in the enterprise.

PAP

PAP is the simplest form of authentication you can use. PAP is the weakest when it comes to security, but the simplest in terms of use and overhead. A PAP authentication message will contain user credentials (such as your password). Since PAP is very weak when it comes to security, the password is sent in cleartext and is vulnerable to any packet sniffer attempting to intercept it. Because of its inherent weaknesses, PAP should never be used.

Kerberos

Kerberos (currently Kerberos v5) is used as the preferred network authentication protocol in many medium and large environments to authenticate users and services requesting access to resources. Kerberos is a network protocol designed to centralize the authentication information for the user or service requesting the resource. This allows authentication of the entity requesting access (user, machine, service, or process) by the host of the resource being accessed through the use of secure and encrypted keys and tickets *(authentication tokens)* from the authenticating Key Distribution Center (KDC). It allows for cross-platform authentication, and will be available in upcoming implementations of various network operating systems. Kerberos is very useful in the distributed computing environments currently used because it centralizes the processing of credentials for authentication. Kerberos utilizes time stamping of its tickets to help ensure they are not compromised by other entities, and uses an overall structure of control that is called a *realm*. Some platforms use the defined terminology, while others such as Windows 2000 use their domain structure to implement the Kerberos concepts.

Kerberos is described in RFC 1510, available on the Web at www.ietf.org/rfc/rfc1510.txt. Developed and owned by the Massachusetts Institute of Technology (MIT), information about the most current and previous releases of Kerberos is available on the Web at http://web.mit.edu/kerberos/www/

Let's look at how the Kerberos process works and how it helps secure authentication activities in a network. First, let's look at Figure 7.20, which shows the default components of a Kerberos v5 realm:

Figure 7.20 Kerberos Required Components

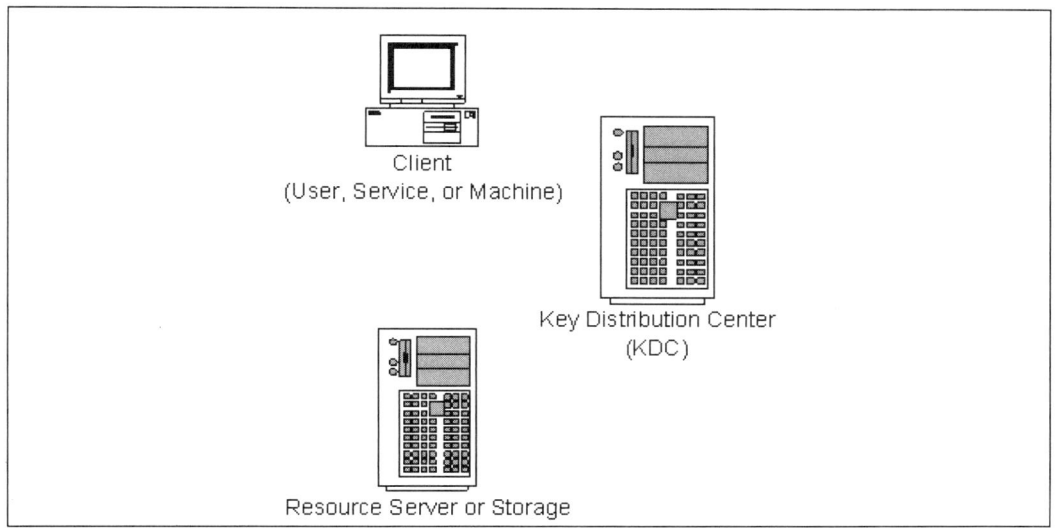

There is an authentication server requirement (the KDC). In a Kerberos realm, whether in a UNIX-based or Windows-based OS, the authentication process is the same. For this purpose, imagine that a client needs to access a resource on the resource server. Look at Figure 7.21 as we proceed to follow the path for the authentication, first for logon, then at Figure 7.22 for the resource access path.

Figure 7.21 Authentication Path for Logon Access in a Kerberos Realm

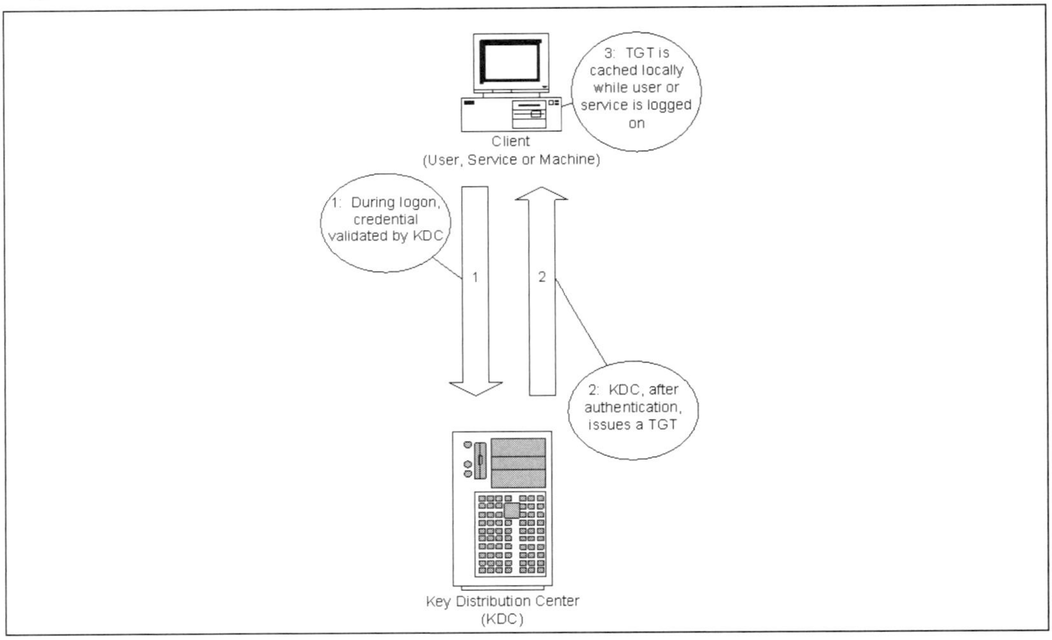

As shown in Figure 7.21, two events are occurring as credentials are presented (password, Smart Card, biometrics) to the KDC for authentication. First, the authentication credential is presented to the KDC. Second, the KDC issues a ticket granting ticket (TGT) that is associated with the access token while you are actively logged in and authenticated. This TGT expires when you (or the service) disconnect or log off the network. This TGT is cached locally for use during the active session.

Figure 7.22 shows the process for resource access in a Kerberos realm. It starts by presenting the previously granted TGT to the authenticating KDC. The authenticating KDC returns a session ticket to the entity wishing access to the resource. This session ticket is then presented to the remote resource server. The remote resource server, after accepting the session ticket, allows the session to be established to the resource.

Figure 7.22 Resource Access in Kerberos Realms

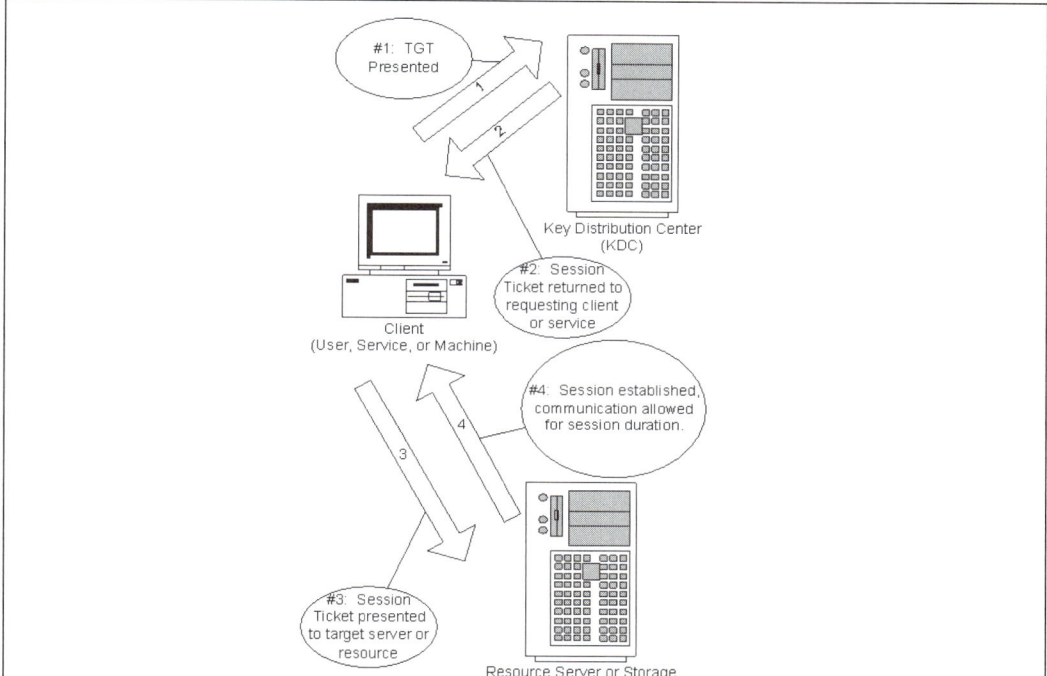

Kerberos uses a time stamp and we need to understand where and when the time stamp is used. Previously mentioned was the concept of *non-repudiation*, which is one reason for the use of the time stamps. In the case of Kerberos, the time stamp is also used to limit the possibility of *replay* or *spoofing* of credentials. Replay is the capture of information, modification of the captured information, and retransmission of the modified information to the entity waiting to receive the communication. If unchecked, this allows for impersonation of credentials when seeking access. Spoofing is the substitution of addressing or authentication information to try to attain access to a resource based on information acceptable to the receiving host, but not truly owned by the sender. The initial time stamp refers to any communication between the entity requesting authentication and the KDC. Normally, this initial time period will not be allowed to exceed five minutes. If clocks are not synchronized between the systems, the credentials (tickets) will not be granted if the time differential exceeds the established limits. Session tickets from the KDC to a resource must be presented within this time period or they will be discarded. The session established between the resource server and the requesting entity is also time-stamped, but generally lasts as long as the entities' logon credentials are valid. This can be affected by system policies like logon hour restrictions, which are defined in the original access token. TGT tickets are not part of the default five-minute period. Rather, they are cached locally on the machine and are valid for the duration of the session.

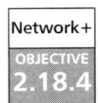

RADIUS

Remote Authentication Dial-In User Service was originally designed as a way to authenticate external users who were dialing in to a company (hence the name). Over the years enhancements have been made to include different types of authentication inside the LAN (firewalls, VPNs, authentication, etc.) RADIUS is designed to carry authentication, authorization, and configuration information between a network device that requires authentication and an authentication server.

As noted in the discussion about 802.1x, users need a centralized entity to handle authentication. Initially, RADIUS was created by Livingston Enterprises to handle dial-in authentication. Then its usage broadened into wireless authentication and VPN authentication. RADIUS is the most popular of all the authentication, authorization, and accounting (AAA) servers, including TACACS, TACACS+, and DIAMETER. An RAS must be able to authenticate a user, authorize the authenticated user to perform specified functions, and log (that is, account for) the actions of users for the duration of the connection.

When users dial into a network, RADIUS is used to authenticate usernames and passwords. A RADIUS server can either work alone or in a distributed environment (known as *distributed RADIUS*) where RADIUS servers are configured in a tiered (hierarchical) structure.

In a distributed RADIUS environment, a RADIUS server forwards the authentication request to an enterprise RADIUS server using a protocol called *proxy RADIUS*. The enterprise RADIUS server handles verification of user credentials and responds back to the service provider's RADIUS server.

One of the reasons that RADIUS is so popular is that it supports a number of protocols including:

- Point-to-Point Protocol
- Password Authentication Protocol
- Challenge Handshake Authentication Protocol

Authentication Process

RADIUS authentication consists of five steps:

1. Users initiate a connection with an ISP RAS or corporate RAS. Once a connection is established, users are prompted for a username and password.

2. The RAS encrypts the username and password using a *shared secret*, and passes the encrypted packet to the RADIUS server.

3. The RADIUS server attempts to verify the user's credentials against a centralized database.

4. If the credentials match those found in the database, the server responds with an *access-accept* message. If the username does not exist or the password is incorrect, the server responds with an *access-reject* message.

5. The RAS then accepts or rejects the message and grants the appropriate rights.

Vulnerabilities

Certain flavors of RADIUS servers and Web servers can be compromised by *buffer-overflow* attacks. A buffer-overflow attack occurs when a buffer is flooded with more information than it can hold. The extra data overflows into other buffers, which may be accessible to hackers.

Head of the Class...

Sometimes You Just Get Lucky...

Once we lock a door, curiosity leads someone to try and see what is behind it. This is the "cat-and-mouse game" that is network security. Many vulnerabilities found in network security are discovered by hackers trying to access systems they are not authorized to use. Sometimes, *whitehat* hackers—security consultants hired to test system vulnerabilities—discover vulnerabilities in their testing. Unlike *blackhat* hackers, whose intentions are malicious, and *grayhat* hackers whose intentions are not malicious), whitehat hackers generally work with companies to fix issues before they become public knowledge. In 2001, RADIUS buffer-overflow attacks were discovered by Internet Security Systems while testing the vulnerabilities of the wireless networks.

TACACS/+

RADIUS is not the only centralized RAS. TACACS is also used in authenticating remote users. TACACS has gone through three major generations: TACACS, XTACACS, and TACACS+. For the Network+ exam, you need to know about TACACS and TACACS+; however, for continuity purposes, XTACACS will also be discussed.

TACACS

TACACS is the "old man" of centralized remote access authentication. TACACS was first developed during the days of (ARPANET), which was the basis for the Internet. TACACS is detailed in RFC 1492, which can be found at www.cis.ohio-state.edu/cgi-bin/rfc/rfc1492.html. Although TACACS offers authentication and authorization, it does not offer any accounting tools. As mentioned earlier, a good RAS must fit all the criteria of the AAA model. Similar to RADIUS, a dial-up user connects to a RAS that prompts the user for their credentials. The credentials are then passed to the TACACS server, which either permits or denies access to the network.

TACACS+

Cisco decided to develop a proprietary version of TACACS known as TACACS+. The driving factor behind TACACS+ was to offer networking professionals the ability to manage all remote access components from a centralized location. TACACS+ is also credited with separating the AAA functions. TACACS+ is considered proprietary because its packet formats are completely different from those in TACACS or XTA-CACS, making TACACS+ incompatible with previous versions. Unlike previous versions of TACACS that used one database for all AAA functions, TACACS+ uses individual databases for each. TACACS+ was the first revision to offer secure communications between the TACACS+ client and the TACACS+ server. Like XTACACS, TACACS+ uses TCP as its transport. TACACS+ continues to gain popularity because it is easy to implement and reasonably priced.

XTACACS

Initially, TACACS utilized the User Datagram Protocol (UDP) to handle communications. The problem with UDP is that it does not provide packet sequencing. Therefore, services such as TACACS must make sure that the entire message has arrived and is intact. To overcome this shortcoming, Cisco Systems developed Extended TACACS (or XTACACS). In XTACACS, the transport protocol was changed from UDP to Transmission Control Protocol (TCP), ensuring that messages would be divided into packets and reassembled when received at the intended destination. XTACACS was a step in the right direction, but it did not provide all of the functionality needed for a centralized remote access authentication solution.

NOTE

XTACACS is rarely deployed in modern installations, and is not a topic of the Network+ exam.

EXAM WARNING

Make sure you understand the difference between TACACS and TACACS+. The most important thing to remember is that TACACS uses UDP as its transport protocol while TACACS+ uses TCP. Also, TACACS+ is a proprietary version owned by Cisco.

Head of the Class...

Decisions To Be Made: RADIUS vs. TACACS+

Both RADIUS and TACACS+ get the job done. Both provide exceptional user authentication, both are transparent to the end user, and both have their share of problems. Specifically, the two issues that differentiate them are separation of duties and the need for reliable transport protocols.

In terms of separation of duties, RADIUS lumps all of the AAA functions into one user profile, whereas TACACS+ separates them. We know that TACACS+ uses TCP for its transport protocol. Both RADIUS and TACACS, on the other hand, use UDP. If reliable transport and sensitivity to packet disruption is important, TACACS+ is the better fit.

EAP

EAP was originally defined under RFC 2284 and then redefined under the IETF Internet draft dated September 13, 2002. EAP is an authentication protocol designed to support several different authentication mechanisms. It runs directly over the Data Link Layer and does not require the use of IP.

EAP comes in several different forms:

- EAP over IP (EAPoIP)
- Message Digest Algorithm/Challenge-Handshake Authentication Protocol (EAP-MD5-CHAP)
- Transport Layer Security (EAP-TLS)
- Tunneled Transport Layer Security (EAP-TTLS)
- RADIUS
- Light Extensible Authentication Protocol (LEAP) Cisco

Each form of EAP has its own characteristics, but for the purpose of the Network+ exam you will only need to know what it is and its different formats.

Summary of Exam Objectives

In this chapter we covered the Network+ exam objectives based around Wide Area Networking technologies such as packet switching, which is the *always on* type of network, and circuit switching, which is a type of network that has to be created each time it is used (such as ISDN). We also covered the fundamentals of ISDN, which is a digital method of transmitting data across copper telephone lines, using service provider ID numbers (also called SPIDS) to connect the network (circuit switched) for the sending and receiving of data. We covered the fundamentals of Frame Relay, MPLS, X.25 and SONET as well as T- and E-level carrier lines.

We discussed the primary ways to get Internet access, such as with DSL. DSL is a digital method of transmitting data over preexisting copper telephone lines. ADSL is a technology that allows for faster download speeds. DSL speeds also vary depending on how far from the central office you are. Cable-based ISPs were also covered, which is generally faster than DSL, but can also become congested if too many subscribers use the shared media all at once. Both are far better when it comes to speed and use than POTS or PSTN. The dial-up method of access using a standard modem is the slowest method of access. Satellite and wireless technologies were also discussed; they afford you the flexibility of use over speed and security.

We also defined the function and use of remote access protocols and services such as VPNs. A VPN is a secure connection created over an insecure network such as the Internet. Protocols used to encapsulate and sometimes secure transmissions include PPP, SLIP, PPPoE, PPTP, and RDP. Other security protocols covered were L2TP (a more secure version of PPTP), SSL, which helps to secure HTTP, as well as wireless security technologies such as WEP and WPA.

To wrap up the chapter we covered commonly used authentication protocols such as PAP, which is weak and easily exploited, to Kerberos, which operates on an entire ticketing system to implement very high-end security.

Exam Objectives Fast Track

Identify the Basic Characteristics of the following WAN (Wide Area Networks) Technologies

- ☑ 2.14.1 Packet switching
- ☑ 2.14.2 Circuit switching
- ☑ 2.14.3 ISDN (Integrated Services Digital Network)
- ☑ 2.14.4 FDDI (Fiber Distributed Data Interface)
- ☑ 2.14.5 T1 (T Carrier level 1) / E1 / J1

☑ 2.14.6 T3 (T Carrier level 3) / E3 / J3

☑ 2.14.7 OCx (Optical Carrier)

☑ 2.14.8 X.25

☑ Most WAN protocols in use today are packet-switched. For technologies such as X.25 and Frame Relay, this means that the packets are sent across links that are always available.

☑ Normal telephone service is based on circuit-switching technology, in which a dedicated line is allocated for transmission between two parties and the circuit is brought up when needed. Circuit switching is ideal when data must be transmitted quickly and must arrive in the same order in which it's sent. Packet switching is more efficient and robust for data that can withstand some delays in transmission.

☑ ISDN is a digital-based circuit-switching technology.

☑ ISDN, an international communications standard for sending voice, video, and data over digital telephone lines or normal telephone wires is commonly seen in the corporate office of companies around the world.

☑ ISDN supports data transfer rates of 64 Kbps (64,000 bits per second).

☑ There are two types of ISDN: BRI and PRI.

☑ Basic Rate Interface (BRI) consists of two 64-KbpsB channels and one D-channel for transmitting control information.

☑ Primary Rate Interface (PRI) consists of 23 B-channels and one D-channel (U.S.) or 30 B-channels and one D-channel (Europe).

☑ The B channel is used for supervisory control.

☑ A T1 is a dedicated phone connection supporting data rates of 1.544Mbits per second.

☑ A T1 line consists of 24 individual channels (DS0), each of which supports 64Kbits per second.

☑ E1 carries signals at 2 Mbps (32 channels at 64Kbps, with 2 channels reserved for signaling and controlling).

☑ A T3 is a dedicated phone connection supporting data rates of about 43 Mbps.

☑ A T3 line consists of 672 individual channels, each of which supports 64 Kbps.

☑ E3 lines carry data at a rate of 34.368 Mbps

Identify the Basic Characteristics of the Following Internet Access Technologies

- ☑ 2.15.1 xDSL (Digital Subscriber Line)
- ☑ 2.15.2 Broadband Cable (Cable modem)
- ☑ 2.15.3 POTS / PSTN (Plain Old Telephone Service / Public Switched Telephone Network)
- ☑ 2.15.4 Satellite
- ☑ 2.15.5 Wireless
- ☑ ADSL is the most common form of DSL and it offers higher download speeds than upload speeds.
- ☑ DSL's performance depends on how far the customer's location is from the central office.
- ☑ DSL technologies use sophisticated modulation schemes to pack data onto copper wires.
- ☑ Broadband cable is faster than DSL in most cases, but is a shared medium that can be affected by too many subscribers.
- ☑ POTS/PSTN refers to the international telephone system based on copper wires carrying analog voice data.
- ☑ Wireless ISPs (WISPs) are known to provide Internet access from anywhere that it has coverage. Many locations that have very little access to a good last mile source utilize this technology to connect to the Internet.
- ☑ Satellite dishes are also starting to gain popularity. Satellite dishes that give access to the Internet via a service provider offer Internet access without having to run the provider's line into your home or business.

Define the Function of the Following Remote Access Protocols and Services

- ☑ 2.16.1 RAS (Remote Access Service)
- ☑ 2.16.2 PPP (Point-to-Point Protocol)
- ☑ 2.16.3 SLIP (Serial Line Internet Protocol)
- ☑ 2.16.4 PPPoE (Point-to-Point Protocol over Ethernet)
- ☑ 2.16.5 PPTP (Point-to-Point Tunneling Protocol)

☑ 2.16.6 VPN (Virtual Private Network)

☑ 2.16.7 RDP (Remote Desktop Protocol)

☑ The Remote Access Service is a feature built into Windows (and other network operating systems) that enables users to log into an LAN using a modem or WAN link. RAS works with several major network protocols, including TCP/IP.

☑ PPP is a protocol used to encapsulate data for transmission. It is more stable than the older SLIP protocol and provides error-checking features.

☑ Working in the Data Link Layer of the OSI model, PPP sends the computer's TCP/IP packets to a server that puts them onto the Internet.

☑ PPP will operate with SLIP (Serial Line Internet Protocol).

☑ SLIP is a protocol used to encapsulate data for transmission. SLIP is rarely used and only works with IP, whereas PPP uses other protocols within its own suite.

☑ PPPoE relies on two widely accepted standards: PPP and Ethernet. PPPoE is a specification for connecting the users on an Ethernet to the Internet through a common broadband medium, such as DSL or cable modem.

☑ PPTP, short for Point-to-Point Tunneling Protocol, is a technology for creating VPNs.

☑ VPNs are used to connect sites or users over insecure public connections (such as the Internet) with encryption that creates a virtual tunnel. This tunnel is used to transmit data securely, hence, a *virtual and private* network.

☑ The Remote Desktop Protocol (RDP) is a Presentation Layer protocol that allows a Windows-based system to communicate with another Windows-based system remotely. RDP allows you to connect to a client computer and to display and input data.

Identify the Following Security Protocols and Describe their Purpose and Function

☑ 2.17.1 IPSec (Internet Protocol Security)

☑ 2.17.2 L2TP (Layer 2 Tunneling Protocol)

☑ 2.17.3 SSL (Secure Sockets Layer)

☑ 2.17.4 WEP (Wired Equivalent Privacy)

☑ 2.17.5 WPA (Wi-Fi Protected Access)

☑ 2.17.6 802.1x

☑ IPSec is a set of protocols developed by the IETF to support secure exchange of packets at the IP layer.

☑ IPSec has been deployed widely to implement VPNs and supports two encryption modes: Transport and Tunnel.

☑ L2TP is an extension to the PPP protocol that enables the operation of VPNs. L2TP merges the best features of two other tunneling protocols: PPTP from Microsoft and L2F from Cisco.

☑ SSL is a protocol developed by Netscape for transmitting private documents via the Internet. SSL works by using a private key to encrypt data that's transferred over the SSL connection.

☑ WEP is a security protocol for wireless local area networks (WLANs) defined in the 802.11b standard. WEP is designed to provide the same level of security as that of a wired LAN, hence the name *Wired Equivalent*.

☑ WPA, short for Wi-Fi Protected Access, is a Wi-Fi standard that was designed to improve upon the security features of WEP. The technology is designed to work with existing Wi-Fi products that have been enabled with WEP 802.1x.

☑ The IEEE 802.1x standard is simply a standard for passing EAP over a wired or wireless LAN. With 802.1x, you package EAP messages in Ethernet frames and don't use PPP.

Identify Authentication Protocols

☑ 2.18.1 CHAP (Challenge Handshake Authentication Protocol)

☑ 2.18.2 MS-CHAP (Microsoft Challenge Handshake Authentication Protocol)

☑ 2.18.3 PAP (Password Authentication Protocol)

☑ 2.18.4 RADIUS (Remote Authentication Dial-In User Service)

☑ 2.18.5 Kerberos

☑ 2.18.6 EAP (Extensible Authentication Protocol)).

☑ CHAP is used for authentication.

☑ MSCHAP authentication is the default authentication method used by the Microsoft Windows 2000 (and above) operating system.

☑ PAP is the most basic form of authentication, in which a user's name and password are transmitted over a network and compared to a table of name-password pairs.

☑ The main weakness of PAP is that both the username and password are transmitted unencrypted.

☑ RADIUS is an authentication and accounting system.

☑ Kerberos is an authentication system designed to enable two parties to exchange private information across an otherwise open network. It works by assigning a unique key, called a ticket, to each user that logs on to the network.

☑ EAP, an extension to PPP, is a general protocol for authentication that also supports multiple authentication methods, such as token cards, Kerberos, one-time passwords, certificates, public key authentication and smart cards.

Self Test

A Quick Answer Key follows the Self Test questions. For complete questions, answers, and explanations to the Self Test questions in this chapter as well as the other chapters in this book, see the **Self Test Appendix**.

1. As the primary lead on your company's helpdesk, you are asked to help resolve a problem call with an ISDN line. A customer wants to upgrade an existing ISDN line because it's currently too slow. Right now, he is using a single BRI ISDN circuit switched B channel. From the available choices, what should his transmission rate be?

   A. 56 Mbps

   B. 64 Kbps

   C. 128 Kbps

   D. 256 Mbps

2. As the network administrator for your company, you are asked by your CIO to design and deploy a data link between two offices of your company. There are 10 employees located in each office. Your main concerns are the speed of the connections, the reliability of transferring of data, and the cost. Which solution should you implement? (Choose one)

   A. Place a modem on a server in each office to so they can connect.

   B. Connect an ISDN circuit to each workstation in both locations.

   C. Use an ISDN circuit connected to a dedicated location or server in each building.

   D. Have each workstation at both locations use a modem to connect to opposite offices.

3. You are the IT manager for rsnetworks.net. As the person responsible for recommending the right technology, what would you select as the solution to provide the fastest connectivity? (Select one)

    A. T3

    B. T1

    C. ISDN BRI

    D. Cable Modem

4. You want to connect a remote office to a corporate network. The only available service is an analog dial-up line provided by the local telephone company. What device would you need to implement to use this analog dial-up solution?

    A. CSU/DSU

    B. ISDN adapter

    C. Modem

    D. NIC

5. As the Network Manager for rsnetworks.net, you need to implement a solution that will allow for sporadic connection to the Internet. Your only requirement is that you find a solution that will provide a connection of up to 128 Kbps to the Internet, only when needed. Which solution should you implement?

    A. T1

    B. T3

    C. 56 Kbps

    D. BRI ISDN

6. As a network manager for your company's high-speed network, you are looking to implement a new line from a remote site (Chicago) to the company's core hub (New York) where the mainframe is located. The mainframe is where all the company's sales orders are placed daily. The hub site is where all sites get their Internet access from, and where they upload and download files to and from. Connection to this mainframe 24 hours a day is essential to meeting the business plan. You have just heard from your systems engineer that users are no longer able to access the mainframe from the remote sites; the users at the core site are still able to access the mainframe. Within minutes the connection is restored and all users are able to access the mainframe once more. From careful analysis you uncover that during the time that the remote users were not able to access the mainframe, one user had been downloading a very large file from the Internet to the remote site user's PC. You find that the user was downloading a legitimate file and will be doing so each day. You cannot

afford this type of network slowdown each day so you decide to allow for the upgrading of the line. It's currently at 128 Kbps using ISDN BRI. You have found that after careful analysis of the remote sites' usage patterns and looking over the documentation of the current network an upgrade of about 1.5 Mbps is needed across all links. Which technology would you implement? (Choose one)

A. ADSL

B. E1

C. LAN adapter.

D. T1

7. The PSTN is the analog-based telephone system we have come to learn to be very familiar with today. What are some of the features of PSTN? (Choose all that apply.)

A. Compared to DSL and ISDN, it is inexpensive.

B. Worldwide installation base in use and readily available.

C. Easy to use and configure.

D. Transfer rates of 64 Kbps.

8. You are a network administrator at your company. Your company has a number of sales and marketing users who work remotely and telecommute from home or from sales meetings. These users dial into a RAS server to access the corporate headquarters. One day, one of the sales users dials up the RAS server to connect to the corporate headquarters network to access a few files. The sales user dials up the RAS server and cannot connect. The sales user when asked reports that there is no dial tone. What is the cause of the problem? (Choose one)

A. Telephone company problem

B. The modem does not support the PC

C. The modem settings are set incorrectly.

D. There are no settings configured within Windows

9. You are the network technician at your company. You are configuring a Windows NT 4.0 laptop for dial-up networking. The laptop will be used by a telecommuter. The telecommuter will use the laptop to dial into a Microsoft Windows NT 4.0 Remote Access Service (RAS) server. Once connected, the telecommuter will need access to a UNIX machine.

    What should you install on the laptop? (Choose two.)
    A. TCP/IP Protocol

    B. RDP

    C. VPN

    D. Dial-Up Networking

10. You are a consultant looking over network documentation for a small company with one core site and two remote sites. Router A shows the location of the corporate headquarters where there is also a link out for Internet access and another remote site configured to also connect to the core. From the figure below, what type of WAN technology is in use based on the information shown for Link A?

Figure 7.23 WAN Technology

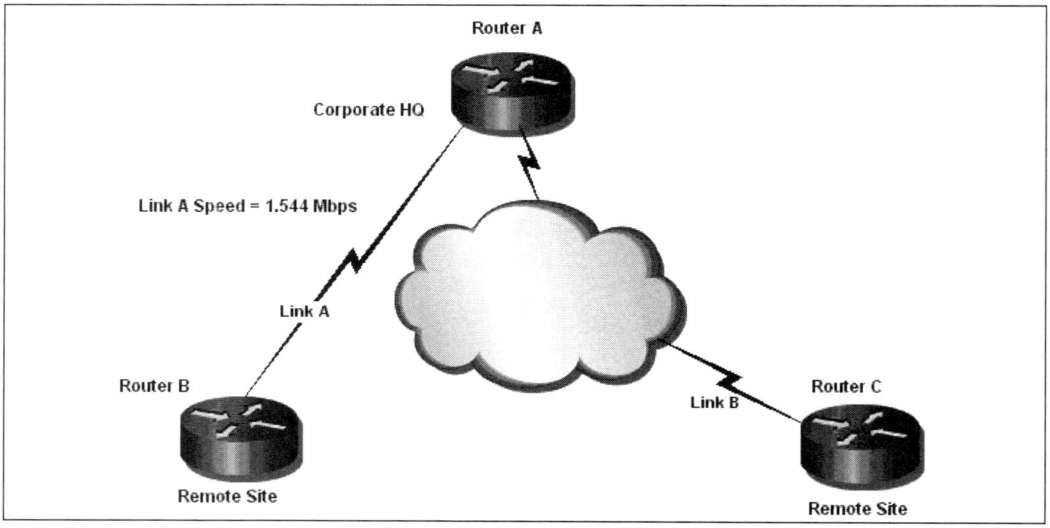

    A. DSL

    B. T3

    C. T1

    D. FDDI

11. You work as an IT consultant. You are currently working for company looking for a secure way to do work over the Internet. There is a need to have secure authentication and encryption for security reasons when accessing the corporate network. You need to use two protocols to implement this solution. From the list provided, what two protocols will allow for secure authentication and encryption over the Internet?

    A. TCP/IP and WEP

    B. TCP/IP and L2TP

    C. TCP/IP and SMTP

    D. TCP/IP and PPP

12. You are an IT consultant. You are asked to implement a solution that provides for security authentication and encryption to a private network for a client machine that needs to connect to a NetWare server inside the private network. Which protocols should you implement to provide this functionality? (Choose all that apply)

    A. DNS

    B. L2TP

    C. RIP

    D. TCP/IP

13. You are a consultant looking over network documentation for a small company with one core site and two remote sites. Router A shows the location of the corporate headquarters where there is also a link out for Internet access and another remote site configured to also connect to the core. From the figure below, what type of WAN technology is in use based on the information seen for Link B?

Figure 7.24 WAN Technology

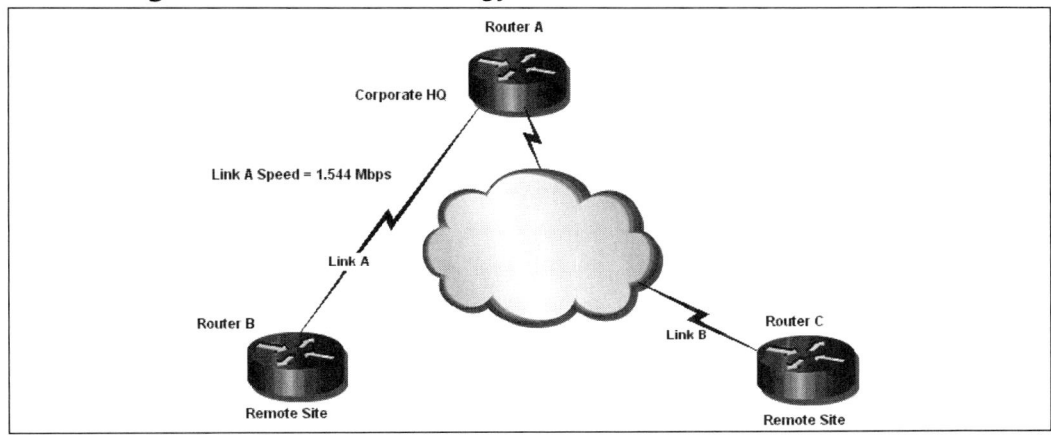

    A. DSL

    B. IPSec

    C. T1

    D. T3

14. HTTPS is a secure protocol used on the Internet. Upon what protocol is it based?

    A. SSH

    B. IPSec

    C. SSL

    D. Kerberos

15. You are a network administrator at your company. You need to implement a secure way to connect to remote hosts and manage them remotely. The way your end users connect today is with Telnet. What is a more secure way for those same users to perform the same tasks ? (Choose one)

    A. SSL

    B. IPSec

    C. SSH

    D. Kerberos

16. You are building a small Windows 2000 network. You have installed 30 Windows XP Professional workstations and two Windows 2003 Server systems. What is the LAN network access security that will be uses on this network by default simply because of using Windows 2003 or XP?

    A. Kerberos

    B. PPTP

    C. WEP

    D. SSL

Self Test Quick Answer Key

For complete questions, answers, and explanations to the Self Test questions in this chapter as well as the other chapters in this book, see the **Self Test Appendix**.

1.	**C**	9.	**A** and **D**	
2.	**C**	10.	**C**	
3.	**A**	11.	**B**	
4.	**C**	12.	**B** and **D**	
5.	**D**	13.	**B**	
6.	**D**	14.	**C**	
7.	**A**, **B** and **C**	15.	**C**	
8.	**A**	16.	**A**	

Chapter 8

NETWORK+

Network Operating Systems

Domain III Objectives in this Chapter:

3.1   Identify the basic capabilities (For example: client support, interoperability, authentication, file and print services, application support and security) of the following server operating systems to access network resources:

    3.1.1   UNIX / Linux / Mac OS X Server

    3.1.2   NetWare

    3.1.3   Windows 3.1

    3.1.4   Appleshare IP (Internet Protocol)

3.2   Identify the basic capabilities needed for client workstations to connect to and use network resources (For example: media, network protocols and peer and server services).

3.3   Identify the appropriate tool for a given wiring task (For example: wire crimper, media tester / certifier, punch down tool or tone generator).

3.4   Given a remote connectivity scenario comprised of a protocol, an authentication scheme, and physical connectivity, configures the connection. Includes connection to the following servers:

    3.4.1   UNIX / Linux / MAC OS X Server

    3.4.2   NetWare

    3.4.3   Windows

    3.4.4   Appleshare IP (Internet Protocol)

Introduction

In this chapter, we will examine the underlying concepts of a network operating system (NOS). Network operating systems have existed in one form or another for several decades. An NOS is designed to provide centralized resource sharing that can be installed on a high-powered *server*, so that these resources can be accessed by multiple *clients* over a network connection. This provides a cost savings for organizations that deploy an NOS, because they can purchase high-powered equipment for only a few central servers running an NOS, and use lower-powered desktop hardware for client computers. Using an NOS also increases productivity for an organization by storing important data and resources centrally, rather than forcing users to keep multiple copies of documents on their local hard drives or to manually transmit files from one person to another using floppy disks. The first network operating system was the UNIX operating system used by many universities and research organizations. This was followed by Novell NetWare in the mid-1980's as one of the first NOSs that gained popularity for commercial use. Microsoft came onto the NOS scene much later, first with Windows for Workgroups and later with Windows NT, and then Windows 2000 and Windows Server 2003.

We will then look at what is required for a client computer to be able to connect to a network server to access shared resources, both for local area network (LAN) connections as well as remote access connections. In addition, we will examine several hardware tools that are available to assist you in installing and troubleshooting network cabling.

Identifying the Basic Capabilities of Network Operating Systems

The primary function of a network operating system is to provide file and print sharing and a centralized user database. In addition, most NOSs provide support for applications like e-mail and Web services. A modern NOS will also be heavily concerned with security, ensuring that only authorized users and groups can gain access to the resources stored on the server that's running the network operating system. In the following sections, we'll examine four of the more popular network operating systems on the market today: Microsoft Windows, Novell NetWare, Linux, and Mac OS X Server.

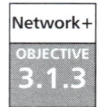

Microsoft Windows

Windows NT 4.0, the first true network operating system offered by Microsoft, found its beginnings in the early 1990's. Windows NT supported both peer-to-peer and domain-based networks, and comes in two distinct versions:

- A workstation version designed to be used primarily as a client operating system.

■ A server version that can operate as a standalone file/print server or as a centralized authentication server (called a *domain controller* in Microsoft networking terminology).

Unlike earlier versions of Windows like Windows 3.1 and Windows 95, Windows NT is multithreaded and can support symmetric multiprocessing (SMP), which allows you to increase the performance of an application by adding more processors (if the application was written to support multiple processors). Windows NT was built with stability and security in mind. 32-bit applications run in their own separate memory spaces, and older Windows 3.*x* and DOS applications run in virtual machines. Thus, the failure of an application cannot bring down the entire OS—the reason why 9*x* machines crash more frequently and have to be rebooted more often than NT machines do. One of the means by which NT remains more stable is by restricting applications from directly accessing the hardware. Applications must interact with the hardware through the Hardware Abstraction Layer (HAL) of the OS. As usual, there is a catch; this extra stability sacrifices compatibility. NT does not work with as many applications and drivers as 9*x* does.

Windows NT was focused on business users, and was built new from the ground up to provide the stability, reliability, and security features needed in the business environment. Until Microsoft comes up with a completely new kernel, all future versions of Windows will be descendants of the NT family line. Just as with the MS-DOS family line, Microsoft started off naming Windows NT with version numbers. Starting with Windows 2000, Windows was named after the year it was released, and the letters NT were removed from the name (although the tag line "built on NT technology" remained on the splash screen). Figure 8.1 shows the structure of the NT family line.

TEST DAY TIP

Just like Windows NT 4.0, Windows 2000 has a workstation operating system called Windows 2000 Professional, in addition to the server operating systems.

Figure 8.1 Following the Windows NT Family Line

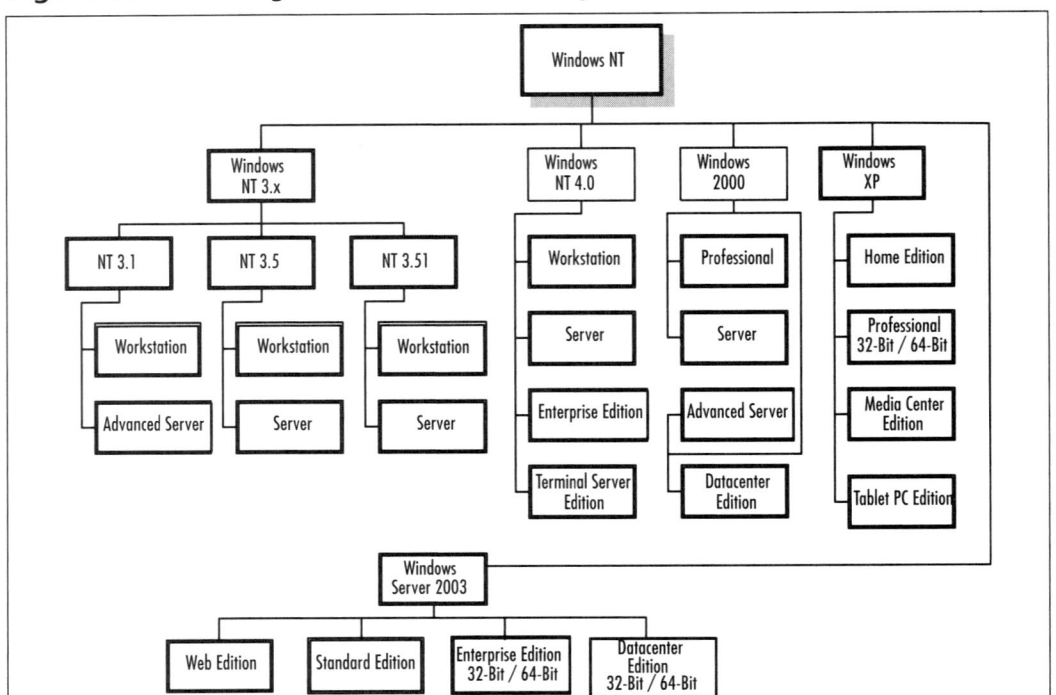

The latest incarnation of Microsoft's server product, Windows Server 2003, offers many new features and improvements that make the network administrator's job easier. This chapter will briefly summarize what's new in 2003 and introduce you to the four members of the Windows Server 2003 family: the Web Edition, the Standard Edition, the Enterprise Edition, and the Datacenter Edition. We'll also discuss how licensing works with Windows Server 2003, and provide a heads up on some of the issues you might encounter when installing the new OS or upgrading from Windows 2000. We'll look at the tools and documentation that come with Windows Server 2003 to familiarize you with new features in this version of the Microsoft operation system.

Windows Server 2003 improves upon previous versions of Windows in the areas of availability, reliability, security, and scalability. Microsoft has enhanced most of the features carried over from Windows 2000 Server and has added some new features for Windows Server 2003.

Installation and Requirements

Unless your company is buying its first Windows server, you are going to have to decide between upgrading and performing a clean install. Each method has advantages and disadvantages:

- Upgrading preserves many of your existing settings, such as users and groups, permissions and rights, and applications.

- Performing a clean installation can improve the performance of your hard drive, as it will be reformatted during installation. This also gives you a chance to change the partition and volume sizes used on your drives. Clean installs ensure that you don't carry over any existing problems that you might have with your current OS. Some administrators (the authors of this book included) prefer clean installs because they have seen many problems related to OS upgrades in the past. There is something comforting about starting from scratch. Microsoft recommends that you perform an upgrade if you will be using existing hardware, and to perform a clean install if you will be purchasing new hardware.

Common Installation Issues

The biggest problems with installing a new operating system are hardware and software incompatibilities. It is important to adhere to the recommended hardware specifications for Windows Server 2003. At a minimum, you need the following hardware configuration:

- 133 MHz processor

- 128MB of RAM (random access memory)

- 1.5GB hard drive

Remember that these are the bare minimums on which Windows Server 2003 will run. Obviously, on such old hardware, performance will suffer. Microsoft recommends at least a 550 MHz processor and 256MB of RAM. The more RAM the better the performance.

You should always verify hardware compatibility before you start your installation. There is a system compatibility check you can run from the Windows Server 2003 CD that will check out your hardware for you automatically via the System Compatibility wizard. Even if all of your hardware is supported, you should always update your machine's BIOS (basic input/output system) to the most recent version, to ensure that your hardware is as up-to-date as possible.

Common Upgrade Issues

Whether you're doing a clean install or an upgrade, you should always verify hardware compatibility and BIOS versions to make sure that they will play well with your new NOS. You should always back up your existing system before you start your upgrade. If you have applications on your server, you should read the release notes on application compatibility.

When upgrading servers from NT 4.0 to Windows Server 2003, you must have Windows NT 4.0 Service Pack 5 or higher installed. You can perform upgrades from all server versions of NT 4.0 (Server, Enterprise Edition, and Terminal Server Edition). Upgrading Windows 2000 machines to Windows Server 2003 doesn't require any service packs to be installed first. Windows 2000 Server can be upgraded to Windows Server 2003 Standard Edition or Enterprise Edition. However, Windows 2000 Advanced Server can only be upgraded to Windows Server 2003 Enterprise Edition, and Windows 2000 Datacenter Server can only be upgraded to Windows Server 2003 Datacenter Edition. You must have at least 2GB of free hard drive space for all upgrades.

Design and Planning

Planning is the first step in building a reliable, secure, high-performance, and highly available Windows Server 2003-based network. In this section, we'll begin with an overview of network infrastructure planning, introducing you to planning strategies and how to use planning tools. We'll also discuss how to develop a test network environment and how to document the planning and network design process.

Proper planning of a network infrastructure is essential to ensuring high performance, availability, and overall satisfaction with your network operations. In order to create a viable network design, you'll need an understanding of both the business requirements of your organization and current and emerging networking technologies. Accurate network planning will allow your organization to maximize the efficiency of its computer operations, lower costs, and enhance your overall business processes. When planning for a new infrastructure or upgrading an existing network, you should take some or all of the following steps:

- Document the business requirements of your client or organization.

- Create a baseline of the performance of any existing hardware and network utilization.

- Determine the necessary capacity for the physical network installation, including client and server hardware, as well as allocating network and Internet bandwidth for network services and applications.

- Select an appropriate network protocol and create an addressing scheme that will provide for the existing size of the network and will allocate room for any foreseeable expansions, mergers, or acquisitions.

- Specify and implement the technologies that will meet the existing needs of your network while allowing room for future growth.

- Plan to upgrade and/or migrate any existing technologies, including server operating systems and routing protocols.

Planning Strategies

When designing a new network or significantly upgrading an existing one, you should first use the business requirements of your organization as the primary source of planning information. You'll need to create a network infrastructure that addresses the needs of your management structure, such as fault tolerance, security, scalability, performance, and cost. You'll need to balance these requirements with the types of services that your users and clients will expect from a modern network, including e-mail, calendaring, project collaboration, Internet access, and file, print, and application services.

After you've determined the business requirements of your network, you should then analyze the technical requirements of your organization. These requirements may apply to any applications that are already in use or that you plan to implement, as well as to the associated hardware and operating system. You should carefully note all of these requirements so that you won't create any difficulties later on during the implementation process. Be sure to analyze and document the existing network, including any hardware, software, and network services that are already in place. This will make it easier to take the existing configuration into account when planning the new or upgraded network.

Finally, any well-formed network plan should make allowances for future changes to the organization, including support for new technologies and operating systems, as well as additional hardware and users. Your organization's business requirements can change—through a merger, an acquisition, or simple growth and expansion. Although it is impossible to foresee all possible changes of this nature, a good network design will be flexible enough to accommodate as many adjustments as possible.

Using Planning Tools

There are a number of tools available to assist you in developing a plan for your network infrastructure. The first and best of these, however, might be the simplest: pencil and paper. As we discussed in the previous section, you should begin your planning by determining the requirements of the business that will be using the network.

After you have a high-level understanding of your company's organizational structure and computing needs, you should inventory the hardware and software that is already in place. This is especially important to ensure existing hardware and software is supported in Windows Server 2003. In a small office environment, you can accomplish this by simply taking a walk to determine the physical layout of network cables, routers, and the like. In a medium- to large-sized enterprise network, you will probably want to rely on automated inventory tools such as Microsoft's Systems Management Server (SMS) or a third-party equivalent. Take as detailed of an inventory as possible, including the hardware configuration of server and workstation machines, as well as vendor names and the version numbers of the operating system and business applications the systems are running.

You can use a network analyzer, such as the Network Monitor utility built into the Windows Server 2003 operating system or the more full-featured version of Network

Monitor included in SMS, to create a baseline of the current utilization of your network bandwidth. If this utilization is already near capacity, you can use this baseline to justify and plan upgrades to your network infrastructure (moving from 10 Mbps Ethernet to 100 Mbps Ethernet, for example). When implementing a new network or computer solution, you should perform a thorough battery of testing before deploying it into production. Although not specific to Windows Server 2003, you should follow a systematic approach to designing a new or upgraded network. This typically includes developing a test environment in which you can test compatibility, usability, connectivity, security settings, and more.

You'll begin the test process in an isolated lab where new technologies will have no chance of adversely affecting the existing computing environment. After you are satisfied with the new technology's performance in the test lab, you can expand testing into a pilot deployment involving a few actual users, analyzing their input and reactions to make any necessary adjustments to your design. Only after you are satisfied with the pilot deployment should you perform a full-scale deployment in your production environment.

Depending on the total number of users you have, you might want to split your full-scale deployment schedule into stages. After each stage, you can verify that your system is accommodating the increased processing load from the additional users as expected, before you begin deploying the next group of users.

The success of any network deployment depends heavily on your ability to develop an effective test environment. This test lab can consist of a single lab or several labs, each of which can test various pieces of the overall design without risking the integrity of your production environment. Working in the test lab will allow you to verify the effectiveness of your design, discover any potential deployment problems, and increase your staff's familiarity with the new technology before it goes live. In short, a well-developed test environment will reduce the risk of errors during the deployment of a new technology, thus minimizing any potential downtime for your clients and users.

Planning the Test Network

Before you begin testing your network design, you need to plan the test network itself. The first step is to determine the hardware resources required to set up the lab. This involves identifying the standard configurations of your existing or new client computers. If you support diverse workstations, do your best to include a representative workstation from each supported configuration. Be sure to include all components and peripherals, including the following:

- BIOS versions
- USB (universal serial bus) adapters
- CD-ROM and DVD-ROM drives
- Sound cards

- Video cards

- Network adapters

- Smart card readers

- Removable storage devices, such as Zip drives or external hard drives

- Small Computer System Interface (SCSI) adapters

- Removable storage devices

- Mouse or trackball devices

- Keyboards

Although using separate hardware devices for your test lab is the ideal, many small- and medium-sized businesses simply cannot afford to buy dozens of computers for the test lab. Using a third-party product such as VMware (www.vmware.com) will allow you to simulate a multiple server/domain environment, as well as multiple desktop operations systems fairly closely without the expense of multiple individual machines. VMware can run multiple operating systems—such as Microsoft Windows, Linux, and Novell NetWare—simultaneously on a single PC, including all networking and connectivity that you would need to perform your testing.

In addition to purchasing hardware or virtual PC environments for the test lab, you need to secure appropriate licensing for all necessary software, including operating systems, service packs, management utilities, and business applications. Make sure that you can obtain or duplicate the following configuration and information when creating a test lab for Windows Server 2003:

- **Network services** Install the same services on a test server that will be used in the actual deployment. This can include Domain Name System (DNS), Dynamic Host Configuration Protocol (DHCP), Windows Internet Name Service (WINS), or any other Windows service.

- **User accounts** Create a domain controller in your test environment to effectively simulate any upgrade procedures.

- **Domain structure** Simulate the domain hierarchy of your proposed environment, including forests, trees, parent and child domains, and all necessary trust relationships. Configure sites as necessary to simulate any WAN (wide area network) testing considerations.

- **Network protocols and topology** Re-create the network technologies that will be used in your production environment as completely as possible. For example, if your production environment will be using 100 Mbps cabling, using Gigabit Ethernet will provide erroneous results when doing performance testing. You should also include routers to test for performance latency as well as replication across WAN links.

■ **Domain authentication** Use the appropriate authentication to mimic the desired production environment, such as using NTLM versus Kerberos client authentication. NTLM stands for New Technology LAN Manager, and is a Microsoft protocol used for authentication purposes. Selecting the appropriate authentication model will allow you to compare apples to apples during testing and avoid any unexpected behavior later. Kerberos is covered in detail in Chapter 7.

One important (but often overlooked) step in the planning process is that of carefully selecting a location for your test lab. Too often, the test lab is relegated to a corner of a server room or whatever room is available in a file or storage area. However, if you will be performing tests for an extended period of time, you should consider allocating a permanent or semi-permanent location for the lab. Be sure to locate the test lab in an area with enough space for all necessary equipment and personnel. If you will be testing network equipment that will be deployed to multiple locations, you should consider deploying a test lab at each site to test WAN links, replication, and site configurations. Also, identify the personnel you'll need to perform testing, as well as whatever training they will need.

Finally, be sure to provide both physical and logical security measures for the equipment and resources of the test lab. This includes isolating the test lab topology from your corporate network using routers, switches, or firewalls, as appropriate. If you need to provide a connection from the test lab to the corporate network, decide in advance how you will control, secure, and monitor that connection, and be sure to devise a way to quickly terminate the connection if something unexpected or adverse occurs.

Documenting the Planning and Network Design Process

The importance of documenting your computing environment after you have deployed a new network design cannot be overemphasized. As you move through the network design and testing processes, you should also keep detailed documentation of each design, product, or vendor decision that you make, including your reasons for choosing one alternative over another. Personnel changes can occur without warning, and a well-maintained design document will quickly answer the question of "Why did we choose Vendor X over Vendor Y?" when it is posed by the new Vice President of IT, who just started last week. Knowing that Vendor Y's product proved incompatible after several hours of troubleshooting will save you from wasting time by repeating portions of the design process.

Because of the effects that ongoing changes can have in a production environment, many organizations use test equipment to test every patch and service pack that is released by their product vendors, so that any potential problems or bugs can be intercepted before the patch is applied globally. Whatever method you use to roll out ongoing updates and changes, you should include detailed documentation, not only of *what* update was rolled out on a given date, but also of *how* the change was applied to client machines or other devices on your network.

When documenting both your test lab and your overall network design, there are a number of items that need to be discussed. Although maintaining network documentation is often relegated to a backseat behind the numerous fires that we must put out on a daily basis as network administrators, comprehensive records in this area will actually help you in whatever troubleshooting issues come up after the new network is placed into production. Include configuration information about the following components of your final network design (although a complete list is limited only by the amount of time you have in the day!):

- Windows Server 2003 domain structure information, including DNS hierarchy and replication information, and AD (Active Directory) structural information.

- Trust relationships, both transitive and explicitly defined.

- Network connectivity hardware (switches, routers, firewalls, and other LAN and WAN connectivity devices).

- Client computer configuration, both hardware and software.

- Line-of-business application inventory and configuration.

- Backup, restore, and disaster recovery procedures.

TEST DAY TIP

Disaster recovery is sometimes referred to simply as DR.

Users and Groups

An important part of the network administrator's job involves management of the network's users and computers. Windows Server 2003 assigns accounts to both users and computers for security and management purposes. User accounts can be further managed by placing them in groups so that tasks—such as assigning permissions—can be applied to an entire group of users simultaneously rather than having to do so for each individual user account. In this section we'll show you how to work with Active Directory user accounts, including the built-in accounts and those you create. You'll also learn to work with group accounts and you'll learn about group types and scopes. You'll learn to use the built in tools—both graphical and command line—to perform the common administrative tasks associated with the users, groups, and computers including creating and managing all three types of accounts.

Security principals get their name because they are Active Directory objects that are assigned *security identifiers* (SIDs) when they are created. The SID is used to control access to resources and by internal processes to identify security principals. Because each SID is unique, unless security is breached, there is no way for accounts to mistakenly gain access to restricted resources when the system is properly configured by an administrator.

SIDs are used because unlike the names associated with objects, SIDs don't change. When the object is created, a unique alphanumeric value is associated with it, and this stays with the object until it is deleted. Such things as changing the object's name or other attributes don't affect the SID. Because the SID is used to determine access, the user's identity remains constant, and any access the user has will be unaffected.

As shown in Figure 8.2, the SID is used as part of the authentication process. When a user logs on to a domain, the Local Security Authority (LSA) is used to authenticate to Active Directory, and create an access token. The access token is used for controlling a user's access to resources, and contains the user's logon name and SID, the names and SIDs for any groups the user is a member of, and privileges assigned to the user. The token is created each time the user logs on, and holds all of the information needed for access control.

Figure 8.2 How Security Identifiers Are Used in Access Control

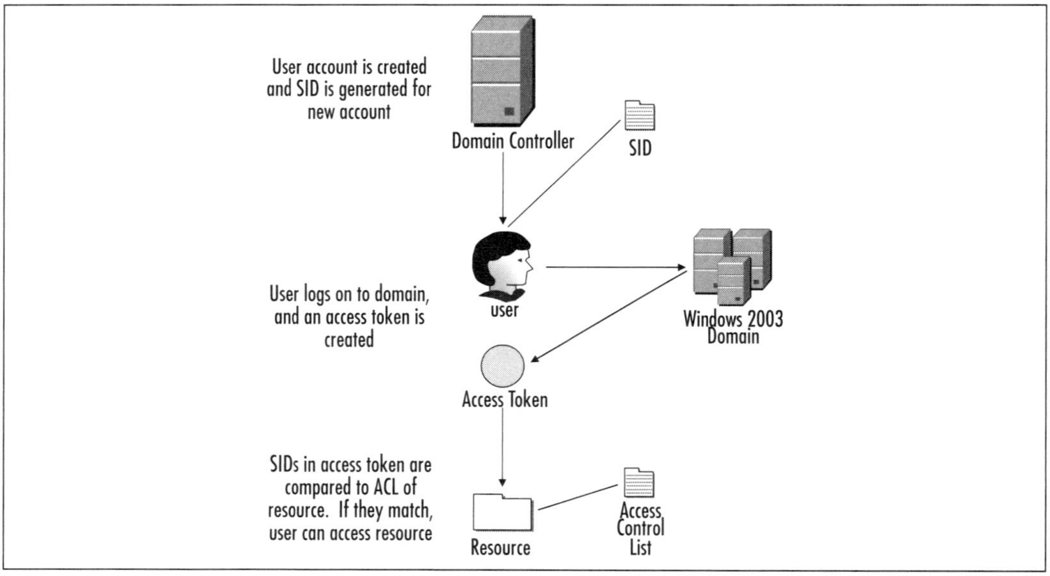

When a user attempts to access a resource, Windows Server 2003 compares the SID with the resource's security descriptor. An access control list (ACL) contains two components, the discretionary access control list (DACL) and the system access control list (SACL). The SACL is used for auditing access to a resource. An entry in an SACL contains information on whether logging should be generated on attempts to access a resource. This logging can be generated when a specified user or group attempts to access a resource and is successful, fails, or both. The DACL is used for a different purpose. DACLs determine whether a security principal is granted or denied access to a resource. The DACL catalogs who has access to the resource and what level of access he or she has. When a user tries to access an object, the user's SID is compared to entries in the DACL. If the user's SID or the SID of a group he or she belongs to matches an entry in the DACL, that user can be either explicitly permitted or denied access to use the resource.

When a security principal attempts to access a resource that is protected by a DACL, each entry in the DACL is analyzed in sequence to determine if access should be allowed or denied. As shown in Figure 8.3, the SID of the user and any groups he or she belongs to is compared to the access control entries (ACEs) in the DACL. Windows Server 2003 will look at each ACE until one of the following occurs:

- An entry is found that explicitly denies access to the resource.

- One or more entries are found that explicitly grants access to the resource.

- The entire DACL is searched, but no ACE is found that explicitly grants or denies access. Since no entry is found, the security principal is implicitly denied access.

In Figure 8.3, one user is granted access while the other is denied access. When the SIDs associated with the access token of the JaneS user is compared with the entries in the DACL, the system will find that she is a member of GroupA (which has read and write access) and GroupB (which has execute access). Because of her membership in these groups, she will be granted read, write, and execute permissions for the resource. When the SIDs associated with the access token of the JohnD user is compared with the DACL, the system will find that he is a member of GroupB, which has execute permission for the resource. However, there is also an ACE that explicitly denies JohnD read, write, and execute access. When the user's SID is compared with this entry, he will be denied access. In general, the most permissive combination of permissions will be allowed when a user accesses a resource, unless an explicit deny is assigned.

Figure 8.3 The User's SID Is Compared with the DACL to Determine Access

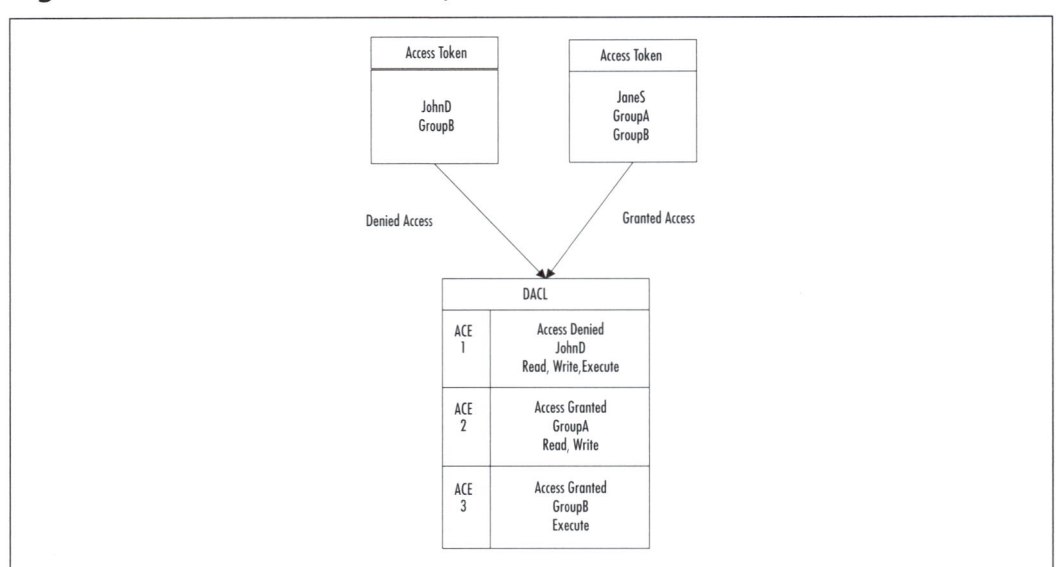

In addition to containing the user's SID and the SIDs of any groups the user is a member of, the access token might also contain additional SIDs that result from group membership the operating system assigns dynamically or other special logon scenarios.

Creating User Accounts

In Windows Server 2003, two different types of user accounts can be created: local and domain-based user accounts. Local user accounts are used to control access to the computer on which you are working. They are created on Windows Server 2003 by using the Local Users and Groups snap-in, or the Users node under the Local Users and Groups node in the Computer Management utility. Once created, the account information is stored in a local database called the *Security Accounts Manager* (SAM). The account information only applies to the local computer, and isn't replicated to other machines within the domain. When a user logs on to the computer, Windows Server 2003 authenticates the user with this information, and either permits or denies access to the machine.

Domain accounts are created in Active Directory and are considerably different from local user accounts. Rather than storing information on the local machine, account information is stored in the directory and replicated to other Active Directory domain controllers or DCs. Domain controllers are computers that are running the Windows NOS that provides for centralized authentication using domain accounts.

As we discussed earlier, when the user logs on to a DC, the account information is used to build an access token. This access token is used for the duration of time that the user is logged on to the network, and determines what the user is allowed to access on the network, and actions he or she can perform.

Active Directory user accounts are created and managed using the Active Directory Users and Computers snap-in. As shown in the Figure 8.4, this snap-in provides a graphical user interface (GUI) that allows you to point-and-click through the various tasks related to administering user objects. The left pane of this tool is the console tree, which contains nodes representing your domain and the container objects within your domain such as OUs (organizational units). Expanding the node of a domain displays the containers, which can be selected to view objects stored within them. These objects within the container are displayed in the right pane of the console.

Figure 8.4 Active Directory Users and Computers

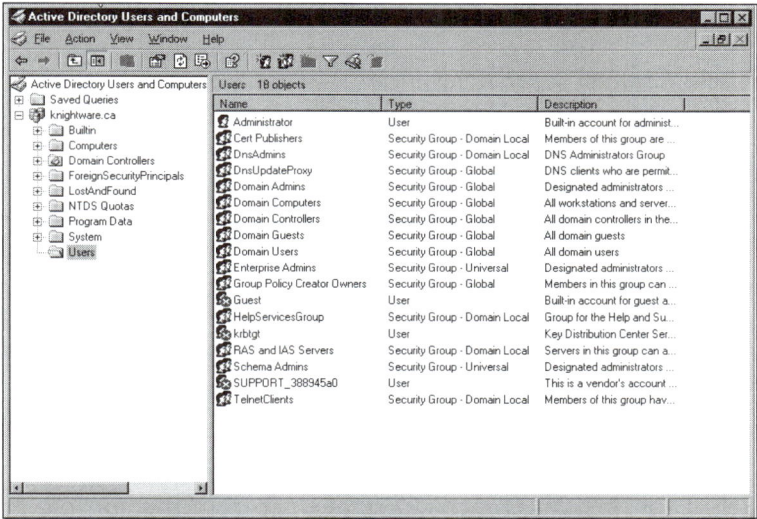

You can manually create user objects for accounts used by users and services within your organization, in addition to those automatically created when Active Directory is first installed. The two most common built-in accounts are stored in the Users container of Active Directory Users and Computers, and are:

- **Administrator** This is the first account that's created when Active Directory is installed, and has the highest level of access of any default account created in Active Directory. It is a member of the Administrators, Domain Admins, Domain Users, Enterprise Admins, Group Policy Creator Owners, and Schema Admins groups. Due to the importance of the Administrator account, it cannot be deleted from Active Directory or removed from the Administrators group. It can, however, depending on which version of Windows you use, be disabled or renamed to make it more difficult for unauthorized or malicious users to use this account by guessing its password.

■   **Guest** The Guest account is another built-in account, but provides the lowest level of access. It is designed to be used by occasional users who need minimal access and don't want to log on with their own account, or users who don't have an account of their own in the domain.

Windows Server 2003 allows you to create users at the command line, as well as using the Active Directory Users and Computers GUI. Active Directory Users and Computers is a tool that is installed on domain controllers and is used by those with the appropriate access to create domain accounts. Only members of the following Windows security groups can create new user accounts by default:

■   Administrators

■   Account Operators

■   Domain Admins

■   Enterprise Admins

EXERCISE 8.1

CREATING ACCOUNTS USING ACTIVE DIRECTORY USERS AND COMPUTERS

1. Access **Start | Administrative Tools | Active Directory Users and Computers.**

2. When the utility opens, expand the console tree so that your domain and the containers within it are visible.

3. Select the **TestOU Organizational Unit** from the console tree. If you did not create a TestOU earlier, create one now by selecting **New | User** from the **Action** menu.

4. When the **New Object - User** dialog box appears, enter the following information in the corresponding fields:

Field	Data to Enter
First name	John
Initials	Q
Last name	Public
Full name	John Public
User logon name	Jpublic
User logon name (pre-Windows 2000)	Jpublic

5. After entering this information, click the **Next** button to continue.

6. Enter a password of your choosing in the **Password** field, and then reenter it in the **Confirm password** field.

7. Clear the **User must change password at next logon** checkbox.

8. Click **Next** to continue. When the summary screen appears, review the settings you have entered and click **Finish** to create the account.

9. From the **Action** menu, select **New | User**.

10. When the **New Object - User** dialog box appears, enter the following information in the corresponding fields:

Field	Data to Enter
First name	Jane
Last name	Doe
Full name	Jane Doe
User logon name	Jdoe
User logon name (pre-Windows 2000)	Jdoe

11. After entering this information, click the **Next** button to continue.

12. Enter a password of your choosing in the **Password** field, and then reenter it in the **Confirm password** field.

13. Click **Next** to continue. When the summary screen appears, review the settings you have entered and click **Finish** to create the account.

14. Log off and then log back on as the jdoe user. Notice that you are required to change the password.

15. Log off and then log back on as the jpublic user. Notice that you aren't required to change the password.

Naming Limitations for User and Group Accounts

When you create a name that's used by the user to log on to Active Directory, certain limitations exist in what you can use in the logon name. The name cannot contain all spaces, and must not contain any leading or trailing spaces, or any of the following characters: " / \ [ ] : ; | = , + * ? < >

Groups also have certain requirements that must be adhered to when they're created. When creating groups in Active Directory, the name cannot be longer than 64 characters. In addition, the name must not contain leading or trailing spaces, trailing periods, or any of the following characters: / [ ] : | = ? * , + " \ < > ;

Security principals also make use of three other types of naming conventions, which are common to all objects in Active Directory:

- Relative distinguished name (RDN)
- Distinguished name (DN)
- Canonical name

Relative distinguished names refer to the name of the object in relation to where it is located in the directory. In other words, it doesn't show the path to where you can find the object in the directory structure. For example, a user object named John Smith would be a valid RDN. In looking at this name, however, you wouldn't know whether it was stored in the Users container or another location.

Because the RDN identifies the object within a container, this name must be unique within the container in which it is stored. In other words, you can't have two users named John Smith in the same OU. If two objects did exist with the same name, confusion could occur as to which object you really wanted to access.

To provide more specific information concerning the exact location of an object within the directory's hierarchy, a *distinguished name* is used. The DN is used to show the *path* to an object. It says that the object is located in a particular domain, and possibly even within a specific OU. This path identifies the name of the object, and the hierarchy to the container in which it is stored. To provide this information, the DN uses the following notations:

- **CN** The common name of the object.
- **OU** An organizational unit that contains the object, or contains another OU in the hierarchical path to the OU that contains the object.
- **DC** A domain component that specifies a DNS name in the hierarchy to the object. Just as with OU objects, there may be multiple domain components in the hierarchical path to the object.

As shown in Figure 8.5, the DN uses these notations to provide a map to how you can find a single object within the structure of Active Directory. In

Continued

Figure 8.5, we see that there are a number of users located in the Accounts Receivable OU, which resides in the Accounting OU of knightware.ca. If you wanted to find a user object named John Doe within this structure, you would use the following DN:

```
CN=John Doe,OU=Accounts Receivable,OU=Accounting,DC=knightware,DC=ca
```

In comparing the DN to Figure 8.5, you can see that it starts with the object, and works its way up to the highest level of the structure.

Figure 8.5 Distinguished Names Are Used to Show Location of Objects

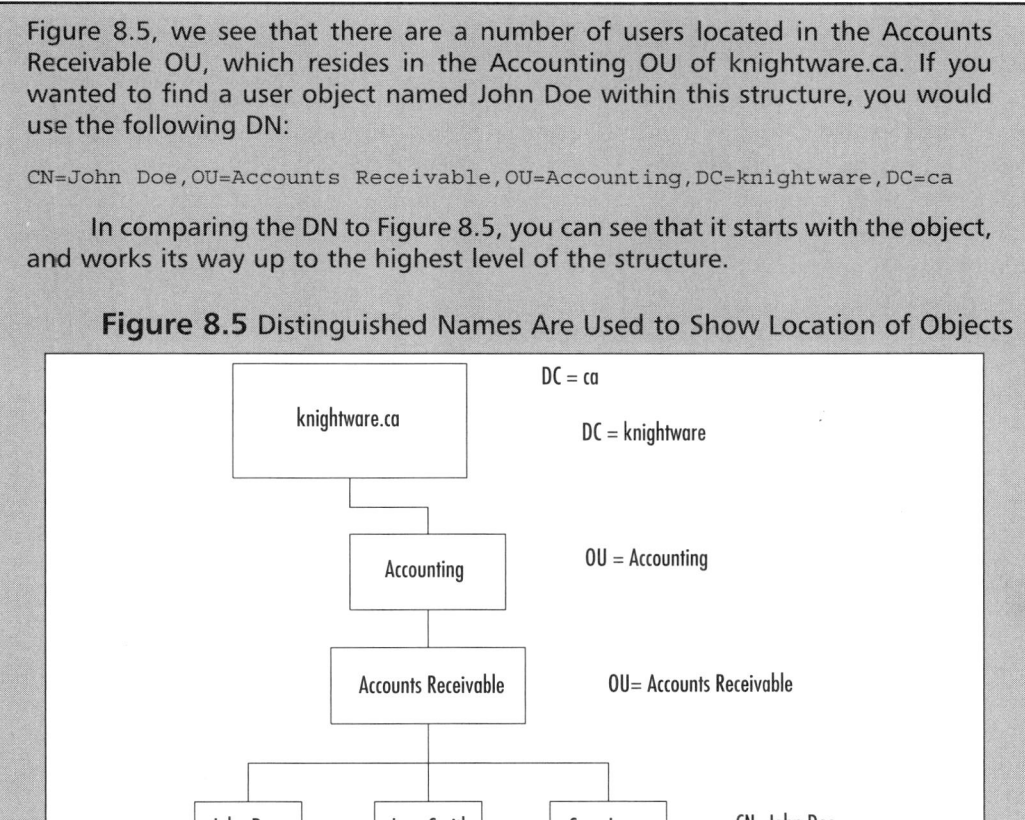

Managing User Accounts

Managing user accounts is done through the properties of the object, which are accessible by using Active Directory Users and Computers. You can access the properties of a user object by selecting the object, and then clicking on **Action | Properties**. You can also right-click on the object and select **Properties** from the context menu.

Upon opening the properties of the user, you will see a number of tabs that allow you to set various options and provide information dealing with the account including general information, settings for Terminal Services, certificate information, and group membership, among others. Individually, each of the tabs allows you to manage different settings related to the user account. However, a number of these tabs are related, in that they deal with particular aspects of user account management. As we'll see in the sections that follow, by using them together, you can configure how the account can be used.

In looking at which properties can be set with these tabs, you will see that there are four tabs that contain personal information about the user: General, Address, Telephones, and Organization. As shown in Figure 8.6, the General tab contains a number of fields that contain information provided when the account was initially created.

In looking at this tab, notice that Telephone and Web page fields have a button beside them named Other. When this button is clicked, a dialog box will open that allows you to enter additional entries. As you might guess, this is because many users might have more than one Web page or telephone number associated with them. If additional entries exist, you can also click the **Other** button to view these entries in the dialog box that appears.

Figure 8.6 General Tab of User's Properties

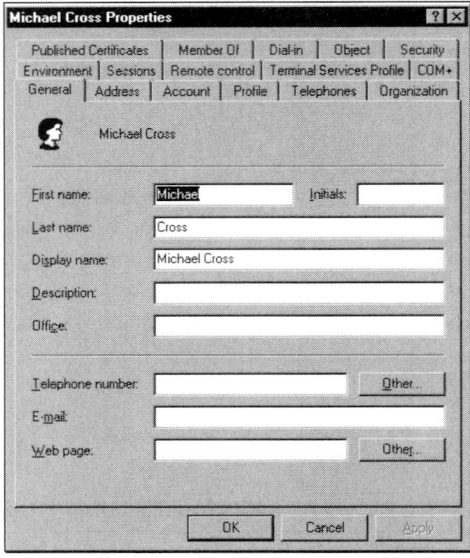

The Address tab is used to store contact information dealing with a user's physical or mailing address, as shown in Figure 8.7.

Figure 8.7 Address Tab of a User's Properties

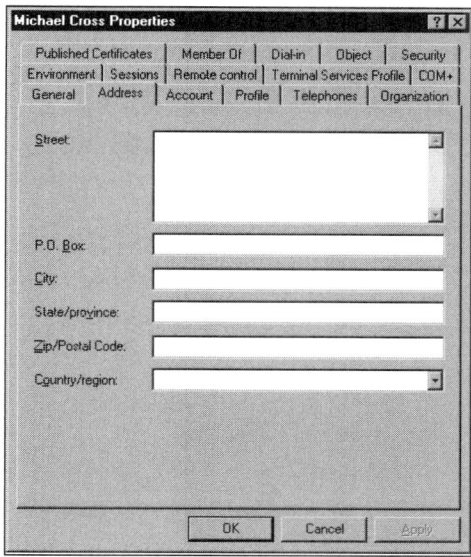

The Telephones tab is another tab that contains personal properties related to the user. As shown in Figure 8.8, this tab provides contact information relating to various methods of verbal or digital communication. Because users might have multiple telephone numbers, pagers, and other methods of communication, each of these fields (except for Notes) also includes an Other button.

Figure 8.8 Telephones Tab of User's Properties

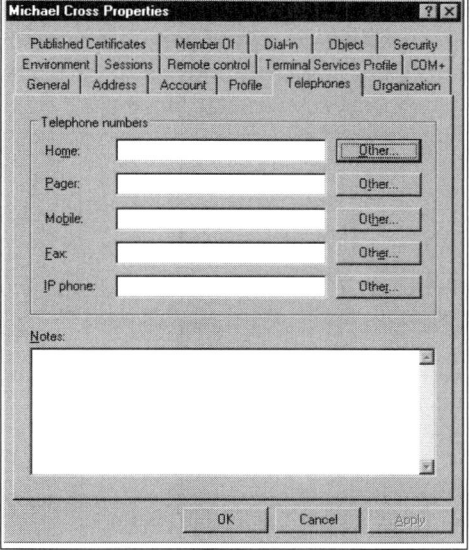

The Organization tab is the final tab that contains personal properties for the user. This tab allows you to enter information relating to the organization in which the user works, as seen in Figure 8.9.

Figure 8.9 Organization Tab of User's Properties

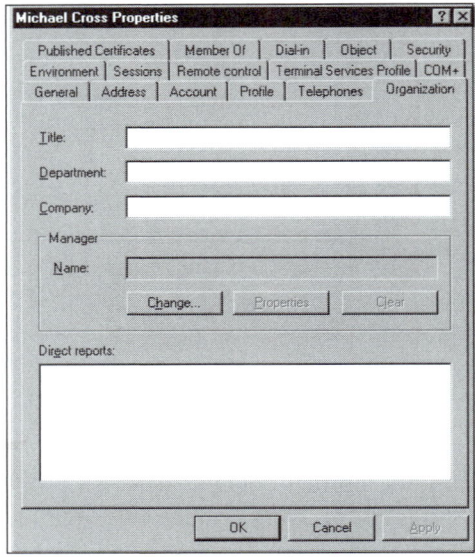

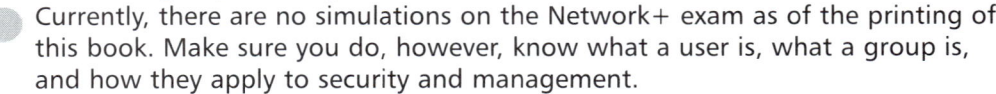

EXAM WARNING

You will be expected to know the concepts behind making users and groups for the Network+ exam. The rest of this information is useful to get you making users and groups... but you will not have to 'make' them on the exam. Currently, there are no simulations on the Network+ exam as of the printing of this book. Make sure you do, however, know what a user is, what a group is, and how they apply to security and management.

Working with Active Directory Group Accounts

Using groups, you can perform a variety of tasks that will affect the accounts and groups that are members. These include:

■ Assigning rights to a group account to authorize them to perform a certain task.

- Assigning permissions on shared resources to a group, so that all members can access the resource in the same manner.

- Distributing bulk e-mail to all members of the group.

System Management

In addition to the Active Directory Users & Computers tool that you've already seen, the majority of Windows management takes place in the Computer Management utility shown in Figure 8.10. This utility provides a one-stop shop to perform any number of Windows management tasks, including:

- Starting and stopping services.

- Managing disk space, including creating and deleting partitions and assigning drive letters.

- Managing user connections to a server.

- Creating shared folders for remote user access.

- Managing specific services such as the Internet Information Service (IIS) Web service, the Microsoft Indexing Service to index files on the server hard drive, etcetera.

- Accessing removable storage such as backup tapes and USB devices.

- Managing and installing hardware devices through the Windows Device Manager. This includes installing new devices and updating device drivers for existing devices.

Figure 8.10 The Windows Computer Management Console

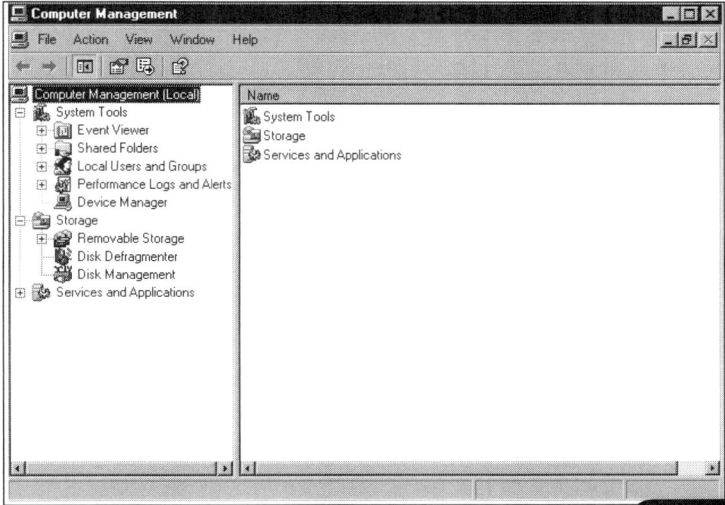

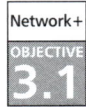

TEST DAY TIP

Make sure you know what the Computer Management console is (as shown in Figure 8.10) and what you can do within it. There are many areas of interest that you should be familiar with, such as Device Manager, Event Viewer, Services, and Local Users and Groups… where we can make users and groups on local systems… this is not the same as the Active Directory Users and Groups console that is used to create domain accounts. In Figure 8.10, this is where local users and groups can be created and managed. Be familiar with what it is you can do in the Computer Management console.

Client Support

The Windows Server family supports a wide variety of both Microsoft and non-Microsoft clients. You can connect to an Active Directory domain controller using a client computer that is running any of the following operating systems:

- MS DOS
- Windows 3.x
- Windows 9x/ME
- Windows NT 4.0
- Windows 2000
- Windows XP
- Macintosh
- UNIX/Linux

In the case of Windows clients, most will be able to connect to an Active Directory server without any special software requirements. Macintosh and UNIX/Linux clients require a special *service* to be running on the Windows Server, either Client Services for Macintosh or Client Services for UNIX. Clients will also need to be running a protocol that is supported by the Windows server. In Windows NT 4.0 and earlier, the default Windows protocol was *NetBEUI*. In Windows 2000 and Windows Server 2003 as well as Windows XP, the default network protocol is *TCP/IP* (Transmission Control Protocol/Internet Protocol).

Interoperability

As you saw in the previous section, Microsoft Windows allows many different client operating systems to connect to a Windows server. Windows NT 4.0 and Active Directory provide similar interoperability for other network operating systems as well.

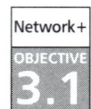

For example, you can use Client Services for UNIX to allow Windows clients to connect to a UNIX server, UNIX clients to access resources on a Windows server, and you can even create a *trust relationship* between a Windows and a UNIX server so that clients can access resources on either one using a single username and password.

You can also install the *Gateway Services for NetWare* (GSNW) on a Windows server to allow Microsoft clients to access files that reside on a NetWare server without having to install NetWare-specific client software. This service is installed on a Windows server and acts as a go-between whenever a client requests a resource that's located on a NetWare server.

Authentication

As you saw earlier, Windows NT 4.0 and earlier versions of Windows use LAN Manager (LM) or NT LAN Manager authentication to allow clients to access resources on the Windows server. Client computers running Windows 3.11, Windows 95/98 or Windows NT 4.0 will always use LM or NTLM to access resources on a Microsoft NOS. NTLM provides the ability to verify the identity of a user who is attempting to log onto a Microsoft server.

With Active Directory, Microsoft introduces a new way of authenticating users through the *Kerberos* authentication method. Kerberos is more flexible than NTLM, as well as being much more secure. Clients running Windows 2000, Windows XP or Windows Server 2003 will use Kerberos to connect to a Windows server whenever possible; however, all Active Directory servers will still support NTLM authentication for backwards compatibility with older clients who do not support Kerberos authentication.

File and Print Services

Practically every organization uses file and print services, as sharing files and printers was the original reason for networking computers together. Microsoft has improved the tools used to manage your file system by making the tools run faster than before; this allows users to get their jobs done in less time and requires less downtime from your servers. The Distributed File System (DFS) and the File Replication Service (FRS) have also been enhanced for Windows Server 2003, and Microsoft has made printing faster and easier to manage.

Enhanced File System Features

Windows Server 2003 supports WebDAV, which was first introduced in Exchange 2000. It allows remote document sharing. Through standard file system calls, clients can access files stored on Web repositories. In other words, clients think they are making requests to their local file systems, but the requests are actually being fulfilled via Web resources.

Microsoft made it easier to manage disks in Windows Server 2003 by including a command-line interface. From the command line, you can do tasks that were only supported from the GUI in Windows 2000, such as managing partitions and volumes, configuring RAID (redundant array of independent disks), and defragmenting your disks. There are also command-line tools for extending basic disk, file system tuning, and shadow copy management.

Disk fragmentation is a problem that commonly plagues file servers. This occurs when data is constantly written to and removed from a drive and moved around the disk. Data is no longer in contiguous blocks, therefore it will take longer to find and reassemble the data for use. Fragmented drives do not perform as well as defragmented drives. Although Windows 2000 (unlike NT) included a disk defragmentation tool, it was notoriously slow. To address this, Microsoft enhanced the defragmenter tool in Windows Server 2003 so that it is much faster than before. In addition, the new tool is not limited to only specific cluster sizes that it can defrag, and it can perform an online defragmentation of the Master file allocation table (FAT).

One of the best file system improvements in Windows Server 2003 is *shadow copies*. After you enable shadow copies on the server and install the shadow copy client software on the desktop computer, end users can right-click on a file and view previous versions that were backed up via shadow copies. They can then keep the current version of the file or roll back to an earlier version. This will remove the burden (to some extent) of simple file restores from your IT staff and allow the users to handle it themselves.

Improved Printing Features

Even though we rely more on electronic communications than ever before, printing is still an important requirement for most companies. One of the more common reasons for small companies to put in a network is for the purpose of sharing printers (a shared Internet connection and e-mail are two other reasons). Microsoft has taken many steps to improve the printing experience in Windows Server 2003. Users who print long documents should notice a performance boost over Windows 2000, because Windows Server 2003 does a better job of file spooling, so print jobs should get to the printer faster.

Microsoft has also made printing easier to manage. Windows Server 2003 has command-line utilities for managing printer configuration, including print queues, print jobs, and driver management. System Monitor has counters for managing print performance.

Installing printers is easy with Windows 2003 because of plug-and-play (PnP) functionality. This allows you to physically connect the printer to the machine and have Windows set it up for you automatically (as long as the printer itself supports PnP). Windows Server 2003 supports over 3800 new print drivers.

Granting Access to Shares Resources

Windows NT, 2000, and 2003 provide clients with the ability to access files and printers that are housed on a remote server just as easily as if the resources were located on the client's local hard drive. To enable access to shared resources, a Windows administrator needs to assign *permissions* to a Windows user or group account. In most cases, you'll assign permissions to groups of users rather than one user at a time, in order to make the administrative process more efficient. Using groups, you can perform a variety of tasks that will affect the accounts and groups that are members. These include:

- Assigning rights to a group account to authorize group members to perform a certain task.

- Assigning permissions on shared resources to a group, so that all members can access the resource in the same manner.

- Distributing bulk e-mail to all members of the group.

The first step in working with group accounts is deciding on the type of group you want to create and work with. In Active Directory, there are two different types, each of which is used for a different purpose:

- Security groups
- Distribution groups

The difference between these groups resides in how they are used. Security groups are designed to be used for security purposes, while distribution groups are designed to be used for sending bulk e-mail to collections of users.

Security Groups

A security group is a collection of users who have specific rights and permissions to resources. Although both can be applied to a group account, *rights* and *permissions* are different from one another. *Rights* are assigned to users and groups, and control the actions a user or member of a group can take. In Windows Server 2003, rights are also sometimes called *privileges*. *Permissions* are used to control access to resources. When permissions are assigned to a group, they determine what the members of the group can do with a particular resource.

Security groups are able to obtain such access because they are given a security identifier when the group account is first created. Because it has a SID, it can be part of a discretionary access control list, which lists the permissions users and groups have to a resource. When the user logs on, an access token is created that includes the user's SID and those of any groups to which the user belongs. When the user tries to access a resource, this access token is compared to the DACL to see which permissions should be given to the user. It is through this process and the use of groups that the user obtains more (and in some cases, less) access than has been explicitly given to his or her account.

Another benefit of a security group is that you can send e-mail to it. When e-mail is sent to a group, every member of the group receives the e-mail. This saves having to send an e-mail message to each individual user.

Distribution Groups

While security groups are used for access control, distribution groups are used for sharing information. This type of group has nothing to do with security. It is used for distributing e-mail messages to groups of users. Rather than sending the same message to one user after another, distribution groups allow applications such as Microsoft Exchange to send e-mails to collections of users.

The reason why distribution groups can't be used for security purposes is because they can't be listed in DACLs. When a new distribution group is created, it isn't given a SID, preventing it from being listed in the DACL. Although users who are members of different security groups can be added to a distribution group, it has no effect on the permissions and rights associated with their accounts.

Application Support

Perhaps the greatest strength of the Microsoft NOS is the fact that it supports an incredibly large number of applications. There are literally thousands of applications that are supported by Windows NT 4.0 and newer Microsoft NOSs, including productivity applications like Microsoft Office, e-mail, and database servers like Microsoft Exchange and Microsoft SQL server, and even complex Enterprise Resource Planning (ERP) and financial management software packages. The Windows NOS versions also support Internet technologies using Microsoft Internet Explorer, as well as numerous third-party browsers.

Security

You might have noticed that Microsoft is paying more attention to security concerns in recent releases of the Windows operating system such as Windows Server 2003. You can now control which software can run on a machine via software restriction policies. These policies can be applied at the domain, site, OU, or locally. You define a default security level that either allows or disallows software to run via the Group Policy Object Editor snap-in. Among other things, software restriction policies can be used to prevent viruses and other harmful programs from running on your PC, and can also be used to limit end users to only running the programs needed for their jobs. You can also use Group Policy Objects (GPOs) to create a consistent desktop setting for your users, which will also increase the overall security of your network.

What about the Everyone Group?

Those who have worked previously with Windows NT–based operating systems will recall that by default, the root of each drive contains a DACL that allows the *Everyone* group full control access to all files and folders on the drive. What's the problem with that? In this default configuration, "Everyone" means just that, and includes anyone accessing the machine from anywhere, including anonymous FTP (File Transfer Protocol) or Web access accounts. Obviously, this isn't acceptable if you want to control access under the concept of *least privilege*, which is the preferred option when assigning access permissions to resources. In a default installation, Windows 2000 continues this default assignment of permissions to the Everyone group. Be sure to eliminate this condition early in your machine setup regimen. See Figure 8.11 for an example of this setting.

Figure 8.11 Default Permissions on the Root of a Drive in Windows 2000

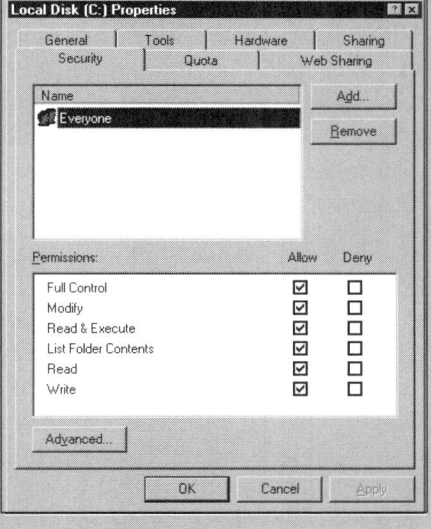

Windows Server 2003 in particular adds a number of new networking technologies that increase the security of your network. For example:

■ It supports IPv6, which was created to overcome the limited number of addresses in IPv4 (previous versions of NT use IPv4). Windows Server 2003 supports IPv4/IPv6 coexistence through technologies such as Intra–Site Automatic Tunnel Addressing Protocol (ISATAP) and 6to4. Internet and remote access functionality has been enhanced in Windows Server 2003.

■ Point-to-Point Protocol over Ethernet (PPPoE) allows making broadband connections to an Internet Service Provider (ISP) without having to load any additional software.

www.syngress.com

- Windows can now use IP Security (IPSec) over a connection that's using Network Address Translation (NAT).

In Windows 2000, IPSec was not supported through a NAT server. This was a serious drawback for some companies, as it meant they could not use a virtual private network (VPN) connection through a NAT device using IPSec or the Layer Two Tunneling Protocol (L2TP). This restriction has been removed in Windows Server 2003. Both IPSec connections and L2TP connections using IPSec are supported over NAT when you have a Server 2003 VPN server. This is done using a technology called *NAT traversal*, or NAT-T. On the client end, the Microsoft L2TP/IPSec VPN client supports NAT-T. It can be downloaded at www.microsoft.com/windows2000/server/evalua-tion/news/bulletins/l2tpclient.asp and can be installed on Windows 98, ME, and NT 4.0 Workstation. The Windows 2000 and Windows XP update can be found at http://support.microsoft.com/default.aspx?scid=kb%3Ben-us%3B818043.

Finally, the Internet Connection Firewall (ICF) functions as a personal software-based firewall and provides protection for computers connected to the Internet or unsecured networks. ICF protects LAN, VPN, dial-up, and PPPoE connections by making it easier to secure your server against attacks. With ICF, only the services that you need to offer are exposed. For example, you can use ICF to filter the network connection of your DNS server so that only DNS requests are passed through. ICF is included with the 32-bit versions of the Standard and Enterprise Editions of Windows Server 2003. It is not included with the Web and Datacenter Editions, or with any of the 64-bit versions.

NetWare

Novell NetWare was one of the first network operating systems to really gain a foothold in corporate networks, and had a near-monopoly on the NOS market before Microsoft released its own NOS. While they have lost a certain amount of their market share to the Microsoft NOSs, Novell NetWare is still a thriving concern in many small and large businesses today. As a part of their plan to continue to compete in the NOS market, Novell has begun offering open source Linux-based solutions for companies who are looking for an alternative to Microsoft Windows products and Active Directory.

Installation and Requirements

To install the most recent release of NetWare, version 6.5, you'll need a computer that meets the following installation requirements:

- A Pentium II processor, though the recommendation is a Pentium III, Pentium 4 or Xeon operating at 700 MB or better.

- 512 MB of RAM, 1GB recommended

- An SVGA display adapter

- A DOS partition with at least 200 MB of available space, 1GB recommended

- 2 GB of free space on another disk partition, 4 GB recommended

If you are installing additional applications on the NetWare server such as ZenWorks, GroupWise, or Border Manager, you should increase the hardware specifications of your server accordingly.

Users and Groups

Novell created Novell Directory Services (NDS) in the early to mid-1990's. This was a hierarchical user database similar to what Microsoft would offer in Active Directory a few years later. As NDS evolved, so did the name. The current NetWare solution for user and group management is eDirectory, which is an open framework that allows NetWare users to access many different applications using a single user object. The NetWare eDirectory can contain two types of objects:

- **Leaf objects** These are objects that do not contain any other types of objects. A printer, a user object, and a group object are all considered leaf objects.

- **Container objects** These are used to group the eDirectory into logical partitions, similar to domains and organizational units in Microsoft Active Directory.

EXAM WARNING

Don't be thrown off-guard: a group object is considered a *leaf object* in Novell NetWare.

System Management

NetWare includes a number of utilities that will allow you to manage all facets of the NetWare environment, from creating and managing users in eDirectory to managing network services such as the Apache Web server. Many, though not all, NetWare utilities run within a Web browser to provide the flexibility of being able to administer a NetWare server from many different platforms and from a remote location.

The most common tools that you'll use to manage a NetWare server are as follows:

- **iManager** A Web-based utility used to manage your NetWare server environment, set up and configure eDirectory and create eDirectory objects, and to configure network services.

- **ConsoneOne** A Java-based tool that allows you to manage the eDirectory and NetWare server resources (though iManager is the preferred tool for performing these tasks).

- **NetWare Remote Manager** A browser-based tool that you can use to manage your NetWare server from a remote location, including monitoring your server's health or performing diagnostics or troubleshooting.

- **Remote Server Management** A Java-based tool that allows for remote management from a remote workstation.

- **OpenSSH** Provides a Secure Shell (SSH) connection to a NetWare server to perform monitoring, maintenance, and troubleshooting. It uses the Novell International Cryptographic Infrastructure (NICI) to encrypt OpenSSH connections.

- **Apache Manager** A Web-based utility to manage the Apache Web server that is bundled with Novell NetWare.

Test Day Tip

Because Novell and Linux have entered into a partnership, you'll see some technologies that overlap between them, such as the Apache Web server that is available on both NetWare and Linux servers.

Client Support

Unlike Microsoft, Novell does not offer a client operating system; there is no such thing as "NetWare 6.5 Professional" or the like. Most NetWare clients are Windows or Linux computers that are running NetWare client software to provide connectivity to NetWare resources. This client software allows users to take advantage of all NetWare services including eDirectory and file and print services. The current release of the NetWare client software is available in two versions: one for Windows 95 and 98, and one for Windows XP and 2000. NetWare clients must be running a network protocol that is supported by the NetWare server. In NetWare version 4 and earlier, the default protocol was IPX/SPX. In version 5 and later, the default NetWare protocol is TCP/IP.

Authentication

Novell NetWare uses the Novell Modular Authentication Service (NMAS) to provide authentication to the NetWare eDirectory and to Novell NDS. NMAS is bundled with NetWare version 6.5 or later, and can be purchased separately for earlier versions of the NOS. NMAS provides users with the ability to use a single username and password to connect to all available NetWare resources, rather than needing to remember multiple logins for different services. The NMAS server allows administrators to choose from three types of logins:

- A username and password
- A biometric device like a fingerprint or retina scanner
- A smart card or other token like a digital certificate.

File and Print Services

Novell uses the Novell Storage Services (NSS) file system, which allows for access control based on user ID, user and directory quotas, and file attributes that allow the administrator to provide extensive file and print services to users and groups. Novell NetWare was one of the first companies to provide file and print services through its NOS, so the technology is well developed and stable. NSS can allow you to manage shared file storage for even a large organization with hundreds of thousands of employees.

Application Support

While NetWare doesn't have quite the level of application support as its Microsoft counterpart, there are still a number of useful applications that provide services to a NetWare network, including the following:

GroupWise = Email, etc.

- Novell GroupWise 6.5 is a collaboration service that provides e-mail and other information sharing capabilities. GroupWise can run on NetWare, Linux and Windows servers, and supports client software for Windows, Linux, Macintosh, as well as a Web-based client.

ZENworks = Software Rollouts

- Novell ZENworks provides administrators with the ability to roll out software and manage settings for desktops, laptops, servers and handheld devices.
- BorderManager provides firewall and VPN technologies for Novell NetWare networks. *BorderManager = Firewall & VPN*

Interoperability

Rather than just providing a way to create and manage user and group objects for NetWare networks, NetWare 6.5 allows you to synchronize information between eDirectory and NT domains, Active Directory, and third-party solutions like PeopleSoft and Lotus Notes. NetWare uses a service called *DirXML* to synchronize information between these different directory services, and you can customize how DirXML will react to new or changed information based on whatever rules you define. These rules can be business rules, or technical constraints based on time of day or available bandwidth. NetWare also offers *PasswordSync*, which allows your users to use a single password to access these different directories: when a password is changed in one location, PasswordSync will automatically change the password in other locations to match.

Security

Novell provides its own certificate server that allows you to deploy public key cryptography services that are directly integrated into eDirectory. This allows you to create, manage, and revoke digital certificates for both users and servers that will protect data as it's transmitted over public networks like the Internet. The Novell Certificate Server integrates with many e-mail clients including GroupWise and Microsoft Outlook.

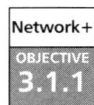

Linux/Unix

In direct contrast with Microsoft, the Linux Network Operating System is distributed as *open source* software, which means that any developer is free to make changes to the source code of the NOS to meet their needs. Linux is not free in the sense that it will cost you absolutely nothing to deploy it—you will still need to invest time and money in having the necessary hardware, software and administrative expertise to administer a Linux network effectively.

Installation and Requirements

In order to install Linux, you'll need to acquire a *distribution* of the Linux software. Because Linux is open source software, there are many distributions, including GenToo, Red Hat, and Novell SUSE out on the market today. You can purchase a copy of Linux just as you would a copy of Windows, or you can download a distribution from the Internet and burn it to a writeable CD. Most Linux distributions contain the basic Linux kernel, as well as a number of add-on utilities and services that add to the usability and security of the operating system.

The hardware requirements for Linux vary depending on which distribution you're using, but most Linux distributions will support being installed on PC hardware. As an example, SUSE Linux recommends the following minimum hardware requirements:

- A Pentium; AMD: Duron, or AMD: Athlon processor

- A minimum of 128 MB of RAM; with 256 MB recommended

- At least 500 MB of disk space to install minimum services, 2.5 GB recommended for a standard installation

Users and Groups

You can create users in Linux from the command line, or by using a GUI utility such as Webmin. Just like with Windows and NetWare, you can organize users into groups to simplify administration. In Linux, the most powerful administrative account is called *root*. This root user can access and control every aspect of the operating system, and perform any function at any time. On university Linux systems in the early '90s, the root user was often named "God", with good reason. Therefore, it is essential that you protect the root account with a strong password, and not use the root account for day-to-day tasks such as checking e-mail or surfing the Web.

TEST DAY TIP

You'll create new users from the Linux command line by using the **useradd** command.

All users that have been created on a Linux server reside in a file called /etc/passwd. You can view the file one page at a time using the **more** command, like this:

```
more /etc/passwd
```

Each line of the etc/password file contains a new user along with parameters such as their home directory and their numerical user ID.

Groups in Linux are organized in much the same way as in Windows or NetWare. You create a group and then add user objects as members of the group. You can then assign rights and permissions to the group instead of to each individual user object. You'll create a new group at the command line with the **groupadd** command, or by using a GUI interface. Groups are stored in a file called /etc/group. To add a user to a group, use the **gpasswd −a** *username* command, specifying the user that you want to add to the group. You can delete a user from a group by using the **gpasswd −d** *username* command. You can also make changes to groups by editing the /etc/group file directly.

System Management

Much of Linux administration happens at the command line, though there are a number of GUI tools that you can also use to perform common administrative tasks. You can run different *consoles* simultaneously on a Linux system, and each console can be run in the *security context* of a different user. This means that you can be doing day-to-day tasks using an everyday user account, and open up a separate console to perform administrative tasks using the root password. Many of the commands that you can use on a Linux server are similar to DOS commands, but there are some differences. Some of the commands that you'll use on an everyday basis include the following:

- **cd** to change to a different directory in the file system
- **ls** to list the files and folders in a directory
- **cp** to copy a file
- **mv** to move a file
- **cat** to view the contents of a text file

- **more** to view a file one screen at a time
- **vi** provides an editor to create and manage text files
- **man** provides the help (or manual) page for all built-in Linux commands.

Client Support

Client access to Linux servers is done using standard protocols and applications such as the following:

- **telnet** will allow you to open a text-based console window on a remote server.
- **ssh** is similar to telnet, but provides a secure connection.
- **ftp** allows you to upload and download files to and from a remote server.
- **sftp** is similar to ftp, but provides a secure connection.

Test Day Tip

When given the choice between two utilities such as **telnet** and **ssh**, you'll want to choose the utility that provides the greatest security, so long as the remote server supports it. If a remote server only supports telnet, for example, then you would not be able to use SSH to access resources on that server.

Authentication

Historically, forms of UNIX authentication have existed for over forty years. From the venerable /etc/passwd to the more modern and secure Password Access Manager (PAM), various methods of authentication have been utilized for Linux workstation logon. This section will examine authentication methodologies that function across the many flavors of Linux. In many cases, this information is also applicable to Solaris, BSD, MacOS, and HP-UX flavors of UNIX.

Understanding LDAP Authentication

Lightweight Directory Application Protocol (LDAP)-based authentication is one of the most widely used cross-platform enterprise authentication technologies. It is versatile, well supported, and features strong encryption. As mentioned above, authentication services frequently integrate with directory services. In the case of LDAP authentication, the authentication service is the directory service. In small companies with simple authentication needs, OpenLDAP is often used as the authentication server for *nix systems.

The security of LDAP authentication can be increased substantially through the use of SASL (Simple Authentication and Security Layer) and TLS/SSL (Transport Layer Security / Secure Sockets Layer). SASL provides a rich set of authentication technologies, and TLS/SSL enables encryption to ensure data and password (hash) privacy.

EXAM WARNING

LDAP operates on TCP port 389. Secure LDAP (LDAPS) operates on TCP port 636.

Understanding /etc/passwd/shadow Authentication

One of the simplest ways of managing authentication is to use a local file containing usernames and passwords. A more secure way of managing local authentication is encrypting the passwords and storing them in a separate file.

In the case of a modern standalone Linux workstation, user information is stored in /etc/passwd, and password information is stored in /etc/shadow. Access control permissions allow anyone to read /etc/passwd, but only allow root to read the password hashes in /etc/shadow. Here you can see the contents of a sample /etc/passwd.

```
root:x:0:0:root:/root:/bin/bash

daemon:x:1:1:daemon:/usr/sbin:/bin/sh

bin:x:2:2:bin:/bin:/bin/sh

lp:x:7:7:lp:/var/spool/lpd:/bin/sh

dallen:x:1000:1000:David Allen,,,:/home/dallen:/bin/bash

nobody:x:65534:65534:nobody:/nonexistent:/bin/sh
```

The following is a sample of /etc/shadow:

```
root:$1$6wDYOdeM$teP1VcO3v9sCG5W4TRbLO.:12655:0:99999:7:::

daemon:*:12590:0:99999:7:::

bin:*:12590:0:99999:7:::

sys:*:12590:0:99999:7:::

lp:*:12590:0:99999:7:::

dallen:$1$hxo7GmPU$kT34Rhw2VV5cOdqjXb.qt.:12655:0:99999:7:::

nobody:*:12590:0:99999:7:::
```

As you can see, the system-level accounts (such as *daemon*, *bin*, and *lp*) do not have a password. The password entries for *root* and *dallen* are hashes of the word "secret".

Understanding PAM

PAM is a flexible abstraction mechanism for user authentication that allows the authentication configuration for each application to be stored in a configuration file. This has the effect of separating the privilege-granting portions of an application into a system that can be dynamically reconfigured to support nearly any type of authentication scheme, without recompilation or reconfiguration of the application itself.

Invented by Sun Microsystems, PAM is used in the current version of Solaris. The Solaris PAM implementation differs slightly from the Linux PAM implementation in file location, error codes, and configuration methodology. In this book, when we refer to PAM, we are referring to Linux PAM. All modern Linux distributions, including Red Hat, Debian, Suse, Mandrake, and others, provide PAM support.

The PAM framework provides a library of functions for user authentication requests. When an application needs to authenticate a user, it calls the appropriate function, and the PAM subsystem handles the request. PAM will attempt to read the PAM configuration file for the application, which is usually stored as /etc/pam.d/*applicationname*. In some cases the configuration may be stored in a single file (/etc/pam.conf). If the /etc/pam.d/ directory exists, most PAM implementations will ignore settings in /etc/pam.conf.

A PAM configuration file is composed of multiple lines listing PAM tokens formatted in this way:

```
service-name    module-type    control-flag    module-path    [args]
```

PAM configuration files separate the authentication functions into four types: user authentication (*auth*), account restriction enforcement (*account*), session startup/teardown (*session*), and password (or authentication token) updating (*password*) functions.

File and Print Services

In the simple form (and in historical UNIX), file-based access control is called the *workgroups system* and consists of only one level and three types of ownership per file or directory (one user, one group, and world) and three types of access control (*read*, *write*, and/or *execute*). User and group identity is traditionally set in /etc/passwd and /etc/group, although user ID (UID) and group ID (GID) can be attained from other areas such as NIS or OpenLDAP. Ownership changes are performed with the commands **chown** and **chgrp** and are controlled with permission bits: nine file-mode bits (*read*, *write*, *execute*) and three special bits (*setuid*, *setgid*, and *sticky*). The command **chmod** can be used to set the permission and special bits, but some commands specifically set the three special bits (*setuid*, *getuid*, *setreuid*, *seteuid*, and *setfsuid*). On a directory, *read* allows you to list the contents, *write* allows you can create files within, and *execute* allows you to search a directory.

ACL attributes are inherited from the parent directory at the time of creation. An ACL entry is composed of a *type* (user, group, mask, or other), a *user/group* or blank, and *permissions*. When no user is specified for a given type, permissions apply to the user or group that owns the file or directory. Permissions resolution is determined in the following non-cumulative order: owner, named user, owning group, named group, other. Table 8.1 shows the terms given to the following types of ACL entries.

Table 8.1 ACL Entry Terms

Term	Text Form	Note
Owner	user::rwx	traditional UNIX owner
named user	user:root:rwx	
owning group	group::rwx	traditional UNIX group
named group	group:admin:rwx	
Mask	mask::rwx	
traditional UNIX other	other::rwx	traditional UNIX other

Effective permissions are calculated by combining the user and mask entry. See Table 8.2 for an example.

Table 8.2 ACL Types, Entries, and Permissions

Type	Entry	Permission
named user	user::rw-	read and write
Mask	mask::r-x	read and execute
Effective permission	r--	Read

Security

When securing a Linux server, providing for physical security should be one of your top priorities. Servers should be housed in locked rooms that can only be accessed by authorized personnel. You should also perform regular backups to protect your critical data. In addition, you can use the built-in Linux firewall called *iptables* to control who is able to access your Linux servers and how.

Mac OS X

The latest version of the Macintosh server operating system, Mac OS X, is similar in operation and management to the Linux and UNIX network operating systems. Mac OS X uses open industry standards from the open-source BSD community, and provides true 64-bit computing support. The current release of OS X is version 10.4, codenamed "Tiger". Tiger integrates numerous open-source applications to provide database, e-mail and spam-filtering technologies.

Users and Groups

The primary tool that you'll use to create and manage user and group objects in OS X is called *Workgroup Manager*. You can run Workgroup Manager from the server console, or you can install it on a client workstation to manage users remotely. You can also create ACLs that will permit or deny access to files and other resources to individual users and groups.

System Management

In addition to Workgroup Manager, Mac OS X also comes with the *Server Admin* tool. This graphical utility allows you to create, manage and monitor network services from any network-connected client. If you prefer to work from the command line, you can also use **ssh** to connect to and administer a Mac OS X server.

Interoperability and Authentication

Because OS X is built on open standards, the Macintosh NOS is compatible with most existing network and computing infrastructures for directory services and file and printer sharing. The Mac OS X NOS relies on Open Directory to provide a user database, and uses Kerberos for secure authentication to server resources. Just like with Active Directory and Linux implementations, Kerberos allows for strong authentication and single sign-on access to Mac resources. Open Directory is an LDAP implementation that can interoperate with UNIX and Linux implementations, and even Active Directory.

File and Print Services

Because OS X relies on industry standard protocols, clients can access Mac server resources without installing any special client software. OS X uses the Linux file permissions that we discussed in the previous section, as well as the access control lists used for Windows resources. OS X Server provides file sharing for all major client operating systems using the following protocols:

- **AFP** for Macintosh clients
- **SMB/CIFS** for Windows computers
- **NFS** for UNIX and Linux clients
- **FTP and WebDAV** for clients connecting via a Web browser

OS X server also uses the Common UNIX Printing Service (CUPS) to deploy print sharing on Macintosh servers.

Application Support

The Macintosh Server NOS offers the following applications to clients accessing the server:

- **Software Update Server** controls how your Macintosh clients will receive software updates from www.apple.com. This gives the administrator control over when and how updates are deployed across a network.

- **iChat Server** is a secure instant messaging platform, which operates with the iChat Macintosh client in addition to several open-source clients available for other operating systems.

- **Weblog Server** creates a system to manage *blogging* within an organization to allow for collaboration and information sharing.

- **SpamAssassin** provides filtering for unsolicited emails sent to the OS X mail server.

- **ClamAV** offers open-source anti-virus detection and quarantine for OS X servers and clients.

Security

Mac OS X uses industry standards to provide network security, including IPSec and 802.1X network authentication. On higher-end server hardware, you can also deploy Virtual LANs (VLANs) to segregate network traffic and prevent sensitive information from traversing a public network such as the Internet. OS X also comes with a built-in firewall and support for access control lists to secure server resources.

Appleshare IP

As you've learned, Mac OS X Server is built around Linux-based open source standards. Prior to OS X, the server NOS that was available from Apple was called *AppleShare IP*. The AppleShare IP NOS offered a number of standard services for both Macintosh and Windows clients: web services, SMTP, POP3, IMAP, Finger, the *NotifyMail* email package, AppleShare for network services (which could use either the proprietary AppleTalk protocol or TCP/IP). AppleShare IP also offered FTP services, a built-in Print Server (again using TCP/IP or AppleTalk), a DNS server service, and File Sharing geared specifically for Windows clients. Each of these applications came with its own proprietary management console to administer the service or application.

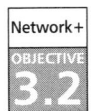

Identifying the Basic Capabilities Needed for Client Workstations to Connect to and Use Network Resources

Regardless of the operating system that's running on the server that a client is connecting to, there are certain components that are necessary to create a network connection. In this section, we'll discuss the hardware and software that's necessary to allow a client workstation to access network resources. When you are troubleshooting a network connectivity scenario, be sure that all of these elements are present and configured correctly.

Networking Hardware

The first element that is required for a network connection is having the appropriate hardware installed and configured. For a client workstation to access network resources, the following hardware must be in place:

- **Network interface card (NIC)** This is the peripheral card that's installed in a computer, which allows you to connect a client to a wired or wireless network. When connecting a client to a network, be sure that the NIC you choose is of a brand and model that is appropriate for the client hardware. For example, in the case of a Windows computer, you can check the *Windows Catalog* to see if your NIC card is listed there. The Windows Catalog is a listing of all hardware that has been certified to operate with the Microsoft Windows operating systems. If you are working with a Linux distribution, there will likely be a readme.txt file or some other type of documentation that comes with the installation files that will list the supported NICs that you can install in your Linux computer.

- **Network media** In the case of a wired network, this is the physical cabling that's used to connect the computer's NIC to a piece of networking hardware. There are many different specifications for network cabling, each with its own restrictions on length and transmission rate. For wireless networks, there is no physical cabling and the wireless NIC communicates with the wireless access point (WAP) using radio frequency (RF) transmissions.

- **Networking hardware** This is the hardware that's used to connect multiple computers to one another. Some of the possibilities for networking hardware are a *hub*, a *switch* or a *router* for a wired network, or a WAP for a wireless network.

Networking Software

Once the appropriate networking hardware is in place, a computer needs to have the necessary software components installed to enable network communications. The two software pieces that are necessary to create a network connection are as follows:

- The network *client* is a software piece that allows a client computer to interact with a server NOS. This client software can be built right into the client's operating system, or it can be an add-on that's installed manually by an administrator. Windows computers come pre-configured with the Microsoft Client for Microsoft Networks, while Novell NetWare requires a separate client that can be installed from the NetWare server installation CD.

- The network *protocol* is the "language" or set of rules two computers use to communicate with one another. You can think of a network protocol as a spoken language: if one person speaks only English and another person speaks only German, then they will not be able to communicate. Likewise, if one computer has only the TCP/IP protocol installed, and another computer has only the IPX/SPX protocol installed, then those two computers will not be able to communicate either. Two computers will need to have at least *one protocol in common* in order to be able to communicate with each other. Linux, Mac OS X, and Microsoft client operating systems running Windows 2000 or later will have TCP/IP enabled by default. Other protocols will need to be installed from the installation media.

When configuring a workstation to access network resources, there are two different types of networks that you will encounter:

- Computers that communicate in a *peer-to-peer* network do not use a dedicated server to host resources. As the name implies, each computer on the network is a peer or an equal; each individual computer can host resources that other computers in the peer-to-peer network can access. A peer-to-peer network also has *no centralized authentication database* in place, which means that users must authenticate to each individual computer to access resources on each one. Peer-to-peer networks are most commonly used for small office networks that cannot afford to invest in a centralized server.

- Computers in a *client-server* network rely on one or more centralized servers to host resources. Client-server networks rely on a *centralized authentication database* so that users only need to remember one username and password to access network resources on the server computers. Because of this centralized authentication database, client-server networks are more efficient for larger networks. One potential disadvantage of a client-server network is that it requires additional hardware for the server computers, as well as requiring additional technical expertise to manage the server hardware and operating system.

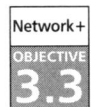

EXAM **WARNING**

A peer-to-peer Windows network is called a *workgroup*. A client-server Windows network requires at least one Windows server, and is called a *domain*.

Identifying the Appropriate Tool for a Wiring Task

In many cases as a network administrator, the network hardware you'll be configuring will be limited to the running a short *patch cable* from a PC to a wall jack that's already been installed by a contractor. However, you may find yourself needing to install your own cabling and even network jacks themselves. In this section, we'll introduce some of the tools that you might encounter when working with network wiring.

Wire Crimper

Network cables consist of one or more wires that are *shielded* by an outer shell made from plastic or PVC coating. You've also learned that cables terminate at some type of connector at the end of the cable, usually an RJ-11 connector (for CAT-3 or telephone wire), or an RJ-45 connector for CAT-5, CAT-6 Ethernet cable. In order for network communications to take place, the wires inside of network cabling have to be configured inside of this connector in a particular order. In most cases, you'll purchase network cables with the ends pre-connected. But if you're running a large amount of cable, it might be more economical to cut lengths of cable and add the connectors yourself. To do this, you'll need to have a *wire crimper* to create a firm connection between the cable and the connector. Most wire crimpers also include a *wire stripper* that will remove the outer plastic/PVC coating from the network cable without damaging the wires inside. Wire crimpers can be purchased from most hardware, electronics or home improvement stores; you can see an example of one in Figure 8.12.

Figure 8.12 A Typical Wire Crimper

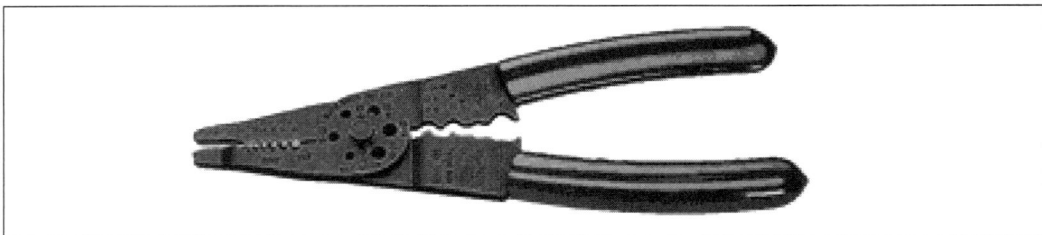

Media Tester/Certifier

You can use a *media tester* to test for any faults or breaks in a network cable. These testers are designed to allow you to plug both ends of a cable into the tester, or one end of the tester can be plugged into a wall jack to confirm that a wall jack is functioning properly. If the cable is in good condition, Light Emitting Diode (LED) lights on the tester will light up. If there is a break in the cable (or if the wires are in the wrong order) the LED lights on the tester will not light. In some more advanced (and expensive) models, the tester will even give you a diagnostic of what is wrong with the cable, displaying something like "Fault at 75 feet". If the cable passes the tester's diagnostics, this will also certify that the cable is functioning properly.

Punch Down (Impact) Tool

You'll use an impact tool (commonly called a *punch down tool*) to connect Ethernet cabling to a wall jack using a series of metal pegs and wires. Punch down tools are primarily used for telephone cables and Token Ring connectors, since they cannot support CAT-5 Ethernet cables. For modern Ethernet cables, the punch down tool has been replaced by the *patch panels* that are installed in network wiring closets. You can see an example of a punch down tool in Figure 8.13.

Figure 8.13 A Typical Punch Down Tool

Tone Generator

If you need to troubleshoot telephone connections when dealing with dial-up modems for a remote access connection, you may find yourself in need of a *tone generator*. This is either a piece of software or a hardware device that generates the tones that are used in a telephone system, including a dial tone, busy signal, and ring tone. You can plug a tone generator into a telephone jack to determine if the jack is functioning and able to make and receive calls. You can see a software-based tone generator in Figure 8.14.

Figure 8.14 Test Tone Generator Software for Windows

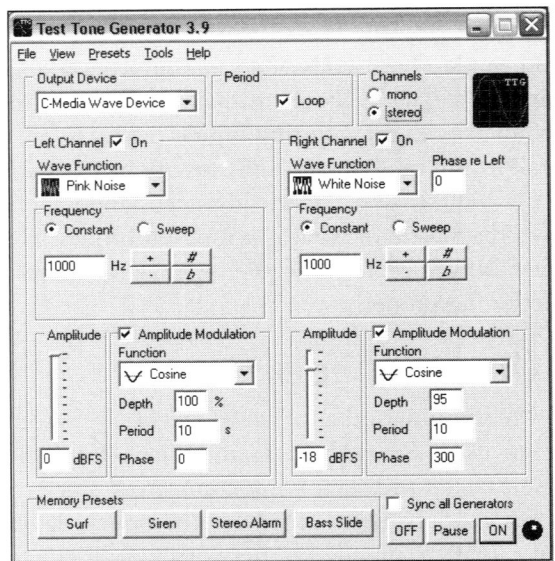

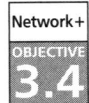 **Network+**

OBJECTIVE

3.4

Configure a Remote Connectivity Scenario

In today's business world, users need access to their company network not only when they're on company premises, but also from home and when they're on the road. An important part of a network administrator's job is to design and implement a strategy for allowing authorized users to connect to network resources without compromising security. All of the server NOSs we've discussed in this chapter include technologies and features that make this easier.

Even if your network is small, chances are you have a need for remote access, whether for traveling employees, telecommuters, or remote branches. You can choose from several methods of remote access, including dial-in access and VPN access through the Internet. Which methods you support and how you configure them will depend on the needs of your organization and its individual users.

When you plan which types of remote access to allow, you should consider how they meet your organization's needs and the needs of the users, the expense and administrative effort involved in implementing each one, and their relative levels of security. In this section we'll look in more detail at each one.

Planning for Dial-In Access

The traditional method of remote access uses a pool of modems and a server running a remote access service such as the Microsoft Routing and Remote Access (RRAS) service. Although there are alternatives, such as VPN access, modems still have some advantages:

■ Dedicated modem lines don't require encryption and communications are more difficult to intercept. This is because the connection is direct and does not go over a public data network. In addition, you can use security features available only in phone systems, such as caller ID verification and callback security.

■ Although modem access is slow, its speed is consistent and unaffected by Internet usage and other issues. Thus, it might be more reliable when high bandwidth is not needed. In some NOSs, you can also use a *multilink* feature to combine multiple modem links into a single faster connection. You can also use ISDN (Integrated Services Digital Network) modems for faster dial-in connections. ISDN lines are highly reliable and provide speeds of up to 128Kbps, almost three times faster than typical analog modem connections.

Test Day Tip

You can use the *Bandwidth Allocation Protocol (BAP)* in conjunction with multilink. BAP is used to manage multilink so that multiple connections are not wasted unnecessarily. Using BAP, a connection can automatically add and remove multilink connections as needed.

■ You might be able to use existing phone lines and modems rather than purchasing or configuring new equipment for VPN access.

■ Adding phone lines for clients is an expense, but additional clients do not increase the bandwidth load in an Internet connection.

Dial-in access typically uses the Point-to-Point Protocol (PPP) for communication. This is an Internet-standard protocol for dial-in connections. PPP assigns an IP address, DNS server addresses, and other critical configuration elements to a remote access client.

NOTE

Before PPP was developed, dial-up clients relied on the Serial Line Internet Protocol, or SLIP. SLIP was a much weaker protocol than PPP that transmitted the username and password in cleartext, rather than using any type of encryption. While SLIP has largely been replaced by the more reliable and secure PPP, it is still used with some older equipment. Most remote access servers will support SLIP for backward compatibility, but you should not enable it for remote access connectivity unless absolutely necessary.

Planning for VPN Access

A VPN uses encryption to create a virtual connection, or *tunnel*, between a remote node and your network, using a public network such as the Internet. You can see an example of this in Figure 8.15.

Figure 8.15 Tunneling Encrypted Traffic Over the Internet

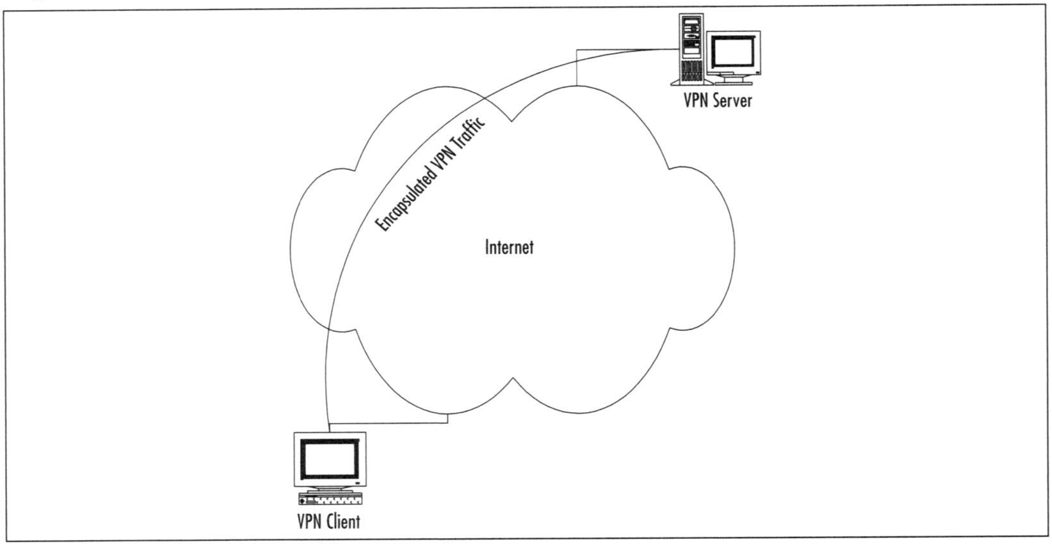

VPN access has a number of advantages over dial-in remote access:

- More bandwidth is available, assuming the client can obtain a broadband Internet connection or has a high-speed dedicated leased line.

- The network can accept unlimited connections from clients through a single Internet connection, without the need to add equipment for additional clients.

- Clients and corporate networks often have existing Internet connections that can be adapted for VPN use with a minimum of effort and expense.

A VPN connection is created through the use of a tunneling protocol, sometimes called a VPN protocol, supported by both the client and the server. Two of the more common VPN protocols are the Point to Point Tunneling Protocol (PPTP) and IPSec combined with L2TP. (You'll often see this written as L2TP/IPSec.) L2TP/IPSec provides better security and performance than PPTP, and should be enabled wherever possible.

Exam Warning

Windows NT 4.0 remote access only supports PPTP. L2TP/IPSec is supported by Windows 2000 Server and later.

In a VPN, you can also control the level of encryption that is allowed for access. By disallowing unencrypted connections or those that use less secure encryption, you can decrease the risk of network snooping. You should mandate the strongest level of encryption that your clients will support, such as the 128-bit encryption offered by Triple DES (3DES). DES (Data Encryption Standard) encryption uses much weaker 56-bit encryption and should not be used unless absolutely necessary. While VPN access has more security risks associated with it because data is transmitted over a public network, most NOSs allow you to mandate encryption for VPN connections so that clients that do not support a minimum level of encryption will not be able to connect to your network.

Choosing Remote Access Authentication Methods

When a user attempts to connect to a remote access server, one or more protocols are used for authentication to verify the user's identity. After the user is authenticated, the remote access service can determine what resources the user is authorized to access.

When you configure a remote access server, you can select which authentication methods will be allowed. You should choose authentication methods based on their relative levels of security. Additionally, the methods you choose will depend on the client operating system and the authentication methods they support. Just like LAN clients need to have a protocol like TCP/IP in common with a server it is attempting to connect to, a remote access client must use an *authentication protocol* that is supported by the remote access server.

A number of the available authentication methods use simple usernames and passwords for authentication. The simplest of these is the Password Authentication Protocol (PAP). In PAP, the client transmits the user's password as unencrypted text. To ensure a secure network, you should disable PAP as well as the Shiva Password Encrypted Protocol (SPAP), another authentication protocol that transmits password information in cleartext. Only the very oldest operating systems still require the use of PAP or SPAP; even clients as old as Windows 95 and 98 can support the stronger authentication mechanisms described next.

The Challenge Handshake Authentication Protocol (CHAP) improves security by creating an encrypted challenge and enabling the client to create a response using the password. This avoids sending the password over the network. However, CHAP stores passwords using reversible encryption, and is therefore also considered insecure. MS-CHAP v1, Microsoft's adaptation of CHAP, improves security but is superseded by the more secure MS-CHAP version 2. In addition to MS-CHAP, you can also enable the Extensible Authentication Protocol (EAP) to allow authentication using a variety of different methods.

To ensure secure remote access, you should disable less-secure authentication methods. In Exercise 8.2, you can see how to disable these insecure authentication methods in Windows Server 2003.

EXERCISE 8.2

DISABLING NON-SECURE REMOTE ACCESS AUTHENTICATION
Follow these steps to disable PAP, CHAP, and MS-CHAP v1 authentication:

1. From the **Start** menu, select **Programs | Administrative Tools | Routing and Remote Access**.

2. Highlight the RRAS server name in the left-hand column.

3. Select **Action | Properties** from the menu.

4. The **Properties** dialog box is displayed. Click the **Security** tab.

5. The **Security** properties are displayed, as shown in Figure 8.16.

Figure 8.16 Security Properties

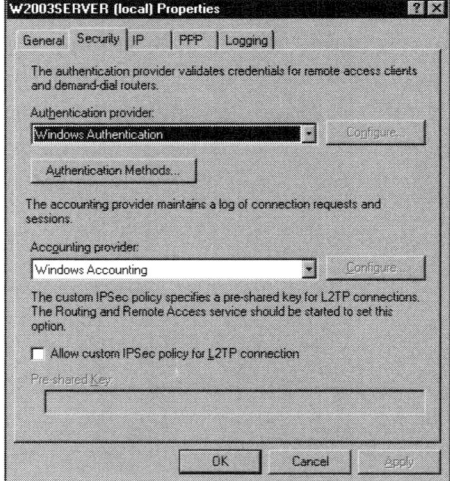

6. Click the **Authentication Methods** button.

7. The Authentication Methods dialog box is displayed. Uncheck the box next to **Microsoft encrypted authentication (MS-CHAP)**.

8. Uncheck the box for **Encrypted authentication (CHAP)**.

9. Uncheck the boxes next to **Shiva Password Authentication Protocol (SPAP)** and **Unencrypted password (PAP)**. Figure 8.17 shows how the dialog box looks with all these options disabled.

Figure 8.17 Authentication Methods

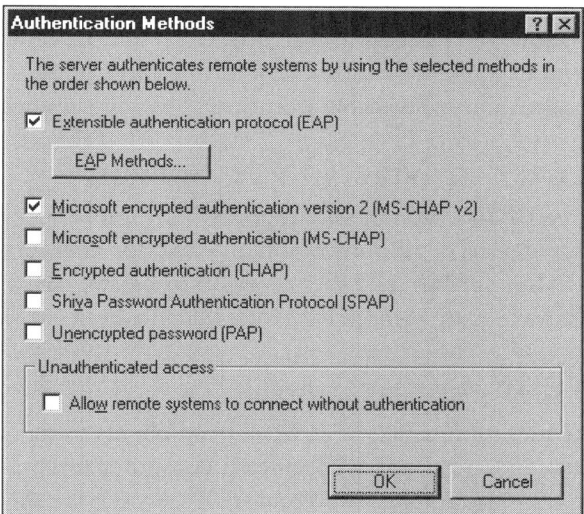

10. Click OK to exit the Authentication Methods dialog box, and then click OK to exit the Properties dialog box and save the changes.

Providing Remote Access for Microsoft Windows

Microsoft Windows (NT 4.0, Windows 2000, and Windows Server 2003) provides a network infrastructure for interconnecting local and remote systems through RRAS. The Windows Server 2003 RRAS service provides interconnectivity for remote users and remote offices using dial-up or VPN access. Windows clients can use a traditional username and password to access an RRAS server, or you can configure additional security by using smart cards or biometric devices such as retina or fingerprint scanners.

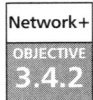

Remote Access in Novell NetWare

Novell NetWare provides remote access using the Border Manager add-on; this functionality isn't built into the server NOS by default. Novell's VPN implementation integrates with the Novell eDirectory that we discussed in a previous section, in order to give remote and mobile employees secure access to network resources. Border Manager uses the built-in Novell Modular Authentication Services authentication mechanism, and allows remote users to authenticate using a username and password, smart cards, or digital certificates.

Providing Remote Access for Linux Servers

Linux servers can allow VPN access using both PPTP and L2TP/IPSec using a number of open-source firewall implementations. One of the most popular implantations is the FreeS/Wan IPSec distribution, available from http://www.freeswan.org.

Remote Access in Mac OS X Server

The Macintosh server NOS offers several options for remote access. OS X uses SSH connections for remote server administration and SSL for encrypted web access. In addition, OS X provides support for L2TP encryption to create Virtual Private Network (VPN) connections for secure remote access to Macintosh networks.

AppleShare IP

AppleShare IP provides remote access to Macintosh clients using *Apple Remote Access (ARA)*. ARA client software allows a Macintosh computer to connect to any AppleShare IP server that's running the AppleShare Remote Access service. ARA is backwards compatible to many older Macintosh operating systems, and can communicate using either TCP/IP or the proprietary AppleTalk protocol, and can communicate over an existing Internet connection or using a direct-dial modem installed in the AppleShare IP server itself.

Summary of Exam Objectives

In Chapter 8, we looked at several popular breeds of the network operating system. The purpose of a NOS is to share files, printers and applications that can be accessed by multiple *clients* over a local area network or remote access connection. The first NOS was the UNIX operating system used by many universities and research organizations, which has given rise to the open-source Linux operating system. UNIX and Linux are still in use today, and provide standards-based access to network services. After UNIX gained popularity in educational and research environments, Novell NetWare gained popularity for commercial use. The current version of NetWare uses TCP/IP as its default protocol, and offers Web-based administration utilities to create and manage network services, users and groups. Microsoft Windows offers its own NOS in Windows NT 4.0 and Active Directory, which use NTLM and Kerberos to authenticate LAN clients. The Windows NOS supports a wide array of business productivity, email, database and Enterprise Resource Planning applications.

We then discussed the requirements for a client computer to be able to connect to a network server to access shared resources, both for LAN connections as well as remote access connections. In order to communicate with a network server, a client must have a network interface card and any necessary cabling installed, or a wireless access point in the case of a wireless client. The client will also need to have the appropriate network client software installed, and a configured network protocol that matches a protocol installed on the server.

VPNs have become a major part of the information technology landscape. As networking has evolved and the Internet has become a major part of corporate communication infrastructure, the need to connect remote users and offices has become increasingly more important. VPNs evolved as an extension of traditional dial-up networking, and the VPN technologies used today evolved from the dial-up networking protocol PPP.

VPN authentication is built upon PPP. The various authentication protocols in use vary in strength and features from PAP authentication with no encryption of passwords or usernames, to the Microsoft Challenge Handshake Authentication Protocol version 2 (MS-CHAP v2), which provides encryption and user and system verification capabilities.

Exam Objectives Fast Track

Explain the Basic Capabilities of Network Operating Systems

☑ Microsoft Windows offers the Windows NT 4.0, Windows 2000 Server, and Windows Server 2003 network operating systems to provide file and print services, application sharing, and centralized user authentication.

☑ Linux is an open-source NOS that is freely obtainable and distributable, and offers services for network clients that are similar to the ones described for Microsoft Windows.

☑ MAC OS X server is built on a UNIX-like platform, and offers many similar services to Linux and UNIX servers including Open SSH and Squirrel Mail for e-mail service.

☑ Novell NetWare was one of the first network operating systems to gain commercial popularity. It offers a centralized user authentication database called eDirectory, as well as several add-on applications like Border Manager for firewalls and VPN and GroupWise for e-mail and collaboration.

Identify the Basic Capabilities Needed for Client Workstations to Connect To and Use Network Resources

☑ A network client needs to have certain hardware installed to be able to communicate on a network, including a network interface card and any necessary cabling.

☑ Once all necessary hardware has been installed, a computer requires network client software to be installed, as well as at least one network protocol.

☑ In order to communicate successfully, a client and server must have at least one network protocol in common.

Identify the Appropriate Tool for a Given Wiring Task

☑ Use a cable tester to verify that a particular length of cable is functioning properly, or to determine if there is a short or fault ay any point along the length of the cable.

☑ A wire crimper is used to attach a cable connector to a length of cable. Most crimpers also come with a wire stripper to remove the outer plastic/PVC coating that surrounds the inner wires of a network cable.

☑ A punch down tool is used to connect Token Ring or telephone cable to a central wiring closet. For CAT-5 Ethernet cable, use a patch panel instead.

☑ Use a tone generator to perform diagnostics on telephone jacks.

Given a Remote Connectivity Scenario Comprised of a Protocol, an Authentication Scheme, and Physical Connectivity, Configures the Connection

☑ Use PPTP or L2TP/IPSec to provide encryption for VPNs.

☑ Dial-up connections rely on the Point-to-Point protocol, as well as various protocols for authentication such as MS-CHAP, MS-CHAPv2 and EAP.

☑ Novell NetWare Border Manager uses the NetWare Modular Authentication Service (NMAS) to provide client authentication.

Exam Objectives Frequently Asked Questions

The following Frequently Asked Questions, answered by the authors of this book, are designed to both measure your understanding of the Exam Objectives presented in this chapter, and to assist you with real-life implementation of these concepts.

Q: Can I mix authentication protocols between client and server?

A: Authentication protocols, VPN protocols, and encryption strength must match in order to establish a VPN connection. However, you can configure the client and/or server to support multiple protocols. As long as they have at least one in common, the connection can be made.

Q: What are smart cards and how are they used?

A: Smart cards are small credit-card-sized cards that usually store encryption keys, public key certificates, and other types of account information. The card is inserted into a card reader attached to the computer, which reads the information stored on the card.

Q: You mention different levels of encryption. What difference does it make if you use stronger encryption?

A: The strength of an encryption protocol is indicated by its *bit number* – 40-bit, 56-bit, 128-bit. The bit number refers to the length of the encryption key. The more digits there are in a key, the longer it will take to guess the key by randomly trying different combinations. Stronger encryption techniques make it more difficult to extract the clear-text password through brute-force attacks. In other words, the stronger the encryption, the longer it should take for an attacker to compromise the encrypted password if every possible combination of passwords is to be tried in a given scenario.

Q: Are PPTP and IPSec proprietary protocols? Do we need to use technologies supplied by only one company if we put PPTP or IPSec in place on our network?

A: PPTP and IPSec are Internet standard protocols; however, Microsoft Routing and Remote Access (RRAS) has implemented its own version of PPTP. It is recommended that you use L2TP/IPSec for VPN encryption if interoperability with non-Microsoft products is a concern.

Q: What type of software do I need to connect my server to a broadband Internet connection like DSL or a cable modem?

A: As long as your server NOS supports PPP-over-Ethernet (PPPoE), you should not need to install any additional software and your NOS should allow a direct connection to your broadband modem. (Windows Server 2003, for example, supports PPoE natively.) If your NOS does not support PPoE, you will need to install proprietary software from your Internet Service Provider.

Q: What is the difference between joining my PC to an Active Directory domain and putting it into a workgroup?

A: If you do not join your PC to an Active Directory domain, you will not have a *machine account* in Active Directory. You will not be able to manage your PC from the domain. For example, Group Policy settings will not apply to your machine. In addition, you will not be able to log onto your PC with a domain user account. Domain user accounts can only log onto machines that are joined to an Active Directory domain.

Self Test

A Quick Answer Key follows the Self Test questions. For complete questions, answers, and explanations to the Self Test questions in this chapter as well as the other chapters in this book, see the **Self Test Appendix**.

1. You are the network administrator for a Novell NetWare network. You have been tasked with providing e-mail and collaboration software for your company's employees. What would be the best choice of software to fill this need?

   A. GroupWise

   B. Exchange

   C. SquirrelMail

   D. Border Manager

2. You are the network administrator for a Windows network. You need to purchase a new computer to be used as a client workstation by one of your users. Which operating system should you configure for the new workstation? (Each answer represents a complete solution. Select all that apply.)

   A. Windows 2000 Professional

   B. Windows NT 4.0 Workstation

   C. Windows Server 2003 Standard Edition

   D. Windows XP Professional

3. You are the network administrator for a Windows network. The user Jane Smith on your network has chosen to return to using her maiden name of Johnson. What do you need to do to accomplish this in the most efficient way?

   A. Rename the user's account to reflect the new last name.

   B. Delete the user's account and create a new one with the new last name.

   C. Copy the user's account and create a new one with the new last name.

   D. Maintain the user account with the original last name.

4. You are the administrator of a Mac OS X network. You have been tasked with deploying Instant Messaging for your corporate network. This IM service must be restricted to only internal users, and must provide encryption of the data being transmitted. How can you meet these requirements?

    A. Deploy the SpamAssassin service.

    B. Create accounts for your users on the AOL Instant Messenger Service.

    C. Deploy the Mac OS X iChat service.

    D. Deploy the Mac OS X Weblog service.

5. You are the administrator of a Windows Server 2003 Active Directory domain. Your network clients are running exclusively Windows XP Professional. What protocol will your LAN clients use for domain authentication?

    A. MS-CHAP

    B. NTLM

    C. SPAP

    D. Kerberos

6. You are the administrator of a Linux server. You want to maintain this server in a secured location while being able to administer it from your desktop PC. What is the best choice to gain access to a console session on the Linux server to perform administration from the command-line?

    A. Telnet

    B. FTP

    C. SSH

    D. NFS

7. You are the administrator of a Windows 2000 Active Directory network. You need to create a number of new user accounts to access resources on your server. What utility will you use to accomplish this?

    A. iManager

    B. Workgroup Manager

    C. Active Directory Users & Computers

    D. Computer Management

8. You are configuring a Windows 2000 Professional workstation to connect to a Novell NetWare 4.11 network installed with default settings. After configuring the NIC and plugging in the network cable, what do you need to install on the client workstation to enable access to the NetWare server? (Choose two.)

    A. IPX/SPX

    B. Gateway Services for NetWare

    C. Client for NetWare networks

    D. TCP/IP

9. You are a consultant who has been tasked with setting up a network for a small graphics design firm. This office consists of only three workstations, and the business owner does not currently have the funds to purchase a dedicated server. How should you configure the computers in this network?

    A. Configure the network as a workgroup.

    B. Purchase a dedicated server and configure the network as a domain.

    C. Configure the network as a domain without a dedicated server.

    D. Use one of the workstations as a server to configure a domain.

10. You are configuring a Windows 2000 Professional workstation to connect to a Windows Server 2003 Active Directory domain installed with default settings. After configuring the NIC and plugging in the network cable, what additional software do you need to install on the client workstation to enable access to the Active Directory domain? (Select all that apply.)

    A. TCP/IP

    B. Client for Microsoft Networks

    C. NetBEUI

    D. None of the above.

11. You have recently been hired as the network administrator for a large medical supply firm. The firm has just leased additional office space in the same building as their current offices, and you need to take an inventory of the network and telephone jacks to determine which ones are functioning. What tools can you use to perform this inventory? (Select all that apply.)

    A. Cable tester

    B. Tone generator

    C. Oscilloscope

    D. Punch down tool

12. You have been hired as a consultant to install new LANs for offices inside of a newly constructed office building. You need to be able to install wiring closets for CAT-5 cabling coming from the various wall jacks. What tool can you use to accomplish this?

    A. Punch down tool

    B. Patch panel

    C. Cable tester

    D. Oscilloscope

13. You are the administrator of a Windows 2000 Active Directory network. You need to configure remote access for file transfers from a business partner. This business partner insists that there be no chance of data being intercepted during transit, regardless of cost. What type of remote access do you need to configure? (Choose all that apply)

    A. Configure a VPN using your company's Internet connection.

    B. Configure a dial-up remote access connection using a dedicated phone line.

    C. Configure a VPN using a dedicated T1 connection between your offices.

    D. Configure a dial-up remote access connection through a dial-up Internet connection.

14. You are configuring your home PC to connect to your company's Windows Server 2003 RRAS server. Your home PC has two modems installed in it, and you would like to be able to use both of these modems to increase the performance of your remote access connection. What feature must your RRAS server support in order for this to happen?

    A. Callback

    B. Caller ID

    C. Multi-link

    D. Virtual private networking

Self Test Quick Answer Key

For complete questions, answers, and explanations to the Self Test questions in this chapter as well as the other chapters in this book, see the **Self Test Appendix**.

1. **A**
2. **A**, **B**, and **D**
3. **A**
4. **C**
5. **D**
6. **C**
7. **C**

8. **A** and **C**
9. **A**
10. **D**
11. **A** and **B**
12. **B**
13. **B** and **C**
14. **C**

NETWORK+
Domain III

Network Implementation

## Chapter 9

NETWORK+

Network Infrastructure and Security

Domain III Objectives in this Chapter:

3.5   Identify the purpose, benefits and characteristics of using a firewall.

3.6   Identify the purpose, benefits and characteristics of using a proxy service.

3.7   Given a connectivity scenario, determine the impact on network functionality of a particular security implementation (For example: port blocking / filtering, authentication and encryption).

3.8   Identify the main characteristics of VLANs (Virtual Local Area Networks).

3.9   Identify the main characteristics and purpose of extranets and intranets.

3.10   Identify the purpose, benefits and characteristics of using antivirus software.

Introduction to Network Infrastructure

In this chapter, we look at what a Network+ technician needs to know about network infrastructure. In Chapter 3, we discussed network devices such as routers, switches, hubs, and bridges. Here we'll expand on the technologies that we covered in Chapter 3 and take a look at some more advanced network components, including firewalls, proxy servers, and demilitarized zones (DMZs).

Figure 9.1 presents an illustration of the various network infrastructure concepts that you'll learn about in preparation for the Network+ exam. A *firewall* sits at the edge of your corporate network, making decisions about what kinds of traffic should (and should not) be allowed to reach your internal hosts. A *proxy server* acts as a go-between to retrieve Web pages and other Internet resources for your internal clients as well as to cache Web content locally so that your clients can access it faster. Within the internal network, you can control network traffic through the use of virtual LANs (VLANs), which are implemented using network switches. Your internal users can access company information and share resources using an *intranet*, which is typically hosted on a Web server located in your company's internal network. To provide access to internal resources for external users such as vendors, business partners, and customers, you can deploy an *extranet* using Web browsers on the client end and secure tunnels such as virtual private networks (VPNs) or Secure Socket Layer (SSL) technology to protect your information as it travels over the Internet.

Figure 9.1 Introducing the Network Infrastructure

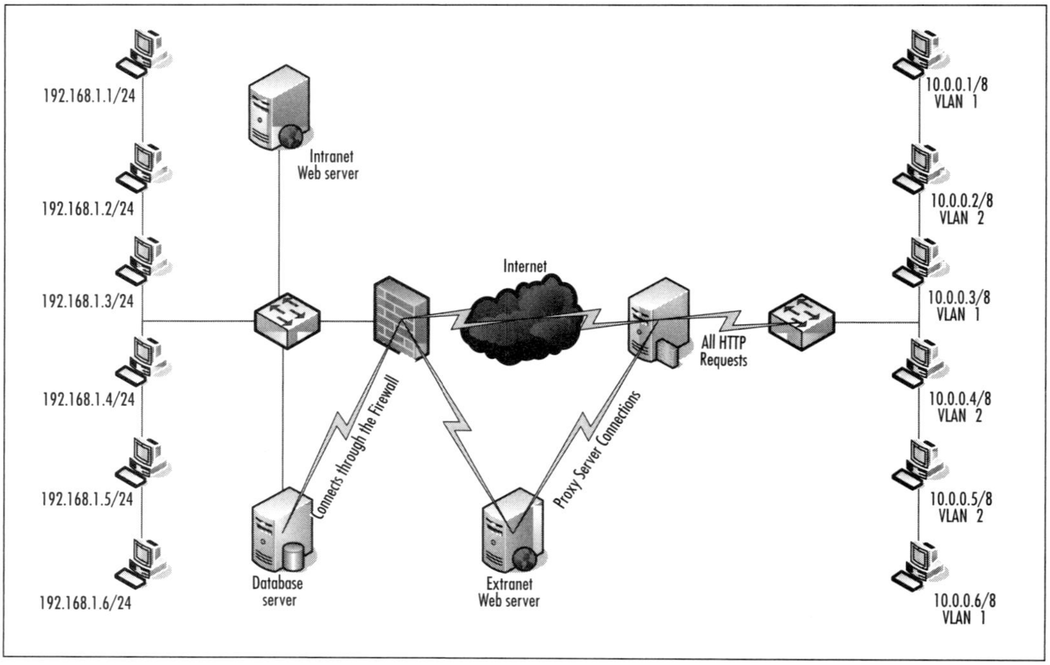

Understanding Firewalls

Although you usually hear the word *firewall* in connection with computer networks, it actually started as a term used by architects and car manufacturers. In buildings or cars, a firewall is an actual physical wall, built from concrete or some other fire-resistant material, that's designed to slow the spread of a fire. In a car, the firewall is placed between the car's engine and the passenger seats so that the people inside the car will be protected if the car's engine catches on fire. Just as physical firewalls are designed to stop the spread of fire, network firewalls are used to prevent unauthorized traffic from reaching inside a private network.

It used to be fairly common for companies with Internet-connected computers to have no firewalls at all and merely rely on the security of the individual computers to protect their data. But as networks get larger and more complex, it becomes more difficult to secure each individual host this way, so many companies today rely on a firewall as a sort of "border guard," protecting the perimeter of their networks from unauthorized traffic. Your network *perimeter* (or *edge*) is the point on your network where you physically connect to a public network such as the Internet, much the way your front door serves as the entry to your house. Figure 9.2 illustrates the concept of deploying a firewall at the edge of your corporate network.

Figure 9.2 Original Basic Firewall Configuration

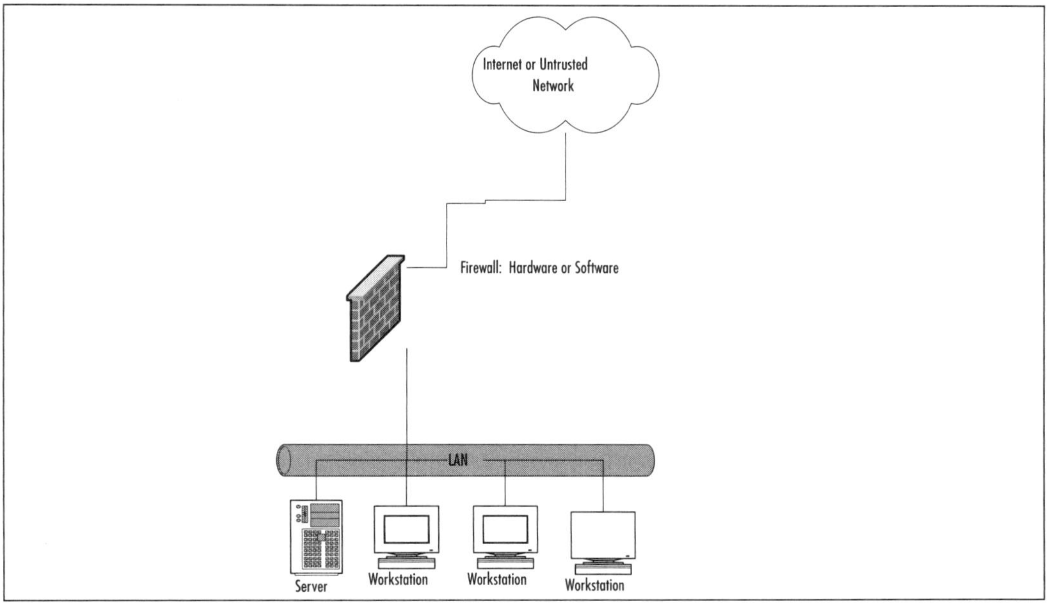

There are many different types of firewalls; some are physical devices, and some are software applications that you can install on computers running the Windows or UNIX operating systems. But regardless of the type of firewall you're using, any firewall is designed to provide several key services. The most essential functions of a firewall are:

- **IP address conservation** As we discussed in Chapter 6, TCP/IP networks can use either *public* or *private* IP addressing schemes. Because public IP addresses are so scarce, many companies are given only a handful of them to use for their Internet-connected machines such as mail and Web servers. So as not to waste public IP addresses, these companies will then use *private* IP addresses for their internal networks and workstations. Using a firewall allows you to make this distinction so that machines on your network that are *behind* the firewall can use private IP addresses. (Remember that this includes addresses such as the 192.168.*x.x* and 10.*x.x.x* address spaces.) You can then assign a *public* IP address to any computer that you want to be accessible from the Internet, such as a Web server that needs to be accessed by customers or vendors outside your internal network. This way, you can create a local area network (LAN) or wide area network (WAN) that has full access to the Internet, even if you only have one public IP address. You'll do this by configuring the computers that are behind your firewall to use private, nonroutable IP addresses. The firewall itself, along with any publicly accessible computers, can be configured with public, routable IP addresses. This process is also referred to as *Network Address Translation (NAT)*. You should understand, however, that a firewall does not necessarily need to provide NAT services to be considered a firewall. Still, many firewalls allow you to choose this feature. You can see an illustration of NAT in Figure 9.3.

Figure 9.3 Network Address Translation

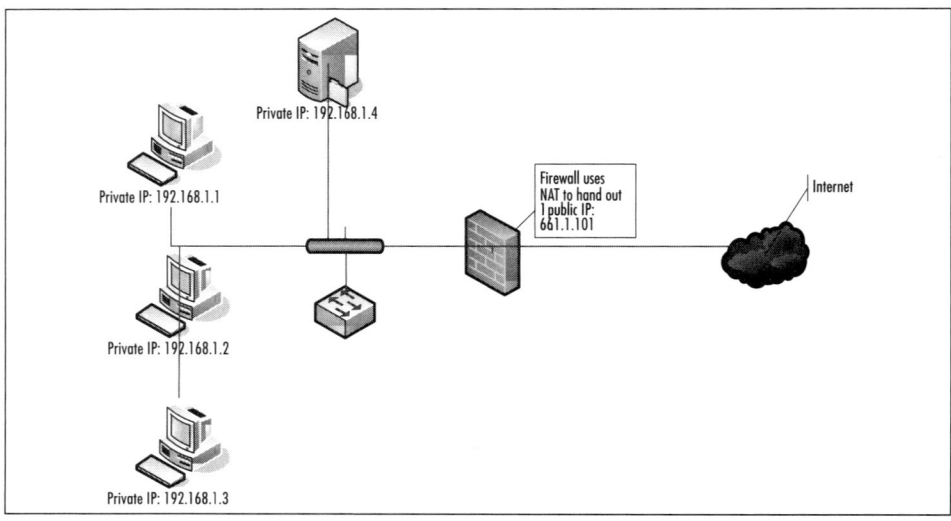

EXAM DAY TIP

Remember that the Internet is nothing more than many different computers attached to a single global network. You can create a WAN connection between two groups of computers using the Internet or using a private connection, as you learned in Chapter 7, "WAN Standards and Remote Access Services."

- **Traffic forwarding** Many firewalls also act as *routers* so that one network (say, a private 10.100.100.0/24 network) can communicate with another network, such as the Internet. You can also use this feature to help control traffic between subnets on your internal network.

- **Network differentiation** Using a firewall is the best way to create a boundary between your internal network and any other network like the Internet. Because the firewall creates a clear distinction (or differentiation) between networks, it helps you manage traffic by making it easy to designate a particular host as *internal* or *external*. You can then create rules that govern how network traffic should be handled between internal machines as well as between internal and external machines. Figure 9.4 provides an example of how network differentiation works.

Figure 9.4 Using a Firewall for Network Differentiation

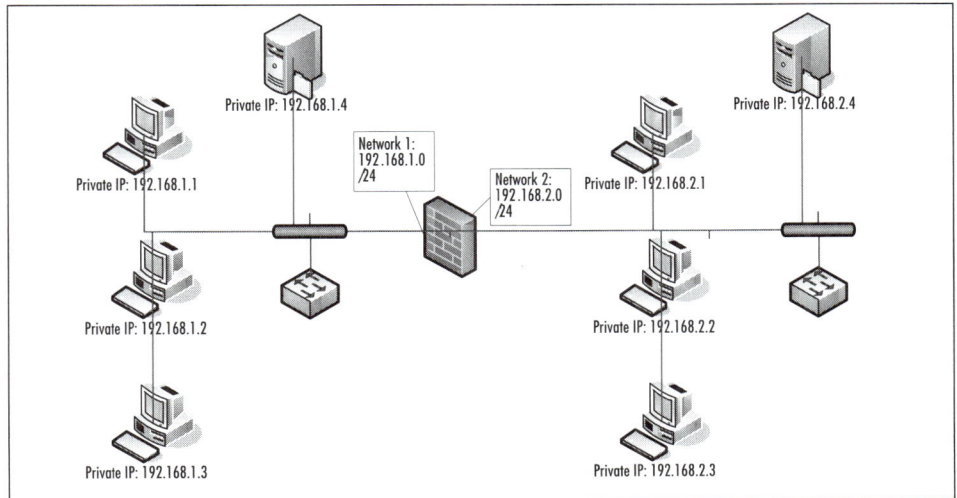

Exam Warning

Remember that a firewall doesn't necessarily need to be deployed *only* between a private network and the Internet. In many cases, a company will deploy a firewall *inside* its network to further protect a sensitive area of the company, such as the research and development or payroll departments, from the rest of the internal network. Firewalls can even be run on other hosts, such as your wireless systems, a home PC, or a corporate server. Routers today are even sold with a "firewall feature set" that allows you to turn on advanced filtering for potential attacks.

■ **Protection against denial of service (DoS), scanning, and sniffing attacks** A firewall acts as a single point of entry to your network. Having a single point of entry creates the ability to *monitor* incoming and outgoing traffic on your network and allows you to check that traffic for viruses as well as hackers' attempts to infiltrate your network. You can then configure your firewall to restrict or block any type of traffic that you choose. The drawback to this single point of entry is that it can create a "choke point" at the perimeter of your network that can slow performance and throughput.

■ **IP and port filtering** This is where we really begin to see the power of a firewall to restrict traffic on your network. A firewall can *filter*, or restrict, TCP/IP traffic based on the IP address of the machine that's sending the traffic as well as the TCP or UDP port that's being used to send information. This filtering function gives a firewall the ability to allow or reject a connection based on IP address and port; this is what most people in IT commonly think of when they hear the word *firewall*. This filtering process is done using *packet filters*, which we talk about later in the chapter. For example, a very basic packet filter can block traffic to your network if it originates from a particular external IP address and port. Packet filtering can become a complex process because a firewall can filter traffic based on its source *and* its destination.

■ **Authentication and encryption** A firewall also has the ability to authenticate users as well as encrypt transmissions between your private network and another network that's connected to the Internet.

■ **Traffic logging** One of the most important—though commonly ignored—benefits of a firewall is that it allows you to examine all details about network packets that pass through it. By paying attention to your log files, you can be alerted to hackers attempting to scan or gain access to your network, as well as monitoring access to your network by legitimate users.

An important thing to keep in mind about firewalls is that they aren't meant to provide every single security function that's needed on your network. You can and should install other systems that handle user authentication, intrusion detection, and remote access services such as VPN. At the end of the day, the firewall serves an important but very specific role on your network: to monitor incoming traffic and decide who should be let in and who should be kept out. Other functions such as remote access and intrusion detection, although crucial to the overall security of your network, should be kept separate from the firewall so that it can be dedicated to acting as your network's "gatekeeper." By combining these various devices to create several layers of protection for your network, you can create *defense in depth*, which is a critical concept when it comes to network security.

Introducing Firewall Concepts

When discussing the security that's provided by network firewalls, it's important to keep in mind some of the fundamentals of the network. We use the *confidentiality, integrity, and availability (CIA)* triad model as a starting point in talking about network security. This CIA triad provides you with a model to evaluate your network's security. For instance, the first leg of the CIA triad calls for *confidentiality*. One of the methods you can use to provide confidentiality for your network resources is to use a proxy server or a firewall as well as Network Address Translation (NAT) between an outside (untrusted) network and your internal (trusted) network. In this scenario, a firewall protects the confidentiality of your resources by separating the two types of network from each other and limiting users from the untrusted network in their attempts to view your internal networks.

TEST DAY TIP

Firewall configurations act primarily to route and restrict traffic flow to and from different network segments.

Identifying Risks to Network Transmissions

When deploying a firewall, you need to be aware of the kinds of threats for which your network is at risk. A firewall can help you maintain the security of the network services that you provide to your users and business. With the growth of the Internet as a means for business communication, it's become normal for a company to provide e-mail, Web, secure online purchasing, and other services directly to individuals and companies, both inside and outside the LAN. Some of the risks to your network services that a firewall can protect you from include:

- DoS attacks
- Unauthorized use of services
- E-mail relaying ("spam")

- Compromise of systems through misconfiguration of services, such as:
    - DNS server zone transfer misconfiguration
    - Telnet service active and unprotected
    - File Transfer Protocol (FTP) server file root unsecured or not otherwise protected
    - Interception or diversion of services or service information
    - Unauthorized remote control of systems

Firewall Definitions and History

As we continue our introduction to the fundamentals of network firewalls, let's discuss some of the terminology and definitions that are related to our work with firewalls and their components. Before we proceed to a more in-depth discussion of the firewall, we need to go over definitions of some terminology as well as a brief history of firewalls. Let's start out with some common terms that we'll use throughout this section. Table 9.1 details and defines some of the important terms that relate to firewalls.

Table 9.1 DMZ Definitions

Term	Definition or Description
DMZ	In computer networks, a demilitarized zone, or DMZ, is a computer host or small network inserted as a "neutral zone" between a company's private network and the outside public network. The DMZ prevents outside users from getting direct access to a server that has company data. (The term comes from the geographic buffer zone that was set up between North Korea and South Korea following the United Nations "police action" in the early 1950s.) A DMZ is an optional and more secure approach to a firewall and effectively acts as a proxy server.
Bastion host (untrusted host)	A machine (usually a server) located in the DMZ with strong host-level protection and minimal services. It is used as a gateway between the inside and the outside of networks. The bastion host is normally *not* the firewall, but a separate machine that is often used as a distraction to lure hackers away from more critical network resources. The notation "untrusted host" may be used because the bastion host is always considered to be potentially compromised and therefore should not be fully trusted by internal network clients.
Firewall	A hardware device or software package that provides filtering and/or rules to allow or deny specific types of network traffic to flow between internal and external networks.

Continued

Table 9.1 continued DMZ Definitions

Term	Definition or Description
Proxy server	An application-based translation of network access requests. Provision for local user authentication for access to untrusted network. Logging and control of port/protocol access may be possible. Normally used to connect two networks.
Network Address Translation (NAT)	A network service that translates private IP addresses (like those on the 10.0.0.x network) to a public IP address. This service is used to share a small number of public IP addresses with a large number of internal clients.
Packet filtering	A technology that uses a set of rules that will open or close ports to specific protocols (such as allowing Transmission Control Protocol [TCP] or User Datagram Protocol [UDP] packets) or protocol ID(s), such as allowing or blocking Internet Control Message Protocol (ICMP).
Stateful packet filtering	The use of a process to inspect packets as they reach the firewall and maintain the state of the connection by allowing or disallowing packets to pass based on the access policy.
Screened subnet	This is an isolated network containing hosts that need to be accessible from both the untrusted external network and the internal network. An example is placing a bastion host in a dual-firewall network, with the bastion host in the network between the firewalls. A screened subnet is often a part of a DMZ implementation.

The use of a firewall and its overall design and implementation can be relatively simple or extremely complex, depending on the needs of the particular business or network system. Network firewalls are used as a way to separate private and public networks; the need for this separation became more acute when we began to provide more access to network services for individuals outside the traditional LAN.

When you're working with a firewall, there are a number of ways that you can configure traffic to flow between the internal network and the external network. In addition to the basic configuration you've already seen, you can add network hosts, such as a bastion host, to increase your network's security, as shown in Figure 9.5.

Figure 9.5 Basic Network, Single Firewall, and Bastion Host (Untrusted Host)

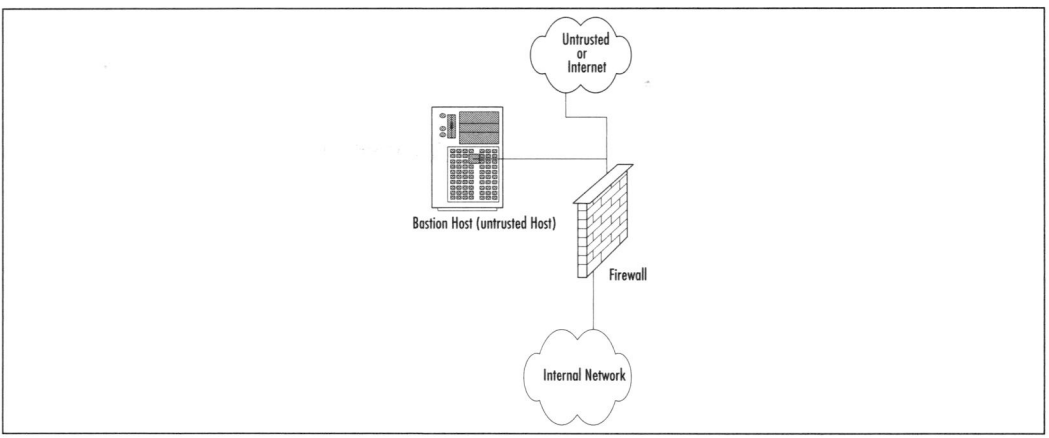

Figure 9.6 shows a network configuration that consists of two firewalls. In this arrangement, network hosts located on the *screened subnet* can be protected from outside threats while allowing connections to or from the internal network. This configuration is common in larger network implementations, where you need to host more than one computer on the screened subnet.

Figure 9.6 A Dual Firewall With a DMZ

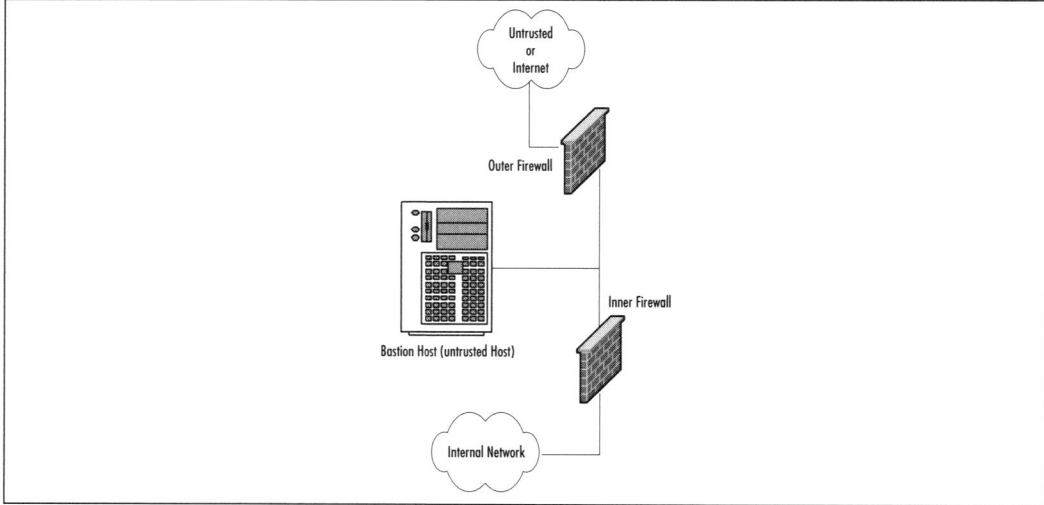

Packet Filters

In its most basic form, a *packet filter* makes decisions about whether to forward a TCP/IP packet based on the the IP, TCP, or UDP information it finds contained within the packet. In this way, packet filtering (and firewalls in general) make routing decisions based on the contents of the packets that are received. However, a packet filter only handles individual packets; it doesn't keep track of any ongoing TCP sessions, such as a session between a client workstation and a Web application. For this reason, a basic packet filter is poorly equipped to handle some types of network attacks. For instance, packet filters have difficulty dealing with *spoofed* packets, which are network packets that come in through an outside interface pretending to be part of the internal network. You can configure packet filters to allow or block traffic according to source and destination IP addresses, source and destination ports, and the type of protocol (TCP, UDP, ICMP, and so on).

So what is the advantage of a packet filter if it does not protect your network against spoofing attacks? The primary benefit of a packet filter is *speed*. Since it does not have to do any inspection of application data, a packet filter can operate nearly as fast as a router. However, the packet filter concept has been improved to include the ability to monitor the state of an application, as we'll see in the next section.

Stateful Inspection Packet Filters

The concept of *stateful inspection* came about in an effort to improve on the capabilities and security of regular packet filters, without impacting on their ability to process packets quickly. A packet filter with stateful inspection is able to keep track of network sessions through the use of a *connection table*. Every time an internal client makes a request to an outside address, the IP of the internal machine is placed in this connection table. When the stateful packet filter receives a TCP packet from the outside, it can look at the destination of this external packet and try to match it up against the entries in the connection table. If it finds a match, the stateful packet filter will allow the packet through. Otherwise, the packet gets dropped. Entries in the connection table are automatically timed out after a certain period of time. In the case of an FTP connection, for example, the server that the user connects to on port 21 will initiate a data connection back on port 20 when a file download is requested. If the firewall hasn't kept track of the FTP control connection that was initially established, it won't allow the connection back in on port 20. This concept also applies to many of the newer multimedia protocols such as RealAudio and NetMeeting.

As you'll recall from Chapter 6, TCP is a connection-oriented protocol, whereas UDP is connectionless. So it would seem impossible for a stateful packet filter to be able to process UDP packets, since they do not maintain state from one packet to the next. But statefulness can also be applied to UDP communication, after a fashion. In the case of UDP, the firewall creates an entry in the connection table when the first UDP packet is transmitted. A UDP packet from a less secure network (a response) will be accepted only if there's a corresponding entry in the connection table.

Application Layer Filtering

Stateful inspection packet filters remain the speed kings of firewalls and are the most flexible where new protocols are concerned, but they are sometimes less secure than application proxies. As the name implies, an application proxy firewall acts as a "go-between" for user network sessions. User-initiated connections actually terminate at the proxy, and the proxy initiates a separate connection to the destination host. In an application proxy, connections are analyzed all the way up to the application layer to determine if they are allowed. It is this characteristic that gives proxies a higher level of security than packet filters, stateful or otherwise.

Figure 9.7 shows how packet processing is handled at the application layer before it is passed on or blocked. However, this additional processing means that application proxies don't have quite the same speed as packet filters, since packet filters only need to examine network traffic as far as the transport layer.

Figure 9.7 Application Proxy Data Flow

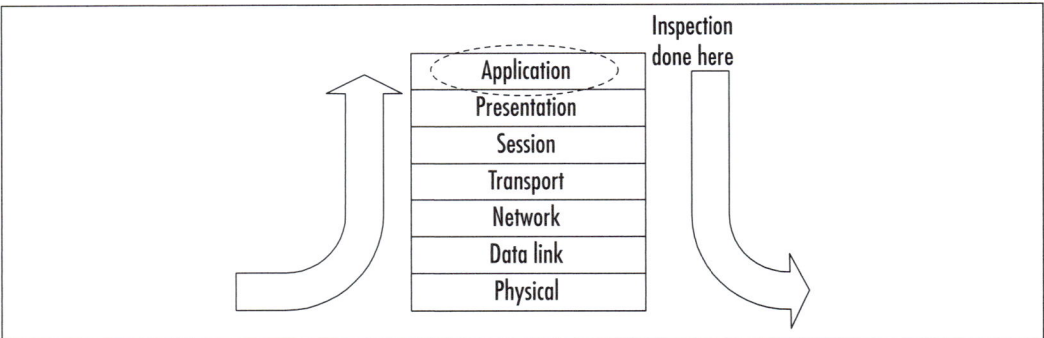

One potentially significant limitation of application proxies is that, as new application protocols are implemented, corresponding proxies need to be developed to handle them. This means that you could be at the mercy of your vendor if a hot new video multicasting technology is introduced, for example, but there is no proxy for it.

Exam Day Tip

Modern proxy-based firewalls often provide the ability to configure generic proxies for IP, TCP, and UDP. Although not as secure as proxies that work at the application layer, these configurable proxies often allow for passing of newer protocols.

Examples of proxy-based firewalls include Gauntlet from Secure Computing (acquired from Network Associates) and Symantec Raptor (also known as Enterprise Firewall).

Firewall Interfaces: Inside, Outside, and DMZ

In its most basic form, a firewall has just two network interfaces: inside and outside. These labels refer to the level of trust you have in the network that's attached to the particular interface. In almost all cases, the outside interface is connected to an untrusted network (often the Internet), and the inside interface is connected to the trusted network. For a firewall deployed within an internal network, the interface referred to as "outside" can be connected to the company's Internet backbone. Although this connection is probably not as untrusted as the Internet, it's still more vulnerable and therefore less trustworthy than a more controlled subnet. For example, you can deploy a firewall within your company's internal network to separate your payroll department from the rest of the network. In this case, the Payroll subnet would be considered the *inside* network, and the connection to the rest of the network would be the *outside* network.

As your company's need for Internet-based resources becomes more complex, you could find some limitations in having only two interfaces for your network. For example, where would you put a Web server for your customers? If you place it outside the firewall, the Web server will be fully exposed to attacks on the outside network. In this case, you're forced to rely on the security of the Web server itself. Another possibility with a two-interface firewall is to place the Web server on the internal network, on the same side of the firewall as your internal network clients. The firewall would be configured to allow Web traffic on port 80 and port 443 for SSL to pass through the firewall to the IP address of the Web server. This configuration will prevent an outsider from directly accessing your Web server. But what happens if the outsider is able to compromise your Web server through port 80 and gain administrative access to the server? At this point, you have a compromised machine residing on your internal network, and the hacker will be free to launch attacks from your Web server on any other host in your internal network, with no restrictions.

The solution is to create a network design that supports multiple interfaces on your firewall, as most commercial systems now do. This solution allows you to create an intermediate zone that's neither inside nor outside your network. These intermediary zones are referred to as *demilitarized zones,* or DMZs. Machines that reside on a DMZ network will be protected from outside users by one firewall while still separated from the internal network, so access to your internal clients will be protected as well. Figure 9.8 illustrates a typical DMZ layout.

Figure 9.8 A DMZ Network

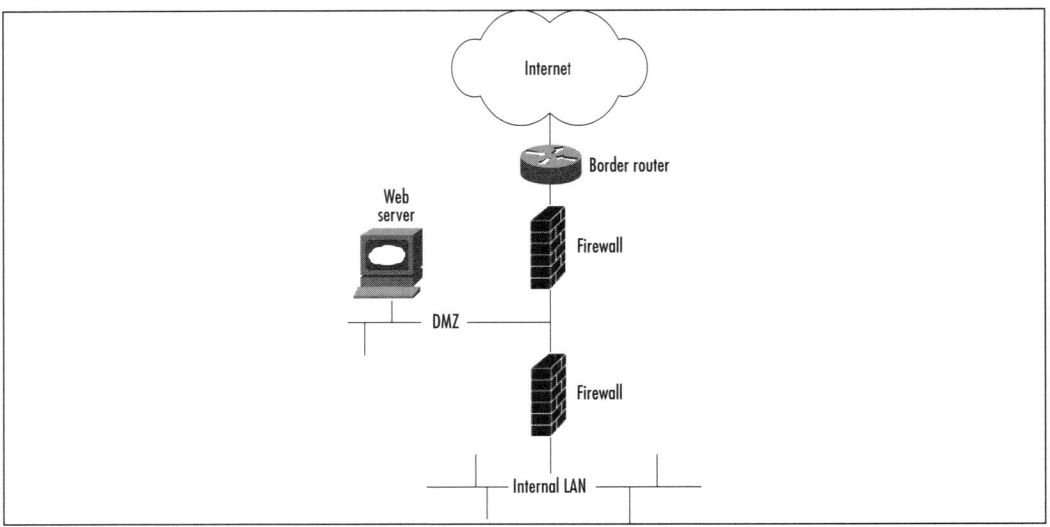

Some companies even implement multiple DMZs, each with a different business purpose and corresponding level of trust. For example, one DMZ segment could contain only servers for public access, whereas another could host servers just for business partners or customers. This approach allows you to create a granular level of control as well as simplifying administration of your network.

Using Network Address Translation

RFC 1918, "Address Allocation for Private Internets," specifies certain IP address ranges that can only be used on private networks and are not routed across the Internet. These reserved ranges are:

> 10.0.0.0–10.255.255.255 (10/8 prefix)
>
> 172.16.0.0–172.31.255.255 (172.16/12 prefix)
>
> 192.168.0.0–192.168.255.255 (192.168/16 prefix)

Because these addresses are private, they do not need to be unique. Your company can use the 10.0.0.0/8 network for its internal computers, and another company across town can use the same private IP address range without causing any conflicts. The primary reason for setting aside these private address ranges was a fear that we were running out of IP addresses. By using these address ranges for private networks, we are able to conserve public IP addresses for situations where they are really needed.

But if these addresses are not routable over the Internet, how do you access the Web from a private network? The source IP of such a connection would be a private address, and the user's connection attempt would just be dropped before it got very far. This is where NAT comes into play. Most organizations connected to the Internet use NAT to hide their internal addresses from the global Internet. This serves as a basic security measure that can make it a bit more difficult for an external attacker to map out the internal network. NAT is typically performed on the Internet firewall and takes two forms, static or dynamic. When NAT is performed, the firewall rewrites the source and/or the destination addresses in the IP header, replacing them with translated addresses. This process is configurable.

In the context of address translation, *inside* refers to the internal, private network. *Outside* is the greater network to which the private network connects (typically the Internet). Within the inside address space, addresses are referred to as *local* addresses that get translated to *global* addresses. These inside global addresses are visible from the Internet and can be routed accordingly. When a client on an internal network needs to access a resource on the Internet, NAT will translate one of these local addresses to a global address. NAT will use either *static* or *dynamic* address translation to translate between these local and global addresses.

Static Address Translation

In static NAT, a permanent one-to-one mapping gets established between a local and a global address. This method is useful when you have a small number of inside hosts that require access to the Internet and have enough global addresses so that each internal client can have their own corresponding global address. When a NAT router or firewall receives a packet from an inside host, it looks to see if there is a matching source address entry in its static NAT table. If there is, it replaces the local source address with the global source address and then forwards the packet. Replies from the outside destination host are simply translated in reverse and routed onto the inside network.

Static translation is also useful to translate outside communications that get initiated to an inside host—if you have a Web server located on your internal network, for example. In this situation, an outside machine sends a packet with a global destination address, which the NAT router translates into the appropriate local address. You can see an example of static NAT in Figure 9.9, where each local inside address (192.168.0.10, 192.168.0.11, and 192.168.0.12) has a matching global inside address (10.0.1.10, 10.0.1.11, and 10.0.1.12, respectively).

Figure 9.9 Static Address Translation

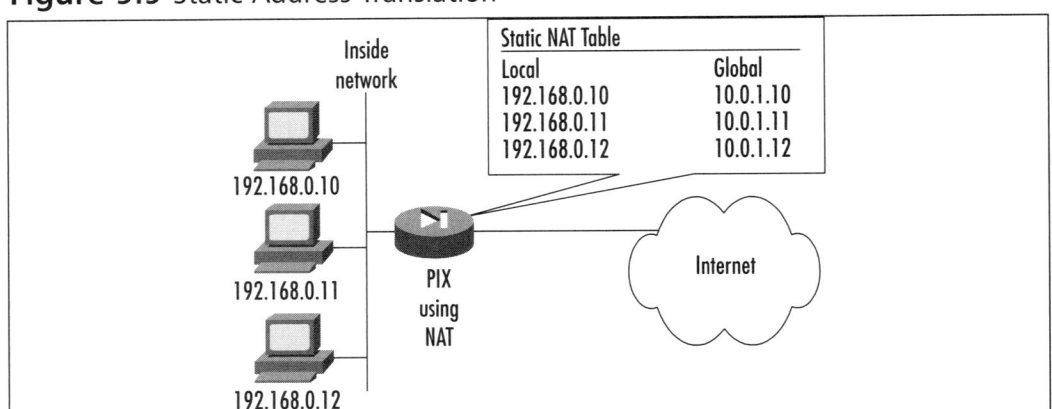

Dynamic Address Translation

The disadvantage of static NAT is that it uses up quite a few public IP addresses, and it's not effective if you have dozens or hundreds of internal clients, with only one or two public IP addresses. In this case, it's much more effective to use dynamic NAT translation. When dynamic NAT is set up, you define a *pool* of inside addresses to be used for outbound translation. When the NAT router or firewall receives a packet from an inside host and dynamic NAT is configured, it selects the next available address from this address pool and maps the address to one of the available public IPs. Dynamic NAT differs from static NAT because these address mappings can change for each new network connection that's requested. Also, only those internal machines that request external resources will be placed into the translation table.

Recognizing Popular Firewalls

There are many players in the firewall market, and naming and describing them all could easily turn into a chapter in itself. Although you won't be expected to be able to configure individual firewalls for the Network+ exam, it's helpful to recognize the more common models in case they come up as an example. Firewalls for a corporate network are usually hardware devices that run a dedicated operating system, but you can install software-based firewalls as well. Table 9.2 introduces some of the major vendors of firewalls and whether they are hardware or software based.

Table 9.2 Firewall Vendors and Types

Firewall Vendor	Hardware or Software?
3Com Corporation and SonicWALL	Hardware
Check Point Software Technologies	Both
Cisco Systems, Inc.	Hardware

Continued

Table 9.2 Firewall Vendors and Types

Firewall Vendor	Hardware or Software?
CyberGuard	Hardware
Microsoft ISA Server	Software
NetScreen	Hardware
Novell Border Manager	Software
Secure Computing	Hardware
Stonesoft, Inc.	Software
Symantec Corporation	Software
WatchGuard Technologies, Inc.	Hardware

As you can see, the Microsoft, Novell, and Symantec firewall products fall into the software category, whereas the other vendors in the table produce hardware-based firewalls. The Check Point firewall falls into both categories: You can install a software-based Check Point firewall onto a Windows or UNIX machine, or you can purchase a dedicated hardware device that runs the Check Point firewall.

Hardware–Based Firewalls

A typical hardware-based firewall uses packet filtering or stateful packet filtering to make decisions about what types of traffic to allow or block. Hardware solutions are available for networks of all sizes. For example, some 3Com products focus on small business and home office users, whereas the Cisco PIX comes in configurations that support up to 250,000 connections.

Hardware-based firewalls are often referred to as *firewall appliances*. A disadvantage of hardware-based firewalls is the proprietary nature of the software they run. Another disadvantage of many of these products, such as Cisco's highly respected PIX, is the high cost. The advantage of hardware-based firewalls is that they tend to be faster and more secure than software-based firewalls, since the hardware appliance is dedicated to running only the firewall software and nothing else. In this section, we'll look at some of the common hardware-based firewalls available today.

> **EXAM WARNING**
>
> When you're running a software-based firewall, the most important thing to do is to harden (or secure) the operating system that the firewall is installed on. This will prevent malicious attackers from bypassing the firewall by exploiting a software vulnerability of the underlying OS.

The Cisco PIX Firewall

The Cisco PIX firewall is designed to meet the needs of small or home networks to enterprise-sized networks. The PIX provides various types of users with the same security level and features, but performance is increased with the larger PIX appliance. The PIX can support many users, and most PIX models have VPN support. Depending on the model, the PIX might have a fixed chassis that cannot be upgraded to support additional interfaces, whereas other PIX models may support many network interfaces.

Some key features of the PIX firewall include the following:

- A user license supports a limited amount of internal IP addresses to access the Internet simultaneously, and the DHCP server feature supports a fixed number of DHCP address assignments. Depending on the model, this may be unlimited.

- Various levels of clear-text throughput, from 10Mbps to 1Gbps.

- Various types of hardware, including rack-mountable, also have many different types of network card support fixed for a small office.

- Optional encryption licenses, which are required if 168-bit 3DES or 56-bit DES VPN tunnels are used.

- An unlimited number of VPN users.

- URL filtering, which can limit the URLs that can be accessed by particular users based on a policy defined by the network administrator or a security policy.

- Content filtering, which can block ActiveX or Java applets, regardless of the source or destination address.

Cisco PIX firewalls run a proprietary operating system similar to the one used by Cisco routers and switches. Because the PIX OS is designed solely for the purpose of operating a firewall, it doesn't share the same vulnerabilities as a software-based firewall running on Windows or UNIX.

Nokia Firewall

The Nokia hardware platform comes with a hardened FreeBSD operating system out of the box. Nokia firewalls are rack-mountable and are easily maintained by using the same firewall software as the Check Point family of firewalls.

Check Point FW-1

Check Point firewalls have a large and powerful feature set that have made them quite popular with larger enterprise networks. The firewalls include most of the features that you would expect from a standard firewall package, including stateful packet filtering, NAT capabilities, and the ability to protect multiple network segments. More powerful

Check Point firewalls can even be configured to provide failover services in the event of loss of one firewall.

Software-Based Firewalls

In addition to firewall appliances, there are various firewall software applications you can install on a regular computer running a standard operating system such as Sun Solaris, Windows, or Linux. Most of these software-based packages use either stateful packet inspection or application layer filtering to make filtering decisions. Some of these software pieces also function as other applications as well; Microsoft ISA server, for example, can serve as both a firewall and a proxy server. (We talk more about proxy servers in another section.)

Microsoft ISA Server

Microsoft's Internet Security and Acceleration (ISA) Server is a pretty comprehensive product, used for firewalling, content filtering, NAT (covered in the previous section), and more. It's meant to be used as an all-in-one security package, offering an application layer firewall, VPN server, and Web caching to improve client Web browsing performance. Because ISA Server is an application layer firewall, it performs a much fuller inspection of network traffic than a simple packet layer firewall and so can detect threats that packet-filtering software might miss. The following code shows the kind of detailed information that ISA Server examines before making a decision to allow or reject a particular network packet rather than simply looking at the TCP or UDP port being used:

```
Host: www.example.com

User-Agent: Mozilla/5.0 (Windows; U; Windows NT 5.1; en-US; rv:1.6)
Geckc/20040113

Accept:
text/xml,application/xml,application/xhtml+xml,text/html;q=0.9,text/plain;q=0.8,i
mage/png,image/jpeg,image/gif;q=0.2,*/*;q=0.1

Accept-Language: en-us,en;q=0.5

Accept-Encoding: gzip,deflate

Accept-Charset: ISO-8859-1,utf-8;q=0.7,*;q=0.7

Keep-Alive: 300

Connection: keep-alive

Referer: http://www.example.com/development.html


Date: Thu, 13 May 2004 10:17:12 GMT

Server: Apache

Last-Modified: Tue, 21 May 2004 17:22:00 GMT

ETag: "9a01a-4696-7e354b00"

Accept-Ranges: bytes
```

```
Content-Length: 18070

Keep-Alive: timeout=15, max=100

Connection: Keep-Alive

Content-Type: text/html; charset=ISO-8859-1
```

ISA Server also includes a number of management utilities and configuration wizards to help you get up and running quickly and securely.

IP Chains and IP Tables

The Linux operating system uses IP Chains and IP Tables to create rules controlling network access to and from a particular machine or network. Like other components of the Linux operating system, IP Chains is freely available software that you can install on an existing Linux machine. Installing and configuring IP Chains or IP Tables requires some previous knowledge of the Linux operating system as well as an understanding of how to write UNIX shell scripts. You won't be expected to know the ins and outs of actually configuring IP Chains, but you should recognize the name and know that it's used as a software-based firewall for Linux and UNIX systems. The following code listing will give you an idea of what a sample IP Tables configuration script might look like. The lines that start with a pound sign (**#**) are comments.

```
# Disable response to ping.
/bin/echo "1" > /proc/sys/net/ipv4/icmp_echo_ignore_all


# Disable response to broadcasts.
/bin/echo "1" > /proc/sys/net/ipv4/icmp_echo_ignore_broadcasts


# Don't accept source routed packets. Attackers can use source routing to
generate
# traffic pretending to be from inside your network, but which is routed back
along
# the path from which it came, namely outside, so attackers can compromise your
# network. Source routing is rarely used for legitimate purposes.
/bin/echo "0" > /proc/sys/net/ipv4/conf/all/accept_source_route


# Disable ICMP redirect acceptance. ICMP redirects can be used to alter your
routing
# tables, possibly to a bad end.
for interface in /proc/sys/net/ipv4/conf/*/accept_redirects; do
    /bin/echo "0" > ${interface}
done
```

```
# Enable bad error message protection.
/bin/echo "1" > /proc/sys/net/ipv4/icmp_ignore_bogus_error_responses
```

IP Security Protocol

The IP Security (IPSec) protocol is an extension of TCP/IP (covered in Chapter 7) that allows you to build some security features directly into TCP/IP network packets. IPSec allows you to perform many typical firewall features such as packet filtering on IP traffic that's being routed to a particular machine, as well as more advanced security features such as enabling digital signatures for TCP/IP traffic. Using digital signatures, you can mandate that any TCP/IP traffic on an IPSec network must be encrypted before it's transmitted. This provides a way to encapsulate TCP/IP data to keep it safe while it's being transmitted. Although the primary purpose of IPSec is to provide these digital signatures for network traffic, it can also be used to create a simple firewall on Windows 2000 and Windows Server 2003.

Creating an IPSec Ruleset

You won't be expected to configure individual firewalls for the Network+ exam, but it's helpful to see one in action to get a good sense of what's going on. In Exercise 9.1, we walk through the steps of configuring a firewall in Windows 2000 using IPSec. Even if this doesn't all make sense because you haven't worked with Windows 2000 before, try to follow along to see how IPSec is being used as a software-level firewall in this case.

WARNING

Do not attempt this exercise in a production environment, since you could affect your clients' ability to connect to resources they need.

EXERCISE 9.1

CONFIGURING A WINDOWS FIREWALL USING IPSEC

1. Click **Start | Administrative Tools | Active Directory Users & Computers**.

2. Right-click your domain and select **Properties**.

3. Go to the Group Policy tab and select the default **Domain Policy. Select Edit**.

4. Navigate to **Computer Configuration | Windows Settings | Security Settings | IP Security Policies**.

5. Right-click **IP Security Policies** and select **Create IP Security Policy**. Click **Next** to bypass the initial Welcome screen.

6. Give your IP Security policy a name and a description, and then click **Next**.

7. The next screen gives you the option to enable the Default Response Rule. In Windows 2000, the Default Response Rule attempts to enable secure communications with any machine that requests a connection. It's usually a good idea to leave this enabled in most settings. Click **Next** to continue.

8. The next screen asks you to specify the authentication method that the Default Response Rule should use. Click **Next** to accept the default authentication method, which is Kerberos.

9. Click **Next** again to begin creating a new firewall rule.

10. To create a new rule, click **Add**, and then click **Next** to bypass the initial Welcome screen.

11. Your first question involves IP tunneling. You can configure IPSec in tunneling mode for a VPN or transport mode for all other communication types. Leave it at transport mode and click **Next** to continue.

12. Next you'll configure whether you want the IPSec encryption to apply to all network interfaces, the LAN interface only, or to remote access connections. In most cases, you'll want to apply your IPSec policy to all network connections. Select **All network interfaces** and click **Next** to continue.

13. Next you'll select the IP filter list that this policy should apply to. The default filter lists are "All ICMP Traffic" and "All IP Traffic." Let's create a new filter list to look for traffic on port 6667, since that's the default port for the Internet Relay Chat (IRC) protocol and a well-known transport mechanism for worms and other malicious code.

14. Click **Add** to create a new IP filter list. Give it a name and a description, then get rid of the check mark next to **Use Add Wizard** to configure a new filter without the wizard. Click **Add** again to configure a specific IP filter. You'll see the screen shown in Figure 9.10.

Figure 9.10 IP Filter Properties

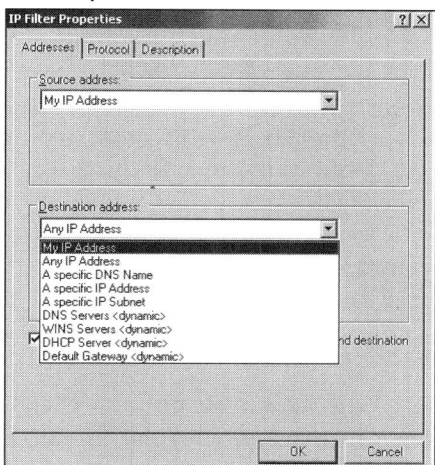

15. When you're configuring an IP filter, you have three tabs: Addresses, Protocol, and Description. As you can see in Figure 9.10, you have a number of options for configuring the Source and Destination IP addresses. The **Protocol** tab will then let you choose the specific TCP/IP protocol that this filter should apply to. Configure a filter with the following properties:

- Source IP Address: Any

- Destination IP Address: My IP address

- Protocol: TCP, Destination Port 6667

16. Once you've finished configuring the IP filter, click **OK** until you're back at the screen shown in Step 3.

17. Your next step will be to configure a filter action—what the firewall will actually do when it encounters traffic on TCP port 6667. Select the IP Filter List you just created, and click **Next**.

18. Click **Add** to configure a filter action. Select the option to **Block traffic that meets the parameters of this IP Filter**, and select **OK**.

You've now configured an IPSec policy that you can use as a software-based firewall on any Windows 2000 or 2003 machine.

Personal Firewall Software

One type of firewall software model that is increasing in popularity is the *personal firewall*. In this case, you'll have firewall software loaded on each individual workstation instead of having one big firewall at the perimeter of your network. This is a popular choice for home-based PCs, especially with the increased popularity of DSL and other "always on" home Internet connections. In Exercise 9.2, we'll enable the personal firewall in Windows XP Professional.

EXERCISE 9.2

ENABLING A PERSONAL FIREWALL

1. Click **Start | Run**. Type **nwc.cpl** and click **OK** to access the Network Connections Control Panel Applet, as shown in Figure 9.11.

Figure 9.11 Viewing Network Connections in the Control Panel

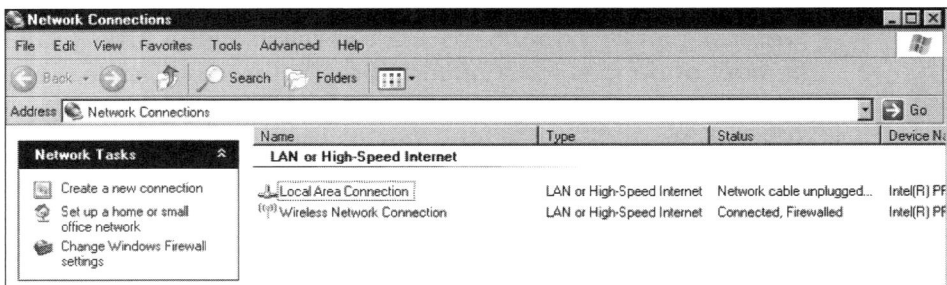

2. Right-click your network connection, and select **Properties**. You can see that this computer has both a wireless card and an RJ-45 network card installed. To enable the Windows firewall for both of these connections, you would need to follow these instructions twice—once for each connection listed in the Network Connections applet.

3. Click the **Advanced** tab, and place a check mark next to **Protect my computer and network by limiting or preventing access to this computer from the Internet**.

4. Click **Settings** to customize the behavior of the Windows firewall. On the **Exceptions** tab (shown in Figure 9.12) you can see the applications that the Windows firewall has been configured to allow. You have the option to add a new program to the list of "allowed" applications, to add a new TCP or UDP port, or to edit or delete an existing entry in the "allowed" list.

Figure 9.12 Configuring the List of Permitted Applications

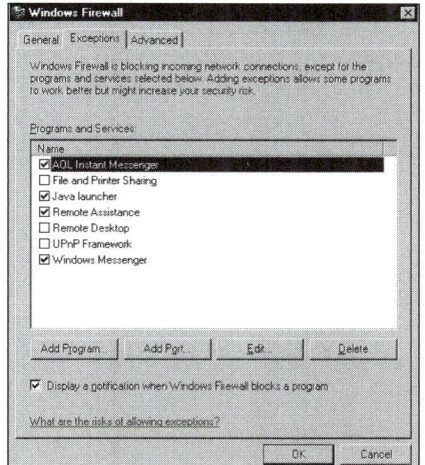

5.   Click **OK** when you've finished configuring the Windows firewall.

Until now, personal firewalls were a bit rarer in corporate settings because each individual workstation would need to have the firewall configured individually. In an attempt to make this technology more appealing to a corporate network, Microsoft has included a personal firewall in Windows XP Service Pack 2 that can be centrally configured by a network administrator. This gives you the additional security of a firewall sitting on each individual workstation while allowing you to manage and configure the firewall settings of each workstation from a single administrative workstation.

Configuring and Implementing Firewalls

Implementing firewalls on any network is always a work in progress. You always need to stay flexible and on your toes to keep your network protection levels up to date and effective. This requires a certain amount of ongoing effort so that your system's security is always as high as you can make it while still allowing users and clients to access the necessary resources on your network. In deploying a firewall, you shouldn't be intimidated by the apparent complexity of it: All it really boils down to is determining what types of traffic should and should not be permitted to enter your internal network. In this section, we'll look at implementing firewalls for a corporate network, paying particular attention to the design process. Once you've determined the overall design of your firewall implementation, you can then turn your attention to deploying specific firewall hardware and software.

Security Alert!

Network Convergence

Even though we're discussing a number of networking technologies—firewalls, proxy servers, DMZs, and the like—as separate entities, you might find as you actually work on a production network that you have a single device that serves more than one of these functions. Routers, switches, firewalls, and intrusion detection devices (along with wireless, telephony, and other technologies) are quickly merging under the hood of a single physical device. In this section we'll talk about configuring and implementing a firewall, but in many cases you can configure a simple router to behave as a simple firewall. The following code shows how you can configure a Cisco Router (2621XM series) with a firewall feature set:

```
ip inspect name firewall tcp

ip inspect name firewall udp

ip inspect name firewall ftp

ip inspect name firewall h323

ip inspect name firewall netshow

ip inspect name firewall fragment maximum 256 timeout 1

ip inspect name firewall rcmd
```

You can also configure logging on the router to provide intrusion detection, which will allow you to monitor your network for any attempted intrusions from malicious users:

```
Jan 19 06:20:48.900: %FW-4-ALERT_ON: getting aggressive, count
(500/500) current 1-min rate: 500

Jan 19 06:29:26.799: %FW-4-ALERT_OFF: calming down, count (0/400)
current 1-min rate: 297

Jan 19 11:05:14.299: %FW-4-ALERT_ON: getting aggressive, count
(500/500) current 1-min rate: 500

Jan 19 11:06:57.998: %FW-4-ALERT_OFF: calming down, count (0/400)
current 1-min rate: 169

Jan 20 12:29:48.757: %FW-4-HOST_TCP_ALERT_ON: Max tcp half-open
connections (50) exceeded for host 10.0.0.1.
```

So, as you prepare to enter the "real world" of administering corporate networks, be sure that you understand how this convergence is becoming more and more prevalent in the world of networking. Hardware vendors are merging different services into a single device to offer better services at better price points. Though we used a Cisco 2600-series router as an example here, Cisco is not the only vendor that is moving toward network convergence. All vendors with a major stake in the networking market are on board. For instance, Juniper

Continued

Networks (www.juniper.net) has recently acquired Trend Micro and will likely be bundling antivirus solutions directly into their routers and firewall devices.

Why the Design Process Is So Important

Designing your firewall implementation is critical to the overall protection of your internal network. Your firewall design can incorporate VPN traffic, Web traffic, extranet and employee connections, and public access to information provided by your organization. It's important to realize that you can't really design a firewall without a clear vision of what you're trying to protect. Will your firewall be protecting a handful of servers that provide basic services to your network? Will it be protecting the entirety of your internal network and its resources? Or somewhere in the middle? To determine this, you must understand the needs of your company, the role that the firewall will play in your overall network infrastructure, the type of traffic it will support, and any plans your company has for future growth.

For example, let's say that, as the network architect for a small company, you are given the task of creating a security solution to protect your infrastructure, your data, and your internal clients while providing external access to a company Web site. The company already has Internet connectivity via a dial-up connection, and now you need to create an Internet presence for your Web server while protecting your internal network resources. You need to begin gathering information, starting with the current environment and the requirements for the upgrade. You can see an illustration of this layout in Figure 9.13.

Figure 9.13 A Sample Network Layout for a Firewall Design

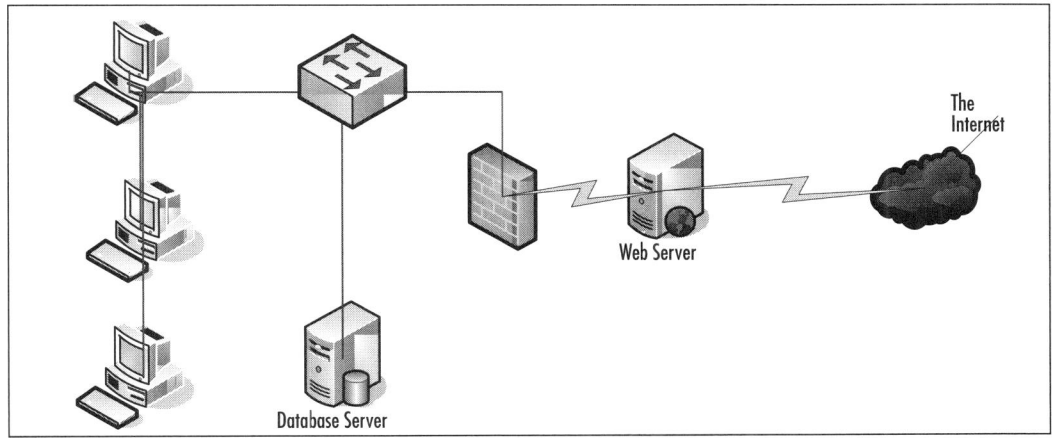

Here is what you know:

- The Web site will start out small but could grow as sales over the Internet increase.

- The site will be a scalable server environment with a single Web/application server and a database server.

- The infrastructure currently in place is not capable of supporting the new Web site.

- The site is estimated to reach 10,000 hits and 1000 transactions a day at first and then grow steadily.

With this information ready, you now need to ask some more questions so that you can move on to designing a solution:

- How much Internet bandwidth is required to support the site?

- What kind of security is needed? Will there be a need for both Web traffic and SSL traffic?

Exam Day Tip

Remember that the SSL protocol is used to secure Web traffic and operates on TCP port 443.

- Does the site require high availability? (We'll be talking more about high availability and disaster recovery concepts in Chapter 10.)

- What are the connectivity requirements among the internal network, the Web/application server, and the database server?

- What is the budget for the firewall?

These are not the only questions that you should ask when designing a firewall, of course, but this list should give you a good starting point to help you gather enough information to create a firewall design to protect your internal network and resources.

Your web developers and business managers come back to you with the answers to these questions. Since the site will only receive 10,000 hits and 1000 transactions a day, you will initially acquire a single T1 line; as the site grows, you'll add more bandwidth. Since the site will be processing credit card transactions, both HTTP (TCP port 80) and SSL (TCP port 443) need to be allowed to access the Web/application server from the Internet. Your product database should only be accessed by the internal LAN and should respond to Web/application server requests for information. Finally, all Web servers and switches are 100Mbps full-duplex-capable devices.

From this information, you can now start to plan, install, and document your firewall solution. Analyzing the requirements, you decide that you will create a DMZ with a firewall on each side that will offer you the most secure and scalable solution. This DMZ allows you to separate the Web server into a firewalled network segment to allow for greater security. The DMZ will contain the Web server, and your internal network will contain the database servers. Because users will only access the Web server, you'll configure firewall rules so that the DMZ is only accessible from the outside network via TCP port 80 (HTTP) and the SSL port, TCP port 443. Your internal network will not allow unsolicited connectivity from the Internet; it will use stateful packet filtering to respond only to requests made for data by the Web server or originating from the internal LAN. Separating the Web server from your internal network allows for greater security in the event the Web/application server is compromised by an intruder, while the second firewall will still protect the Web server from external threats. Figure 9.14 shows the final result of your firewall planning.

Figure 9.14 The Result of Firewall Planning

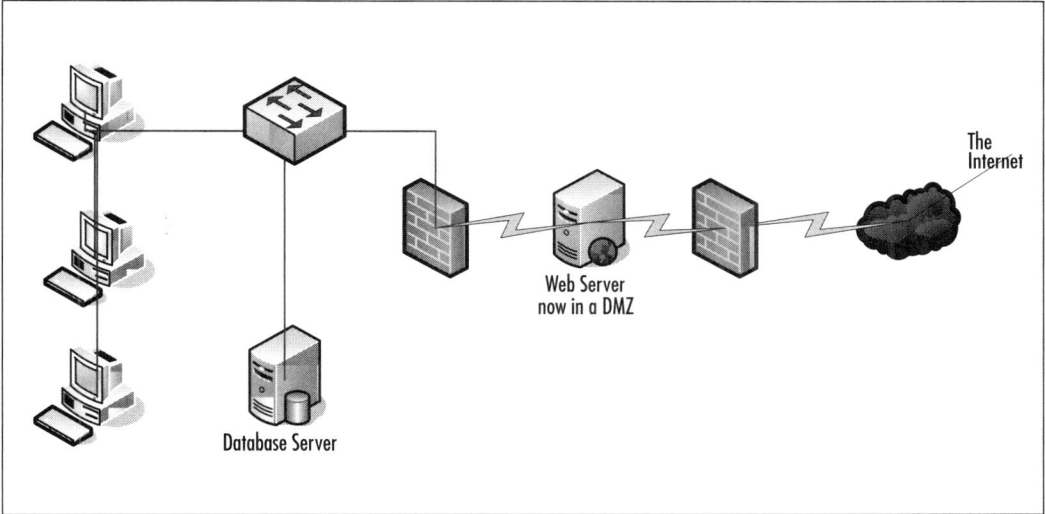

EXAM WARNING

Be careful not to fall into the trap of thinking that having a firewall means that your security troubles are over. You need to apply the principle of *defense in depth*, providing multiple layers of defense to secure your network.

Designing Your Firewall to Protect Your TCP/IP Clients

The current implementation of the TCP/IP protocol suite, IP version 4 (or IP v4, for short) contains a number of well-documented flaws that affect the design of both your security plan and your firewall implementation. Some of these problems have been corrected in IP version 6, but since implementation of this technology still isn't widespread, you need to protect your network against the weaknesses of the existing protocols when you implement your firewall design.

NOTE

The newest version of the IP protocol, commonly called IPv6, makes several improvements over the existing implementation, IPv4. The most noticeable improvement is the number of IP addresses that are available in version 6. In the new version of IP, we move from a 32-bit addressing scheme in IPv4 to a 128-bit address space in IPv6. In moving to a 128-bit address space, we've gone from having 4 billion IP addresses available to around 1033 possible addresses—an improvement of several orders of magnitude. IPv6 also includes many built-in security measures that make it more inherently secure than the current implementation of TCP/IP.

You can read more about IPv6 in RFC 2460, available at www.ietf.org/rfc/rfc2460.txt.

Therefore, you need to plan against certain known weaknesses in IP v4:

- Data that is sent in clear-text packets, especially passwords and other sensitive information that can be easily "sniffed" or captured on your network and exploited

- Vulnerabilities to DoS from SYN attacks

- IP spoofing

- Forged packets created by sequence guessing; refer back to Chapter 6 for more information on TCP/IP sequence numbering and windowing

- Man-in-the-middle (MITM) attacks

- Lack of authentication

The design that you create for your firewall needs to accommodate the weaknesses of the IP protocol and to provide the necessary protection to prevent these types of attacks. To accomplish this, you need to implement protection against these attacks using IPSec and other types of safeguards.

Understanding TCP/IP Vulnerabilities

To protect your network from intruders, you should have an understanding of the types of attack that TCP/IP is vulnerable to. In this section, we discuss some of the more common types of hack attacks:

- DoS attacks
- Scanning and spoofing
- Source routing and other protocol exploits
- Software and system exploits

When you have a basic understanding of how these types of attack work, you will be better prepared to guard against them.

NOTE

In this section, we use the words *attacker, intruder,* or *hacker* to refer to a person who compromises the security of a network by gaining unauthorized access or who compromises the accessibility of a network by preventing authorized access.

Denial-of-Service (DoS) Attacks

In February 2000, massive DoS attacks brought down several of the biggest Web sites, including Yahoo.com and Buy.com. DoS attacks are one of the most popular choices for Internet hackers who want to disrupt a network's operations. Although they do not destroy or steal data as some other types of attack do, the objective of DoS attackers is to bring down a network, denying service to its legitimate users. DoS attacks are easy to initiate; software that will allow anyone to launch a DoS attack with little or no technical expertise is readily available from hacker Web sites.

The purpose of a DoS attack is to render a network inaccessible by generating a type or amount of network traffic that will crash the servers, overwhelm the routers, or otherwise prevent the network's devices from functioning properly. DoS can be accomplished by tying up the server's resources—for example, by overwhelming the CPU and memory resources. In other cases, a particular user or machine can be the target of DoS attacks that hang up the client machine and require it to be rebooted.

Distributed Denial-of-Service Attack

Distributed DoS (DDoS) attacks use intermediary computers, called *agents,* on which programs called *zombies* have previously been surreptitiously installed. The hacker activates these zombie programs remotely, causing the intermediary computers (which can number in the hundreds or even thousands) to simultaneously launch the actual attack. Because the attack comes from the computers running the zombie programs, which could be on networks anywhere in the world, the hacker is able to conceal the true origin of the attack.

It is important to note that DDoS attacks pose a two-layer threat. Not only could your network be the target of a DoS attack that crashes your servers and prevents incoming and outgoing traffic, but your computers could be used as the "innocent middlemen" to launch a DoS attack against another network or site.

Ping of Death

Another type of DoS attack is the *ping of death* (also known as the *large packet ping*). The ping-of-death attack is launched by creating an IP packet (sometimes referred to as a *killer packet*) larger than 65,536 bytes, which is the maximum allowed by the IP specification. This can cause the target system to crash, hang, or reboot.

Teardrop

The *teardrop attack* works a little differently from the ping of death but with similar results. The teardrop program creates IP fragments, which are pieces of an IP packet into which an original packet can be divided as it travels through the Internet. The problem is that the offset fields on these fragments, which are supposed to indicate the portion (in bytes) of the original packet that is contained in the fragment, overlap.

For example, normally two fragments' offset fields might appear as shown here:

Fragment 1: (offset) 100–300

Fragment 2: (offset) 301–600

This indicates that the first fragment contains bytes 100 through 300 of the original packet, and the second fragment contains bytes 301 through 600.

Overlapping offset fields would appear something like this:

Fragment 1: (offset) 100–300

Fragment 2: (offset) 200–400

When the destination computer tries to reassemble these packets, it is unable to do so and could crash, hang, or reboot.

Ping or ICMP Flood

The *ping flood* or *ICMP flood* is a means of tying up a specific client machine. It is caused by an attacker sending a large number of ping packets (ICMP echo request packets) to the Winsock or dialer software. This action prevents the software from responding to server ping activity requests, which causes the server to eventually time out the connection. A symptom of a ping flood is a huge amount of modem activity, as indicated by flashing modem lights. This attack is also referred to as a *ping storm*.

Mail Bomb Attack

A *mail bomb* is a means of overwhelming a mail server, causing it to stop functioning and thus denying service to users. This is a relatively simple form of attack, accomplished by sending a massive quantity of e-mail to a specific user or system. Programs available on hacking sites on the Internet allow a user to easily launch a mail bomb attack, automatically sending floods of e-mail to a specified address while protecting the attacker's identity.

A variation on the mail bomb program automatically subscribes a targeted user to hundreds or thousands of high-volume Internet mailing lists, subsequently filling the user's mailbox and/or the mail server. Bombers call this attack *list linking*. Examples of these mail bomb programs include Unabomber, Extreme Mail, Avalanche, and Kaboom.

The solution to repeated mail bomb attacks is to block traffic from the originating network using packet filters. Unfortunately, this solution does not work with list linking, because the originator's address is obscured; the deluge of traffic comes from the mailing lists to which the victim has been subscribed.

Scanning and Spoofing

The term *scanner,* in the context of network security, refers to a software program that hackers use to remotely determine the TCP/UDP ports that are open on a given system and thus vulnerable to attack. Scanners are also used by administrators to detect vulnerabilities in their own systems so that they can correct the vulnerabilities before an intruder finds them. Network diagnostic tools include sophisticated port-scanning capabilities. A good scanning program can locate a target computer on the Internet (one that is vulnerable to attack), determine the TCP/IP services running on the machine, and probe those services for security weaknesses.

Port Scanning

Port scanning refers to a means of locating "listening" TCP or UDP ports on a computer or router and obtaining as much information as possible about the device from the listening ports. TCP and UDP services and applications use a number of *well-known ports*, which are widely published. The hacker uses his knowledge of these commonly used ports to extrapolate information.

For example, Telnet normally uses port 23. If a hacker finds that port open and listening, she knows that Telnet is probably enabled on the machine. She can then try to infiltrate the system by, for example, guessing the appropriate password in a brute-force attack.

NOTE

Packet sniffers are also called *protocol analyzers* or *network analyzers*. Sniffer and Sniffer Pro are two packet-sniffer products marketed by Network Associates.

Using Firewalls to Protect Network Resources

Firewalls are not the only part of the network security design, but they do play a major role in allowing you to control traffic more completely, thus providing a higher level of protection for your internal resources. Deploying a firewalls is a major part of providing defense in depth for your network. Part of the design process includes evaluating the requirements and performance of different hardware- and software-based firewall products. We've already discussed some of the most-used technologies, such as Check Point NG, Cisco PIX, Nokia, and Microsoft's ISA Server. As you begin to deploy your firewall, you must first be clear about what the firewall is intended to protect.

A design that is only intended to superficially limit internal users' access to the Internet, for example, requires much less planning and design work than a system protecting resources from multiple access points or providing multiple services to the public network or users from remote locations. An appropriate path to follow for your design path might look like this:

- Perform baseline security analysis of existing infrastructure, including OS and application analysis

- Perform baseline network mapping and performance monitoring

- Identify risk to resources and appropriate mitigation processes

- Identify potential security threats, both external and internal

- Identify needed access points from external sources:

    - Public networks

    - VPN access

    - Extranets

    - Remote access services

- Identify critical services

A firewall would not serve any purpose if it blocked all traffic. To properly protect a network environment, network traffic must be filtered both outbound and inbound. The key to configuring a firewall is to ensure that it only allows the traffic you want to allow and only blocks the traffic you want blocked. In some cases, this is not an easy task. Securing *inbound* traffic means ensuring that only trusted hosts on an external network (such as the Internet) are allowed to make connections to machines residing inside the firewall. This can include roaming users connecting to internal resources or external clients attaching to a Web server that's hosted behind a firewall. Securing outbound traffic requires you to determine how your internal clients are permitted to connect to the resources on the Internet or on another untrusted network.

Understanding the TCP and UDP ports that are used in network communication becomes an extremely important part of your ability to filter network access and protect assets using a firewall. You'll recall that ports 0 through 1023 are reserved for specific uses but that some network applications can use other ports from 1024 through 49151. Ports between 49152 and 65535 are *unregistered* ports, used for private applications, client-side processes, or other processes that dynamically allocate port numbers.

EXAM DAY TIP

The entire list of common TCP and UDP ports can be found at www.iana.org/port-numbers. Some of the more common ones that you should be aware of are:

- ftp on port 21
- telnet on port 23
- smtp on port 25
- tftp on port 69
- http on port 80
- kerberos on port 88
- pop3 on port 110
- nntp on port 119

Once you understand which ports should be allowed and disallowed on your network, you can incorporate rules that block all unnecessary or unauthorized traffic. Generally, this involves creating a rule set or an *access control list (ACL)* that restricts or blocks all unused ports. The following code demonstrates how you can block TCP port 445 on a Cisco router. Port 445 is a common attack point for viruses and malware.

```
ip access-list extended black-list-1
  deny    tcp host 10.1.1.80 any eq 445
  deny    tcp any host 10.1.1.80 eq 445
  deny    ip host 10.1.1.80 any
  deny    ip any host 10.1.1.80
  permit tcp any any eq 445
  permit tcp any any
  permit udp any any
  permit icmp any any
  permit ip any any
ip access-list extended black-list-1.1
  permit ip host 10.1.1.7 any
  permit ip any host 10.1.1.7
  permit ip 10.1.1.0 0.0.0.255 any
```

```
  permit ip any 10.1.1.0 0.0.0.255
  permit ip host 10.1.1.36 any
  permit ip any host 10.1.1.36
  deny    tcp any any eq 445
  deny    udp any any eq netbios-dgm
  deny    udp any any eq netbios-ns
  deny    udp any any eq netbios-ss
  deny    tcp any any eq 139
  permit tcp any any
  permit udp any any
  permit icmp any any
  permit ip any any
ip access-list extended black-list-1.2
  deny    tcp host 10.1.1.71 any eq 445
  deny    tcp any host 10.1.1.71 eq 445
  deny    ip host 10.1.1.71 any
  deny    ip any host 10.1.1.71
  permit tcp any any eq 445
  permit tcp any any
  permit udp any any
  permit icmp any any
  permit ip any any
```

You'll typically begin the design process from one of two "all or nothing" configurations: Either you'll configure all ports to be open and close them only as problems occur, or you'll configure all ports to be closed by default, opening required ports only as necessary. You can use either approach, but the latter is heavily recommended since it provides a much higher level of default security for your network.

There are a number of common ports that most security authorities recommend be blocked in a secure firewall configuration. These ports are all commonly known points of entry for a Windows or UNIX system, and they often have known vulnerabilities associated with them that make them easy prey for a hacker who's looking for an unpatched machine. Table 9.3 lists some of the most common ports that should be blocked in a firewall configuration.

Table 9.3 Common Ports to Block

Service Type	TCP Port(s)	UDP Port(s)
Login Services	Telnet: 23; SSH: 22; FTP: 21; NetBIOS: f139; rlogin: 512, 513, 514	N/A
RPC and NFS	Portmap/rpcbind: 111; NFS: 2049; lockd: 4045	Portmap/rpcbind: 111; NFS: 2049; lockd: 4045
NetBIOS in Windows NT and W2K and XP	135, 139, 445(W2K and XP)	135, 137, 138, 445 (W2K and XP)
X Windows	6000 through 6255	N/A
Naming Services	DNS: Block zone transfers (TCP 53) except from external secondaries	DNS: Block UDP 53 to all machines that are not DNS servers
	LDAP: 389	LDAP: 389
Mail	SMTP: 25 to all machines that are not external mail relays POP: 109, 110 IMAP: 143	N/A
Web	HTTP: 80; SSL: 443, except to external Web servers. Also consider common high-order HTTP port choices, such as 8000, 8080, 8888	N/A
Miscellaneous	Finger: 79; NNTP: 119; LPD: 515; SNMP: 161, 162; BGP: 179; SOCKS: 1080	TFTP: 69; NTP: 123; syslog: 514; SNMP: 161, 162
ICMP	Blocks incoming echo request (ping and traceroute), outgoing echo replies, time exceeded, and destination unreachable messages, *except* "packet too big" messages (Type 3, Code 4)	*Note:* This setting will block known malicious uses, but also will restrict your legiti-mate use of the ICMP echo request

Configuring Your Firewall to Filter Network Packets

Creating packet-filtering rules can become somewhat involved, mainly because you have to spend a great deal of time determining the source and destination IP addresses and ports. You also need to be familiar with how connections are made, managed, and ended.

However, some simple rules can help you create a packet filter as soon as possible. As far as outgoing traffic is concerned, you should take the following steps:

1. Configure your firewall to deny all outgoing traffic unless explicitly allowed. This means that your firewall will deny all services to your end users, unless you allow it by creating a rule allowing a specific traffic type.

2. Configure your firewall to allow your internal network to use ports that are higher than 1023. Most network clients use these ports to establish connections to network services.

3. Identify the ports that are used by any services that you want to allow access to. If, for example, you want to allow end users to access the Web, you must create a rule allowing all local network hosts to access all remote systems at ports 80 and 443. Likewise, if you want your local clients to use remote POP3 servers, you will have to allow local hosts to access remote systems at port 110.

As far as incoming traffic is concerned, you have a number of options. Many systems administrators want to create a firewall that forbids all incoming traffic except for the TCP and UDP packets used by remote clients to connect to the firewall. For example, if you want to allow internal clients to access the Web, you need to allow remote hosts (Web servers) to make connections to your firewall. This involves allowing remote hosts to open their local ports above 1023 to access your systems at ports above 1023. Therefore, you should take the following steps:

1. Configure your firewall to prohibit all incoming traffic from accessing any services below port 1023. The most secure firewall will not allow any connections to these ports.

2. Forbid all incoming traffic unless it is part of an already established session by using stateful packet filtering. This will instruct your firewall to match any incoming packet with the client that requested it and allow the traffic to pass. Any unsolicited packets sent directly to an internal host and not to the firewall itself will be dropped.

3. Disable all incoming ICMP traffic to protect yourself against DoS attacks. This step is optional, of course, because disabling this feature makes network troubleshooting more difficult, since tools like *ping* and *tracert* rely on ICMP to function.

4. Enable logging to troubleshoot your firewall operations as well as to determine if you are in the midst of an intrusion attempt.

Using a Proxy Server

When you're the network administrator for a company that makes heavy use of the Internet, you might need to implement a *proxy server* to optimize and secure Internet access for your internal users. Similar to a firewall, a proxy server helps separate your internal network from the outside world. But unlike a firewall, which only filters traffic, a proxy server actually acts as a "go-between" for your internal users. This means that the proxy server will receive a request for Internet access from an internal user and then forward the request to the Internet. You can see an example of this process in Figure 9.15.

Figure 9.15 Proxy Servers Send Web Requests on Behalf of Internal Clients

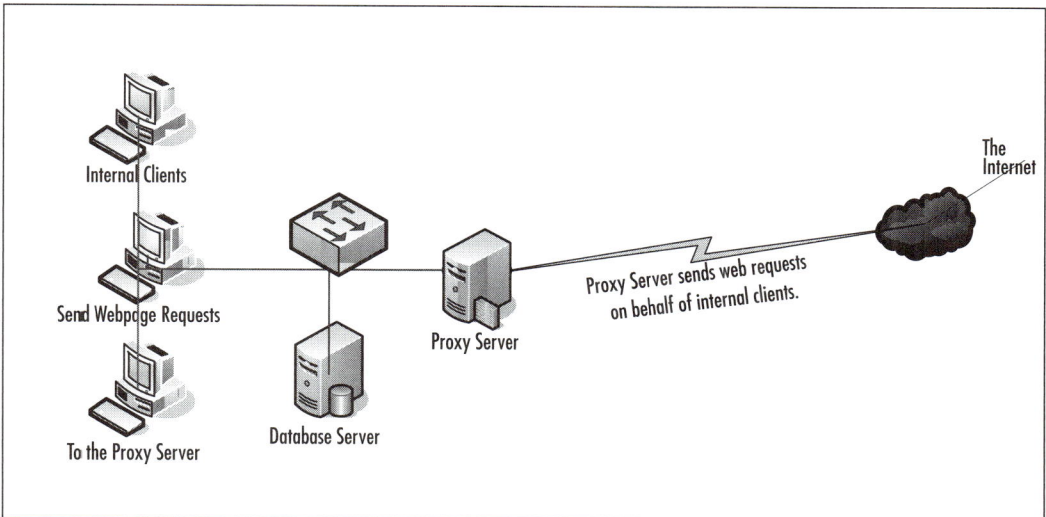

A proxy server will hide the computers on your LAN from the outside network so that only the IP address of the proxy server will be visible on the Internet; your internal computers will use private IP addresses that can't be reached from the other side of the proxy.

Before it forwards the request out to the Internet, the proxy server will check its local cache to see if it already has a local copy of the page being requested. If the page isn't in the proxy server's cache, the proxy server will make the request on behalf of the client and then return the requested page to the user. From an end user's perspective, the proxy server is basically transparent. Any Internet requests get returned to the client as though they were being returned directly. Proxy servers increase the efficiency of an enterprise network by caching frequently requested pages so that users can retrieve them more quickly. Although the functionality of a proxy server can be bundled with a firewall, proxy servers have several functions that are specific to them:

www.syngress.com

- **Content filtering** Proxy servers are generally the only types of firewall that manage and control traffic by inspecting URL and page content. If configured properly, a proxy server or a proxy firewall can identify and block content that you consider objectionable.

- **Packet redirection** Sometimes it is necessary for a firewall to send traffic to another port or another host altogether. For example, suppose that you have installed a proxy server on a host, separate from your firewall. It is likely that you will want to have your firewall automatically forward all traffic sent to ports 80 and 443 (the standard HTTP and HTTPS ports) to your proxy server for additional processing.

- **Content caching** In many cases, users visit the same Web sites on a regular basis, or multiple users within the organization visit the same sites and view the same pages. Web caching provides a way to reduce network traffic for both outbound Web requests from your internal users to Web servers on the Internet and for inbound Web requests from external users to the Web servers you host on your internal network.

Head of the Class…

Popular Proxy Server Products

When deploying a proxy server for your company's network, you have a number of options to choose from for both Windows and UNIX-based operating systems. Regardless of the operating system, you should look for a proxy server that will fill the functional requirements that we've talked about in this section. Here are two of the more popular choices:

- **Microsoft Internet Security & Acceleration (ISA) Server** This is the Microsoft product that began simply as the Microsoft Proxy Server, but it was expanded to incorporate firewall functions while maintaining the functionality of a proxy server. It allows for Web caching to improve user access to the Internet and can make filtering decisions that will deny access to certain types of content or that can restrict Internet access to specific groups of users.

- **Squid** This freeware proxy server implementation runs on UNIX- and Linux-based servers. Squid is a full-featured Web proxy and caching service that supports proxying and caching of HTTP, FTP, SSL, and DNS traffic as well as the ability to string several Squid servers together in a hierarchical caching design.

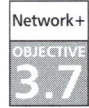

Implementing Network Filtering

You could find yourself administering a corporate network where all your users reside in fixed locations and everyone exists in close proximity to the resources that they're trying to access, but this is becoming more an exception than the rule. To avoid overburdening your company's network bandwidth, as well as to increase security, you'll probably need to implement some type of network-filtering solution to control how external users can access your internal resources. In a larger network, you might even need to fine-tune how *internal* traffic gets transmitted so that users can access their files and resources in an efficient manner. Some of the ways you can do this include virtual LANs (VLANs), extranets, and intranets.

Using a Virtual LAN

If you're administering a network where all your users are grouped together so that you can place the resources they need in close physical proximity to them, you can usually rely on network switches to segment your network, since switches are more than sufficient to isolate and optimize network traffic for this type of departmental or workgroup environment. But how about a situation where your users are spread further apart than that? Maybe you have a group of users who need to collaborate closely and share the same resources, but they're physically scattered across different floors of a single building or even different buildings within an office complex? As your users become further and further distant from one another, using only network switching becomes less effective in segmenting your network traffic. This is because switches are useful only in controlling *unicast* traffic—traffic that's sent directly from one computer to another. Switches are incapable of controlling *broadcast* or *multicast* traffic, and on a large network this can create bandwidth problems by causing "broadcast storms." You can use routers to control broadcast traffic, but they are much slower than switches and can create traffic bottlenecks.

EXAM WARNING

Remember that switches operate at the *data link* layer of the OSI model, whereas routers operate at the *network* layer. Layer 3 switches (switches that have a router module installed in them) combine the features of both a switch and a router, and the benefits are huge since you don't need to traverse the network for a routing decision. If a particular switch can't find a host, it can look in the routing information table (RIT) and then forward the packet from inside the switch.

One possible alternative to this problem is to configure your switches to use virtual LANs (VLANs). A VLAN allows a group of machines to communicate as though they were connected to a single LAN segment, even if in reality they're spread out across multiple network segments or locations. VLANs also operate at the data link layer and so can transmit traffic faster than using routers that rely on complex routing tables. You can see the difference between a standard switched network and one that uses VLANs in Figures 9.16 and 9.17. In Figure 9.16, you can see that all the workstations on the segment will receive broadcast and multicast traffic from any other machine. In Figure 9.17, we've split the segment into three separate VLANs. Now users in the same VLAN will receive only traffic that's destined for that VLAN, which cuts down on bandwidth utilization for your network.

Figure 9.16 A Common Configuration of a Switched Network

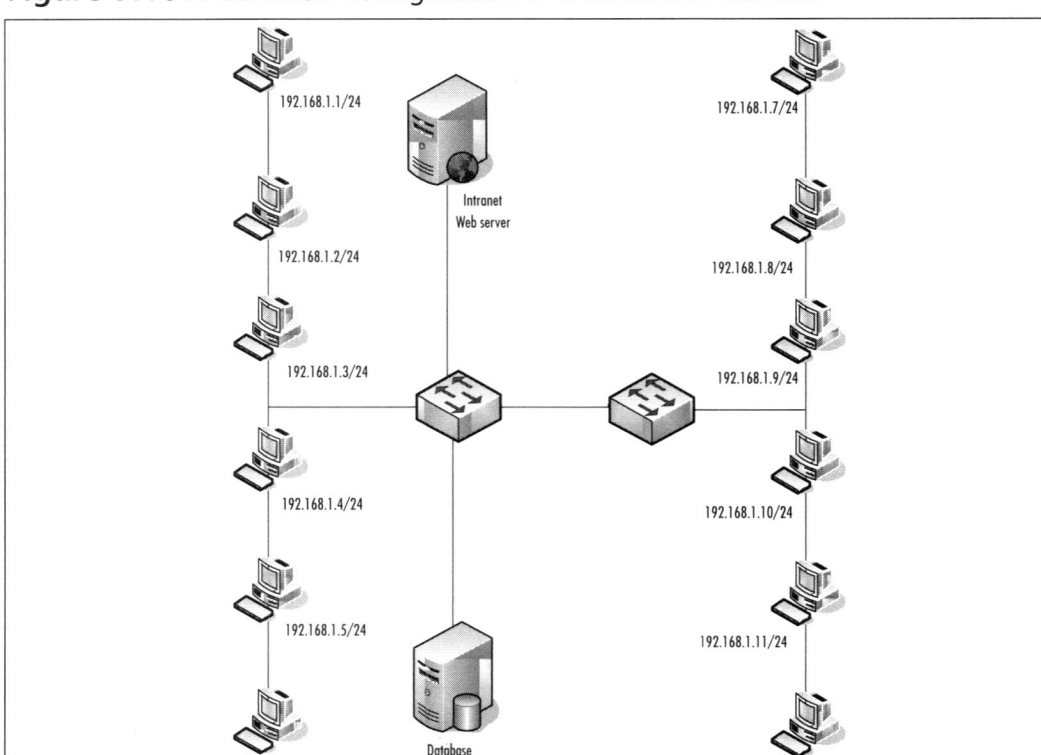

So how does a particular VLAN know which machines belong to it? You'll control how traffic is routed across VLANs based on VLAN *memberships* in one or more VLANs. You'll configure VLAN membership based on a few possible criteria:

- **Port number** You can specify VLAN membership based on the number assigned to the physical port that a particular computer is plugged into. This membership assignment is typically controlled by management software that's loaded on the switch. For example, you can specify that ports 1 and 2 correspond to the Human Resources VLAN; 3, 4, 9 and 10 belong to the IT VLAN; and all remaining ports belong to the Accounting VLAN, as you can see in Figure 9.17. If you need to move a particular port from one VLAN to another, you can just make the change from the management software.

Figure 9.17 Configuring VLAN Membership on a Switched Network

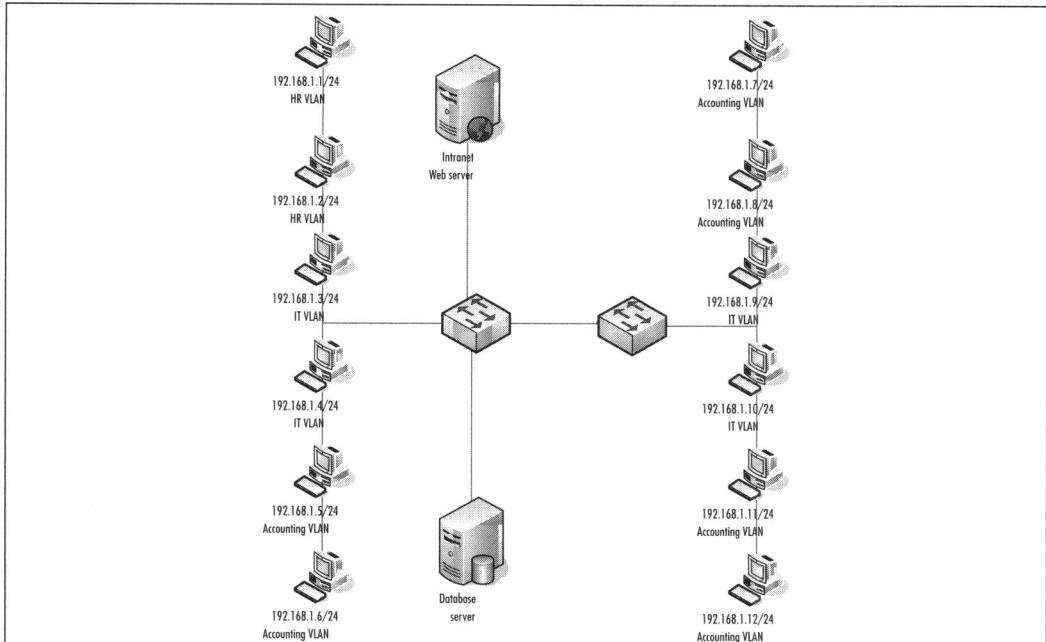

- **MAC address** You can assign a specific MAC address to belong to a particular VLAN so that a particular workstation can maintain its VLAN membership even if it moves from one location to another. This is particularly useful in the case of roaming users who need to plug into your network from multiple locations.

- **802.1q** This is a protocol VLANs use that embeds VLAN membership information directly into a network packet so that the switch will make routing decisions based on the content of the packet that's being sent.

- **Inter-Switch Link (ISL)** This is a proprietary protocol used on Cisco switches that support VLAN technology.

Segmenting your user population using VLANs offers you two major advantages over using network switches without the use of VLANs. The first is improved performance, since you can use VLANs to control not only unicast but also multicast and broadcast traffic. In this way, broadcast traffic that needs to be seen by only a few machines can be confined to those machines, rather than taking up bandwidth for your entire network by broadcasting traffic to everyone on the network segment. The second advantage of a VLAN is that it simplifies how you administer your network, since you can configure and reconfigure VLANs using software installed on the VLAN-capable switch rather than needing to physically move network cables from one switch to another. This also makes VLAN creation extremely flexible, since you can reconfigure VLAN membership on the fly, usually with a few clicks of your mouse. VLANs are also *extensible*, since a single VLAN can span multiple switches to encompass computers across a wide geographical area. The most common way to configure this is through the VLAN Trunking Protocol (VTP), which allows you to disseminate configuration information between multiple switches.

NOTE

It's often necessary to configure *multiple* VLAN memberships for machines such as file and print servers, since they need to be accessible by users in multiple workgroups or departments. This requires the use of the 802.1q protocol, since it's quite difficult to configure a single MAC address to belong to multiple VLANs.

In preparing for the Network+ exam, be sure that you have an understanding of what a VLAN is and how it operates within a network. Be aware of the ways that VLAN memberships can be assigned as well as the benefits of configuring a VLAN on your network.

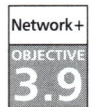

Deploying an Extranet

In our increasingly Internet-connected business world, you could find yourself in a situation where you need to provide access to internal network resources over an unsecured connection. This is often the case in situations where you enter into a business partnership or a research project with another company. One of the challenges that this presents is the question of how to appropriately allow connectivity between organizations while still maintaining proper authentication and security for all involved parties. Many of the basic firewall designs we've discussed can provide partial solutions to these issues, but you might also need to look at alternative solutions to provide remote access for users from other companies while still adhering to your own company's security requirements. Figure 9.18 shows a typical extranet configuration between two separate companies.

Figure 9.18 A Typical Extranet Configuration

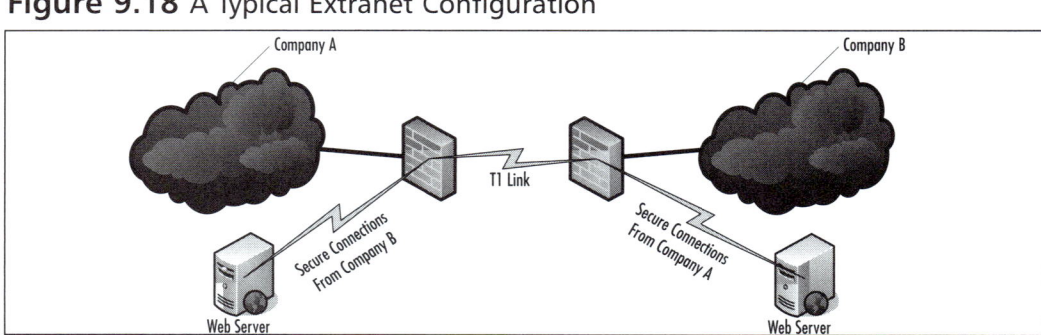

Of all the ways to provide connectivity for external business partners, *extranets* often provide the greatest flexibility for use in an enterprise network. An extranet is a portion of your internal network that you make available over the Internet so that you can share your business information with suppliers, vendors, customers, or other business partners. You can use an extranet to exchange data with a business partner, share product information with vendors or wholesalers, and collaborate with other companies on joint business or research ventures. Extranets can be Web browser-based information stores that allow customers to look up product information in an online catalog and can allow real-time (or nearly so) tracking of shipments as well as inventory management. Additionally, you can configure an extranet for collaborative efforts between business partners to allow these partnerships to share information while working on joint projects.

One of the most critical facets of deploying an extranet is that of security. On the client side, extranet applications most commonly take the form of Web browser-based applications, which can be protected using SSL encryption for the transmission of sensitive data. You can also consider deploying a VPN, using IPSec or another type of encryption, to create a secure tunnel over the Internet. You'll typically place extranet servers on isolated network segments to isolate them from your internal network. These isolated segments host machines that allow these external users to access information without actually providing them with access to your internal network.

Using an Intranet

Though it sounds like they should be opposites, intranets and extranets are actually pretty similar concepts. The main purpose of an intranet is to share company information, typically through a Web site hosted on your company's internal Web server. You can also use an intranet for more advanced features such as document collaboration and shared calendaring, which can help your company facilitate online project teams and teleconferences. You can use an intranet to provide your employees with access to company documents, software, and calendars as well as access to companywide information such as human resources information and health insurance forms. Much as with an extranet, you can use security mechanisms like SSL encryption and VPNs to secure this information for internal employees who need to access the intranet remotely or to connect one portion of your company's network with another.

> **! EXAM WARNING**
>
> The largest difference between an extranet and an intranet is that an intranet is primarily concerned with sharing resources and information among your *internal* employees. An extranet is used to share information from your internal network with *external* vendors or customers.

Network+
OBJECTIVE
3.10
Protecting Your Network From Viruses

As computers became increasingly essential in the home and workplace, computer viruses will often follow them in through the door. Viruses are nothing more than small programs designed to disrupt and alter the functionality of a computer. In earlier days, the most common way for a virus to spread between computers was through floppy disks. Today, it's much more common for computer viruses to spread through corporate and personal e-mail systems and through online file-sharing services such as Kazaa. Regardless of how the virus is transmitted, all viruses have one thing in common: They will copy themselves from one machine to another to spread the virus infection, much like a virus in the medical world.

You'll often hear viruses referred to as *malicious software*, or *malware* for short. Thousands of viruses are floating around the networks of the world, and most of them carry some type of destructive or disruptive capabilities. A destructive virus is one that actually damages or deletes data on your hard drive, attempting to delete your documents or operating system files. A disruptive virus is one that doesn't delete any data but attempts to clog up a network by creating a DoS attack. DoS attacks are attempts to overwhelm a server or a router by sending thousands of bogus requests to it. If the server has no way of knowing that a request is bogus, it will try to service all these malicious requests to the point that legitimate users will not be able to access the server or service.

We'll start this section with a look at different types of malicious software that can threaten your network and then move on to ways to protect yourself from them.

Understanding Malware

Malware comes from the phrase "*mal*icious soft*ware*." This is sort of a blanket term that covers an entire scope of aggressive software such as Trojan horses and worms. Though malware's definition varies, the term basically describes any software or code that is specifically designed to damage and/or disrupt a system. People create malware for any number of reasons: as a prank, to gain notoriety and publicity, or simply to wreak havoc on other people's computers. Because the motivations of malware writers are so varied, the effects of malware range from somewhat annoying to downright devastating. Some viruses simply clog up your e-mail inbox; others actually try to destroy or alter information on your computer. But no matter how you perceive the damage caused by malware, it is fair to say that most viruses—worms, Trojan horses, and macro viruses alike—meet the definition of malware. Let's look at a few of the more common types of malware.

Viruses

The largest distinguishing characteristic of a virus is that, to be able to perform the malicious tasks that its creators intended, it somehow needs to be executed or run on the target machine. Once the virus has been executed, it attempts to replicate itself throughout the computer and ultimately onto other network-connected computers.

Viruses are activated when an infected program is loaded into memory and executed either by its own code or by the actions of the user.

Whether a computer virus is disruptive or destructive, all viruses have a similar reason for being, and that is to disrupt the normal flow of data processing for a personal computer or for an entire network. For this reason alone, you should take every step possible to eradicate these threats and prevent them from attacking your systems. Most viruses attach themselves to other programs that are routinely executed, especially executable files such as EXE, VBS, and DLL. These files can enter your systems via users downloading infected files from a Web site or bulletin board or inserting infected disks into a diskette drive.

Exam Day Tip

The malicious code released by a virus is referred to as the virus *payload*.

Worms

A *worm* is a program of which the primary function is to replicate its code. The main difference between a virus and a worm is that a worm can replicate itself *without user intervention*. A virus depends on a user opening an e-mail attachment or running an infected executable to be able to spread, but a worm can run under its own power and actively seek out other network-attached machines to infect. Worms will often spread as a result of flaws in a computer operating system, like the Code Red and Nimda worms that spread because of a flaw in the Microsoft Web server software. Worms are designed to replicate themselves throughout a system's disks and memory, attempting to use up all the infected machine's resources and, if successful, eventually crash the system.

Logic Bombs

When discussing worms, you also need to talk about *logic bombs*. These are program routines that destroy data whenever certain conditions are met. For example, a logic bomb may reformat your hard disk or insert random code into files on a predetermined date. The most infamous example of a logic bomb was the Michelangelo virus, which was programmed to execute a destructive payload on the Renaissance artist's birthday every year.

Macro Viruses

Another type of computer virus is the *macro virus*. Macro viruses are very simple programs that are usually written in VBScript or another easy-to-learn scripting language. Macro viruses became quite prevalent after Microsoft introduced Visual Basic into its release of Office 97, because even low-level hackers were provided with a tool that allowed for the creation of malicious code that was simple to write and easy to deploy.

Macro viruses are Visual Basic for Applications (VBA) script files that provide easy access into a computer. Although macro viruses were originally designed to infect Microsoft applications such as Word, Excel, and Access, newer macro viruses have been written to infect other programs as well. The two most well-known macro viruses from recent years have been the Melissa (W97M.melissa) and ILOVEYOU (VBS.LoveLetter) viruses, which brought Internet traffic to a near halt when they first began circulating.

Trojan Horses

Trojan horses are best described by the age-old analogy of "a wolf in sheep's clothing." A Trojan horse masquerades as a file that contains useful content, perhaps a system utility or a game. But once a user opens the file and the Trojan horse is unleashed, it releases its destructive payload. Trojan horses exhibit behaviors similar to other viruses, deleting, altering, or destroying your data. Perhaps the most dangerous aspect of the Trojan horse is that it can even allow a malicious user to take control of your computer, accessing and even stealing your sensitive data and information. The largest difference between Trojan horses and their virus and worm counterparts is that Trojan horses do not replicate themselves. Rather, these programs remain in memory on a particular computer until they're eradicated. (And the eradication process often requires reformatting and rein- stalling the operating system of the computer that's been compromised.)

Probably the most notable example of a Trojan is the program Back Orifice, which was released by a hacker organization as a way to take control of remote machines using nothing but an Internet connection. This Trojan breaks down into two functional parts: a small and virtually invisible "server" piece that runs on the recipient's system and a client-end piece that runs on the hacker's computer. The server software is a small pro- gram that secretly installs itself on a recipient's system and runs even after a system reboot. It can attach itself to any Windows executable, which will run normally after its installation. This means the server-side piece can creep in just like any virus, completely undetected. Back Orifice will run over any User Datagram Protocol (UDP) port but will default to port 31337.

Once this Trojan is installed, hackers can initiate numerous commands, such as get- ting a list of the files stored on the remote machine's hard drive, terminating processes that are running, or logging the keystrokes that a user on the remote machine types at the keyboard. So if you have a traveling user at your company who has access to a great deal of sensitive documentation and financial records on your network, and if this user's laptop becomes infected with this Trojan horse, a hacker would be able to record every- thing that this remote user typed into his or her keyboard. For a user with access to sen- sitive information, this can provide a hacker with data such as bank account numbers and balances as well as administrative passwords to critical network systems.

Backdoor.SubSeven is another Trojan horse that is quite similar to Back Orifice. It grants a hacker (or any unauthorized individual) access to a computer over the Internet. When the server portion of the program is properly installed and running on a computer, it is possible for the hacker to accomplish tasks such as editing the Registry, setting up the computer as an FTP server, browsing its file system, taking screen shots, opening and closing programs, editing a currently running program's information, and even restarting the system.

Other Types of Malicious Programs

Though they're becoming less common, you should also be aware of *boot sector* and *master boot record viruses* when you're protecting your network against malicious software. Both of these boot viruses are memory-resident viruses that were primarily written for DOS. However, no matter what operating system is in use, all computers are potential targets for these types of viruses. A boot sector virus functions by taking over the system area of a diskette or a hard drive by attaching itself to a small program within the boot record that is run each time you start the computer from the disk. Once the virus has planted itself into the boot record, it can cause damage to other disks on your system. After that, whenever you put a diskette that isn't write-protected into your computer, that diskette will receive a copy of the boot virus so that it can spread the virus to other computers.

Security Alert!

Virus Hoaxes

As a network administrator, you need to be aware of not only the threats posed by computer viruses but also the less technical (but still dangerous) threat presented by *virus hoaxes*. Virus hoaxes are false (and usually quite ridiculous) messages that are almost always sent via e-mail. In most cases, they amount to little more than a bad Internet chain letter. These hoaxes are most commonly forwarded by someone who, though well meaning, doesn't understand how true viruses actually work. These messages are usually sent out of fear and in the hopes of warning friends of possible danger. In reality, all that a virus hoax does is clog up inboxes and sometimes even coax an unknowing user into deleting a critical file from his or her hard drive. Some common phrases used in hoaxes are:

- If you have accidentally received an e-mail titled (*name of hoax*), do not open it!
- Delete immediately!
- The virus will delete everything on your hard drive!
- Today (*any reputable organization*) announced the threat of this new virus …
- Forward this to everyone in your address book!

There is nothing worse than your end users receiving such an e-mail, which panics them into deleting system files from their computers. You might have heard of the Teddy Bear virus hoax e-mail that circulated some time ago— but unfortunately, a user on my corporate network had not. It all started with an

Continued

e-mail that read as follows: "I found this little bear in my machine, and because of that I am sending this message in order for you to find it in your machine. The procedure is very simple: The objective of this e-mail is to warn all Hotmail users about a new virus that is spreading by MSN Messenger. The name of this virus is jdbgmgr.exe and it is sent automatically by the Messenger and by the address book, too. The virus is not detected by McAfee or Norton and it stays quiet for 14 days before damaging the system." The e-mail goes on to warn the recipient of how they desperately need to *delete* this item from their computer before it does any damage. The file referenced by the hoax is Jdbgmgr.exe, which happens to be the Microsoft Debugger Registrar for Java. In most cases, deleting Jdbgmgr.exe on the average computer will have no adverse effects, and reinstalling it is actually quite simple. However, what if the e-mail referenced a critical system file?

As a network administrator, you should be sure to warn your end users to ignore virus threats that come from any source other than their own IT department. Most hoax e-mail warnings rarely stray from this simple pattern. If you need to verify the authenticity of a virus for one of the users on your network, search for the potential virus name with Symantec's Security Response Hoax page at www.symantec.com/avcenter/hoax.html or at www.snopes.com.

Deploying Antivirus Software

To help protect yourself against these types of malicious software, you should install an *antivirus program* to guard the computers on your network from viruses, worms, and Trojan horses. Antivirus programs are designed to recognize potential viruses as they attempt to enter your computer systems. Antivirus software uses two methods to protect your computer:

- **Virus signatures** Each virus that is catalogued by an antivirus software manufacturer has a unique digital signature that allows antivirus software to recognize it. As new computer viruses are created, new signatures need to be installed to help your antivirus software recognize these new threats. So in addition to installing antivirus software, you also need to keep it up to date by downloading new antivirus signatures on a regular basis.

Exam Day Tip

Antivirus signature updates are also called antivirus *definitions*. Be sure to update the antivirus definitions for your network on a regular basis. New viruses are discovered every week, and your antivirus software needs constant updating to be able to protect your network against the newest viruses.

- **Heuristics** This is a way for antivirus software to recognize a very new virus threat even before a signature has been developed for it. Heuristics work by looking for "virus-like" behavior on the part of anything that's executing on your computer. For example, heuristics would probably look at a VBScript file that was trying to send 10,000 e-mails from your computer or that was trying to delete the entire contents of your C:\ drive and would flag this file as containing a potential virus. Heuristics provide something of a fail-safe mechanism to help you deal with the newest viruses until your antivirus software can be updated.

Just as with firewalls, there are any number of commercially available antivirus programs that you can use to secure your network. You won't need to recognize specific antivirus applications for the Network+ exam, but it's helpful to be aware of your available options to protect a corporate network. Programs such as Norton AntiVirus 2005, which is intended for the home Internet user, retails for around $50. You can also purchase a corporate solution such as Symantec Antivirus Corporate Edition (SAVCE) or a number of other similar products to protect an entire network.

Computer Associates Software

Computer Associates (CA) offers a variety of antivirus solutions. InoculateIT Advanced Edition and eTrust InoculateIT are the current antivirus contenders CA offers. Advanced Edition is designed for midsize to large organizations that have multiple servers and workstations. It provides centralized management functionality designed to ease the protection of large networks against virus attacks. With Advanced Edition, large-scale deployment is simplified through the single-point remote installation of all servers, clients, and antivirus agents.

eTrust InoculateIT is CA's award-winning antivirus solution. eTrust InoculateIT has been designed to reduce virus infections and simplify and automate updating virus signatures. Extensive features include multiple scanning engine support, real-time detection with system cure, and centralized event logging and alerting. eTrust InoculateIT addresses all the potential points of entry for virus attacks, from desktops to servers.

Network Associates Software

Network Associates is better known to the computer purchasing public for its wildly popular McAfee line of products. Current programs offered by Network Associates are VirusScan Professional and the Total Virus Defense (TVD) Suite. VirusScan Professional was created for small businesses and home networks that have multiple computers. It allows users to protect their computers and safeguard their business and personal data. It is a more "network-oriented" version of the popular McAfee VirusScan and protects up to five PCs. The TVD Suite is a more enterprise-oriented product that allows you to protect numerous networked PCs from a single administrative point.

Deploying Antivirus for an Enterprise Network

Making a standalone personal computer with Internet connections impervious to viruses is a simple enough task. All you really need in most cases is a CD-ROM drive, the software, and about five minutes to click "Next" a few times. However, securing an enterprise network consisting of numerous servers and hundreds if not thousands of clients can be a daunting task. Enterprise antivirus solutions such as SAVCE are designed to ease the deployment of such a scenario. These powerful enterprise solutions not only facilitate the deployment of the product to your servers and clients without having to physically visit each individual computer, they provide numerous features for hassle-free management and up-to-date virus protection throughout your network.

Regardless of which product you use to manage antivirus protection for your network, your enterprise solution should create a manageable collection of servers and workstations that you can configure easily and efficiently. There should be some centralized mechanism that will allow you to propagate changes to your antivirus configuration to all members of your network with no additional effort. You also need to be able to perform antivirus-related tasks, such as scheduling regular hard disk scans and performing ad hoc virus sweeps of an entire network.

Depending on your clients' physical location and network connectivity, you can manage antivirus software for them in a number of different ways. Client machines that are connected to the same LAN as your antivirus server can be managed through a centralized administrative console since they can communicate quite frequently with the antivirus servers to receive updates and send alerts regarding virus infections. You can manage clients that are not well connected to the same network using configuration files that are stored on the local workstation or by delegating the responsibility of updating virus definitions to the computer users themselves.

Summary of Exam Objectives

In this chapter, we looked at several different technologies that you can use to protect and enhance the security of your network. First we examined firewalls, which you can use to filter the types of traffic that are allowed to reach your internal users. A packet-filtering firewall can filter traffic based on the source or destination IP address of a particular network packet as well as the TCP or UDP port number that it's transmitting on. Packet-filtering firewalls make filtering decisions based on the information they find at the network layer and transport layer, but they won't examine network packets any further than that.

There are also application-level (or circuit-level) firewalls that more fully examine incoming traffic to ensure that it is not malicious or harmful in any way. This process involves examining a network packet's contents to determine if they are malicious or not, rather than just making decisions based on the IP address or port that the traffic is destined for.

Firewalls can also function as Network Address Translation (NAT) devices, which allow you to use private IP addresses for your internal clients while still enabling access to a public network such as the Internet. Static NAT filtering creates a one-to-one mapping between private and public IP addresses and is useful for a network with only a few internal hosts. For a network that has many internal hosts and only a few public IP addresses to go around, you can enable dynamic NAT translation, where private-to-public IP address mappings take place on the fly.

Another option for protecting your network is a proxy server, which acts as a go-between for your internal clients whenever they need to request a resource from the Internet or another untrusted network. Proxy servers can also make filtering decisions similar to firewalls, allowing or disallowing a particular user's request based on the content of that request, time of day, or security groups that the user belongs to. Proxy servers can also cache repeated requests for the same Web resources so that users can access them more quickly over the local network.

If your company has an active Internet presence, you might also need to use an extranet to provide secure access to your internal resources for external business partners, vendors, or customers. This involves creating a secure connection to your internal resources, usually by using a virtual private network or an SSL-encrypted Web connection. External users will access your extranet using Web browsers or a VPN client.

You can also configure an intranet to provide easier access to your internal resources for your employees, especially ones that travel or telecommute. An intranet is typically an internal Web server that provides a single place to access resources from the various departments or divisions in your company, protected by SSL encryption to provide secure access for traveling or telecommuting users.

Finally, we talked about computer viruses and how to protect your company's network from them. Viruses, worms, and Trojan horses are all malicious computer programs that attempt to either damage the data or disrupt the operations of a single computer or an entire network. You can protect your network from viruses by installing antivirus software and keeping your definition files up to date. Antivirus software uses signature files to recognize known viruses and uses heuristics to respond to malicious behavior from a new virus that might be included in the most recent definitions.

Exam Objectives Fast Track

Implementing Firewalls

☑ Use a firewall at the perimeter of your network to protect your internal resources.

☑ Network Address Translation (NAT) helps you share a small number of public IP addresses between a large number of internal clients.

☑ Application layer firewalls examine traffic at the application layer of the OSI model. Packet-filtering firewalls operate at the transport layer.

☑ Create firewall rules to allow or deny traffic to enter your internal network based on source or destination IP address as well as the TCP or UDP port that's being used.

Using Proxy Servers

☑ Proxy servers improve your network performance by caching frequently requested Web pages and serving them up to your users at LAN speeds.

☑ You can use forward caching to speed up Web browsing for your internal users and reverse caching to improve Web site availability for your clients and business partners.

☑ Proxy servers can be standalone devices or they can be bundled with the features of a firewall as well.

Using Network Filtering

☑ Use VLANs to control broadcast traffic on your network without dealing with the overhead of complex routing tables.

☑ An extranet allows your business partners, customers, and vendors to securely access your company's internal resources from the Internet.

☑ Using a corporate intranet can improve collaboration and information sharing for your company's internal users, even those who are accessing information remotely.

Protecting Your Network From Viruses

☑ Viruses are a particular breed of malicious software that, when launched, attempt to replicate to other computers through e-mail or network connections.

☑ Worms are similar to viruses except that they can spread over network connections with no user interaction whatsoever.

☑ When implementing antivirus protection for your network, keep your AV definitions and signature files up to date to avoid the latest virus threats.

Exam Objectives Frequently Asked Questions

The following Frequently Asked Questions, answered by the authors of this book, are designed to both measure your understanding of the Exam Objectives presented in this chapter, and to assist you with real-life implementation of these concepts. You will also gain access to thousands of other FAQs at ITFAQnet.com.

Q: Is there any reason to deploy a proxy server by itself, or should I always use a proxy server in combination with a firewall?

A: You can deploy proxy servers for a number of purposes, including installing one or more proxy servers that are only used to do Web caching to improve bandwidth usage on your network. In this case, you can use a proxy server by itself without adding the overhead of deploying a firewall along with it.

Q: Will antivirus software protect my users from adware and other forms of spyware?

A: Viruses and spyware are two very different things, and most antivirus software is not designed to recognize or combat spyware that gets installed on a system. Most of the major antivirus vendors have also begun to release spyware detection utilities, which you should include as a part of your overall protection scheme.

Q: I have configured three VLANs on one network segment to cut down on network traffic. But now the machines in the different VLANs are unable to communicate with each other. How can I correct this?

A: You need to deploy a router to be able to transmit traffic between multiple VLANs.

Q: Is there a particular advantage in using a hardware-based firewall over using a software-based one?

A: Each type of firewall has its own advantages and disadvantages. Hardware-based firewalls tend to be faster and more powerful since they are dedicated hardware devices that perform only firewall functions. However, these devices also tend to be more expensive and aren't always appropriate for a company that's on a tight budget. Software-based firewalls tend to be less expensive (or free) to deploy, but you are running the risk of the firewall being circumvented if the operating system of the machine that it's running on becomes compromised.

Q: One of my users is reporting strange behavior on her machine that started after she opened an e-mail attachment. I've downloaded the latest antivirus definitions, but nothing on this machine is showing up as a virus when I scan the hard drive. How can I figure out if this is a new virus?

A: All the major antivirus vendors have a mechanism in place for you to transmit suspected new viruses so that they can analyze them and provide new antivirus definitions to combat them. Check your antivirus vendor's Web site to learn how to submit a suspected file for analysis.

Self Test

A Quick Answer Key follows the Self Test questions. For complete questions, answers, and explanations to the Self Test questions in this chapter as well as the other chapters in this book, see the Self Test Appendix.

1. You are the network administrator for a financial services company. Your company has a single Web server that contains an intranet that is accessed by internal employees while also providing information to the general public. You would like to secure access to this Web server without preventing the necessary users from accessing it. What is the best way to do this?

    A. Install a single firewall. Place the Web server on your company's internal network.

    B. Install a single firewall. Place the Web server outside the firewall with a direct connection to the Internet.

    C. Install a proxy server to handle requests from your internal users.

    D. Install the Web server into a demilitarized zone (DMZ).

2. You are the network administrator for a bank that has several branch offices located throughout a single city. Each branch office contains 25 workstations and one file server that should be accessed only by users internal to the branch. You have been provided with three public IP addresses for your company's Web server, firewall, and proxy server, and now you need to configure IP addresses for your branch offices. Which range of IP addresses can you use to configure the workstations and servers in each branch? (Select all that apply.)

   A. 192.168.1.0/24

   B. 10.0.0.0/8

   C. 66.195.34.0/24

   D. 172.16.0.0/16

   E. 127.0.0.0/8

3. You are the new network administrator for a medium-sized law firm that runs its own Web server and DNS that are configured with public IP addresses. To increase the security of your externally reachable machines, you place both servers inside a DMZ. You need to configure the external firewall so that only HTTP and SSL traffic can reach the Web server and only DNS traffic can reach the DNS server. What rules should you configure on your firewall? (Select all that apply.)

   A. Create a firewall rule that allows only TCP port 80 and TCP port 443 to reach the Web server.

   B. Create a firewall rule that allows only TCP port 80 and TCP port 110 to reach the Web server.

   C. Create a firewall rule that allows only TCP port 53 to reach the DNS server.

   D. Create a firewall rule that allows only TCP port 443 to reach the DNS server.

4. Different firewall implementations operate at different layers of the OSI model. Match the firewall implementation with the layer of the OSI model at which it operates. (Choose two.)

   A. Circuit-level firewall: Application layer

   B. Stateful inspection packet filter: Transport layer

   C. Circuit-level firewall: Transport layer

   D. Stateful inspection packet filter: Network layer

5. You are the network administrator for a public library in a major city. You have configured several computers on the main floor of the library to allow patrons to browse the Web and check their e-mail. The library's board of directors is concerned that patrons will use the kiosks to view objectionable content. They are especially concerned because the library is frequented by children and young adults who will be accessing the kiosks without parental supervision. You suggest that the library deploy a proxy server to help address this issue. What functionality of a proxy server will help ensure that no objectionable content can be accessed from the library kiosks?

   A. Packet filtering

   B. Packet redirection

   C. Content filtering

   D. Content caching

6. You are the network administrator for a large medical supply company with sales offices located in several states. Each sales office has a proxy server installed to allow Internet access for the office, since sales reps pull up pricing for the products they sell from the company intranet. Some of these offices are connected to the main office using only 56K dialup lines, and you have received complaints that accessing these Web pages is taking too long. You do not have funds to increase the connection speed for these offices. How can you improve Web site access for your remote offices?

   A. Install a packet filter on the proxy server so that only requests to the corporate Web server are allowed.

   B. Enable content caching on the proxy server.

   C. Install a copy of the company's inventory database at each local office.

   D. Disable antivirus software on the proxy server to improve performance.

7. You are the network administrator for a financial services company with offices in several cities. You would like to create a VPN between the offices to allow for secure file access. What technology will you use to create a VPN between your company's branch offices?

   A. SSL

   B. Packet filtering

   C. IPSec

   D. HTTP

8. You are the network administrator for an Internet service provider. You have configured an FTP server so that your customers can upload Web files to their respective Web directories. To increase security for the FTP server, you want to configure a firewall to protect both inbound and outbound traffic. Which ports should you allow on the firewall protecting the FTP server? (Choose all.)

   A. TCP port 21 inbound

   B. TCP port 20 inbound

   C. TCP port 21 outbound

   D. TCP port 20 outbound

9. You are the network administrator for a small marketing firm. You begin to receive reports that network performance has become incredibly slow over the last few days. In attempting to track down the source of the problem, you use a network sniffer to determine how much bandwidth is being used on your network. You discover that your network is being bombarded by half-open TCP connections from several machines located on different networks attached to the Internet. What type of network attack are you experiencing right now?

   A. Virus

   B. Trojan horse

   C. IP spoofing

   D. Distributed denial of service

10. You are in the planning stages of a project to deploy VLANs on your corporate network. What methods are available for you to assign VLAN membership to the computers on your network? (Select all that apply.)

    A. Port number

    B. MAC address

    C. IP address

    D. 802.1q

11. You are the network administrator for a large financial services company. Your accounting department relies on a mission-critical financial application that uses TCP/IP broadcast packets to send notifications to users of the application when they receive information that they should be aware of. This wasn't a problem when the company was small and contained only a few dozen workstations, but with hundreds of machines on the same network, you have begun to receive complaints that network performance is unacceptably slow. How can you improve performance for the users on your network while allowing members of the accounting

department to continue to use their mission-critical application? (Each choice represents a complete solution. Choose two.)

A.   Decrease the available bandwidth on your LAN.

B.   Configure a VLAN for the computers in the accounting department.

C.   Place the computers in the accounting department on a separate subnet.

D.   Install an intranet to allow the accounting department to use the application.

12.   You are assisting with the planning of a new VLAN implementation for your network. You create a test lab containing two VLANs, called VLAN1 and VLAN2, connected to a single switch. After some testing, you realize that traffic from VLAN1 is unable to reach VLAN2. How can you correct this problem?

A.   Install a router to transmit traffic between the two VLANs.

B.   Update the routing table on the switch.

C.   Install a separate switch for each VLAN.

D.   Configure one computer that is a member of both VLANs to transmit information between them.

13.   You are the network administrator for a large university that is involved in several joint research projects with the federal government. You need to be able to allow government researchers access to your researchers' project data, without allowing them access to other internal network resources. What is the best way to accomplish this goal?

A.   Grant each government researcher a logon to the servers on your LAN.

B.   Install a Web server on your DMZ to host the joint data using an extranet.

C.   Install a Web server on your private network to host the joint data using an intranet.

D.   Create a VPN between your university and the government office where the researchers are located.

14.   You have installed a Web server to function as an extranet for your company's customers, allowing them to look up inventory levels for your products as well as the current status of any orders they've placed. Customers will access this extranet using their Web browsers. You need to ensure that any customer data is encrypted as it passes from your extranet server to the customers' Web browsers so that information cannot be stolen by a hacker or a competing company. How can you ensure the security of your extranet data as it's being transmitted to your customers?

    A. Use IPSec to protect Web connections to the extranet server.

    B. Use SSL to protect Web connections to the extranet server.

    C. Use a firewall to protect Web connections to the extranet server.

    D. Use a proxy server to protect Web connections to the extranet server.

15. You are the network administrator for a small law firm that is in the process of being acquired by a larger firm in the same city. During the acquisition process, all your network data needs to be accessible by the larger firm so that both firms can begin the process of transitioning information to the larger firm's servers. Both firms are connected to the Internet via high-speed T1 links. Each firm's data needs to remain secure while being accessed by the other firm's users. What is the best way to provide this type of access between the two company networks?

    A. Create a filtering rule on each firewall that allows each firm's public IP address to go through the firewall.

    B. Create an extranet that will allow each firm to view the other firm's data using a Web browser.

    C. Place the servers containing each firm's data into a DMZ between the two firms.

    D. Create a VPN between the two firms.

16. You are a consultant who has been contracted by a small company to set up its network. The owner of the company has purchased a copy of a popular antivirus program for each workstation on the network. After you have installed the antivirus software on each computer, what is the most important thing to configure?

    A. Configure the software to e-mail an administrator whenever it encounters a virus.

    B. Configure the software to download the most recent antivirus definitions on a regular basis.

    C. Configure the software to scan a file only when a user double-clicks on it.

    D. Configure the software to immediately delete any virus-infected files that it finds.

17. You are working on the network help desk for a financial services company. You receive a phone call from a user who complains that her computer is acting strangely, rebooting at random intervals and crashing with the Blue Screen of Death. As you attempt to figure out how this occurred, she tells you that she recently received an e-mail from a friend that contained an attachment that ran a

cute Snowman Bowling game. What do you suspect is the most likely cause of her problem?

A. The driver for her network card has become corrupted.

B. Her computer has been infected with a Trojan horse.

C. She has disabled her personal firewall software.

D. Her computer is configured with an incorrect IP address.

18. You are the junior network administrator for a small publishing company. The senior network administrator is on vacation, and you receive a support call from the CEO of the company. The CEO has received an e-mail from a trusted friend that is advising him to delete certain system files on his computer that indicate a virus infection and to forward the e-mail to everyone in his address book so that they can be protected as well. Your network uses an enterprise antivirus solution that automatically pushes out new antivirus updates to all network computers every day. What advice would you give the CEO in this situation?

A. The e-mail is legitimate and his PC is infected. He should delete the files mentioned in the e-mail right away.

B. The e-mail is legitimate and his PC might be infected. He should copy the files mentioned in the e-mail to a network share so that you can scan them for viruses.

C. The e-mail is a virus "hoax" that is trying to "con" the CEO into deleting important system files from his computer. The instructions in the e-mail should be disregarded.

D. The e-mail contains a virus and should be deleted right away.

Self Test Quick Answer Key

For complete questions, answers, and explanations to the Self Test questions in this chapter as well as the other chapters in this book, see the Self Test Appendix.

1.	**D**	10.	**A**, **B**, and **D**
2.	**A**, **B**, and **D**	11.	**B** and **C**
3.	**A** and **C**	12.	**A**
4.	**A** and **B**	13.	**B**
5.	**C**	14.	**B**
6.	**B**	15.	**D**
7.	**C**	16.	**B**
8.	**A** and **D**	17.	**B**
9.	**D**	18.	**C**

## Chapter 10

NETWORK+

Fault Management and Disaster Recovery

Domain III Objectives in this Chapter:

Introduction

In today's high-speed networks, data is relied upon for just about everything. If you want to send an e-mail, you need to have an e-mail server that is available to process the incoming and outgoing messages, if you want to access a file, the file server must be available and functioning as it should. Although this is common sense, it is only really realized when a disaster occurs. It is common sense that the systems that provide you with the service you need should be set up to avert catastrophe, and even more so, to survive it. You may not know it, but most computer parts are made with the possibility that they will fail. Look at hard disks for example; most, if not all of them, come with a mean time between failure (MTBF) value associated with them so that you can prepare for the unlikely event that they will cease to function properly. This is where a redundant array of independent disks (RAID), or perhaps the use of a cluster, comes in to save the day.

All of this and more will be covered in this chapter, as the Network+ exam requires that you know how to deal with disasters or prepare for them and avoid them completely. In this chapter we will talk about the fundamentals of fault tolerance and disaster recovery. We will cover the basics of how to plan for and apply disaster recovery and fault tolerance in your network. Well-thought-out plans and documents provide information that is used to create a successful redundant solution. Without them, organizations would find it difficult to deal with incidents or to avoid problems that can adversely affect a company. As a Network+ technician, you will be expected to understand the fundamental concepts of disaster recovery planning and fault tolerance implementation.

This chapter examines the concepts storage systems, sites that can be used if your primary site is destroyed or rendered useless, as well as how to implement layers of protection to help you keep your systems up to achieve whatever your desired *uptime* is.

We will also briefly cover DRPs. A disaster recovery plan is a set of documents used to identify potential threats and outline the procedures necessary to deal with different types of threats, disasters, and anything else not of the norm and clearly defined with action in the plan. When creating a disaster recovery plan, administrators should try to identify all the different types of threats that may affect the company. For example, a company in California would not need to worry about blizzards, but would need to be concerned about earthquakes, fire, flooding, power failures, and other kinds of disasters. Once the administrator has determined what disasters their company could face, they can then create procedures to minimize the risk of such disasters. The end of this chapter will cover the importance of documenting your network. In an emergency, having an up-to-date and accurate set of documentation is very important. Let us now take a serious look into applying fault tolerance and disaster recovery into your network and prepare for the Network+ exam.

etwork+
BJECTIVE
3.11

Fault Tolerance

A single point of failure can be the Achilles heel that brings down a system. Imagine a single road with a bridge that provides the only way to enter or exit a town. If the bridge fell down, no one would be able to come into or leave the town. Just as the bridge provides a single point of failure that can cut off people from the outside world, a single point of failure in a system can sever a company's ability to perform normal business functions.

Because there are so many components making up a network, something failing to function properly is inevitable. Hard drives can crash, power can go out, network connections can go down, and any number of other events can take down individual computers or the network as a whole. Until the problem is fixed, employees may be unable to do their jobs, and the company loses money. To minimize the impact, networks must be fault tolerant.

Fault tolerance is the ability of a system, device or network to continue functioning despite a malfunction or an event that causes failure. When a component fails, another component will automatically take over, or procedures can be followed to have another system take its place. In other words, every important system has a backup system. Redundant systems and fault tolerance allow systems and services to be available in the event of a failure, so that there is little or no loss of service.

There are many ways to protect a business and its systems, but the first step in planning for a possible problem is determining what's important in your network. It might be nice to have everything duplicated on a network so that if any component fails there's another one to take its place, but the cost of actually doing this would be astronomical in most situations. Besides, not everything is that important. While one company's employees may use online programs to do their jobs, another company may only use their intranet's Web server to post a corporate newsletter and some reference material. In this case, the first company could benefit by having a second Web server that they could switch to in the event of a failure, where the second company might not even notice their Web server was gone. What's important varies from company to company. You will need to determine what's important to your network, and what always needs to be available and protected.

Since networks can be unique, having different devices and services, the task of identifying what needs to be fault tolerant can seem overwhelming. However, there are several areas of a network that should be evaluated in terms of fault tolerance:

- Power
- Link Redundancy
- Storage
- Services

As we'll see in the sections that follow, once you've identified the systems in these categories that need to be fault tolerant, you can then implement measures to keep them available if a failure occurs.

Fault Tolerant Power

On August 14, 2003, the largest blackout in North American history shut down cities across the northeastern United States and in Ontario, Canada. In the day or more that followed without power, people found themselves without light, air conditioning, or other systems that relied on electricity. People were trapped in elevators and subway trains, while food spoiled in refrigerators and grocery stores. It was a sobering reminder of how dependent our society is on electrical energy and how easy it is to fail us, leaving us somewhat stranded and in disbelief that this could happen in the first place. Where were the backup systems? As with most issues of this size and complexity, that remained to be seen at the time.

For those in computer-related professions, this event also served as a wake-up call and stressed the importance of fault tolerance, as well as disaster recovery. When utility companies are unable to provide electricity consistently, measures must be in place to provide power to essential computers and devices if problems occur. Included are servers that provide key services and data storage, workstations that will be used during the power outage, and equipment needed to network them together. The methods you choose to power these components will depend on how long they'll need an alternate source of power.

An uninterruptible power supply (UPS) is used to provide regulated battery power to devices when normal sources of electricity become unavailable. When normal power is available, it will charge the UPS's battery. The UPS will generally provide such functions as surge protection and noise filtering for the devices plugged into it. When power to the UPS fails, it will revert to battery power, and continue supplying electricity for a limited amount of time, usually enough time for you (or the UPS itself if configured properly) to power the equipment down safely.

Sudden power losses not only prevent people from using computers and other equipment, but can also corrupt data and damage hardware. By having computers, printers, and other devices plugged into the UPS, you are given a window of opportunity to shut them down properly, and avoid any damage. The components plugged into the UPS during a power outage continue receiving power from the UPS's battery for a limited amount of time (often ranging from 10 to 45 minutes) until normal power is restored. While this isn't a solution for continuing business during long blackouts, it does provide enough time to properly shut down systems plugged into the UPS, or for continuing work during temporary losses of power.

UPSs were traditionally expensive enough that network administrators limited their use. In recent years, the cost of these devices have dropped to the point that many people use them for home computer systems, and companies are implementing them to provide emergency power to a wider range of equipment.

When power is out for lengthy periods of time, additional measures may be necessary to supply electricity to equipment. Power generators can run on gasoline, kerosene, or other fuels for a specific period of time, extended by the refueling of the generator. The capacity of these generators varies, with some being able to provide power to a small office or home, while others can provide energy to an entire building. With larger generators, power outlets within the building may be connected to the generator so that any systems plugged into these special outlets will receive power when normal power is lost.

Security Alert!

Becoming Powerless

During the 2003 blackout, many network administrators and computer-related professionals were surprised at what was overlooked in terms of preparation. Some were honest oversights that were rectified afterward, while others were situations that few could have foreseen.

While servers, workstations and network devices may have been hooked up to UPSs and generator power, less obvious choices of equipment were left without power. Situations arose when air conditioning became unavailable. Servers and equipment stored in secured closets lost the air conditioning of the general office area, while some network administrators discovered the air conditioning systems in their server rooms weren't hooked up to the generator. Equipment continued running under generator power, lending heat to the rising temperatures of their surrounding areas. Because the blackout happened during the hot and humid days of August, computer personnel scrambled to find fans to cool the devices before they overheated. Some missed the mark and had to replace systems that had fried up like an egg on a frying pan.

While many businesses didn't have generators to provide an alternate source of power, those who did found another dilemma. Generators that ran on gasoline needed to be refueled, but most of the gas stations were closed. While there was plenty of gas in the tanks beneath the stations, the gas pumps ran on electricity so there was no way to pump it out. Ironically, those who didn't have a supply of gasoline found their alternate source of power running out of power.

Another issue came when computers tried to connect to the outside world. While laptops could run on battery power, home computers on UPSs, and corporate computers on generators, many found that the Internet was suddenly unavailable to them. Internet Service Providers (ISPs) who were unprepared for massive power failures couldn't provide services. Similarly, companies who were internetworked with other organizations found that while their network was operational, the same could not be said for others they connected to.

When all was said and done, the blackout became a minor footnote in history and generally held an interesting tale for those involved. However, the smart ones didn't simply dismiss the events when the lights came back on; they had learned from them. Plans and procedures on how the power failure was handled needed to be reviewed and in many cases, updated or altered. As an example, network administrators needed to ensure the air conditioning in their server rooms was hooked up to generator power, and that generators had sufficient fuel available for significant outages. Devices that were left without power, but necessary to business functions needed to be attached to UPSs and generators, while those that had power, but were unnecessary needed to be reevaluated.

Continued

Training issues had to be explored, and many found they needed to ensure that changes were made in other businesses (such as ISPs), so that the same issues wouldn't repeat themselves.

EXERCISE 10.1

CONFIGURING A UPS ON A WINDOWS 2000 PROFESSIONAL COMPUTER

This exercise requires you to be logged onto a Windows 2000 Professional computer that has a UPS attached to it. You must also be using an Administrator account or an account that allows you to modify the power options of the computer.

1. From the **Start** menu, select **Settings** and then click **Control Panel**.

2. Double-click **Power Options**.

3. Click the **UPS** tab. A screen similar to that shown in Figure 10.1 will be displayed.

Figure 10.1 Power Options—UPS Tab

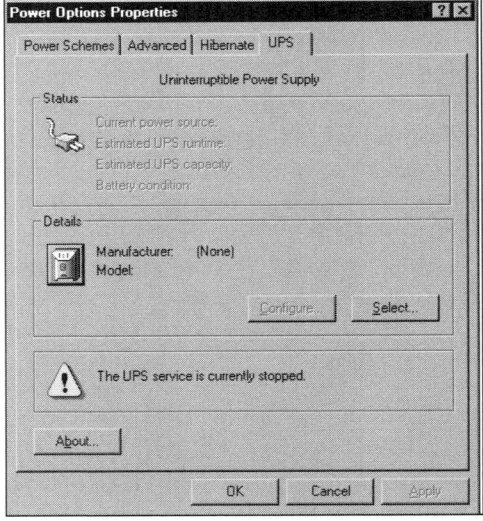

4. In the Details section, click Select. The UPS Selection dialog box will be displayed (Figure 10.2).

Figure 10.2 UPS Selection Dialog Box

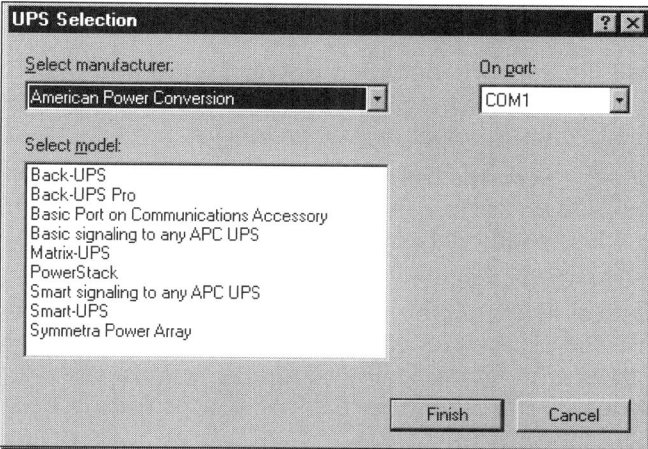

5. Use the **Select manufacturer** drop-down list to select the name of the company that manufactured your UPS.

6. Use the **Select model** drop-down list to select the model of your UPS.

7. Use the **On port** drop-down list to select the communication port that your UPS is attached to. The cable connecting the UPS to the COM port of your computer allows the UPS to send notifications of power failures to the computer.

8. Click **Finish** to return to the previous screen.

9. In the **Details** section of the UPS tab, click **Configure**. The UPS Configuration dialog box will be displayed (Figure 10.3).

Figure 10.3 UPS Configuration Dialog Box

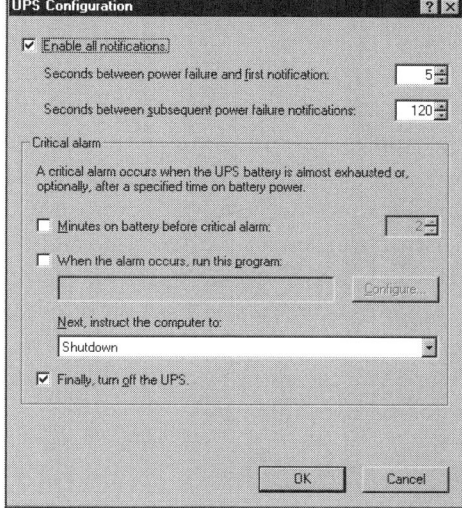

10. Ensure that the **Enable all notifications** option is enabled. This will activate the computer's ability to accept notifications of a power failure from the UPS.

11. Use the **Seconds between power failure and first notification** drop-down list to set the number of seconds that will elapse between when the UPS loses power and when you are notified.

12. Use the **Seconds between subsequent power failure notifications** drop-down list to specify how long (in seconds) the UPS will wait before sending additional notifications of the power failure.

13. In the **Critical alarm** section, enable the **Minutes on battery before critical alarm** option, then set the number of minutes your UPS can provide power. This will allow the computer to run on the battery power without doing any additional actions, such as running a specific program. If this time limit is met, a critical alarm occurs.

14. Use the **Next, instruct the computer to** drop-down list to select the action that you want the computer to take when a critical alarm occurs. Your options are for the computer to **Shutdown**, or to **Hibernate**.

15. Ensure that the **Finally, turn off the UPS** option is enabled. The computer will signal the UPS to shut down when the computer either hibernates or shuts down.

16. Click **OK**.

17. Click **OK** again.

Fault Tolerant Link Redundancy

Fault tolerance can also be found in the network connections between different sites, such as when multiple sites are connected together on a wide area network (WAN). In organizations with branch offices, pools of buildings, or various divisions spread over a geographic area, the network is often interconnected between locations. These smaller local area networks (LANs) might share data or other resources, or may require access to specific servers in other locations. For example, sales offices might need to enter orders and invoices into a database on a server at the main office. If the network connection between these locations went down, orders for products couldn't be processed. Losing the link between two locations on a network can result in different possible outcomes: the business could suffer losses or a redundant link could be used to resume connectivity.

Link redundancy simply means that when one method of communication between sites fails, another can be used to maintain a link. Network lines may be used to connect two sites, with a separate network line set up in case the first goes down. If this first link fails, the network can still use the second link.

The way the network determines which link to use is based on a priority system that you configure; a link with high priority is used before a low priority link. For example, let's say you had a T1 line and an ISDN (Integrated Services Digital Network) line connecting two sites together (similar to Figure 10.4). Network traffic between the two sites goes over the T1 line, but if it fails, then a backup line (here we are using an ISDN line) is used. This means the T1 line is configured as high priority and the ISDN link is configured as low priority. The ISDN line is redundant and only used if the T1 line fails, thereby allowing network traffic to continue between these sites while a problem exists, and then when the problem is solved, the traffic resumes its normal path through the network.

Figure 10.4 A Network Using Redundant Links

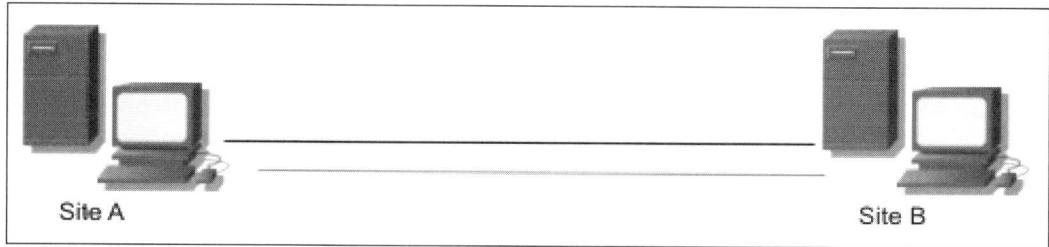

Another way of providing redundancy is to ensure that there is more than one route that can be used to send data over the network. Additional lines between sites provide redundant paths for network traffic to travel. For example, suppose that site A is connected to site B, which is connected to site C. These two links connect the three sites together, but if either of the links fails, then one of the sites will be unable to communicate with the others, and vice versa. To provide high availability, a third link can be set up between site A and C. As shown in Figure 10.5, the additional link allows the three sites to communicate with one another if any one link fails.

Figure 10.5 A Network with Multiple Routes

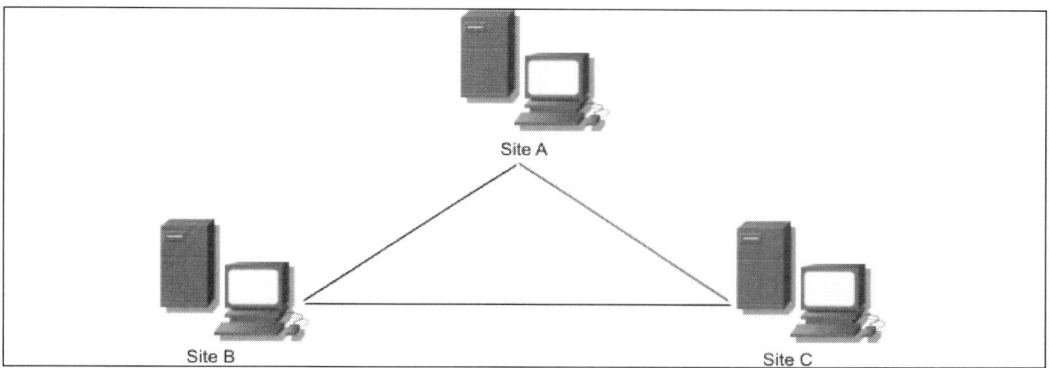

Such redundancy not only applies to a corporate network, but can also extend to the Internet. Many companies depend on Internet connectivity almost as much as network connectivity. In some cases, such as e-commerce business, they depend on it even more. A redundant ISP can be used to provide connectivity when the organization's primary ISP's service becomes unavailable. The link to the secondary ISP can be configured as a low priority route, while your primary ISP is advertised as high priority. Such a configuration will have users using the primary ISP for normal usage, but automatically switching over to the low priority connection when the first one fails. If a secondary ISP isn't desired, then you should ensure that the ISP uses two different *points of presence*. A point of presence is an access point to the Internet, and multiple ones will allow access to the Internet if one goes down.

TEST DAY TIP

Some of the questions on the Network+ exam will test you using a combination of scenarios and diagrams. A picture or diagram may be used in conjunction with a question to show you the layout of a network or other important information. Pay special attention to these diagrams, as they can often hold the key to correctly answering the question. By quickly glancing at the diagram or ignoring it completely, you may be unable to answer the question correctly.

EXAM WARNING

The full mesh network topology discussed in Chapter 1, "Network Fundamentals," is an example of fault tolerance and link redundancy.

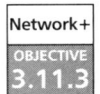

Network+

OBJECTIVE
3.11.3

Fault Tolerant Storage

One of the most precious commodities of any business using computers is its data. Much of the work performed in offices today is stored as individual files (such as documents or spreadsheets) or in databases. Because of its importance, the areas in which the data is stored also need to be fault tolerant.

A way that data can be recovered after a catastrophic problem is by restoring data from backups. Backups are a source of fault tolerance; you have multiple copies of the same data, therefore if data is accidentally erased, it can be retrieved from a copy. Backups allow a single file or an entire hard disk to be restored if the one currently being used is damaged or destroyed.

Another way you can recover from a serious problem would be to have fault tolerant hard disks in your server. Fault tolerant disks allow a computer to recover from a disaster so that data isn't lost or corrupted. As we'll see later in this chapter, there are several ways in which hard disks can be made fault tolerant by using multiple disks. Data can be written to multiple disks at once or across several disks, so that if one fails, the data can still be recovered. These methods are referred to as different levels of *RAID*.

Although adding a level of redundancy will provide you with some fault tolerance, you may also experience a small amount of latency due to the added systems and/or hardware. As well, with RAID and backups, there is also a delay during which employees must wait until network administrators can fix the problem when one occurs and recover from the fault as well as to check and restore the data if need be. The wait time to restore data is a minor consequence however, when you consider that data stored on the disks isn't lost due to a hard drive crash or other problems.

Fault Tolerant Services

Users of networks rely on specific services to perform their jobs. E-mail, databases, websites available over the Internet or local intranet, and other services are vital to many organizations. If certain services aren't available, the company's employees are limited in the work they can complete and may be unable to perform specific tasks. Because of the consequences of failure of these services, it's important to identify which services are mission critical to the business so that measures can be taken to make them available in the event of a failure.

A method of making services fault tolerant involves duplicating services on multiple computers. This group of machines is called a cluster, and has the benefit of sharing the load of work that would otherwise be performed by a single server. Each server in the cluster is called a node, and together they act and appear as a single machine on the network. If one computer fails, users of the network can continue using the services available through the cluster because the other nodes are still running. Clustering is discussed in more detail later in this chapter.

Computer systems may also make use of failsafe computers, which are two computers that are essentially identical to one another, and provide the same services. While the primary computer runs normally, it provides services to users of the network. A secondary computer called a *failsafe*, monitors the primary computer, and routinely checks to see if it's operational. If the primary computer fails, the failsafe computer will take over. For users of the network, there is a short absence of services during the time that the failsafe computer detects that the primary computer is unavailable and takes over its role.

RAID

RAID was developed to prevent the loss of data and/or improve performance by writing data across a set of hard disks, or writing a duplicate of data from one hard disk to another. The methods used by RAID that provide fault tolerance allow data to be restored if a single disk fails. If more than one disk fails however, the data cannot be restored, and you'll have to resort to recovering data from a backup.

Each method of storing data is referred to as a level of RAID. The levels of RAID are used for different purposes, with each one offering different mixes of performance, reliability, and cost. Because not every level of RAID offers improved performance or fault tolerance, it is important to choose the level of RAID that suits your needs.

As shown in Table 10.1, there are a number of similarities and differences among the different levels of RAID. RAID 0 offers no fault tolerance, but offers improved performance over using a single hard disk, because it writes data across a set of hard disks. This method is called *striping*, which we'll discuss later in more detail. Because data is read or written across several disks in the striped set, it is able to read and write the data faster. RAID 1 (which we'll also discuss in greater detail later in this chapter) uses two disks. When data is written to one disk it is also written to the other disk in the set, so that each disk is a duplicate of the other. If one of the disks fails, the data still resides on the other disk. Other levels of RAID (2, 3, 4, 5, 10, and 53) use striping, but also provide fault tolerance. In some of these levels, redundant information is written to one of the disks in the set, while others write redundant information to each disk in the set. If one of the disks fails, the redundant information enables regeneration of the data that was on the failed disk.

Table 10.1 RAID Levels

RAID Level	Description
RAID 0	Disk striping. Data is written (striped) across two or more disks, but no copies of the data are made. This improves performance because data is read from multiple disks, but there is no fault tolerance if a disk fails.
RAID 0 + 1	Disk striping with mirroring. This level combines features of RAID 0 and RAID 1. It allows four or more disks to be used as a set, but provides full redundancy and the same fault tolerance as RAID 5.
RAID 1	Disk mirroring or duplexing. Data that's written to one disk is also written to another, so that each drive has an exact copy of the data. In other words, one disk's data is a mirror image of the other's. Additional fault tolerance is achieved by using separate disk controllers for each disk, which is called duplexing. If one of the disks fails, or (in the case of duplexing) if a controller fails, the data is still available through the other disk in the pair. Because data from one disk is mirrored to another, a minimum of two disks must be used to implement RAID 1.
RAID 2	Disk striping across disks. Also maintains error correction codes across the disks. This level is similar to RAID 0, except that error correction codes are used for drives that don't have built-in error detection.

Continued

Table 10.1 continued RAID Levels

RAID Level	Description
RAID 3	Same as level 2, except the error correction information is stored as parity information on one disk. Data is striped across three or more drives, but one drive is used to store the parity bits for each byte that's written to the other disks. When a disk fails, it can be replaced and data can be restored to it from the parity information. If two or more disks in the set fail, then data cannot be recovered.
RAID 4	Employs striping data in much larger blocks than in levels 2 and 3. Parity information is kept on a single disk. This level is similar to RAID 3, but stripes data in larger blocks. As with RAID 3, if one disk fails, data can be recovered. However, if more than one disk fails, data cannot be recovered. Three or more hard disks are required to implement RAID 4.
RAID 5	Disk striping with parity across multiple drives. Data is striped across three or more disks, but parity information is stored across multiple drives.
RAID 10	Allows four or more drives to be used in an array, and has data striped across them with the same fault tolerance as RAID 1.
RAID 53	Allows a minimum of five disks to be used in an array, but provides the same fault tolerance as RAID 3.

RAID is available through hardware or software. Hardware RAID will generally support more levels of RAID, and will provide higher performance. This type of RAID can also support *hot swapping*, in which a disk can be removed from the server without having to take the server down. Software RAID is provided through operating systems, such as Windows 2000 and 2003 Server. When RAID is provided through the software, the levels of RAID supported may be limited and will also take a higher toll on the system, as RAID functions must run through the operating system running on the machine. Because of this, hot swapping is often unsupported, so you'll need to take down the system to replace a disk.

EXAM WARNING

Don't expect to see many questions dealing with RAID 0+1, 10, or 53 on the exam. You will probably see questions dealing with levels 0 and 1 through 5 of RAID. Of the various levels, pay particular attention to disk striping (RAID 0), disk mirroring (RAID 1), and disk striping with parity (RAID5). These are levels of RAID that aren't only supported by hardware, but also by most software.

Mirroring and Duplexing

One of the more common ways to provide fault tolerance in hard disks is to create a mirrored copy of the data on another disk. Data that's written to one disk is also written to another, so that each drive has an exact copy of the data. In other words, one disk's data is a mirror image of the other's. If one of the physical disks fails, the server can continue operating by using the other disk.

Because data from one hard disk is mirrored to another, a minimum of two disks must be used. The second disk (which is the mirrored disk) must be at least the same size as the first drive, because information from the first drive has to be written to it. If the second disk was smaller than the first, then there is the potential that all of the data on the first drive couldn't be copied to the second.

As shown in Figure 10.6, when mirrored volumes are created, the disk controller writes the same data simultaneously to separate disks. If one of these disks fails, the mirrored volume must be *broken*, meaning that each disk in the mirrored set is now considered to be a single entity. For example, on Windows servers, the Disk Management tool would be used to break the mirror so that each disk is now considered a separate volume. Each disk would then have its own drive letter, so data could be read from and written to them individually.

Figure 10.6 Mirroring

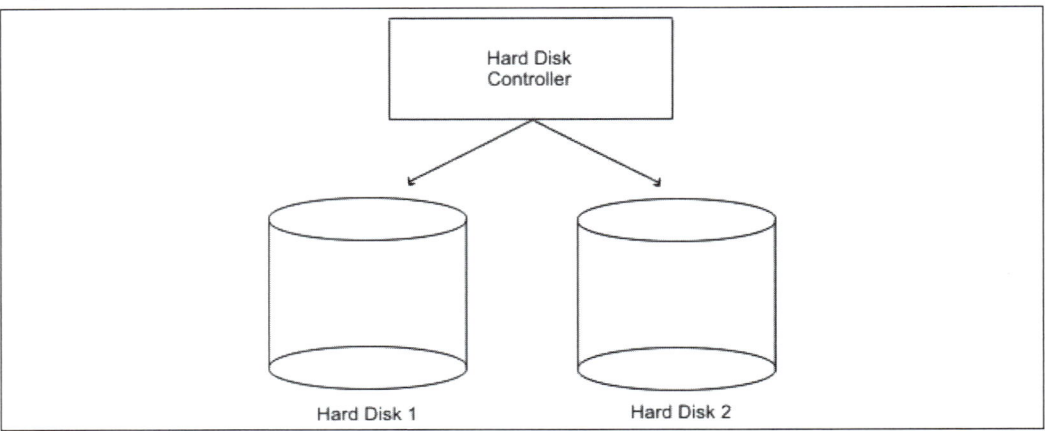

Mirroring disks not only provides fault tolerance, but can also impact performance. Multiple reads and writes to the disks are performed each time new data is accessed or saved. Because data is read from both mirrored volumes, this can increase performance because two different disks are reading the data at the same time. However, when data is written to the mirrored disks, there is a decrease in performance, because both disks must have the same data written to them.

Another drawback to disk mirroring is cost. For every hard disk the company wants mirrored, a second hard disk must be purchased. Since this means that the cost of purchasing hard disks doubles, you should determine which computers are necessary to numerous users, or are mission critical to business functions. While many servers in an organization might benefit from being mirrored, mirroring every computer on the network would be expensive and generally unnecessary.

A variation of mirroring that provides greater fault tolerance is duplexing. Duplexing ensures fault tolerance not just with your data, but also with your disk controller. With traditional mirroring there is one disk controller. If the controller fails, both disks become unavailable until that component is replaced. As shown in Figure 10.7, duplexing has each disk installed on a different controller. If one of the disks fails or a controller fails, the data is still available through the other disk in the pair.

Figure 10.7 Duplexing

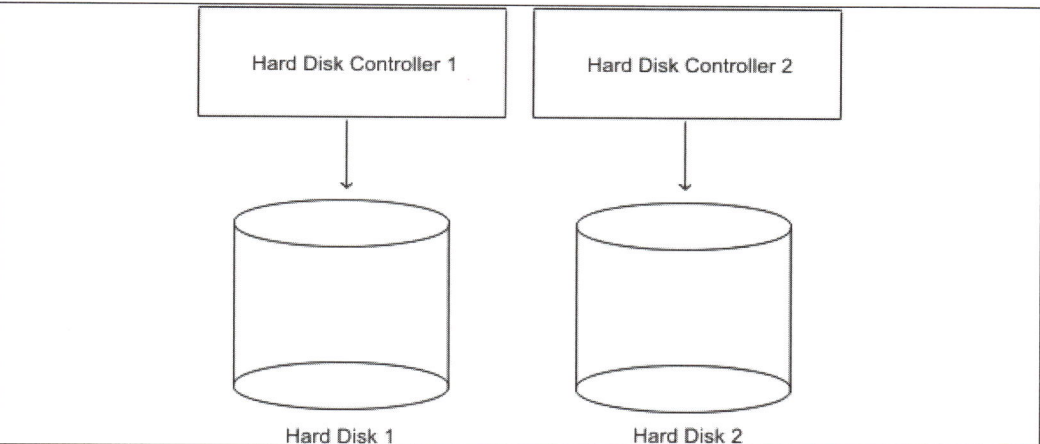

Duplexing also provides an added benefit over mirroring in terms of performance. Because each hard disk uses its own controller, this can speed up response time when writing to disk. With mirroring, added performance is only seen when data is being read from both disks. With duplexing, there is added performance in both reading from and writing to the disk.

EXAM WARNING

The difference between disk mirroring and duplexing is in the disk controllers. With disk mirroring, one controller is used for the disks in the mirrored set. With disk duplexing, there is one controller for each disk. Duplexing provides added fault tolerance, because if one of the controllers fails, the other controller will still be able to access data on one of the disks in the mirrored set.

Striping With and Without Parity

Disk striping is used to write data across a set of disks. In disk striping, data is written in stripes across a volume that has been created from areas of free space. These areas are all the same size and spread over an array of up to 32 disks. Data is spread out across the disks, thereby improving performance because data is read from and written to multiple disks. Rather than data being stored on one drive, striping has multiple drives all acting to get a piece of data.

When data is written across multiple hard disks using disk striping, data is divided into blocks that are spread equally over all disks. Each stripe is the size of the smallest partition on the set of disks, so if you have three hard disks of different sizes, the stripe will be the size of the smallest partition. For example, if you had a 1 GB hard disk, a 200 MB hard disk, and a 100 MB hard disk, then the largest amount of data on each disk in the stripe set would be 100 MB. For this reason, it's important to use hard disks that are all the same size (so that space on the hard disks won't be wasted).

In disk striping with parity, data is written across three or more disks, parity information is kept on the drives. Parity is a calculated value that's used to restore data from the other drives if one of the drives in the set fails. It determines the number of odd and even bits in a number, and can use this to reconstruct data if a sequence of numbers is lost, which is the case if one of the disks fails. Fault tolerance is achieved through the parity information stored on the stripe set of hard disks.

When deciding between striping with or without parity, you are essentially weighing performance against fault tolerance. Since parity information has to be calculated, the performance of a server can decrease when data is written. However, because data is still read from multiple disks at once, performance during reads is the same for both types of striping. The major deciding factor comes when considering what will happen if a problem occurs with one of the disks. If striping without parity is used, the data is unrecoverable from all disks in the stripe set. If striping with parity is used, when a disk fails, the performance decreases because the server must reconstruct the data from parity information on the other disks. However, the data can be recovered.

Head of the Class…

Losing Data in Stripe Sets

Stripe sets can be useful for storing data, but it is important to realize the worst case scenario of what you're dealing with. In the event of a single disk failure, all of the data on a stripe set without parity is lost. If disk striping with parity is used, then you can reconstruct the data from parity information on the other disks. However, if more than a single disk fails, the data cannot be reconstructed, meaning that all of the data on the stripe set is lost.

You should also consider limiting the number of disks used in a stripe set. Although 32 disks could be added to a stripe set, using fewer will reduce the odds of an unrecoverable failure. Put simply, the more disks you add, the greater the chance that one will fail. Using fewer disks minimizes the odds of one of them failing, or that a second disk will fail before the first can be replaced.

> To prevent losing everything, it is important that you still back up data. Even if striping with parity is used, you shouldn't simply rely on reconstructing the data if there is a failure. Since up to 32 disks can be used with disk striping, this means that a considerable amount of data can be lost. Imagine losing that much data, and you'll see the need to take precautions.

TEST DAY TIP

You need to remember the fault tolerance Network+ objectives: Power is made fault tolerant with a UPS. Links are made redundant with other links to avoid an issue if a line drops and no communication can take place. Another link us used to keep that from happening, if one link goes down, the other one takes over in its place. Also, setting up a hot site, which we will be covering later in the chapter, is part of disaster recovery planning. Ensure that you know the differences between fault tolerance and disaster recovery; you should know what fault tolerance is comprised of, as well as what you can do to provide disaster recovery.

Clustering and Load Balancing

While it's important to provide fault tolerance for data, power and other elements of your network, the servers that are critical to an organization shouldn't be overlooked in your fault tolerance plans. A common method of making servers fault tolerant and improving their performance is *clustering*.

Server clustering is a method of grouping individual computers together. Each of these computers works together as a unit, and appears to the network as a single system. By being clustered, the servers are able to handle a shared workload and gain fault tolerance.

Each computer that is part of a cluster is called a *node*. These nodes communicate with one another by sending out messages called *heartbeats*. If the other computers in a cluster fail to detect the heartbeat of one of the other computers, it considers this computer to be unavailable. At this point, a failover occurs, whereby the resources of the failed computer are taken offline and another computer begins providing those services.

Because the cluster appears as a single system on the network, users of the network don't notice such failures. The cluster simply appears to users as a server that's highly available. If a service is requested from one server that normally provides the service, and that server isn't available, the service is transparently provided by one of the other servers in the network. This makes it appear to users of the network as if nothing was wrong with the server, and that everything is functioning normally.

Servers can be configured as part of a cluster through software packages, or possibly through a service provided with the network operating system (NOS). While clustering isn't available in every operating system, some do provide cluster services. For example, Windows 2003 Server Enterprise and Datacenter editions allow up to eight computers to be part of a cluster. Depending on the NOS on your servers, the ability to create a cluster may already exist in your network.

In addition to making resources in the cluster highly available, a server cluster can also be used for *load balancing*. Load balancing allows the normal workload of a server to be divided among multiple computers. This improves performance because more than one computer is processing requests and providing services.

The load balancing features of a cluster are particularly important when large numbers of network users access the same services or resources, or where the number of users is difficult to predict. For example, a Web server may host a website that gets a significant number of hits. Because of the number of people visiting this site, too many hits could overwhelm the server's ability to serve requests and could potentially cause the server to crash. By having the Web server as part of a cluster, requests are distributed among multiple servers in the cluster, improving performance and increasing the ability to service requests.

Disaster Recovery Plan

In the last few years, there have been a number of disasters or potential threats that businesses have faced. The Y2K bug caused programmers and other computer personnel to rewrite code and upgrade equipment, and brought the need for disaster recovery and business continuity to the forefront. The need for such planning gained emphasis when massive power failures, terrorism, tsunamis, earthquakes, and numerous other events bankrupted businesses and cost billions of dollars in damage. With some of these events, equipment, data, and personnel were destroyed, and the economic ripples were felt internationally. While some companies experienced varying levels of downtime, some never recovered. Many of these events were extreme circumstances that were difficult or impossible to predict, and numerous companies relied on disaster recovery plans for guidance on how to deal with the incidents as they occurred.

Many thoughts about disasters are associated with catastrophic events in nature. Disaster recovery plans actually deal with a multitude of incidents that could negatively impact on the company's ability to function. As we discussed previously, disasters can stem from human, environmental, internal, external, intentional, or accidental causes. Because of the variety of sources that can cause a disaster, it is important that as many potential causes as possible are addressed in the documentation.

In the same way, it is also vital that the disaster recovery plan recognizes the elements that are needed to restore the business and may be affected by a disaster. Elements that must be considered are:

- Data, which consists of any business-related information stored on servers or other computers in the company.

- Equipment, which includes any devices necessary to the organization, including servers, workstations, or other hardware technology (such as x-ray machines in hospitals or a transmission tower used to dispatch ambulances).

- Software, which includes operating systems, applications, and other programs that are required for normal practices.

- Personnel, which are the people employed and involved with the company. Since certain members of the organization (or those under contract to perform specific services) may have distinct skills, it would be a major loss if they became unavailable.

- Facilities, which consists of offices or other locations. Facilities are necessary to house the previous elements we've discussed.

In looking at these elements of the business, it is easy to see that omitting any of these issues could prove detrimental to restoring the business, and must be addressed before any of these areas of the business are lost. Preparation for disaster recovery begins long before a disaster actually occurs, and will reference a number of other policies, procedures, and documents. As we discussed earlier, notification documentation is required to outline who is to be called to deal with certain incidents, while other procedures provide information on how to restore specific business functions. This includes procedures on backing up and restoring data, alternate sites and equipment, and other activities we'll discuss later in this chapter. While it is hoped that such preparation is never needed, it is vital that these strategies are already in place to deal with incidents if they occur.

Security Alert!

Cutting Corners

Although it's tempting to restore certain elements of a business by cutting corners in a disaster, it's imperative that you determine which practices have to be followed to the letter of the law. When creating disaster recovery plans, it is important that the plans don't violate any existing policies, regulations, or laws. Some companies must adhere to certain rules or guidelines if they are to remain in business, and failing to meet these requirements can cause more harm than the disaster itself. For example, a hospital may be required to use certain technologies or adhere to certain criteria so that patient information is kept confidential. If the IT staff was restoring the network and didn't adhere to these requirements, its possible that lawsuits could result. In other situations, the business might even be shut down for failing to abide by certain regulations or legislation.

Another important corner not to cut involves identifying vulnerabilities, especially in the case where a hacker or malicious software attacks systems in your organization. If a virus or Trojan Horse infected your network, you might

Continued

> need to reinstall software and restore data from backup tapes after removing the offending program. However, if you didn't update your anti-virus files, the same virus could infect your network over and over again. In the same way, if a hacker exploited a particular vulnerability on a server and hacked your network, he or she could continue breaking into your network after you repaired the damage from the first attack. By fixing vulnerabilities, you are preventing the same disaster from repeatedly occurring.

Backup and Restore

Backing up data is a fundamental part of any disaster recovery plan. When data is backed up, it is copied to a type of media that can be stored in a separate location. The type of media will vary depending on the amount of data being copied, but can include digital audio tape (DAT), digital linear tape (DLT), compact disks (CDR/CD-RW), or even floppy disks. If on-site data is destroyed, it can then be restored as if nothing had happened.

When making backups, you need to decide which data will be copied to alternative media. Critical data, such as trade secrets that the business relies on to function, and other important data crucial to the business needs must be backed up. Other data, such as temporary files, applications, and other data may not be backed up, as they can easily be reinstalled or missed in a backup. Such decisions, however, will vary from company to company.

Once you've decided on which information has to be backed up, you can then determine the type of backup that will be performed. Depending on the type of backup selected in the software you're using, the archive bit on files may be read and modified. The archive bit is an attribute of the file, and is used by the backup software to determine whether a file has changed since a previous backup. When a file is opened and used, the bit is turned on to indicate that it has to be included in the next backup. When the file is backed up, the archive bit is turned off to indicate the file has been backed up. Depending on the type of backup performed, the backup utility may look at the archive bit to back up only files that have been modified since the last backup. Common backup types include:

- Full backup, which backs up all data in a single backup job. Generally, this will include all data, system files, and software on a system. When each file is backed up, the archive bit is changed to indicate that the file was backed up.

- Incremental backup, which backs up all data that was changed since the last full, incremental or differential backup. Because only files that have changed are backed up, this type of backup takes the least amount of time to perform. When each file is backed up, the archive bit is changed.

- Differential backup, which backs up all data that has changed since the last full backup. When this type of backup is performed, the archive bit isn't changed, so data on one differential backup will contain the same information as the previous differential backup plus any additional files that have changed.

- Copy backup, which makes a full backup but doesn't change the archive bit. Because the archive bit isn't marked, it will not affect any incremental or differential backups that are performed.

Because different types of backups will copy different types of data, the methods used to back up data will vary between businesses. One company may make daily full backups, while another may use a combination of full and incremental backups (or full and differential backups). As we'll see in later sections, this will affect how data is recovered. Regardless of the type used, however, it is important that data is backed up on a daily basis, so large amounts of data won't be lost in the event of a disaster.

TEST DAY TIP

The archive bit is the key to understanding the various types of backups that may be performed. Remember that the archive bit is an attribute of the file (just as *read-only* or *hidden* are file attributes).

Full backups and copy backups will both back up everything, but a copy backup won't change the archive bit on each file. Incremental backups back up everything that has changed, and will change the archive bit on each file it backs up. Differential backups back up everything since the last full backup, but won't change the archive bit.

Rotation Schemes

As we'll see in the next section, it is important to keep at least one set of backup tapes offsite so that all of the tapes aren't kept in a single physical location. If backup tapes were kept in the same location as the servers that were backed up, all of the data (on the server and the backup tapes) could be destroyed in a disaster (such as a fire or flood). By rotating sets of backups, data isn't always being backed up to the same tapes, and a previous set is always available in another location.

A popular rotation scheme is the Grandfather-Father-Son (GFS) rotation, which organizes rotation into a daily, weekly, and monthly set of tapes. With a GFS backup schedule, at least one full backup is performed per week, with differential or incremental backups performed on other days of the week. At the end of the week, the daily and weekly backups are stored offsite, and another set is used through the next week. To understand this better, let's assume a company is open from Monday to Friday. As shown in Table 10.2, a full backup of the server's volumes is performed every Monday, with differential backups performed Tuesday through Friday. On Friday, the tapes are then moved to another location, and another set of tapes is used for the following week.

Table 10.2 Sample Weekly Backup Schedule

Monday	Tuesday	Wednesday	Thursday	Friday
Full Backup	Differential	Differential	Differential	Differential, with week's tapes moved offsite

Because it would be too expensive to continually be using new tapes, old tapes are reused for backups. A tape set for each week in the month would be rotated back into service and reused. For example, at the beginning of each month, the tape set for the first week of the previous month would be rotated back into service, and used for that week's backup jobs. Because one set of tapes are used for each week of the month, this means that you have most sets of tapes kept offsite. Even if one set was corrupted, the set of tapes for the week previous to this could still be used to restore data.

In the Grandfather-Father-Son rotation scheme, the full backup is considered the *Father*, and the daily backup is considered the *Son*. The *Grandfather* segment of the GFS rotation is an additional full backup that's performed monthly, and stored offsite. The Grandfather tape isn't reused, but is permanently stored offsite. Each of the Grandfather tapes can be kept for a specific amount of time (such as a year), so that data can be restored from previous backups, even after the Father and Son tapes have been rotated back into service. If someone needed data restored from several months ago, the Grandfather tape enables a network administrator to retrieve the required files.

While it is important to be diligent in backing up data, it is important to realize that a backup is only as good as its ability to be restored. Too often, backup jobs are routinely performed, but the network administrator never knows whether the backup was performed properly until the data has to be restored. To ensure that data is being backed up properly, and can be restored correctly, you should perform test restores of data to the server. This can be as simple as attempting to restore a directory or small group of files from the backup tape to another location on the server.

EXERCISE 10.3

PERFORMING A FULL BACKUP

1. Log onto Windows 2000 using an account that has administrator access or is a member of the Backup Operators group.

2. Click **Start | Programs | Accessories | System Tools | Backup**.

3. Click **Backup Wizard**.

4. When the Backup Wizard appears, you will see a Welcome screen. Click **Next** to continue.

5. Select the **Back up everything on my computer**, option, then click **Next** to continue

6. Select the type of media you will back up to and the name of the media. This will determine where data will be backed up (for example, tape or CD). Click **Next** to continue.

7. When the Summary screen appears, click **Advanced**.

8. Select the type of backup that will be performed. For this exercise, select **Copy** so that a full backup of data is performed, but normal backup operations won't be affected. Click **Next**.

9. Enable the **Verify the data after backup** and **Use Hardware Compression** options. Click **Next**.

10. Select the option to **Replace the data on the media with this backup**. Click **Next** to continue.

11. Begin scheduling the job by selecting **Later** from the **When to Back Up** dialog box, and then provide the name and password of an account that has administrator access or is a member of the Backup Operators group. Click **OK**.

12. Provide a name for the job, and then click the button labeled **Set Schedule**. Select the date and time that the backup is to take place. Click **OK**, then click **Next**.

13. Review the information on the Summary screen, and then click **Finish** to confirm your settings.

Restoring Backups

Because the entire point of backing up data is so that you can restore it at some later point, it is important to learn how to properly restore the data. Data from a backup may be restored to the same or a different computer. When it is restored, the type of backup that was used will affect how it is restored, and will determine the time it will take to perform this task.

Full and copy backups take longer to perform, but are the fastest to restore. When only full or copy backups are performed, all of the files are backed up, regardless of whether they've changed since the last full backup. As these types of backup jobs can fit on a single tape (or set of tapes), you only need to restore the last backup tape or set that was used.

Incremental backups take the longest amount of time to restore, but they're the fastest method of backing up the data. Incremental backups contain all data that has changed since the last full or incremental backup. Because of this, if it has been a while since the last full backup was created, many tapes may be used to store a large number of different incremental backup jobs. When this type of backup is used, you need to restore the last full backup and each incremental backup that was made since. Therefore, if a full backup was created every week and incremental backups were created every night after, you would have to restore the tape with the full backup, and then restore the six incremental backup jobs that took place afterward.

Differential backups take less time and fewer tapes to restore than incremental backups. Because differential backups will back up all data that was changed since the last full backup, only two tapes are needed to restore a system. You need to restore the tape containing the last full backup and the tape containing a last differential backup job.

Since different types of backups have their own advantages and disadvantages, you will need to consider which type of backup will be suitable for your needs. Some types take longer than others to back up or restore, so you will need to decide whether you want data backed up quickly or restored quickly when needed. To aid you in your decision, Table 10.3 provides information on different aspects of backup types.

Table 10.3 Advantages and Disadvantages of Different Backup Types

Backup Type	Backup Speed	Restoration Speed	Disadvantages
Daily full backups	Takes longer than using weekly full backups with either daily incremental or daily differential backups.	Fastest to restore, as only the last full backup is needed.	Takes considerably longer to backup data, as all files are backed up.
Full backup with daily incremental backups	Fastest method of backing up data, as only files that have changed since the last full or incremental backup are backed up.	Slowest to restore, as the last full backup and each incremental backup made since that time needs to be restored.	Requires more tapes than differential backups.

Continued

Table 10.3 continued Advantages and Disadvantages of Different Backup Types

Backup Type	Backup Speed	Restoration Speed	Disadvantages
Full backup with daily differential backups	Takes longer to back up data than incremental backups	Faster to restore than incremental backups, as only the last full backup and differential backup are needed to perform the restore.	Each time a backup is performed, all data modified since the last full backup (including that which was backed up in the last differential backup) is backed up to tape. This means that data contained in the last differential backup is also backed up in the next differential backup.

Offsite Storage

Once backups have been performed, you shouldn't keep all the backup tapes in the same location as the machines you've backed up. After all, a major reason you're performing backups is to have the backed up data available in case of a disaster. If a fire or flood occurred and destroyed the server room, any backup tapes in that room could also be destroyed. This would make it pointless to have gone through the work of backing up data. To protect your data, you should store the backups in a different location so that they'll be safe until they're needed.

Offsite storage can be achieved in a number of ways. If your company has multiple buildings, such as in different cities, the backups from other sites can be stored in one of those buildings and the backups for servers in that building can be stored in another building. If this isn't possible, you can consider using a firm that provides offsite storage facilities. The key is to keep the backups away from the physical location of the original data.

When deciding on an offsite storage facility, you should ensure that it is secure and has the environmental conditions necessary to keep the backups safe. You should also ensure that the site has air conditioning and heating, as temperature changes may affect the integrity of data. It should also be protected from moisture and flooding, and have fire protection in case a disaster befalls the storage facility. The backups have to be locked up and there should be strict policies on who can pick up the data when needed. You don't want someone posing as a member of your organization and taking off with your data. Conversely, you want the data to be accessible when needed so that you can acquire the data from the facility right away without having to wait until the next time the building is open for business.

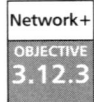

Hot and Cold Spares

While its important to have data available to be restored through backups, you will also want backup equipment available. Spare equipment allows you to replace existing equipment if a problem occurs. If a system fails or if the equipment is damaged or destroyed, the replacement can be switched in automatically, booted up manually, or set up from scratch. There are two different types of spares that can be used in these situations:

- Hot Spares
- Cold Spares

Hot spares are replacement devices that are already running and can be used as soon as a problem occurs. If the current system fails, the hot spare can be used with little to no work on the part of the network administrator. In some cases, a computer providing an essential service to a network may have a failover computer running in parallel. The failover computer routinely checks the first machine to see that it's running. If the failover machine doesn't receive a response to its checks, it automatically takes over the role of the first machine. In other cases, a hot spare may be an identically configured server or other device that is offline that can simply be powered up to replace the original computer or device. Regardless of how the hot spare is implemented, it is always ready to be used immediately.

Cold spares are more commonly used in computer environments because there is less management and lower costs. Rather than running or storing a redundant machine that must be updated with identical hardware, software, and configuration settings, a cold spare is simply a computer or device that can be set up to replace an existing machine or component. When a problem occurs, the cold spare is installed and configured to replace the failed device. For example, if a server fails, another computer can be set up and configured, then loaded with data from a recent backup of the failed server. Needless to say, the drawback to using a cold spare is that it takes longer to implement in a disaster.

Hot, Warm, and Cold Sites

Just as replacement equipment may be necessary in a disaster, facilities may also be damaged or destroyed so that a substitute site is needed. Alternate sites are important to certain companies so they experience minimal downtime or almost no downtime at all. When a disaster occurs, the company will require a temporary facility in which data can be restored to servers, and business functions can resume. Without such a facility, the company would need to scout for a new business location, purchase new equipment, set it up, and then go live. When the company is not prepared, such activities could take so long that the disaster could put them out of business.

As is the case with spare equipment, there are different flavors of sites that may be used in a disaster. They are:

- Hot sites, which are set up with everything necessary to resume normal business functions immediately, or almost immediately.

- Warm sites, which are partially set up to resume normal operations, but require additional work to make everything operational.

- Cold sites, in which very little has been set up, and significant work is required to resume normal functions.

A hot site is a facility that has the necessary hardware, software, phone lines, and network connectivity to allow a business to resume normal functions almost immediately. This can be a branch office or data centre, but must be online and connected to the production network. A copy of data is held on a server at that location so little or no data is lost. The site may also have servers configured to have replication of data from production servers occurring in real time so that an exact duplicate of the system is ready when needed. In other instances, the bulk of data is stored on servers and only a minimal amount of data has to be restored. This allows business functions to resume very quickly, with almost zero downtime.

A warm site is not as equipped as a hot site, but has part of the necessary hardware, software, and other office needs to restore normal business functions. Such a site may have most of the equipment necessary, but will still need work to bring it online so that it can support the needs of the business. With such a site, the bulk of data will have to be restored to servers and additional work (such as activating phone lines or other services) will have to be done. With this type of site, no data is replicated to the server, so backup tapes must be restored so that data on the servers is recent.

A cold site requires the most work to set up, as it is neither online nor part of the production network. It may have all or part of the necessary equipment and resources needed to resume business activities, but installation is required and data has to be restored to servers. Additional work (such as activating phone lines and other services) will also have to be done. The major difference between a cold site and hot site is that a hot site can be used immediately when a disaster occurs, while a cold site must be built from scratch.

When deciding on appropriate locations for such sites, it is important that they be in different geographical locations. If the alternate site is not a significant distance from the primary site, it can fall victim to the same disaster. Imagine having a cold site across the road from a company when an earthquake happens. Both sites would experience the same disaster, so now there would be no alternate site available to resume business. On the other hand, you don't want the alternate site so far away that it will significantly add to downtime. If the IT staff needs to get on a plane and fly overseas to another office, this can increase the downtime and result in additional losses. Designate a site that's close enough to work from (such as 100 miles away), but not so far that its distance will become a major issue when a disaster occurs.

Test Day Tip

The way to remember the differences between hot and cold spares, and hot, warm, and cold sites is by using the levels of warmth. The same way you might gauge how close your dinner is to being fully cooked by how hot it is, that's how you gauge the level of work needed to use spare equipment or an alternate site. If it's hot, it's ready to go. If it's warm, it's getting there. If it's cold, it's not done yet.

Business Continuity Plan

A business continuity plan (BCP) is used to ensure that a business can continue to function despite any disasters or other threats. The business continuity plan identifies the key functions of a business and the risks that are most likely to endanger it. Once these threats are identified, a series of procedures are created to ensure that the normal functions of the business won't be interrupted, or at least won't be interrupted for very long. In doing so, the organization gains the ability to operate under almost any circumstances.

Business continuity planning involves creating a collection of plans that address different areas of the business, and focus on restoring the business as a whole. If a threat becomes an actual problem, the procedures provide instructions on how to recover so the organization can continue providing services or selling its product to the public. By taking a proactive approach to various threats, the company is better able to recover from disasters when they occur. Some of the plans that may be incorporated into a business continuity plan include:

- A disaster recovery plan, which provides procedures for recovering from a disaster after it occurs.

- A business recovery plan, which addresses how the functions of the business will resume after a disaster, such as using an alternate facility to conduct business.

- A business resumption plan, which addresses how critical systems and key functions will be maintained during a crisis.

- A contingency plan, which addresses the actions that can be taken to restore normal business activities after a disaster or accidents or additional problems occur during this process. If problems occur while implementing the other plans, a contingency plan can be used to continue the process of restoring the business.

Before these plans can be created, you first need to understand what is important to the business. Business continuity plans begin by identifying the key functions of departments within the company and the components that must exist for people to do their jobs. Each department in the company should identify the requirements that are critical for them to continue functioning and determine which functions they perform that are critical to the company as a whole. If a disaster occurs, the business continuity plan can then be used to restore those functions.

Identifying these functions and necessities of different departments can be a long and ongoing process. Meetings must be held with managers and key personnel from every department within the company, and they must state what functions they perform in the organization and what items are necessary to perform their jobs. For example, a call center would provide the function of phone soliciting. At a bare minimum, they would need phones, lists of phone numbers for potential clients or customers, and scripts that the sales people would refer to when making calls. While they may use computers, automated calling systems, and other tools, you are seeking the bare elements needed to perform their jobs.

It is crucial that you filter the requirements and functions of each department down to what is critical to the company's ability to operate. This is difficult because everyone considers himself or herself necessary to a business, even if he or she are not. For example, the maintenance staff may see themselves as a vital part of the company, but people can clean and empty their own trashcans during a crisis. This would not be the case in a cleaning company however, where the cleaners would be essential. From this, you can see that the key functions and fundamental personnel vary from one company to another.

While many issues will vary during this analysis from company to company, there are some elements that will remain consistent. Personnel will need facilities to perform their duties, methods of communication with the outside world (such as cell phones, land lines, and e-mail), items to document information (such as office supplies like pens and paper, or computer systems), and other components that the business absolutely requires to function. By looking at what is needed to conduct business, contingency plans can then be set in place to allow those functions to resume in the face of catastrophe.

Once key functions of the organization have been identified, it is important that budgets be created to establish how much money will be assigned to individual components. To put it simply, this involves putting money away for a rainy day. The budgets provide a method for the company to continue functioning in a limited capacity, while rebuilding or restructuring the business to its previous state. When a system is being recovered to a previous state, it doesn't mean that things will be exactly the same as they were before. It will take time and money to bring the business back to normal.

> **N**OTE
>
> For the Network+ exam you will not need to know the details of BCP, although understanding it will help you to see the bigger picture when it comes to disaster recovery planning and why it is so important in production (if not all) environments. Fault tolerance and disaster recovery, however, are two topics you must know intimately for the Network+ exam.

Configuration Management

Unless you're dealing with a small network of only a few computers, once a computer or other piece of equipment has been configured, management of the device is necessary. Configuration management is a practice that involves documentation of a device's configuration, as well as keeping that documentation up to date so that any future changes can be controlled and tracked. While this seems at face value like a straightforward, easy to follow practice, it is one that often falls by the wayside.

Configuration management is useful for a number of reasons. The documentation created on the network can be quickly referenced, allowing you to identify how a device was configured, its location on the network, and other detailed information about the device. By having this information, you can replace devices and make changes to the network quickly.

By compiling information on the components of your network, you create an inventory, which can be used to track items that need to be replaced or upgraded. Most organizations have a life cycle for computer equipment, and replace older machines every three or four years. Network devices like routers and switches may last longer, but they will eventually need to be replaced with newer and faster equipment. Keeping a database allows you to schedule upgrades and replacements more easily, because you can monitor when the item was installed on the network and whether it is approaching the end of its life cycle.

Managing software and hardware in this fashion also provides a record of computer assets that are owned by the company. This information can be useful in budgeting replacements and determining insurance needs. If a disaster occurs, the documented information can also be used for insurance purposes, allowing you to identify what was destroyed or damaged.

As we'll see late in this chapter, disasters are an important issue in network administration, and to businesses as a whole. If a disaster occurs, the configuration information can be used to replace damaged devices, so that they are configured the same as their predecessors. For example, if a server was destroyed, you could replace that server with another, give it the same name and IP (Internet Protocol) address, and have it provide the same services. Except for the time taken to replace the server, users of the network might be unaware that a problem even existed.

Documenting Configurations

Configuration management starts by performing an inventory of network components and documenting information about each device. How much data you compile is subjective, but you should include as many specifics as possible about the machine. Information included in a database or series of documents might include:

- The date that the document was last modified, so you can determine whether you're looking at the most recent information.

- The asset number, which is a unique number that your organization may assign to an asset so that it can be identified within the company. A sticker may be used to affix to an item so it can easily be matched to information within a database.

- The name of the device, which is the name that a computer, printer, or other device is given so that it can be identified on a network.

- The IP address, which is a unique network number that identifies a computer or device on a TCP/IP (Transmission Control Protocol/Internet Protocol) network.

- The MAC (Media Access Control) address, which is a unique hardware number that identifies the computer on a network.

- The make and model, which identifies who made the device, as well as its model number.

- The serial number and product ID, which are numbers or alphanumeric combinations that appear on devices. They can be used to identify a particular device when several are in one location, and may be required when calling manufacturers, help desks, or service representatives when a problem arises.

- The location, so you can determine the building, floor, and room in which a device is located.

- The person who has been issued the device. This is useful when computers, PDAs (personal digital assistants) or other devices are issued to a specific person. This provides a contact person, and can make it easier to locate the device.

- The purchase date, which indicates when the company bought the device.

- The warranty information, including how long the device is under warranty, and whether it includes parts and labor, onsite service, etcetera.

- The operating system, which should include the manufacturer, name, and version information (for example, Microsoft Windows 2000 Professional 5.0.2195

Service Pack 4 Build 2195). This will not only indicate the operating system installed, but also whether the latest service packs have been applied.

■ Memory, which refers to the amount of physical memory installed on a computer. This will allow you to determine whether software or upgrades to a newer operating system can be installed on a particular machine.

■ The processor type, which will often determine whether the computer needs to be upgraded, and also whether upgrades of software are possible.

■ Hard disk information, including the sizes and number of hard disks, which is useful when replacing a RAID array.

■ Common and special software. This includes the names and versions of major software packages that are used throughout your organization (such as Microsoft Office or Internet Explorer), as well as applications that are only used on that computer or certain machines in your company.

■ Components installed or associated with the device, such as modems, PCI (Peripheral Component Interconnect) cards issued with a laptop, or other components that were added after the initial purchase of the machine.

There are a number of methods and tools available to help you acquire most of the information to be included in your hardware database. Obviously, the location of the device and to whom it was issued are things that a program can't tell you, but other information can be acquired using configuration utilities that come with the device or those offered by a computer's operating system. Some of these tools are discussed in greater detail in Chapter 11, and not only serve as troubleshooting tools, but can be used to acquire data about the computer being used and various devices on your network. These tools include:

■ ipconfig

■ ifconfig

■ winipcfg

■ ping

■ System Information

ipconfig is a command line tool that allows you to view information about a Microsoft Windows NT, 2000, 2003, or XP computer's TCP/IP configuration. On UNIX and Linux machines, a similar tool called *ifconfig* is used to display this information. By typing **ipconfig** at the command line (or **ifconfig** on UNIX/Linux computers), you can see how each network card or modem on a computer is configured, including the IP address, subnet mask, and default gateway, as well as other important information about the network adapter. As shown in Figure 10.8, to view additional information, including the physical address (MAC address), DHCP (Dynamic Host Configuration Protocol) and DNS (Domain Name System) information, you would type **ipconfig /ALL**.

Figure 10.8 Using ipconfig /ALL on a Windows System

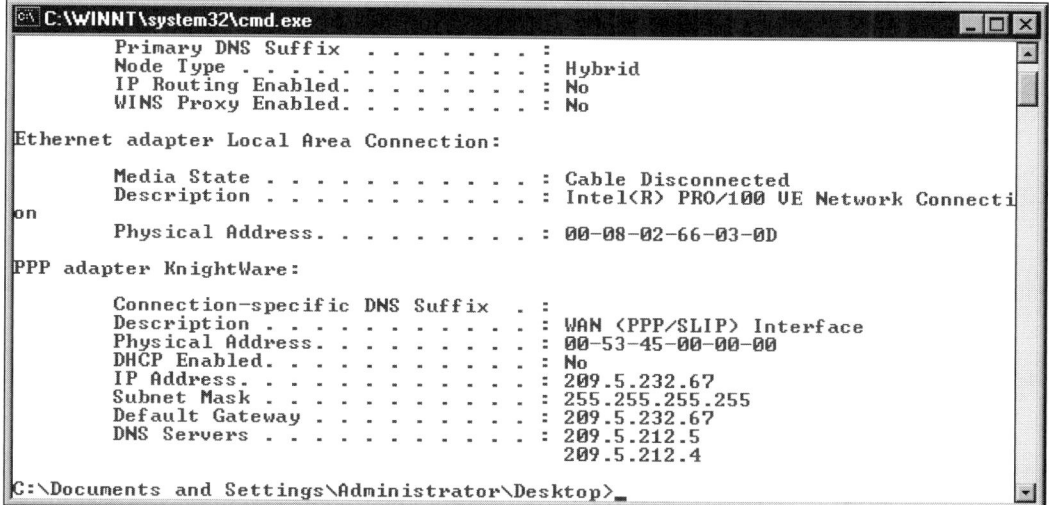

On most UNIX and Linux distributions, you can use the ifconfig command to report the status of the network adapters currently installed on the system. You can also use the ifconfig command with the **–a** argument. As shown in Figure 10.9, you can see both versions of the command in use, one reporting interfaces that are up and in use, and the other (ifconfig –a), showing all the adapters currently installed, whether they are up and in use or down and not in use.

Figure 10.9 Using ifconfig on a Linux/UNIX System

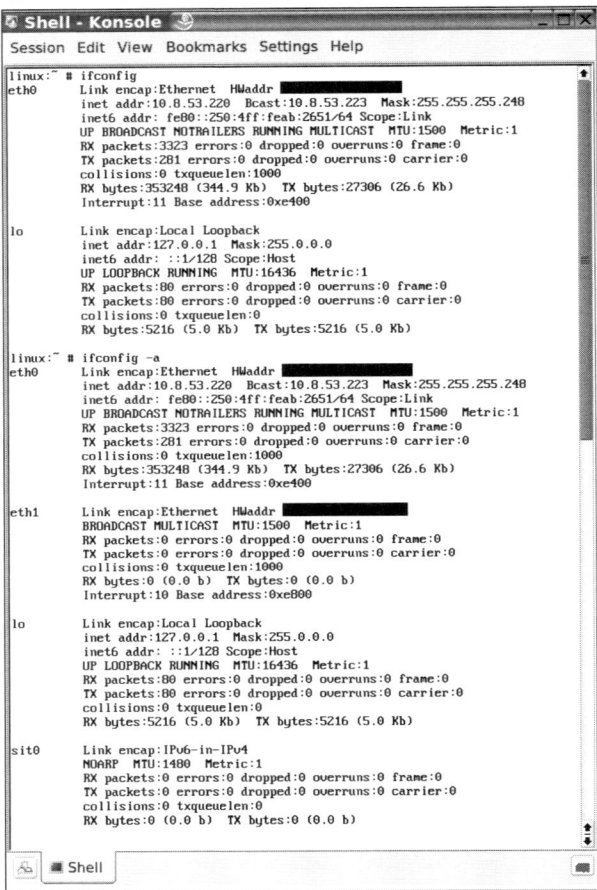

winipcfg is a tool that provides similar information about computers running Windows 9x and Windows ME. Like ipconfig, it provides information about the TCP/IP configuration of a machine, but does so through a GUI interface. While this tool is only available in a limited number of operating systems, it is still another source for creating your database of configuration information.

ping is a tool that's used to test the connectivity of a device that's on a TCP/IP network, but can also be used to acquire information about a device on a network using DNS. Because DNS resolves names to IP addresses, ping can be used to display the IP address of a device. For example, if you know the name of a server, network printer, or other component of your network, you can type **ping** followed by the name of that device. If the device is found, its IP address will be displayed along with information that will help you determine if it is connected to the network.

EXAM WARNING

Remember for the Network+ exactly what each tool does and which operating systems support each specific tool. ifconfig is used in Linux/UNIX, ipconfig is used in Windows NT, 2000, 2003, and XP, and winipcfg is supported by Windows 9x and ME.

A large amount of the information about servers and workstations can be acquired through the System Information tool. As shown in Figure 10.10, this tool provides information about the make and model of the computer, as well as its name, operating system, memory, hard disks, and other installed devices and software. By using this tool, the bulk of information needed for your hardware database can be acquired.

Figure 10.10 System Information Tool

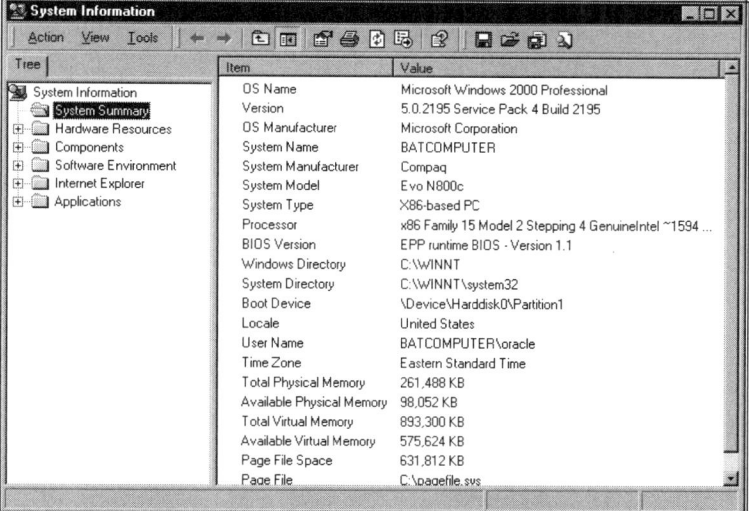

EXERCISE 10.2

ACQUIRING CONFIGURATION INFORMATION FROM A WINDOWS 2000 PROFESSIONAL COMPUTER

This exercise requires that you log onto a Windows 2000 Professional computer, using an Administrator account or an account that allows access to the Run command and system tools.

1. Select **Start | Run**. When the Run dialog box opens, type **CMD** in the **Open** field, and then click **OK**. The Command Prompt tool will open, providing you with a command-line interface.

2. Type **ipconfig /ALL** and press **Enter**. Information about each of the network adapters on your computer will be displayed.

3. Document the following items about your computer:
    - Hostname (the name of your computer)
    - IP address
    - Subnet mask
    - Default gateway
    - Physical (MAC) address

4. When you have completed documenting the configuration information about your computer, exit from the Command Prompt tool by typing **Exit** and pressing **Enter**.

5. On the **Start** menu, select **Programs | Accessories | System Tools | System Information**.

6. In the left pane, click on the **System Summary** node. The right pane of the program will display information about your system.

7. From the **View** menu, click on **Advanced**. This will display information that is not displayed in the default basic view.

8. Document the following items about your computer:
    - OS name (the name of the operating system)
    - Version (the version of the operating system)
    - System manufacturer (who made your computer)
    - System model
    - Processor
    - Total physical memory

9. In the left pane, expand the **Components** node, and then expand the **Storage** node. Click on the **Drives** node to display information about hard drives installed on your computer.

10. Look through the list of drive information on your computer. As shown in Figure 10.11, if multiple hard disks are connected to your computer, they will be separated by a space in the listing. The **Drive** entry in the listing will display the letter associated with that drive, while the **Description** entry will display whether it is a network connection (mapped drive to a server) or a local fixed disk.

Figure 10.11 Drive Information Displayed by the Windows System Information Tool

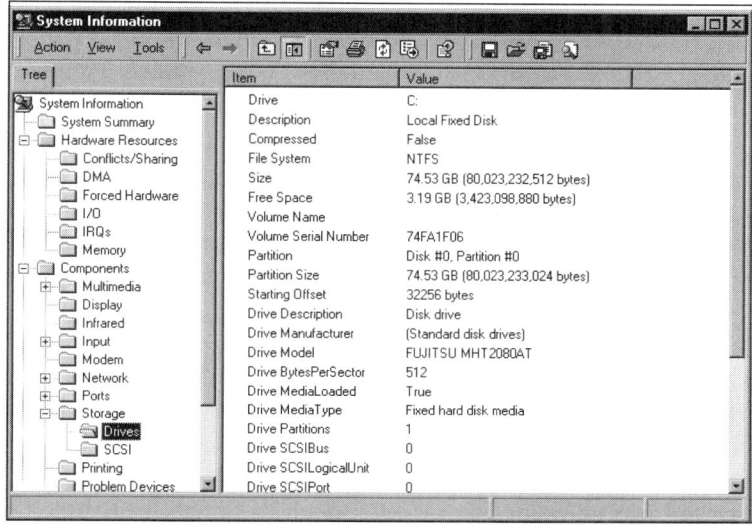

11. For each drive listed in the **Drives** node, document the size of each local fixed disk on your computer. The size of the disk appears as a value for the **Size** entry under each drive letter.

12. Close the System Information tool.

Change Control Documentation

One of the benefits of compiling information about devices on your network is that it can allow you to see which devices will be affected by a network change. For example, let's say you were planning on changing the IP address of a router, which serves as the default gateway for workstations. Since these computers use the router to connect to other portions of a network, when this change is made, the default gateway setting of these workstations would no longer be valid. By searching your hardware database, you can determine which computers use the router as a default gateway and will therefore be affected by the change. This allows you to see which computers will have to have configuration settings changed so that their settings match the router's new IP address. As you can see, one change can cause numerous other changes across the network.

Because change is inevitable and possibly far-reaching, it's important to maintain information about changes. Configuration information stored in a hardware database has to be kept up to date. In addition to this, you should also maintain documentation on changes that have been made.

Change control documentation provides a record of changes that have been made to a system, which can be used in troubleshooting problems and upgrading systems. When creating a change control document, you should begin by describing the change that was made and explaining why this change occurred. Changes should not appear to be for the sake of change, but have good reasons, such as fixing security vulnerabilities, hardware no longer being supported by vendors, new functionality, or any number of other reasons. The documentation should then outline how these changes were made, detailing the steps you performed.

By providing details in this manner, you also create a document that gives you back-out steps on how to restore a system to its previous state. At times, you will need to undo the changes and restore the system to a previous state because of issues resulting from a change. In such cases, the change documentation can be used as a reference for backtracking the steps taken.

The procedures you document are a valuable resource when you are recovering from a disaster and/or need to install another device or software in the same way. Rather than leaving someone to guess at how something should be installed, your documentation on the steps you performed can be used to duplicate the installation. Because the same steps can be followed, a computer or other device can be set up and configured identically to the one it's replacing.

Logs

Just as documentation on configurations and changes can be helpful in solving problems with your network, so can the logs generated by the software running on these machines. Logs are records of events that have occurred and actions that were taken. Many systems will provide logs that will give automated information on events that have occurred, including accounts that were used to log on, activities performed by users and by the system, and problems that transpired. These details make logs a valuable tool when troubleshooting problems and identifying adverse incidents (such as intrusions to the system).

On many systems, the logs may be simple text files that are saved to a location on the local hard drive or a network server. In other cases, the system will provide a specific tool for viewing the information. For example, in Windows NT, 2000, 2003, and XP, a tool called Event Viewer is used to view a series of logs generated by the operating system. As shown in Figure 10.12, Event Viewer allows you to view data stored in the following:

- Application log, which contains events that are logged by individual programs or applications installed on the operating system.

- Security log, which displays possible security issues that the operating system monitors. This includes valid and invalid logon attempts, the use of a specific resource by an audited user, and other actions related to security.

■ System log, which displays events logged by the system components of the operating system. Information stored in this log includes facts about drivers that failed to load properly, warnings on low disk space and memory, remote access attempts and other information on the system itself.

Figure 10.12 Event Viewer

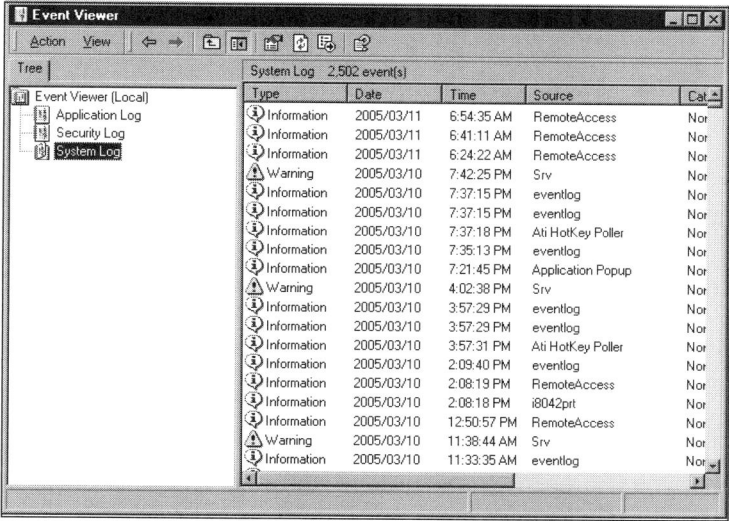

Each of the logs in Event Viewer can be accessed by clicking on the corresponding node in the left pane of the application. When a log is selected, the individual events recorded in the log are displayed in the right pane of the application. To view specific information about an event, you simply double-click its entry in the right pane.

Logs are also created by other software and devices installed on a computer, or generated by devices that have been configured to write information to a file stored on a particular computer. For example, firewall software installed on a server would maintain its own records of users accessing specific websites, downloaded files, attempts to access restricted resources, and other information. In the same way, a door lock system may require a PIN number, biometrics, or a card key before access is granted to the building. Such systems commonly record authorized and denied entry attempts to a file or series of files on a specific computer. In each of these cases, the logs provide a record that can be reviewed in the event of a security breach or other problems.

Password Lists

Passwords are access codes that use alphanumeric and special characters that allow you to log onto operating systems, software, or specific files. Over the years, you've probably heard that passwords shouldn't be written down, and should only be remembered. This is generally true in most cases, as it would be unwise to have passwords written on little pieces of paper and carried in wallets, left on desks, or stuck to the monitors of computers. However, there may be times when you're unavailable and other members of the IT staff need a particular password to fix a problem. Because of this, passwords should also be documented so others can use them.

Password lists should contain all of the passwords used to perform administrative or maintenance tasks on the network. This includes passwords for:

- The Administrator account on servers and workstations

- Accounts that have access to modify other accounts, in case management of network accounts are needed

- Setup and configuration utilities on computers and other devices

- Administrative features in software

- Files, such as those containing other passwords or documentation containing procedures

Once this list is prepared, it should be stored in a secure location that is known to key personnel and that can be accessed only by them. This might be a safe, locked cabinet in a branch office where tape backups are stored, or a safe deposit box at a bank. In an emergency, this list can then be used to perform tasks that are necessary while you're unavailable, or that you can't perform because of unforeseen circumstances in a disaster situation.

Notification Documentation

If security is compromised or another major problem occurs, it's important that the right people are notified as soon as possible. Notification is vital to dealing with a crisis swiftly so that problems aren't left unresolved for an extended period of time, allowing them to increase in severity. When critical incidents, such as system failures or intrusions occur, it is important that the appropriate person(s) to deal with the situation be called in.

Notification documentation includes contact information for specific people in an organization, their roles, and when they should be called. Having this documentation helps to ensure that the appropriate person is called at the appropriate times to deal with issues. For example, during regular business hours, the network administrator might be called to deal with any issues dealing with the network. After work and on weekends however, the members of the IT department may rotate the duty of being on-call, so that a different member of the staff is responsible for fixing problems during off-hours. If the organization calls the on-call person, and he or she is unable to fix the problem, it is at that point that the on-call person would contact the network administrator. In doing so, the right person for the right job is called in the right order.

Having a call order or chain of command is important to notification procedures. After all, while the bosses of a company may claim they want to be notified of problems, chances are they won't appreciate being called in the middle of the night because someone forgot a password. At the same time, you don't want everyone in the organization being able to contact you directly, or you might get dozens of phone calls at home about the same problem. Even worse, you may get calls about inane problems that don't warrant your being called at home (such as someone needing their maiden name changed to their married name on a system, or someone being unable to find a particular Web page on the corporate intranet).

During off-hours, people need to know that problems are to go through a particular person or group of people who have a list of people to notify. This might be a help desk, receptionists, dispatchers, or others who have a twenty-four hour shift rotation (or are at least there when you're not). The person or department who has the notification list acts as a filter for problems, and has the responsibility of determining who to call, or if it's necessary to call someone in after normal business hours are over.

Those responsible for notifying people need to have up-to-date information on how to contact members of the IT staff and certain other employees within the organization. If the problem is catastrophic, such as a fire at a particular office building, then management and various IT staff members may need to be called in. Those who are called in to solve a problem can then determine if additional persons need to be contacted.

The contact information included in notification documentation should provide several methods of contacting the appropriate person. The list of people to contact might include each person's name, role in the organization, and pager number. Extensive information might include phone extension within the company, home phone number, cell phone number, address, and other information that will ensure the person can be contacted. If such extensive information isn't included with the notification documentation, then it should reference where additional contact information should also be available, such as an employee database.

Notification procedures should also include contact information for certain outside parties who are contracted to support specific systems. For example, if there is a problem with the air conditioner in a server room, then a heating/cooling company that's under contract might be called in to fix the system. However, when outside parties are called in on an emergency basis, it's important to remember that other procedures and practices are still followed (such as signing them in and out of secure areas). Except in extreme circumstances, the policies of a company shouldn't be ignored in a crisis. Although notification procedures may be a starting point in a disaster, other plans, policies and procedures also come into play.

Summary of Exam Objectives

Problems can happen when you least expect it, making it important to have safeguards in place that allow a business to function in the worst of cases. Fault tolerance is used to allow components of a network to continue functioning when a malfunction or disaster causes failure. Fault tolerant systems can be created by implementing UPSs and generators to provide power during an outage, redundant links to provide a second method of communication between sites, RAID for fault tolerant storage, and clustering to allow services to be available if a particular server fails. Using these methods increases the availability of systems by providing secondary systems or procedures to deal with failures as they occur.

Business continuity plans must be created before a disaster occurs. A business continuity plan identifies key functions of an organization and the threats that most likely endanger them, and creates processes and procedures that ensure these functions won't be interrupted in the face of an incident. A business continuity plan consists of a disaster recovery plan, a business recovery plan that addresses how business functions will resume at an alternate site, and a business resumption plan that addresses how critical systems and key functions of the business will be maintained. Contingency plans may also be created to outline the actions that can be performed to restore normal business activities after a disaster and actions that can be taken if an initial plan fails.

Disaster recovery plans provide procedures for restoring technologies and other functions necessary to the business after a disaster occurs. They also provide insight into methods for preparing for the recovery should the need arise. Because preparation for disaster recovery begins long before a disaster actually occurs, the plan will address such issues as proper methods for backing up data, offsite storage, alternate sites, and replacement equipment needed for restoring systems to their previous state. Together, these documents and methods provide a proactive approach to dealing with incidents before they occur.

Preparing for failures in systems or other disasters requires documentation to be made well in advance. Configuration documentation should contain information on computers and other devices on the network, while notification lists should contain contact information on people to contact in the event of a disaster. If a problem occurs, password lists that are stored in secure locations, and logs generated by operating systems and other software on the network may be used to restore systems. For these documents to be effective however, they must be generated and maintained prior to an actual crisis.

Exam Objectives Fast Track

Fault Tolerance

☑ Fault tolerance is the ability of a system, device, or network to continue functioning despite a malfunction or an event that causes failure.

☑ Uninterruptible power supplies (UPSs) are used to provide battery power to devices when normal sources of electricity become unavailable.

☑ Link redundancy is used to provide redundant paths of communication between sites so that if one network connection between sites fails, another can be used to maintain a link.

☑ RAID is a technology that was developed to prevent the loss of data and/or improve performance by writing data across a set of hard disks, or writing a duplicate of data from one hard disk to another.

☑ Disk mirroring ensures that data written to one hard disk is also written to another, so that each drive has an exact copy of the data. Disk duplexing also does this, but each disk drive has its own controller.

☑ Disk striping is used to write data across a set of disks. When the data is written across multiple hard disks, it is divided into blocks, which are spread equally over all disks.

☑ Clustering is a method of grouping individual computers together. Each of these computers works together as a unit and appear to the network as a single system.

☑ Load balancing allows the normal workload of a server to be divided among multiple computers.

☑ Clustering provides fault tolerance for servers. If one computer in a cluster fails, then other computers in that cluster can continue to provide services and other resources to users.

Disaster Recovery Plan

☑ Disaster recovery plans are collections of procedures and other documents that address recovery from a disaster after it occurs.

☑ Backups are used to make copies of data that can be restored to a computer if a problem occurs. Data can be backed up to various media, but tape backups are most common.

☑ Backups should be performed using a rotation scheme, with one or more of the backups stored offsite.

☑ Hot spares are replacement devices that are running and can be used as soon as a problem occurs, while cold spares require setup and configuration.

☑ Alternate sites may be used during a disaster when a company's current facilities are unavailable or uninhabitable. Hot sites have everything necessary to resume normal business functions immediately, or almost immediately, while warm sites require some additional work. Cold sites have very little pre-existing setup, and require significant work to be functional.

☑ Business continuity plans are developed using a process that identifies key functions of an organization and the threats most likely to endanger them. Processes and procedures are then developed to ensure these functions won't be interrupted (or interrupted for very long) in the event of a disaster.

Exam Objectives Frequently Asked Questions

The following Frequently Asked Questions, answered by the authors of this book, are designed to both measure your understanding of the Exam Objectives presented in this chapter, and to assist you with real-life implementation of these concepts.

Q: Brownouts are common in the area where the taxi cab company I work for is located. I want to implement fault tolerance for power by plugging computers and certain other devices into UPSs. The company has several hundred computers on the network, and can't afford to purchase UPSs for all of them. What should I do?

A: Have servers and devices required for the network to operate attached to UPSs. This will protect the servers and the data stored on them from being damaged by improperly shutting down from a loss of power. Try to have as many workstations as possible hooked up to UPSs, so that people don't lose their work from a brownout, but ensure that the workstations that are used for work essential to the organization are attached to UPSs. This will vary from company to company, but in the case of a taxi company, this might include computers used by dispatchers, the bookkeeper's workstation, and other systems that could negatively affect the business if data was corrupted or the computers were unavailable.

Q: I've implemented RAID for fault tolerance my server's operating system, but still have to shut down the system to remove and replace a failed hard disk. Is there any way to implement RAID without having to shut down the server when a disk needs replacing?

A: RAID can be implemented through hardware, which can support *hot swapping*, in which a disk can be removed from the server without having to shut the server down. Software RAID takes a higher toll on the system, as RAID functions must run through the operating system running on the machine. Because of this, hot swapping is often unsupported through the operating system, which is why you must take down the system to replace a disk.

Q: I work for a small company that only has one facility, so storing backup tapes at another site isn't an option. What can I do to keep the backup tapes safe in case of a disaster?

A: There are many options for storing backup tapes offsite. A safety deposit box could be rented at a bank to store the backup tapes, or a firm that provides storage facilities for backups could be hired. When deciding on a storage facility, ensure that it's secure and has protection against fires and other disasters. You don't want to store your backups in a location that has a higher likelihood of risk than your own facilities.

Q: The company I work for can't afford to have an alternate site with additional computers and other equipment installed, which may never be used. What can I do to provide a disaster recovery plan that provides an alternate site?

A: Large companies are the only ones who can generally afford hot sites. Small- to medium-sized companies may opt for warm or cold sites, where more work is required to set up equipment and other necessities of the business in a disaster. If even this is out of reach for the company, then try to implement as many other items in a disaster recovery plan as you can, and create an emergency budget that will allow you to rent facilities and purchase equipment if a disaster occurs. Even if you can't do everything, some preparation is better than none.

Q: I have developed a disaster recovery plan, but I'm not completely certain that the plans and procedures will be effective during a disaster. How can I be sure?

A: Perform dry runs of the disaster recovery plan to ensure that developed strategies work as expected, and revise any steps that are ineffective.

Self Test

A Quick Answer Key follows the Self Test questions. For complete questions, answers, and explanations to the Self Test questions in this chapter as well as the other chapters in this book, see the **Self Test Appendix**.

1. As shown in the following illustration, a company has its main office in Manhattan and branch offices in Brooklyn and Queens. A T1 line connects Brooklyn to Manhattan, while another T1 line connects Manhattan to Queens. Because Brooklyn and Queens are both connected to Manhattan, this enables them to exchange data with one another. You have concerns that if either of the T1 lines go down, the business will be unable to function normally. Because of the importance of each of these sites communicating with one another, fault tolerance for the links between them is necessary but cost is a concern. Which of the following will you do to implement fault tolerance?

Figure 10.13 Links Between Offices

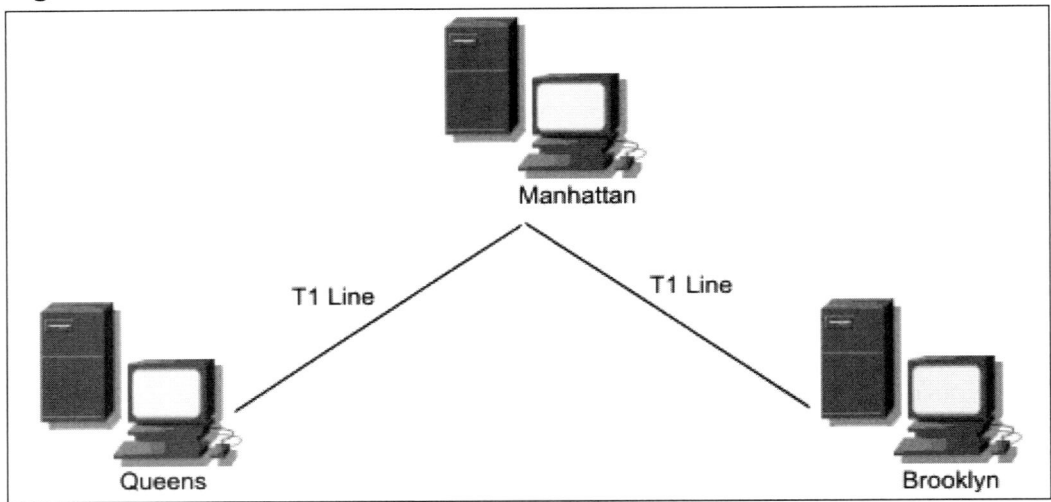

A. Install an ISDN line between Manhattan and Brooklyn, which can be used if the T1 line goes down.

B. Install an ISDN line between Manhattan and Queens, which can be used if the T1 line goes down.

C. Install an ISDN line between Brooklyn and Queens.

D. Install a T1 connection between Brooklyn and Queens.

2. You currently use RAID for fault tolerance on a server, so that data from one disk is copied to another. When data is written to one disk, it is duplicated on another disk in the set. You are concerned that if the disk controller fails, then neither of the disks will be able to be accessed. Which of the following will you do to improve fault tolerance?

   A. Implement disk striping by using RAID level 0.

   B. Implement disk mirroring by using RAID level 1.

   C. Implement disk duplexing by using RAID level 1.

   D. Implement disk striping with parity using RAID level 0.

3. You have decided to implement a RAID for fault tolerance, and want data to be striped across multiple disks with parity information stored on multiple drives. Which of the following levels of RAID will you use?

   A. RAID 0

   B. RAID 1

   C. RAID 3

   D. RAID 5

4. You are creating configuration documentation for a computer on your network that is using Linux as its operating system. In creating this documentation, you need the IP address, subnet mask, and default gateway of the computer. Which of the following tools would you use to acquire this information?

   A. ipconfig

   B. ifconfig

   C. System Information

   D. winipcfg

5. You believe that someone has been attempting to hack into a Windows 2000 Server on your network by guessing the Administrator password. You set up auditing of this account, and then check Event Viewer each morning to view logs on this server. Which log would you use to view information about valid and invalid logon attempts using this account?

   A. Application Log

   B. Security Log

   C. System Log

   D. None. Event Viewer isn't used to view logs.

6. You are concerned about the impact of various risks to your company. You have learned from your insurance company that businesses that can be infected with a virus may experience an hour of downtime to remove the virus from a server, and that an average of two viruses a year may infect a system with security comparable to yours. If you consider that an hour of downtime costs your company $1000, what would the Annual Loss Expectancy of this risk be to your company?

   A. $1000

   B. $2000

   C. $3000

   D. $4000

7. An intruder has gained access to your website through a service on the server, and damaged a number of files needed by the company. The service isn't necessary to the Web server's functionality, and as near as you can tell isn't used by any software or users of the company. This Web server is used to provide a presence for the company on the Internet, and is used for public relations as well as to provide information on the company's products. During the intrusion, you were working on upgrading a router in another part of the building, which is why you didn't notice audit notifications sent to your e-mail address. These audit notifications could have tipped you off about suspicious activity on the server, but now that you're aware of the problem, you're concerned that a repeat attack may occur while you're fixing the problem. Which of the following actions will you immediately take in resolving this situation?

   A. Recover data files that were damaged in the attack.

   B. Continue upgrading the router so that you can focus on audit notifications that may occur.

   C. Remove the unneeded services running on the server.

   D. Remove the Web server from the Internet until there is no further risk of being hacked.

8. During a disaster, you don't want to spend a significant amount of time restoring a series of tapes from previous backups of production servers. At the same time, you don't want backups to take a significantly long period of time to perform each night. Currently, you back up all data on the servers once a week, and then each night you perform a backup of data that has changed during the day. To make it faster to restore data in a disaster, you're willing to change the current backup plan. Based on these factors, which of the following backup plans would you use?

   A. Perform a full backup each night of the servers. This will mean that only one tape will be needed per server to restore all the current data.

   B. Perform full backups weekly and incremental backups each night afterwards of the servers.

   C. Perform copy backups nightly. This will mean that only one tape will be needed per server to restore all the current data.

   D. Perform a full backup weekly and differential backups each night afterward.

9. You are the administrator of a network that is spread between a main building and a remote site several miles away. You make regular backups of the data on servers, which are centrally located in the main building. Where should you store the backup tapes so they are available when needed in the case of a disaster? Choose all that apply.

   A. Keep the backup tapes in the server room within the main building so they are readily at hand. If a disaster occurs, you will be able to obtain these tapes quickly, and restore the data to servers.

   B. Keep the backup tapes in another section of the main building, so they are readily at hand.

   C. Keep the backup tapes in the remote site.

   D. Keep the backup tapes with a firm that provides offsite storage facilities.

10. A fire has destroyed the server room where file servers are located. Having prepared for this possibility, you move operations to a branch office of the company. The office is part of the production network, and has a copy of the data on servers at this location. What type of alternate site is being used for disaster recovery?

   A. Cold site

   B. Warm site

   C. Hot site

   D. Hot spare

11. You are setting up a series of servers that can be used in case one of the production servers fails. Each of the servers is identical to its counterparts on the production network. If one of the servers fails at this site, a replacement server can simply be powered up and run on the network. What type of equipment is this?

    A. Cold spare

    B. Hot spare

    C. Cold site

    D. Hot site

12. You want to make a Web server's services fault tolerant, and you also want improve the performance of these services when people visit the websites hosted by this server. Which of the following can be used to meet these needs? Choose all that apply

    A. Disk striping

    B. Load balancing

    C. Clustering

    D. Hot spares

13. You have four nodes that are part of a cluster. The nodes listening for heartbeats fail to detect this signal from one of the other nodes. Which of the following will happen?

    A. The node that isn't sending the heartbeat will be considered available.

    B. The other nodes in the cluster will begin providing services that were offered by the node that is no longer sending the heartbeat.

    C. The cluster will fail and notification will be sent to other computers on the network.

    D. The cluster will appear as a single server on the network, so users don't recognize that a failure has occurred.

Self Test Quick Answer Key

For complete questions, answers, and explanations to the Self Test questions in this chapter as well as the other chapters in this book, see the **Self Test Appendix**.

1.	**C**	8.	**D**
2.	**C**	9.	**C** and **D**
3.	**D**	10.	**C**
4.	**B**	11.	**B**
5.	**B**	12.	**B** and **C**
6.	**B**	13.	**B**
7.	**C**		

NETWORK+
Domain IV

Network Support

Chapter 11

NETWORK+

Network Troubleshooting Tools

Domain IV Objectives in this Chapter:

4.1   Given a troubleshooting scenario, select the appropriate network utility from the following:

         4.1.1   Tracert / traceroute

         4.1.2   ping

         4.1.3   arp

         4.1.4   netstat

         4.1.5   nbtstat

         4.1.6   ipconfig / ifconfig

         4.1.7   winipcfg

         4.1.8   nslookup / dig

4.2   Given output from a network diagnostic utility (for example, those utilities listed in objective 4.1), identify the utility and interpret the output.

4.3   Given a network scenario, interpret visual indicators (for example, link LEDs and collision LEDs) to determine the nature of a stated problem.

Introduction

Throughout this exam guide, we've talked about the fundamentals of network protocols and network operating systems. In this chapter, we'll bring together that knowledge to help you in troubleshooting any errors or problems that occur on your network. We'll begin by talking about the overall methodology that you'll use to troubleshoot a network. This begins with gathering information about a problem to try to determine its cause. You'll then use your understanding of networking concepts, as well as your knowledge of how your particular network is configured, to isolate the point where the problem is occurring. By eliminating points of failure in a systematic fashion, you can eliminate trouble spots, one by one, until you've located the cause of the problem. Maintaining accurate documentation of the physical layout of your network is essential for this process, as is having a firm grasp of the layers of the OSI (Open Systems Interconnect) model and the devices that operate at the various layers.

To help you in troubleshooting your network, there are many software utilities for both the Windows and Linux operating systems that will help you pinpoint the exact nature of a failure. You'll start with tools that will test basic network connectivity to determine if two computers can communicate with each other in any way. You can then move onto more detailed tools that will show you every detail about the path that a network packet takes to travel from one computer to another, or to gather detailed information about name resolution issues. You also have access to a wide range of testers for physical network components like network cables and wall jacks. By combining a broad understanding of networking concepts with specific knowledge of the different troubleshooting tools available to you, you will be able to effectively troubleshoot any issues you might face when administering a network.

Methodology

Before we talk about specific tools and utilities that you can use to troubleshoot your network, it's important that you have an overall structure in place that will help you perform that troubleshooting. Unfortunately, networking technologies haven't advanced to the point that a router will flash up an error message like, "My default gateway is misconfigured, please correct this." Instead, it is up to you to determine *what* a problem is before you'll be able to go about fixing it. When you're troubleshooting a problem relating to network connectivity, you need to have an understanding of your network as a whole so that you can determine where the trouble is occurring. One of the key factors in network troubleshooting is *isolating* the issue to figure out whether it's being caused by a single workstation or cable, or if it's a larger issue affecting numerous users on your network.

You can break down the troubleshooting process into two major steps:

- Gathering information
- Analyzing the information you've gathered

Gathering Information About a Problem

In order to troubleshoot a problem, you first need to identify the problem. This can be a challenge when you're trying to gather information from different users on your network, especially if you're dealing with a situation where you're receiving reports of multiple problems at the same time. You need to determine which component of your network is causing the issue; this can be a physical component like a network cable, or a logical component like the IP (Internet Protocol) configuration for a particular NIC (network interface card). You'll use the information you gather to determine which component of your network has failed or is misconfigured.

Your first step should be to gather information from your users about the nature of the problem. Some questions you'll probably want to ask include the following:

1. **What is the exact nature of the problem?** Try to be as specific as possible when making this determination. For example, you may get a report that your users are unable to browse external hosts on the Internet. To get a better understanding of the problem, you need to determine if they have lost all physical connectivity to the outside world, or if it's only a specific application that isn't functioning. Your troubleshooting steps will be different if a user can ping outside hosts, but not connect to a specific Web server, versus not being able to connect to the outside world in any way.

   How many computers are affected by this problem? If the issue is isolated to a single computer, it is likely that the cause of the problem will be related to the computer itself. If it is affecting all computers on a particular subnet or those connected to a particular hub or switch, you can use this information to help you in the troubleshooting process. You can probably tell from this that your troubleshooting will be far more successful if you have detailed information about your network's physical network topology. Because of this, one of the most critical documents you can have on hand when troubleshooting is a network diagram detailing the physical layout of your network. You should also maintain some type of database containing the IP address configuration of your routers, switches, servers, and workstations.

2. **When did the problem begin to occur?** More specifically, you should find out what *changed* on the network when the issues first began. If your users began to experience connectivity issues after you installed a new router, your first step will be to check the configuration of the router. Sometimes this can take a certain amount of investigation, since you may not be aware of every-

thing that's being administered or modified on a large network. Your Internet Service Provider (ISP) might have made some changes that you're not aware of, which might be causing the connectivity failures.

Analyzing and Responding to a Problem

Now that you've collected information about the problem, you need to analyze all of it to determine the cause of the problem. You should examine every layer in the OSI model, starting at Layer 1. Check your Physical Layer connectivity, like cables, patch panels, wall jacks, and hubs. Then work your way up to Layer 2, verifying that any switches or switch ports are configured properly. At Layer 3 you'll verify that your routers are configured and functioning properly, and then move onto troubleshooting the actual application itself at the Transport Layer and beyond. In almost all cases, it's best to start at the Physical Layer and work your way up so that you're eliminating the lowest common denominator as a potential issue before moving onto more complex troubleshooting problems. If two computers aren't communicating simply because a cable is unplugged, you can save yourself quite a bit of time by starting with the Physical Layer and working up from there.

You'll then want to determine the proper troubleshooting tool to use. We'll spend the majority of this chapter talking about the different tools available for your use, but as a rule you should start with basic connectivity tools like *ping*, moving on to other tools once you've determined that basic connectivity is in place. The reason we start with ping is because it is simple to use and lets you determine at a glance if two nodes on your network are able to communicate with each other at the most basic level. It also very effectively slices the OSI model in half for you in terms of troubleshooting, since ping operates at the Network Layer. For example, if you are able to ping a remote host but you cannot FTP (File Transfer Protocol) to it, then you know that the issue lies somewhere above the Network Layer, because otherwise ping would not be successful. If the ping is unsuccessful, then you know that the issue lies in the Network, Data Link, or Physical Layers.

In Exercise 11.1, we'll look at a common situation where you might use ping to investigate a connectivity problem between two computers. Let's say that you're troubleshooting a connectivity problem between Computer A, with an IP address of 192.168.1.1 and subnet mask of 255.255.255.0, and Computer B with an IP address of 192.168.2.5 and a subnet mask of 255.255.255.0 – this is illustrated in Figure 11.1. These two computers were able to communicate with each other yesterday, but the two computers haven't been able to connect since some changes were made on the network yesterday.

Figure 11.1 Connectivity Diagram

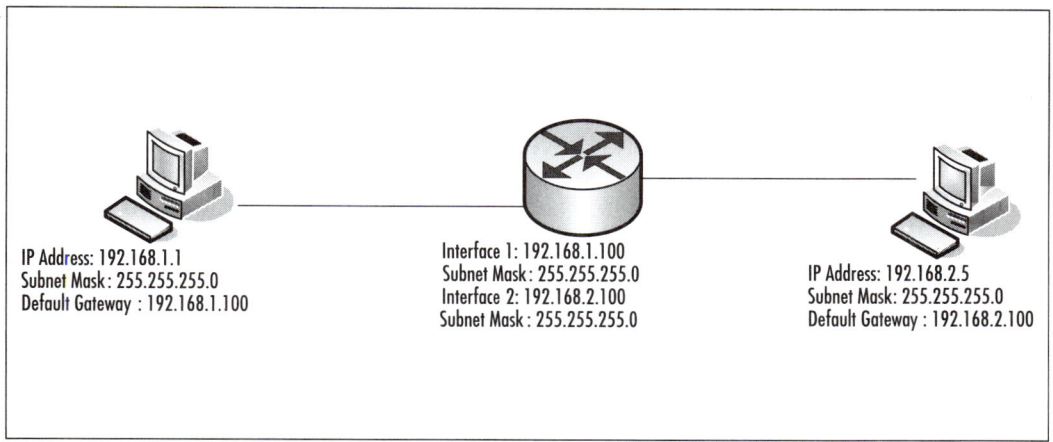

IP Address: 192.168.1.1
Subnet Mask: 255.255.255.0
Default Gateway : 192.168.1.100

Interface 1: 192.168.1.100
Subnet Mask: 255.255.255.0
Interface 2: 192.168.2.100
Subnet Mask: 255.255.255.0

IP Address: 192.168.2.5
Subnet Mask: 255.255.255.0
Default Gateway : 192.168.2.100

EXERCISE 11.1

TROUBLESHOOTING A CONNECTIVITY ISSUE

1. The first thing you should do is go to Computer A and check things out for yourself. Use Computer A to ping 192.168.2.5, the IP address of Computer B, to confirm that the two computers are unable to communicate.

2. If you don't receive a response from Computer B, you need to isolate where the failure is taking place. So your next step is to ping the loopback address, 127.0.0.1. You should remember that the loopback address is a *virtual* IP address that's used for troubleshooting the TCP/IP (Transmission Control Protocol/Internet Protocol) installation on a local PC. If you are unable to ping the loopback address, then TCP/IP is either not installed or has become corrupted on the local computer. If this ping is successful, the problem does not lie in the TCP/IP stack of Computer A.

3. Next, try pinging another machine on the same network segment as Computer A, such as 192.168.1.2. If you get a response from another machine on the same segment, you know that your local machine's TCP/IP stack is functioning properly, and that Computer A is able to connect to other computers on the same subnet—this rules out a malfunctioning NIC or network cable at the Physical Layer. Next, ping the default gateway for Computer A to determine if the default gateway is functioning.

4. If your default gateway responds, try pinging another host on the same network segment as Computer B, the computer that's failing to respond. If you get a response from another computer on Computer B's network segment, you know that there are no problems related to Computer B's network segment itself.

5. If all of your tests thus far have been successful, but you are still unable to contact Computer B, then you have isolated the problem to Computer B itself. Perhaps the network cable connecting Computer B to the network has gone bad, its network card has failed or needs a new driver installed, or its IP configuration is incorrect.

By approaching the problem systematically, you were able to trace the network connectivity from one end of the path (Computer A) to the other (Computer B). Testing at each step of the journey allowed you to isolate exactly where the problem was occurring.

Configuring & Implementing

Prioritizing Multiple Issues

Sometimes, you'll encounter a troubleshooting situation where you have several problems happening all at once. In fact, this is not uncommon because multiple problems will often be created by the same root cause. When multiple problems occur simultaneously, it's important to focus on the problem that has the greatest impact on users. For example, if some of your users are reporting a complete inability to access any resources, and others are reporting that their network access is only slightly slow, the two problems may or may not be related. You should troubleshoot the computers that are experiencing a total lack of network access first, because restoring network connectivity is more critical than removing the occasional occurrence of lag on an otherwise working connection.

Network Discovery

Now, in a perfect world you'll be administering a network that someone has already created detailed configuration diagrams for, so that you'll know exactly what you're working with when you need to troubleshoot a problem. In reality, though, we're usually not that lucky, and network administrators often find themselves taking over networks that have little or no documentation in place, or documentation that hasn't been kept up to date. Luckily, there are a number of tools that you can use to perform *network discovery*, which will help you to automatically generate documentation about the devices on your network and how they are configured. These network discovery tools will examine a single IP address or an entire subnet and gather as much information about the devices on that subnet as possible, including their IP addresses, MAC (media access control) addresses, what type of operating system the device is running, and even what types of applications are installed on the device if it is a server or a workstation computer.

There are a number of products available that will perform network discovery for you, though the majority of them are paid commercial software and are not available as free downloads. One such product is a suite of tools from SolarWinds that includes an IP Network Browser to perform automatic network discovery, in Figure 11.2. If you are taking over a network that has poor or nonexistent network documentation in place, it's strongly advisable to invest in one of these network discovery tools; the amount of time it will save you in troubleshooting network connectivity issues will more than pay for the cost of the tool.

Figure 11.2 SolarWinds IP Network Browser

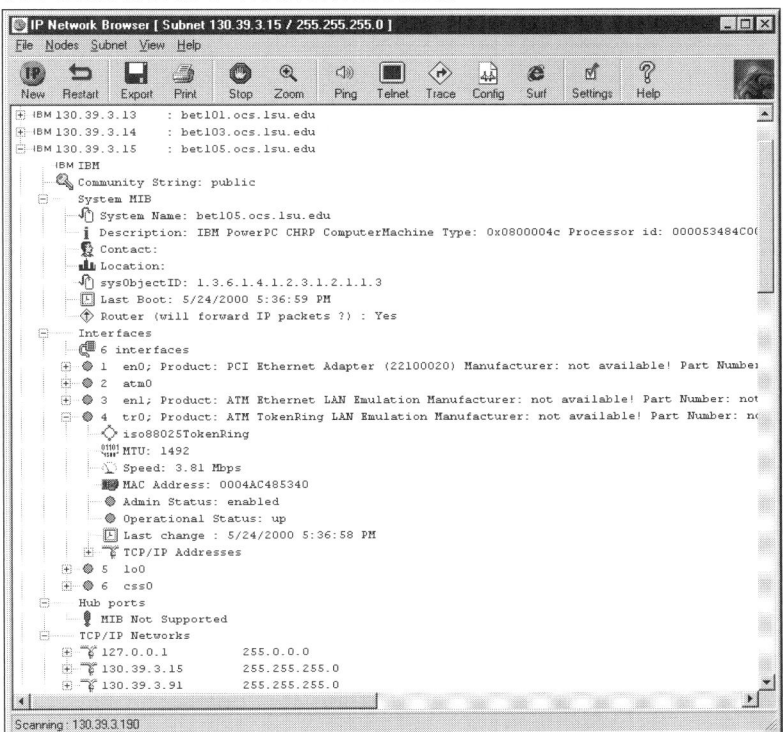

OSI Model

As you learned in Chapter 5, the OSI model creates a framework that defines how networking protocols like TCP/IP communicate. Network packets are passed from the Physical Layer up to the Application Layer, with each layer adding its own header to the packet. When a network packet is passed from one host to another, the receiving host will read or analyze the packet one layer at a time, with the Application Layer reading the Application Layer header, the Presentation Layer reading the header from the Presentation Layer, and so forth.

You can use your understanding of the OSI model to improve your troubleshooting techniques. It's important to understand what takes place at each layer of the OSI model, and which devices operate at these layers. When it comes to network troubleshooting, the most important layers of the model are the Physical, Data Link, Network, and Transport Layers. Let's take a look at each of these layers in turn.

> **NOTE**
>
> We are only going to touch on the function of each layer here—refer back to Chapter 5 for an in-depth look at the layers of the OSI model.

The Physical Layer

The Physical Layer is the lowest layer of the OSI model, and involves the actual electrical signals that are going from the network cables into the NIC of a computer, switch, router, or hub. A failure at the hardware level will usually involve the physical components of a computer or device, such as the cable that connects the computer to the network or the network card itself. Network hubs also operate at the Physical Layer, so a failure in a network hub could also lead to connectivity issues that occur at the Physical Layer. The Physical Layer is responsible for a number of different functions, including:

- The type of signal transmission used
- The cable type
- The actual layout or path of the network wiring
- The voltage and electrical signals being used by the network cabling.

When using the OSI model for troubleshooting, you should know which devices operate at which layer. The following physical devices function at the Physical Layer of the OSI model:

- Network cabling
- Network interface cards
- Active and passive hubs
- Repeaters

When troubleshooting at the Physical Layer, be on the lookout for issues with NIC drivers, as well as physical failures of a NIC, hub, or length of cabling.

TEST DAY TIP

An *active hub* will boost the signal that's being sent before transmitting it to the nodes attached to the hub. A *passive hub* will simply transmit the information without any sort of boost.

The Data Link Layer

The Data Link Layer is responsible for taking the information from the Physical Layer and organizing it into *frames*. The Data Link Layer takes the information that it receives from higher up in the OSI model and passes it down to the Physical Layer to be transmitted across the wire. The functions of the Data Link Layer include error checking, where the Data Link Layer will add error-checking information onto each *frame* of data that it transmits. The Data Link Layer is also responsible for error-free delivery of these data frames, as well as maintaining the reliability of the communications between two computers.

The two types of devices that operate at the Data Link Layer of the OSI model are *switches* and *bridges*. Bridges are able to divide a network into multiple segments, but they aren't able to actually subnet a network the way that a router does. So if you use a bridge to physically separate two areas of the network, it will still appear to be one big network to higher-level protocols in the Network Layer, Transport Layer, and above. Bridges and switches are useful for cutting down on network congestion because they can do some basic filtering of data traffic based on the MAC address of the destination computer. When a transmission reaches the bridge, the bridge will not pass it across to the other side of the network if the MAC address of the destination computer is known to be on the same side of the network as the sending computer. As a part of this process, the bridge or switch will build *tables* (similar to a routing table) indicating which addresses are on which side, and uses them to determine whether to let the transmission across.

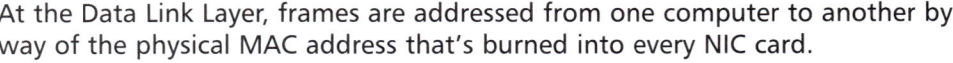

TEST DAY TIP

At the Data Link Layer, frames are addressed from one computer to another by way of the physical MAC address that's burned into every NIC card.

The Network Layer

The Network Layer is where the majority of troubleshooting issues will occur. The Network Layer takes the frames it receives from the Data Link Layer and organizes them into *packets*. The Network Layer is also the layer where physical MAC addresses are translated into IP addresses. Unlike MAC addresses, which are physically assigned to each NIC and can never be changed, IP addresses are *logical* addresses that can be added, modified, and removed as often as you want. This allows a single computer to be moved and reconfigured to belong to many different IP subnets throughout the course of its life. This flexibility comes at a price, though, since these IP addresses are assigned by human administrators and are therefore somewhat prone to misconfiguration and error. If you misconfigure a network card's IP address or subnet mask by even a single digit, that computer will experience connectivity issues in connecting with local and remote computers. The most important physical device at the Network Layer is the *router*. This is the device that uses the logical IP addresses of the Network Layer to transmit network packets from one subnet to another.

Depending on where the problem occurs, failures at the Network Layer can create connectivity issues for a single client or an entire subnet. When this happens, the devices in question will not be able to communicate with another portion of a network, either because of a physical device failure or because a router has been configured with an incorrect route, subnet mask, or some other key piece of information. Because Network Layer issues can render a computer entirely unable to communicate on a routed network, they tend to be the most visible troubleshooting issues, so you should have a firm grasp of the functions of the Network Layer and the tools you can use to troubleshoot here. The best tools to check connectivity at the Network Layer are **ping**, **tracert**, **traceroute**, and **pathping**, which we'll discuss in a later section.

The Transport Layer

One a packet has left the Network Layer, the Transport Layer takes over. This is where network packets are even further differentiated by the *port number* that they are using to communicate—these port numbers can be for either connection-oriented TCP communications or low-overhead connectionless UDP (User Datagram Protocol) applications. Any application that has to communicate between two networked computers will have to use a particular port number, and the most common services all have well-known port numbers that have been assigned by the Internet Assigned Numbers Authority, or

IANA. Firewalls and proxy servers will often work at the Transport Layer to filter traffic based on the TCP or UDP port that it's using. If you're having issues at the Transport Layer, you'll probably find individual network applications that aren't functioning properly—like a user who can Telnet to a particular host, but is unable to connect to the Web server running on the same computer.

The Transport Layer is responsible for making sure that data sent by one computer arrives at its intended destination in good condition. Sending and receiving computers also need a way to differentiate between different communications that may be addressed to different applications on the same computer, which is where TCP and UPD port numbers become useful. Troubleshooting the Transport Layer is quite similar to working at the Application Layer, since the TCP and UDP protocols form the basis of the ports that are used by all network applications. So you can use **telnet** to see if a particular port is listening on the destination machine, and you can use the *netstat* utility (which we'll discuss in the next section) to see a list of all ports that are listening on a particular machine.

Windows Tools

Because TCP/IP has become the default network protocol for Windows operating systems, it's important to have a good understanding of TCP/IP troubleshooting when working with any of the Microsoft operating systems. Windows computers have a number of built-in utilities that will assist you in troubleshooting TCP/IP problems relating to basic connectivity and name resolution. The most common tools that you should be aware of include the following:

- ping
- nslookup
- tracert
- arp
- ipconfig
- nbtstat
- netstat
- pathping (new to Windows 2000 and Windows XP)

In this section, we'll take a detailed look at each of these tools, including what the tool is used for and what type of output it produces. We'll also look at some examples of how to apply these tools (and other more advanced tools that won't necessarily appear on the Network+ exam) to troubleshoot a particular problem.

ping

The *ping* command, which stands for Packet INternet Groper and uses *ICMP (Internet Control Message Protocol) echo* messages to communicate with other computers. You'll usually use the ping command to test basic TCP/IP connectivity between two computers. You can ping a computer using either its IP address or its hostname. The ping command has the following switches:

- **ping –t** will ping a specified host continuously until you stop it by typing **Ctrl + C**. Typing **Ctrl + Break** will show you statistics on the ping results and then continue.

- **–a** resolves IP addresses to hostnames. For example, if you ping a computer with the IP address 192.168.1.101 and you need to find out its DNS (Domain Name System) name, you can ping using the –a switch to produce the following output:

```
C:\Documents and Settings\Laura>ping -a 192.168.1.101

Pinging WWW.MYCOMPANY.COM [192.168.1.101] with 32 bytes of data:

Reply from 192.168.1.101: bytes=32 time=90ms TTL=245
Reply from 192.168.1.101: bytes=32 time=85ms TTL=245
Reply from 192.168.1.101: bytes=32 time=24ms TTL=242
Reply from 192.168.1.101: bytes=32 time=24ms TTL=242

Ping statistics for 192.168.1.101:
    Packets: Sent = 4, Received = 4, Lost = 0 (0% loss), Approximate round trip
times in milli-seconds:
    Minimum = 24ms, Maximum = 90ms, Average = 55ms
```

- **–n** will let you specify the number of ping packets to send. For example, the command **ping –n 10 192.168.1.101** will send 10 ping packets to the specified host.

- **–w** specifies how long each packet should wait before it times out and returns a "Request timed out" error. The default value is 1000 milliseconds.

- **–i** will change the default Time To Live (TTL) for the ICMP echo messages used by the ping command. By default, the TTL is 252, which means that a ping command can pass through 252 router *hops* before the packet is dropped. You can alter this value by using the –i switch.

Head of the Class…

Understanding ICMP

The Internet Control Message Protocol (ICMP) is documented in RFC 792, which you can read online at www.freesoft.org/CIE/RFC/792/index.htm. ICMP is part of the TCP/IP protocol suite that operates at the Network Layer. ICMP messages are primarily used to send messages related to network troubleshooting, so an understanding of ICMP is a critical part of the network troubleshooting process. Some of ICMP's main functions are as follows:

- **Reporting network connectivity issues**, like a particular computer or a larger portion of a network that has become unavailable or unreachable. Whenever a computer or router forwards an IP datagram to a remote host, the forwarding device will decrement the TTL field of an IP header by one. If this TTL ever reaches 0, ICMP will create a "Time to live exceeded in transit" message and send it back to the host that initiated the message.

- **Inform users of network congestion.** If a router is receiving too many packets to process efficiently, it will create an ICMP *Source Quench* message and forward this message to the host that is sending the large number of packets. This message will cause the source machine to slow down how quickly it is sending packets to allow the router to "catch up".

- **Provide Information for Network Troubleshooting.** Most common network utilities use ICMP to communicate, including *ping*, *tracert*, and *traceroute*. These utilities will look for ICMP "Time to live exceeded in transit" messages, as well as "Destination unreachable" messages, to determine whether a particular host or group of hosts is reachable.

etwork+
BJECTIVE
1.1.1

tracert

The *tracert* utility allows you to trace the *path* that a network packet will take from one host to another. A network packet will often have to pass through several routers or hops to reach its destination, and you can use tracert to determine whether one of these routers, or a link between two routers, is overloaded or has failed. The tracert utility works by sending a series of ICMP echo requests, much like the ping utility. For example, when you type **tracert www.digitalthink.com** at the command prompt, you'll see output that resembles the following:

```
C:\>tracert www.digitalthink.com

Tracing route to www.digitalthink.com [216.35.144.147]

over a maximum of 30 hops:

1  <10 ms <10 ms <10 ms stablazer.tacteam.net [192.168.1.16]

2  70 ms 80 ms 70 ms dal-colo13.dallas.net [209.44.40.13]
```

```
3  80 ms  91 ms  110 ms  grf-dal-ge002.dallas.net [209.44.40.9]

4  70 ms  120 ms  100 ms  atm9-0-04.CR-1.usdlls.savvis.net [209.44.32.9]

5  120 ms  120 ms  170 ms  tm9-0-013.CR-1.ussntc.savvis.net [209.83.222.41]

6  120 ms  140 ms  120 ms  209.144.160.142

7  110 ms  131 ms  330 ms  bbr01-g6-0.sntc01.exodus.net [216.33.147.35]

8  140 ms  130 ms  120 ms  bbr01-p2-0.sntc02.exodus.net [209.185.249.110]

9  170 ms  130 ms  161 ms  bbr02-p3-0.sntc04.exodus.net [209.1.169.254]

10 130 ms  141 ms  120 ms  dcr01-g2-0.sntc04.exodus.net [216.34.2.33]

11 121 ms  130 ms  170 ms  rsm11-vlan920.sntc04.exodus.net [216.34.2.154]

12 131 ms  140 ms  150 ms  216.35.142.250

13 150 ms  140 ms  141 ms  www.digitalthink.com [216.35.144.147]

Trace complete.
```

Each line in the tracert output indicates one hop on the path between your local computer and the destination. The three numbers at the beginning of each line indicate the round-trip response time for a single ping to get to that router and back. As you can see in the example above, this ping is sent three times to each router. There are also some command line switches that you can use to customize the tracert output:

- **tracert −d** will instruct tracert not to resolve IP addresses to hostnames (this will increase the speed of the tracert).

- **tracert −h** *maximum_hops* will indicate the maximum number of hops that tracert will use to search for a target. If tracert reaches this maximum number and hasn't reached the target yet, it will quit. The default value is 30 hops.

- **tracert −w** *timeout* indicates the amount of time each ping will wait for each reply, in milliseconds. The default value is 1000 milliseconds.

Exam Warning

Do not get confused between tracert and traceroute; they are essentially the same tools with different names. tracert maps to Microsoft Windows and traceroute maps to other vendors such as Cisco's IOS (Internetwork Operating System) as well as UNIX and Linux.

pathping

The *pathping* utility is new with Windows 2000 and Windows Server 2003, and is an updated and expanded version of ping. The pathping utility will send ICMP echo request messages to each router along the path to the destination host, and will calculate how long it takes each router to reply. The pathping tool combines the capabilities of both tracert and ping, and gives you additional information that you can't get easily from using either tool individually. pathping will calculate the following information each time it runs:

- The amount of time it takes the ping packet to get to the destination host and back, called the *round-trip*.

- The amount of time it takes to ping each individual router.

- The percent of ping requests that are lost at each router.

- The percent of ping requests lost between the routers.

pathping provides some interesting statistics for network troubleshooting because it gives you information regarding *where* packet loss is taking place, which can indicate that a particular router may be overloaded or malfunctioning. For example, when you enter the command **pathping 192.168.1.101**, you'll see the following output:

```
Tracing route to www.mycompany.com [192.168.1.101] over a maximum of 30 hops:
  0   IBM-A38375FF22E [192.168.1.100]
  1   10.7.94.1
  2   192.81.10.1
  3   so-0-2-0-0.BB-RTR1.PHIL.network.net [192.81.7.217]
  4   so-3-0-0-0.BB-RTR1.NWRK.network.net [192.81.7.242]
  5   so-0-0-0-0.BB-RTR2.NWRK.network.net [192.81.19.3]
  6   so-5-0-0-0.BB-RTR1.NY5030.network.net [192.81.7.189]
  7   so-6-0-0-0.BB-RTR1.NY325.network.net [192.81.7.89]
  8   so-6-0-0-0.PEER-RTR1.NY111.network.net [192.81.17.129]
  9   so-2-0-0-0.PEER-RTR2.NY111.network.net [192.81.4.2]
 10   192.81.15.14
 11   p14-0.core02.jfk02.atlas.company.com [10.54.1.165]
 12   p14-0.core01.phl01.atlas.company.com [10.28.4.2]
 13   demarc.company.com [10.28.30.202]
 14   seo1-ge2.router.mycompany.com [192.168.217.12]
 15   sfs-systems2.sfs.upenn.edu [192.168.1.101]


Computing statistics for 375 seconds...
                Source to Here   This Node/Link
Hop   RTT     Lost/Sent = Pct   Lost/Sent = Pct   Address
```

```
  0                                               IBM-A38375FF22E
[192.168.1.100]
                                 0/ 100 =  0%   |
  1    18ms      0/ 100 =  0%    0/ 100 =  0%  10.7.94.1
                                 0/ 100 =  0%   |
  2    22ms      0/ 100 =  0%    0/ 100 =  0%  192.81.10.1
                                 0/ 100 =  0%   |
  3    23ms      0/ 100 =  0%    0/ 100 =  0%  so-0-2-0-0.BB-
RTR1.PHIL.network.net [192.81.7.217]
                                 0/ 100 =  0%   |
  4    22ms      0/ 100 =  0%    0/ 100 =  0%  so-3-0-0-0.BB-
RTR1.NWRK.network.net [192.81.7.242]
                                 0/ 100 =  0%   |
  5    23ms      0/ 100 =  0%    0/ 100 =  0%  so-0-0-0-0.BB-
RTR2.NWRK.network.net [192.81.19.3]
                                 0/ 100 =  0%   |
  6    25ms      0/ 100 =  0%    0/ 100 =  0%  so-5-0-0-0.BB-
RTR1.NY5030.network.net [192.81.7.189]
                                 0/ 100 =  0%   |
  7    23ms      0/ 100 =  0%    0/ 100 =  0%  so-6-0-0-0.BB-
RTR1.NY325.network.net [192.81.7.89]
                                 0/ 100 =  0%   |
  8    24ms      0/ 100 =  0%    0/ 100 =  0%  so-6-0-0-0.PEER-
RTR1.NY111.network.net [192.81.17.129]
                                 0/ 100 =  0%   |
  9    23ms      0/ 100 =  0%    0/ 100 =  0%  so-2-0-0-0.PEER-
RTR2.NY111.network.net [192.81.4.2]
                                 0/ 100 =  0%   |
 10    ---     100/ 100 =100%  100/ 100 =100%  192.81.15.14
                                 0/ 100 =  0%   |
 11    22ms      0/ 100 =  0%    0/ 100 =  0%  p14-
0.core02.jfk02.atlas.company.
com [10.54.1.165]
                                 0/ 100 =  0%   |
 12    25ms      0/ 100 =  0%    0/ 100 =  0%  p14-
0.core01.phl01.atlas.company.
com [10.28.4.2]
                                 0/ 100 =  0%   |
```

```
 13    25ms      0/ 100 =  0%     0/ 100 =  0%   demarc.company.com
[10.28.30.202]

                                  0/ 100 =  0%   |
 14    24ms      1/ 100 =  1%     1/ 100 =  1%   seo1-ge2.router.mycompany.com
[192.168.217.12]

                                  0/ 100 =  0%   |
 15    25ms      0/ 100 =  0%     0/ 100 =  0%   www.mycompany.com
[192.168.1.101]
Trace complete.
```

You should notice that pathping first runs a tracert to the remote host and identifies all of the routers along the path to the destination, and shows you a list of those routers in the first section of the output. Then, pathping provides statistics about each router and each link between the routers. From this information, you can assess whether an individual router is being overworked, or whether there is congestion on a link between routers. You can see an illustration of this in Figure 11.3.

Figure 11.3 Following a Packet Through a Large Network

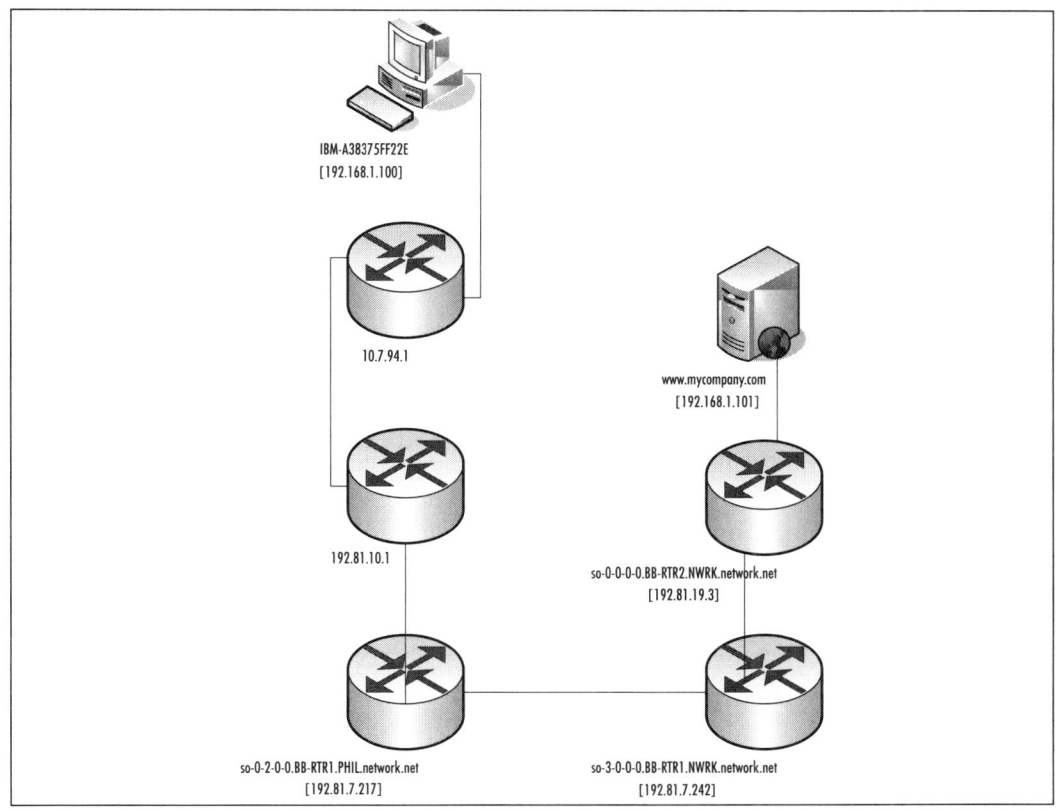

The last two columns of the pathping output provide the most useful information when you're troubleshooting routers and the links between them. Notice in the last column you can see the name of the router, the IP address, and a percentage listed to the left of the router. If this percentage is a high number, it means that a large number of ping packets are being lost when they're sent to that router. This is an indication that the router itself may be overloaded.

In between the names of the routers in a tracert output, you see a "|" (pipe) character like this one:

```
13    25ms       0/ 100 =   0%      0/ 100 =   0%   demarc.company.com [10.28.30.202]
                                    0/ 100 =   0%   |
14    24ms       1/ 100 =   1%      1/ 100 =   1%   seo1-ge2.router.mycompany.com
[192.168.217.12]
```

This represents the link between the router and the next-hop router. When there is a large percentage of lost pings for the *link*, it indicates congestion on the network between hops. In this case, you would want to investigate problems with network congestion, rather than with the router itself.

arp

The *arp* utility allows you to view and manipulate entries in the TCP/IP *arp cache*. The arp cache is a list of MAC addresses for computers that have been recently contacted, so that their IP-to-MAC address mapping has been stored by the local computer so it can be located again quickly. The arp utility is helpful when troubleshooting problems that are related to duplicate IP addresses or duplicate MAC addresses on a particular network segment.

For example, suppose that Computer A and Computer B have inadvertently been given the same IP address: 192.168.1.10. Computer A is supposed to be 192.168.1.10, and Computer B is supposed to be 192.168.1.11. When machines on the same segment as these two computers try to contact 192.168.1.10, they'll send an *arp broadcast* to resolve the IP address to a MAC address. Depending on which computer responds first, that will be the computer that they connect to. However, because there are two machines with the same IP address, you might connect to different machines at different times. You can see the contents of the arp cache by typing **arp −a** at the command prompt. You'll see output similar to the following:

```
Interface: 192.168.1.3 on Interface 0x1000003
Internet Address  Physical Address  Type
192.168.1.1 00-00-1c-3a-64-68 dynamic
192.168.1.2 00-40-05-37-c6-18 dynamic
192.168.1.16 00-40-f6-54-d7-43 dynamic
192.168.1.185 00-50-da-0d-f5-2d dynamic
```

The arp utility also allows you to add and delete entries in the arp cache. When you add an entry into the arp cache, you create a *static entry*. A static entry will be listed with "static" in the type field when you view the arp cache. You might want to create static arp entries for frequently accessed servers on the segment, or perhaps for the default gateway. When you create static entries, the source machine won't need to issue arp broadcasts to resolve IP addresses to MAC addresses.

Security Alert!

The Dangers of Static ARP Entries

Though they have their uses, static arp entries can get you in trouble. I was once consulted to assess why no machines on a particular segment were able to contact a particular server. Each client on the segment was able to connect to any other client on the segment, and the server itself was able to connect to any of the clients. The only problem was that the clients were unable to connect to the server itself. To reduce arp broadcast traffic on the network, the administrator had created a batch file that automatically placed static entries for each server on the same segment, as well as the default gateway for the segment. He then placed the batch file in each computer's startup folder, so that when a machine was restarted, the entries would be placed in the arp cache again.

The problems began for this company when they replaced the NIC on the server. Because the MAC address of a computer is tied to the NIC that's installed, this meant that the static arp entries became incorrect and had to be updated. However, for some reason, nobody remembered the batch file that was still populating the arp cache of each machine with these static entries that were now incorrect. Because of this, most clients on the network became unable to connect to the new server until the batch file was discovered and brought up to date.

---

etwork+
BJECTIVE
4.1.4

netstat

The *netstat* utility will give you a great deal of useful information about the active connections on a particular computer. It provides you detailed information about each protocol and port on a computer that is listening or that has established a connection with another computer. You should remember from Chapters 5 and 6 that TCP/IP-based applications like FTP and Telnet will communicate using a particular TCP or UDP port. When one of these programs or services is running on a computer, it means that port is listening for new connection attempts from other computers. A connection listed in netstat can be in one of four states:

- **Listening** means that a particular port is open and waiting for connections, but no active connections have been made to it.

- **Established** means that a particular connection is active—an FTP client has connected to an FTP server, a client's Web browser has connected to a World Wide Web (WWW) service, and the like.

- **Time_Wait** means that a connection has been made, but it hasn't received any data for some time and is in the process of timing out.

- **Close_Wait** means that an active connection is being closed.

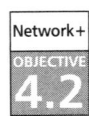

The netstat command has a number of command-line switches that will produce different types of troubleshooting output. The full syntax of netstat is as follows:

```
NETSTAT [-a] [-b] [-e] [-n] [-o] [-p proto] [-r] [-s] [-v] [interval]
```

- **netstat -a** displays all TCP/IP connections and listening ports on the local computer, and produces output similar to the following:

```
Active Connections
Proto Local Address Foreign Address State
TCP 0.0.0.0:21 0.0.0.0:0 LISTENING
TCP 0.0.0.0:25 0.0.0.0:0 LISTENING
TCP 0.0.0.0:42 0.0.0.0:0 LISTENING
TCP 0.0.0.0:53 0.0.0.0:0 LISTENING
TCP 0.0.0.0:80 0.0.0.0:0 LISTENING
TCP 0.0.0.0:119 0.0.0.0:0 LISTENING
TCP 0.0.0.0:135 0.0.0.0:0 LISTENING
TCP 0.0.0.0:443 0.0.0.0:0 LISTENING
TCP 0.0.0.0:445 0.0.0.0:0 LISTENING
TCP 0.0.0.0:563 0.0.0.0:0 LISTENING
TCP 0.0.0.0:1045 0.0.0.0:0 LISTENING
TCP 0.0.0.0:1047 0.0.0.0:0 LISTENING
TCP 0.0.0.0:1056 0.0.0.0:0 LISTENING
TCP 0.0.0.0:1063 0.0.0.0:0 LISTENING
TCP 0.0.0.0:1064 0.0.0.0:0 LISTENING
TCP 0.0.0.0:1066 0.0.0.0:0 LISTENING
TCP 0.0.0.0:1077 0.0.0.0:0 LISTENING
TCP 0.0.0.0:1104 0.0.0.0:0 LISTENING
TCP 0.0.0.0:1109 0.0.0.0:0 LISTENING
TCP 0.0.0.0:1111 0.0.0.0:0 LISTENING
TCP 0.0.0.0:1113 0.0.0.0:0 LISTENING
TCP 0.0.0.0:1114 0.0.0.0:0 LISTENING
TCP 0.0.0.0:1123 0.0.0.0:0 LISTENING
TCP 0.0.0.0:1124 0.0.0.0:0 LISTENING
TCP 0.0.0.0:1133 0.0.0.0:0 LISTENING
TCP 0.0.0.0:1135 0.0.0.0:0 LISTENING
```

```
TCP 0.0.0.0:1139 0.0.0.0:0 LISTENING
TCP 0.0.0.0:1141 0.0.0.0:0 LISTENING
TCP 0.0.0.0:1142 0.0.0.0:0 LISTENING
TCP 0.0.0.0:1154 0.0.0.0:0 LISTENING
TCP 0.0.0.0:1268 0.0.0.0:0 LISTENING
TCP 0.0.0.0:1270 0.0.0.0:0 LISTENING
TCP 0.0.0.0:1503 0.0.0.0:0 LISTENING
TCP 0.0.0.0:1720 0.0.0.0:0 LISTENING
TCP 0.0.0.0:1755 0.0.0.0:0 LISTENING
TCP 0.0.0.0:2057 0.0.0.0:0 LISTENING
TCP 0.0.0.0:2826 0.0.0.0:0 LISTENING
TCP 0.0.0.0:3074 0.0.0.0:0 LISTENING
TCP 0.0.0.0:3372 0.0.0.0:0 LISTENING
TCP 0.0.0.0:3762 0.0.0.0:0 LISTENING
TCP 0.0.0.0:3934 0.0.0.0:0 LISTENING
TCP 0.0.0.0:3937 0.0.0.0:0 LISTENING
TCP 0.0.0.0:3969 0.0.0.0:0 LISTENING
TCP 0.0.0.0:6666 0.0.0.0:0 LISTENING
TCP 0.0.0.0:7007 0.0.0.0:0 LISTENING
TCP 0.0.0.0:7778 0.0.0.0:0 LISTENING
TCP 127.0.0.1:15841 0.0.0.0:0 LISTENING
TCP 192.168.1.3:42 192.168.1.185:3919 ESTABLISHED
TCP 192.168.1.3:135 192.168.1.2:1651 ESTABLISHED
TCP 192.168.1.3:135 192.168.1.2:1653 ESTABLISHED
TCP 192.168.1.3:135 192.168.1.2:1656 ESTABLISHED
TCP 192.168.1.3:139 0.0.0.0:0 LISTENING
TCP 192.168.1.3:1063 192.168.1.16:42 ESTABLISHED
TCP 192.168.1.3:1064 192.168.1.185:42 ESTABLISHED
TCP 192.168.1.3:1109 192.168.1.2:135 ESTABLISHED
TCP 192.168.1.3:1111 192.168.1.2:135 ESTABLISHED
TCP 192.168.1.3:1113 192.168.1.2:1089 ESTABLISHED
TCP 192.168.1.3:1114 192.168.1.2:1089 ESTABLISHED
TCP 192.168.1.3:1123 192.168.1.2:1654 ESTABLISHED
TCP 192.168.1.3:1124 192.168.1.2:1089 ESTABLISHED
TCP 192.168.1.3:1129 0.0.0.0:0 LISTENING
TCP 192.168.1.3:1129 192.168.1.16:139 ESTABLISHED
TCP 192.168.1.3:1133 192.168.1.16:1057 ESTABLISHED
TCP 192.168.1.3:1135 192.168.1.16:1057 ESTABLISHED
```

```
TCP 192.168.1.3:1139 192.168.1.16:1074 ESTABLISHED
TCP 192.168.1.3:1141 192.168.1.2:135 ESTABLISHED
TCP 192.168.1.3:1142 192.168.1.2:135 ESTABLISHED
TCP 192.168.1.3:1154 192.168.1.16:1074 ESTABLISHED
TCP 192.168.1.3:1268 192.168.1.185:3389 ESTABLISHED
TCP 192.168.1.3:1270 192.168.1.2:5631 ESTABLISHED
TCP 192.168.1.3:1448 0.0.0.0:0 LISTENING
TCP 192.168.1.3:1448 192.168.1.185:139 ESTABLISHED
TCP 192.168.1.3:1569 0.0.0.0:0 LISTENING
TCP 192.168.1.3:1569 192.168.1.1:139 ESTABLISHED
TCP 192.168.1.3:2057 192.168.1.16:5631 ESTABLISHED
TCP 192.168.1.3:2826 192.168.1.2:1089 ESTABLISHED
TCP 192.168.1.3:3762 209.185.128.149:1863 ESTABLISHED
TCP 192.168.1.3:3934 192.168.1.185:389 ESTABLISHED
TCP 192.168.1.3:3937 192.168.1.185:389 ESTABLISHED
TCP 192.168.1.3:3968 192.168.1.186:1002 TIME_WAIT
TCP 192.168.1.3:3969 192.168.1.185:445 ESTABLISHED
TCP 192.168.1.3:3976 192.168.1.185:389 TIME_WAIT
UDP 0.0.0.0:42 *:*
UDP 0.0.0.0:135 *:*
UDP 0.0.0.0:161 *:*
UDP 0.0.0.0:445 *:*
```

EXAM WARNING

Make sure you understand what you are looking at when you see the output of the netstat command:

TCP 192.168.1.3:42 192.168.1.185:3919 ESTABLISHED

This means that the computer has *ESTABLISHED* or created a connection that's using the *TCP* protocol. The connection has been made between *192.168.1.3:42* and *168.1.185:3919*, which means that the computer at IP address 192.168.1.3 is sending information using TCP port 42, and 168.1.185 is receiving information using port 3919.

- **netstat –b** displays the name of the executable that created each connection or listening port, like this:

```
Active Connections

   Proto    Local Address              Foreign Address           State           PID
   TCP      IBM-A38375FF22E:1747     dc1.mycompany.com:1025    ESTABLISHED     130
[OUTLOOK.EXE]

   TCP      IBM-A38375FF22E:1750     dc2.mycompany.com:1026    ESTABLISHED     1320
[OUTLOOK.EXE]

   TCP      IBM-A38375FF22E:2665     mail.mycompany.com:1225 ESTABLISHED
   1320  [OUTLOOK.EXE]
```

- **netstat –e** displays Ethernet statistics for the local computer. This command produces the following output:

```
Interface Statistics

                              Received            Sent
Bytes                        139699480        23384356
Unicast packets                 330830          290527
Non-unicast packets              23358            6586
Discards                             0               0
Errors                               0               0
Unknown protocols                    9
```

- **netstat -p** *protocol* will show you the same information displayed by the **–a** option, restricted to a specific protocol. You can restrict your output to TCP, UDP, TCPv6, or UDPv6. You can combine the **–p** switch with the **–s** switch to display three additional protocols, IP, ICMP, and ICMPv6. For example, **netstat –p TCP** produces the following output:

```
Active Connections

   Proto    Local Address              Foreign Address           State
   TCP      IBM-A38375FF22E:1747     dc1.mycompany.com:1025    ESTABLISHED
   TCP      IBM-A38375FF22E:1750     dc2.mycompany.com:1026    ESTABLISHED
   TCP      IBM-A38375FF22E:2665     mail.mycompany.com:1225 ESTABLISHED
```

- **netstat –n** diplays addresses and port numbers in numerical form instead of using hostnames.
- **netstat –r** displays the routing table for the local computer, like this:

```
Route Table
===========================================================================
Interface List
0x1 ......................... MS TCP Loopback interface
0x2 ...00 0e 35 1a e2 8d ...... Intel(R) PRO/Wireless 2200BG Network Connection
===========================================================================
Active Routes:
Network Destination        Netmask          Gateway       Interface  Metric
          0.0.0.0          0.0.0.0      192.168.1.1   192.168.1.100     30
        127.0.0.0        255.0.0.0        127.0.0.1       127.0.0.1      1
      192.168.1.0    255.255.255.0    192.168.1.100   192.168.1.100     30
    192.168.1.100  255.255.255.255        127.0.0.1       127.0.0.1     30
    192.168.1.255  255.255.255.255    192.168.1.100   192.168.1.100     30
        224.0.0.0        240.0.0.0    192.168.1.100   192.168.1.100     30
  255.255.255.255  255.255.255.255    192.168.1.100   192.168.1.100      1
  255.255.255.255  255.255.255.255    192.168.1.100               3      1
Default Gateway:       192.168.1.1
===========================================================================
Persistent Routes:
  None
```

- **netstat −s** provides detailed statistics about the local computer's network connections. You can restrict which statistics are displayed by combining this with
  the **-p** option and specifying a particular protocol. The command **netstat −s**
  will produce the following information:

```
IPv4 Statistics
  Packets Received               = 352283
  Received Header Errors         = 0
  Received Address Errors        = 7
  Datagrams Forwarded            = 0
  Unknown Protocols Received     = 0
  Received Packets Discarded     = 17828
  Received Packets Delivered     = 334455
  Output Requests                = 296841
  Routing Discards               = 0
  Discarded Output Packets       = 16
  Output Packet No Route         = 0
```

```
Reassembly Required                 = 0
Reassembly Successful               = 0
Reassembly Failures                 = 0
Datagrams Successfully Fragmented   = 0
Datagrams Failing Fragmentation     = 0
Fragments Created                   = 0


ICMPv4 Statistics

                          Received     Sent
  Messages                1494         1557
  Errors                  47           0
  Destination Unreachable 18           8
  Time Exceeded           14           0
  Parameter Problems      0            0
  Source Quenches         0            0
  Redirects               0            0
  Echos                   0            1549
  Echo Replies            1415         0
  Timestamps              0            0
  Timestamp Replies       0            0
  Address Masks           0            0
  Address Mask Replies    0            0


TCP Statistics for IPv4
  Active Opens                = 1609
  Passive Opens               = 29
  Failed Connection Attempts  = 22
  Reset Connections           = 477
  Current Connections         = 3
  Segments Received           = 264193
  Segments Sent               = 232274
  Segments Retransmitted      = 591


UDP Statistics for IPv4
  Datagrams Received  = 68746
  No Ports            = 1491
  Receive Errors      = 0
  Datagrams Sent      = 62415
```

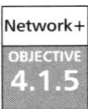

nbtstat

Network+
OBJECTIVE
4.1.5

nbtstat is quite similar to netstat, except that it displays information specifically relating to NetBIOS over TCP (NetBT). nbtstat will show you NetBT protocol statistics and NetBIOS name tables for local and remote computers. nbtstat will also allow you to display and refresh the NetBIOS cache. nbtstat uses the following command-line switches:

- **nbtstat −a** *Computername* will display the NetBIOS name cache for a remote computer, specified by the computer's NetBIOS hostname. The command **nbtstat −a DC1** will display the following information:

```
Node IpAddress: [192.168.1.100] Scope Id: []

           NetBIOS Remote Machine Name Table

       Name                Type           Status
    -------------------------------------------------

    DC2               <00>   UNIQUE     Registered
    DC2               <20>   UNIQUE     Registered
    MYCOMPANY         <00>   GROUP      Registered
    MYCOMPANY         <1C>   GROUP      Registered
    DC2               <03>   UNIQUE     Registered
    DC2               <6A>   UNIQUE     Registered
    DC2               <87>   UNIQUE     Registered
    JSMITH            <03>   UNIQUE     Registered
    DC2               <01>   UNIQUE     Registered
    MEVANS            <03>   UNIQUE     Registered
    MAC Address = 00-40-8A-0C-A2-9E
```

- **nbtstat −A** *IP Address* will display the same information as nbtstat −a, but will allow you to specify the target machine by IP address instead of NetBIOS name.

- **nbtstat -c** will display the NetBIOS name cache of NetBIOS names that have already been resolved on the local computer. This command will show you a table of NetBIOS names and their associated IP addresses, as follows:

```
Node IpAddress: [192.168.1.100] Scope Id: []

              NetBIOS Remote Cache Name Table

       Name             Type     Host Address    Life [sec]
    ----------------------------------------------------------

    App1          <20>  UNIQUE    10.0.0.101        277
    DC2           <20>  UNIQUE    10.0.0.102        277
    DC3           <20>  UNIQUE    10.0.0.102        277
```

- **nbtstat –n** displays the NetBIOS names that are registered for the local computer. The command **nbtstat –n** displays information in the following format:

```
Node IpAddress: [192.168.1.100] Scope Id: []


              NetBIOS Local Name Table

    Name                 Type        Status

----------------------------------------------

  IBM-A38375FF22E    <00>  UNIQUE      Registered
  IBM-A38375FF22E    <20>  UNIQUE      Registered
  WORKGROUP          <00>  GROUP       Registered
```

- **nbtstat –r** will display NetBIOS statistics for the local computer. This will display the number of NetBIOS names that have been registered using broadcast and a WINS (Windows Internet Name Service) server, and the number of NetBIOS names that have been *resolved* using both of these methods. The **–r** switch displays information in the following format:

```
NetBIOS Names Resolution and Registration Statistics

---------------------------------------------------


Resolved By Broadcast     = 27
Resolved By Name Server   = 55


Registered By Broadcast   = 0
Registered By Name Server = 9
```

- **nbtstat –R** will *purge* the current contents of the NetBIOS cache on the local machine. In addition to removing any entries in the local cache, nbtstat –R will also re-load any entries in the local LMHOSTS file that have the "#PRE" tag. Remember that "#PRE" is used in the LMHOSTS file to *pre-load* a NetBIOS name mapping into a machine's NetBIOS cache when it first starts up.

- **nbtstat –RR** will release and refresh any NetBIOS names that are registered on the local computer.

TEST DAY TIP

The **nbtstat –RR** command is especially useful for troubleshooting, since you may encounter a situation where a computer's NetBIOS name has been updated and you need to quickly remove any cached entries.

■   **nbtstat –s** will display any existing NetBIOS sessions, producing output that resembles the following:

```
                        NetBIOS Connection Table


Local Name              State    In/Out  Remote Host      Input   Output
----------------------------------------------------------------------


DC1             <03>  Listening

JSMITH          <03>  Listening

MEVANS          <03>  Listening

CKLINE          <03>  Listening
```

■   **nbtstat –S** will display the same information as using the **-s** switch, but it will display the local name as an IP address only.

ipconfig

The *ipconfig* utility works at the command line to provide you with IP configuration data for all NICs installed on your local computer. You can simply type **ipconfig** by itself to see basic information about the NICs in your computer, or you can use a number of switches to retrieve more detailed information. At its most basic, the output for the ipconfig command will resemble the following:

```
Windows IP Configuration
Ethernet adapter Wireless Network Connection:
        Connection-specific DNS Suffix  . :
        IP Address. . . . . . . . . . . . : 192.168.1.100
        Subnet Mask . . . . . . . . . . . : 255.255.255.0
        Default Gateway . . . . . . . . . : 192.168.1.1


Ethernet adapter Local Area Connection:
        Media State . . . . . . . . . . . : Media disconnected
```

As you can see, the basic ipconfig command provides you the IP address, subnet mask, and default gateway for the NICs installed on a particular machine. This information can be handy as a quick reference when trying to figure out what IP address and subnet mask has been assigned to a particular computer, particularly if it receives its IP configuration from DHCP (Dynamic Host Configuration Protocol). You can get more detailed information by using the **ipconfig /all** command, as you can see here:

```
Windows IP Configuration

        Host Name . . . . . . . . . . . . : IBM-A38375FF22E

        Primary Dns Suffix  . . . . . . . :

        Node Type . . . . . . . . . . . . : Hybrid

        IP Routing Enabled. . . . . . . . : No

        WINS Proxy Enabled. . . . . . . . : No


Ethernet adapter Wireless Network Connection:

        Connection-specific DNS Suffix  . :

        Description . . . . . . . . . . . : Intel(R) PRO/Wireless 2200BG
Network Connection

        Physical Address. . . . . . . . . : 00-8E-36-4A-E5-8D

        Dhcp Enabled. . . . . . . . . . . : Yes

        Autoconfiguration Enabled . . . . : Yes

        IP Address. . . . . . . . . . . . : 192.168.1.100

        Subnet Mask . . . . . . . . . . . : 255.255.255.0

        Default Gateway . . . . . . . . . : 192.168.1.1

        DHCP Server . . . . . . . . . . . : 192.168.1.1

        DNS Servers . . . . . . . . . . . : 151.197.0.38

                                            151.197.0.39

        Lease Obtained. . . . . . . . . . : Wednesday, February 16, 2005
9:27:37 AM

        Lease Expires . . . . . . . . . . : Thursday, February 17, 2005
9:27:37 AM


Ethernet adapter Local Area Connection:


        Media State . . . . . . . . . . . : Media disconnected

        Description . . . . . . . . . . . : Intel(R) PRO/1000 MT Mobile
Connection

        Physical Address. . . . . . . . . : 09-AD-69-CF-35-09
```

By using the ipconfig /all command, you get information about the DNS and WINS servers that your computer has been configured with, as well as the MAC address of each installed NIC. If you're troubleshooting DNS-related problems, for example, this is a quick way to determine the hostname and primary DNS suffix that your machine is using.

TEST DAY TIP

You can also use **ipconfig /release** and **ipconfig /renew** to force a DHCP client to request a new IP address lease from a DHCP server.

You can use the **ipconfig /flushdns** command to clear the DNS cache on the local computer. This will force the computer to contact a DNS server for any hostnames that it tries to connect to. This is particularly useful if you've recently made changes to your DNS records so that your clients can access the most up-to-date DNS information. **ipconfig /displaydns** will show you the *contents* of the local DNS cache. After typing **ipconfig /displaydns** at the command prompt, you'll see output similar to the following:

```
Windows IP Configuration

        1.0.0.127.in-addr.arpa

        ----------------------------------------
        Record Name . . . . . : 1.0.0.127.in-addr.arpa.
        Record Type . . . . . : 12
        Time To Live  . . . . : 311660
        Data Length . . . . . : 4
        Section . . . . . . . : Answer
        PTR Record  . . . . . : localhost


        Record Name . . . . . : dbru.br.ns.els-gms.att.net
        Record Type . . . . . : 1
        Time To Live  . . . . : 53255
        Data Length . . . . . : 4
        Section . . . . . . . : Additional
        A (Host) Record . . . : 199.191.128.106


        Record Name . . . . . : dmtu.mt.ns.els-gms.att.net
        Record Type . . . . . : 1
        Time To Live  . . . . : 53255
        Data Length . . . . . : 4
```

```
Section . . . . . . . : Additional
A (Host) Record . . . : 12.127.16.70


localhost

---------------------------------------
Record Name . . . . . : localhost
Record Type . . . . . : 1
Time To Live  . . . . : 311660
Data Length . . . . . : 4
Section . . . . . . . : Answer
A (Host) Record . . . : 127.0.0.1
```

ipconfig /registernds will refresh DHCP leases for all NICs on the machine, and will re-register the machine's hostname and IP address with the DNS server. The is a helpful switch to use when you've made changes to the local machine's IP address configuration and need to quickly re-register the new information with the DNS server.

winipcfg

winipcfg (shown in Figure 11.4) is the graphical equivalent of the ipconfig command that's available in earlier versions of Windows. This will display the same information shown by ipconfig, and provides you a one-click shortcut to release and renew DHCP information.

Figure 11.4 Using Winipcfg

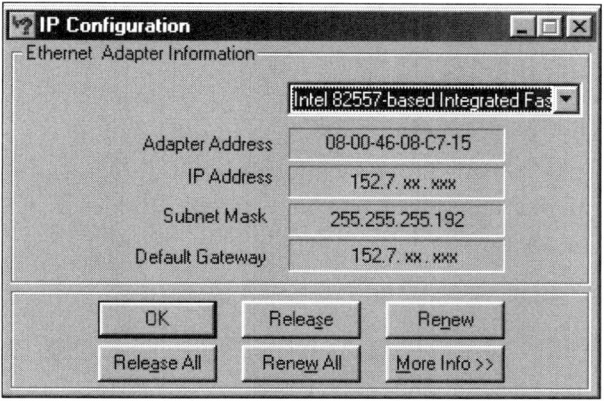

www.syngress.com

EXAM WARNING

winipcfg is not available in more recent versions of the Windows OS like Windows 2000 and Windows XP. winipcfg is primarily used on Windows 95 and Windows 98 workstations.

nslookup

The *nslookup* utility allows you to test and query the records stored in your DNS server. You can use nslookup in *command mode* to perform a single query, or in *interactive mode* to perform multiple queries. For example, if you enter the command **nslookup defiant.tacteam.net**, you'll see the following output (you can use another hostname in place of the one listed in this example to see nslookup in action):

```
Server: constellation.tacteam.net

Address: 192.168.1.185

Name: defiant.tacteam.net

Address: 192.168.1.2

C:\>
```

As you can see, you get returned to the command prompt once you receive the information – this is typical of using nslookup in command mode. To enter interactive mode, just type **nslookup** at the command prompt, and your output will look like this:

```
C:\>nslookup

Default Server: constellation.tacteam.net

Address: 192.168.1.185

>
```

Notice that you're not returned to the command prompt, but to the nslookup command's interactive prompt. Once you enter interactive mode, you can use the **set** commands to control the information that's returned by your queries. The set commands available in nslookup are as follows:

- **set all**   Prints options, current server, and host.
- **set [no]debug**   Prints debugging information. **set debug** turns debugging on, **set no debug** turns debugging off.
- **set [no]d2**   Prints the most exhaustive debugging information possible.
- **set domain=NAME**   Sets the default domain name for any queries.
- **set root=NAME**   Sets the root server being used.

- **set srchlist=N1[/N2/.../N6]** Sets the DNS domains used to search for a particular host.

- **set retry=X** Sets the number of retries.

- **set timeout=X** Sets the initial timeout interval for DNS queries.

- **set [no]defname** Appends the default domain name to each query.

- **set [no]recurse** Performs a recursive query or a non-recursive (iterative) query.

- **set [no]search** Uses the domain search list configured on the client.

- **set querytype=X** Restricts the query type so that it only returns a particular type of records. You can restrict nslookup queries to look for CNAME records, MX records, NS and SRV records, and more.

When you're ready to leave the interactive mode and return to the command prompt, just type **exit**.

TEST DAY TIP

Be sure that you're familiar with the different query types that you can use with nslookup. In particular, be aware of how to search for mail server records using the **MX** option, and DNS servers using the **NS** option.

route

You can use the *route* command to manipulate and display the routing table for the local computer. The **route print** command produces the same results as the netstat –r command – it produces a copy of the local computer's routing table, like the one shown here:

```
Route Table
===========================================================================
Interface List
0x1 ......................... MS TCP Loopback interface
0x2 ...00 0e 35 1a e2 8d ..... Intel(R) PRO/Wireless 2200BG Network Connection
===========================================================================
Active Routes:
Network Destination        Netmask          Gateway       Interface  Metric
          0.0.0.0          0.0.0.0      192.168.1.1    192.168.1.100       30
        127.0.0.0        255.0.0.0      127.0.0.1        127.0.0.1        1
```

www.syngress.com

```
      192.168.1.0      255.255.255.0    192.168.1.100   192.168.1.100        30
    192.168.1.100    255.255.255.255        127.0.0.1       127.0.0.1        30
    192.168.1.255    255.255.255.255    192.168.1.100   192.168.1.100        30
        224.0.0.0          240.0.0.0    192.168.1.100   192.168.1.100        30
  255.255.255.255    255.255.255.255    192.168.1.100   192.168.1.100         1
  255.255.255.255    255.255.255.255    192.168.1.100               3         1
Default Gateway:        192.168.1.1
=============================================================================
Persistent Routes:
  None
```

You can also use the route command to add, change, or delete routes that are defined on the local computer. To specify the route to a remote host using the route command, you need to configure the following information:

1. **Destination** The destination that this route statement is designed to reach. This can be a single host, a network address, or the *default route* for this computer, indicated by the syntax **0.0.0.0**. The default route dictates where network packets will be sent if the routing table doesn't have a more specific entry for them.

2. **Mask** This indicates the subnet mask for the route's destination. If the destination is a single IP address, the mask will be 255.255.255.255. For a network address, this will be the subnet mask of the destination network. The mask for the default route is 0.0.0.0.

3. **Gateway** The IP address that packets will be forwarded to for this route. This has to be an IP address that's on the same subnet as the local computer.

4. **Metric** This specifies the metric or *cost* of a particular route, from 1 to 9999. The higher the metric, the less likely the computer is to use a particular route. This is particularly useful if you're creating multiple routes to the same network as a fault tolerance measure; configure one route with a metric of 1 and another with a metric of 50. The local computer will use the first route unless it's not available, at which point it will revert to the second route.

5. **Interface** This indicates the IP address of the NIC that should be used to reach the destination specified in this route. If you have two NICs installed that are attached to two different networks, you'll need to specify which NIC the route command should use to reach its destination.

EXAM WARNING

In most cases, you'll only add routes in this fashion on a server that's attached to multiple networks. Workstations will simply rely on their default gateway to route network traffic.

To add a route to a remote network, issue the following command at the command line:

```
route add 172.16.1.0 255.255.0.0 192.168.1.101 1
```

To change the metric of the route you just created, use the **route change** command:

```
route change 172.16.1.0 255.255.0.0 192.168.1.101 10
```

To delete a route that you've created, use **route delete**:

```
route delete 172.16.1.0 255.255.0.0 192.168.1.101 10
```

The route command has two additional switches that you should be aware of as you're preparing for the Network+ exam:

- **route –f** will clear any routes to destination networks that are currently in the routing table. If you use the –f switch while creating or changing a route, the route command will clear the routing table and then add the new route you specify.

- **route –p** will make the entry you're adding to the routing table *persistent*. By default, any routes that you add manually will only stay in the routing table until the computer reboots. Using the –p switch ensures that the route will remain in memory until you manually delete it.

SNMP

The Simple Network Management Protocol (SNMP) is a protocol used to communicate status messages from computers and devices on your network. These messages are sent to machines configured to receive these status messages. Machines that send these messages run *SNMP agent software*, and the machines that receive the status messages run *SNMP management software*. One way to remember how this works is to think of the agent software as a "secret agent" that gets information about a network device, and then reports the information to his "manager" at headquarters.

While the name of the SNMP protocol would lead you to believe that its primary function is to allow you to manage objects on your network, the management that's happening here has more to do with *monitoring* your network, rather than actually making any changes to the devices themselves. SNMP allows you to audit the activities of servers, workstations, routers, bridges, intelligent hubs, and just about any network-connected device that supports SNMP agent software. For example, the agent software available with Windows 2000 implementation allows to you monitor the Windows 2000 Server and Professional operating system, as well as Windows services like DHCP, WINS, Routing and Remote Access Service (RRAS), and others. All of these Windows 2000 services can be monitored remotely by SNMP management software.

In order for the SNMP agent software to collect information regarding a particular service, a Management Information Base (MIB) must be created. The MIB is a database that describes which kinds of information should be gathered from a particular device. The MIBs included with Windows 2000 allow the agent software to communicate a wide range of information. The agent software is responsible for reporting the information gathered by the MIB. However, agents rarely volunteer information spontaneously. Rather, the SNMP agent must be *queried* by an SNMP management system. There is, however, an exception to this: a *trap* message. A trap message is sent spontaneously by an SNMP agent to the SNMP management system when an important event occurs. For example, you could configure a trap message to indicate that the World Wide Web service has become unresponsive on a particular machine. We would then configure the agent to send a trap message to the IP address of a computer running the SNMP management software so that an administrator can quickly respond to this event. SNMP trap messages are sent to UDP port 162.

There are two other types of messages associated with SNMP. A *GET* message is a request that is sent from an SNMP management system that requests information from an agent. A *SET* message will allow the SNMP management system to write changes to an MIB, and therefore extend its information-gathering abilities. SNMP GET and SET messages communicate on UDP port 161.

SNMP is a fairly open protocol that doesn't have many security features. To control which machines receive SNMP trap messages, you will configure an SNMP *community name*. In addition, you'll configure a *trap destination*, which is the hostname or IP address of the computer running the SNMP management software. In order for a system to report to an SNMP management system, you first need to install the agent software on the target computer. In Exercise 11.2, we'll install and configure the SNMP agent software on a Windows XP machine.

EXERCISE 11.2

INSTALL AND CONFIGURE THE SNMP AGENT

1. Click **Start | Control Panel | Add/Remove Programs.**
2. Click **Add/Remove Windows Components**. You'll see the screen shown in Figure 11.5.

Figure 11.5 Adding a New Component to Microsoft Windows

Windows Components Wizard

Windows Components
You can add or remove components of Windows XP.

To add or remove a component, click the checkbox. A shaded box means that only part of the component will be installed. To see what's included in a component, click Details.

Components:

☐ 🔧 Management and Monitoring Tools	2.0 MB
☐ 📧 Message Queuing	0.0 MB
☐ 🌐 MSN Explorer	20.7 MB
☐ 🔧 Networking Services	0.3 MB
☐ 🔧 Other Network File and Print Services	0.0 MB

Description: Includes Windows Accessories and Utilities for your computer.

Total disk space required: 56.7 MB
Space available on disk: 21928.1 MB   [Details...]

[< Back] [Next >] [Cancel]

3. Scroll down to **Management and Monitoring Tools** and select **Details**.

4. Enable the **Simple Network Management Protocol** option.

5. Click **Next** to begin the file copy process, and **Finish** when the process is complete.

6. To configure the SNMP community, click **Start | Control Panel | Administrative Tools | Services**.

7. Scroll down to the SNMP service. Right-click on the service and select **Properties**.

8. Click the **Traps** tab. You'll see the screen shown in Figure 11.6.

Figure 11.6 Configuring the SNMP Community

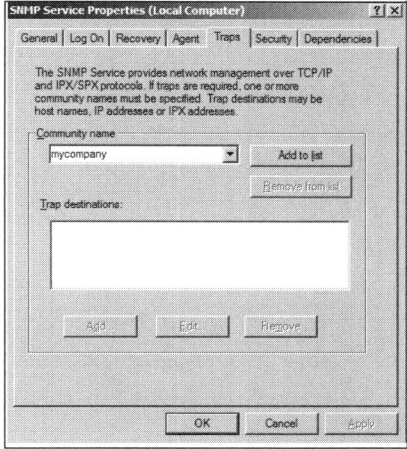

SNMP Service Properties (Local Computer)

General | Log On | Recovery | Agent | Traps | Security | Dependencies

The SNMP Service provides network management over TCP/IP and IPX/SPX protocols. If traps are required, one or more community names must be specified. Trap destinations may be host names, IP addresses or IPX addresses.

Community name
mycompany   [Add to list]
     [Remove from list]

Trap destinations:

[Add...] [Edit...] [Remove]

[OK] [Cancel] [Apply]

9. In the **Community Name** drop-down list, enter the name of the SNMP community and click **Add**.

10. Under **Trap Destinations**, enter the hostname or IP address of the computer running the SNMP management software and click **Add**.

11. Click **OK** to finish configuring the SNMP Agent.

Linux Tools

While you may be spending a great deal of your "real world" troubleshooting time working on Windows computers, you should also be aware of the troubleshooting tools that are available for Linux- and UNIX-based computers. This is especially important since large organizations often employ these open-source operating systems as Web servers, firewalls, and other components of the network infrastructure. Many of the troubleshooting tools available for Linux and UNIX are similar or even identical to tools we've already covered for Windows: you can use the ping command from both a Windows and a UNIX computer, for example. In this section, we'll look at some tools that are specific to Linux- and UNIX-based operating systems.

ifconfig

You'll use the *ifconfig* command to configure the NICs installed in a Linux computer, as well as to view information about any configured interfaces. Like most Linux tools, you'll work with ifconfig from the command line. The most basic syntax and output for ifconfig is to simply type **ipconfig**, which will produce the following output:

```
eth0      Link encap:Ethernet  HWaddr 00:80:C8:F8:4A:51
          inet addr:192.168.99.35  Bcast:192.168.99.255  Mask:255.255.255.0
          UP BROADCAST RUNNING MULTICAST  MTU:1500  Metric:1
          RX packets:190312 errors:0 dropped:0 overruns:0 frame:0
          TX packets:86955 errors:0 dropped:0 overruns:0 carrier:0
          collisions:0 txqueuelen:100
          RX bytes:30701229 (29.2 Mb)  TX bytes:7878951 (7.5 Mb)
          Interrupt:9 Base address:0x5000

lo        Link encap:Local Loopback
          inet addr:127.0.0.1  Mask:255.0.0.0
          UP LOOPBACK RUNNING  MTU:16436  Metric:1
          RX packets:306 errors:0 dropped:0 overruns:0 frame:0
          TX packets:306 errors:0 dropped:0 overruns:0 carrier:0
```

```
collisions:0 txqueuelen:0
RX bytes:29504 (28.8 Kb)  TX bytes:29504 (28.8 Kb)
```

Even if you haven't worked with Linux before, you should be able to recognize the two adapters that ifconfig is displaying information for: an Ethernet adapter called "eth0", and the Loopback Adapter. You can see the following information listed for the eth0 interface:

- **HWaddr 00:80:C8:F8:4A:50** is the MAC address of the Ethernet adapter.

- **addr:192.168.99.35 Bcast:192.168.99.255 Mask:255.255.255.0** indicates the IP address, broadcast address, and subnet mask.

- **Interrupt:9 Base address:0x5000** give you information about the hardware resources being used by the Ethernet adapter.

- **RX packets** indicate the number of packets received by this adapter. **TX packets** show the number of packets transmitted.

You can quickly disable the Ethernet NIC on this Linux computer by typing **ifconfig eth0 down**. If you re-issue the ifconfig command after you've brought the Ethernet adapter down, you'll only see configuration information for the loopback adapter:

```
ifconfig

lo          Link encap:Local Loopback
            inet addr:127.0.0.1  Mask:255.0.0.0
            UP LOOPBACK RUNNING  MTU:16436  Metric:1
            RX packets:306 errors:0 dropped:0 overruns:0 frame:0
            TX packets:306 errors:0 dropped:0 overruns:0 carrier:0
            collisions:0 txqueuelen:0
            RX bytes:29504 (28.8 Kb)  TX bytes:29504 (28.8 Kb)
```

Bringing an adapter back online is slightly more complicated, since you need to have the IP address and subnet mask ready to configure the adapter with. To configure the Ethernet adapter with the same IP address it had before, you'll issue the following command (notice the **up** at the end of the statement, which brings the NIC online after assigning it an IP address):

```
ifconfig eth0 192.168.99.35 netmask 255.255.255.0 up
```

If you enter the ifconfig command again after configuring the Ethernet adapter, you'll once again see configuration information for eth0 in the output, as follows:

```
eth0        Link encap:Ethernet   HWaddr 00:80:C8:F8:4A:51
            inet addr:192.168.99.35   Bcast:192.168.99.255   Mask:255.255.255.0
            UP BROADCAST RUNNING MULTICAST   MTU:1500   Metric:1
            RX packets:190312 errors:0 dropped:0 overruns:0 frame:0
            TX packets:86955 errors:0 dropped:0 overruns:0 carrier:0
            collisions:0 txqueuelen:100
            RX bytes:30701229 (29.2 Mb)   TX bytes:7878951 (7.5 Mb)
            Interrupt:9 Base address:0x5000


lo          Link encap:Local Loopback
            inet addr:127.0.0.1   Mask:255.0.0.0
            UP LOOPBACK RUNNING   MTU:16436   Metric:1
            RX packets:306 errors:0 dropped:0 overruns:0 frame:0
            TX packets:306 errors:0 dropped:0 overruns:0 carrier:0
            collisions:0 txqueuelen:0
            RX bytes:29504 (28.8 Kb)   TX bytes:29504 (28.8 Kb)
```

TEST DAY TIP

ifconfig will configure a NIC in a Linux machine at the command line in the same way that the Network applet in Control Panel works on a Windows computer.

Network+
OBJECTIVE
4.1.8

dig

The *dig* command is the Linux equivalent to nslookup in Windows – it's used to send name resolution queries to DNS servers to troubleshoot name resolution on a Linux-based client computer. The syntax of the dig command is as follows:

```
dig [@server] [-b address] [-c class] [-f filename] [-k filename] [ -n ] [-p
port#] [-t type] [-x addr] [-y name:key] [name] [type] [class] [queryopt...]


dig [-h]


dig [global-queryopt...] [query...]
```

Unlike nslookup, there is no interactive mode for nslookup; you'll specify all of the necessary command line switches each time you issue the command. Each of these switches specifies certain behavior for the dig command, as follows:

- **@server** This is the name of the computer you're querying for. Unlike nslookup, dig requires you to use the Fully Qualified Domain Name (FQDN) of the host you're looking for. Therefore, **dig server1.mycompany.com** is correctly formatted, while **dig server1** would return an error.

- **-b address** If you have multiple NICs installed on your computer, this switch will specify the IP address that you want the query to be sent from. This is useful if you have NICs attached to different networks and you are trying to isolate which network is experiencing the name resolution failure.

- **-t type** This specifies the type of record you're looking for, like an MX or SRV record.

- **-f filemane** This will allow dig to operate in *batch mode*, where it will perform multiple queries that it reads in from a text file.

- **-p port** This will issue a DNS query on a non-standard port.

EXAM WARNING

Remember that the default DNS port is 53. DNS *queries* use UDP port 53, and DNS *zone transfers* use TCP port 53.

- **+ [no] tcp** Specifies whether to use TCP or UDP when performing a DNS query. **dig www.mycompany.com + tcp** will perform the query using TCP. **dig www.mycompny.com +no tcp** will issue the query using UDP.

- **+domain=*domainname*** Searches for a host using only the domain name that you specify, rather than using the search list that the Linux computer is configured with.

- **+ [no] recursive** Specifies whether to use an iterative or a recursive query. Dig queries are *recursive* by default, so issuing the **dig www.mycompany.com +no recursive** would instruct dig to use an iterative query.

- **+time=*Time*** Specifies the time (in seconds) that dig should wait before deciding that a query has timed out. The default value is 5 seconds.

traceroute

As you can probably guess, *traceroute* is the Linux and UNIX equivalent to tracert on a Windows computer. By typing **traceroute www.mycompany.com** from the command prompt of a Linux computer, you'll see output similar to the following:

```
traceroute to library.airnews.net (10.66.12.202), 30 hops max, 40 byte packets
  1   rbrt3 (192.225.64.50)   4.867 ms   4.893 ms   3.449 ms
  2   519.Hssi.ALTER.NET (10.130.0.17)   6.918 ms   8.721 ms   16.476 ms
  3   113.ATM3.ALTER.NET (172.188.176.38)   6.323 ms   6.123 ms   7.011 ms
  4   192.ATM2-0.ALTER.NET (192.188.176.82)   6.955 ms   15.400 ms   6.684 ms
  5   105.ATM6FW4.ALTER.NET (192.188.136.245)   49.105 ms   49.921 ms   47.371 ms
  6   298.XR2.DFW4.ALTER.NET (192.188.240.77)   48.162 ms   48.052 ms   47.565 ms
  7   194.GW1.DFW1.ALTER.NET (192.188.240.45)   47.886 ms   47.380 ms   50.690 ms
  8   iadfstomer.ALTER.NET (172.39.138.74)   69.827 ms   68.112 ms   66.859 ms
  9   libnews.net (10.66.12.202)   174.853 ms   163.945 ms   147.501 ms
```

Exam Warning

As you can see, the output of the traceroute and tracert commands are nearly identical. Just remember that you'll use *traceroute* on a Linux or UNIX computer, and *tracert* on a Windows computer.

NetWare Tools

When troubleshooting client connectivity to NetWare servers, especially Microsoft Windows clients using the NWLink protocol, the most common culprit tends to be the Ethernet *frame type* that's in use. When you install NWLink on a Windows PC, NWLink will be configured to use an *Auto Detect* feature to determine the correct frame type. In most cases, Auto Detect detects the correct frame type and network number. However, you can run into connectivity issues if your network is using multiple frame types or if a particular machine has the incorrect frame type set. By default, NWLink will set the Ethernet frame type to 802.2. You can verify that the frame type is set correctly as follows:

1. Access the **Local Area Connection** dialog box on the Windows PC. Right-click the desired LAN connection and select **Properties**.

2. Double-click **NWLink IPX/SPX/NetBIOS Compatible Transport Protocol**.

3. On the **General** tab, you can either verify that Auto Detect has been selected in the **Frame type** field, or else manually specify the frame type that should be used.

TEST DAY TIP

You can verify the network number and frame type on a Windows PC by typing **ipxroute config** at the command prompt.

Other Network Troubleshooting Tools

All of the troubleshooting tools we've discussed so far have been concerned with the networking *software* installed on a computer, especially the TCP/IP stack. However, there are a number of tools that you can use to test the physical connectivity on your network. Some of these are tools that you can build yourself, like an Ethernet crossover cable, and some are more sophisticated, like high-powered hardware testers such as an oscilloscope or a tone generator. In this section, we'll look at the different types of hardware testers that you should be familiar with.

Crossover Cables

A standard Ethernet cable will connect the NIC installed in a server or workstation to a wall jack or directly into a hub, switch, or router. For troubleshooting situations, though, you may need to connect two computers directly together In this case, you'll need to create a *crossover cable*, also called a *null modem* cable. You can also use crossover cables to identify which wall plate corresponds to a particular port on a switch or a hub—this is useful if you've taken over administration of a network that doesn't have a good diagram of the physical network layout. The easiest way to create a crossover cable is to cut one end off of a standard Ethernet cable, and then re-arrange the wires on one end of the cable so that they are in the following order (starting at pin 1):

1. White/green
2. Green
3. White/orange
4. White/brown
5. Brown
6. Orange
7. Blue
8. White/blue

Oscilloscope

For in-depth troubleshooting of your network cabling, you can use an oscilloscope to monitor the electrical signal levels as they pass through the Ethernet cable. An oscilloscope displays a small graph that shows how electrical signals change over time. This helps you determine the voltage and frequency of an electrical signal, and if any malfunctioning hardware components are distorting the signal. You can see an illustration of an oscilloscope in Figure 11.7.

Figure 11.7 Display and Controls of An Oscilloscope

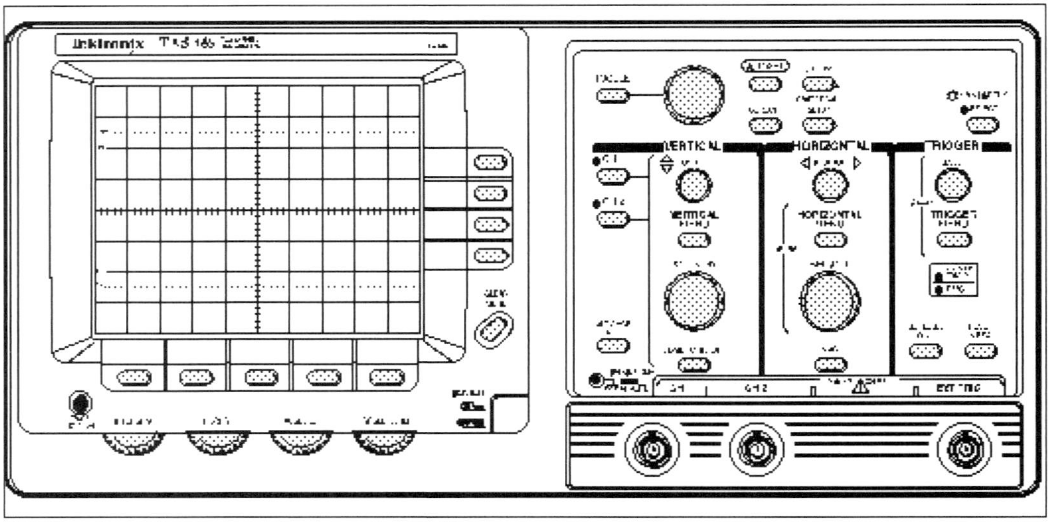

Tone Generator

If you need to troubleshoot telephone connections, especially when dealing with modem connections, you may find yourself in need of a *tone generator*. This is either a piece of software or a hardware device that generates the tones that are used in a telephone system, including a dial tone, busy signal, and ring tone. You can plug a tone generator into a telephone jack to determine if the jack is functioning and able to make and receive calls. You can see a software-based tone generator in Figure 11.8.

Figure 11.8 Test Tone Generator Software for Windows

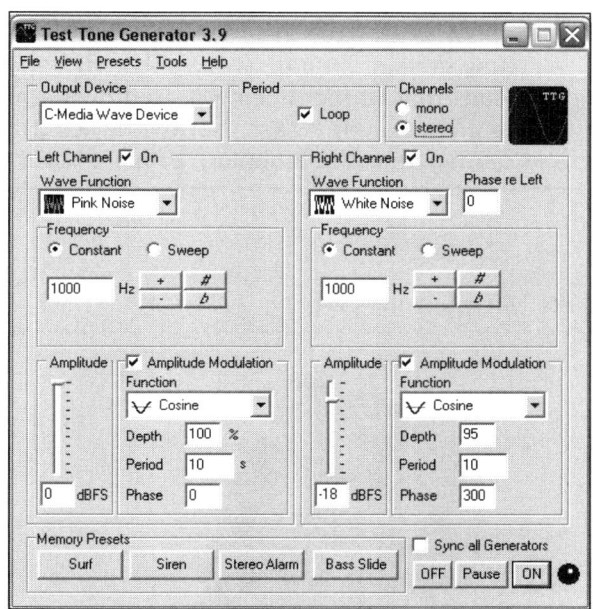

Cable Testers

As you saw when we talked about creating a crossover cable, the wires in Ethernet cables are arranged in pairs, as follows:

- White/orange
- Orange
- White/green
- Blue
- White/blue
- Green
- White/brown
- Brown

You can use a *cable tester* to test for any faults or breaks in an Ethernet cable. Cable testers are designed to allow you to plug both ends of a cable into the tester. If the cable is in good condition, Light Emitting Diode (LED) lights on the tester will light up. If there is a break in the cable (or if the wires are in the wrong order) the LED lights on the tester will not light. You can see an illustration of a Fluke cable tester in Figure 11.9.

NICs, hubs, routers, and switches have their own LED lights that you can use for troubleshooting. A steady green light indicates a solid network connection. A blinking green light means that traffic is being passed over a particular connection. An amber (orange-brown) light means that the device (NIC, router port, hub port, etcetera) is damaged, malfunctioning, or has encountered an error.

Figure 11.9 The Fluke MicroScanner Pro

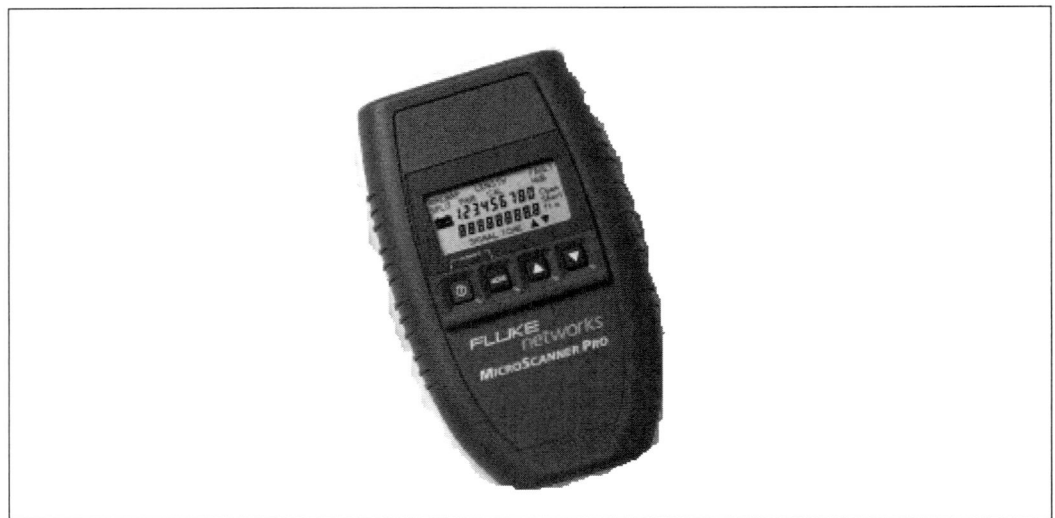

Importance of Network Documentation

After you've done all of the necessary troubleshooting to solve a problem, documenting your troubleshooting activities is vitally important. Putting down on paper the steps you go through, as you perform them, serves several purposes.

First, it helps you to stay organized and perform those steps methodically. If you're writing it down, you're less likely to skip steps, because it's all there in front of you, in visual form. You don't have to wonder, "Did I test that cable segment?" or "Did I check the default gateway setting?" Documenting your actions also provides a valuable record if you end up having to call in an outside consultant or otherwise request someone else's assistance with the problem. You'll save time and money with an outside consultant if you can provide detailed information about what you tried, how you proceeded, and what the results were.

Many network administrators lull themselves into a state of complacency about not documenting their behavior because they see the documentation process as too time-consuming. However, if a mistake occurs because of a failure to document what you've done, or what you were planning to do, the amount of time lost far exceeds the time you would have spent actually writing things down in the first place.

Finally, you should document the troubleshooting and problem resolution process for a very practical reason: History tends to repeat itself, and human memory is imperfect. As you wipe the perspiration off your brow and breathe a silent sigh of relief at having finally tracked down and solved your connectivity problem, you may think that there is no way you will ever, ever forget what you did to fix it—not after going through all of that agony. But a year later, when the same thing occurs again, it's likely that you'll remember only, "This happened before and I fixed it … somehow." The details tend to get lost unless you write them down.

One last caveat on documentation: It's great to have a nice, neatly typed (and maybe even illustrated) troubleshooting log, but if you do your record-keeping on the computer instead of on paper, it's a good idea not only to back it up to tape, floppy, writable CD, or other media, but also to print out a hard copy. It should be a given, but sometimes folks forget that when the computers go down, computerized documents may be inaccessible as well.

Summary of Exam Objectives

In this chapter we talked about the different troubleshooting tools available for you to track down and isolate connectivity problems on your network. We started by looking at the importance of having an overall framework or methodology for tackling networking issues. Before you think about the different tools available for troubleshooting, you first need to determine what the problem actually is. To do this, you need to gather as much information as possible from your users, as well as gathering information from system logs of any devices that are having trouble. You need to figure out what the problem actually is – users can't access the Internet, they can't communicate with another subnet, or maybe they're only having trouble with a particular application. You also need to determine how widespread the failure is—if a problem is only affecting a single computer, the cause will probably be quite different than if it is affecting an entire subnet or your whole network.

To help you further isolate the cause of a problem that you're troubleshooting, you have a number of utilities available in the Windows and Linux operating systems. To test basic TCP/IP connectivity between two hosts, you can use the ping command – this is the equivalent of sending a message saying "Hey, can you hear me?" If you're unable to ping the destination host, you can ping any number of devices along the way to determine where TCP/IP connectivity is failing—start by pinging a computer on the same subnet as the source host, then pinging the default gateway of the source host, and then pinging another host on the same segment as the destination host. You can also use the tracert command on a Windows computer or traceroute on Linux to view the actual path that network traffic takes between two hosts. tracert will ping each router that a network packet travels over to reach its destination to see how well it is responding. You can see the IP address of each router that's between you and your destination, and whether any of these hops is unavailable or slow to respond. On Windows 2000 and XP, you can use the pathping command, which combines the features of ping and tracert into a single utility.

To troubleshoot name resolution issues, you can use nslookup on a Windows computer and dig on Linux. These commands will allow you to verify that your DNS servers are functioning properly and have the correct information with which to answer client queries. For Windows-based computers that rely on NetBIOS, you can use the nbtstat command to troubleshoot NetBIOS name resolution. There are other tools that you can use to release and refresh IP address information that's been assigned by a DHCP server, including ipconfig and winipcfg. To troubleshoot the physical components of your network, including network cables and wall jacks, you should also be familiar with the purpose of an Ethernet crossover cable, as well as cable testers that are designed to test Ethernet cables for flaws or breaks.

Exam Objectives Fast Track

Troubleshooting Methodology

- ☑ When troubleshooting network connectivity, gather as much information from your users as possible.

- ☑ Use your knowledge of your network's physical layout to isolate connectivity issues.

- ☑ Documentation of your network's physical and logical layout is critical in performing troubleshooting in an efficient manner.

The OSI Model

- ☑ A solid understanding of the OSI model will help you troubleshoot connectivity issues that occur at all layers of the model, especially the Physical, Data Link, Network, and Transport Layers.

- ☑ Physical Layer difficulties are often associated with bad network cables, network interface cards, or hubs.

- ☑ The Network Layer usually creates the largest number of troubleshooting issues, since IP address configuration is assigned by an administrator and can change over time, unlike the MAC addresses of the Data Link Layer that typically doesn't change.

Windows Tools

- ☑ Use ping to test basic network connectivity between two hosts.

- ☑ tracert will show you the actual path that network packets take when traveling from one computer to another, and how well these intermediary hops are functioning.

- ☑ nslookup will allow you to troubleshoot name resolution issues relating to DNS. nbtstat is useful for troubleshooting NetBIOS-related issues.

Linux Tools

- ☑ ifconfig is used to configure the network adapter on a Linux or UNIX–based computer, much like the **Network Connections** applet on a Windows computer.

☑   dig is quite similar to nslookup in Windows, and is used to test DNS name resolution for Linux computers

☑   traceroute is the Linux equivalent to tracert in Windows, and produces nearly identical output.

Exam Objectives
Frequently Asked Questions

The following Frequently Asked Questions, answered by the authors of this book, are designed to both measure your understanding of the Exam Objectives presented in this chapter, and to assist you with real-life implementation of these concepts. You will also gain access to thousands of other FAQs at ITFAQnet.com.

Q: I'm working on a Linux computer and have forgotten the syntax of the ifconfig command. Is there any way to quickly look it up without an Internet connection?

A: Use the command **man ifconfig**. man is short for *manual page*, and will produce a help file for many Linux and UNIX-based commands. Use **man ifconfig | more** to force the man output to pause after every full screen.

Q: What is the difference between a recursive DNS query and an iterative query?

A: Iterative queries are used by DNS servers to look up records on behalf of clients. An iterative query is basically a big game of "whisper down the lane", where one DNS server will refer to several other servers to find the answer to a query. A recursive query is performed by a DNS client, where the client will send a query to a server and wait patiently for an answer.

Q: I have a Windows Server 2003 server that runs the World Wide Web service. I want to prevent outside users from being able to ping this server. Money is tight at our company, so we can't afford to buy a physical firewall device to protect this server. How can I protect this server?

A: Enable the built-in firewall that comes with Windows Server 2003. You can configure this firewall to block any ICMP requests to the server, which will prevent outside users from being able to ping the server.

Q: I have recently upgraded my copy of Microsoft Visio to Visio 2003. I used to have the ability to perform an automatic network discovery from the **Tools** menu in Visio. Where is this option in Visio 2003?

A: Unfortunately, Microsoft removed the automatic network discovery feature from Visio 2003. You'll need to purchase a third-party tool like Solar Winds or LAN MapShot. If you are still running Visio 2000 or 2003, you have access to a basic network discovery tool that will map out the IP addresses and hostnames of computers within a Windows domain.

Q: I'm having a hard time remembering the different switches that are available for all of these troubleshooting utilities. Is there an easy way to look these up when I need to use them?

A: Yes. Almost all Windows and Linux command-line utilities have a Help switch, which you can access by using the **–?** or **/?** switch after typing in the name of the command.

Self Test

A Quick Answer Key follows the Self Test questions. For complete questions, answers, and explanations to the Self Test questions in this chapter as well as the other chapters in this book, see the Self Test Appendix.

1. You have been called in to troubleshoot a connectivity issue for a desktop computer running Windows 98. You would like to quickly determine the IP address, subnet mask and default gateway assigned to this computer. Which utility would be the best one to use?

   A. route print

   B. tracert

   C. winipcfg

   D. netstat

2. You are the network administrator for your company. Your predecessor configured a NetWare 4.1 server to provide file and print services for your Windows 2000 and XP clients. You need to determine the frame type that the NetWare server uses to communicate over IPX/SPX so that you can configure a new client to connect to the server. How can you determine what frame type is in use on your network?

A. Type **ipxroute config** from a client that can successfully connect to the NetWare server.

B. Type **netstat** from a client that can successfully connect to the NetWare server.

C. Type **route print** from a client that can successfully connect to the NetWare server.

D. Ping the IP address of the NetWare server from a client that can successfully connect to the NetWare server.

3. You are the network administrator for a small company. Your company relies on LMHOSTS files installed on each individual machine to provide NetBIOS name resolution to communicate with servers and other clients. You have determined that one workstation has a typo in the LMHOSTS file that is preventing it from connecting to the server. You correct the entry in the LMHOSTS file, and now need to allow this client to connect to the server with a minimum amount of disruption for the user. What should you do?

A. Reboot the workstation.

B. Access the command prompt and issue the nbtstat –RR command.

C. Log the user out of the workstation and have them log back in.

D. Access the command prompt and issue the ipconfig command.

4. You are the network administrator for a company that uses a mixture of Windows and Linux computers. One of your Windows 2000 servers is running the WINS service, and you have created static WINS entries for your Linux computers. A NIC in one of the Linux computers fails and has to be replaced by a technician, however, the technician did not provide you with the MAC address of the new NIC before he left. The replacement NIC has already been assigned an IP address. From the console of the Linux computer, what utility can you use to determine the MAC address of the new NIC to update your WINS server entries?

A. ifconfig

B. dig

C. nbtstat

D. nslookup

5. You are the network administrator for an IIS web server running Windows 2000. You have recently configured a new firewall and are attempting to determine if clients are still able to connect to the Web server. You run the netstat –A command and see the following output:

```
Active Connections


Proto    Local Address       Foreign Address        State
TCP      example:http        204.96.18.5:26861      ESTABLISHED
TCP      example:http        204.96.18.115:28246    ESTABLISHED
TCP      example:http        215.96.18.45:28890     ESTABLISHED
TCP      example:http        151.96.14.62:29097     ESTABLISHED
TCP      example:http        204.96.18.5:29477      ESTABLISHED
TCP      example:http        204.96.18.5:29759      ESTABLISHED
TCP      example:http        204.96.18.5:29860      ESTABLISHED
```

What can you determine from this output?

A. Network clients are unable to connect to your Web server.

B. Your Web server is listening for client connections on non-standard ports like 26861 and 28246.

C. Network clients are successfully connecting to port 21 on your Web server.

D. Network clients are successfully connecting to port 80 on your Web server.

6. You are troubleshooting network connectivity on a Windows 2000 Professional workstation. You issue the route print command to view the workstation's routing table, and see the following information:

```
=============================================================================
Interface List
0x1 ......................... MS TCP Loopback interface
0x2 ...00 0e 35 1a e2 8d ..... Intel(R) PRO/Wireless 2200BG Network Connection
=============================================================================
Active Routes:
Network Destination        Netmask          Gateway        Interface  Metric
          0.0.0.0          0.0.0.0      192.168.1.1    192.168.1.100       30
        127.0.0.0        255.0.0.0        127.0.0.1        127.0.0.1        1
      192.168.1.0    255.255.255.0    192.168.1.100    192.168.1.100       30
    192.168.1.100  255.255.255.255        127.0.0.1        127.0.0.1       30
    192.168.1.255  255.255.255.255    192.168.1.100    192.168.1.100       30
        224.0.0.0        240.0.0.0    192.168.1.100    192.168.1.100       30
  255.255.255.255  255.255.255.255    192.168.1.100    192.168.1.100        1
  255.255.255.255  255.255.255.255    192.168.1.100                3        1
Default Gateway:       192.168.1.1
=============================================================================
```

In this routing table, what does *224.0.0.0* in the *Network Destination* column indicate?

A. The multicast address

B. The local broadcast address

C. The default gateway

D. The subnet mask

7. You are working on the help desk for a small company that has a router with the IP address 192.168.1.100. You use tracert to determine why you cannot access a particular website, and see the following output:

```
1    <1 ms     <1 ms     <1 ms    [192.168.72.1]
2    <1 ms     <1 ms     <1 ms    [192.168.1.100]
3      *         *         *       Request timed out.
4      *         *         *       Request timed out.
5      *         *         *       Request timed out.
6      *         *         *       Request timed out.
```

You are able to access other remote websites successfully, as well as accessing resources on the internal LAN. Based on this output, what is a possible reason why you cannot access this remote website?

A. Your workstation has been configured with the incorrect subnet mask.

B. The remote Web server is down or overloaded.

C. Your router is down or overloaded.

D. Your router has been configured with the incorrect default gateway.

8. You are the network administrator of a small company. You have just purchased a new PC for the president of your company, and you need to connect it directly to his old PC in order to transfer her files before making the switch. Which tool will allow you to do this?

A. Standard Ethernet cable

B. Cable tester

C. Crossover cable

D. Tone generator

9. You are the help desk manager for a large multi-site office. You receive several calls stating that users are unable to connect to a particular file server. You ping the server from your desk and receive several "Request Timed Out" messages. You walk over to the server, check the NIC on the back of the server and notice that one of the LED lights is glowing amber. The server's desktop is available and the keyboard and mouse are responsive. Other hosts on the same subnet as this server are accessible by users. What is the most likely cause of this connectivity failure?

A. The operating system has crashed and the server should be rebooted.

B. The network cable connecting the server to its hub is damaged and should be replaced.

C. The NIC installed in the server is damaged and should be repaired or replaced.

D. The NIC installed in the server should be configured for full duplex operations.

10. You are the new network administrator for a Windows network. As part of your administrative duties, you are responsible for maintaining your company's telephone and PBX systems. Your company has recently purchased the office building adjacent to the current facility to allow for expansion. There are a number of telephone jacks in the new facility that are not listed on any network diagrams, and you need to determine if they are functional. Which tool should you use to determine this?

    A. Null model cable

    B. Tone generator

    C. Oscilloscope

    D. Crossover cable

11. You are troubleshooting a remote user's home computer after she reports to you that she is unable to browse any websites. You would like to determine whether her cable modem is functional. You examine the LED lights on the cable modem, and see one light that is a solid green and a second light that is flickering green. What can you determine from the status of these LED lights?

    A. The cable modem has a network connection and is passing network traffic.

    B. The cable modem has a network connection, but is not passing any network traffic.

    C. The cable modem has no network connection and is not passing any network traffic.

    D. The cable modem is experiencing a hardware malfunction and is not passing any network traffic.

12. You are the network administrator for a small health services company. Your company's network uses a DHCP server to provide IP addressing configuration for 50 workstations, using an address range from 192.168.99.1 through 192.168.99.254, with a Class C subnet mask and a default gateway of 192.168.99.1. You have recently configured a Linux server to operate as the web server for your company's Internet presence, and you need this server to have a statically assigned IP address. Once you configure the IP address for this server, you attempt to access your company's Web page and are unable to do so. You use the ifconfig command to verify the IP configuration of the Linux server. Based on the output below, which configuration item do you need to change?

```
eth0        Link encap:Ethernet   HWaddr 00:80:C8:F8:4A:51

            inet addr:192.168.98.35  Bcast:192.168.99.255  Mask:255.255.255.0

            UP BROADCAST RUNNING MULTICAST  MTU:1500  Metric:1

            RX packets:190312 errors:0 dropped:0 overruns:0 frame:0

            TX packets:86955 errors:0 dropped:0 overruns:0 carrier:0

            collisions:0 txqueuelen:100

            RX bytes:30701229 (29.2 Mb)  TX bytes:7878951 (7.5 Mb)

            Interrupt:9 Base address:0x5000
```

   A. HWaddr

   B. Inet addr

   C. Bcast

   D. Mask

13. You are the network administrator for a small office containing five workstations and a single file server. You are troubleshooting a connectivity failure on a single workstation that is unable to browse the Internet; all other workstations are able to communicate without issue. As your first troubleshooting step, you ping the loopback interface of the workstation that is experiencing trouble and you receive the output shown here. Based on this output, what is the most likely cause of the connectivity failure?

```
Pinging IBM-A38375FF22E [127.0.0.1] with 32 bytes of data:

Request timed out.

Request timed out.

Request timed out.

Request timed out.


Ping statistics for 127.0.0.1:

    Packets: Sent = 4, Received = 0, Lost = 4 (100% loss),
```

   A. The workstation is configured with the incorrect IP address.

   B. The TCP/IP stack on the workstation has become corrupted and has to be re-installed.

   C. The workstation is configured with the incorrect default gateway.

   D. The router for your company's network is unresponsive.

Self Test Quick Answer Key

For complete questions, answers, and explanations to the Self Test questions in this chapter as well as the other chapters in this book, see the Self Test Appendix.

1. **C**		8. **C**
2. **A**		9. **C**
3. **B**		10. **B**
4. **A**		11. **A**
5. **D**		12. **B**
6. **A**		13. **B**
7. **B**		

## Chapter 12

NETWORK+

Network Troubleshooting Methodology

Domain IV Objectives in this Chapter:

4.4 Given a troubleshooting scenario involving a client accessing remote network services, identify the cause of the problem (for example, file services, print services, authentication failure, protocol configuration, physical connectivity, and Small Office/Home Office router).

4.5 Given a troubleshooting scenario between a client and the following server environments, identify the cause of a stated problem:

4.5.1 UNIX / Linux / Mac OS X Server

4.5.2 NetWare

4.5.3 Windows

4.5.4 Appleshare IP

4.6 Given a scenario, determine the impact of modifying, adding or removing network services (for example, DHCP, DNS, and WINS) for network resources and users.

4.7 Given a troubleshooting scenario involving a network with a particular physical topology (for example, bus, star, mesh, or ring) and including a network diagram, identify the network area affected and the cause of the stated failure.

4.8 Given a network troubleshooting scenario involving an infrastructure (for example, wired or wireless) problem, identify the cause of a stated problem (for example, bad media, interference, network hardware, or environment).

4.9 Given a network problem scenario, select an appropriate course of action based on a logical troubleshooting strategy. This strategy can include the following steps:

4.9.1 Identify the symptoms and potential causes

Introduction

Congratulations! You've made it almost all the way through the Network+ exam preparation guide. You've learned all about the physical and logical components that make up a network, and how to install and configure the TCP/IP (Transmission Control Protocol/Internet Protocol) protocol suite. You've also learned about the different protocols that make up the TCP/IP suite as well as how they map to the OSI (Open Systems Interconnect) model. This includes the Internet Protocol, which is the workhorse of the TCP/IP suite that handles the "heavy lifting" of routing TCP/IP traffic from one host to another. You've also learned about TCP/IP's two session layer protocols: TCP, and the User Datagram Protocol (UDP). TCP is a connection-oriented protocol that's used when each Session Layer packet has to be acknowledged by the computer it's being sent to. UDP is connectionless, which is useful for low-overhead connections where speed is at a premium. Both are Transparent Layer Protocol. You've also seen the Internet Control Message Protocol (ICMP), which is used for TCP/IP troubleshooting. In our last chapter, we talked extensively about the various utilities that are available to troubleshoot connectivity problems on a network. In our final chapter, we'll take the information from Chapter 11 and learn how to use it in a real-world situation to troubleshoot network connectivity issues. We'll revisit the OSI model and the TCP/IP-based DoD (Department of Defense) model. We'll also review the components of the suite of protocols that make up the TCP/IP stack and how common connectivity devices, such as repeaters, bridges, routers, and switches are used to expand or segment TCP/IP networks. All of this is critical information to have at your fingertips when you're troubleshooting because, just as a physician is better able to treat a sick patient if he knows the person's background, characteristics, and how the patient normally behaves when he is not ill, you will be at a big advantage when you're confronted with "sick" or badly functioning networks if you understand your network's "anatomy" and components well. And the TCP/IP suite of protocols that most networks depend on to communicate is one of the most important "body parts."

The objective of this chapter is to give you a detailed review of TCP/IP that will allow you to recognize symptoms of network troubles and to diagnose and correct any errors or misconfigurations that you find. We all know that a healthy network makes for a happy network administrator, and the information you find in this chapter will help you in preparing both for the Network+ exam and for your journey into the real world of network administration and troubleshooting. To help you with this, we'll go through each layer of the OSI model and talk about the different troubleshooting steps you can take at each one. For example, the Physical Layer is concerned with physical connectivity between two computers, so here you'll look for broken cables or a malfunctioning NIC (network interface card) or hub. The Data Link layer is where switches, bridges, and Ethernet frame types operate, so you'll troubleshoot this layer by examining all of these entities. We'll start at the Physical Layer, which is the lowest layer of the OSI model, and work all the way up to the Application Layer. This chapter will help you put together all of the concepts you've learned throughout this study guide, to help you use them in troubleshooting real-world issues that you might encounter on a network.

Exam Warning

Be sure that you really understand what is really happening at each layer of the OSI model. It's important for the Network+ exam that you're able to recognize the different network protocols and devices that operate at each level, rather than just memorizing the "Please Do Not Throw Sausage Pizza Away" or "All People Seem To Need Data Processing" mnemonics

How to Use the OSI Model in Troubleshooting

As a network administrator, you should be familiar with the common networking models. In Chapter 5 we initially covered the OSI and DoD models. In this chapter we will learn how to map those layers to troubleshooting that may be performed at each level. For example, if you had a problem with a wireless access point (WAP), which layer would you start with? Why would you select that layer and what could be the issue? What if you had misconfigured your encryption settings for WEP (Wireless Encryption Protocol), and cannot connect to the wireless network? We'll look at examples like these to see how each layer of the OSI model fits into an overall troubleshooting strategy as you prepare for the Network+ exam.

The Purpose of Networking Models

In Chapter 5 we covered network models in depth. We also covered why they are important. One of the main reasons why using network models is so important is to give you the ability to isolate issues to specific layers of a protocol stack to help you troubleshoot a problem on a network. You'll often hear the OSI model referenced when you're troubleshooting a problem, such as, "We have a Layer 3 switch problem." Because understanding the OSI model is so critical to the network troubleshooting process, it's imperative that you master the OSI model's layering.

A network protocol is a set of rules used by computers to communicate. Protocols had to be developed so that two computers attempting to transfer data back and forth would be able to understand one another. Some people will describe protocols as "languages," but this isn't entirely accurate and can cause confusion, since computer languages are an entirely different concept. A *protocol* is more like the *syntax* of the language, which refers to the order in which the words are put together, rather than the language itself.

The first networking protocols were proprietary; that is, each networking vendor developed its own set of rules. Computers using an individual vendor's protocol would be able to communicate with each other, but not with computers that were using the networking product of a different vendor. This had the effect of locking a business into a particular product; the business would always have to use the same vendor's products in order to maintain compatibility.

The solution to this problem was the development of protocols based on *open standards*. Organizations such as the ISO (International Organization for Standardization) were charged with overseeing the definition and control of these standards and publishing them so they would be available to any vendor that wanted to create products that adhered to them. The advantage to the consumer is that no longer is he forced to patronize a single vendor. The advantage to the vendor is that its products are more widely compatible, and therefore can be used in networks that started out using a different vendor's products.

A *model* provides an easy-to-understand description of the networking architecture and serves as the framework for the standards. The OSI model has become a common reference point for discussion of network protocols and connection devices.

As we look at the OSI and DoD models, you'll see that they both use *layers* to represent areas of functionality. In OSI terms, each of the layered specifications uses the services of the layer below it to build an *enriched service*. The layered approach provides a logical division of responsibility, where each layer handles only the functions that are specific to that layer. You can think of this like the teamwork exhibited by a good assembly-line crew that's building an automobile. One worker may be responsible for fitting a wheel onto the axis, another for inserting and tightening the screws, and so forth. There are several advantages to this type of working model:

- Each worker only has to be concerned with his or her own area of responsibility.

- Each worker becomes extremely proficient at his or her particular job through constant repetition.

- Working together in sequence, the team of workers is able to produce the final product much more quickly and efficiently than one person or than a group of people with no assigned responsibilities could.

- If something goes wrong (for instance, if a particular part was put on incorrectly), the supervisor knows who to blame for the problem.

Likewise, when the networking protocols are divided into layers, communication generally flows more smoothly, and when it doesn't, troubleshooting is easier because you are better able to narrow down the source of the problem to a specific layer. We'll be using the ISO's OSI model to help us in troubleshooting network connectivity issues.

Reviewing the OSI Model

You should remember that the OSI model consists of seven layers. When one computer communicates with another one, data at the sending computer is passed from one layer to the next until the Physical Layer finally puts it out onto the network cable. At the receiving end, it travels back up in reverse order. Although the data travels down the layers on one side and up the layers on the other, the logical communication link is between each layer and its matching counterpart, as shown in Figure 12.1.

Figure 12.1 Each Layer of the OSI Model Communicates with the Corresponding Layer

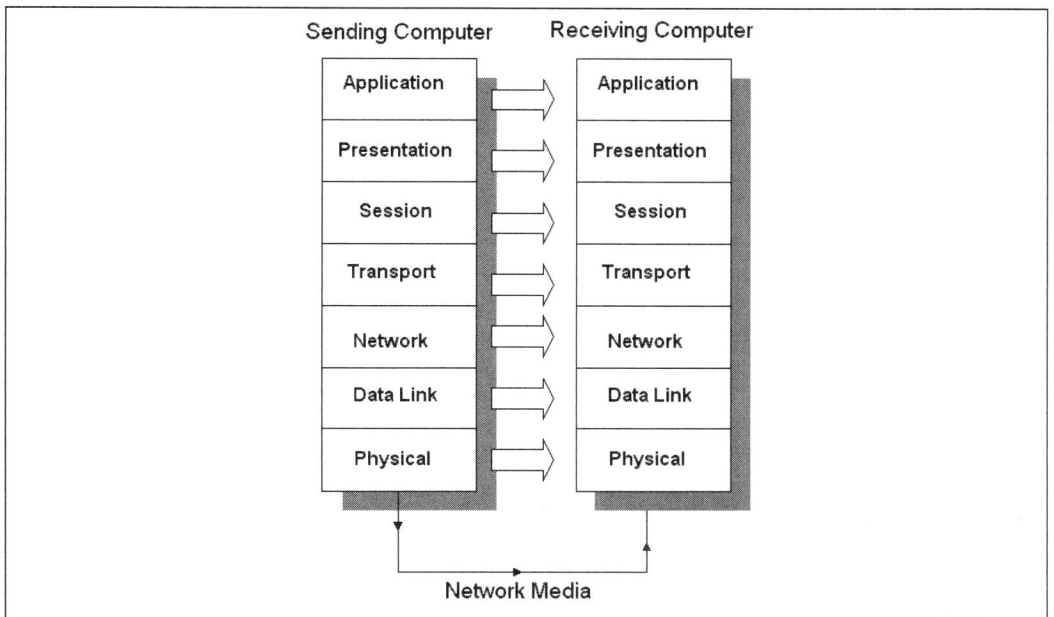

Here's how it works: as the data goes down through the layers, it is *encapsulated* or enclosed within a larger unit as each layer adds its own header information. When it reaches the receiving computer, the process occurs in reverse; the information is passed upward through each layer, and as it does so, the encapsulation information is evaluated and then stripped off one layer at a time. The information added by the Network Layer, for example, will be read and processed by the Network Layer on the receiving side. After processing, each layer removes the header information that was added by its corresponding layer on the sending side. It is finally presented to the Application Layer, and then to the user's application at the receiving computer. At this point, the data is in the form it was in when sent by the user application at the source machine. Figure 12.2 illustrates how the header information is added to the data as it progresses down through the layers.

Figure 12.2 Each Layer Adds its Own Header Information

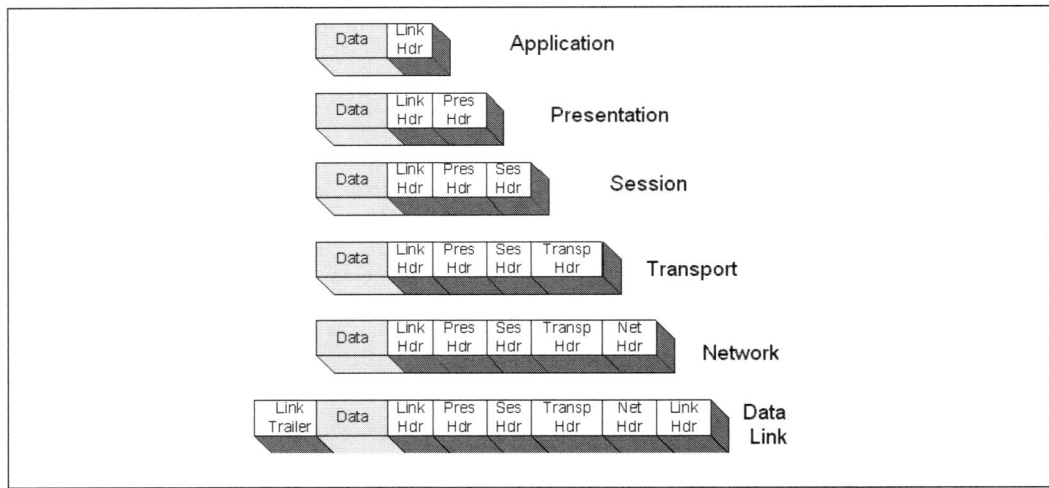

 # Establishing a Troubleshooting Strategy

This chapter will provide a number of examples of how to troubleshoot network issues. The most important thing that you can do when troubleshooting is to be organized and methodical in your approach to solving problems. If you work in a rushed fashion, you're likely to miss a crucial troubleshooting step or forget what you did to solve the problem the next time it occurs.

In general, you can break down the steps necessary to troubleshoot a network issue into the following seven steps:

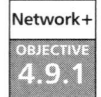 1. **Identify the symptoms and potential causes** The first step is determining exactly what's wrong, and if there's actually a problem at all. For

example, if you upgrade the speed of your company's Internet connection so that a file transfer that used to take 30 seconds now takes no time at all, a user might think that the file transfer didn't work. In this case there really wasn't an error, but the user *thought* that there was a problem because something she was used to had suddenly changed. So your first step should be in determining the exact symptoms of the problem. Is a user unable to access the Internet entirely, or is it only that she is unable to receive her e-mail while Web browsing is working fine? Having this information at hand will help you determine the potential causes of an issue.

etwork+
BJECTIVE
1.9.2

2. **Identify the affected area**   Is only one user having trouble accessing the Internet, or is there an issue that's affecting an entire subnet or your entire network? If all users on a particular subnet are experiencing connectivity troubles, you might suspect the default gateway or the network connection between that subnet and the rest of your network. If the issue is restricted to a single user, you'll be more likely to examine the specific user's workstation to check for hardware failures or software misconfigurations.

etwork+
BJECTIVE
1.9.3

3. **Establish what has changed**   Once you've determined what the problem is, you should try to find out if anything has changed on the local computer, or on the router or switch if the problem is affecting multiple computers. I can't tell you the number of times I've scratched my head trying to solve a connectivity problem only to find out that my router administrators were "messing with the routers this morning" and changed a critical setting that created the outage that I was experiencing. Knowing what has changed on a network will usually give you a good starting point from which you can begin the troubleshooting process.

etwork+
BJECTIVE
1.9.4

4. **Select the most probable cause**   Based on the information you gathered in the first three steps, and using the troubleshooting tools we covered in Chapter 11, try to determine the most likely reason why you are experiencing a connectivity failure. Keep in mind that your first guess might be incorrect and that there may be more than one cause at work, so don't get discouraged if you need to eliminate your first, second, and even third guesses.

twork+
BJECTIVE
.9.5

5. **Implement an action plan and solution, including potential effects**   The first part of this seems straightforward enough – "Fix the problem!" But many administrators will overlook the second half of the statement, which is just as important: you don't want to do something to fix one problem that will only end up causing another (potentially worse) problem. So think carefully about the potential effects of any troubleshooting steps that you are going to take, especially if it involves steps that you're taking on a server, router, or other device that many users rely on. For example, you may decide that you need to stop and restart the WWW publishing service on your Microsoft Web server

to solve an issue being experienced by one particular user, but you need to plan this carefully since it will affect every user that's connected to the Web server. You should be even more careful in changing any configuration items on a server or router so that the change you're making doesn't create more issues than it corrects.

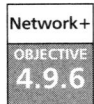

6. **Test the result** In addition to determining if your solution actually fixed the problem you were experiencing, you should also look at the overall connectivity on your network to make sure that you didn't inadvertently create another issue by implementing the fix you chose in Step 5.

7. **Identify the results and document the solution and process** Even though you probably think that you'll never forget how to fix this problem, especially if it's one that you had to work at solving for hours and hours, the simple fact of the matter is that if you don't write down your solution, odds are quite good that you won't remember if the issue recurs many months down the line or won't be able to reproduce it precisely. You should document the information that you gathered in each of these steps: how the problem manifested itself, the systems that were affected, the solution and how you implemented it, and any side effects that came about as a result of implementing the fix. Taking a few minutes to do this now can save you hours down the line when you find that you need to retrace your steps.

Troubleshooting the Physical Layer

In many ways, the Physical Layer is the easiest to troubleshoot because it deals with devices and concepts that are concrete and tangible—you can actually *see* the network cabling and NICs that exist at the Physical Layer, whereas nobody has ever been able to tell me what an IP address looks like. The Physical Layer deals with such things as the type of signal transmission used, the cable type, and the actual layout or path of the network wiring. These are things we can see, touch, or at least easily represent with a drawing or diagram. Because of this, the functions of the Physical Layer devices (NICs, cables, connectors, hubs, and repeaters) are also relatively easy to understand.

Physical Layer devices are mostly items that you'll find in any networking equipment catalog. The basics are deceptively simple: you insert a network card into an expansion slot on each computer, plug a piece of cable into each network card, and plug the other end of each cable into a hub. But leafing through any type of an equipment catalog will reveal that Physical Layer issues are a little more complex. Some cable manufacturers offer literally thousands of different cables, and the variety of available network cards and connectivity devices is just as overwhelming. Getting a network up and running at the Physical Layer requires a good bit of knowledge about what works with what and which hardware type is best for your particular situation.

The NIC is the hardware device most essential to establishing communication between computers. Although there are ways to connect computers without a NIC (using a modem over the phone lines or via a serial null modem cable, for instance), in most cases where there is a network, there is a NIC (or more accurately, at least one NIC for each participating computer). The bottom line when selecting a NIC for any device is this: the NIC must match the bus type for which you have an open slot in the computer, it must be of the correct media access type, it must have the correct connector for the cable your network uses, and it must be rated to transfer data at the proper speed. Ethernet normally transmits at 10, 100, or 1000 Mbps, and Token Ring runs at 4 or 16 Mbps.

The network *media* is the cable or wireless technology on which the signal is sent. Cable types include thin and thick coaxial cable (similar to cable TV cable), twisted-pair (such as used for modern telephone lines, available in both shielded and unshielded types), or fiber optic (which sends pulses of light through thin strands of glass or plastic for fast, reliable communication, but is expensive and difficult to work with). Wireless media include radio waves, laser, infrared, and microwave.

Hubs and *repeaters* are devices that operate at the Physical Layer. Repeaters connect two network segments (usually thin or thick coax) and boost the signal so the distance of the cabling can be extended past the normal limits at which attenuation, or weakening, interferes with the reliable transmission of the data. Hubs are generally used with Ethernet twisted-pair cable, and most modern hubs are repeaters with multiple ports. Hubs also strengthen the signal before passing it back out to the computers attached to it. Hubs can be categorized as follows:

- Active hubs are the ones just described. They serve as both a connection point and a signal booster. Data that comes in is passed back out on all ports.

- Passive hubs serve as connection points only; they do not boost the signal before passing it on. Passive hubs do not require electricity and thus won't have a power cord as active hubs do.

- Intelligent or "smart" hubs include a microprocessor chip with diagnostic capabilities, so you can monitor the transmission on individual ports.

The NIC is another device that functions at the Physical Layer, and is responsible for preparing the data to be sent out over the network media. Exactly how that preparation is done depends on which media is being used; a Token Ring NIC is different from an Ethernet NIC, for example. It logically would have to be, since they use different access methods. And even though 10Base2, 10Base5, and 10BaseT Ethernet networks all use CSMA/CD (Carrier Sense Multiple Access/Collision Detection) as their access method, they use different cable and connector types; however, it is possible to get a "combo" card that has connectors for all three.

Another consideration at the Physical Layer is whether the signaling method will use the entire bandwidth of the cable to transmit the data, or only use one frequency.

When all frequencies are used, the transmission method is called *baseband*. If only part of the bandwidth is used (thus allowing other signals to share the bandwidth), it is referred to as *broadband*. Traditionally, baseband transmission has been associated with digital signaling and broadband with analog, but this does not always hold true. For instance, Digital Subscriber Line (DSL) is a high-speed technology offered by many telephone companies for Internet connectivity. DSL is a broadband technology because it uses only a part of the wire to transmit data. Voice communication can take place simultaneously on the same cable, using a different frequency than is being used by the data communications. Cable television is another example of broadband transmission, bringing dozens of different channels into your home on just one coaxial cable.

Another important Physical Layer issue is the layout, or topology, of the network. This refers to whether the cables are arranged in a line going directly from computer to computer (bus), in a circle going from computer to computer with the last connecting back to the first (ring), or in a spoke-like fashion with each connecting directly to a central hub (star). A fourth topology, the mesh, is used when every computer is connected to every other computer, creating redundant data pathways and high fault tolerance, at the cost of increasing complexity as the network grows. Wireless communications can use the cellular topology that is widely used for wireless telephone networks. In this case, an area is divided into slightly overlapping cells, representing connection points.

The physical layout of the network will influence other factors, such as which media access method (and thus which cable type) is used. All of the Physical Layer factors (cable type, access method, topology, etcetera), when considered together, define the *architecture* of the network. Popular network architectures include Ethernet, ARCnet, Token Ring, and AppleTalk.

Layer 1 Troubleshooting

When troubleshooting the Physical Layer, you'll be most concerned with NICs, network cables, and hubs. We'll start by looking at potential issues with NICs, and ways to troubleshoot and correct them. Configuring the NIC at the Physical Layer is the first step in creating a TCP/IP connection. Although an improperly configured card is not a protocol-specific issue, it may be mistaken for one, and you can lose a great deal of time trying to troubleshoot TCP/IP when the problem actually lies with the NIC itself. Thus, it's important for you to know how to determine when a TCP/IP connection is failing due to a lower-level problem such as one with the NIC or with physical cabling.

One easy way to determine that the problem lies at the Physical Layer, and not with a specific protocol, is to attempt to establish a connection using a different protocol. If your computer is unable to communicate with others on the network using TCP/IP, but can make the connection when NetBEUI or NWLink is installed on the machines, you can surmise that the problem lies in the way that TCP/IP is configured, and you can start troubleshooting the protocol configuration accordingly. If you still have no luck in making a connection with other network transport protocols, it is likely that you have a problem with the hardware or the hardware drivers. This simple test can save you much time and effort when you begin the troubleshooting process.

In addition, when you are troubleshooting physical devices like cables or NICs, it's also helpful to have spare equipment to swap out so that you can quickly determine the cause of the problem. If you suspect that the network cable is at fault, switch it with one that you know works; if connectivity is restored, then you know that the cable was the culprit. If switching the cable doesn't help, try using a different wall jack or another port on the switch or hub. If switching to a different port solves the problem, then you have isolated the point of failure.

The Role of the NIC

The NIC (also sometimes called the network adapter, or just the network card) plays an essential role in TCP/IP and other network communications. The NIC is the device that physically joins the computer and the cable or other network media, but its function is more complex than that. Network cards also have memory chips, called *buffers*, in which information is stored so that if the data comes in or goes out too quickly, it can "rest" there while the bottleneck clears until there is room for it to pass onto the cable or up into the computer's components.

It is essential that you ensure that the NIC installed in the computer is the proper type for both the media and architecture used by your network. For instance, Ethernet and Token Ring require different types of NICs. This is because of the different ways in which the media access methods function. And, of course, the card must have the proper connector for the cable type being used. These are basic, relatively straightforward issues, but don't overlook them when troubleshooting connectivity problems.

If you are installing a NIC on a Windows-based computer, be sure to check the Windows Hardware Compatibility List (HCL) or Windows Catalog to ensure that your card is supported. The list can be accessed from the Microsoft website at www.microsoft.com/hcl. Although devices not listed may still work with Windows, if your card is on the list you can be confident that it has been tested and is compatible with the operating system.

Driver Issues

Like other hardware devices, the NIC requires a software driver to provide the interface between the operating system and the card. Be sure the driver that is designated for your specific model of NIC is installed and that it is the most recent version. In many cases, simply installing an updated NIC driver can solve countless connection problems.

Recent Windows operating systems like 2000, XP, and 2003, support a large number of common brands and models of NICs, and the drivers are included on the Windows installation CDs. However, these may not be the latest versions. Always check the manu-facturer's website for a download area where you can obtain the latest drivers. Since Windows 2000, XP, and 2003, unlike NT 4.0, are plug-and-play operating systems, sup-ported cards are more likely to be automatically detected and the drivers installed from the Windows installation files (or you will be prompted to supply the disk or network location). Be cautioned again, however, that the drivers installed by the operating system may be outdated. In Exercise 12.1, we'll walk through the steps of updating a driver for a NIC installed on a Windows 2000 PC.

EXERCISE 12.1

UPDATING DRIVERS

1. Click **Start | Settings | Control Panel | System**. Select the **Hardware** tab, and click **Device Manager**. The list of installed devices will be dis-played, as shown in Figure 12.3.

Figure 12.3 Windows 2000 Device Manager

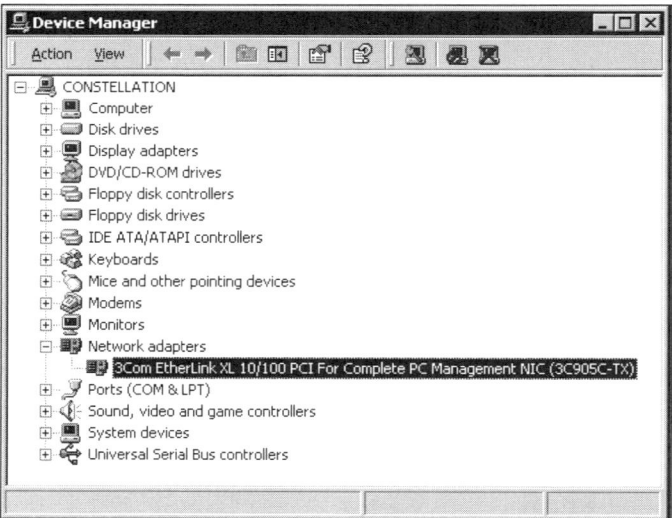

2. Click the **+** sign next to **Network Adapters**. Double-click the NIC installed in this computer and select the **Driver** tab. You'll see a screen similar to the one shown in Figure 12.4

Figure 12.4 Updating the Device Driver

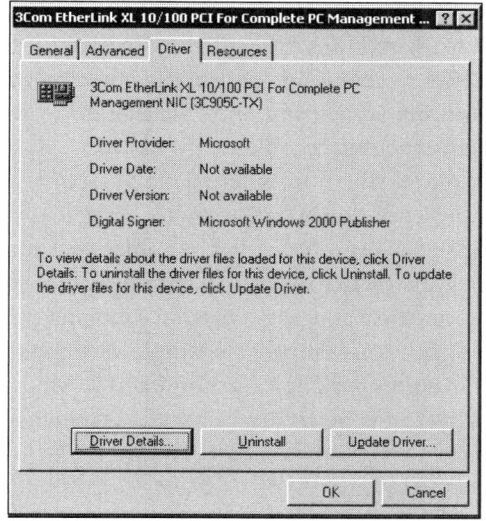

3. Click **Update Driver** and follow the prompts to update the driver to the latest version.
4. Click **OK** when you're finished, and reboot your PC.

Problems with Cables and Other Network Media

Another type of problem that can mimic TCP/IP protocol configuration problems is damaged, defective, or improperly installed cables or other network media. Broken or shorted cables can be detected with a cable tester. Some of the more sophisticated (and more expensive) LAN (local area network) testers will even pinpoint the exact location of the break.

As a network administrator, you may have other personnel who handle hardware and cabling. It is important, however, that you are able to recognize the symptoms of Physical Layer problems so that you will know when to call in the technicians, rather than spend your time attempting to "fix what isn't broken." Damage to the media is not the only factor when considering Physical Layer problems. All network architectures, for example, Ethernet, Token Ring, and AppleTalk, include specifications that must be met concerning networking equipment and media. If those rules are ignored, connectivity may be lost completely or you may experience intermittent problems.

Some instances in which ignoring these specifications can result in difficulties in establishing or maintaining a connection include cable type and grade, and the limitations on the allowable segment length for various network/cable types. Be sure that the cabling for your network meets specifications for the particular architecture. For instance, a 10Base2 network requires not just thin coaxial cable, but a particular type of thin coax: RG-58 A/U (the cable grade is usually indicated on the side of the cable itself). Don't try to substitute something else that is close or looks similar; you will be setting yourself up for connectivity problems if you do.

You may even run into a situation where a cable technician (or perhaps an administrator with little hardware experience) attempts to replace a broken or bad length of thin coax cable with RG-58 U or even RG-59 (the cable used for cable TV). Therefore, in checking the Physical Layer for the source of a connectivity problem, be certain not only that the cable is connected and appears to be undamaged, but that the cable type meets the necessary specifications. Another example of improper cable type would be substituting Category 3 twisted-pair for Cat 5 on a 100 Mbps (100BaseT) or Gigabit Ethernet network. Cable type is generally indicated on the cable itself.

Cable Length Issues

You are aware that because of the susceptibility of copper cabling to *attenuation*, or signal loss over distance, network specifications place limits on the acceptable length of a segment of cable, depending on the architecture and cable type. Violating the length specifications may be tempting, especially if you only need to go "a tiny bit further" in order to get the cable to a specific office or other location. You might get away with it—the cable does not just automatically stop working when you exceed the specified distance. But going beyond these limitations can cause you to have connectivity problems that you might easily mistake for software- or protocol-related problems when the real trouble is at the Physical Layer.

Troubleshooting Physical Layer Devices

Usually the type of device we associate with an internetwork is the router, which works at the Network Layer in the OSI model. But we also should remember that there are other, lower-level devices that can be used for such purposes as:

- Extending the distance limitations of network cable.
- Connecting network segments that use different media types, for instance, thin coax and UTP (unshielded twisted-pair).
- Segmenting the network to reduce traffic without dividing the network into separate IP subnets.

Because repeaters and hubs operate at the Physical Layer, problems affecting these devices will be physical problems, or hardware problems. This layer is not concerned with high-level protocols like TCP and IP, and problems with these devices will interfere with communications regardless of the network transport protocols being used.

However, Physical Layer device problems can mimic TCP/IP protocol configuration problems. Because of this, you should always consider the Physical Layer when troubleshooting connectivity problems. If the hardware itself doesn't work, all the software reconfiguration in the world won't solve the problem.

Locate the Source of the Problem

If you are unable to establish a connection between computers, you need to first verify that TCP/IP is properly installed (by pinging the loopback address as discussed in Chapter 11), check the configuration and operability of the NIC as we discussed earlier in this section, and confirm that there are no shorts, breaks, or other problems with the cable. If you still are unable to connect, look at your connectivity devices such as repeaters and hubs:

- Ensure that the device has power.

- Ensure that the computers' NICs are communicating with the device (by checking status lights).

- Ensure that devices are installed in accordance with the IEEE (Institute of Electrical and Electronic Engineers) specifications for the particular network architecture.

- Ensure that all ports on the device are functional by checking for a green LED (light emitting diode) lights when you attach a computer to the port via a network cable.

The last includes compliance with any distance limitations for the media being used and, for coax networks, the restrictions imposed by the *5-4-3 rule*. This rule states that on a 10Base2 or 10Base5 network (using coax cable and a bus configuration), you should have no more than five segments, connected by no more than four repeaters, and that only three of those segments should be populated. A populated node is one that has nodes (computers or other network devices) attached to it. In this context, a network segment is the length of the cable between repeaters.

Troubleshooting the hubs that connect a 10BaseT network will depend in part on the type of hub being used. *Passive hubs* are simply connection points and give you few clues as to whether they are operating correctly. Fortunately, because it is a simple, non-powered device, not much can go wrong with a passive hub. The pins and wiring inside the hub or a damaged female RJ-45 jack could create connection problems. This can be prevented by ensuring that the hubs are handled properly, since most such damage is caused by human mistreatment. An *active hub* (sometimes called a multiport repeater) does give you a few clues to help you in troubleshooting connectivity problems. The pretty flashing lights that indicate network communication (or collisions) on each port are a starting point. By observing the status lights, you can ascertain if one port is "dead" or unlit, indicating either a problem with the jack or cable at that port or a problem originating with the computer attached to it.

The intelligent or *smart* hub (also called a managed hub) is a bit more helpful. This type of hub runs software with which you can communicate with the hub from a terminal or across the network. In this case, the software program will provide information about port status, and in some cases will run diagnostic applications to assist you in troubleshooting connectivity problems.

TEST DAY TIP

You'll also use the tools we discussed in the previous chapter—the oscilloscope, and cable tester cable—to perform testing at the Physical Layer.

Troubleshooting the Data Link Layer

The Data Link Layer takes the datagram passed down to it from the Network Layer and repackages it into a unit called a *frame*. This frame includes error checking information, which is processed by the Data Link Layer on the receiving computer when the frame reaches its destination. The Data Link Layer is responsible for error-free delivery of the data frames. It's also responsible for maintaining the reliability of the physical link between two computers, which is handled by the Physical Layer just below it. The Data Link Layer is the only layer of the OSI model that is divided into sub-layers: the Logical Link Control (LLC) and the Media Access Control (MAC) sublayers. We will look at each of these individually.

The LLC sublayer is charged with ensuring the reliability of the link or the connection. IEEE 802.2 is an LLC standard that operates using both CSMA/CD and Token Ring media access standards. Point-to-Point Protocol (PPP) also operates at the LLC level. The MAC sublayer deals with the logical topology of the network, which may or may not be the same as the physical topology or layout. For instance, IBM Token Ring networks use a physical *star* topology where all computers connect to a central hub (called an MSAU, or Multistation Access Unit). However, the logical topology is a ring, because inside the MSAU, the wiring is set up such that the data travels in a circle. A 10BaseT network connecting to an Ethernet hub, on the other hand, uses a physical star configuration, but is logically a bus (which is why it is sometimes called a star bus).

The IEEE has developed a number of standards to govern the transmissions that take place at the Data Link and Physical Layers. When preparing for the Network+ exam, you should be aware of the following standards:

- 802.2 establishes standards for the implementation of the LLC sublayer of the Data Link Layer.

- 802.3 sets specifications for an Ethernet network using CSMA/CD, a linear or star bus topology, and baseband transmission.

- 802.5 sets standards for a token passing network using a physical star/logical ring topology such as Token Ring.

- 802.7 establishes criteria for networks using broadband transmission.

- 802.8 sets specifications for using fiber optic as a network medium.

- 802.11 establishes standards for wireless networking.

Understanding Data Link Access Control Methods

MAC-level protocols govern the access control method, or how the data accesses the transmission media. The popular methods are grouped in three categories:

- Contention methods

- Token passing

- Polling methods

Contention methods include CSMA/CD, used in Ethernet networks, and Carrier Sense Multiple Access Collision Avoidance (CSMA/CA), used in AppleTalk networks (used in wireless networks). In both cases, computers that want to transmit data on the network must compete for the use of the wire or other media. A collision occurs if two stations attempt to send at the same time. CSMA/CD and CSMA/CA differ how they address this collision problem. With CSMA/CD, data collisions are detected and the data is sent again after a random amount of time. With CSMA/CA, an "intent to transmit" message is put out as a "feeler" before the computer transmits the actual data.

TEST DAY TIP

I learned to remember the difference between Collision Detection and Collision Avoidance in this way: with CSMA/CD, you want to cross a busy street. So you start to walk across the street, and if you get hit by a car you wait for a little while and then try again. With CSMA/CA, you want to cross that same busy street, so you send a remote controlled car across the street before you start walking. If the little toy car makes it across safely, you decide that it's safe to cross yourself. If the toy car gets hit, you wait a little while and then try to send the toy across again.

Token passing methods eliminate the possibility of collision by using a circulating signal called a *token* to determine which computer is allowed to transmit information across the wire, where only one computer (the computer that has the token) is allowed to transmit at any given time. So a computer on a token passing network is more polite than one on a network using contention methods. Rather than blurting out its transmission whenever it has something to say, it waits patiently for its turn (when the token gets around to it) and sends data only when it "has the floor."

Polling methods are similar in some ways to token passing, except that instead of the group of computers policing themselves by passing around a token, there is a central unit that acts as a "chairperson." This "presiding" unit asks members of the "committee" in turn whether they have something to say. Since all computers follow these "rules of parliamentary procedure," data transmission proceeds in an orderly fashion.

Understanding MAC Addressing

Although the permanent address burned into the NIC is sometimes called the physical address, its proper name is the *Media Access Control* address. The MAC sublayer of the Data Link Layer also handles MAC addressing functions. MAC addresses on Ethernet cards are expressed as 12-digit hexadecimal numbers, which represent 4-bit (6-byte) binary numbers. The first three bytes contain a *manufacturer code*, which is assigned by the IEEE. The last three bytes are assigned by the manufacturer and represent that particular card. Each computer must have a MAC address that is unique on the network.

Higher-level protocols will translate IP addresses (also called logical addresses) into MAC addresses, which represent the physical network location of a particular device. These lower-level protocols cannot recognize or use IP addresses. Think of it this way: a city or county may assign a street name and house number to a structure, but this is really only a "logical" address. Logical addresses can be more easily changed. A neighborhood group will petition to have a street renamed, or the city council will change the numbering scheme to facilitate emergency response or to accommodate new construction. The location where the building stands also has a "physical" address: its geographic coordinates. When the land is surveyed, it will be identified by degrees of longitude and latitude, and these will remain constant regardless of changes to the street name and number. That physical address is like the NIC's MAC address; it will (almost always) remain the same.

Configuring & Implementing

Changing a MAC Address

Some network card manufacturers have made NICs that allow you to change the MAC address by *flashing* the card with a special software program. This is a precaution in case you have duplicate MAC addresses on a network because those manufacturers have begun to recycle their addresses. This is typically done through a software utility that will automate the change process, rather than forcing you to enter many different complicated commands. Being able to access and edit MAC addresses is also useful from a security standpoint, since it is possible for a hacker to spoof MAC addresses on a network. As you learned in Chapter 9, *spoofing* refers to masquerading as a legitimate host, in this case a legitimate MAC address, in order to gain access to a network. Many wireless networks are restricted based on the MAC address of legitimate NICs, and hackers will attempt to spoof a legitimate MAC address to gain access to a wireless network.

Recognizing Data Link Layer Devices

The two types of devices that operate at the Data Link Layer of the OSI model are *switches* and *bridges*. Bridges can separate a network into segments, but they don't subnet the network as routers do. In other words, if you use a bridge to physically separate two areas of the network, it will still appear to be all one network to higher-level protocols. Bridges can cut down on network congestion because they can do some basic filtering of data traffic based on the MAC address of the destination computer. When a transmission reaches the bridge, the bridge will not pass it across to the other side of the network if the MAC address of the destination computer is known to be on the same side of the network as the sending computer. The bridge builds tables indicating which addresses are on which side, and uses them to determine whether to let the transmission across.

Sometimes even experienced network administrators become confused about network bridges. This confusion comes in because there are different types of bridges. Although all of them operate at the Data Link Layer, some operate at the lower MAC sublayer and others at the higher LLC sublayer. There are some important differences. One practical question is whether you can use a bridge to connect network segments that use different media access methods (for instance, an Ethernet segment and a Token Ring segment). The answer is, unfortunately, "It depends." Specifically, this depends on which type of bridge you're referring to. A bridge that operates at the Logical Link Control sublayer, sometimes called a *translation bridge*, can connect segments using different access methods. However, a lower-level bridge (one that operates at the MAC sublayer) cannot perform this type of translation. But both types of bridges can connect segments that use different physical media, like a segment cabled with thin coax and a segment running on unshielded twisted-pair.

Another device that operates at the Data Link Layer is the *switch*, or switching hub, which has become very popular on Ethernet networks. Like the hubs that operate at the Physical Layer, these switches are multi-port devices that you can plug numerous devices into. Like bridges, a switch will maintain a table of MAC addresses, showing which computer is connected to which port. When data comes into the switch, instead of just sending it back out to all the computers as a hub does, the switch examines the destination address in the header, consults the table, and sends it only out the port to which the corresponding computer is attached. This cuts down overall network traffic considerably, and helps to prevent collisions. Some types of switches are even more sophisticated than this and can perform basic routing functions like dividing networks into virtual LANs (VLANs), in addition to the type of switching described here.

As you saw in the previous section, this is also the layer where *wireless access points* reside, and so it is the layer at which you'll start troubleshooting wireless connectivity issues. This includes verifying the Service Set Identifier (SSID), which is the network name for a given wireless access point, and ensuring that your wireless hardware all supports the same 802.11 specification: 802.11a, 802.11b and/or 802.11g.

Layer 2 Troubleshooting

Bridges and switches are useful devices for segmenting a network and controlling the amount of traffic. However, they introduce an extra layer of complexity and thus the potential for several different types of problems. The primary reason for using a bridge or a switch to divide your network is to increase network performance. However, it is possible that bridging or switching itself can have the opposite effect if it is not implemented correctly. You will find that bridging or switching a network, while cutting down on overall traffic, will also slightly increase *latency* for those communications that must cross the bridge or switch. This term refers to delays in transmission of the data in route to the destination computer.

The reason for this is the way in which the bridge or switch decides whether to forward traffic across the network; it must first analyze the header information in the data frame to find out the destination computer's MAC address, and then it must look up that address in its routing table. This takes some time, although in most cases the performance hit will not be significant and will be offset by the overall reduction in network traffic. By following a few simple guidelines, you can prevent any noticeable performance degradation from being created.

One popular networking guideline pertaining to the use of bridges and switches is the *80/20 rule*. This states that 80 percent of network traffic should be local (occurring on the same side of the bridge or switch), and no more than 20 percent should cross the bridge or switch. For best performance, ensure that those computers that communicate with one another most often are on the same side of the bridge or switch. Frequently accessed file or print servers should be placed on the same side of the bridge or switch as those clients that use them most often. Before implementing a bridging or switching solution, you should carefully analyze the normal flow of network traffic and try to group nodes so that most communication, and especially transfer of large amounts of data, takes place without the need to cross the bridge.

Identifying the Cause of an Infrastructure Problem

Another issue that sometimes occurs with bridges and switches is *looping*. This can occur when there is more than one active bridge or switch on a network. In a loop, when the bridges and switches don't know the location of a destination computer, they send the data frame across the bridge or switch. This results in multiple copies of the same data frame on the network, causing unnecessary congestion—but it gets even worse than that.

As each device detects the frame sent by the other bridge or switch, it passes the frame back across to the other side. The frames coming from the other bridge cause each bridge or switch to make incorrect entries in its switching table for the destination computer, and this in turn intermittently prevents the destination computer from receiving data. (A switch maintains a *switching table* in much the same way that a router maintains a routing table.) The problem is intermittent because the bridges keep resetting the entries in the switching table, based on where the data frames are coming from. This can go on forever in an endless loop, hence the term *looping*. See Figure 12.5 for an example of how this can happen.

Figure 12.5 Looping Can Occur on a Bridged or Switched Network

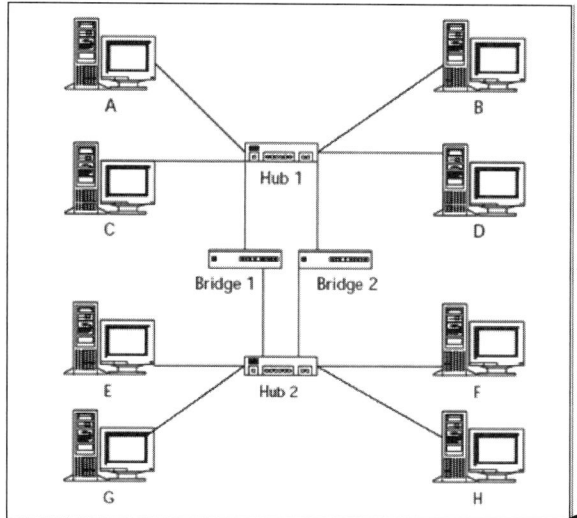

In the scenario shown in Figure 12.5, if Computer B sends a message to Computer A, both bridges would detect the data frame. Neither bridge knows where Computer A is located, so both bridges would transmit the frame to the other segment. They would put an entry in the switching tables identifying Computer B as being off the left-side port. Two copies of the data frame have now been transmitted onto the right-side bridge port. Now each bridge will also detect the copy of the data frame sent by the other bridge on the right-side port. They see the source address and think this is Computer B sending Computer A another frame. They will now pass the frame back to the left-side port. Assuming Computer B is now on the right-side port, they change the table to reflect that status. This can go on forever, with both bridges detecting each other's transmitted frames and passing them across, then changing Computer B's status in the table from the right- to the left-side port over and over again.

When the switching table is incorrectly set, Computer B will not be able to receive any data. When the table changes again and Computer B is identified as being on the correct bridge port, it will be able to receive data, but only until the tables are changed once more. The problem here is that a bridge looks at the source and destination addresses, but cannot identify duplicate frames.

This does not mean that you can't have two bridges on a network. In fact, redundancy is a good idea, in case one bridge "dies." So how do you prevent the looping behavior? By using the *Spanning Tree Protocol*. If your bridge supports and is configured to use this protocol, it will be able to communicate with other bridges on the network. The two bridges will then work cooperatively, with one functioning in active mode and the other on standby unless or until it detects a failure of the first bridge. At that point, the second bridge will take over passing data frames. With only a single pathway available at any given time, there is no possibility of a loop.

Troubleshooting the Network Layer

Both TCP and UDP, which operating at the Transport Layer, rely on the Internet Protocol to actually move data from the sending to the receiving computer. As you've worked through this guide, you've learned that *routing* takes place at the Network Layer, and routing is all about recognizing network and host addresses and mapping out the most efficient way to get from one address to another. You would be performing a function similar to that of the Network Layer if you took on the job of navigator on a cross-country automobile trip. Just as TCP and IP, working together, have different responsibilities, you and the driver could divide the duties so that the journey goes more smoothly. It's the driver's job to get the car to the destination safely and all in one piece (somewhat like the Transport Layer protocols). It's the job of the navigator to consult a map, determine exactly which highways will take you there, where to turn off one road and onto another, and to consider such factors as the size of each thoroughfare, known areas of congestion, and anything else that might make one route more desirable than another. This is similar to the job of the Network Layer; it is responsible for finding a path through a network to the destination computer. It is also responsible for translating *logical addresses* (the IP addresses assigned by an administrator or a DHCP [Dynamic Host Configuration Protocol] server) into *physical addresses*. The physical, or MAC, address is burned into a chip on the network interface card by its manufacturer.

IP routes messages based on the network number of the destination address. Every computer has a table of network numbers, known as a *routing table*. If there is an entry in the routing table for the destination network ID, the computer sends it to a *gateway* address, which represents the first router in the path to the destination. A default gateway address is included in the routing table to send packets to when a specific route to the destination network ID isn't found in the routing table. The default gateway must be on the same network as the source computer. Each gateway or router that the message must go through on the way to its destination is called a *hop*. You might say that a journey of a thousand hops begins with a single step: the gateway address listed in the routing table for a particular network number.

The Network Layer can use either *static* or *dynamic* routing to find a path from a source to a destination computer. It's easy to map out a *static* route to a friend's house that is four blocks away—the path that you take will likely never change, and it's a simple one to remember. However, if you're trying to get to the home of a relative who lives in the backwoods in another state, you may need more than a good map. You may need to call ahead and get directions from someone who has traveled there recently. As networks become larger and more complex, it becomes more difficult to manually maintain routing tables. When this happens, you will want to use a *dynamic routing protocol*. Dynamic routing protocols automatically update routes on all routers on the network. The most common dynamic routing protocols available are the Routing Information Protocol (RIP) and the Open Shortest Path First (OSPF) protocol.

TEST DAY TIP

Remember that routers, whether they are dedicated hardware devices or routing software running on a Windows server, all operate at the Network Layer.

The TCP/IP protocol suite includes several protocols that operate at the Network Layer of the OSI model, including one of the two major components of the suite: the Internet Protocol. IP handles addressing and routing at the Network Level, relying on logical (IP) addresses. It can use packet switching methods to route different packets, which are all part of the same message, via different pathways. It can use dynamic routing protocols to determine the most efficient routes on a per-packet basis. IP is a *connectionless* protocol; it depends on TCP at the Transport Layer above it to provide a connection, if necessary. However, it is able to use number sequencing to break down and reassemble messages, and uses a checksum to perform error checking on the IP header.

Head of the Class…

Packet Switching and Circuit Switching—Deciphering the Terminology

Many people easily confuse the terms *packet switching* and *circuit switching*. Even experienced network administrators, if they haven't had much exposure to the conceptual and hardware sides of WAN technology, find them a little mysterious. They sound like the same thing, but they're not.

Circuit switching technology is something we use all the time, whether we're aware of it or not. The public telephone system (which is formally called PSTN, or Public Switched Telephone Network) is the most familiar example of switched-circuit communication. An end-to-end communication link is established when you place a telephone call, and that same physical path from one end (your telephone) to the other (Aunt Mary's telephone in Boise, Idaho, for example) is maintained for the duration of that call. The path is reserved until you break the connection by hanging up.

If you call Aunt Mary again next week, the pathway (also called the circuit) used may be completely different. That's where the switching comes in, and that explains why sometimes when you talk to Aunt Mary, the connection is clear, while other times there's so much noise and static on the line that you have to ask her to repeat herself when she tells you whose quilt won first prize at this year's county fair.

Packet switching is different in that there is no dedicated pathway or circuit established. It is known as a *connectionless* technology for that reason. If you send data from your computer to your company's national headquarters in New York over a packet-switched network, each individual packet, or chunk of data, can take a different physical route to get there. Most traffic sent across the Internet uses packet switching.

Another type of digital packet switching network called X.25 can also support *virtual circuits*, in which a dedicated logical connection is established between two parties for a certain duration. A *permanent virtual circuit*, or *PVC*, creates an ongoing, dedicated logical connection between two locations, even though the physical network connection can be shared by more than one logical connection.

Two additional TCP/IP protocols that operate at the Network Layer are the Address Resolution Protocol (ARP) and the Reverse Address Resolution Protocol (RARP). ARP's job is to translate logical IP addresses to physical MAC addresses. ARP discovers this information by way of *broadcasts*, and keeps a table of IP-to-MAC entries. This table is referred to as the *ARP cache*. RARP is a similar protocol that does the opposite of ARP; instead of starting with an IP address and finding the matching MAC address, it uses the MAC address to find the IP address. This is somewhat like a reverse-lookup telephone directory.

The Internet Control Message Protocol (ICMP) is known as a maintenance protocol and is invaluable in TCP/IP troubleshooting. It allows two computers on an IP network to share IP status and error information. ICMP is used by the *ping* and *tracert* utilities that we discussed in Chapter 11, as well as the *traceroute* utility for UNIX and Linux computers. Computers and routers using IP can report errors and exchange control and status information via ICMP. And finally, the Internet Group Management Protocol (IGMP) allows computers on a network such as the Internet to participate in IP multicasting. A *multicast address* allows an application to send a message to a large number of recipients without requiring the source computer to know the addresses of all the recipients. Network routers use IGMP to translate the multicast address into host addresses. This works because each computer involved in a multicast group will use IGMP to report its *multicast group memberships* to the necessary routers in order to receive the appropriate multicast messages. For example, if you sign up for a real-time webcast from your laptop computer, your laptop will use IGMP to register with the multicast router that will be transmitting the webcast. When the webcast starts, the webcast application will send its information to the multicast router, which will use IGMP to send the webcast to any computers who signed up for it (including yours).

Configuring & Implementing

The 6to4 Protocol

The Internet Engineering Task force (IETF) has created a new protocol called *6to4*, the purpose of which is to encapsulate IPv6 packets inside IPv4 packets. This will allow networks that migrate to IPv6 early to be able to send their data across the Internet, even if the ISPs (Internet Service Providers) they use don't yet support the new version of IP.

Many ISPs are now using Network Address Translation (NAT) to allow for the translation of multiple private IP addresses that don't have to be registered, to a smaller number of public assigned addresses. For this reason, many ISPs have not been in a hurry to implement IPv6 support. Reconfiguring all of their equipment to use IPv6 addresses would be a big project, requiring a great deal of time and effort. The recent popularity of NAT devices and software implementations of NAT (along with inexpensive proxy software) has taken the edge off of the urgency of upgrading, at least for some companies. NAT is built into Windows 2000 Server products, and a simple, lighter version of NAT called Internet Connection Sharing (ICS) is included in the Windows 2000, Windows 98SE, Windows XP, and Windows Server 2003 operating systems. Using one of these operating systems, all of the computers on a network can access the Internet using just one public registered IP address.

The new 6to4 protocol will solve the compatibility problem for those corporate networks that do wish to adopt IPv6 sooner rather than later and may make migration more attractive for others as well. The 6to4 protocol is installed on a

Continued

www.syngress.com

router that serves as a gateway from the IPv6 network to the Internet. It works by automatically assigning a prefix to each IPv6 address, which identifies it as a 6to4 address. The 6to4 protocol then establishes a tunnel over IPv6 network.

Layer 3 Troubleshooting

You'll spend quite a bit of time troubleshooting at the Network Layer, since this is the layer that really governs whether two computers can communicate with one another. A failure at the Network Layer can create connectivity issues where a single client or an entire subnet cannot communicate with another portion of a network, either because of a physical device failure or because of some type of misconfiguration.

Especially when you're troubleshooting IP connectivity issues on a large network, it's helpful to have documentation of the physical and logical network design available so that you can understand how traffic *should* be flowing on your network, and potentially compare that to the path that it is actually taking. You'll recall that network routes are measured in hops, where each hop represents a single router between the source and destination computer. Because of this, you have the potential for failure at every hop along the way, and so you may need to test connectivity at every single hop.

When troubleshooting Network Layer issues, there are a few common situations that tend to be the source of most connectivity issues. If a source computer is trying to send information to a destination computer, and the source computer's default gateway does not have a *route* to the destination, the packet will never reach the destination computer because the gateway doesn't know where to send it. This can happen, not only at the default gateway, but at every router along the path. There might also be a physical connectivity issue between the source and destination computers, where either a router or a network link that's required to transmit the information has failed or gone offline. The best tools to check connectivity at the Network Layer are ping, tracert, and pathping for Windows systems, and ping and traceroute for UNIX/Linux systems. Troubleshooting tools are covered in Chapter 11.

You should also check for configuration issues on each router along the path to ensure that nothing has changed or been configured incorrectly. A common misconfiguration, especially when new routers or network links are added to a network, is a *routing loop*, which occurs in this fashion:

1. A source computer on Network A is trying to reach a destination computer on Network C. The source computer sends the packet to its default gateway, let's call it Router A.

2. Router A checks its routing table to figure out how to reach Network C. Router A sees that the next hop to Network C is Router B. So Router A sends the packet to Router B.

3. Router B receives the packet that's intended for Network C. Router B checks its routing table, and sees that the *next hop* to Network C…is *Router A*. So it sends the packet *back* to Router A.

4. I bet you can guess what happens next: Router A receives the packet that's intended for Network C. It checks its routing table, and sends the packet to Router B, which then proceeds to send it *back* to Router A, and the process repeats itself until the Time-to-Live (TTL) of the packet has been exceeded and the packet is dropped.

The good news is that a routing loop is easy to detect by using the tracert or traceroute command, since you'll see the path that the packet is taking bounce back and forth between the same two routers over and over again as follows:

```
 9      29 ms      29 ms      28 ms   p10-0.sjc01.atlas.cogentco.com [154.54.2.1]

10      30 ms      29 ms      40 ms   p4-0.sfo01.atlas.cogentco.com [66.28.4.93]

11      29 ms      29 ms      28 ms   p10-0.sjc01.atlas.cogentco.com [154.54.2.1]

12      30 ms      29 ms      40 ms   p4-0.sfo01.atlas.cogentco.com [66.28.4.93]

13      29 ms      29 ms      28 ms   p10-0.sjc01.atlas.cogentco.com [154.54.2.1]

14      30 ms      29 ms      40 ms   p4-0.sfo01.atlas.cogentco.com [66.28.4.93]

15      29 ms      29 ms      28 ms   p10-0.sjc01.atlas.cogentco.com [154.54.2.1]

16      30 ms      29 ms      40 ms   p4-0.sfo01.atlas.cogentco.com [66.28.4.93]
```

If the connectivity failure is limited to a single workstation, use the *ipconfig* command to verify that the IP address, subnet mask and default gateway have been configured correctly. You can also use the *route* command to verify that the default gateway and other routing table entries are correct for an individual PC.

TEST DAY TIP

If all physical links and routers are functioning between a source and destination computer, but traffic is still not getting through, verify that a *packet filter* hasn't been configured on a router or firewall between the two computers that is preventing traffic from getting through.

Troubleshooting the Transport Layer

The Transport Layer's main purpose in life is ensuring reliability. The Transport Layer must verify that any data sent by one computer arrives at its intended destination in good condition. It also needs a way to differentiate between different communications that may be addressed to different applications that are being served up by the same IP address. This is accomplished through the use of *port numbers*. Thanks to the multitasking capabilities of Windows 2000 and other modern operating systems, you can use more than one network application simultaneously. For example, you can use your Web browser to access your company's homepage at the same time your e-mail software is downloading your e-mail. You already know that TCP/IP uses an IP address to identify your computer on the network, and get the messages to the correct system, but how does it separate the response to your browser's request from your incoming mail when both messages arrive at the same IP address?

This is where ports come in. The two parts of an IP address that represent the network address and the host address are somewhat like a street name and an individual street number. In this analogy, the port number would identify the specific apartment or suite within the building.

TCP and UDP, the Transport Layer protocols, assign port numbers to each application so the data intended for the Web browser in Apartment A doesn't get sent to the e-mail program living in Apartment B. The Transport Layer uses two types of connection services: connection-oriented and connectionless. Which type of connection is most appropriate for sending a particular message depends on whether you are more concerned with reliability or speed. In TCP/IP communications, data is sent over the network as a sequence of *datagrams*. A datagram is a collection of data sent as a single message. Each datagram is sent across the network individually.

A connection-oriented protocol such as TCP offers better error control, but can't send information as quickly because it needs to confirm that each datagram has reached its destination successfully. A connectionless protocol such as UDP, on the other hand, suffers in the reliability department but has better speed since it doesn't need to confirm the delivery of any datagrams that it sends.

The easiest way to differentiate between connection-oriented and connectionless communications is by looking at the different ways you can send a letter from your local post office. If you need to send an important report to the manager of your company's branch office in El Paso, you could put it in an envelope, affix the required amount of postage, and drop it in the corner mailbox. This would be the easiest, quickest way to take care of the task, but you would have no idea whether or when the report reached its destination. On the other hand, you could go to the post office and fill out a card to send the report via registered, certified mail, with a return receipt requested. This would cost more and it would take more time and effort on your part, but it would be a more reliable form of communication. You would get back an acknowledgment when the package was delivered, showing that it was indeed received by the person to whom it was addressed.

Connection-oriented services are more like the second example, although they actually go one step further: They establish the connection before sending the data. This would be as if, before you sent your certified mail, you first got on the telephone with the El Paso manager and let him know the report was coming so he could be on the lookout for its arrival. If you're really detail-minded (or paranoid), you could even ask that he call you back when it gets there, and let you know that all the pages are there in sequence and it wasn't damaged along the way. You've taken pains to make sure your communication is as reliable as possible, but at a cost in terms of time (and long distance charges) to both you and the intended recipient.

EXAM WARNING

As a provider of connection-oriented services, TCP first establishes a *virtual connection* between the sending and receiving computers. This is done through the use of acknowledgments and response messages.

Understanding TCP

TCP works on the Transport Layer of the TCP/IP model, providing connection-based communication with other IP hosts. When an application passes data to the Transport Layer, it is often too much data to transmit in one packet, so TCP segments the data on the sending side and reassembles it at the receiving end according to sequence information that is packaged with the packet. TCP sends acknowledgments to confirm successful delivery and analyzes each packet according to checksum information to ensure data integrity.

TCP uses a system of ports to manage communication. Applications bind to a specific TCP port, and any inbound traffic delivered to that port will be picked up by the application. This enables multiple applications on one host to use TCP at the same time, and also standardizes the way a client can connect to a given service on a server. For instance, Telnet's standard TCP port is 23, so Telnet clients try to establish connections on port 23 by default. Port assignments are flexible; that is, you can change the port a client or server uses for a specific application if needed. Although Web servers typically use port 80 for HTTP (HyperText Transfer Protocol) communication, the Web server application can be bound to a different port. You should be aware of the default TCP ports that are used by major applications when you're troubleshooting network issues at the Transport Layer. Table 12.1 illustrates some of the more common TCP applications and the ports they use:

Table 12.1 Well-Known TCP Ports

Port Number	Application
20	FTP (data)
21	FTP(control)
22	SSH
23	Telnet
25	SMTP
53	DNS Zone Transfers
80	HTTP
88	Kerberos
110	POP3
119	NNTP
139	NetBIOS
443	SSL

Head of the Class…

The Three-Way Handshake

Computers using TCP to communicate have both a *send* window and a *receive* window. At the beginning of a TCP communication, the protocol uses a three-way handshake to establish the session between the two computers. Because TCP (unlike its Transport Layer sibling, UDP) is connection-oriented, a session, or direct one-to-one communication link, must be created prior to sending and receiving of data. The client computer initiates the communication with the server (the computer whose resources it wants to access). The handshake includes the following steps:

1. A SYN (synchronization request) segment is sent by the client machine. An initial sequence number, sometimes just referred to as the ISN, is generated by the client and sent to the server, along with the port number the client is requesting to connect to on the server.

2. An ACK message and a SYN message are sent back to the client from the server. The ACK segment is the client's original ISN plus 1, and the server's SYN is an unrelated number generated by the server itself. The ACK acknowledges the client's SYN request, and the server's SYN indicates the intent to establish a session with the client. The client and server machines must synchronize one another's sequence numbers.

3. An ACK is sent from the client back to the server, acknowledging the server's request for synchronization. This ACK from the client is, as you might have guessed, the server's ISN plus 1. When both machines have acknowledged each other's requests by returning

Continued

ACK messages, the handshake has been successfully completed and a connection is established between the two.

You can see an example of this three-way handshake in Figure 12.6.

Figure 12.6 The TCP Three-Way Handshake

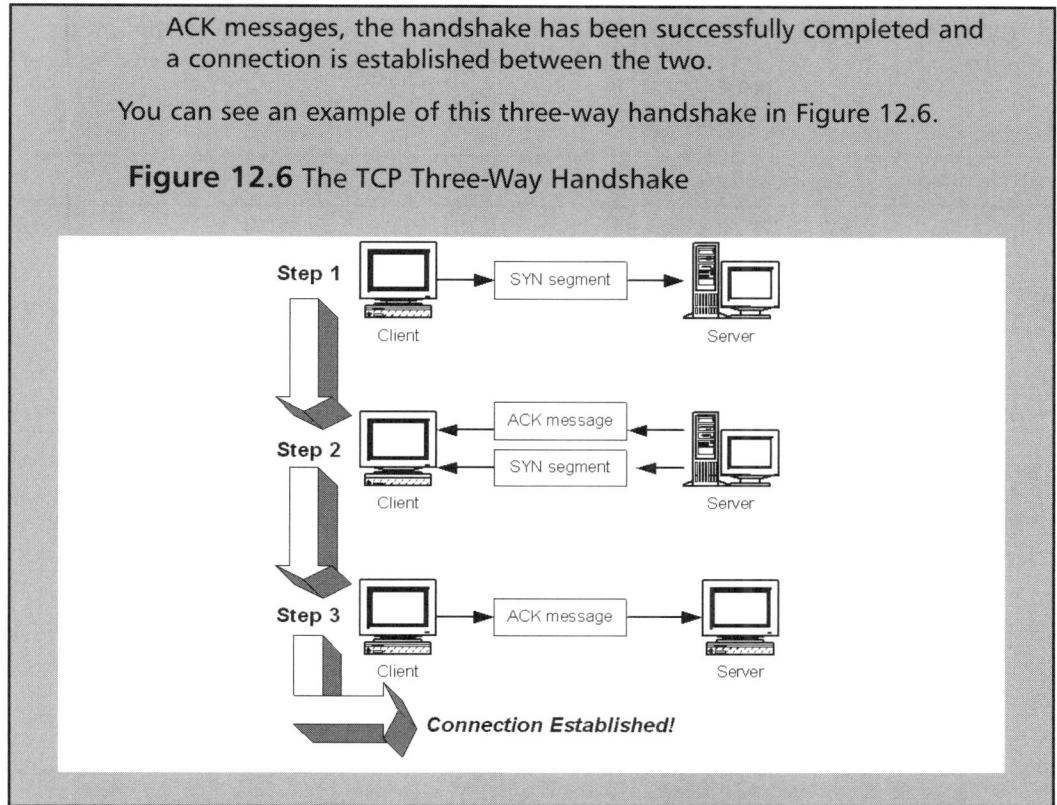

Understanding UDP

A *connectionless* transport protocol like UDP doesn't provide the same acknowledgment of receipt process as the connection-oriented TCP does. Since UDP doesn't sequence the packets that the data arrives in, an application program that uses UDP has to be able to make sure that the entire message has arrived and is in the right order. To save processing time, network applications that have very small data units to exchange, and thus very little message reassembling to do, may use UDP instead of TCP. For example, DNS (Domain Name System) hostname lookup messages that will always fit in a single datagram can effectively use UDP. For these very short queries, you don't need all the complexity of TCP; if you don't receive an answer after a few seconds, you can just ask again.

UDP doesn't split data into multiple datagrams, as TCP does. It also doesn't keep track of what it has sent. Data can be resent if needed, and UDP doesn't guarantee delivery or protect against duplication. However, it is not completely irresponsible: it does provide for a checksum capability to ensure that data arrives intact, and it provides port numbers to distinguish between the requests sent by different user applications. Examples of applications that use UDP for communication include Trivial File Transfer Protocol (TFTP), RIP, RADIUS accounting, and some implementations of Kerberos authentication. Table 12.2 illustrates some of the more common UDP-based applications and ports:

Table 12.2 Well-Known UDP Ports

Port Number	Application
7	Echo
53	DNS query
69	TFTP
123	Network Time Protocol
161	SNMP

Layer 4 Troubleshooting

Troubleshooting the Transport Layer is quite similar to working at the Application Layer, since the TCP and UDP protocols form the basis of the *ports* that are used by all network applications. So you can use the **telnet** command to see if a particular port is listening on the destination machine, and you can use the **netstat** utility to see a list of all ports that are listening on a particular machine. You should remember from Chapter 11 that you can use **netstat –a** to do this, with results similar to the following:

```
Active Connections

  Proto   Local Address                Foreign Address            State
  TCP     IBM-A38375FF22E:epmap        IBM-A38375FF22E:0        LISTENING
  TCP     IBM-A38375FF22E:microsoft-ds IBM-A38375FF22E:0        LISTENING
  TCP     IBM-A38375FF22E:netbios-ssn  IBM-A38375FF22E:0        LISTENING
  TCP     IBM-A38375FF22E:1202         112.25.12.64.in-addr.arpa:5190
                                                                 ESTABLISHED
  TCP     IBM-A38375FF22E:1299         workstation.office.com:3389
                                                                 ESTABLISHED
  TCP     IBM-A38375FF22E:1025         IBM-A38375FF22E:0        LISTENING
  TCP     IBM-A38375FF22E:5180         IBM-A38375FF22E:0        LISTENING
  UDP     IBM-A38375FF22E:snmp         *:*
  UDP     IBM-A38375FF22E:microsoft-ds *:*
  UDP     IBM-A38375FF22E:isakmp       *:*
  UDP     IBM-A38375FF22E:1032         *:*
  UDP     IBM-A38375FF22E:1033         *:*
  UDP     IBM-A38375FF22E:1048         *:*
  UDP     IBM-A38375FF22E:1300         *:*
```

```
UDP     IBM-A38375FF22E:2361            *:*
UDP     IBM-A38375FF22E:4500            *:*
UDP     IBM-A38375FF22E:ntp             *:*
UDP     IBM-A38375FF22E:netbios-ns  *:*
UDP     IBM-A38375FF22E:netbios-dgm *:*
UDP     IBM-A38375FF22E:1900            *:*
UDP     IBM-A38375FF22E:ntp             *:*
UDP     IBM-A38375FF22E:1305            *:*
UDP     IBM-A38375FF22E:1311            *:*
UDP     IBM-A38375FF22E:1900            *:*
UDP     IBM-A38375FF22E:2242            *:*
UDP     IBM-A38375FF22E:2313            *:*
UDP     IBM-A38375FF22E:4519            *:*
```

If you run the **netstat –a** command on a server that's functioning as a Web server, you should see at least one entry in the netstat output to indicate that it's listening on port 80; if it's not, the WWW service might be stopped or disabled.

TEST DAY TIP

It's important to remember that you can't pick and choose which applications use TCP versus UDP. A test question might try to trip you up by talking about configuring HTTP to use UDP to solve a troubleshooting issue. This simply isn't possible, since HTTP uses TCP port 80 and not UDP. Be very aware of the well-known ports listed throughout this guide as you prepare for the exam.

Troubleshooting the Session Layer

The Session Layer handles the task of establishing a one-to-one session between the sending and the receiving computers. The Session Layer sets up and tears down application-to-application dialogs, and synchronizes the data flow for the applications. The Session Layer also controls whether a transmission is established as *half-duplex* or *full-duplex*. Full-duplex is bi-directional communication in which both sides can send and receive simultaneously. Half-duplex is also bi-directional communication, but the signals can flow in only one direction at a time. To illustrate the difference, think of how a telephone conversation works. Both parties can talk at the same time, and you can still hear the other person's voice while you're talking. That's full-duplex. But with most two-way radios like walkie-talkies, when you key the microphone to speak, you can't hear anything the other person might be saying while you're speaking. This means that only one of you can broadcast over the channel at a time. That's half-duplex.

Another important responsibility of the Session Layer is to define the rules for data exchange between the applications. In this respect, you might think of the Session Layer as a referee or mediator who makes sure both parties (the sending and receiving computers) are aware of and agree to follow the "rules of the game" for that particular session. When two family members are at odds and seek counseling to help them communicate with one another, a good counselor or mediator will start the visit by getting both people to agree to certain rules. These might include who gets to talk first, and for how long, as well as the "format" of the communication (for example, no yelling, screaming, or name-calling). Although computers aren't known for getting emotional, before they can communicate effectively they also need to negotiate communications guidelines. Otherwise, they may bombard each other with too much data to be processed, or both try to "talk" at the same time. The Session Layer controls this flow of conversation so that the message will get through clearly. In this way, the Session Layer provides for *flow control*.

The most common protocols that exist at the Session Layer are usually Application Program Interfaces, or APIs, that control how an application will set up, manage, and tear down sessions between two computers. The most common APIs you'll encounter are NetBIOS, TCP/IP Sockets, and Remote Procedure Calls. These three APIs make it easier for software developers to create applications that can function over a network connection by *standardizing* how such an application should behave. You've already heard of TCP/IP *sockets* as the combination of an IP address and port number that's used by one computer to communicate with another: this is the Session Layer at work.

Layer 5 Troubleshooting

Just as the functions of the Presentation Layer are often swallowed up by Application Layer protocols, the functions of TCP/IP protocols from the Session Layer up to the Application layer will often span all three layers—the difference between them can sometimes get a bit fuzzy. Because of this, it's not particularly common to perform troubleshooting that's geared *only* toward the Session Layer of the OSI model.

The most common issues you'll see at the Session Layer involve slow network transmissions between two computers, which is caused by one computer in a connection using a half-duplex connection instead of a full-duplex connection. This is especially troublesome on Windows PCs since they will default to using auto-detect, where the network interface card will attempt to automatically detect the duplex type that it should be using. In Exercise 12.2, we'll configure a NIC on a Windows XP workstation to use a full-duplex connection.

EXERCISE 12.2

CONFIGURING FULL DUPLEX

1. Click **Start | Connect To | Show All Connections**.

2. Right-click the **Local Area Connection** icon and select **Properties**.

3. On the **General** tab, click **Configure** to configure the NIC.

4. Access the **Advanced** tab and scroll to **Link Speed & Duplex**. You'll see the screen shown in Figure 12.7. By default, this is set to **Auto Detect**. Change the setting to **100Mbps/Full Duplex** to force the NIC to use a 100Mbps connection that allows the sending and receiving computers to communicate simultaneously.

Figure 12.7 Configuring a Full Duplex Connection

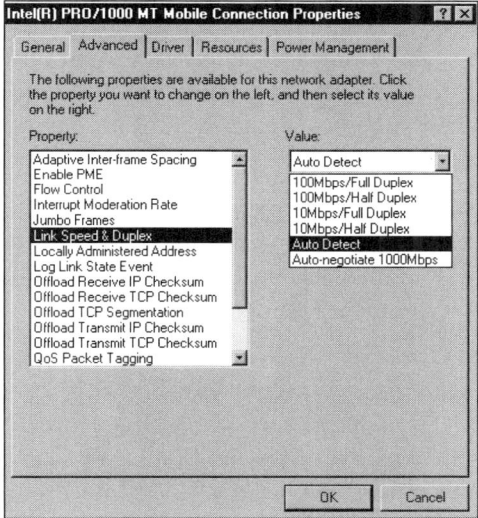

5. Click **OK** to save your changes.

Troubleshooting the Presentation Layer

No, the Presentation Layer doesn't turn your data into PowerPoint slides! However, as the name suggests, it is responsible for the way in which data is presented, or formatted. The Presentation Layer handles such things as encryption (presenting the data in such a way as to keep it from being readable by unauthorized persons) and compression (packaging the data in such a way as to get more of it through at a time). On the receiving side, the Presentation Layer is responsible for translating data into a format understandable by the application, and then presenting it to the Application Layer.

Identifying the Cause of Client and Various Server Environment Problems:

Since the Presentation Layer handles the very important task of protocol translation, this layer is where many *gateways* operate. One of the purposes of a network protocol is to provide a single "language" that different computers can use in order to talk to each other. In this case, a gateway acts as a translator between two separate protocols, so that computers that are running different protocols can communicate with each other. Gateways allow this process to take place transparently, so that Computer A doesn't realize that it needs a translator to communicate with Computer B; from the end user's perspective it just works automatically. Examples of gateways include:

- **E-mail gateway** This software translates the messages from diverse, non-compatible e-mail systems into a common Internet format such as the Simple Mail Transfer Protocol (SMTP). Thus, Cousin Mary is able to read your letter even though you were using Microsoft Outlook with an Exchange server and she is on a NetWare network using GroupWise e-mail.

- **SNA gateway** Systems Network Architecture (SNA) is a proprietary IBM architecture used in mainframe computer systems such as the AS/400. An SNA gateway allows personal computers on a local area network to access files and applications on the mainframe computer.

- **Gateway Services for NetWare (GSNW)** This software is included with the Windows 2000 and Windows NT Server operating systems to allow the Windows server's clients to access files on a Novell NetWare server. It translates between the SMB (Server Message Block) file sharing protocol used on Microsoft networks and NCP (NetWare Core Protocol), the file sharing protocol used by the NetWare networks.

There are almost as many gateway products available as there are different protocol combinations, and more are being developed all the time as interoperability becomes increasingly important to connect the diverse systems that are available. For example, there are services that you can install on a Windows server or client to allow access to the AppleTalk protocol for Macintosh and OS X resources, UNIX and Linux servers and clients, as well as the Gateway Services for NetWare.

Another common function of the Presentation Layer is translating text and graphics from one format to another. So the Presentation Layer might translate text from a computer using EBCDIC (Extended Binary-Coded Decimal Interchange Code) encoding so that it can be understood by a computer using ASCII (American Standard Code for

Information Interchange) encoding, and vice versa. The following are some types of text and image encoding operate at the Presentation Layer:

- EBCDIC
- ASCII
- JPEG
- MPEG

EXAM WARNING

You should remember from the previous chapter that the *Ethernet frame type* is often a common culprit when tracking down connectivity issues with a NetWare server. Versions of NetWare prior to version 4 used Ethernet 802.3 as their default frame type. NetWare 4.0 and later use 802.2 as the default.

Layer 6 Troubleshooting

You won't run into a great many problems with troubleshooting at the Presentation Layer, since most of the duties handled by this layer are stable technologies that have been around for decades. Additionally, the functions of the Presentation Layer will often actually be performed by a protocol that you would normally think of as functioning at the Application Layer, so that troubleshooting will all take place using the steps we'll describe in the next section.

TEST DAY TIP

Remember that the OSI model is just that: a *model*. Some protocols will map to more than one layer of the OSI model, and some layers of the model won't be used at all in some cases.

Some examples of problems you may find at the Presentation Layer include:

- An image file becomes garbled or corrupted when it's sent via e-mail from one person to another.
- E-mail messages between two different server types (Exchange and GroupWise, for example) become scrambled or unreadable.

■   You are unable to copy or move files between two different network types, usually Microsoft and Novell, or you are unable to open a file once it's been copied.

In most cases, you can resolve these issues by restarting or re-installing the gateway service that's creating these errors: restarting the Gateway Services for NetWare on your Windows 2000 server, for example.

Troubleshooting the Application Layer

Especially where the application is concerned, be sure to keep in mind that the OSI model describes only the logical networking components, not any specific programs that you'll use like Internet Explorer or Microsoft Outlook. By remembering this, you won't make the common mistake of thinking the Application Layer actually represents user application software.

What the Application Layer really does to is define how a user's application will interact with a network protocol. In other words, Application Layer protocols accept user data to be transmitted on the network, that is, the data that's created by the user application that's operating above the networking layers. For example, if you want to send an e-mail message, your user application might be Microsoft Outlook. A user sending e-mail will see only the application interface, not any underlying protocols. They can type their letters to Cousin Mary, perhaps attach graphics files containing photos of the grizzly bear who almost ate Uncle Joe from their last family outing to Yellowstone National Park, and then click **Send**. Assuming that they typed the correct e-mail address in the "to" field, they've configured their e-mail software properly, their hardware is working, their phone lines aren't down, and their ISP is on the ball (quite a lot of assumptions, to be sure), the message goes through and lands in Mary's e-mail Inbox. Neither the user sending the message nor Cousin Mary needs to know anything about what the networking components of their respective operating systems are doing in order to communicate via e-mail. That's because the application itself (Outlook) sends the data (the message they typed) to the Application Layer, and the Application Layer takes it from there. The Application Layer adds header information, which will be used by the Application Layer on the receiving end, and then passes the information down to the Presentation Layer. The Application Layer is the top level of the OSI model, and is the layer that resides closest to the user. The Application Layer is different from the lower layers of the model because it doesn't provide services to any other OSI layer. Instead, it provides network services to user applications such as spreadsheet programs, word processing, and e-mail programs.

Application Layer Protocols

TCP/IP provides several protocols that operate at the Application Layer to provide services such as news, mail and file transfer, and monitoring/diagnostics capability. The most common protocols that operate at the Application layer are as follows:

- **FTP**   The File Transfer Protocol (FTP) is used for copying files from one computer to another. Windows 2000, XP, and Windows Server 2003 include both a command-line FTP *client* program, and the FTP *server* service that is installed as part of the Microsoft Internet Information Server (IIS). If you haven't installed the FTP server service on a Windows computer, you will only have access to the FTP client, which is available from the Windows command line when TCP/IP is installed.

- **SNMP**   The Simple Network Management Protocol (SNMP) provides a way to gather statistical and troubleshooting information about devices such as PCs, routers, switches, and hubs. An SNMP management system sends requests to an SNMP agent, and the information is stored in a Management Information Base (MIB). The MIB is a database that holds information about a networked computer (for example, how much hard disk space is available). In order to install the SNMP service on a Windows computer, you need to be logged on as a member of the Administrators group. The SNMP agent software is installed as a Windows Component and runs as a service.

Exam Warning

SNMP management software is not currently included with the Windows operating system and has to be purchased and installed separately.

- **Telnet**   Telnet is a TCP/IP-based service that allows users to log onto a computer from a remote location, run character-mode or command-line utilities on the remote computer or device, and view files on a remote device. Windows 2000 and 2003 Server computers include both Telnet server and Telnet client software, while Windows client operating systems such as Windows 2000 and XP Professional only include the Telnet client. Telnet differs from FTP in that you cannot transfer files from one computer to another (upload or download). Telnet is often used to access a UNIX shell account on an ISP's server and delete e-mail messages directly from the server without downloading them to the local machine. The Telnet server service uses TCP port 25 to listen for Telnet requests.

EXAM DAY TIP

Because it usually sends usernames and passwords in *clear-text* the use of Telnet has been almost entirely superseded by Secure Shell Host (SSH). If you are troubleshooting a remote device like a router or a switch, you'll want to use SSH for better security whenever possible.

- **SMTP** The Simple Mail Transfer Protocol is used for sending e-mail messages, typically across the Internet. SMTP is a simple ASCII protocol and is not vendor-specific. Because SMTP has limited capability in queuing messages at the receiving end, most e-mail client programs use SMTP for *sending* e-mail only, and either POP3 (Post Office Protocol version 3) or IMAP (Internet Message Access Protocol) for storing any messages that are received by an e-mail server. The SMTP service uses TCP port 25 to send messages using SMTP.

- **HTTP** The HyperText Transfer Protocol is perhaps the most familiar of the Application Layer protocols because it is used on the World Wide Web, the most popular Internet service. HTTP allows computers to exchange files in various formats (text, graphic images, sound, video, and other multimedia files) via client software called a *Web browser.* A computer running a Web server program, such as Microsoft's Internet Information Server, stores files in HyperText Markup Language (HTML) format that can be accessed by the client browser. These HTML *pages* often contain hyperlinks for quickly and automatically connecting to other files on the Internet, on an intranet, or on the local machine. The HTTP protocol uses TCP port 80 to send and receive information to Web servers and clients.

- **NNTP** Network News Transfer Protocol (NNTP) is used for managing messages posted to private and public *newsgroups*. NNTP servers provide for storage of newsgroup posts, which can be downloaded by client software called a *newsreader.* Windows 2000 and 2003 Server include an NNTP server as a part of IIS. Outlook Express, which is part of the Internet Explorer software included with Windows 2000, XP, and 2003, provides both an e-mail client and a newsreader. The NNTP service defaults to using TCP oort 119.

- **DNS** The Domain Name System is used by most of the other applications in the TCP/IP protocol suite to resolve hostnames to IP addresses. A Web browser, for example, cannot establish a connection to a Web server unless it knows the IP address of the server. DNS is used to resolve hostnames, such as www.microsoft.com, to IP addresses. DNS is a distributed database that is essential for TCP/IP to be used on a massive Internet-sized scale. It provides a function that hides the complexity of IP addresses from users, and makes things such as e-mail and the World Wide Web much easier to use.

■ **DHCP** The Dynamic Host Configuration Protocol is used to dynamic assign TCP/IP addresses and configuration information to clients and servers. IP addressing information is *leased* by a DHCP server for a specific period of time, usually three days, before the lease must be renewed by the client. You can also use a DHCP server to centrally configure TCP/IP client options such as the default gateway, subnet mask, and DNS servers for your DHCP clients. This is particularly convenient because if you need to change one of these options you can change it *once* on the DHCP server rather than needing to make a change on every single client in your environment. Windows NT, 2000, 2003, and UNIX/Linux servers can act as a DHCP server; all Windows and UNIX/Linux can act as clients. You can use the **ipconfig /release** and **ipconfig /renew** commands to refresh the DHCP configuration on a particular workstation.

Exam Warning

Windows DHCP clients are able to use *Automatic Private IP Addressing* (APIPA) if they are unable to contact a DHCP server. This allows for limited connectivity using the 169.254.0.0 Class B address that does not include DNS name resolution or a default gateway.

Determining Impact of Modifying, Adding or Removing Network Services for Network Resources and Users

Because the Application Layer is the layer at which name resolution services like DNS and WINS (Windows Internet Naming Service) function, this is the layer you'll be working at if you run into a troubleshooting scenario involving clients that cannot access resources using their Fully Qualified Domain Names (FQDNs) or NetBIOS names. This builds from the troubleshooting that you performed at all of the layers below: at the Physical Layer, you looked for broken cables or malfunctioning NICs to isolate physical connectivity problems. At the Network Layer, you used ping and tracert (or traceroute for a UNIX/Linux computer) to determine if network packets were being properly routed from one host to another. Troubleshooting the Application Layer means that all of the underlying layers are functioning properly, but your clients are still running into problems. If you can ping a remote host using its IP address, but pinging its

FQDN returns a "Request Timed Out" error, then you have an issue with DNS name resolution. You can use *nslookup* or *dig* to troubleshoot an existing DNS server, as we discussed in the previous chapter. If, on the other hand, you are working on an internal network that doesn't have a DNS server in place, you should consider implementing one so that your clients can access remote resources by using easy-to-remember hostnames rather than IP addresses.

Likewise, if your clients are unable to access remote hosts using their NetBIOS names, but they are able to access computers using their associated IP addresses, then you need to put a mechanism in place to allow your clients to perform NetBIOS name resolution. This is especially necessary to allow access to file and print services on a Windows network, since these services rely heavily on NetBIOS name resolution. On a small network with only two or three hosts, you can do this by placing an lmhosts file on each computer. An lmhosts file is a plain text file that includes the IP address of the host in question, followed by its NetBIOS name, as you can see here:

```
10.0.0.8        SERVER1
10.0.0.1        SERVER2
10.0.0.105      SERVER3
```

Once you go beyond a small number of clients and hosts, though, lmhosts files become difficult to manage. For larger networks, you should install a WINS server to provide NetBIOS name resolution on a larger scale, and configure your network clients to use this WINS server to register their NetBIOS names so that other clients can locate the resources that they need. You can think of a WINS server as performing the same function for NetBIOS name resolution that DNS does for Internet-based name resolution.

Test Day Tip

For a small number of clients, you can use a hosts file for basic DNS resolution as well. A hosts file will take the same format as an lmhosts file, except that it will use FQDNs instead of NetBIOS names.

Layer 7 Troubleshooting

You'll probably spend quite a bit of time troubleshooting Application Layer issues, since these are the most visible to an end user. This can be something as simple as "My Internet Explorer won't work" to troubleshooting mail routing issues for an e-mail server that's running SMTP. One of the most useful utilities for troubleshooting Application Layer protocols is Telnet, since you can use this tool to connect to many different application layer services by specifying the *port* that's used by the service. So you can Telnet to a Web server, specifying port 80, to see if the Web server is *listening* on that port. If the Web server doesn't respond, then you know that something is wrong with the Web service on that particular server. On the other hand, if you can successfully Telnet to port 80, then you know that the problem lies elsewhere and you can concentrate your troubleshooting efforts on problems with client configuration or name resolution.

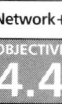

EXAM DAY TIP

To troubleshoot name resolution problems, you can use the nslookup utility that we discussed at length in Chapter 11.

Identifying a Client's Remote Network Access Problem

Network+
OBJECTIVE
4.4

In Exercise 12.3, we'll go through the steps of troubleshooting the SMTP service on an e-mail server by using Telnet.

EXERCISE 12.3

USING TELNET TO TROUBLESHOOT FTP

1. Click **Start | Programs | Accessories | Command Prompt** to access the Windows command prompt.

2. Type **telnet** *servername 25. Servername* indicates the IP address or DNS name of the e-mail server that you are troubleshooting. 25 specifies that you are Telnetting to port 25 of that server. So to connect to the mail.example.com server, you would type **telnet mail.example.com 25** at the command prompt. If this is successful, you'll see something like this:

```
220 mail.example.com Microsoft Exchange Internet Mail Connector
```

3. From here, you can try to send a test e-mail message directly from the Telnet window. Begin by typing the following (substitute the domain of a valid email address for *example.com*):

```
HELO example.com
```

4. If this command works, you'll see the following:

```
250 OK
```

5. Next, specify the e-mail address that the test message is from by entering the following, using a valid e-mail address:

```
MAIL FROM:user@example.com
```

6. If this was successful, you'll see the following:

```
250 OK - MAIL FROM user@example.com
```

7. Next, specify the e-mail address to send the test message to. Type the following, using a valid recipient address that's located on the server you're testing (so if you're troubleshooting the example.com email server, try sending a test message to jenny@example.com rather than joe@mycompany.com). Use the following syntax to specify the recipient's e-mail address:

```
RCPT TO: jenny@example.com
```

8. If this was successful, you'll see the following:

```
250 OK - Recipient jenny@example.com
```

9. Type **DATA** to begin entering the text of your message. Then type the text of the test message that you want to send.

10. To let the SMTP server know that you're finished, type a period (.) on a blank line and then press **Enter**. If the message was created successfully, you'll see the following:

```
250 OK
```

11. Type **QUIT** to exit the Telnet session. Verify that the recipient received the test message. If it did not, you can check the error logs generated by the e-mail server, as well as the configuration of the recipient's e-mail client.

Summary of Exam Objectives

Troubleshooting TCP/IP and other network connectivity issues is made easier if you follow the Ten Commandments of Troubleshooting:

1. Know thy network.
2. Use the tools of the trade.
3. Take it one change at a time.
4. Isolate the problem.
5. Recreate the problem.
6. Don't overlook the obvious.
7. Try the easy way first.
8. Document what you do.
9. Practice the art of patience.
10. Seek help from others when you need it.

There is a great deal of troubleshooting information for TCP/IP and other network issues. Be sure to take advantage of the following:

- Microsoft documentation, including Help files, the Resource Kits, white papers, TechNet, official newsgroups, and the Microsoft website.
- Third-party documentation, including Internet mailing lists, Usenet public newsgroups, Web resources, local user groups, and books and magazines.

Following an organized set of troubleshooting steps allows you to organize the troubleshooting process and makes it less likely that you will overlook something important along the way. The problem-solving models used by other professions can be applied to network troubleshooting as well. Gathering information is always one of the first steps in problem solving. In network troubleshooting, as in most areas, this involves asking questions. Which questions to ask (and of whom) vary according to the situation, but the following can serve as a guideline to get you started:

- Exactly what task were you trying to perform when the problem occurred?
- Were you doing anything else in addition to this primary task at the time?
- What error message(s), if any, were displayed?
- Is anyone else on the network experiencing the same problem?
- Have you ever been able to perform this task on this computer?
- When was the last time you were able to do so?
- What changes have occurred since the last time you were able to do so?

In order to make a diagnosis or analysis of the information, you must organize it in a logical manner. This means learning to sift through and discard irrelevant information, and looking for patterns in the data. This also means setting priorities according to such factors as who is affected by the problem, how many are affected by the problem, what production activities are affected by the problem, and how often the problem occurs. Solutions, once formulated, should also be prioritized according to cost, time involved, longevity, and long-term effect on performance.

Exam Objectives Fast Track

Application Layer Troubleshooting

- ☑ The Application Layer is the top layer of the OSI model, and provides services to actual end user applications on the desktop or server.

- ☑ Be sure you understand the difference between the Application Layer protocol, like HTTP, and the actual application that it supports, like Internet Explorer.

- ☑ You can use Telnet to connect to specific ports on a server to see if the HTTP, SMTP, and FTP protocols are functioning.

Presentation Layer Troubleshooting

- ☑ The Presentation Layer handles the way that data is formatted between different systems, such as translating text from a system that uses EBCDIC encoding and one that uses ASCII.

- ☑ In many cases, the function of the Presentation Layer is handled by the Application Layer service like HTTP, so isolating Presentation Layer problems can be difficult.

- ☑ Certain types of gateways also function at the Presentation Layer, such as Gateway Service for NetWare in Windows 2000 Server.

Session Layer Troubleshooting

- ☑ The Session Layer controls how two computers will create, maintain and tear down a conversation (also called a session) between them.

- ☑ The Session Layer also controls whether a connection is full-duplex (able to transmit in both directions simultaneously), or half-duplex (only able to transmit in one direction at a time).

☑ A mismatch in full-versus half-duplex can create significant performance degradation between two computers that are attempting to communicate.

Transport Layer Troubleshooting

☑ The Transport Connection Protocol (TCP) and the User Datagram Protocol (UDP) both exist at the Transport Layer, which controls whether communications between computers are connection-oriented and acknowledged, or connectionless with low overhead.

☑ Use **netstat –a** to see a list of which TCP and UDP ports are currently listening on a particular server.

☑ You can use Telnet to test connectivity at the Transport Layer in addition to testing the Application Layer.

Network Layer Troubleshooting

☑ A great deal of your troubleshooting time will be spent at the Network Layer, since this actually controls how traffic is transmitted or *routed* between two computers.

☑ The most important device that operates at the Network Layer is the router, and router troubleshooting will include troubleshooting the physical device as well as how it is configured.

☑ ICMP operates at the Network Layer, and is used to provide troubleshooting information for TCP/IP troubleshooting utilities such as ping, tracert, and traceroute.

Data Link Layer

☑ The Data Link layer is responsible for taking the information it gets from the Physical layer and organizing it into *frames*.

☑ The devices that operate at the Data Link Layer are switches and bridges. Troubleshooting these devices includes verifying that the correct frame type is being used and that any virtual LANs (VLANs) are configured correctly.

☑ The Spanning Tree Protocol (STP) can be used to prevent the possibility of loops on a switched or bridged network.

Physical Layer

☑   The Physical Layer is the lowest layer of the OSI model, and is concerned with the physical cabling and network devices that connect you to the network.

☑   Troubleshooting often begins at the Physical Layer, where you need to determine if your network cards, hubs, and cabling are functioning and connected correctly.

☑   Be sure that you are using the correct type of NIC for your network type and the correct cabling to allow for network connectivity.

Exam Objectives Frequently Asked Questions

The following Frequently Asked Questions, answered by the authors of this book, are designed to both measure your understanding of the Exam Objectives presented in this chapter, and to assist you with real-life implementation of these concepts. You will also gain access to thousands of other FAQs at ITFAQnet.com.

Q: Is it possible for me to disable NetBIOS over TCP/IP (NetBT)?

A: Microsoft states that you can remove NetBT once you have a pure Windows 2000 environment. Since WINS relies on NetBT, you cannot disable NetBT until you are no longer relying on WINS for name resolution. Additionally, legacy applications and logon scripts often use NetBIOS names, and these must be modified to use DNS name resolution before you can remove NetBT. You can disable NetBT via DHCP on Windows 2000 clients when you are ready to make the change.

Q. What types of networks are most likely to use OSPF instead of RIP?

A: Large enterprise networks and very large internetworks, such as corporate campuses and global networks. Microsoft documentation generally recommends that OSPF be used for internetworks that include more than 50 networks. OSPF is also appropriate for networks in which the topology changes frequently, and those that include more than one path between pairs of endpoints.

Q. What is a gateway, and why would I need one?

A. The word *gateway* has many different meanings in the IT world. A *protocol-translating gateway* translates between different protocols. Think of it as the United Nations interpreter of the networking world. If the President of the United States needs to exchange information with the Chancellor of Germany, but neither speaks the other's language, they can call in someone who is fluent in both to help them get their messages across. Similarly, if a mainframe system and a Windows 2000 computer need to communicate with one another—perhaps the mainframe has important files that need to be accessed by the PC—but they don't know how to "talk" to each other, you can install a gateway to clear up the confusion. The gateway is even more skilled than the interpreter is; it actually fools the mainframe into believing it's communicating with another mainframe, and makes the PC think it is having a "conversation" with a fellow PC. *Gateway* is also the term used to refer to the address of a router that connects your network to another, acting as the gateway to the "outside world."

Q: What is the difference between TCP and UDP if they both operate at the Transport Layer?

A: Although both TCP and UDP are Transport Layer protocols and provide the same basic function, TCP is a connection-oriented protocol, which means a session is established before data is transmitted, and acknowledgments are sent back to the sending computer to verify that the data did arrive and was accurate and complete. UDP is connectionless; no session or one-to-one connection is established prior to data transmission. This makes UDP the faster of the two, while TCP is the more reliable.

Self Test

A Quick Answer Key follows the Self Test questions. For complete questions, answers, and explanations to the Self Test questions in this chapter as well as the other chapters in this book, see the Self Test Appendix.

1. You are a network consultant specializing in supporting Small Office Home Office (SOHO) networks. One of your clients maintains an office consisting of three workstations configured in a peer-to-peer workgroup. This office does not have a server computer at this time. One of the workstations, \\OFFICE1, has an IP address of 192.168.1.100 and hosts a file share that the other three workstations are able to access using the following syntax: \\OFFICE1\share. Your client has called you in to troubleshoot a new workstation that they have recently installed that is unable to access this share. When you arrive on site, you find that the workstation is able to ping OFFICE1 by its IP address, but not by its NetBIOS name. What is the best way for you to allow the new workstation to access the file share located on OFFICE1?

A. Upgrade OFFICE1 to Windows 2000 server and configure the WINS Server service.

B. Add an entry to the lmhosts file on the new workstation.

C. Add an entry to the hosts file on the new workstation.

D. Upgrade OFFICE1 to Windows 2000 server and configure the DNS service.

2. You are troubleshooting network connectivity issues on a network that is running Windows servers and clients. Users are reporting that they are unable to send e-mail, though they have been receiving messages from external users without a problem. During your troubleshooting, you see the following configuration item on the Windows server. Based on this information, how can you correct the issue that this office is reporting?

Figure 12.8 Network Connectivity Configuration

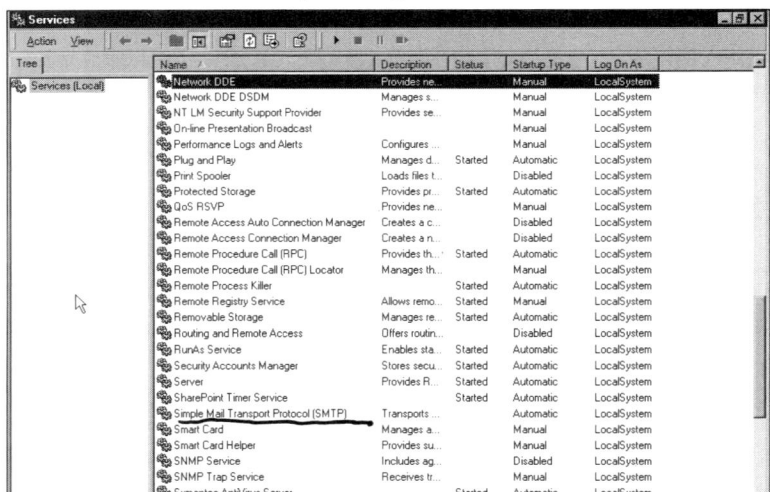

A. Install and configure the POP3 service.

B. Change the startup type of the SNMP Trap Service to **Automatic**.

C. Start the Simple Mail Transport Protocol (SMTP) service.

D. Start the Routing and Remote Access Service.

3. You are a network consultant and have been called in to troubleshoot a connectivity issue on a UNIX network. From the client's UNIX workstations, which of the following utilities can you use to perform network troubleshooting? (Select all that apply.)

A. ping

B. tracert

C. pathping

D. traceroute

E. nslookup

F. dig

4. You are the network administrator for a network that employs a Windows 2000 server and 30 Windows XP Professional workstations. The Windows 2000 server runs the DHCP service to provide TCP/IP configuration information to the Windows XP clients. You receive a call from one of your users stating that he is unable to browse any internal network resources or Internet websites. Other users on the same subnet are able to browse without difficulty. You run the **ipconfig** command on the problem workstation and see the following output:

```
Windows IP Configuration

        Host Name . . . . . . . . . . .    : IBM-A38375FF22E

        Primary Dns Suffix  . . . . . . .  :

        Node Type . . . . . . . . . . .    : Hybrid

        IP Routing Enabled. . . . . . ..   : No

        WINS Proxy Enabled. . . . . .      : No

Ethernet adapter Wireless Network Connection :

        Connection-specific DNS Suffix  .  :

        Description . . . . . . . . . .    : Intel(R) PRO/Wireless 2200BG
        Network Connection

        Physical Address. . . . . . . .    : 00-1E-25-1A-D3-5A

        Dhcp Enabled. . . . . . . . . .    : Yes

        Autoconfiguration Enabled . . . . .  : Yes

        IP Address. . . . . . . . . . .    : 169.254.1.96

        Subnet Mask . . . . . . . . . .    : 255.255.0.0

        Default Gateway . . . . . . . .    :

        DHCP Server . . . . . . . . . .    :

        DNS Servers . . . . . . . . . .    :

        Lease Obtained. . . . . . . .   .  : Tuesday, March 29, 2005 1:00:10
        PM

        Lease Expires . . . . . . . . .    : Wednesday, March 30, 2005 1:00:10
        PM
```

Based on this output, why is this workstation unable to browse any network resources?

A.   The default gateway is unavailable.

B.   The workstation could not contact a DHCP server.

C.   The workstation is configured with the incorrect default gateway.

D.   The workstation's DHCP lease has expired.

5.   You are the network administrator for a sales office. Until now, this has been a small peer-to-peer network consisting of five Windows 2000 professional workstations using lmhosts files on each workstation to perform DNS name resolution. The sales force has recently expanded significantly, requiring you to purchase a Windows Server 2003 server and fifteen additional workstations. You have encountered numerous troubleshooting situations where a workstation's lmhosts file was missing or out of date, preventing name resolution from taking place. How can you improve the name resolution process for your network?

A.   Install the DNS service on the Windows 2000 server.

B.   Install the WINS service on the Windows 2000 server.

C.   Install the DHCP service on the Windows 2000 server.

D.   Install the DNS service on each Windows XP workstation.

6.   You are the network administrator for a large pharmaceutical company that has over 1,000 workstations. To simplify TCP/IP configuration for these numerous clients, you installed a DHCP server over a year ago to automatically configure your clients with an IP address, as well as the following common configuration information:

```
Subnet Mask:      255.255.0.0
Default Gateway:  172.16.0.1
DNS Servers:      172.16.0.100
                  172.16.0.101
```

As part of a recent network redesign, you had to change the default gateway used by your clients to a different IP address: 172.16.1.1. You made the necessary change on the DHCP server, and most of your clients were updated automatically. After you make this change, you receive a call from one user who no longer able to browse the Internet. You examine the TCP/IP configuration of her LAN connection and see the following:

Figure 12.9 Internal Protocol Properties

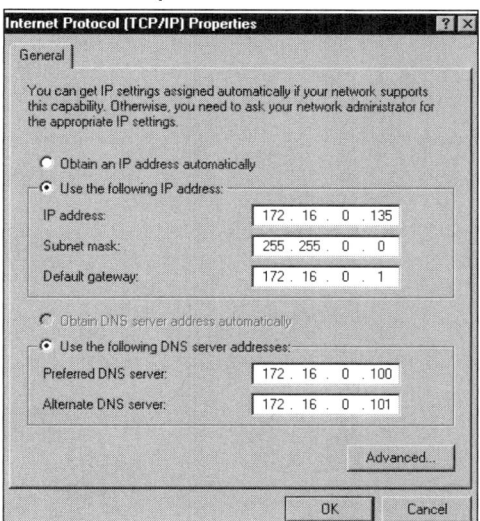

How can you configure this workstation with the correct default gateway information? (Each choice represents a complete solution. Choose two.)

A. Delete the manually configured information and select **Obtain an IP address automatically**.

B. Run **ipconfig /renew** from the command prompt.

C. Manually update the IP address of the default gateway.

D. Run **ipconfig /release** from the command prompt.

7. You are the administrator for the network shown in the following figure. Based on the information in this figure, which computer is configured incorrectly?

Figure 12.10 Incorrect Configuration on Network

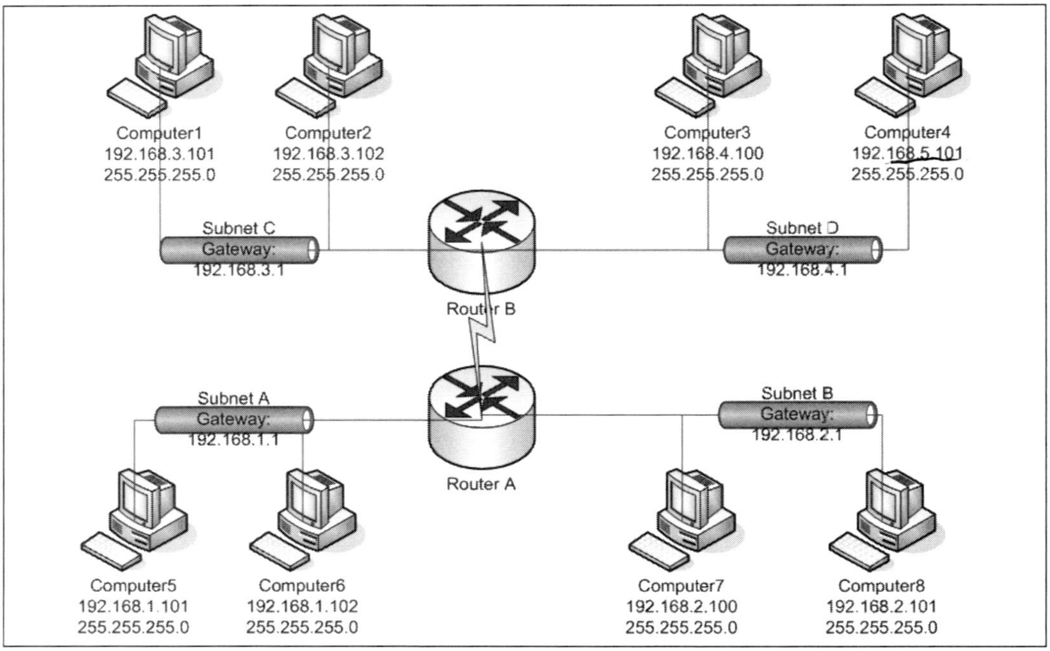

A. Computer1

B. Computer2

C. Computer3

D. Computer4

E. Computer5

F. Computer6

G. Computer7

H. Computer8

8. You are the network administrator for the network shown in the following figure. You have recently purchased a new Windows XP workstation called Computer9 that you now need to add to Subnet C. Which of the following would be a valid IP address that would allow Computer9 to access resources on all four subnets?

Figure 12.11 Valid IP Address for Accessing Resources

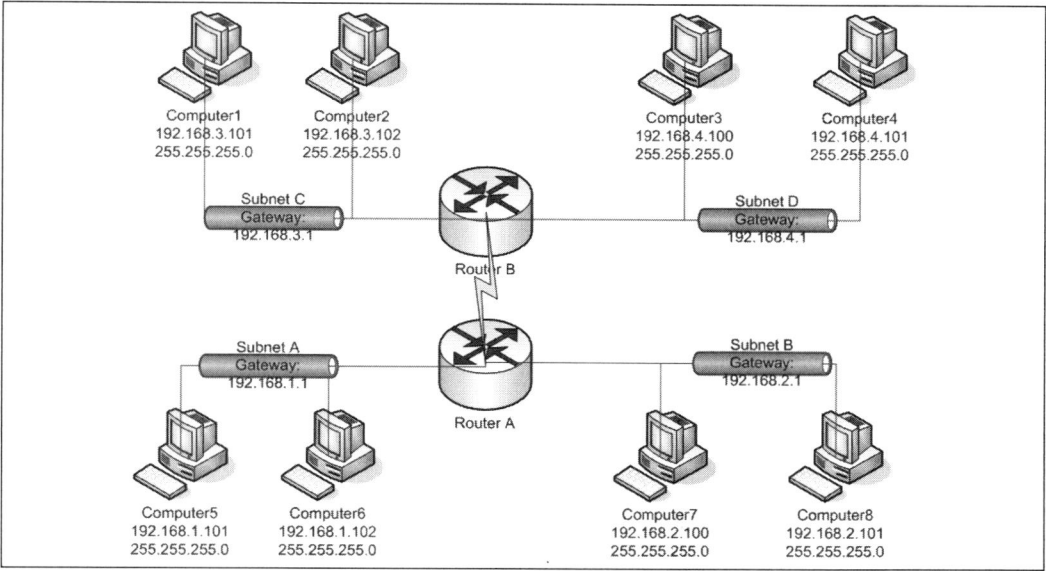

A. 192.168.3.155

B. 192.168.3.1

C. 192.168.3.0

D. 192.168.3.255

9. You are the administrator for the network shown in the following figure. You receive a help desk call from the user of Computer8, stating that she cannot browse the Internet or access a shared folder located on Computer5. Upon investigating the issue, you find that Computer7 is able to access the Internet and other shared resources, but Computer8 cannot ping any other hosts on the network. Based on this information, which of the following are likely points of failure that you should investigate? (Each selection represents a complete choice. Select all that apply.)

Figure 12.12 Likely Points of Failure on the Network

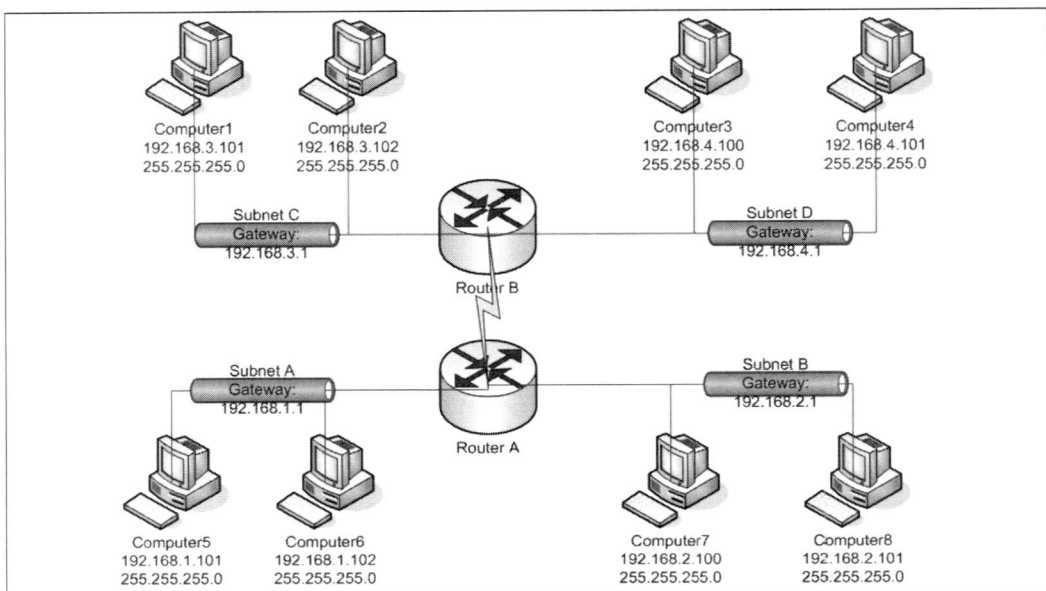

A. The NIC installed in Computer8

B. The network cable attaching Computer8 to the network

C. The NIC installed in RouterA attached to Subnet B

D. The TCP/IP configuration of Computer7

10. You are the administrator of the network shown in the following figure. The firewall in the exhibit was installed by an outside consultant a few weeks ago. Once a
month, one of your company's employees needs to access the FTP site of one of
your company's business partners, ftp.airplanes.com, in order to download large PDF
files containing product marketing information. You receive a help desk call from
this employee, stating that he is now unable to access this FTP site. The last time he
performed this task was before the firewall was installed, and he says that it worked
fine then. You are able to ping the ftp.airplanes.com DNS name, and you can access
www.airplanes.com, which is located on the same physical machine. What is the
best way to restore this employee's access to the ftp.airplanes.com FTP site?

Figure 12.13 Restoring FTP Access After Firewall Installation

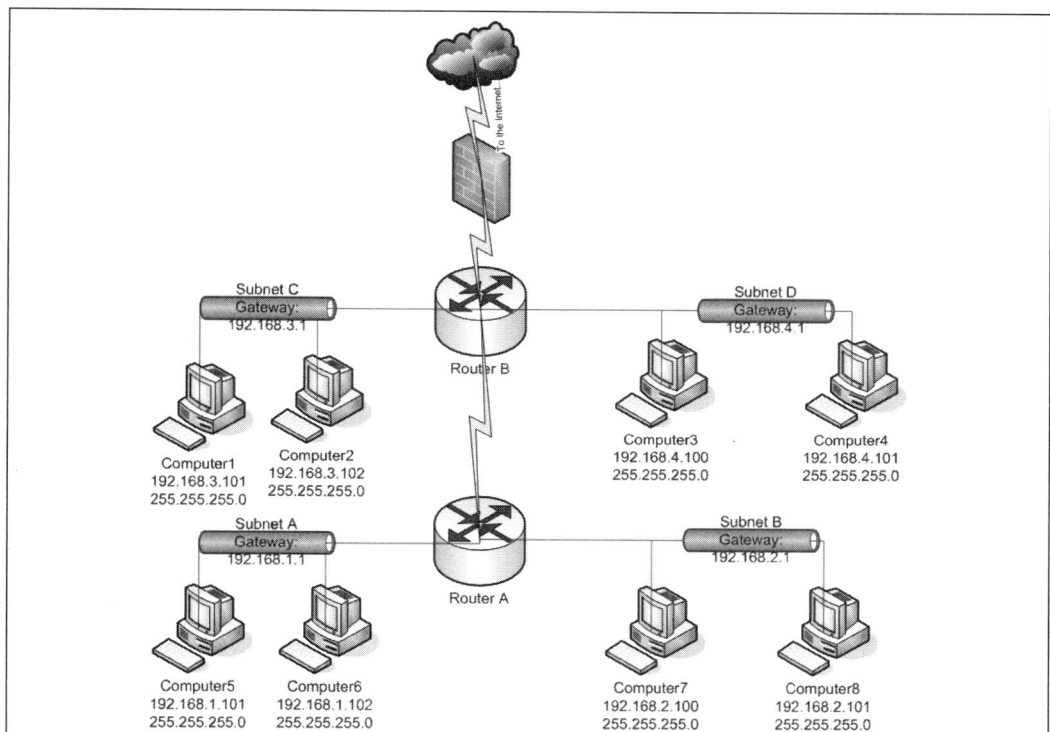

A. Configure a firewall rule allowing traffic to TCP ports 20 and 21.

B. Configure a firewall rule allowing traffic to TCP ports 25 and 110.

C. Configure a firewall rule allowing all TCP traffic to this employee's workstation.

D. Configure a firewall rule allowing traffic to TCP ports 80 and 443.

11. You are the network administrator for a medium-sized law firm. You have recently deployed a wireless access point (WAP) for use by your internal support staff and attorneys. You have been charged with ensuring that only legitimate users of your company network will be able to access these wireless access points. What are some steps you can take to enable network connectivity to your wireless access point so that only legitimate users will be able to obtain access? (Each choice represents a complete answer. Choose all that apply.)

A. Enable MAC address filtering.

B. Enable the default SSID broadcast.

C. Enable WEP or WPA encryption.

D. Enable the DHCP server on the wireless access point.

12. You are the administrator of the network shown in the following figure. You receive a call from the users of Computer5 and Computer6, stating that they cannot access any resources on the Internet. No other users on the network are reporting outages. Based on this diagram, what is most likely causing this connectivity issue?

Figure 12.14 Connectivity Issued with Computer5 and Computer6

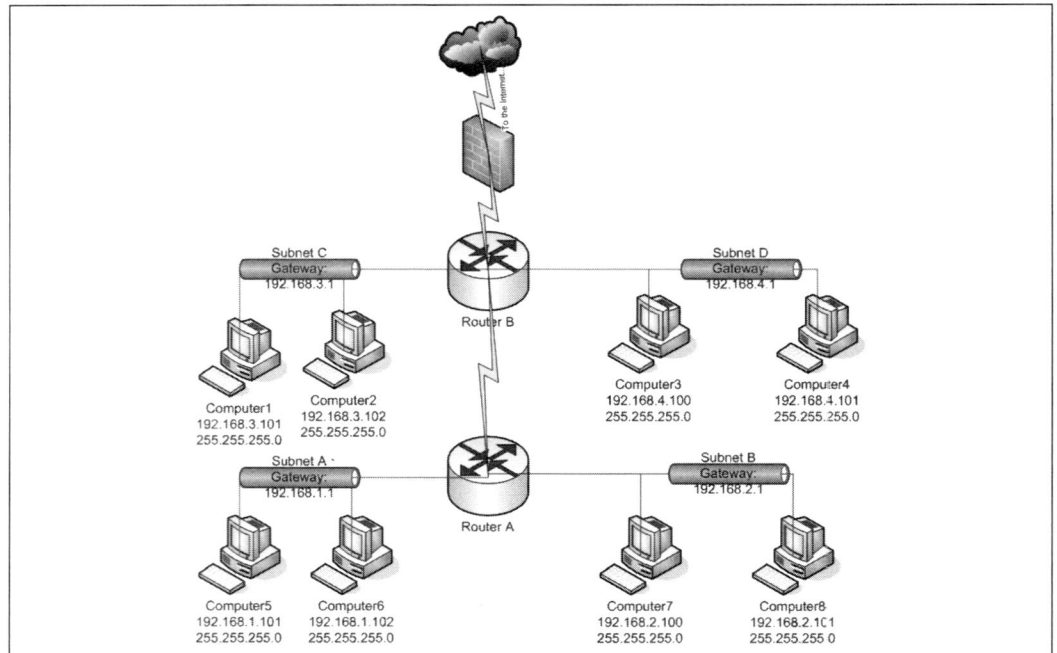

A. The network cable attaching Computer5 to the network.

B. The 192.168.1.1 interface on Router A.

C. The 192.168.4.1 interface on Router B.

D. The 192.168.5.1 interface on Router A

13. You are the administrator of the network shown in the following figure. The user of Computer1 is unable to access a shared resource located on Computer3. Computer1 is able to access shared resources on other subnets on the internal network as well as the Internet. Computer3 is able to access shared resources on Computer5 and Computer7, as well as resources on the Internet. When you ping Computer1 from Computer3, you receive a "Request Timed Out" message. Based on this information, what is the most likely cause of the connectivity issue?

Figure 12.15 "Request Timed Out" on Computer1 and Computer3

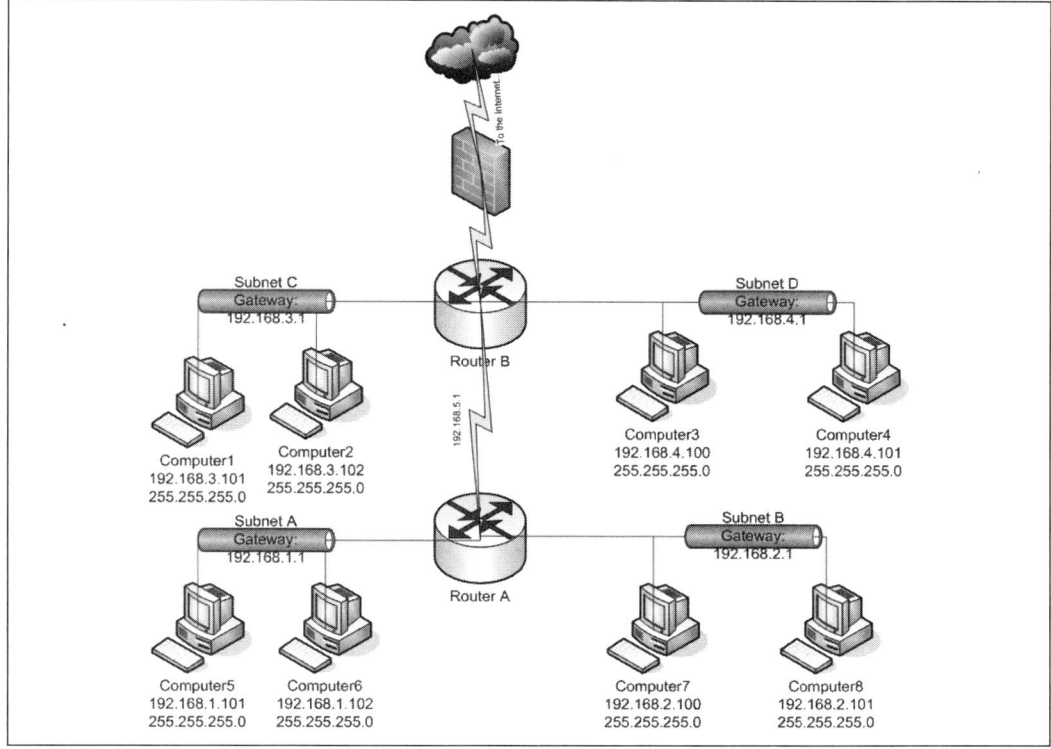

A. The router interface attached to Subnet D is malfunctioning.

B. The router interface attached to Subnet C is malfunctioning.

C. Router B does not have a route from Subnet C to the Internet.

D. Router B does not have a route from Subnet C to Subnet D.

Self Test Quick Answer Key

For complete questions, answers, and explanations to the Self Test questions in this chapter as well as the other chapters in this book, see the Self Test Appendix.

1. **B**

2. **C**

3. **A**, **D**, and **F**

4. **B**

5. **B**

6. **A** and **C**

7. **D**

8. **A**

9. **A** and **B**

10. **A**

11. **A** and **C**

12. **B**

13. **D**

NETWORK+

Self Test Appendix

Chapter 1 Network Fundamentals

1. You are creating a network for a small business with only four employees. Because employees often leave the office to visit clients, a minimum of one person is in the office and using a computer at any given time. Currently there are two computers in the office, but the company is willing to purchase more if needed. Based on this information, what is the minimum number of computers that you'll need to create a network?

   A. One

   B. Two

   C. Three

   D. Four

   ☑ **B**. Two. A network can exist when two or more computers are connected together to form a network. While additional computers can be used to create the network, a minimum of two is needed so the computers can communicate and exchange data.

   ☒ **A**, **C**, **D**. Answer **A** is incorrect because at least two computers are necessary to create a network. If there is only one computer, it would be a standalone, and not connected to a network of other computers. Answers **C** and **D** are incorrect because the question asks for the minimum number of computers needed to create a network.

2. The LAN used by your organization is on a single floor of a building. The network has servers and other resources that are kept in a secure server room. You are the only network administrator in the organization, and have sole responsibility for managing these resources and administration of network security for all of the users who are distributed throughout the network. What type of network model is being used?

   A. Centralized

   B. Decentralized

   C. Distributed

   D. Peer-to-peer

   ☑ **A**. Centralized. Centralized network models have resources that are centrally located and administered. In this situation, there is one network administrator that is responsible for managing servers and other resources that are centrally located.

☒ **B, C, D**. Answers **B** and **C** are incorrect because decentralized and distributed networks have resources and administration that spans the entire network. They are not centrally located, but various system administrators or designated users provide management of resources in various areas of the network. Answer **D** is incorrect because servers are used, making this a client/server model.

3. Your company's network is on several floors of a building. Due to the amount of data being stored, there are three file servers, a Web server for the intranet, an e-mail server for internal e-mail, and a SQL server that is used for several databases that have been developed in house. Due to security reasons, floppy disks and other devices to transfer or transmit data to and from the computer have been removed and aren't permitted. What type of network model is being used?

A. Client/server

B. Peer-to-peer

C. MAN

D. PAN

☑ **A**. Client/server. Computers on this network act as clients by requesting data and other services from dedicated servers. The Client/Server model involves dedicated servers that provide services and data to clients, without making similar requests of them. It consists of high-end computers serving clients on a network, by providing them with specific services upon request.

☒ **B, C, D**. Answer **B** is incorrect because servers are being used, so this isn't a peer-to-peer network. On a peer-to-peer network, computers on the network are equals and aren't in the role of dedicated servers. Answers **C** and **D** are incorrect because these aren't network models, they are types of networks. Because the network doesn't extend across a metropolitan area, it isn't a MAN, and because personal devices aren't being used to network with computers or other network devices, it isn't a PAN.

4. A company has hired you to create a network for their small business. Security isn't an issue, and there isn't enough money to hire or train a permanent network administrator. Users of the network routinely work on similar projects, and need to access one another's data on a regular basis. What type of network model will you use?

A. Client/server

B. Peer-to-peer

C. Client

D. Server

☑   **B**. Peer-to-Peer. On a peer-to-peer network, computers on the network are equals and have the ability to access data and services they've been permitted to use on other machines, as well as to provide services and data to others.

☒   **A, C, D**. Answer **A** is incorrect because the requirements specified in the question define a peer-to-peer network model. A client/server model provides increased security, which isn't needed for this network, and also generally requires someone to be hired or trained as a network administrator. Answers **C** and **D** are incorrect because these aren't network models, but are roles on a client/server network. A client requests data and resources, while a server provides them.

5. A company has multiple offices that are internetworked. Office A has a single computer that has the ability to dial into the Internet, but isn't connected to the other offices. Office B is in another part of the country from the other offices, but doesn't have its network interconnected to the other offices. Offices C and D are in separate states, but have a dedicated connection between them. Office C has twenty computers that access each other's machines, and provide services and data to one another. Office D has fifty computers that log onto the network using a single server. Based on this information, which of the offices are part of both a LAN and a WAN?

    A.   Offices A and B

    B.   Offices B and C

    C.   Offices C and D

    D.   The entire network (Offices A, B, C, and D)

    ☑   **C**. Offices C and D. Both of these offices have LANs. Office C has a peer-to-peer network, while Office D has a client/server network. They are interconnected to one another, and thereby part of a WAN.

    ☒   **A, B, D**. Answer **A** is incorrect because Office A doesn't have a network, but only an Internet connection, and because Office B isn't part of a WAN. Answer **B** is incorrect because although Office B has a LAN, it isn't connected to the other networks and therefore isn't part of the WAN. Answer **D** is incorrect because not every office has a LAN, and the others connected together form a WAN.

6. An organization has offices in two countries. Office A is a small field office with two networked computers and is internetworked with Office B, which is across the road and has ten networked computers. Because they are a subsidiary of the main company, and perform different services from the rest of the organization, neither of these offices has been internetworked with the other offices, and is awaiting Internet

connectivity to be provided next month. Office C is another field office that has a single computer, isn't networked with other offices, and only has an Internet connection. Office D is the headquarters of the company, has one hundred network users who are awaiting Internet connectivity to be added to the network, and has a network connection to Office E in London, which is their European office. Based on this information, which of the offices is connected to the largest WAN?

   A. Office A

   B. Office B

   C. Office C

   D. Office D

   ☑ **C**. Office C. Office C is connected to the Internet, which is the largest WAN.

   ☒ **A, B, D**. Answers **A** and **B** are incorrect because Office A and Office B are networked together, but are across the road from one another, and have the smallest number of network users (except for Office C, which has no users who are part of this network). Answer **D** is incorrect because although they have a WAN connecting the LANs in each country, Office D doesn't have a connection to the Internet (which is the largest WAN).

7. A company wants to create a WAN between two networks in different cities. To connect them, you want to have the fastest possible connection to meet their needs. Each network has massive amounts of data being sent between floors of their existing networked building, and you determine that at maximum, 1Mbps of data will have to be transmitted during normal business hours. Although they are a large business, and cost is not a major issue, they don't want to waste money on getting a solution with a bandwidth that's higher than they need. What type of connection will you choose in connecting these networks?

   A. Dial-up modem

   B. ISDN

   C. T1

   D. T3

   ☑ **C**. T1. Office C is connected to the Internet, which is the largest Wide Area Network. The company needs to send a maximum of 1Mbps, which is below the T1 speed of 1.544Mbps. While slower than T3 (which is more expensive), it meets the needs of the company.

⊠ **A, B, D**. Answer **A** is incorrect because a dial-up modem has a maximum speed of 56Kbps, which is well below what they need. Answer **B** is incorrect because it, too, has a lower bandwidth than they need. ISDN has a maximum speed of 128Kbps. Answer **D** is incorrect because a T3 connection provides speeds ranging from 3Mbps to 44.736Mbps, which makes it faster than required for their needs. It is also the most expensive, meaning that a T3 would be a waste of money.

8.   A company has several offices that are networked together across the city. Each of the sales representatives uses PDAs to keep track of appointments with clients. The company has just implemented a new system where the appointments taken by receptionists are automatically uploaded to the PDAs whenever the sales staff enters the main reception area. What types of networks are being used in this environment? Choose all that apply.

A. MAN

B. SAN

C. CAN

D. PAN

☑ **A** and **D**. MAN and PAN. A MAN is a metropolitan area network and consists of a group of LANs that are internetworked within a local geographical area, such as a city. A PAN is a personal area network, which allows wireless transmission of information between computers and devices like PDAs.

⊠ **C, D**. Answer **C** is incorrect because a SAN is a storage area network, in which storage devices are networked together on a segment of the network so that computers on a LAN can view and store data on them. Answer **D** is incorrect because the network is more dispersed than a CAN. A CAN is a campus area network, which internetworks buildings that are closely situated together.

9.   You have been hired by a company that uses the topology shown below. In looking at the physical layout of your network, which of the following types of topologies is being used?

Figure 1.9 Network Topology

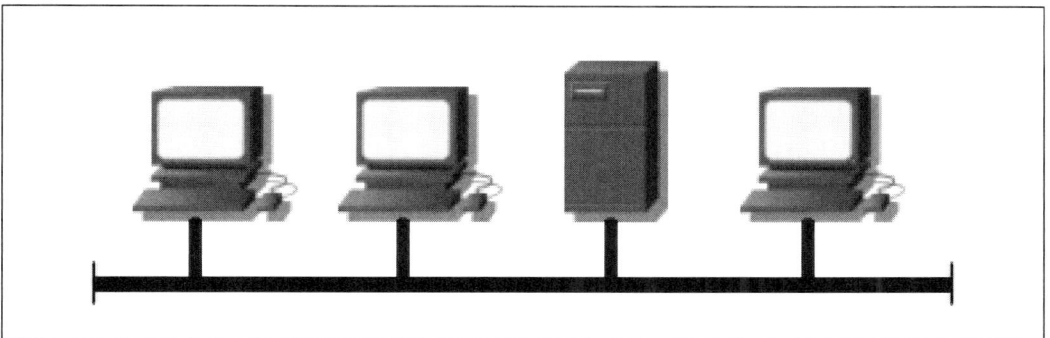

A. Bus

B. Star

C. Mesh

D. Ring

☑ **A.** Bus. In a bus topology, all of the computers are connected together using a single cable, which is called a trunk, backbone, or segment.

☒ **B, C, D.** Answer **B** is incorrect because a star topology has computer connected to a central hub or switch. Answer **C** is incorrect because a mesh topology has every component of the network connected directly to every other component. Answer **D** is incorrect because a ring topology has computers connected to cables in a physical ring arrangement.

10. Your network uses cells to send and receive data to and from computers. This allows computers in different buildings to be networked together so they can access data from servers in either building. A topology map has been created, using circles to identify the areas that computers can be placed to access the network. Based on this information, which of the following topologies is being used?

A. Star

B. Mesh

C. Wireless

D. Ring

☑ **C.** Wireless. A wireless topology uses transmitters called cells, which broadcast the packets using radio frequencies. The cells extend a radio sphere around the transmitter in the shape of a bubble that can extend to multiple rooms and possibly different floors in a building.

☒ **A, B, D**. Answer **A** is incorrect because a star network doesn't use cells to send and receive data to and from computers. It cables computers to a centralized hub. Answer **B** is incorrect because a mesh topology also doesn't use cells, but uses a greater amount of cable than any other topology due to multiple connections between a computer and other computers on the network. Answer **D** is incorrect because a ring topology also doesn't use cells, but has computers connected to a looped cable.

11. You are training a new member of the IT staff, and decide to explain the topology of the existing network, shown below. What topology is currently being used?

A. Bus

B. Star

C. Mesh

D. Ring

☑ **C**. Mesh. A mesh topology has every component of the network connected directly to every other component. This creates an extremely fault tolerant network, but is expensive and difficult to maintain.

☒ **A, B, D**. Answer **A** is incorrect because in a bus topology, all of the computers are connected using a single cable, which is called a trunk, backbone, or segment. Answer **B** is incorrect because a star topology has computers connected to a central hub or switch. Answer **D** is incorrect because a ring topology has computers connected to each other in a physical ring arrangement.

12. You are reviewing different topologies that will be used for a small network within your company. You want to ensure that all computers on the network have equal access. You also want to use a topology that is relatively easy to troubleshoot if a cable fails or breaks. Based on these criteria, which of the following topologies would you choose?

A. Bus

B. Mesh

C. Wireless

D. Ring

☑ **D**. Ring. In a ring topology, every computer has equal access to communicate on the network. An electronic signal called a token is passed around the network. When computer has the token, it has the option of communicating over the network, and will then pass it to the next computer in the loop.

☒ **A, B, C.** Incorrect Answers & Explanations: **A, B, C**. Answer **A** is incorrect because a bus topology requires computers to contend for access to the network. Answer **B** is also incorrect for this reason, because a mesh topology uses the most amount of cabling, as every network component is cabled to every other network component. Answer **C** is incorrect because clients access a wireless network using wireless technology, so all computers wouldn't be cabled to the network.

13. The IEEE 802 standards split a lower layer of the OSI model into two sublayers. One of these sublayers is used to establish connections between computers, and used by other protocols defined by the 802 committee. Which sublayer performs these actions, and which OSI layer is it part of?

   A. Media Access Control, which is part of the Data Link Layer

   B. Logical Link Control, which is part of the Data Link Layer

   C. Physical Layer, which is part of the Data Link Layer

   D. Data Link Layer, which is part of the Logical Link Control Layer

   ☑ **B**. Logical Link Control, which is part of the Data Link Layer. The LLC is covered by the 802.2 standard, and is one of two sublayers that correspond to the Data Link Layer of the OSI model. The Logical Link Control is used to establish connections between computers, and is used by other protocols defined by the 802 committee.

   ☒ **A, C, D**. Answer **A** is incorrect because the Media Access Control is not used to establish connections. The MAC allows multiple devices to share the media (coaxial cable, twisted-pair, etcetera) that data is being sent over. Answer **C** is incorrect because the Physical Layer of the OSI model isn't used to establish connections, but instead deals with how data is moves on and off the network media. Answer **D** is incorrect because the Logical Link Control is a sublayer of the Data Link Layer, not the other way around.

14. The network used in your organization uses the IEEE 802.3 standard. Before sending data onto the network, a computer will listen to ensure the network is clear so that two computers don't send data onto the cable at the same time. When two computers send out data at the same time, which of the following is true?

   A. A critical network error will have occurred from a collision, and the network will crash.

   B. The computer detecting the collision will send out a signal to all other computers. Because the collision has been detected, all devices will stop transmitting data for a random period of time, listen to see if the network is free of traffic, and then begin sending data again.

C.   The computer detecting the collision will send out a signal to all the other computers. Because it detected the problem, it now has precedence over the other computers, and can send its data before any other computer.

D.   None of the above. This cannot happen because the computers listen for network traffic before sending, which prevents data collisions from ever occurring.

☑   **B**. A network using Carrier Sense Multiple Access with Collision Detection or Ethernet is being discussed in this situation. If two devices transmit at the same time, a collision occurs. Each device stops transmitting and sends a signal to alert other nodes about the collision. Then, all the nodes stop transmitting and wait a random amount of time before listening to see if the network is clear so they can send data again.

☒   **A, C, D**. Answer **A** is incorrect because the network will not crash in the event of a collision. Collisions are normal in Ethernet. It is when collisions are excessive and the network is unable to function properly that it becomes a problem. Answer **C** is incorrect because sending data on an Ethernet network isn't a lottery of who can detect a collision so they can now send data. Precedence isn't given to computers who detect a collision. Answer **D** is incorrect because although computers do listen to see if the cable is clear of traffic, collisions can still occur. CSMA/CD minimizes collisions, but it doesn't prevent them completely.

15.   Your network uses a ring topology in which computers are connected to a closed loop of cabling. A secondary ring of cabling is also used. If the primary ring of cabling has a break, what will happen?

A.   The network will fail.

B.   The secondary ring will be used, but the primary ring won't be used.

C.   The primary ring will be used, but the secondary ring won't be used.

D.   Both rings will be used.

☑   **D**. Both rings will be used. The primary ring in a FDDI ring topology always uses the primary ring. If a break occurs in the ring, then the secondary ring is used. The data is passed off the primary ring to the secondary ring, so that it continues to loop around the ring topology.

☒   **A, B, C**. Answer **A** is incorrect because the network will not fail. Answers **B** and **C** are incorrect because the data will be passed off the primary ring to the secondary ring, so that a continuous loop still exists.

16. You are designing a network for an organization that will have all components of the network connected to every other component. In designing this network, you need to determine the number of connections that will be necessary to achieve this topology. You find that there are 20 computers on this network. Based on this information, how many connections will be needed?

    A. 20

    B. 40

    C. 150

    D. 190

    ☑ **D**. 190 connections would be needed. The scenario describes a mesh network, in which every component of the network is connected to every other component. To determine the number of connections required, the formula $Ln=n(n-1)/2$ would be used, where *n* is the number of computers. This would mean that for a network of twenty computers, the formula would be $20(20-1)/2$, which equals 190.

    ☒ **A, B, C**. Answer **A** is incorrect because this is the number of computers on the network. Answer **B** and **C** are incorrect because a mesh network of twenty computers would require 190 connections.

Chapter 2 Network Media

1. You are the network administrator of a 10BaseT network. On the weekend, when few people are working, you run 110 meters of cable to a new server that is being used as a file server. The cable is installed in a new section of the building, where no cabling currently exists. When you attempt to access files on the server, they are experiencing errors and corrupt data. Which of the following is most likely the cause of this problem?

    A. Bandwidth

    B. Attenuation

    C. Crosstalk from a neighboring cable

    D. CSMA/CD issues

    ☑ **B**. Attenuation. Attenuation occurs when data transmitted over media weakens over distance. The scenario states that the cable length is 110 meters, which is 10 meters longer than the maximum distance for 10BaseT.

    ☒ **A, C, D**. Answer **A** is incorrect because bandwidth is a measurement of the amount of data that can be passed over a cable in a given amount of time. Answer **C** is incorrect because the cable is being installed in a section of the building where no other cabling currently exists. Crosstalk occurs when the electromagnetic field of one wire interferes with the transmission of another. Answer **D** is incorrect because Carrier Sense Multiple Access with Collision Detection (CSMA/CD) prevents devices from interfering with one another during transmission by detecting collisions of data. It is not a cause for data to weaken or be corrupt.

2. Your company uses UTP cable for all of its network connections including workstations and servers. The users have reported problems connecting to one of the most important servers on the network and you have been called in to look at it, due to a possible physical security breach by a former employee. While examining the server, you find that a small battery-powered motor has been placed and is running next to the server's network connection. What is causing the network problem?

   A. Electromagnetic interference

   B. Static electricity

   C. Transceivers

   D. Unknown, but the motor is probably unrelated

   ☑ **A**. Electromagnetic interference (EMI) is a low voltage, low current, high frequency signal that can interfere with the electronic signals transmitted over cabling. The motor is powered by electromagnets whose presence can interfere with the flow of electrons along the UTP cable.

   ☒ **B**, **C**, **D**. Answer **B** is incorrect because static electricity may cause damage to network cards and other electronics, but will not interfere with network traffic on a UTP cable. Answer **C** is incorrect because transceivers are the portion of a network interface that transmits and receives electrical signals across the transmission media. It is unlikely that this is a cause of the problem. Answer **D** is incorrect because the small motor is most likely to be the source of this interference. Anytime a UTP cable is near electromagnetic interference there will be communications problems.

3. You are designing a new network and are concerned about interference from other wires. Which of the following is most susceptible to transmission errors due to crosstalk?

   A. Coaxial

   B. UTP

   C. STP

   D. Fiber optic

☑ **B**. UTP. Unshielded twisted-pair is most vulnerable to crosstalk. Crosstalk refers to the unwanted electrical fields induced by neighboring cables. These electrical fields generate false signals. Since the UTP cable is unshielded, it is more susceptible to transmission errors caused by crosstalk than any other given cable types.

☒ **A, C, D**. Answer **A** is incorrect because the coaxial cable is shielded and is less prone to errors cause by crosstalk. Answer **C** is incorrect because STP (shielded twisted-pair) is shielded, and thereby is also more protected against crosstalk. Answer **D** is incorrect because the fiber optic cable works on light signals and is not affected by either electrical or magnetic signals.

4. You are designing a new network for a grocery store. Cabling will have to run along the ceiling, where there are a significant number of florescent lights. You are concerned about interference from these lights. Which of the following cable types could be used, which would not be susceptible to this type of interference?

    A. Coaxial

    B. UTP

    C. STP

    D. Fiber optic

☑ **D**. Fiber Optic. Fiber optic cabling is the only type of cabling that is immune to electromagnetic interference. Fiber optic cable carries digital data signals in the form of modulated pulses of light, which isn't effected by EMI.

☒ **A, B, C**. Answers **A**, **B**, and **C** are incorrect, because each of these use copper wiring that is susceptible to EMI.

5. Your network uses vampire taps and AUI connectors to access data from the network cable. Which of the following cabling types is being used?

    A. Thinnet

    B. Thicknet

    C. STP

    D. Fiber optic

☑ **B**. Thicknet. Thicknet is a term for cabling used in 10Base5 networks. Thicknet coaxial cable can transfer data over longer distances than the 10Base2 Thinnet cable, and requires vampire taps to connect to the network interface card with the AUI (Adapter Unit Interface) connector. Thicknet is not a common cabling type and is only used in backbones.

☒ **A, C, D.** Answer **A** is incorrect because the Thinnet is a 10Base2 cable. Answer **C** is incorrect because STP is a twisted-pair cable that uses an RJ-45 connector, and not a vampire tap or AUI connector. Answer **D** is also incorrect because fiber optic cable doesn't use vampire taps or AUI connectors.

6. You are designing a 10Base2 network. In creating this network, what distance limitation will you be facing when installing the cabling?

    A.   100 meters

    B.   185 meters

    C.   500 meters

    D.   2 km

☑ **B.** 185. 10Base2 (Thinnet) has a distance limitation of 185 meters. 10Base5 (Thicknet) has a distance limitation of 500 meters, and 10BaseT has a distance limitation of 100 meters.

☒ **A, C, D.** Answer **A** is incorrect because 100 meters is a limitation for 10BaseT. Answer **C** is incorrect because 500 meters is a distance limitation for 10Base5 networks. Answer **D** is incorrect because 2 km is a distance limitation for fiber optic cable.

7. Examine the following illustration:

Figure 2.14 Determine Connectors for a 10Base2 Network

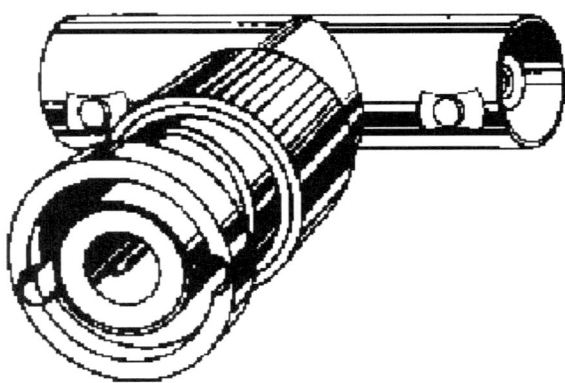

Your network is a 10Base2 network, and uses these connectors to attach to the network. Which of the following types of connectors is being used?

A. RJ-11

B. DIX

C. BNC Barrel Connector

D. BNC T-Connector

☑ **D**. BNC T-Connector. The connector shown in the illustration is a BNC T-Connector, which is circular and T-shaped. It is used to connect workstations to a 10Base2 (Thinnet) network.

☒ **A**, **B**, **C**. Answer **A** is incorrect because an RJ-11 connector is used to connect devices to a telephone line. An RJ-11 connector is a small square-shaped connector with a locking clip and several wire places inside the connector itself. Answer **B** is incorrect, because a DIX connector is D-shaped and has 15 pins. Answer **D** is incorrect because a BNC barrel connector is round or barrel-shaped.

8. You have been hired by a small company to cable its network. The company has offices in two buildings that are 300 meters apart. Both of the offices have about 15 computers and the numbers are expected to grow in near future. All of the computers are within 90 meters of one another. You need to decide on the cabling that will be used both in the individual buildings, and which will be used to connect the buildings LANs together. Which of the following will you do?

A. Use UTP cabling in each of the buildings, and connect the two buildings together using 10BaseT cabling.

B. Use fiber optic cabling in each of the buildings, and connect the two buildings together using 10Base2 cabling.

C. Use 10BaseT cabling in each of the buildings, and connect the two buildings together using 10Base5 cabling.

D. Use 100BaseFX cabling in each of the buildings, and connect the two buildings together using 10BaseT cabling.

☑ **C**. Use 10BaseT cabling in each of the buildings, and connect the two buildings together using 10Base5 cabling. The two offices can be connected using thick coaxial cable (10Base5), which can transfer data up to 500 meters. 10BaseT can be used within the buildings because it supports distances of 100 meters.

☒ **A**, **B**, **D**. Answer **A** is incorrect because 10BaseT has a distance limitation of 100 meters. This means that the two buildings can't be connected together. Answer **B** is incorrect because 10Base2 has a distance limitation of 185 meters, which is too short for the two buildings. Answer **D** is also incorrect because 10BaseT has a distance limitation of 100 meters.

9. Your network uses 100BaseFX so that data can be transferred at higher speeds and up to distances of 400 meters. During transmission, data can travel in both directions, but only in one direction at a given time. Which of the following transmission methods is used?

    A. Simplex

    B. FireWire

    C. Half-Duplex

    D. Full Duplex

    ☑   **C.** Half-Duplex. 100BaseFX is an Ethernet standard that uses fiber optic cabling. It can transmit data at speeds of 100 Mbps, but if communication is half-duplex, it can transmit data across cable segments that are up to 400 meters in length. If full duplex is used, then it can transmit data up to 2 kilometers. Because data travels both ways on the medium but in only one direction at a time, half-duplex is being described.

    ☒   **A, B, D.** Answer **A** is incorrect because simplex refers to data moving in a single direction. Answer **B** is incorrect because FireWire is a proprietary name for IEEE1394, which is an external bus that supports fast data transfer rates of 400Mbps and 800Mbps. Answer **D** is incorrect because full duplex refers to data traveling in both directions simultaneously.

10. Examine the following illustration:

Figure 2.15 Determine Connectors in Star Topology

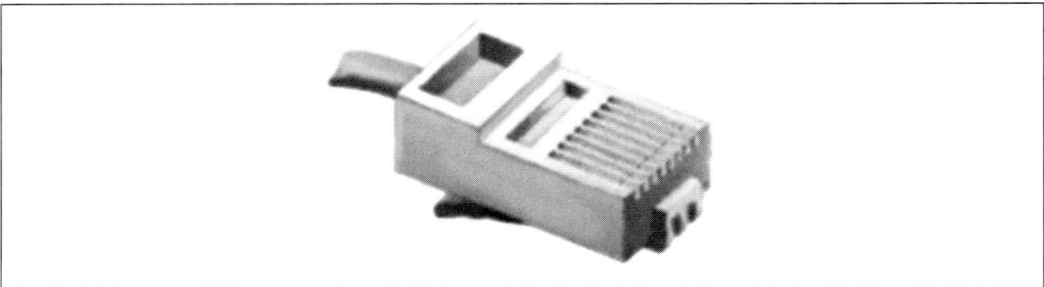

    Your network uses UTP cabling in a star topology. Which of the following types of connectors is being used?

    A. RJ-45

    B. BNC

    C. ST

    D. SC

☑   **A**. RJ-45. The illustration shows an RJ-45 connector. This type of connector is used in UTP (Unshielded Twisted-Pair) cabling, and commonly used for networks that use a star topology. An RJ-45 cable has 8 pins and is rectangular is shape with a plastic lock on one side.

☒   **B**, **C**, **D**. Answer **B** is incorrect, because a BNC Barrel connector is round or barrel shaped, while a BNC T connector is circular and T-shaped. Neither of these types of connectors is used on with UTP. Answer **C** and **D** are incorrect, because both ST and SC connectors are used with fiber optic cabling.

11. As a Network technician for 123 LLC, you are asked by your CIO about the access method of Gigabit Ethernet. Which of the following access methods does Gigabit Ethernet use?

A. FDDI

B. CSMA/CD

C. CSMA/CA

D. Token passing

☑   **B**. CSMA/CD. Gigabit Ethernet has evolved from Ethernet which uses the Carrier Sense Multiple Access with Collision Detection (CSMA/CD) access method.

☒   **A**, **C**, **D**: FDDI is a technology used to create high-speed backbone connections and uses token passing. It is not an access method. CSMA/CA is primarily used for Wireless technologies. Token Passing is another access method, used with Token Ring networks and FDDI.

12. You are the network engineer assigned to implement a new 100 Mbps network connection. You need to select the correct cabling, as well as the correct standard. From the selections below; choose which 100 Mbps networking standard makes use of only two pairs of a Category 5 UTP cable.

A. 10BaseT

B. 100BaseFL

C. 100BaseTX

D. 100BroadT4

☑   **C**. 100BaseTX uses two UTP pairs (four wires) in a Category 5 UTP cable.

☒   **A**, **B**, **D**. Answer **A** is incorrect because 10BaseT requires Category 3 UTP and only operates at 10 Mbps. Answer **B** is incorrect because 100BaseFL doesn't exist, it's really 10BaseFL, and it requires 10 Mbps fiber optic cable. Answer **D** is incorrect because 100BoardT4 is not a legitimate networking standard.

Chapter 3 Network Devices

1. Cables from workstations are connected to a central network connectivity device that takes data from one port and resends it to all of the other ports. In doing so, the data is regenerated so it is as strong as when it was originally sent. Which of the following devices is being used?

   A. Active hub

   B. Passive hub

   C. Switching hub

   D. Switch

   ☑ **A**. Active hub. An active hub will take data sent to it and resend it to all ports on the hub. An active hub also works as a repeater for all data received on its ports, as the signal is regenerated before it is transmitted on all ports of the hub.

   ☒ **B**, **C**, **D**. Answer **B** is incorrect because the function of a passive hub is simply to receive data from one port of the hub and send it out to the other ports. It does not regenerate the data. Answers **C** and **D** are incorrect because a switch or switching hub will take the data sent to it on one port and then send it to a specific port that will send the data only to the destination computer or device.

2. Your network consists of a single large LAN that is in a star topology configuration. You have found that there are a significant number of collisions occurring on the network, and want to segment it into two smaller LANs. Which of the following devices will you use to segment this network, allowing each LAN to communicate with the other?

   A. NIC

   B. MAU

   C. Bridge

   D. Repeater

   ☑ **C**. Bridge. A bridge is a network connectivity device that connects two different networks and makes them appear to be one network, and allows a larger LAN to be segmented into two smaller halves. The bridge filters local traffic between the two networks and copies all other traffic to the other side of the bridge.

   ☒ **A**, **B**, **D**. Answer **A** is incorrect because a NIC is simply a network interface card, which is installed on a PC or other network device, to allow it to communicate on the network. Answer **B** is incorrect because a MAU is a device that multiple workstations are connected to in order to communicate on a Token Ring network. Answer **D** is incorrect because a repeater is used to con-nect segments of cable and repeat the data it receives so that it won't weaken along the cable.

3. You want to get Internet access for a computer that is used by the IT staff to download drivers and updated software from the Internet. Because of the amount of data that is going to be downloaded, you want to use the fastest possible method of downloading data. Which of the following will you use?

    A. Analog modem with dial-up access to an ISP

    B. ISDN Digital Subscriber Line

    C. Consumer Digital Subscriber Line

    D. Very High Digital Subscriber Line

    ☑ **D**. Very High Digital Subscriber Line. A Very High Digital Subscriber Line has a downstream speed of 12.9 to 52.8 Mbps, and an upstream speed of 1.5 to 2.3 Mbps. Of the choices offered, this is the fastest choice for accessing the Internet.

    ☒ **A**, **B**, **C**. Answer **A** is incorrect because an analog modem with dial-up access is limited to a maximum speed of 56 Kbps. Answer **B** is incorrect because an ISDN Digital Subscriber Line has a maximum speed of 128 Kbps. Answer **D** is incorrect because a Consumer Digital Subscriber Line has a maximum speed of 1 Mbps.

4. You are looking into purchasing a new switch for your network. You want the switch to be able to route packets of data based on the uniform resource locator included with the packet. Which switch type should you buy?

    A. Layer 2 Switch

    B. Layer 3 Switch

    C. Layer 4 Switch

    D. Layer 5 Switch

    ☑ **D**. Layer 5 Switch. Layer 5 switches use information from the Session Layer, allowing it to route packets using uniform resource locators (URLs).

    ☒ **A**, **B**, **C**. Answer **A** is incorrect because Layer 2 Switches work at the Data Link Layer, and look at the MAC address of the packet to determine where it is to be sent. Answer **B** is incorrect because Layer 3 switches work at the Network Layer of the OSI model, and have an integrated router function that allows it to make decisions as to where the data should be sent. Answer **D** is incorrect because Layer 4 switches use information in the packet that identifies the application it belongs to, so that priorities can be set in routing the packets to the destination computer.

5. You have installed new cabling to accommodate a new section of the building that is being networked. Once computers are installed, you find that they are unable to connect to the network. You believe the problem is that the length of the cabling has exceeded the maximum distance allowed. You want to fix the problem with the least amount of cost and work. Which of the following will you do?

   A. Remove the cabling and install cable that supports a longer distance.

   B. Install a passive hub to increase the distance that data can travel along the cable.

   C. Install a NIC to increase the distance that data can travel along the cable.

   D. Install a switch to increase the distance that data can travel along the cable.

   ☑ **D**. Install a switch to increase the distance that data can travel along the cable. Switches can perform the same functions that repeaters used to, by regenerating the data so that it is sent out from the switch at its original strength.

   ☒ **A**, **B**, **C**. Answer **A** is incorrect because removing the cabling and replacing it with another kind is not only costly, but a considerable amount of work. Answer **B** is incorrect because a passive hub won't regenerate the data when it is sent out from its ports. Answer **C** is incorrect because a NIC is used as an interface to communicate on the network. It isn't used as a means of regenerating data so that the network can be extended.

6. What will happen if the default gateway is not specified on your computer and you are trying to reach another network?

   A. The packet will ask every router if they know the path to reach the destination.

   B. The packet will broadcast for the IP address of the nearest router.

   C. The packet will be forwarded to the DNS server.

   D. The packet will not be sent.

   ☑ **D**. The packet will not be sent. Without that default gateway, you are stuck on the local network. The subnet mask, which you will learn about in the next chapter, is also very important. Without a properly configured subnet mask to determine which subnet your computer is on, your computer will be unable to communicate outside of the local network.

☒ **A**, **B**, **C**. Answer **A** is incorrect because the PC will not know the addresses of the routers to send the data packets to or even inquire about router addresses or destination addresses. Answer **B** is incorrect for the same reason. Answer **C** is incorrect because the DNS server is used for name-to-IP address resolution and not IP addresses of routers.

7. You need to connect two networks that work on two different network protocols. Which of the following should be used?

A. DMZ

B. Firewall

C. Gateway

D. NAS

☑ **C**. Gateway. If two networks work on different communication systems, they will not be able to talk to each other. A gateway functions as a translator between two dissimilar networks so that both are able to communicate. For example, if your Ethernet network is to be connected to a Token Ring network, you will need to have a gateway so that hosts in the two networks are able to communicate.

☒ **A**, **B**, **D**. Answer **A** is incorrect because a DMZ is a neutral network segment where systems accessible to the public Internet are housed, which offers some basic levels of protection against attacks. Answer **B** is incorrect because a firewall provides protection by filtering traffic from the external network to the internal network, and vice versa. Answer **D** is incorrect because a NAS is a system of devices that are dedicated to providing storage of data on the network.

8. You have replaced all the hubs in your network with 10/100 Mbps switches. The switch ports are configured to work by automatically sensing the network speed. Most of the workstations already had 10/100 Mbps network adapters. Which of the following will you need to do in order to upgrade the speed of the entire network to 100 Mbps?

A. Replace all 10 Mbps network adapters to 10/100 Mbps in the remaining workstations.

B. Reconfigure all the ports on the switch to operate only at 100 Mbps.

C. Reconfigure the 10 Mbps adapters in remaining workstations to operate only at 100 Mbps.

D. None of the above.

☑ **A**. Replace all 10 Mbps network adapters to 10/100 Mbps in the remaining workstations. Since the switch ports are configured to automatically sense the network speed, the workstations with 100 Mbps network adapters will communicate with the switch at 100 Mbps and others at 10 Mbps. This will affect the overall network speed. In order to have a complete 100 Mbps network, you should replace the 10 Mbps adapters with 10/100 Mbps network adapters in the remaining workstations.

☒ **B**, **C**, **D**. Answer **B** is incorrect because even if the switch ports are configured to operate at 100 Mbps, the communication with workstations with 10 Mbps adapters will be at 10 Mbps. Answer **C** is incorrect because 10 Mbps adapters cannot be configured to operate at 100 Mbps. Answer **D** is incorrect because answer A is a legitimate solution.

9. You are implementing a firewall for a small company that wishes to establish an Internet presence. The company wants to use its dedicated Internet connection to allow employees to access the Internet as well as host a Web server. What is the best type of firewall to use in this situation?

   A. A packet filtering firewall

   B. A stateful inspection firewall

   C. An application layer gateway

   D. No firewall is necessary

   ☑ Answer **A** is the correct. A packet-filtering firewall will fill the needs of the company, cost the least, and perform the fastest without adding unnecessary processing overhead that would slow down traffic.

   ☒ A stateful inspection firewall (**B**) would serve the company's needs, but because it is a small company and does not plan on allowing incoming connections other than to its Web server, the cost is not worth the benefits. An application layer gateway (**C**) would cost more and provide much more functionality than the company needs. Both stateful inspection firewalls and application layer gateways would slow down the company's Internet connection slightly. Answer **D** is incorrect because any time you have a constant-on Internet connection, you need to protect the system that is using that connection.

10. What is the area of the network that typically contains public DNS servers and Web servers?

    A. Firewall

    B. DMZ

    C. VLAN

    D. VPN

☑ Answer **B** is correct. The DMZ is typically where publicly accessible DNS servers, Web servers, and e-mail servers are found. These servers are protected against a large number of attacks by being placed in the DMZ, but can still perform their functions. A second firewall is located on the internal side of the DMZ to further restrict connection attempts to the intranet.

☒ Answer **A** is incorrect, because a firewall device can be used to create a DMZ, but is not a network area by itself. Answer **C** is incorrect, because a VLAN may contain publicly accessible servers, but not in most cases. Answer **D** is incorrect, because a VPN is a secure tunnel created over an insecure medium, such as the Internet, that can be used to pass traffic with security and authenticity.

11. Hannah wants to configure a VLAN on her network. What advantage can Hannah expect to get out of a VLAN?

A. It will segment traffic on the internal network for increased security.

B. It will create a DMZ to protect her Web servers from attacks.

C. It will hide her internal network IP addresses from being seen on the Internet.

D. It will provide a secure tunnel from her intranet to the intranet of a partner company.

☑ Answer **A** is correct. VLANs can be used to physically segment network traffic on the intranet, thus allowing you to keep traffic segmented by purpose.

☒ Answer **B** is incorrect, because a DMZ is not created by a VLAN. Answer **C** is incorrect, because a NAT device is not created by a VLAN. Answer **D** is incorrect, because a VPN is not created by a VLAN.

12. To allow its employees remote access to the corporate network, a company has implemented a hardware VPN solution. Why is this considered a secure remote access solution?

A. Because only the company's employees will know the address to connect to in order to use the VPN.

B. Because VPNs use the Internet to transfer data.

C. Because a VPN uses compression to make its data secure.

D. Because a VPN uses encryption to make its data secure.

☑ Answer **D** is the correct answer. A VPN uses encryption to secure the data it is tunneling over the Internet. By implementing secure encryption technology, VPNs make it very difficult to read what data is being sent between the client and the host.

☒ Restricting the knowledge of which address to access in order to use the VPN (**A**) is not why VPNs are considered secure. This uses the concept of "security through obscurity," which rarely works. Using the Internet to transfer data (**B**) is not secure. Many VPNs use compression (**C**) to make data transfer faster, but this does not make it secure.

13. You have installed an Active IDS system onto your network. When an attack occurs and is detected by your new IDS, what might you expect it to do? (Choose all that apply)

    A. Inform the attacker that his or her actions may be monitored as part of the network AUP.

    B. Disable a service or services.

    C. Terminate the connection after a predefined amount of time.

    D. Shut down a server or servers.

    ☑ Answers **B**, **C**, and **D** are correct. An Active IDS will not only collect data about the attack, but it will also seek to prevent damage to the network it is protecting. Thus, you might expect an active IDS to disable services, disconnect a session, or even shut down servers if required to protect the network from compromise.

    ☒ Answer **A** is incorrect, because informing the user that their actions may be monitored is not part of the IDSs job.

14. You have an IDS system running only on one computer in your network. What type of IDS system is this?

    A. Active

    B. Host

    C. Network

    D. Anomaly

    ☑ Answer **B** is correct. This is a host-based IDS system, as it is running on only one computer.

    ☒ Answer **A** is incorrect, because an Active IDS is one that responds actively to attacks against the network or system, which is not part of this question. Answer **C** is incorrect, because a network-based IDS is run from a central location and monitors the entire network. Answer **D** is incorrect, because anomalies are used for detecting attacks, not to classify where an IDS is run.

Chapter 4 Wireless Technologies

1. What is the name of the behavior that occurs when the strength of an electromagnetic wave is changed, such as by an antenna?

   A. Refraction

   B. Absorption

   C. Gain

   D. Scattering

   ☑ **C**. Gain occurs when a signal has its strength increased, such as by passing it through an amplifier.

   ☒ **A, B, D**. When a wave is refracted, it passes through a medium and changes course with some of the original wave being reflected away from the original wave's path, thus Answer **A** is incorrect. Absorption occurs when an electromagnetic wave impacts an object that does not pass it on through any means (reflection, refraction or diffraction), thus Answer **B** is incorrect. Scattering occurs when an incoming electromagnetic wave hits a surface that is small compared to its wavelength, thus Answer **D** is incorrect.

2. What is the name of the behavior that occurs when an electromagnetic wave is redirected in multiple directions, possibly resulting in a complete loss of usable signal at the destination?

   A. Reflection

   B. Scattering

   C. Refraction

   D. Loss

   ☑ **B**. When an incoming electromagnetic wave hits a surface that is small compared to its wavelength, scattering will occur. The incoming signal is degraded, and in some cases, completely destroyed, before arriving at the intended destination. Typical sources of scattering include trees, street signs and atmospheric conditions.

   ☒ **A, C, D**. Reflection occurs when an electromagnetic radio frequency wave has impacted upon a surface that has a much larger cross section than that of the wave itself, thus Answer **A** is incorrect. When a wave is refracted, it passes through a medium and changes course with some of the original wave being reflected away from the original wave's path, thus Answer **C** is incorrect. Loss occurs when a signal has its strength decreased, either intentionally through the use of a device such as an attenuator or unintentionally such as through resistance losses in a cable, thus Answer **D** is incorrect.

3. You suspect that your long range outdoor wireless link may be losing signal strength due to blockage of the Fresnel Zone by trees and buildings. At what percent Fresnel Zone blockage can you expect to start seeing signal loss?

    A. 50%

    B. 40%

    C. 30%

    D. 20%

    ☑   **D**. At Fresnel Zone blockage of 20%, you can reasonably expect to start seeing RF signal loss from source to destination, thus Answer **D** is correct.

    ☒   **A, B, C**. RF signal loss can start to occur at as low as 20% Fresnel Zone blockage, thus Answers **A, B**, and **C** are all incorrect.

4. What design feature causes an antenna to become an amplification device?

    A. It focuses the RF energy into a smaller beam.

    B. It focuses the RF energy into a broad beam.

    C. It is made of a ferrous metal.

    D. It is cylindrical in shape.

    ☑   **A**. Amplification occurs in an antenna due to the fact that an antenna focuses the RF energy into a smaller beam, thus Answer **A** is correct. Different antenna types result in different shapes of the RF signal output, and thus varying amounts of amplification.

    ☒   **B, C, D**. A broader beam would result in a lowering of signal strength, thus Answer **B** is incorrect. While the physical construction of the antenna itself may at times play a role in how the output signal will relate to the input signal, neither the metal used nor the shape of the antenna are the overriding factors that cause antennas to be passive amplification devices, thus Answers **C** and **D** are incorrect.

5. In long outdoor links, refraction of RF signals becomes a problem. Which of the following conditions is typically the reason for refraction in long outdoor links?

    A. Curvature of the Earth

    B. Rain or snow

    C. Differing air density

    D. Trees or buildings

☑ **C**. Long outdoor links may travel through areas of differing air density, which result in refraction of the RF signal, thus Answer **C** is correct.

☒ **A**, **B**, **D**. The curvature of the Earth is typically responsible for causing reflection or Fresnel Zone blockage, not refraction, thus Answer **A** is incorrect. Rain or snow typically cause scattering to occur, thus Answer **B** is incorrect. Trees and buildings are also typically responsible for Fresnel Zone blockage, thus Answer **D** is incorrect.

6. In the United States, how many channels are available for usage by 802.11b and 802.11g wireless networks?

   A. 1

   B. 11

   C. 13

   D. 83

   ☑ **B**. There are 11 channels available for usage by 802.11b and 802.11g devices in the United States, thus Answer **B** is correct.

   ☒ **A**, **C**, **D**. There are 11 channels available for usage by 802.11b and 802.11g devices in the United States, thus Answers **A**, **C** and **D** are incorrect.

7. If you were implementing a new 802.11b or 802.11g wireless network in your large warehouse, what three channels could you safely use without having overlap? (Choose three correct answers)

   A. 1

   B. 2

   C. 4

   D. 5

   E. 6

   F. 10

   G. 11

   ☑ **A**, **E**, **G**. Channels 1, 6, and 11 can safely be used in a single location without fear of overlap, thus Anwers **A**, **E** and **G** are correct.

   ☒ **B**, **C**, **D**, **F**. Channels 2, 4 and 5 could not be used in this scenario as they would overlap with Channels 1 and 6, thus Answers **B**, **C** and **D** are incorrect. Channel 10 could not be used in this scenario, as it would overlap with Channels 6 and 11, thus Answer **F** is incorrect.

8. Your supervisor has charged you with determining which 802.11 authentication method to use when deploying the new wireless network. Given your knowledge of the 802.11 specification, which of the following is the most secure 802.11 authentication method?

   A. Shared-Key Authentication

   B. EAP-TLS

   C. EAP-MD5

   D. Open Authentication

   ☑ **D.** Open authentication is actually more secure than shared key authentication because it is not susceptible to a known plaintext attack, to which the shared-key authentication method is susceptible.

   ☒ **A, B, C.** Shared-key authentication is susceptible to a known plaintext attack if the attacker can capture the random challenge sent by the AP to the client, as well as the encrypted response from the client. The attacker can then use try to brute force the WEP key by trying to decrypt the encrypted response and comparing it to the random challenge sent by the AP, thus Answer **A** is incorrect. EAP-TLS and EAP-MD5 are authentication methods specified in the 802.1x standard, not the 802.11 standard, thus Answers **C** and **D** are incorrect.

9. What are the two WEP key sizes available in 802.11 networks?

   A. 64-bit and 104-bit keys

   B. 24-bit and 64-bit keys

   C. 64-bit and 128-bit keys

   D. 24-bit and 104-bit keys

   ☑ **C.** The 802.11 specification calls for 64-bit keys for use in WEP. Later the specification was amended to allow for 128-bit keys as well.

   ☒ **A, B, D.** The actual key size of the secret key is 40-bits and 104-bits. When added to the 24-bit initialization vector, you wind up with WEP key sizes of 64-bits and 128-bits, thus Answers **A, B** and **D** are incorrect.

10. Which of the following is a weakness in WEP related to the initialization vector (IV)? (Choose all that apply)

    A. The IV is a static value, which makes it relatively easy for an attacker to brute force the WEP key from captured traffic.

    B. The IV is transmitted in plaintext and can be easily seen in captured traffic.

    C. The IV is only 24-bits in size which makes it possible that two or more data frames will be transmitted with the same IV, thereby resulting in an IV collision that an attacker can use to determine information about the network.

    D. There is no weakness in WEP related to the IV.

    ☑ **B, C.** The IV is transmitted in plaintext because the AP or the other adhoc participants in the network must know its value in order to be able to recreate the WEP key to decrypt traffic. Because of the small size of the IV space allows for the potential of IV collisions that an attack can use to XOR out the keystream used to encrypt the traffic and thereby possibly recover information such as IP address information from packets.

    ☒ **A, D.** The IV is not a static value, it is randomly determined, thus Answer **A** is incorrect. There are weaknesses associated with WEP that are directly attributable to the short length of the IV as mentioned previously, thus Answer **D** is incorrect.

11. Bill, the network administrator, wishes to deploy a wireless network and use open authentication. His problem is that he also wants to make sure that the network is not accessible by anyone. How can he authenticate users without a shared-key authentication mechanism (choose the best answer)?

    A. Use MAC address filters to restrict which wireless network cards can associate to the network.

    B. Deploy a RADIUS server and require the use of EAP.

    C. Set a WEP key on the access points and use it as the indirect authenticator for users.

    D. Use IP filters to restrict access to the wireless network.

    ☑ **C.** Use the WEP key as an indirect authenticator for open networks. Unlike shared-key authentication, open authentication does not provide for a challenge/response exchange and therefore does not expose the WEP key to a known-plaintext cryptographic attack.

    ☒ **A, B, D.** MAC filtering does not absolutely authenticate a user as MAC addresses are easily spoofed. Additionally, MAC filtering is an administrative burden, thus Answer **A** is incorrect. Deploying RADIUS server or IP filters are both beyond the scope of the question being asked, thus Answers **B** and **D** are incorrect.

12. The 802.1*x* standard specifies a series of exchanges between the supplicant and the authentication server. Which of the following is not part of the 802.1*x* authentication exchange?

    A. Association Request

    B. EAPoL Start

    C. RADIUS-Access-Request

    D. EAP-Success

    ☑ **A.** The Association Request is part of the 802.11 standard and not the 802.1*x* standard.

    ☒ **B, C, D.** The EAPoL start, RADIUS Access Request and EAP-Success messages are all part of the 802.1*x* authentication exchange, thus Answers **B**, **C** and **D** are incorrect.

13. 802.1*x* provides for mutual authentication of the supplicant and the authenticator. Which of the following 802.1*x* methods support mutual authentication?

    A. EAP-MD5

    B. EAP-PWD

    C. EAP-RC4

    D. EAP-TLS

    ☑ **D.** EAP-TLS provides for mutual authentication through the use of certificates.

    ☒ **A, B, C.** EAP-MD5 does not provide for mutual authentication of the supplicant and the authenticator, thus Answer **A** is incorrect. EAP-PWD and EAP-RC4 are not EAP authentication methods, thus Answers **B** and **C** are incorrect.

14. The 802.1*x* standard requires the use of an authentication server to allow access to the wireless LAN. You are deploying a wireless network and will use EAP-TLS as your authentication method. What is the most likely vulnerability in your network?

    A. Unauthorized users accessing the network by spoofing EAP-TLS messages.

    B. Denial of Service attacks occurring because 802.11 management frames are not authenticated.

    C. Attackers cracking the encrypted traffic.

    D. None of the above.

☑ **B**. One of the biggest problems identified in a paper discussing 802.1*x* security is the lack of authentication in the 802.11 management frames and that 802.1*x* does not address this problem.

☒ **A, C, D**. Spoofing EAP-TLS is not possible as the attacker needs the user's certificate and passphrase, thus Answer A is incorrect. Cracking encrypted traffic is possible but unlikely since EAP-TLS allows for WEP key rotation, thus Answer **C** is incorrect. The lack of authentication in 802.11 is the most likely vulnerability, thus Answer **B** is incorrect.

15. The tool NetStumbler detects wireless networks based on what feature?

    A. SSID.

    B. WEP Key.

    C. MAC Address.

    D. CRC-32 Checksum.

    ☑ **A**. NetStumbler detects wireless networks by looking for SSIDs.

    ☒ **B, C, D**. NetStumbler does identify networks with WEP enabled but does not use that fact in identifying the network, thus Answer **B** is incorrect. NetStumbler does detect clients and APs based on their MAC but does not use this information for identifying wireless networks, thus Answer **C** is incorrect. CRC-32 Checksums are of no concern to NetStumbler, thus Answer **D** is incorrect.

16. Some Denial of Service (DoS) attacks are unintentional. Your wireless network at home has been having sporadic problems. The wireless network is particularly susceptible in the afternoon and the evenings. This is most likely due to which of the following possible problems?

    A. The AP is flaky and needs to be replaced.

    B. Someone is flooding your AP with traffic in a DoS attack.

    C. The wireless network is misconfigured.

    D. Your cordless phone is using the same frequency as the wireless network and whenever someone calls or receives a call the phone jams the wireless network.

    ☑ **D**. The most likely problem is that a cordless phone (or a microwave or one of many other wireless devices) is jamming the wireless signal because it uses the same frequency. This is becoming more and more common as cordless phone manufacturers use the 2.4GHz frequency.

    ☒ **A, B, C**. Bad hardware is something to be concerned with, but should not be considered the sole reason for problems until further investigation has been done to determine the source of the problem, thus Answer **A** is incorrect. It is possible, but not likely, that someone is launching a DoS attack against you, thus Answer **B** is incorrect. If a device is not configured properly, it would not work at all times, not just sporadically, thus Answer **D** is incorrect.

17. You suspect that someone is stealing data from your company, due to the fact that your closest competitor routinely seems to make it to market weeks before you on every product you introduce. You have conducted sweeps of your organization's campus looking for surreptitious users and user actions, but have yet to locate anything out of the ordinary. What type of wireless network attack are you most likely being subjected to?

    A. Spoofing.

    B. Jamming.

    C. Sniffing.

    D. Man-in-the-middle.

    ☑ **C.** You are being subjected to a sniffing attack whereby an attack can simply sit passively and capture your wireless network traffic without giving an indication of suspicious activity. You would, in this case, need to investigate strong wireless network security, starting with the implementation of WEP immediately followed up by a solution such as TKIP and LEAP.

    ☒ **A, B, D**. Spoofing attacks are those where the attacker tricks the network hardware into thinking that he or she is an authorized user, such as MAC spoofing, thus Answer **A** is incorrect. Jamming attacks are those where high power RF waves are targeted at a wireless network installation with the hopes of knocking it out of operation by overpowering it, thus Answer **B** is incorrect. A man-in-the-middle attack is one where an attacker sits between two communicating parties, intercepting and manipulating both sides of the transmission to suit his or her own needs, thus Answer **D** is incorrect.

18. Your wireless network does use WEP to authorize users. You do, however, make use of MAC filtering to ensure that only preauthorized client can associate with your access points. On Monday morning, you reviewed the AP association table logs for the previous weekend and noticed that the MAC address assigned to the network adapter in your portable computer had associated with your access points several times over the weekend. Your portable computer spent the weekend on you dining room table and was not connected to your corporate wireless network during this period of time. What type of wireless network attack are you most likely being subjected to?

A. Spoofing.

B. Jamming.

C. Sniffing.

D. Man-in-the-middle.

☑ **A.** You are the victim of a MAC spoofing attack where an attacker has captured valid MAC addresses by sniffing your wireless network. The fact that you have no other protection in place has made becoming associated with your access points an easy task for this attacker.

☒ **B, C, D.** Jamming attacks are those where high power RF waves are targeted at a wireless network installation with the hopes of knocking it out of operation by overpowering it, thus Answer **B** is incorrect. While your network has been sniffed previously to obtain the valid MAC address, you are currently being attacked using a spoofing attack, thus Answer **C** is incorrect. A man-in-the-middle attack is one where an attacker sits between two communicating parties, intercepting and manipulating both sides of the transmission to suit his or her own needs, thus Answer **D** is incorrect.

19. The major weakness of WEP has to do with the fact that there are only a limited number of what available?

A. IVs

B. Packets

C. Frames

D. Beacons

☑ **A.** There are only 2^{24} IVs available, which might seem like a lot until you realize that every frame or packet requires a unique IV. The entire stock of IVs could be exhausted in a short amount of time, perhaps just several hours, on a busy wireless network. This gives an attacker the opportunity to capture multiple frames using the same numerical IV, which is a large first step towards cracking the WEP key.

☒ **B, C, D.** There are only 2^{24} IVs available, which might seem like a lot until you realize that every frame or packet requires a unique IV. The entire stock of IVs could be exhausted in a short amount of time, perhaps just several hours, on a busy wireless network. This gives an attacker the opportunity to capture multiple frames using the same numerical IV which is a large first step towards cracking the WEP key, thus Answers **B**, **C** and **D** are incorrect.

20. In Windows 2000, how do you configure WEP protection for a wireless client?

   A. Open the network adapter properties page and configure WEP from the Wireless Networks tab.

   B. Install the high security encryption pack from Microsoft.

   C. Issue the computer a digital certificate from a Windows 2000 Certificate Authority.

   D. Use the utilities provided by the manufacturer of the network adapter.

   ☑ **D**. Windows 2000 does not provide integrated control and management of wireless network adapters, thus you will need to perform all configuration by using the vendor supplied utilities.

   ☒ **A**, **B**, **C**. Windows 2000 does not have a Wireless Networks tab in the network adapter properties page, thus Answer **A** is incorrect. Installing the high encryption pack from Microsoft just raises the encryption strength supported by the computer itself to 128-bits, thus Answer **B** is incorrect. Issuing the computer a digital certificate will not configure it for WEP protection in a wireless network, thus Answer **C** is incorrect.

21. In Windows XP, how do you configure WEP protection for a wireless client?

   A. Open the network adapter properties page and configure WEP from the Wireless Networks tab.

   B. Install the high security encryption pack from Microsoft.

   C. Issue the computer a digital certificate from a Windows 2000 Certificate Authority.

   D. Use the utilities provided by the manufacturer of the network adapter.

   ☑ **A**. In about 95% or more of the cases, Windows XP integrates control and management of wireless network adapters into the network adapter properties page.

   ☒ **B**, **C**, **D**. Installing the high encryption pack from Microsoft just raises the encryption strength supported by the computer itself to 128-bits, thus Answer **B** is incorrect. Issuing the computer a digital certificate will not configure it for WEP protection in a wireless network, thus Answer **C** is incorrect. In about 95% or better of the cases, Windows XP integrates control and management of wireless network adapters into the network adapter Properties page, thus you cannot configure network adapters using the manufacturer's utilities, thus Answer **D** is incorrect.

22. You are attempting to configure a client computer wireless network adapter in Windows XP. You have installed and launched the utility program that came with the adapter but you cannot configure the settings from it. What is the source of your problem?

    A. You are not a member of the Network Configuration Operators group.

    B. You do not have the correct Windows Service Pack installed.

    C. You do not configure wireless network adapters in Windows XP through manufacturer's utilities.

    D. Your network administrator has disabled SSID broadcasting for the wireless network.

    ☑ **C**. In Windows XP, you must use the network adapter properties page to perform wireless network configuration.

    ☒ **A**, **B**, **D**. Being a member of the Network Configuration Operators group is not required to make configuration changes to a wireless network adapter properties, thus Answer **A** is incorrect. The Service Pack level has no bearing to being able to configure the network adapter properties, thus Answer **B** is incorrect. Closed networks, those that do not broadcast the SSID, have no effect on being able to configure the network adapter properties, thus Answer **D** is incorrect.

Chapter 5 OSI Model

1. What is the unique physical address (Burned in Address – BIA) that is found on all NICs called?

    A. DNS Address

    B. NAT Address

    C. IP Address

    D. MAC Address

    ☑ **D**. Every network adapter has a unique Media Access Control (MAC) address assigned to it. The MAC address is the unique ID serial number of the Ethernet card in one's computer. MAC addresses are needed in a LAN for computers to communicate; therefore, Answer **D** is correct. Note that MAC addresses have nothing to do with Apple Macintosh computers

    ☒ Answer **A** is incorrect because a DNS address is a logical address, not a physical address. Answer **B** is incorrect because network adapters have MAC addresses, whereas NAT is a logical configuration to translate one address into another address. Answer **C** is incorrect because a network adapter could be configured with different IP addresses, multiple IP addresses and IP addresses are logically assigned, they are not burned into the card. It should be noted that MAC addresses can in fact be changed, although it is highly uncommon to do it, and is usually only done with very old cards that may have survived all this time. In this case, the old cards may have duplicate numbers, and you may have to update the BIA on the card to use it.

2. Which of the following is a valid MAC address?

    A. 00:05:J6:0D:91:K1

    B. 10.0.0.1 – 255.255.255.0

    C. 00:05:J6:0D:91:B1

    D. 00:D0:A0:5C:C1:B5

    ☑ **D.** A MAC address consists of six hexadecimal numbers. The highest possible hexadecimal number is FF:FF:FF:FF:FF:FF, which denotes a broadcast. The first three bytes contain a manufacturer code and the last three bytes contain a unique station ID. Therefore, Answer **D** is correct. You have to understand hexadecimal in order to be able to solve this, as decimal is base10, binary is a base2 system, and hex is base16. The numbers are counted from 0 to 9, then lettered A to F before adding another digit. The letters A through F represent decimal numbers 10 through 15, respectively. Since F is the highest, then obviously an answer like C is easy to eliminate, as a quick scan of the hex shows a letter 'J' used, which is not in the base16 numbering system. You will learn more about the numbering systems in Chapter 6.

    ☒ Answer **A** is incorrect because there is a K, which does not convert to base16 math. Answer **B** is incorrect because 255.255.255.0 is an IP address/subnet mask, not a MAC address. Answer **C** is incorrect because there is a J, which does not convert to base16 math. Remember, it's 0-9, A-F, which, when added up, equal 16, hence base16. A letter G would equal 17, which is not acceptable; therefore anything above an F cannot be used.

3. When working with MAC addresses, which layer of the OSI model do MAC addresses, frames and switches associate to?

    A. Data Link

    B. Host to Host

    C. Presentation

    D. Application

☑ **A.** The Data Link layer contains two sublayers, the MAC and LLC sublayers. The LLC or Logical Link Control sublayer is responsible for providing the logic for the data link, thus it controls the synchronization, flow control, and error checking functions of the Data Link layer. The MAC sublayer is responsible for providing control for accessing the transmission medium. It is responsible for moving data packets from one NIC to another, across a shared transmission medium such as an Ethernet or fiber optic transmission medium. Physical addressing is addressed at the MAC sublayer. Every NIC has a unique MAC address, also called the physical address, which identifies that specific NIC on the network. The MAC address of a NIC usually is burned into a read-only memory (ROM) chip on the NIC card. Therefore, Answer **A** is correct.

☒ Answer **B** is incorrect because the Host-to-Host layer (of the DoD model) maps to the Transport layer of the OSI, which does not deal with MAC addressing. Answer **C** is incorrect because the Presentation layer of the OSI model does not deal with MAC addressing. Answer **D** is incorrect because the Application layer of the OSI model does not deal with MAC addressing.

4. You are the system administrator for a small company that runs two Windows servers (Windows Server 2003) and two Linux servers (SUSE Linux). You need to lock down the connections to the switch via port security; this essentially means you will need to retrieve the MAC addresses on the systems. MAC addresses are found on Linux server by issuing which command?

A. ipconfig /a

B. ifconfig /a

C. winipcfg /a

D. ifconfig –a

☑ **D.** It is very easy to confuse this with other system commands as they are very similar, but Answer **D** is correct. Do not forget that Linux is ifconfig; Windows is either winipcfg or ipconfig.

☒ Answer **A** is incorrect because ipconfig /a is not a command. The proper command (in Windows) would be ipconfig /all. Answer **B** is incorrect because ifconfig is not used with the /a switch, it's used with the –a switch instead. Answer **C** is incorrect because winipcfg is a GUI interface and does not launch with the /a switch.

5. You are the system administrator for a small company that runs two Windows servers (Windows Server 2003) and two Linux servers (SUSE Linux). You need to lock down the connections to the switch via port security; this essentially means you will need to retrieve the MAC addresses on the systems. MAC addresses are found on Windows Server 2003 systems by issuing which command?

A. ipconfig /a

B. ifconfig /all

C. winipcfg /all

D. ipconfig /all

☑ **D**. It is very easy to confuse this with other system commands, as they are very similar. Windows systems such as NT, 2000, XP and 2003 all use ipconfig to get basic IP addressing information. The /all switch adds more information to the output seen, such as the physical hardware address, or MAC address; therefore, Answer **D** is correct. Do not forget that Linux is ifconfig; Windows is either winipcfg or ipconfig .

☒ Answer **A** is incorrect because ipconfig /a is not a valid command. Answer **B** is incorrect because ifconfig is not used on Windows systems; it's used on Linux systems. The command should also be ifconfig –a, if it was to be used on a Linux system to retrieve the MAC address. Answer **C** is incorrect because winipcfg /all is not a command; winipcfg is a GUI interface and does not launch with the /a switch. Winipcfg is used on Windows ME and Windows 9x systems.

6. You are the system administrator for a small company that runs two Windows servers (Windows Server 2003) and two Linux servers (SUSE Linux). You have 20 desktop systems, half of which are running Windows 98 SE. You need to lock down the connections to the switch via port security for the Windows 9x systems; this essentially means you will need to retrieve the MAC addresses on the systems. MAC addresses are found on Windows 9x systems by issuing which command?

A. ipconfig /a

B. ifconfig /a

C. winipcfg

D. ifconfig –a

☑ **C**. winipcfg is a small program that launches with its own GUI. This is commonly seen on older Windows systems such as Windows ME or 9x systems. Since the requirements for the question were to ensure that you can retrieve MAC address information from your Windows 9x systems, you will definitely need to use winipcfg; therefore, Answer **D** is correct. Do not forget that Linux is ifconfig; Windows is either winipcfg or ipconfig.

☒ Answer **A** is incorrect because ipconfig /a is not a valid command. Answer **B** is incorrect because ifconfig is not used with the /a switch, it's used with a –a switch for Linux. Answer **D** is incorrect because ifconfig -a (although the correct Linux command to retrieve MAC address information) will not help you with your Windows 9x systems.

7. From the list of choices, which of the following media access methods is used for an IEEE 802.5 network?

   A. Direct sequence

   B. Token passing

   C. CSMA /CD

   D. CSMA /CA

   ☑ **B**. The 802.5 standard defines a Token Ring network. Token Ring uses token passing as its method of communicating on the network, therefore, Answer **B** is correct.

   ☒ Answer **A** is incorrect because direct sequence is not an access method at all. Answer **C** is incorrect because CSMA/CD is used on multiple access networks as defined in the IEEE 802.3 specification. Using this method, devices that have data to transmit listen for an opening on the line before transmitting (Carrier Sense). That is, they wait for a time when there are no signals traveling on the cable. When a device detects an opening, it transmits its data. Answer **D** is incorrect because CSMA/CA is a media access protocol that is used on multiple access networks such as token passing or wireless topologies. With CSMA/CA, a device listens for an opportunity to transmit its data just as devices do on CSMA/CD networks. However, when the device senses an opening, it does not immediately transmit the data; instead it transmits a signal notifying other devices that it is transmitting (a sort of warning message) before actually sending the data. This means data packets will never collide (although warning packets may).

8. Which of the following provides NetBIOS name to IP address resolution?

   A. hosts

   B. lmhosts

   C. services

   D. protocols

   ☑ **B**. The lmhosts file contains NetBIOS name-to-IP address mappings. It is stored on local Windows workstations and acts much like a hosts file, but instead of working within DNS, the lmhosts file works with NetBIOS name to IP address name resolution. Therefore, Answer **B** is correct.

   ☒ Answer **A** is incorrect because a host's file contains hostname-to-IP address mappings which is not what the question is asking for, it's looking for NetBIOS names-to-IP address mappings, therefore A is incorrect, hosts files work with DNS. Answer **C** is incorrect because services has nothing to do with name resolution, whether it be DNS or NetBIOS-based. Answer **D** is

www.syngress.com

incorrect because protocols has nothing to do with name resolution, whether it be DNS or NetBIOS based.

9. Which OSI model layer is responsible for frame sequencing?

A. The Physical Layer

B. The Transport Layer

C. The Data Link Layer

D. The Application Layer

☑ **C.** The Data Link layer combines bits into bytes and bytes into frames, provides access to media using MAC addresses, and error detection. Furthermore, it provides sequencing of frames. Therefore, Answer **C** is correct.

☒ Answer **A** is incorrect because the physical layer is responsible to move bits between devices and specifies voltage, wire speed and pin-out cables. Answer **B** is incorrect because the transport layer provides for both reliable and unreliable delivery and error correction at the layer 4 of the OSI. Answer **D** is incorrect because the Application layer is where the user/applications access the network.

10. POP3 is identified by which TCP/IP port number?

A. UDP Port 21

B. TCP Port 23   *POP3 = 110*

C. UDP Port 25

D. TCP Port 110

☑ **D.** POP use TCP port 110. Therefore, Answer **D** is correct.

☒ Answer **A** is incorrect because FTP uses TCP port 21. Answer **B** is incorrect because Telnet use TCP port 23. Answer **C** is incorrect because SMTP uses TCP port 25. For the exam, don't get hung up on extra distractions added to the question like whether it uses TCP or UDP. For example, POP3 uses port TCP 110. Answers A, B and C could never be right, regardless of whether they specified UDP or TCP.

11. Standards for CSMA/CD are specified by which IEEE 802 sublayer?

A. 802.1

B. 802.2

C. 802.3

D. 802.5

☑ **C.** CSMA/CD is used on multiple access networks as defined in the IEEE 802.3 specification. Using this method, devices that have data to transmit listen for an opening on the line before transmitting (Carrier Sense). That is, they wait for a time when there are no signals traveling on the cable. When a device detects an opening, it transmits its data. Therefore, Answer **C** is correct.

☒ Answer **A** is incorrect because 802.1 maps to internetworking standards that deal with the management of LANs and MANs, including bridges and the spanning tree algorithm used by bridges to prevent looping. Answer **B** is incorrect because 802.2 maps to the LLC sublayer. Answer **D** is incorrect because 802.5 maps to Token Ring, the technology developed by IBM that uses a physical star and logical ring topology with twisted-pair cabling (shielded or unshielded) and the token passing access method. For the Network+ exam, it's imperative that you know how to differentiate between the 802 standards. Remember, when working with 802.3, CSMA/CD is the media access control method used on Ethernet networks.

12. From the choices listed, which of the following protocols represents e-mail protocols? Please choose two from the list below.

    A. POP3

    B. SMNP

    C. IMAP4   *EMAIL*

    D. Telnet

    ☑ **A** and **C.** POP3, IMAP4 and SMTP are common e-mail based protocols. Therefore, Answers **A** and **C** are correct.

    ☒ Answer **B** is incorrect because SMNP is not a valid protocol name (even though its spelling resembles SNMP and SMTP). Answer **D** is incorrect because Telnet is associated with terminal emulation, not e-mail.

13. From the following protocols listed, select the protocol that network management applications use to monitor network devices remotely.

    A. SNMP

    B. DNS

    C. SMTP

    D. DHCP

    ☑ **A.** SNMP is used for communications between a network management console and the network's devices, such as bridges, routers, and hubs. This protocol facilitates the sharing of network control information with the management console. SNMP employs a management system/agent framework to share relevant network management information. This information is stored in a MIB and contains a set of objects, each of which represents a particular type of network information such as an event, an error, or an active session. SNMP employs UDP datagram's to send messages between the management console and the agents. Therefore, Answer **A** is correct.

☒ Answer **B** is incorrect because DNS stands for Domain Name System and resolves hostnames and IP address. Answer **C** is incorrect because the Simple Mail Transfer Protocol handles sending and receiving of e-mail messages. Answer **D** is incorrect because Dynamic Host Configuration Protocol handles the automatic (dynamic) assignment of IP's so that you do not have to assign them statically.

14. Which of the following can you use to connect with a UNIX server using terminal emulation software?

   A. Web Browser

   B. FTP

   C. Telnet

   D. NNTP

   ☑ **C.** Telnet is used for remote login using terminal emulation. Therefore, Answer **C** is correct.

   ☒ Answer **A** is incorrect because any Web browser (Internet Explorer, etc.) by default is not made to be a *terminal emulation client* like Telnet is. In fact, don't get messed up on the Network+ exam, as Netscape cannot be used as terminal emulator, but could be with additional software. As an example, Netscape 7.x includes cutting-edge add-on applications that help you get more from the Internet including Java for running Web applets and many other services and features. Don't get hung up on reading into the question - make sure you know that *terminal emulation* is Telnet, no matter what could be added on, or taken away as an extra component. Answer **B** is incorrect because although also commonly seen as a command line tool, FTP is a file transfer program, made to send and receive files, whereas Telnet was created to perform terminal emulation. Answer **D** is incorrect because NNTP is used for news, not terminal emulation.

15. When discussing the OSI model and the DoD model, which layers of the OSI model handle what you would find in the Application layer of the DoD model? Choose all that apply.

    A. Application

    B. Presentation

    C. Transport

    D. Session

    ☑ **A, B** and **D**. The OSI model has seven layers, and the DoD model has four. The top layer of the DoD model is the Application layer, but it also maps cleanly to the OSI model's top three layers, Application, Presentation, and Session.

    ☒ Answer **C** is incorrect because the Transport layer is layer 4 of the OSI model and maps to layer 3 of the DoD model, the Host-to-Host layer. Make sure you are intimately familiar with the OSI model, as you are sure to be tested on its layers on the Network+ exam.

16. You are a network administrator looking to implement technology into a company. You are told you need to build a network utilizing the IEEE 802.11 standard. From the list below, the IEEE 802.11 standard maps to which of the following? (Select only one answer).

    A. Token Ring

    B. Wired Ethernet

    C. Metropolitan Area Network (MAN)

    D. Wireless in Infrastructure mode

    ☑ **D**. 802.11 Standards such as 802.11, 802.11b 802.11a, and 802.11g all related to wireless networking. Wireless technologies and infrastructure mode are covered in depth in Chapter 4, "Wireless Technologies". For this chapter, you need to master the memorization of these standards; the Network+ exam focuses on wireless technologies more now than in the past, so make sure you review this section completely.

    ☒ Answer **A** is incorrect because Token Ring maps to 802.5. Answer **B** is incorrect because Ethernet maps to 802.3. Answer **C** is incorrect because Metropolitan Area Networks (MANs) map to 802.6.

17. You are a network technician assigned to install a new network hub. Which layer of the OSI model does a standard hub operate at? Select only one answer.

    A. Physical Layer

    B. Data Link Layer

    C. Network Layer

    D. Transport Layer

    ☑ **A**. Hubs operate at the Physical layer of the OSI model. Therefore, Answer **A** is correct.

    ☒ Answer **B** is incorrect because hubs operate at the Physical layer. Switches, NICs, and bridges operate at the Data Link layer. Answer **C** is incorrect because this is where routing takes place, with routers and so on. A hub is a layer 1 device, with very little intelligence in it. It broadcasts out all ports and floods up your network, whereas a switch (at layer 2) is more intelligent, as it can memorize port assignments and MAC address information. A router operates at layer 3, and again, is even more intelligent. Answer **D** is incorrect because layer 4 switches, but not hubs, operate at the Transport layer.

18. You are a network technician assigned to install a new network switch. Which layer of the OSI model does a standard switch (or bridge) operate at? Select only one answer.

    A. Physical Layer

    B. Data Link Layer

    C. Network Layer

    D. Transport Layer

    ☑ **B**. Switches and bridges operate at the Data Link Layer of the OSI model. Therefore, Answer **B** is correct.

    ☒ Answer **A** is incorrect because hubs operate at the Physical layer. Answer **C** is incorrect because routers operate at the Network layer. Answer **D** is incorrect because layer 4 switches operate at the Transport layer.

19. You are a network technician assigned to install a new network Router. Which layer of the OSI model does a standard router operate at? Choose all that apply.

    A. Physical Layer

    B. Data Link Layer

    C. Network Layer

    D. Transport Layer

☑ **C**. Routers operate at the Network layer of the OSI model. Therefore, Answer **C** is correct. Don't get caught up with "choose all that apply", as it's only a distracter. Pay close attention to wording such as this on the Network+ exam, navigating tricky wording is also another skill that you are learning while reading this publication. Pay attention to all the layers, where they lay in the model, what happens at each layer, and which devices operate where.

☒ Answer **A** is incorrect because hubs operate at the Physical layer. Answer **B** is incorrect because switches operate at the Data Link layer. Answer **D** is incorrect because layer 4 switches operate at the Transport layer.

20. You are a network technician assigned to install a new NIC in a PC. Which layer of the OSI model does a NIC operate at? Select only one answer.

A. Physical Layer

B. Data Link Layer

C. Network Layer

D. Transport Layer

☑ **B**. NICs operate at the Data Link layer of the OSI model. Therefore, Answer **B** is correct.

☒ Answer A is incorrect because hubs operate at the Physical layer. Answer C is incorrect because routers operate at the Network layer. Answer D is incorrect because layer 4 switches operate at the Transport layer.

Chapter 6 Network Protocols

1. You are the network administrator assigned to building a new network within a new facility. You want to implement a protocol that identifies nodes through the use of the MAC address as part of its address scheme. You need to choose the best protocol to suit the job. Which protocol should you use?

A. TCP/IP

B. IPX/SPX

C. AppleTalk

D. NetBEUI

☑ **B**. The address of an IPX frame is 80 bits. The network portion of an IPX address is 32 bits long. The host portion of an IPX address is taken from the station's 48 bit MAC address, therefore, Answer **B** is correct. Although you will most likely not be installing a new IPX/SPX network anytime soon, consider that the Network+ exam will at minimum test you on your understanding of how the protocol operates so that you can distinguish it from other network protocols you may encounter.

☒ Answer **A** is incorrect because although you would most likely want to install a new network with TCP/IP (which could also lead you into reading the question too quickly and providing an incorrect answer), this question asks you to pick the best protocol to suit the job, and IPX/SPX does that. Answer **C** is incorrect because AppleTalk does not identify nodes through the use of the MAC address; AppleTalk uses a 2 byte network number, a 1 byte node number and a 1 byte socket number. Answer **D** is incorrect, because NetBEUI was originally designed for very small, non-routable networks, is broadcast based, is not routable and has such low overhead, the addressing is covered by NetBIOS names broadcast to all nodes on the network. Remember for the Network+ exam, you will be expected to know the differences between the network protocols.

2. Which protocol from the options shown is non-routable by design?

A. TCP/IP

B. IPX/SPX

C. AppleTalk

D. NetBEUI

☑ **D**. NetBEUI was originally designed for very small, non-routable networks, is broadcast-based, and has such low overhead that the addressing is covered by NetBIOS names broadcast to all nodes on the network. Therefore, Answer **D** is correct.

☒ Answer **A** is incorrect because TCP/IP is routable by design, statically as well as dynamically. Answer **B** is incorrect because just like TCP/IP, IPX/SPX is also routable by design. Answer **C** is incorrect because AppleTalk is also routable. Make sure you review this fact before taking the Network+ exam.

3. Your computer seems to have a problem with name resolution and you decide the problem may be in your hosts file. Your computer's IP address is 66.212.14.8. You open the hosts file and spot the likely problem. Which line from the hosts file is the most likely the cause of your name resolution problem?

A. 66.214.41.1 router1

B. 127.0.0.1 localhost

C. 191.87.221.2 server.company.com pisces

D. 66.212.14.8 localhost

☑ **D**. 66.212.14.8 is the IP address of your computer. However, the localhost is a loopback address that is a reserved network IP address of 127.0.0.0. This entry should not be in the hosts file; therefore Answer **D** is correct.

☒ Answer **A** is incorrect because you may have selected this answer thinking that the router was not on your network. However, since we don't know the subnet mask, we are not exactly sure where this router is. Therefore, this is not the best answer. Answer **B** is incorrect because this is the localhost loopback address. If you use the ping utility and type **ping 127.0.0.1**, you will send a ping message to your own computer internally. This is useful to verify that your own computer's TCP/IP function is working properly. Answer **C** is incorrect because this listing is a legitimate entry for a hosts.txt file. The IP address is followed by a Fully Qualified Domain Name (FQDN) and a hostname "pisces."

4. You've just accepted a job at a small company as the IT Manager. The company network is not yet connected to the Internet and you've been asked to make this your top priority. You examine the IP addresses on several computers and find these addresses in use: 192.168.0.4, 192.168.0.19, and 192.168.0.11. What is the next step you would have to take to connect your network to the Internet?

A. Purchase, configure, and install a server to act as a firewall for Internet connectivity.

B. Apply to the InterNIC for the appropriate IP address assignment.

C. Install and configure the common Internet protocols including SMTP, FTP, and HTTP.

D. Subnet the current network configuration using a custom Class C subnet mask.

☑ **B**. The 192.168.0.0/16 address range is a private Class C network configuration, therefore Answer **B** is correct. This can provide up to 256 Class C networks or the 16 bits can be used for host address spaces. In either case, this address range is reserved for private use and cannot connect to the Internet, nor can it be reached via the Internet. You would need to contact the InterNIC for a unique public address assignment.

☒ Answer **A** is incorrect because when you have a public network address, you should certainly install and configure a firewall to prevent unauthorized network access via the Internet. However, that is not the first step involved. Answer **C** is incorrect because when you have a legitimate public address, you can install and configure Internet-related services on a server. This is not the first step you would have to take for Internet connectivity. Answer **D** is incorrect because the current network configuration may be subnetted, but this has little to do with connecting the network to the Internet. As configured, it cannot be connected because the company elected to use a private network address, which must first be changed to a public network address.

5. A user contacts you to let you know his computer won't connect to the corporate network. You ask the user to go into his Network Connections properties and tell you both his IP address and subnet mask. He tells you his IP address is 180.10.254.36 and his subnet mask is 255.255.240.0. Based on this information, what is the correct binary representation of the network ID to which this user is connected?

   A. 10110100.00001001.11110000.00000000

   B. 10110100.00001010.11100000.00000000

   C. 10110110.00001010.11110000.00000000

   D. 10110100.00001010.11110000.00000000

☑ **D.** The user's IP address is 180.10.254.36 and the subnet mask is 255.255.240.0. To find the underlying network address, you need to use bit-wise ANDing and compare the bits in the IP address to the bits in the subnet mask to find the underlying IP address. In this case, the bits look like this:
180.10.254.36 = 10110100.00001010.11111110.00100100
255.255.240.0 = 11111111.11111111.11110000.00000000
Network ID =   10110100.00001010.11110000.00000000 = 180.10.240.0

☒ Answer **A** is incorrect because the dotted decimal representation of this number is 180.9.240.0. The ANDing comparison between the user's IP address and subnet mask yields 10 in the second octet, not 9. Answer **B** is incorrect because the dotted decimal representation of this number is 180.10.224.0. The subnet mask sets the four left-most bits of the third octet to 1. The user's ID also has the four left-most bits of the third octet set to 1. ANDing these would result in 240, not 224. Answer **C** is incorrect because the first octet in this answer equals 182 not 180. Bitwise ANDing the user's IP address and subnet mask results in the first octet being equal to 180, not 182.

6. Another IT staff person, Mike, tells you about a problem he's troubleshooting. He says that Jake's computer doesn't connect to the corporate network. The network uses DHCP to automatically assign IP addresses to computers, so he believes the IP address is correct and unique. He's tried pinging the localhost and that works fine, but when he pings a server that is on the same subnet as Jake's computer, he gets an error message. What is the most likely cause of this problem?

   A. Mike's NIC card has a duplicate IP address.

   B. Mike's NIC card has a duplicate MAC address.

C. Mike's NIC card has no IP address.

D. Mike's Ethernet cable is loose.

☑ **D**. Although there could be a number of reasons that Mike's computer is having trouble connecting to the network, Answer **D** is the best answer. The success of the localhost ping indicates the computer's TCP/IP stack and NIC are functioning properly.

☒ Answer **A** is incorrect because Mike would not be able to connect to the network with an invalid IP address. However, since the network is set to use DHCP, the IP address automatically assigned to Mike's computer is most likely correct and unique, unless Mike changed his computer's settings. Answer **B** is incorrect because unless there was a manufacturer's error or the NIC was purchased on the black market, each NIC has a unique MAC address and cannot be duplicated. This is not the likely cause of the problem. Answer **C** is incorrect, because the network employs DHCP to dynamically assign IP addresses, so Mike's computer probably has an IP address. If Mike inadvertently deleted the IP address, he may not have an IP address but he'd probably either tell you this or he'd reboot before calling you. Rebooting would cause his computer to request an IP address using the DHCP process. Therefore, this is not the most likely cause of the problem.

7. You're designing a network scheme from a Class A network address. You want to be able to have about 16,000 hosts on each subnet. Based on this, what is the maximum number of host address bits you can take to still allow up to 16,000 hosts per subnet?

A. 8

B. 16

C. 24

D. 17

☑ **B**. There are a number of ways to calculate this answer. One way is to start with your knowledge that bit 8 (left-most) of the first octet is equal to 128. As we move to the left, each bit is twice the value of the one to its right. Thus, the string becomes (bit 9 =256), (bit 10 = 512)…(bit 16 = 16,384), (bit 17 = 32,768). Therefore, we need no fewer than 16 bits for our host address space to allow for up to 16,382 addresses per subnet.

☒ Answer **A** is incorrect because eight bits would give us only 254 address spaces (128 + 64 + 32 + 16 + 8 + 4 + 2 + 1 = 256 − 2 − 254). Answer **C** is incorrect because 24 bits would allow us far too many host address spaces (2^{24} = 16,277,214 useable addresses). Answer **D** is incorrect because 17 bits would give us just about double the number we need, 32,766; It's one more bit than we need. It's more common to take one more network bit than you think you need versus taking one more host bit, as it's typically better to have fewer hosts on more subnets for faster, more efficient networks.

8. The company for which you work has three locations in three different states. The WAN links are dedicated T1 lines, which are heavily utilized. Your current network ID is 166.12.0.0. The subnet mask is 255.255.192.0. Each location has grown significantly over the past three years and the network at each site is slow. Given this information, what is the most effective change you could make that would increase network speed for all users?

   A. Replace static routers with dynamic routers.

   B. Subdivide each of the three sites into smaller subnets.

   C. Add additional bandwidth between the sites.

   D. Reduce the number of hosts on each subnet.

   ☑ **B**. Subnets can be subnetted again, therefore Answer **B** is correct. If the number of hosts per current subnet is straining the segment's capacity, it should be subnetted. Although this can be a cumbersome process (changing IP addresses and subnet masks for hosts), it will allow for future expansion.

   ☒ Answer **A** is incorrect because dynamic routers may make routing more efficient, but alone will not likely reduce network traffic. Adding routers may help alleviate some of the traffic problems, but adding routers typically means you've subnetted your network and those subnets require routers in order to keep local traffic local. Answer **C** is incorrect because additional bandwidth between the sites might help the speed of WAN communications, but will not reduce local network traffic. Answer **D** is incorrect because reducing the number of hosts per subnet is certainly the answer to reducing local traffic, but short of removing computers from your network, the only way to reduce the number of hosts on the network is to create smaller subnets. Thus, Answer **B** is still the better answer because it effectively reduces the number of hosts on the network by creating smaller networks (subnets).

9. You receive an e-mail from your supervisor, Lisa. She says that the IT director decided to go ahead with one of the subnetting plans you and Lisa developed. Lisa's e-mail simply says, "Let's use the 132.12.0.0/21 configuration we discussed. Please work up the network address ranges as soon as possible. I'll get to work on a list of the devices using static addresses we'll need to change. Thanks, Lisa." Based on Lisa's e-mail, what is the last (highest) network ID that will be created?

A. 132.12.0.0

B. 132.12.224.0

C. 132.12.248.0

D. 132.12.240.0

☑ **C**. 132.12.0.0 is a Class B network ID because it uses the first two octets for the network address space and is in the Class B network range of 128.0.y.z to 191.255.y.z, therefore Answer **C** is correct. You know you're using the first two octets, 16 bits, for the network address space. The notation Lisa used, /21, indicates that you're going to take five bits from the address space to create your subnets. Using the five high-order bits from the third octet (y) yields 248. Therefore, your highest network address would be 132.12.248.0.

☒ Answer **A** is incorrect because 132.12.0.0 is your original network ID and would be the first network address, not the last. Answer **B** is incorrect because this network address is within your new range, but is not the highest network ID. This network ID has the following configuration in the third octet: 11100000, putting it near the middle of your address ranges. Answer **D** is incorrect because this network address is not the last. It uses only the four high-order bits, so the third octet would be 11110000. This is the second-to-last network address.

10. The company for which you work has three locations in three different states. You were assigned a Class B network ID from the InterNIC and your predecessor subdivided the network for better efficiency. Your current network ID is 166.12.0.0. The subnet mask is 255.255.192.0. Given this information, how many subnets did your predecessor create at the time he subdivided the network?

A. 192

B. 3 to 4

C. 16,382

D. 2

☑ **B**. The subnet mask identified how many bits are used for the network address space. In this case, 192 = 128 + 64. Thus two bits were used. Two bits can have the following combinations: 00, 01, 10, 11. Therefore, up to four networks could be created using this subnet mask, so Answer **B** is correct.

☒ Answer **A** is incorrect because 192 is the dotted decimal value of the bits used to extend the network address space. This is the value of the bits used, but not the number of subnets created. Answer **C** is incorrect because 16,382 is the number of host addresses available per subnet after the network address space is extended by two bits. Answer **D** is incorrect because two bits are used to create the subnetted addresses but this is not the *number of subnets* that result from the use of those two bits.

11. From the list of IP addresses shown, which IP address is a public IP address?

    A. 11.1.1.1

    B. 10.0.1.1

    C. 192.168.1.1

    D. 172.17.1.1

    ☑ **A**. 11.1.1.1, therefore Answer **A** is correct. 11.1.1.1 is an IP address that falls in the public range of IP addresses. The other answers all fall in the private block of IP addresses that are reserved for use within networks and not used at all on the public Internet. It's very important to not only remember the difference between public and private addresses on the Network+ exam, but to also know which IP ranges fall within which class as well as what the default subnet mask is for each. Make sure you review this information before exam day.

    ☒ Answer **B** is incorrect because 10.0.1.1 falls in the Class A range of private addresses: 10.0.0.0 – 10.255.255.255. Answer **C** is incorrect because 192.168.1.1 falls in the Class C range of private addresses: 192.168.0.0–192.168.255.255. Answer **D** is incorrect because 172.17.1.1 falls in the Class B range of private addresses: 172.16.0.0–172.31.255.255.

12. You are the technician assigned to deploy a Windows Server 2003 server and 20 Windows XP Professional clients all with default installations. Your DHCP server is currently down and all your XP clients are complaining that they cannot surf the Internet, whereas 60 minutes ago they could. You see that all your clients currently have addresses in the 169.254.xx.xx range. What is most likely the problem?

    A. There is a duplicate DHCP server on the network with a scope in the 169.254.xx.xx range.

    B. The DHCP server is currently not available so APIPA is used.

    C. You suspect that static addressing was configured without your knowledge.

    D. The 169.254.xx.xx range is automatically configured by a service called Zeroconf.

    ☑ **B**. APIPA is used, therefore Answer **B** is correct. The workstation is using an IP address in the 169.254.xx.xx range. This is via Microsoft's APIPA, which stands for Automatic Private IP Addressing. When the DHCP server is down, APIPA is the next solution used. Remember, APIPA must be disabled if you do not want to use it, otherwise it's automatically used if a DHCP server is not available to service requests.

☒ Answer **A** is incorrect because although a common problem on some networks, the 169.254.xx.xx range does specifically point to APIPA in use, therefore this is not likely the problem, and the 169.254.xx.xx range is a privately used range and should never be used in a DHCP server scope and leased out. Answer **C** is incorrect because it is not likely that anyone came in and changed a dynamic environment into a static one, especially using the APIPA range as its static range. Answer **D** is incorrect because although Zeroconf can help with the configuration of systems automatically, it should not be confused with APIPA, which is based on a similar concept, but very specific to the scenario we just looked at. If a DHCP server is not available, by default, your 2003 servers and XP workstations will immediately use APIPA. Do not confuse the two for the Network+ exam.

13. You are a network administrator at your company. Your company has a firewall that blocks all communication. You need to allow users in your organization to send e-mail messages as part of their daily business activities. Which protocol should you allow through the firewall so that users can send e-mail messages?

    A. FTP

    B. TFTP

    C. POP3

    D. SMTP

    ☑ **D**. SMTP, therefore Answer **D** is correct. The Simple Mail Transfer Protocol (SMTP) in most e-mail programs is used to send e-mail messages. POP3 is used to *receive* e-mail messages (do not confuse the two). You will need to master the concept of protocols and ports as you move into the world of network security, allowing protocols through your firewall by their port assignment, such as TCP port 25 for SMTP.

    ☒ Answer **A** is incorrect because FTP transfers files, not e-mail messages. Answer **B** is incorrect because TFTP (the UDP-based version of FTP) is also not used to send e-mail messages. Answer **C** is incorrect because POP3 is used to *receive* messages, whereas SMTP is used to *send* them.

14. You are the network administrator at your company. Your company's network includes a Web server and an SMTP server. The network has a permanent connection to the Internet protected by a network firewall. Because you are concerned about the threat of hackers gaining access from the Internet, you decide to enforce HTTPS on your Web server, which is SSL over HTTP. After configuring HTTPS, your Web server is no longer accessible from the Internet, but can still be accessed by your internal network users. What is the likely cause of this problem?

A. Your DNS server is down.

B. Your Web server address has changed.

C. Your firewall is blocking port 389.

D. Your firewall is blocking port 443.

☑ **D**. HTTPS uses port 443 for communication, therefore Answer **D** is correct. HTTPS (the SSL protocol) uses port 443. The firewall might be blocking this port and you may need to allow the connection through by altering the configuration on the firewall.

☒ Answer **A** is incorrect because your DNS server being down will stop the connection both internally and externally. Answer **B** is incorrect because if the Web server changed its address, again, you would have problems on both sides of the network, internally and externally. Answer **C** is incorrect because 389 is the port for LDAP, not HTTP. For the Network+ exam you must memorize port and protocol assignments.

15. You are developing a new application for your company. This application needs to send and receive data across the corporate network. In order to make this application work correctly, you need to be sure that the data sent is accurately received on the other end and that data sent from the other side is accurately received. Which TCP/IP protocol would you implement to accomplish this?

A. ICMP

B. TCP/IP

C. IP

D. TCP

☑ **D**. In order to ensure that data is reliably sent and received at both ends of the network communication, TCP is used, therefore Answer **D** is correct. This is a connection-based protocol that utilizes the acknowledgement message (ACK) to verify receipt of data.

☒ Answer **A** is incorrect because the Internet Control Message Protocol is used for error handling related to internetwork communications. This does not provide data transport services nor does it provide acknowledgement messages to ensure reliable delivery of data. Answer **B** is incorrect because TCP/IP is the entire protocol suite, which includes many different protocols. Although TCP is one of the protocols in this suite, this answer includes all of the protocols in TCP/IP, many of which have nothing to do with reliable data transfers. Answer **C** is incorrect because the Internet Protocol is used to address messages, but is not directly responsible for transporting the data, nor is it involved with sending and receiving messages to verify accurate packet delivery.

16. You work as a network administrator at your company. The company's local network includes multiple services and has a permanent connection to the Internet. You are concerned about hackers gaining access to the local network from the Internet. You decide to implement a firewall and configure it to filter ports 100 through 150. Which service might be affected by the firewall?

    A. FTP

    B. NTP

    C. HTTP

    D. SMTP

    ☑ **B**. NTP might be affected, therefore Answer **B** is correct. NTP operates via UDP port 123. Since you have blocked ports 100 through 150, port 123 will also be blocked.

    ☒ Answer **A** is incorrect because FTP uses port 21, which is not in the filtered range. Answer **C** is incorrect because HTTP uses port 80, which is not in the filtered range. Answer **D** is incorrect because SMTP uses port 25, which is not in the filtered range. You must know all the common ports for the Network+ exam so that you can figure out scenario questions that incorporate them.

17. POP3 is identified by which TCP/IP port number?

    A. 80

    B. 110

    C. 25

    D. 21

    ☑ **B**. POP3 uses port 110 for communication, therefore Answer **B** is correct. POP3 uses TCP port 110 to receive e-mail from a server to a POP3 client as an example. Some questions on the Network+ exam are scenario-based and somewhat long, or fairly short and to the point, looking to see if you understand the concept.

    ☒ Answer **A** is incorrect because port 80 is associated with HTTP. Answer **C** is incorrect because port 25 is associated with SMTP. Answer **D** is incorrect because port 21 is associated with FTP.

18. Telnet is identified by which TCP/IP port number?

    A. 80

    B. 23

    C. 119

    D. 161

☑ **B**. 23, therefore Answer **B** is correct. Telnet uses TCP port 23 for communications.

☒ Answer **A** is incorrect because port 80 is associated with HTTP. Answer **C** is incorrect because port 119 is associated with NNTP. Answer **D** is incorrect because port 161 is associated with SNMP.

19. You've just upgraded from Windows 2000 Server to Windows Server 2003 Enterprise Edition. Your client computers are configured to use WINS for resolving NetBIOS names on the network. However, users are complaining that they can't reach certain resources on the network now. What is the most likely cause of the problem?

A. The Enterprise Edition of Windows Server 2003 no longer supports WINS.

B. The WINS service is not enabled.

C. The WINS service can be enabled only on the client side to allow for NetBIOS name resolution.

D. The WINS client must be enabled on client computers first.

☑ **B**. By default, the WINS service is not enabled upon installation of Windows Server 2003 (or on any edition), therefore Answer **B** is correct. WINS must be enabled before it will work. By default, DNS is used to resolve names in Windows Server 2003, but WINS is provided for backward compatibility.

☒ Answer **A** is incorrect because the Enterprise Edition of Windows Server 2003 still supports WINS, but does not enable the service by default. Answer **C** is incorrect because the WINS service runs on a computer that will act as a name resolver (server). The WINS server function is not enabled on client computers. Answer **D** is incorrect because the WINS client function is automatically installed on the client and does not need to be enabled manually for WINS to work. A WINS server service must be available on the network for the WINS client to work.

Chapter 7

1. As the primary lead on your company's helpdesk, you are asked to help resolve a problem call with an ISDN line. A customer wants to upgrade an existing ISDN line because it's currently too slow. Right now, he is using a single BRI ISDN circuit switched B channel. From the available choices, what should his transmission rate be?

A. 56 Mbps

B. 64 Kbps

C. 128 Kbps

D. 256 Mbps

☑ **C.** When working with ISDN technology, always remember that the transmission rate of a single BRI ISDN B channel is 64Kbps.

☒ **A, B, D.** Answer **A** is incorrect because the rate is 64 Kbps, not 56 Mbps. Answer **B** is incorrect because the rate is 64 Kbps, not 128 kbps. Answer **C** is incorrect because the rate is 64 Kbps, not 256 Mbps.

2. As the network administrator for your company, you are asked by your CIO to design and deploy a data link between two offices of your company. There are 10 employees located in each office. Your main concerns are the speed of the connections, the reliability of transferring of data, and the cost. Which solution should you implement? (Choose one)

A. Place a modem on a server in each office to so they can connect.

B. Connect an ISDN circuit to each workstation in both locations.

C. Use an ISDN circuit connected to a dedicated location or server in each building.

D. Have each workstation at both locations use a modem to connect to opposite offices.

☑ **C.** ISDN provides better speed, connection time, and reliability compared than a modem. ISDN can be connected to systems in many ways because of the different adapters that can be used with it. ISDN circuits will be terminated on a device or within a location, not on a modem, or on individual workstations using modems.

☒ **A, B, D.** Answer **A** is incorrect because ISDN circuits will be terminated on a device or within a location, not on a modem, or on individual workstations using modems. Answer **B** is incorrect because ISDN circuits do not terminate on workstations. Answer **D** is incorrect because ISDN circuits will be terminated on a device or within a location, not on a modem, or on individual workstations using modems.

3. You are the IT manager for rsnetworks.net. As the person responsible for recommending the right technology, what would you select as the solution to provide the fastest connectivity? (Select one)

A.   T3

B.   T1

C.   ISDN BRI

D.   Cable Modem

☑   **A**. T3. The T3 provides the fastest connectivity T3s provide access up to 45 Mbps.

☒   **B**, **C**, **D**. Answer **B** is incorrect because a T1 provides up to 1.544 Mbps. Answer **C** is incorrect because ISDN BRI provides up to 128Kbps. Answer **D** is incorrect because a cable modem network is generally up to 10 Mbps.

4.   You want to connect a remote office to a corporate network. The only available service is an analog dial-up line provided by the local telephone company. What device would you need to implement to use this analog dial-up solution?

A.   CSU/DSU

B.   ISDN adapter

C.   Modem

D.   NIC

☑   **C**. A modem is used to connect to the Internet using the local telephone company's telephone lines.

☒   **A**, **B**, **D**. Answer **A** is incorrect because a CSU/DSU is a multiplexer generally used with T1 access. Answer **B** is incorrect because an ISDN adapter is used for digital service, not analog. Answer **D** is incorrect because a NIC is used for connecting a system to a local area network.

5.   As the Network Manager for rsnetworks.net, you need to implement a solution that will allow for sporadic connection to the Internet. Your only requirement is that you find a solution that will provide a connection of up to 128 Kbps to the Internet, only when needed. Which solution should you implement?

A.   T1

B.   T3

C.   56 Kbps

D.   BRI ISDN

☑   **D**. ISDN BRI provides up to 128 Kbps.

☒   **A**, **B**, **C**. Answer **A** is incorrect because a T1 is a dedicated connection, it's always on, and you always pay for its use. It's also 1.544 Mbps. Answer **B** is incorrect because a T3, much like a T1, is a dedicated connection providing up to 45 Mbps. Answer **C** is incorrect because a 56 Kbps leased line will only provide up to 56 Kbps.

6. As a network manager for your company's high-speed network, you are looking to implement a new line from a remote site (Chicago) to the company's core hub (New York) where the mainframe is located. The mainframe is where all the company's sales orders are placed daily. The hub site is where all sites get their Internet access from, and where they upload and download files to and from. Connection to this mainframe 24 hours a day is essential to meeting the business plan. You have just heard from your systems engineer that users are no longer able to access the mainframe from the remote sites; the users at the core site are still able to access the mainframe. Within minutes the connection is restored and all users are able to access the mainframe once more. From careful analysis you uncover that during the time that the remote users were not able to access the mainframe, one user had been downloading a very large file from the Internet to the remote site user's PC. You find that the user was downloading a legitimate file and will be doing so each day. You cannot afford this type of network slowdown each day so you decide to allow for the upgrading of the line. It's currently at 128 Kbps using ISDN BRI. You have found that after careful analysis of the remote sites' usage patterns and looking over the documentation of the current network an upgrade of about 1.5 Mbps is needed across all links. Which technology would you implement? (Choose one)

A. ADSL

B. E1

C. LAN adapter.

D. T1

☑ **D.** T1.

☒ **A**, **B**, **C**. Answer **A** is incorrect because ADSL is not good for uploading, just for downloading, and it is not fast enough to meet the required needs. Answer **B** is incorrect because an E1 doesn't even apply; this technology is European-based and the company is located in the United States. Answer **C** is incorrect because a LAN adapter, which can deliver amazing speeds, is a LAN-based technology, not a WAN-based technology, which is what is used to connect the remote sites to the core.

7. The PSTN is the analog-based telephone system we have come to learn to be very familiar with today. What are some of the features of PSTN? (Choose all that apply.)

A. Compared to DSL and ISDN, it is inexpensive.

B. Worldwide installation base in use and readily available.

C. Easy to use and configure.

D. Transfer rates of 64 Kbps.

☑   **A, B, C**. Answers A, B, and C are all correct because the PSTN is a readily available, easy to use, and is a relatively inexpensive method to dial up to an ISP and connect to the Internet.

☒   **D**. Answer **D** is incorrect because the PSTN has a transfer rate of 56 Kbps, whereas the answer specified 64 Kbps.

8. You are a network administrator at your company. Your company has a number of sales and marketing users who work remotely and telecommute from home or from sales meetings. These users dial into a RAS server to access the corporate headquarters. One day, one of the sales users dials up the RAS server to connect to the corporate headquarters network to access a few files. The sales user dials up the RAS server and cannot connect. The sales user when asked reports that there is no dial tone. What is the cause of the problem? (Choose one)

A. Telephone company problem

B. The modem does not support the PC

C. The modem settings are set incorrectly.

D. There are no settings configured within Windows

☑   **A**. If there is no dial tone on the line, you will not be able to dial out to the RAS server to connect to your corporate network. For the network+ exam you will be expected to troubleshoot many scenarios so make sure you read them very carefully. .

☒   **B, C, D**. Answer **B** is incorrect because neither the modem nor the PC is the problem; the problem is with the carrier. There is no dial tone, therefore you will not be able to dial out. Answer **C** is incorrect because the modem settings are not the root cause of the problem. Answer **D** is incorrect because the Windows Operating system is installed on a PC, which has nothing to do with the absence of dial tone.

9. You are the network technician at your company. You are configuring a Windows NT 4.0 laptop for dial-up networking. The laptop will be used by a telecommuter. The telecommuter will use the laptop to dial into a Microsoft Windows NT 4.0 Remote Access Service (RAS) server. Once connected, the telecommuter will need access to a UNIX machine.

What should you install on the laptop? (Choose two.)

A. TCP/IP Protocol

B. RDP

C. VPN

D. Dial-Up Networking

☑ **A** and **D**. You will need to have dial-up networking and the TCP/IP protocol installed on your Windows system to dial into a Windows NY 4.0 RAS server.

☒ **B** and **C**. Answer **B** is incorrect because RDP (Remote Desktop Protocol) it not needed for connectivity to a RAS server. RDP is used to make connections to remote hosts. Answer **C** is incorrect because a VPN is a secure network created over an insecure one (namely the Internet).

10. You are a consultant looking over network documentation for a small company with one core site and two remote sites. Router A shows the location of the corporate headquarters where there is also a link out for Internet access and another remote site configured to also connect to the core. From the figure below, what type of WAN technology is in use based on the information shown for Link A?

Figure 7.23 WAN Technology

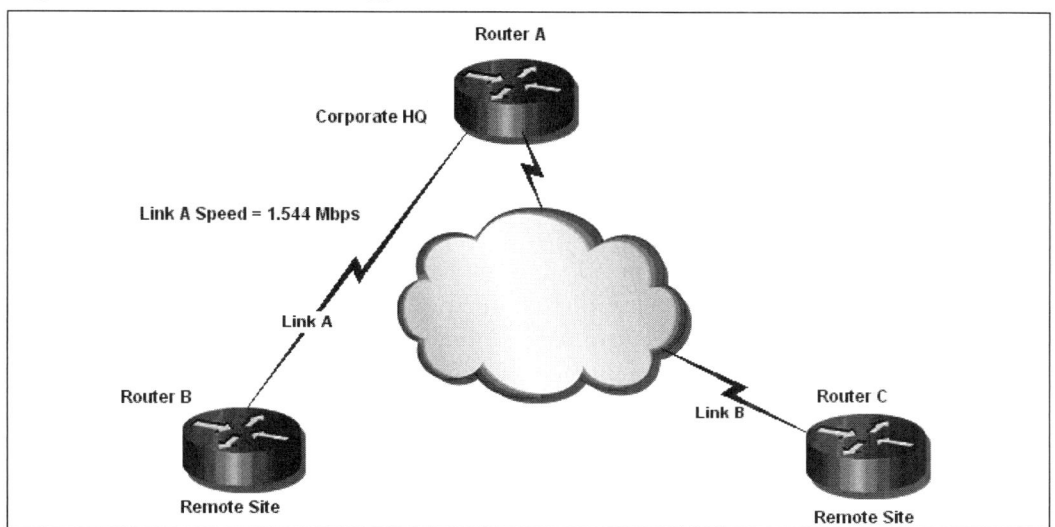

A. DSL

B. T3

C. T1

D. FDDI

☑ **C.** Based on the information given, it is clear that a T1 is in use.

☒ **A, B, D.** Answer **A** is incorrect because DSL does not operate in a point to point fashion, nor does it operate at the speed shown in the illustration. Answer **B** is incorrect because a T3 operates at 45 Mbps, not 1.544. Answer **D** is incorrect because a cable network is a shared network that supports speed up to 10 Mbps.

11. You work as an IT consultant. You are currently working for company looking for a secure way to do work over the Internet. There is a need to have secure authentication and encryption for security reasons when accessing the corporate network. You need to use two protocols to implement this solution. From the list provided, what two protocols will allow for secure authentication and encryption over the Internet?

A. TCP/IP and WEP

B. TCP/IP and L2TP

C. TCP/IP and SMTP

D. TCP/IP and PPP

☑ **B.** You can use TCP/IP and PPTP to provide secure access over the Internet.

☒ **A, C, D.** Answer **A** is incorrect because you can't use TCP/IP and WEP to provide secure access over the Internet, WEP is a wireless security protocol. Answer **C** is incorrect because you can't use TCP/IP and SMTP to provide secure access over the Internet, as SMTP is a mail protocol used for sending e-mail messages. Answer **D** is incorrect because you can't use TCP/IP and PPP to provide secure access over the Internet, as PPP does not provide for any security.

12. You are an IT consultant. You are asked to implement a solution that provides for security authentication and encryption to a private network for a client machine that needs to connect to a NetWare server inside the private network. Which protocols should you implement to provide this functionality? (Choose all that apply)

A. DNS

B. L2TP

C. RIP

D. TCP/IP

☑ **B** and **D.** L2TP and TCP/IP are both used to provide secure access to the Internet.

☒ **A** and **C**. Answer **A** is incorrect because DNS is used for resolving fully quali-fied domain names to IP addresses. Answer **C** is incorrect because RIP is a routing protocol used to keep routing tables updated between peers on a WAN. RIP is a protocol used to help update the routing tables.

13. You are a consultant looking over network documentation for a small company with one core site and two remote sites. Router A shows the location of the cor-porate headquarters where there is also a link out for Internet access and another remote site configured to also connect to the core. From the figure below, what type of WAN technology is in use based on the information seen for Link B?

Figure 7.24 WAN Technology

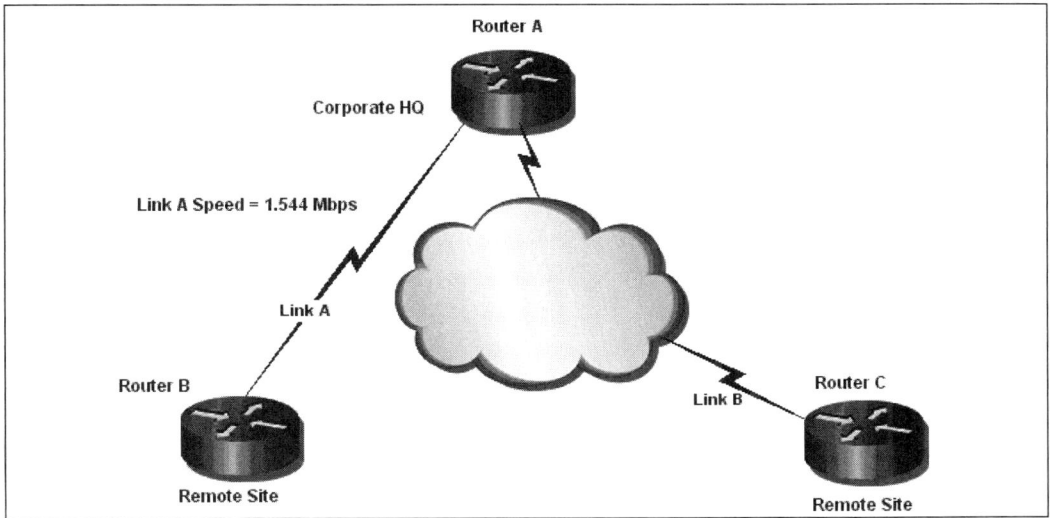

A. DSL

B. IPsec

C. T1

D. T3

☑ **B**. Based on the information given, it is clear that IPsec encryption is being used.

☒ **A, C, D**. Answer **A** is incorrect because although a DSL line could be in use, its IPSec that is building the usable link to the core through the Internet. Answer **C** is incorrect because much like DSL, the T1 will not be able to con-nect Router C to Router A to provide resources. Answer **D** is incorrect because a T3 operates at 45 Mbps and does little to build an encrypted tunnel to the core from the remote site.

14.   HTTPS is a secure protocol used on the Internet. Upon what protocol is it based?

    A. SSH

    B. IPsec

    C. SSL

    D. Kerberos

    ☑ **C**. SSL (secure socket layer) is a protocol that encrypts otherwise vulnerable Web-based traffic to allow safe transactions over the Internet. HTTPS is based on the Secure Socket Layer protocol (SSL).

    ☒ Answer **A** is incorrect because SSH (Secure Shell) an encrypted Telnet session used for safe remote management of systems. Answer **B** is incorrect because IPsec is used to create a virtual tunnel of encryption over an unsafe network (such as the Internet); it has nothing to do with HTTP. Answer **D** is incorrect because Kerberos is a ticketing system used to secure infrastructure.

15.   You are a network administrator at your company. You need to implement a secure way to connect to remote hosts and manage them remotely. The way your end users connect today is with Telnet. What is a more secure way for those same users to perform the same tasks ? (Choose one)

    A. SSL

    B. IPsec

    C. SSH

    D. Kerberos

    ☑ **C**. SSH is nothing more than encrypted Telnet. SSH is used to provide secure communication between the client and the server. Make sure that you use SSH whenever possible since it's virtually the same as using Telnet, except it's secure.

    ☒ **A**, **B**, **D**. Answer **A** is incorrect because SSL is used to ensure secure Web-based communications normally working within HTTP and port 80. Answer **B** is incorrect because IPsec is a method for building encrypted tunnels between hosts to ensure secure communications. Answers **D** is incorrect because Kerberos is a ticket system and is not used to remotely manage systems.

16. You are building a small Windows 2000 network. You have installed 30 Windows XP Professional workstations and two Windows 2003 Server systems. What is the LAN network access security that will be uses on this network by default simply because of using Windows 2003 or XP?

   A. Kerberos

   B. PPTP

   C. WEP

   D. SSL

   ☑ **A**. Make sure you read the questions carefully when taking the Network+ exam, as it's very easy to miss things if you read too quickly or haphazardly. In this question, it's very important to remember that you are talking about the LAN network access security, where every host on the network functions off the ticket granting system. Kerberos is a LAN-based authentication protocol that can help add another level of security to your internal infrastructure and systems.

   ☒ **B**, **C**, **D**. Answer **B** is incorrect because PPTP is used to secure remote access connections between a server and a client for example. Answer **C** is incorrect because WEP is used to secure wireless transmissions, not LAN access. Answer **D** is incorrect because SSL is used to secure web transactions, not LAN access.

Chapter 8 Network Operating Systems

1. You are the network administrator for a Novell NetWare network. You have been tasked with providing e-mail and collaboration software for your company's employees. What would be the best choice of software to fill this need?

   A. GroupWise

   B. Exchange

   C. SquirrelMail

   D. Border Manager

   ☑ **A**. GroupWise is the Novell application used to provide e-mail and collaboration for users of NetWare networks. Therefore, Answer **A** is correct.

   ☒ **B**, **C**, **D**. Microsoft Exchange is the Microsoft Windows e-mail and collaboration package, it does not run on Novell NetWare. Therefore, Answer **B** is incorrect. SquirrelMail is a Linux/UNIX-based email package that is used on Linux and Mac OS X servers. Therefore, Answer **C** is incorrect. Border

Manager is the Novell application used to provide firewall and VPN access to NetWare networks, not to provide email and collaboration software. Therefore, Answer **D** is incorrect.

2. You are the network administrator for a Windows network. You need to purchase a new computer to be used as a client workstation by one of your users. Which operating system should you configure for the new workstation? (Each answer represents a complete solution. Select all that apply.)

    A. Windows 2000 Professional

    B. Windows NT 4.0 Workstation

    C. Windows Server 2003 Standard Edition

    D. Windows XP Professional

    ☑   **A**, **B**, **D**. Windows 2000 Professional is the workstation edition of the Windows 2000 product line. Therefore, Answer **A** is correct. Windows NT 4.0 Workstation is the workstation edition of the Windows NT 4.0 product line. Therefore, Answer **B** is correct. Windows XP Professional is appropriate for use by a corporate user as a desktop client operating system. Therefore, Answer **D** is correct.

    ☒   **C**. Windows Server 2003, Standard Edition, is a server NOS used to provide file and print sharing, application sharing and remote access to multiple client workstations. It is not appropriate for use as a desktop workstation. Therefore, Answer **C** is incorrect.

3. You are the network administrator for a Windows network. The user Jane Smith on your network has chosen to return to using her maiden name of Johnson. What do you need to do to accomplish this in the most efficient way?

    A. Rename the user's account to reflect the new last name.

    B. Delete the user's account and create a new one with the new last name.

    C. Copy the user's account and create a new one with the new last name.

    D. Maintain the user account with the original last name.

    ☑   **A**. The security identifier (SID) built into Windows user accounts is used to assign rights and permissions to a user account. This SID remains in place even if the account is renamed. Therefore, Answer **A** is correct.

    ☒   **B**, **C**, **D**. Deleting the user's account and creating a new one would generate a new SID, which would require you to assign permissions to the new account all over again. Therefore, Answer **B** is incorrect. Copying the user's account and creating a new one would generate a new SID, which would require you to assign permissions to the new account. Therefore, Answer **C** is incorrect.

Because the SID will remain in place when the account is renamed, you are not required to maintain the account with the original last name. Therefore, Answer **D** is incorrect.

4. You are the administrator of a Mac OS X network. You have been tasked with deploying Instant Messaging for your corporate network. This IM service must be restricted to only internal users, and must provide encryption of the data being transmitted. How can you meet these requirements?

    A. Deploy the SpamAssassin service.

    B. Create accounts for your users on the AOL Instant Messenger Service.

    C. Deploy the Mac OS X iChat service.

    D. Deploy the Mac OS X Weblog service.

    ☑ **C**. Mac OS X includes an instant messaging service that provides secure IM traffic for a corporate network. Therefore, Answer **C** is correct.

    ☒ **A, B, D**. SpamAssassin is used to reduce the impact of unwanted commercial email on a Mac OS X mail server. Therefore, Answer **A** is incorrect. Commercial Instant Messaging services like AIM cannot be restricted to your internal corporate users, and cannot provide encryption for your information. Therefore, Answer **B** is incorrect. The Weblog service is used to create *blog* pages for your internal users for information sharing and collaboration; it is not used for instant messaging services. Therefore, Answer **D** is incorrect.

5. You are the administrator of a Windows Server 2003 Active Directory domain. Your network clients are running exclusively Windows XP Professional. What protocol will your LAN clients use for domain authentication?

    A. MS-CHAP

    B. NTLM

    C. SPAP

    D. Kerberos

    ☑ **D**. Windows Server 2003 supports Kerberos authentication for improved security and single sign-on. By default, Windows 2000, XP and 2003 clients will use Kerberos authentication. Therefore, Answer **D** is correct.

    ☒ **A, B, C**. MS-CHAP is an authentication protocol used for remote access connections, not for LAN clients. Therefore, Answer **A** is incorrect. NTLM was the authentication protocol used by Windows NT 4.0, and is used by down-level clients such as Windows NT 4.0, Windows 95 and Windows 98. Therefore, Answer **B** is incorrect. SPAP is a legacy remote access protocol that transmits username and password information in clear-text. It is not used for LAN connections. Therefore, Answer **D** is incorrect.

6. You are the administrator of a Linux server. You want to maintain this server in a secured location while being able to administer it from your desktop PC. What is the best choice to gain access to a console session on the Linux server to perform administration from the command-line?

   A. Telnet

   B. FTP

   C. SSH

   D. NFS

   ☑ **C**. Secure Shell (SSH) will open up a command prompt on a remote server, allowing you to perform command-line administration of the server over a secured connection. Therefore, Answer **C** is correct.

   ☒ **A**, **B**, **D**. Telnet will open up a command prompt on a remote server, but it does not provide encryption and passes information over the network in clear text. Therefore, Answer **A** is incorrect. FTP is used to transfer files to and from a remote host, not to perform command-line administration. Therefore, Answer **B** is incorrect. NFS is the file system used by Linux and UNIX servers; it does not enable remote administration of a server. Therefore, Answer **D** is incorrect.

7. You are the administrator of a Windows 2000 Active Directory network. You need to create a number of new user accounts to access resources on your server. What utility will you use to accomplish this?

   A. iManager

   B. Workgroup Manager

   C. Active Directory Users & Computers

   D. Computer Management

   ☑ **C**. To create domain user accounts in Active Directory, you will use the Active Directory Users & Computers utility. Therefore, Answer **C** is correct.

   ☒ **A**, **B**, **D**. iManager is used to create and manage user accounts in Novell NetWare's eDirectory, not in Active Directory. Therefore, Answer **A** is incorrect. Workgroup Manager is used to create and manage users for Mac OS X server, not within Active Directory. Answer **B** is incorrect. The Computer Management utility is used to manage local user accounts on a Windows 2000 computer, not domain accounts in Active Directory. Therefore, Answer **D** is incorrect.

8. You are configuring a Windows 2000 Professional workstation to connect to a Novell NetWare 4.11 network installed with default settings. After configuring the NIC and plugging in the network cable, what do you need to install on the client workstation to enable access to the NetWare server? (Choose two.)

    A. IPX/SPX

    B. Gateway Services for NetWare

    C. Client for NetWare networks

    D. TCP/IP

    ☑ **A, C.** The default protocol for a NetWare server running version 4 or earlier is IPX/SPX. Therefore, Answer **A** is correct. To connect to a NetWare network, the client workstation requires the Client for NetWare networks to be installed. Therefore, Answer **C** is correct.

    ☒ **B, D.** The Gateway Services for NetWare is installed on a Windows server to allow clients who are part of a Windows domain to access resources on a NetWare server. Therefore, Answer **B** is incorrect. By default, NetWare 4.11 uses the IPX/SPX protocol, not TCP/IP. Therefore, Answer **D** is incorrect.

9. You are a consultant who has been tasked with setting up a network for a small graphics design firm. This office consists of only three workstations, and the business owner does not currently have the funds to purchase a dedicated server. How should you configure the computers in this network?

    A. Configure the network as a workgroup.

    B. Purchase a dedicated server and configure the network as a domain.

    C. Configure the network as a domain without a dedicated server.

    D. Use one of the workstations as a server to configure a domain.

    ☑ **A.** For a small office such as this one, you should configure the clients in a peer-to-peer configuration, which is called a workgroup in Microsoft terminology. Therefore, Answer **A** is correct.

    ☒ **B, C, D.** The business owner has stated that she does not currently have the funds to purchase a dedicated server for this network. Therefore, Answer **B** is incorrect. To configure a Windows domain, you need to have at least one computer that is running the Windows server NOS. Therefore, Answer **C** is incorrect. To configure a Windows domain, you need to have at least one computer that is running the Windows server NOS. Therefore, Answer **D** is incorrect.

10. You are configuring a Windows 2000 Professional workstation to connect to a Windows Server 2003 Active Directory domain installed with default settings. After configuring the NIC and plugging in the network cable, what additional software

do you need to install on the client workstation to enable access to the Active Directory domain? (Select all that apply.)

A. TCP/IP

B. Client for Microsoft Networks

C. NetBEUI

D. None of the above.

☑ **D**. Windows 2000 Professional has TCP/IP and the Client for Microsoft Networks installed by default. No additional software has to be installed to enable a connection to an Active Directory domain. Therefore, Answer **D** is correct.

☒ **A**, **B**, **C**. TCP/IP is installed by default on Windows 2000 Professional. Therefore, Answer **A** is incorrect. The Client for Microsoft Networks is installed by default on Windows 2000 Professional. Therefore, Answer **B** is incorrect. The default protocol used by Windows Server 2003 Active Directory is TCP/IP, not NetBEUI. Therefore, Answer **C** is incorrect.

11. You have recently been hired as the network administrator for a large medical supply firm. The firm has just leased additional office space in the same building as their current offices, and you need to take an inventory of the network and telephone jacks to determine which ones are functioning. What tools can you use to perform this inventory? (Select all that apply.)

A. Cable tester

B. Tone generator

C. Oscilloscope

D. Punch down tool

☑ **A**, **B**. You can use a cable tester to determine if a network cable or a wall jack is functioning correctly. The LED lights on the tester will light up if it is able to transmit information. Therefore, Answer **A** is correct. A tone generator is used to perform diagnostics on telephone jacks, including determining if a jack is "live" and able to make and receive calls. Therefore, Answer **B** is correct.

☒ **C**, **D**. An oscilloscope is used to measure the level of electrical current that's being passed through a length of cable. Therefore, Answer **C** is incorrect. A punch down tool is used to connect telephone or token ring cabling to a panel in a wiring closet. Therefore, Answer **D** is incorrect.

12. You have been hired as a consultant to install new LANs for offices inside of a newly constructed office building. You need to be able to install wiring closets for CAT-5 cabling coming from the various wall jacks. What tool can you use to accomplish this?

    A. Punch down tool

    B. Patch panel

    C. Cable tester

    D. Oscilloscope

    ☑ **B.** A patch panel is used to connect CAT-5 or CAT-6 Ethernet cables to a panel in a wiring closet. Therefore, Answer **B** is correct.

    ☒ **A, C, D.** A punch down tool is used to connect token ring or telephone cabling to a panel in a wiring closet – it will not support CAT-5 or CAT-6 Ethernet cabling. Therefore, Answer **A** is incorrect. A cable tester is used to verify that a piece of cable or a wall jack is functioning correctly. Therefore, Answer **C** is incorrect. An oscilloscope is used to measure the level of electrical current that's being passed through a length of cable. Therefore, Answer **D** is incorrect.

13. You are the administrator of a Windows 2000 Active Directory network. You need to configure remote access for file transfers from a business partner. This business partner insists that there be no chance of data being intercepted during transit, regardless of cost. What type of remote access do you need to configure? (Choose all that apply)

    A. Configure a VPN using your company's Internet connection.

    B. Configure a dial-up remote access connection using a dedicated phone line.

    C. Configure a VPN using a dedicated T1 connection between your offices.

    D. Configure a dial-up remote access connection through a dial-up Internet connection.

    ☑ **B, C.** To create a remote access connection with little to no chance of data being intercepted in transit, use a dedicated dial-up connection that does not transmit data over the Internet or another public network. Therefore Answer **B** is correct. To create a remote access connection with little to no chance of data being intercepted in transit, you can use a VPN connection over a dedicated leased line that does not transmit data over the Internet or another public network. Therefore Answer **C** is correct.

    ☒ **A, D.** Even though a VPN will encrypt information sent across an Internet connection, it still does not have the same level of security as using a dedicated connection. Therefore, Answer **A** is incorrect. Using a simple dial-up Internet connection will not provide any encryption at all for any data transmitted over the connection. Therefore, Answer **D** is incorrect.

14. You are configuring your home PC to connect to your company's Windows Server 2003 RRAS server. Your home PC has two modems installed in it, and you would like to be able to use both of these modems to increase the performance of your remote access connection. What feature must your RRAS server support in order for this to happen?

    A. Callback

    B. Caller ID

    C. Multi-link

    D. Virtual private networking

    ☑ **C**. Multi-link is a feature in remote access servers that will allow a client to use more than one modem to increase the bandwidth of their connection. Therefore, Answer **C** is correct.

    ☒ **A**, **B**, **D**. The callback feature will cause a remote access server to automatically disconnect when a client dials in, and then call that client back at a specified number. This feature will not allow you to use more than one modem to create a connection. Therefore, Answer **A** is incorrect. Caller ID is used by remote access servers to only allow connections from a specific list of incoming phone numbers. Therefore, Answer **B** is incorrect. Virtual private networking creates a secure tunnel over an existing public connection such as the Internet. Therefore, Answer **D** is incorrect.

Chapter 9

1. You are the network administrator for a financial services company. Your company has a single Web server that contains an intranet that is accessed by internal employees while also providing information to the general public. You would like to secure access to this Web server without preventing the necessary users from accessing it. What is the best way to do this?

    A. Install a single firewall. Place the Web server on your company's internal network.

    B. Install a single firewall. Place the Web server outside the firewall with a direct connection to the Internet.

    C. Install a proxy server to handle requests from your internal users.

    D. Install the Web server into a demilitarized zone (DMZ).

☑ **D.** The most appropriate firewall configuration for this Web server would be a DMZ. In a DMZ, the Web server is located between two firewalls—an external firewall to protect the Web server against malicious outsiders and a firewall between the Web server and the internal network to protect internal network resources. Therefore, Answer **D** is correct.

☒ **A**, **B**, **D.** Although installing a single firewall and placing the Web server on your company's internal network will protect the Web server to an extent, it does not provide the best level of protection, since you need to allow outside users access to your internal network through the firewall. Therefore, Answer **A** is incorrect. Placing the Web server outside a single firewall will protect your internal network from malicious outsiders, but it does nothing to protect the Web server itself from attack. Therefore, Answer **B** is incorrect. Using only a proxy server would not be appropriate in this scenario, since a proxy server by itself would not provide the protection against network attacks that a firewall would. Therefore, Answer **C** is incorrect.

2. You are the network administrator for a bank that has several branch offices located throughout a single city. Each branch office contains 25 workstations and one file server that should be accessed only by users internal to the branch. You have been provided with three public IP addresses for your company's Web server, firewall, and proxy server, and now you need to configure IP addresses for your branch offices. Which range of IP addresses can you use to configure the workstations and servers in each branch? (Select all that apply.)

A. 192.168.1.0/24

B. 10.0.0.0/8

C. 66.195.34.0/24

D. 172.16.0.0/16

E. 127.0.0.0/8

☑ **A, B, D.** IP version 4 allows for three private IP address ranges. These private addresses are not routable and can be used without registering them with an Internet registrar. The Class C private address range is 192.168.1.0/24. Therefore, Answer **A** is correct. The Class A private address range is 10.0.0.0/8. Therefore, Answer **B** is correct. The Class B private address range is 172.16.0.0/16. Therefore, Answer **D** is correct.

☒ **C, E.** The range 66.195.34.0 is a public IP address range that must be registered with an Internet registrar and is probably already owned by another corporation, so your company cannot use it. Therefore, Answer **C** is incorrect. The range 127.0.0.0/8 is the loopback range that is reserved for TCP/IP troubleshooting, diagnostics, and testing. Therefore, Answer **E** is incorrect.

3. You are the new network administrator for a medium-sized law firm that runs its own Web server and DNS that are configured with public IP addresses. To increase the security of your externally reachable machines, you place both servers inside a DMZ. You need to configure the external firewall so that only HTTP and SSL traffic can reach the Web server and only DNS traffic can reach the DNS server. What rules should you configure on your firewall? (Select all that apply.)

A. Create a firewall rule that allows only TCP port 80 and TCP port 443 to reach the Web server.

B. Create a firewall rule that allows only TCP port 80 and TCP port 110 to reach the Web server.

C. Create a firewall rule that allows only TCP port 53 to reach the DNS server.

D. Create a firewall rule that allows only TCP port 443 to reach the DNS server.

☑ **A, C.** HTTP traffic uses TCP port 80, and SSL traffic uses TCP port 443. These two ports should be enabled to allow outside users to reach both secure and nonsecure Web pages on your company's Web server. Therefore, Answer **A** is correct. DNS uses TCP port 53. This port should be enabled to allow outside users to perform DNS queries against your company's DNS server. Therefore, Answer **C** is correct.

☒ **B, D.** HTTP traffic uses TCP port 80, but TCP port 110 is used by the POP3 protocol. With this configuration, users would not be able to access SSL-encrypted resources on your Web server. Therefore, Answer **B** is incorrect. DNS uses TCP port 53, not 443. In this configuration, users would not be able to perform DNS queries against your company's DNS server. Therefore, Answer **D** is incorrect.

4. Different firewall implementations operate at different layers of the OSI model. Match the firewall implementation with the layer of the OSI model at which it operates. (Choose two.)

A. Circuit-level firewall: Application layer

B. Stateful inspection packet filter: Transport layer

C. Circuit-level firewall: Transport layer

D. Stateful inspection packet filter: Network layer

☑ **A, B.** Circuit-level firewalls perform an in-depth scan of incoming network packets at the application layer to look for harmful or malicious content. Therefore, Answer **A** is correct. Packet-filtering firewalls, both stateful and otherwise, base their decisions on the TCP or UDP port being used, which operates at the transport layer. Therefore, Answer **B** is correct.

☒   **C, D**. Circuit-level firewalls operate at the application layer of the OSI model, not the transport layer. Therefore, Answer **C** is incorrect. Stateful inspection packet filters operate at the transport layer, not the network layer. Therefore, Answer **D** is incorrect.

5. You are the network administrator for a public library in a major city. You have configured several computers on the main floor of the library to allow patrons to browse the Web and check their e-mail. The library's board of directors is concerned that patrons will use the kiosks to view objectionable content. They are especially concerned because the library is frequented by children and young adults who will be accessing the kiosks without parental supervision. You suggest that the library deploy a proxy server to help address this issue. What functionality of a proxy server will help ensure that no objectionable content can be accessed from the library kiosks?

    A. Packet filtering

    B. Packet redirection

    C. Content filtering

    D. Content caching

    ☑   **C**. A proxy server can examine Web requests sent to it and filter those requests so that certain types of content can be disallowed. Therefore, Answer C is correct.

    ☒   **A**, **B**, **D**. Packet filtering is used by firewalls to allow or disallow network packets based on the TCP or UDP ports in use, not by the content of a Web page being requested. Therefore, Answer A is incorrect. Packet redirection is used to direct external user requests to a Web server or other computer located inside a proxy server-protected network. This feature does not filter content requested by internal users. Therefore, Answer B is incorrect. Content caching is used to store frequently accessed Web pages on a local server so that they can be accessed more quickly by internal users. This feature does not block Web pages based on objectionable or disallowed content. Therefore, Answer D is incorrect.

6. You are the network administrator for a large medical supply company with sales offices located in several states. Each sales office has a proxy server installed to allow Internet access for the office, since sales reps pull up pricing for the products they sell from the company intranet. Some of these offices are connected to the main office using only 56K dialup lines, and you have received complaints that accessing these Web pages is taking too long. You do not have funds to increase the connection speed for these offices. How can you improve Web site access for your remote offices?

A.   Install a packet filter on the proxy server so that only requests to the corporate Web server are allowed.

B.   Enable content caching on the proxy server.

C.   Install a copy of the company's inventory database at each local office.

D.   Disable antivirus software on the proxy server to improve performance.

☑   **B**. One feature of proxy servers is content caching, which stores frequently accessed Web pages locally so that they can be accessed more quickly by local users. Therefore, Answer B is correct.

☒   **A**, **C**, **D**. Packet filtering is a function of a firewall device, not a proxy server. Therefore, Answer A is incorrect. Installing a local copy of the inventory database at each site would be inefficient and would lead to inconsistent data. Therefore, Answer C is incorrect. Disabling antivirus software on the proxy server would leave the server vulnerable to virus infections and would not improve the speed with which the server could retrieve Web pages over a slow link. Therefore, Answer D is incorrect.

7.   You are the network administrator for a financial services company with offices in several cities. You would like to create a VPN between the offices to allow for secure file access. What technology will you use to create a VPN between your company's branch offices?

A.   SSL

B.   Packet filtering

C.   IPSec

D.   HTTP

☑   **C**. IPSec is an extension of TCP/IP that is used to provide encryption and authentication for site-to-site VPNs. Therefore, Answer **C** is correct.

☒   **A**, **B**, **D**. SSL is Secure Sockets Layer technology, used to encrypt traffic between a Web server and a Web browser. Therefore, Answer **A** is incorrect. Packet filtering is used by firewalls to allow or disallow traffic based on TCP or UDP port numbers. Therefore, Answer **B** is incorrect. HTTP is used to pass unencrypted traffic between a Web server and a web browser. Therefore, Answer **D** is incorrect.

8.   You are the network administrator for an Internet service provider. You have configured an FTP server so that your customers can upload Web files to their respective Web directories. To increase security for the FTP server, you want to configure a firewall to protect both inbound and outbound traffic. Which ports should you allow on the firewall protecting the FTP server? (Choose two.)

A. TCP port 21 inbound

B. TCP port 20 inbound

C TCP port 21 outbound

D. TCP port 20 outbound

    ☑   **A**, **D**. FTP uses TCP port 21 for inbound connections to the FTP server. Therefore, Answer **A** is correct. FTP uses TCP port 20 for outbound connections to return to the FTP client. Therefore, Answer **D** is correct.

    ☒   **B**, **C**. FTP uses TCP port 20 for outbound connections to the client, not inbound connections to the server. Therefore, Answer **B** is incorrect. FTP uses TCP port 21 for inbound connections to the server, not outbound connections back to the client. Therefore, Answer **C** is incorrect.

9. You are the network administrator for a small marketing firm. You begin to receive reports that network performance has become incredibly slow over the last few days. In attempting to track down the source of the problem, you use a network sniffer to determine how much bandwidth is being used on your network. You discover that your network is being bombarded by half-open TCP connections from several machines located on different networks attached to the Internet. What type of network attack are you experiencing right now?

A. Virus

B. Trojan horse

C. IP spoofing

D. Distributed denial of service

    ☑   **D**. A distributed denial-of-service attack occurs when several "zombie machines" are taken over by a malicious attacker to overwhelm a target network (in this case, yours) with useless network traffic, denying service to legitimate users. Therefore, Answer D is correct.

    ☒   **A**, **B**, **C**. A virus is a small piece of computer code that will replicate itself using e-mail attachments or diskettes. Therefore, Answer A is incorrect. A Trojan horse is a malicious program that piggy-backs on top of another executable such as a game or an e-mail attachment. Therefore, Answer B is incorrect. IP spoofing occurs when a flaw in your network router allows an attacker to transmit network packets from an outside network but pass them off as though they originated on your local network. Therefore, Answer C is incorrect.

10. You are in the planning stages of a project to deploy VLANs on your corporate network. What methods are available for you to assign VLAN membership to the computers on your network? (Select all that apply.)

    A. Port number

    B. MAC address

    C. IP address

    D. 802.1q

    ☑ **A**, **B**, **D**. You can assign VLAN membership based on the switch port that a particular client is plugged into. Therefore, Answer **A** is correct. You can assign VLAN membership based on the MAC address assigned to the NIC installed in a particular computer. Therefore, Answer **B** is correct. The 802.1q method inserts a "tag" in the TCP/IP frame at the data link layer, indicating which VLAN the packet should be sent to. Therefore, Answer **D** is correct.

    ☒ **C**. VLANs are functions of switches, which operate at Layer 2 of the OSI model. IP addresses are a function of the network layer, which is Layer 3. Therefore, you cannot assign VLAN membership based on IP addresses, so Answer **C** is incorrect.

11. You are the network administrator for a large financial services company. Your accounting department relies on a mission-critical financial application that uses TCP/IP broadcast packets to send notifications to users of the application when they receive information that they should be aware of. This wasn't a problem when the company was small and contained only a few dozen workstations, but with hundreds of machines on the same network, you have begun to receive complaints that network performance is unacceptably slow. How can you improve performance for the users on your network while allowing members of the accounting department to continue to use their mission-critical application? (Each choice represents a complete solution. Choose two.)

    A. Decrease the available bandwidth on your LAN.

    B. Configure a VLAN for the computers in the accounting department.

    C. Place the computers in the accounting department on a separate subnet.

    D. Install an intranet to allow the accounting department to use the application.

    ☑ **B**, **C**. Configuring a separate VLAN for the accounting department will restrict the broadcast traffic from the accounting application to only the computers in that department. Therefore, Answer **B** is correct. You can also reduce the impact of broadcast traffic by separating your network into different subnets, since broadcast traffic does not pass beyond a router. Therefore, Answer **C** is correct.

☒ **A**, **D**. Decreasing the available bandwidth on your LAN will only make network performance issues worse, rather than improving them. Therefore, Answer **A** is incorrect. Installing an intranet will not do anything to reduce the impact of broadcast traffic from the accounting application. Therefore, Answer **D** is incorrect.

12. You are assisting with the planning of a new VLAN implementation for your network. You create a test lab containing two VLANs, called VLAN1 and VLAN2, connected to a single switch. After some testing, you realize that traffic from VLAN1 is unable to reach VLAN2. How can you correct this problem?

A. Install a router to transmit traffic between the two VLANs.

B. Update the routing table on the switch.

C. Install a separate switch for each VLAN.

D. Configure one computer that is a member of both VLANs to transmit information between them.

☑ **A**. After you install VLANs, you need to use a router to transmit information between them. Therefore, Answer A is correct.

☒ **B**, **C**, **D**. Switches do not contain routing tables; only routers have this feature. Therefore, Answer B is incorrect. You can configure a single switch to host multiple VLANs, but you need to install a router to move traffic between them. Therefore, Answer C is incorrect. A single computer can belong to multiple VLANs, but configuring a machine in this way will not allow it to transmit information between the VLANs. Therefore, Answer D is incorrect.

13. You are the network administrator for a large university that is involved in several joint research projects with the federal government. You need to be able to allow government researchers access to your researchers' project data, without allowing them access to other internal network resources. What is the best way to accomplish this goal?

A. Grant each government researcher a logon to the servers on your LAN.

B. Install a Web server on your DMZ to host the joint data using an extranet.

C. Install a Web server on your private network to host the joint data using an intranet.

D. Create a VPN between your university and the government office where the researchers are located.

☑ **B**. Extranets are useful in granting access to a specific portion of your internal network data to outside users and business partners, without granting access to the rest of your internal network. Therefore, Answer B is correct.

☒ **A, C, D**. Granting a logon to each government researcher would be tedious and would grant the researchers more access to your internal network resources than is necessary for this situation. Therefore, Answer A is incorrect. An intranet is used to create a centralized display of information for your internal employees, including human resources information and interdepartmental data. It is not used to grant access to external users such as customers or business partners. Therefore, Answer C is incorrect. Creating a VPN would grant more access to the government office than is required in this situation, since the researchers only need access to data pertaining to specific projects. Therefore, Answer D is incorrect.

14. You have installed a Web server to function as an extranet for your company's customers, allowing them to look up inventory levels for your products as well as the current status of any orders they've placed. Customers will access this extranet using their Web browsers. You need to ensure that any customer data is encrypted as it passes from your extranet server to the customers' Web browsers so that information cannot be stolen by a hacker or a competing company. How can you ensure the security of your extranet data as it's being transmitted to your customers?

    A. Use IPSec to protect Web connections to the extranet server.

    B. Use SSL to protect Web connections to the extranet server.

    C. Use a firewall to protect Web connections to the extranet server.

    D. Use a proxy server to protect Web connections to the extranet server.

    ☑ **B**. To encrypt Web traffic, you should use Secure Sockets Layer (SSL) technology, which uses TCP port 443. Therefore, Answer B is correct.

    ☒ **A, C, D**. IPSec is used to create VPNs, not to protect Web browser data. Therefore, Answer A is incorrect. Although a firewall can make packet-filtering decisions as to which traffic should and should not reach your extranet server, it cannot encrypt data that's being sent to your customers' Web browsers. Therefore, Answer C is incorrect. A proxy server is used to make requests for Web pages on behalf of internal network clients, but it does not encrypt any traffic being sent from an extranet Web server. Therefore, Answer D is incorrect.

15. You are the network administrator for a small law firm that is in the process of being acquired by a larger firm in the same city. During the acquisition process, all your network data needs to be accessible by the larger firm so that both firms can begin the process of transitioning information to the larger firm's servers. Both firms are connected to the Internet via high-speed T1 links. Each firm's data needs

to remain secure while being accessed by the other firm's users. What is the best way to provide this type of access between the two company networks?

A. Create a filtering rule on each firewall that allows each firm's public IP address to go through the firewall.

B. Create an extranet that will allow each firm to view the other firm's data using a Web browser.

C. Place the servers containing each firm's data into a DMZ between the two firms.

D. Create a VPN between the two firms.

☑ **D**. For the level of access required in this scenario, you should create a VPN to allow the two offices to securely access each other's data. Therefore, Answer D is correct.

☒ **A, B, C**. "Poking a hole" in the firewall will reduce the security of each individual network and will not secure any data that is transmitted between the two. Therefore, Answer A is incorrect. An extranet would not be applicable for this situation, since the two firms need to directly access each other's servers and data processes to prepare for the acquisition process. Therefore, Answer B is incorrect. Placing the firms' servers into a demilitarized zone would leave them open to attack by malicious outsiders, since they would be accessible via a public IP address on the Internet. Therefore, Answer C is incorrect.

16. You are a consultant who has been contracted by a small company to set up its network. The owner of the company has purchased a copy of a popular antivirus program for each workstation on the network. After you have installed the antivirus software on each computer, what is the most important thing to configure?

A. Configure the software to e-mail an administrator whenever it encounters a virus.

B. Configure the software to download the most recent antivirus definitions on a regular basis.

C. Configure the software to scan a file only when a user double-clicks on it.

D. Configure the software to immediately delete any virus-infected files that it finds.

☑ **B**. Antivirus software needs to be regularly updated with the most recent antivirus definition files so that it can recognize new viruses that have been created. Therefore, Answer B is correct.

☒ **A, C, D**. It might be useful for an administrator to be made aware of virus-infected files on a computer, but it is far more important to configure regular antivirus definition updates to ensure that antivirus software is as effective as possible. Therefore, Answer A is incorrect. Antivirus software should use real-time protection to scan all files on a user's hard drive, regardless of whether the user is actively using the file or not. Therefore, Answer C is incorrect. When antivirus software encounters a virus-infected file, it should first attempt to repair the file and remove the virus to try to prevent data loss for the user. Deleting the file immediately does not meet this aim. Therefore, Answer D is incorrect.

17. You are working on the network help desk for a financial services company. You receive a phone call from a user who complains that her computer is acting strangely, rebooting at random intervals and crashing with the Blue Screen of Death. As you attempt to figure out how this occurred, she tells you that she recently received an e-mail from a friend that contained an attachment that ran a cute Snowman Bowling game. What do you suspect is the most likely cause of her problem?

A. The driver for her network card has become corrupted.

B. Her computer has been infected with a Trojan horse.

C. She has disabled her personal firewall software.

D. Her computer is configured with an incorrect IP address.

☑ **B.** A Trojan horse is a type of virus that piggy-backs on top of a legitimate-looking program to infect a target machine. This user's computer was likely infected with a Trojan horse when she opened the Snowman Bowling attachment. Therefore, Answer B is correct.

☒ **A, C, D.** Although a corrupted NIC driver can sometimes cause operating system instability, it is far more likely that this user's computer has been infected with a virus due to downloading an infected e-mail attachment. Therefore, Answer A is incorrect. Disabling personal firewall software will not in and of itself cause a computer to experience system failures. Therefore, Answer C is incorrect. Configuring a computer with an incorrect IP address will cause connectivity issues in reaching network resources, not system instability and crashes. Therefore, Answer D is incorrect.

18. You are the junior network administrator for a small publishing company. The senior network administrator is on vacation, and you receive a support call from the CEO of the company. The CEO has received an e-mail from a trusted friend that is advising him to delete certain system files on his computer that indicate a virus infection and to forward the e-mail to everyone in his address book so that they can be protected as well. Your network uses an enterprise antivirus solution

that automatically pushes out new antivirus updates to all network computers every day. What advice would you give the CEO in this situation?

A. The e-mail is legitimate and his PC is infected. He should delete the files mentioned in the e-mail right away.

B. The e-mail is legitimate and his PC might be infected. He should copy the files mentioned in the e-mail to a network share so that you can scan them for viruses.

C. The e-mail is a virus "hoax" that is trying to "con" the CEO into deleting important system files from his computer. The instructions in the e-mail should be disregarded.

D. The e-mail contains a virus and should be deleted right away.

☑ **C.** This is a common example of a virus hoax that is sent by (usually well-meaning) people through e-mail. The malicious purpose of a virus hoax is to convince an unknowing computer user to delete important system files from his or her PC. Therefore, Answer C is correct.

☒ **A, B, D.** This type of e-mail is indicative of a virus hoax; the CEO's PC is not virus-infected, and he should not delete the files referenced in the e-mail. Therefore, Answer A is incorrect. If the CEO's PC is virus-infected, you should run a virus scan on his local computer, not copy potentially infected files to a shared location where they might be able to infect other computers on your network. Therefore, Answer B is incorrect. Virus hoaxes don't usually contain viruses themselves; rather, they are designed to frighten unknowing computer users into deleting important files from their hard drives. Therefore, Answer D is incorrect.

Chapter 10 Fault Management and Disaster Recovery

1. As shown in the following illustration, a company has its main office in Manhattan and branch offices in Brooklyn and Queens. A T1 line connects Brooklyn to Manhattan, while another T1 line connects Manhattan to Queens. Because Brooklyn and Queens are both connected to Manhattan, this enables them to exchange data with one another. You have concerns that if either of the T1 lines go down, the business will be unable to function normally. Because of the importance of each of these sites communicating with one another, fault tolerance for the links between them is necessary but cost is a concern. Which of the following will you do to implement fault tolerance?

Figure 10.13 Links Between Offices

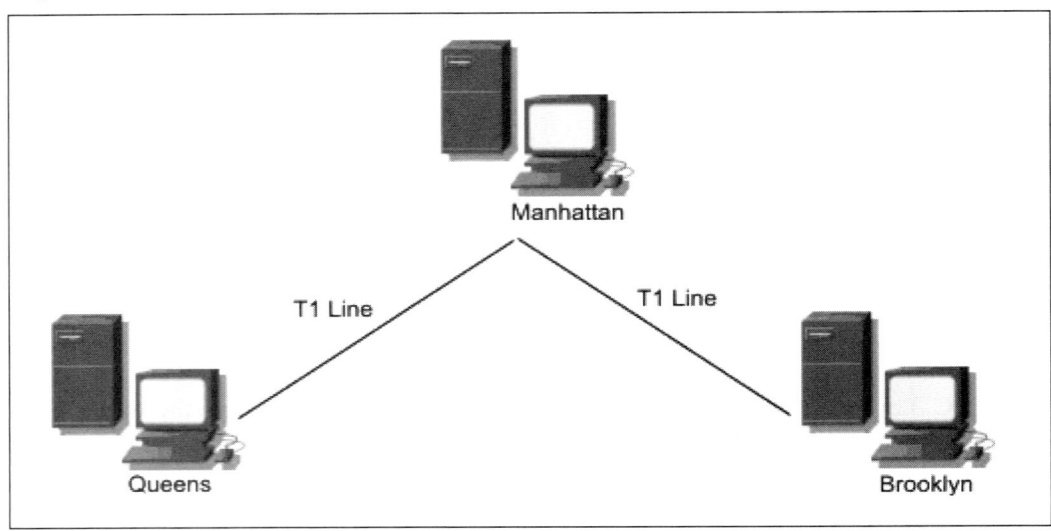

A. Install an ISDN line between Manhattan and Brooklyn, which can be used if the T1 line goes down.

B. Install an ISDN line between Manhattan and Queens, which can be used if the T1 line goes down.

C. Install an ISDN line between Brooklyn and Queens.

D. Install a T1 connection between Brooklyn and Queens.

☑ **C**. Install an ISDN line between Brooklyn and Queens. Under the current configuration, Brooklyn can communicate with Queens (and vice versa) using their mutual connections with Manhattan. By installing an ISDN line between Brooklyn and Queens, the three can continue to communicate with one another if either of the T1 lines goes down.

☒ **A, B, D**. Answer **A** is incorrect because if the T1 line goes down between Manhattan and Queens, then Queens will be separated from the network. Implementing the ISDN line between Manhattan and Brooklyn will only provide fault tolerance between these two sites. Answer **B** is incorrect for similar reasons. If the T1 line goes down between Manhattan and Brooklyn, then Brooklyn will be separated from the network. Implementing the ISDN line between Manhattan and Queens will only provide fault tolerance between these two sites. Answer **D** is incorrect because the scenario states that cost is a concern. Installing an ISDN line between Queens and Brooklyn is cheaper than installing a new T1 line.

2. You currently use RAID for fault tolerance on a server, so that data from one disk is copied to another. When data is written to one disk, it is duplicated on another disk in the set. You are concerned that if the disk controller fails, then neither of the disks will be able to be accessed. Which of the following will you do to improve fault tolerance?

   A. Implement disk striping by using RAID level 0.

   B. Implement disk mirroring by using RAID level 1.

   C. Implement disk duplexing by using RAID level 1.

   D. Implement disk striping with parity using RAID level 0.

   ☑ **C**. Implement disk duplexing by using RAID level 1. RAID 1 is mirroring or duplexing. The question indicates that mirroring is currently being used, but there is a fear of disk controllers failing. Additional fault tolerance by using separate controllers for each disk, which is called duplexing. If one of the disks fail or a controller fails, the data can still be available through the other disk in the pair.

   ☒ **A, B**, **D**. Answer **A** is incorrect because implementing RAID 0 (disk striping) would actually remove fault tolerance from the current system. Answer **B** is incorrect because the question indicates that mirroring is already being used. Answer **D** is incorrect because disk striping with parity is RAID 5.

3. You have decided to implement a RAID for fault tolerance, and want data to be striped across multiple disks with parity information stored on multiple drives. Which of the following levels of RAID will you use?

   A. RAID 0

   B. RAID 1

   C. RAID 3

   D. RAID 5

   ☑ **D**. RAID 5. RAID 5 is disk striping with parity. Data is striped across multiple disks, but parity information is stored across multiple drives. It provides fault tolerance because a single disk that fails in the set can be restored from the parity information on the other disks.

   ☒ **A, B**, **C**. Answer **A** is incorrect because RAID 0 provides no fault tolerance. Data is written (striped) across multiple disks, but no copies of the data are made. This improves performance because data is read from multiple disks, but the data on the entire set will be lost if one disk fails. Answer **B** is incorrect because RAID 1 is disk mirroring or duplexing. Data that's written to one disk is also written to another, so that one disk's data is a mirror image of the other's. Parity information is not stored on multiple drives with this method.

Answer **C** is incorrect because RAID 3 has data striped across several drives, but one drive is used to store the parity bits for each byte that's written to the other disks. When a disk fails, it can be replaced and data can be restored to it from the parity information.

4. You are creating configuration documentation for a computer on your network that is using Linux as its operating system. In creating this documentation, you need the IP address, subnet mask, and default gateway of the computer. Which of the following tools would you use to acquire this information?

   A. ipconfig

   B. ifconfig

   C. System Information

   D. winipcfg

   ☑ **B**. ifconfig. ifconfig is a command-line tool in Linux that displays information on the TCP/IP configuration of the computer. By typing **ifconfig**, you can display the IP address, subnet mask, and default gateway that's been configured on the machine.

   ☒ **A**, **C**, **D**. Answer **A** is incorrect because ipconfig isn't used on Linux computers; ifconfig is. ipconfig is a more commonly used version of the ifconfig utility that runs on Windows operating systems. Answer **C** is incorrect because System Information is a utility that is available on Windows-based computers. Answer **D** is incorrect because although winipcfg provides this information, it isn't available on Linux. It is used on computers running Windows 95, Windows 98 or Windows ME operating systems.

5. You believe that someone has been attempting to hack into a Windows 2000 Server on your network by guessing the Administrator password. You set up auditing of this account, and then check Event Viewer each morning to view logs on this server. Which log would you use to view information about valid and invalid logon attempts using this account?

   A. Application Log

   B. Security Log

   C. System Log

   D. None. Event Viewer isn't used to view logs.

   ☑ **B**. Security Log. The Security log displays possible security issues that the operating system monitors. This includes valid and invalid logon attempts, and other actions related to security.

☒ **A**, **C**, **D**. Answer **A** is incorrect because the application log contains events that are logged by individual programs or applications installed on the operating system. Answer **C** is incorrect because the system log displays events logged by the system components of the operating system. Answer **D** is incorrect because Event Viewer is a tool that is used to view logs.

6. You are concerned about the impact of various risks to your company. You have learned from your insurance company that businesses that can be infected with a virus may experience an hour of downtime to remove the virus from a server, and that an average of two viruses a year may infect a system with security comparable to yours. If you consider that an hour of downtime costs your company $1000, what would the Annual Loss Expectancy of this risk be to your company?

   A. $1000

   B. $2000

   C. $3000

   D. $4000

   ☑ **B**. $2000. Calculating the Annual Loss Expectency (ALE) uses the formula ALE=ARO x SLE. In this case we know that a single incident would cost the company $1000 for 1 hour of downtime. This gives us the Single Loss Expectancy (SLE). The Annualized Rate of Occurrence (ARO) for this incident is 2 incidents per year. Therefore by multiplying the SLE (1 x $1000) by the ARO (2), we get $2000.

   ☒ **A**, **C**, **D**. Answer **A** is incorrect, because $1000 is the Single Loss Expectancy of the risk. Answer **C** and **D** are incorrect, because the correct answer of using the formula ALE = ARO (2) x SLE ($1000) is $2000.

7. An intruder has gained access to your website through a service on the server, and damaged a number of files needed by the company. The service isn't necessary to the Web server's functionality, and as near as you can tell isn't used by any software or users of the company. This Web server is used to provide a presence for the company on the Internet, and is used for public relations as well as to provide information on the company's products. During the intrusion, you were working on upgrading a router in another part of the building, which is why you didn't notice audit notifications sent to your e-mail address. These audit notifications could have tipped you off about suspicious activity on the server, but now that you're aware of the problem, you're concerned that a repeat attack may occur while you're fixing the problem. Which of the following actions will you immediately take in resolving this situation?

    A. Recover data files that were damaged in the attack.

    B. Continue upgrading the router so that you can focus on audit notifications that may occur.

    C. Remove the unneeded services running on the server.

    D. Remove the Web server from the Internet until there is no further risk of being hacked.

    ☑ **C**. Remove the unneeded services running on the server. The service is a vulnerability to the Web server. Since the attack was made possible through this service, removing it eliminates the method of entry into the system. Once you've identified vulnerabilities, you should remove or deal with these weaknesses as soon as possible. Failing to do so could leave your system open to repeat attacks, or make damage caused by disasters more significant.

    ☒ **A**, **B**, **D**. Answer **A** is incorrect because recovering the data files that were damaged won't prevent a repeat attack. Any files that were damaged can be restored from backups after you've secured the server. Answer **B** is incorrect because the router upgrade is unimportant to the situation of securing the Web server. Answer **D** is incorrect because the risk of being hacked will always exist, unless you permanently take down your website. Since you know the vulnerability, removing the service from the server will prevent future attacks in the same manner.

8. During a disaster, you don't want to spend a significant amount of time restoring a series of tapes from previous backups of production servers. At the same time, you don't want backups to take a significantly long period of time to perform each night. Currently, you back up all data on the servers once a week, and then each night you perform a backup of data that has changed during the day. To make it faster to restore data in a disaster, you're willing to change the current backup plan. Based on these factors, which of the following backup plans would you use?

    A. Perform a full backup each night of the servers. This will mean that only one tape will be needed per server to restore all the current data.

    B. Perform full backups weekly and incremental backups each night afterwards of the servers.

    C. Perform copy backups nightly. This will mean that only one tape will be needed per server to restore all the current data.

    D. Perform a full backup weekly and differential backups each night afterward.

    ☑ **D**. Perform a full backup weekly and differential backups each night afterward. The full backup will back up everything on the server, and change the archive bit on each file to show it was backed up. The differential backup will back up all data that has changed since the last full backup, but won't change the archive bit. Therefore, when you restore the backups, only the tape with the full backup and the tape with the last differential backup are needed to restore all the data.

☒ **A**, **B**, **C**. Answer **A** is incorrect because the scenario states that you don't want nightly backups to take significantly longer to perform. Full and copy backups take the longest to perform because they back up everything. Answer **B** is incorrect because this describes the current backup plan. Answer **C** is incorrect for the same reason that **A** is incorrect. Copy backups take longer to perform because all data on the server is backed up, just like a full backup. The difference between the two is that the archive bit isn't changed. Aside from this, full and copy backups both take the longest to perform because they backup everything.

9. You are the administrator of a network that is spread between a main building and a remote site several miles away. You make regular backups of the data on servers, which are centrally located in the main building. Where should you store the backup tapes so they are available when needed in the case of a disaster? Choose all that apply.

   A. Keep the backup tapes in the server room within the main building so they are readily at hand. If a disaster occurs, you will be able to obtain these tapes quickly, and restore the data to servers.

   B. Keep the backup tapes in another section of the main building, so they are readily at hand.

   C. Keep the backup tapes in the remote site.

   D. Keep the backup tapes with a firm that provides offsite storage facilities.

   ☑ **C** and **D**. Keep the backup tapes in the remote site, or with a firm that provides offsite storage facilities. Since the company has a remote location that is miles from the main building, the tapes can be kept there for safekeeping. A firm can also be hired to keep the tapes in a storage facility. When a disaster occurs, you can then retrieve these tapes and restore the data.

   ☒ **A** and **B**. Answer **A** and **B** are incorrect, because a disaster that effects the server room or main building could also destroy the backup tapes if they were stored in these locations.

10. A fire has destroyed the server room where file servers are located. Having prepared for this possibility, you move operations to a branch office of the company. The office is part of the production network, and has a copy of the data on servers at this location. What type of alternate site is being used for disaster recovery?

A. Cold site

B. Warm site

C. Hot site

D. Hot spare

☑ **C**. Hot site. A hot site takes the least amount of work to set up, as it is online and part of the production network. A copy of the data may be stored on a server at that location so that minimal setup is required to resume operations.

☒ **A, B, D**. Answer **A** is incorrect because a cold site is neither online nor part of the production network. It may have all or part of the necessary equipment and resources needed to resume business activities, but installation is required and data has to be restored to servers. Answer **B** is incorrect because a warm site only has part of the necessary equipment, software, and other requirements to resume normal business operations. Answer **D** is incorrect because a hot spare is equipment and not a facility.

11. You are setting up a series of servers that can be used in case one of the production servers fails. Each of the servers is identical to its counterparts on the production network. If one of the servers fails at this site, a replacement server can simply be powered up and run on the network. What type of equipment is this?

A. Cold spare

B. Hot spare

C. Cold site

D. Hot site

☑ **B**. Hot spare. Hot spares are replacement devices that are running and can be used as soon as a problem occurs. If the current system fails, the hot spare can be used with little to no work on the part of the network administrator.

☒ **A, C, D**. Answer **A** is incorrect because cold spares are not fully configured and require setup and possibly installation of software before they can be used on a production network. Answers **C** and **D** are incorrect because neither hot sites nor cold sites are redundant or replacement equipment. They are facilities that can be used in a disaster.

12. You want to make a Web server's services fault tolerant, and you also want improve the performance of these services when people visit the websites hosted by this server. Which of the following can be used to meet these needs? Choose all that apply.

A. Disk striping

B. Load balancing

C. Clustering

D. Hot spares

☑ **B** and **C**. Clustering and Load balancing. Clustering provides fault tolerance by grouping computers together, so that they work as a single unit. If one of these computers fails, the others will continue to provide services. Clustering also provides load balancing by sharing the workload between the computers, which improves performance.

☒ **A** and **D**. Answer **A** is incorrect because while disk striping may provide improvements in the performance of reading and writing to a hard disk, it does not improve performance or provide fault tolerance to services running on a network's servers. Answer **D** is incorrect because hot spares are used to replace equipment when it fails. They do not improve performance.

13. You have four nodes that are part of a cluster. The nodes listening for heartbeats fail to detect this signal from one of the other nodes. Which of the following will happen?

A. The node that isn't sending the heartbeat will be considered available.

B. The other nodes in the cluster will begin providing services that were offered by the node that is no longer sending the heartbeat.

C. The cluster will fail and notification will be sent to other computers on the network.

D. The cluster will appear as a single server on the network, so users don't recognize that a failure has occurred.

☑ **B**. The other nodes in the cluster will begin providing services that were offered by the computer that is no longer sending the heartbeat. The nodes (computers) in a cluster communicate with one another by sending out messages called heartbeats. If the computers in a cluster fail to detect the heartbeat of one of the other computers, they consider that computer to be unavailable. At this point, a failover occurs, where the resources of the failed computer are taken offline and another computer begins providing its services.

☒ **A, C, D**. Answer **A** is incorrect because when a computer no longer sends out a heartbeat signal to other computers in the cluster, that computer is considered unavailable. Answer **C** is incorrect because a cluster provides fault tolerance, so services won't become unavailable if one of the computers in the cluster fails. Answer **D** is incorrect because a cluster of computers will always appear as a single server on the network.

Chapter 11 Network Troubleshooting Tools

1. You have been called in to troubleshoot a connectivity issue for a desktop computer running Windows 98. You would like to quickly determine the IP address, subnet mask and default gateway assigned to this computer. Which utility would be the best one to use?

   A. route print

   B. tracert

   C. winipcfg

   D. netstat

   ☑ **C**. On a Windows 95 or Windows 98 PC, winipcfg will show you a graphical interface that gives you at-a-glance access to the IP address, subnet mask, and default gateway of the Windows client. Therefore, Answer **C** is correct.

   ☒ **A**, **B**, **D**. route print will show the contents of the routing table for a Windows-based PC; it does not provide an easy way to see the IP address, subnet mask and default gateway that are assigned to it. Therefore, Answer **A** is incorrect. tracert is used to test the route between a source and a destination PC, to determine if any hops along the way are overloaded or failing. Therefore, Answer **B** is incorrect. netstat shows the active Ethernet connections on a particular PC, but not the IP configuration of that PC. Therefore, Answer **D** is incorrect.

2. You are the network administrator for your company. Your predecessor configured a Netware 4.1 server to provide file and print services for your Windows 2000 and XP clients. You need to determine the frame type that the Netware server uses to communicate over IPX/SPX so that you can configure a new client to connect to the server. How can you determine what frame type is in use on your network?

   A. Type **ipxroute config** from a client that can successfully connect to the Netware server.

   B. Type **netstat** from a client that can successfully connect to the Netware server.

   C. Type **route print** from a client that can successfully connect to the Netware server.

   D. Ping the IP address of the Netware server from a client that can successfully connect to the Netware server.

☑ **A.** The ipxroute config command will give you the frame type and network name that's in use on a Windows client. Therefore, Answer **A** is correct.

☒ **B, C, D.** netstat shows the active Ethernet connections on a particular PC, but not the Ethernet frame type that is in use. Therefore, Answer **B** is incorrect. route print will show the contents of the routing table for a Windows-based PC. It does not show the Ethernet frame type that's in use. Therefore, Answer **C** is incorrect. Using ping will verify that TCP/IP is functional on the Netware server, but it will not show you the Ethernet frame type that is in use. Therefore, Answer **D** is incorrect.

3. You are the network administrator for a small company. Your company relies on LMHOSTS files installed on each individual machine to provide NetBIOS name resolution to communicate with servers and other clients. You have determined that one workstation has a typo in the LMHOSTS file that is preventing it from connecting to the server. You correct the entry in the LMHOSTS file, and now need to allow this client to connect to the server with a minimum amount of disruption for the user. What should you do?

A. Reboot the workstation.

B. Access the command prompt and issue the nbtstat -RR command.

C. Log the user out of the workstation and have them log back in.

D. Access the command prompt and issue the ipconfig command.

☑ **B.** nbtstat –RR will release and renew all NetBIOS registrations on a computer, including refreshing the entries from the LMHOSTS file. If you need to quickly update a computer's NetBIOS information, this is the utility to use. Therefore, Answer **B** is correct.

☒ **A, C, D.** Rebooting the workstation would refresh the entries in the LMHOSTS file, but would unnecessarily disrupt the user's work. Therefore, Answer **A** is incorrect. Logging the user out of their workstation would not refresh the entries in the LMHOSTS file, as well as unnecessarily disrupting the user's work. Therefore, Answer **C** is incorrect. Using ipconfig by itself will not update any information, it will only display the current IP configuration of the computer. Therefore, Answer **D** is incorrect.

4. You are the network administrator for a company that uses a mixture of Windows and Linux computers. One of your Windows 2000 servers is running the WINS service, and you have created static WINS entries for your Linux computers. A NIC in one of the Linux computers fails and has to be replaced by a technician, however, the technician did not provide you with the MAC address of the new NIC before he left. The replacement NIC has already been assigned an IP address.

From the console of the Linux computer, what utility can you use to determine the MAC address of the new NIC to update your WINS server entries?

A. ifconfig

B. dig

C. nbtstat

D. nslookup

☑ **A**. ifconfig will provide configuration information about the installed NICs in a Linux computer, including the IP address, subnet mask, default gateway and hardware (MAC) address. Therefore, Answer **A** is correct,

☒ **B, C, D**. dig is used to look up entries on a DNS server from a Linux PC, not to look up the physical MAC address of a NIC. Therefore, Answer **B** is incorrect. nbtstat is used to view NetBIOS information for a Windows PC. Therefore, Answer **C** is incorrect. nslookup is used to look up entries on a DNS server from a Windows PC, not to look up the physical MAC address of a NIC. Therefore, Answer **D** is incorrect.

5. You are the network administrator for an IIS web server running Windows 2000. You have recently configured a new firewall and are attempting to determine if clients are still able to connect to the Web server. You run the netstat −A command and see the following output:

```
Active Connections

Proto   Local Addres   Foreign Address                State
TCP     example:http      204.96.18.5:26861       ESTABLISHED
TCP     example:http      204.96.18.115:28246     ESTABLISHED
TCP     example:http      215.96.18.45:28890      ESTABLISHED
TCP     example:http      151.96.14.62:29097      ESTABLISHED
TCP     example:http      204.96.18.5:29477       ESTABLISHED
TCP     example:http      204.96.18.5:29759       ESTABLISHED
TCP     example:http      204.96.18.5:29860       ESTABLISHED
```

What can you determine from this output?

A. Network clients are unable to connect to your Web server.

B. Your Web server is listening for client connections on non-standard ports like 26861 and 28246.

C. Network clients are successfully connecting to port 21 on your Web server.

D. Network clients are successfully connecting to port 80 on your Web server.

☑ **D.** The "example:http" entry means that your Web server is listening for client connections on the HTTP (Hypertext Transfer Protocol) port, which is TCP port 80. Established connections on the HTTP port means that clients are able to connect to your Web server. Therefore, Answer **D** is correct.

☒ **A**, **B**, **C**. If clients were unable to connect to your web server, you would not see "ESTABLISHED" connections listed in the netstat output. Therefore, Answer **A** is incorrect. The non-standard port numbers listed in the output are the ones used by the client computers, not the server. Again, "example:http" indicates that the server is listening on the default HTTP port. Therefore, Answer **B** is incorrect. The default HTTP port is TCP port 80. Port 21is the default port for FTP, not HTTP. Therefore, Answer **D** is incorrect.

6. You are troubleshooting network connectivity on a Windows 2000 Professional workstation. You issue the route print command to view the workstation's routing table, and see the following information:

```
===========================================================================
Interface List
0x1 ........................ MS TCP Loopback interface
0x2 ...00 0e 35 1a e2 8d ...... Intel(R) PRO/Wireless 2200BG Network Connection
===========================================================================
Active Routes:
Network Destination        Netmask          Gateway        Interface    Metric
        0.0.0.0          0.0.0.0       192.168.1.1   192.168.1.100        30
      127.0.0.0        255.0.0.0       127.0.0.1       127.0.0.1          1
    192.168.1.0    255.255.255.0     192.168.1.100   192.168.1.100        30
  192.168.1.100  255.255.255.255     127.0.0.1       127.0.0.1          30
  192.168.1.255  255.255.255.255   192.168.1.100   192.168.1.100        30
      224.0.0.0        240.0.0.0     192.168.1.100   192.168.1.100        30
255.255.255.255  255.255.255.255   192.168.1.100   192.168.1.100          1
255.255.255.255  255.255.255.255   192.168.1.100               3          1
Default Gateway:       192.168.1.1
===========================================================================
```

In this routing table, what does *224.0.0.0* in the *Network Destination* column indicate?

A. The multicast address

B. The local broadcast address

C. The default gateway

D. The subnet mask

☑ **A**. 224.0.0.0 is a Class D address, which is used for multicast traffic. Therefore, Answer **A** is correct.

☒ **B, C, D**. The local broadcast address in this routing table is indicated by 192.168.1.255, where 192.168.1 is the network address, and 255 indicates that traffic will be sent to everyone in that network. Therefore, Answer **B** is incorrect. The default gateway in this routing table is indicated at the bottom of the table; it is 192.168.1.1. Therefore, Answer **C** is incorrect. The subnet mask for a Class C address is 255.255.255.0, not 224.0.0.0. Therefore, Answer **D** is incorrect.

7. You are working on the help desk for a small company that has a router with the IP address 192.168.1.100. You use tracert to determine why you cannot access a particular website, and see the following output:

```
1    <1 ms     <1 ms     <1 ms    [192.168.72.1]
2    <1 ms     <1 ms     <1 ms    [192.168.1.100]
3    *         *         *        Request timed out.
4    *         *         *        Request timed out.
5    *         *         *        Request timed out.
6    *         *         *        Request timed out.
```

You are able to access other remote websites successfully, as well as accessing resources on the internal LAN. Based on this output, what is a possible reason why you cannot access this remote website?

A. Your workstation has been configured with the incorrect subnet mask.

B. The remote Web server is down or overloaded.

C. Your router is down or overloaded.

D. Your router has been configured with the incorrect default gateway.

☑ **B**. Since you are able to access other remote sites successfully, the most likely cause of your connectivity issues is the particular site that you are unable to access. Though more troubleshooting is necessary to determine the exact answer, the remote site is not responding to your tracert, which means that it is likely down or unreachable for some reason. Therefore, Answer **B** is incorrect.

☒ **A**, **C**, **D**. If your workstation had been configured with an incorrect subnet mask, you would be having difficulty in accessing internal and external resources beyond a single website. Therefore, Answer **A** is incorrect. If your router was down or overloaded, you would not be able to access other websites. In addition, the tracert is returning <1 millisecond response times from the router, indicating that it is functioning very well. Therefore, Answer **C** is incorrect. If your router had been configured with the incorrect default gateway, you would not be able to access other remote websites. Therefore, Answer **D** is incorrect.

8. You are the network administrator of a small company. You have just purchased a new PC for the president of your company, and you need to connect it directly to his old PC in order to transfer her files before making the switch. Which tool will allow you to do this?

A. Standard Ethernet cable

B. Cable tester

C. Crossover cable

D. Tone generator

☑ **C**. You'll use a crossover cable to connect two computers, one directly to the other, rather than connecting both PCs to a hub. Therefore, Answer **C** is correct.

☒ **A**, **B**, **D**. You'll use a standard Ethernet cable to connect a computer to a hub, switch, or a router, not directly to another PC. Therefore, Answer **A** is incorrect. You'll use a cable tester to determine if a length of Ethernet cable is functioning properly or if it has experienced any type of short or break. Therefore, Answer **B** is incorrect. You'll use a tone generator to perform troubleshooting of telephone systems, not to connect two PCs directly to each other. Therefore, Answer **D** is incorrect.

9. You are the help desk manager for a large multi-site office. You receive several calls stating that users are unable to connect to a particular file server. You ping the server from your desk and receive several "Request Timed Out" messages. You walk over to the server, check the NIC on the back of the server and notice that one of the LED lights is glowing amber. The server's desktop is available and the keyboard and mouse are responsive. Other hosts on the same subnet as this server are accessible by users. What is the most likely cause of this connectivity failure?

A. The operating system has crashed and the server should be rebooted.

B. The network cable connecting the server to its hub is damaged and should be replaced.

C. The NIC installed in the server is damaged and should be repaired or replaced.

D. The NIC installed in the server should be configured for full duplex operations.

☑ **C.** An amber LED light indicates that a device (in this case a NIC) has begun to malfunction, and should be repaired or replaced. Therefore, Answer **C** is correct.

☒ **A, B, D.** If the operating system had crashed, you would have seen an error on the server desktop like the "Blue Screen of Death". Since the server desktop is responsive, this is not the cause of the problem. Therefore, Answer **B** is incorrect. An amber LED light on the NIC means that the NIC is physically malfunctioning, so changing the duplex mode of the card will not correct this issue. Therefore, Answer **D** is incorrect.

10. You are the new network administrator for a Windows network. As part of your administrative duties, you are responsible for maintaining your company's telephone and PBX systems. Your company has recently purchased the office building adjacent to the current facility to allow for expansion. There are a number of telephone jacks in the new facility that are not listed on any network diagrams, and you need to determine if they are functional. Which tool should you use to determine this?

A. Null model cable

B. Tone generator

C. Oscilloscope

D. Crossover cable

☑ **B.** A tone generator is a device that can perform diagnostics on telephone equipment, including determining if a telephone jack is receiving any signal. Therefore, Answer **B** is correct.

☒ **A, C, D.** A null model cable is used to connect a computer's serial cable to a device such as a router in order to configure or troubleshoot the device without using a network connection. Therefore, Answer **A** is incorrect. An oscilloscope is used to measure electrical current, not to troubleshoot telephone equipment. Therefore, Answer **C** is incorrect. A crossover cable is used to connect two computers or other devices directly to one another without a hub or a switch between them. Therefore, Answer **D** is incorrect.

11. You are troubleshooting your mother's home computer after she reports to you that she is unable to browse any websites. You would like to determine whether her cable modem is functional. You examine the LED lights on the cable modem, and see one light that is a solid green and a second light that is flickering green. What can you determine from the status of these LED lights?

    A. The cable modem has a network connection and is passing network traffic.

    B. The cable modem has a network connection, but is not passing any network traffic.

    C. The cable modem has no network connection and is not passing any network traffic.

    D. The cable modem is experiencing a hardware malfunction and is not passing any network traffic.

    ☑ **A**. Most network devices have two LED lights: one to indicate whether there is an active network connection and one to indicate whether traffic is being passed by the device. The solid green LED light indicates a good network connection, and the flickering green LED indicates that traffic is being passed. Therefore, Answer **A** is correct.

    ☒ **B**, **C**, **D**. If one LED light was solid green and the other was not lit at all, this would indicate an established network connection that was not passing any traffic. Therefore, Answer **B** is incorrect. If neither LED light was lit, this would indicate that there was not an established network connection, either because of a faulty cable or some other reason. Therefore, Answer **C** is incorrect. If the cable modem was experiencing a hardware problem, one of the LED lights would be lit with a solid amber or orange color. Therefore, Answer **D** is incorrect.

12. You are the network administrator for a small health services company. Your company's network uses a DHCP server to provide IP addressing configuration for 50 workstations, using an address range from 192.168.99.1 through 192.168.99.254, with a Class C subnet mask and a default gateway of 192.168.99.1. You have recently configured a Linux server to operate as the web server for your company's Internet presence, and you need this server to have a statically assigned IP address. Once you configure the IP address for this server, you attempt to access your company's Web page and are unable to do so. You use the ifconfig command to verify the IP configuration of the Linux server. Based on the output below, which configuration item do you need to change?

```
eth0        Link encap:Ethernet  HWaddr 00:80:C8:F8:4A:51
            inet addr:192.168.98.35  Bcast:192.168.99.255  Mask:255.255.255.0
            UP BROADCAST RUNNING MULTICAST  MTU:1500  Metric:1
            RX packets:190312 errors:0 dropped:0 overruns:0 frame:0
            TX packets:86955 errors:0 dropped:0 overruns:0 carrier:0
            collisions:0 txqueuelen:100
            RX bytes:30701229 (29.2 Mb)  TX bytes:7878951 (7.5 Mb)
            Interrupt:9 Base address:0x5000
```

    A. HWaddr

    B. Inet addr

    C. Bcast

    D. Mask

    ☑ **B**. Given the IP configuration of this network, this computer's IP address should be on the 192.168.99.0 network. ifconfig indicates that you made a typo and configured it for the 192.168.98.0 network. This will render the server unable to communicate on this network; therefore, Answer **B** is correct.

    ☒ **A**, **C**, **D**. The HWaddr setting is the MAC address of the NIC card, which does not have to be changed in this situation. Therefore, Answer **A** is incorrect. The BCast setting indicates the local broadcast address for this computer, which is correct for this configuration. Therefore, Answer **C** is incorrect. This network uses the default Class C subnet mask, so the mask setting of 255.255.255.0 is correct for this scenario. Therefore, Answer **D** is incorrect.

13. You are the network administrator for a small office containing five workstations and a single file server. You are troubleshooting a connectivity failure on a single workstation that is unable to browse the Internet; all other workstations are able to communicate without issue. As your first troubleshooting step, you ping the loop-back interface of the workstation that is experiencing trouble and you receive the output shown here. Based on this output, what is the most likely cause of the connectivity failure?

```
Pinging IBM-A38375FF22E [127.0.0.1] with 32 bytes of data:
Request timed out.
Request timed out.
Request timed out.
Request timed out.


Ping statistics for 127.0.0.1:
    Packets: Sent = 4, Received = 0, Lost = 4 (100% loss),
```

A. The workstation is configured with the incorrect IP address.

B. The TCP/IP stack on the workstation has become corrupted and has to be re-installed.

C. The workstation is configured with the incorrect default gateway.

D. The router for your company's network is unresponsive.

☑ **B.** The loopback interface is a virtual IP address that exists on any computer that's running TCP/IP and is used for troubleshooting and diagnostics. If you do not receive a response from pinging the loopback interface, it means that the TCP/IP protocol on this particular computer has become corrupted and has to be re-installed. Therefore, Answer **B** is correct.

☒ **A, C, D.** If you receive no response from the loopback interface, it means that the TCP/IP stack is corrupted. Even if the workstation has been configured with the correct IP address, the unresponsive loopback address means that the TCP/IP stack is corrupted. Therefore, Answer **A** is incorrect. If you receive no response from the loopback interface, it means that the TCP/IP stack is corrupted. Even if the workstation has been configured with the correct default gateway, the unresponsive loopback address means that the TCP/IP stack is corrupted. Therefore, Answer **B** is incorrect. If other workstations on the network are able to access Internet-based resources, then the router used by the office is not the point of failure. Therefore, Answer **D** is incorrect.

Chapter 12 Network Troubleshooting Methodology

1. You are a network consultant specializing in supporting Small Office Home Office (SOHO) networks. One of your clients maintains an office consisting of three workstations configured in a peer-to-peer workgroup. This office does not have a server computer at this time. One of the workstations, \\OFFICE1, has an IP address of 192.168.1.100 and hosts a file share that the other three workstations are able to access using the following syntax: \\OFFICE1\share. Your client has called you in to troubleshoot a new workstation that they have recently installed that is unable to access this share. When you arrive on site, you find that the workstation is able to ping OFFICE1 by its IP address, but not by its NetBIOS name. What is the best way for you to allow the new workstation to access the file share located on OFFICE1?

   A. Upgrade OFFICE1 to Windows 2000 server and configure the WINS Server service.

   B. Add an entry to the lmhosts file on the new workstation.

   C. Add an entry to the hosts file on the new workstation.

   D. Upgrade OFFICE1 to Windows 2000 server and configure the DNS service.

   ☑ **B**. For a SOHO environment such as this one, you can use lmhosts files to provide IP address-to-NetBIOS name mappings for a small number of work-stations. The new workstation probably does not have the correct lmhosts file in place, which is why it is unable to browse network resources. Therefore, Answer **B** is correct.

   ☒ **A, C, D**. While installing a WINS server will provide NetBIOS name resolu-tion, it is overkill in this scenario because this is only a small office – creating a server environment just to provide name resolution is not necessary. Therefore, Answer **A** is incorrect. The hosts file is used to provide DNS name resolution, not NetBIOS. lmhosts is used to provide NetBIOS name resolution. Therefore, Answer **C** is incorrect. Installing a DNS server will not provide name resolu-tion, and would be overkill for this scenario anyway. Therefore, Answer **D** is incorrect.

2. You are troubleshooting network connectivity issues on a network that is running Windows servers and clients. Users are reporting that they are unable to send e-mail, though they have been receiving messages from external users without a problem. During your troubleshooting, you see the following configuration item on the Windows server. Based on this information, how can you correct the issue that this office is reporting?

Figure 12.8 Network Connectivity Configuration

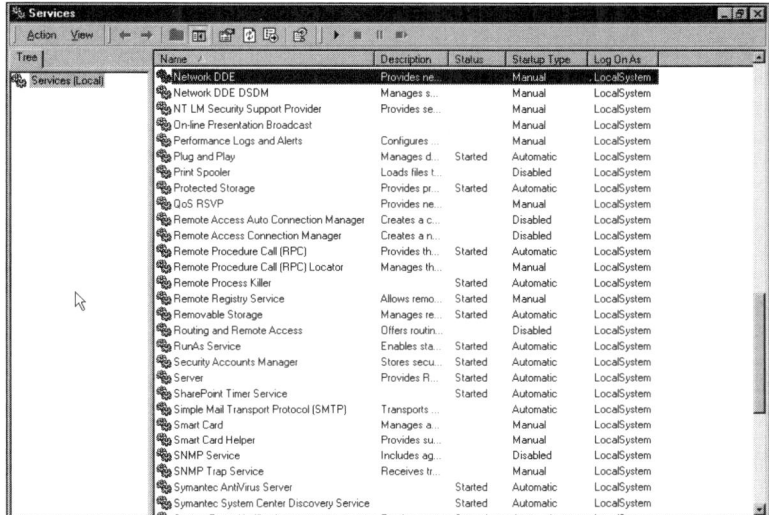

A. Install and configure the POP3 service.

B. Change the startup type of the SNMP Trap Service to **Automatic**.

C. Start the Simple Mail Transport Protocol (SMTP) service.

D. Start the Routing and Remote Access Service.

☑ **C.** The Simple Mail Transport Protocol (SMTP) operates at the Application Layer and is used to send e-mail messages to other e-mail servers. If this service is not running, e-mail delivery will not function. Therefore, Answer **C** is correct.

☒ **A**, **B**, **D.** The POP3 service is used to create a local mailbox to allow clients to receive email; it is not used to send e-mail. Therefore, Answer **A** is incorrect. The SNMP Trap Service is used to send SNMP diagnostic information to an SNMP management agent; it is not used to send e-mail. Therefore, Answer **B** is incorrect. The Routing and Remote Access Service is used to provide remote access services such as dial-up and VPN access, not to send e-mail. Therefore, Answer **D** is incorrect.

3. You are a network consultant and have been called in to troubleshoot a connectivity issue on a UNIX network. From the client's UNIX workstations, which of the following utilities can you use to perform network troubleshooting? (Select all that apply.)

A. ping

B. tracert

C. pathping

D. traceroute

E. nslookup

F. dig

☑ **A**, **D**, **F**. **ping** is a troubleshooting command that is available on both Windows and UNIX/Linux workstations to determine basic network connectivity. Therefore, Answer **A** is correct. **traceroute** is a utility that is available to map the path between two network hosts, available on a UNIX or linux workstation. Therefore, Answer **D** is correct. **dig** is a utility available on UNIX and linux workstations to troubleshoot DNS name resolution. Therefore, Answer **F** is correct.

☒ **B**, **C**, **E**. The **tracert** command is available on Windows workstations and servers, not on UNIX or Linux servers. Therefore, Answer **B** is incorrect. The **pathping** command is available on Windows workstations and servers, not on UNIX or Linux servers. Therefore, Answer **C** is incorrect. The **nslookup** command is available on Windows workstations and servers to troubleshoot DNS name resolution, not on UNIX or Linux servers. Therefore, Answer **E** is incorrect.

4. You are the network administrator for a network that employs a Windows 2000 server and 30 Windows XP Professional workstations. The Windows 2000 server runs the DHCP service to provide TCP/IP configuration information to the Windows XP clients. You receive a call from one of your users stating that he is unable to browse any internal network resources or Internet websites. Other users on the same subnet are able to browse without difficulty. You run the **ipconfig** command on the problem workstation and see the following output:

```
Windows IP Configuration
        Host Name . . . . . . . . . . . . : IBM-A38375FF22E
        Primary Dns Suffix  . . . . . . . :
        Node Type . . . . . . . . . . . . : Hybrid
        IP Routing Enabled. . . . . . . . : No
        WINS Proxy Enabled. . . . . . . . : No
Ethernet adapter Wireless Network Connection:
        Connection-specific DNS Suffix  . :
        Description . . . . . . . . . . . : Intel(R) PRO/Wireless 2200BG
Network Connection
        Physical Address. . . . . . . . . : 00-1E-25-1A-D3-5A
        Dhcp Enabled. . . . . . . . . . . : Yes
        Autoconfiguration Enabled . . . . : Yes
        IP Address. . . . . . . . . . . . : 169.254.1.96
        Subnet Mask . . . . . . . . . . . : 255.255.0.0
        Default Gateway . . . . . . . . . :
        DHCP Server . . . . . . . . . . . :
        DNS Servers . . . . . . . . . . . :
        Lease Obtained. . . . . . . . . . : Tuesday, March 29, 2005 1:00:10 PM
        Lease Expires . . . . . . . . . . : Wednesday, March 30, 2005 1:00:10
PM
```

Based on this output, why is this workstation unable to browse any network resources?

A. The default gateway is unavailable.

B. The workstation could not contact a DHCP server.

C. The workstation is configured with the incorrect default gateway.

D. The workstation's DHCP lease has expired.

☑ **B.** This workstation is configured using Automatic Private IP Addressing (APIPA), which is used by Windows workstations when they are unable to contact a DHCP server. APIPA provides limited IP connectivity with no default gateway or DNS name resolution. Therefore, Answer **B** is correct.

☒ **A, C, D.** A workstation configured with APIPA does not have a default gateway. If other workstations on the same subnet are able to communicate, this indicates that the problem does not lie with the default gateway. Therefore, Answer **A** is incorrect. A workstation configured with APIPA is configured with the default Class B subnet mask. This workstation's inability to communicate stems from its inability to contact a DHCP server and is not related to its subnet mask. Therefore, Answer **C** is incorrect. This workstation's inability

www.syngress.com

communicate stems from its inability to contact a DHCP server and is not related to the length of its DHCP lease. Therefore, Answer **D** is incorrect.

5. You are the network administrator for a sales office. Until now, this has been a small peer-to-peer network consisting of five Windows 2000 professional workstations using lmhosts files on each workstation to perform DNS name resolution. The sales force has recently expanded significantly, requiring you to purchase a Windows Server 2003 server and fifteen additional workstations. You have encountered numerous troubleshooting situations where a workstation's lmhosts file was missing or out of date, preventing name resolution from taking place. How can you improve the name resolution process for your network?

    A. Install the DNS service on the Windows 2000 server.

    B. Install the WINS service on the Windows 2000 server.

    C. Install the DHCP service on the Windows 2000 server.

    D. Install the DNS service on each Windows XP workstation.

    ☑ **B**. The Windows Internet Naming Service (WINS) will provide centralized NetBIOS name-to-IP address mapping and name resolution for a client-server environment. Therefore, Answer **B** is correct.

    ☒ **A, C, D**. The WINS service provides for centralized Internet hostname resolution; it is not a replacement for lmhosts files. Therefore, Answer **A** is incorrect. The DHCP service provides automatic IP address configuration for client computers; it does not provide name resolution. Therefore, Answer **C** is incorrect. The DNS service runs on Windows server computers; it is not available on Windows XP Professional workstations. Therefore, Answer **D** is incorrect.

6. You are the network administrator for a large pharmaceutical company that has over 1,000 workstations. To simplify TCP/IP configuration for these numerous clients, you installed a DHCP server over a year ago to automatically configure your clients with an IP address, as well as the following common configuration information:

```
Subnet Mask: 255.255.0.0
Default Gateway: 172.16.0.1
DNS Servers:   172.16.0.100
               172.16.0.101
```

As part of a recent network redesign, you had to change the default gateway used by your clients to a different IP address: 172.16.1.1. You made the necessary change on the DHCP server, and most of your clients were updated automatically. After you make this change, you receive a call from one user who no longer able to browse the Internet. You examine the TCP/IP configuration of her LAN connection and see the following:

Figure 12.9 Internal Protocol Properties

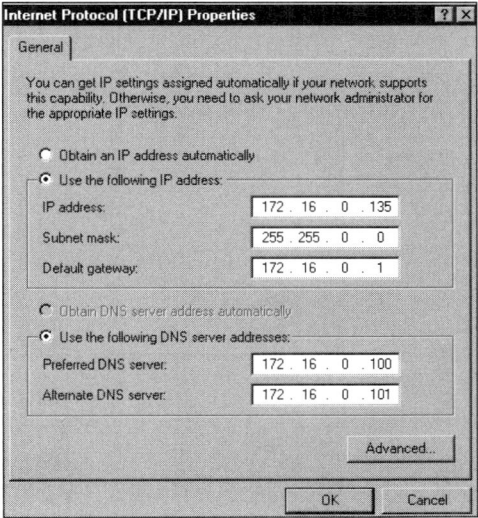

How can you configure this workstation with the correct default gateway information? (Each choice represents a complete solution. Choose two.)

A. Delete the manually configured information and select **Obtain an IP address automatically**.

B. Run **ipconfig /renew** from the command prompt.

C. Manually update the IP address of the default gateway.

D. Run **ipconfig /release** from the command prompt.

☑ **A, C.** A computer that has its TCP/IP configuration manually configured will not be updated when you make changes to the configuration being handed out by a DHCP server. To allow this client to receive these updates automatically, you must remove the manually configured information and configure the workstation to obtain an IP address automatically. Therefore, Answer **A** is correct. If a computer's TCP/IP configuration is manually configured, it will not be updated when you make changes to the configuration being handed out by a DHCP server. You must manually update the default gateway that this computer is configured with in order to restore connectivity. Therefore, Answer **C** is correct.

☒ **B, D.** This computer is configured with a static IP address, so the **ipconfig /renew** command will have no effect. Therefore, Answer **B** is incorrect. This computer is configured with a static IP address, so the **ipconfig /release** command will have no effect. Therefore, Answer **D** is incorrect.

7. You are the administrator for the network shown in the following figure. Based on the information in this figure, which computer is configured incorrectly?

Figure 12.10 Incorrect Configuration on Network

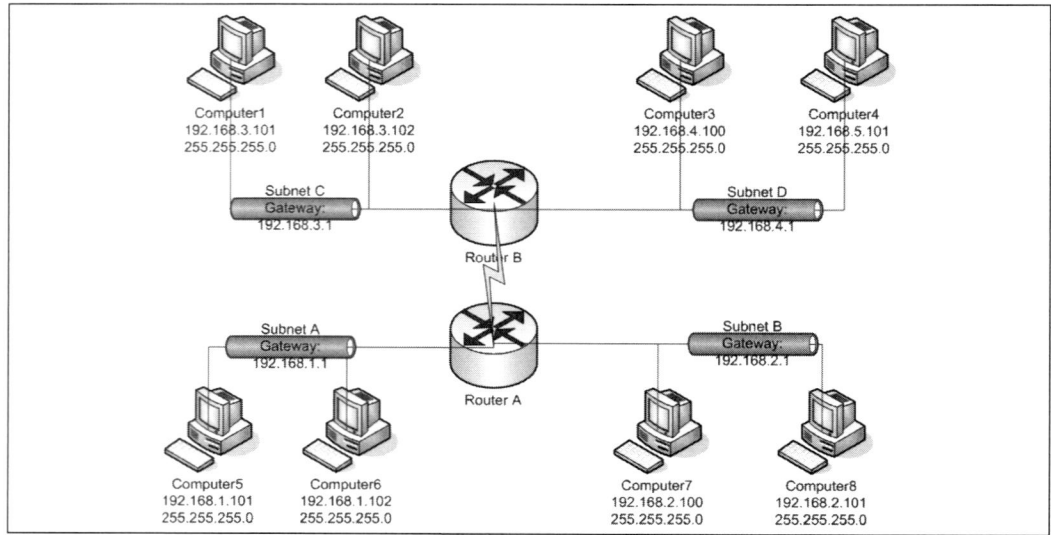

A. Computer1

B. Computer2

C. Computer3

D. Computer4

E. Computer5

F. Computer6

G. Computer7

H. Computer8

☑ **D.** Based on the subnet mask and default gateway information, Computer4 is configured incorrectly. An IP address of 192.168.5.101 with a subnet mask of 255.255.255.0 will not be able to communicate correctly on the 192.168.4.0 network. Therefore Answer **D** is correct.

☒ **A, B, C, E, F, G, H**. Based on the information in this figure, Computer1 is configured correctly. Therefore, Answer **A** is incorrect. Based on the information in this figure, Computer2 is configured correctly. Therefore, Answer **B** is incorrect. Based on the information in this figure, Computer3 is configured correctly. Therefore, Answer **C** is incorrect. Based on the information in this figure, Computer5 is configured correctly. Therefore, Answer **E** is incorrect. Based on the information in this figure, Computer6 is configured correctly. Therefore, Answer **F** is incorrect. Based on the information in this figure, Computer7 is configured correctly. Therefore, Answer **G** is incorrect. Based on the information in this figure, Computer8 is configured correctly. Therefore, Answer **H** is incorrect.

8. You are the network administrator for the network shown in the following figure. You have recently purchased a new Windows XP workstation called Computer9 that you now need to add to Subnet C. Which of the following would be a valid IP address that would allow Computer9 to access resources on all four subnets?

Figure 12.11 Valid IP Address for Accessing Resources

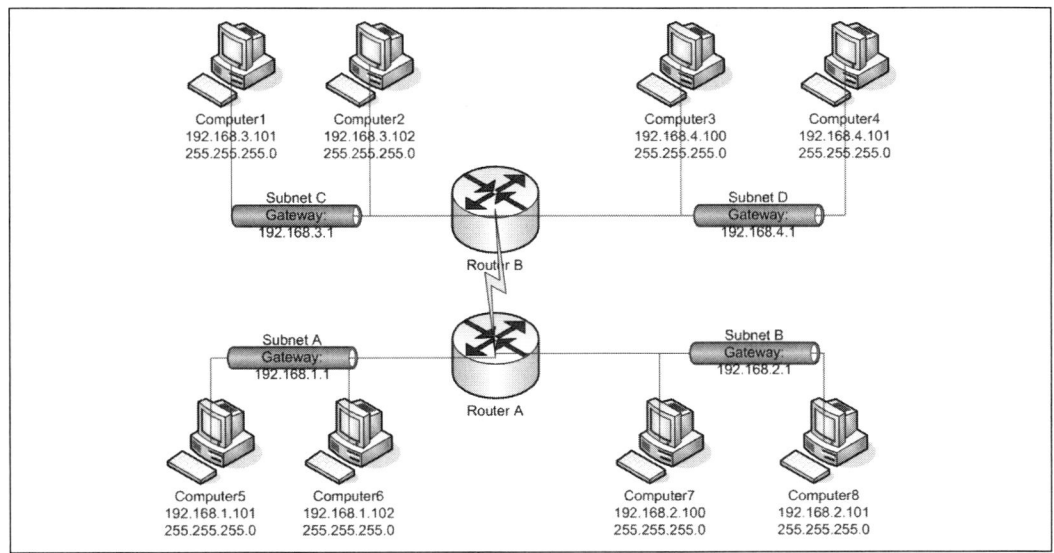

A. 192.168.3.155

B. 192.168.3.1

C. 192.168.3.0

D. 192.168.3.255

☑ **A.** 192.168.3.155 would be a valid IP address for the 192.168.3.0 Class C network since it is an unused address in the range of 192.168.3.1-192.168.3.254. Therefore, Answer **A** is correct.

☒ **B, C, D.** 192.168.3.1 is in the correct address range for Subnet C, but it is already in use as the default gateway for Subnet C. Assigning a duplicate IP address in this manner would cause connectivity issues for the entire subnet. Therefore, Answer **B** is incorrect. 192.168.3.0 is the network address for the 192.168.3.0 Class C network, and cannot be assigned to an individual host. Therefore, Answer **C** is incorrect. 192.168.3.255 is the broadcast address for the 192.168.3.0 Class C network, and should not be assigned to an individual computer. Therefore, Answer **D** is incorrect.

9. You are the administrator for the network shown in the following figure. You receive a help desk call from the user of Computer8, stating that she cannot browse the Internet or access a shared folder located on Computer5. Upon investigating the issue, you find that Computer7 is able to access the Internet and other shared resources, but Computer8 cannot ping any other hosts on the network. Based on this information, which of the following are likely points of failure that you should investigate? (Each selection represents a complete choice. Select all that apply.)

Figure 12.12 Likely Points of Failure on the Network

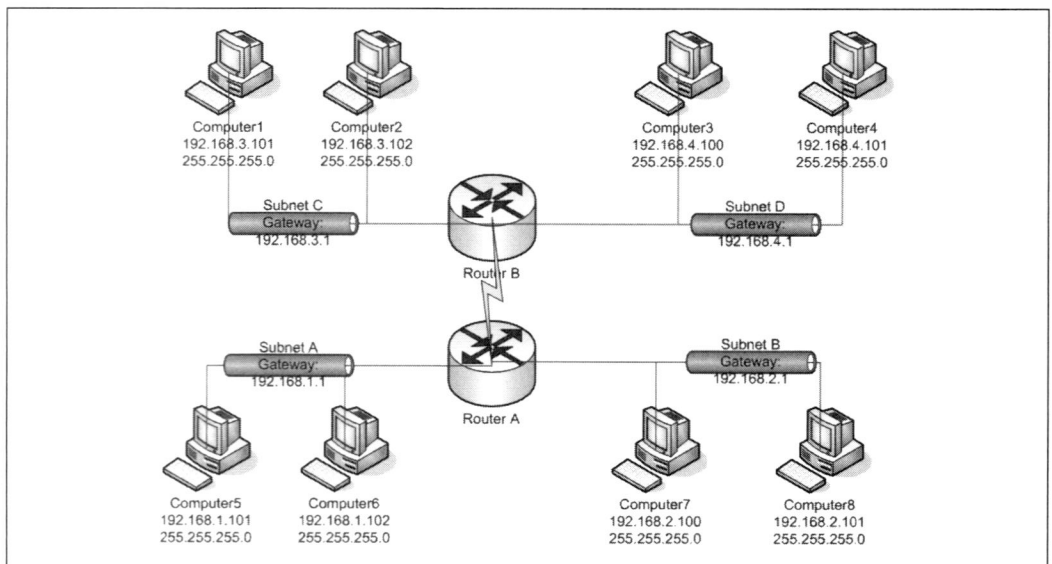

A. The NIC installed in Computer8

B. The network cable attaching Computer8 to the network

C. The NIC installed in RouterA attached to Subnet B

D. The TCP/IP configuration of Computer7

☑ **A, B**. Based on the situation described here, it appears that the network connectivity issue is isolated to Computer8. It is therefore logical to troubleshoot the physical network hardware that is installed in Computer8 such as the NIC. Therefore, Answer **A** is correct. Based on the situation described here, it appears that the network connectivity issue is isolated to Computer8. It is therefore logical to troubleshoot the physical network hardware that is attached to Computer8 such as the network cable. Therefore, Answer **B** is correct.

☒ **C, D**. If Router A was experiencing a hardware failure, Computer7 would be experiencing connectivity issues along with Computer8. Since the connectivity failure seems to be limited to Computer8, this does not appear to be the case. Therefore, Answer **C** is incorrect. In the scenario described in this question, Computer7 is not experiencing any network connectivity issues, so the TCP/IP configuration of Computer7 does not require troubleshooting. Therefore, Answer **D** is incorrect.

10. You are the administrator of the network shown in the following figure. The firewall in the exhibit was installed by an outside consultant a few weeks ago. Once a month, one of your company's employees needs to access the FTP site of one of your company's business partners, ftp.airplanes.com, in order to download large PDF files containing product marketing information. You receive a help desk call from this employee, stating that he is now unable to access this FTP site. The last time he performed this task was before the firewall was installed, and he says that it worked fine then. You are able to ping the ftp.airplanes.com DNS name, and you can access www.airplanes.com, which is located on the same physical machine. What is the best way to restore this employee's access to the ftp.airplanes.com FTP site?

Figure 12.13 Restoring FTP Access After Firewall Installation

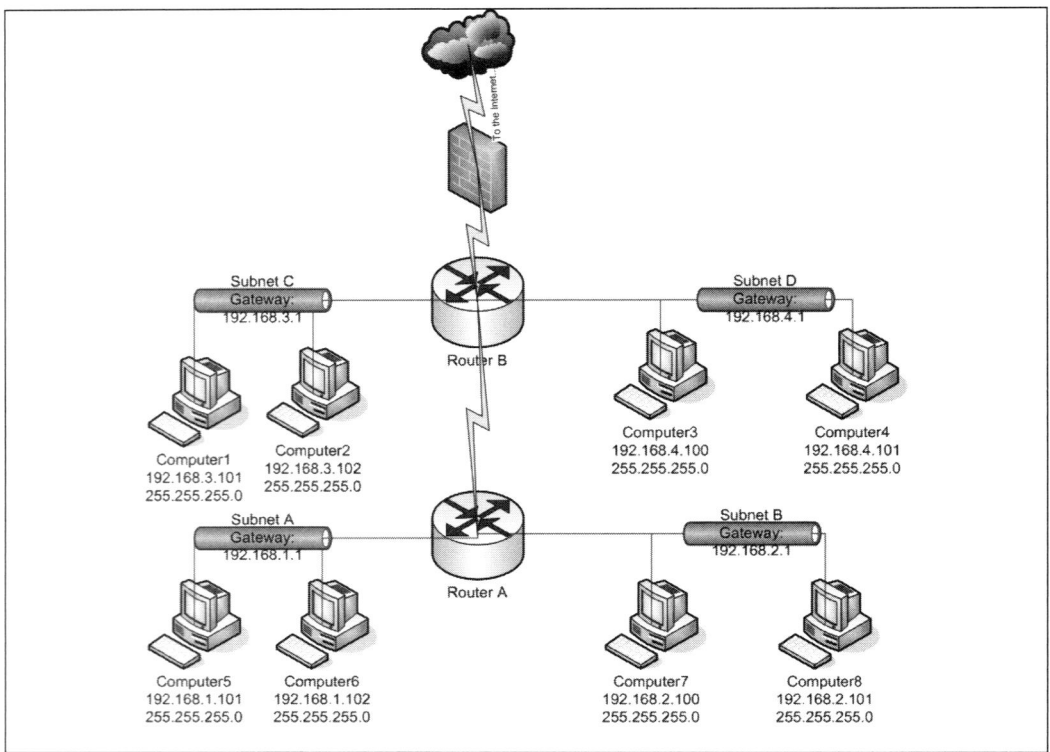

A. Configure a firewall rule allowing traffic to TCP ports 20 and 21.

B. Configure a firewall rule allowing traffic to TCP ports 25 and 110.

C. Configure a firewall rule allowing all TCP traffic to this employee's workstation.

D. Configure a firewall rule allowing traffic to TCP ports 80 and 443.

☑ **A**. FTP uses TCP ports 20 and 21 to transmit and receive information. When the firewall was installed, the consultant apparently did not permit any FTP traffic to pass between your internal network and the Internet. Creating a firewall rule to allow these two ports will restore the employee's access to FTP. Therefore, Answer **A** is correct.

☒ **B**, **C**, **D**. TCP port 25 is used for the Simple Mail Transfer Protocol (SMTP), and TCP port 110 is used for the Post Office Protocol (POP3). These two protocols are used to send and receive e-mail, not to allow FTP file transfers. Therefore, Answer **B** is incorrect. While allowing all TCP traffic to pass through to this employee's workstation will restore his access to the ftp.airplanes.com FTP server, it will also unnecessarily expose his computer and the rest of your network to security threats and is therefore not the best choice in this scenario. Therefore, Answer **C** is incorrect. TCP port 80 is used for HTTP traffic and TCP port 443 is used for SSL encrypted traffic, not for sending and receiving FTP file transfers. Therefore, Answer **D** is incorrect.

11. You are the network administrator for a medium-sized law firm. You have recently deployed a wireless access point (WAP) for use by your internal support staff and attorneys. You have been charged with ensuring that only legitimate users of your company network will be able to access these wireless access points. What are some steps you can take to enable network connectivity to your wireless access point so that only legitimate users will be able to obtain access? (Each choice represents a complete answer. Choose all that apply.)

    A. Enable MAC address filtering.

    B. Enable the default SSID broadcast.

    C. Enable WEP or WPA encryption.

    D. Enable the DHCP server on the wireless access point.

    ☑ **A, C**. By enabling MAC address filtering, you are restricting network connectivity on your wireless access point to only those MAC addresses that you specify. Therefore, Answer **A** is correct. By enabling WEP or WPA encryption, you are restricting network connectivity on your wireless access point to only those people who know the numeric WEP key or the WPA password. Therefore, Answer **C** is correct.

    ☒ **B, D**. By enabling the default Security Set Identifier (SSID) broadcast, you are leaving your wireless access point available to anyone within range of the wireless signal whose wireless device is configured to connect to any available network. Therefore, Answer **B** is incorrect. By enabling the DHCP server on the wireless access point, you are enabling the WAP to provide TCP/IP configuration to anyone who connects to the WAP; this does nothing to restrict who has access to your wireless network. Therefore, Answer **D** is incorrect.

12. You are the administrator of the network shown in the following figure. You receive a call from the users of Computer5 and Computer6, stating that they cannot access any resources on the Internet. No other users on the network are reporting outages. Based on this diagram, what is most likely causing this connectivity issue?

Figure 12.14 Connectivity Issued with Computer5 and Computer6

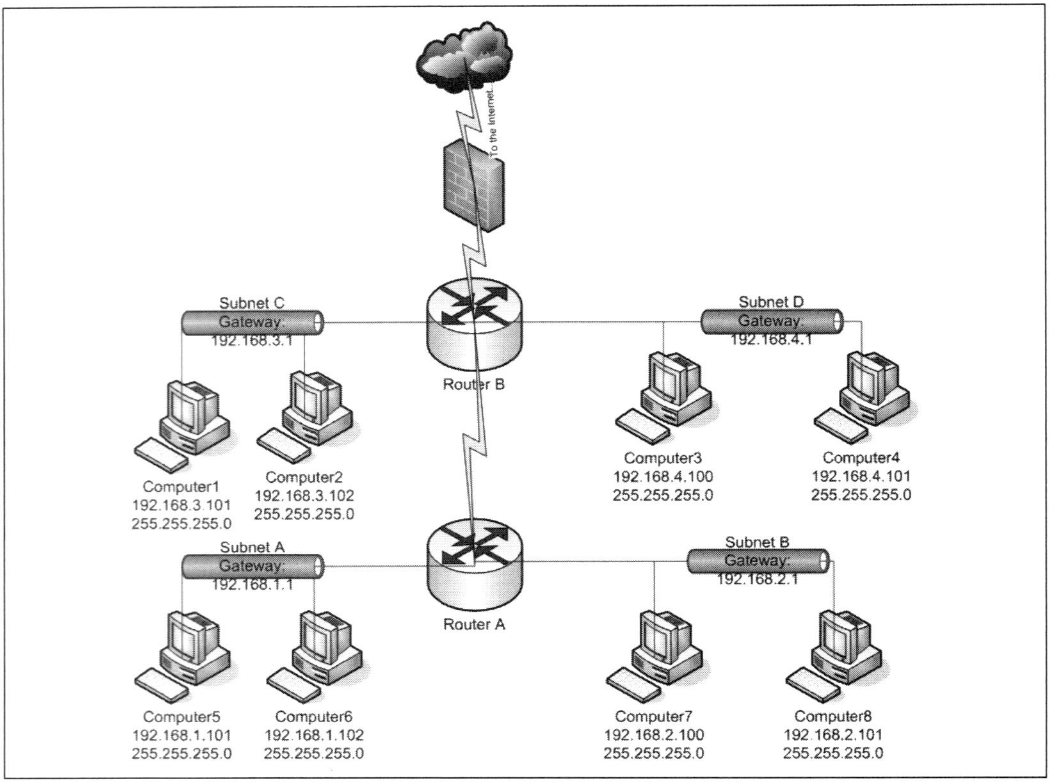

A. The network cable attaching Computer5 to the network.

B. The 192.168.1.1 interface on Router A.

C. The 192.168.4.1 interface on Router B.

D. The 192.168.5.1 interface on Router A

☑ **B**. Computer5 and Computer6 are connected to the 192.168.1.1 interface of Router A, so a failure of this interface would create an outage for both PCs. Therefore, Answer **B** is correct.

☒ **A, C, D**. A failed network cable on Computer5 would not create a connectivity issue for both Computer5 and Computer6. Therefore, Answer **A** is incorrect. The 192.168.4.1 interface of Router B is attached to Subnet D, and does not connect Computer5 and Computer6 to the Internet. Based on this diagram, an outage on Subnet D would not affect Internet connectivity for Subnet A. Therefore, Answer **C** is incorrect. The 192.168.5.1 interface connects Router A to Router B. If this network segment was down, both Subnet A and

Subnet B would be unable to access the Internet. Since no other computers on the network are reporting any outages, Answer **D** is incorrect.

13. You are the administrator of the network shown in the following figure. The user of Computer1 is unable to access a shared resource located on Computer3. Computer1 is able to access shared resources on other subnets on the internal network as well as the Internet. Computer3 is able to access shared resources on Computer5 and Computer7, as well as resources on the Internet. When you ping Computer1 from Computer3, you receive a "Request Timed Out" message. Based on this information, what is the most likely cause of the connectivity issue?

Figure 12.15 "Request Timed Out" on Computer1 and Computer3

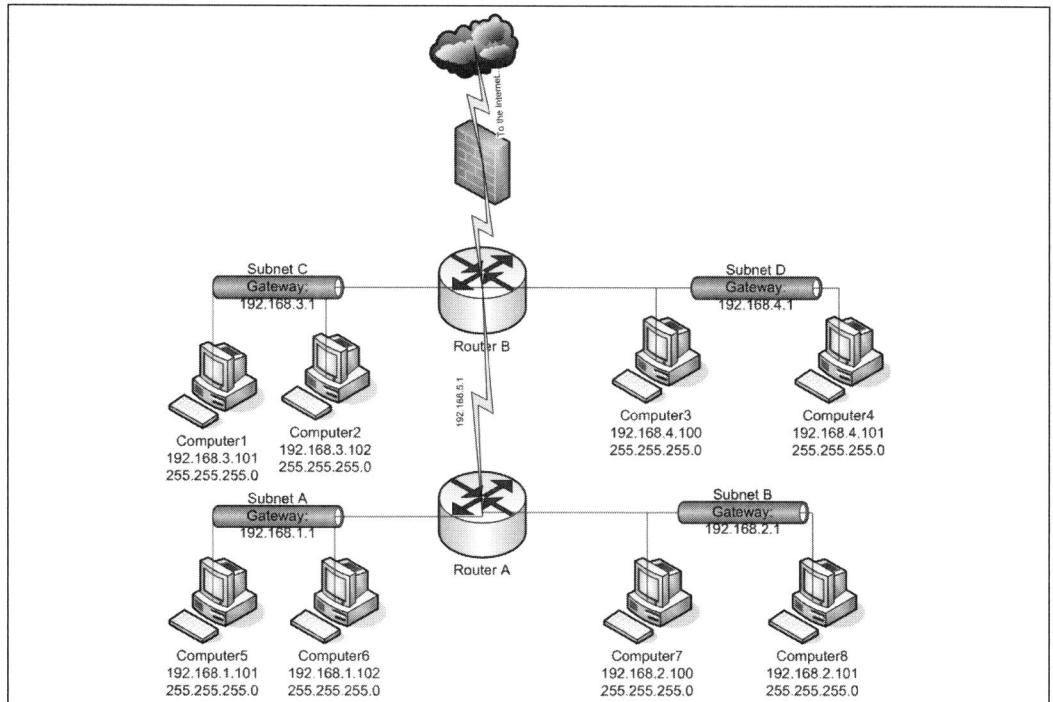

A. The router interface attached to Subnet D is malfunctioning.

B. The router interface attached to Subnet C is malfunctioning.

C. Router B does not have a route from Subnet C to the Internet.

D. Router B does not have a route from Subnet C to Subnet D.

☑ **D**. If two subnets are attached by a single router with no hops in between, and these two subnets cannot communicate with each other, it is likely that the router does not have a route configured between the two subnets. Therefore, Answer **D** is correct.

☒ **A, B, C**. If the router interface attached to Subnet D was malfunctioning, Computer3 would not be able to access resources outside of Subnet D. Since this is not the case, Answer **A** is incorrect. If the router interface attached to Subnet C was malfunctioning, Computer1 would not be able to access resources outside of Subnet C. Since this is not the case, Answer **B** is incorrect. If Router B did not have a route from Subnet C to the Internet, Computer1 would not be able to access the Internet. Since this is not the case, Answer **C** is incorrect.

Index

A

AAA (authentication, authority, and accountability), 207
AARP requests and AppleTalk, 326
absorption, RF behavior, 185–186
access
  control. *See* access control
  dial-in, planning for, 539–540
  element of networks, 6
  Internet, WAN methods, 446–452, 482
  to internetworks, 7–8
  remote. *See* remote access
  in ring topologies, 32–33
  unauthorized, 215–217
  VPN, planning for, 540–541
access control
  Data Link methods, 749
  media, 252–253
  methods for, 284
access control lists (ACLs) and switches, 268
access points. *See* APs
acknowledgement (ACK)
  and CSMA/CD, 192
  described, 292–293
  and negative acknowledgment (NACK), 208
  TCP, 762
ACLs (access control lists)
  controlling access with, 160
  described, 591
  entries, permissions, 530–531
Active Directory
  described, 17
  domains, and workgroups, 548
  group accounts, 514–515
Active Directory Users and Computers snap-in, 507–509, 511–516
active hubs, 127, 683, 741, 747
active monitor on Token Ring network, 32–33
ad-hoc networks, 197–198
adapters
  ISND, 135–136
  terminal (TAs), 139
address classes, 342–346
Address Resolution Protocol. *See* ARP
address translation, dynamic and static, 571–572
addresses
  aggregatable global unicast, 332
  IP. *See* IP addresses
  MAC. *See* MAC addresses
  multicast, 369–370
  physical vs. logical, 267

private, static and dynamic assignments, 361–366, 374
  resolving to MAC address, 386
addressing, 325
  AppleTalk, 325–327
  classful and classless, 342
  dotted decimal format, 328
  IPv6, 331
  IPX, 321–323
ADSL technology, 447
Advanced Research Projects Agency network (ARPNET), 7–8
adware, 611
AFP (AppleTalk File Protocol), 327, 415, 425
Aiken, Howard, 10
AirSnort, 209, 216, 228
Allen, Paul, 12
Altair 8800, 12
American Institute of Electrical Engineers (AIEE), 37
analog modems, 133–134
analog vs. digital signaling, 259–262
AND operator, 349
ANDing, bitwise, 349–351
antennas
  characteristics of, 186–187
  using for site surveys, 228
  and wireless networks, 34
  Yagi-type, 210
antivirus software
  deploying, 606–608
  updating, 612
Apache Manager, 524
APIPA (Automatic Private Internet Protocol Addressing), 422
Apple Computers
  development of GUI, 13
  early development at, 13
  Mac OSX, 531–533
AppleTalk described, addressing, 323–327
AppleTalk File Protocol (AFP), 415
application layer filtering, firewalls, 568–569
Application Layer, OSI model
  described, 271–272
  protocols, TCP/IP, 310, 426
  troubleshooting, 770–776, 778
application level firewalls, 156–157
Application Program Interface boundary layer, 276
applications
  user, and Application Layer, 770
  and user mode services, 276
  and well-known TCP ports (table), 762

APs (access points)
  connecting, 231
  costs of, 181
  and flooding attacks, 217
  locating, 229
  rogue access points, 215, 220, 235
  uncovering unauthorized, 219
  in wireless networks, 182
architecture
  bus types and NICs, 143
  distributed systems, 255–256
  firewall, 154
  network, and troubleshooting, 745
  Systems Network Architecture (SNA), 271
archive bits, and backups, 641
Arnet networks, 92
ARP (Address Resolution Protocol)
  address table and, 220
  cache, process, 384
  described, 289, 423
  Inverse (InARP), 386
  and IPX addresses, 321
  and Network Layer, OSI model, 756
  and RARP, 402
arp utility, troubleshooting with, 692–693
ARPANET (Advanced Research Projects Agency network), 7–8, 11, 15, 249, 309–310
Asynchronous Transfer Mode (ATM), 438
Atanasoff, John, 9
attackers described, 587
attacks
  See also exploits *and specific attack*
  Denial of Service (DoS). See Denial of Service attacks
  dictionary, 208
  Distributed DoS, 264, 587–588
  flooding, 217–219
  jamming, 222
  known-plaintext, 204
  man-in-the-middle (MITM), 207, 219–221
attenuation of signals, 74, 261–262, 746
authentication
  in 802.11 standards, 203–208
  domain, Windows Server 2003, 502
  IPSec, 460–461
  Kerberos, 473–475, 763
  LDAP, 529–531
  Mac OSX operating system, 532
  mixing protocols, 547

Syngress: *The Definition of a Serious Security Library*

Syn·gress (sin–gres): *noun, sing.* Freedom from risk or danger; safety. See *security*.

AVAILABLE NOW
order @
www.syngress.com

Dr. Tom Shinder's Configuring ISA Server 2004
Dr. Thomas W. Shinder, Debra Littlejohn Shinder

Dr. Tom and Deb Shinder have become synonymous with Microsoft's flagship firewall product ISA Server, as a result of his prominent role as a member of the beta development team, and his featured placement on both Microsoft's ISA Server Web site and ISAserver.org. TTom's unparalleled technical expertise combined with prime on-line marketing opportunities will make this the #1 book again in the ISA Server market.

ISBN: 1-931836-19-1

Price: $49.95 US $72.95 CAN

Microsoft Log Parser Toolkit
Gabriele Giuseppini and Mark Burnett

AVAILABLE NOW
order @
www.syngress.com

Do you want to find Brute Force Attacks against your Exchange Server? Would you like to know who is spamming you? Do you need to monitor the performance of your IIS Server? Are there intruders out there you would like to find? Would you like to build user logon reports from your Windows Server? Would you like working scripts to automate all of these tasks and many more for you? If so, "Microsoft Log Parser Toolkit" is the book for you...

ISBN: 1-932266-52-6

Price: $39.95 US $57.95 CAN

Ethereal Packet Sniffing
Angela Orebaugh, Gilbert Ramirez

AVAILABLE NOW
order @
www.syngress.com

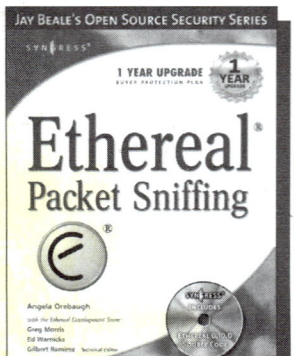

Ethereal offers more protocol decoding and reassembly than any free sniffer out there and ranks well among the commercial tools. You've all used tools like tcpdump or windump to examine individual packets, but Ethereal makes it easier to make sense of a stream of ongoing network communications. Ethereal not only makes network troubleshooting work far easier, but also aids greatly in network forensics, the art of finding and examining an attack, by giving a better "big picture" view. Ethereal Packet Sniffing will show you how to make the most out of your use of Ethereal.

ISBN: 1-932266-82-8

Price: $49.95 U.S. $77.95 CAN

SYNGRESS